Oracle Press™

OCA/OCP
Oracle Database 11g
All-in-One
Exam Guide

(Exam 1Z0-051, 1Z0-052, and 1Z0-053)

About the Authors

John Watson (Oxford, UK) works for BPLC Management Consultants, teaching and consulting throughout Europe and Africa. He was with Oracle University for several years in South Africa, and before that worked for a number of companies, government departments, and NGOs in England and Europe. He is OCP qualified in both database and application server administration. John is the author of several books and numerous articles on technology and has 25 years of experience in IT.

Roopesh Ramklass (South Africa), OCP, is an Oracle specialist who has worked in a range of contexts. He was part of Oracle's Support team and taught at Oracle University in South Africa for many years. As an independent consultant and manager of his own consulting business, he designed and developed software and training courses based on a wide spectrum of Oracle technologies., including the database, application server, and business intelligence products. Roopesh is a co-author of the *OCA Oracle Database 11g: SQL Fundamentals I Exam Guide* (Oracle Press, 2008) and has more than 12 years of experience in the IT industry.

About the Technical Editors

Gavin Powell (Cartersville, GA) is a consultant and technical writer with 20 years of experience in the IT industry. He has worked as a programmer, developer, analyst, data modeler, and database administrator in numerous industries.

Bruce Swart (South Africa) works for 2Cana Solutions and has over 14 years of experience in IT. While maintaining a keen interest for teaching others, he has performed several roles, including developer, analyst, team leader, administrator, project manager, consultant, and lecturer. He is OCP qualified in both database and developer roles. He has taught at Oracle University in South Africa for several years and has also spoken at numerous local Oracle User Group conferences. His passion is helping others achieve greatness.

April Wells (Austin, TX) is an experienced Oracle DBA who holds multiple DBA OCP certifications. She currently manages Oracle databases and Oracle data warehouses at NetSpend corporation in Austin, Texas. Previously, April has worked for Oracle Corporation in Austin, Texas, as on-site support at Dell, at Corporate Systems in Amarillo, Texas, and at U.S. Steel in Pennsylvania and Minnesota.

Oracle Press™

OCA/OCP
Oracle Database 11*g*
All-in-One
Exam Guide

(Exam 1Z0-051, 1Z0-052, and 1Z0-053)

John Watson
Roopesh Ramklass

New York • Chicago • San Francisco • Lisbon
London • Madrid • Mexico City • Milan • New Delhi
San Juan • Seoul • Singapore • Sydney • Toronto

The **McGraw·Hill** Companies

Cataloging-in-Publication Data is on file with the Library of Congress

McGraw-Hill books are available at special quantity discounts to use as premiums and sales promotions, or for use in corporate training programs. To contact a representative, please e-mail us at bulksales@mcgraw-hill.com.

OCA/OCP Oracle Database 11g All-in-One Exam Guide (Exams 1Z0-051, 1Z0-052, and 1Z0-053)

7890 DOC /DOC 154

ISBN Book P/N 978-0-07-162919-5 and CD p/n 978-0-07-162920-1
of set 978-0-07-162918-8

MHID Book p/n 0-07-162919-X and CD p/n 0-07-162920-3
of set 0-07-162918-1

Sponsoring Editor Timothy Green	**Indexer** Rebecca Plunkett
Editorial Supervisor Janet Walden	**Production Supervisor** Jean Bodeaux
Project Editor LeeAnn Pickrell	**Composition** Apollo Publishing Sevices
Acquisitions Coordinator Meghan Riley	**Illustration** Apollo Publishing Services, Lyssa Wald
Technical Editors Gavin Powell, Bruce Swart, April Wells	**Art Director, Cover** Jeff Weeks
Copy Editor Robert Campbell	**Cover Designer** Pattie Lee
Proofreader Paul Tyler	

Thank you, Silvia, for helping me do this (and for giving me a reason for living).

—John

Ameetha, a more loving and caring companion to share this journey through life, I could not have found.

—Roopesh

CONTENTS AT A GLANCE

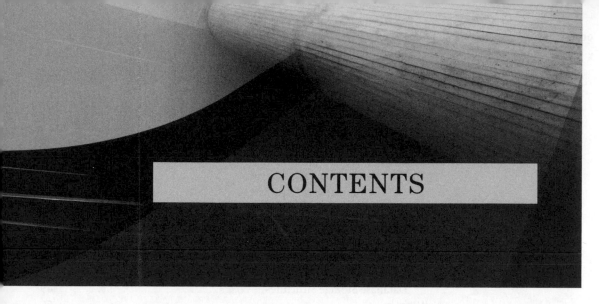

CONTENTS

Part II	SQL

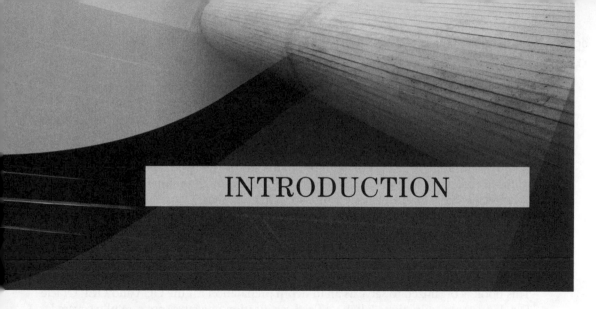

INTRODUCTION

There is an ever increasing demand for staff with IT industry certification. The benefits to employers are significant—they can be certain that staff have a certain level of competence—and the benefits to the individuals, in terms of demand for their services, are equally great. Many employers are now requiring technical staff to have certifications, and many IT purchasers will not buy from firms that do not have certified staff. The Oracle certifications are among the most sought after. But apart from rewards in a business sense, knowing that you are among a relatively small pool of elite Oracle professionals and have proved your competence is a personal reward well worth attaining.

Your studies of the fascinating world of Oracle database administration are about to begin—you can continue these studies for the rest of your working life. Enjoy!

Oracle Certification

There are several Oracle certification *tracks*—this book is concerned with the Oracle Database Administration certification track, specifically for release 11g of the database. There are three levels of DBA certification: Certified Associate (OCA), Certified Professional (OCP), and Certified Master (OCM). The OCA qualification is based on two examinations; the OCP qualification requires passing a third examination. These examinations can be taken at any Prometric Center and typically consist of 60 or 70 questions to be completed in 90 minutes, with 60–70 percent correct needed as the passing score. The OCM qualification requires completing a further two-day evaluation at an Oracle testing center, involving simulations of complex environments and use of advanced techniques that are not covered in this book.

To prepare for the OCA/OCP examinations, you can attend Oracle University instructor-led training courses, you can study Oracle University online learning material, or you can read this book. In all cases, you should also refer to the Oracle Documentation Library for details of syntax. This book will be a valuable addition to other study methods, but it is also sufficient by itself. It has been designed with the examination objectives in mind, though it also includes a great deal of information that will be useful in the course of your work.

However, it is not enough to buy the book, place it under your pillow, and assume that knowledge will permeate the brain by a process of osmosis: you must read it thoroughly, work through the exercises and sample questions, and experiment further with various commands. As you become more familiar with the Oracle environment, you will realize that there is one golden rule: When it doubt, try it out.

In a multitude of cases, you will find that a simple test that takes a couple of minutes can save hours of speculation and poring through manuals. If anything is ever unclear, construct an example and see what happens.

This book was developed using Windows and Linux, but to carry out the exercises and your further investigations, you can use any platform that is supported for Oracle.

In This Book

This book is organized to serve as an in-depth preparation for the OCA and OCP Oracle Database 11g examinations. All the official certification objectives are carefully covered in the book. There are three parts, which in effect build up a case study of configuring a database application from nothing to a fully functional system. Part I assumes no prior knowledge or software installed and goes through the basics of installing the Oracle software and creating a database. Then Part II covers the SQL language, using it to create and use an application in the database created in Part I. Part III deals with the maintenance phase of running the database application (matters such as backup and tuning), and some more advanced database capabilities.

On the CD-ROM

The CD-ROM contains the entire contents of the book in electronic form, as well as practice tests that simulate each of the real Oracle Database 11g OCA/OCP certification tests. For more information on the CD-ROM, please see the appendix.

Exam Readiness Checklist

At the end of this introduction, you will find an Exam Readiness Checklist. We constructed this table to allow you to cross-reference the official exam objectives with the certification objectives as we present and cover them in this book. This has a reference for each objective exactly as Oracle Corporation presents it, with the study guide chapter in which the objective is covered.

There is no need to sit the three examinations in order. You can take them whenever you please, but you will probably gain the highest marks if you sit all three after completing the book. This is because the content of the exams builds up slowly, and there is considerable overlap of objectives between the exams. Topics dealt with later will revisit and reinforce topics dealt with previously.

In Every Chapter

This book includes a set of chapter components that call your attention to important items, reinforce important points, and provide helpful exam-taking hints. Take a look at what you'll find in every chapter:

- **Opening bullets** at the beginning of every chapter are the official exam objectives (by number) covered in the chapter. Because the exams have overlapping objectives, any one chapter may cover objectives from more than one of the exams.

- **Exam Tips** call attention to information about, and potential pitfalls in, the exam.

- **Exercises** are interspersed throughout the chapters; they allow you to get the hands-on experience you need in order to pass the exams. They help you master skills that are likely to be an area of focus on the exam. Don't just read through the exercises; they are hands-on practice that you should be comfortable completing. Learning by doing is an effective way to increase your competency with a product.

- **Tips** describe the issues that come up most often in real-world settings. They provide a valuable perspective on certification- and product-related topics. They point out common mistakes and address questions that have arisen from on-the-job discussions and experience.

- The **Two-Minute Drill** at the end of every chapter is a checklist of the exam objectives covered in the chapter. You can use it for a quick, last-minute review before the test.

- The **Self Test** offers questions similar to those found on the certification exam. The answers to these questions, as well as explanations of the answers, can be found at the end of each chapter. By taking the Self Test after completing each chapter, you'll reinforce what you've learned from that chapter, while becoming familiar with the structure of the exam questions.

Some Pointers

Once you've finished reading this book, set aside some time to do a thorough review. You might want to return to the book several times and make use of all the methods it offers for reviewing the material:

- **Reread all the Two-Minute Drills or have someone quiz you**   You also can use the drills as a way to do a quick cram before the exam. You might want to make some flash cards out of 3 × 5 index cards that have the Two-Minute Drill material on them.

- **Reread all the Exam Tips**   Remember that these notes are based on the exams. The authors have tried to draw your attention to what you should expect—and what you should be on the lookout for.

- **Retake the Self Tests**   It is a good idea to take the Self Test right after you've read the chapter because the questions help reinforce what you've just learned.

- **Complete the Exercises**   Did you do the chapter exercises when you read each chapter? If not, do them! These exercises are designed to cover exam topics, and there's no better way to get to know this material than by practicing. Be sure you understand why you are performing each step in each exercise. If there is something you are not completely clear about, reread that section in the chapter.

Exam Readiness Checklist: Exams 1Z0-051, 1Z0-052, and 1Z0-053

Examination 1Z0-051, Oracle Database 11g: SQL Fundamentals I, Objectives

Examination 1Z0-052, Oracle Database 11g: Administration I, Objectives

ID	Name	Chapter
052.3	*Creating an Oracle Database*	
052.3.1	Create a database by using the Database Configuration Assistant (DBCA)	2
052.4	*Managing the Oracle Instance*	
052.4.1	Setting database initialization parameters	3
052.4.2	Describe the stages of database startup and shutdown	3
052.4.3	Using alert log and trace files	3
052.4.4	Using data dictionary and dynamic performance views	3
052.5	*Configuring the Oracle Network Environment*	
052.5.1	Configure and manage the Oracle network	4
052.5.2	Using the Oracle Shared Server architecture	4
052.6	*Managing Database Storage Structures*	
052.6.1	Overview of tablespace and datafiles	5
052.6.2	Create and manage tablespaces	5
052.6.3	Space management in tablespaces	5
052.7	*Administering User Security*	
052.7.1	Create and manage database user accounts	6
052.7.2	Grant and revoke privileges	6
052.7.3	Create and manage roles	6
052.7.4	Create and manage profiles	6
052.8	*Managing Schema Objects*	
052.8.1	Create and modify tables	7
052.8.2	Manage constraints	7
052.8.3	Create indexes	7
052.8.4	Create and use temporary tables	7
052.9	*Managing Data and Concurrency*	
052.9.1	Manage data using DML	8
052.9.2	Identify and administer PL/SQL objects	8
052.9.3	Monitor and resolve locking conflicts	8
052.10	*Managing Undo Data*	
052.10.1	Overview of undo	8
052.10.2	Transactions and undo data	8
052.10.3	Managing undo	8
052.11	*Implementing Oracle Database Security*	
052.11.1	Database security and the principle of least privilege	6

Examination 1Z0-053, Oracle Database 11g: Administration II, Objectives

PART I

Oracle Database 11*g* Administration

CHAPTER 1

Architectural Overview of Oracle Database 11*g*

Exam Objectives

In this chapter you will learn to

- 052.1.1 Explain the Memory Structures
- 052.1.2 Describe the Process Structures
- 052.1.3 Identify the Storage Structures

This guide is logically structured to enable a thorough understanding of the Oracle server product and the fundamentals of SQL (Structure Query Language, pronounced *sequel*). The authors seek to relate your learning as much to the real world as possible to concretize some of the abstract concepts to follow, by introducing a hypothetical scenario that will be systematically expanded as you progress through the book. This approach involves nominating you as the DBA in charge of setting up an online store. You will appreciate the various roles a DBA is expected to fulfill as well as some of the technology areas with which a DBA is expected to be familiar.

The nonexaminable discussion of the Oracle product stack is followed by considering several prerequisites for fully understanding the tasks involved in setting up an Oracle 11*g* database system. This discussion leads into the examinable objectives in this chapter, which are the Single-Instance Architecture and the Memory, Process, and Storage Structures.

Oracle Product Stack

No Oracle guide is complete without contextualizing the product under study. This section discusses the three core product families currently available from Oracle Corporation. End users of Oracle technology typically use a subset of the available products that have been clustered into either the server, development tools, or applications product families.

Oracle Server Family

The three primary groupings of products within the server technology family consist of the database, application server, and enterprise manager suites. These form the basic components for Oracle's vision of grid computing. The concept underlying the Grid is *virtualization*. End users request a service (typically from a web-based application), but they neither know nor need to know the source of that service. Simplistically, the database server is accessible to store data, the application server hosts the infrastructure for the service being requested by the end user, and the enterprise manager product provides administrators with the management interface. The platforms or physical servers involved in supplying the service are transparent to the end user. Virtualization allows resources to be optimally used, by provisioning servers to the areas of greatest requirement in a manner transparent to the end user.

Database Server

The database server comprises Oracle instances and databases with many features like Streams, Partitioning, Warehousing, Replication, and Real Application Clusters (RAC), but ultimately it provides a reliable, mature, robust, high-performance enterprise-quality data store, built on an object-relational database system. Historically, one of the projects undertaken in the late 1970s to animate the relational theory proposed by Dr. E.F. Codd resulted in the creation of a relational database management system (RDBMS) that later became known as the Oracle Server. The Oracle Server product is well established in the worldwide database market, and the product is central to

Oracle Corporation's continued growth, providing the backbone for many of its other products and offerings. This book is dedicated to describing the essential features of the Oracle Server and the primary mechanisms used to interact with it. It covers the aspects that are measured in the certification exams, but by no means explores the plethora of features available in the product.

An Oracle database is a set of files on disk. It exists until these files are deleted. There are no practical limits to the size and number of these files, and therefore no practical limits to the size of a database. Access to the database is through the Oracle instance. The *instance* is a set of processes and memory structures: it exists on the CPU(s) and in the memory of the server node, and its existence is temporary. An instance can be started and stopped. Users of the database establish sessions against the instance, and the instance then manages all access to the database. It is absolutely impossible in the Oracle environment for any user to have direct contact with the database. An Oracle instance with an Oracle database makes up an Oracle server.

The processing model implemented by the Oracle server is that of client-server processing, often referred to as *two-tier*. In the client-server model, the generation of the user interface and much of the application logic is separated from the management of the data. For an application developed using SQL (as all relational database applications will be), this means that the client tier generates the SQL commands, and the server tier executes them. This is the basic client-server split, usually with a local area network dividing the two tiers. The network communications protocol used between the user process and the server process is Oracle's proprietary protocol, Oracle Net.

The client tier consists of two components: the users and the user processes. The server tier has three components: the server processes that execute the SQL, the instance, and the database itself. Each user interacts with a user process. Each user process interacts with a server process, usually across a local area network. The server processes interact with the instance, and the instance with the database. Figure 1-1 shows this relationship diagrammatically. A *session* is a user process in communication with a server process. There will usually be one user process per user and one server process per user process. The user and server processes that make up sessions are launched on demand by users and terminated when no longer required; this is the log-on and log-off cycle. The instance processes and memory structures are launched by the database administrator and persist until the administrator deliberately terminates them; this is the database startup and shutdown cycle.

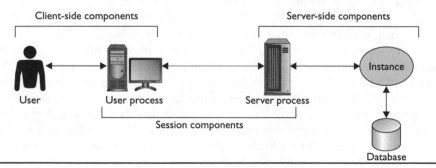

Figure I-I   The indirect connection between a user and a database

The user process can be any client-side software that is capable of connecting to an Oracle server process. Throughout this book, two user processes will be used extensively: SQL*Plus and SQL Developer. These are simple processes provided by Oracle for establishing sessions against an Oracle server and issuing ad hoc SQL. What the user process actually is does not matter to the Oracle server at all. When an end user fills in a form and clicks a SUBMIT button, the user process will generate an INSERT statement (detailed in Chapter 8) and send it to a server process for execution against the instance and the database. As far as the server is concerned, the INSERT statement might just as well have been typed into SQL*Plus as what is known as ad hoc SQL.

Never forget that all communication with an Oracle server follows this client-server model. The separation of user code from server code dates back to the earliest releases of the database and is unavoidable. Even if the user process is running on the same machine as the server (as is the case if, for example, one is running a database on one's own laptop PC for development or training purposes), the client-server split is still enforced, and network protocols are still used for the communications between the two processes. Applications running in an application server environment (described in the next section) also follow the client-server model for their database access.

Application Server

With the emergence of the Web as the de facto standard platform for delivering applications to end users has arisen the need for application servers. An application server allows client-side software, traditionally installed on end-user computers, to be replaced by applications hosted and executing from a centralized location. The application user interface is commonly exposed to users via their web browsers. These applications may make use of data stored in one or more database servers.

Oracle Application Server provides a platform for developing, deploying, and managing *web applications*. A web application can be defined as any application with which users communicate via HTTP. Web applications usually run in at least three tiers: a database tier manages access to the data, the client tier (often implemented via a web browser) handles the local window management for communications with the users, and an application tier in the middle executes the program logic that generates the user interface and the SQL calls to the database.

It is possible for an application to use a one-to-one mapping of end-user session to database session: each user will establish a browser-based session against the application server, and the application server will then establish a session against the database server on the user's behalf. However, this model has been proven to be highly inefficient when compared to the *connection pooling* model. With connection pooling, the application server establishes a relatively small number of persistent database sessions and makes them available on demand (queuing requests if necessary) to a relatively large number of end-user sessions against the application server. Figure 1-2 illustrates the three-tier architecture using connection pooling.

From the point of view of the database, it makes no difference whether a SQL statement comes from a client-side process such as SQL*Plus or Microsoft Access or from a pooled session to an application server. In the former case, the user process occurs on one machine; in the latter, the user process has been divided into two tiers: an applications tier that generates the user interface and a client tier that displays it.

Figure 1-2
The connection
pooling model

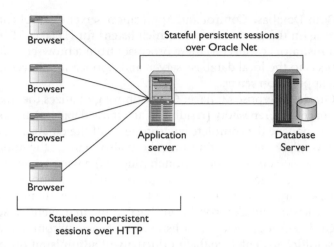

 TIP DBAs often find themselves pressed into service as Application Server administrators. Be prepared for this. There is a separate OCP curriculum for Application Server, for which it may well be worth studying.

Enterprise Manager

The increasing size and complexity of IT installations can make management of each component quite challenging. Management tools can make the task easier, and consequently increase staff productivity.

Oracle Enterprise Manager comes in three forms:

- Database Control
- Application Server Control
- Grid Control

Oracle Enterprise Manager Database Control is a graphical tool for managing one database, which may be a Real Application Clusters (RAC) clustered database. RAC databases are covered in more advanced books; they are mentioned here because they can be managed through the tool. Database Control has facilities for real-time management and monitoring, for running scheduled jobs such as backup operations, and for reporting alert conditions interactively and through e-mail. A RAC database will have a Database Control process running on each node where there is a database instance; these processes communicate with each other, so that each has a complete picture of the state of the RAC.

Oracle Enterprise Manager Application Server Control is a graphical tool for managing one or more application server instances. The technology for managing multiple instances is dependent on the version. Up to and including Oracle Application Server 10g release 2, multiple application servers were managed as a *farm*, with a metadata repository (typically residing in an Oracle database) as the central management point. This is an excellent management model and offers superb capabilities for deploying and maintaining applications, but it is proprietary to Oracle. From Application Server 10g release 3 onward, the technology is based on J2EE clustering, which is not proprietary to Oracle.

Both Database Control and Application Server Control consist of a Java process running on the server machine, which listens for HTTP or HTTPS connection requests. Administrators connect to these processes from a browser. Database Control then connects to the local database server, and Application Server Control connects to the local application server.

Oracle Enterprise Manager Grid Control globalizes the management environment. A management repository (residing in an Oracle database) and one or more management servers manage the complete environment: all the databases and application servers, wherever they may be. Grid Control can also manage the nodes, or machines, on which the servers run, and (through plug-ins) a wide range of third-party products. Each managed node runs an agent process, which is responsible for monitoring the managed targets on the node: executing jobs against them and reporting status, activity levels, and alert conditions back to the management server(s).

Grid Control provides a holistic view of the environment and, if well configured, can significantly enhance the productivity of administration staff. It becomes possible for one administrator to manage effectively hundreds or thousands of targets. The inherent management concept is management by exception. Instead of logging on to each target server to check for errors or problems, Grid Control provides a summary graphic indicating the availability of targets in an environment. The interface supports honing into the targets that are generating exceptions, using drill-down web links, thereby assisting with expedient problem identification.

 EXAM TIP Anything that can be done with OEM can also be done through SQL statements. The OCP examinations test the use of SQL for administration work extensively. It is vital to be familiar with command-line techniques.

Oracle Development Tools

Oracle provides several tools for developing applications and utility programs, and supports a variety of languages. The programming languages that are parsed and executed internally within the Oracle Server are Structured Query Language (SQL), Procedural SQL (PL/SQL), and Java. Oracle development technologies written externally to the database include products found in Oracle Developer Suite (Forms, Reports, and Discoverer), Oracle Application Server, and other third-generation languages (3GLs). There is also a wide variety of third-party tools and environments that can be used for developing applications that will connect to an Oracle database; in particular .NET from Microsoft, for which Oracle provides a comprehensive developers' toolkit.

Internal Languages

SQL is used for data-related activities but cannot be used on its own for developing complete applications. It has no real facilities for developing user interfaces, and it also lacks the procedural structures needed for advanced data manipulation. The other two languages available within the database fill these gaps. They are PL/SQL and Java. PL/SQL is a 3GL proprietary to Oracle. It supports the regular procedural constructs (such as conditional branching based on if-then-else and iterative looping) and facilities for user interface design. SQL calls may be embedded in the PL/SQL code. Thus, a PL/SQL application might use SQL to retrieve one or more rows from the database, perform various actions based on their content, and then issue more SQL to write rows back to the database. Java offers a similar capability to embed SQL calls within the Java code. This is industry-standard technology: any Java programmer should be able to write code that will work with an Oracle database (or indeed with any other Java-compliant database).

All Oracle DBAs must be fully acquainted with SQL and PL/SQL. This is assumed, and required, knowledge.

Knowledge of Java is not assumed and indeed is rarely required. A main reason for this is that bespoke Java applications are now rarely run within the database. Early releases of Oracle's application server could not run some of the industry-standard Java application components, such as servlets and Enterprise JavaBeans (EJBs). To get around this serious divergence from standards, Oracle implemented a Java engine within the database that did conform to the standards. However, from Oracle Application Server release 9i, it has been possible to run servlets and EJBs where they should be run: on the application server middle tier. Because of this, it has become less common to run Java within the database.

The DBA is likely to spend a large amount of time tuning and debugging SQL and PL/SQL. Oracle's model for the division of responsibility here is clear: the database administrator identifies code with problems and passes it to the developers for fixing. But in many cases, developers lack the skills (or perhaps the inclination) to do this and the database administrator has to fill this role.

TIP All DBAs must be fully acquainted with SQL and with PL/SQL. Knowledge of Java and other languages is not usually required but is often helpful.

External Languages

Other languages are available for developing client-server applications that run externally to the database. The most commonly used are C and Java, but it is possible to use most of the mainstream 3GLs. For most languages, Oracle provides the OCI (Oracle Call Interface) libraries that let code written in these languages connect to an Oracle database and invoke SQL commands.

Applications written in C or other procedural languages make use of the OCI libraries to establish sessions against the database server. These libraries are proprietary to Oracle. This means that any code using them will be specifically written for Oracle, and would have to be substantially rewritten before it could run against any other database. Java applications can avoid this problem. Oracle provides database connectivity for both *thick* and *thin* Java clients.

A thick Java client is Oracle aware. It uses the supplied OCI class library to connect to the database. This means that the application can make use of all the database's capabilities, including features that are unique to the Oracle environment. Java thick-client applications can exploit the database to the full. But they can never work with a third-party product, and they require the OCI client software to be installed.

A thin Java client is not aware of the database against which it is running: it works with a virtual database defined according to the Java standard, and it lets the container within which it is running map this virtual database onto the Oracle database. This gives the application portability across database versions and providers: a thin Java client application could be deployed in a non-Oracle environment without any changes. But any Oracle features that are not part of the Java database connectivity (JDBC) standard will not be available.

The choice between thick and thin Java clients should be made by a team of informed individuals and influenced by a number of factors, including performance; the need for Oracle-specific features; corporate standards; application portability; and programmer productivity. Oracle's JDeveloper tool can be used to develop both thick- and thin-client Java applications.

Oracle Developer Suite

Some organizations do not want to use a 3GL to develop database applications. Oracle Corporation provides rapid application development tools as part of the Oracle Developer Suite. Like the languages, these application development tools end up doing the same thing: constructing SQL statements that are sent to the database server for execution.

Oracle Forms Developer builds applications that run on an Oracle Application Server middle tier and display in a browser. Forms applications are generally quick to develop and are optimized for interfacing with database objects. Specialized triggers and components support feature-rich web-based database applications.

Oracle Reports is a tool for generating and formatting reports, either on demand or according to a schedule. Completed reports can be cached for distribution. Oracle Reports, like Forms, is a full development environment and requires a programmer to generate specialized reports. The huge advantage provided by Oracle Reports is that the output is infinitely customizable and end users can get exactly what they requested.

Oracle Discoverer is a tool for ad hoc report generation that empowers end users to develop reports themselves. Once Oracle Discoverer, which runs on an Oracle Application Server middle tier, has been appropriately configured, programmer input is not needed, since the end users do their own development.

Oracle Applications

The number of Oracle Applications products has increased substantially in recent years due to a large number of corporate acquisitions, but two remain predominant. The Oracle E-Business Suite is a comprehensive suite of applications based around an accounting engine, and Oracle Collaboration Suite is a set of office automation tools.

Oracle E-Business Suite, based around a core set of financial applications, includes facilities for accounting; human resources; manufacturing; customer relationship management; customer services; and much more. All the components share a common data model. The current release has a user interface written with Oracle Developer Forms and Java; it runs on Oracle Application Server and stores data in an Oracle database.

Oracle Collaboration Suite includes (among other things) servers for e-mail, diary management, voicemail and fax, web conferencing, and (perhaps most impressive) file serving. There is complete integration between the various components. The applications run on Oracle Application Servers, and can be accessed through a web interface from browsers or made available on mobile wireless devices.

Exercise 1-1: Investigate DBMSs in Your Environment   This is a paper-based exercise, with no specific solution.

Identify the applications, application servers, and databases used in your environment. Then, concentrating on the databases, try to get a feeling for how big and busy they are. Consider the number of users; the volatility of the data; the data volumes. Finally, consider how critical they are to the organization: how much downtime or data loss can be tolerated for each applications and database? Is it possible to put a financial figure on this?

The result of this exercise should indicate the criticality of the DBA's role.

Prerequisite Concepts

The Oracle Database Server product may be installed on a wide variety of hardware platforms and operating systems. Most companies prefer one of the popular Unix operating systems or Microsoft Windows. Increasingly, information technology graduates who opt to pursue a career in the world of Oracle Server technologies lack the exposure to Unix, and you are strongly advised (if you are in such a position), to consider courses on Unix fundamentals, shell scripting, and system administration. In smaller organizations, a DBA may very well concurrently fulfill the roles of system administrator and database administrator (and sometimes even, software developer). As organizations grow in size, IT departments become very segmented and specialized and it is common to have separate Operating Systems, Security, Development, and DBA departments. In fact, larger organizations often have DBA Teams working only with specific operating systems.

This section discusses several basic concepts you need to know to get up and running with an installation of the Oracle database. The actual installation is covered in Chapter 2.

Oracle Concepts

The Oracle Database Server comprises two primary components called the Instance and the Database. It is easy to get confused since the term "Database" is often used synonymously with the term "Server." The instance component refers to a set of operating system processes and memory structures initialized upon startup, while the database component refers to the physical files used for data storage and database operation. You must therefore expect your Oracle Server installation to consume memory, process, and disk resources on your server. Oracle supplies many tools you may use when interacting with the database, the most common of which are: Oracle Universal Installer (OUI), which is used to install and remove Oracle software;

Database Configuration Assistant (DBCA), which may be used to create, modify, or delete databases; and SQL*Plus and SQL Developer, which provide interfaces for writing and executing SQL. These tools are described in Chapter 2.

SQL Concepts

SQL is a powerful language integral to working with Oracle databases. We introduce the concepts of tables, rows, columns, and basic SQL queries here to support your learning as you perform the basic DBA tasks. A complete and thorough discussion of these concepts is detailed in Part 2 of this guide.

Tables, Rows, and Columns

Data in an Oracle database is primarily stored in two-dimensional relational tables. Each table consists of rows containing data that is segmented across each column. A table may contain many rows but has a fixed number of columns. Data about the Oracle Server itself is stored in a special set of tables known as *data dictionary* tables. Figure 1-3 shows the DICTIONARY table comprising two columns called TABLE_NAME and COMMENTS. Thirteen rows of data have been retrieved from this table.

Relational tables conform to certain rules that constrain and define the data. At the column level, each column must be of a certain data type, such as numeric, date-time, or character. The character data type is the most generic and allows the storage of any character data. At the row level, each row usually has some uniquely identifying characteristic: this could be the value of one column, such as the TABLE_NAME shown in the example just given, that cannot be repeated in different rows.

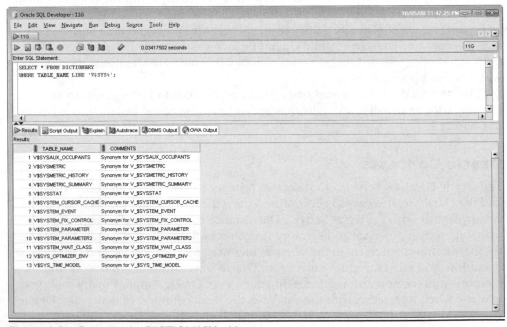

Figure 1-3   Querying the DICTIONARY table

Basic Queries

Figure 1-3 introduces a classic SQL query executed using the SQL Developer tool supplied by Oracle. There are many tools that provide a SQL interface to the database, the most common of which is SQL*Plus. Although the details of SQL queries are discussed in Part 2, they are generally intuitive, and for your immediate needs it is sufficient to interpret the query in Figure 1-3 as follows. The keywords in the statement are SELECT, FROM, WHERE, and LIKE. The asterisk in the first line instructs Oracle to retrieve all columns from the table called DICTIONARY. Therefore both columns, called TABLE_NAME and COMMENTS respectively, are retrieved. The second line contains a conditional WHERE clause that restricts the rows retrieved to only those which have a data value beginning with the characters "V$SYS" in the TABLE_NAME column.

Operating System Concepts

The database installation will consume physical disk storage, and you are encouraged to start considering the hardware you have earmarked for your installation. The two primary disk space consumers are Oracle program files and Oracle database *datafiles*. The program files are often referred to as the Oracle *binaries*, since they collectively represent the compiled C programs essential for creating and maintaining databases. Once the Oracle 11*g binaries* are installed, they consume about 3GB of disk space, but this usage remains relatively stable. The datafiles, however, host the actual rows of data and shrink and grow as the database is used. The default seed database that is relatively empty consumes about 2GB of disk space. Another important hardware consideration is memory (RAM). You will require a minimum of 512MB of RAM, but at least 1GB is required for a usable system.

Most Unix platforms require preinstallation tasks, which involve ensuring that operating system users, groups, patches, kernel parameters, and swap space are adequately specified. Consult with an operating system specialist if you are unfamiliar with these tasks. The superuser (or root) privilege is required to modify these operating system parameters. Commands for checking these resources are described in Chapter 2.

Single-Instance Architecture

In this book, you will deal largely with the most common database environment: one instance on one computer, opening a database stored on local disks. The more complex distributed architectures, involving multiple instances and multiple databases, are beyond the scope of the OCP examination (though not the OCM qualification), but you may realistically expect to see several high-level summary questions on distributed architectures.

Single-Instance Database Architecture

The instance consists of memory structures and processes. Its existence is transient, in your RAM and on your CPU(s). When you shut down the running instance, all trace of its existence goes away at the same time. The database consists of physical files, on disk. Whether running or stopped, these remain. Thus the lifetime of the instance is only as long as it exists in memory: it can be started and stopped. By contrast, the database, once created, persists indefinitely—until you deliberately delete the files that are associated with the database.

The processes that make up the instance are known as *background* processes because they are present and running at all times while the instance is active. These processes are for the most part completely self-administering, though in some cases it is possible for the DBA to influence the number of them and their operation.

The memory structures, which are implemented in shared memory segments provided by the operating system, are known as the *system global area,* or SGA. This is allocated at instance startup and released on shutdown. Within certain limits, the SGA in the 11g instance and the components within it can be resized while the instance is running, either automatically or in response to the DBA's instructions.

User sessions consist of a user process running locally to the user machine connecting to a server process running locally to the instance on the server machine. The technique for launching the server processes, which are started on demand for each session, is covered in Chapter 4. The connection between user process and server process is usually across a local area network and uses Oracle's proprietary Oracle Net protocol layered on top of an industry-standard protocol (usually TCP). The user process–to–server process split implements the client-server architecture: user processes generate SQL; server processes execute SQL. The server processes are sometimes referred to as *foreground* processes, in contrast with the background processes that make up the instance. Associated with each server process is an area of nonsharable memory, called the *program global area,* or PGA. This is private to the session, unlike the system global area, which is available to all the foreground and background processes. Note that background processes also have a PGA. The size of any one session's PGA will vary according to the memory needs of the session at any one time; the DBA can define an upper limit for the total of all the PGAs, and Oracle manages the allocation of this to sessions dynamically.

TIP You will sometimes hear the term *shadow process*. Be cautious of using this. Some people use it to refer to foreground processes; others use it for background processes.

Memory management in 11g can be completely automated: the DBA need do nothing more than specify an overall memory allocation for both the SGA and the PGA and let Oracle manage this memory as it thinks best. Alternatively, the DBA can determine memory allocations. There is an in-between technique, where the DBA defines certain limits on what the automatic management can do.

EXAM TIP SGA memory is shared across all background and foreground processes; PGA memory can be accessed only by the foreground process of the session to which it has been allocated. Both SGA and PGA memory can be automatically managed.

The physical structures that make up an Oracle database are the datafiles, the redo log, and the controlfile. Within the visible physical structure of the datafiles lie the logical structures seen by end users (developers, business analysts, data warehouse architects, and so on). The Oracle architecture guarantees abstraction of the logical from the physical: there is no need for a programmer to know the physical location of any data, since they only interact with logical structures, such as tables. Similarly, it is impossible for a system administrator to know what data resides in any physical structure: the operating system files, not their contents, are all that is visible. It is only you, the database administrator, who is permitted (and required) to see both sides of the story.

Data is stored in *datafiles*. There is no practical limit to the number or size of datafiles, and the abstraction of logical storage from physical storage means that datafiles can be moved or resized and more datafiles can be added without end users being aware of this. The relationship between physical and logical structures is maintained and documented in the data dictionary, which contains metadata describing the whole database. By querying certain views in the data dictionary, the DBA can determine precisely where every part of every table is located.

The *data dictionary* is a set of tables stored within the database. There is a recursive problem here: the instance needs to be aware of the physical and logical structure of the database, but the information describing this is itself within the database. The solution to this problem lies in the staged startup process, which is detailed in Chapter 3.

A requirement of the RDBMS standard is that the database must not lose data. This means that it must be backed up, and furthermore that any changes made to data between backups must be captured in such a manner that they can be applied to a restored backup. This is the forward recovery process. Oracle implements the capture of changes through the *redo log*. The redo log is a sequential record of all *change vectors* applied to data. A change vector is the alteration made by a DML (Data Manipulation Language: INSERT, UPDATE, or DELETE) statement. Whenever a user session makes any changes, the data itself in the data block is changed, and the change vector is written out to the redo log, in a form that makes it repeatable. Then in the event of damage to a datafile, a backup of the file can be restored and Oracle will extract the relevant change vectors from the redo log and apply them to the data blocks within the file. This ensures that work will never be lost—unless the damage to the database is so extensive as to lose not only one or more datafiles, but also either their backups or the redo log.

The *controlfile* stores the details of the physical structures of the database and is the starting point for the link to the logical structures. When an instance opens a database, it begins by reading the controlfile. Within the controlfile is information the instance can then use to connect to the rest of the database, and the data dictionary within it.

The architecture of a single-instance database can be summarized as consisting of four interacting components:

- A user interacts with a user process.
- A user process interacts with a server process.
- A server process interacts with an instance.
- An instance interacts with a database.

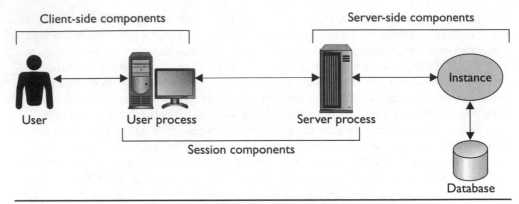

Client-side components

Server-side components

User

User process

Server process

Instance

Session components

Database

Figure 1-4   The indirect connection between a user and a database

Figure 1-4 represents this graphically.

It is absolutely impossible for any client-side process to have any contact with the database: all access must be mediated by server-side processes. The client-server split is between the user process, which generates SQL, and the server process, which executes it.

Distributed Systems Architectures

In the single-instance environment, one instance opens one database. In a distributed environment, there are various possibilities for grouping instances and databases. Principally:

- Real Application Clusters (RAC), where multiple instances open one database
- Streams, where multiple Oracle servers propagate transactions between each other
- Dataguard, where a primary database updates a standby database

Combinations of these options can result in a system that can achieve the goals of 100 percent uptime and no data loss, with limitless scalability and performance.

Real Application Clusters (RAC)

RAC provides amazing capabilities for performance, fault tolerance, and scalability (and possibly cost savings) and is integral to the Oracle's concept of the Grid. With previous releases, RAC (or its precursor, Oracle Parallel Server) was an expensive add-on option, but from database release 10g onward, RAC is bundled with the Standard Edition license. This is an indication of how much Oracle Corporation wants to push users toward the RAC environment. Standard Edition RAC is limited to a certain number of computers and a certain number of CPUs and cores per computer, but even within these limitations it gives access to a phenomenally powerful environment. RAC is an extra-cost option for the Enterprise Edition, where the scalability becomes effectively limitless: bounded only by the clustering capacity of the underlying operating system and hardware.

A RAC database can be configured for 100 percent uptime. One instance can be brought down (either for planned maintenance, or perhaps because the computer on which it is running crashes) and the database will remain accessible through a surviving instance on another machine. Sessions against the failed instance can be reestablished against a surviving instance without the end user being aware of any disruption.

Transparent scalability comes from the ability to add instances, running on different machines, to a RAC dynamically. They will automatically take on some of the workload without users needing to be aware of the fact that now more instances are available.

Some applications will have a performance benefit from running on a RAC. Parallel processing can improve the performance of some work, such as long-running queries and large batch updates. In a single-instance database, assigning multiple parallel execution servers to such jobs will help—but they will all be running in one instance on one machine. In a RAC database, the parallel execution servers can run on different instances, which may get around some of the bottlenecks inherent in single-instance architecture. Other work, such as processing the large number of small transactions typically found in an OLTP system, will not gain a performance benefit.

 TIP Don't convert to RAC just because you can. You need to be certain of what you want to achieve before embarking on what is a major exercise that may not be necessary.

Streams

There are various circumstances that make it desirable to transfer data from one database to another. Fault tolerance is one: if an organization has two (or more) geographically separated databases, both containing identical data and both available at all times for users to work on, then no matter what goes wrong at one site, work should be able to continue uninterrupted at the other. Another reason is tuning: the two databases can be configured for different types of work, such as a transaction processing database and a data warehouse.

Keeping the databases synchronized will have to be completely automatic, and all changes made at either site will need to be propagated in real or near-real time to the other site. Another reason could be maintenance of a data warehouse. Data sets maintained by an OLTP database will need to be propagated to the warehouse database, and subsequently these copies will need to be periodically refreshed with changes. The data might then be pushed further out, perhaps to a series of data marts, each with a subset of the warehouse. Streams is a facility for capturing changes made to tables and applying them to remote copies of the tables.

Streams can be bidirectional: identical tables at two or more sites, with all user transactions executed at each site broadcast to and applied at the other sites. This is the streaming model needed for fault tolerance. An alternative model is used in the data warehouse example, where data sets (and ensuing changes made to them) are extracted from tables in one database and pushed out to tables in another database. In this model, the flow of information is more likely to be unidirectional, and the table structures may well not be identical at the downstream sites.

Dataguard

Dataguard systems have one primary database against which transactions are executed, and one or more standby databases used for fault tolerance or for query processing. The standbys are instantiated from a backup of the primary, and updated (possibly in real time) with all changes applied to the primary.

Standbys come in two forms. A *physical* standby is byte-for-byte identical with the primary, for the purpose of zero data loss. Even if the primary is totally destroyed, all data will be available on the standby. The change vectors applied to the primary are propagated to the physical standby in the form of redo records, and applied as though a restored backup database were being recovered. A *logical* standby contains the same data as the primary, but with possibly different data structures, typically to facilitate query processing. The primary database may have data structures (typically indexes) optimized for transaction processing, while the logical standby may have structures optimized for data warehouse type work. Change vectors that keep the logical standby in synch with the primary are propagated in the form of SQL statements, using the Streams mechanism.

Exercise 1-2: Determine if the Database Is Single Instance or Part of a Distributed System   In this exercise, you will run queries to determine whether the database is a self-contained system, or if it is part of a larger distributed environment. Either SQL Developer or SQL*Plus may be used. If you do not have access to an Oracle database yet to practice this exercise, you can skip to Chapter 2, complete an installation, and return to this exercise.

1. Connect to the database as user SYSTEM.

2. Determine if the instance is part of a RAC database:

```
select parallel from v$instance;
```

This will return NO if it is a single-instance database.

3. Determine if the database is protected against data loss by a standby database:

```
select protection_level from v$database;
```

This will return UNPROTECTED if the database is indeed unprotected.

4. Determine if Streams has been configured in the database:

```
select * from dba_streams_administrator;
```

This will return no rows, if Streams has never been configured.

Instance Memory Structures

An Oracle instance consists of a block of shared memory known as the system global area, or SGA, and a number of background processes. The SGA contains three mandatory data structures:

- The database buffer cache
- The log buffer
- The shared pool

It may, optionally, also contain

- A large pool
- A Java pool
- A Streams pool

These memory structures are depicted in Figure 1-5, and the three primary structures are detailed in the sections that follow.

User sessions also need memory on the server side. This is nonsharable and is known as the program global area, or PGA. Each session will have its own, private PGA.

Managing the size of these structures can be largely automatic, or the DBA can control the sizing himself. It is generally good practice to use the automatic management.

EXAM TIP Which SGA structures are required, and which are optional? The database buffer cache, log buffer, and shared pool are required; the large pool, Java pool, and Streams pool are optional.

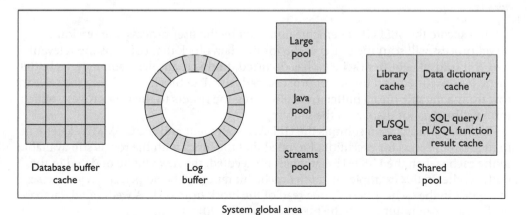

Figure 1-5   The key memory structures present in the SGA

The Database Buffer Cache

The *database buffer cache* is Oracle's work area for executing SQL. When updating data, users' sessions don't directly update the data on disk. The data blocks containing the data of interest are first copied into the database buffer cache (if they are not already there). Changes (such as inserting new rows and deleting or modifying existing rows) are applied to these copies of the data blocks in the database buffer cache. The blocks will remain in the cache for some time afterward, until the buffer they are occupying is needed for caching another block.

When querying data, the data also goes via the cache. The session works out which blocks contain the rows of interest and copies them into the database buffer cache (if they are not already there); the relevant rows are then transferred into the session's PGA for further processing. And again, the blocks remain in the database buffer cache for some time afterward.

Take note of the term *block*. Datafiles are formatted into fixed-sized blocks. Table rows, and other data objects such as index keys, are stored in these blocks. The database buffer cache is formatted into memory buffers each sized to hold one block. Unlike blocks, rows are of variable length; the length of a row will depend on the number of columns defined for the table, whether the columns actually have anything in them, and if so, what. Depending on the size of the blocks (which is chosen by the DBA) and the size of the rows (which is dependent on the table design and usage), there may be several rows per block or possibly a row may stretch over several blocks. The structure of a data block will be described in the section "Database Storage Structures" later in this chapter.

Ideally, all the blocks containing data that is frequently accessed will be in the database buffer cache, therefore minimizing the need for disk I/O. As a typical use of the database buffer cache, consider a sales rep in the online store retrieving a customer record and updating it, with these statements:

```
select customer_id, customer_name from customers;
update customers set customer_name='Sid' where customer_id=100;
commit;
```

To execute the SELECT statement submitted by the user process, the session's server process will scan the buffer cache for the data block that contains the relevant row. If it finds it, a buffer cache *hit* has occurred. In this example, assume that a buffer cache *miss* occurred and the server process reads the data block containing the relevant row from a datafile into a buffer, before sending the results to the user process, which formats the data for display to the sales rep.

The user process then submits the UPDATE statement and the COMMIT statement to the server process for execution. Provided that the block with the row is still available in the cache when the UPDATE statement is executed, the row will be updated in the buffer cache. In this example, the buffer cache hit ratio will be 50 percent: two accesses of a block in the cache, but only one read of the block from disk. A well-tuned database buffer cache can result in a cache hit ratio well over 90 percent.

A buffer storing a block whose image in the cache is not the same as the image on disk is often referred to as a *dirty* buffer. A buffer will be *clean* when a block is first copied into it: at that point, the block image in the buffer is the same as the block image on disk. The buffer will become dirty when the block in it is updated. Eventually, dirty buffers must be written back to the datafiles, at which point the buffer will be clean again. Even after being written to disk, the block remains in memory; it is possible that the buffer will not be overwritten with another block for some time.

Note that there is no correlation between the frequency of updates to a buffer (or the number of COMMITs) and when it gets written back to the datafiles. The write to the datafiles is done by the database writer background process.

The size of the database buffer cache is critical for performance. The cache should be sized adequately for caching all the frequently accessed blocks (whether clean or dirty), but not so large that it caches blocks that are rarely needed. An undersized cache will result in excessive disk activity, as frequently accessed blocks are continually read from disk, used, overwritten by other blocks, and then read from disk again. An oversized cache is not so bad (so long as it is not so large that the operating system has to swap pages of virtual memory in and out of real memory) but can cause problems; for example, startup of an instance is slower if it involves formatting a massive database buffer cache.

TIP Determining the optimal size of the database buffer cache is application specific and a matter of performance tuning. It is impossible to give anything but the vaguest guidelines without detailed observations, but it is probably true to say that the majority of databases will operate well with a cache sized in hundreds of megabytes up to a few gigabytes. Very few applications will perform well with a cache smaller than this, and not many will need a cache of hundreds of gigabytes.

The database buffer cache is allocated at instance startup time. Prior to release 9i of the database it was not possible to resize the database buffer cache subsequently without restarting the database instance, but from 9i onward it can be resized up or down at any time. This resizing can be either manual or (from release 10g onward) automatic according to workload, if the automatic mechanism has been enabled.

TIP The size of the database buffer cache can be adjusted dynamically and can be automatically managed.

The Log Buffer

The *log buffer* is a small, short-term staging area for change vectors before they are written to the redo log on disk. A *change vector* is a modification applied to something; executing DML statements generates change vectors applied to data. The redo log is the database's guarantee that data will never be lost. Whenever a data block is changed, the change vectors applied to the block are written out to the redo log, from which they can be extracted and applied to datafile backups if it is ever necessary to restore a datafile.

Redo is not written directly to the redo log files by session server processes. If it were, the sessions would have to wait for disk I/O operations to complete whenever they executed a DML statement. Instead, sessions write redo to the log buffer, in memory. This is much faster than writing to disk. The log buffer (which may contain change vectors from many sessions, interleaved with each other) is then written out to the redo log files. One write of the log buffer to disk may therefore be a batch of many change vectors from many transactions. Even so, the change vectors in the log buffer are written to disk in very nearly real time—and when a session issues a COMMIT statement, the log buffer write really does happen in real time. The writes are done by the log writer background process, the LGWR.

The log buffer is small (in comparison with other memory structures) because it is a very short-term storage area. Change vectors are inserted into it and are streamed to disk in near real time. There is no need for it to be more than a few megabytes at the most, and indeed making it much bigger than the default value can be seriously bad for performance. The default is determined by the Oracle server and is based on the number of CPUs on the server node.

It is not possible to create a log buffer smaller than the default. If you attempt to, it will be set to the default size anyway. It is possible to create a log buffer larger than the default, but this is often not a good idea. The problem is that when a COMMIT statement is issued, part of the commit processing involves writing the contents of the log buffer to the redo log files on disk. This write occurs in real time, and while it is in progress, the session that issued the COMMIT will hang. Commit processing is a critical part of the Oracle architecture. The guarantee that a committed transaction will never be lost is based on this: the commit-complete message is not returned to the session until the data blocks in the cache have been changed (which means that the transaction has been completed) and the change vectors have been written to the redo log on disk (and therefore the transaction could be recovered if necessary). A large log buffer means that potentially there is more to write when a COMMIT is issued, and therefore it may take a longer time before the commit-complete message can be sent, and the session can resume work.

TIP Raising the log buffer size above the default may be necessary for some applications, but as a rule start tuning with the log buffer at its default size.

The log buffer is allocated at instance startup, and it cannot be resized without restarting the instance. It is a circular buffer. As server processes write change vectors to it, the current write address moves around. The log writer process writes the vectors out in batches, and as it does so, the space they occupied becomes available and can be overwritten by more change vectors. It is possible that at times of peak activity, change vectors will be generated faster than the log writer process can write them out. If this happens, all DML activity will cease (for a few milliseconds) while the log writer clears the buffer.

The process of flushing the log buffer to disk is one of the ultimate bottlenecks in the Oracle architecture. You cannot do DML faster than the LGWR can flush the change vectors to the online redo log files.

TIP If redo generation is the limiting factor in a database's performance, the only option is to go to RAC. In a RAC database, each instance has its own log buffer, and its own LGWR. This is the only way to parallelize writing redo data to disk.

EXAM TIP The size of the log buffer is static, fixed at instance startup. It cannot be automatically managed.

The Shared Pool

The *shared pool* is the most complex of the SGA structures. It is divided into dozens of substructures, all of which are managed internally by the Oracle server. This discussion of architecture will briefly discuss only four of the shared pool components:

- The library cache
- The data dictionary cache
- The PL/SQL area
- The SQL query and PL/SQL function result cache

Several other shared pool structures are described in later chapters. All the structures within the shared pool are automatically managed. Their size will vary according to the pattern of activity against the instance, within the overall size of the shared pool. The shared pool itself can be resized dynamically, either in response to the DBA's instructions or through being managed automatically.

EXAM TIP The shared pool size is dynamic and can be automatically managed.

The Library Cache

The *library cache* is a memory area for storing recently executed code, in its parsed form. *Parsing* is the conversion of code written by programmers into something executable, and it is a process which Oracle does on demand. By caching parsed code in the shared pool, it can be reused greatly improving performance. Parsing SQL code takes time. Consider a simple SQL statement:

```
select * from products where product_id=100;
```

Before this statement can be executed, the Oracle server has to work out what it means, and how to execute it. To begin with, what is products? Is it a table, a synonym, or a view? Does it even exist? Then the "*"—what are the columns that make up the products table (if it is a table)? Does the user have permission to see the table? Answers to these questions and many others have to be found by querying the data dictionary.

TIP The algorithm used to find SQL in the library cache is based on the ASCII values of the characters that make up the statement. The slightest difference (even something as trivial as SELECT instead of select) means that the statement will not match but will be parsed again.

Having worked out what the statement actually means, the server has to decide how best to execute it. Is there an index on the product_id column? If so, would it be quicker to use the index to locate the row, or to scan the whole table? More queries against the data dictionary? It is quite possible for a simple one-line query against a user table to generate dozens of queries against the data dictionary, and for the parsing of a statement to take many times longer than eventually executing it. The purpose of the library cache of the shared pool is to store statements in their parsed form, ready for execution. The first time a statement is issued, it has to be parsed before execution—the second time, it can be executed immediately. In a well-designed application, it is possible that statements may be parsed once and executed millions of times. This saves a huge amount of time.

The Data Dictionary Cache

The data dictionary cache is sometimes referred to as the row cache. Whichever term you prefer, it stores recently used object definitions: descriptions of tables, indexes, users, and other metadata definitions. Keeping such definitions in memory in the SGA, where they are immediately accessible to all sessions, rather than each session having to read them repeatedly from the data dictionary on disk, enhances parsing performance.

The data dictionary cache stores object definitions so that when statements do have to be parsed, they can be parsed quickly—without having to query the data dictionary. Consider what happens if these statements are issued consecutively:

```
select sum(order_amount) from orders;
select * from orders where order_no=100;
```

Both statements must be parsed because they are different statements—but parsing the first SELECT statement will have loaded the definition of the orders table and its columns into the data dictionary cache, so parsing the second statement will be faster than it would otherwise have been, because no data dictionary access will be needed.

 TIP Shared pool tuning is usually oriented toward making sure that the library cache is the right size. This is because the algorithms Oracle uses to allocate memory in the SGA are designed to favor the dictionary cache, so if the library cache is correct, then the dictionary cache will already be correct.

The PL/SQL Area

Stored PL/SQL objects are procedures, functions, packaged procedures and functions, object type definitions, and triggers. These are all stored in the data dictionary, as source code and also in their compiled form. When a stored PL/SQL object is invoked by a session, it must be read from the data dictionary. To prevent repeated reading, the objects are then cached in the PL/SQL area of the shared pool.

The first time a PL/SQL object is used, it must be read from the data dictionary tables on disk, but subsequent invocations will be much faster, because the object will already be available in the PL/SQL area of the shared pool.

 TIP PL/SQL can be issued from user processes, rather than being stored in the data dictionary. This is called *anonymous* PL/SQL. Anonymous PL/SQL cannot be cached and reused but must be compiled dynamically. It will therefore always perform worse than stored PL/SQL. Developers should be encouraged to convert all anonymous PL/SQL into stored PL/SQL.

The SQL Query and PL/SQL Function Result Cache

The result cache is a release 11g new feature. In many applications, the same query is executed many times, by either the same session or many different sessions. Creating a result cache lets the Oracle server store the results of such queries in memory. The next time the query is issued, rather than running the query the server can retrieve the cached result.

The result cache mechanism is intelligent enough to track whether the tables against which the query was run have been updated. If this has happened, the query results will be invalidated and the next time the query is issued, it will be rerun. There is therefore no danger of ever receiving an out-of-date cached result.

The PL/SQL result cache uses a similar mechanism. When a PL/SQL function is executed, its return value can be cached, ready for the next time the function is executed. If the parameters passed to the function, or the tables that the function queries, are different, the function will be reevaluated; otherwise, the cached value will be returned.

By default, use of the SQL query and PL/SQL function result cache is disabled, but if enabled programmatically, it can often dramatically improve performance. The cache is within the shared pool, and unlike the other memory areas described previously, it does afford the DBA some control, as a maximum size can be specified.

Sizing the Shared Pool

Sizing the shared pool is critical for performance. It should be large enough to cache all the frequently executed code and frequently needed object definitions (in the library cache and the data dictionary cache) but not so large that it caches statements that have only been executed once. An undersized shared pool cripples performance because server sessions have repeatedly to grab space in it for parsing statements, which are then overwritten by other statements and therefore have to be parsed again when they are reexecuted. An oversized shared pool can impact badly on performance because it takes too long to search it. If the shared pool is less than the optimal size, performance will degrade. But there is a minimum size below which statements will fail.

Memory in the shared pool is allocated according to an LRU (least recently used) algorithm. When the Oracle server needs space in the shared pool, it will overwrite the object that has been unused for the longest time. If the object is later needed again, it will have to be reloaded—possibly displacing another object in the shared pool.

TIP Determining the optimal size is a matter for performance tuning, but it is probably safe to say that most databases will need a shared pool of several hundred megabytes. Some applications will need more than a gigabyte, and very few will perform adequately with less than a hundred megabytes.

The shared pool is allocated at instance startup time. Prior to release 9*i* of the database it was not possible to resize the shared pool subsequently without restarting the database instance, but from 9*i* onward it can be resized up or down at any time. This resizing can be either manual or (from release 10*g* onward) automatic according to workload, if the automatic mechanism has been enabled.

 EXAM TIP The shared pool size is dynamic and can be automatically managed.

The Large Pool

The large pool is an optional area that, if created, will be used automatically by various processes that would otherwise take memory from the shared pool. One major use of the large pool is by shared server processes, described in Chapter 4 in the section "Use the Oracle Shared Server Architecture." Parallel execution servers will also use the large pool, if there is one. In the absence of a large pool, these processes will use memory on the shared pool. This can cause contention for the shared pool, which may have negative results. If shared servers or parallel servers are being used, a large pool should always be created. Some I/O processes may also make use of the large pool, such as the processes used by the Recovery Manager when it is backing up to a tape device.

Sizing the large pool is not a matter for performance. If a process needs the large pool of memory, it will fail with an error if that memory is not available. Allocating more memory than is needed will not make statements run faster. Furthermore, if a large pool exists, it will be used: it is not possible for a statement to start off by using the large pool, and then revert to the shared pool if the large pool is too small.

From 9*i* release 2 onward it is possible to create and to resize a large pool after instance startup. With earlier releases, it had to be defined at startup and was a fixed size. From release 10*g* onward, creation and sizing of the large pool can be completely automatic.

 EXAM TIP The large pool size is dynamic and can be automatically managed.

The Java Pool

The Java pool is only required if your application is going to run Java stored procedures within the database: it is used for the heap space needed to instantiate the Java objects. However, a number of Oracle options are written in Java, so the Java pool is considered standard nowadays. Note that Java code is not cached in the Java pool: it is cached in the shared pool, in the same way that PL/SQL code is cached.

The optimal size of the Java pool is dependent on the Java application, and how many sessions are running it. Each session will require heap space for its objects. If the Java pool is undersized, performance may degrade due to the need to continually reclaim space. In an EJB (Enterprise JavaBean) application, an object such as a stateless session bean may be instantiated and used, and then remain in memory in case it is needed again: such an object can be reused immediately. But if the Oracle server has had to destroy the bean to make room for another, then it will have to be reinstantiated next time it is needed. If the Java pool is chronically undersized, then the applications may simply fail.

From 10g onward it is possible to create and to resize a large pool after instance startup; this creation and sizing of the large pool can be completely automatic. With earlier releases, it had to be defined at startup and was a fixed size.

 EXAM TIP The Java pool size is dynamic and can be automatically managed.

The Streams Pool

The Streams pool is used by Oracle Streams. This is an advanced tool that is beyond the scope of the OCP examinations or this book, but for completeness a short description follows.

The mechanism used by Streams is to extract change vectors from the redo log and to reconstruct statements that were executed from these—or statements that would have the same net effect. These statements are executed at the remote database. The processes that extract changes from redo and the processes that apply the changes need memory: this memory is the Streams pool. From database release 10g it is possible to create and to resize the Streams pool after instance startup; this creation and sizing can be completely automatic. With earlier releases it had to be defined at startup and was a fixed size.

 EXAM TIP The Streams pool size is dynamic and can be automatically managed.

Exercise 1-3: Investigate the Memory Structures of the Instance   In this exercise, you will run queries to determine the current sizing of various memory structures that make up the instance. Either SQL Developer or SQL*Plus may be used.

1. Connect to the database as user SYSTEM.

2. Show the current, maximum, and minimum sizes of the SGA components that can be dynamically resized:

```
select COMPONENT,CURRENT_SIZE,MIN_SIZE,MAX_SIZE
from v$sga_dynamic_components;
```

This illustration shows the result on an example database:

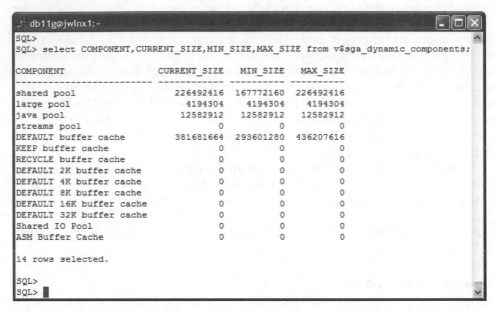

```
db11g@jwlnx1:~                                                        _ □ X
SQL>
SQL> select COMPONENT,CURRENT_SIZE,MIN_SIZE,MAX_SIZE from v$sga_dynamic_components;

COMPONENT                  CURRENT_SIZE   MIN_SIZE    MAX_SIZE
-------------------------  ------------   ----------  ----------
shared pool                  226492416    167772160   226492416
large pool                     4194304      4194304     4194304
java pool                     12582912     12582912    12582912
streams pool                         0            0           0
DEFAULT buffer cache         381681664    293601280   436207616
KEEP buffer cache                    0            0           0
RECYCLE buffer cache                 0            0           0
DEFAULT 2K buffer cache              0            0           0
DEFAULT 4K buffer cache              0            0           0
DEFAULT 8K buffer cache              0            0           0
DEFAULT 16K buffer cache             0            0           0
DEFAULT 32K buffer cache             0            0           0
Shared IO Pool                       0            0           0
ASM Buffer Cache                     0            0           0

14 rows selected.

SQL>
SQL>
```

The example shows an instance without Streams, hence a Streams pool of size zero. Neither the large pool nor the Java pool has changed since instance startup, but there have been changes made to the sizes of the shared pool and database buffer cache. Only the default pool of the database buffer cache has been configured; this is usual, except in highly tuned databases.

3. Determine how much memory has been, and is currently, allocated to program global areas:

```
select name,value from v$pgastat
where name in ('maximum PGA allocated','total PGA allocated');
```

Instance Process Structures

The instance background processes are the processes that are launched when the instance is started and run until it is terminated. There are five background processes that have a long history with Oracle; these are the first five described in the sections that follow: System Monitor (SMON), Process Monitor (PMON), Database Writer (DBWn), Log Writer (LGWR), and Checkpoint Process (CKPT). A number of others have been introduced with the more recent releases; notable among these are Manageability Monitor (MMON) and Memory Manager (MMAN). There are also some that are not essential but will exist in most instances. These include Archiver (ARCn) and Recoverer (RECO). Others will exist only if certain options have been enabled. This last group includes the processes required for RAC and Streams. Additionally, some processes exist that are not properly documented (or are not documented at all). The processes described here are those that every OCP candidate will be expected to know.

Figure 1-6 provides a high-level description of the typical interaction of several key processes and SGA memory structures. The server process is representative of the server side of a client-server connection, with the client component consisting of a user session and user process described earlier. The server process interacts with the datafiles to fetch a data block into the buffer cache. This may be modified by some DML, dirtying the block in the buffer cache. The change vector is copied into the circular log buffer that is flushed in almost real-time by the log writer process (LGWR) to the online redo log files. If archivelog mode of the database is configured, the archiver process (ARCn) copies the online redo log files to an archive location. Eventually, some condition may cause the database writer process (DBWn) to write the dirty block to one of the datafiles. The mechanics of the background processes and their interaction with various SGA structures are detailed in the sections that follow.

There is a platform variation that must be cleared up before discussing processes. On Linux and Unix, all the Oracle processes are separate operating system processes, each with a unique process number. On Windows, there is one operating system process (called ORACLE.EXE) for the whole instance: the Oracle processes run as separate threads within this one process.

SMON, the System Monitor

SMON initially has the task of mounting and opening a database. The steps involved in this are described in detail in Chapter 3. In brief, SMON *mounts* a database by locating and validating the database controlfile. It then *opens* a database by locating and validating all the datafiles and online log files. Once the database is opened and in use, SMON is responsible for various housekeeping tasks, such as coalescing free space in datafiles.

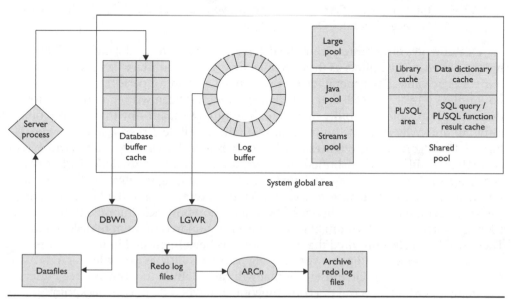

Figure 1-6   Typical interaction of instance processes and the SGA

PMON, the Process Monitor

A user session is a user process that is connected to a server process. The server process is launched when the session is created and destroyed when the session ends. An orderly exit from a session involves the user logging off. When this occurs, any work done will be completed in an orderly fashion, and the server process will be terminated. If the session is terminated in a disorderly manner (perhaps because the user's PC is rebooted), then the session will be left in a state that must be cleared up. PMON monitors all the server processes and detects any problems with the sessions. If a session has terminated abnormally, PMON will destroy the server process, return its PGA memory to the operating system's free memory pool, and roll back any incomplete transaction that may have been in progress.

 EXAM TIP If a session terminates abnormally, what will happen to an active transaction? It will be rolled back, by the PMON background process.

DBWn, the Database Writer

Always remember that sessions do not as a general rule write to disk. They write data (or changes to existing data) to buffers in the database buffer cache. It is the database writer that subsequently writes the buffers to disk. It is possible for an instance to have several database writers (up to a maximum of twenty), which will be called DBW0, DBW1, and so on: hence the use of the term DBWn to refer to "the" database writer. The default is one database writer per eight CPUs, rounded up.

 TIP How many database writers do you need? The default number may well be correct. Adding more may help performance, but usually you should look at tuning memory first. As a rule, before you optimize disk I/O, ask why there is any need for disk I/O.

DBWn writes dirty buffers from the database buffer cache to the datafiles—but it does not write the buffers as they become dirty. On the contrary: it writes as few buffers as possible. The general idea is that disk I/O is bad for performance, so don't do it unless it really is needed. If a block in a buffer has been written to by a session, there is a reasonable possibility that it will be written to again—by that session, or a different one. Why write the buffer to disk, if it may well be dirtied again in the near future? The algorithm DBWn uses to select dirty buffers for writing to disk (which will clean them) will select only buffers that have not been recently used. So if a buffer is very busy, because sessions are repeatedly reading or writing it, DBWn will not write it to disk. There could be hundreds or thousands of writes to a buffer before DBWn cleans it. It could be that in a buffer cache of a million buffers, a hundred thousand of them are dirty—but DBWn might only write a few hundred of them to disk at a time. These will be the few hundred that no session has been interested in for some time.

DBWn writes according to a very lazy algorithm: as little as possible, as rarely as possible. There are four circumstances that will cause DBWn to write: no free buffers, too many dirty buffers, a three-second timeout, and when there is a checkpoint.

EXAM TIP What will cause DBWR to write? No free buffers, too many dirty buffers, a three-second timeout, or a checkpoint.

First, when there are no free buffers. If a server process needs to copy a block into the database buffer cache, it must find a *free buffer*. A free buffer is a buffer that is neither dirty (updated, and not yet written back to disk) nor pinned (a pinned buffer is one that is being used by another session at that very moment). A dirty buffer must not be overwritten because if it were changed, data would be lost, and a pinned buffer cannot be overwritten because the operating system's memory protection mechanisms will not permit this. If a server process takes too long (this length of time is internally determined by Oracle) to find a free buffer, it signals the DBWn to write some dirty buffers to disk. Once this is done, these will be clean, free, and available for use.

Second, there may be too many dirty buffers—"too many" being another internal threshold. No one server process may have had a problem finding a free buffer, but overall, there could be a large number of dirty buffers: this will cause DBWn to write some of them to disk.

Third, there is a three-second timeout: every three seconds, DBWn will clean a few buffers. In practice, this event may not be significant in a production system because the two previously described circumstances will be forcing the writes, but the timeout does mean that even if the system is idle, the database buffer cache will eventually be cleaned.

Fourth, there may be a checkpoint requested. The three reasons already given will cause DBWn to write a limited number of dirty buffers to the datafiles. When a checkpoint occurs, all dirty buffers are written. This could mean hundreds of thousands of them. During a checkpoint, disk I/O rates may hit the roof, CPU usage may go to 100 percent, end user sessions may experience degraded performance, and people may start complaining. Then when the checkpoint is complete (which may take several minutes), performance will return to normal. So why have checkpoints? The short answer is, don't have them unless you have to.

 EXAM TIP What does DBWn do when a transaction is committed? It does absolutely nothing.

The only moment when a checkpoint is absolutely necessary is as the database is closed and the instance is shut down—a full description of this sequence is given in Chapter 3. A checkpoint writes all dirty buffers to disk: this synchronizes the buffer cache with the datafiles, the instance with the database. During normal operation, the datafiles are always out of date, as they may be missing changes (committed and uncommitted). This does not matter, because the copies of blocks in the buffer cache are up to date, and it is these that the sessions work on. But on shutdown, it is necessary to write everything to disk. Automatic checkpoints only occur on shutdown, but a checkpoint can be forced at any time with this statement:

```
alter system checkpoint;
```

Note that from release 8i onward, checkpoints do not occur on log switch (log switches are discussed in Chapter 14).

The checkpoint described so far is a full checkpoint. Partial checkpoints occur more frequently; they force DBWn to write all the dirty buffers containing blocks from just one or more datafiles rather than the whole database: when a datafile or tablespace is taken offline; when a tablespace is put into backup mode; when a tablespace is made read only. These are less drastic than full checkpoints and occur automatically whenever the relevant event happens.

To conclude, the DBWn writes on a very lazy algorithm: as little as possible, as rarely as possible—except when a checkpoint occurs, when all dirty buffers are written to disk, as fast as possible.

LGWR, the Log Writer

LGWR writes the contents of the log buffer to the online log files on disk. A write of the log buffer to the online redo log files is often referred to as *flushing* the log buffer.

When a session makes any change (by executing INSERT, UPDATE, or DELETE commands) to blocks in the database buffer cache, before it applies the change to the block it writes out the change vector that it is about to apply to the log buffer. To avoid loss of work, these change vectors must be written to disk with only minimal delay. To this end, the LGWR streams the contents of the log buffer to the online redo log files on disk in very nearly real-time. And when a session issues a COMMIT, the LGWR writes in real-time: the session hangs, while LGWR writes the buffer to disk. Only then is the transaction recorded as committed, and therefore nonreversible.

LGWR is one of the ultimate bottlenecks in the Oracle architecture. It is impossible to perform DML faster than LGWR can write the change vectors to disk. There are three circumstances that will cause LGWR to flush the log buffer: if a session issues a COMMIT; if the log buffer is one-third full; if DBWn is about to write dirty buffers.

First, the write-on-commit. To process a COMMIT, the server process inserts a commit record into the log buffer. It will then hang, while LGWR flushes the log buffer to disk. Only when this write has completed is a commit-complete message returned to the session, and the server process can then continue working. This is the guarantee that transactions will never be lost: every change vector for a committed transaction will be available in the redo log on disk and can therefore be applied to datafile backups. Thus, if the database is ever damaged, it can be restored from backup and all work done since the backup was made can be redone.

 TIP It is in fact possible to prevent the LGWR write-on-commit. If this is done, sessions will not have to wait for LGWR when they commit: they issue the command and then carry on working. This will improve performance but also means that work can be lost. It becomes possible for a session to COMMIT, then for the instance to crash before LGWR has saved the change vectors. Enable this with caution! It is dangerous, and hardly ever necessary. There are only a few applications where performance is more important than data loss.

Second, when the log buffer is one-third full, LGWR will flush it to disk. This is done primarily for performance reasons. If the log buffer is small (as it usually should be) this one-third-full trigger will force LGWR to write the buffer to disk in very nearly real time even if no one is committing transactions. The log buffer for many applications will be optimally sized at only a few megabytes. The application will generate enough redo to fill one third of this in a fraction of a second, so LGWR will be forced to stream the change vectors to disk continuously, in very nearly real time. Then, when a session does COMMIT, there will be hardly anything to write: so the COMMIT will complete almost instantaneously.

Third, when DBWn needs to write dirty buffers from the database buffer cache to the datafiles, before it does so it will signal LGWR to flush the log buffer to the online redo log files. This is to ensure that it will always be possible to reverse an uncommitted transaction. The mechanism of transaction rollback is fully explained in Chapter 8. For now, it is necessary to know that it is entirely possible for DBWn to write an uncommitted transaction to the datafiles. This is fine, so long as the undo data needed to reverse the transaction is guaranteed to be available. Generating undo data also generates change vectors. As these will be in the redo log files before the datafiles are updated, the undo data needed to roll back a transaction (should this be necessary) can be reconstructed if necessary.

Note that it can be said that there is a three-second timeout that causes LGWR to write. In fact, the timeout is on DBWR—but because LGWR will always write just before DBWn, in effect there is a three-second timeout on LGWR as well.

EXAM TIP When will LGWR flush the log buffer to disk? On COMMIT, when the buffer is one-third full; just before DBWn writes.

CKPT, the Checkpoint Process

The purpose of the CKPT changed dramatically between release 8 and release 8i of the Oracle database. In release 8 and earlier, checkpoints were necessary at regular intervals to make sure that in the event of an instance failure (for example, if the server machine should be rebooted) the database could be *recovered* quickly. These checkpoints were initiated by CKPT. The process of recovery is repairing the damage done by an instance failure; it is fully described in Chapter 14.

After a crash, all change vectors referring to dirty buffers (buffers that had not been written to disk by DBWn at the time of the failure) must be extracted from the redo log, and applied to the data blocks. This is the recovery process. Frequent checkpoints would ensure that dirty buffers were written to disk quickly, thus minimizing the amount of redo that would have to be applied after a crash and therefore minimizing the time taken to recover the database. CKPT was responsible for signaling regular checkpoints.

From release 8i onward, the checkpoint mechanism changed. Rather than letting DBWn get a long way behind and then signaling a checkpoint (which forces DBWn to catch up and get right up to date, with a dip in performance while this is going on) from 8i onward the DBWn performs *incremental checkpoints* instead of full checkpoints. The incremental checkpoint mechanism instructs DBWn to write out dirty buffers at a constant rate, so that there is always a predictable gap between DBWn (which writes blocks on a lazy algorithm) and LGWR (which writes change vectors in near real time). Incremental checkpointing results in much smoother performance and more predictable recovery times than the older full checkpoint mechanism.

TIP The faster the incremental checkpoint advances, the quicker recovery will be after a failure. But performance will deteriorate due to the extra disk I/O, as DBWn has to write out dirty buffers more quickly. This is a conflict between minimizing downtime and maximizing performance.

The CKPT no longer has to signal full checkpoints, but it does have to keep track of where in the redo stream the incremental checkpoint position is, and if necessary instruct DBWn to write out some dirty buffers in order to push the checkpoint position forward. The current checkpoint position, also known as the RBA (the redo byte address), is the point in the redo stream at which recovery must begin in the event of an instance crash. CKPT continually updates the controlfile with the current checkpoint position.

EXAM TIP When do full checkpoints occur? Only on request, or as part of an orderly database shutdown.

MMON, the Manageability Monitor

MMON is a process that was introduced with database release 10g and is the enabling process for many of the self-monitoring and self-tuning capabilities of the database.

The database instance gathers a vast number of statistics about activity and performance. These statistics are accumulated in the SGA, and their current values can be interrogated by issuing SQL queries. For performance tuning and also for trend analysis and historical reporting, it is necessary to save these statistics to long-term storage. MMON regularly (by default, every hour) captures statistics from the SGA and writes them to the data dictionary, where they can be stored indefinitely (though by default, they are kept for only eight days).

Every time MMON gathers a set of statistics (known as a *snapshot*), it also launches the Automatic Database Diagnostic Monitor, the ADDM. The ADDM is a tool that analyses database activity using an expert system developed over many years by many DBAs. It observes two snapshots (by default, the current and previous snapshots) and makes observations and recommendations regarding performance. Chapter 5 describes the use of ADDM (and other tools) for performance tuning.

EXAM TIP By default, MMON gathers a snapshot and launches the ADDM every hour.

As well as gathering snapshots, MMON continuously monitors the database and the instance to check whether any alerts should be raised. Use of the alert system is covered in the second OCP exam and discussed in Chapter 24. Some alert conditions (such as warnings when limits on storage space are reached) are enabled by default; others can be configured by the DBA.

MMNL, the Manageability Monitor Light

MMNL is a process that assists the MMON. There are times when MMON's scheduled activity needs to be augmented. For example, MMON flushes statistical information accumulated in the SGA to the database according to an hourly schedule by default. If the memory buffers used to accumulate this information fill before MMON is due to flush them, MMNL will take responsibility for flushing the data.

MMAN, the Memory Manager

MMAN is a process that was introduced with database release 10g. It enables the automatic management of memory allocations.

Prior to release 9i of the database, memory management in the Oracle environment was far from satisfactory. The PGA memory associated with session server processes was nontransferable: a server process would take memory from the operating system's free memory pool and never return it—even though it might only have been needed for a short time. The SGA memory structures were static: defined at instance startup time, and unchangeable unless the instance was shut down and restarted.

Release 9i changed that: PGAs can grow and shrink, with the server passing out memory to sessions on demand while ensuring that the total PGA memory allocated stays within certain limits. The SGA and the components within it (with the notable exception of the log buffer) can also be resized, within certain limits. Release 10g automated the SGA resizing: MMAN monitors the demand for SGA memory structures and can resize them as necessary.

Release 11g takes memory management a step further: all the DBA need do is set an overall target for memory usage, and MMAN will observe the demand for PGA memory and SGA memory, and allocate memory to sessions and to SGA structures as needed, while keeping the total allocated memory within a limit set by the DBA.

 TIP The automation of memory management is one of the major technical advances of the later releases, automating a large part of the DBA's job and giving huge benefits in performance and resource utilization.

ARCn, the Archiver

This is an optional process as far as the database is concerned, but usually a required process by the business. Without one or more ARCn processes (there can be from one to thirty, named ARC0, ARC1, and so on) it is possible to lose data in the event of a failure. The process and purpose of launching ARCn to create archive log files is described in detail in Chapter 14. For now, only a summary is needed.

All change vectors applied to data blocks are written out to the log buffer (by the sessions making the changes) and then to the *online* redo log files (by the LGWR). There are a fixed number of online redo log files of a fixed size. Once they have been filled, LGWR will overwrite them with more redo data. The time that must elapse before this happens is dependent on the size and number of the online redo log files, and the amount of DML activity (and therefore the amount of redo generated) against the database. This means that the online redo log only stores change vectors for recent activity. In order to preserve a complete history of all changes applied to the data, the online log files must be copied as they are filled and before they are reused. The ARCn process is responsible for doing this. Provided that these copies, known as *archive* redo log files, are available, it will always be possible to recover from any damage to the database by restoring datafile backups and applying change vectors to them extracted from all the archive log files generated since the backups were made. Then the final recovery, to bring the backup right up to date, will come by using the most recent change vectors from the online redo log files.

 EXAM TIP LGWR writes the online log files; ARCn reads them. In normal running, no other processes touch them at all.

Most production transactional databases will run in *archive log mode,* meaning that ARCn is started automatically and that LGWR is not permitted to overwrite an online log file until ARCn has successfully archived it to an archive log file.

 TIP The progress of the ARCn processes and the state of the destination(s) to which they are writing must be monitored. If archiving fails, the database will eventually hang. This monitoring can be done through the alert system.

RECO, the Recoverer Process

A *distributed* transaction involves updates to two or more databases. Distributed transactions are designed by programmers and operate through database links. Consider this example:

```
update orders set order_status=complete where customer_id=1000;
update orders@mirror set order_status=complete where customer_id=1000;
commit;
```

The first update applies to a row in the local database; the second applies to a row in a remote database identified by the database link MIRROR.

The COMMIT command instructs both databases to commit the transaction, which consists of both statements. A full description of commit processing appears in Chapter 8. Distributed transactions require a *two-phase commit.* The commit in each database must be coordinated: if one were to fail and the other were to succeed, the data overall would be in an inconsistent state. A two-phase commit prepares each database by instructing its LGWRs to flush the log buffer to disk (the first phase), and once this is confirmed, the transaction is flagged as committed everywhere (the second phase). If anything goes wrong anywhere between the two phases, RECO takes action to cancel the commit and roll back the work in all databases.

Some Other Background Processes

It is unlikely that processes other than those already described will be examined, but for completeness descriptions of the remaining processes usually present in an instance follow. Figure 1-7 shows a query that lists all the processes running in an instance on a Windows system. There are many more processes that may exist, depending on what options have been enabled, but those shown in the figure will be present in most instances.

The processes not described in previous sections are

- **CJQ0, J000** These manage jobs scheduled to run periodically. The job queue coordinator, CJQn, monitors the job queue and sends jobs to one of several job queue processes, Jnnn, for execution. The job scheduling mechanism is measured in the second OCP examination and covered in Chapter 22.

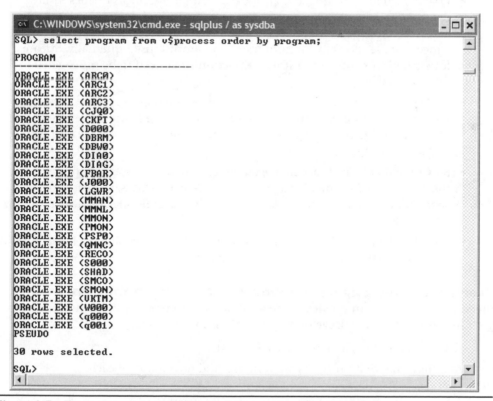

Figure I-7   The background processes typically present in a single instance

- **D000** This is a dispatcher process that will send SQL calls to shared server processes, Snnn, if the shared server mechanism has been enabled. This is described in Chapter 4.

- **DBRM** The database resource manager is responsible for setting resource plans and other Resource Manager–related tasks. Using the Resource Manager is measured in the second OCP examination and covered in Chapter 21.

- **DIA0** The diagnosability process zero (only one is used in the current release) is responsible for hang detection and deadlock resolution. Deadlocks, and their resolution, are described in Chapter 8.

- **DIAG** The diagnosability process (not number zero) performs diagnostic dumps and executes oradebug commands (oradebug is a tool for investigating problems within the instance).

- **FBDA** The flashback data archiver process archives the historical rows of tracked tables into flashback data archives. This is a facility for ensuring that it is always possible to query data as it was at a time in the past.

- **PSP0** The process spawner has the job of creating and managing other Oracle processes, and is undocumented.

- **QMNC, Q000** The queue manager coordinator monitors queues in the database and assigns Qnnn processes to enqueue and dequeue messages to and from these queues. Queues can be created by programmers (perhaps as a means for sessions to communicate) and are also used internally. Streams, for example, use queues to store transactions that need to be propagated to remote databases.

- **SHAD** These appear as TNS V1–V3 processes on a Linux system. They are the server processes that support user sessions. In the figure there is only one, dedicated to the one user process that is currently connected: the user who issued the query.

- **SMCO, W000** The space management coordinator process coordinates the execution of various space management–related tasks, such as proactive space allocation and space reclamation. It dynamically spawns slave processes (Wnnn) to implement the task.

- **VKTM** The virtual keeper of time is responsible for keeping track of time and is of particular importance in a clustered environment.

Exercise 1-4: Investigate the Processes Running in Your Instance In this exercise you will run queries to see what background processes are running on your instance. Either SQL Developer or SQL*Plus may be used.

1. Connect to the database as user SYSTEM.

2. Determine what processes are running, and how many of each:

```
select program from v$session order by program;
select program from v$process order by program;
```

These queries produce similar results: each process must have a session (even the background processes), and each session must have a process. The processes that can occur multiple times will have a numeric suffix, except for the processes supporting user sessions: these will all have the same name.

3. Demonstrate the launching of server processes as sessions are made, by counting the number of server processes (on Linux or any Unix platform) or the number of Oracle threads (on Windows). The technique is different on the two platforms, because on Linux/Unix, the Oracle processes are separate operating system processes, but on Windows they are threads within one operating system process.

   A. On Linux, run this command from an operating system prompt:

   ```
   ps -ef|grep oracle|wc -1
   ```

   This will count the number of processes running that have the string oracle in their name; this will include all the session server processes (and possibly a few others).

   Launch a SQL*Plus session, and rerun the preceding command. You can use the host command to launch an operating shell from within the SQL*Plus session. Notice that the number of processes has increased. Exit the session, rerun the command, and you will see that the number has dropped down again. The illustration shows this fact:

```
db11g@jwlnx1:~
[db11g@jwlnx1 ~]$
[db11g@jwlnx1 ~]$ ps -ef | grep oracle | wc -1
4
[db11g@jwlnx1 ~]$ sqlplus system/oracle

SQL*Plus: Release 11.1.0.6.0 - Production on Thu Oct 25 09:51:35 2007

Copyright (c) 1982, 2007, Oracle.  All rights reserved.


Connected to:
Oracle Database 11g Enterprise Edition Release 11.1.0.6.0 - Production
With the Partitioning, OLAP, Data Mining and Real Application Testing options

SQL> host
[db11g@jwlnx1 ~]$ ps -ef | grep oracle | wc -1
5
[db11g@jwlnx1 ~]$ exit
exit

SQL> exit
Disconnected from Oracle Database 11g Enterprise Edition Release 11.1.0.6.0 - Produ
ction
With the Partitioning, OLAP, Data Mining and Real Application Testing options
[db11g@jwlnx1 ~]$ ps -ef | grep oracle | wc -1
4
[db11g@jwlnx1 ~]$
```

Observe in the illustration how the number of processes changes from 4 to 5 and back again: the difference is the launching and terminating of the server process supporting the SQL*Plus session.

B. On Windows, launch the task manager. Configure it to show the number of threads within each process: from the View menu, choose Select Columns and tick the Thread Count check box. Look for the ORACLE.EXE process, and note the number of threads. In the next illustration, this is currently at 33.

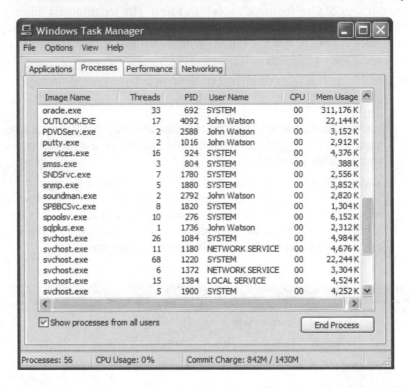

Launch a new session against the instance, and you will see the thread count increment. Exit the session, and it will decrement.

Database Storage Structures

The Oracle database provides complete abstraction of logical storage from physical. The logical data storage is in *segments*. There are various segment types; a typical segment is a table. The segments are stored physically in datafiles. The abstraction of the logical storage from the physical storage is accomplished through tablespaces. The relationships between the logical and physical structures, as well as their definitions, are maintained in the data dictionary.

There is a full treatment of database storage, logical and physical, in Chapter 5.

The Physical Database Structures

There are three file types that make up an Oracle database, plus a few others that exist externally to the database and are, strictly speaking, optional. The required files are the controlfile, the online redo log files, and the datafiles. The external files that will usually be present (there are others, needed for advanced options) are the initialization parameter file, the password file, the archive redo log files, and the log and trace files.

 EXAM TIP What three file types must be present in a database? The controlfile, the online redo log files, and any number of datafiles.

The Controlfile

First a point of terminology: some DBAs will say that a database can have multiple controlfiles, while others will say that it has one controlfile, of which there may be multiple copies. This book will follow the latter terminology, which conforms to Oracle Corporation's use of phrases such as "multiplexing the controlfile," which means to create multiple copies.

The controlfile is small but vital. It contains pointers to the rest of the database: the locations of the online redo log files and of the datafiles, and of the more recent archive log files if the database is in archive log mode. It also stores information required to maintain database integrity: various critical sequence numbers and timestamps, for example. If the Recovery Manager tool (described in Chapters 15, 16, and 17) is being used for backups, then details of these backups will also be stored in the controlfile. The controlfile will usually be no more than a few megabytes big, but your database can't survive without it.

Every database has one controlfile, but a good DBA will always create multiple copies of the controlfile so that if one copy is damaged, the database can quickly be repaired. If all copies of the controlfile are lost, it is possible (though perhaps awkward) to recover, but you should never find yourself in that situation. You don't have to worry about keeping multiplexed copies of the controlfile synchronized—Oracle will take care of that. Its maintenance is automatic—your only control is how many copies to have, and where to put them.

If you get the number of copies, or their location, wrong at database creation time, you can add or remove copies later, or move them around—but you should bear in mind that any such operations will require downtime, so it is a good idea to get it right at the beginning. There is no right or wrong when determining how many copies to have. The minimum is one; the maximum possible is eight. All organizations should have a DBA standards handbook, which will state something like "all production databases will have three copies of the controlfile, on three separate devices," three being a number picked for illustration only, but a number that many organizations are happy with. There is no rule that says two copies is too few, or seven copies is too many; there are only corporate standards, and the DBA's job is to ensure that the databases conform to these.

Damage to any controlfile copy will cause the database instance to terminate immediately. There is no way to avoid this: Oracle Corporation does not permit operating a database with less than the number of controlfiles that have been requested. The techniques for multiplexing or relocating the controlfile are covered in Chapter 14.

The Online Redo Log Files

The redo log stores a chronologically ordered chain of every change vector applied to the database. This will be the bare minimum of information required to reconstruct, or redo, all work that has been done. If a datafile (or the whole database) is damaged or destroyed, these change vectors can be applied to datafile backups to redo the work, bringing them forward in time until the moment that the damage occurred. The redo log consists of two file types: the online redo log files (which are required for continuous database operation) and the archive log files (which are optional for database operation, but mandatory for point-in-time recovery).

Every database has at least two online redo log files, but as with the controlfile, a good DBA creates multiple copies of each online redo log file. The online redo log consists of groups of online redo log files, each file being known as a *member*. An Oracle database requires at least two groups of at least one member each to function. You may create more than two groups for performance reasons, and more than one member per group for security (an old joke: this isn't just data security, it is job security). The requirement for a minimum of two groups is so that one group can accept the current changes, while the other group is being backed up (or *archived*, to use the correct term).

 EXAM TIP Every database must have at least two online redo log file groups to function. Each group should have at least two members for safety.

One of the groups is the *current* group: changes are written to the current online redo log file group by LGWR. As user sessions update data in the database buffer cache, they also write out the minimal change vectors to the redo log buffer. LGWR continually flushes this buffer to the files that make up the current online redo log file group. Log files have a predetermined size, and eventually the files making up the current group will fill. LGWR will then perform what is called a log switch. This makes the second group current and starts writing to that. If your database is configured appropriately, the ARCn process(es) will then archive (in effect, back up) the log file members making up the first group. When the second group fills, LGWR will switch back to the first group, making it current, and overwriting it; ARCn will then archive the second group. Thus, the online redo log file groups (and therefore the members making them up) are used in a circular fashion, and each log switch will generate an archive redo log file.

As with the controlfile, if you have multiple members per group (and you should!) you don't have to worry about keeping them synchronized. LGWR will ensure that it writes to all of them, in parallel, thus keeping them identical. If you lose one member of a group, as long as you have a surviving member, the database will continue to function.

The size and number of your log file groups are a matter of tuning. In general, you will choose a size appropriate to the amount of activity you anticipate. The minimum size is fifty megabytes, but some very active databases will need to raise this to several gigabytes if they are not to fill every few minutes. A very busy database can generate megabytes of redo a second, whereas a largely static database may generate only a few megabytes an hour. The number of members per group will be dependent on what level of fault tolerance is deemed appropriate, and is a matter to be documented in corporate standards. However, you don't have to worry about this at database creation time. You can move your online redo log files around, add or drop them, and create ones of different sizes as you please at any time later on. Such operations are performed "online" and don't require downtime—they are therefore transparent to the end users.

The Datafiles

The third required file type making up a database is the datafile. At a minimum, you must have two datafiles, to be created at database creation time. With previous releases of Oracle, you could create a database with only one datafile—10g and 11g require two, at least one each for the SYSTEM tablespace (that stores the data dictionary) and the SYSAUX tablespace (that stores data that is auxiliary to the data dictionary). You will, however, have many more than that when your database goes live, and will usually create a few more to begin with.

Datafiles are the repository for data. Their size and numbers are effectively unlimited. A small database, of only a few gigabytes, might have just half a dozen datafiles of only a few hundred megabytes each. A larger database could have thousands of datafiles, whose size is limited only by the capabilities of the host operating system and hardware

The datafiles are the physical structures visible to the system administrators. Logically, they are the repository for the *segments* containing user data that the programmers see, and also for the segments that make up the data dictionary. A segment is a storage structure for data; typical segments are tables and indexes. Datafiles can be renamed, resized, moved, added, or dropped at any time in the lifetime of the database, but remember that some operations on some datafiles may require downtime.

At the operating system level, a datafile consists of a number of operating system blocks. Internally, datafiles are formatted into Oracle *blocks*. These blocks are consecutively numbered within each datafile. The block size is fixed when the datafile is created, and in most circumstances it will be the same throughout the entire database. The block size is a matter for tuning and can range (with limits depending on the platform) from 2KB up to 64KB. There is no relationship between the Oracle block size and the operating system block size.

TIP Many DBAs like to match the operating system block size to the Oracle block size. For performance reasons, the operating system blocks should never be larger than the Oracle blocks, but there is no reason not have them smaller. For instance, a 1KB operating system block size and an 8KB Oracle block size is perfectly acceptable.

Within a block, there is a header section and a data area, and possibly some free space. The header section contains information such as the row directory, which lists the location within the data area of the rows in the block (if the block is being used for a table segment) and also row locking information if there is a transaction working on the rows in the block. The data area contains the data itself, such as rows if it is part of a table segment, or index keys if the block is part of an index segment.

When a user session needs to work on data for any purpose, the server process supporting the session locates the relevant block on disk and copies it into a free buffer in the database buffer cache. If the data in the block is then changed (the buffer is dirtied) by executing a DML command against it, eventually DBWn will write the block back to the datafile on disk.

 EXAM TIP Server processes read from the datafiles; DBWn writes to datafiles.

Datafiles should be backed up regularly. Unlike the controlfile and the online redo log files, they cannot be protected by multiplexing (though they can, of course, be protected by operating system and hardware facilities, such as RAID). If a datafile is damaged, it can be restored from backup and then *recovered* (to recover a datafile means to bring it up to date) by applying all the redo generated since the backup was made. The necessary redo is extracted from the change vectors in the online and archive redo log files. The routines for datafile backup, restore, and recovery are described in Chapters 15–18.

Other Database Files

These files exist externally to the database. They are, for practical purposes, necessary—but they are not strictly speaking part of the database.

- **The instance parameter file** When an Oracle instance is started, the SGA structures initialize in memory and the background processes start according to settings in the parameter file. This is the only file that needs to exist in order to start an instance. There are several hundred parameters, but only one is required: the DB_NAME parameter. All others have defaults. So the parameter file can be quite small, but it must exist. It is sometimes referred to as a pfile or spfile, and its creation is described in Chapter 3.

- **The password file** Users establish sessions by presenting a username and a password. The Oracle server authenticates these against user definitions stored in the data dictionary. The data dictionary is a set of tables in the database; it is therefore inaccessible if the database is not open. There are occasions when you need to be authenticated before the data dictionary is available: when you need to start the database, or indeed create it. An external password file is one means of doing this. It contains a small number (typically less than half a dozen) of user names and passwords that exist outside the data dictionary, and which can therefore be used to connect to an instance before the data dictionary is available. Creating the password file is described in Chapter 3.

- **Archive redo log files** When an online redo log file fills, the ARCn process copies it to an archive redo log file. Once this is done, the archive log is no longer part of the database in that it is not required for continued operation of the database. It is, however, essential if it is ever necessary to recover a datafile backup, and Oracle does provide facilities for managing the archive redo log files.

- **Alert log and trace files** The alert log is a continuous stream of messages regarding certain critical operations affecting the instance and the database. Not everything is logged: only events that are considered to be really important, such as startup and shutdown; changes to the physical structures of the database; changes to the parameters that control the instance. Trace files are generated by background processes when they detect error conditions, and sometimes to report specific events.

The Logical Database Structures

The physical structures that make up a database are visible as operating system files to your system administrators. Your users see logical structures such as tables. Oracle uses the term *segment* to describe any structure that contains data. A typical segment is a table, containing rows of data, but there are more than a dozen possible segment types in an Oracle database. Of particular interest (for examination purposes) are table segments, index segments, and undo segments, all of which are investigated in detail later on. For now, you need only know that tables contain rows of information; that indexes are a mechanism for giving fast access to any particular row; and that undo segments are data structures used for storing the information that might be needed to reverse, or roll back, any transactions that you do not wish to make permanent.

Oracle abstracts the logical from the physical storage by means of the *tablespace*. A tablespace is logically a collection of one or more segments, and physically a collection of one or more datafiles. Put in terms of relational analysis, there is a many-to-many relationship between segments and datafiles: one table may be cut across many datafiles, one datafile may contain bits of many tables. By inserting the tablespace entity between the segments and the files, Oracle resolves this many-to-many relationship.

A number of segments must be created at database creation time: these are the segments that make up the data dictionary. These segments are stored in two tablespaces, called SYSTEM and SYSAUX. The SYSAUX tablespace was new with release 10g: in previous releases, the entire data dictionary went into SYSTEM. The database creation process must create at least these two tablespaces, with at least one datafile each, to store the data dictionary.

EXAM TIP The SYSAUX tablespace must be created at database creation time in Oracle 10g and later. If you do not specify it, one will be created by default.

A segment consists of a number of blocks. Datafiles are formatted into blocks, and these blocks are assigned to segments as the segments grow. Because managing space one block at a time would be a time-consuming process, blocks are grouped into *extents*. An extent is a contiguous series of blocks that are consecutively numbered within a datafile, and segments will grow by an extent at a time. These extents need not be adjacent to each other, or even in the same datafile; they can come from any datafile that is part of the tablespace within which the segment resides.

Figure 1-8 shows the Oracle data storage hierarchy, with the separation of logical from physical storage.

The figure shows the relationships between the storage structures. Logically, a tablespace can contain many segments, each consisting of many extents. An *extent* is a set of Oracle blocks. Physically, a datafile consists of many operating system blocks. The two sides of the model are connected by the relationships showing that one tablespace can consist of multiple datafiles, and at the lowest level that one Oracle block consists of one or more operating system blocks.

The Data Dictionary

The data dictionary contains metadata that describes the database, both physically and logically, and its contents. User definitions, security information, integrity constraints, and (with release 10g and later) performance monitoring information are all stored in the data dictionary. It is stored as a set of segments in the SYSTEM and SYSAUX tablespaces.

In many ways, the segments that make up the data dictionary are segments like any other: just tables and indexes. The critical difference is that the data dictionary tables are generated at database creation time, and you are not allowed to access them directly. There is nothing to stop an inquisitive DBA from investigating the data dictionary directly, but if you do any updates to it, you may cause irreparable damage to your database, and certainly Oracle Corporation will not support you. Creating a data

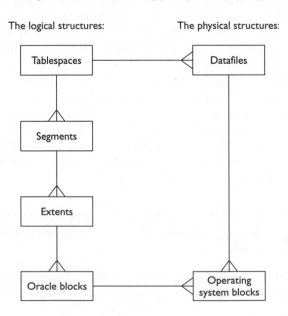

Figure 1-8
The Oracle logical and physical storage hierarchy

dictionary is part of the database creation process. It is maintained subsequently by data definition language commands. When you issue the CREATE TABLE command, you are in fact inserting rows into data dictionary tables, as you are with commands such as CREATE USER or GRANT.

To query the dictionary, Oracle provides a set of views. Most of these views come in three forms, prefixed DBA_, ALL_, or USER_. Any view prefixed USER_ will describe objects owned by the user querying the view. So no two distinct users will see the same contents while querying a view prefixed with USER_. If user JOHN queries USER_TABLES, he will see information about his tables; if you query USER_TABLES, you will see information about your tables. Any view prefixed ALL_ will display rows describing objects to which you have access. So ALL_TABLES shows rows describing your own tables, plus rows describing tables belonging to other users that you have permission to see. Any view prefixed DBA_ has rows for every object in the database, so DBA_TABLES has one row for every table in the database, no matter who created it. These views are created as part of the database creation process, along with a large number of PL/SQL packages that are provided by Oracle to assist database administrators in managing the database and programmers in developing applications. PL/SQL code is also stored in the data dictionary.

 EXAM TIP Which view will show you ALL the tables in the database? DBA_ TABLES, not ALL_TABLES.

The relationship between tablespaces and datafiles is maintained in the database controlfile. This lists all the datafiles, stating which tablespace they are a part of. Without the controlfile, there is no way that an instance can locate the datafiles and then identify those that make up the SYSTEM tablespace. Only when the SYSTEM tablespace has been opened is it possible for the instance to access the data dictionary, at which point it becomes possible to open the database.

SQL code always refers to objects defined in the data dictionary. To execute a simple query against a table, the Oracle server must first query the data dictionary to find out if the table exists, and the columns that make it up. Then it must find out where, physically, the table is. This requires reading the extent map of the segment. The extent map lists all the extents that make up the table, with the detail of which datafile each extent is in, what block of the datafile the extent starts at, and how many blocks it continues for.

Exercise 1-5: Investigate the Storage Structures in Your Database
In this exercise you will create a table segment, and then work out where it is physically. Either SQL Developer or SQL*Plus may be used.

1. Connect to the database as user SYSTEM.

2. Create a table without nominating a tablespace—it will be created in your default tablespace, with one extent:

```
create table tab24 (c1 varchar2(10));
```

3. Identify the tablespace in which the table resides, the size of the extent, the file number the extent is in, and which block of the file the extent starts at:

```
select tablespace_name, extent_id, bytes, file_id, block_id
from dba_extents where owner='SYSTEM' and segment_name='TAB24';
```

4. Identify the file by name: substitute the file_id from the previous query when prompted:

```
select name from v$datafile where file#=&file_id;
```

5. Work out precisely where in the file the extent is, in terms of how many bytes into the file it begins. This requires finding out the tablespace's block size. Enter the block_id and tablespace_name returned by the query in Step 3 when prompted.

```
select block_size * &block_id from dba_tablespaces
where tablespace_name='&tablespace_name';
```

The illustration that follows shows these steps, executed from SQL*Plus:

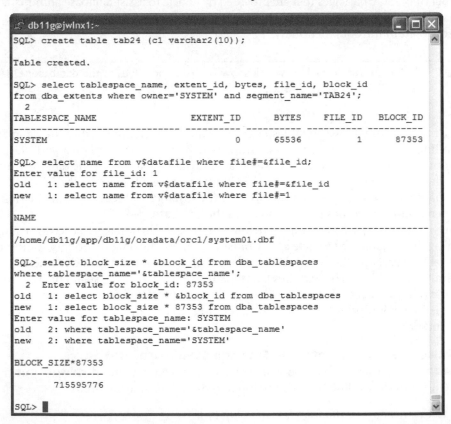

The illustration shows that the table exists in one extent that is 64KB large. This extent is in the file `/home/db11g/app/db11g/oradata/orcl/system01.dbf` and begins about 700MB into the file.

Two-Minute Drill

Single-Instance Architecture

- An Oracle server is an instance connected to a database.
- An instance is a block of shared memory and a set of background processes.
- A database is a set of files on disk.
- A user session is a user process connected to a server process.

Instance Memory Structures

- The instance shared memory is the system global area (the SGA).
- A session's private memory is its program global area (the PGA).
- The SGA consists of a number of substructures, some of which are required (the database buffer cache, the log buffer, and the shared pool) and some of which are optional (the large pool, the Java pool, and the Streams pool).
- The SGA structures can be dynamically resized and automatically managed, with the exception of the log buffer.

Instance Process Structures

- Session server processes are launched on demand when users connect.
- Background processes are launched at instance startup and persist until shutdown.
- Server processes read from the database; background processes write to the database.
- Some background processes will always be present (in particular SMON, PMON, DBWn, LGWR, CKPT, and MMON); others will run depending on what options have been enabled.

Database Storage Structures

- There are three required file types in a database: the controlfile, the online redo log files, and the datafiles.
- The controlfile stores integrity information and pointers to the rest of the database.
- The online redo logs store recent change vectors applied to the database.
- The datafiles store the data.
- External files include the parameter file, the password file, archive redo logs, and the log and trace files.

- Logical data storage (segments) is abstracted from physical data storage (datafiles) by tablespaces.

- A tablespace can consist of multiple datafiles.

- Segments consist of multiple extents, which consist of multiple Oracle blocks, which consist of one or more operating system blocks.

- A segment can have extents in several datafiles.

Self Test

1. Which statements regarding instance memory and session memory are correct? (Choose two answers.)

   A. SGA memory is private memory segments; PGA memory is shared memory segments.

   B. Sessions can write to the PGA, not the SGA.

   C. The SGA is written to by all sessions; a PGA is written by one session.

   D. The PGA is allocated at instance startup.

   E. The SGA is allocated at instance startup.

2. How do sessions communicate with the database? (Choose the best answer.)

   A. Server processes use Oracle Net to connect to the instance.

   B. Background processes use Oracle Net to connect to the database.

   C. User processes read from the database and write to the instance.

   D. Server processes execute SQL received from user processes.

3. What memory structures are a required part of the SGA? (Choose three answers.)

   A. The database buffer cache

   B. The Java pool

   C. The large pool

   D. The log buffer

   E. The program global area

   F. The shared pool

   G. The Streams pool

4. Which SGA memory structure(s) cannot be resized dynamically after instance startup? (Choose one or more correct answers.)

   A. The database buffer cache

   B. The Java pool

   C. The large pool

   D. The log buffer

   E. The shared pool

    F. The Streams pool

    G. All SGA structures can be resized dynamically after instance startup

5. Which SGA memory structure(s) cannot be resized automatically after instance startup? (Choose one or more correct answers.)

    A. The database buffer cache

    B. The Java pool

    C. The large pool

    D. The log buffer

    E. The shared pool

    F. The Streams pool

    G. All SGA structures can be resized automatically after instance startup

6. When a session changes data, where does the change get written? (Choose the best answer.)

    A. To the data block in the cache, and the redo log buffer

    B. To the data block on disk, and the current online redo log file

    C. The session writes to the database buffer cache, and the log writer writes to the current online redo log file

    D. Nothing is written until the change is committed

7. Which of these background processes is optional? (Choose the best answer.)

    A. ARCn, the archive process

    B. CKPT, the checkpoint process

    C. DBWn, the database writer

    D. LGWR, the log writer

    E. MMON, the manageability monitor

8. What happens when a user issues a COMMIT? (Choose the best answer.)

    A. The CKPT process signals a checkpoint.

    B. The DBWn process writes the transaction's changed buffers to the datafiles.

    C. The LGWR flushes the log buffer to the online redo log.

    D. The ARCn process writes the change vectors to the archive redo log.

9. An Oracle instance can have only one of some processes, but several of others. Which of these processes can occur several times? (Choose three answers.)

    A. The archive process

    B. The checkpoint process

    C. The database writer process

    D. The log writer process

    E. The session server process

10. How can one segment can be spread across many datafiles? (Choose the best answer.)

    A. By allocating an extent with blocks in multiple datafiles

    B. By spreading the segment across multiple tablespaces

    C. By assigning multiple datafiles to a tablespace

    D. By using an Oracle block size that is larger than the operating system block size

11. Which statement is correct regarding the online redo log? (Choose the best answer.)

    A. There must be at least one log file group, with at least one member.

    B. There must be at least one log file group, with at least two members.

    C. There must be at least two log file groups, with at least one member each.

    D. There must be at least two log file groups, with at least two members each.

12. Where is the current redo byte address, also known as the incremental checkpoint position, recorded? (Choose the best answer.)

    A. In the controlfile

    B. In the current online log file group

    C. In the header of each datafile

    D. In the system global area

Self Test Answers

1. ☑ C and E. The SGA is shared memory, updated by all sessions; PGAs are private to each session. The SGA is allocated at startup time (but it can be modified later).

   ☒ A, B, and D. A is wrong because it reverses the situation: it is the SGA that exists in shared memory, not the PGA. B is wrong because sessions write to both their own PGA and to the SGA. D is wrong because (unlike the SGA) the PGA is only allocated on demand.

2. ☑ D. This is the client-server split: user processes generate SQL; server processes execute SQL.

   ☒ A, B, and C. A and B are wrong because they get the use of Oracle Net wrong. Oracle Net is the protocol between a user process and a server process. C is wrong because it describes what server processes do, not what user processes do.

3. ☑ A, D, and F. Every instance must have a database buffer cache, a log buffer, and a shared pool.

☒   B, C, E, and G. B, C, and G are wrong because the Java pool, the large pool, and the Streams pool are only needed for certain options. E is wrong because the PGA is not part of the SGA at all.

4. ☑   D. The log buffer is fixed in size at startup time.

  ☒   A, B, C, E, F, and G. A, B, C, E, and F are wrong because these are the SGA's resizable components. G is wrong because the log buffer is static.

5. ☑   D. The log buffer cannot be resized manually, never mind automatically.

  ☒   A, B, C, E, F, and G. A, B, C, E, and F are wrong because these SGA components can all be automatically managed. G is wrong because the log buffer is static.

6. ☑   A. The session updates the copy of the block in memory and writes out the change vector to the log buffer.

  ☒   B, C, and D. B is wrong, because while this will happen, it does not happen when the change is made. C is wrong because it confuses the session making changes in memory with LGWR propagating changes to disk. D is wrong because all changes to data occur in memory as they are made—the COMMIT is not relevant.

7. ☑   A. Archiving is not compulsory (though it is usually a good idea).

  ☒   B, C, D, and E. CKPT, DBWn, LGWR, and MMON are all necessary processes.

8. ☑   C. On COMMIT, the log writer flushes the log buffer to disk. No other background processes need do anything.

  ☒   A, B, and D. A is wrong because checkpoints only occur on request, or on orderly shutdown. B is wrong because the algorithm DBWn uses to select buffers to write to the datafiles is not related to COMMIT processing, but to how busy the buffer is. D is wrong because ARCn only copies filled online redo logs; it doesn't copy change vectors in real time.

9. ☑   A, C, and E. A and C are correct because the DBA can choose to configure multiple archive and database writer processes. E is correct because one server process will be launched for every concurrent session.

  ☒   B and D. These are wrong because an instance can have only one log writer process and only one checkpoint process.

10. ☑   C. If a tablespace has several datafiles, segments can have extents in all of them.

  ☒   A, B, and D. A is wrong because one extent consists of consecutive block in one datafile. B is wrong because one segment can only exist in one tablespace (though one tablespace can contain many segments). D is wrong because while this can certainly be done, one block can only exist in one datafile.

11. ☑   C. Two groups of one member is the minimum required for the database to function.

   ☒   A, B, and D. A and B are wrong because at least two groups are always required. D is wrong because while it is certainly advisable to multiplex the members, it is not a mandatory requirement.

12. ☑   A. The checkpoint process writes the RBA to the controlfile.

   ☒   B, C, and D. The online logs, the datafiles, and SGA have no knowledge of where the current RBA is.

CHAPTER 2

Installing and Creating a Database

Exam Objectives

In this chapter you will learn to

- 052.2.1   Identify the Tools for Administering an Oracle Database
- 052.2.2   Plan an Oracle Database Installation
- 052.2.3   Install the Oracle Software by Using Oracle Universal Installer (OUI)
- 052.3.1   Create a Database by Using the Database Configuration Assistant (DBCA)

Perhaps the simplest yet most important strategic task in the life of an Oracle database occurs at the planning and installation phase. Although the decisions you make at this point are not cast in stone, they will often be complex to undo. For example, choosing a database name, the locations of the installation binaries, and those of other important files might seem trivial, but once you have committed to these settings, they are usually permanent. It is therefore well worth the effort to consider the key factors that influence planning, installing, and creating a database.

This chapter begins by introducing the essential bread-and-butter tools used by Oracle DBAs and proceeds to discuss planning a database installation. Once the plan is made, installing the Oracle software is described and the chapter culminates with you creating your very own database.

Identify the Tools for Administering an Oracle Database

Oracle Corporation provides a number of tools for managing the Oracle environment. First there is the Oracle Universal Installer (OUI) used (as its name suggests) to install any Oracle software. Second is the Database Configuration Assistant (DBCA), the tool for creating a database. A related tool used during upgrades is the Database Upgrade Assistance (DBUA), but a discussion of DBUA is beyond the scope of the exams. These can be launched from the OUI or run separately. Third, the OUI will install a number of other tools for managing a database and related components, notably SQL*Plus. Depending on the installation type chosen, it may also install SQL Developer.

Oracle Enterprise Manager (OEM) Database Control is also installed by the OUI and will be used extensively in this book.

The Oracle Universal Installer

Historically, managing Oracle software could be a painful task. This was because the DBA was largely responsible for ensuring that incompatible products were kept separate. It was not uncommon to install one product, a second, and a third satisfactorily—then installation of a fourth would break the other three. The problem of incompatibilities lies in the use of the *base libraries*. The base libraries provide facilities that are common to all Oracle products. For example, all Oracle products use the Oracle Net communications protocol; it is impossible to install a product without it. If two products are built on the same version of the base libraries, then (theoretically) they can coexist in the same *Oracle Home*. An Oracle Home is the location of an Oracle product installation: a set of files in a directory structure. Before the Oracle Universal Installer, each product had its own self-contained installation routine, which was sometimes not too clever at identifying incompatibilities with already installed products.

The OUI is written in Java, using JDK/JRE1.5. This means that it is the same on all platforms. The OUI can be installed as a self-contained product in its own Oracle Home, but this is not usually necessary, as it is shipped with every Oracle product and can be launched from the product installation media; it will install itself into the

Oracle Home along with the product. There are different versions of the OUI, and if a product comes with an earlier version than one already installed on the machine, then it will usually be a good idea (and may indeed be necessary) to install the product using the already-installed version. When the OUI prompts for the location of a `products.xml` file, specify the media with the product you want to install.

 TIP Always use the latest version of the OUI that you have available. There can be issues with updating the OUI inventory if you try to revert to earlier versions after using a later version.

The OUI Inventory

Central to the OUI is the *inventory*. This is a set of files that should ideally exist outside any Oracle Home. The inventory stores details of all the Oracle products installed on the machine, including the exact version, the location, and in some cases details of patches that have been applied. Every run of the OUI will check the inventory for incompatibilities before permitting an install into an existing Oracle Home to proceed, and will then update the inventory with details of all products installed or upgraded. The location of the Unix inventory can be chosen by the DBA the first time the OUI (any version) is run on the machine. On Windows, the location is always created in

```
%SystemRoot%\Program files\Oracle\Inventory
```

All platforms have a hard-coded, platform-specific location where the OUI will search for an existing inventory pointer. On Linux this is a file:

```
/etc/oraInst.loc
```

On Solaris it is also a file:

```
/var/opt/oracle/oraInst.loc
```

On Windows it is a key in the registry:

```
HKEY_LOCAL_MACHINE\SOFTWARE\ORACLE\inst_loc
```

When the OUI starts, it will look for this file (or registry key). If it does not exist, OUI assumes that there has never been any Oracle software installed on the machine, and it will create the file (or registry key) and write to it the location of the new inventory that is to be created. All subsequent runs of the OUI, no matter what version, will then be able to find the inventory.

This mechanism for creating an inventory pointer does raise an issue with operating system privileges: on Linux or Unix, the user running the installer for the first time will need permission to write to the appropriate directory. Usually only the root user can write to `/etc` or `/var`. As it is not acceptable for security reasons to run the OUI as the root user, OUI will generate a script (the `orainstRoot.sh` script) to be run by the root user that will create the `oraInst.loc` file. On Windows, the user running the OUI will need privileges to create the registry key.

TIP To relocate the inventory, first copy it (the whole directory system to which the inventory pointer is pointing) to the new location, and then edit the pointer file (or registry key). Sometimes, you may want to create a new inventory but keep the old one. On Linux, simply delete the `oraInst.loc` file, run the OUI, and choose a location for the new inventory. From then on, edit `oraInst.loc` to switch between the two inventories.

The Prerequisite Tests

The OUI checks certain requirements on the server machine before it will run. These are platform specific and are provided in this file on the installation media:

- `/install/oraparam.ini` (Unix)
- `\install\oraparam.ini` (Windows)

The requirements are not too demanding, doing little more than checking that the graphics device on which the installer is displaying can show at least 256 colors.

The `oraparam.ini` file also specifies the location of the file `products.xml`, which is the file with details of all the products that can be installed from this media. Each product will have its own requirements, and these may be demanding (or irritating, if you know they actually don't matter). The product requirements are listed in a set of XML files. Typical of these is

- `/stage/prereq/db/refhost.xml` (Unix)
- `\stage\prereq\db\refhost.xml` (Windows)

The Windows file is usually very simple, specifying little more than a calculation for necessary swap space, and the operating system release:

```
<SYSTEM>
  <MEMORY>
  <PHYSICAL_MEMORY VALUE="256" UNIT="MB"/>
  <!--AVAILABLE_MEMORY VALUE="512" UNIT="MB"/-->
        <SWAP_SIZE>
  <STEP NAME="PHYSICAL_MEMORY" ATLEAST="0" ATMOST="256"
UNIT="MB" MULTIPLE="3"/>
  <STEP NAME="PHYSICAL_MEMORY" GREATER_THAN="256" ATMOST="512"
UNIT="MB" MULTIPLE="2"/>
  <STEP NAME="PHYSICAL_MEMORY" GREATER_THAN="512" ATMOST="2048"
UNIT="MB" MULTIPLE="1.5"/>
  <STEP NAME="PHYSICAL_MEMORY" GREATER_THAN="2048" ATMOST="8192"
UNIT="MB" MULTIPLE="1"/>
  <STEP NAME="PHYSICAL_MEMORY" GREATER_THAN="8192"
UNIT="MB" MULTIPLE="0.75"/>
  </SWAP_SIZE>
  </MEMORY>
  </SYSTEM>
  <CERTIFIED_SYSTEMS>
  <OPERATING_SYSTEM>
  <VERSION VALUE="5.0"/>
  <SERVICE_PACK VALUE="1"/>
  </OPERATING_SYSTEM>
```

```
<OPERATING_SYSTEM>
<VERSION VALUE="5.1"/>
<SERVICE_PACK VALUE="1"/>
</OPERATING_SYSTEM>
<OPERATING_SYSTEM>
<VERSION VALUE="5.2"/>
</OPERATING_SYSTEM>
<!--Microsoft Windows Vista-->
<OPERATING_SYSTEM>
<VERSION VALUE="6.0"/>
</OPERATING_SYSTEM>
</CERTIFIED_SYSTEMS>
```

It is worth noting the swap space calculation, which is based on the amount of main memory detected. For instance, if OUI detects physical memory of 512MB–2048MB, it will demand a swap file of 1.5 times the amount of physical memory. OUI is not intelligent enough to realize that Windows can resize its swap file, so that even if the present size is far less than this, it could expand to far more. Also note that the Windows Vista base version (Windows version 6.0) is listed, but not with any service packs.

The Unix prerequisites are more demanding, in that as well as a calculation for required swap space they specify a whole list of packages and kernel settings, with several sections for the various supported Unix versions. Following is a print of a typical section:

```
<PACKAGES>
  <PACKAGE NAME="make" VERSION="3.81" />
  <PACKAGE NAME="binutils" VERSION="2.17.50.0.6" />
  <PACKAGE NAME="gcc" VERSION="4.1.1" />
  <PACKAGE NAME="libaio" VERSION="0.3.106" />
  <PACKAGE NAME="libaio-devel" VERSION="0.3.106" />
  <PACKAGE NAME="libstdc++" VERSION="4.1.1" />
  <PACKAGE NAME="elfutils-libelf-devel" VERSION="0.125" />
  <PACKAGE NAME="sysstat" VERSION="7.0.0" />
  <PACKAGE NAME="compat-libstdc++-33" VERSION="3.2.3" />
  <PACKAGE NAME="libgcc" VERSION="4.1.1" />
  <PACKAGE NAME="libstdc++-devel" VERSION="4.1.1" />
  <PACKAGE NAME="unixODBC" VERSION="2.2.11" />
  <PACKAGE NAME="unixODBC-devel" VERSION="2.2.11" />
</PACKAGES>
<KERNEL>
  <PROPERTY NAME="semmsl" NAME2="semmsl2" VALUE="250" />
  <PROPERTY NAME="semmns" VALUE="32000" />
  <PROPERTY NAME="semopm" VALUE="100" />
  <PROPERTY NAME="semmni" VALUE="128" />
  <PROPERTY NAME="shmmax" VALUE="536870912" />
  <PROPERTY NAME="shmmni" VALUE="4096" />
  <PROPERTY NAME="shmall" VALUE="2097152" />
  <PROPERTY NAME="file-max" VALUE="65536" />
  <PROPERTY NAME="VERSION" VALUE="2.6.18" />
  <PROPERTY NAME="ip_local_port_range" ATLEAST="1024" ATMOST="65000" />
  <PROPERTY NAME="rmem_default" VALUE="4194304" />
  <PROPERTY NAME="rmem_max" VALUE="4194304" />
  <PROPERTY NAME="wmem_default" VALUE="262144" />
  <PROPERTY NAME="wmem_max" VALUE="262144" />
</KERNEL>
```

Obtaining the required packages can be a quite challenging for some Unix distributions. Also, some of the kernel settings (such as the `ip_local_port_range`) may conflict with local system administration policies. If you cannot get your system into a state where it will pass the prerequisite tests, you have three options. First, you can edit the `oraparam.ini` file or the `refhost.xml` file to change the value or to remove the test entirely. This will "fix" the problem permanently. Second, you can run the OUI with a switch that tells it to ignore the prerequisite tests. Third, you can run the OUI and during the run tell it to ignore any failures. This last option can only work when running OUI interactively, not when doing a silent install.

If at all possible, do not do any of these! In practice, often the problem is not that the products will not work. For example, on Linux, some of the kernel settings and packages are not really needed for an entry-level installation. The problem, however, lies with the supportability of your installation. If you ever raise an SR (an SR is a Service Request, passed to Oracle Support Services through MetaLink) and your system does not conform to the prerequisites, the support analysts may well refuse to help you. So if you have to break one of the rules to get an installation through, fix it as soon as possible afterward.

Running the OUI

Oracle products are shipped on CDs or DVDs, or can be downloaded from Oracle Corporation's web site. The installation can be done directly from the CD or DVD, but it is usually better to copy the CD or DVD to disk first (this is called staging), and install from there. This does save time, since you aren't prompted to insert different media during the installation. The downloaded versions are usually ZIP files, or for Linux and Unix compressed TAR or CPIO files. Use whatever operating system utility is appropriate to expand them.

To launch the OUI, on Windows run the `setup.exe` file in the root directory, on Linux and Unix, run the `runInstaller` shell script.

Database Creation and Upgrade Tools

The Database Configuration Assistant (DBCA) is a graphical tool used for creating and modifying a database. Creating a database is not a big deal using DBCA. The wizard-driven approach guides you through the database creations options, allowing you to determine parameter values and file location options. DBCA then generates the appropriate scripts to create a database with the options you have chosen. DBCA ensures there are no syntax errors and proceeds to run these scripts. Everything that DBCA does can also be done manually using a command-line utility. DBCA is commonly launched by OUI. When you opt for this, OUI instantiates the Oracle Home and then goes on to run DBCA.

As with database creation, database upgrade can be done manually or through a graphical tool. The graphical tool is the Database Upgrade Assistant (DBUA). It, too, can be called by OUI, if OUI detects an existing database Oracle Home of an earlier version. The DBUA will ensure that no steps are missed, but many DBAs prefer to do upgrades manually. They believe that it gives them more control, and in some cases a manual upgrade can be quicker.

Both DBCA and DBUA are written in Java and therefore require a graphics terminal to display.

Tools for Issuing Ad Hoc SQL: SQL*Plus and SQL Developer

There are numerous tools that can be used to connect to an Oracle database. Two of the most basic are SQL*Plus and SQL Developer. These are provided by Oracle Corporation and are perfectly adequate for much of the work that a database administrator needs to do. The choice between them is partly a matter of personal preference, partly to do with the environment, and partly to do with functionality. SQL Developer undoubtedly offers far more function than SQL*Plus, but it is more demanding in that it needs a graphical terminal, whereas SQL*Plus can be used on character-mode devices.

SQL*Plus

SQL*Plus is available on all platforms to which the database has been ported, and it is installed into both Oracle database and Oracle client Oracle Homes. On Linux, the executable file is `sqlplus`. The location of this file will be installation specific but will typically be something like

```
/u01/app/oracle/product/db_1/bin/sqlplus
```

Your Linux account should be set up appropriately to run SQL*Plus. There are some environment variables that will need to be set. These are

- ORACLE_HOME
- PATH
- LD_LIBRARY_PATH

The PATH must include the `bin` directory in the Oracle Home. The LD_LIBRARY_PATH should include the `lib` directory in the Oracle Home, but in practice you may get away without setting this. Figure 2-1 shows a Linux terminal window and some tests to see if the environment is correct.

In Figure 2-1, first the `echo` command checks whether the three variables have been set up correctly: there is an ORACLE_HOME, and the `bin` and `lib` directories in it have been set as the first elements of the PATH and LD_LIBRARY_PATH variables. Then `which` confirms that the SQL*Plus executable file really is available, in the PATH. Finally, SQL*Plus is launched with a username, a password, and a connect identifier passed to it on the command line.

Following the logon, the next lines of text display the version of SQL*Plus being used, which is 11.1.0.6.0, the version of the database to which the connection has been made (which happens to be the same as the version of the SQL*Plus tool), and which options have been installed within the database. The last line is the prompt to the user, `SQL>`, at which point they can enter any SQL*Plus or SQL command.

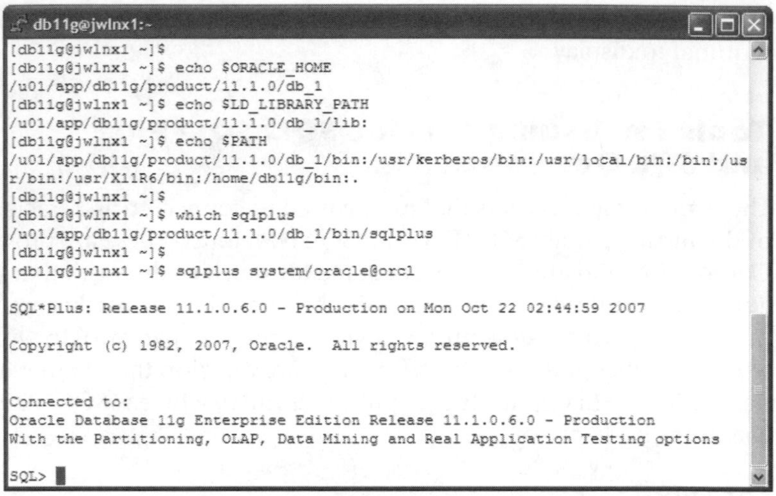

Figure 2-1
Checking the Linux
session setup

```
db11g@jwlnx1:~
[db11g@jwlnx1 ~]$
[db11g@jwlnx1 ~]$ echo $ORACLE_HOME
/u01/app/db11g/product/11.1.0/db_1
[db11g@jwlnx1 ~]$ echo $LD_LIBRARY_PATH
/u01/app/db11g/product/11.1.0/db_1/lib:
[db11g@jwlnx1 ~]$ echo $PATH
/u01/app/db11g/product/11.1.0/db_1/bin:/usr/kerberos/bin:/usr/local/bin:/bin:/us
r/bin:/usr/X11R6/bin:/home/db11g/bin:.
[db11g@jwlnx1 ~]$
[db11g@jwlnx1 ~]$ which sqlplus
/u01/app/db11g/product/11.1.0/db_1/bin/sqlplus
[db11g@jwlnx1 ~]$
[db11g@jwlnx1 ~]$ sqlplus system/oracle@orcl

SQL*Plus: Release 11.1.0.6.0 - Production on Mon Oct 22 02:44:59 2007

Copyright (c) 1982, 2007, Oracle.  All rights reserved.


Connected to:
Oracle Database 11g Enterprise Edition Release 11.1.0.6.0 - Production
With the Partitioning, OLAP, Data Mining and Real Application Testing options

SQL>
```

Historically, there were always two versions of SQL*Plus for Microsoft Windows: the character version and the graphical version. The character version is the executable file `sqlplus.exe`, the graphical version was `sqlplusw.exe`; with the current release the graphical version no longer exists, but many DBAs will prefer to use it, and the versions shipped with earlier releases are perfectly good tools for working with an 11g database. There are no problems with mixing client versions: an 11g SQL*Plus client can connect to a 9i database, and a 9i SQL*Plus client can connect to an 11g database; changes in Oracle Net may make it impossible to go back further than 9i. Following a default installation of either the Oracle database or just the Oracle client on Windows, SQL*Plus will be available as a shortcut on the Windows Start menu.

The tests of the environment and the need to set the variables if they are not correct, previously described for a Linux installation, are not usually necessary on a Windows installation. This is because the variables are set in the Windows registry by the Oracle Universal Installer when the software is installed. If SQL*Plus does not launch successfully, check the registry variables. Figure 2-2 shows the relevant section of the registry, viewed with the Windows `regedit.exe` registry editor utility. Within the registry editor, navigate to the key

```
HKEY_LOCAL_MACHINE\SOFTWARE\ORACLE\KEY_OraDb11g_home1
```

The final element of this navigation path will have a different name if there have been several 11g installations on the machine.

SQL Developer

SQL Developer is a tool for connecting to an Oracle database (or, in fact, some non-Oracle databases too) and issuing ad hoc SQL commands. It can also manage PL/SQL objects. Unlike SQL*Plus, it is a graphical tool with wizards for commonly needed actions. SQL Developer is written in Java, and requires a Java Runtime Environment (JRE) to run. It is available on all platforms that support the appropriate version of the JRE. SQL Developer does not need to be installed with the Oracle Universal

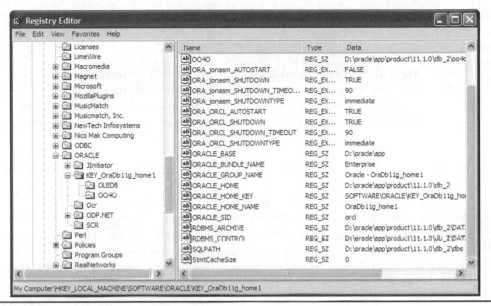

Figure 2-2 The Oracle registry variable

Installer. It is not installed in an Oracle Home but is completely self-contained. The latest version can be downloaded from Oracle Corporation's web site.

To install SQL Developer, unzip the ZIP file. That's all. It does require at least JRE release 1.5, to be available. If a JRE is not available on the machine being used, there are downloadable versions of SQL Developer for Windows that include it. (These versions include a Java Developers Kit or JDK which includes the JRE.) For platforms other than Windows, JRE1.5 must be preinstalled. Download it from Sun Microsystem's web site, and install it according to the platform-specific directions. To check that the JRE is available and its version, run the following command from an operating system prompt:

```
java -version
```

This should return something like

```
java version 1.5.0_13
Java(TM) 2 Runtime Environment, Standard Edition (build 1.5.0_13-b05)
Java HotSpot(TM) Client VM (build 1.5.0_13-b05, mixed mode, sharing)
```

If the version number returned is not what you expect, using `which java` may help identify the problem: the search path could be locating an incorrect version.

Once SQL Developer has been unzipped, change your current directory to the directory in which SQL Developer was unzipped, and launch it. On Windows, the executable file is `sqldeveloper.exe`. On Linux, it is the `sqldeveloper.sh` shell script. Remember to check that the DISPLAY environment variable has been set to a suitable value (such as 127.0.0.1:0.0, if SQL Developer is being run on the system console) before running the shell script.

Any problems with installing the JRE and launching SQL Developer should be referred to your system administrator.

TIP Database 11g does ship with a release of SQL Developer, and OUI will unzip it into a directory in the Oracle Home, but this will not be the up-to-date version. As of the time of writing, the version shipped with the production release of the 11g database is version 1.1, but the current version is 1.5.

Figure 2-3 shows the SQL Developer User Interface after connecting to a database and issuing a simple query.

The general layout of the SQL Developer window comprises a left pane for navigation around objects, and a right pane to display and enter information.

In the figure, the left-hand pane shows that a connection has been made to a database. The connection is called orcl_sys. This name is just a label chosen when the connection was defined, but most developers will use some sort of naming convention—in this case, the name chosen is the database identifier, which is orcl, and the name of the user the connection was made as, which was sys. The branches beneath list all the possible object types that can be managed. Expanding the branches would list the objects themselves. The

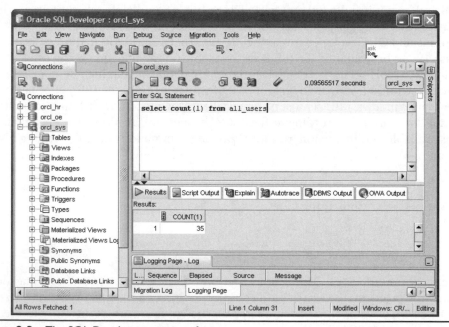

Figure 2-3 The SQL Developer user interface

right-hand pane has an upper part prompting the user to enter a SQL statement, and a lower part that will display the result of the statement. The layout of the panes and the tabs visible on them are highly customizable.

The menu buttons across the top menu bar give access to standard facilities:

- **File**   A normal Windows-like file menu, from where one can save work and exit from the tool.

- **Edit**   A normal Windows-like edit menu, from where one can undo, redo, copy, paste, find, and so on.

- **View**   The options for customizing the SQL Developer user interface.

- **Navigate**   Facilities for moving between panes, and also for moving around code that is being edited.

- **Run**   Forces execution of the SQL statements, SQL script, or PL/SQL block that is being worked on.

- **Debug**   Rather than running a whole block of code, step through it line by line with breakpoints.

- **Source**   Options for use when writing SQL and PL/SQL code, such as keyword completion and automatic indenting.

- **Migration**   Tools for converting applications designed for third-party databases (Microsoft Access and SQL Server, and MySQL) to the Oracle environment.

- **Tools**   Links to external programs, including SQL*Plus.

- **Help**   It's pretty good.

SQL Developer can be a very useful tool, and it is very customizable. Experiment with it, read the Help, and set up the user interface the way that works best for you.

Exercise 2-1: Install SQL Developer on Windows   In this exercise, you will install SQL Developer on a Windows machine.

1. Download the current version of SQL Developer. The URL is

   `http://www.oracle.com/technology/software/products/sql/index.html`

   Click the radio button to accept the license agreement, and then select the file that includes the JDK (if you do not already have this) or without the JDK if it already available on the machine.

   The file will be called something like `sqldeveloper-1.2.1.3213.zip`, depending on the version.

2. Move the file to an empty directory, and expand it. You will need WinZip or a similar utility installed to do this. The next illustration shows the contents

of the directory into which the file was unzipped, viewed from a command window.

```
C:\WINDOWS\system32\cmd.exe                                    _ □ ×
C:\sqldev\sqldeveloper>dir /ogn
 Volume in drive C is ACER
 Volume Serial Number is 389D-543B

 Directory of C:\sqldev\sqldeveloper

26/10/2007  09:46    <DIR>          .
26/10/2007  09:46    <DIR>          ..
26/10/2007  09:40    <DIR>          ide
26/10/2007  09:40    <DIR>          j2ee
26/10/2007  09:40    <DIR>          jdbc
26/10/2007  09:40    <DIR>          jdev
26/10/2007  09:41    <DIR>          jdk
26/10/2007  09:41    <DIR>          jlib
26/10/2007  09:41    <DIR>          lib
26/10/2007  09:41    <DIR>          rdbms
26/10/2007  09:41    <DIR>          sqldeveloper
21/08/2007  16:55             1,404 icon.png
21/08/2007  16:58            14,154 readme.html
21/08/2007  16:54               489 sqlcli
21/08/2007  16:54               577 sqlcli.bat
21/08/2007  16:55            84,432 sqldeveloper.exe
21/08/2007  16:54                71 sqldeveloper.sh
              6 File(s)        101,127 bytes
             11 Dir(s)  1,569,353,728 bytes free

C:\sqldev\sqldeveloper>_
```

Note the presence of the `readme.html` file. This contains the product release notes—open it in a browser, and read them.

3. Confirm success of your installation by running the `sqldeveloper.exe` executable file, either from the command prompt or by double-clicking it in Windows Explorer.

Oracle Enterprise Manager

The version of Oracle Enterprise Manager relevant to the OCP examination is Database Control. This is a tool for managing one database (which can be a RAC database), whereas Grid Control can manage many databases (and more). Database Control is installed into the Oracle Home. It consists of a Java process that monitors a port for incoming connection requests. If there are several database instances running off the same Oracle Home, each instance will be accessible through Database Control on a different port.

Database Control connects to the database on behalf of the user. It has built-in monitoring capability and will display real-time information regarding alert conditions, activity, and resource usage. It also gives access to many wizards that can make database management and tuning tasks feasible for novice DBAs, and quick to carry out for experienced DBAs.

Starting and stopping the Database Control process is described in Chapter 3; using it for management tasks is demonstrated in most subsequent chapters.

 TIP Oracle Enterprise Manager can be a very useful tool, but never use it without understanding what it is doing. Many DBAs like to work from the SQL*Plus or SQL Developer command line to understand exactly how to do something, and then use Enterprise Manager to make doing it easy. It is also a nice tool for checking syntax for a command you've forgotten.

Other Administration Tools

There are a number of other utilities that will be used in the course of this book. In many cases, there are both graphical and command-line interfaces. All of these are installed into the Oracle Home.

Oracle Net Manager, Oracle Net Configuration Assistant

These are two Java graphical tools for configuring the Oracle networking environment. There is considerable overlap in their functionality, but each does have some capability lacking in the other. Most network administration tasks can also be done through Database Control, and all can be done by editing configuration files by hand.

Historically, manual editing of the Oracle Net configuration files could be an extremely dodgy business: many DBAs believed that the files were very sensitive to trifling variations in format such as use of white spaces, abbreviations, and case. For this reason alone, the graphical tools have always been popular. Recent releases of Oracle Net appear to be less sensitive to such issues, but the graphical tools are still useful for preventing silly syntax errors.

Data Loading and Unloading Utilities

The classical utilities for transferring data between Oracle databases are the Export and Import tools. Export runs queries against a database to extract object definitions and data, and writes them out to an operating system file as a set of DDL and DML commands. Import reads the file and executes the DDL and DML statements to create the objects and enter the data into them. These utilities were very useful for transferring data between databases, because the transfer could go across operating systems and Oracle versions, but because they work through regular user sessions (they are client-server tools), they were not always suitable for large-scale operations. Export files can only be read by Import.

The replacement for Export and Import is Data Pump, introduced with release 10g. Functionally, Data Pump is very similar: it extracts data from one database, writes it out to a file, and inserts it into another database (possibly a different version, on a different platform). But the implementation is completely different. Data Pump uses background processes, not server sessions, to read and write data. This makes it much faster. Launching, controlling, and monitoring Data Pump jobs is done through client-server sessions, but the job itself all happens within the instance. Export and Import are still supported, but Data Pump is the preferred utility. Data Pump–generated files can only be read by Data Pump: there is no compatibility with Export and Import.

SQL*Loader is a tool for loading large amounts of data into an Oracle database from operating system files. These files can be laid out in a number of formats. There are restrictions on the formats SQL*Loader can use, but it is a pretty versatile tool and can be configured to parse many file layouts. Typical usage is the regular upload of data into an Oracle database from a third-party feeder system: the third-party database will write the data out in an agreed format, and SQL*Loader will then load it.

 EXAM TIP Data Pump can read only files generated by Data Pump, but SQL*Loader can read files generated by any third-party product, so long as the file is formatted in a way that can be parsed.

Data Pump and SQL*Loader are described in Chapter 23. Both utilities have command-line interfaces and a graphical interface through Database Control.

 TIP Export and Import will be useful for a long time to come. Data Pump is available only for releases 10g and 11g, so whenever it is necessary to transfer data to or from 9i and earlier databases, the older utilities will still be needed. It is well worth getting familiar with them.

Backup Utilities

It is possible to back up an Oracle database using operating system utilities. Operating system backups (known as *user-managed* backups) are fully supported, and there are circumstances when they may be the best option. But the preferred tool is RMAN, the Recovery Manager. RMAN backups are known as *server-managed* backups. RMAN is introduced and used for simple backup and restore operations in Chapters 15–17.

RMAN server-managed backups have capabilities that user-managed backups cannot provide. These include incremental backups, where only the changed blocks of a datafile are backed up; block-level restore and recovery, where if the damage to a file is only to a small part of the file, just that part can be repaired; the application of an incremental backup to full backup, to roll it forward; and validating the datafiles to detect corruptions before end users hit them.

 TIP The degree of knowledge of backup and recovery techniques tested by the OCP examinations may not be adequate for a DBA to be considered fully competent. Remember that the OCP curriculum is only an introduction to database administration. Backup is a critical task and will require further study.

The Oracle Secure Backup facility lets the DBA manage backup of the entire environment: Oracle Application Servers, remote clients, and operating system files, as well as the database. It is developed by Oracle in conjunction with operating system and hardware vendors.

Plan an Oracle Database Installation

Before running OUI, it is necessary to confirm adequate hardware and operating system resources, to make a decision about where to install the software, and to consider setting some environment variables.

Choice of Operating System

Some people become almost religiously attached to their favorite operating system. Try to avoid this. All operating systems have good and bad points: none are suitable for all applications. In general, Oracle Corporation supports all the mainstream platforms, including

• Linux on Intel and AMD

- Microsoft Windows on Intel and AMD
- Solaris on SPARC
- AIX on POWER
- HPUX on PA-RISC

These platforms are probably the most common, but there are many others. Some operating systems are available in both 32-bit and 64-bit versions to support different popular machine architectures. Usually, Oracle ports the database to both. When selecting an operating system, the choice should be informed by many factors, including

- Cost
- Ease of use
- Choice of hardware
- Available skills
- Scalability
- Fault tolerance
- Performance

There are other factors, and not only technical ones. Corporate standards will be particularly important.

Linux deserves a special mention. Oracle Corporation has made a huge commitment to Linux, and Linux is used as the development platform for many products (including database release 11g). Linux comes in several distributions. The most popular for Oracle servers are Red Hat and SUSE, but do not ignore the Oracle distribution: Enterprise Linux. This is very well packaged and fully supported by Oracle Corporation. This means you can have one support line for the entire server technology stack.

Hardware and Operating System Resources

Determining the necessary hardware resources for an Oracle database server requires knowledge of the anticipated data volumes and transaction workload. There are sizing guides available on MetaLink. The minimum hardware requirements for a usable system are

- 1GB RAM
- 1.5GB swap space
- 400MB in the TEMP location
- 1.5GB–3.5GB for the Oracle Home
- 1.5GB for the demonstration seed database
- 2.4GB for the flash recovery area
- A single 1GHz CPU

The wide range in space for the Oracle Home is because of platform variations. Around 2.5GB is typical for the Windows NTFS file system, 3.5GB for the Linux ext3 file system. The flash recovery area is optional. Even if defined, there is no check made as to whether the space is actually available. Machines of a lower specification than that just given can be used for learning or development but would not be suitable for anything else. The TEMP location is a directory specified by the TEMP environment variable.

The server operating system must be checked for compliance with the Oracle certified platforms, bearing in mind these issues:

- That some operating systems come in 32-bit and 64-bit versions
- Correct version and patch level
- Required packages
- Kernel parameters

These prerequisite factors will be checked by the OUI.

Exercise 2-2: Confirm Available Hardware Resources   In this exercise, you will check what resources are available, first for Windows and second for Linux.

Windows:

1. Right-click My Computer, and bring up the Properties dialog box. Note the amount of RAM. This should be at least 512MB, preferable 1GB.

2. Choose the Advanced tab, and then in the Performance section click the SETTINGS button.

3. In the Performance Options dialog box select the Advanced tab. Note the virtual memory setting. This should be at least one and a half times the memory reported in Step 1.

4. Open a command window, and find the location of your temporary data directory with this command:

   ```
   C:\> echo %TEMP%
   ```

   This will return something like

   ```
   C:\ Temp
   ```

   Check that there is at least 400MB free space on the file system returned (in this example, it is drive C:).

5. Identify a file system with 5GB free space for the Oracle Home and a database. This must be a local disk, not on a file server. If you want to stage the installation media (you probably do), that will need another 1.5GB, which can be on a file server.

Linux:

1. From an operating system prompt, run `free` to show main memory and swap space, which should ideally both be at least 1GB. These are the values in the total column. In the illustration that follows, they are both about 2GB.

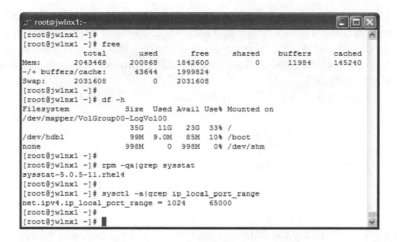

```
root@jwlnx1:~
[root@jwlnx1 ~]#
[root@jwlnx1 ~]# free
              total       used       free     shared    buffers     cached
Mem:        2043468     200868    1842600          0      11984     145240
-/+ buffers/cache:       43644    1999824
Swap:       2031608          0    2031608
[root@jwlnx1 ~]#
[root@jwlnx1 ~]# df -h
Filesystem          Size  Used Avail Use% Mounted on
/dev/mapper/VolGroup00-LogVol00
                     35G   11G   23G  33% /
/dev/hdb1            99M  9.0M   85M  10% /boot
none                998M     0  998M   0% /dev/shm
[root@jwlnx1 ~]#
[root@jwlnx1 ~]# rpm -qa|grep sysstat
sysstat-5.0.5-11.rhel4
[root@jwlnx1 ~]#
[root@jwlnx1 ~]# sysctl -a|grep ip_local_port_range
net.ipv4.ip_local_port_range = 1024        65000
[root@jwlnx1 ~]#
[root@jwlnx1 ~]#
```

2. Run df -h to show the free space in each mounted file system. Confirm that there is a file system with 5GB free for the Oracle Home and the database. Confirm that there is 400MB free in /tmp if it exists as a separate file system; if there is no specific file system for /tmp (as is the case in the illustration), you can assume that it is in the root file system. In the illustration, there is 23GB free in the root file system.

3. Use rpm to check that all required packages are installed, at the correct (or later) version. In the illustration, the sysstat package is being checked.

4. Use sysctl to check that all the required kernel settings have been made—you may need to have root privilege to do this. In the illustration, the IP port range is being checked.

Optimal Flexible Architecture

The Oracle Home will need a file system into which it can be installed. Oracle Corporation has designed OFA, the Optimal Flexible Architecture, as a file system directory structure that should make maintaining multiple versions of multiple Oracle products straightforward. The heart of OFA is two environment variables: ORACLE_BASE and ORACLE_HOME. The ORACLE_BASE directory is one directory on the server, beneath which all the Oracle software (all products, all versions) should be installed. Each version of each product will then have its own ORACLE_HOME, beneath the ORACLE_BASE. This structure should ensure that many databases can be created and upgraded without ever ending up with files in inappropriate locations.

The Linux and Unix OFA standard for ORACLE_BASE is that it should be a directory named according the template /pm/h/u, where p is a string constant such as u, m is a numeric constant such as 01, h is a standard directory name such as app, and u is the operating system account that will own all the Oracle software, such as oracle.

The Windows OFA standard for ORACLE_BASE is \oracle\app off the root of any suitable drive letter.

The OFA standard for the database ORACLE_HOME is $ORACLE_BASE/*product*/*v*/ *db_n*, where *product* is the constant product, *v* is the release number of the product such as 11.1.0, and *db_n* is a name derived by the installer based on which product it is, such as db for database, and an incrementing number for each installation of that product, such as 1.

Typical Linux values for ORACLE_BASE and ORACLE_HOME are

```
/u01/app/oracle
/u01/app/oracle/product/11.1.0/db_1
```

and typical Windows values are

```
D:\oracle\app
D:\oracle\app\product\11.1.0\db_1
```

The OFA location for the database itself is ORACLE_BASE/*q*/*d*, where *q* is the string oradata and *d* is the name of the database. A Linux example for a database called orcl is

```
/u01/app/oracle/oradata/orcl
```

Within the database directory, the controlfile copies, online redo logfiles, and datafiles should be named as follows:

File Type	Name	Variable	Examples
Controlfile	control*nn*.ctl	*nn* is a unique number	control01.ctl, control02.ctl
Redo logfiles	redo*nn*.log	*nn* is the online redo logfile group number	redo01.log, redo02.log
Datafiles	*tablespacenamenn*.dbf	the datafile's tablespace name and a number	system01.dbf, system02.dbf

 TIP OFA does not specify the naming convention for multiplexed online redo logfiles. Many DBAs suffix the OFA name with a letter to differentiate members in the same group: redo01a.log, redo01b.log.

Environment Variables

One significant difference between Windows and Unix operating systems is in the way in which environment variables are set. Within the Unix family, there are further variations depending on the shell being used. On Windows operating systems, there is the registry: Unix has no equivalent of this.

The Oracle database makes use of several environment variables, some of which can be set before even running the OUI. The OUI will prompt for them, using the preset values as defaults. On Linux, the one variable that must be set before the installer can run is DISPLAY.

Variables in Windows

Variables can be set at various levels with various degrees of persistence on a Windows system, ranging from permanent, system-wide variables set in the Windows registry to variables set interactively within a command shell. As a general rule, variables set at a higher level (such as within the registry) can be overruled at a lower level (such as within a shell).

The highest level for variables is in the registry. The OUI creates a key in the registry,

```
HKEY_LOCAL_MACHINE\SOFTWARE\ORACLE
```

and defines variables for each installed Oracle product beneath this. Figure 2-2 earlier shows the variables set for the ORACLE key, and then those set one level down, in the key `KEY_OraDb11g_home1`.

At the `ORACLE` level, the variable `inst_loc` defines the location of the OUI inventory, described previously. Beneath this level there are keys for each installed product. In the example shown, there are two products installed: JInitiator (which is Oracle's client-side JVM for running the Forms viewing applet—two versions have been installed on the system) and Database 11*g*. In the key `KEY_OraDb11g_home1` there are a number of variables, two of the more significant being the ORACLE_BASE and the ORACLE_HOME. Others specify the locations of various components and the options Windows should use for automatic startup and shutdown of a database instance called ORCL.

 TIP There is no easy way to query the value of a Windows registry variable, other than by looking at the registry with a tool such as the `regedit.exe` registry editing tool. For this reason, many DBAs like to set variables at the session level, from where they can be easily retrieved and used. Figure 2-4 shows an example of doing this.

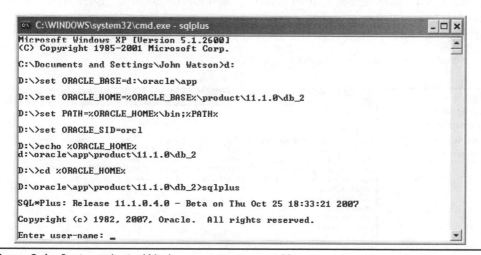

Figure 2-4   Setting and using Windows environment variables

The commands for setting up the environment in the manner desired would usually be specified in a batch file that could be invoked from the command line or as a login script.

Variables in Linux

The syntax for setting and reading environment variables varies from one shell to another. The examples that follow are for the bash shell, because that is possibly the most widely used Linux shell.

Linux environment variables are always session specific. They must all be set up for each session—there is no equivalent of the Windows registry setting up variables with a scope that can include all sessions. To simulate setting what might be thought of as "global" variables applying to all sessions by all users, set them in the /etc/ profile file, which is executed at each logon.

Figure 2-5 shows examples of setting and using bash shell environment variables.

Note that in Figure 2-5 two more variables are being set on Linux than in Figure 2-4 on Windows. The LD_LIBRARY_PATH variable should include all dynamically linked libraries that may be needed, and the DISPLAY must be set to point to the terminal on which the user is working.

 EXAM WATCH If the DISPLAY variable is not set appropriately, OUI will not be able to open any windows and will throw an error.

Install the Oracle Software by Using the Oracle Universal Installer (OUI)

To run the OUI for the first time, log on to the server machine as an operating system user with permission to read the installation media (or the directory to which it has been staged) and to write to the directory chosen for the ORACLE_BASE. Then launch the OUI by running

setup.exe (Windows)

runInstaller.sh (Linux)

Figure 2-5

Setting and using environment variables in the bash shell

```
db11g@jwlnx1:~
[db11g@jwlnx1 ~]$
[db11g@jwlnx1 ~]$
[db11g@jwlnx1 ~]$
[db11g@jwlnx1 ~]$ export ORACLE_BASE=/u01/app
[db11g@jwlnx1 ~]$ export ORACLE_HOME=$ORACLE_BASE/db11g/product/11.1.0/db_1
[db11g@jwlnx1 ~]$ export PATH=$ORACLE_HOME/bin:$PATH
[db11g@jwlnx1 ~]$ export LD_LIBRARY_PATH=$ORACLE_HOME/lib:$LD_LIBRARY_PATH
[db11g@jwlnx1 ~]$ export DISPLAY=jwacer.bplc.co.za:0.0
[db11g@jwlnx1 ~]$ export ORACLE_SID=orcl11g
[db11g@jwlnx1 ~]$
[db11g@jwlnx1 ~]$ which sqlplus
/u01/app/db11g/product/11.1.0/db_1/bin/sqlplus
[db11g@jwlnx1 ~]$
[db11g@jwlnx1 ~]$ echo $ORACLE_SID
orcl11g
[db11g@jwlnx1 ~]$
[db11g@jwlnx1 ~]$
```

To bypass the prerequisite checks (not advised, but may be useful), add a switch:

```
runinstaller -ignoreSysPrereqs
```

It is possible to do an unmanaged installation known as a silent install. This will be necessary if there is no graphics device, and is very convenient if you are performing many identical installs on identical machines. Also, it becomes possible to embed an Oracle installation within the routine for deploying a packaged application. A silent install requires a response file, which includes answers to all the prompts that would usually be manually given. The syntax for running the OUI in this way is

```
runInstaller -silent -responsefile responsefilename
```

The response file can be created manually (there are examples in the /response directory on the installation media), or it can be recorded by OUI during an interactive install:

```
runInstaller -record -destinationFile responsefilename
```

Before doing a silent install, the inventory pointer file (/etc/oraInst.loc on Linux) must have been created, or OUI will not be able to locate (or create if necessary) the inventory.

Exercise 2-3: Install the Oracle Home In this exercise, install an Oracle Home on Linux using the OUI.

1. Log on to Linux as a user who is a member of the dba group. In the following example, the operating system user is db11g. Confirm the username and group membership with the id command, as in this illustration:

```
db11g@jwlnx1:~
login as: db11g
Sent username "db11g"
db11g@10.0.0.4's password:
Last login: Sat Oct 27 00:57:19 2007 from 10.0.0.12
[db11g@jwlnx1 ~]$
[db11g@jwlnx1 ~]$ id
uid=501(db11g) gid=501(dba) groups=100(users),501(dba)
[db11g@jwlnx1 ~]$
[db11g@jwlnx1 ~]$ su -
Password:
[root@jwlnx1 ~]# mkdir -p /u02/app/db11g
[root@jwlnx1 ~]# chown db11g:dba /u02/app/db11g
[root@jwlnx1 ~]# chmod 770 /u02/app/db11g
[root@jwlnx1 ~]# exit
logout
[db11g@jwlnx1 ~]$ export DISPLAY=10.0.0.12:0.0
[db11g@jwlnx1 ~]$
[db11g@jwlnx1 ~]$ /home/db11g/db11g_dvd/runInstaller
Starting Oracle Universal Installer...
```

2. Switch to the root user with su and create an OFA-compliant directory for the Oracle Base with the mkdir command. In the example, this is /u02/app/ db11g. Change the ownership and access modes of the directory such that the db11g user has full control of it with the chown and chmod commands, as in the preceding illustration, and exit back to the Oracle user.

3. If you are not working on the console machine, set your DISPLAY variable to point to an X Window server on the machine on which you are working. In the illustration, this is 10.0.0.12:0.0.

4. Launch the OUI by running the `runInstaller` shell script from the root of the installation media. In the example, the installation media has been copied into the directory `/home/db11g/db11g_dvd`.

5. The first OUI window will appear, as in the illustration that follows:

   A. Select the Basic Installation radio button.

   B. Specify the Oracle Base as the directory created in Step 2. The Oracle Home will default to an OFA-compliant name beneath it.

   C. Select the Enterprise Edition installation type.

   D. Select dba as the Unix DBA group.

   E. De-select the option to create a database.

   F. Click NEXT.

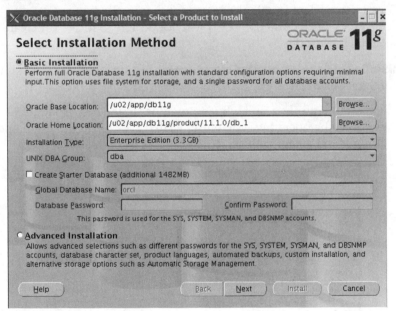

6. If this is the first Oracle install on the machine, the next window will prompt for the location of the OUI inventory. Be sure to specify a directory to which the db11g user has write permission.

7. The OUI will then perform its prerequisite checks. If they pass, click NEXT to continue. If any fail, take note and fix them if possible. Then use the RETRY button to rerun the test. If the check really cannot be fixed, you can click NEXT to proceed anyway at your own risk.

8. The next window will be a summary of what the OUI is going to do. Click NEXT, and it will do it. This should take twenty minutes or so (highly variable, depending on the machine).

9. Toward the end of the install, the window shown in the illustration that follows will appear. This prompts you to run two scripts as the root user: the `orainstRoot.sh` script that will write the `/etc/oraInst.loc` file, and the `root.sh` script that adjusts permissions on files in the new Oracle home. If this is not the first time the OUI has run on the machine, there will not be a prompt for `orainstRoot.sh`. Run the script(s) as root from an operating system prompt (accept defaults for any prompts) and then click OK.

10. The installer will return a message stating that "The installation of Oracle Database 11g was successful." Congratulations! Click EXIT.

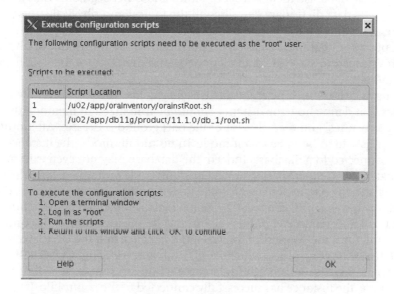

Create a Database by Using the Database Configuration Assistant

This one OCP examination objective is in fact a large task, comprising several steps. It is not large in terms of the practicalities (creating a database can be quick and simple—a single two-word command will do it, and it may take less than ten minutes), but there are many prerequisite concepts you should understand:

- The instance, the database, and the data dictionary
- Using the DBCA to create a database
- The instance parameter file
- The CREATE DATABASE command
- Post-creation scripts
- The DBCA's other functions

The Instance, the Database, and the Data Dictionary

An Oracle server consists of an instance and a database; the two are separate, but connected. The instance comprises memory structures and processes, stored in your machine's RAM and executing on its CPU(s); its existence is transient; it can be started and stopped. The database comprises files on disk; once created, it persists until it is deleted. Creating an instance is nothing more than building the memory structures and starting the processes. Creating a database is done by the instance as a once-off operation, and the instance can then open and close it many times subsequently. The database is inaccessible without the instance.

Within the database there is a set of tables and other segments called the *data dictionary*. The data dictionary describes all the logical and physical structures in the database, including all the segments that store user data.

The process of database creation establishes the bare minimum of physical structures needed to store the data dictionary, and then creates the data dictionary within them.

An instance is defined by an instance *parameter file*. The parameter file contains directives that define how the instance should be initialized in memory: the size of the memory structures, and the behavior of the background processes. After building the instance, it is said to be in *no mount* mode. In no mount mode, the instance exists but has not connected to a database. Indeed, the database may not even exist at this point.

All parameters, either specified by the parameter file or implied, have default values, except for one: the parameter DB_NAME. The DB_NAME parameter names the database to which the instance will connect. This name is also embedded in the controlfile. The CONTROL_FILES parameter points the instance to the location of the controlfile. This parameter defines the connection between the instance and the database. When the instance reads the controlfile (which it will find by reading the CONTROL_FILES parameter) if there is a mismatch in database names, the database will not *mount*. In mount mode, the instance has successfully connected to the controlfile. If the controlfile is damaged or nonexistent, it will be impossible to mount the database. The controlfile is small, but vital.

Within the controlfile, there are pointers to the other files (the online redo logfiles and the datafiles) that make up the rest of the database. Having mounted the database, the instance can *open* the database by locating and opening these other files. An open database is a database where the instance has opened all the available online redo logfiles and datafiles. Also within the controlfile, there is a mapping of datafiles to tablespaces. This lets the instance identify the datafile(s) that make(s) up the SYSTEM tablespace within which it will find the data dictionary. The data dictionary lets the instance resolve references to objects referred to in SQL code to the segments in which they reside, and work out where, physically, the objects are.

The creation of a database server must therefore involve these steps:

- Create the instance.
- Create the database.
- Create the data dictionary.

In practice, the steps are divided slightly differently:

- Create the instance.
- Create the database and the data dictionary objects.
- Create the data dictionary views.

The data dictionary as initially created with the database is fully functional but unusable. It has the capability for defining and managing user data but cannot be used by normal human beings because its structure is too abstruse. Before users (or DBAs) can actually use the database, a set of views must be created on top of the data dictionary that will render it understandable by humans.

The data dictionary itself is created by running a set of SQL scripts that exist in the ORACLE_HOME/rdbms/admin directory. These are called by the CREATE DATABASE command. The first is sql.bsq, which then calls several other scripts. These scripts issue a series of commands that create all the tables and other objects that make up the data dictionary.

The views and other objects that make the database usable are generated by additional scripts in the ORACLE_HOME/rdbms/admin directory, prefixed with "cat". Examples of these are catalog.sql and catproc.sql, which should always be run immediately after database creation. There are many other optional "cat" scripts that will enable certain features—some of these can be run at creation time; others might be run subsequently to install these features at a later date.

Using the DBCA to Create a Database

These are the steps to follow to create a database:

1. Create a parameter file and (optionally) a password file.
2. Use the parameter file to build an instance in memory.
3. Issue the CREATE DATABASE command. This will generate, as a minimum, a controlfile; two online redo logfiles; two datafiles for the SYSTEM and SYSAUX tablespaces; and a data dictionary.
4. Run SQL scripts to generate the data dictionary views and the supplied PL/SQL packages.
5. Run SQL scripts to generate the objects used by Enterprise Manager Database Control, and any other database options chosen to be enabled.

On Windows systems, there is an additional step because Oracle runs as a Windows service. Oracle provides a utility, oradim.exe, to assist you in creating this service.

These steps can be executed interactively from the SQL*Plus prompt or through a GUI tool, the Database Configuration Assistant (DBCA). Alternatively, you can automate the process by using scripts or start the DBCA with a response file.

Whatever platform you are running on, the easiest way to create a database is through the DBCA. You may well have run this as part of the installation: OUI can launch the DBCA, which prompts you and walks you through the whole process. It creates a parameter file and a password file and then generates scripts that will start the instance; create the database; and generate the data dictionary, the data dictionary views, and Enterprise Manager Database Control. Alternatively, you can create the parameter file and password file by hand, and then do the rest from a SQL*Plus session. Many DBAs combine the two techniques: use the DBCA to generate the files and scripts, and then look at them and perhaps edit them before running them from SQL*Plus.

The DBCA is written in Java—it is therefore the same on all platforms. On Unix, you run the DBCA on the machine where you wish to create the database, but you can launch and control it from any machine that has an X server to display the DBCA windows. This is standard X Window System—you set an environment variable DISPLAY to tell the program where to send the windows it opens. For example,

```
export DISPLAY=10.10.10.65:0.0
```

will redirect all X windows to the machine identified by IP address 10.10.10.65, no matter which machine you are actually running the DBCA on.

To launch the DBCA on Windows, take the shortcut on the Start menu. The navigation path will be

1. Start
2. Programs
3. Oracle – OraDB11g_home3
4. Configuration and Migration Tools
5. Database Configuration Assistant

Note that the third part of the path will vary, depending on the name given to the Oracle Home at install time.

To launch the DBCA on Linux, first set the environment variables that should always be set for any Linux DBA session: ORACLE_BASE, ORACLE_HOME, PATH, and LD_LIBRARY_PATH. This is an example of a script that will do this:

```
export ORACLE_BASE=/u02/app/db11g
export ORACLE_HOME=$ORACLE_BASE/product/11.1.0/db_1
export PATH=$ORACLE_HOME/bin:$PATH
export LD_LIBRARY_PATH=$ORACLE_HOME/lib:$LD_LIBRARY_PATH
```

Note that the Base and Home will vary according to choices made at install time. To launch the DBCA, run the dbca shell script, located in the $ORACLE_HOME/bin directory.

TIP Be sure to have the $ORACLE_HOME/bin directory at the start of your search path, in case there are any Linux executables with the same name as Oracle executables. A well-known case in point is rman, which is both an Oracle tool and a SUSE Linux utility.

Remember that (with one exception) every choice made at database creation time can be changed later, but that some changes are awkward and may involve downtime. It is not therefore vital to get everything right—but the more right it can be, the better.

If the database to be created is going to use Enterprise Manager Database Control, there is an additional step that should be carried out before launching the DBCA: configuring a database listener. This requirement is because Database Control always connects to its database through a listener, and the DBCA checks whether one is available. The configuration is a simple task, described in detail in Chapter 4. For now, do this with the Net Configuration Assistant, accepting defaults all the way.

To launch the Net Configuration Assistant on Windows, take the shortcut on the Start menu. The navigation path will be

1. Start

2. Programs

3. Oracle – OraDB11g_home3

4. Configuration and Migration Tools

5. Net Configuration Assistant

To launch the assistant on Linux, run the `netca` shell script, located in the `$ORACLE_HOME/bin` directory.

Exercise 2-4: Use the DBCA to Create a Database   In this exercise you will create a database listener (if one does not exist already) and then create a database to be called ocp11g using the DBCA, on either Windows or Linux. There is no significant difference between platforms. The illustrations that follow happen to be from Windows.

1. Launch the Net Configuration Assistant. The radio button for Listener Configuration will be selected.

2. Click NEXT three times. If there is a message stating that a listener already exists, you can exit the tool immediately by clicking CANCEL and FINISH, and proceed to Step 3. Otherwise, click NEXT another four times to define the default listener, and then FINISH to exit the tool.

3. Launch the Database Configuration Assistant.

4. On the DBCA Welcome dialog box, click NEXT.

5. The next dialog box has radio buttons for

   • Create a Database

   • Configure Database Options

   • Delete a Database

   • Manage Templates

   • Configure Automatic Storage

The second and third options will be grayed out, unless the DBCA detects an existing database running off this Oracle Home. Select the Create A Database radio button, and click NEXT.

6. The Database Templates dialog box has radio buttons for selecting a template on which to base the new database. Select the Custom Database radio button, as this will present all possible options. Click NEXT.

7. In the Database Identification dialog box, enter a global database name, and a System Identifier (a SID), which will be used as the instance name. These will default to the same thing, which is often what is wanted. For this exercise, enter **ocp11g** for both names. Click NEXT.

8. The Management Options dialog box has a check box for configuring the database with Enterprise Manager. Select this. Then there are radio buttons for either Grid Control or Database Control. The Grid Control radio button will be grayed out if the DBCA does not detect a Grid Control agent running on the machine. Select Database Control. There are check boxes for Enable Email Notifications and Enable Daily Backup; do not select these. Click NEXT. It is at this point that the DBCA will give an error if there is no listener available.

9. The Database Credentials dialog box prompts for passwords for four users in the database: SYS (who owns the data dictionary), SYSTEM (used for most DBA work), DBSNMP (used for external monitoring), and SYSMAN (used by Enterprise Manager). Select the radio button for Use The Same Password For All Accounts. Enter **oracle** as the password, twice, and click NEXT.

10. In the Security Settings dialog box, accept the default, which is 11g security, and click NEXT.

11. The Storage Options dialog box offers a choice between file system, ASM, or raw devices. Select File System, and click NEXT.

12. The Database File Locations dialog box prompts for a root directory for the database. Select Use Database File Locations From Template. Click the FILE LOCATION VARIABLES button to see where the database will be created. It will be the OFA location ORACLE_BASE/oradata/DB_NAME. Click NEXT.

13. In the Recovery Configuration dialog box, accept the default configuration for the flash recovery area (which will be 2GB in ORACLE_BASE/flash_recovery_area) and do not enable archiving. Click NEXT.

14. In the Database Content dialog box, deselect all options except Enterprise Manager Repository. The others are not needed for this database and will increase the creation time. Some options will be grayed out; this will be because they have not been installed into the Oracle Home. Click the STANDARD DATABASE COMPONENTS button, and deselect these as well. Don't worry about a warning that the XML DB is used by other components. Click NEXT.

15. The Initialization Parameters dialog box has four tabs. Leave the default values, but examine all the tabs. The Memory tab shows the memory that will be allocated to the instance, based on a percentage of the main memory detected. The Sizing tab shows the database block size, defaulting to 8KB. This is the one thing that can never be changed after creation. The Character Sets tab shows the character set to be used within the database, which will have a default value based on the operating system. This can be very awkward to change afterward. The Connection Mode tab determines how user sessions will be managed. Click NEXT.

16. The Database Storage dialog box shows, via a navigation tree on the left, the files that will be created. Navigate around this, and see the names and sizes of the files. These are usually nowhere near adequate for a production system but will be fine for now. Click NEXT.

17. In the Creation Options dialog box, select the check boxes for Create Database and Generate Database Creation Scripts. Note the path for the scripts; it will be `ORACLE_BASE/admin/ocp11g/scripts`. Click FINISH.

18. The Confirmation dialog box shows what the DBCA is about to do. Click OK.

19. The DBCA will generate the creation scripts (which should only take a few minutes). Click OK, and the DBCA will create the database. The illustration that follows shows the progress dialog box. Note the location of the DBCA logs—`ORACLE_BASE/cfgtoollogs/dbca/ocp11g`—it may be necessary to look at the logs if anything fails. The creation will typically take fifteen to forty minutes, depending on the machine.

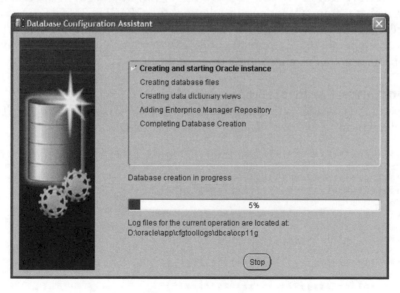

20. When the DBCA completes, it will present the dialog box shown in the illustration that follows. Take note of all the information given, in particular the URL given for database control:

```
https://jwacer.bplc.co.za:1158/em
```

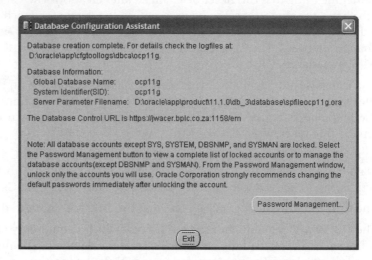

The Scripts and Other Files Created by the DBCA

While the DBCA is creating the database, inspect the scripts generated. They will be in the directory ORACLE_BASE/admin/DB_NAME/scripts. In the example that follow, which is from a Windows installation, the ORACLE_BASE is d:\oracle\app and the database name (the global name, without the domain suffix) is ocp11g, so the scripts are therefore in d:\oracle\app\admin\ocp11g\scripts. Navigate to the appropriate directory, and study the files therein.

The Instance Parameter File

The first file to consider is the instance parameter file, named init.ora. This is a print of a typical init.ora file, as generated by the DBCA:

```
######################################################################
# Copyright (c) 1991, 2001, 2002 by Oracle Corporation
######################################################################
##########################################
# Cache and I/O
##########################################
db_block_size=8192
##########################################
# Cursors and Library Cache
##########################################
open_cursors=300
##########################################
# Database Identification
##########################################
db_domain=""
db_name=ocp11g
```

```
##########################################
# File Configuration
##########################################
control_files=("D:\oracle\app\oradata\ocp11g\control01.ctl",
"D:\oracle\app\oradata\ocp11g\control02.ctl",
"D:\oracle\app\oradata\ocp11g\control03.ctl")
db_recovery_file_dest=D:\oracle\app\flash_recovery_area
db_recovery_file_dest_size=2147483648
##########################################
# Job Queues
##########################################
job_queue_processes=10
##########################################
# Miscellaneous
##########################################
compatible=11.1.0.0.0
diagnostic_dest=D:\oracle\app
##########################################
# NLS
##########################################
nls_language="ENGLISH"
nls_territory="UNITED KINGDOM"
##########################################
# Processes and Sessions
##########################################
processes=150
##########################################
# SGA Memory
##########################################
sga_target=318767104
##########################################
# Security and Auditing
##########################################
audit_file_dest=D:\oracle\app\admin\ocp11g\adump
audit_trail=db
remote_login_passwordfile=EXCLUSIVE
##########################################
# Shared Server
##########################################
dispatchers="(PROTOCOL=TCP) (SERVICE=ocp11gXDB)"
##########################################
# Sort, Hash Joins, Bitmap Indexes
##########################################
pga_aggregate_target=105906176
##########################################
# System Managed Undo and Rollback Segments
##########################################
undo_management=AUTO
undo_tablespace=UNDOTBS1
```

Any line beginning with a # symbol is a comment and can be ignored. There are about 300 parameters, but the file generated by the DBCA sets only a few. Most of these are covered in detail in later chapters. Two parameters to emphasize at this point are DB_BLOCK_SIZE and CONTROL_FILES. DB_BLOCK_SIZE determines the size of the buffers in the database buffer cache. When the instance is instructed to create a database, this size will also be used to format the datafiles that make up the SYSTEM and SYSAUX tablespaces. It can never be changed after database creation. CONTROL_FILES is the pointer that allows the instance to find all the multiplexed copies of the database controlfile. At this stage, the controlfile does not exist; this parameter will tell the instance where to create it. Some of the other parameters are self-explanatory and can be easily related back to the options taken when going through the steps of the exercise, but eventually you must refer to the Oracle Documentation Library (the volume you need is titled "Reference") and read up on all of them. All! Those necessary for examination purposes will be described at the appropriate point.

 EXAM TIP What is the only instance parameter for which there is no default? It is DB_NAME. A parameter file must exist with at least this one parameter, or you cannot start an instance. The DB_NAME can be up to eight characters long, letters and digits only, beginning with a letter.

The Database Creation Shell Script

This is the file the DBCA executes to launch the database creation process. It is a batch file on Windows, and a shell script on Linux. A Windows example:

```
mkdir D:\oracle\app
mkdir D:\oracle\app\admin\ocp11g\adump
mkdir D:\oracle\app\admin\ocp11g\dpdump
mkdir D:\oracle\app\admin\ocp11g\pfile
mkdir D:\oracle\app\cfgtoollogs\dbca\ocp11g
mkdir D:\oracle\app\flash_recovery_area
mkdir D:\oracle\app\oradata\ocp11g
mkdir D:\oracle\app\product\11.1.0\db_3\database
set ORACLE_SID=ocp11g
set PATH=%ORACLE_HOME%\bin;%PATH%
D:\oracle\app\product\11.1.0\db_3\bin\oradim.exe -new -sid OCP11G
-startmode manual -spfile
D:\oracle\app\product\11.1.0\db_3\bin\oradim.exe -edit -sid OCP11G
-startmode auto -srvcstart system
D:\oracle\app\product\11.1.0\db_3\bin\sqlplus /nolog
 @D:\oracle\app\admin\db11g\scripts\ocp11g.sql
```

First, the script creates a few directories in the Oracle Base. Then it sets the ORACLE_SID environment variable (more of this later) and prepends the ORACLE_HOME/bin directory to the search path.

The two commands that use oradim.exe will not appear on a Linux system. On Windows, an Oracle instance runs as a Windows service. This service must be created. The oradim.exe utility is run twice. The first time will define a new service in the Windows registry, with the system identifier OCP11G, and put the service on manual start. The -spfile switch refers to the type of initialization parameter file to be used. The second use of oradim.exe edits the service, to set it to start automatically whenever Windows starts. Figure 2-6 shows the resulting service defined in the registry. To see this, use the regedit.exe registry editor (or some similar tool) to navigate to the key

```
HKEY_LOCAL_MACHINE/SYSTEM/currentControlSet/Services/OracleServiceOCP11G
```

Each database instance that can run on a Windows machine will be a service, named after the name of the instance (in this case, OCP11G) that was provided in Exercise 2-4, Step 7.

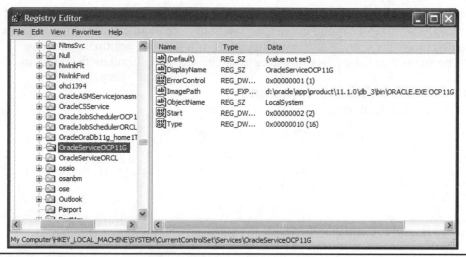

Figure 2-6 The Windows service defining an Oracle instance

After the service creation, the script launches SQL*Plus and runs the SQL script `ocp11g.sql` which will control the creation of the database:

```
set verify off
PROMPT specify a password for sys as parameter 1;
DEFINE sysPassword = &1
PROMPT specify a password for system as parameter 2;
DEFINE systemPassword = &2
PROMPT specify a password for sysman as parameter 3;
DEFINE sysmanPassword = &3
PROMPT specify a password for dbsnmp as parameter 4;
DEFINE dbsnmpPassword = &4
host D:\oracle\app\product\11.1.0\db_3\bin\orapwd.exe
file=D:\oracle\app\product\11.1.0\db_3\database\PWDocp11g.ora
password=&&sysPassword force=y
@D:\oracle\app\admin\ocp11g\scripts\CreateDB.sql
@D:\oracle\app\admin\ocp11g\scripts\CreateDBFiles.sql
@D:\oracle\app\admin\ocp11g\scripts\CreateDBCatalog.sql
@D:\oracle\app\admin\ocp11g\scripts\emRepository.sql
@D:\oracle\app\admin\ocp11g\scripts\postDBCreation.sql
```

At the top of the script, there are prompts for passwords for four critical accounts. These will be provided by the password entered in Exercise 2-4, Step 9.

Then, using host to spawn an operating system shell, the script runs the `orapwd` `.exe` utility (just called `orapwd` on Linux.) This will create an external password file for the database. The name of the file must be

```
%ORACLE_HOME%\database\PWD<db_name>.ora
```

on Windows, or

```
$ORACLE_HOME/dbs/orapw<db_name>
```

on Linux, where *<db_name>* is the name of the database. This is the name provided for the global database name in Exercise 2-4, Step 7, but without any domain suffix. Usually, this is the same as the instance name—but they are not the same thing.

The script then calls `CreateDB.sql`, which will actually create the database.

The CREATE DATABASE Command

This is an example of the `CreateDB.sql` script:

```
connect "SYS"/"&&sysPassword" as SYSDBA
set echo on
spool D:\oracle\app\admin\ocp11g\scripts\CreateDB.log
startup nomount pfile="D:\oracle\app\admin\ocp11g\scripts\init.ora";
CREATE DATABASE "ocp11g"
MAXINSTANCES 8
MAXLOGHISTORY 1
MAXLOGFILES 16
MAXLOGMEMBERS 3
MAXDATAFILES 100
DATAFILE 'D:\oracle\app\oradata\ocp11g\system01.dbf'
SIZE 300M REUSE AUTOEXTEND ON NEXT 10240K MAXSIZE UNLIMITED
EXTENT MANAGEMENT LOCAL
SYSAUX DATAFILE 'D:\oracle\app\oradata\ocp11g\sysaux01.dbf'
SIZE 120M REUSE AUTOEXTEND ON NEXT 10240K MAXSIZE UNLIMITED
SMALLFILE DEFAULT TEMPORARY TABLESPACE TEMP TEMPFILE
'D:\oracle\app\oradata\ocp11g\temp01.dbf' SIZE 20M REUSE
AUTOEXTEND ON NEXT 640K MAXSIZE UNLIMITED
SMALLFILE UNDO TABLESPACE "UNDOTBS1" DATAFILE
'D:\oracle\app\oradata\ocp11g\undotbs01.dbf' SIZE 200M REUSE
AUTOEXTEND ON NEXT 5120K MAXSIZE UNLIMITED
CHARACTER SET WE8MSWIN1252
NATIONAL CHARACTER SET AL16UTF16
LOGFILE GROUP 1 ('D:\oracle\app\oradata\ocp11g\redo01.log') SIZE 51200K,
GROUP 2 ('D:\oracle\app\oradata\ocp11g\redo02.log') SIZE 51200K,
GROUP 3 ('D:\oracle\app\oradata\ocp11g\redo03.log') SIZE 51200K
USER SYS IDENTIFIED BY "&&sysPassword"
USER SYSTEM IDENTIFIED BY "&&systemPassword";
spool off
```

The script connects to the instance, using the syntax for password file authentication (this is fully described in Chapter 3). Let's consider the script line by line.

The `echo` and `spool` commands cause SQL*Plus to write out a log of everything that happens next.

The STARTUP NOMOUNT command builds the instance in memory, using the static parameter file we saw earlier. The significance of "NOMOUNT" will be dealt with in Chapter 3; for now, let it suffice that it is necessary, as there is no database to mount and open. After this completes, there will be an instance running with an SGA and the background processes. The SGA will have been sized according to the parameters in the nominated `init.ora` file.

The CREATE DATABASE command, which continues to the semicolon at the end of the file, is followed by the database name (which is ocp11g). The first section of the command sets some overall limits for the database. These can all be changed subsequently, but if they are clearly inappropriate, it is a good idea to change them now, before creation.

TIP With the current release, some of these limits (such as the number of datafiles) are only soft limits, and therefore of little significance.

Datafile specifications are provided for the SYSTEM, SYSAUX, and UNDO tablespaces. Tempfile specifications for a TEMPORARY tablespace are also provided.

The database character set used for storing data dictionary data and table columns of type VARCHAR2, CHAR, and CLOB is specified followed by the national character set (which is used for columns of type NVARCHAR2, NCHAR, and NCLOB). It is possible to change the character set after creation with SQL*Plus. Choice and use of character sets, and other aspects of globalization, are covered in detail in Chapter 26.

TIP Until version 9i of the database, there was no supported means for changing the database character set after creation: it was therefore vital to get this right. With 9i and later, it is possible to change it afterward, but this is not an operation to embark on lightly. Get it right now!

The logfile clause specifies three log file groups, each consisting of one member. This is an example of the DBCA defaults perhaps not doing a perfect job. It would be better practice to multiplex the redo log: to create at least two members for each group. Not a problem—this can be fixed later (in Chapter 14). The online redo log will always require substantial tuning; the defaults are applicable to virtually no production systems.

Finally, SYS and SYSTEM passwords are initialized, and spooling to the log is switched off.

This one file with the CREATE DATABASE command will create a database. After its successful execution, you will have an instance running in memory, and a database consisting of a controlfile and copies as specified by the CONTROL_FILES initialization parameter, and the datafiles and redo logs specified in the CREATE DATABASE command. A data dictionary will have been generated in the SYSTEM tablespace. But although the database has been created, it is unusable. The remaining scripts called by `ocp11g.sql` make the database usable. The CREATE DATABASE command has many options, all of which have defaults. For example, if you do not specify a datafile for the SYSTEM or SYSAUX tablespace, one will be created anyway. If you do not specify a character set, there is a default, which will depend on the operating system configuration (it may not be a very helpful default—commonly, it is US7ASCII, which is inadequate for many applications). There are also defaults for the online redo logfiles. There are no defaults for the TEMP and UNDO tablespaces; if these are not specified, the database will be created without them. Not a problem—they can be added later.

TIP The CREATE DATABASE command can be extremely long and complicated—but there are defaults for everything. You can create a database from a SQL*Plus prompt with two words: CREATE DATABASE.

Post-Creation Scripts

The other SQL scripts called by `ocp11g.sql` to complete the database creation will depend on the options chosen when going through the DBCA. In this example, as all options except for Enterprise Manager Database control were deselected, there are only four:

- **CreateDBfiles.sql** This is of minor significance. It creates a small tablespace, USERS, to be used as the default location for any objects created by users.

- **CreateDBCatalog.sql** This is vital. It runs a set of scripts in the `$ORACLE_HOME/rdbms/admin` directory that construct views on the data dictionary and create many PL/SQL packages. It is these views and packages that make it possible to manage an Oracle database.

- **emRepository.sql** This runs the script to create the objects needed by Enterprise Manager Database Control. It is run because this was selected in Exercise 2-4, Step 8.

- **postDBCreation.sql** This generates a server parameter file from the `init.ora` file (more of this in Chapter 3), unlocks the DBSNMP and SYSMAN accounts used by Enterprise Manager, and runs the Enterprise Manager configuration Assistant (which is `emca.bat` on Windows, `emca` on Linux) to configure Database Control for the new database.

The DBCA's Other Functions

The opening screen of the DBCA gives you five options:

- Create a database
- Configure database options
- Delete a database
- Manage templates
- Configure automatic storage management

"Configure Database Options" helps you change the configuration of a database you have already created. In the preceding exercise, you deselected all the options: this was to make the creation as quick and simple as possible.

 TIP By deselecting all the options, particularly those for "standard database components," creation time is reduced dramatically.

If you decide subsequently to install some optional features, such as Java or OLAP, running the DBCA again is the simplest way to do it. An alternative method is to run the scripts to install the options by hand, but these are not always fully documented and it is possible to make mistakes—the DBCA is better.

The Delete A Database radio button will prompt you for which database you wish to delete, and then give you one more chance to back out before it deletes all the files that make up the database and (for a Windows system) invokes `oradim.exe` to delete the instance's service from the Windows registry as well.

> **TIP** Behind the scenes, Delete A Database invokes the SQL*Plus command DROP DATABASE. There is some protection for this command: the database cannot be open at the time; it must be in mount mode.

Manage Templates allows you to store database creation options for later use. Remember that in the exercise, you chose to create a "Custom" database. A custom database is not preconfigured—you chose it in order to see all the possibilities as you worked your way through the DBCA. But apart from "Custom," there were options for "Data Warehouse" and "General Purpose or Transaction Processing." If you choose either of these, the DBCA suggests different defaults with which to create a database. These defaults will be partly optimized for decision support systems (DSS, the data warehouse option) or for online transaction processing systems (OLTP, the transaction processing option). These templates do not create a database from the beginning; they expand a set of compressed datafiles and modify these. The final question when you created your database gave you the possibility of saving it as a template—i.e., not to create it at all, but to save the definition for future use. The DBCA will let you manage templates, either the supplied ones or new templates you create yourself, by creating, copying, modifying, or deleting them. Templates can be extremely useful if you are in a position where you are frequently creating and re-creating databases that are very similar.

Finally, the Configure Automatic Storage Management option launches a wizard that will create an ASM instance. An ASM instance does not open a database; it manages a pool of disks, used for database storage. This is covered in Chapter 20.

Two-Minute Drill

Identify the Tools for Administering an Oracle Database

- Installation: the OUI
- Database creation and upgrade: DBCA, DBUA
- For issuing ad hoc SQL: SQL*Plus, SQL Developer
- Backup: RMAN, Oracle Secure Backup
- Network administration: Oracle Net Manager, Oracle Net Configuration Assistant
- Data load and unload utilities: Data Pump, SQL*Loader
- Management: Oracle Enterprise Manager, Database Control, and Grid Control

Plan an Oracle Database Installation

- Hardware requirements
  - Disk space
  - Main memory
    - Swap space
    - Temporary space
    - A graphics terminal
- Operating system requirements
  - Certified version
  - Necessary packages
  - Kernel settings
- OFA: an appropriate directory for the Oracle Base

Install the Oracle Software by Using the Oracle Universal Installer (OUI)

- Use a suitable operating system account.
- Set necessary environment variables (Linux, Unix).
- Provide access to the root account (Linux, Unix).
- Make either an interactive or silent install.

Create a Database by Using the Database Configuration Assistant

- A database can be created with the DBCA or from the SQL*Plus command line.
- The DBCA can create a database from a saved template.
- The DBCA and SQL*Plus commands can delete a database.
- An instance must be created before the database can be created.
- Any options not selected at creation time can be added later.

Self Test

1. Which of these tools is not usually installed with the Oracle Universal Installer? (Choose the best answer.)

   A. The Oracle Universal Installer itself

   B. SQL*Plus

   C. SQL Developer

   D. Oracle Enterprise Manager Grid Control

2. Which tools can be used to create a database? (Choose three correct answers.)

   A. Database Configuration Assistant

   B. Database Upgrade Assistant

   C. SQL*Plus

   D. Oracle Universal Installer

   E. Oracle Enterprise Manager Database Control

3. Oracle provides the ability to back up the entire environment, not just the Oracle Database. What tool can do this? (Choose the best answer.)

   A. Recovery Manager

   B. Oracle Secure Backup

   C. User-managed backups, carried out with operating system commands

4. What statement best describes the relationship between the Oracle Base and the Oracle Home? (Choose the best answer.)

   A. The Oracle Base exists inside the Oracle Home.

   B. The Oracle Base can contain Oracle Homes for different products.

   C. One Oracle Base is required for each product, but versions of the product can exist in their own Oracle Homes within their Oracle Base.

   D. The Oracle Base is created when you run the `orainstRoot.sh` script, and contains a pointer to the Oracle Home.

5. What does Optimal Flexible Architecture (OFA) describe? (Choose the best answer.)

   A. A directory structure

   B. Distributed database systems

   C. Multitier processing architecture

   D. OFA encompasses all the above

6. What environment variable must be set on Linux before running the Oracle Universal Installer? (Choose the best answer.)

   A. ORACLE_HOME

   B. ORACLE_BASE

   C. ORACLE_SID

   D. DISPLAY

7. If the OUI detects that a prerequisite has not been met, what can you do? (Choose the best answer.)

   A. You must cancel the installation, fix the problem, and launch OUI again.

   B. A silent install will fail; an interactive install will continue.

   C. Instruct the OUI to continue (at your own risk).

   D. The options will depend on how far into the installation the OUI is when the problem is detected.

8. What type of devices can the OUI install an Oracle Home onto? (Choose one or more correct answers.)

    A. Regular file systems

    B. Clustered file systems

    C. Raw devices

    D. ASM disk groups

9. Which command-line switch can be used to prevent the OUI from stopping when prerequisite tests fail? (Choose the best answer.)

    A. -silent

    B. -record

    C. -responsefile

    D. -ignoresysprereqs

10. When does an OUI inventory get created? (Choose the best answer.)

    A. Every time a new Oracle Home is created

    B. Every time a new Oracle Base is created

    C. Before the first run of the OUI

    D. During the first run of the OUI

11. To create a database, in what mode must the instance be? (Choose the best answer.)

    A. Not started

    B. Started in NOMOUNT mode

    C. Started in MOUNT mode

    D. Started in OPEN mode

12. The SYSAUX tablespace is mandatory. What will happen if you attempt to issue a CREATE DATABASE command that does not specify a datafile for the SYSAUX tablespace? (Choose the best answer.)

    A. The command will fail.

    B. The command will succeed, but the database will be inoperable until the SYSAUX tablespace is created.

    C. A default SYSAUX tablespace and datafile will be created.

    D. The SYSAUX objects will be created in the SYSTEM tablespace.

13. Is it necessary to have a database listener created before creating a database? (Choose the best answer.)

    A. No.

    B. Yes.

    C. It depends on whether the database is created with the DBCA or SQL*Plus.

    D. It depends on whether the Database Control option is selected in the DBCA.

14. Several actions are necessary to create a database. Place these in the correct order:

    1. Create the data dictionary views.

    2. Create the parameter file.

    3. Create the password file.

    4. Issue the CREATE DATABASE command.

    5. Issue the STARTUP command.

    (Choose the best answer.)

    A. 2, 3, 5, 4, 1

    B. 3, 5, 2, 4, 1

    C. 5, 3, 4, 2, 1

    D. 2, 3, 1, 5, 4

15. What instance parameter cannot be changed after database creation? (Choose the best answer.)

    A. All instance parameters can be changed after database creation.

    B. All instance parameters can be changed after database creation, if it is done while the instance is in MOUNT mode.

    C. CONTROL_FILES.

    D. DB_BLOCK_SIZE.

16. What files are created by the CREATE DATABASE command? (Choose one or more correct answers.)

    A. The controlfile

    B. The dynamic parameter file

    C. The online redo log files

    D. The password file

    E. The static parameter file

    F. The SYSAUX tablespace datafile

    G. The SYSTEM tablespace datafile

17. What will happen if you do not run the CATALOG.SQL and CATPROC.SQL scripts after creating a database? (Choose the best answer.)

    A. It will not be possible to open the database.

    B. It will not be possible to create any user tables.

    C. It will not be possible to use PL/SQL.

    D. It will not be possible to query the data dictionary views.

    E. It will not be possible to connect as any users other than SYS and SYSTEM.

18. What tools can be used to manage templates? (Choose one or more correct answers.)

    A. The Database Configuration Assistant

    B. The Database Upgrade Assistant

    C. SQL*Plus

    D. Database Control

    E. The Oracle Universal Installer

19. At what point can you choose or change the database character set? (Choose two correct answers.)

    A. At database creation time, if you are not using any template

    B. At database creation time, if you are using a template that does not include datafiles

    C. At database creation time, whether or not you are using a template

    D. After database creation, with the DBCA

    E. After database creation, with SQL*Plus

20. If there are several databases created off the same Oracle Home, how will Database Control be configured? (Choose the best answer.)

    A. Database Control will give access to all the databases created from the one Oracle Home through one URL.

    B. Database Control will give access to each database through different ports.

    C. Database Control need only be configured in one database and can then be used to connect to all of them.

    D. Database Control can only manage one database per Oracle Home.

Self Test Answers

1. ☑ C. SQL Developer is not installed with the OUI; it is delivered as a ZIP file that just needs to be unzipped.

   ☒ A, B, and D. All other products (even the OUI) are installed with the OUI.

2. ☑ A, C, and D. DBCA is meant for creating databases, but they can also be created from SQL*Plus or by instructing the OUI to create a database after installing the Oracle Home.

   ☒ B and E. B is wrong because DBUA can only upgrade an existing database. E is wrong because Database Control is available only after the database is created.

3. ☑ B. Oracle Secure Backup is the enterprise backup facility.

   ☒ A and C. These are both wrong because they are limited to backing up database files only.

PART I

4. ☑ B. The Oracle Base directory contains all the Oracle Homes, which can be any versions of any products.

   ☒ A, C, and D. A is wrong because it inverts the relationship. C is wrong because there is no requirement for a separate base for each product. D is wrong because it confuses the oraInst.loc file and the OUI with the OFA.

5. ☑ A. The rather grandly named Optimal Flexible Architecture is nothing more than a naming convention for directory structures.

   ☒ B, C, and D. These are wrong because they go way beyond OFA.

6. ☑ D. Without a DISPLAY set, the OUI will not be able to open any windows.

   ☒ A, B, and C. These are wrong because while they can be set before launching the OUI, the OUI will prompt for values for them.

7. ☑ C. Perhaps not advisable, but you can certainly do this.

   ☒ A, B, and D. A is wrong because while it might be a good idea, it is not something you have to do. B is wrong because the interactive installation will halt. D is wrong because all prerequisites are checked at the same time.

8. ☑ A and B. The Oracle Home must exist on a file system, but it can be local or clustered.

   ☒ C and D. Raw devices and ASM devices can be used for databases, but not for an Oracle Home.

9. ☑ D. The -ignoresysprereqs switch stops OUI from running the tests.

   ☒ A, B, and C. A is wrong because this will suppress generation of windows, not running tests. B is wrong because this is the switch to generate a response file. C is wrong because this is the switch to read a response file.

10. ☑ D. If the OUI cannot find an inventory, it will create one.

   ☒ A, B, and C. A and B are wrong because one inventory stores details of all Oracle Base and Oracle Home directories. C is wrong because it is not possible to create an inventory before running the OUI.

11. ☑ B. The CREATE DATABASE command can only be issued in NOMOUNT mode.

   ☒ A, C, and D. A is wrong, because if the instance is not started, the only possible command is STARTUP. C and D are wrong because it is impossible to mount a database if there is no controlfile, and it cannot be opened if there is no redo log and SYSTEM tablespace.

12. ☑ C. There are defaults for everything, including the SYSAUX tablespace and datafile definitions.

   ☒ A, B, and D. A is wrong because the command will succeed. B and D are wrong because these are not the way the defaults work.

13. ☑ **D.** The only time a listener is required is if the DBCA is used, and Database Control is selected. The DBCA will not continue if it cannot detect a listener.

☒ **A, B,** and **C. A** is wrong because there is a circumstance where a listener is required; **B** is wrong because in all other circumstances a listener is not required. **C** is wrong because it does not go far enough: The DBCA will not require a listener, if Database Control is not selected.

14. ☑ **A.** This is the correct sequence (though 2 and 3 could be done the other way round).

☒ **B, C,** and **D.** None of these are possible.

15. ☑ **D.** This is the one parameter that can never be changed after creation.

☒ **A, B,** and **C. A** and **B** are wrong because DB_BLOCK_SIZE cannot be changed no matter when you try to do it. **C** is wrong because the CONTROL_FILES parameter can certainly be changed, though this will require a shutdown and restart.

16. ☑ **A, C, F,** and **G.** All of these will always be created, by default if they are not specified.

☒ **B, D,** and **E. B** and **D** are wrong because these should exist before the instance is started. **E** is wrong because the conversion of the static parameter file to a dynamic parameter file only occurs, optionally, after the database is created.

17. ☑ **D.** The database will function, but without the data dictionary views and PL/SQL packages created by these scripts it will be unusable.

☒ **A, B, C,** and **E. A** is wrong because the database will open; in fact, it must be open to run the scripts. **B** is wrong because tables and other objects can certainly be created. **C** is wrong because PL/SQL will be available; it is the supplied packages that will be missing. **E** is completely irrelevant to these scripts.

18. ☑ **A.** The DBCA is the only tool that can manage templates.

☒ **B, C, D,** and **E.** These are all wrong because only the DBCA offers template management.

19. ☑ **C** and **E. C** is right because the character set can be set at creation time, no matter how the creation is done. **E** is right because it is possible to change character sets after creation (though you don't want to do this unless it is really necessary).

☒ **A, B,** and **D. A** and **B** are wrong because templates are not relevant. If the template includes datafiles, the DBCA will change the character set behind the scenes. **D** is wrong because the DBCA does not offer an option to do this.

20. ☑ **B.** Database Control can be used for each database and will be configured with a different port for each one.

☒ **A, C,** and **D. A** is wrong because this is what Grid Control can do. **C** is wrong because Database Control must be installed in every database that will use it. **D** is wrong because while a Database Control is only for one database, every database can have its own.

CHAPTER 3

Instance Management

Exam Objectives

In this chapter you will learn to

- 052.4.1 Set Database Initialization Parameters
- 052.4.2 Describe the Stages of Database Startup and Shutdown
- 052.4.3 Use Alert Log and Trace Files
- 052.4.4 Use Data Dictionary and Dynamic Performance Views

You should now have a database installed on your learning environment and be ready to investigate and demystify your Oracle instance. There are many benefits to learning in a playpen environment, the most important of which is that as you experiment and explore you will inevitably make a mistake, and the authors find that resolving such mistakes provides the best opportunity for learning. You could always deinstall and reinstall the software if you believe you have damaged it irreparably, but even such a nonheroic solution still provides valuable OUI experience.

The database and instance are governed by a set of initialization parameters. There are a vast number of them, of which only about 33 are really important to know. These parameters determine settings like the amount of memory your instance will request the operating system to allocate at instance startup time, the location of the controlfiles and redo logfiles, and the database name. The default parameter values won't suit most production environments, but they are general enough to acceptably run your learning environment. Many DBAs are slightly afraid of modifying these parameters, but there is nothing scary here, just a bunch of settings that once configured hardly ever change. If you change them during the course of a performance tuning exercise, or while trying to multiplex your controlfiles, and the database behaves worse, it is a simple matter to revert your changes. These initialization settings are stored in a parameter file without which your instance will not start.

The stages of database startup and shutdown will be examined, and although they are quite simple, these fundamental stages have important implications for understanding how the mechanism for instance crash recovery operates and how some of the instance background processes interact with the database.

The value provided by alert log and trace files cannot be overemphasized when problems arise, and Oracle has contrived a convenient set of initialization parameters used to quickly locate the relevant files. This is especially useful when high-powered company executives are intently watching you resolve problems after your company's production database has just decided to go for a loop. The alert log file is probably the most important file to a DBA, as it contains a living record of the critical events that occur on your instance, recording events like startups, shutdowns, and serious error conditions. The trace files are usually generated by background and server processes and, just like the alert log file, provide a mixture of informational and error messaging. Familiarity with these files is vital and will be discussed.

The chapter closes with a discussion of the database dictionary and the dynamic performance views. These objects are interrogated by SQL queries and provide vital information on the current state of your system. One of the authors once had a manager who insisted that all DBA support staff memorize the data dictionary objects. And they did. Thankfully, the manager left when Oracle 7 was the current version. The Oracle 11g dictionary is significantly larger and can be intimidating, but fortunately, you do not have to memorize the plethora of information available. Knowing the nature of the information available is, however, important and very useful. The data available in the dynamic performance views will not persist across instance shutdown and startup cycles. These views report on the current database activity and help both the instance and the DBA keep abreast of the happenings in the system. Using and befriending these objects will greatly simplify your task of understanding what the database is really about.

Set Database Initialization Parameters

An instance is defined by the parameters used to build it in memory. Many, though not all parameters, can be changed after startup. Some are fixed at startup time and can only be changed by shutting down the instance and starting again.

The parameters used to build the instance initially come either from the parameter file (which may be a static pfile or a dynamic spfile) or from defaults. Every parameter has a default value, except for the DB_NAME parameter; this must always be specified. In total there are close to three hundred parameters (the exact number will vary between releases and platforms) that it is acceptable for the DBA to set. There are in fact about another fifteen hundred parameters, known as "hidden" parameters, that the DBA is not supposed to set; these are not usually visible and should only be set on the advice of Oracle Support.

The (approximately) three hundred parameters are divided into "basic" and "advanced." The idea is that most database instances will run well with default values for the advanced parameters. Only about thirty-three (the exact number may vary between versions) are "basic." So setting parameters is not an enormous task. But it is enormously important.

Static and Dynamic Parameters and the Initialization Parameter File

To view the parameters and their current values, you may query the V$PARAMETER view:

```
select name,value from v$parameter order by name;
```

A query that may give slightly different results is

```
select name,value from v$spparameter order by name;
```

The difference is the view from which the parameter names and values are taken. V$PARAMETER shows the parameter values currently in effect in the running instance. V$SPPARAMETER shows the values stored in the spfile on disk. Usually, these will be the same. But not always. Some parameters can be changed while the instance is running; others, known as static parameters, are fixed at instance startup time. A change made to the changeable parameters will have an immediate effect on your running instance and can optionally be written out to the spfile. If this is done, then the change will be permanent: the next time the instance is stopped and started, the new value will be read from the spfile. If the change is not saved to the spfile, then the change will only persist until the instance is stopped. To change a static parameter, the change must be written to the spfile, but it will only come into effect at the next startup. If the output of the two preceding queries differs, this will typically be because the DBA has done some tuning work but not yet made it permanent, or has found it necessary to adjust a static parameter and hasn't yet restarted the instance.

The other columns in V$PARAMETER and V$SPPARAMETER are self-explanatory. They show information such as whether the parameter can be changed (for a session or for the whole instance), whether it has been changed, and whether it has been specified at all or is on default.

The views can also be seen through Database Control. From the database home page, take the Server tab and the Initialization Parameters link. On the window following, shown in Figure 3-1, there are two subtabs: Current shows the values currently in effect in the running instance and may be obtained by querying the V$PARAMETER view, while the SPFile tab shows those values recorded in the spfile and may be obtained by querying the V$SPPARAMETER view.

The changeable parameters can be adjusted through the same window. The values for the first four parameters shown (CLUSTER_DATABASE, COMPATIBLE, CONTROL_FILES, and DB_BLOCK_SIZE) cannot be dynamically changed; they are static. But the next parameter, DB_CREATE_FILE_DEST, can be dynamically changed. In the figure, it has not been set—but it can be, by entering a value in the box in the column headed "Value." To change the static parameters, it is necessary to navigate to the SPFile tab, and make the changes there.

To change a parameter from SQL*Plus, use the ALTER SYSTEM command. Figure 3-2 shows several examples.

The first query in Figure 3-2 shows that the values for the parameter DB_CREATE_FILE_DEST are the same in the running instance in memory, and in the spfile on disk. The next two commands adjust the parameter in both places to different values, by using the SCOPE keyword. The results are seen in the second query. The final command uses SCOPE=BOTH to change both the running and the stored value with one command. The BOTH option is the default, if the SCOPE keyword is not specified.

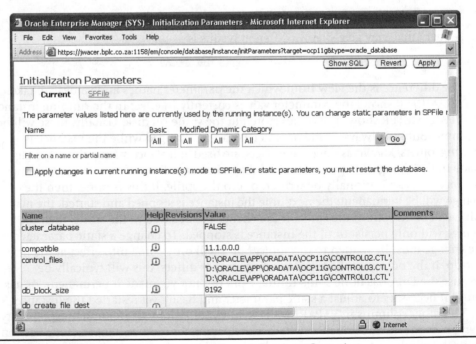

Figure 3-1   Initialization parameters, as seen through Database Control

```
C:\WINDOWS\system32\cmd.exe - sqlplus / as sysdba

SQL> select p.value,s.value from v$parameter p join v$spparameter s
  2  on p.name =s.name where p.name='db_create_file_dest';

VALUE                                VALUE
------------------------------------ ------------------------------------
c:\oradata                           c:\oradata

SQL> alter system set db_create_file_dest='c:\oraone' scope=memory;

System altered.

SQL> alter system set db_create_file_dest='c:\oratwo' scope=spfile;

System altered.

SQL> select p.value,s.value from v$parameter p join v$spparameter s
  2  on p.name =s.name where p.name='db_create_file_dest';

VALUE                                VALUE
------------------------------------ ------------------------------------
c:\oraone                            c:\oratwo

SQL> alter system set db_create_file_dest='c:\oradata' scope=both;

System altered.

SQL> _
```

Figure 3-2 Changing and querying parameters with SQL*Plus

 EXAM TIP An attempt to change a static parameter will fail unless the SCOPE is specified as SPFILE. The default SCOPE is BOTH the running instance and the spfile. If the instance is started with a pfile, then SCOPE=SPFILE will fail.

As was seen in Chapter 2, when a database instance is first created, it is built with a pfile. This may be converted to an spfile using this command:

```
create spfile [='spfilename'] from pfile [='pfilename'];
```

If names are not given for *spfilename* or *pfilename*, then the default names based on the ORACLE_HOME and the SID will be assumed. To reverse-engineer an spfile into a pfile, the command is

```
create pfile [='pfilename'] from spfile [='spfilename'] ;
```

The CREATE PFILE and CREATE SPFILE commands can be run from SQL*Plus at any time, even before the instance has been started.

The Basic Parameters

The instance parameters considered to be "basic" are those that should be considered for every database. In some cases, the default values will be fine—but it is good practice to always consider the values of the basic parameters in your database. The basic parameters and their current values may be queried using

```
select name,value from  v$parameter where isbasic='TRUE' order by name;
```

A query that may give slightly different results is

```
select s.name,s.value
from v$spparameter s join v$parameter p on s.name=p.name
where p.isbasic='TRUE' order by name;
```

Any differences are because some parameter changes may have been applied to the instance but not the spfile (or vice versa). The necessity for the join is because there is no column on V$SPPARAMETER to show whether a parameter is basic or advanced. Table 3-1 summarizes the basic parameters.

Parameter	Purpose
cluster_database	Is the database a RAC or a single instance? That this is basic indicates that RAC is considered a standard option
compatible	The version that the instance will emulate. Normally this would be the actual version, but it can look like older versions
control_files	The name and location of the controlfile copies
db_block_size	The default block size for formatting datafiles
db_create_file_dest	The default location for datafiles
db_create_online_log_dest_1	The default location for online redo logfiles
db_create_online_log_dest_2	The default location for online redo logfiles multiplexed copies
db_domain	The domain name that can be suffixed to the db_name to generate a globally unique name
db_name	The name of the database (the only parameter with no default)
db_recovery_file_dest	The location of the flash recovery area
db_recovery_file_dest_size	The amount of data that may be written to the flash recovery area
db_unique_name	A unique identifier necessary if two databases with the same db_name are on the same machine
instance_number	Used to distinguish two or more RAC instances opening the same database. Another indication that RAC is considered standard
job_queue_processes	The number of processes available to run scheduled jobs
log_archive_dest_1	The destination for archiving redo logfiles
log_archive_dest_2	The destination for multiplexed copies of archived redo logfiles
log_archive_dest_state_1	An indicator for whether the destination is enabled or not
log_archive_dest_state_2	An indicator for whether the destination is enabled or not
nls_language	The language of the instance (provides many default formats)
nls_territory	The geographical location of the instance (which provides even more default formats)
open_cursors	The number of SQL work areas that a session can have open at once
pga_aggregate_target	The total amount of memory the instance can allocate to PGAs
processes	The maximum number of processes (including session server processes) allowed to connect to the instance

Table 3-1   The Basic Parameters

Parameter	Purpose
remote_listener	The addresses of listeners on other machines with which the instance should register; another parameter that is only relevant for a RAC
remote_login_passwordfile	Whether or not to use an external password file, to permit password file authentication
rollback_segments	Almost deprecated—superseded by the UNDO parameters that follow
sessions	The maximum number of sessions allowed to connect to the instance
sga_target	The size of the SGA, within which Oracle will manage the various SGA memory structures
shared_servers	The number of shared server processes to launch, for sessions that are not established with dedicated server processes
star_transformation_enabled	Whether to permit the optimizer to rewrite queries that join the dimensions of a fact table
undo_management	Whether undo data should be automatically managed in an undo tablespace, or manually managed in rollback segments
undo_tablespace	If using automatic undo management, where the undo data should reside

Table 3-1   The Basic Parameters (continued)

All of these basic parameters, as well as some of the advanced parameters, are discussed in the appropriate chapters.

Changing Parameters

The static parameters can only be changed using an ALTER SYSTEM command with a SCOPE=SPFILE clause. Remember this command updates the spfile. Static parameters cannot, by definition, take immediate effect. An example of a static parameter is LOG_BUFFER. If you want to resize the log buffer to 6MB, you may issue the command:

```
alter system set log_buffer=6m;
```

It will fail with the message "ORA-02095: specified initialization parameter cannot be modified." It must be changed with the SCOPE=SPFILE clause. The command will succeed, but the instance must be restarted for the new value to take effect.

 TIP The default log buffer size is probably correct. If you raise it, you may find that commit processing takes longer. If you make it smaller than its default value, it will in fact be internally adjusted up to the default size.

Certain parameters affect the entire system, individual sessions, or both. An example of a parameter that applies to the whole instance but can also be adjusted for individual sessions is OPTIMIZER_MODE. This influences the way in which Oracle will execute statements. A common choice is between the values ALL_ROWS and FIRST_ROWS. ALL_ROWS instructs the optimizer to generate execution plans that will run the statement to completion as quickly as possible, whereas FIRST_ROWS instructs it to generate plans that will get something back to the user as soon as possible, even if the complete execution of the statement ultimately takes longer to complete. So if your database is usually used for long DSS-type queries but some users use it for interactive work, you might issue the command

```
alter system set optimizer_mode=all_rows;
```

and let those individual users issue

```
alter session set optimizer_mode=first_rows;
```

There are a few parameters that can only be modified at the session level. Principal among these is NLS_DATE_FORMAT. This parameter, which controls the display of date and time values, can be specified in the parameter file but cannot be changed with ALTER SYSTEM. So it is static, as far as the instance is concerned. But it can be adjusted at the session level:

```
alter session set nls_date_format='dd-mm-yy hh24:mi:ss';
```

This will change the current session's date/time display to the European norm without affecting any other sessions.

Exercise 3-1: Query and Set Initialization Parameters   In this exercise, use either SQL*Plus or SQL Developer to manage initialization parameters.

1. Connect to the database (which must be open!) as user SYS, with the SYSDBA privilege. Use either operating system authentication or password file authentication.

2. Display all the basic parameters, checking whether they have all been set or are still on default:

```
select name,value,isdefault from v$parameter where isbasic='TRUE'
order by name;
```

3. Any basic parameters that are on default should be investigated to see if the default is appropriate. In fact, all the basic parameters should be considered. Read up on all of them in the Oracle documentation. The volume you need is titled *Oracle Database Reference*. Part 1, Chapter 1 has a paragraph describing every initialization parameter.

4. Change the PROCESSES parameter to 200. This is a static parameter which means its value cannot be changed in memory with immediate effect. It must be set in the static pfile, or if you are using an spfile, it can be set as described in the illustration by specifying "scope=spfile" and then restarting the database.

```
cx  C:\WINDOWS\system32\cmd.exe - sqlplus system/oracle              - □ ×
SQL>
SQL> alter system set processes=200;
alter system set processes=200
                      *
ERROR at line 1:
ORA-02095: specified initialization parameter cannot be modified


SQL> alter system set processes=200 scope=spfile;

System altered.

SQL> startup force;
ORACLE instance started.

Total System Global Area   330616832 bytes
Fixed Size                   1328428 bytes
Variable Size              109054676 bytes
Database Buffers           213909504 bytes
Redo Buffers                 6324224 bytes
Database mounted.
Database opened.
SQL>
```

5. Rerun the query from Step 3. Note the new value for PROCESSES, and also for SESSIONS. PROCESSES limits the number of operating system processes that are allowed to connect to the instance, and SESSIONS limits the number of sessions. These figures are related, because each session will require a process. The default value for SESSIONS is derived from PROCESSES, so if SESSIONS was on default, it will now have a new value.

6. Change the value for the NLS_LANGUAGE parameter for your session. Choose whatever mainstream language you want (Oracle supports many languages: 67 at the time of writing), but the language must be specified in English (e.g., use "German," not "Deutsch"):

```
alter session set nls_language=German;
```

7. Confirm that the change has worked by querying the system date:

```
select to_char(sysdate,'day') from dual;
```

You may want to change your session language back to what it was before (such as English) with another ALTER SESSION command. If you don't, be prepared for error messages to be in the language your session is now using.

8. Change the OPTIMIZER_MODE parameter, but restrict the scope to the running instance only; do not update the parameter file. This exercise enables the deprecated rule-based optimizer, which might be needed while testing some old code.

```
alter system set optimizer_mode=rule scope=memory;
```

9. Confirm that the change has been effected, but not written to the parameter file:

```
select value from v$parameter where name='optimizer_mode'
union
select value from v$spparameter where name='optimizer_mode';
```

10. Return the OPTIMIZER_MODE to its standard value, in the running instance:

```
alter system set optimizer_mode=all_rows scope=memory;
```

Describe the Stages of Database Startup and Shutdown

Oracle Corporation's recommended sequence for starting a database is to start Database Control, then the database listener, and then the database. Starting the database is itself a staged process. There is no necessity to follow this sequence, and in more complex environments such as clustered systems or those managed by Enterprise Manager Grid Control there may well be additional processes too. But this sequence will suffice for a simple single-instance environment.

Starting and Connecting to Database Control

Database Control is a tool for managing one database (though this database can be clustered). If there are several database instances running off the same Oracle Home, each instance will have its own Database Control instance. The tool is written in Perl and Java, and accessed from a browser. There is no need to have a Java Runtime Environment or a Perl interpreter installed on the system; both are provided in the Oracle Home and installed by the OUI. All communications with Database Control are over HTTPS, the secure sockets variant of HTTP, and there should therefore be no problems with using Database Control from a browser anywhere in the world—the communications will be secure, and any firewall proxy servers will have no problem routing them. The only configuration needed on the firewall will be making it aware of the port on which Database Control is listening for connection requests.

The configuration of Database Control is done at database creation time. This configuration includes two vital bits of information: the hostname of the computer on which Database Control is running, and the TCP port on which it will be listening. If it is ever necessary to change either of these, Database Control will need to be reconfigured.

To start Database Control, use the emctl utility located in the ORACLE_HOME/bin directory. The three commands to start or stop Database Control and to check its status are

```
emctl start dbconsole
emctl stop dbconsole
emctl status dbconsole
```

For these commands to work, three environment variables must be set: PATH, ORACLE_HOME, and ORACLE_SID. PATH is needed to allow the operating system to find the emctl utility. The ORACLE_HOME and ORACLE_SID are needed so that emctl can find the Database Control configuration files. These are in three places: the directory ORACLE_HOME/sysman/config has general configuration directives that will apply to all Database Control instances running from the Oracle Home (one per database). The ORACLE_HOME/*hostname_sid*/sysman/config and a similarly named directory beneath ORACLE_HOME/oc4j/j2ee contain details for the Database Control that manages one particular database (hostname is the *hostname* of the machine, and *sid* is the value of the ORACLE_SID variable).

Figure 3-3 shows the startup of Database Control, after a couple of problems.

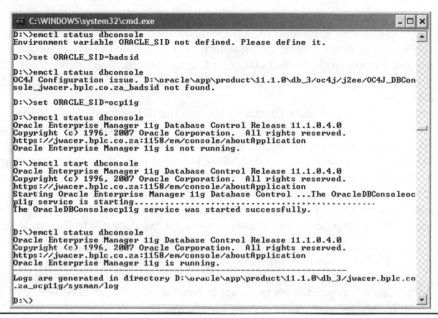

Figure 3-3 Database Control startup, on a Windows system

In Figure 3-3, the first attempt to query the status of Database Control fails because the ORACLE_SID environment variable is not set. Without this, the `emctl` utility can't find the necessary configuration files. This is further demonstrated by setting the ORACLE_SID to a nonexistent instance name; the `emctl status dbconsole` command uses this environment variable to construct a directory path that does not exist. After setting the ORACLE_SID correctly, to ocp11g, the `emctl` executable is located and its status can be queried. The nature of this query is nothing more than accessing a URL; this URL can also be accessed from any browser as a simple test. As Database Control is not running, the example in the figure continues with starting it, and then again queries the status—this time successfully. Because this example is on a Windows system, the startup involves starting a Windows service, called OracleDBConsoleocp11g.

To connect to Database Control using your web browser, navigate to the URL

```
https://hostname:port/em
```

where *hostname* is the name of the machine on which Database Control is running, and *port* is the TCP port on which it is listening for incoming connection requests. If the host has several names or several network interface cards, any will do. You can even use a loopback address, such as 127.0.0.1, because the Database Control process does listen on all addresses. To identify the port, you can use `emctl`. As shown in Figure 3-3, the output of `emctl status dbconsole` shows the port on which Database Control should be running. Alternatively, you can look in the file ORACLE_HOME/install/portlist.ini, which lists all the ports configured by the OUI and DBCA.

As Database Control (the current version, not the one released with 10g) requires the use of HTTPS for security reasons, when you connect from your browser with the URL just given, you may (depending on your local security settings) receive a message regarding the digital certificate that Database Control is returning to your browser. This certificate was generated by Oracle when the Oracle Home was installed and the database created.

Your browser performs three checks on the validity of the certificate. The first check is that the certificate is issued by a certificate issuing authority that your browser is prepared to trust. If you view the details of the certificate, you will see that the certificate was issued by the computer on which the Oracle installation was made. Presumably this is a trustworthy source, so that is not a problem. The second check is for the validity dates of the certificate. The third check is whether the host requested in the URL is the same as the host to which the certificate was issued. These will usually be the same, but if the machine has several hostname aliases or network interface cards, they may not be.

 TIP The mechanism for managing certificates and HTTPS will vary depending on your browser and how it is configured. For Database Control, the certificate really doesn't matter; you do not need secure sockets for authentication, only for encryption.

Once past any SSL certificate issue (which may not arise, depending on local security configuration), you will see the Database Control logon window, if the database listener is running. If the listener is not running, you will see the screen in Figure 3-4, which is presented when Database Control cannot detect the listener or the database instance.

Starting the Database Listener

The database listener is a process that monitors a port for database connection requests. These requests (and all subsequent traffic once a session is established) use Oracle Net, Oracle's proprietary communications protocol. Oracle Net is a layered protocol running over whatever underlying network protocol is in use, usually TCP/IP. Managing the listener is fully described in Chapter 4, but it is necessary to know how to start it now.

There are three ways to start the database listener:

- With the `lsnrctl` utility
- With Database Control
- As a Windows service (Windows only, of course)

The `lsnrctl` utility is located in the `ORACLE_HOME/bin` directory. The key commands are

```
lsnrctl start [listener]
lsnrctl status [listener]
```

where *listener* is the name of listener. This will have defaulted to LISTENER, which is correct in most cases. You will know if you have created a listener with another name. Figure 3-5 shows the output of the `lsnrctl status` command when the listener is running.

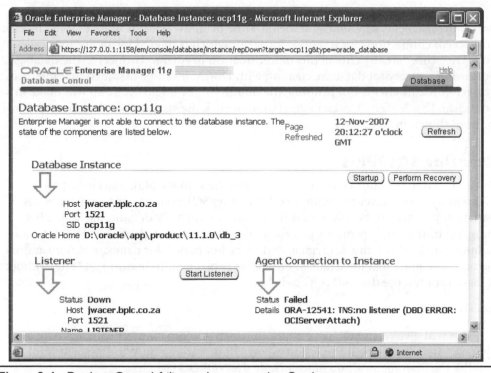

Figure 3-4   Database Control, failing to detect any other Oracle processes

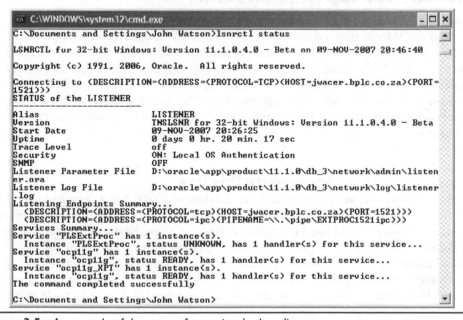

Figure 3-5   An example of the status of a running database listener

Note the third line of the output in the figure shows the host address and port on which the listener is listening, and the fifth line from the bottom states that the listener will accept connections for a service "ocp11g", which is offered by an instance called "ocp11g". These are the critical bits of information needed to connect to the database. Following a successful database creation with DBCA, it can be assumed that they are correct. If the listener is not running, the output of `lsnrctl status` will make this very clear. Use `lsnrctl start` to start it, or click the START LISTENER Database Control button, shown in Figure 3-4.

Starting SQL*Plus

As discussed in previous chapters, this couldn't be simpler. SQL*Plus is just an elementary client-server program used for issuing SQL commands to a database. A variation you need to be aware of is the NOLOG switch. By default, the SQL*Plus program immediately prompts you for an Oracle username, password, and database connect string. This is fine for regular end users, but useless for database administrators because it requires that the database must already be open. To launch SQL*Plus without a login prompt, use the /NOLOG switch:

```
sqlplus /nolog
```

This will give you a SQL prompt, from which you can connect with a variety of syntaxes, detailed in the next section. Many DBAs working on Windows will want to modify the Start menu shortcut to include the NOLOG switch.

Database Startup and Shutdown

If one is being precise (always a good idea, if you want to pass the OCP examinations), one does not start or stop a database: an instance may be started and stopped; a database is mounted and opened, and then dismounted and closed. This can be done from either SQL*Plus, using the STARTUP and SHUTDOWN commands, or through Database Control. On a Windows system, it may also be done by controlling the Windows service within which the instance runs. The alert log will give details of all such operations, however they were initiated. Startup and shutdown are critical operations. As such, they are always recorded and can only be carried out by highly privileged users.

Connecting with an Appropriate Privilege

Ordinary users cannot start up or shut down a database. This is because an ordinary user is authenticated against the data dictionary. It is logically impossible for an ordinary user to start up an instance and open (or create) a database, since the data dictionary cannot be read until the database is open. You must therefore connect with some form of external authentication: you must be authenticated either by the operating system, as being a member of the group that owns the Oracle software, or by giving a username/ password combination that exists in an external password file. You tell Oracle that you wish to use external authentication by using appropriate syntax in the CONNECT command that you submit in your user process.

If you are using SQL*Plus, the syntax of the CONNECT command tells Oracle what type of authentication you wish to use: the default of data dictionary authentication, password file authentication, or operating system authentication. These are the possibilities after connecting using the /NOLOG switch as described previously:

```
connect user/pwd[@connect_alias]
connect user/pwd[@connect_alias] as sysdba
connect user/pwd[@connect_alias] as sysoper
connect / as sysdba
connect / as sysoper
```

In these examples, *user* is the username and *pwd* is the password. The *connect_alias* is a network identifier, fully described in Chapter 4. The first example is normal, data dictionary authentication. Oracle will validate the username/password combination against values stored in the data dictionary. The database must be open, or the connect will fail. Anyone connecting with this syntax cannot, no matter who they are, issue startup or shutdown commands. The second two examples instruct Oracle to go to the external password file to validate the username/password combination. The last two examples use operating system authentication; Oracle will go to the host operating system and check whether the operating system user running SQL*Plus is a member of the operating system group that owns the Oracle software, and if the user passes this test, they will be logged on as SYSDBA or SYSOPER without any need to provide a username and password. A user connecting with any of the bottom four syntaxes will be able to issue startup and shutdown commands and will be able to connect no matter what state the database is in—it may not even have been created yet. Note that the first three examples can include a network identifier string; this is necessary if the connection is to be made across a network. Naturally, this is not an option for operating system authentication, because operating system authentication relies on the user being logged on to the machine hosting the Oracle server: they must either be working on it directly or have logged in to it with telnet, secure shell, or some similar utility.

TIP From an operating system prompt, you can save a bit of time and typing by combining the launch of SQL*Plus and the CONNECT into one command. Here are two examples:
```
sqlplus / as sysdba
sqlplus sys/oracle@orcl as sysdba
```

Database Control will, by default, attempt to connect through a listener, but it can also use operating system authentication. If the situation is that depicted in Figure 3-4, clicking the STARTUP button will require operating system logon credentials to be entered in order to proceed. If the listener is running, Database Control will present the login window shown in Figure 3-6. The Connect As list of values lets you choose whether to make a normal connection or a SYSDBA connection.

Figure 3-6
The Database
Control login
window, when a
listener has been
detected

```
Oracle Enterprise Manager - Microsoft Internet Explorer

File   Edit   View   Favorites   Tools   Help

Address  https://127.0.0.1:1158/em/console/logon/logon

ORACLE Enterprise Manager 11g                              Help
Database Control

Login
```

Login to Database:ocp11g

```
            * User Name   [                    ]
            * Password    [                    ]
            Connect As    [Normal  v]
                                        ( Login )
```

Copyright © 1996, 2007, Oracle. All rights reserved.
Oracle, JD Edwards, PeopleSoft, and Retek are registered trademarks of Oracle Corporation and/or its affiliates. Other names
Unauthorized access is strictly prohibited.

SYSOPER and SYSDBA

These are privileges with special capabilities. They can only be enabled when users are connecting with an external authentication method: either operating system or password file. SYSOPER has the ability to issue these commands:

```
STARTUP
SHUTDOWN
ALTER DATABASE [MOUNT | OPEN | CLOSE | DISMOUNT]
ALTER [DATABASE | TABLESPACE] [BEGIN | END] BACKUP
RECOVER
```

The SYSDBA privilege includes all of these, but in addition has the ability to create a database, to perform incomplete recovery, and to create other SYSOPER and SYSDBA users.

 EXAM TIP SYSDBA and SYSOPER are not users; they are privileges that can be granted to users. By default, only user SYS has these privileges until they are deliberately granted to other users.

You may be wondering what Oracle user you are actually logging on as when you use operating system authentication. To find out, from a SQL*Plus prompt connect using the operating system authentication syntax already shown, and then issue the `show user` command (which can be abbreviated to `sho user`—never underestimate the importance of saving keystrokes) as shown in the examples in Figure 3-7.

Use of the SYSDBA privilege logs you on to the instance as user SYS, the most powerful user in the database and the owner of the data dictionary. Use of the SYSOPER privilege connects you as user PUBLIC. PUBLIC is not a user in any normal sense—it is a notional user with administration privileges, but (by default) has no privileges that lets it see or manipulate data. You should connect with either of these privileges only when you need to carry out procedures that no normal user can perform.

```
C:\WINDOWS\system32\cmd.exe - sqlplus /nolog                    - □ ×
C:\>set ORACLE_SID=ocp11g

C:\>sqlplus /nolog

SQL*Plus: Release 11.1.0.4.0 - Beta on Mon Nov 12 21:14:02 2007

Copyright (c) 1982, 2007, Oracle.  All rights reserved.

SQL> connect / as sysdba
Connected.
SQL> show user
USER is "SYS"
SQL> conn / as sysoper
Connected.
SQL> sho user
USER is "PUBLIC"
SQL> connect sys/oracle@jwacer.bplc.co.za:1521/ocp11g as sysdba
Connected.
SQL> show user
USER is "SYS"
SQL> conn sys/oracle @ocp11g as sysoper
Connected.
SQL> show user
USER is "PUBLIC"
SQL>
```

Figure 3-7   Use of operating system and password file authentication

Startup: NOMOUNT, MOUNT, and OPEN

Remember that the instance and the database are separate entities that exist independently of each other. When an instance is stopped, no memory structures or background processes exist and the instance ceases to exist, but the database (consisting of files) endures. Indeed, in a RAC environment other instances on other nodes could exist and connect to the database.

The startup process is therefore staged: first you build the instance in memory, second you enable a connection to the database by mounting it, and third you open the database for use. At any moment, a database will be in one of four states:

- SHUTDOWN
- NOMOUNT
- MOUNT
- OPEN

When the database is SHUTDOWN, all files are closed and the instance does not exist. In NOMOUNT mode, the instance has been built in memory (the SGA has been created and the background processes started, according to whatever is specified in its parameter file), but no connection has been made to a database. It is indeed possible that the database does not yet exist. In MOUNT mode, the instance locates and reads the database control file. In OPEN mode, all database files are located and opened and the database is made available for use by end users. The startup process is staged: whenever you issue a startup command, it will go through these stages. It is possible to stop the startup partway. For example, if your control file is damaged, or a multiplexed copy is missing, you will not be able to mount the database, but by stopping in NOMOUNT mode you may be able to repair the damage. Similarly, if there are problems with any datafiles or redo logfiles, you may be able to repair them in MOUNT mode before transitioning the database to OPEN mode.

At any stage, how does the instance find the files it needs, and exactly what happens? Start with NOMOUNT. When you issue a startup command, Oracle will attempt to locate a parameter file using a systematic ordered search as depicted in Figure 3-8.

There are three default filenames. On Unix they are

```
$ORACLE_HOME/dbs/spfileSID.ora
$ORACLE_HOME/dbs/spfile.ora
$ORACLE_HOME/dbs/initSID.ora
```

and on Windows,

```
%ORACLE_HOME%\database\SPFILESID.ORA
%ORACLE_HOME%\database\SPFILE.ORA
%ORACLE_HOME%\database\INITSID.ORA
```

Figure 3-8
Sequential search for an instance parameter file during STARTUP

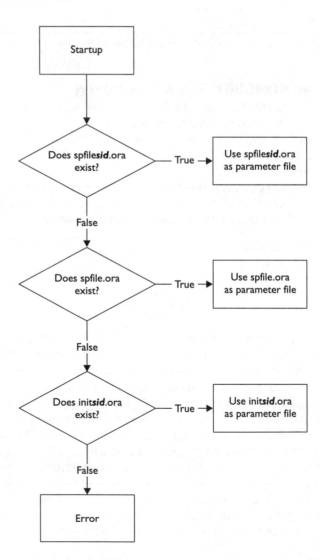

TIP spfile*SID*.ora is undoubtedly the most convenient file to use as your parameter file. Normally, you will only use spfile.ora in a RAC environment, where one file may be used to start several instances. You will generally only use an init*SID*.ora file if for some reason you need to make manual edits using a text editor; spfiles are binary files and cannot be edited by hand.

In all cases, *SID* refers to the name of the instance that the parameter file will start. The preceding order is important! Oracle will work its way down the list, using the first file it finds and ignoring the rest. If none of them exist, the instance will not start.

The only files used in NOMOUNT mode are the parameter file and the alert log. The parameters in the parameter file are used to build the SGA in memory and to start the background processes. Entries will be written out to the alert log describing this process. Where is the alert log? In the location given by the BACKGROUND_DUMP_DEST parameter, that can be found in the parameter file or by running

```
sho parameter background_dump_dest
```

from a SQL*Plus prompt once connected as a privileged user. If the alert log already exists, it will be appended to. Otherwise, it will be created. If any problems occur during this stage, trace files may also be generated in the same location.

EXAM TIP An "init" file is known as a "static" parameter file or a pfile, because it is only read once, at instance startup. An "spfile" is known as a dynamic parameter file, because Oracle continuously reads and updates it while the instance is running. A parameter file of one sort or the other is essential, because there is one parameter without a default value: the DB_NAME parameter.

Once the instance is successfully started in NOMOUNT mode, it may be transitioned to MOUNT mode by reading the controlfile. It locates the controlfile by using the CONTROL_FILES parameter, which it knows from having read the parameter file used when starting in NOMOUNT mode. If the controlfile (or any multiplexed copy of it) is damaged or missing, the database will not mount and you will have to take appropriate action before proceeding further. All copies of the controlfile must be available and identical if the mount is to be successful.

As part of the mount, the names and locations of all the datafiles and online redo logs are read from the controlfile, but Oracle does not yet attempt to find them. This happens during the transition to OPEN mode. If any files are missing or damaged, the database will remain in MOUNT mode and cannot be opened until you take appropriate action. Furthermore, even if all the files are present, they must be synchronized before the database opens. If the last shutdown was orderly, with all database buffers in the database buffer cache being flushed to disk by DBWn, then everything will be synchronized: Oracle will know that that all committed transactions are safely stored in the datafiles, and that no uncommitted transactions are hanging about waiting to be rolled back. However, if the last shutdown was disorderly (such as from a loss of power, or the server being accidently rebooted), then Oracle must repair the damage and the database is considered to be in an inconsistent state. The mechanism for this is described in Chapter 14. The process that mounts and opens the database (and carries out repairs, if the previous shutdown was disorderly) is the SMON process. Only once the database has been successfully opened will Oracle permit user sessions to be established. The startup process just described is graphically summarized in Figure 3-9.

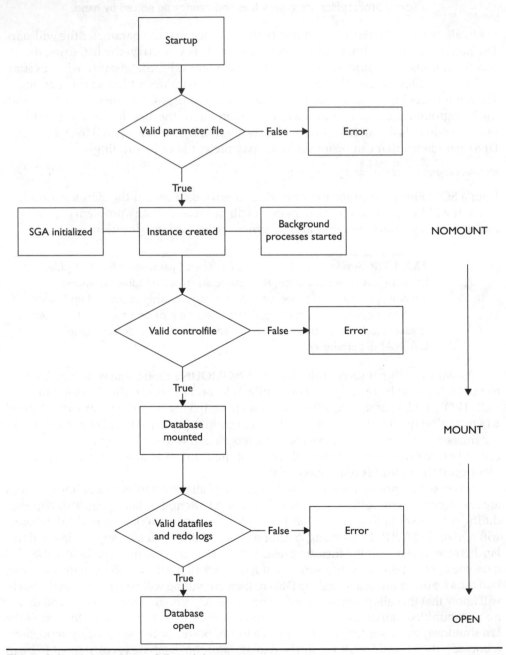

Figure 3-9 High-level steps followed during an instance startup

Shutdown should be the reverse of startup. During an orderly shutdown, the database is first closed, then dismounted, and finally the instance is stopped. During the close phase, all sessions are terminated: active transactions are rolled back by PMON, completed transactions are flushed to disk by DBWn, and the datafiles and redo logfiles are closed. During the dismount, the controlfile is closed. Then the instance is stopped by deallocating the SGA memory and terminating the background processes.

TIP If someone were in the middle of a long-running uncommitted statement (for example, they were loading tables for a data warehouse), when you had to shut down the database, the rollback phase, and therefore the time it takes the database to close and shut down cleanly, could be a very *long* time.

Shutdown: NORMAL, TRANSACTIONAL, IMMEDIATE, and ABORT

There are options that may be used on the shutdown command, all of which require either a SYSDBA or a SYSOPER connection:

```
shutdown [normal | transactional | immediate | abort]
```

Normal: This is the default. No new user connections will be permitted, but all current connections are allowed to continue. Only once all users have (voluntarily!) logged off, will the database actually shut down.

TIP Typically, a normal shutdown is useless: there is always someone logged on, even if it is only the Database Control process.

Transactional: No new user connections are permitted; existing sessions that are not actively performing a transaction will be terminated; sessions currently involved in a transaction are allowed to complete the transaction and will then be terminated. Once all sessions are terminated, the database will shut down.

Immediate: No new sessions are permitted, and all currently connected sessions are terminated. Any active transactions are rolled back, and the database will then shut down.

Abort: As far as Oracle is concerned, this is the equivalent of a power failure. The instance terminates immediately. Nothing is written to disk, no file handles are closed, and there is no attempt to terminate transactions that may be in progress in any orderly fashion.

TIP A shutdown abort will not damage the database, but some operations (such as backups) are not advisable after an abort.

The "normal," "immediate," and "transactional" shutdown modes are usually referred to as "clean," "consistent," or "orderly" shutdowns. After all sessions are terminated, PMON will roll back any incomplete transactions. Then a checkpoint is issued (remember the CKPT process from Chapter 1), which forces the DBWn process to write all updated data from the database buffer cache down to the datafiles. LGWR also flushes any change vectors still in memory to the logfiles. Then the file headers are updated, and the file handles closed. This means that the database is in a "consistent" state: all committed transactions are in the datafiles, there are no uncommitted transactions hanging about that need to be rolled back, and all datafiles and logfiles are synchronized.

The "abort" mode, sometimes referred to as a "disorderly" shutdown, leaves the database in an "inconsistent" state: it is quite possible that committed transactions have been lost, because they existed only in memory and DBWn had not yet written them to the datafiles. Equally, there may be uncommitted transactions in the datafiles that have not yet been rolled back. This is a definition of a corrupted database: it may be missing committed transactions, or storing uncommitted transactions. These corruptions must be repaired by instance recovery (described in Chapter 14). It is exactly as though the database server had been switched off, or perhaps rebooted, while the database was running.

 TIP There is a startup command `startup force` that can save time. It is two commands in one: a `shutdown abort` followed by a `startup`.

An orderly shutdown is a staged process, and it is possible to control the stages using the SQL*Plus:

```
alter database close;
alter database dismount;
```

These commands are exactly the reverse of the startup sequence. In practice, however, there is little value to them; a `shutdown` is generally all any DBA will ever use. The staged shutdown commands are not even available through Database Control.

Exercise 3-2: Conduct a Startup and a Shutdown Use SQL*Plus to start an instance and open a database, then Database Control to shut it down. If the database is already open, do this in the other order. Note that if you are working on Windows, the Windows service for the database must be running. It will have a name of the form OracleService*SID*, where *SID* is the name of the instance.

1. Log on to the computer as a member of the operating system group that owns the ORACLE_HOME, and set the environment variables appropriately for ORACLE_HOME and PATH and ORACLE_SID, as described in Chapter 2.

2. Check the status of the database listener, and start it if necessary. From an operating system prompt:

   ```
   lsnrctl status
   lsnrctl start
   ```

3. Check the status of the Database Control console, and start it if necessary. From an operating system prompt:

```
emctl status dbconsole
emctl start dbconsole
```

4. Launch SQL*Plus, using the /nolog switch to prevent an immediate logon prompt:

```
sqlplus /nolog
```

5. Connect as SYS with operating system authentication:

```
connect / as sysdba
```

6. Start the instance only. Then query the V$INSTANCE view and examine its STATUS column. Note that the status of the instance is "STARTED".

```
startup nomount;
select status from v$instance;
```

7. Mount the database and query the instance status. The database has now been "MOUNTED" by the instance.

```
alter database mount;
select status from v$instance;
```

8. Open the database:

```
alter database open;
```

9. Confirm that the database is open by querying V$INSTANCE. The database should now be "OPEN".

```
select status from v$instance;
```

10. From a browser, connect to the Database Control console. The hostname and port will have been shown in the output of the `emctl status dbconsole` command in Step 3. The URL will be of the format: `https://hostname: port/em`.

11. Log on as SYS with the password selected at database creation, and choose SYSDBA from the Connect As drop-down box.

12. On the database home page, click the SHUTDOWN button.

13. The next window prompts for host credentials, which will be your operating system username and password, and database credentials, which will be the SYS username and password. If you want to save these to prevent having to enter them repeatedly, check the box Save As Preferred Credential. Click OK.

Use the Alert Log and Trace Files

The alert log is a continuous record of critical operations applied to the instance and the database. Its location is determined by the instance parameter BACKGROUND_DUMP_DEST, and its name is `alert_SID.log`, where SID is the name of the instance.

The critical operations recorded in the alert log include

- All startup and shutdown commands, including intermediate commands such as ALTER DATABASE MOUNT
- All errors internal to the instance (for example, any ORA-600 errors)
- Any detected datafile block corruptions
- Any record locking deadlocks that may have occurred
- All operations that affect the physical structure of the database, such as creating or renaming datafiles and online redo logfiles
- All ALTER SYSTEM commands that adjust the values of initialization parameters
- All log switches and log archives

The alert log entry for a startup shows all the nondefault initialization parameters. This information, together with the subsequent record of changes to the instance made with ALTER SYSTEM commands and to the database physical structures made with ALTER DATABASE commands, means that it is always possible to reconstruct the history of changes to the database and the instance. This can be invaluable when trying to backtrack in order to find the source of a problem.

 TIP For many DBAs, the first thing they do when they are asked to look at a database for the first time is locate the alert log and scan through it, just to get an idea of what has been going on.

Trace files are generated by the various background processes, usually when they encounter an error. These files are located in the BACKGROUND_DUMP_DEST directory, along with the alert log. If a background process has failed because of an error, the trace file generated will be invaluable in diagnosing the problem.

Exercise 3-3: Use the Alert Log   In this exercise, locate the alert log and find the entries for the parameter changes made in Exercise 3-1 and the startups and shutdowns in Exercise 3-2.

1. Connect to your database with either SQL*Plus or SQL Developer, and find the value of the BACKGROUND_DUMP_DEST parameter:

```
select value from v$parameter where name='background_dump_dest';
```

Note that this value can also be found with Database Control.

2. Using whatever operating system tool you please (such as Windows Explorer, or whatever file system browser your Linux session is using), navigate to the directory identified in Step 1.

3. Open the alert log. It will be a file called `alert_SID.log`, where SID is the name of the instance. Use any editor you please (but note that on Windows, Notepad is not a good choice because of the way carriage returns are handled. WordPad is much better).

4. Go to the bottom of the file. You will see the ALTER SYSTEM commands of Exercise 3-1 and the results of the startup and shutdowns.

Use Data Dictionary and Dynamic Performance Views

An Oracle database is defined by its data dictionary. The data dictionary is not very comprehensible. For this reason, Oracle provides a set of views onto the data dictionary that are much easier to understand. These views provide the DBA with a tool for understanding what is happening in the database. The instance also has a set of tables (which are in fact C data structures) that are not easily understandable. These are externalized as the dynamic performance views that are key to understanding what is happening within the instance.

The Data Dictionary Views

The data dictionary contains metadata: that is, data about data. It describes the database, both physically and logically, and its contents. User definitions, security information, integrity constraints, and (from release 10*g* onward) performance monitoring information are all part of the data dictionary. It is stored as a set of segments in the SYSTEM and SYSAUX tablespaces.

In many ways, the segments that make up the data dictionary are like other regular table and index segments. The critical difference is that the data dictionary tables are generated at database creation time, and you are not allowed to access them directly. There is nothing to stop an inquisitive DBA from investigating the data dictionary directly, but if you do any updates to it you may cause irreparable damage to your database, and certainly Oracle Corporation will not support you. Creating a data dictionary is part of the database creation process. It is maintained subsequently by Data Definition Language (DDL) commands. When you issue the CREATE TABLE command, you are not only creating a data segment to store your data in its rows, your DDL command has the side effect of inserting rows into many data dictionary tables that keep track of segment-related information including tablespace, extent, column and ownership related properties.

To query the dictionary, Oracle provides a set of views which come in three forms, prefixed with: DBA_, ALL_, or USER_. Most of the views come in all three forms. Any view prefixed USER_ will be populated with rows describing objects owned by the user querying the view. So no two users will see the same contents. When user JOHN queries USER_TABLES, he will see information about only his tables; if you query USER_TABLES, you will see information about only your tables. Any view prefixed ALL_ will be populated with rows describing objects to which you have access. So ALL_TABLES will contain rows describing your own tables, plus rows describing tables belonging to anyone else that you have been given permission to see. Any view prefixed DBA_ will have rows for every object in the database, so DBA_TABLES will have one row for every table in the database, no matter who created it. Figure 3-10 describes the underlying concept represented by the three forms of dictionary views. The USER_ views sit in the middle of the concentric squares and only describe an individual user's objects. The ALL_ views in the middle display all the contents of the USER_ views, and in addition describe objects that belong to other schemas but to which your user has been granted access. The DBA_ views describe all objects in the database. Needless to say, a user must have DBA privileges to access the DBA_ views.

Figure 3-10
The overlapping
structure of the
three forms of the
dictionary views

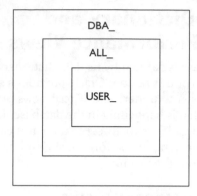

These views are created as part of the database creation process, along with a large number of PL/SQL packages that are provided by Oracle to assist database administrators in managing the database and programmers in developing applications.

 TIP Which view will show you ALL the tables in the database? DBA_TABLES, not ALL_TABLES.

There are hundreds of data dictionary views. Some of those commonly used by DBAs are

- **DBA_OBJECTS** A row for every object in the database
- **DBA_DATA_FILES** A row describing every datafile
- **DBA_USERS** A row describing each user
- **DBA_TABLES** A row describing each table
- **DBA_ALERT_HISTORY** Rows describing past alert conditions

There are many more than these, some of which will be used in later chapters. Along with the views, there are public synonyms onto the views. A query such as this,

```
select object_name,owner, object_type from dba_objects
where object_name='DBA_OBJECTS';
```

shows that there is, in fact, a view called DBA_OBJECTS owned by SYS, and a public synonym with the same name.

The Dynamic Performance Views

There are more than three hundred dynamic performance views. You will often hear them referred to as the "Vee dollar" views, because their names are prefixed with "V$". In fact, the "Vee dollar" views are not views at all—they are synonyms to views that are prefixed with "V_$", as shown in Figure 3-11.

Figure 3-11
A V_$ view and
its V$ synonym

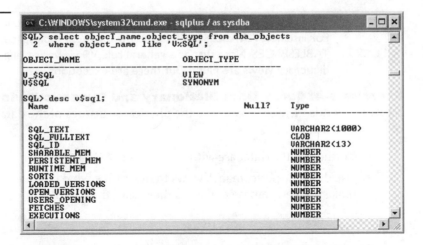

```
C:\WINDOWS\system32\cmd.exe - sqlplus / as sysdba

SQL> select objecT_name,object_type from dba_objects
  2  where object_name like 'U%SQL';

OBJECT_NAME                              OBJECT_TYPE
-------------------------------          --------------------
U_$SQL                                   UIEW
U$SQL                                    SYNONYM

SQL> desc v$sql;
 Name                                    Null?    Type
 ------------------------------          ------   -----------------

 SQL_TEXT                                         UARCHAR2<1000>
 SQL_FULLTEXT                                     CLOB
 SQL_ID                                           UARCHAR2<13>
 SHARABLE_MEM                                     NUMBER
 PERSISTENT_MEM                                   NUMBER
 RUNTIME_MEM                                      NUMBER
 SORTS                                            NUMBER
 LOADED_UERSIONS                                  NUMBER
 OPEN_UERSIONS                                    NUMBER
 USERS_OPENING                                    NUMBER
 FETCHES                                          NUMBER
 EXECUTIONS                                       NUMBER
```

The figure shows V$SQL, which has one row for every SQL statement currently stored in the shared pool, with information such as how often the statement has been executed.

The dynamic performance views give access to a phenomenal amount of information about the instance, and (to a certain extent) about the database. The majority of the views are populated with information from the instance; while the remaining views are populated from the controlfile. All of them provide real-time information. Dynamic performance views that are populated from the instance, such as V$INSTANCE or V$SYSSTAT, are available at all times, even when the instance is in NOMOUNT mode. Dynamic performance views that are populated from the controlfile, such as V$DATABASE or V$DATAFILE, cannot be queried unless the database has been mounted, which is when the controlfile is read. By contrast, the data dictionary views (prefixed DBA, ALL, or USER) can only be queried after the database—including the data dictionary—has been opened.

 EXAM TIP Dynamic performance views are populated from the instance or the controlfile; DBA_, ALL_, and USER_ views are populated from the data dictionary. This difference determines which views can be queried at the various startup stages.

The dynamic performance views are created at startup, updated continuously during the lifetime of the instance, and dropped at shutdown. This means they will accumulate values since startup time; if your database has been open for six months nonstop, they will have data built up over that period. After a shutdown/startup, they will be initialized. While the totals may be interesting, they do not directly tell you anything about what happened during certain defined periods, when there may have been performance issues. For this reason, it is generally true that the dynamic performance views give you statistics, not metrics. The conversion of these statistics into metrics is a skillful and sometimes time-consuming task, made much easier by the self-tuning and monitoring capabilities of the database.

TIP There is some overlap between V$ views and data dictionary views. For instance, V$TABLESPACE has a row for every tablespace, as does DBA_ TABLESPACES. Note that as a general rule, V$ views are singular and data dictionary views are plural. But there are exceptions.

Exercise 3-4: Query Data Dictionary and Dynamic Performance Views In this exercise, investigate the physical structures of the database by querying views.

1. Connect to the database with SQL*Plus or SQL Developer.

2. Use dynamic performance views to determine what datafiles and tablespaces make up the database as well as the size of the datafiles:

```
select t.name,d.name,d.bytes from v$tablespace t join
v$datafile d on t.ts#=d.ts# order by t.name;
```

3. Obtain the same information from data dictionary views:

```
select tablespace_name,file_name,bytes from dba_data_files
order by tablespace_name;
```

4. Determine the location of all the controlfile copies. Use two techniques:

```
select * from v$controlfile;
select value from v$parameter where name='control_files';
```

5. Determine the location of the online redo logfile members, and their size. As the size is an attribute of the group, not the members, you will have to join two views:

```
select m.group#,m.member,g.bytes from v$log g join v$logfile m
on m.group#=g.group# order by m.group#,m.member;
```

Two-Minute Drill

Describe the Stages of Database Startup and Shutdown

- The stages are NOMOUNT, MOUNT, and OPEN.
- NOMOUNT mode requires a parameter file.
- MOUNT mode requires the controlfile.
- OPEN mode requires the datafiles and online redo logfiles.

Set Database Initialization Parameters

- Static parameters cannot be changed without a shutdown/startup.
- Other parameters can be changed dynamically, for the instance or a session.
- Parameters can be seen in the dynamic performance views V$PARAMETER and V$SPPARAMETER.

Use the Alert Log and Trace Files

- The alert log contains a continuous stream of messages regarding critical operations.
- Trace files are generated by background processes, usually when they encounter errors.

Use Data Dictionary and Dynamic Performance Views

- The dynamic performance views are populated from the instance and the controlfile.
- The data dictionary views are populated from the data dictionary.
- Dynamic performance views accumulate values through the lifetime of the instance, and are reinitialized at startup.
- Data dictionary views show information that persists across shutdown and startup.
- Both the data dictionary views and the dynamic performance views are published through synonyms.

Self Test

1. You issue the URL https.//127.0.0.1:5500/em and receive an error. What could be the problem? (Choose three answers.)

   A. You have not started the database listener.

   B. You have not started the dbconsole.

   C. The dbconsole is running on a different port.

   D. You are not logged on to the database server node.

   E. You have not started the Grid Control agent.

   F. You have not started the database.

2. Which files must be synchronized for a database to open? (Choose the best answer.)

   A. Datafiles, online redo logfiles, and controlfile

   B. Parameter file and password file

   C. All the multiplexed controlfile copies

   D. None—SMON will synchronize all files by instance recovery after opening the database

3. During the transition from NOMOUNT to MOUNT mode, which files are required? (Choose the best answer.)

   A. Parameter file

   B. Controlfile

   C. Online redo logfiles

   D. Datafiles

   E. All of the above

4. You shut down your instance with SHUTDOWN IMMEDIATE. What will happen on the next startup? (Choose the best answer.)

   A. SMON will perform automatic instance recovery.

   B. You must perform manual instance recovery.

   C. PMON will roll back uncommitted transactions.

   D. The database will open without recovery.

5. You have created two databases on your computer and want to use Database Control to manage them. Which of the following statements are correct? (Choose two answers.)

   A. You cannot use Database Control, because it can only manage one database per computer.

   B. You must use Grid Control, as you have multiple databases on the computer.

   C. You can use Database Control, if you contact it on different ports for each database.

   D. You must set the ORACLE_SID variable appropriately before starting each Database Control console.

6. You issue the command SHUTDOWN, and it seems to hang. What could be the reason? (Choose the best answer.)

   A. You are not connected as SYSDBA or SYSOPER.

   B. There are other sessions logged on.

   C. You have not connected with operating system or password file authentication.

   D. There are active transactions in the database; when they complete, the SHUTDOWN will proceed.

7. What action should you take after terminating the instance with SHUTDOWN ABORT? (Choose the best answer.)

   A. Back up the database immediately.

B. Open the database, and perform database recovery.

C. Open the database, and perform instance recovery.

D. None—recovery will be automatic.

8. What will be the setting of the OPTIMIZER_MODE parameter for your session after the next startup if you issue these commands:

```
alter system set optimizer_mode=all_rows scope=spfile;
alter system set optimizer_mode=rule;
alter session set optimizer_mode=first_rows;
```

A. all_rows

B. rule

C. first_rows

(Choose the best answer.)

9. The LOG_BUFFER parameter is a static parameter. How can you change it? (Choose the best answer.)

A. You cannot change it, because it is static.

B. You can change it only for individual sessions; it will return to the previous value for all subsequent sessions.

C. You can change it within the instance, but it will return to the static value at the next startup.

D. You can change it in the parameter file, but the new value will only come into effect at the next startup.

10. Which of these actions will not be recorded in the alert log? (Choose two answers.)

A. ALTER DATABASE commands

B. ALTER SESSION commands

C. ALTER SYSTEM commands

D. Archiving an online redo logfile

E. Creating a tablespace

F. Creating a user

11. Which parameter controls the location of background process trace files? (Choose the best answer.)

A. BACKGROUND_DUMP_DEST

B. BACKGROUND_TRACE_DEST

C. DB_CREATE_FILE_DEST

D. No parameter—the location is platform specific and cannot be changed

12. Which of these views can be queried successfully in nomount mode? (Choose all correct answers.)

A. DBA_DATA_FILES

B. DBA_TABLESPACES

C. V$DATABASE

D. V$DATAFILE

E. V$INSTANCE

F. V$SESSION

13. Which view will list all tables in the database? (Choose the best answer.)

A. ALL_TABLES

B. DBA_TABLES

C. USER_TABLES, when connected as SYS

D. V$FIXED_TABLE

Self Test Answers

1. ☑ **B, C, and D.** There will always be an error if the database console process has not been started or it is on a different port, and since the URL used a loopback address, there will be an error if the browser is not running on the same machine as the console.

☒ **A, E, and F.** A and F are wrong because these are not a problem; the listener and the database can both be started if the console is accessible. E is wrong because the Grid Control agent is not necessary for Database Control.

2. ☑ **A.** These are the files that make up a database, and must all be synchronized before it can be opened.

☒ **B, C, and D.** B is wrong because these files are not, strictly speaking, part of the database at all. C is wrong because an error with the controlfile will mean the database cannot even be mounted, never mind opened. E is wrong because SMON can only fix problems in datafiles, not anything else.

3. ☑ **B.** Mounting the database entails the opening of all copies of the controlfile.

☒ **A, C, D, and E.** A is wrong because the parameter file is only needed for NOMOUNT. C, D, and E are wrong because these file types are only needed for open mode.

4. ☑ **D.** An immediate shutdown is clean, so no recovery will be required.

☒ **A, B, and C.** These are wrong because no recovery or rollback will be required; all the work will have been done as part of the shutdown.

5. ☑ C and D. Database Control will be fine but must be started for each database and contacted on different ports for each database.

☒ A and B. A is wrong because you can use Database Console, but you will need separate instances for each database. B is wrong because while Grid Control may be a better tool, it is by no means essential.

6. ☑ B. The default shutdown mode is SHUTDOWN NORMAL, which will hang until all sessions have voluntarily disconnected.

☒ A, C, and D. A and C are wrong because these would cause an error, not a hang. D is wrong because it describes SHUTDOWN TRANSACTIONAL, not SHUTDOWN NORMAL.

7. ☑ D. There is no required action; recovery will be automatic.

☒ A, B, and C. A is wrong because this is one thing you should not do after an ABORT. B is wrong because database recovery is not necessary, only instance recovery. C, instance recovery, is wrong because it will occur automatically in mount mode at the next startup.

8. ☑ B. The default scope of ALTER SYSTEM is both memory and spfile.

☒ A and C. A is wrong because this setting will have been replaced by the setting in the second command. C is wrong because the session-level setting will have been lost during the restart of the instance.

9. ☑ D. This is the technique for changing a static parameter.

☒ A, B, and C. A is wrong because static parameters can be changed—but only with a shutdown. B and C are wrong because static parameters cannot be changed for a running session or instance.

10. ☑ B and F. Neither of these affects the structure of the database or the instance; they are not important enough to generate an alert log entry.

☒ A, C, D, and E. All of these are changes to physical or memory structures, and all such changes are recorded in the alert log.

11. ☑ A. This is the parameter used to determine the location of background trace files.

☒ B, C, and D. B is wrong because there is no such parameter. C is wrong because this is the default location for datafiles, not trace files. D is wrong because while there is a platform-specific default, it can be overridden with a parameter.

12. ☑ E and F. These views are populated from the instance and will therefore be available at all times.

☒ A, B, C, and D. A and B are data dictionary views, which can only be seen in open mode. C and D are dynamic performance views populated from the controlfile, and therefore only available in mount mode or open mode.

13. ☑ **B.** The DBA views list every appropriate object in the database.

☒ **A, C,** and **D. A** is wrong because this will list only the tables the current user has permissions on. **C** is wrong because it will list only the tables owned by SYS. **D** is wrong because this is the view that lists all the dynamic performance views, not all tables.

CHAPTER 4

Oracle Networking

Exam Objectives

In this chapter you will learn to

- 052.5.1   Configure and Manage the Oracle Network
- 052.5.2   Use the Oracle Shared Server Architecture

Networking is an integral part of the client-server database architecture that is fundamental to all modern relational databases. The Oracle database had the potential for client-server computing from the beginning (version 1, released in 1978, made a separation between the Oracle code and the user code), but it was only with version 4 in 1984 that Oracle introduced interoperability between PC and server. True client-server support came with version 5, in 1986. This chapter introduces the Oracle Net services. Oracle Net was previously known as Sqlnet, and you will still hear many DBAs refer to it as such.

The default Oracle Net configuration is dedicated server. In a dedicated server environment, each user process is connected to its own server process. An alternative is shared server, where a number of user processes make use of a pool of server processes that are shared by all the sessions. Generally speaking, DBAs have been reluctant to use shared server, but there are indications that Oracle Corporation would like more sites to move to it, and certainly knowledge of the shared server architecture is vital for the OCP examination.

Configure and Manage the Oracle Network

Oracle Net is the enabling technology for Oracle's client-server architecture. It is the mechanism for establishing sessions against a database instance. There are several tools that can be used for setting up and administering Oracle Net, though it can be done with nothing more than a text editor. Whatever tool is used, the end result is a set of files that control a process (the database listener, which launches server processes in response to connection requests) and that define the means by which a user process will locate the listener.

Oracle Net and the Client-Server Paradigm

There are many layers between the user and the database. In the Oracle environment, no user ever has direct access to the database—nor does the process that the user is running. Client-server architecture guarantees that all access to data is controlled by the server.

A user interacts with a user process: this is the software that is run on their local terminal. For example, it could be Microsoft Access plus an ODBC driver on a Windows PC; it could be something written in C and linked with the Oracle Call Interface (or OCI) libraries; it could even be your old friend SQL*Plus. Whatever it is, the purpose of the user process is to prompt the user to enter information that the process can use to generate SQL statements. In the case of SQL*Plus, the process merely waits for you to type something in—a more sophisticated user process will present a proper data entry screen, will validate your input, and then when you click the Submit button will construct the statement and send it off to the server process.

The server process runs on the database server machine and executes the SQL it receives from the user process. This is your basic client-server split: a user process generating SQL, that a server process executes. The execution of a SQL statement goes through four stages: parse, bind, execute, and fetch. In the parse phase your server

PART I

process works out what the statement actually means, and how best to execute it. Parsing involves interaction with the shared pool of the instance: shared pool memory structures are used to convert the SQL into something that is actually executable. In the bind phase, any variables are expanded to literal values. Then the execute phase will require more use of the instance's SGA, and possibly of the database. During the execution of a statement, data in the database buffer cache will be read or updated and changes written to the redo log buffer, but if the relevant blocks are not in the database buffer cache, your server process will read them from the datafiles. This is the only point in the execution of a statement where the database itself is involved. And finally, the fetch phase of the execution cycle is where the server process sends the result set generated by the statement's execution back to the user process, which should then format it for display.

Oracle Net provides the mechanism for launching a server process to execute code on behalf of a user process. This is referred to as establishing a session. Thereafter, Oracle Net is responsible for maintaining the session: transmitting SQL from the user process to the server process, and fetching results from the server process back to the user process.

Figure 4-1 shows the various components of a session. A user interacts with a user process; a user process interacts with a server process, via Oracle Net; a server process interacts with the instance; and the instance, via its background processes, interacts with the database. The client-server split is between the user process generating SQL and the server process executing it. This split will usually be physical as well as logical: there will commonly be a local area network between the machines hosting the user processes and the machine hosting the server processes. But it is quite possible for this link to be over a wide area network, or conversely to run the user processes on the server machine. Oracle Net is responsible for establishing a session, and then for the ongoing communication between the user process and the server process.

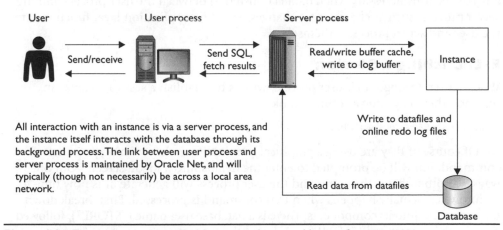

Figure 4-1 The database is protected from users by several layers of segregation.

A Word on Oracle Net and Communication Protocols

Oracle Net is a layered protocol: it runs on top of whatever communications protocol is supported by your operating system. Historically, Sqlnet could work with all the popular protocols (with the exception of NetBIOS/NetBEUI, which has limited functionality and cannot be used for large database systems: it cannot be routed), but in release 11g Oracle's network support is limited to TCP, TCP with secure sockets, Windows Named Pipes (or NMP), and the newer Sockets Direct Protocol (or SDP) over Infiniband high-speed networks. This reduction in protocol support is in line with industry standards. All operating systems also have an Inter-Process Communication (or IPC) protocol proprietary to the operating system—this is also available to Oracle Net for local connections where the user process is on the same machine as the server.

This layering of Oracle Net on top of whatever is provided by your operating system provides Oracle platform independence. You, as DBA, do not need to know anything about the underlying network; you configure Oracle Net to use whatever protocol has been configured by your network administrators. You need not concern yourself with what is happening at a lower networking layer. TCP is, for better or worse, undoubtedly the most popular protocol worldwide, so that is the one used in the examples that follow. The use of industry standard protocols means that there need be no dependency between the server-side and the client-side platforms. There is no reason why, for example, a client on Windows cannot talk to a database on Unix. As long as the platform can offer a TCP layer 4 interface, then Oracle Net can use it.

With regard to conformance with the Open Systems Interconnection (or OSI) seven-layer model to which all IT vendors are supposed to comply, Oracle Net maps on to layers 5, 6, and 7: the session, presentation, and application layers. The protocol adapters installed with the standard Oracle installation provide the crossover to layer 4, the transport layer, provided by your operating system. Thus Oracle Net is responsible for establishing sessions between the end systems once TCP (or whatever else you are using) has established a layer 4 connection. The presentation layer functions are handled by the Oracle Net Two Task Common (or TTC) layer. TTC is responsible for any conversions necessary when data is transferred between the user process and the server process, such as character set changes. Then the application layer functions are the user and server processes themselves.

Establishing a Session

When a user, through their user process, wishes to establish a session against an instance, they may issue a command like

```
CONNECT STORE/ADMIN123@ORCL11G
```

Of course, if they are using a graphical user interface, they won't type in that command. but will be prompted to enter the details into a logon screen—but one way or another that is the command the user process will generate. It is now time to go into what actually happens when that command is processed. First, break down the command into its components. There is a database user name ("STORE"), followed by a database password ("ADMIN123"), and the two are separated by a "/" as a delimiter. Then there is an "@" symbol, followed by a connect string, "ORCL11G". The "@" symbol is an indication to the user process that a network connection is required. If the "@" and the connect string are omitted, then the user process will assume that the instance you wish to connect to is running on the local machine, and that the always-available IPC protocol can be used. If the "@" and a connect string are included, then the user process will assume that you are requesting a network connection to an instance on a remote machine—though in fact, you could be bouncing off the network card and back to the machine on to which you are logged.

Connecting to a Local Instance

Even when you connect to an instance running on your local machine, you still use Oracle Net. All Oracle sessions use a network protocol to implement the separation of user code from server code, but for a local connection the protocol is IPC: this is the protocol provided by your operating system that will allow processes to communicate within the host machine. This is the only type of connection that does not require a database listener; indeed, local connections do not require any configuration at all. The only information needed is to tell your user process which instance you want to connect to. Remember that there could be several instances running on your local computer. You give the process this information through an environment variable. Figure 4-2 shows examples of this on Linux, and Figure 4-3 shows how to connect to a local database on Windows.

Figure 4-2 Local database connections—Linux	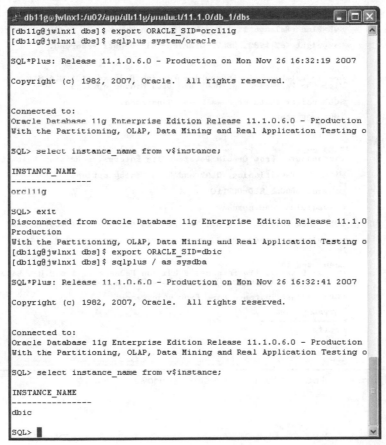

Remember that the only difference between platforms is the syntax for setting environment variables, as demonstrated in Figures 4-2 and 4-3.

Name Resolution

When connecting using Oracle Net, the first stage is to work out exactly what it is you want to connect to. This is the process of name resolution. If your connect statement includes the connect string "@orcl11g", Oracle Net has to work out what is meant by "orcl11g". This means that the string has to be resolved into certain pieces of information: the protocol you want to use (assume that this is TCP), the IP address on which the database listener is running, the port that the listener is monitoring for incoming connection requests, and the name of the instance (which need not be the same as the connect string) to which you wish to connect. There are variations: rather than an IP address, the connect string can include a hostname, which then gets further resolved to an IP address by a DNS server. Rather than specifying an instance by name, the connect string can include the name of a service, which (in a RAC environment) could be made up of a number of instances. In a single-instance environment, services can

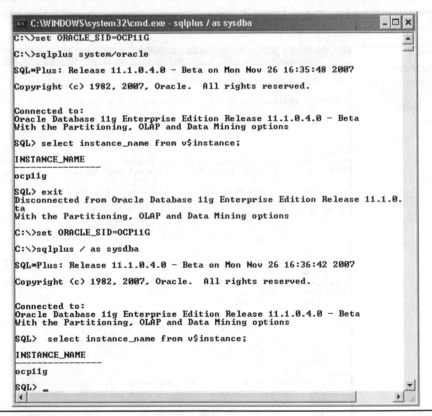

Figure 4-3 Local database connections—Windows

PART I

still be used—perhaps to assist with tracking the workload imposed on the database by different groups of users. You can configure a number of ways of resolving connect strings to address and instance names, but one way or another the name resolution process gives your user process enough information to go across the network to a database listener and request a connection to a particular instance.

Launching a Server Process

The database listener, running on the server machine, uses one or more protocols to monitor one or more ports on one or more network interface cards for incoming connection requests. You can further complicate matters by running multiple listeners on one machine, and any one listener can accept connection requests for a number of instances. When it receives a connect request, the listener must first validate whether the instance requested is actually available. Assuming that it is, the listener will launch a new server process to service the user process. Thus if you have a thousand users logging on concurrently to your instance, you will be launching a thousand server processes. This is known as the dedicated server architecture. Later in this chapter you'll see the shared server alternative where each user process is handled by a dedicated dispatcher process, but shared by multiple user processes.

In the TCP environment, each dedicated server process launched by a listener will acquire a unique TCP port number. This will be assigned at process startup time by your operating system's port mapping algorithm. The port number gets passed back to the user process by the listener (or on some operating systems the socket already opened to the listener is transferred to the new port number), and the user process can then communicate directly with its server process. The listener has now completed its work and waits for the next connect request.

 EXAM TIP If the database listener is not running, no new server processes can be launched—but this will not affect any existing sessions that have already been established.

Creating a Listener

A listener is defined in a file: the `listener.ora` file, whose default location is in the ORACLE_HOME/network/admin directory. As a minimum, the `listener.ora` file must include a section for one listener, which states its name and the protocol and listening address it will use. You can configure several listeners in the one file, but they must all have different names and addresses.

 TIP You can run a listener completely on defaults, without a `listener.ora` file at all. It will listen on whatever address resolves to the machine's hostname, on port 1521. Always configure the `listener.ora` file, to make your Oracle Net environment self-documenting.

As with other files used to configure Oracle Net, the `listener.ora` file can be very fussy about seemingly trivial points of syntax, such as case sensitivity, white spaces, and abbreviations. For this reason, many DBAs do not like to edit it by hand (though there is no reason not to). Oracle provides three graphical tools to manage Oracle Net: Enterprise Manager (Database Control or Grid Control), the Net Manager, and the Net Configuration Assistant. The latter two tools are both written in Java. There is considerable overlap between the functionality of these tools, though there are a few things that can only be done in one or another.

This is an example of a `listener.ora` file:

```
LISTENER =
  (DESCRIPTION =
    (ADDRESS = (PROTOCOL = TCP)(HOST = jwlnx1)(PORT = 1521))
  )
LIST2 =
  (DESCRIPTION =
    (ADDRESS_LIST =
        (ADDRESS = (PROTOCOL = TCP)(HOST = 127.0.0.1)(PORT = 1522))
        (ADDRESS = (PROTOCOL = TCP)(HOST = jwlnx1.bplc.co.za)(PORT = 1522))
    )
  )
```

The first section of this file defines a listener called LISTENER, monitoring the local hostname on the default port, 1521. The second section defines another listener called LIST2. This listener monitors port 1522 on both the hostname address and a loopback address.

To create the listener, you need do nothing more than create an entry in the `listener.ora` file, and start it. Under Windows the listener will run as a Windows service, but there is no need to create the service explicitly; it will be created implicitly the first time the listener is started. From then, if you wish, it can be started and stopped like any other Windows service.

Figure 4-4 shows the Net Manager's view of the listener LIST2, and Figure 4-5 shows it through the Net Configuration Assistant.

Note that the Net Manager lets you configure multiple listening addresses for a listener (Figure 4-4 shows the loopback address), whereas the Net Configuration Assistant does not: it can only see the one address of the hostname; there is no prompt for creating or viewing any other.

Database Registration

A listener is necessary to spawn server processes against an instance. In order to do this, it needs to know what instances are available on the computer on which it is running. A listener finds out about instances by the process of "registration."

 EXAM TIP The listener and the instance must be running on the same computer, unless you are using RAC. In a RAC environment, any listener on any computer in the cluster can connect you to any instance on any computer.

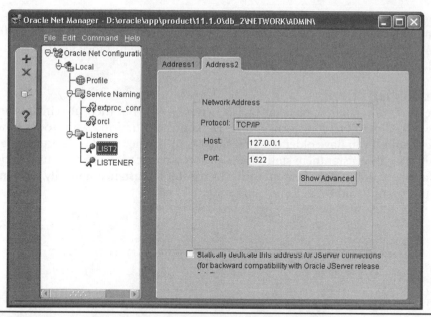

Figure 4-4 A listener definition as created or viewed with the Net Manager

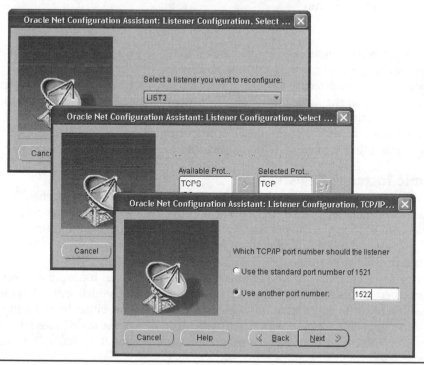

Figure 4-5 A listener definition as created or viewed with the Net Configuration Assistant

There are two methods for registering an instance with a database: static and dynamic registration. For static registration, you hard-code a list of instances in the `listener.ora` file. Dynamic registration means that the instance itself, at startup time, locates a listener and registers with it.

Static Registration

As a general rule, dynamic registration is a better option, but there are circumstances when you will resort to static registration. Dynamic registration was introduced with release 8i, but if you have older databases that your listener must connect users to, you will have to register them statically. Also some applications may require static registration: typically management tools. To register an instance statically, add an appropriate entry to the `listener.ora` file:

```
LIST2 =
  (DESCRIPTION_LIST =
    (DESCRIPTION =
        (ADDRESS = (PROTOCOL = TCP)(HOST = 127.0.0.1)(PORT = 1522))
    )
  )

SID_LIST_LIST2 =
  (SID_LIST =
    (SID_DESC =
      (ORACLE_HOME = /u01/oracle/app/product/11.1.0/db_1)
      (SID_NAME = ocp11g)
    )
  )
```

This entry will configure the listener called LIST2 to accept connection requests for an instance called ocp11g. It says nothing about whether the instance is running or even exists at all. The directive `ORACLE_HOME` is only required if the database listener is not running from the same Oracle Home as the instance. If this is the case, then this directive will let the listener find the executable file that it must run to launch a server process. Usually, this is only necessary if configuring a listener to make connections to instances of a different version, which have to be running off a different home.

Dynamic Instance Registration

This is the preferred method by which an instance will register with a listener. The initialization parameter `local_listener` tells the instance the network address that it should contact to find a listener with which to register. At instance startup time, the PMON process will use this parameter to locate a listener, and inform it of the instance's name and the names of the service(s) that the instance is offering. The instance name is defined by the `instance_name` parameter, and the `service_names` parameter will have defaulted to this suffixed by the `db_domain` parameter, which will default to null. It is possible to create and start additional services at any time, either by changing the value of the `service_names` parameter (which can be a comma-delimited list, if the instance is to offer several services) or programmatically using the DBMS_SERVICE package.

Any change to the services must be registered with the local listener. If this is not done, the listener won't know what services are being offered, and will therefore not be able to set up sessions to them. The PMON process will register automatically once a minute, but at any time subsequent to instance startup you can force a re-registration by executing the command

```
SQL> alter system register;
```

 TIP You will need to register your instance with the listener with `alter system register` if you have restarted the listener, or if you started the database instance before starting the listener or you can wait a minute for PMON to register.

Dynamic registration is a better option than static registration because it ensures that only running instances and available services are registered with the listener, and also that there are no errors in the instance and service names. It is all too easy to make mistakes here, particularly if you are editing the `listener.ora` file by hand. Also, when the instance shuts down, it will deregister from the listener automatically.

From release 9*i* onward, dynamic registration requires no configuration at all if your listener is running on the default port, 1521. All instances will automatically look for a listener on the local host on that port, and register themselves if they find one. However, if your listener is not running on the default port on the address identified by the hostname, you must specify where the listener is by setting the parameter `local_listener` and re-registering, for example,

```
SQL> alter system set local_listener=list2;
SQL> alter system register;
```

In this example, the `local_listener` has been specified by name. This name needs to be resolved into an address in order for the instance to find the listener and register itself, as described in the following section. An alternative technique is to hard-code the listener's address in the parameter:

```
SQL> alter system set
 local_listener='(address=(protocol=tcp)(host=127.0.0.1)(port=1522))';
```

This syntax is perfectly acceptable, but the use of a name that can be resolved is better practice, as it places a layer of abstraction between the logical name and the physical address. The abstraction means that if the listening address ever has to be changed, one need only change it in the name resolution service, rather than having to change it in every instance that uses it.

Techniques for Name Resolution

At the beginning of this chapter you saw that to establish a session against an instance, your user process must issue a connect string. That string resolves to the address of a listener and the name of an instance or service. In the discussion of dynamic instance registration, you saw again the use of a logical name for a listener, which needs to be resolved into a network address in order for an instance to find a listener with which to register. Oracle provides four methods of name resolution: easy connect, local naming, directory naming, and external naming. It is probably true to say that the majority of Oracle sites use local naming, but there is no question that directory naming is the best method for a large and complex installation.

Easy Connect

The Easy Connect name resolution method was introduced with release 10g. It is very easy to use—it requires no configuration at all. But it is limited to one protocol: TCP. The other name resolution methods can use any of the other supported protocols, such as TCP with secure sockets, or Named Pipes. Another limitation is that Easy Connect cannot be used with any of Oracle Net's more advanced capabilities, such as load balancing or connect-time failover across different network routes. It is fair to say that Easy Connect is a method you as the DBA will find very handy to use, but that it is not a method of much use for your end users. Easy Connect is enabled by default. You invoke it with connect string syntax such as

```
SQL> connect store/admin123@jwlnx1.bplc.co.za:1522/ocp11g
```

In this example, SQL*Plus will use TCP to go to port 1522 on the IP address to which the hostname resolves. Then if there is a listener running on that port and address, it will ask the listener to spawn a server process against an instance that is part of the service called ocp11g. Easy Connect can be made even easier:

```
SQL> connect store/admin123@jwlnx1.bplc.co.za
```

This syntax will also work, but only if the listener running on this hostname is using port 1521, and the service name registered with the listener is jwlnx1.bplc.co.za, the same as the computer name.

Local Naming

With local naming the user supplies an alias, known as an Oracle Net service alias, for the connect string, and the alias is resolved by a local file into the full network address (protocol, address, port, and service or instance name). This local file is the infamous tnsnames.ora file, which has caused DBAs much grief over the years. Consider this example of a tnsnames.ora file:

```
ocp11g =
  (DESCRIPTION =
    (ADDRESS_LIST =
      (ADDRESS = (PROTOCOL = TCP)(HOST = jwlnx1.bplc.co.za)(PORT = 1522))
    )
    (CONNECT_DATA =
      (service_name = ocp11g)
    )
  )
test =
  (DESCRIPTION =
    (ADDRESS_LIST =
      (ADDRESS = (PROTOCOL = TCP)(HOST = serv2.bplc.co.za)(PORT = 1521))
    )
    (CONNECT_DATA =
```

```
        (sid = testdb)
    )
  )
```

This `tnsnames.ora` file has two Oracle Net service aliases defined within it: ocp11g and test. These aliases are what your users will provide in their connect statements. The first entry, ocp11g, simply says that when the connect string "@ocp11g" is issued, your user process should use the TCP protocol to go the machine jwlnx1.bplc.co.za, contact it on port 1522, and ask the listener monitoring that port to establish a session against the instance with the service name ocp11g. The second entry, test, directs users to a listener on a different machine and asks for a session against the instance called testdb.

TIP There need be no relationship between the alias, the service name, and the instance name, but for the sake of your sanity you will usually keep them the same.

Local naming supports all protocols and all the advanced features of Oracle Net, but maintaining `tnsnames.ora` files on all your client machines can be an extremely time-consuming task. The `tnsnames.ora` file is also notoriously sensitive to apparently trivial variations in layout. Using the GUI tools will help avoid such problems.

Directory Naming and External Naming

Directory naming points the user toward an LDAP directory server to resolve aliases. LDAP (the Lightweight Directory Protocol) is a widely used standard that Oracle Corporation (and other mainstream software vendors) is encouraging organizations to adopt. To use directory naming, you must first install and configure a directory server somewhere on your network. Oracle provides an LDAP server (the Oracle Internet Directory) as part of the Oracle Application Server, but you do not have to use that—if you already have a Microsoft Active Directory, that will be perfectly adequate. IBM and Novell also sell directory servers conforming to the LDAP standard.

Like local naming, directory naming supports all Oracle Net features—but unlike local naming, it uses a central repository, the directory server, for all your name resolution details. This is much easier to maintain than many `tnsnames.ora` files distributed across your whole user community.

External naming is conceptually similar to directory naming, but it uses third-party naming services such as Sun's Network Information Services (NIS+) or the Cell Directory Services (CDS) that are part of the Distributed Computing Environment (DCE).

The use of directories and external naming services is beyond the scope of the OCP syllabus.

The Listener Control Utility

You can start and stop listeners through Database Control, but there is also a command-line utility, `lsnrctl` (it is `lsnrctl.exe` on Windows). The `lsnrctl` commands can be run directly from an operating system prompt, or through a simple user interface. For all the commands, you must specify the name of the listener, if it is not the default name of LISTENER. Figures 4-6 and 4-7 show how to check the status of a listener and to stop and start it, issuing the commands either from the operating system prompt or from within the user interface.

Note that the `status` command always tells you the address on which the listener accepts connection requests, the name and location of the `listener.ora` file that defines the listener, and the name and location of the log file for the listener. Also, in the examples shown in the figures, the listener LIST2 "supports no services." This is because there are no services statically registered in the `listener.ora` file for that listener, and no instances have dynamically registered either. Figure 4-8 uses the `services` command to show the state of the listener after an instance has registered dynamically.

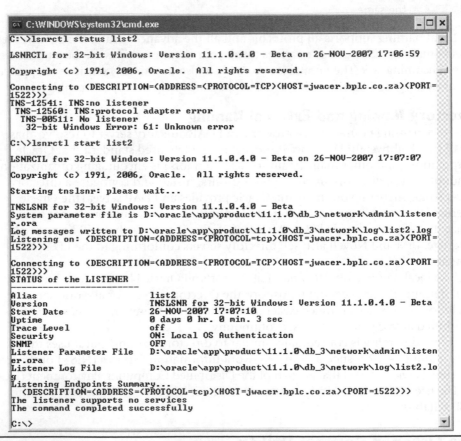

Figure 4-6 Using `lsnrctl` commands from the operating system prompt to check the status and then start the listener LIST2

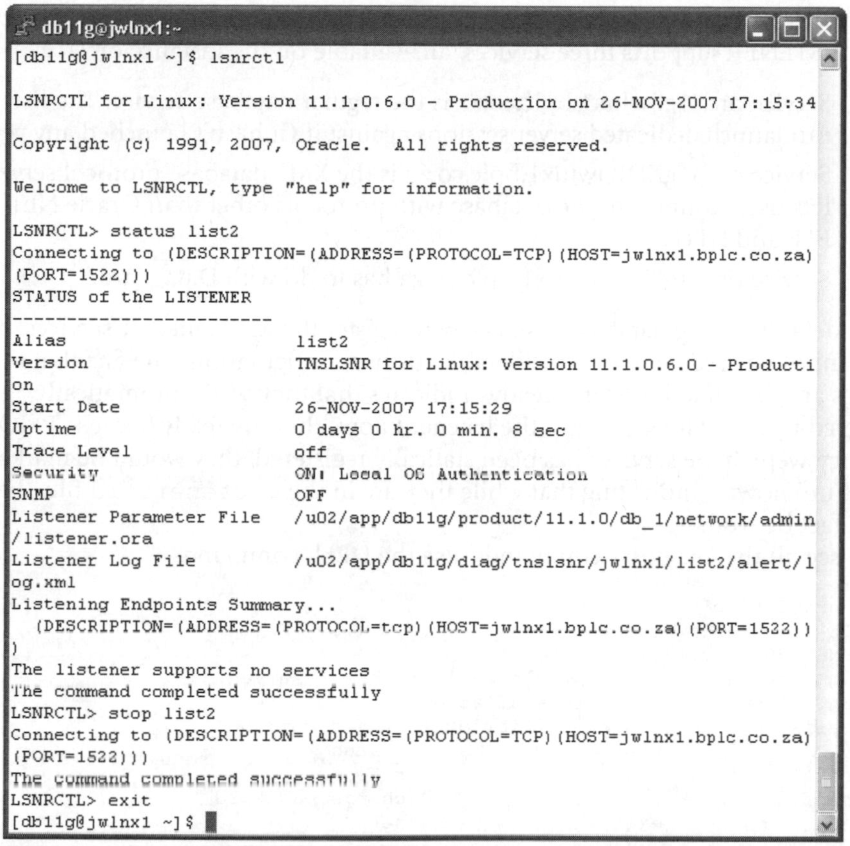

PART I

```
db11g@jwlnx1:~                                                    _ □ ✕
[db11g@jwlnx1 ~]$ lsnrctl

LSNRCTL for Linux: Version 11.1.0.6.0 - Production on 26-NOV-2007 17:15:34

Copyright (c) 1991, 2007, Oracle.  All rights reserved.

Welcome to LSNRCTL, type "help" for information.

LSNRCTL> status list2
Connecting to (DESCRIPTION=(ADDRESS=(PROTOCOL=TCP)(HOST=jwlnx1.bplc.co.za)
(PORT=1522)))
STATUS of the LISTENER
-----------------------
Alias                     list2
Version                   TNSLSNR for Linux: Version 11.1.0.6.0 - Producti
on
Start Date                26-NOV-2007 17:15:29
Uptime                    0 days 0 hr. 0 min. 8 sec
Trace Level               off
Security                  ON: Local OS Authentication
SNMP                      OFF
Listener Parameter File   /u02/app/db11g/product/11.1.0/db_1/network/admin
/listener.ora
Listener Log File         /u02/app/db11g/diag/tnslsnr/jwlnx1/list2/alert/l
og.xml
Listening Endpoints Summary...
  (DESCRIPTION=(ADDRESS=(PROTOCOL=tcp)(HOST=jwlnx1.bplc.co.za)(PORT=1522))
)
The listener supports no services
The command completed successfully
LSNRCTL> stop list2
Connecting to (DESCRIPTION=(ADDRESS=(PROTOCOL=TCP)(HOST=jwlnx1.bplc.co.za)
(PORT=1522)))
The command completed successfully
LSNRCTL> exit
[db11g@jwlnx1 ~]$
```

Figure 4-7   Using the `lsnrctl` user interface to check the status and then stop the listener LIST2

Figure 4-8
The `services`
command shows the
services for which
the listener will
accept connections.

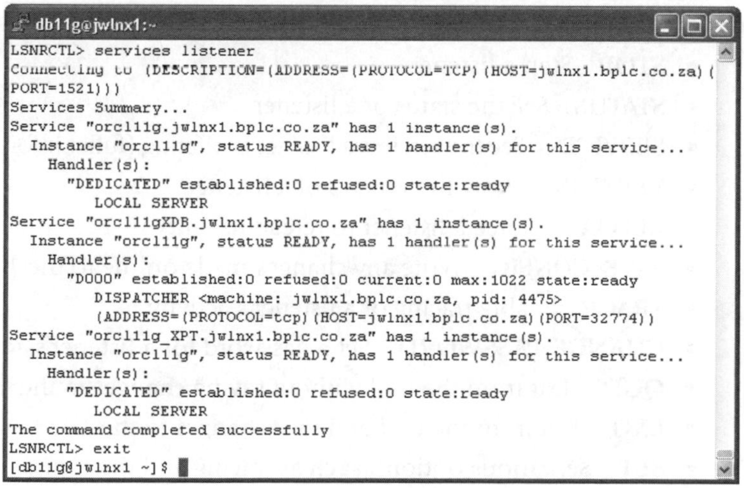

```
db11g@jwlnx1:~                                                    _ □ ✕
LSNRCTL> services listener
Connecting to (DESCRIPTION=(ADDRESS=(PROTOCOL=TCP)(HOST=jwlnx1.bplc.co.za)(
PORT=1521)))
Services Summary...
Service "orcl11g.jwlnx1.bplc.co.za" has 1 instance(s).
  Instance "orcl11g", status READY, has 1 handler(s) for this service...
    Handler(s):
      "DEDICATED" established:0 refused:0 state:ready
         LOCAL SERVER
Service "orcl11gXDB.jwlnx1.bplc.co.za" has 1 instance(s).
  Instance "orcl11g", status READY, has 1 handler(s) for this service...
    Handler(s):
      "D000" established:0 refused:0 current:0 max:1022 state:ready
         DISPATCHER <machine: jwlnx1.bplc.co.za, pid: 4475>
         (ADDRESS=(PROTOCOL=tcp)(HOST=jwlnx1.bplc.co.za)(PORT=32774))
Service "orcl11g_XPT.jwlnx1.bplc.co.za" has 1 instance(s).
  Instance "orcl11g", status READY, has 1 handler(s) for this service...
    Handler(s):
      "DEDICATED" established:0 refused:0 state:ready
         LOCAL SERVER
The command completed successfully
LSNRCTL> exit
[db11g@jwlnx1 ~]$
```

In Figure 4-8, the output of the `status` command tells you that the listener called LISTENER supports three services, all available on the instance orcl11g:

- Service orcl11g.jwlnx1.bplc.co.za is the regular database service. The listener can launch dedicated server sessions against it (it hasn't launched any yet).

- Service orcl11gXDB.jwlnx1.bplc.co.za is the XML database protocol server. This lets users connect to the database with protocols other than Oracle NET, such FTP and HTTP.

- Service orcl11g_XPT.jwlnx1.bplc.co.za has to do with Dataguard.

By default, an 11g database instance will register the XDP and XPT services, but they cannot be used without considerable further configuration. The fact that the services are shown to be "status ready" indicates that they were automatically registered by the PMON process: the listener knows they are ready because PMON said they were. If the services has been statically registered, they would be marked as "status unknown," indicating that while they are in the `listener.ora` file, they may not in fact be working.

To see all the `lsnrctl` commands, use the HELP command:

```
C:\>lsnrctl help
LSNRCTL for 32-bit Windows: Version 11.1.0.4.0 - Beta
on 26-NOV-2007 17:47:16
Copyright (c) 1991, 2006, Oracle.  All rights reserved.
The following operations are available
An asterisk (*) denotes a modifier or extended command:
start                   stop                    status
services                version                 reload
save_config             trace                   change_password
quit                    exit                    set*
show*
```

In summary, these commands are

- **START**   Start a listener.
- **STOP**   Stop a listener.
- **STATUS**   See the status of a listener.
- **SERVICES**   See the services a listener is offering (fuller information than STATUS).
- **VERSION**   Show the version of a listener.
- **RELOAD**   Force a listener to reread its entry in `listener.ora`.
- **SAVE_CONFIG**   Write any changes made online to the `listener.ora` file.
- **TRACE**   Enable tracing of a listener's activity.
- **CHANGE_PASSWORD**   Set a password for a listener's administration.
- **QUIT**   Exit from the tool without saving changes to the `listener.ora` file.
- **EXIT**   Exit from the tool and save changes to the `listener.ora` file.
- **SET**   Set various options, such as tracing and timeouts.
- **SHOW**   Show options that have been set for a listener.

Note that all these commands should be qualified with the name of the listener to which the command should be applied. If a name is not supplied, the command will be executed against the listener called LISTENER.

Configuring Service Aliases

Having decided what name resolution method to use, your next task is to configure the clients to use it. You can do this through Database Control, but since Database Control is a server-side process, you can use it only to configure clients running on the database server. An alternative is to use the Net Manager. This is a stand-alone Java utility, shipped with all the Oracle client-side products.

To launch the Net Manager, run `netmgr` from a Unix prompt, or on Windows you will find it on the Start menu.

The Net Manager navigation tree has three branches. The Profile branch is used to set options that may apply to both the client and server sides of Oracle Net and can be used to influence the behavior of all Oracle Net connections. This is where, for example, you can configure detailed tracing of Oracle Net sessions. The Service Naming branch is used to configure client-side name resolution, and the Listeners branch is used to configure database listeners.

When you select the Profile branch as shown in Figure 4-9, you are in fact configuring a file called `sqlnet.ora`. This file exists by default in your `ORACLE_HOME/network/admin` directory. It is optional, as there are defaults for every `sqlnet.ora` directive, but you will usually configure it if only to select the name resolution method.

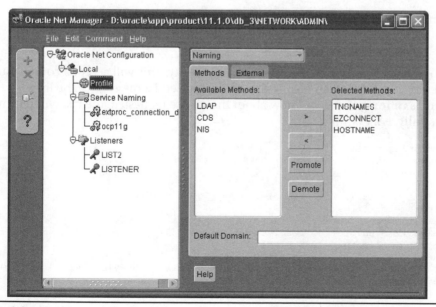

Figure 4-9 Net Manager's Profile editor

In the Profile branch, you will see all the available naming methods, with three (TNSNAMES and EZCONNECT and HOSTNAME) selected by default: these are Local Naming and Easy Connect and Host Naming. The external methods are NIS and CDS. LDAP is Directory Naming. Host Naming is similar to Easy Connect and retained for backward compatibility.

Then you need to configure the individual Oracle Net service aliases. This is done in the Service Naming branch, which in fact creates or edits the Local Naming `tnsnames.ora` file that resides by default in your `ORACLE_HOME/network/admin` directory. If you are fortunate enough to be using Directory Naming, you do not need to do this; choosing LDAP in the Profile as your naming method is enough.

A typical entry in the `tnsnames.ora` file would be

```
OCP11G =
  (DESCRIPTION =
    (ADDRESS_LIST =
      (ADDRESS = (PROTOCOL = TCP)(HOST = jwacer.bplc.co.za)(PORT = 1521))
    )
    (CONNECT_DATA =
      (SERVICE_NAME = ocp11g)
    )
  )
```

If a user enters the connect string "ocp11g", this entry will resolve the name to a listener running on the address jwlnx1.bplc.co.za monitoring port 1521, and ask the listener for a session against an instance offering the service ocp11g. To connect with this, use

```
sqlplus system/oracle@ocp11g
```

The equivalent with Easy Connect would be

```
sqlplus system/manager@jwacer.bplc.co.za:1521/ocp11g
```

To test a connect string, use the TNSPING utility. This will accept a connect string, locate the Oracle Net files, resolve the string, and send a message to the listener. If the listener is running and does know about the service requested, the test will return successfully. For example,

```
C:\> tnsping ocp11g
TNS Ping Utility for 32-bit Windows: Version 11.1.0.4.0 - Beta
on 27-NOV-2007 11
:49:55
Copyright (c) 1997, 2006, Oracle.  All rights reserved.
Used parameter files:
D:\oracle\app\product\11.1.0\db_3\network\admin\sqlnet.ora
Used TNSNAMES adapter to resolve the alias
Attempting to contact (DESCRIPTION =
(ADDRESS_LIST = (ADDRESS = (PROTOCOL = TCP)
(HOST = 127.0.0.1)(PORT = 2521))) (CONNECT_DATA = (SERVICE_NAME = ocp11g)))
OK (40 msec)
```

Note that the output of TNSPING shows the `sqlnet.ora` file used, the name resolution method used, and then the details of the address contacted. The tool does not go further than the listener; it will not check whether the instance is actually working.

Filenames and the TNSADMIN Environment Variable

There are three critical files involved in configuring Oracle Net:

- The `listener.ora` file is a server-side file that defines database listeners. It includes the protocols, addresses, and ports on which they will listen for incoming connection requests, and (optionally) a hard-coded list of instances against which they will launch sessions.

- The `tnsnames.ora` file is a client-side file used for name resolution. It is used by user processes to locate database listeners. It may also be used by the instance itself, to locate a listener with which to register.

- The `sqlnet.ora` file is optional and may exist (possibly with different settings) on the server side, the client side, or both. It contains settings that apply to all connections and listeners, such as security rules and encryption.

The three Oracle Net files by default exist in the directory `ORACLE_HOME/network/ admin`. It is possible to relocate them with an environment variable: TNS_ADMIN. An important use of this is on systems that have several Oracle Homes. This is a very common situation. A typical Oracle server machine will have at least three homes: one for the Enterprise Manager Grid Control Agent, one for launching database instances, and one for launching Automatic Storage Management (ASM) instances. (ASM is covered in the second OCP examination.) Client machines may well have several Oracle Homes as well, perhaps one each for the 10g and 11g clients. Setting the TNS_ADMIN variable to point to one set of files in one of the Oracle home directories (or indeed in a different directory altogether) means that instead of having to maintain multiple sets of files, you need maintain only one set. To set the variable, on Windows you can use the SET command to set it for one session,

```
set TNS_ADMIN=c:\oracle\net
```

though it will usually be better to set it in the registry, as a string value key in the Oracle Home branch. On Linux and Unix, the syntax will vary depending on the shell, but something like this will usually do:

```
set TNS_ADMIN=/u01/oracle/net; export TNS_ADMIN
```

This command could be placed in each user's `.profile` file, or in the `/etc/ profile` where every user will pick it up.

Figure 4-10 traces the flow of logic utilized to resolve a typical client connection request.

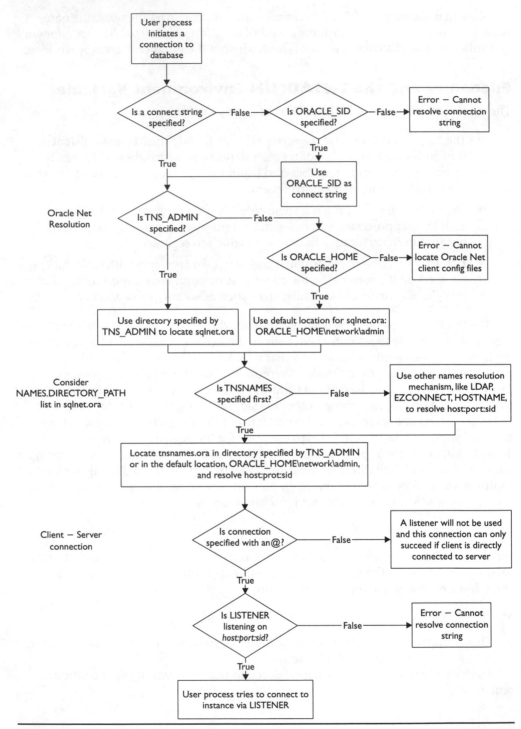

Figure 4-10 Typical resolution logic for client connection request

A user typically initiates a connection to the database server by providing a username, a password, and a connect string. If a connect string is absent, the Oracle Net client layer tries to use the ORACLE_SID environment variable or registry variable as a default connect string value. If this is not set, an error usually results. If a connect string is available, the Oracle Net client then tries to figure out what mechanism to utilize to resolve the connect string and it does this by trying to locate the relevant `sqlnet.ora` file, either in the directory specified by the TNS_ADMIN variable or in the `ORACLE_HOME/network/admin` directory. If neither the TNS_ADMIN nor ORACLE_HOME variable is set, an error is returned.

Typically, `sqlnet.ora` contains a NAMES.DIRECTORY_PATH directive, which lists, in order of preference, the different connection name resolution mechanisms, like TNSNAMES, LDAP, and EZCONNECT. If TNSNAMES is listed as the first preferred mechanism, Oracle Net then tries to locate the infamous `tnsnames.ora` file either in the directory specified by the TNS_ADMIN variable or in the `ORACLE_HOME/network/admin` directory. The `tnsnames.ora` file is then used to obtain the network address of the connection string, typically yielding a `hostname:port:sid` or `hostname:port:servicename` triad.

The Oracle Net client is finally in a position to bind the user process that initiated the connection to the database server. If the connection string contained the "@" symbol, then the listener on the hostname is contacted on the relevant port, for access to the specified instance or service. If the listener is functioning correctly, the user process tries to negotiate a server connection, or else an error is returned. If the connection string does not contain the "@" symbol, a local IPC connection is attempted. If the instance or service is available on the same server as the client user process, then the connection may be successfully made.

Database Links

So far, Oracle Net has been discussed in the context of users connecting to database instances. Oracle Net can also be used for communications between databases: a user session against one database can execute SQL statements against another database. This is done through a database link. There are several options for creating database links (all to do with security), but a simple example is

```
create database link prodstore
connect to store identified by admin123 using 'prod';
```

This defines a database link from the current database to a remote database identified by the connect string PROD. The link exists in and can only be used by the current user's schema. When a statement such as

```
select * from orders@prodstore;
```

is issued, the user's session will launch a session against the remote database, log on to it transparently as user STORE, and run the query there. The results will be sent back to the local database and then returned to the user.

Any SQL statements can be executed through a link, provided that the schema to which the link connects has appropriate permissions. For example, consider this scenario:

There is a production database, identified by the connect string PROD, which contains a schema STORE, with two tables: ORDERS and PRODUCTS. There is a link to this database as just defined. There is also a development database, identified by the connect string DEV, which also contains the schema STORE. You are connected to a third database called TEST. You need to update the development schema with the production data.

First, define a database link to the development database:

```
create database link devstore
connect to store identified by devpasswd using 'dev';
```

Then update the development schema to match the production schema:

```
truncate table orders@devstore;
truncate table customers@devstore;
insert into orders@devstore select * from orders@prodstore;
insert into customers@devstore select * from customers@prodstore;
commit;
```

To check whether any rows have been inserted in the production system since the last refresh of development and, if so, insert them into development, you could run this statement:

```
insert into orders@devstore
(select * from orders@prodstore  minus select * from orders@devstore);
```

If it were necessary to change the name of a customer, you could do it in both databases concurrently with

```
update customers@prodstore set customer_name='Coda' where customer_id=10;
update customers@devstore customer_name='Coda' where customer_id=10;
commit;
```

When necessary, Oracle will always implement a two-phase commit to ensure that a *distributed transaction* (which is a transaction that affects rows in more than one database) is treated as an atomic transaction: the changes must succeed in all databases or be rolled back in all databases. Read consistency is also maintained across the whole environment.

Exercise 4-1: Configure Oracle Net   In this exercise, you will set up a complete Oracle Net environment, using graphical and command-line tools. Differences between Windows and Linux will be pointed out.

1. Create a directory to be used for the Oracle Net configuration files, and set the TNS_ADMIN variable to point to this. It doesn't matter where the directory is, as long as the Oracle user has permission to create, read, and write it.

   On Linux:

   ```
   mkdir /u01/oracle/net
   export TNS_ADMIN=/u01/oracle/net
   ```

Ensure that all work from now is done from a session where the variable has been set.

On Windows:

```
mkdir d:\oracle\net
```

Create and set the key TNS_ADMIN as a string variable in the registry in the Oracle Home branch. This will typically be

```
HKEY_LOCAL_MACHINE\SOFTWARE\ORACLE\KEY_OraDb11g_home1
```

2. Check that the variable is being read by using the TNSPING command from an operating system prompt:

```
tnsping orcl
```

This will return an error "TNS-03505: Failed to resolve name" because there are no files in the TNS_ADMIN directory. On Windows, you may need to launch a new command prompt to pick up the new TNS_ADMIN value from the registry.

3. Start the Net Manager. On Linux, run `netmgr` from an operating system prompt; on Windows, launch it from the Start menu. The top line of the Net Manager window will show the location of the Oracle Net files. If this is not the new directory, then the TNS_ADMIN variable has not been set correctly.

4. Create a new listener: expand the Local branch of the navigation tree, highlight Listeners, and click the + icon.

5. Enter a listener name, **NEWLIST**, and click OK.

6. Click Add Address.

7. For Address 1, choose TCP/IP as the protocol and enter **127.0.0.1** as the host, **2521** as the port. The illustration that follows shows the result.

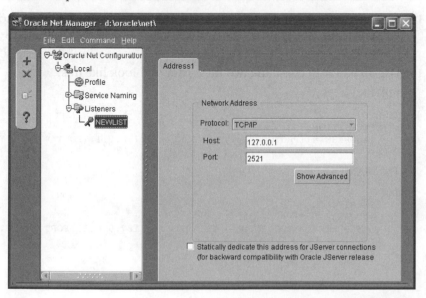

8. Create a new service name: highlight Service Naming in the navigation tree, and click the + icon.

9. Enter **NEW** as the net service name, and click Next.

10. Select TCP/IP as the protocol, and click Next.

11. Enter **127.0.0.1** as the host name and **2521** as the port and click Next.

12. Enter **SERV1** as the service name, and click Next.

13. Click Finish. If you try the test, it will fail at this time. The illustration that follows shows the result.

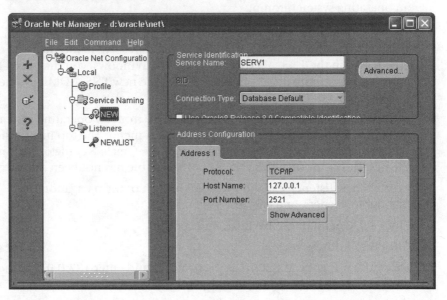

14. Save the configuration by clicking File and Save Network Configuration. This will create the `listener.ora` and `tnsnames.ora` files in the TNS_ADMIN directory.

15. Use an editor to check the two files. They will look like this:

LISTENER.ORA:

```
NEWLIST =
  (DESCRIPTION =
    (ADDRESS = (PROTOCOL = TCP)(HOST = 127.0.0.1)(PORT = 2521))
  )
```

TNSNAMES.ora:

```
NEW =
  (DESCRIPTION =
    (ADDRESS_LIST =
      (ADDRESS = (PROTOCOL = TCP)(HOST = 127.0.0.1)(PORT = 2521))
    )
    (CONNECT_DATA =
      (SERVICE_NAME = SERV1)
    )
  )
```

16. From an operating system prompt, start the listener with `lsnrctl start newlist`.

17. From an operating system prompt, test the connect string with `tnsping new`.

18. Connect to your database using operating system authentication, bypassing any listener, with `sqlplus / as sysdba`.

19. Set the `service_names` and `local_listener` parameters for the running instance (memory only, not the parameter file) and register the new service name with the new listener:

```
alter system set service_names=serv1 scope=memory;
alter system set local_listener=new scope=memory;
alter system register;
```

20. From an operating system prompt, confirm that the new service has registered with the new listener with `lsnrctl services newlist`.

21. Confirm that the new network environment is functional by logging on:

```
sqlplus system/oracle@new
```

Use the Oracle Shared Server Architecture

The standard dedicated server architecture requires that the database listener should spawn a dedicated server process for each concurrent connection to the instance. These server processes will persist until the session is terminated. On Unix-type platforms, the server processes are real operating system processes; on Windows, they are threads within the one ORACLE.EXE process. This architecture does not scale easily to support a large number of user processes on some platforms. An alternative is the *shared server* architecture, known as the multithreaded server (or MTS) in earlier releases.

The Limitations of Dedicated Server Architecture

As more users log on to your instance, more server processes get launched. This is not a problem as far as Oracle is concerned. The database listener can launch as many processes as required, though there may be limits on the speed with which it can launch them. If you have a large number of concurrent connection requests, your listener will have to queue them up. You can avoid this by running multiple listeners on different ports, and load-balancing between them. Then once the sessions are established, there is no limit to the number that PMON can manage. But your operating system may well have limits on the number of processes that it can support, limits to do with context switches and with memory.

A computer can only do one thing at once unless it is an SMP machine, in which case each CPU can only do one thing at once. The operating system simulates concurrent processing by using an algorithm to share CPU cycles across all the currently executing processes. This algorithm, often referred to as a time slicing or time sharing algorithm, takes care of allocating a few CPU cycles to each process in turn. The switch of taking one process off CPU in order to put another process on CPU is called a *context switch*. Context switches are very expensive: the operating system has to do a lot of work to restore the state of each process as it is brought on to CPU and then save its state when it is switched off the CPU. As more users connect to the instance, the operating system has to context-switch between more and more server processes. Depending on your operating system, this can cause a severe degradation in performance. A decent mainframe operating system can context-switch between tens of thousands of processes without problems, but newer (and simpler) operating systems such as Unix and Windows may not be good at running thousands, or even just hundreds, of concurrent processes. Performance degrades dramatically, because a large proportion of the computer's processing capacity is taken up with managing the context switches, leaving a relatively small amount of processing capacity available for actually doing work.

There may also be memory problems that occur as more sessions are established. The actual server processes themselves are not an issue, because all modern operating systems use shared memory when the same process is loaded more than once. So launching a thousand server processes should take no more memory than launching one. The problem comes with the program global area, or PGA. The PGA is a block of memory associated with each server process, to maintain the state of the session and as a work area for operations such as sorting rows. Clearly, the PGAs cannot be in shared memory: they contain data unique to each session. In many operating systems, as memory thresholds are reached, they make use of swap space or paging areas on disk, and memory pages are swapped out to disk to make room for memory requirements of other processes. When the memory pages that have been swapped out to disk are required, they are swapped back into memory and something else is swapped out to disk. Excessive swapping can be catastrophic for the performance of your system. Due to the PGA requirements of each session, your system may begin to swap as more users log on.

So in the dedicated server environment, performance may degrade if your operating system has problems managing a large number of concurrent processes, and the problem will be exacerbated if your server machine has insufficient memory. Note that it doesn't really matter whether the sessions are actually doing anything or not. Even if the sessions are idle, the operating system must still bring them on and off CPU, and possibly page the appropriate PGA into main memory from swap files, according to its time slicing algorithm. There comes a point when, no matter what you do in the way of hardware upgrades, performance begins to degrade because of operating system inefficiencies in managing context switches and paging. These are not Oracle's problems, but to overcome them Oracle offers the option of the shared server architecture. This allows a large number of user processes to be serviced by a relatively small number of shared server processes, thus reducing dramatically the number of processes that the server's operating system has to manage. As a fringe benefit, memory usage may also reduce.

Always remember that the need for a shared server is very much platform and installation specific. Some operating systems will hardly ever need it. For example, a mainframe computer can time-share between many thousands of processes with no problems—it is usually simpler operating systems like Windows or Unix that are more likely to have problems.

The Shared Server Architecture

One point to emphasize immediately is that shared server is implemented purely on the server side. The user process and the application software have no way of telling that anything has changed. The user process issues a connect string that must resolve to the address of a listener and the name of a service (or of an instance). In return, it will receive the address of a server-side process that it will think is a dedicated server. It will then proceed to send SQL statements and receive back result sets; as far as the user process is concerned, absolutely nothing has changed. But the server side is very different.

Shared server is implemented by additional processes that are a part of the instance. They are background processes, launched at instance startup time. There are two new process types, dispatchers and shared servers. There are also some extra queue memory structures within the SGA, and the database listener modifies its behavior for shared server. When an instance that is configured for shared server starts up, in addition to the usual background processes one or more dispatcher processes also start. The dispatchers, like any other TCP process, run on a unique TCP port allocated by your operating system's port mapper: they contact the listener and register with it, using the local_ listener parameter to locate the listener. One or more shared server processes also start. These are conceptually similar to a normal dedicated server process, but they are not tied to one session. They receive SQL statements, parse and execute them, and generate a result set—but they do not receive the SQL statements directly from a user process, they read them from a queue that is populated with statements from any number of user processes. Similarly, the shared servers don't fetch result sets back to a user process directly—instead, they put the result sets onto a response queue.

The next question is, how do the user-generated statements get onto the queue that is read by the server processes, and how do results get fetched to the users? This is where the dispatchers come in. When a user process contacts a listener, rather than launching a server process and connecting it to the user process, the listener passes back the address of a dispatcher. If there is only one dispatcher, the listener will connect it to all the user processes. If there are multiple dispatchers, the listener will load-balance incoming connection requests across them, but the end result is that many user processes will be connected to each dispatcher. Each user process will be under the impression that it is talking to a dedicated server process, but it isn't: it is sharing a dispatcher with many other user processes. At the network level, many user processes will have connections multiplexed through the one port used by the dispatcher.

 EXAM TIP A session's connection to a dispatcher persists for the duration of the session, unlike the connection to the listener, which is transient.

When a user process issues a SQL statement, it is sent to the dispatcher. The dispatcher puts all the statements it receives onto a queue. This queue is called the *common* queue, because all dispatchers share it. No matter which dispatcher a user process is connected to, all statements end up on the common queue.

All the shared server processes monitor the common queue. When a statement arrives on the common queue, the first available shared server picks it up. From then execution proceeds through the usual parse-bind-execute cycle, but when it comes to the fetch phase, it is impossible for the shared server to fetch the result set back to the user process: there is no connection between the user process and the shared server. So instead, the shared server puts the result set onto a *response* queue that is specific to the dispatcher that received the job in the first place. Each dispatcher monitors its own response queue, and whenever any results are put on it, the dispatcher will pick them up and fetch them back to the user process that originally issued the statement. Figure 4-11 depicts three user processes making use of shared server mode.

User processes 1 and 2 try to connect to an instance or service and are handed over to Dispatcher 1 by the listener, while user process 3 interacts with the instance via Dispatcher 2.

A	User process 1 submits a statement for execution.
B	Dispatcher 1 places the statement onto the common queue.
C	A shared server process picks up the statement from the common request queue, parses it, executes it, and generates a result set.
D	The shared server places the result set in Dispatcher 1's response queue.
E	Dispatcher 1 fetches the result set from its response queue.
F	Dispatcher 1 returns the results to User process 1.
G–L	These steps are identical to steps A–F but apply to User process 2. Note that Dispatcher 1 services both these user processes.
M	User process 3 submits a statement for execution.
N	Dispatcher 2 places the statement onto the common queue.
O	A shared server process picks up the statement from the common request queue, parses it, executes it, and generates a result set.
P	The shared server places the result set in Dispatcher 2's response queue. Note that this shared server process could be the very same process that performed preceding steps C, I, O, D and J.
Q	Dispatcher 2 fetches the result set from its response queue.
R	Dispatcher 2 returns the results to User process 3.

 EXAM TIP There is a common input queue shared by all dispatchers, but each dispatcher has its own response queue.

A result of the mechanism of dispatchers and queues is that any statement from any user process could be executed by any available shared server. This raises the question of how the state of the session can be maintained. It would be quite possible

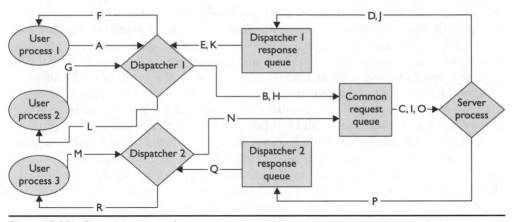

Figure 4-11 Shared server mode

for a user process to issue, for example, a SELECT FOR UPDATE, a DELETE, and a COMMIT. In a normal dedicated server connection, this isn't a problem because the PGA (which is tied to the one server process that is managing the session) stores information about what the session was doing, and therefore the dedicated server will know what to COMMIT and what locks to release. The PGA for a dedicated server session will store the session's session data, its cursor state, its sort space, and its stack space. But in the shared server environment, each statement might be picked off the common queue by a different shared server process, which will have no idea what the state of the transaction is. To get around this problem, a shared server session stores most of the session data in the SGA, rather than in a PGA. Then whenever a shared server picks a job off the common queue, it will go to the SGA and connect to the appropriate block of memory to find out the state of the session. The memory used in the SGA for each shared server session is known as the user global area (the UGA) and includes all of what would have been in a PGA with the exception of the session's stack space. This is where the memory saving will come from. Oracle can manage memory in the shared pool much more effectively than it can in many separate PGAs.

The part of the SGA used for storing UGAs is the large pool. This can be configured manually with the `large_pool_size` parameter, or it can be automatically managed.

EXAM TIP In shared server, what PGA memory structure does not go into the SGA? The stack space.

Configuring Shared Server

Being a server-side capability, no additional client configuration is needed beyond the regular client-side Oracle Net (the `tnsnames.ora` and `sqlnet.ora` files) as detailed previously. On the server side, shared server has nothing to do with the database—only the instance. The listener will be automatically configured for shared server through dynamic instance registration. It follows that shared server is configured though instance initialization parameters. There are a number of relevant parameters, but two are all that are usually necessary: dispatchers and shared_servers.

The first parameter to consider is shared_servers. This controls the number of shared servers that will be launched at instance startup time. Shared server uses a queuing mechanism, but the ideal is that there should be no queuing: there should always be a server process ready and waiting for every job that is put on the common queue by the dispatchers. Therefore, shared_servers should be set to the maximum number of concurrent requests that you expect. But if there is a sudden burst of activity, you don't have to worry too much, because Oracle will dynamically launch additional shared servers, up to the value specified by max_shared_servers. By default, shared_servers is one if dispatchers is set. If the parameter max_shared_servers is not set, then it defaults to one eighth of the processes parameter.

The dispatchers parameter controls how many dispatcher processes to launch at instance startup time, and how they will behave. This is the only required parameter. There are many options for this parameter, but usually two will suffice: how many to start, and what protocol they should listen on. Among the more advanced options are ones that allow you to control the port and network card on which the dispatcher will listen, and the address of the listener(s) with which it will register, but usually you can let your operating system's port mapper assign a port, and use the local_listener parameter to control which listener they will register with. The max_dispatchers parameter sets an upper limit to the number of dispatchers you can start, but unlike with shared servers, Oracle will not start extra dispatchers on demand. You can, however, manually launch additional dispatchers at any time up to this limit.

For example, to enable the shared server architecture, adjust the two critical parameters as follows:

```
SQL> alter system set dispatchers='(dispatchers=2)(protocol=tcp)';
SQL> alter system set shared_servers=20;
```

Tuning the shared server is vital. There should always be enough shared servers to dequeue requests from the common queue as they arrive, and enough dispatchers to service incoming requests as they arrive and return results as they are enqueued to the response queues. Memory usage by shared server sessions in the SGA must be monitored. After converting from dedicated server to shared server, the SGA will need to be substantially larger.

When to Use the Shared Server

You will not find a great deal of hard advice in the Oracle documentation on when to use shared server, or how many dispatchers and shared servers you'll need. The main point to hang on to is that shared server is a facility you use because you are forced to, not something you use automatically. It increases scalability, but it could potentially reduce performance. It is quite possible that any one statement will take longer to execute in a shared server environment than if it were executing on a dedicated server, because it has to go via queues. It may also take more CPU resources because of the enqueuing and dequeuing activity. But overall, the scalability of your system will increase dramatically. Even if each request is marginally slower, you will be able to carry out many more requests per second through the instance.

TIP It is often said that you should think about using shared server when your number of concurrent connections is in the low hundreds. If you have less than a hundred concurrent connections, you almost certainly don't need it. But if you have more than a thousand, you probably do. The critical factor is whether your operating system performance is beginning to degrade.

Consider an OLTP environment, such as one where the application supports hundreds of telephone operators in a call center. Each operator may spend one or two minutes per call, collecting the caller details and entering them into the user process (their application session). Then when the Submit button is clicked, the user process constructs an insert statement and sends it off to the server process. The server process might go through the whole parse/bind/execute/fetch cycle for the statement in just a few hundredths of a second. Clearly, no matter how fast the clerks work, their server processes are idle 99.9 percent of the time. But the operating system still has to switch all those processes on and off CPU, according to its time sharing algorithm. By contrast, consider a data warehouse environment. Here, users submit queries that may run for a long time. The batch uploads of data will be equally long running. Whenever one of these large jobs is submitted, the server process for that session could be working flat out for hours on just one statement.

It should be apparent that shared server is ideal for managing many sessions doing short transactions, where the bulk of the work is on the client side of the client-server divide. In these circumstances, one shared server will be able to service dozens of sessions. But for batch processing work, dedicated servers are much better. If you submit a large batch job through a shared server session, it will work—but it will tie up one of your small pool of shared server processes for the duration of the job, leaving all your other users to compete for the remaining shared servers. The amount of network traffic involved in batch uploads from a user process and in fetching large result sets back to a user process will also cause contention for dispatchers.

A second class of operations that are better done through a dedicated server is database administration work. Index creation, table maintenance operations, and backup and recovery work through the Recovery Manager will perform much better through a dedicated server. And it is logically impossible to issue startup or shutdown commands through a shared server: the shared servers are part of the instance and thus not available at the time you issue a startup command. So the administrator should always have a dedicated server connection.

TIP If the default mode has been changed to shared server mode, batch and administration user processes can ensure that they are serviced by dedicated server processes, by modifying their client-side `tnsnames.ora` by adding the entry: (`SERVER=DEDICATED`).

Exercise 4-2: Set Up a Shared Server Environment   In this exercise, which continues from Step 21 of Exercise 4-1, you will configure the shared server and prove that it is working.

1. Set the `dispatchers` and `shared_servers` parameters and register with the listener as follows:

```
alter system set dispatchers='(protocol=tcp)(dispatchers=2)'
scope=memory;
alter system set shared_servers=4 scope=memory;
alter system register;
```

2. Confirm that the dispatchers and shared servers have started by querying the view V$PROCESS. Look for processes named S000, S001, S002, S003, D000, and D001:

```
select program from v$process order by program;
```

3. From an operating system prompt, confirm that the dispatchers have registered with the listener:

```
lsnrctl services newlist
```

4. Connect through the listener, and confirm that the connection is through the shared server mechanism:

```
connect system/oracle@new;
select d.name,s.name from v$dispatcher d,v$shared_server s, v$circuit c
where d.paddr=c.dispatcher and s.paddr=c.server;
```

This query will show the dispatcher to which your season is connected, and the shared server process that is executing your query.

5. Tidy up the environment, by returning to the original configuration:

```
alter system set local_listener='' scope=memory;
alter system set service_names='' scope=memory;
alter system set dispatchers='' scope=memory;
alter system set shared_servers=0 scope=memory;
alter system register;
```

Stop the listener from an operating system prompt with `lsnrctl stop newlist`.

Unset the TNS_ADMIN variable: on Linux, export TNS_ADMIN=" or on Windows, remove the TNS_ADMIN registry key.

Two-Minute Drill

Configure and Manage the Oracle Network

- The server-side files are the `listener.ora` and (optionally) `sqlnet.ora` files.

- The client-side files are the `tnsnames.ora` and (optionally) `sqlnet.ora` files.

- The Oracle Net files live by default in `ORACLE_HOME/network/admin`, or in whatever directory the TNS_ADMIN variable points to.

- Name resolution can be local (with a `tnsnames.ora` file) or central (with an LDAP directory).

- Easy Connect does not need any name resolution.

- One listener can listen for many databases.

- Many listeners can connect to one database.

- Instance registration with listeners can be static (by coding details in the `listener.ora` file) or dynamic (by the PMON process updating the listener).

- Each user process has a persistent connection to its dedicated server process.

Use the Oracle Shared Server Architecture

- User processes connect to dispatchers; these connections are persistent.

- All dispatchers place requests on a common queue.

- Shared server processes dequeue requests from the common queue.

- Each dispatcher has its own response queue.

- Shared server processes place results onto the appropriate dispatcher's response queue.

- The dispatchers fetch results back to the appropriate user process.

- Shared server is configured with (as a minimum) two instance parameters: `dispatchers` and `shared_servers`.

Self Test

1. Which protocols can Oracle Net 11*g* use? (Choose all correct answers.)

   A. TCP

   B. UDP

   C. SPX/IPX

   D. SDP

   E. TCP with secure sockets

   F. Named Pipes

   G. LU6.2

   H. NetBIOS/NetBEUI

2. Where is the division between the client and the server in the Oracle environment? (Choose the best answer.)

   A. Between the instance and the database

   B. Between the user and the user process

   C. Between the server process and the instance

   D. Between the user process and the server process

   E. The client-server split varies depending on the stage of the execution cycle

3. Which of the following statements about listeners is correct? (Choose the best answer.)

   A. A listener can connect you to one instance only.

   B. A listener can connect you to one service only.

   C. Multiple listeners can share one network interface card.

   D. An instance will only accept connections from the listener specified on the local_listener parameter.

4. You have decided to use Local Naming. Which files must you create on the client machine? (Choose the best answer.)

   A. `tnsnames.ora` and `sqlnet.ora`

   B. `listener.ora` only

   C. `tnsnames.ora` only

   D. `listener.ora` and `sqlnet.ora`

   E. None—you can rely on defaults if you are using TCP and your listener is running on port 1521

5. If you stop your listener, what will happen to sessions that connected through it? (Choose the best answer.)

   A. They will continue if you have configured failover.

   B. They will not be affected in any way.

   C. They will hang until you restart the listener.

   D. You cannot stop a listener if it is in use.

   E. The sessions will error out.

6. Study this `tnsnames.ora` file:

```
test =
  (description =
    (address_list =
      (address = (protocol = tcp)(host = serv2)(port = 1521))
    )
    (connect_data =
      (service_name - prod)
    )
  )
prod =
  (description =
    (address_list =
      (address = (protocol = tcp)(host = serv1)(port = 1521))
    )
    (connect_data =
      (service_name = prod)
    )
  )
dev =
  (description =
    (address_list =
      (address = (protocol = tcp)(host = serv2)(port = 1521))
    )
    (connect_data =
      (service_name = dev)
    )
  )
```

Which of the following statements is correct about the connect strings test, prod, and dev? (Choose all correct answers.)

A. All three are valid.

B. All three can succeed only if the instances are set up for dynamic instance registration.

C. The test connection will fail, because the connect string doesn't match the service name.

D. There will be a port conflict on serv2, because prod and dev try to use the same port.

7. Consider this line from a `listener.ora` file:

   `L1=(description=(address=(protocol=tcp)(host=serv1)(port=1521)))`

   What will happen if you issue this connect string?

   `connect scott/tiger@L1 (Choose the best answer)`

   A. You will be connected to the instance L1.

   B. You will only be connected to an instance if dynamic instance registration is working.

   C. The connection attempt will fail.

   D. If you are logged on to the server machine, IPC will connect you to the local instance.

   E. The connection will fail if the listener is not started.

8. Which of these memory structures is not stored in the SGA for a shared server session? (Choose the best answer.)

   A. Cursor state

   B. Sort space

   C. Stack space

9. Match the object to the function:

Object	Function
a. Common queue	A. Connects users to dispatchers
b. Dispatcher	B. Stores jobs waiting for execution
c. Large pool	C. Executes SQL statements
d. Listener	D. Stores results waiting to be fetched
e. Response queue	E. Receives statements from user processes
f. Shared server	F. Stores UGAs accessed by all servers

10. Which of the following is true about dispatchers? (Choose all correct answers.)

   A. Dispatchers don't handle the work of users' requests; they only interface between user processes and queues.

   B. Dispatchers share a common response queue.

   C. Dispatchers load-balance connections between themselves.

   D. Listeners load-balance connections across dispatchers.

   E. You can terminate a dispatcher, and established sessions will continue.

11. Which of the following statements about shared servers are true? (Choose the best answer.)

    A. All statements in a multistatement transaction will be executed by the same server.

    B. If one statement updates multiple rows, the work may be shared across several servers.

    C. The number of shared servers is fixed by the SHARED_SERVERS parameter.

    D. Oracle will spawn additional shared servers on demand.

Self Test Answers

1. ☑ A, D, E, and F. TCP, SDP, TCPS, and NMP are the supported protocols with the current release.

    ☒ B, C, G, and H. B and H are wrong because UDP and NetBIOS/NetBEUI have never been supported. C and G are wrong because SPX and LU6.2 are no longer supported.

2. ☑ D. The client-server split is between user process and server process.

    ☒ A, B, C, and E. These all misrepresent the client-server architecture.

3. ☑ C. Many listeners can shared one address, if they use different ports.

    ☒ A, B, and D. A is wrong because one listener can launch sessions against many instances. B is wrong because a listener can connect you to a registered service. D is wrong because the `local_listener` parameter controls which listener the instance will register with dynamically; it will also accept connections from any listener that has it statically registered.

4. ☑ C. This is the only required client-side file for local naming.

    ☒ A, B, D, and E. A is wrong because `sqlnet.ora` is not essential. B and D are wrong because they refer to server-side files. E is wrong because some configuration is always necessary for local naming (though not for Easy Connect).

5. ☑ B. The listener establishes connections but is not needed for their maintenance.

    ☒ A, C, D, and E. These are all incorrect because they assume that the listener is necessary for the continuance of an established session.

6. ☑ A and B. All three are valid but will only work if the services are registered with the listeners.

    ☒ C and D. C is wrong because there need be no connection between the alias used in a connect string and the service name. D is wrong because many services can be accessible through a single listening port.

7. ☑ C. The CONNECT_DATA that specifies a SID or service is missing.

☒ A, B, D, and E. A is wrong because L1 is the connect string, not an instance or service name. B is wrong because dynamic registration is not enough to compensate for a missing CONNECT_DATA clause. D is wrong because the use of IPC to bypass the listener is not relevant. E is wrong because (while certainly true) it is not the main problem.

8. ☑ C. Stack space is not part of the UGA and therefore does not go into the SGA.

☒ A and B. These are UGA components and therefore do go into the SGA.

9. ☑ a – B, b – E, c – F, d – A, e – D, f – C
These are the correct mappings of objects to functions.

10. ☑ A and D. Dispatchers maintain the connection to user processes, place requests on the common queue, and retrieve result sets from response queues.

☒ B, C, and E. B is wrong because each dispatcher has its own response queue. C is wrong because it is the listener that load-balances, not the dispatchers. E is wrong because the connections to a dispatcher are persistent: if it dies, they will be broken.

11. ☑ D. To prevent queueing on the common queue, Oracle will launch additional shared servers—but only up to the `max_shared_servers` value.

☒ A, B, and C. A is wrong because each statement may be picked up by a different server. B is wrong because any one statement can be executed by only one server. C is wrong because this parameter controls the number of servers initially launched, which may change later.

CHAPTER 5

Oracle Storage

Exam Objectives

In this chapter you will learn to

- 052.6.1 Work with Tablespaces and Datafiles
- 052.6.2 Create and Manage Tablespaces
- 052.6.3 Handle Space Management in Tablespaces

The preceding two chapters dealt with the instance and the sessions against it: processes and memory structures. This chapter begins the investigation of the database itself. All data processing occurs in memory, in the instance, but data storage occurs in the database on disk. The database consists of three file types: the controlfile, the online redo log files, and the datafiles. Data is stored in the datafiles.

Users never see a physical datafile. All they see are logical segments. System administrators never see a logical segment. All they see are physical datafiles. The Oracle database provides an abstraction of logical storage from physical. This is one of the requirements of the relational database paradigm. As a DBA, you must be aware of the relationship between the logical and the physical storage. Monitoring and administering these structures, a task often described as *space management*, used to be a huge part of a DBA's workload. The facilities provided in recent releases of the database can automate space management to a certain extent, and they can certainly let the DBA set up storage in ways that will reduce the maintenance workload considerably.

Overview of Tablespaces and Datafiles

Data is stored logically in segments (typically tables) and physically in datafiles. The *tablespace* entity abstracts the two: one tablespace can contain many segments and be made up of many datafiles. There is no direct relationship between a segment and a datafile. The datafiles can exist as files in a file system or (from release 10g onward) on Automatic Storage Management (ASM) devices.

The Oracle Data Storage Model

The separation of logical from physical storage is a necessary part of the relational database paradigm. The relational paradigm states that programmers should address only logical structures and let the database manage the mapping to physical structures. This means that physical storage can be reorganized, or the whole database moved to completely different hardware and operating system, and the application will not be aware of any change.

Figure 5-1 shows the Oracle storage model sketched as an entity-relationship diagram, with the logical structures to the left and the physical structures to the right.

There is one relationship drawn in as a dotted line: a many-to-many relationship between segments and datafiles. This relationship is dotted, because it shouldn't be there. As good relational engineers, DBAs do not permit many-to-many relationships. Resolving this relationship into a normalized structure is what the storage model is all about. The following discussion takes each of the entities in Figure 5-1 one by one.

The *tablespace* entity resolves the many-to-many relationship between segments and datafiles. One tablespace can contain many segments and be made up of many datafiles. This means that any one segment may be spread across multiple datafiles, and any one datafile may contain all of or parts of many segments. This solves many storage challenges. Some older database management systems used a one-to-one

Figure 5-1
The Oracle storage
model

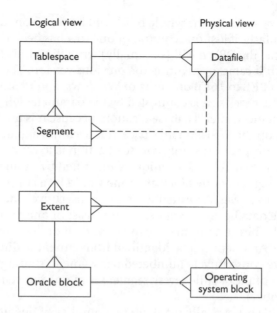

relationship between segments and files: every table or index would be stored as a
separate file. This raised two dreadful problems for large systems. First, an application
might well have thousands of tables and even more indexes; managing many
thousands of files was an appalling task for the system administrators. Second, the
maximum size of a table is limited by the maximum size of a file. Even if modern
operating systems do not have any practical limits, there may well be limitations
imposed by the underlying hardware environment. Use of tablespaces bypasses both
these problems. Tablespaces are identified by unique names in the database.

The *segment* entity represents any database object that stores data and therefore
requires space in a tablespace. Your typical segment is a table, but there are other
segment types, notably index segments (described in Chapter 7) and undo segments
(described in Chapter 8). Any segment can exist in only one tablespace, but the
tablespace can spread it across all the files making up the tablespace. This means that
the tables' sizes are not subject to any limitations imposed by the environment on
maximum file size. As many segments can share a single tablespace, it becomes
possible to have far more segments than there are datafiles. Segments are schema
objects, identified by the segment name qualified with the owning schema name.
Note that programmatic schema objects (such as PL/SQL procedures, views, or
sequences) are not segments: they do not store data, and they exist within the data
dictionary.

The *Oracle block* is the basic unit of I/O for the database. Datafiles are formatted
into Oracle blocks, which are consecutively numbered. The size of the Oracle blocks
is fixed for a tablespace (generally speaking, it is the same for all tablespaces in the
database); the default (with release 11*g*) is 8KB. A row might be only a couple
hundred bytes, and so there could be many rows stored in one block, but when

a session wants a row, the whole block will be read from disk into the database buffer cache. Similarly, if just one column of one row has been changed in the database buffer cache, the DBWn will (eventually) write the whole block back into the datafile from which it came, overwriting the previous version. The size of an Oracle block can range from 2KB to 16KB on Linux or Windows, and to 32KB on some other operating systems. The block size is controlled by the parameter DB_BLOCK_SIZE. This can never be changed after database creation, because it is used to format the datafile(s) that make up the SYSTEM tablespace. If it becomes apparent later on that the block size is inappropriate, the only course of action is to create a new database and transfer everything into it. A block is uniquely identified by its number within a datafile.

Managing space one block at a time would be a crippling task, so blocks are grouped into *extents*. An extent is a set of consecutively numbered Oracle blocks within one datafile. Every segment will consist of one or more extents, consecutively numbered. These extents may be in any and all of the datafiles that make up the tablespace. An extent can be identified from either the dimension of the segment (extents are consecutively numbered per segment, starting from zero) or the dimension of the datafile (every segment is in one file, starting at a certain Oracle block number).

A *datafile* is physically made up of a number of operating system blocks. How datafiles and the operating system blocks are structured is entirely dependent on the operating system's file system. Some file systems have well-known limitations and are therefore not widely used for modern systems (for example, the old MS-DOS FAT file system could handle files up to only 4GB, and only 512 of them per directory). Most databases will be installed on file systems with no practical limits, such as NTFS on Windows or ext3 on Linux. The alternatives to file systems for datafile storage are raw devices or Automatic Storage Management (ASM). Raw devices are now very rarely used for datafile storage because of manageability issues. ASM is detailed in Chapter 20.

An *operating system block* is the basic unit of I/O for your file system. A process might want to read only one byte from disk, but the I/O system will have to read an operating system block. The operating system block size is configurable for some file systems (for example, when formatting an NTFS file system you can choose from 512B to 64KB), but typically system administrators leave it on default (512B for NTFS, 1KB for ext3). This is why the relationship between Oracle blocks and operating system blocks is usually one-to-many, as shown in Figure 5-1. There is no reason not to match the operating system block size to the Oracle block size if your file system lets you do this. The configuration that should always be avoided would be where the operating system blocks are bigger than the Oracle blocks.

Segments, Extents, Blocks, and Rows

Data is stored in segments. The data dictionary view DBA_SEGMENTS describes every segment in the database. This query shows the segment types in a simple database:

```
SQL> select segment_type,count(1) from dba_segments group by segment_type
  2  order by segment_type;
SEGMENT_TYPE          COUNT(1)
------------------    ----------
CLUSTER                     10
INDEX                     3185
INDEX PARTITION            324
LOB PARTITION                7
LOBINDEX                   760
LOBSEGMENT                 760
NESTED TABLE                29
ROLLBACK                     1
TABLE                     2193
TABLE PARTITION            164
TYPE2 UNDO                  10
11 rows selected.
SQL>
```

In brief, and in the order they are most likely to concern a DBA, these segments types are

- **TABLE** These are heap-structured tables that contain rows of data. Even though a typical segment is a table segment, never forget that the table is not the same as the segment, and that there are more complex table organizations that use other segment types.

- **INDEX** Indexes are sorted lists of key values, each with a pointer, the ROWID, to the physical location of the row. The ROWID specifies which Oracle block of which datafile the row is in, and the row number within the block.

- **TYPE2 UNDO** These are the undo segments (no one refers to them as "type2 undo" segments) that store the pre-change versions of data that are necessary for providing transactional integrity: rollback, read consistency, and isolation.

- **ROLLBACK** Rollback segments should not be used in normal running from release 9i onward. Release 9i introduced automatic undo management, which is based on undo segments. There will always be one rollback segment that protects the transactions used to create a database (this is necessary because at that point no undo segments exist), but it shouldn't be used subsequently.

- **TABLE PARTITION** A table can be divided into many partitions. If this is done, the partitions will be individual segments, and the partitioned table itself will not be a segment at all: it will exist only as the sum total of its partitions. Each table partition of a heap table is itself structured as a heap table, in its own segment. These segments can be in different tablespaces, meaning that it becomes possible to spread one table across multiple tablespaces.

- **INDEX PARTITION** An index will by default be in one segment, but indexes can also be partitioned. If you are partitioning your tables, you will usually partition the indexes on those tables as well.

- **LOBSEGMENT, LOBINDEX, LOB PARTITION** If a column is defined as a large object data type, then only a pointer is stored in the table itself: a pointer to an entry in a separate segment where the column data actually resides. LOBs can have indexes built on them for rapid access to data within the objects, and LOBs can also be partitioned.

- **CLUSTER** A cluster is a segment that can contain several tables. In contrast with partitioning, which lets you spread one table across many segments, clustering lets you denormalize many tables into one segment.

- **NESTED TABLE** If a column of a table is defined as a user-defined object type that itself has columns, then the column can be stored in its own segment, as a nested table.

Every segment is comprised of one or more extents. When a segment is created, Oracle will allocate an initial extent to it in whatever tablespace is specified. Eventually, as data is entered, that extent will fill. Oracle will then allocate a second extent, in the same tablespace but not necessarily in the same datafile. If you know that a segment is going to need more space, you can manually allocate an extent. Figure 5-2 shows how to identify precisely the location of a segment.

In the figure, the first command creates the table HR.NEWTAB, relying completely on defaults for the storage. Then a query against DBA_EXTENTS shows that the

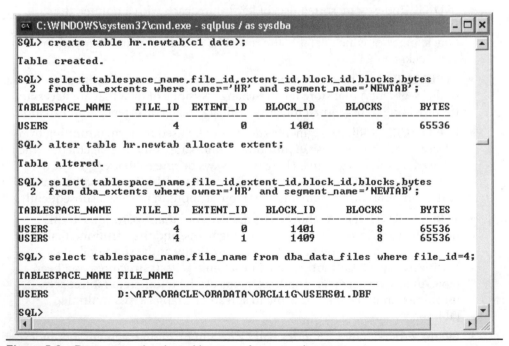

Figure 5-2 Determining the physical location of a segment's extents

segment consists of just one extent, extent number zero. This extent is in file number 4 and is 8 blocks long. The first of the 8 blocks is block number 1401. The size of the extent is 64KB, which shows that the block size is 8KB. The next command forces Oracle to allocate another extent to the segment, even though the first extent is not full. The next query shows that this new extent, number 1, is also in file number 4 and starts immediately after extent zero. Note that it is not clear from this example whether or not the tablespace consists of multiple datafiles, because the algorithm Oracle uses to work out where to assign the next extent does not simply use datafiles in turn. If the tablespace does consist of multiple datafiles, you can override Oracle's choice with this syntax:

```
ALTER TABLE tablename ALLOCATE EXTENT STORAGE (DATAFILE 'filename');
```

TIP Preallocating space by manually adding extents can deliver a performance benefit but is a huge amount of work. You will usually do it for only a few tables or indexes that have an exceptionally high growth rate, or perhaps before bulk loading operations.

The last query in Figure 5-2 interrogates the view DBA_DATA_FILES to determine the name of the file in which the extents were allocated, and the name of the tablespace to which the datafile belongs. To identify the table's tablespace, one could also query the DBA_SEGMENTS view.

TIP You can query DBA_TABLES to find out in which tablespace a table resides, but this will only work for nonpartitioned tables—not for partitioned tables, where each partition is its own segment and can be in a different tablespace. Partitioning lets one table (stored as multiple segments) span tablespaces.

An extent consists of a set of consecutively numbered blocks. Each block has a header area and a data area. The header is of variable size and grows downward from the top of the block. Among other things, it contains a row directory (that lists where in the block each row begins) and row locking information. The data area fills from the bottom up. Between the two there may (or may not) be an area of free space. Events that will cause a block's header to grow include inserting and locking rows. The data area will initially be empty and will fill as rows are inserted (or index keys are inserted, in the case of a block of an index segment). The free space does get fragmented as rows are inserted, deleted, and updated (which may cause a row's size to change), but that is of no significance because all this happens in memory, after the block has been copied into a buffer in the database buffer cache. The free space is coalesced into a contiguous area when necessary, and always before the DBWn writes the block back to its datafile.

File Storage Technologies

Datafiles can exist on four device types: local file systems, clustered file systems, raw devices, and ASM disk groups:

- **Files on a file local system** These are the simplest datafiles; they exist as normal operating system files in a directory structure on disks directly accessible to the computer running the instance. On a PC running Windows or Linux, these could be internal IDE or SATA drives. On more sophisticated hardware, they would usually be SCSI disks, or external drives.

- **Files on a clustered file system** A clustered file system is usually created on external disks, mounted concurrently on more than one computer. The clustered file system mediates access to the disks from processes running on all the computers in the cluster. Using clustered file systems is one way of implementing RAC: the database must reside on disks accessible to all the instances that are going to open it. Clustered file systems can be bought from operating system vendors, or Oracle Corporation's OCFS (Oracle Clustered File System) is an excellent alternative. OCFS was first written for Linux and Windows (for which there were no proper clustered file systems) and bundled with database release 9*i*; with 10*g* it was ported to all the other mainstream operating systems.

- **Files on raw devices** It is possible to create datafiles on disks with no file system at all. This is still supported but is really only a historical anomaly. In the bad old days before clustered file systems (or ASM) existed, raw devices were the only way to implement a Parallel Server database. Parallel Server itself was replaced with RAC in database release 9*i*.

- **Files on ASM devices** ASM is Automatic Storage Management, a facility introduced with database release 10*g*. This is an alternative to file system–based datafile storage and covered in detail in Chapter 20.

 TIP Some people claim that raw devices give the best performance. With contemporary disk and file system technology, this is almost certainly not true. And even if it were true, they are so awkward to manage that no sane DBA wants to use them.

ASM is tested in detail in the second OCP examination, but an understanding of what it can do is expected for the first examination. ASM is a logical volume manager provided by Oracle and bundled with the database. The general idea is that you take a bunch of raw disks, give them to Oracle, and let Oracle get on with it. Your system administrators need not worry about creating file systems at all.

A logical volume manager provided by the operating system, or perhaps by a third party such as Veritas, will take a set of *physical volumes* and present them to the operating system as *logical volumes.* The physical volumes could be complete disks, or they could be partitions of disks. The logical volumes will look to application software like disks, but the underlying storage of any one logical volume might not be one physical volume but several. It is on these logical volumes that the file systems are then created.

A logical volume can be much larger than any of the physical volumes of which it is composed. Furthermore, the logical volume can be created with characteristics that exploit the performance and safety potential of using multiple physical volumes. These characteristics are striping and mirroring of data. Striping data across multiple physical volumes gives huge performance gains. In principle, if a file is distributed across two disks, it should be possible to read it in half the time it would take if it were all on one disk. The performance will improve geometrically, in proportion to the number of disks assigned to the logical volume. Mirroring provides safety. If a logical volume consists of two or more physical volumes, then every operating system block written to one volume can be written simultaneously to the other volume. If one copy is damaged, the logical volume manager will read the other. If there are more than two physical volumes, a higher degree of mirroring becomes possible, providing fault tolerance in the event of multiple disk failures.

Some operating systems (such as AIX) include a logical volume manager as standard; with other operating systems it is an optional (and usually chargeable) extra. Historically, some of the simpler operating systems (such as Windows and Linux) did not have much support for logical volume managers at all. If a logical volume manager is available, it may require considerable time and skill to set up optimally.

ASM is a logical volume manager designed for Oracle database files. The definition of "database file" is broad. Apart from the true database files (controlfile, online redo log files, and datafiles), ASM can also store backup files, archived redo log files, and Data Pump files (all these files will be detailed in later chapters). It cannot be used for the Oracle Home, or for the alert log and trace files.

 EXAM TIP ASM can store only database files, not the binaries. The Oracle Home must always be on a conventional file system.

Exercise 5-1: Investigate the Database's Data Storage Structures In this exercise, you will run queries to document a database's physical structure. The commands could be run interactively from SQL*Plus or Database Control, but it would make sense to save them as a script that (with suitable refinements for display format and for site specific customizations) can be run against any database as part of the regular reports on space usage.

1. Connect to the database as user SYSTEM.
2. Determine the name and size of the controlfile(s):

```
select name,block_size*file_size_blks bytes from v$controlfile;
```

3. Determine the name and size of the online redo log file members:

```
select member,bytes from v$log join v$logfile using (group#);
```

4. Determine the name and size of the datafiles and the tempfiles:

```
select name,bytes from v$datafile
union all
select name,bytes from v$tempfile;
```

Create and Manage Tablespaces

Tablespaces are repositories for schema data, including the data dictionary (which is the SYS schema). All databases must have a SYSTEM tablespace and a SYSAUX tablespace, and (for practical purposes) a temporary tablespace and an undo tablespace. These four will usually have been created when the database was created. Subsequently, the DBA may create many more tablespaces for user data, and possible additional tablespaces for undo and temporary data.

Tablespace Creation

To create a tablespace with Enterprise Manager Database Control, from the database home page take the Server tab and then the Tablespaces link in the Storage section. Figure 5-3 shows the result for the default database.

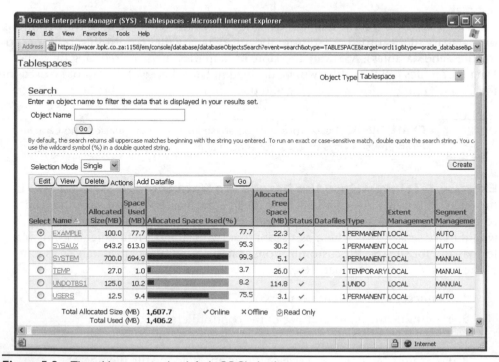

Figure 5-3   The tablespaces in the default ORCL database

There are six tablespaces shown in the figure. For each tablespace, identified by name, the window shows

- **Allocated size**   This is the current size of the datafile(s) assigned to the tablespace. It is based on the current size, not the maximum size to which it may be allowed to expand.

- **Space used**   This is the space occupied by segments in the tablespace that cannot be reclaimed.

- **Allocated space used (%)**   A graphical representation of the preceding two figures.

- **Allocated free space**   The space currently available within the tablespace.

- **Status**   A green tick indicates that the tablespace is online, and therefore that the objects within it should be accessible. An offline tablespace would be indicated with a red cross.

- **Datafiles**   The number of datafiles (or tempfiles for temporary tablespaces, if one is being precise) that make up the tablespace.

- **Type**   The type of objects that can be stored in the tablespace. A permanent tablespace stores regular schema objects, such as tables and indexes. A temporary tablespace stores only system-managed temporary segments, and an undo tablespace stores only system-managed undo segments.

- **Extent management**   The technique used for allocating extents to segments. LOCAL is the default and should always be used.

- **Segment management**   The technique used for locating blocks into which data insertions may be made. AUTO is the default and is recommended for all user data tablespaces.

This information could be also be gleaned by querying the data dictionary views DBA_TABLESPACES, DBA_DATA_FILES, DBA_SEGMENTS, and DB_FREE_SPACE as in this example:

```
SQL> select t.tablespace_name name, d.allocated, u.used, f.free,
  2  t.status, d.cnt, contents, t.extent_management extman,
  3  t.segment_space_management segman
  4  from dba_tablespaces t,
  5  (select sum(bytes) allocated, count(file_id) cnt from dba_data_files
  6  where tablespace_name='EXAMPLE') d,
  7  (select sum(bytes) free from dba_free_space
  8  where tablespace_name='EXAMPLE') f,
  9  (select sum(bytes) used from dba_segments
 10  where tablespace_name='EXAMPLE') u
 11  where t.tablespace_name='EXAMPLE';

NAME      ALLOCATED      USED       FREE STATUS  CNT CONTENTS  EXTMAN SEGMAN
-------   ----------  ---------  --------- ------ ---- --------- ------ ------
EXAMPLE   104857600   81395712   23396352 ONLINE    1 PERMANENT LOCAL  AUTO
```

Click the CREATE button to create a tablespace. The Create Tablespace window prompts for a tablespace name, and the values for Extent Management, Type, and Status. In most circumstances, the defaults will be correct: Local, Permanent, and Read Write. Then the ADD button lets you specify one or more datafiles for the new tablespace. Each file must have a name and a size, and can optionally be set to *autoextend* up to a maximum file size. The autoextend facility will let Oracle increase the size of the datafile as necessary, which may avoid out-of-space errors.

Figures 5-4 and 5-5 show the Database Control interfaces for creating a tablespace NEWTS with one datafile.

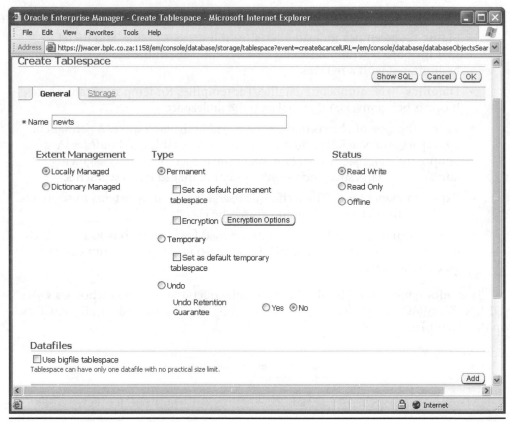

Figure 5-4 The Create Tablespace window

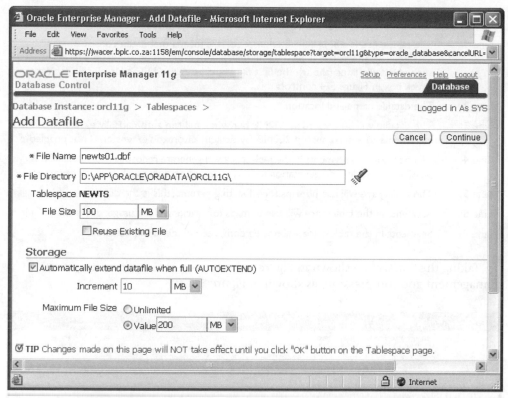

Figure 5-5 The Add Datafile window

Clicking the SHOW SQL button would display this command (the line numbers have been added manually):

```
1    CREATE SMALLFILE TABLESPACE "NEWTS"
2    DATAFILE 'D:\APP\ORACLE\ORADATA\ORCL11G\newts01.dbf'
3    SIZE 100M AUTOEXTEND ON NEXT 10M MAXSIZE 200M
4    LOGGING
5    EXTENT MANAGEMENT LOCAL
6    SEGMENT SPACE MANAGEMENT AUTO
7    DEFAULT NOCOMPRESS;
```

Consider this command line by line:

Line 1	The tablespace is a SMALLFILE tablespace. This means that it can consist of many datafiles. The alternative is BIGFILE, in which case it would be impossible to add a second datafile later (though the first file could be resized.) The Use Bigfile Tablespace check box in Figure 5-4 controls this.
Line 2	The datafile name and location.
Line 3	The datafile will be created as 100MB but when full can automatically extend in 10MB increments to a maximum of 200MB. By default, automatic extension is not enabled.
Line 4	All operations on segments in the tablespace will generate redo; this is the default. It is possible to disable redo generation for a very few operations (such as index generation).
Line 5	The tablespace will use bitmaps for allocating extents; this is the default.
Line 6	Segments in the tablespace will use bitmaps for tracking block usage; this is the default.
Line 7	Segments in the tablespace will not be compressed; this is the default.

Taking the Storage tab shown in Figure 5-4 gives access to options for extent management and compression, as shown in Figure 5-6.

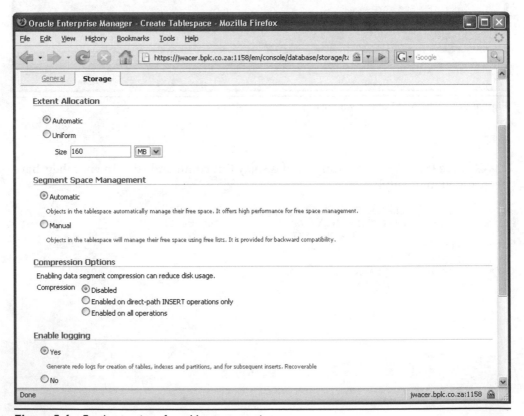

Figure 5-6 Further options for tablespace creation

When using local extent management (as all tablespaces should), it is possible to enforce a rule that all extents in the tablespace should be the same size. This is discussed in the following section. If enabling compression, then it can be applied to data only when it is bulk-loaded, or as a part of all DML operations. If logging is disabled, this provides a default for the very few operations where redo generation can be disabled, such as index creation. Whatever setting is chosen, all DML operations will always generate redo.

 TIP All tablespaces should be locally managed. The older mechanism, known as dictionary managed, was far less efficient and is only supported (and only just) for backward compatibility. It has been possible to create locally managed tablespaces, and to convert dictionary-managed tablespaces to locally managed, since release 8*i*.

A typical tablespace creation statement as executed from the SQL*Plus command line is shown in Figure 5-7, with a query confirming the result.

The tablespace STORETABS consists of two datafiles, neither of which will autoextend. The only deviation from defaults has been to specify a uniform extent size of 5MB. The first query in the figure shows that the tablespace is not a bigfile tablespace—if it were, it would not have been possible to define two datafiles.

The second query in the figure investigates the TEMP tablespace, used by the database for storing temporary objects. It is important to note that temporary tablespaces use *tempfiles,* not datafiles. Tempfiles are listed in the views V$TEMPFILE

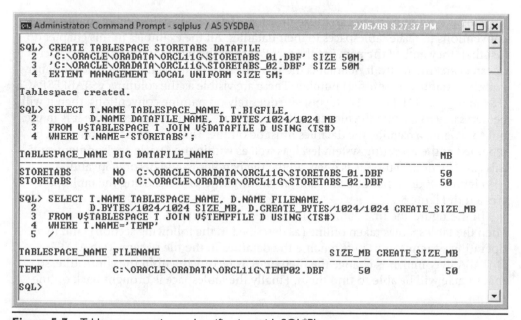

Figure 5-7   Tablespace creation and verification with SQL*Plus

and DBA_TEMP_FILES, whereas datafiles are listed in V$DATAFILE and DBA_DATA_ FILES. Also note that the V$ views and the DBA views give different information. As the query shows, you can query V$TABLESPACE to find if a tablespace is a bigfile table and V$TEMPFILE (or V$DATAFILE) to find how big a file was at creation time. This information is not shown in the DBA views. However, the DBA views give the detail of extent management and segment space management. The different information available in the views is because some information is stored only in the controlfile (and therefore visible only in V$ views) and some is stored only in the data dictionary (and therefore visible only in DBA views). Other information is duplicated.

Altering Tablespaces

The changes made to tablespaces after creation are commonly

- Renaming
- Taking online and offline
- Flagging as read-write or read only
- Resizing
- Changing alert thresholds

Rename a Tablespace and Its Datafiles

The syntax is

```
ALTER TABLESPACE tablespaceoldname RENAME TO tablespacenewname;
```

This is very simple but can cause problems later. Many sites rely on naming conventions to relate tablespaces to their datafiles. All the examples in this chapter do just that: they embed the name of the tablespace in the name of the datafiles. Oracle doesn't care: internally, it maintains the relationships by using the tablespace number and the datafile (or tempfile) number. These are visible as the columns V$TABLESPACE .TS# and V$DATAFILE.FILE#. If your site does rely on naming conventions, then it will be necessary to rename the files as well. A tablespace can be renamed while it is in use, but to rename a datafile, the datafiles must be offline. This is because the file must be renamed at the operating system level, as well as within the Oracle environment, and this can't be done if the file is open: all the file handles would become invalid.

Figure 5-8 demonstrates an example of the entire process, using the tablespace created in Figure 5-7.

In the figure, the first command renames the tablespace. That's the easy part. Then the tablespace is taken offline (as described in the following section), and two operating system commands rename the datafiles in the file system. Two ALTER DATABASE commands change the filenames as recorded within the controlfile, so that Oracle will be able to find them. Finally the tablespace is brought back online.

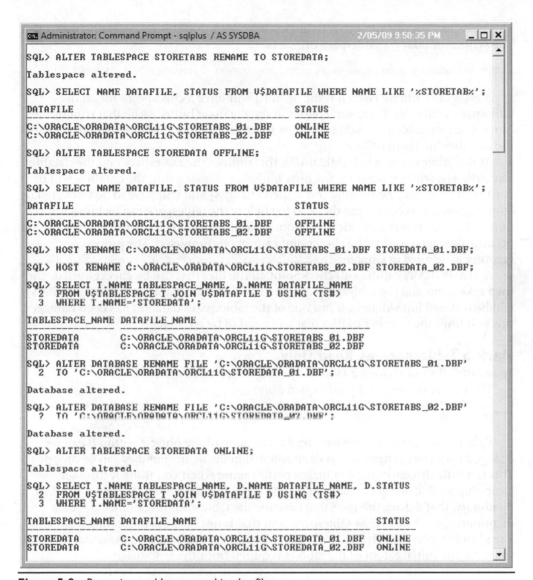

```
Administrator: Command Prompt - sqlplus / AS SYSDBA          2/05/09 9:50:35 PM    _ □ ✕

SQL> ALTER TABLESPACE STORETABS RENAME TO STOREDATA;

Tablespace altered.

SQL> SELECT NAME DATAFILE, STATUS FROM V$DATAFILE WHERE NAME LIKE '%STORETAB%';

DATAFILE                                            STATUS
--------------------------------------------        -------
C:\ORACLE\ORADATA\ORCL11G\STORETABS_01.DBF          ONLINE
C:\ORACLE\ORADATA\ORCL11G\STORETABS_02.DBF          ONLINE

SQL> ALTER TABLESPACE STOREDATA OFFLINE;

Tablespace altered.

SQL> SELECT NAME DATAFILE, STATUS FROM V$DATAFILE WHERE NAME LIKE '%STORETAB%';

DATAFILE                                            STATUS
--------------------------------------------        -------
C:\ORACLE\ORADATA\ORCL11G\STORETABS_01.DBF          OFFLINE
C:\ORACLE\ORADATA\ORCL11G\STORETABS_02.DBF          OFFLINE

SQL> HOST RENAME C:\ORACLE\ORADATA\ORCL11G\STORETABS_01.DBF STOREDATA_01.DBF;

SQL> HOST RENAME C:\ORACLE\ORADATA\ORCL11G\STORETABS_02.DBF STOREDATA_02.DBF;

SQL> SELECT T.NAME TABLESPACE_NAME, D.NAME DATAFILE_NAME
  2  FROM V$TABLESPACE T JOIN V$DATAFILE D USING (TS#)
  3  WHERE T.NAME='STOREDATA';

TABLESPACE_NAME DATAFILE_NAME
--------------- ------------------------------------------
STOREDATA       C:\ORACLE\ORADATA\ORCL11G\STORETABS_01.DBF
STOREDATA       C:\ORACLE\ORADATA\ORCL11G\STORETABS_02.DBF

SQL> ALTER DATABASE RENAME FILE 'C:\ORACLE\ORADATA\ORCL11G\STORETABS_01.DBF'
  2  TO 'C:\ORACLE\ORADATA\ORCL11G\STOREDATA_01.DBF';

Database altered.

SQL> ALTER DATABASE RENAME FILE 'C:\ORACLE\ORADATA\ORCL11G\STORETABS_02.DBF'
  2  TO 'C:\ORACLE\ORADATA\ORCL11G\STOREDATA_02.DBF';

Database altered.

SQL> ALTER TABLESPACE STOREDATA ONLINE;

Tablespace altered.

SQL> SELECT T.NAME TABLESPACE_NAME, D.NAME DATAFILE_NAME, D.STATUS
  2  FROM V$TABLESPACE T JOIN V$DATAFILE D USING (TS#)
  3  WHERE T.NAME='STOREDATA';

TABLESPACE_NAME DATAFILE_NAME                                       STATUS
--------------- ------------------------------------------------    -------
STOREDATA       C:\ORACLE\ORADATA\ORCL11G\STOREDATA_01.DBF          ONLINE
STOREDATA       C:\ORACLE\ORADATA\ORCL11G\STOREDATA_02.DBF          ONLINE
```

Figure 5-8   Renaming a tablespace and its datafiles

Taking a Tablespace Online or Offline

An *online* tablespace or datafile is available for use; an *offline* tablespace or datafile
exists as a definition in the data dictionary and the controlfile but cannot be used. It
is possible for a tablespace to be online but one or more of its datafiles to be offline.

This is a situation that can produce interesting results and should generally be avoided. The syntax for taking a tablespace offline is

```
ALTER TABLESPACE tablespacename OFFLINE [NORMAL | IMMEDIATE | TEMPORARY];
```

A NORMAL offline (which is the default) will force a checkpoint for all the tablespace's datafiles. Every dirty buffer in the database buffer cache that contains a block from the tablespace will be written to its datafile, and then the tablespace and the datafiles are taken offline.

At the other extreme is IMMEDIATE. This offlines the tablespace and the datafiles immediately, without flushing any dirty buffers. Following this, the datafiles will be corrupted (they may be missing committed changes) and will have to be recovered by applying change vectors from the redo log before the tablespace can be brought back online. Clearly, this is a drastic operation. It would normally be done only if a file has become damaged so that the checkpoint cannot be completed. The process of recovery is detailed in Chapter 16.

A TEMPORARY offline will checkpoint all the files that can be checkpointed, and then take them and the tablespace offline in an orderly fashion. Any damaged file(s) will be offlined immediately. If just one of the tablespaces datafiles has been damaged, this will limit the number of files that will need to be recovered.

Mark a Tablespace as Read Only

To see the effect of making a tablespace read only, study Figure 5-9.

The syntax is completely self-explanatory:

```
ALTER TABLESPACE tablespacename [READ ONLY | READ WRITE];
```

Following making a tablespace read only, none of the objects within it can be changed with DML statements, as demonstrated in the figure. But they can be dropped. This is a little disconcerting but makes perfect sense when you think it through. Dropping a table doesn't actually affect the table. It is a transaction against the data dictionary, that deletes the rows that describe the table and its columns; the data dictionary is in the SYSTEM tablespace, and that is not read only. Creating a table in a read-only tablespace also fails, since although it is a DDL statement, actual physical space for the initial extent of the table is required from the tablespace.

 TIP Making a tablespace read only can have advantages for backup and restore operations. Oracle will be aware that the tablespace contents cannot change, and that it may not therefore be necessary to back it up repeatedly.

Resize a Tablespace

A tablespace can be resized either by adding datafiles to it or by adjusting the size of the existing datafiles. The datafiles can be resized upward automatically as necessary if

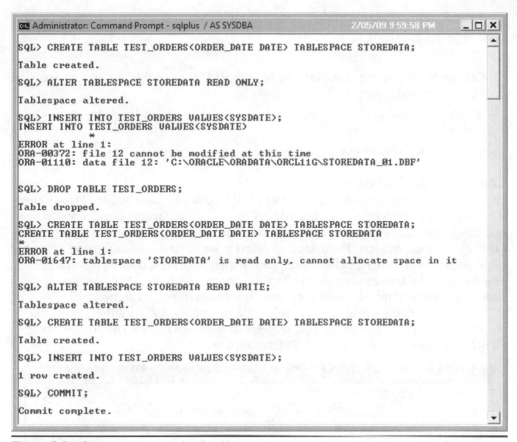

```
SQL> CREATE TABLE TEST_ORDERS(ORDER_DATE DATE) TABLESPACE STOREDATA;

Table created.

SQL> ALTER TABLESPACE STOREDATA READ ONLY;

Tablespace altered.

SQL> INSERT INTO TEST_ORDERS VALUES(SYSDATE);
INSERT INTO TEST_ORDERS VALUES(SYSDATE)
            *
ERROR at line 1:
ORA-00372: file 12 cannot be modified at this time
ORA-01110: data file 12: 'C:\ORACLE\ORADATA\ORCL11G\STOREDATA_01.DBF'

SQL> DROP TABLE TEST_ORDERS;

Table dropped.

SQL> CREATE TABLE TEST_ORDERS(ORDER_DATE DATE) TABLESPACE STOREDATA;
CREATE TABLE TEST_ORDERS(ORDER_DATE DATE) TABLESPACE STOREDATA
*
ERROR at line 1:
ORA-01647: tablespace 'STOREDATA' is read only, cannot allocate space in it

SQL> ALTER TABLESPACE STOREDATA READ WRITE;

Tablespace altered.

SQL> CREATE TABLE TEST_ORDERS(ORDER_DATE DATE) TABLESPACE STOREDATA;

Table created.

SQL> INSERT INTO TEST_ORDERS VALUES(SYSDATE);

1 row created.

SQL> COMMIT;

Commit complete.
```

Figure 5-9   Operations on a read-only tablespace

the AUTOEXTEND syntax was used at file creation time. Otherwise, you have to do it manually with an ALTER DATABASE command:

```
ALTER DATABASE DATAFILE filename RESIZE n[M|G|T];
```

The M, G, or T refer to the units of size for the file: megabytes, gigabytes, or terabytes. For example,

```
alter database datafile '/oradata/users02.dbf' resize 10m;
```

From the syntax, you do not know if the file is being made larger or smaller. An upward resize can only succeed if there is enough space in the file system; a resize downward can only succeed if the space in the file that would be released is not already in use by extents allocated to a segment.

To add another datafile of size 50MB to a tablespace,

```
alter tablespace storedata
add datafile ' C:\ORACLE\ORADATA\ORCL11G\STOREDATA_03.DBF' size 50m;
```

Clauses for automatic extension can be included, or to enable automatic extension later use a command such as this:

```
alter database datafile ' C:\ORACLE\ORADATA\ORCL11G\STOREDATA_03.DBF'
autoextend on next 50m maxsize 2g;
```

This will allow the file to double in size, increasing 50MB at a time.

Change Alert Thresholds

The use of the server-generated alert system will be described in Chapter 24. For now, it is only necessary to know that the MMON process of the instance monitors, in near real time, how full every tablespace is. If a tablespace fills up beyond a certain point, MMON will raise an alert. The default alert levels are to raise a warning alert when a tablespace is over 85 percent full, and a critical alert when it is over 97 percent full. The alerts can be seen in several ways, but the easiest is to look at the database home page of Database Control, where they are displayed in the Alerts section.

To view or change the alert levels, select the tablespace and click the EDIT button, visible in Figure 5-3, then in the Edit Tablespace window take the Thresholds tab. Figure 5-10 shows this for the EXAMPLE tablespace.

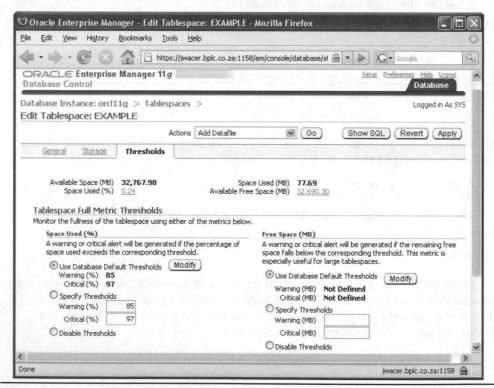

Figure 5-10   The alert thresholds for the EXAMPLE tablespace

In the figure, the "Available Space" in the tablespace is reported as 32GB. This is clearly incorrect, because the Allocated Space, as displayed in Figure 5-3, is only 100MB. The answer lies in datafile autoextension. If AUTOEXTEND is enabled for a datafile and no MAXSIZE is specified, then the file can grow to a platform-dependent limit, in this case 32GB. Of course, this says nothing about whether the file system has room for a file that size. The alert system uses the maximum possible size of the tablespace as the basis for its calculations, which is meaningless if the tablespace's datafiles were created with the syntax AUTOEXTEND ON MAXSIZE UMLIMITED, or if a MAXSIZE was not specified.

It should be apparent that when using automatic extension, it is good practice to set a maximum limit. This can be done from the command line with an ALTER DATABASE command, or through Database Control.

Dropping Tablespaces

To drop a tablespace, use the DROP TABLESPACE command. The syntax is

```
DROP TABLESPACE tablespacename
[INCLUDING CONTENTS [AND DATAFILES] ] ;
```

If the INCLUDING CONTENTS keywords are not specified, the drop will fail if there are any objects in the tablespace. Using these keywords instructs Oracle to drop the objects first, and then to drop the tablespace. Even this will fail in some circumstances, such as if the tablespace contains a table that is the parent in a foreign key relationship with a table in another tablespace.

If the AND DATAFILES keywords are not specified, the tablespace and its contents will be dropped but the datafiles will continue to exist on disk. Oracle will know nothing about them anymore, and they will have to be deleted with operating system commands.

 TIP On Windows systems, you may find the datafiles are still there after using the INCLUDING CONTENTS AND DATAFILES clause. This is because of the way Windows flags files as "locked." It may be necessary to stop the Windows Oracle service (called something like OracleServiceORCL) before you can delete the files manually.

Oracle-Managed Files (OMF)

Use of OMF is intended to remove the necessity for the DBA to have any knowledge of the file systems. The creation of database files can be fully automated. To enable OMF, set some or all of these instance parameters:

```
DB_CREATE_FILE_DEST
DB_CREATE_ONLINE_LOG_DEST_1
DB_CREATE_ONLINE_LOG_DEST_2
DB_CREATE_ONLINE_LOG_DEST_3
DB_CREATE_ONLINE_LOG_DEST_4
DB_CREATE_ONLINE_LOG_DEST_5
DB_RECOVERY_FILE_DEST
```

The DB_CREATE_FILE_DEST parameter specifies a default location for all datafiles. The DB_CREATE_ONLINE_LOG_DEST_n parameters specify a default location for online redo log files. DB_RECOVERY_FILE_DEST sets up a default location for archive redo log files and backup files. As well as setting default file locations, OMF will generate filenames and (by default) set the file sizes. Setting these parameters can greatly simplify file-related operations. Having enabled OMF, it can always be overridden by specifying a datafile name in the CREATE TABLESPACE command.

Exercise 5-2: Create, Alter, and Drop Tablespaces   In this exercise, you will create tablespaces and change their characteristics. Then enable and use OMF. The exercise can be done through Database Control, but if so, be sure to click the SHOW SQL button at all stages to observe the SQL statements being generated.

1. Connect to the database as user SYSTEM.

2. Create a tablespace in a suitable directory—any directory on which the Oracle owner has write permission will do:

```
create tablespace newtbs
datafile '/home/db11g/oradata/newtbs_01.dbf' size 10m
extent management local autoallocate
segment space management auto;
```

This command specifies the options that are the default. Nonetheless, it may be considered good practice to do this, to make the statement self-documenting.

3. Create a table in the new tablespace, and determine the size of the first extent:

```
create table newtab(c1 date) tablespace newtbs;
select extent_id,bytes from dba_extents
where owner='SYSTEM' and segment_name='NEWTAB';
```

4. Add extents manually, and observe the size of each new extent by repeatedly executing this command,

```
alter table newtabs allocate extent;
```

followed by the query from Step 3. Note the point at which the extent size increases.

5. Take the tablespace offline, observe the effect, and bring it back online. This is shown in the following illustration.

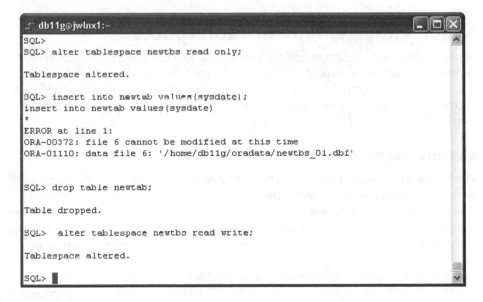

```
db11g@jwlnx1:~
SQL>
SQL> alter tablespace newtbs offline;

Tablespace altered.

SQL> insert into newtab values(sysdate);
insert into newtab values(sysdate)
                 *
ERROR at line 1:
ORA-00376: file 6 cannot be read at this time
ORA-01110: data file 6: '/home/db11g/oradata/newtbs_01.dbf'


SQL> alter tablespace newtbs online;

Tablespace altered.

SQL> insert into newtab values(sysdate);

1 row created.

SQL>
```

6. Make the tablespace read only, observe the effect, and make it read-write again. This is shown in the next illustration.

```
db11g@jwlnx1:~
SQL>
SQL> alter tablespace newtbs read only;

Tablespace altered.

SQL> insert into newtab values(sysdate);
insert into newtab values(sysdate)
*
ERROR at line 1:
ORA-00372: file 6 cannot be modified at this time
ORA-01110: data file 6: '/home/db11g/oradata/newtbs_01.dbf'


SQL> drop table newtab;

Table dropped.

SQL>  alter tablespace newtbs read write;

Tablespace altered.

SQL>
```

7. Enable Oracle-Managed Files for datafile creation:

```
alter system set db_create_file_dest='/home/db11g/oradata';
```

8. Create a tablespace, using the minimum syntax now possible:

```
create tablespace omftbs;
```

9. Determine the characteristics of the OMF file:

```
select file_name,bytes,autoextensible,maxbytes,increment_by
from dba_data_files where tablespace_name='OMFTBS';
```

Note the file is initially 100MB, autoextensible, with no upper limit.

10. Adjust the OMF file to have more sensible characteristics. Use whatever system-generated filename was returned by Step 9:

```
alter database datafile
'/oradata/ORCL11G/datafile/o1_mf_omftbs_3olpn462_.dbf'
resize 500m;
alter database datafile
'/home/db11g/oradata/ORCL11G/datafile/o1_mf_omftbs_3olpn462_.dbf'
autoextend on next 100m maxsize 2g;
```

11. Drop the tablespace, and use an operating system command to confirm that the file has indeed gone:

```
drop tablespace omftbs including contents and datafiles;
```

Space Management in Tablespaces

Space management occurs at several levels. First, space is assigned to a tablespace. This is done by sizing the datafiles, as already described. Second, space within a tablespace is assigned to segments. This is done by allocating extents. Third, space within a segment is assigned to rows. This is done by maintaining bitmaps that track how much space is free in each block.

Extent Management

The extent management method is set per tablespace and applies to all segments in the tablespace. There are two techniques for managing extent usage: *dictionary management* or *local management*. The difference is clear: local management should always be used; dictionary management should never be used. Dictionary-managed extent management is still supported, but only just. It is a holdover from previous releases.

Dictionary extent management uses two tables in the data dictionary. SYS.UET$ has rows describing used extents, and SYS.FET$ has rows describing free extents. Every time the database needs to allocate an extent to a segment, it must search FET$ to find an appropriate bit of free space, and then carry out DML operations against FET$ and UET$ to allocate it to the segment. This mechanism causes negative problems with performance, because all space management operations in the database (many of which could be initiated concurrently) must serialize on the code that constructs the transactions.

Local extent management was introduced with release 8*i* and became default with release 9*i*. It uses bitmaps stored in each datafile. Each bit in the bitmap covers a range of blocks, and when space is allocated, the appropriate bits are changed from zero to one. This mechanism is far more efficient than the transaction-based mechanism of dictionary management. The cost of assigning extents is amortized across bitmaps in every datafile that can be updated concurrently, rather than being concentrated (and serialized) on the two tables.

When creating a locally managed tablespace, an important option is *uniform size*. If uniform is specified, then every extent ever allocated in the tablespace will be that size. This can make the space management highly efficient, because the block ranges covered by each bit can be larger: only one bit per extent. Consider this statement:

```
create tablespace large_tabs datafile 'large_tabs_01.dbf' size 10g
extent management local uniform size 160m;
```

Every extent allocated in this tablespace will be 160MB, so there will be about 64 of them. The bitmap needs only 64 bits, and 160MB of space can be allocated by updating just one bit. This should be very efficient—provided that the segments in the tablespace are large. If a segment were created that needed space for only a few rows, it would still get an extent of 160MB. Small objects need their own tablespace:

```
create tablespace small_tabs datafile 'small_tabs_01.dbf' size 1g
extent management local uniform size 160k;
```

The alternative (and default) syntax would be

```
create tablespace any_tabs datafile 'any_tabs_01.dbf' size 10g
extent management local autoallocate;
```

When segments are created in this tablespace, Oracle will allocate a 64KB extent. As a segment grows and requires more extents, Oracle will allocate extents of 64KB up to 16 extents, from which it will allocate progressively larger extents. Thus fast-growing segments will tend to be given space in ever-increasing chunks.

 TIP Oracle Corporation recommends AUTOALLOCATE, but if you know how big segments are likely to be and can place them accordingly, UNIFORM SIZE may well be the best option.

It is possible that if a database has been upgraded from previous versions, it will include dictionary-managed tablespaces. You can verify this with the query:

```
select tablespace_name, extent_management from dba_tablespaces;
```

Any dictionary-managed tablespaces should be converted to local management with the provided PL/SQL program, which can be executed as follows:

```
execute dbms_space_admin.tablespace_migrate_to_local('tablespacename');
```

TIP Converting tablespaces to local management is quick and easy, except for the SYSTEM tablespace, where some extra steps are required. These are well documented in the System Administrator's guide available as part of the product documentation.

Segment Space Management

The segment space management method is set per tablespace and applies to all segments in the tablespace. There are two techniques for managing segment space usage: *manual* or *automatic*. The difference is clear: automatic management should always be used; manual management should never be used. Manual segment space management is still supported but never recommended. Like dictionary-managed extent management, it is a holdover from previous releases.

Automatic segment space management was introduced with release 9*i* and has become the default with release 11*g*. Every segment created in an automatic management tablespace has a set of bitmaps that describe how full each block is. There are five bitmaps for each segment, and each block will appear on exactly one bitmap. The bitmaps track the space used in bands or ranges: there is a bitmap for full blocks; and there are bitmaps for blocks that are 75 percent to 100 percent used; 50 percent to 75 percent used; 25 percent to 50 percent used; and 0 percent to 25 percent used. When searching for a block into which to insert a row, the session server process will look at the size of the row to determine which bitmap to search. For instance, if the block size is 4KB and the row to be inserted is 1500 bytes, an appropriate block will be found by searching the 25 percent to 50 percent bitmap. Every block on this bitmap is guaranteed to have at least 2KB of free space. As rows are inserted, deleted, or change size through updates, the bitmaps get updated accordingly.

The old manual space management method used a simple list, known as the *free list,* which listed which blocks were available for inserts but without any information on how full they were. This method could cause excessive activity, as blocks had to be tested for space at insert time, and often resulted in a large proportion of wasted space.

To verify if any tablespaces are using manual management, you can run the query:

```
select tablespace_name,segment_space_management from dba_tablespaces;
```

It is not possible to convert a tablespace from manual to automatic segment space management. The only solution is to create a new tablespace using automatic segment space management, move the segments into it (at which point the bitmaps will be generated), and drop the old tablespaces.

Exercise 5-3: Change Tablespace Characteristics   In this exercise, you will create a tablespace using the nondefault manual space management, to simulate the need to convert to automatic segment space management after an upgrade.

1. Connect to your database as user SYSTEM.
2. Create a tablespace using manual segment space management. As OMF was enabled in Exercise 5-2, there is no need for any datafile clause:

```
create tablespace manualsegs segment space management manual;
```

3. Confirm that the new tablespace is indeed using the manual technique:

```
select segment_space_management from dba_tablespaces
where tablespace_name='MANUALSEGS';
```

4. Create a table and an index in the tablespace:

```
create table mantab (c1 number) tablespace manualsegs;
create index mantabi on mantab(c1) tablespace manualsegs;
```

These segments will be created with freelists, not bitmaps.

5. Create a new tablespace that will (by default) use automatic segment space management:

```
create tablespace autosegs;
```

6. Move the objects into the new tablespace:

```
alter table mantab move tablespace autosegs;
alter index mantabi rebuild online tablespace autosegs;
```

7. Confirm that the objects are in the correct tablespace:

```
select tablespace_name from dba_segments
where segment_name like 'MANTAB%';
```

8. Drop the original tablespace:

```
drop tablespace manualsegs including contents and datafiles;
```

9. Rename the new tablespace to the original name. This is often necessary, because some application software checks tablespace names:

```
alter tablespace autosegs rename to manualsegs;
```

10. Tidy up by dropping the tablespace, first with this command:

```
drop tablespace manualsegs;
```

Note the error caused by the tablespace not being empty, and fix it:

```
drop tablespace manualsegs including contents and datafiles;
```

Two-Minute Drill

Overview of Tablespaces and Datafiles

- One tablespace can be physically represented by many datafiles.
- One tablespace can contain many segments.
- One segment comprises one or more extents.
- One extent is many consecutive blocks, in one datafile.
- One Oracle block should be one or more operating system blocks.
- The Oracle block is the granularity of database I/O.

Create and Manage Tablespaces

- A SMALLFILE tablespace can have many datafiles, but a BIGFILE tablespace can have only one.

- Tablespaces default to local extent management, automatic segment space management, but not to a uniform extent size.

- OMF datafiles are automatically named, initially 100MB, and can autoextend without limit.

- A tablespace that contains segments cannot be dropped—unless an INCLUDING CONTENTS clause is specified.

- Tablespaces can be online or offline, read-write or read only.

- Tablespaces can store one of three types of objects: permanent objects, temporary objects, or undo segments.

Space Management in Tablespaces

- Local extent management tracks extent allocation with bitmaps in each datafile.

- The UNIFORM SIZE clause when creating a tablespace forces all extents to be the same size.

- The AUTOALLOCATE clause lets Oracle determine the next extent size, which is based on how many extents are being allocated to a segment.

- Automatic segment space management tracks the free space in each block of an extent using bitmaps.

- It is possible to convert a tablespace from dictionary extent management to local extent management, but not from freelist segment management to automatic management.

Self Test

1. This illustration shows the Oracle storage model, with four entities having letters for names. Match four of the following entities to the letters A, B, C, D:

    DATAFILE

    EXTENT

    ORACLE BLOCK

    ROW

    SEGMENT

    TABLE

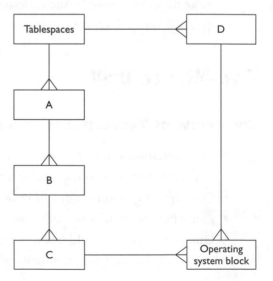

2. Which statements are correct about extents? (Choose all correct answers.)

   A. An extent is a consecutive grouping of Oracle blocks.

   B. An extent is a random grouping of Oracle blocks.

   C. An extent can be distributed across one or more datafiles.

   D. An extent can contain blocks from one or more segments.

   E. An extent can be assigned to only one segment.

3. Which of these are types of segment? (Choose all correct answers.)

   A. Sequence

   B. Stored procedure

   C. Table

   D. Table partition

   E. View

4. If a tablespace is created with this syntax:

   ```
   create tablespace tbs1 datafile 'tbs1.dbf' size 10m;
   ```

   which of these characteristics will it have? (Choose all correct answers.)

   A. The datafile will autoextend, but only to double its initial size.

   B. The datafile will autoextend with MAXSIZE UNLIMITED.

   C. The extent management will be local.

   D. Segment space management will be with bitmaps.

   E. The file will be created in the DB_CREATE_FILE_DEST directory.

5. How can a tablespace be made larger? (Choose all correct answers.)

   A. Convert it from a SMALLFILE tablespace to a BIGFILE tablespace.

   B. If it is a SMALLFILE tablespace, add files.

   C. If it is a BIGFILE tablespace, add more files.

   D. Resize the existing file(s).

6. Which of these commands can be executed against a table in a read-only tablespace? (Choose the best answer.)

   A. DELETE

   B. DROP

   C. INSERT

   D. TRUNCATE

   E. UPDATE

7. What operation cannot be applied to a tablespace after creation? (Choose the best answer.)

    A. Convert from dictionary extent management to local extent management.

    B. Convert from manual segment space management to automatic segment space management.

    C. Change the name of the tablespace.

    D. Reduce the size of the datafile(s) assigned to the tablespace.

    E. All the above operations can be applied.

8. By default, what thresholds are set for space warnings on a tablespace? (Choose the best answer.)

    A. 85 percent and 97 percent.

    B. This will depend on whether AUTOEXTEND has been enabled.

    C. This will depend on whether it is a SMALLFILE or a BIGFILE tablespace.

    D. By default, no warnings are enabled.

9. When the database is in mount mode, what views must be queried to identify the datafiles and tablespaces that make up the database? (Choose all correct answers.)

    A. DBA_DATA_FILES

    B. DBA_TABLESPACES

    C. DBA_TEMP_FILES

    D. V$DATABASE

    E. V$DATAFILE

    F. V$TABLESPACE

10. Which views could you query to find out about the temporary tablespaces and the files that make them up? (Choose all correct answers.)

    A. DBA_DATA_FILES

    B. DBA_TABLESPACES

    C. DBA_TEMP_TABLESPACES

    D. DBA_TEMP_FILES

    E. V$DATAFILE

    F. V$TABLESPACE

    G. V$TEMPTABLESPACE

    H. V$TEMPFILE

Self Test Answers

1. ☑ **A** is SEGMENT; **B** is EXTENT; **C** is ORACLE BLOCK; **D** is DATAFILE.

   ☒ Neither ROW nor TABLE is included in the model.

2. ☑ **A** and **E**. One extent is several consecutive Oracle blocks, and one segment consists of one or more extents.

   ☒ **B, C,** and **D**. **B, C,** and **D** are all wrong because they misinterpret the Oracle storage model.

3. ☑ **C** and **D**. A table can be a type of segment, as is a table partition (in which case the partitioned table is not a segment).

   ☒ **A, B,** and **E**. **A, B,** and **E** are wrong because they exist only as objects defined within the data dictionary. The data dictionary itself is a set of segments.

4. ☑ **C** and **D**. With release 11g, local extent management and automatic segment space management are enabled by default.

   ☒ **A** and **B**. **A** and **B** are both wrong because by default autoextension is disabled.
   E is wrong because providing a filename will override the OMF mechanism.

5. ☑ **B** and **D**. A small file tablespace can have many files, and all datafiles can be resized upward.

   ☒ **A** and **C**. **A** is wrong because you cannot convert between a SMALLFILE and a BIGFILE. **C** is wrong because a BIGFILE tablespace can have only one file.

6. ☑ **B**. Objects can be dropped from read-only tablespaces.

   ☒ **A, C, D,** and **E**. All of these commands will fail because they require writing to the table, unlike a DROP, which only writes to the data dictionary.

7. ☑ **B**. It is not possible to change the segment space management method after creation.

   ☒ **A C, D,** and **E**. **A** and **C** are wrong because a tablespace can be converted to local extent management or renamed at any time. **D** is wrong because a datafile can be resized downward—though only if the space to be freed up has not already been used. **E** is wrong because you cannot change the segment space management method without re-creating the tablespace.

8. ☑ **A**. 85 percent and 97 percent are the database-wide defaults applied to all tablespaces.

   ☒ **B, C,** and **D**. **B** is wrong because AUTOEXTEND does not affect the warning mechanism (though it may make it pointless). **C** is wrong because the warning mechanism considers only the tablespace, not the files. **D** is wrong because by default the space warning is enabled.

9. ☑ E and F. Joining these views will give the necessary information.

☒ A, B, C, and D. A and B are wrong because these views will not be available in mount mode. C is wrong because it is not relevant to datafiles (and is also not available in mount mode). D is wrong because there is no datafile or tablespace information in V$DATABASE.

10. ☑ B, D, F, and H. V$TABLESPACE and DBA_TABLESPACES will list the temporary tablespaces, and V$TEMPFILE and DBA_TEMP_FILES will list their files.

☒ A, C, E, and G. A and E are wrong because V$DATAFILE and DBA_DATA_FILES do not include tempfiles. C and G are wrong because there are no views with these names.

CHAPTER 6

Oracle Security

Exam Objectives

In this chapter you will learn to

- 052.7.1   Create and Manage Database User Accounts
- 052.7.2   Grant and Revoke Privileges
- 052.7.3   Create and Manage Roles
- 052.7.4   Create and Manage Profiles
- 052.11.1 Implement Database Security and Principle of Least Privilege
- 052.11.2 Work with Standard Database Auditing

Security is an issue of vital concern at all sites. All organizations should have a security manual documenting rules and procedures. If your organization does not have such a manual, someone should be writing it—perhaps that someone should be you. In security, there is no right or wrong; there is only conformance or nonconformance to agreed procedures. If administrators follow the rules and advise on what those rules should be, then any breach of security is not their fault. But unfortunately, history shows that when something goes wrong in the security arena, there is a great desire to blame individuals. It is vitally important that administration staff should be able to point to a rule book that lays down the procedures they should follow, and to routines and logs that demonstrate that they did indeed follow them. This devolves the responsibility to the authors of the rule book, the security manual. If no such manual exists, then any problems are likely to be dumped on the most convenient scapegoat. This is often the database administrator. You have been warned.

The Oracle product set provides many facilities for enforcing security up to and beyond the highest standards specified by any legislation. Many of the facilities (such as data encryption) are beyond the scope of the first OCP examination, where the treatment of security is limited to the use of privileges and auditing. This chapter discusses the basic security model governing user accounts and their authentication. The differences between a schema and a user (terms often used synonymously) are explored along with the use of privileges to permit access to as few items as necessary and the grouping of privileges into roles for ease of administration. Profiles used to manage passwords and resources to a limited extent are covered before delving into the powerful auditing features available.

Create and Manage Database User Accounts

When a user logs on to the database, they connect to a *user account* by specifying an account name followed by some means of authentication. The user account defines the initial access permissions and the attributes of the session. Associated with a user account is a *schema*. The terms "user," "user account," and "schema" can often be used interchangeably in the Oracle environment, but they are not the same thing. A user is a person who connects to a user account by establishing a session against the instance and logging on with the user account name. A schema is a set of objects owned by a user account, and is described in Chapter 7. The way the account was created will set up a range of attributes for the session, some of which can be changed later, while the session is in progress. A number of accounts are created at database creation time, and the DBA will usually create many more subsequently.

In some applications, each user has their own database user account. This means that the database is fully aware of who is the real owner of each session. This security model works well for small applications but is often impractical for larger systems with many hundreds or thousands of users. For large systems, many users will connect to the same account. This model relies on the application to map the real end user to a database user account, and it can make session-level security and auditing more complex. This chapter assumes that every user is known to the database: they each have their own user account.

User Account Attributes

A user account has a number of attributes defined at account creation time. These will be applied to sessions that connect to the account, though some can be modified by the session or the DBA while the session is running. These attributes are

- Username
- Authentication method
- Default tablespace
- Tablespace quotas
- Temporary tablespace
- User profile
- Account status

All of these should be specified when creating the user, though only username and authentication methods are mandatory; the others have defaults.

Username

The username must be unique in the database and must conform to certain rules. A username must begin with a letter, must have no more than 30 characters, and can consist of only letters, digits, and the characters dollar ($) and underscore (_). A user name may not be a reserved word. The letters are case sensitive but will be automatically converted to uppercase. All these rules (with the exception of the length) can be broken if the username is specified within double quotes, as shown on Figure 6-1.

```
C:\WINDOWS\system32\cmd.exe - sqlplus / as sysdba

SQL> create user john identified by pa55w0rd;

User created.

SQL> create user "john" identified by pa55w0rd;

User created.

SQL> create user "john%#" identified by pa55w0rd;

User created.

SQL> create user "table" identified by pa55w0rd;

User created.

SQL> select username,created from dba_users where lower(username) like 'john%';

USERNAME                    CREATED
--------------------------  --------------------
JOHN                        18-12-07 10:24:49
john                        18-12-07 10:24:56
john%#                      18-12-07 10:25:04

SQL> select username,created from dba_users where username='table';

USERNAME                    CREATED
--------------------------  --------------------
table                       18-12-07 10:25:18
```

Figure 6-1   How to create users with nonstandard names

In the first example in the figure, a username JOHN is created. This was entered in lowercase, but is converted to uppercase, as can be seen in the first query. The second example uses double quotes to create the user with a name in lowercase. The third and fourth examples use double quotes to bypass the rules on characters and reserved words; both of these would fail without the double quotes. If a username includes lowercase letters or illegal characters or is a reserved word, then double quotes must always be used to connect to the account subsequently.

TIP It is possible to use nonstandard usernames, but this may cause dreadful confusion. Some applications rely on the case conversion; others always use double quotes. It is good practice to always use uppercase and only the standard characters.

A username can never be changed after creation. If it is necessary to change it, the account must be dropped and another account created. This is a drastic action, because all the objects in the user's schema will be dropped along with the user.

Default Tablespace and Quotas

Every user account has a *default tablespace*. This is the tablespace where any schema objects (such as tables or indexes) created by the user will reside. It is possible for a user to create (own) objects in any tablespace on which they have been granted a quota, but unless another tablespace is specified when creating the object, it will go into the user's default tablespace.

There is a database-wide default tablespace that will be applied to all user accounts if a default tablespace is not specified when creating the user. The default can be set when creating the database and changed later with:

```
ALTER DATABASE DEFAULT TABLESPACE tablespace_name ;
```

If a default tablespace is not specified when creating the database, it will be set to the SYSTEM tablespace.

TIP After creating a database, do not leave the default tablespace as SYSTEM; this is very bad practice as nonsystem users could potentially fill up this tablespace, thus hampering the operation of the data dictionary and consequently the entire database. Change it as soon as you can.

A *quota* is the amount of space in a tablespace that the schema objects of a user are allowed to occupy. You can create objects and allocate extents to them until the quota is reached. If you have no quota on a tablespace, you cannot create any objects at all. Quotas can be changed at any time by an administrator user with sufficient privileges. If a user's quota is reduced to below the size of their existing objects (or even reduced to zero), the objects will survive and will still be usable, but they will not be permitted to get any bigger.

Figure 6-2 shows how to investigate and set quotas.

Figure 6-2
Managing user
quotas

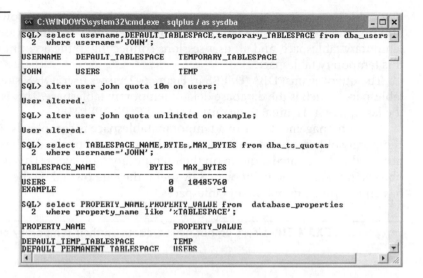

The first command queries DBA_USERS and determines the default and temporary tablespaces for the user JOHN, created in Figure 6-1. DBA_USERS has one row for every user account in the database. User JOHN has picked up the database defaults for the default and temporary tablespaces, which are shown in the last query against DATABASE_PROPERTIES.

The two ALTER USER commands in Figure 6-2 give user JOHN the capability to use up to 10MB of space in the USERS tablespace, and an unlimited amount of space in the EXAMPLE tablespace. The query against DBA_TS_QUOTAS confirms this, the number "–1" represents an unlimited quota. At the time the query was run, JOHN had not created any objects, so the figures for BYTES are zeros, indicating that he is not currently using any space in either tablespace.

EXAM TIP Before you can create a table, you must have both permission to execute CREATE TABLE and quota on a tablespace in which to create it.

TIP Most users will not need any quotas, because they will never create objects. They will only have permissions against objects owned by other schemas. The few object-owning schemas will probably have QUOTA UNLIMITED on the tablespaces where their objects reside.

Temporary Tablespace

Permanent objects (such as tables) are stored in permanent tablespaces; temporary objects are stored in temporary tablespaces. A session will need space in a temporary tablespace if it needs space for certain operations that exceed the space available in the session's PGA. Remember that the PGA is the program global area, the private memory allocated to the session. Operations that need temporary space (in memory if possible, in a temporary tablespace if necessary) include sorting rows, joining tables, building indexes, and using temporary tables. Every user account is assigned a temporary tablespace, and all user sessions connecting to the account will share this temporary tablespace.

The query against DBA_USERS in Figure 6-2 shows user JOHN's temporary tablespace, which is the database default temporary tablespace. This is shown by the last query in Figure 6-2, against DATABASE_PROPERTIES.

Space management within a temporary tablespace is completely automatic. Temporary objects are created and dropped as necessary by the database. A user does not need to be granted a quota on their temporary tablespace. This is because the objects in it are not actually owned by them; they are owned by the SYS user, who has an unlimited quota on all tablespaces.

 EXAM TIP Users do not need a quota on their temporary tablespace.

To change a user's temporary tablespace (which will affect all future sessions that connect to that account), use an ALTER USER command:

```
ALTER USER username TEMPORARY TABLESPACE tablespace_name;
```

 TIP If many users are logging on to the same user account, they will share the use of one temporary tablespace. This can be a performance bottleneck, which may be avoided by using temporary tablespace groups.

Profile

A user's profile controls their password settings and provides a limited amount of control over resource usage. Use of profiles is detailed in the later section "Create and Manage Profiles."

Profiles are a useful way of managing passwords and resources but can really only apply in an environment where every application user has their own database user account. For example, if many users connect to the same database user account, you would not want the password to be invalidated by one of them, because that would lock out everyone else. Similarly, resource usage will often need to be managed on a per-session basis rather than for the account as a whole.

Account Status

Every user account has a certain status, as listed in the ACCOUNT_STATUS column of DBA_USERS. There are nine possibilities:

- **OPEN**   The account is available for use.
- **LOCKED**   This indicates that the DBA deliberately locked the account. No user can connect to a locked account.

- **EXPIRED** This indicates that the password lifetime has expired. Passwords can have a limited lifetime. No user can connect to an EXPIRED account until the password is reset.

- **EXPIRED & LOCKED** Not only has the account been locked, but its password has also expired.

- **EXPIRED (GRACE)** This indicates that the *grace period* is in effect. A password need not expire immediately when its lifetime ends; it may be configured with a grace period during which users connecting to the account have the opportunity to change the password.

- **LOCKED (TIMED)** This indicates that the account is locked because of failed login attempts. An account can be configured to lock automatically for a period after an incorrect password is presented a certain number of times.

- **EXPIRED & LOCKED (TIMED)**

- **EXPIRED (GRACE) & LOCKED**

- **EXPIRED (GRACE) & LOCKED (TIMED)**

To lock and unlock an account, use these commands:

```
ALTER USER username ACCOUNT LOCK ;
ALTER USER username ACCOUNT UNLOCK ;
```

To force a user to change their password, use this command:

```
ALTER USER username PASSWORD EXPIRE;
```

This will immediately start the grace period, forcing the user to make a password change at their next login attempt (or one soon after). There is no such command as "alter . . . unexpire." The only way to make the account fully functional again is to reset the password.

Authentication Methods

A user account must have an authentication method: some means whereby the database can determine if the user attempting to create a session connecting to the account is allowed to do so. The simplest technique is by presenting a password that will be matched against a password stored within the database, but there are alternatives. The possibilities are

- Operating system authentication
- Password file authentication
- Password authentication
- External authentication
- Global authentication

The first two techniques are used only for administrators; the last requires an LDAP directory server. The LDAP directory server may be the Oracle Internet Directory, shipped as a part of the Oracle Application Server.

Operating System and Password File Authentication

To enable operating system and password file authentication (the two go together) for an account, you must grant the user either the SYSDBA or the SYSOPER privilege:

```
GRANT [sysdba | sysoper ] TO username ;
```

Granting either (or both) of these privileges will copy the user's password from the data dictionary into the external password file, where it can be read by the instance even if the database is not open. It also allows the instance to authenticate users by checking whether the operating system user attempting the connection is a member of the operating system group that owns the Oracle Home installation. Following database creation, the only user with these privileges is SYS.

To use password file authentication, the user can connect with this syntax using SQL*Plus:

```
CONNECT username / password [@db_alias] AS [ SYSOPER | SYSDBA ] ;
```

Note that password file authentication can be used for a connection to a remote database over Oracle Net.

To use operating system authentication, the user must be first logged on to the database server after being authenticated as an operating system user with access to the Oracle binaries before connecting with this syntax using SQL*Plus:

```
CONNECT / AS [ SYSOPER | SYSDBA ] ;
```

The operating system password is not stored by Oracle, and therefore there are no issues with changing passwords.

The equivalent of these syntaxes is also available when connecting with Database Control, by selecting SYSDBA from the Connect As drop-down box on the Database Control login window. To determine to whom the SYSDBA and SYSOPER privileges have been granted, query the view V$PWFILE_USERS. Connection with operating system or password file authentication is always possible, no matter what state the instance and database are in, and is necessary to issue STARTUP or SHUTDOWN commands.

A third privilege that operates in the same manner as SYSDBA and SYSOPER is SYSASM. This is a privilege that is only applicable to ASM instances and is detailed in Chapter 20.

TIP All user sessions must be authenticated. There is no such thing as an "anonymous" login, and some authentication method must be used.

Password Authentication

The syntax for a connection with password authentication using SQL*Plus is

```
CONNECT username / password [@db_alias] ;
```

Or with Database Control, select NORMAL from the Connect As drop-down box.

When connecting with password authentication, the instance will validate the password given against that stored with the user account in the data dictionary. For this to work, the database must be open; it is therefore logically impossible to issue STARTUP or SHUTDOWN commands when connected with password authentication. The user SYS is not permitted to connect with password authentication; only password file, operating system, or LDAP authentication is possible for SYS.

Usernames are case sensitive but are automatically converted to uppercase unless specified within double quotes. In previous releases of the database, passwords were not case sensitive at all. With release 11g, passwords are case sensitive and there is no automatic case conversion. It is not necessary to use double quotes, the password will always be read exactly as entered.

When a connection is made across a network, release 11g will always encrypt it using the AES algorithm before transmission. To use encryption for the ongoing traffic between the user process and the server process requires the Advanced Security Option, but password encryption is standard.

Any user can change their user account password at any time, or a highly privileged user (such as SYSTEM) can change any user account password. The syntax (whether you are changing your own password or another one) is

```
ALTER USER username IDENTIFIED BY password ;
```

External Authentication

If a user account is created with external authentication, Oracle will delegate the authentication to an external service; it will not prompt for a password. If the Advanced Security Option has been licensed, then the external service can be a Kerberos server, a RADIUS server, or (in the Windows environment) the Windows native authentication service. When a user attempts to connect to the user account, rather than authenticating the user itself, the database instance will accept (or reject) the authentication according to whether the external authentication service has authenticated the user. For example, if using Kerberos, the database will check that the user does have a valid Kerberos token.

Without the Advanced Security Option, the only form of external authentication that can be used is operating system authentication. This is a requirement for SYSDBA and SYSOPER accounts (as already discussed) but can also be used for normal users. The technique is to create an Oracle user account with the same name as the operating system user account but prefixed with a string specified by the instance parameter OS_AUTHENT_PREFIX. This parameter defaults to the string OPS$. To check its value, use a query such as

```
select value from v$parameter where name='os_authent_prefix';
```

On Linux or Unix, external operating system authentication is very simple. Assuming that the OS_AUTHENT_PREFIX is on default and that there is an operating system user called `jwatson`, then create an oracle user and grant the CREATE SESSION privilege as follows:

```
create user ops$jwatson identified externally;
grant create session to ops$jwatson;
```

A user logged on to Unix as `jwatson` will be able to issue the command:

```
sqlplus /
```

from an operating system prompt, and will be connected to the database user account `ops$jwatson`.

Under Windows, when Oracle queries the operating system to identify the user, Windows will usually (depending on details of Windows security configuration) return the username prefixed with the Windows domain. Assuming that the Windows logon ID is `John Watson` (including a space) and that the Windows domain is JWACER (which happens to be the machine name) and that the OS_AUTHENT_PREFIX is on default, the command will be

```
create user "OPS$JWACER\JOHN WATSON" identified externally;
```

Note that the username must be in uppercase, and because of the illegal characters (a backslash and a space) must be enclosed in double quotes.

TIP Using external authentication can be very useful, but only if the users actually log on to the machine hosting the database. Users will rarely do this, so the technique is more likely to be of value for accounts used for running maintenance or batch jobs.

Global Authentication

An emerging standard for identity management makes use of LDAP servers. An LDAP-compliant directory server, the Oracle Internet Directory, is distributed by Oracle Corporation as part of Oracle Application Server. A *global user* is a user who is defined within the LDAP directory, and *global authentication* is a means of delegating user authentication to the directory.

There are two techniques for global authentication:

- The users can be defined in the directory, and also in the database. A user will be connected to a user account with the same name as the user's common name in the directory.

- The users can be defined only in the directory. The database will be aware of the users' global names but connects all users to the same database user account.

Neither of these techniques requires the user to present a password to the database. The connection will happen without any prompts if the directory accounts and the database user accounts are set up correctly.

Creating Accounts

The CREATE USER command has only two mandatory arguments: a username and a method of authentication. Optionally, it can accept a clause to specify a default tablespace and a temporary tablespace, one or more quota clauses, a named profile, and commands to lock the account and expire the password. A typical example (with line numbers added) would be

```
1     create user scott identified by tiger
2     default tablespace users temporary tablespace temp
3     quota 100m on users, quota unlimited on example
4     profile developer_profile
5     password expire
6     account unlock;
```

Only the first line is required; there are defaults for everything else. Taking the command line by line:

1. Provide the username, and a password for password authentication.
2. Provide the default and temporary tablespaces.
3. Set up quotas on the default and another tablespace.
4. Nominate a profile for password and resource management.
5. Force the user to change his password immediately.
6. Make the account available for use (which would have been the default).

Every attribute of an account can be adjusted later with ALTER USER commands, with the exception of the name. To change the password:

```
alter user scott identified by lion;
```

To change the default and temporary tablespaces:

```
alter user scott default tablespace store_data temporary tablespace temp;
```

To change quotas:

```
alter user scott quota unlimited on store_data, quota 0 on users;
```

To change the profile:

```
alter user scott profile prod_profile;
```

To force a password change:

```
alter user scott password expire;
```

To lock the account:

```
alter user scott account lock;
```

Having created a user account, it may be necessary to drop it:

```
drop user scott;
```

This command will only succeed if the user does not own any objects: if the schema is empty. If you do not want to identify all the objects owned and drop them first, they can be dropped with the user by specifying CASCADE:

```
drop user scott cascade;
```

To manage accounts with Database Control, from the database home page take the Schema tab and then the Users link in the Security section. This will show all the user accounts in the database. Figure 6-3 shows these, sorted in reverse order of creation. To change the sort order, click the appropriate column header.

The first "user" in the figure is PUBLIC. This is a notional user to whom privileges can be granted if you wish to grant them to every user. The CREATE button will present a window that prompts for all the user account attributes. The DELETE button will drop an account, with the CASCADE option if necessary—but it will give an "Are you sure?" prompt before proceeding.

To adjust the attributes of an account, select it and click EDIT. This will take you to the Edit User window, shown in Figure 6-4. This interface can be used to change all

Figure 6-3   Users shown by Database Control

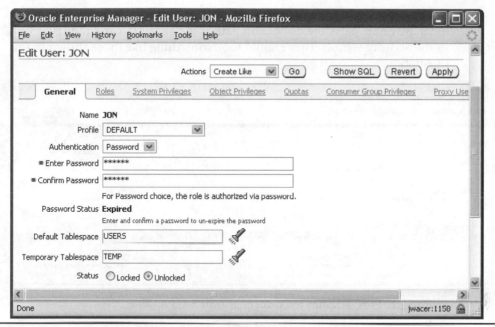

Figure 6-4 The Edit User Database Control window

aspects of the account except for tablespace quotas, which have their own tabs. It also
has tabs for granting and revoking privileges and roles.

Exercise 6-1: Create Users   In this exercise, you will create some users to be
used for the remaining exercises in this chapter. It is assumed that there is a permanent
tablespace called STOREDATA and a temporary tablespace called TEMP. If these don't
exist, either create them or use any other suitable tablespaces.

1. Connect to your database with SQL*Plus as a highly privileged user, such as
   SYSTEM or SYS.

2. Create three users:

```
create user sales identified by sales
default tablespace storedata password expire;
create user webapp identified by oracle
default tablespace storedata quota unlimited on storedata;
create user accounts identified by oracle;
```

3. Confirm that the users have been created with Database Control. From the database home page, the navigation path is the Server tab and the Users link in the Security section. They should look something like those shown in this illustration:

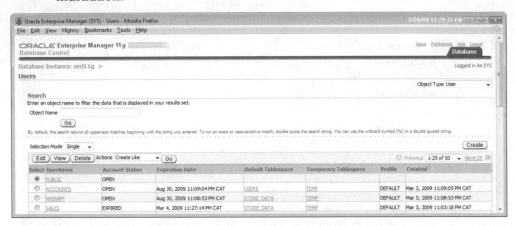

4. From SQL*Plus, attempt to connect as user SALES:

```
connect sales/sales
```

5. When prompted, select a new password (such as "oracle"). But it won't get you anywhere, because user SALES does not have the CREATE SESSION privilege.

6. Refresh the Database Control window, and note that the status of the SALES account is no longer EXPIRED but OPEN, because the password has been changed.

Grant and Revoke Privileges

By default, no unauthorized user can do anything in an Oracle database. A user cannot even connect without being granted a privilege. And once this has been done, you still can't do anything useful (or dangerous) without being given more privileges. Privileges are assigned to user accounts with a GRANT command and withdrawn with a REVOKE. Additional syntax can give a user the ability to grant any privileges they have to other users. By default only the database administrators (SYS and SYSTEM) have the right to grant any privileges. The user that grants one or more privileges to another user is referred to as the *grantor* while the recipient is referred to as the *grantee*.

Privileges come in two groups: system privileges that (generally speaking) let users perform actions that affect the data dictionary, and object privileges that let users perform actions that affect data.

System Privileges

There are about two hundred system privileges. Most apply to actions that affect the data dictionary, such as creating tables or users. Others affect the database or the instance, such as creating tablespaces, adjusting instance parameter values, or establishing a session. Some of the more commonly used privileges are

- **CREATE SESSION**   This lets the user connect. Without this, you cannot even log on to the database.

- **RESTRICTED SESSION**   If the database is started with STARTUP RESTRICT, or adjusted with ALTER SYSTEM ENABLE RESTRICTED SESSION, only users with this privilege will be able to connect.

- **ALTER DATABASE**   Gives access to many commands necessary for modifying physical structures.

- **ALTER SYSTEM**   Gives control over instance parameters and memory structures.

- **CREATE TABLESPACE**   With the ALTER TABLESPACE and DROP TABLESPACE privileges, these will let a user manage tablespaces.

- **CREATE TABLE**   Lets the grantee create tables in their own schema; includes the ability to alter and drop them, to run SELECT and DML commands on them, and to create, alter, or drop indexes on them.

- **GRANT ANY OBJECT PRIVILEGE**   Lets the grantee grant object permissions on objects they don't own to others—but not to themselves.

- **CREATE ANY TABLE**   The grantee can create tables that belong to other users.

- **DROP ANY TABLE**   The grantee can drop tables belonging to any other users.

- **INSERT ANY TABLE, UPDATE ANY TABLE, DELETE ANY TABLE**   The grantee can execute these DML commands against tables owned by all other users.

- **SELECT ANY TABLE**   The grantee can SELECT from any table in the database.

The syntax for granting system privileges is

```
GRANT privilege [, privilege...] TO username ;
```

After creating a user account, a command such as this will grant the system privileges commonly assigned to users who will be involved in developing applications:

```
grant create session, alter session,
create table, create view, create synonym, create cluster,
create database link, create sequence,
create trigger, create type, create procedure, create operator
to username ;
```

These privileges will let you connect and configure your session, and then create objects to store data and PL/SQL objects. These objects can only exist in your own schema; you will have no privileges against any other schema. The object creation will also be limited by the quota(s) you may (or may not) have been assigned on various tablespaces.

A variation in the syntax lets the grantee pass their privilege on to a third party. For example:

```
connect system/oracle;
grant create table to scott with admin option;
connect scott/tiger;
grant create table to jon;
```

This gives SCOTT the ability to create tables in his own schema, and also to issue the GRANT command himself. In this example, he lets user JON create tables too—but JON will only be able to create them in the JON schema. Figure 6-5 shows the result of the grant as depicted by Database Control; the same information could be garnered by querying the view DBA_SYS_PRIVS.

If a system privilege is revoked from you, any actions you performed using that privilege (such as creating tables) remain intact. Also, if you had been granted the privilege with the ADMIN OPTION, any users to whom you passed on the privilege will retain it, even after it was revoked from you. There is no record kept of the grantor of a system privilege, so it is not possible for a REVOKE to cascade as illustrated in Figure 6-6.

 EXAM TIP Revocation of a system privilege will not cascade (unlike revocation of an object privilege).

The ANY privileges give permissions against all relevant objects in the database. Thus,

```
grant select any table to scott;
```

will let SCOTT query every table in every schema in the database. It is often considered bad practice to grant the ANY privileges to any user other than the system administration staff.

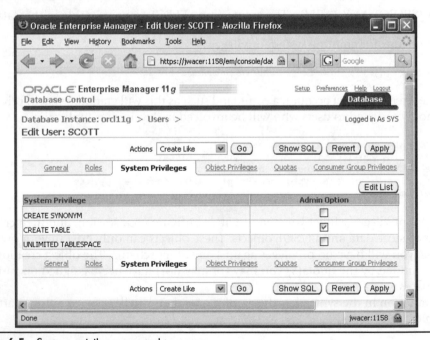

Figure 6-5 System privileges granted to a user

Figure 6-6
GRANT and
REVOKE from
SQL*Plus

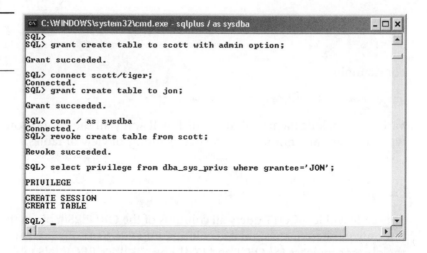

```
 C:\WINDOWS\system32\cmd.exe - sqlplus / as sysdba          _ □ ×
SQL>
SQL> grant create table to scott with admin option;

Grant succeeded.

SQL> connect scott/tiger;
Connected.
SQL> grant create table to jon;

Grant succeeded.

SQL> conn / as sysdba
Connected.
SQL> revoke create table from scott;

Revoke succeeded.

SQL> select privilege from dba_sys_privs where grantee='JON';

PRIVILEGE
----------------------------------------------------------------
CREATE SESSION
CREATE TABLE

SQL> _
```

TIP In fact, ANY is not as dangerous now as with earlier releases. It no longer includes tables in the SYS schema, so the data dictionary is still protected. But ANY should still be used with extreme caution, as it removes all protection from user tables.

Object Privileges

Object privileges provide the ability to perform SELECT, INSERT, UPDATE, and DELETE commands against tables and related objects, and to execute PL/SQL objects. These privileges do not exist for objects in the users' own schemas; if users have the system privilege CREATE TABLE, they can perform SELECT and DML operations against the tables they create with no further need for permissions.

EXAM TIP The ANY privileges, that grant permissions against objects in every user account in the database, are not object privileges—they are system privileges.

The object privileges apply to different types of object:

Privilege	Granted on
SELECT	Tables, views, sequences, synonyms
INSERT	Tables, views, synonyms
UPDATE	Tables, views, synonyms
DELETE	Tables, views, synonyms
ALTER	Tables, sequences
EXECUTE	Procedures, functions, packages, synonyms

The syntax is

```
GRANT privilege ON [schema.]object TO username [WITH GRANT OPTION] ;
```

For example,

```
grant select on store.customers to scott;
```

Variations include the use of ALL, which will apply all the permissions relevant to the type of object, and nominate particular columns of view or tables:

```
grant select on store.orders to scott;
grant update (order_status) on store.orders to scott;
grant all on store.regions to scott;
```

This code will let SCOTT query all columns of the ORDERS table in the STORE schema but only write to one nominated column, ORDER_STATUS. Then SCOTT is given all the object privileges (SELECT and DML) on STORE's REGIONS table. Figure 6-7 shows the result of this, as viewed in Database Control.

 TIP Granting privileges at the column level is often said to be bad practice because of the massive workload involved. If it is necessary to restrict peoples' access to certain columns, creating a view that shows only those columns will often be a better alternative.

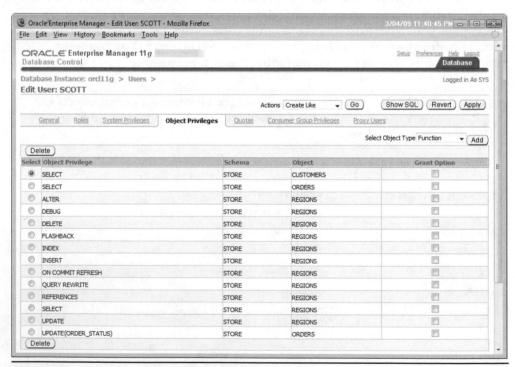

Figure 6-7 Object privilege management with Database Control

Using WITH GRANT OPTION (or with Database Control, selecting the Grant Option check box shown in Figure 6-7) lets a user pass their object privilege on to a third party. Oracle retains a record of who granted object privileges to whom; this allows a REVOKE of an object to cascade to all those in the chain. Consider this sequence of commands:

```
connect store/admin123;
grant select on customers to sales with grant option;
connect sales/sales;
grant select on store.customers to webapp with grant option;
conn webapp/oracle;
grant select on store.customers to scott;
connect store/admin123;
revoke select on customers from sales;
```

At the conclusion of these commands, neither SALES nor WEBAPP nor SCOTT has the SELECT privilege against STORE.CUSTOMERS.

 EXAM TIP Revocation of an object privilege will cascade (unlike revocation of a system privilege).

Exercise 6-2: Grant Direct Privileges   In this exercise, you will grant some privileges to the users created in Exercise 6-1 and prove that they work.

1. Connect to your database as user SYSTEM with SQL*Plus.

2. Grant CREATE SESSION to user SALES:

   ```
   grant create session to sales;
   ```

3. Open another SQL*Plus session, and connect as SALES. This time, the login will succeed:

   ```
   connect sales/oracle
   ```

4. As SALES, attempt to create a table:

   ```
   create table t1 (c1 date);
   ```

   This will fail with the message "ORA-01031: insufficient privileges."

5. In the SYSTEM session, grant SALES the CREATE TABLE privilege:

   ```
   grant create table to sales;
   ```

6. In the SALES session, try again:

   ```
   create table t1 (c1 date);
   ```

   This will fail with the message "ORA-01950: no privileges on tablespace STOREDATA."

7. In the SYSTEM session, give SALES a quota on the STOREDATA tablespace:

   ```
   alter user sales quota 1m on storedata;
   ```

8. In the SALES session, try again. This time, the creation will succeed.

9. As SALES, grant object privileges on the new table:

   ```
   grant all on t1 to webapp;
   grant select on t1 to accounts;
   ```

10. Connect to Database Control as user SYSTEM.

11. Confirm that the object privileges have been granted. The navigation path from the database home page is as follows: On the Schema tab click the Tables link in the Database Objects section. Enter **SALES** as the Schema and **T1** as the Table and click GO. In the Actions drop-down box, select Object Privileges. As shown in the illustration, ACCOUNTS has only SELECT, but WEBAPP has everything else. Note that the window also shows by whom the privileges were granted, and that none of them were granted WITH GRANT OPTION.

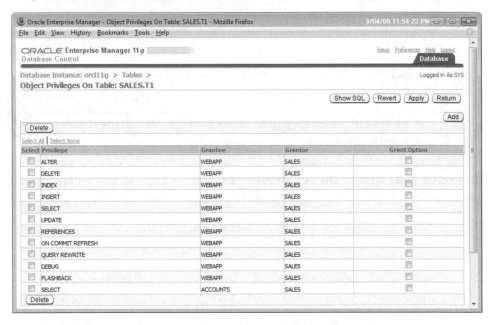

12. With Database Control, confirm which privileges have granted to SALES. The navigation path from the database home page is as follows: On the Server tab click the Users link in the Security section. Select the radio button for SALES, and click VIEW. You will see that he has two system privileges (CREATE SESSION and CREATE TABLE) without the ADMIN OPTION, a 1MB quota on STOREDATA, and nothing else.

13. Retrieve the same information shown in Steps 11 and 12 with SQL*Plus. As SYSTEM, run these queries:

```
select grantee,privilege,grantor,grantable from dba_tab_privs
where owner='SALES' and table_name='T1';
select * from dba_sys_privs where grantee='SALES';
```

14. Revoke the privileges granted to WEBAPP and ACCOUNTS:

```
revoke all on sales.t1 from webapp;
revoke all on sales.t1 from accounts;
```

Confirm the revocations by rerunning the first query from Step 13.

Create and Manage Roles

Managing security with directly granted privileges works but has two problems. First, it can be a huge workload: an application with thousands of tables and users could need millions of grants. Second, if a privilege has been granted to a user, that user has it in all circumstances: it is not possible to make a privilege active only in certain circumstances. Both these problems are solved by using *roles*. A role is a bundle of system and/or object privileges that can be granted and revoked as a unit, and having been granted can be temporarily activated or deactivated within a session.

Creating and Granting Roles

Roles are not schema objects: they aren't owned by anyone and so cannot be prefixed with a username. However, they do share the same namespace as users: it is not possible to create a role with the same name as an already-existing user, or a user with the same name as an already-existing role.

Create a role with the CREATE ROLE command:

```
CREATE ROLE rolename ;
```

Then grant privileges to the role with the usual syntax, including WITH ADMIN or WITH GRANT OPTION if desired.

For example, assume that the HR schema is being used as a repository for data to be used by three groups of staff. Managerial staff have full access, senior clerical staff have limited access, and junior clerical staff have very restricted access. First create a role that might be suitable for the junior clerks; all they can do is answer questions by running queries:

```
create role hr_junior;
grant create session to hr_junior;
grant select on hr.regions to hr_junior;
grant select on hr.locations to hr_junior;
grant select on hr.countries to hr_junior;
grant select on hr.departments to hr_junior;
grant select on hr.job_history to hr_junior;
grant select on hr.jobs to hr_junior;
grant select on hr.employees to hr_junior;
```

Anyone granted this role will be able to log on to the database and run SELECT statements against the HR tables. Then create a role for the senior clerks, who can also write data to the EMPLOYEES and JOB_HISTORY tables:

```
create role hr_senior;
grant hr_junior to hr_senior with admin option;
grant insert, update, delete on hr.employees to hr_senior;
grant insert, update, delete on hr.job_history to hr_senior;
```

This role is first granted the HR_JUNIOR role (there is no problem granting one role to another) with the syntax that will let the senior users assign the junior role to others. Then it is granted DML privileges on just two tables. Then create the manager's role, which can update all the other tables:

```
create role hr_manager;
grant hr_senior to hr_manager with admin option;
grant all on hr.regions to hr_manager;
grant all on hr.locations to hr_manager;
grant all on hr.countries to hr_manager;
grant all on hr.departments to hr_manager;
grant all on hr.job_history to hr_manager;
grant all on hr.jobs to hr_manager;
grant all on hr.employees to hr_manager;
```

This third role is given the HR_SENIOR role with the ability to pass it on, and then gets full control over the contents of all the tables. But note that the only system privilege this role has is CREATE_SESSION, acquired through HR_SENIOR, which acquired it through HR_JUNIOR. Not even this role can create or drop tables; that must be done by the HR user, or an administrator with CREATE ANY TABLE and DROP ANY TABLE.

Note the syntax WITH ADMIN OPTION, which is the same as that for granting system privileges. As with system privileges, revocation of a role will not cascade; there is no record kept of who has granted a role to whom.

Finally, grant the roles to the relevant staff. If SCOTT is a manager, SUE is a senior clerk, and JON and ROOP are junior clerks, the flow could be as in Figure 6-8.

Predefined Roles

There are at least 50 predefined roles in an Oracle database (possibly many more, depending on what options have been installed). Roles that every DBA should be aware of are

- **CONNECT**   This only exists for backward compatibility. In previous releases it had the system privileges necessary to create data storing objects, such as tables. Now it has only the CREATE SESSION privilege.

Figure 6-8
Granting roles
with SQL*Plus

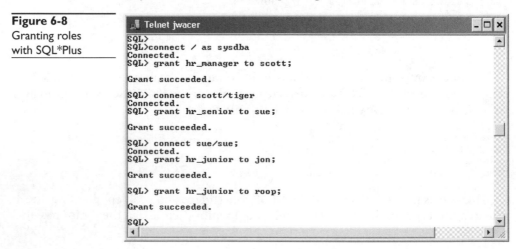

```
SQL>
SQL>connect / as sysdba
Connected.
SQL> grant hr_manager to scott;

Grant succeeded.

SQL> connect scott/tiger
Connected.
SQL> grant hr_senior to sue;

Grant succeeded.

SQL> connect sue/sue;
Connected.
SQL> grant hr_junior to jon;

Grant succeeded.

SQL> grant hr_junior to roop;

Grant succeeded.

SQL>
```

- **RESOURCE** Also for backward compatibility, this role can create both data objects (such as tables) and procedural objects (such PL/SQL procedures). It also includes the UNLIMITED TABLESPACE privilege.

- **DBA** Has most of the system privileges, and several object privileges and roles. Any user granted DBA can manage virtually all aspects of the database, except for startup and shutdown.

- **SELECT_CATALOG_ROLE** Has over 2000 object privileges against data dictionary objects, but no system privileges or privileges against user data. Useful for junior administration staff who must monitor and report on the database but not be able to see user data.

- **SCHEDULER_ADMIN** Has the system privileges necessary for managing the Scheduler job scheduling service.

There is also a predefined role PUBLIC, which is always granted to every database user account. It follows that if a privilege is granted to PUBLIC, it will be available to all users. So following this command:

```
grant select on hr.regions to public;
```

all users will be able to query the HR.REGIONS table.

 TIP The PUBLIC role is treated differently from any other role. It does not, for example, appear in the view DBA_ROLES. This is because the source code for DBA_ROLES, which can be seen in the `cdsec.sql` script called by the `catalog.sql` script, specifically excludes it.

Enabling Roles

By default, if a user has been granted a role, then the role will be *enabled*. This means that the moment a session is established connecting to the user account, all the privileges (and other roles) granted to the role will be active. This behavior can be modified by making the role nondefault. Following the example given in the preceding section, this query shows what roles have been granted to JON:

```
SQL> select * from dba_role_privs where grantee='JON';
GRANTEE                         GRANTED_ROLE     ADM DEF
------------------------------- ---------------- --- ---
JON                             HR_JUNIOR        NO  YES
```

JON has been granted HR_JUNIOR. He does not have administration on the role (so he cannot pass it on to anyone else), but it is a default role—he will have this role whenever he connects. This situation may well not be what you want. For example, JON has to be able to see the HR tables (it's his job) but that doesn't mean that you want him to be able to dial in from home, at midnight, and hack into the tables with SQL*Plus. You want to arrange things such that he can only see the tables when he is at a terminal in the Personnel office, running the HR application, in working hours.

To change the default behavior:

```
alter user jon default role none;
```

Now when JON logs on, he will not have any roles enabled. Unfortunately, this means he can't log on at all—because it is only HR_JUNIOR that gives him the CREATE SESSION system privilege. Easily fixed:

```
SQL> grant connect to jon;
Grant succeeded.
SQL> alter user jon default role connect;
User altered.
SQL> select * from dba_role_privs where grantee='JON';
GRANTEE                        GRANTED_ROLE     ADM DEF
------------------------------ ---------------- --- ---
JON                            HR_JUNIOR        NO  NO
JON                            CONNECT          NO  YES
```

Now when JON connects, only his CONNECT role is enabled—and the current version of CONNECT is not dangerous at all. Within the application, software commands can be embedded to enable the HR_JUNIOR role. The basic command to enable a role within a session is

```
SET ROLE rolename ;
```

which can be issued by the user at any time. So no security yet. But if the role is created with this syntax:

```
CREATE ROLE rolename IDENTIFIED USING procedure_name ;
```

then the role can only be enabled by running the PL/SQL procedure nominated by *procedure_name*. This procedure can make any number of checks, such as checking that the user is working on a particular TCP/IP subnet; or that they are running a particular user process (probably not SQL*Plus); or that the time is in a certain range; and so on. Embedding calls to the enabling procedures at appropriate points in an application can switch roles on and off as required, while leaving them disabled at all times when a connection is made with an ad hoc SQL tool such as SQL*Plus.

 TIP It can be very difficult to work out why you can see certain data. You may have been granted the SELECT privilege on specific objects; you may have been granted the ALL privilege; you may have SELECT ANY; SELECT may have been granted to PUBLIC; or you may have a role to which SELECT has been granted. You may have all of these, in which case they would all have to be revoked to prevent you from seeing the data.

Exercise 6-3: Create and Grant Roles   In this exercise, you will create some roles, grant them to the users, and demonstrate their effectiveness.

1. Connect to your database with SQL*Plus as user SYSTEM.

2. Create two roles as follows:

   ```
   create role usr_role;
   create role mgr_role;
   ```

3. Grant some privileges to the roles, and grant USR_ROLE to MGR_ROLE:

   ```
   grant create session to usr_role;
   grant select on sales.t1 to usr_role;
   grant usr_role to mgr_role with admin option;
   grant all on sales.t1 to mgr_role;
   ```

4. As user SYSTEM, grant the MGR_ROLE to WEBAPP:

   ```
   grant mgr_role to WEBAPP;
   ```

5. Connect to the database as user WEBAPP:

   ```
   connect webapp/oracle;
   ```

6. Grant the USR_ROLE to ACCOUNTS, and insert a row into SALES.T1:

   ```
   grant usr_role to accounts;
   insert into sales.t1 values(sysdate);
   commit;
   ```

7. Confirm the ACCOUNTS can connect and query SALES.T1 but do nothing else. The INSERT statement that follows should fail with an ORA-01031: insufficient privileges error.

   ```
   connect accounts/oracle
   select * from sales.t1;
   insert into sales.t1 values(sysdate);
   ```

8. As user SYSTEM, adjust ACCOUNTS so that by default the user can log on but do nothing else:

   ```
   connect system/oracle
   grant connect to accounts;
   alter user accounts default role connect;
   ```

9. Demonstrate the enabling and disabling of roles. The first time SALES tries to query the SALES.T1 table, it will receive an "ORA-00942: table or view does not exist" error. Once the USR_ROLE is activated, the same query succeeds.

   ```
   connect accounts/oracle
   select * from sales.t1;
   set role usr_role;
   select * from sales.t1;
   ```

10. Use Database Control to inspect the roles. The navigation path from the database home page is: On the Server tab click the Roles link in the Security section. Click the links for the two new roles to see their privileges. This illustration shows the MGR_ROLE:

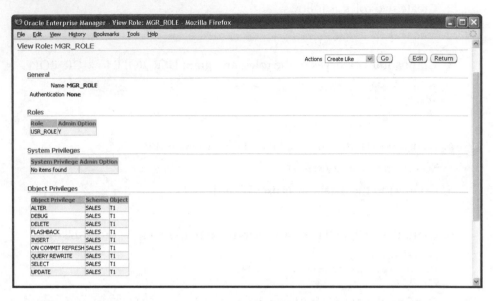

11. To see to whom a role has been granted, in the Actions drop-down box shown in the preceding illustration, select Show Grantees and click GO. This illustration shows the result for USR_ROLE:

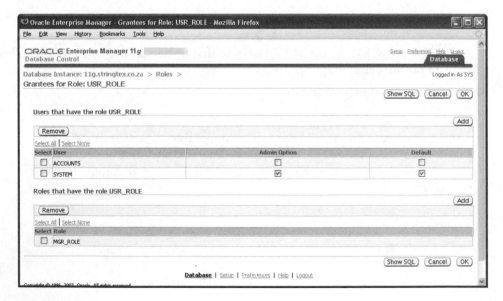

12. Obtain the same information retrieved in Steps 10 and 11 with these queries:

```
select * from dba_role_privs
where granted_role in ('USR_ROLE','MGR_ROLE');
select grantee,owner,table_name,privilege,grantable
from dba_tab_privs where grantee in ('USR_ROLE','MGR_ROLE')
union all
select grantee,to_char(null),to_char(null),privilege,admin_option
from dba_sys_privs  where grantee in ('USR_ROLE','MGR_ROLE')
order by grantee;
```

Create and Manage Profiles

A *profile* has a dual function: to enforce a password policy and to restrict the resources a session can consume. Password controls are always enforced; resource limits are only enforced if the instance parameter RESOURCE_LIMIT is on TRUE—by default, it is FALSE. Profiles are used automatically, but the default profile (applied by default to all users, including SYS and SYSTEM) does very little.

 EXAM TIP Profile password limits are always enforced; profile resource limits are enforced only if the instance parameter RESOURCE_LIMIT is TRUE.

Password Management

The limits that can be applied to passwords are

- **FAILED_LOGIN_ATTEMPTS**   Specifies the number of consecutive errors on a password before the account is locked. If the correct password is given before this limit is reached, the counter is reset to zero.
- **PASSWORD_LOCK_TIME**   The number of days to lock an account after FAILED_LOGIN_ATTEMPTS is reached.
- **PASSWORD_LIFE_TIME**   The number of days before a password expires. It may still be usable for a while after this time, depending on PASSWORD_GRACE_TIME.
- **PASSWORD_GRACE_TIME**   The number of days following the first successful login after the password has expired that prompts to change the password will be generated. The old password is still usable during this time.
- **PASSWORD_REUSE_TIME**   The number of days before a password can be reused.
- **PASSWORD_REUSE_MAX**   The number of times a password can be reused.
- **PASSWORD_VERIFY_FUNCTION**   The name of a function to run whenever a password is changed. The purpose of the function is assumed to be checking the new password for a required degree of complexity, but it can do pretty much anything you want.

Resource Limits

The limits that can be applied to resource usage (also known as *kernel* limits) are

- **SESSIONS_PER_USER**   The number of concurrent logins that can be made to the same user account. Sessions attempting to log in with the same user name when this limit is reached will be blocked.

- **CPU_PER_SESSION**   The CPU time (in centiseconds) that a session's server process is allowed to use before the session is forcibly terminated.

- **CPU_PER_CALL**   The CPU time (in centiseconds) that a session's server process is allowed to use to execute one SQL statement before the statement is forcibly terminated.

- **LOGICAL_READS_PER_SESSION**   The number of blocks that can be read by a session (irrespective of whether they were in the database buffer cache or read from disk) before the session is forcibly terminated.

- **LOGICAL_READS_PER_CALL**   The number of blocks that can be read by a single statement (irrespective of whether they were in the database buffer cache or read from disk) before the statement is forcibly terminated.

- **PRIVATE_SGA**   For sessions connected through the shared server architecture, the number of kilobytes that the session is allowed to take in the SGA for session data.

- **CONNECT_TIME**   In minutes, the maximum duration of a session before the session is forcibly terminated.

- **IDLE_TIME**   In minutes, the maximum time a session can be idle before the session is forcibly terminated.

- **COMPOSITE_LIMIT**   A weighted sum of CPU_PER_SESSION, CONNECT_TIME, LOGICAL_READS_PER_SESSION, and PRIVATE_SGA. This is an advanced facility that requires configuration beyond the scope of the OCP examination.

Resource limits will not be applied unless an instance parameter has been set:

```
alter system set resource_limit=true;
```

This defaults to FALSE.

When a session is terminated because a resource limit has been reached, if there was a transaction in progress it will be rolled back. If a statement is terminated, the work done by the statement will be rolled back, but any earlier statements will remain intact and uncommitted.

 TIP Profiles can be used to limit resource usage, but a much more sophisticated tool is the Resource Manager discussed in Chapter 21.

Creating and Assigning Profiles

Profiles can be managed through Database Control or from SQL*Plus. To see which profile is currently assigned to each user, run this query:

```
select username,profile from dba_users;
```

By default, all users (with the exception of two internal users, DBSNMP and WKSYS) will be assigned the profile called DEFAULT. Then the view that will display the profiles themselves is DBA_PROFILES:

```
select * from dba_profiles where profile='DEFAULT';
```

Or with Database Control, from the database home page take the Server tab, and then click the Users link in the Security section to see which profile each user has. Select a user and click EDIT to assign a different profile. To see how the profiles are set up, click the Profiles link in the Security section.

The DEFAULT profile has no resource limits at all, but there are some password limits:

Resource Name	Limit
FAILED_LOGIN_ATTEMPTS	10
PASSWORD_LOCK_TIME	I
PASSWORD_LIFE_TIME	180
PASSWORD_GRACE_TIME	7

These restrictions are not too strict: a password can be entered incorrectly ten consecutive times before the account is locked for one day, and a password will expire after about six months with a one-week grace period for changing it after that.

The simplest way to enable more sophisticated password management is to run the Oracle-supplied script. On Unix or Linux it is

```
$ORACLE_HOME/rdbms/admin/utlpwdmg.sql
```

On Windows it is

```
%ORACLE_HOME%\rdbms\admin\utlpwdmg.sql
```

On either platform, the script creates two functions called VERIFY_FUNCTION and VERIFY_FUNCTION_11G, and runs this command:

```
ALTER PROFILE DEFAULT LIMIT
PASSWORD_LIFE_TIME 180
PASSWORD_GRACE_TIME 7
PASSWORD_REUSE_TIME UNLIMITED
PASSWORD_REUSE_MAX UNLIMITED
FAILED_LOGIN_ATTEMPTS 10
PASSWORD_LOCK_TIME 1
PASSWORD_VERIFY_FUNCTION verify_function_11G;
```

This command will adjust the profile called DEFAULT. Any users with the DEFAULT profile (which is all users, by default) will immediately pick up the new values. Following a standard database creation, the only change will be the specification of the PASSWORD_VERIFY_FUNCTION. The function nominated, VERIFY_FUNCTION_11G, makes a set of simple tests and will reject a password change if it does not pass all of them:

- The new password must be at least eight characters long.
- The new password cannot be the same as the username (spelled backward or forward) or the name of the database, in upper- or lowercase.
- A few simple and commonly used passwords (such as "oracle") will be rejected.
- The new password must have at least one letter and at least one digit.
- The password must differ in at least three characters from the preceding password.

The script should be viewed as an example script (certainly the function is very elementary) and should be edited to suit the needs of the organization. Most organizations will need to go further than this and create a set of profiles to be applied to different users.

To create a profile with SQL*Plus, use the CREATE PROFILE command, setting whatever limits are required. Any limits not specified will be picked up from the current version of the DEFAULT profile. For example, it could be that the rules of the organization state that no users should be able to log on more than once, except for administration staff, who can log on as many concurrent sessions as they want and must change their passwords every week with one-day grace, and the programmers, who can log on twice. To do this, first adjust the DEFAULT profile:

```
alter profile default limit sessions_per_user 1;
```

Create a new profile for the DBAs, and assign it:

```
create profile dba_profile limit sessions_per_user unlimited
password_life_time 7 password_grace_time 1;
alter user system profile dba_profile;
```

Create a profile for the programmers, and assign it:

```
create profile programmers_profile limit sessions_per_user 2;
alter user jon profile programmers_profile;
alter user sue profile programmers_profile;
```

To let the resource limit take effect, adjust the instance parameter:

```
alter system set resource_limit=true;
```

Assuming that the instance is using an SPFILE, this change will be propagated to the parameter file and will therefore be permanent.

A profile cannot be dropped if it has been assigned to users. They must be altered to a different profile first. Once done, drop the profile with

```
DROP PROFILE profile_name ;
```

Alternatively, use this syntax:

```
DROP PROFILE profile_name CASCADE ;
```

which will automatically reassign all users with *profile_name* back to the DEFAULT profile.

Exercise 6-4: Create and Use Profiles   In this exercise, create, assign, and test a profile that will force some password control.

1. Connect to your database with SQL*Plus as user system.

2. Create a profile that will lock accounts after two wrong passwords:

   ```
   create profile two_wrong limit failed_login_attempts 2;
   ```

3. Assign this new profile to SALES:

   ```
   alter user sales profile two wrong;
   ```

4. Deliberately enter the wrong password for SALES a few times. You will get an "ORA-28000: the account is locked" message after the third failed attempt.

   ```
   connect sales/wrongpassword
   ```

5. As user SYSTEM, unlock the SALES account:

   ```
   alter user sales account unlock;
   ```

6. Check that SALES can now connect:

   ```
   connect sales/oracle
   ```

   The next illustration shows the sequence of events.

7. Tidy up by dropping the profile, the roles, and the users. Note the use of CASCADE when dropping the profile to remove it from SALES, and on the DROP USER command to drop their table as well. Roles can be dropped even if they are assigned to users. The privileges granted on the table will be revoked as the table is dropped.

```
connect system/oracle
drop profile two_wrong cascade;
drop role usr_role;
drop role mgr_role;
drop user sales cascade;
drop user accounts;
drop user webapp;
```

Database Security and Principle of Least Privilege

The safest principle to follow when determining access to computer systems is that of *least privilege*: no one should have access to anything beyond the absolute minimum needed to perform their work, and anything not specifically allowed is forbidden. The Oracle database conforms to this, in that by default no one can do anything at all, with the exception of the two users SYS and SYSTEM. No other users can even connect—not even those created by the standard database creation routines.

In addition to the use of password profiles, there are best practices that should be followed to assist with implementing the least-privilege principle, particularly regarding privileges granted to the PUBLIC account and certain instance parameters.

Public Privileges

The PUBLIC role is implicitly granted to every user. Any privileges granted to PUBLIC have, in effect, been granted to everyone who can connect to the database; every account you create will have access to these privileges. By default, PUBLIC has a large number of privileges. In particular, this role has execute permission on a number of PL/SQL utility packages, as shown in Figure 6-9.

You should always consider revoking the execution privileges on the UTL packages, but remember that application software may assume that the privilege is there. Execution privilege may be revoked as follows:

```
SQL> revoke execute on utl_file from public;
```

Some of the more dangerous packages listed in Figure 6-9 are

- **UTL_FILE** Allows users to read and write any file and directory that is accessible to the operating system Oracle owner. This includes all the database files, and the ORACLE_HOME directory. On Windows systems, this is particularly dangerous, as many Windows databases run with Administrator privileges. The package is to a certain extent controlled by the UTL_FILE_DIR instance parameter, discussed in the next section.

```
C:\WINDOWS\system32\cmd.exe - sqlplus / as sysdba                    _ □ ×
SQL>
SQL> select count(*) from dba_tab_privs where grantee='PUBLIC';

  COUNT(*)
----------
     27477

SQL> select table_name from dba_tab_privs where grantee='PUBLIC'
  2  and privilege='EXECUTE' and table_name like 'UTL%';

TABLE_NAME
--------------------------------
UTL_TCP
UTL_HTTP
UTL_FILE
UTL_INADDR
UTL_SMTP
UTL_URL
UTL_ENCODE
UTL_GDK
UTL_COMPRESS
```

Figure 6-9   Privileges granted to PUBLIC

- **UTL_TCP**   Allows users to open TCP ports on the server machine for connections to any accessible address on the network. The interface provided in the package only allows connections to be initiated by the PL/SQL program; it does not allow the PL/SQL program to accept connections initiated outside the program. Nonetheless, it does allow malicious users to use your database as the starting point for launching attacks on other systems, or for transmitting data to unauthorized recipients.

- **UTL_SMTP**   Written using UTL_TCP calls, this package lets users send mail messages. It is restricted by the UTL_SMTP_SERVER instance parameter, which specifies the address of the outgoing mail server, but even so you probably do not want your database to be used for exchange of mail messages without your knowledge.

- **UTL_HTTP**   Allows users to send HTTP messages and receive responses—in effect, converting your database into a web browser. This package also makes use of UTL_TCP subprograms.

Always remember that, by default, these packages are available to absolutely anyone who has a logon to your database, and furthermore that your database may have a number of well-known accounts with well-known passwords.

 EXAM TIP PUBLIC is a role that is granted to everyone—but when connecting to the instance using the AS SYSOPER syntax, you will appear to be connected to an account PUBLIC.

Security-Critical Instance Parameters

Some parameters are vital to consider for securing the database. The defaults are usually fine, but in some circumstances (for which there should always be a good business case), you may need to change them. All of the parameters described here are static: you must restart the instance for a change to take effect. This is intended to provide extra security, as it reduces the likelihood that they can be changed temporarily to an inappropriate setting without the DBA being aware of it.

UTL_FILE_DIR

The UTL_FILE_DIR instance parameter defaults to NULL and is therefore not a security problem. But if you need to set it, take care. This parameter gives PL/SQL access to the file system of the server machine, through the UTL_FILE supplied package. The package has procedures to open a file (either a new file or an existing one) and read from and write to it. The only limitation is that the directories listed must be accessible to the Oracle owner.

The difficulty with this parameter is that, being set at the instance level, it offers no way to allow some users access to some directories and other users access to other directories. All users with execute permission on the UTL_FILE package have access to all the directories listed in the UTL_FILE_DIR parameter.

The parameter takes a comma-separated list of directories and is static. To set it, follow the syntax in this example, which gives access to two directories, and restart the instance:

```
SQL> alter system set utl_file_dir='/oracle/tmp','/oracle/interface' scope=spfile;
```

 TIP The UTL_FILE_DIR parameter can include wildcards. Never set it to '*', because that will allow all users access to everything that the database owner can see, including the ORACLE_HOME and all the database files.

REMOTE_OS_AUTHENT and OS_AUTHENT_PREFIX

The REMOTE_OS_AUTHENT instance parameter defaults to FALSE. This controls whether a user can connect to the database from a remote computer without the need to supply a password. The reasons for wanting to do this have largely disappeared with modern computer systems, but the capability is still there.

In the days before all users had intelligent terminals, such as PCs, it was customary for users to log on directly to the database server machine and therefore to be authenticated by the server's operating system. They would then launch their user process on the server machine and connect to the database. In order to avoid the necessity for users to provide usernames and passwords twice (once for the operating system logon, and again for the database logon), it was common to create the Oracle users with this syntax:

```
SQL> create user jon identified externally;
```

This delegates responsibility for authentication to the server's operating system. Any person logged on to the server machine as operating system user "jon" will be able to connect to the database without the need for any further authentication:

```
$ sqlplus /
Connected to:
Oracle Database 11g Enterprise Edition Release 11.1.0.6.0 - Production
```

```
SQL> show user;
USER is "JON"
SQL>
```

This is secure, as long as your server's operating system is secure. As networking became more widespread, it became common to separate the user process workload from the server process workload by having users log on to a different machine dedicated to running user processes, which would connect to the server over Oracle Net (or SQL*Net, as it was then known). Since the user no longer logs on to the server's operating system, external authentication can't be used—unless you use the REMOTE_OS_AUTHENT parameter. Setting this to TRUE means that user JON can connect without a password from any machine where he is logged on as operating system user "jon". An example of the syntax is

```
sqlplus connect /@orcl11g
```

This will log the user on to the database identified in the connect string ORCL11G, passing through his operating system username on his local machine as the database username. This is only secure if you trust the operating systems of all machines connected to the network. An obvious danger is PCs: it is common for users to have administration rights on their PCs, and they can therefore create user accounts that match any Oracle account name.

 TIP It is generally considered bad practice to enable remote operating system authentication.

The OS_AUTHENT_PREFIX instance parameter is related to external authentication, either local or remote. It specifies a prefix that must be applied to the operating system username before it can be mapped onto an Oracle username. The default is "OPS$". In the preceding example, it is assumed that this parameter has been cleared, with

```
SQL> alter system set os_authent_prefix='' scope=spfile;
```

Otherwise, the Oracle username would have had to be OPS$JON.

O7_DICTIONARY_ACCESSIBILITY

The O7_DICTIONARY_ACCESSIBILITY instance parameter controls the effect of granting object privileges with the ANY keyword. It defaults to FALSE. You can give user JON permission to see any table in the database with

```
SQL> grant select any table to jon;
```

but do you want him to be able to see the data dictionary tables as well as user tables? Probably not—some of them contain sensitive data, such as unencrypted passwords or source code that should be protected.

O7_DICTIONARY_ACCESSIBILITY defaults to false, meaning that the ANY privileges exclude objects owned by SYS, thus protecting the data dictionary; JON can see all the user data, but not objects owned by SYS. If you change the parameter to TRUE, then ANY really does mean ANY—and JON will be able to see the data dictionary as well as all user data.

It is possible that some older application software may assume that the ANY privileges include the data dictionary, as was always the case with release 7 of the Oracle database (hence the name of the parameter). If so, you have no choice but to change the parameter to TRUE until the software is patched up to current standards.

 TIP Data dictionary accessibility is sometimes a problem for application installation routines. You may have to set O7_DICTIONARY_ACCESSIBILITY to TRUE while installing a product, and then put it back on default when the installation is finished.

If you have users who really do need access to the data dictionary, rather than setting O7_DICTIONARY_ACCESSIBILITY to true, consider granting them the SELECT ANY DICTIONARY privilege. This will let them see the data dictionary and dynamic performance views, but they will not be able to see any user data—unless you have specifically granted them permission to do so. This might apply, for example, to the staff of an external company you use for database administration support: they need access to all the data dictionary information, but they have no need to view your application data.

REMOTE_LOGIN_PASSWORDFILE

The remote REMOTE_LOGIN_PASSWORDFILE instance parameter controls whether it is possible to connect to the instance as a user with the SYSDBA or SYSOPER privilege over the network. With this parameter on its default of NONE, the only way to get a SYSDBA connection is to log on to the operating system of the server machine as a member of the operating system group that owns the Oracle software. This is absolutely secure—as long as your server operating system is secure, which it should be.

Setting this parameter to either EXCLUSIVE or SHARED gives users another way in: even if they are not logged on to the server as a member of the Oracle owning group, or even if they are coming in across the network, they can still connect as SYSDBA if they know the appropriate password. The passwords are embedded, in encrypted form, in an operating system file in the Oracle home directory: $ORACLE_ HOME/dbs on Unix, or %ORACLE_HOME%\database on Windows. A setting of SHARED means that all instances running of the same Oracle home directory will share a common password file. This will have just one password within it for the SYS user that is common to all the instances. EXCLUSIVE means that the instance will look for a file whose name includes the instance name: PWDinstance_name.ora on Windows, orapwinstance_name on Unix, where instance_name is the instance name. This file will have instance-specific passwords.

Create the password file by running the `orapwd` utility from an operating system prompt. This will create the file and embed within it a password for the SYS user. Subsequently, you can add other users' passwords to the file, thus allowing them to connect as SYSDBA or SYSOPER as well. Review the scripts in Chapter 2 for an example of the syntax for creating a password file. To add another user to the file, grant them either the SYSDBA or SYSOPER privilege, as in Figure 6-10. The V$PWFILE_USERS view shows you which users have their passwords entered in the password file, and whether they have the SYSOPER privilege, the SYSDBA privilege, or both.

Note that when connecting as SYSDBA, even though you use a username and password, you end up connected as user SYS; when connecting as SYSOPER, you are in fact connected as the PUBLIC user.

Enabling a password file does not improve security; it weakens it, by giving users another way of obtaining a privileged connection (in addition to local operating system authentication, which is always available). It is, however, standard practice to enable it, because without a password file it may be very difficult to manage the database remotely.

TIP Some computer auditors do not understand operating system and password file authentication. They may even state that you must create a password file, to improve security. Just do as they say—it is easier than arguing.

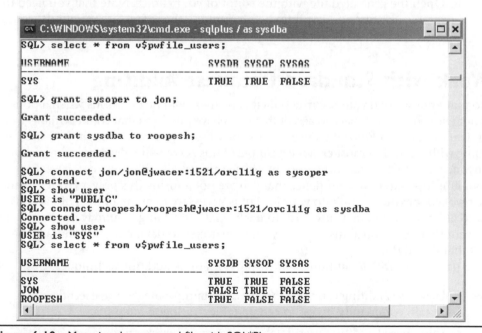

Figure 6-10   Managing the password file with SQL*Plus

Exercise 6-5: Remove Some Potentially Dangerous Privileges In this exercise, you will generate a script that could be used (possibly after edits, depending on local requirements) to remove some of the more dangerous privileges from PUBLIC. Use SQL*Plus.

1. Connect to your database as user SYSTEM.

2. Adjust SQL*Plus to remove extraneous characters from its output:

```
set heading off
set pagesize 0
set feedback off
```

3. Start spooling output to a file in a suitable directory. Following are examples for Unix and Windows:

```
spool $HOME/oracle/scripts/clear_public_privs.sql
spool c:\oracle\scripts\clear_public_privs.sql
```

4. Generate the SQL command file by running this statement:

```
select 'revoke execute on '||table_name||' from public;'
from dba_tab_privs where table_name like 'UTL_%';
```

5. Stop the spooling of output:

```
spool off
```

6. Open the generated file with the editor of your choice. Note that you need to remove the first and last lines before running the script. Site variations would determine which (if any) privileges could not actually be revoked.

Work with Standard Database Auditing

No matter how good your security policies are, there will be occasions when a policy is not enough. You will have to accept that users have privileges that could be dangerous. All you can do is monitor their use of those privileges, and track what they are actually doing with them. The most extreme example of this is you—the database administrator. Anyone with the SYSDBA privilege can do anything at all within the database. For your employers to have confidence that you are not abusing this power (which cannot be revoked, or you couldn't do your job), it is necessary to audit all SYSDBA activity. For regular users, you may also wish to track what they doing. You may not be able to prevent them from breaking company rules on access to data, but you can track the fact that they did it.

Apart from SYSDBA auditing, Oracle provides three auditing techniques:

- Database auditing can track the use of certain privileges, the execution of certain commands, access to certain tables, or logon attempts.

- Value-based auditing uses database triggers. Whenever a row is inserted, updated, or deleted, a block of PL/SQL code will run that can (among other things) record complete details of the event.

- Fine-grained auditing allows tracking access to tables according to which rows (or which columns of the rows) were accessed. It is much more precise than either database auditing or value-based auditing, and it can limit the number of audit records generated to only those of interest.

TIP Auditing of any type increases the amount of work that the database must do. In order to limit this workload, you should focus your auditing closely and not track events of minimal significance.

Auditing SYSDBA Activity

If the instance parameter AUDIT_SYS_OPERATIONS is set to TRUE (the default is FALSE), then every statement issued by a user connected AS SYSDBA or AS SYSOPER is written out to the operating system's audit trail. This contains a complete record of all work done by the DBA. Clearly, the audit trail must be protected; if it were possible for the DBA to delete the audit records, there would be no point in creating them. This brings up the question of *separation of duties.* Your system needs to be configured in such a way that the DBA has no access to the audit records that track their activity; they should only be accessible to the computer's system administrator. If the DBA is also the system administrator, then the auditing is useless. For this reason, a decent computer auditor will always state that the DBA must not have the Unix "root" password (or the Windows "Administrator" password).

The destination of the SYS audit records is platform specific. On Windows, it is the Windows Application log, on Unix it is controlled by the AUDIT_FILE_DEST parameter. This parameter should point to a directory on which the Oracle owner has write permission (so that the audit records can be written by the instance) but that the Unix ID used by the DBA does not, so that they cannot adjust the audit records by hand.

Database Auditing

Before setting up database auditing, the AUDIT_TRAIL instance parameter must be set. This has six possible values:

- **NONE (or FALSE)**   Database auditing is disabled, no matter what auditing you attempt to configure.
- **OS**   Audit records will be written to the operating system's audit trail—the Application Log on Windows, or the AUDIT_FILE_DEST directory on Unix.
- **DB**   The audit records are written to a data dictionary table, SYS.AUD$. There are views that let you see the contents of this table.
- **DB_EXTENDED**   As DB, but including the SQL statements with bind variables that generated the audit records.
- **XML**   As OS, but formatted with XML tags.
- **XML_EXTENDED**   As XML, but with the SQL statements and bind variables.

Having set the AUDIT_TRAIL parameter, you can use database auditing to capture login attempts, use of system and object privileges, and execution of SQL commands. Furthermore, you can specify whether to audit these events when they succeeded, when they failed because of insufficient privileges, or both. Auditing commands that did not succeed can be particularly valuable: any records produced will tell you that users are attempting to break their access rights.

Database auditing is configured using the AUDIT command.

Use of privileges can be audited with, for example,

```
SQL> audit create any trigger;
SQL> audit select any table by session;
```

Your programmers will have been granted the CREATE ANY TRIGGER privilege because they will be creating triggers on other schemas' tables as part of their work, but it is a dangerous privilege that could be used maliciously. So you certainly need to know when they use it, in order that you can demand to see the code. Similarly, some staff will need the SELECT ANY TABLE and UPDATE ANY TABLE privileges in order to sort out problems with transactions that have gone wrong, but whenever they use these privileges, a record must be kept so that they will be deterred from accessing data unless they have a legitimate reason.

By default, auditing will generate one audit record for every session that violates an audit condition, irrespective of the number of times it violates the condition. This is equivalent to appending BY SESSION to the AUDIT command. Appending the keywords BY ACCESS to the AUDIT command will generate one record for every violation.

 TIP The default BY SESSION clause will often not be what you want, but it does reduce the volume of audit records produced to a more manageable number.

Auditing can also be oriented toward objects:

```
SQL> audit insert on ar.hz_parties whenever successful;
SQL> audit all on ar.ra_interface_lines_all;
```

The first of these commands will generate audit records if a session inserts a row into the named table. The WHENEVER SUCCESSFUL keywords restrict audit records to those where the operation succeeded; the alternative syntax is WHENEVER NOT SUCCESSFUL. By default, all operations (successful or not) are audited. The second example will audit every session that executes and SELECT, DML, or DDL statements against the named table.

Database Control has a graphical interface to the auditing system. Figure 6-11 shows the interface after executing the two preceding commands. Note that the window has tabs for displaying, adding, and removing auditing of privileges, objects, and statements. In the figure, you can see the auditing of objects owned by user AR.

In the Configuration section of the window shown in Figure 6-11, there are links for setting the audit parameter previously described.

Figure 6-11 Managing standard auditing with Database Control

Logons are audited with AUDIT SESSION. For example,

```
SQL> audit session whenever not successful;
```

This is equivalent to auditing the use of the CREATE SESSION privilege. Session
auditing records each connection to the database. The NOT SUCCESFUL keywords
restrict the output to only failed attempts. This can be particularly useful: recording
failures may indicate if attempts are being made to break into the database.

If auditing is to the operating system (because the AUDIT_TRAIL instance
parameter is set to OS or XML), then view the files created in the operating system
audit trail to see the results of the audits with an appropriate editor. If auditing is
directed to the database (AUDIT_TRAIL=DB or DB_EXTENDED), then the audit
records are written to a table in the data dictionary: the SYS.AUD$ table. It is possible
to query this directly, but usually you will go through views. The critical view is the
DBA_AUDIT_TRAIL view. This will show all audit trail entries, no matter whether the
audited event was use of a privilege, execution of a statement, or access to an object.
Of necessity, the view is very generic, and not all columns (41 in all) will be populated
for each audit trail entry. Table 6-1 lists the more commonly used columns.

Column	Description
OS_USERNAME	Operating system name of the user performing the action
USERNAME	Oracle username of the user performing the action
USERHOST	The name of the machine running the user process
TIMESTAMP	When the audited event occurred
OWNER, OBJ_NAME	Schema and name of the object affected
ACTION_NAME	The action audited
PRIV_USED	System privilege used (if any)
SQL_TEXT	The statement executed

Table 6-1   Common Columns in the DBA_AUDIT_TRAIL View

The other audit views (DBA_AUDIT_OBJECT, DBA_AUDIT_STATEMENT, and DBA_AUDIT_SESSION) each show a subset of the DBA_AUDIT_TRAIL view, only displaying certain audit records and the columns relevant to them.

Value-Based Auditing with Triggers

The database auditing just described can catch the fact that a command was executed against a table, but not necessarily the rows that were affected. For example, issuing AUDIT INSERT ON HR.EMPLOYEES will cause an audit record to be generated whenever a row is inserted into the named table, but the record will not include the actual values of the row that was inserted. On occasion, you may want to capture these. This can be done by using database triggers.

A *database trigger* is a block of PL/SQL code that will run automatically whenever an INSERT, UPDATE, or DELETE is executed against a table. A trigger can do almost anything—in particular, it can write out rows to other tables. These rows will be part of the transaction that caused the trigger to execute, and they will be committed when the rest of the transaction is committed. There is no way that a user can prevent the trigger from firing: if you update a table with an update trigger defined, that trigger will execute.

Consider this trigger creation statement:

```
SQL> CREATE OR REPLACE TRIGGER system.creditrating_audit
  2  AFTER UPDATE OF creditrating
  3  ON store.customers
  4  REFERENCING NEW AS NEW OLD AS OLD
  5  FOR EACH ROW
  6  BEGIN
  7  IF :old.creditrating != :new.creditrating THEN
  8  INSERT INTO system.creditrating_audit
  9  VALUES (sys_context('userenv','os_user'),
 10  sys_context('userenv','ip_address'),
 11  :new.customer_id ||' credit rating changed from
 12  '||:old.creditrating||
 13  ' to '||:new.creditrating);
 14  END IF;
 15  END;
 16  /
```

The first line names the trigger, which is in the SYSTEM schema. Lines 2 and 3 specify the rule that determines when the trigger will execute: every time the CREDITRATING column of a row in STORE's CUSTOMERS table is updated. There could be separate triggers defined to manage inserts and deletes, or actions on other columns. Line 7 supplies a condition: if the CREDITRATING column were not actually changed, then the trigger will exit without doing anything. But if the CREDITRATING column were updated, then a row is inserted into another table designed for trapping audit events. Lines 9 and 10 use the SYS_CONTEXT function to record the user's operating system user name and the IP address of the terminal in use when the update is executed. Lines 11, 12, and 13 record the customer number of the row updated, and the old and new values of the CREDITRATING column. Database auditing as described in the preceding section could have captured all this information, except for the actual values: which customer was updated, and what the data change actually was.

 TIP   Auditing through triggers is a slower process than database auditing, but it does give you more information and let you implement sophisticated business rules.

Fine-Grained Auditing (FGA)

Database auditing can record all statement accesses to a table, whether SELECT or for DML. But it cannot distinguish between rows, even though it might well be that only some rows contain sensitive information. Using database auditing, you may have to sift through a vast number of audit records to find the few that have significance. Fine-grained auditing, or FGA, can be configured to generate audit records only when certain rows are accessed, or when certain columns of certain rows are accessed. It can also run a block of PL/SQL code when the audit condition is breached.

FGA is configured with the package DBMS_FGA. To create an FGA audit policy, use the ADD_POLICY procedure, which takes these arguments:

Argument	Description
OBJECT_SCHEMA	The name of the user who owns the object to be audited. This defaults to the user who is creating the policy.
OBJECT_NAME	The name of the table to be audited.
POLICY_NAME	Every FGA policy created must be given a unique name.
AUDIT_CONDITION	An expression to determine which rows will generate an audit record. If left NULL, access to any row is audited.
AUDIT_COLUMN	A list of columns to be audited. If left NULL, then access to any column is audited.
HANDLER_SCHEMA	The username that owns the procedure to run when the audit condition is met. The default is the user who is creating the policy.
HANDLER_MODULE	A PL/SQL procedure to execute when the audit condition is met.
ENABLE	By default, this is TRUE: the policy will be active and can be disabled with the DISABLE_POLICY procedure. If FALSE, then the ENABLE_POLICY procedure must be used to activate the policy.

Argument	Description
STATEMENT_TYPES	One or more of SELECT, INSERT, UPDATE, or DELETE to define which statement types should be audited. Default is SELECT only.
AUDIT_TRAIL	Controls whether to write out the actual SQL statement and its bind variables to the FGA audit trail. The default is to do so.
AUDIT_COLUMN_OPTS	Determines whether to audit if a statement addresses any or all of the columns listed in the AUDIT_COLUMNS argument. Options are DBMS_FGA.ANY_COLUMNS, the default, or DBMS_FGA_ALL_COLUMNS.

The other DBMS_FGA procedures are to enable, disable, or drop FGA policies. To see the results of fine-grained auditing, query the DBA_FGA_AUDIT_TRAIL view:

```
SQL> describe dba_fga_audit_trail;
 Name                             Null?    Type
 -------------------------------- -------- ---------------------------
 SESSION_ID                       NOT NULL NUMBER
 TIMESTAMP                                 DATE
 DB_USER                                   VARCHAR2(30)
 OS_USER                                   VARCHAR2(255)
 USERHOST                                  VARCHAR2(128)
 CLIENT_ID                                 VARCHAR2(64)
 EXT_NAME                                  VARCHAR2(4000)
 OBJECT_SCHEMA                             VARCHAR2(30)
 OBJECT_NAME                               VARCHAR2(128)
 POLICY_NAME                               VARCHAR2(30)
 SCN                                       NUMBER
 SQL_TEXT                                  NVARCHAR2(2000)
 SQL_BIND                                  NVARCHAR2(2000)
 COMMENT$TEXT                              VARCHAR2(4000)
 STATEMENT_TYPE                            VARCHAR2(7)
 EXTENDED_TIMESTAMP                        TIMESTAMP(6) WITH TIME ZONE
 PROXY_SESSIONID                           NUMBER
 GLOBAL_UID                                VARCHAR2(32)
 INSTANCE_NUMBER                           NUMBER
 OS_PROCESS                                VARCHAR2(16)
 TRANSACTIONID                             RAW(8)
 STATEMENTID                               NUMBER
 ENTRYID                                   NUMBER
```

This procedure call will create a policy POL1 that will record all SELECT statements that read the SALARY column of the HR.EMPLOYEES table, if at least one of the rows retrieved is in department 80:

```
SQL>  execute dbms_fga.add_policy(-
> object_schema=>'HR',-
> object_name=>'EMPLOYEES',-
> policy_name=>'POL1',-
> audit_condition=>'department_id=80',-
> audit_column=>'SALARY');
```

In addition to the DBA_AUDIT_TRAIL view, which shows the results of standard database auditing, and the DBA_FGA_AUDIT_TRAIL view, which shows the results of fine-grained auditing, the DBA_COMMON_AUDIT_TRAIL view shows audit events from both types of auditing.

 EXAM TIP Which views show the audit trail? DBA_AUDIT_TRIAL is used for standard database auditing; DBA_FGA_AUDIT_TRAIL is used for fine-grained auditing; while DBA_COMMON_AUDIT_TRAIL is used for both. To see the results of auditing with triggers, you must create your own views that address your own tables.

Exercise 6-6: Use Standard Database Auditing In this exercise you will enable standard database auditing and see the results, using either Database Control or SQL*Plus. If you use Database Control, be sure to click the SHOW SQL button whenever possible to see the SQL statements being generated.

1. Connect to your database as user SYSTEM and create a user and a table to be used for the exercise:

```
create user auditor identified by oracle;
create table system.audi as select * from all_users;
grant create session, select any table to auditor;
grant select on audi to auditor;
```

2. Enable auditing of AUDITOR's use of SELECT ANY PRIVILEGE, and of all accesses to the table AUDI. With SQL*Plus:

```
audit select any table by access;
audit all on system.audi by access;
```

With Database Control, this can be done from the Audit Settings window.

3. Connect to the database as user SYS. This is necessary, as this step involves restarting the instance. Set the audit trail destination to DB and enable auditing of privileged users, and bounce the instance. Using SQL*Plus:

```
alter system set audit_trail='DB_EXTENDED' scope=spfile;
alter system set audit_sys_operations=true scope =spfile;
startup force;
```

Using Database Control, a possible navigation path from the database home page is to take the Server tab, and then the Audit Settings link in the Security section. Clicking the link labeled Audit Trail in the Configuration section will take you to a window where you can modify the parameter settings in the spfile. Alternatively, go directly to the Initialization Parameters window from the Server tab by taking the Initialization Parameters link in the Database Configuration section.

Set the two parameters in the spfile, and then from the database home page shut down and restart the database.

4. While connected as SYS, all statements will be audited. Run this statement:

```
select count(*) from system.audi;
```

5. If using Linux or Unix, identify the location of the system audit trail by querying the parameter AUDIT_FILE_DEST. This will be used for the auditing of SYS operations, irrespective of the setting for AUDIT_DEST. With SQL*Plus:

```
select value from v$parameter where name='audit_file_dest';
```

Using an operating system utility, navigate to this directory and open the most recently created file.

If using Microsoft Windows, open the Application Log in the Event Viewer. Either way, you will see the SELECT statement that you executed as SYS, with details of the operating system user and hostname.

6. Connect to the database as AUDITOR, and run these queries:

```
select count(*)from system.audi;
select count(*) from system.product_user_profile;
```

7. As user SYSTEM, run this query to see the audit events:

```
select sql_text,priv_used,action_name from dba_audit_trail
where username='AUDITOR';
```

Note that the lowest possible privilege is used: access to the AUDI table was through the SELECT object privilege, not through the much more powerful (SELECT ANY TABLE) system privilege that was needed to get to PRODUCT_USER_PROFILE.

8. Tidy up:

```
drop user auditor;
drop table system.audi;
```

Two-Minute Drill

Create and Manage Database User Accounts

- Users connect to a user account, which is coupled with a schema.
- All users must be authenticated before they can connect.
- A user must have a quota on a tablespace before they create any objects.
- A user who owns objects cannot be dropped, unless the CASCADE keyword is used.

Grant and Revoke Privileges

- By default, a user can do nothing. You can't even log on.
- Direct privileges are always enabled.
- A revocation of a system privilege does not cascade; a revocation of an object privilege does.

Create and Manage Roles

- Roles are not schema objects.
- Roles can contain both system and object privileges, and other roles.
- A role can be enabled or disabled for a session.

Create and Manage Profiles

- Profiles can manage passwords and resource limits.
- Password limits are always enforced; resource limits are dependent on an instance parameter.
- Every user is associated with a profile, which by default is the DEFAULT profile.

Database Security and Principle of Least Privilege

- Everything not specifically permitted should be forbidden.
- The database administrator and the system administrator should not be the same person.
- Privileges granted to the PUBLIC role must be monitored.
- Security-critical instance parameters must be monitored and cannot be changed without restarting the instance.

Work with Standard Database Auditing

- Database auditing can be oriented toward privileges, commands, or objects.
- Audit records can be directed toward a database table or an operating system file.
- Database audit records are stored in the SYS.AUD$ data dictionary table.
- Fine-grained auditing can be directed toward particular rows and columns.
- Auditing can also be implemented with database triggers.

Self Test

1. How can you permit users to connect without requiring them to authenticate themselves? (Choose the best answer.)

    A. Grant CREATE SESSION to PUBLIC.

    B. Create a user such as this, without a password:

```
CREATE USER ANON IDENTIFIED BY '';
```

    C. Create a profile that disables password authentication and assign it to the users.

    D. You cannot do this because all users must be authenticated.

2. You create a user with this statement:

```
create user jon identified by oracle default tablespace example;
```

What more must be done before he can create a table in the EXAMPLE tablespace? (Choose all correct answers.)

A. Nothing more is necessary.

B. Give him a quota on EXAMPLE.

C. Grant him the CREATE TABLE privilege.

D. Grant him the CREATE SESSION privilege.

E. Grant him the MANAGE TABLESPACE privilege.

3. If a user owns tables in a tablespace, what will be the effect of attempting to reduce their quota on the tablespace to zero? (Choose the best answer.)

A. The tables will survive, but INSERTs will fail.

B. The tables will survive but cannot get bigger.

C. The attempt will fail unless the tables are dropped first.

D. The tables will be dropped automatically if the CASCADE keyword is used.

4. If you create a user without specifying a temporary tablespace, what temporary tablespace will be assigned? (Choose the best answer.)

A. You must specify a temporary tablespace

B. SYSTEM

C. TEMP

D. The database default temporary tablespace

E. The user will not have a temporary tablespace

5. You issue these commands:

```
a.  grant select on hr.regions to jon;
b.  grant all on hr.regions to jon;
c.  grant dba to jon;
d.  grant select on hr.regions to public;
```

Which grants could be revoked to prevent JON from seeing the contents of HR.REGIONS? (Choose all correct answers.)

A. a, b, c, and d

B. a, c, and d

C. b, c, and d

D. c and d

E. a, b, and c

6. Which of these statements about system privileges are correct? (Choose all correct answers.)

A. Only the SYS and SYSTEM users can grant system privileges.

    B. If a system privilege is revoked from you, it will also be revoked from all users to whom you granted it.

    C. If a system privilege is revoked from you, it will not be revoked from all users to whom you granted it.

    D. CREATE TABLE is a system privilege.

    E. CREATE ANY TABLE is a system privilege.

7. Study this script (line numbers have been added):

```
1     create role hr_role identified by pass;
2     grant create table to hr_role;
3     grant select table to hr_role;
4     grant connect to hr_role;
```

    Which line will cause an error? (Choose the best answer.)

    A. Line 1, because only users, not roles, have passwords.

    B. Line 2, because only users, not roles, can create and own tables.

    C. Line 3, because SELECT TABLE is not a privilege.

    D. Line 4, because a role cannot have a system privilege in addition to table privileges.

8. Which of these statements is incorrect regarding roles? (Choose the best answer.)

    A. You can grant object privileges and system privileges and roles to a role.

    B. A role cannot have the same name as a table.

    C. A role cannot have the same name as a user.

    D. Roles can be enabled or disabled within a session.

9. You have created a profile with LIMIT SESSIONS_PER_USER 1 and granted it to a user, but you find that they are still able to log on several times concurrently. Why could this be? (Choose the best answer.)

    A. The user has been granted CREATE SESSION more than once.

    B. The user has been granted the DBA role.

    C. The RESOURCE_LIMIT parameter has not been set.

    D. The RESOURCE_MANAGER_PLAN parameter has not been set.

10. Which of these can be controlled by a password profile? (Choose all correct answers.)

    A. Two or more users choosing the same password

    B. Preventing the reuse of a password by the same user

    C. Forcing a user to change password

    D. Enabling or disabling password file authentication

11. Under what circumstances should you set the REMOTE_LOGIN_PASSWORDFILE instance parameter to EXCLUSIVE? (Choose two correct answers.)

    A. You need a SYSDBA connection when you are logged on to a machine other than the server.

    B. You want to disable operating system authentication.

    C. You want to add users to the password file.

    D. You want to prevent other users from being added to the password file.

12. If you execute this command as user SYSTEM, it will fail. Why? (Choose the best answer.)

    ```
    alter system set audit_sys_operations=false;
    ```

    A. The parameter can only be changed by the SYS user.

    B. The parameter can only be adjusted in NOMOUNT or MOUNT mode, and SYSTEM can only connect when the database is OPEN.

    C. The principle of "separation of duties" means that only the system administrator, not the database administrator, can change this parameter.

    D. The parameter is a static parameter.

13. What conditions must hold before a database session can create a file stored by the operating system of the server? (Choose three correct answers.)

    A. The session must be connected to a database account with execute permission on the package UTL_FILE.

    B. The session must be connected to a database account with execute permission on the package DBMS_OUTPUT.

    C. The parameter UTL_FILE_DIR must have been set.

    D. The parameter DB_WRITER_PROCESSES must be set to greater than zero.

    E. The parameter DB_CREATE_FILE_DEST must be set.

    F. The operating system account under which the Oracle instance is running must have write permission on the directory that will store the file.

14. If you want a block of PL/SQL code to run whenever certain data is accessed with a SELECT statement, what auditing technique could you use? (Choose the best answer.)

    A. Database auditing

    B. Fine-grained auditing

    C. Database triggers

    D. You cannot do this

15. What is necessary to audit actions done by a user connected with the SYSDBA privilege? (Choose the best answer.)

    A. Set the AUDIT_SYS_OPERATIONS instance parameter to TRUE.

    B. Use database auditing to audit use of the SYSDBA privilege.

C. Set the REMOTE_LOGIN_PASSWORDFILE instance parameter to NONE, so that SYSDBA connections can only be made with operating system authentication. Then set the AUDIT_TRIAL parameter to OS, and make sure that the DBA does not have access to it.

D. This is not possible: any user with SYSDBA privilege can always bypass the auditing mechanisms.

16. Where can you see the results of standard database auditing? (Choose all correct answers.)

A. In the DBA_AUDIT_TRAIL view, if the AUDIT_TRAIL parameter is set to DB

B. In the DBA_COMMON_AUDIT_TRAIL view, if the AUDIT_TRAIL parameter is set to DB

C. In the operating system audit trail, if the AUDIT_TRAIL parameter is set to OS

D. In the operating system audit trail, if the AUDIT_TRAIL parameter is set to XML

17. You issue this statement:

```
audit select on hr.emp by access;
```

but when you issue the command:

```
select * from hr.emp where employee_id=0;
```

no audit record is generated. Why might this be? (Choose the best answer.)

A. You are connected as SYS, and the parameter AUDIT_SYS_OPERATIONS is set to FALSE.

B. The AUDIT_TRAIL parameter is set to NONE.

C. The statement did not access any rows; there is no row with EMPLOYEE_ID equal to zero.

D. The instance must be restarted before any change to auditing comes into effect.

Self Test Answers

1. ☑ D. All users must be authenticated.
   ☒ A, B, C. A is wrong because while this will give all users permission to connect, they will still have to authenticate. B is wrong because a NULL is not acceptable as a password. C is wrong because a profile can only manage passwords, not disable them.

2. ☑ B, C, and D. All these actions are necessary.
   ☒ A and E. A is wrong because without privileges and quota, JON cannot connect and create a table. E is wrong because this privilege lets you manage a tablespace, not create objects in it.

3. ☑ **B.** It will not be possible to allocate further extents to the tables.

☒ **A, C, and D.** A is wrong because inserts will succeed as long as there is space in the extents already allocated. C is wrong because there is no need to drop the tables. D is wrong because CASCADE cannot be applied to a quota command.

4. ☑ **D.** There is always a database-wide default, which (by default) is SYSTEM. In many cases, it will have been set to TEMP.

☒ **A, B, C, and E.** A is wrong because there is a default. B is wrong because the default may not be SYSTEM (though it is by default). C is wrong because while TEMP is a frequently used default, it may not be. E is wrong because all user accounts must have a temporary tablespace.

5. ☑ **A, B, and C.** Any of these will prevent the access.

☒ **D and E.** D is wrong because the grants in (a) and (b) will remain in effect. Note that ALL is implemented as a set of grants (or revokes) of each privilege, so it is not necessary to grant or revoke SELECT as well as ALL. E is wrong because the grant to PUBLIC in (d) will remain in effect.

6. ☑ **C, D, and E.** C is correct because the revocation of a system privilege does not cascade. D and E are correct because any action that updates the data dictionary is a system privilege.

☒ **A and B.** A is wrong because system privileges can be granted by any user who has been granted the privilege WITH ADMIN OPTION. B is wrong because the revocation of a system privilege does not cascade.

7. ☑ **C.** There is no such privilege as SELECT TABLE; it is granted implicitly with CREATE TABLE.

☒ **A, B, and D.** A is wrong because roles can be password protected. B is wrong because even though tables must be owned by users, permission to create them can be granted to a role. D is wrong because a role can have any combination of object and system privileges.

8. ☑ **B.** Roles are not schema objects, and so can have the same names as tables.

☒ **A, C, and D.** A is wrong because roles can have any combination of system, object, and role privileges. C is wrong because roles cannot have the same names as users. D is wrong because roles can be enabled and disabled at any time.

9. ☑ **C.** The RESOURCE_LIMIT parameter will default to FALSE, and without this resource limits are not enforced.

☒ **A, B, and D.** A is wrong because this privilege controls whether users can connect to the account at all, not how many times. B is wrong because no role can exempt a user from profile limits. D is wrong because this parameter controls which Resource Manager plan is active, which is not relevant to whether resource limits are enforced.

10. ☑   B and C. These are both password limits.

   ☒   A and D. A is wrong because this cannot be prevented by any means. D is wrong because profiles only apply to password authentication; password file authentication is managed separately.

11. ☑   A and C. Password file authentication is necessary if SYSDBA connections need to be made across a network, and if you want to grant SYSDBA or SYSOPER to any other database users.

   ☒   B and D. B is wrong because operating system authentication can never be disabled. D is wrong because EXCLUSIVE doesn't exclude users; it means one password file per instance.

12. ☑   D. No matter who you are connected as, the parameter is static and will therefore require a SCOPE=SPFILE clause when changing it.

   ☒   A, B, and C. A is wrong because SYSTEM can adjust the parameter (as can anyone to whom the ALTER SYSTEM privilege has been granted). B is wrong because the parameter can be changed in any mode—if the SCOPE is SPFILE. C is wrong because the system administrator cannot change parameters: only a database administrator can do this.

13. ☑   A, C, and F. The necessary conditions are that the session must be able to execute the UTL_FILE procedures, and that the UTL_FILE_DIR parameter must point to a directory on which the Oracle user has the necessary permissions.

   ☒   B, D, and E. B is wrong because DBMS_OUTPUT is used to write to the user process, not to the operating system. D is wrong because DB_WRITER_PROCESSES controls the number of database writers. E is wrong because DB_CREATE_FILE_DEST sets a default location for datafiles.

14. ☑   B. A fine-grained auditing policy can nominate a PL/SQL function to run whenever the audit condition is violated.

   ☒   A, C, and D. A is wrong because database auditing can do no more than record events. C is wrong because database triggers can only be defined for DML and not for SELECT statements. D is wrong because FGA can indeed do this.

15. ☑   A. Setting this parameter is all that is necessary, though on Unix and Linux you may want to adjust AUDIT_FILE_DEST as well.

   ☒   B, C, and D. B is wrong because this is a privilege whose use cannot be audited, because it can apply before the database is open. C is wrong because the method of gaining SYSDBA access is not relevant to whether it is audited. D is wrong because SYS cannot bypass this audit technique.

16. ☑   A, B, C, and D. These are all correct.

   ☒   None.

17. ☑ **B.** If AUDIT_TRAIL is set to NONE, there will be no standard database auditing.

☒ **A, C,** and **D. A** is wrong because auditing the SYS user is in addition to standard database auditing. **C** is wrong because standard database auditing will record access to the object, regardless of whether any rows were retrieved. **D** is wrong because audits of parameter changes require an instance restart, not audits of commands.

PART II

SQL

CHAPTER 7

DDL and Schema Objects

Exam Objectives

In this chapter you will learn to

- 051.10.1   Categorize the Main Database Objects
- 051.10.2   Review the Table Structure
- 051.10.3   List the Data Types That Are Available for Columns
- 051.10.4   Create a Simple Table
- 051.10.5   Explain How Constraints Are Created at the Time of Table Creation
- 051.10.6   Describe How Schema Objects Work
- 052.8.1   Create and Modify Tables
- 052.8.2   Manage Constraints
- 052.8.3   Create Indexes
- 052.8.4   Create and Use Temporary Tables
- 051.11.1   Create Simple and Complex Views
- 051.11.2   Retrieve Data from Views
- 051.11.3   Create, Maintain, and Use Sequences
- 051.11.4   Create and Maintain Indexes
- 051.11.5   Create Private and Public Synonyms

In terms of the sheer number of exam objectives covered in this chapter, it looks horrific. Do not worry: there is some duplication in the objectives, and many of the objectives are revisited in other chapters as well.

Understanding the primitive data types and the standard heap-organized table structure is the first topic. Then the chapter moves on to defining the object types that are dependent on tables (indexes, constraints, and views), and then sequences and synonyms. Objects of all these types will be used throughout the remainder of this book, sometimes with more detail provided.

Categorize the Main Database Objects

There are various object types that can exist within a database, many more with the current release than with earlier versions. All objects have a name and a type, and each object is owned by a *schema*. Various common object types and the rules to which they must conform will be discussed.

Object Types

This query lists (in a neatly formatted output), the count by object types for the objects that happen to exist in this particular database:

```
SQL> select object_type,count(object_type) from dba_objects
     group by object_type order by object_type;
```

OBJECT_TYPE	COUNT(OBJECT_TYPE)	OBJECT_TYPE	COUNT(OBJECT_TYPE)
CLUSTER	10	PACKAGE	1240
CONSUMER GROUP	12	PACKAGE BODY	1178
CONTEXT	6	PROCEDURE	118
DIMENSION	5	PROGRAM	17
DIRECTORY	9	QUEUE	37
EDITION	1	RESOURCE PLAN	7
EVALUATION CONTEXT	13	RULE	1
FUNCTION	286	RULE SET	21
INDEX	3023	SCHEDULE	2
INDEX PARTITION	342	SEQUENCE	204
INDEXTYPE	12	SYNONYM	26493
JAVA CLASS	22018	TABLE	2464
JAVA DATA	322	TABLE PARTITION	199
JAVA RESOURCE	820	TRIGGER	413
JOB	11	TYPE	2630
JOB CLASS	11	TYPE BODY	231
LIBRARY	177	UNDEFINED	6
LOB	769	VIEW	4669
LOB PARTITION	7	WINDOW	9
MATERIALIZED VIEW	3	WINDOW GROUP	4
OPERATOR	60	XML SCHEMA	93

```
42 rows selected.
```

This query addresses the view DBA_OBJECTS, which has one row for every object in the database. The numbers are low, because the database is a very small one used only for teaching. A database used for a business application might have hundreds of thousands of objects. You may not be able to see the view DBA_OBJECTS, depending on what permissions your account has. Alternate views are USER_OBJECTS, which will show all the objects owned by you, and ALL_OBJECTS, which will show all the objects to which you have been granted access (including your own). All users have access to these views.

The objects of greatest interest to a SQL programmer are those that contain, or give access to, data. These include: Tables, Views, Synonyms, Indexes, and Sequences.

Tables basically store data in rows segmented by columns. A view is a stored SELECT statement that can be referenced as though it were a table. It is nothing more than a query, but rather than running the statement itself, the user issues a SELECT statement against the view instead. In effect, the user is selecting from the result of another selection. A synonym is an alias for a table (or a view). Users can execute SQL statements against the synonym, and the database will map them into statements against the object to which the synonym points. Indexes are a means of improving access times to rows in tables. If a query requires only one row, then rather than scanning the entire table to find the row, an index can provide a pointer to the row's exact location. Of course, the index itself must be searched, but this is often faster than scanning the table. A sequence is a construct that generates unique numbers. There are many cases where unique numbers are needed. Sequences issue numbers in order, on demand: it is absolutely impossible for the same number to be issued twice.

The remaining object types are less commonly relevant to a SQL programmer. Their use falls more within the realm of PL/SQL programmers and database administrators.

Naming Schema Objects

A schema object is owned by a user and must conform to certain rules:

- The name may be between 1 to 30 characters long (with the exception of database link names that may be up to 128 characters long).
- Reserved words (such as SELECT) cannot be used as object names.
- All names must begin with a letter of the alphabet.
- Object names can only include letters, numbers, the underscore (_), the dollar sign ($), or the hash symbol (#).
- Lowercase letters will be automatically converted to uppercase.

By enclosing the name within double quotes, all these rules (with the exception of the length) can be broken, but to get to the object subsequently, it must always be specified with double quotes, as in the examples in Figure 7-1. Note that the same restrictions also apply to column names.

 EXAM TIP Object names must be no more than 30 characters. The characters can be letters, digits, underscore, dollar, or hash.

```
C:\WINDOWS\system32\cmd.exe - sqlplus                              _ □ ×
SQL> create table "with space" ("-Hyphen" date);

Table created.

SQL> insert into "with space" values(sysdate);

1 row created.

SQL> select * from with space;
select * from with space
                   *
ERROR at line 1:
ORA-00903: invalid table name


SQL> select -Hyphen from "with space";
select -Hyphen from "with space"
         *
ERROR at line 1:
ORA-00904: "HYPHEN": invalid identifier


SQL> select "-Hyphen" from "with space";

-Hyphen
----------
16-NOV-07

SQL> _
```

Figure 7-1   Using double quotes to use nonstandard names

Although tools such as SQL*Plus and SQL Developer will automatically convert lowercase letters to uppercase unless the name is enclosed within double quotes, remember that object names are always case sensitive. In this example, the two tables are completely different:

```
SQL> create table lower(c1 date);
Table created.
SQL> create table "lower"(col1 varchar2(2));
Table created.
SQL> select table_name from dba_tables where lower(table_name) = 'lower';
TABLE_NAME
------------------------------
lower
LOWER
```

 TIP While it is possible to use lowercase names and nonstandard characters (even spaces), it is considered bad practice because of the confusion it can cause.

Object Namespaces

It is often said that the unique identifier for an object is the object name, prefixed with the schema name. While this is generally true, for a full understanding of naming it is necessary to introduce the concept of a *namespace*. A namespace defines a group of object types, within which all names must be uniquely identified—by schema and name. Objects in different namespaces can share the same name.

These object types all share the same namespace:

Tables	Views	Sequences
Private synonyms	Stand-alone procedures	Stand-alone stored functions
Packages	Materialized views	User-defined types

Thus it is impossible to create a view with the same name as a table—at least, it is impossible if they are in the same schema. And once created, SQL statements can address a view as though it were a table. The fact that tables, views, and private synonyms share the same namespace means that you can set up several layers of abstraction between what the users see and the actual tables, which can be invaluable for both security and for simplifying application development.

These object types each have their own namespace:

Indexes	Constraints	Clusters
Database triggers	Private database links	Dimensions

Thus it is possible (though perhaps not a very good idea) for an index to have the same name as a table, even within the same schema.

 EXAM TIP Within a schema, tables, views, and synonyms cannot have the same names.

Exercise 7-1: Determine What Objects Are Accessible to Your
Session In this exercise, query various data dictionary views as user HR to determine what objects are in the HR schema and what objects in other schemas HR has access to.

1. Connect to the database with SQL*Plus or SQL Developer as user HR.

2. Determine how many objects of each type are in the HR schema:

```
select object_type,count(*) from user_objects group by object_type;
```

The USER_OBJECTS view lists all objects owned by the schema to which the current session is connected, in this case HR.

3. Determine how many objects in total HR has permissions on:

```
select object_type,count(*) from all_objects group by object_type;
```

The ALL_OBJECTS view lists all objects to which the user has some sort of access.

4. Determine who owns the objects HR can see:

```
select distinct owner from all_objects;
```

List the Data Types That Are Available for Columns

When creating tables, each column must be assigned a data type, which determines the nature of the values that can be inserted into the column. These data types are also used to specify the nature of the arguments for PL/SQL procedures and functions. When selecting a data type, you must consider the data that you need to store and the operations you will want to perform upon it. Space is also a consideration: some data types are fixed length, taking up the same number of bytes no matter what data is actually in it; others are variable. If a column is not populated, then Oracle will not give it any space at all. If you later update the row to populate the column, then the row will get bigger, no matter whether the data type is fixed length or variable.

The following are the data types for alphanumeric data:

VARCHAR2	Variable-length character data, from 1 byte to 4KB. The data is stored in the database character set.
NVARCHAR2	Like VARCHAR2, but the data is stored in the alternative national language character set, one of the permitted Unicode character sets.
CHAR	Fixed-length character data, from 1 byte to 2KB, in the database character set. If the data is not the length of the column, then it will be padded with spaces.

TIP For ISO/ANSI compliance, you can specify a VARCHAR data type, but any columns of this type will be automatically converted to VARCHAR2.

The following are the data types for numeric data, all variable length:

NUMBER	Numeric data, for which you can specify precision and scale. The precision can range from 1 to 38, the scale can range from –84 to 127.
FLOAT	This is an ANSI data type, floating-point number with precision of 126 binary (or 38 decimal). Oracle also provides BINARY_FLOAT and BINARY_DOUBLE as alternatives.
INTEGER	Equivalent to NUMBER, with scale zero.

The following are the data types for date and time data, all fixed length:

DATE	This is either length zero, if the column is empty, or 7 bytes. All DATE data includes century, year, month, day, hour, minute, and second. The valid range is from January 1, 4712 BC to December 31, 9999 AD.
TIMESTAMP	This is length zero if the column is empty, or up to 11 bytes, depending on the precision specified. Similar to DATE, but with precision of up to 9 decimal places for the seconds, 6 places by default.
TIMESTAMP WITH TIMEZONE	Like TIMESTAMP, but the data is stored with a record kept of the time zone to which it refers. The length may be up to 13 bytes, depending on precision. This data type lets Oracle determine the difference between two times by normalizing them to UTC, even if the times are for different time zones.
TIMESTAMP WITH LOCAL TIMEZONE	Like TIMESTAMP, but the data is normalized to the database time zone on saving. When retrieved, it is normalized to the time zone of the user process selecting it.
INTERVAL YEAR TO MONTH	Used for recording a period in years and months between two DATEs or TIMESTAMPs.
INTERVAL DAY TO SECOND	Used for recording a period in days and seconds between two DATEs or TIMESTAMPs.

The following are the large object data types:

CLOB	Character data stored in the database character set, size effectively unlimited: 4GB multiplied by the database block size.
NCLOB	Like CLOB, but the data is stored in the alternative national language character set, one of the permitted Unicode character sets.
BLOB	Like CLOB, but binary data that will not undergo character set conversion by Oracle Net.
BFILE	A locator pointing to a file stored on the operating system of the database server. The size of the files is limited to 4GB.
LONG	Character data in the database character set, up to 2GB. All the functionality of LONG (and more) is provided by CLOB; LONGs should not be used in a modern database, and if your database has any columns of this type, they should be converted to CLOB. There can only be one LONG column in a table.
LONG RAW	Like LONG, but binary data that will not be converted by Oracle Net. Any LONG RAW columns should be converted to BLOBs.

The following are RAW and ROWID data types:

RAW	Variable-length binary data, from 1 byte to 4KB. Unlike the CHAR and VARCHAR2 data types, RAW data is not converted by Oracle Net from the database's character set to the user process's character set on SELECT or the other way on INSERT.
ROWID	A value coded in base 64 that is the pointer to the location of a row in a table. Within it is the exact physical address. ROWID is an Oracle proprietary data type, not visible unless specifically selected.

 EXAM TIP All examinees will be expected to know about these data types: VARCHAR2, CHAR, NUMBER, DATE, TIMESTAMP, INTERVAL, RAW, LONG, LONG RAW, CLOB, BLOB, BFILE, and ROWID. Detailed knowledge will also be needed for VARCHAR2, NUMBER, and DATE.

The VARCHAR2 data type must be qualified with a number indicating the maximum length of the column. If a value is inserted into the column that is less than this, it is not a problem: the value will only take up as much space as it needs. If the value is longer than this maximum, the INSERT will fail with an error. If the value is updated to a longer or shorter value, the length of the column (and therefore the row itself) will change accordingly. If is not entered at all or is updated to NULL, then it will take up no space at all.

The NUMBER data type may optionally be qualified with a precision and a scale. The precision sets the maximum number of digits in the number, and the scale is how many of those digits are to the right of the decimal point. If the scale is negative, this has the effect of replacing the last digits of any number inserted with zeros, which do not count toward the number of digits specified for the precision. If the number of digits exceeds the precision, there will be an error; if it is within the precision but outside the scale, the number will be rounded (up or down) to the nearest value within the scale.

The DATE data type always includes century, year, month, day, hour, minute, and second—even if all these elements are not specified at insert time. Year, month, and day must be specified; if the hours, minutes, and seconds are omitted, they will default to midnight.

Exercise 7-2: Investigate the Data Types in the HR Schema   In this exercise, find out what data types are used in the tables in the HR schema, using two techniques.

1. Connect to the database as user HR with SQL*Plus or SQL Developer.

2. Use the DESCRIBE command to show the data types in some tables:

```
describe employees;
describe departments;
```

3. Use a query against a data dictionary view to show what columns make up the EMPLOYEES table, as the DESCRIBE command would:

```
select column_name,data_type,nullable,data_length,data_precision,data_scale
from user_tab_columns where table_name='EMPLOYEES';
```

The view USER_TAB_COLUMNS shows the detail of every column in every table in the current user's schema.

Create a Simple Table

Tables can be stored in the database in several ways. The simplest is the *heap* table. A heap table contains variable-length rows in random order. There may be some correlation between the order in which rows are entered and the order in which they are stored, but this is not guaranteed and should not be relied upon. More advanced table structures, such as the following, may impose ordering and grouping on the rows or force a random distribution:

Index organized tables	Store rows in the order of an index key.
Index clusters	Can denormalize tables in parent-child relationships so that related rows from different table are stored together.
Hash clusters	Force a random distribution of rows, which will break down any ordering based on the entry sequence.
Partitioned tables	Store rows in separate physical structures, the partitions, allocating rows according to the value of a column.

Using the more advanced table structures has no effect whatsoever on SQL. Every SQL statement executed against tables defined with these options will return exactly the same results as though the tables were standard heap tables, so use of these features will not affect your code. But while their use is transparent to programmers, they can provide enormous benefits in performance.

Creating Tables with Column Specifications

To create a standard heap table, use this syntax:

```
CREATE TABLE [schema.]table [ORGANIZATION HEAP]
(column datatype [DEFAULT expression]
[,column datatype [DEFAULT expression]]);
```

As a minimum, specify the table name (it will be created in your own schema, if you don't specify someone else's) and at least one column with a data type. There are very few developers who ever specify ORGANIZATION HEAP, as this is the default and is industry-standard SQL. The DEFAULT keyword in a column definition lets you provide an expression that will generate a value for the column when a row is inserted if a value is not provided by the INSERT statement.

Consider this statement:

```
CREATE TABLE SCOTT.EMP
(EMPNO NUMBER(4),
ENAME VARCHAR2(10),
HIREDATE DATE DEFAULT TRUNC(SYSDATE),
SAL NUMBER(7,2),
COMM NUMBER(7,2) DEFAULT 0.03);
```

This will create a table called EMP in the SCOTT schema. Either user SCOTT has to issue the statement (in which case nominating the schema would not actually be necessary), or another user could issue it if they have been granted permission to create tables in SCOTT's schema. Taking the columns one by one:

- EMPNO can be four digits long, with no decimal places. If any decimals are included in an INSERT statement, they will be rounded (up or down) to the nearest integer.

- ENAME can store up to ten characters.

- HIREDATE will accept any date, optionally with the time, but if a value is not provided, today's date will be entered as at midnight.

- SAL, intended for the employee's salary, will accept numeric values with up to seven digits. If any digits over seven are to the right of the decimal point, they will be rounded off.

- COMM (for commission percentage) has a default value of 0.03, which will be entered if the INSERT statement does not include a value for this column.

Following creation of the table, these statements insert a row and select the result:

```
SQL> insert into scott.emp(empno,ename,sal) values(1000,'John',1000.789);
1 row created.
SQL> select * from emp;
     EMPNO ENAME      HIREDATE       SAL       COMM
---------- ---------- --------- ---------- ----------
      1000 John       19-NOV-07   1000.79        .03
```

Note that values for the columns not mentioned in the INSERT statement have been generated by the DEFAULT clauses. Had those clauses not been defined in the table definition, the column values would have been NULL. Also note the rounding of the value provided for SAL.

 TIP The DEFAULT clause can be useful, but it is of limited functionality. You cannot use a subquery to generate the default value: you can only specify literal values or functions.

Creating Tables from Subqueries

Rather than creating a table from nothing and then inserting rows into it (as in the preceding section), tables can be created from other tables by using a subquery. This technique lets you create the table definition and populate the table with rows with just one statement. Any query at all can be used as the source of both the table structure and the rows. The syntax is as follows:

```
CREATE TABLE [schema.]table AS subquery;
```

All queries return a two-dimensional set of rows; this result is stored as the new table. A simple example of creating a table with a subquery is

```
create table employees_copy as select * from employees;
```

This statement will create a table EMPLOYEES_COPY, which is an exact copy of the EMPLOYEES table, identical in both definition and the rows it contains. Any not-null and check constraints on the columns will also be applied to the new table, but any primary key, unique, or foreign key constraints will not be. (Constraints are discussed in a later section.) This is because these three types of constraints require indexes that might not be desired.

The following is a more complex example:

```
create table emp_dept as select
last_name ename,department_name dname,round(sysdate - hire_date) service
from employees natural join departments order by dname,ename;
```

The rows in the new table will be the result of joining the two source tables, with two of the selected columns having their names changed. The new SERVICE column will be populated with the result of the arithmetic that computes the number of days since the employee was hired. The rows will be inserted in the order specified. This ordering will not be maintained by subsequent DML, but assuming the standard HR schema data, the new table will look like this:

```
SQL> select * from emp_dept where rownum < 5;
ENAME           DNAME              SERVICE
--------------- --------------- ----------
Gietz           Accounting            4914
De Haan         Executive             5424
Kochhar         Executive             6634
Chen            Finance               3705
4 rows selected.
```

The subquery can of course include a WHERE clause to restrict the rows inserted into the new table. To create a table with no rows, use a WHERE clause that will exclude all rows:

```
create table no_emps as select * from employees where 1=2;
```

The WHERE clause 1=2 can never return TRUE, so the table structure will be created ready for use, but no rows will be inserted at creation time.

Altering Table Definitions after Creation

There are many alterations that can be made to a table after creation. Those that affect the physical storage fall into the domain of the database administrator, but many changes are purely logical and will be carried out by the SQL developers. The following are examples (for the most part self-explanatory):

- Adding columns:

  ```
  alter table emp add (job_id number);
  ```

- Modifying columns:

  ```
  alter table emp modify (commission_pct number(4,2) default 0.05);
  ```

- Dropping columns:

  ```
  alter table emp drop column commission_pct;
  ```

- Marking columns as unused:

  ```
  alter table emp set unused column job_id;
  ```

- Renaming columns:

  ```
  alter table emp rename column hire_date to recruited;
  ```

- Marking the table as read-only:

  ```
  alter table emp read only;
  ```

All of these changes are DDL commands with a built-in COMMIT. They are therefore nonreversible and will fail if there is an active transaction against the table. They are also virtually instantaneous with the exception of dropping a column. Dropping a column can be a time-consuming exercise because as each column is dropped, every row must be restructured to remove the column's data. The SET UNUSED command, which makes columns nonexistent as far as SQL is concerned, is often a better alternative, followed when convenient by

```
ALTER TABLE tablename DROP UNUSED COLUMNS;
```

which will drop all the unused columns in one pass through the table.

Marking a table as read-only will cause errors for any attempted DML commands. But the table can still be dropped. This can be disconcerting but is perfectly logical when you think it through. A DROP command doesn't actually affect the table: it affects the tables in the data dictionary that define the table, and these are not read-only.

Dropping and Truncating Tables

The TRUNCATE TABLE command (discussed in detail in Chapter 8) has the effect of removing every row from a table, while leaving the table definition intact. DROP TABLE is more drastic in that the table definition is removed as well. The syntax is as follows:

```
DROP TABLE [schema.]tablename ;
```

If *schema* is not specified, then the table called *tablename* in your currently logged-on schema will be dropped.

As with a TRUNCATE, SQL will not produce a warning before the table is dropped, and furthermore, as with any DDL command, it includes a COMMIT. A DROP is therefore generally nonreversible. Under certain conditions, a DROP may be reversed using flashback and other recovery techniques (discussed in Chapter 19). But there are some restrictions: if any session (even your own) has a transaction in progress that includes a row in the table, then the DROP will fail, and it is also impossible to drop a table that is referred to in a foreign key constraint defined for another table. This table (or the constraint) must be dropped first.

Exercise 7-3: Create Tables   This exercise marks the formal beginning of the case study. By now, you should have a database installed on one of your machines, and if you completed the exercises in Chapter 5, you should have a tablespace called STOREDATA; otherwise, create it now.

In this exercise, use SQL Developer to create a heap table, insert some rows with a subquery, and modify the table. Do some more modifications with SQL*Plus, and then drop the table.

1. Connect to the database as user SYSTEM and create the WEBSTORE user with default tablespace STOREDATA and temporary tablespace TEMP. Grant the WEBSTORE user unlimited quota on the STOREDATA tablespace as well as the privileges to create a session and create a table. The WEBSTORE schema will be used in subsequent exercises.

2. Using SQL Developer, connect as the WEBSTORE user. Right-click the Tables branch of the navigation tree, and click NEW TABLE.

3. Name the new table **CUSTOMERS**, and use the ADD COLUMN button to set it up as in the following illustration:

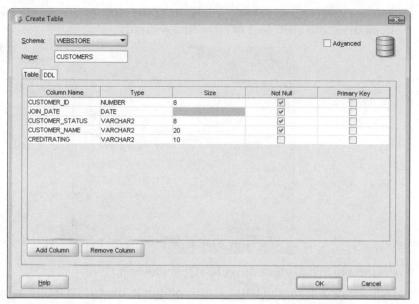

4. Click the DDL tab to see if the statement has been constructed. It should look like this:

```
CREATE TABLE CUSTOMERS
(
  CUSTOMER_ID NUMBER(8, 0) NOT NULL,
  JOIN_DATE DATE NOT NULL,
  CUSTOMER_STATUS VARCHAR2(0) NOT NULL,
  CUSTOMER_NAME VARCHAR2(20) NOT NULL,
  CREDITRATING VARCHAR2(10)
)
;
```

Return to the Table tab (as in the preceding illustration) and click OK to create the table.

5. Run these statements:

```
insert into customers(customer_id, customer_status, customer_name, creditrating)
values (1, 'NEW', 'Ameetha', 'Platinum');
insert into customers(customer_id, customer_status, customer_name, creditrating)
values (2, 'NEW', 'Coda', 'Bronze');
```

and commit the insert:

```
commit;
```

6. Right-click the CUSTOMERS table in the SQL Developer navigator; click COLUMN and ADD.

7. Define a new column EMAIL, type VARCHAR2(50), as in the following illustration; and click APPLY to create the column.

8. Connect to the database as WEBSTORE with SQL*Plus.

9. Define a default for the JOIN_DATE column in the CUSTOMERS table:

```
alter table customers modify (join_date default sysdate);
```

10. Insert a row without specifying a value for JOIN_DATE and check that the new row does have a JOIN_DATE date but that the other rows do not:

```
insert into customers(customer_id, customer_status, customer_name,
creditrating) values (3, 'NEW', 'Sid', 'Gold');
select join_date, count(1) from customers group by join_date;
```

11. Create three additional tables as in the following illustration:

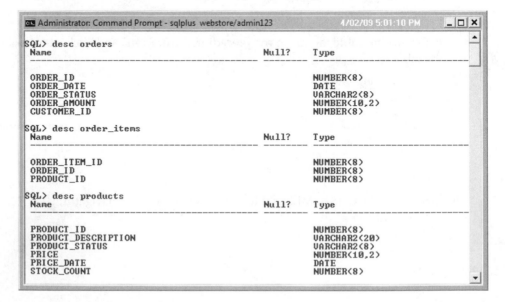

12. Add a column called QUANTITY with datatype NUMBER to the ORDER_
    ITEMS table:

```
alter table order_items add (quantity number);
```

Create and Use Temporary Tables

A *temporary* table has a definition that is visible to all sessions, but the rows within it
are private to the session that inserted them. Programmers can use them as a private
storage area for manipulating large amounts of data. The syntax is

```
CREATE GLOBAL TEMPORARY TABLE temp_tab_name
(column datatype [,column datatype] )
[ON COMMIT {DELETE | PRESERVE} ROWS] ;
```

The column definition is the same as a regular table and can indeed be supplied
from a subquery. The optional clause at the end determines the lifetime of any rows
inserted. The default is to remove the rows the moment the transaction that inserted
them completes, but this behavior can be changed to preserve them until the session
that inserted them ends. Whichever option is chosen, the data will be private to each
session: different users can insert their own rows into their own copy of the table, and
they will never see each other's rows.

In many ways, a temporary table is similar to a permanent table. You can execute
any DML or SELECT command against it. It can have indexes, constraints, and triggers
defined. It can be referenced in views and synonyms, or joined to other tables. The
difference is that the data is transient and private to the session, and that all SQL
commands against it will be far faster than commands against permanent tables.

The first reason for the speed is that temporary tables are not segments in permanent
tablespaces. Ideally, they exist only in the PGAs of the sessions that are using them, so
there is no disk activity or even database buffer cache activity involved. If the PGA cannot
grow sufficiently to store the temporary table (which will be the case if millions of rows
are being inserted—not unusual in complex report generation), then the table gets
written out to a temporary segment in the user's temporary tablespace. I/O on temporary
tablespaces is much faster than I/O on permanent tablespaces, because it does not go
via the database buffer cache; it is all performed directly on disk by the session's server
process.

A second reason for speed is that DML against temporary tables does not generate
redo. Since the data only persists for the duration of a session (perhaps only for the
duration of a transaction), there is no purpose in generating redo. This gives the dual
benefit of fast DML for the session working on the table, and taking the strain off the
redo generation system, which can be a bad point of contention on busy multiuser
databases.

Figure 7-2 shows the creation and use of a temporary table with SQL*Plus. The
Database Control Table Creation Wizard can also create temporary tables.

```
 C:\WINDOWS\system32\cmd.exe - sqlplus scott/tiger                    _ □ ✕

SQL> create global temporary table tmp_emp (dept number,salary number);

Table created.

SQL> insert into tmp_emp (select deptno,sal from emp);

14 rows created.

SQL> update tmp_emp set salary=salary*1.1;

14 rows updated.

SQL> select sum(salary) from tmp_emp;

SUM(SALARY)
-----------
    31927.5

SQL> commit;

Commit complete.

SQL> select sum(salary) from tmp_emp;

SUM(SALARY)
-----------

SQL>
```

Figure 7-2   Creation and use of a temporary table

Exercise 7-4: Create and Use Temporary Tables   In this exercise, create a temporary table to be used for reporting on current employees. Demonstrate, by using two SQL*Plus sessions, that the data is private to each session.

1. Connect to your database with SQL*Plus as user HR.

2. Create a temporary table as follows:

   ```
   create global temporary table tmp_emps on commit preserve rows
   as select * from employees where 1=2;
   ```

3. Insert some rows and commit them:

   ```
   insert into tmp_emps select * from employees where department_id=30;
   commit;
   ```

4. Start a second SQL*Plus session as HR.

5. In the second session, confirm that the first insert is not visible, even though it was committed in the first session, and insert some different rows:

   ```
   select count(*) from tmp_emps;
   insert into tmp_emps select * from employees where department_id=50;
   commit;
   ```

6. In the first session, truncate the table:

   ```
   truncate table tmp_emps;
   ```

7. In the second session, confirm that there are still rows in that session's copy of the table:

   ```
   select count(*) from tmp_emps;
   ```

8. In the second session, demonstrate that terminating the session does clear the rows. This will require disconnecting and connecting again:

```
disconnect;
connect hr/hr
select count(*) from tmp_emps;
```

9. Tidy up the environment by dropping the tables in both sessions.

Indexes

Indexes have two functions: to enforce primary key and unique constraints, and to improve performance. An application's indexing strategy is critical for performance. There is no clear demarcation of whose domain index management lies within. When the business analysts specify business rules that will be implemented as constraints, they are in effect specifying indexes. The database administrators will be monitoring the execution of code running in the database, and will make recommendations for indexes. The developer, who should have the best idea of what is going on in the code and the nature of the data, will also be involved in developing the indexing strategy.

Why Indexes Are Needed?

Indexes are part of the constraint mechanism. If a column (or a group of columns) is marked as a table's primary key, then every time a row is inserted into the table, Oracle must check that a row with the same value in the primary key does not already exist. If the table has no index on the column(s), the only way to do this would be to scan right through the table, checking every row. While this might be acceptable for a table of only a few rows, for a table with thousands or millions (or billions) of rows this is not feasible. An index gives (near) immediate access to key values, so the check for existence can be made virtually instantaneously. When a primary key constraint is defined, Oracle will automatically create an index on the primary key column(s), if one does not exist already.

A unique constraint also requires an index. It differs from a primary key constraint in that the column(s) of the unique constraint can be left null. This does not affect the creation and use of the index. Foreign key constraints are enforced by indexes, but the index must exist on the parent table, not necessarily on the table for which the constraint is defined. A foreign key constraint relates a column in the child table to the primary key or to a unique key in the parent table. When a row is inserted in the child table, Oracle will do a lookup on the index on the parent table to confirm that there is a matching row before permitting the insert. However, you should always create indexes on the foreign key columns within the child table for performance reasons: a DELETE on the parent table will be much faster if Oracle can use an index to determine whether there are any rows in the child table referencing the row that is being deleted.

Indexes are critical for performance. When executing any SQL statement that includes a WHERE clause, Oracle has to identify which rows of the table are to be selected or modified. If there is no index on the column(s) referenced in the WHERE clause, the only way to do this is with a *full table scan*. A full table scan reads every row of the table, in order to find the relevant rows. If the table has billions of rows, this can take hours. If there is an index on the relevant column(s), Oracle can search the index instead. An index is a sorted list of key values, structured in a manner that makes the search very efficient. With each key value is a pointer to the row in the table. Locating relevant rows via an index lookup is far faster than using a full table scan, if the table is over a certain size and the proportion of the rows to be retrieved is below a certain value. For small tables, or for a WHERE clause that will retrieve a large fraction of the table's rows, a full table scan will be quicker: you can (usually) trust Oracle to make the correct decision regarding whether to use an index, based on statistical information the database gathers about the tables and the rows within them.

A second circumstance where indexes can be used is for sorting. A SELECT statement that includes the ORDER BY, GROUP BY, or UNION keyword (and a few others) must sort the rows into order—unless there is an index, which can return the rows in the correct order without needing to sort them first.

A third circumstance when indexes can improve performance is when tables are joined, but again Oracle has a choice: depending on the size of the tables and the memory resources available, it may be quicker to scan tables into memory and join them there, rather than use indexes. The *nested loop join* technique passes through one table using an index on the other table to locate the matching rows; this is usually a disk-intensive operation. A *hash join* technique reads the entire table into memory, converts it into a hash table, and uses a hashing algorithm to locate matching rows; this is more memory and CPU intensive. A *sort merge join* sorts the tables on the join column and then merges them together; this is often a compromise among disk, memory, and CPU resources. If there are no indexes, then Oracle is severely limited in the join techniques available.

 TIP Indexes assist SELECT statements, and also any UPDATE, DELETE, or MERGE statements that use a WHERE clause—but they will slow down INSERT statements.

Types of Index

Oracle supports several types of index, which have several variations. The two index types of concern here are the B*Tree index, which is the default index type, and the bitmap index. As a general rule, indexes will improve performance for data retrieval but reduce performance for DML operations. This is because indexes must be maintained. Every time a row is inserted into a table, a new key must be inserted into every index on the table, which places an additional strain on the database. For this reason, on transaction processing systems it is customary to keep the number of indexes as low as possible (perhaps no more than those needed for the constraints) and on query-intensive systems such as a data warehouse to create as many as might be helpful.

B*Tree Indexes

A B*Tree index (the "B" stands for "balanced") is a tree structure. The root node of the tree points to many nodes at the second level, which can point to many nodes at the third level, and so on. The necessary depth of the tree will be largely determined by the number of rows in the table and the length of the index key values.

 TIP The B*Tree structure is very efficient. If the depth is greater than three or four, then either the index keys are very long or the table has billions of rows. If neither if these is the case, then the index is in need of a rebuild.

The leaf nodes of the index tree store the rows' keys, in order, each with a pointer that identifies the physical location of the row. So to retrieve a row with an index lookup, if the WHERE clause is using an equality predicate on the indexed column, Oracle navigates down the tree to the leaf node containing the desired key value, and then uses the pointer to find the row location. If the WHERE clause is using a nonequality predicate (such as: LIKE, BETWEEN, >, or <), then Oracle can navigate down the tree to find the first matching key value and then navigate across the leaf nodes of the index to find all the other matching values. As it does so, it will retrieve the rows from the table, in order.

The pointer to the row is the *rowid*. The rowid is an Oracle-proprietary pseudocolumn, which every row in every table has. Encrypted within it is the physical address of the row. As rowids are not part of the SQL standard, they are never visible to a normal SQL statement, but you can see them and use them if you want. This is demonstrated in Figure 7-3.

The rowid for each row is globally unique. Every row in every table in the entire database will have a different rowid. The rowid encryption provides the physical address of the row; from which Oracle can calculate which operating system file, and where in the file the row is, and go straight to it.

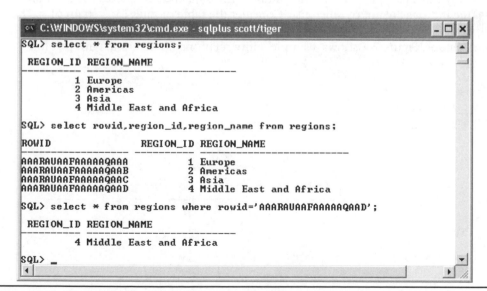

Figure 7-3 Displaying and using rowids

B*Tree indexes are a very efficient way of retrieving rows if the number of rows needed is low in proportion to the total number of rows in the table, and if the table is large. Consider this statement:

```
select count(*) from employees where last_name between 'A%' and 'Z%';
```

This WHERE clause is sufficiently broad that it will include every row in the table. It would be much slower to search the index to find the rowids and then use the rowids to find the rows than to scan the whole table. After all, it is the whole table that is needed. Another example would be if the table were small enough that one disk read could scan it in its entirety; there would be no point in reading an index first.

It is often said that if the query is going to retrieve more than two to four percent of the rows, then a full table scan will be quicker. A special case is if the value specified in the WHERE clause is NULL. NULLs do not go into B*Tree indexes, so a query such as

```
select * from employees where last_name is null;
```

will always result in a full table scan. There is little value in creating a B*Tree index on a column with few unique values, as it will not be sufficiently selective: the proportion of the table that will be retrieved for each distinct key value will be too high. In general, B*Tree indexes should be used if

- The cardinality (the number of distinct values) in the column is high, and
- The number of rows in the table is high, and
- The column is used in WHERE clauses or JOIN conditions.

Bitmap Indexes

In many business applications, the nature of the data and the queries is such that B*Tree indexes are not of much use. Consider the table of sales for a chain of supermarkets, storing one year of historical data, which can be analyzed in several dimensions. Figure 7-4 shows a simple entity-relationship diagram, with just four of the dimensions.

Figure 7-4
A fact table with
four dimensions

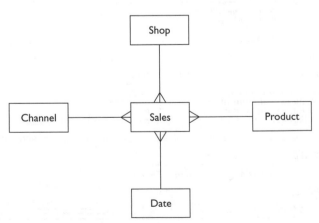

The cardinality of each dimension could be quite low. Make these assumptions:

SHOP	There are four shops.
PRODUCT	There are two hundred products.
DATE	There are 365 days.
CHANNEL	There are two channels (walk-in and delivery).

Assuming an even distribution of data, only two of the dimensions (PRODUCT and DATE) have a selectivity that is better than the commonly used criterion of 2 percent to 4 percent, which makes an index worthwhile. But if queries use range predicates (such as counting sales in a month, or of a class of ten or more products), then not even these will qualify. This is a simple fact: B*Tree indexes are often useless in a data warehouse environment. A typical query might want to compare sales between two shops by walk-in customers of a certain class of product in a month. There could well be B*Tree indexes on the relevant columns, but Oracle would ignore them as being insufficiently selective. This is what bitmap indexes are designed for.

A bitmap index stores the rowids associated with each key value as a bitmap. The bitmaps for the CHANNEL index might look like this:

```
WALK-IN      11010111000101011100010101.....
DELIVERY     00101000111010100010100010.....
```

This indicates that the first two rows were sales to walk-in customers, the third sale was a delivery, the fourth sale was a walk-in, and so on.

The bitmaps for the SHOP index might be

```
LONDON     11001001001001101000010000.....
OXFORD     00100010010000010001001000.....
READING    00010000000100000100100010.....
GLASGOW    00000100100010000010000101.....
```

This indicates that the first two sales were in the London shop, the third was in Oxford, the fourth in Reading, and so on. Now if this query is received:

```
select count(*) from sales where channel='WALK-IN' and shop='OXFORD';
```

Oracle can retrieve the two relevant bitmaps and add them together with a Boolean AND operation:

```
WALK-IN            11010111000101011100010101.....
OXFORD             00100010010000010001001000.....
WALKIN & OXFORD    00000001000000010000001000.....
```

The result of the bitwise-AND operation shows that only the seventh and sixteenth rows qualify for selection. This merging of bitmaps is very fast and can be used to implement complex Boolean operations with many conditions on many columns using any combination of AND, OR, and NOT operators. A particular advantage that bitmap indexes have over B*Tree indexes is that they include NULLs. As far as the bitmap index is concerned, NULL is just another distinct value, which will have its own bitmap.

In general, bitmap indexes should be used if

- The cardinality (the number of distinct values) in the column is low, and
- The number of rows in the table is high, and
- The column is used in Boolean algebra operations.

 TIP If you knew in advance what the queries would be, then you could build B*Tree indexes that would work, such as a composite index on SHOP and CHANNEL. But usually you don't know, which is where the dynamic merging of bitmaps gives great flexibility.

Index Type Options

There are six commonly used options that can be applied when creating indexes:

- Unique or nonunique
- Reverse key
- Compressed
- Composite
- Function based
- Ascending or descending

All these six variations apply to B*Tree indexes, but only the last three can be applied to bitmap indexes.

A *unique* index will not permit duplicate values. Nonunique is the default. The unique attribute of the index operates independently of a unique or primary key constraint: the presence of a unique index will not permit insertion of a duplicate value even if there is no such constraint defined. A unique or primary key constraint can use a nonunique index; it will just happen to have no duplicate values. This is in fact a requirement for a constraint that is deferrable, as there may be a period (before transactions are committed) when duplicate values do exist. Constraints are discussed in the next section.

A *reverse key* index is built on a version of the key column with its bytes reversed: rather than indexing "John", it will index "nhoJ". When a SELECT is done, Oracle will automatically reverse the value of the search string. This is a powerful technique for avoiding contention in multiuser systems. For instance, if many users are concurrently inserting rows with primary keys based on a sequentially increasing number, all their index inserts will concentrate on the high end of the index. By reversing the keys, the consecutive index key inserts will tend to be spread over the whole range of the index. Even though "John" and "Jules" are close together, "nhoJ" and "seluJ" will be quite widely separated.

A *compressed* index stores repeated key values only once. The default is not to compress, meaning that if a key value is not unique, it will be stored once for each occurrence, each having a single rowid pointer. A compressed index will store the key once, followed by a string of all the matching rowids.

A *composite* index is built on the concatenation of two or more columns. There are no restrictions on mixing datatypes. If a search string does not include all the columns, the index can still be used—but if it does not include the leftmost column, Oracle will have to use a skip-scanning method that is much less efficient than if the leftmost column is included.

A *function-based* index is built on the result of a function applied to one or more columns, such as `upper(last_name)` or `to_char(startdate, 'ccyy-mm-dd')`. A query will have to apply the same function to the search string, or Oracle may not be able to use the index.

By default, an index is *ascending,* meaning that the keys are sorted in order of lowest value to highest. A descending index reverses this. In fact, the difference is often not important: the entries in an index are stored as a doubly linked list, so it is possible to navigate up or down with equal celerity, but this will affect the order in which rows are returned if they are retrieved with an index full scan.

Creating and Using Indexes

Indexes are created implicitly when primary key and unique constraints are defined, if an index on the relevant column(s) does not already exist. The basic syntax for creating an index explicitly is

```
CREATE [UNIQUE | BITMAP] INDEX [ schema.]indexname
ON [schema.]tablename (column [, column...] ) ;
```

The default type of index is a nonunique, noncompressed, non–reverse key B*Tree index. It is not possible to create a unique bitmap index (and you wouldn't want to if you could—think about the cardinality issue). Indexes are schema objects, and it is possible to create an index in one schema on a table in another, but most people would find this somewhat confusing. A *composite* index is an index on several columns. Composite indexes can be on columns of different data types, and the columns do not have to be adjacent in the table.

 TIP Many database administrators do not consider it good practice to rely on implicit index creation. If the indexes are created explicitly, the creator has full control over the characteristics of the index, which can make it easier for the DBA to manage subsequently.

Consider this example of creating tables and indexes, and then defining constraints:

```
create table dept(deptno number,dname varchar2(10));
create table emp(empno number, surname varchar2(10),
forename varchar2(10), dob date, deptno number);
create unique index dept_i1 on dept(deptno);
create unique index emp_i1 on emp(empno);
create index emp_i2 on emp(surname,forename);
create bitmap index emp_i3 on emp(deptno);
alter table dept add constraint dept_pk primary key (deptno);
alter table emp add constraint emp_pk primary key (empno);
alter table emp add constraint emp_fk
foreign key (deptno) references dept(deptno);
```

The first two indexes created are flagged as UNIQUE, meaning that it will not be possible to insert duplicate values. This is not defined as a constraint at this point but is true nonetheless. The third index is not defined as UNIQUE and will therefore accept duplicate values; this is a composite index on two columns. The fourth index is defined as a bitmap index, because the cardinality of the column is likely to be low in proportion to the number of rows in the table.

When the two primary key constraints are defined, Oracle will detect the preexisting indexes and use them to enforce the constraints. Note that the index on DEPT.DEPTNO has no purpose for performance because the table will in all likelihood be so small that the index will never be used to retrieve rows (a scan will be quicker), but it is still essential to have an index to enforce the primary key constraint.

Once created, indexes are used completely transparently and automatically. Before executing a SQL statement, the Oracle server will evaluate all the possible ways of executing it. Some of these ways may involve using whatever indexes are available; others may not. Oracle will make use of the information it gathers on the tables and the environment to make an intelligent decision about which (if any) indexes to use.

 TIP The Oracle server should make the best decision about index use, but if it is getting it wrong, it is possible for a programmer to embed instructions, known as optimizer hints, in code that will force the use (or not) of certain indexes.

Modifying and Dropping Indexes

The ALTER INDEX command cannot be used to change any of the characteristics described in this chapter: the type (B*Tree or bitmap) of the index; the columns; or whether it is unique or nonunique. The ALTER INDEX command lies in the database administration domain and would typically be used to adjust the physical properties of the index, not the logical properties that are of interest to developers. If it is necessary to change any of these properties, the index must be dropped and recreated. Continuing the example in the preceding section, to change the index EMP_I2 to include the employees' birthdays,

```
drop index emp_i2;
create index emp_i2 on emp(surname,forename,dob);
```

This composite index now includes columns with different data types. The columns happen to be listed in the same order that they are defined in the table, but this is by no means necessary.

When a table is dropped, all the indexes and constraints defined for the table are dropped as well. If an index was created implicitly by creating a constraint, then dropping the constraint will also drop the index. If the index had been created explicitly and the constraint created later, then if the constraint were dropped the index would survive.

Exercise 7-5: Create Indexes In this exercise, add some indexes to the CUSTOMERS table.

1. Connect to your database with SQL*Plus as user WEBSTORE.

2. Create a compound B*Tree index on the customer names and status:

```
create index cust_name_i on customers (customer_name, customer_status);
```

3. Create bitmap indexes on a low-cardinality column:

```
create bitmap index creditrating_i on customers(creditrating);
```

4. Determine the name and some other characteristics of the indexes just created by running this query.

```
select index_name,column_name,index_type,uniqueness
from user_indexes natural join user_ind_columns
where table_name='CUSTOMERS';
```

Constraints

Table constraints are a means by which the database can enforce business rules and guarantee that the data conforms to the entity-relationship model determined by the systems analysis that defines the application data structures. For example, the business analysts of your organization may have decided that every customer and every order must be uniquely identifiable by number, that no orders can be issued to a customer before that customer has been created, and that every order must have a valid date and a value greater than zero. These would implemented by creating primary key constraints on the CUSTOMER_ID column of the CUSTOMERS table and the ORDER_ID column of the ORDERS table, a foreign key constraint on the ORDERS table referencing the CUSTOMERS table, a not-null constraint on the DATE column of the ORDERS table (the DATE data type will itself ensure that that any dates are valid automatically—it will not accept invalid dates), and a check constraint on the ORDER_AMOUNT column on the ORDERS table.

If any DML executed against a table with constraints defined violates a constraint, then the whole statement will be rolled back automatically. Remember that a DML statement that affects many rows might partially succeed before it hits a constraint problem with a particular row. If the statement is part of a multistatement transaction, then the statements that have already succeeded will remain intact but uncommitted.

 EXAM TIP A constraint violation will force an automatic rollback of the entire statement that hit the problem, not just the single action within the statement, and not the entire transaction.

The Types of Constraint

The constraint types supported by the Oracle database are

- UNIQUE
- NOT NULL
- PRIMARY KEY
- FOREIGN KEY
- CHECK

Constraints have names. It is good practice to specify the names with a standard naming convention, but if they are not explicitly named, Oracle will generate names.

Unique Constraints

A *unique* constraint nominates a column (or combination of columns) for which the value must be different for every row in the table. If the constraint is based on a single column, this is known as the *key* column. If the constraint is composed of more than one column (known as a *composite key* unique constraint), the columns do not have to be the same data type or be adjacent in the table definition.

An oddity of unique constraints is that it is possible to enter a NULL value into the key column(s); it is indeed possible to have any number of rows with NULL values in their key column(s). So selecting rows on a key column will guarantee that only one row is returned—unless you search for NULL, in which case all the rows where the key columns are NULL will be returned.

 EXAM TIP It is possible to insert many rows with NULLs in a column with a unique constraint. This is not possible for a column with a primary key constraint.

Unique constraints are enforced by an index. When a unique constraint is defined, Oracle will look for an index on the key column(s), and if one does not exist, it will be created. Then whenever a row is inserted, Oracle will search the index to see if the values of the key columns are already present; if they are, it will reject the insert. The structure of these indexes (known as B*Tree indexes) does not include NULL values, which is why many rows with NULL are permitted: they simply do not exist in the index. While the first purpose of the index is to enforce the constraint, it has a secondary effect: improving performance if the key columns are used in the WHERE clauses of SQL statements. However, selecting WHERE `key_column` IS NULL cannot use the index (because it doesn't include the NULLs) and will therefore always result in a scan of the entire table.

Not-Null Constraints

The *not-null* constraint forces values to be entered into the key column. Not-null constraints are defined per column and are sometimes called mandatory columns; if the business requirement is that a group of columns should all have values, you cannot define one not-null constraint for the whole group but must define a not-null constraint for each column.

Any attempt to insert a row without specifying values for the not-null-constrained columns results in an error. It is possible to bypass the need to specify a value by including a DEFAULT clause on the column when creating the table, as discussed in the earlier section "Creating Tables with Column Specifications."

Primary Key Constraints

The *primary key* is the means of locating a single row in a table. The relational database paradigm includes a requirement that every table should have a primary key: a column (or combination of columns) that can be used to distinguish every row. The Oracle database deviates from the paradigm (as do some other RDBMS implementations) by permitting tables without primary keys.

The implementation of a primary key constraint is in effect the union of a unique constraint and a not-null constraint. The key columns must have unique values, and they may not be null. As with unique constraints, an index must exist on the constrained column(s). If one does not exist already, an index will be created when the constraint is defined. A table can have only one primary key. Try to create a second, and you will get an error. A table can, however, have any number of unique constraints and not-null columns, so if there are several columns that the business analysts have decided must be unique and populated, one of these can be designated the primary key, and the others made unique and not null. An example could be a table of employees, where e-mail address, social security number, and employee number should all be required and unique.

EXAM TIP Unique and primary key constraints need an index. If one does not exist, one will be created automatically.

Foreign Key Constraints

A *foreign key* constraint is defined on the child table in a parent-child relationship. The constraint nominates a column (or columns) in the child table that corresponds to the primary key column(s) in the parent table. The columns do not have to have the same names, but they must be of the same data type. Foreign key constraints define the relational structure of the database: the many-to-one relationships that connect the table, in their third normal form.

If the parent table has unique constraints as well as (or instead of) a primary key constraint, these columns can be used as the basis of foreign key constraints, even if they are nullable.

EXAM TIP A foreign key constraint is defined on the child table, but a unique or primary key constraint must already exist on the parent table.

Just as a unique constraint permits null values in the constrained column, so does a foreign key constraint. You can insert rows into the child table with null foreign key columns—even if there is not a row in the parent table with a null value. This creates *orphan* rows and can cause dreadful confusion. As a general rule, all the columns in a unique constraint and all the columns in a foreign key constraint are best defined with not-null constraints as well; this will often be a business requirement.

Attempting to insert a row in the child table for which there is no matching row in the parent table will give an error. Similarly, deleting a row in the parent table will give an error if there are already rows referring to it in the child table. There are two techniques for changing this behavior. First, the constraint may be created as ON DELETE CASCADE. This means that if a row in the parent table is deleted, Oracle will search the child table for all the matching rows and delete them too. This will happen automatically. A less drastic technique is to create the constraint as ON DELETE SET NULL. In this case, if a row in the parent table is deleted, Oracle will search the child table for all the matching rows and set the foreign key columns to null. This means that the child rows will be orphaned but will still exist. If the columns in the child table also have a not-null constraint, then the deletion from the parent table will fail.

It is not possible to drop or truncate the parent table in a foreign key relationship, even if there are no rows in the child table. This still applies if the ON DELETE SET NULL or ON DELETE CASCADE clause was used.

A variation on the foreign key constraint is the *self-referencing* foreign key constraint. This defines a condition where the parent and child rows exist in the same table. An example would be a table of employees, which includes a column for the employee's manager. The manager is himself an employee and must exist in the table. So if the primary key is the EMPLOYEE_ID column, and the manager is identified by a column MANAGER_ID, then the foreign key constraint will state that the value of the MANAGER_ID column must refer back to a valid EMPLOYEE_ID. If an employee is his own manager, then the row would refer to itself.

Check Constraints

A *check* constraint can be used to enforce simple rules, such as that the value entered in a column must be within a range of values. The rule must be an expression that will evaluate to TRUE or FALSE. The rules can refer to absolute values entered as literals, or to other columns in the same row, and they may make use of some functions. As many check constraints as you want can be applied to one column, but it is not possible to use a subquery to evaluate whether a value is permissible, or to use functions such as SYSDATE.

 TIP The not-null constraint is in fact implemented as a preconfigured check constraint.

Defining Constraints

Constraints can be defined when creating a table, or added to the table later. When defining constraints at table creation time, the constraint can be defined in line with the column to which it refers, or at the end of the table definition. There is more flexibility to using the latter technique. For example, it is impossible to define a foreign key constraint that refers to two columns or a check constraint that refers to any column other than that being constrained if the constraint is defined in line, but both these are possible if the constraint is defined at the end of the table.

For the constraints that require an index (the unique and primary key constraints), the index will be created with the table if the constraint is defined at table creation time.

Consider these two table creation statements (to which line numbers have been added):

```
1     create table dept(
2     deptno number(2,0) constraint dept_deptno_pk primary key
3     constraint dept_deptno_ck check (deptno between 10 and 90),
4     dname varchar2(20) constraint dept_dname_nn not null);
5     create table emp(
```

```
6     empno number(4,0) constraint emp_empno_pk primary key,
7     ename varchar2(20) constraint emp_ename_nn not null,
8     mgr number (4,0) constraint emp_mgr_fk references emp (empno),
9     dob date,
10    hiredate date,
11    deptno number(2,0) constraint emp_deptno_fk references dept(deptno)
12    on delete set null,
13    email varchar2(30) constraint emp_email_uk unique,
14    constraint emp_hiredate_ck check (hiredate >= dob + 365*16),
15    constraint emp_email_ck
16    check ((instr(email,'@') > 0) and (instr(email,'.') > 0)));
```

Taking these statements line by line:

1. The first table created is DEPT, intended to have one row for each department.

2. DEPTNO is numeric, two digits, no decimals. This is the table's primary key. The constraint is named DEPT_DEPTNO_PK.

3. A second constraint applied to DEPTNO is a check limiting it to numbers in the range 10 to 90. The constraint is named DEPT_DEPTNO_CK.

4. The DNAME column is variable-length characters, with a constraint DEPT_DNAME_NN making it not nullable.

5. The second table created is EMP, intended to have one row for every employee.

6. EMPNO is numeric, up to four digits with no decimals. Constraint EMP_EMPNO_PK marks this as the table's primary key.

7. ENAME is variable-length characters, with a constraint EMP_ENAME_NN making it not nullable.

8. MGR is the employee's manager, who must himself be an employee. The column is defined in the same way as the table's primary key column of EMPNO. The constraint EMP_MGR_FK defines this column as a self-referencing foreign key, so any value entered must refer to an already-extant row in EMP (though it is not constrained to be not null, so it can be left blank).

9. DOB, the employee's birthday, is a date and not constrained.

10. HIREDATE is the date the employee was hired and is not constrained. At least, not yet.

11. DEPTNO is the department with which the employee is associated. The column is defined in the same way as the DEPT table's primary key column of DEPTNO, and the constraint EMP_DEPTNO_FK enforces a foreign key relationship; it is not possible to assign an employee to a department that does not exist. This is nullable, however.

12. The EMP_DEPTO_FK constraint is further defined as ON DELETE SET NULL, so if the parent row in DEPT is deleted, all matching child rows in EMPNO will have DEPTNO set to NULL.

13. EMAIL is variable-length character data and must be unique if entered (though it can be left empty).

14. This defines an additional table level constraint EMP_HIREDATE_CK. The constraint checks for use of child labor, by rejecting any rows where the date of hiring is not at least 16 years later than the birthday. This constraint could not be defined in line with HIREDATE, because the syntax does not allow references to other columns at that point.

15. An additional constraint EMP_EMAIL_CK is added to the EMAIL column, which makes two checks on the e-mail address. The INSTR functions search for "@" and "." characters (which will always be present in a valid e-mail address) and if it can't find both of them, the check condition will return FALSE and the row will be rejected.

The preceding examples show several possibilities for defining constraints at table creation time. Further possibilities not covered include:

- Controlling the index creation for the unique and primary key constraints
- Defining whether the constraint should be checked at insert time (which it is by default) or later on, when the transaction is committed
- Stating whether the constraint is in fact being enforced at all (which is the default) or is disabled

It is possible to create tables with no constraints and then to add them later with an ALTER TABLE command. The end result will be the same, but this technique does make the code less self-documenting, as the complete table definition will then be spread over several statements rather than being in one.

Constraint State

At any time, every constraint is either enabled or disabled, and validated or not validated. Any combination of these is syntactically possible:

- **ENABLE VALIDATE**   It is not possible to enter rows that would violate the constraint, and all rows in the table conform to the constraint.
- **DISABLE NOVALIDATE**   Any data (conforming or not) can be entered, and there may already be nonconforming data in the table.
- **ENABLE NOVALIDATE**   There may already be nonconforming data in the table, but all data entered now must conform.
- **DISABLE VALIDATE**   An impossible situation: all data in the table conforms to the constraint, but new rows need not. The end result is that the table is locked against DML commands.

The ideal situation (and the default when a constraint is defined) is ENABLE VALIDATE. This will guarantee that all the data is valid, and no invalid data can be entered. The other extreme, DISABLE NOVALIDATE, can be very useful when uploading large amounts of data into a table. It may well be that the data being uploaded does not conform to the business rules, but rather than have a large upload fail because of a few bad rows, putting the constraint in this state will allow the upload to succeed. Immediately following the upload, transition the constraint into the ENABLE NOVALIDATE state. This will prevent the situation from deteriorating further while the data is checked for conformance before transitioning the constraint to the ideal state.

As an example, consider this script, which reads data from a source table of live data into a table of archive data. The assumption is that there is a NOT NULL constraint on a column of the target table that may not have been enforced on the source table:

```
alter table sales_archive modify constraint sa_nn1 disable novalidate;
insert into sales_archive select * from sales_current;
alter table sales_archive modify constraint sa_nn1 enable novalidate;
update sales_archive set channel='NOT KNOWN' where channel is null;
alter table sales_archive modify constraint sa_nn1 enable validate;
```

Constraint Checking

Constraints can be checked as a statement is executed (an IMMEDIATE constraint) or when a transaction is committed (a DEFERRED constraint). By default, all constraints are IMMEDIATE and not deferrable. An alternative approach to the previous example would have been possible had the constraint been created as deferrable:

```
set constraint sa_nn1 deferred;
insert into sales_archive select * from sales_current;
update sales_archive set channel='NOT KNOWN' where channel is null;
commit;
set constraint sa_nn1 immediate;
```

For the constraint to be deferrable, it must have been created with appropriate syntax:

```
alter table sales_archive add constraint sa_nn1
check (channel is not null) deferrable initially immediate;
```

It is not possible to make a constraint deferrable later, if it was not created that way. The constraint SA_NN1 will by default be enforced when a row is inserted (or updated), but the check can be postponed until the transaction commits. A common use for deferrable constraints is with foreign keys. If a process inserts or updates rows in both the parent and the child tables, if the foreign key constraint is not deferred the process may fail if rows are not processed in the correct order.

Changing the status of a constraint between ENABLED/DISABLED and VALIDATE/ NOVALIDATE is an operation that will affect all sessions. The status change is a data dictionary update. Switching a deferrable constraint between IMMEDIATE and DEFERRED is session specific, though the initial state will apply to all sessions.

 EXAM TIP By default, constraints are enabled and validated, and they are not deferrable.

Exercise 7-6: Manage Constraints In this exercise, use SQL Developer and SQL*Plus to define and adjust some constraints on the table created in Exercise 7-3.

1. In SQL Developer, navigate to the listing of WEBSTORE's tables and click the CUSTOMERS table.

2. Take the Constraints tab to view the four NOT NULL constraints that were created with the table. Note that their names are not helpful—this will be fixed in Step 8.

3. Click the Actions button and choose Constraints: Add Primary Key.

4. In the Add Primary Key window name the constraint: PK_CUSTOMER_ID, choose the CUSTOMER_ID column, and click Apply.

5. Choose the Show SQL tab to see the constraint creation statement, and then click the Apply button to run the statement.

6. Connect to your database as user WEBSTORE with SQL*Plus.

7. Run this query to find the names of the constraints:

```
select constraint_name,constraint_type,column_name
from user_constraints natural join user_cons_columns
where table_name='CUSTOMERS';
```

8. Rename the constraints to something more meaningful, using the original constraint names retrieved in Step 7, with ALTER TABLE commands:

```
ALTER TABLE CUSTOMERS RENAME CONSTRAINT old_name TO new_name ;
```

9. Add the following constraints to the WEBSTORE schema:

```
alter table ORDERS add constraint PK_ORDER_ID primary key(ORDER_ID);
alter table PRODUCTS add constraint PK_PRODUCT_ID primary key(PRODUCT_ID);
alter table ORDER_ITEMS add constraint FK_PRODUCT_ID foreign key(PRODUCT_ID)
references PRODUCTS(PRODUCT_ID);
alter table ORDER_ITEMS add constraint FK_ORDER_ID foreign key(ORDER_ID)
references ORDERS(ORDER_ID);
alter table ORDERS add constraint FK_CUSTOMER_ID foreign key(CUSTOMER_ID)
references CUSTOMERS(CUSTOMER_ID);
```

Views

To the user, a view looks like a table: a two-dimensional structure of rows of columns, against which the user can run SELECT and DML statements. The programmer knows the truth: a view is just a named SELECT statement. Any SELECT statement returns a two-dimensional set of rows. If the SELECT statement is saved as a view, then whenever the users query or update rows in the view (under the impression that it is a table), the statement runs, and the result is presented to users as though it were a table. The SELECT statement on which a view is based can be anything. It can join tables, perform aggregations, or do sorts; absolutely any legal SELECT command can be used as the basis for a view.

 EXAM TIP Views share the same namespace as tables: anywhere that a table name can be used, a view name is also syntactically correct.

Why Use Views at All?

Possible reasons include: security, simplifying user SQL statements, preventing errors, improving performance, and making data comprehensible. Table and column names are often long and pretty meaningless. The view and its columns can be much more obvious.

Views to Enforce Security

It may be that users should only see certain rows or columns of a table. There are several ways of enforcing this, but a view is often the simplest. Consider the HR.EMPLOYEES table. This includes personal details that should not be visible to staff outside the personnel department. But finance staff will need to be able to see the costing information. This view will depersonalize the data:

```
create view hr.emp_fin as select
hire_date,job_id,salary,commission_pct,department_id from hr.employees;
```

Note the use of schema qualifiers for the table as the source of the data (often referred to as either the *base* or the *detail* table) and the view: views are schema objects and can draw their data from tables in the same schema or in other schemas. If the schema is not specified, it will of course be in the current schema.

Finance staff can then be given permission to see the view but not the table and can issue statements such as this:

```
select * from emp_fin where department_id=50;
```

They will see only the five columns that make up the view, not the remaining columns of EMPLOYEES with the personal information. The view can be joined to other tables or aggregated as though it were a table:

```
select department_name, sum(salary) from departments natural join emp_fin
group by department_name;
```

A well-constructed set of views can implement a whole security structure within the database, giving users access to data they need to see while concealing data they do not need to see.

Views to Simplify User SQL

It will be much easier for users to query data if the hard work (such as joins or aggregations) is done for them by the code that defines the view. In the last example, the user had to write code that joined the EMP_FIN view to the DEPARTMENTS table and summed the salaries per department. This could all be done in a view:

```
create view dept_sal as
select d.department_name, sum(e.salary) from
departments d left outer join employees e on d.department_id=e.department_id
group by department_name order by department_name;
```

Then the users can select from DEPT_SAL without needing to know anything about joins, or even how to sort the results:

```
select * from dept_sal;
```

In particular, they do not need to know how to make sure that all departments are listed, even those with no employees. The example in the preceding section would have missed these.

Views to Prevent Errors

It is impossible to prevent users from making errors, but well-constructed views can prevent some errors arising from a lack of understanding of how data should be interpreted. The preceding section already introduced this concept by constructing a view that will list all departments, whether or not they currently have staff assigned to them.

A view can help to present data in a way that is unambiguous. For example, many applications never actually delete rows. Consider this table:

```
create table emp(empno number constraint emp_empno_pk primary key,
ename varchar2(10),deptno number,active varchar2(1) default 'Y');
```

The column ACTIVE is a flag indicating that the employee is currently employed and will default to 'Y' when a row is inserted. When a user, through the user interface, "deletes" an employee, the underlying SQL statement will be an update that sets ACTIVE to 'N'. If users who are not aware of this query the table, they may severely misinterpret the results. It will often be better to give them access to a view:

```
create view current_staff as select * from emp where active='Y';
```

Queries addressed to this view cannot possibly see "deleted" staff members.

Views to Make Data Comprehensible

The data structures in a database will be normalized tables. It is not reasonable to expect users to understand normalized structures. To take an example from the Oracle E-Business Suite, a "customer" in the Accounts Receivable module is in fact an entity consisting of information distributed across the tables HZ_PARTIES, HZ_PARTY_SITES, HZ_CUST_ACCTS_ALL, and many more. All these tables are linked by primary key–to–foreign key relationships, but these are not defined on any identifiers visible to users (such as a customer number): they are based on columns the users never see that have values generated internally from sequences. The forms and reports used to retrieve customer information never address these tables directly; they all work through views.

As well as presenting data to users in a comprehensible form, the use of views to provide a layer of abstraction between the objects seen by users and the objects stored within the database can be invaluable for maintenance work. It becomes possible to redesign the data structures without having to recode the application. If tables are changed, then adjusting the view definitions may make any changes to the SQL and PL/SQL code unnecessary. This can be a powerful technique for making applications portable across different databases.

Views for Performance

The SELECT statement behind a view can be optimized by programmers, so that users don't need to worry about tuning code. There may be many possibilities for getting the same result, but some techniques can be much slower than others. For example, when joining two tables there is usually a choice between the *nested loop* join and the *hash* join. A nested loop join uses an index to get to individual rows; a hash join reads the whole table into memory. The choice between the two will be dependent on the state of the data and the hardware resources available.

Theoretically, one can always rely on the Oracle optimizer to work out the best way to run a SQL statement, but there are cases where it gets it wrong. If the programmers know which technique is best, they can instruct the optimizer. This example forces use of the hash technique:

```
create view dept_emp as
select /*+USE_HASH (employees departments)*/ department_name, last_name
from departments natural join employees;
```

Whenever users query the DEPT_EMP view, the join will be performed by scanning the detail tables into memory. The users need not know the syntax for forcing use of this join method. You do not need to know it, either: this is beyond the scope of the OCP examination, but the concept of tuning with view design should be known.

Simple and Complex Views

For practical purposes, classification of a view as *simple* or *complex* is related to whether DML statements can be executed against it: simple views can (usually) accept DML statements; complex views cannot. The strict definitions are as follows:

- A simple view draws data from one detail table, uses no functions, and does no aggregation.

- A complex view can join detail tables, use functions, and perform aggregations.

Applying these definitions shows that of the four views used as examples in the preceding section, the first and third are simple and the second and fourth are complex.

It is not possible to execute INSERT, UPDATE, or DELETE commands against a complex view. The mapping of the rows in the view back to the rows in the detail table(s) cannot always be established on a one-to-one basis, which is necessary for DML operations. It is usually possible to execute DML against a simple view but not always. For example, if the view does not include a column that has a NOT NULL constraint, then an INSERT through the view cannot succeed (unless the column has a default value). This can produce a disconcerting effect because the error message will refer to a table and a column that are not mentioned in the statement, as demonstrated in the first example in Figure 7-5.

The first view in the figure, RNAME_V, does conform to the definition of a simple view, but an INSERT cannot be performed through it because it is missing a mandatory column. The second view, RUPPERNAME_V, is a complex view because it includes a function. This makes an INSERT impossible, because there is no way the database can work out what should actually be inserted: it can't reverse-engineer the effect of the UPPER function in a deterministic fashion. But the DELETE succeeds, because that is not dependent on the function.

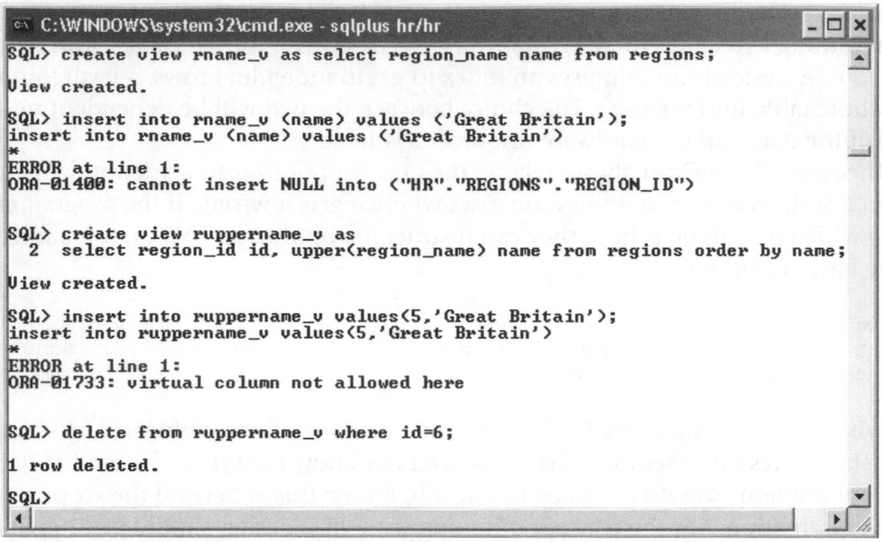

```
C:\WINDOWS\system32\cmd.exe - sqlplus hr/hr                          _ □ ×

SQL> create view rname_v as select region_name name from regions;

View created.

SQL> insert into rname_v (name) values ('Great Britain');
insert into rname_v (name) values ('Great Britain')
*
ERROR at line 1:
ORA-01400: cannot insert NULL into ("HR"."REGIONS"."REGION_ID")


SQL> create view ruppername_v as
  2  select region_id id, upper(region_name) name from regions order by name;

View created.

SQL> insert into ruppername_v values(5,'Great Britain');
insert into ruppername_v values(5,'Great Britain')
*
ERROR at line 1:
ORA-01733: virtual column not allowed here


SQL> delete from ruppername_v where id=6;

1 row deleted.

SQL>
```

Figure 7-5 DML against simple and complex views

CREATE VIEW, ALTER VIEW, and DROP VIEW

The syntax to create a view is as follows:

```
CREATE [OR REPLACE] [FORCE | NOFORCE] VIEW
[schema.]viewname [(alias [,alias]…)]
AS subquery
[WITH CHECK OPTION [CONSTRAINT constraintname]]
[WITH READ ONLY [CONSTRAINT constraintname]] ;
```

Note that views are schema objects. There is no reason not to have a view owned by one user referencing detail tables owned by another user. By default, the view will be created in the current schema. The optional keywords, none of which have been used in the examples so far, are as follows:

- **OR REPLACE**   If the view already exists, it will be dropped before being created.
- **FORCE or NOFORCE**   The FORCE keyword will create the view even if the detail table(s) in the subquery does not exist. NOFORCE is the default and will cause an error if the detail table does not exist.
- **WITH CHECK OPTION**   This has to do with DML. If the subquery includes a WHERE clause, then this option will prevent insertion of rows that wouldn't be seen in the view or updates that would cause a row to disappear from the view. By default, this option is not enabled, which can give disconcerting results.
- **WITH READ ONLY**   Prevents any DML through the view.
- **CONSTRAINT** *constraintname*   This can be used to name the WITH CHECK OPTION and WITH READ ONLY restrictions so that error messages when the restrictions cause statements to fail will be more comprehensible.

In addition, a set of alias names can be provided for the names of the view's columns. If not provided, the columns will be named after the table's columns or with aliases specified in the subquery.

The main use of the ALTER VIEW command is to compile the view. A view must be compiled successfully before it can be used. When a view is created, Oracle will check that the detail tables and the necessary columns on which the view is based do exist. If they do not, the compilation fails and the view will not be created—unless you use the FORCE option. In that case, the view will be created but will be unusable until the tables or columns to which it refers are created and the view is successfully compiled. When an invalid view is queried, Oracle will attempt to compile it automatically. If the compilation succeeds because the problem has been fixed, users won't know there was ever a problem—except that their query may take a little longer than usual. Generally speaking, you should manually compile views to make sure they do compile successfully, rather than having users discover errors.

It is not possible to adjust a view's column definitions after creation in the way that a table's columns can be changed. The view must be dropped and recreated. The DROP command is as follows:

```
DROP VIEW [schema.]viewname ;
```

By using the OR REPLACE keywords with the CREATE VIEW command, the view will be automatically dropped (if it exists at all) before being created.

Exercise 7-7: Create Views   In this exercise, you will create some simple and complex views, using data in the HR schema. Either SQL*Plus or SQL developer can be used.

1. Connect to your database as user HR.

2. Create views on the EMPLOYEES and DEPARTMENT tables that remove all personal information:

   ```
   create view emp_anon_v as
   select hire_date, job_id,salary,commission_pct,department_id from employees;
   create view dept_anon_v as
   select department_id,department_name,location_id from departments;
   ```

3. Create a complex view that will join and aggregate the two simple views. Note that there is no reason not to have views of views.

   ```
   create view dep_sum_v as
   select e.department_id,count(1) staff, sum(e.salary) salaries,
   d.department_name from emp_anon_v e join dept_anon_v d
   on e.department_id=d.department_id
   group by e.department_id,d.department_name;
   ```

4. Confirm that the view works by querying it.

Synonyms

A *synonym* is an alternative name for an object. If synonyms exist for objects, then any SQL statement can address the object either by its actual name or by its synonym. This may seem trivial. It isn't. Use of synonyms means that an application can function for any user, irrespective of which schema owns the views and tables or even in which database the tables reside. Consider this statement:

```
select * from hr.employees@prod;
```

The user issuing the statement must know that the employees table is owned by the HR schema in the database identified by the database link PROD (do not worry about database links—they are a means of accessing objects in a database other than that onto which you are logged). If a public synonym has been created with this statement:

```
create public synonym emp for hr.employees@prod;
```

then all the user (any user!) need enter is the following:

```
select * from emp;
```

This gives both data independence and location transparency. Tables and views can be renamed or relocated without ever having to change code; only the synonyms need to be adjusted.

As well as SELECT statements, DML statements can address synonyms as though they were the object to which they refer.

Private synonyms are schema objects. Either they must be in your own schema, or they must be qualified with the schema name. Public synonyms exist independently of a schema. A public synonym can be referred to by any user to whom permission has been granted to see it without the need to qualify it with a schema name. Private synonyms must have unique names within their schema. Public synonyms can have the same name as schema objects. When executing statements that address objects without a schema qualifier, Oracle will first look for the object in the local schema, and only if it cannot be found will it look for a public synonym. Thus, in the preceding example, if the user happened to own a table called EMP it would be this that would be seen—not the table pointed to by the public synonym.

The syntax to create a synonym is as follows:

```
CREATE [PUBLIC] SYNONYM synonym FOR object ;
```

A user will need to have been granted permission to create private synonyms and further permission to create public synonyms. Usually, only the database administrator can create (or drop) public synonyms. This is because their presence (or absence) will affect every user.

 EXAM TIP The "public" in "public synonym" means that it is not a schema object and cannot therefore be prefixed with a schema name. It does not mean that everyone has permissions against it.

To drop a synonym:

```
DROP [PUBLIC] SYNONYM synonym ;
```

If the object to which a synonym refers (the table or view) is dropped, the synonym continues to exist. Any attempt to use it will return an error. In this respect, synonyms behave in the same way as views. If the object is recreated, the synonym must be recompiled before use. As with views, this will happen automatically the next time the synonym is addressed, or it can be done explicitly with

```
ALTER SYNONYM synonym COMPILE;
```

Exercise 7-8: Create and Use Synonyms   In this exercise, you will create and use private synonyms, using objects in the HR schema. Either SQL*Plus or SQL developer can be used.

1. Connect to your database as user HR.

2. Create synonyms for the three views created in Exercise 7-7:

```
create synonym emp_s for emp_anon_v;
create synonym dept_s for dept_anon_v;
create synonym dsum_s for dep_sum_v;
```

3. Confirm that the synonyms are identical to the underlying objects:

```
describe emp_s;
describe emp_anon_v;
```

4. Confirm that the synonyms work (even to the extent of producing the same errors) by running the statements in Exercise 7-7 against the synonyms instead of the views:

```
select * from dsum_s;
insert into dept_s values(99,'Temp Dept',1800);
insert into emp_s values(sysdate,'AC MGR',10000,0,99);
update emp_s set salary=salary*1.1;
rollback;
select max(salaries / staff) from dsum_s;
```

5. Drop two of the views:

```
drop view emp_anon_v;
drop view dept_anon_v;
```

6. Query the complex view that is based on the dropped views:

```
select * from dep_sum_v;
```

Note that the query fails.

7. Attempt to recompile the broken view:

```
alter view dep_sum_v compile;
```

This will fail as well.

8. Drop the DEP_SUM_V view:

```
drop view dep_sum_v;
```

9. Query the synonym for a dropped view:

```
select * from emp_s;
```

This will fail.

10. Recompile the broken synonym:

```
alter synonym emp_s compile;
```

Note that this does not give an error, but rerun the query from Step 9. It is definitely still broken.

11. Tidy up by dropping the synonyms:

```
drop synonym emp_s;
drop synonym dept_s;
drop synonym dsum_s;
```

Sequences

A sequence is a structure for generating unique integer values. Only one session can read the next value and thus force it to increment. This is a point of serialization, so each value generated will be unique.

Sequences are an invaluable tool for generating primary keys. Many applications will need automatically generated primary key values. Examples in everyday business data processing are customer numbers or order numbers: the business analysts will have stated that every order must have a unique number, which should continually increment. Other applications may not have such a requirement in business terms, but it will be needed to enforce relational integrity. Consider a telephone billing system: in business terms the unique identifier of a telephone is the telephone number (which is a string) and that of a call will be the source telephone number and the time the call began (which is a timestamp). These data types are unnecessarily complex to use as primary keys for the high volumes that go through a telephone switching system. While this information will be recorded, it will be much faster to use simple numeric columns to define the primary and foreign keys. The values in these columns can be sequence based.

The sequence mechanism is independent of tables, the row locking mechanism, and commit or rollback processing. This means that a sequence can issue thousands of unique values a minute—far faster than any method involving selecting a column from a table, updating it, and committing the change.

Figure 7-6 shows two sessions selecting values from a sequence SEQ1.

Note that in the figure, each selection of SEQ1.NEXTVAL generates a unique number. The numbers are issued consecutively in order of the time the selection was made, and the number increments globally, not just within one session.

Creating Sequences

The full syntax for creating a sequence is as follows:

```
CREATE SEQUENCE [schema.]sequencename
[INCREMENT BY number]
[START WITH number]
[MAXVALUE number | NOMAXVALUE]
[MINVALUE number | NOMINVALUE]
[CYCLE | NOCYCLE]
[CACHE number | NOCACHE]
[ORDER | NOORDER] ;
```

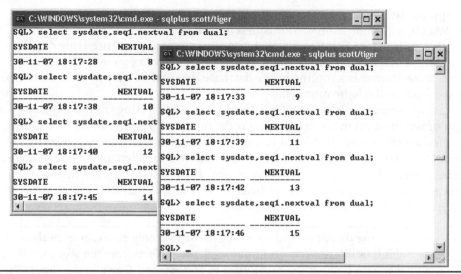

Figure 7-6   Use of a sequence by two sessions concurrently

It can be seen that creating a sequence can be very simple. For example, the sequence used in Figure 7-6 was created with

```
create sequence seq1;
```

The options are shown in the following table.

INCREMENT BY	How much higher (or lower) than the last number issued should the next number be? Defaults to +1 but can be any positive number (or negative number for a descending sequence).
START WITH	The starting point for the sequence: the number issued by the first selection. Defaults to 1 but can be anything.
MAXVALUE	The highest number an ascending sequence can go to before generating an error or returning to its START WITH value. The default is no maximum.
MINVALUE	The lowest number a descending sequence can go to before generating an error or returning to its START WITH value. The default is no minimum.
CYCLE	Controls the behavior on reaching MAXVALUE or MINVALUE. The default behavior is to give an error, but if CYCLE is specified the sequence will return to its starting point and repeat.
CACHE	For performance, Oracle can preissue sequence values in batches and cache them for issuing to users. The default is to generate and cache the next 20 values.
ORDER	Only relevant for a clustered database: ORDER forces all instances in the cluster to coordinate incrementing the sequence, so that numbers issued are always in order even when issued to sessions against different instances.

Appropriate settings for INCREMENT BY, START WITH, and MAXVALUE or MINVALUE will come from your business analysts.

It is very rare for CYCLE to be used, because it lets the sequence issue duplicate values. If the sequence is being used to generate primary key values, CYCLE only makes sense if there is a routine in the database that will delete old rows faster than the sequence will reissue numbers.

Caching sequence values is vital for performance. Selecting from a sequence is a point of serialization in the application code: only one session can do this at once. The mechanism is very efficient: it is much faster than locking a row, updating the row, and then unlocking it with a COMMIT. But even so, selecting from a sequence can be a cause of contention between sessions. The CACHE keyword instructs Oracle to pregenerate sequence numbers in batches. This means that they can be issued faster than if they had to be generated on demand.

TIP The default number of values to cache is only 20. Experience shows that this is usually not enough. If your application selects from the sequence 10 times a second, then set the cache value to 50 thousand. Don't be shy about this.

Using Sequences

To use a sequence, a session can select either the next value with the NEXTVAL pseudocolumn, which forces the sequence to increment, or the last (or "current") value issued to that session with the CURRVAL pseudocolumn. The NEXTVAL will be globally unique: each session that selects it will get a different, incremented value for each SELECT. The CURRVAL will be constant for one session until it selects NEXTVAL again. There is no way to find out what the last value issued by a sequence was: you can always obtain the next value by incrementing it with NEXTVAL, and you can always recall the last value issued to your session with CURRVAL, but you cannot find the last value issued.

EXAM TIP The CURRVAL of a sequence is the last value issued to the current session, not necessarily the last value issued. You cannot select the CURRVAL until after selecting the NEXTVAL.

A typical use of sequences is for primary key values. This example uses a sequence ORDER_SEQ to generate unique order numbers and LINE_SEQ to generate unique line numbers for the line items of the order. First create the sequences, which is a once-off operation:

```
create sequence order_seq start with 10;
create sequence line_seq start with 10;
```

Then insert the orders with their lines as a single transaction:

```
insert into orders (order_id,order_date,customer_id)
values (order_seq.nextval,sysdate,'1000');
insert into order_items (order_id,order_item_id,product_id)
values (order_seq.currval,line_seq.nextval,'A111');
insert into order_items (order_id,order_item_id,product_id)
values (order_seq.currval,line_seq.nextval,'B111');
commit;
```

The first INSERT statement raises an order with a unique order number drawn from the sequence ORDER_SEQ for customer number 1000. The second and third statements insert the two lines of the order, using the previously issued order number from ORDER_SEQ as the foreign key to connect the line items to the order, and the next values from LINE_SEQ to generate a unique identifier for each line. Finally, the transaction is committed.

A sequence is not tied to any one table. In the preceding example, there would be no technical reason not to use one sequence to generate values for the primary keys of the order and of the lines.

A COMMIT is not necessary to make the increment of a sequence permanent: it is permanent and made visible to the rest of the world the moment it happens. It can't be rolled back, either. Sequence updates occur independently of the transaction management system. For this reason, there will always be gaps in the series. The gaps will be larger if the database has been restarted and the CACHE clause was used. All numbers that have been generated and cached but not yet issued will be lost when the database is shut down. At the next restart, the current value of the sequence will be the last number generated, not the last issued. So, with the default CACHE of 20, every shutdown/startup will lose up to 20 numbers.

If the business analysts have stated that there must be no gaps in a sequence, then another means of generating unique numbers must be used. For the preceding example of raising orders, the current order number could be stored in this table and initialized to 10:

```
create table current_on(order_number number);
insert into current_on values(10);
commit;
```

Then the code to create an order would have to become:

```
update current_on set order_number=order_number + 1;
insert into orders (order_number,order_date,customer_number)
values ((select order_number from current_on),sysdate,'1000');
commit;
```

This will certainly work as a means of generating unique order numbers, and because the increment of the order number is within the transaction that inserts the order, it can be rolled back with the insert if necessary: there will be no gaps in order numbers, unless an order is deliberately deleted. But it is far less efficient than using a sequence, and code like this is famous for causing dreadful contention problems. If many sessions try to lock and increment the one row containing the current number, the whole application will hang as they queue up to take their turn.

After creating and using a sequence, it can be modified. The syntax is as follows:

```
ALTER SEQUENCE sequencename
[INCREMENT BY number]
[START WITH number]
[MAXVALUE number | NOMAXVALUE]
[MINVALUE number | NOMINVALUE]
[CYCLE | NOCYCLE]
[CACHE number | NOCACHE]
[ORDER | NOORDER] ;
```

This ALTER command is the same as the CREATE command, with one exception: there is no way to set the starting value. If you want to restart the sequence, the only way is to drop it and recreate it. To adjust the cache value from default to improve performance of the preceding order entry example:

```
alter sequence order_seq cache 1000;
```

However, if you want to reset the sequence to its starting value, the only way is to drop it:

```
drop sequence order_seq;
```

and create it again.

Exercise 7-9: Create and Use Sequences   In this exercise, you will create some sequences and use them. You will need two concurrent sessions, either SQL Developer or SQL*Plus.

1. Log on to your database twice, as WEBSTORE in separate sessions. Consider one to be your A session and the other to be your B session.

2. In your A session, create a sequence as follows:
   ```
   create sequence seq1 start with 10 nocache maxvalue 15 cycle;
   ```
   The use of NOCACHE is deleterious to performance. If MAXVALUE is specified, then CYCLE will be necessary to prevent errors when MAXVALUE is reached.

3. Execute the following commands in the appropriate session in the correct order to observe the use of NEXTVAL and CURRVAL and the cycling of the sequence:

	In Your A Session	In Your B Session
1st	select seq1.nextval from dual;	
2nd		select seq1.nextval from dual;
3rd	select seq1.nextval from dual;	
4th		select seq1.nextval from dual;
5th	select seq1.currval from dual;	
6th		select seq1.nextval from dual;
7th	select seq1.nextval from dual;	
8th		select seq1.currval from dual;
9th	select seq1.nextval from dual;	
10th		select seq1.nextval from dual;

4. Create a table with a primary key:
   ```
   create table seqtest(c1 number,c2 varchar2(10));
   alter table seqtest add constraint seqtest_pk primary key (c1);
   ```

5. Create a sequence to generate primary key values:
   ```
   create sequence seqtest_pk_s;
   ```

6. In your A session, insert a row into the new table and commit:

```
insert into seqtest values(seqtest_pk_s.nextval,'first');
commit;
```

7. In your B session, insert a row into the new table and do not commit it:

```
insert into seqtest values(seqtest_pk_s.nextval,'second');
```

8. In your A session, insert a third row and commit:

```
insert into seqtest values(seqtest_pk_s.nextval,'third');
commit;
```

9. In your B session, roll back the second insertion:

```
rollback;
```

10. In your B session, see the contents of the table:

```
select * from seqtest;
```

This demonstrates that sequences are incremented and the next value published immediately, outside the transaction control mechanism.

11. Tidy up:

```
drop table seqtest;
drop sequence seqtest_pk_s;
drop sequence seq1;
```

12. Connect to the WEBSTORE schema with either SQL Developer or SQL*Plus and create three sequences which will be used in later exercises. (You may have to connect first as a privileged user like SYSTEM and grant the "CREATE SEQUENCE" privilege to the WEBSTORE user.)

```
create sequence prod_seq;
create sequence cust_seq;
create sequence order_seq;
```

Two-Minute Drill

Categorize the Main Database Objects

- Some objects contain data, principally tables and indexes.
- Programmatic objects such as stored procedures and functions are executable code.
- Views and synonyms are objects that give access to other objects.
- Tables are two-dimensional structures, storing rows defined with columns.
- Tables exist within a schema. The schema name together with the table name makes a unique identifier.

List the Data Types That Are Available for Columns

- The most common character data types are VARCHAR2, NUMBER, and DATE.
- There are many other data types.

Create a Simple Table

- Tables can be created from nothing or with a subquery.
- After creation, column definitions can be added, dropped, or modified.
- The table definition can include default values for columns.

Create and Use Temporary Tables

- Rows in a temporary table are visible only to the session that inserted them.
- DML on temporary tables does not generate redo.
- Temporary tables exist only in sessions' PGAs or in temporary segments.
- A temporary table can keep rows for the duration of a session or of a transaction, depending on how it was created.

Constraints

- Constraints can be defined at table creation time or added later.
- A constraint can be defined inline with its column or at the table level after the columns.
- Table-level constraints can be more complex than those defined inline.
- A table may only have one primary key but can have many unique keys.
- A primary key is functionally equivalent to unique plus not null.
- A unique constraint does not stop insertion of many null values.
- Foreign key constraints define the relationships between tables.

Indexes

- Indexes are required for enforcing unique and primary key constraints.
- NULLs are not included in B*Tree indexes but are included in bitmap indexes.
- B*Tree indexes can be unique or nonunique, which determines whether they can accept duplicate key values.
- B*Tree indexes are suitable for high cardinality columns, bitmap indexes for low cardinality columns.
- Bitmap indexes can be compound, function based, or descending; B*Tree indexes can also be unique, compressed, and reverse key.

Views

- A simple view has one detail (or base) table and uses neither functions nor aggregation.
- A complex view can be based on any SELECT statement, no matter how complicated.

- Views are schema objects. To use a view in another schema, the view name must be qualified with the schema name.

- A view can be queried exactly as though it were a table.

- Views can be joined to other views or to tables, they can be aggregated, and in some cases they can accept DML statements.

- Views exist only as data dictionary constructs. Whenever you query a view, the underlying SELECT statement must be run.

Synonyms

- A synonym is an alternative name for a view or a table.

- Private synonyms are schema objects; public synonyms exist outside user schemas and can be used without specifying a schema name as a qualifier.

- Synonyms share the same namespace as views and tables and can therefore be used interchangeably with them.

Sequences

- A sequence generates unique values—unless either MAXVALUE or MINVALUE and CYCLE have been specified.

- Incrementing a sequence need not be committed and cannot be rolled back.

- Any session can increment the sequence by reading its next value. It is possible to obtain the last value issued to your session but not the last value issued.

Self Test

1. If a table is created without specifying a schema, in which schema will it be? (Choose the best answer.)

   A. It will be an *orphaned* table, without a schema.

   B. The creation will fail.

   C. It will be in the SYS schema.

   D. It will be in the schema of the user creating it.

   E. It will be in the PUBLIC schema.

2. Several object types share the same namespace and therefore cannot have the same name in the same schema. Which of the following object types is not in the same namespace as the others? (Choose the best answer.)

   A. Index

   B. PL/SQL stored procedure

   C. Synonym

   D. Table

   E. View

3. Which of these statements will fail because the table name is not legal? (Choose two answers.)

A. `create table "SELECT" (col1 date);`

B. `create table "lowercase" (col1 date);`

C. `create table number1 (col1 date);`

D. `create table 1number(col1 date);`

E. `create table update(col1 date);`

4. What are distinguishing characteristics of heap tables? (Choose two answers.)

A. A heap table can store variable-length rows.

B. More than one table can store rows in a single heap.

C. Rows in a heap are in random order.

D. Heap tables cannot be indexed.

E. Tables in a heap do not have a primary key.

5. Which of the following data types are variable length? (Choose all correct answers.)

A. BLOB

B. CHAR

C. LONG

D. NUMBER

E. RAW

F. VARCHAR2

6. Study these statements:

```
create table tab1 (c1 number(1), c2 date);
alter session set nls_date_format='dd-mm-yy';
insert into tab1 values (1.1,'31-01-07');
```

Will the insert succeed? (Choose the best answer.)

A. The insert will fail because the 1.1 is too long.

B. The insert will fail because the '31-01-07' is a string, not a date.

C. The insert will fail for both reasons A and B.

D. The insert will succeed.

7. Which of the following is not supported by Oracle as an internal data type? (Choose the best answer.)

A. CHAR

B. FLOAT

C. INTEGER

D. STRING

8. Consider this statement:

```
create table t1 as select * from regions where 1=2;
```

What will be the result? (Choose the best answer.)

A. There will be an error because of the impossible condition.

B. No table will be created because the condition returns FALSE.

C. The table T1 will be created but no rows inserted because the condition returns FALSE.

D. The table T1 will be created and every row in REGIONS inserted because the condition returns a NULL as a row filter.

9. When a table is created with a statement such as the following:

```
create table newtab as select * from tab;
```

will there be any constraints on the new table? (Choose the best answer.)

A. The new table will have no constraints, because constraints are not copied when creating tables with a subquery.

B. All the constraints on TAB will be copied to NEWTAB.

C. Primary key and unique constraints will be copied, but not check and not-null constraints.

D. Check and not-null constraints will be copied, but not unique or primary keys.

E. All constraints will be copied, except foreign key constraints.

10. Which types of constraint require an index? (Choose all that apply.)

A. CHECK

B. NOT NULL

C. PRIMARY KEY

D. UNIQUE

11. A transaction consists of two statements. The first succeeds, but the second (which updates several rows) fails partway through because of a constraint violation. What will happen? (Choose the best answer.)

A. The whole transaction will be rolled back.

B. The second statement will be rolled back completely, and the first will be committed.

C. The second statement will be rolled back completely, and the first will remain uncommitted.

D. Only the one update that caused the violation will be rolled back, everything else will be committed.

E. Only the one update that caused the violation will be rolled back, everything else will remain uncommitted.

12. Which of the following statements is correct about indexes? (Choose the best answer.)

    A. An index can be based on multiple columns of a table, but the columns must be of the same datatype.

    B. An index can be based on multiple columns of a table, but the columns must be adjacent and specified in the order that they are defined in the table.

    C. An index cannot have the same name as a table, unless the index and the table are in separate schemas.

    D. None of the above statements is correct.

13. Which of the following options can be applied to B*Tree indexes, but not to bitmap indexes? (Choose all correct answers.)

    A. Compression

    B. Descending order

    C. Function-based key expressions

    D. Reverse key indexing

    E. Uniqueness

    F. Use of compound keys

14. Data in temporary tables has restricted visibility. If a user logs on as HR and inserts rows into a temporary table, to whom will the rows be visible?

    A. To no session other than the one that did the insert

    B. To all sessions connected as HR

    C. To all sessions, until the session that inserted them terminates

    D. To all sessions, until the session that inserted them commits the transaction

15. Where does the data in a temporary table get written to disk? (Choose the best answer.)

    A. It is never written to disk

    B. To the user's temporary tablespace

    C. To the temporary tablespace of the user in whose schema the table resides

    D. To a disk local to the session's user process

16. Which of these is a defining characteristic of a complex view, rather than a simple view? (Choose one or more correct answers.)

    A. Restricting the projection by selecting only some of the table's columns

    B. Naming the view's columns with column aliases

    C. Restricting the selection of rows with a WHERE clause

    D. Performing an aggregation

    E. Joining two tables

17. Consider these three statements:

```
create view v1 as select department_id,department_name,last_name from
departments join employees using (department_id);
select department_name,last_name from v1 where department_id=20;
select d.department_name,e.last_name from departments d, employees e
where d.department_id=e.department_id and
d.department_id=20;
```

The first query will be quicker than the second because (choose the best answer):

A. The view has already done the work of joining the tables.

B. The view uses ISO standard join syntax, which is faster than the Oracle join syntax used in the second query.

C. The view is precompiled, so the first query requires less dynamic compilation than the second query.

D. There is no reason for the first query to be quicker.

18. Study this view creation statement:

```
create view dept30 as
select department_id,employee_id,last_name from employees
where department_id=30 with check option;
```

What might make the following statement fail? (Choose the best answer.)

```
update dept30 set department_id=10 where employee_id=114;
```

A. Unless specified otherwise, views will be created as WITH READ ONLY.

B. The view is too complex to allow DML operations.

C. The WITH CHECK OPTION will reject any statement that changes the DEPARTMENT_ID.

D. The statement will succeed.

19. There is a simple view SCOTT.DEPT_VIEW on the table SCOTT.DEPT. This insert fails with an error:

```
SQL> insert into dept_view values('SUPPORT','OXFORD');
insert into dept_view values('SUPPORT','OXFORD')
*
ERROR at line 1:
ORA-01400: cannot insert NULL into ("SCOTT"."DEPT"."DEPTNO")
```

What might be the problem? (Choose the best answer.)

A. The INSERT violates a constraint on the detail table.

B. The INSERT violates a constraint on the view.

C. The view was created as WITH READ ONLY.

D. The view was created as WITH CHECK OPTION.

20. What are distinguishing characteristics of a public synonym rather than a private synonym? (Choose two correct answers.)

    A. Public synonyms are always visible to all users.

    B. Public synonyms can be accessed by name without a schema name qualifier.

    C. Public synonyms can be selected from without needing any permissions.

    D. Public synonyms can have the same names as tables or views.

21. Consider these three statements:

```
create synonym s1 for employees;
create public synonym s1 for departments;
select * from s1;
```

    Which of the following statements is correct? (Choose the best answer.)

    A. The second statement will fail because an object S1 already exists.

    B. The third statement will show the contents of EMPLOYEES.

    C. The third statement will show the contents of DEPARTMENTS.

    D. The third statement will show the contents of the table S1, if such a table exists in the current schema.

22. A view and a synonym are created as follows:

```
create view dept_v as select * from dept;
create synonym dept_s for dept_v;
```

    Subsequently the table DEPT is dropped. What will happen if you query the synonym DEPT_S? (Choose the best answer.)

    A. There will not be an error because the synonym addresses the view, which still exists, but there will be no rows returned.

    B. There will not be an error if you first recompile the view with the command ALTER VIEW DEPT_V COMPILE FORCE;.

    C. There will be an error because the synonym will be invalid.

    D. There will be an error because the view will be invalid.

    E. There will be an error because the view will have been dropped implicitly when the table was dropped.

23. A sequence is created as follows:

```
create sequence seq1 maxvalue 50;
```

    If the current value is already 50, when you attempt to select SEQ1.NEXTVAL what will happen? (Choose the best answer.)

    A. The sequence will cycle and issue 0.

    B. The sequence will cycle and issue 1.

    C. The sequence will reissue 50.

    D. There will be an error.

24. You create a sequence as follows:

```
create sequence seq1 start with 1;
```

After selecting from it a few times, you want to reinitialize it to reissue the numbers already generated. How can you do this? (Choose the best answer.)

A. You must drop and re-create the sequence.

B. You can't. Under no circumstances can numbers from a sequence be reissued once they have been used.

C. Use the command ALTER SEQUENCE SEQ1 START WITH 1; to reset the next value to 1.

D. Use the command ALTER SEQUENCE SEQ1 CYCLE; to reset the sequence to its starting value.

Self Test Answers

1. ☑ D. The schema will default to the current user.

   ☒ A, B, C, and E. A is wrong because all tables must be in a schema. B is wrong because the creation will succeed. C is wrong because the SYS schema is not a default schema. E is wrong because while there is a notional user PUBLIC, he does not have a schema at all.

2. ☑ A. Indexes have their own namespace.

   ☒ B, C, D, and E. Stored procedures, synonyms, tables, and views exist in the same namespace.

3. ☑ D and E. D violates the rule that a table name must begin with a letter, and E violates the rule that a table name cannot be a reserved word. Both rules can be bypassed by using double quotes.

   ☒ A, B, and C. These are wrong because all will succeed (though A and B are not exactly sensible).

4. ☑ A and C. A heap is a table of variable-length rows in random order.

   ☒ B, D, and E. B is wrong because a heap table can only be one table. D and E are wrong because a heap table can (and usually will) have indexes and a primary key.

5. ☑ A, C, D, E, and F. All these are variable-length data types.

   ☒ B. CHAR columns are fixed length.

6. ☑ D. The number will be rounded to one digit, and the string will be cast as a date.

   ☒ A, B, and C. Automatic rounding and typecasting will correct the "errors," though ideally they would not occur.

7. ☑ D. STRING is not an internal data type.

   ☒ A, B, and C. CHAR, FLOAT, and INTEGER are all internal data types, though not as widely used as some others.

8. ☑ C. The condition applies only to the rows selected for insert, not to the table creation.

   ☒ A, B, and D. A is wrong because the statement is syntactically correct. B is wrong because the condition does not apply to the DDL, only to the DML. D is wrong because the condition will exclude all rows from selection.

9. ☑ D. Check and not-null constraints are not dependent on any structures other than the table to which they apply and so can safely be copied to a new table.

   ☒ A, B, C, and E. A is wrong because not-null and check constraints will be applied to the new table. B, C, and E are wrong because these constraints need other objects (indexes or a parent table) and so are not copied.

10. ☑ C and D. Unique and primary key constraints are enforced with indexes.

    ☒ A and B. Check and not-null constraints do not rely on indexes.

11. ☑ C. A constraint violation will force a rollback of the current statement but nothing else.

    ☒ A, B, D, and E. A is wrong because all statements that have succeeded remain intact. B and D are wrong because there is no commit of anything until it is specifically requested. E is wrong because the whole statement will be rolled back, not just the failed row.

12. ☑ D. All the statements are wrong.

    ☒ A, B, and C. A is wrong because compound indexes need not be on columns of the same datatype. B is wrong because the columns in a compound index need not be physically adjacent. C is wrong because indexes and tables do not share the same namespace.

13. ☑ A, D, and E. Compression, reverse key, and unique can only be applied to B*Tree indexes.

    ☒ B, C, and F. Descending, function-based, and compound indexes can be either B*Tree or bitmap.

14. ☑ A. Rows in a temporary table are visible only to the inserting session.

    ☒ B, C, and D. All these incorrectly describe the scope of visibility of rows in a temporary table.

15. ☑ B. If a temporary table cannot fit in a session's PGA, it will be written to the session's temporary tablespace.

    ☒ A, C, and D. A is wrong because temporary tables can be written out to temporary segments. C is wrong because the location of the temporary segment is session specific, not table specific. **D** is wrong because it is the session server process that writes the data, not the user process.

16. ☑   **D** and **E**. Aggregations and joins make a view complex and make DML impossible.

    ☒   **A**, **B**, and **C**. Selection and projection or renaming columns does not make the view complex.

17. ☑   **D**. Sad but true. Views will not help performance, unless they include tuning hints.

    ☒   **A**, **B**, and **C**. **A** is wrong because a view is only a SELECT statement; it doesn't prerun the query. **B** is wrong because the Oracle optimizer will sort out any differences in syntax. **C** is wrong because, although views are precompiled, this doesn't affect the speed of compiling a user's statement.

18. ☑   **C**. The WITH CHECK OPTION will prevent DML that would cause a row to disappear from the view.

    ☒   **A**, **B**, and **D**. **A** is wrong because views are by default created read/write. **B** is wrong because the view is a simple view. **D** is wrong because the statement cannot succeed because the check option will reject it.

19. ☑   **A**. There is a NOT NULL or PRIMARY KEY constraint on DEPT.DEPTNO.

    ☒   **B**, **C**, and **D**. **B** is wrong because constraints are enforced on detail tables, not on views. **C** and **D** are wrong because the error message would be different.

20. ☑   **B** and **D**. Public synonyms are not schema objects and so can only be addressed directly. They can have the same names as schema objects.

    ☒   **A** and **C**. These are wrong because users must be granted privileges on a public synonym before they can see it or select from it.

21. ☑   **B**. The order of priority is to search the schema namespace before the public namespace, so it will be the private synonym (to EMPLOYEES) that will be found.

    ☒   **A**, **C**, and **D**. **A** is wrong because a synonym can exist in both the public namespace and the schema namespace. **C** is wrong because the order of priority will find the private synonym first. **D** is wrong because it would not be possible to have a table and a private synonym in the same schema with the same name.

22. ☑   **D**. The synonym will be fine, but the view will be invalid. Oracle will attempt to recompile the view, but this will fail.

    ☒   **A**, **B**, **C**, and **E**. **A** is wrong because the view will be invalid. **B** is wrong because the FORCE keyword can only be applied when creating a view (and it would still be invalid, even so). **C** is wrong because the synonym will be fine. **E** is wrong because views are not dropped implicitly (unlike indexes and constraints).

23. ☑ **D.** The default is NOCYCLE, and the sequence cannot advance further.

☒ **A, B,** and **C. A** and **B** are wrong because CYCLE is disabled by default. If it were enabled, the next number issued would be 1 (not zero) because 1 is the default for START WITH. **C** is wrong because under no circumstances will a sequence issue repeating values.

24. ☑ **A.** It is not possible to change the next value of a sequence, so you must re-create it.

☒ **B, C,** and **D. B** is wrong because, while a NOCYCLE sequence can never reissue numbers, there is no reason why a new sequence (with the same name) cannot do so. **C** is wrong because START WITH can only be specified at creation time. **D** is wrong because this will not force an instant cycle, it will only affect what happens when the sequence reaches its MAXVALUE or MINVALUE.

CHAPTER 8

DML and Concurrency

Exam Objectives

In this chapter you will learn to

Data in a relational database is managed with the DML (Data Manipulation Language) commands of SQL. These are INSERT, UPDATE, DELETE, and (with more recent versions of SQL) MERGE. This chapter discusses what happens in memory, and on disk, when you execute INSERT, UPDATE, or DELETE statements—the manner in which changed data is written to blocks of table and index segments and the old version of the data is written out to blocks of an undo segment. The theory behind this, summarized as the ACID test, which every relational database must pass, is explored, and you will see the practicalities of how undo data is managed.

The transaction control statements COMMIT and ROLLBACK, which are closely associated with DML commands, are explained along with a discussion of some basic PL/SQL objects. The chapter ends with a detailed examination of concurrent data access and table and row locking.

Data Manipulation Language (DML) Statements

Strictly speaking, there are five DML commands:

- SELECT
- INSERT
- UPDATE
- DELETE
- MERGE

In practice, most database professionals never include SELECT as part of DML. It is considered to be a separate language in its own right, which is not unreasonable when you consider that the next five chapters are dedicated to describing it. The MERGE command is often dropped as well, not because it isn't clearly a data manipulation command but because it doesn't do anything that cannot be done with other commands. MERGE can be thought of as a shortcut for executing either an INSERT or an UPDATE or a DELETE, depending on some condition. A command often considered with DML is TRUNCATE. This is actually a DDL (Data Definition Language) command, but as the effect for end users is the same as for a DELETE (though its implementation is totally different), it does fit with DML.

INSERT

Oracle stores data in the form of rows in tables. Tables are *populated* with rows (just as a country is *populated* with people) in several ways, but the most common method is with the INSERT statement. SQL is a set-oriented language, so any one command can affect one row or a set of rows. It follows that one INSERT statement can insert an individual row into one table or many rows into many tables. The basic versions of the statement do insert just one row, but more complex variations can, with one command, insert multiple rows into multiple tables.

TIP There are much faster techniques than INSERT for populating a table with large numbers of rows. These are the SQL*Loader utility, which can upload data from files produced by an external feeder system, and Data Pump, which can transfer data in bulk from one Oracle database to another, either via disk files or through a network link.

EXAM TIP An INSERT command can insert one row, with column values specified in the command, or a set of rows created by a SELECT statement.

The simplest form of the INSERT statement inserts one row into one table, using values provided in line as part of the command. The syntax is as follows:

```
INSERT INTO table [(column [,column...])] VALUES (value [,value...]);
```

For example:

```
insert into hr.regions values (10,'Great Britain');
insert into hr.regions (region_name, region_id) values ('Australasia',11);
insert into hr.regions (region_id) values (12);
insert into hr.regions values (13,null);
```

The first of the preceding commands provides values for both columns of the REGIONS table. If the table had a third column, the statement would fail because it relies upon *positional notation*. The statement does not say which value should be inserted into which column; it relies on the position of the values: their ordering in the command. When the database receives a statement using positional notation, it will match the order of the values to the order in which the columns of the table are defined. The statement would also fail if the column order was wrong: the database would attempt the insertion but would fail because of data type mismatches.

The second command nominates the columns to be populated and the values with which to populate them. Note that the order in which columns are mentioned now becomes irrelevant—as long as the order of the columns is the same as the order of the values.

The third example lists one column, and therefore only one value. All other columns will be left null. This statement will fail if the REGION_NAME column is not nullable. The fourth example will produce the same result, but because there is no column list, some value (even a NULL) must be provided for each column.

TIP It is often considered good practice not to rely on positional notation and instead always to list the columns. This is more work but makes the code self-documenting (always a good idea!) and also makes the code more resilient against table structure changes. For instance, if a column is added to a table, all the INSERT statements that rely on positional notation will fail until they are rewritten to include a NULL for the new column. INSERT code that names the columns will continue to run.

PART II

To insert many rows with one INSERT command, the values for the rows must come from a query. The syntax is as follows:

```
INSERT INTO table [column [, column...] ] subquery;
```

Note that this syntax does not use the VALUES keyword. If the column list is omitted, then the subquery must provide values for every column in the table. To copy every row from one table to another, if the tables have the same column structure, a command such as this is all that is needed:

```
insert into regions_copy select * from regions;
```

This presupposes that the table REGIONS_COPY does exist. The SELECT subquery reads every row from the source table, which is REGIONS, and the INSERT inserts them into the target table, which is REGIONS_COPY.

 EXAM TIP Any SELECT statement, specified as a subquery, can be used as the source of rows passed to an INSERT. This enables insertion of many rows. Alternatively, using the VALUES clause will insert one row. The values can be literals or prompted for as substitution variables.

To conclude the description of the INSERT command, it should be mentioned that it is possible to insert rows into several tables with one statement. This is not part of the OCP examination, but for completeness here is an example:

```
insert all
when 1=1 then
  into emp_no_name (department_id,job_id,salary,commission_pct,hire_date)
  values (department_id,job_id,salary,commission_pct,hire_date)
when department_id <> 80 then
  into emp_non_sales (employee_id,department_id,salary,hire_date)
  values (employee_id,department_id,salary,hire_date)
when department_id = 80 then
  into emp_sales (employee_id,salary,commission_pct,hire_date)
  values (employee_id,salary,commission_pct,hire_date)
select employee_id,department_id,job_id,salary,commission_pct,hire_date
from employees where hire_date > sysdate - 30;
```

To read this statement, start at the bottom. The subquery retrieves all employees recruited in the last 30 days. Then go to the top. The ALL keyword means that every row selected will be considered for insertion into all the tables following, not just into the first table for which the condition applies. The first condition is 1=1, which is always true, so every source row will create a row in EMP_NO_NAME. This is a copy of the EMPLOYEES table with the personal identifiers removed. The second condition is DEPARTMENT_ID <> 80, which will generate a row in EMP_NON_SALES for every employee who is not in the sales department; there is no need for this table to have the COMMISSION_PCT column. The third condition generates a row in EMP_SALES for all the salesmen; there is no need for the DEPARTMENT_ID column, because they will all be in department 80.

This is a simple example of a multitable insert, but it should be apparent that with one statement, and therefore only one pass through the source data, it is possible to populate many target tables. This can take an enormous amount of strain off the database.

Exercise 8-1: Use the INSERT Command   In this exercise, use various techniques to insert rows into a table.

1. Connect to the WEBSTORE schema with either SQL Developer or SQL*Plus.

2. Query the PRODUCTS, ORDERS, and ORDER_ITEMS tables, to confirm what data is currently stored:

```
select * from products;
select * from orders;
select * from order_items;
```

3. Insert two rows into the PRODUCTS table, providing the values in line:

```
insert into products values (prod_seq.nextval, '11G SQL Exam Guide',
'ACTIVE',60,sysdate, 20);
insert into products
values (prod_seq.nextval, '11G All-in-One Guide',
'ACTIVE',100,sysdate, 40);
```

4. Insert two rows into the ORDERS table, explicitly providing the column names:

```
insert into orders (order_id, order_date, order_status, order_amount, customer_id)
values (order_seq.nextval, sysdate, 'COMPLETE', 3, 2);
insert into orders (order_id, order_date, order_status, order_amount, customer_id)
values (order_seq.nextval, sysdate, 'PENDING', 5, 3);
```

5. Insert three rows into the ORDER_ITEMS table, using substitution variables:

```
insert into order_items values (&item_id, &order_id, &product_id, &quantity);
```

When prompted, provide the values: {1, 1, 2,5}, {2,1,1,3}, and {1,2,2,4}.

6. Insert a row into the PRODUCTS table, calculating the PRODUCT_ID to be 100 higher than the current high value. This will need a scalar subquery:

```
insert into products values ((select max(product_id)+100 from products),
'11G DBA2 Exam Guide', 'INACTIVE', 40, sysdate-365, 0);
```

7. Confirm the insertion of the rows:

```
select * from products;
select * from orders;
select * from order_items;
```

8. Commit the insertions:

```
commit;
```

The following illustration shows the results of the exercise, using SQL*Plus:

```
Administrator: Command Prompt - sqlplus  webstore/admin123        4/04/09 12:04:09 AM   _ □ ×

SQL> select * from products;
PRODUCT_ID PRODUCT_DESCRIPTION  PRODUCT_      PRICE PRICE_DAT STOCK_COUNT
---------- -------------------- --------- --------- --------- -----------
         1 11G SQL Exam Guide   ACTIVE           60 03-APR-09          20
         2 11G All-in-One Guide ACTIVE          100 03-APR-09          40
       102 11G DBA2 Exam Guide  INACTIVE         40 04-APR-08           0
SQL> select * from orders;
  ORDER_ID ORDER_DAT ORDER_ST ORDER_AMOUNT CUSTOMER_ID
---------- --------- -------- ------------ -----------
         1 03-APR-09 COMPLETE            3           2
         2 03-APR-09 PENDING             5           3
SQL> select * from order_items;
ORDER_ITEM_ID    ORDER_ID PRODUCT_ID   QUANTITY
------------- ----------- ---------- ----------
            1           1          2          5
            2           1          1          3
            1           2          2          4
SQL> commit;
Commit complete.
SQL>
```

UPDATE

The UPDATE command is used to change rows that already exist—rows that have been created by an INSERT command, or possibly by a tool such as Data Pump. As with any other SQL command, an UPDATE can affect one row or a set of rows. The size of the set affected by an UPDATE is determined by a WHERE clause, in exactly the same way that the set of rows retrieved by a SELECT statement is defined by a WHERE clause. The syntax is identical. All the rows updated will be in one table; it is not possible for a single update command to affect rows in multiple tables.

When updating a row or a set of rows, the UPDATE command specifies which columns of the row(s) to update. It is not necessary (or indeed common) to update every column of the row. If the column being updated already has a value, then this value is replaced with the new value specified by the UPDATE command. If the column was not previously populated—which is to say, its value was NULL—then it will be populated after the UPDATE with the new value.

A typical use of UPDATE is to retrieve one row and update one or more columns of the row. The retrieval will be done using a WHERE clause that selects a row by its primary key, the unique identifier that will ensure that only one row is retrieved. Then the columns that are updated will be any columns other than the primary key column. It is very unusual to change the value of the primary key. The lifetime of a row begins when it is inserted, then may continue through several updates, until it is deleted. Throughout this lifetime, it will not usually change its primary key.

To update a set of rows, use a less restrictive WHERE clause than the primary key. To update every row in a table, do not use any WHERE clause at all. This set behavior can be disconcerting when it happens by accident. If you select the rows to be updated with any column other than the primary key, you may update several rows, not just one. If you omit the WHERE clause completely, you will update the whole table—perhaps millions of rows updated with just one statement—when you meant to change just one.

EXAM TIP One UPDATE statement can change rows in only one table, but it can change any number of rows in that table.

An UPDATE command must honor any constraints defined for the table, just as the original INSERT would have. For example, it will not be possible to update a column that has been marked as mandatory to a NULL value or to update a primary key column so that it will no longer be unique. The basic syntax is the following:

```
UPDATE table SET column=value [,column=value...] [WHERE condition];
```

The more complex form of the command uses subqueries for one or more of the column values and for the WHERE condition. Figure 8-1 shows updates of varying complexity, executed from SQL*Plus.

The first example is the simplest. One column of one row is set to a literal value. Because the row is chosen with a WHERE clause that uses the equality predicate on the table's primary key, there is an absolute guarantee that at most only one row will be affected. No row will be changed if the WHERE clause fails to find any rows at all.

The second example shows use of arithmetic and an existing column to set the new value, and the row selection is not done on the primary key column. If the selection is not done on the primary key, or if a nonequality predicate (such as BETWEEN) is used, then the number of rows updated may be more than one. If the WHERE clause is omitted entirely, the update will be applied to every row in the table.

The third example in Figure 8-1 introduces the use of a subquery to define the set of rows to be updated. A minor additional complication is the use of a replacement variable to prompt the user for a value to use in the WHERE clause of the subquery.

```
C:\WINDOWS\system32\cmd.exe - sqlplus hr/hr                        _ □ ×
SQL> update employees set salary=10000 where employee_id=206;

1 row updated.

SQL> update employees set salary=salary*1.1 where last_name='Cambrault';

2 rows updated.

SQL> update employees set salary=salary*1.1
  2  where department_id in
  3  (select department_id from departments
  4  where department_name like '%&Which_department%');
Enter value for which_department: IT
old   4: where department_name like '%&Which_department%')
new   4: where department_name like '%IT%')

5 rows updated.

SQL> update employees
  2  set department_id=80,
  3  commission_pct=(select min(commission_pct) from employees
  4  where department_id=80)
  5  where employee_id=206;

1 row updated.

SQL>
```

Figure 8-1 Examples of using the UPDATE statement

In this example, the subquery (lines 3 and 4) will select every employee who is in a department whose name includes the string 'IT' and increment their current salary by 10 percent (unlikely to happen in practice).

It is also possible to use subqueries to determine the value to which a column will be set, as in the fourth example. In this case, one employee (identified by primary key, in line 5) is transferred to department 80 (the sales department), and then the subquery in lines 3 and 4 sets his commission rate to whatever the lowest commission rate in the department happens to be.

The syntax of an update that uses subqueries is as follows:

```
UPDATE table
SET column=[subquery] [,column=subquery...]
WHERE column = (subquery) [AND column=subquery...] ;
```

There is a rigid restriction on the subqueries using update columns in the SET clause: the subquery must return a *scalar* value. A scalar value is a single value of whatever data type is needed: the query must return one row, with one column. If the query returns several values, the UPDATE will fail. Consider these two examples:

```
update employees
set salary=(select salary from employees where employee_id=206);
update employees
set salary=(select salary from employees where last_name='Abel');
```

The first example, using an equality predicate on the primary key, will always succeed. Even if the subquery does not retrieve a row (as would be the case if there were no employee with EMPLOYEE_ID equal to 206), the query will still return a scalar value: a null. In that case, all the rows in EMPLOYEES would have their SALARY set to NULL—which might not be desired but is not an error as far as SQL is concerned. The second example uses an equality predicate on the LAST_NAME, which is not guaranteed to be unique. The statement will succeed if there is only one employee with that name, but if there were more than one it would fail with the error "ORA-01427: single-row subquery returns more than one row." For code that will work reliably, no matter what the state of the data, it is vital to ensure that the subqueries used for setting column values are scalar.

 TIP A common fix for making sure that queries are scalar is to use MAX or MIN. This version of the statement will always succeed:
```
update employees
set salary=(select max(salary) from employees where
last_name='Abel');
```
However, just because it will work, doesn't necessarily mean that it does what is wanted.

The subqueries in the WHERE clause must also be scalar, if it is using the equality predicate (as in the preceding examples) or the greater/less than predicates. If it is using the IN predicate, then the query can return multiple rows, as in this example which uses IN:

```
update employees
set salary=10000
where department_id in (select department_id from departments
where department_name like '%IT%');
```

This will apply the update to all employees in a department whose name includes the string 'IT'. There are several of these. But even though the query can return several rows, it must still return only one column.

 EXAM TIP The subqueries used to SET column values must be scalar subqueries. The subqueries used to select the rows must also be scalar, unless they use the IN predicate.

Exercise 8-2: Use the UPDATE Command In this exercise, use various techniques to update rows in a table. It is assumed that the WEBSTORE.PRODUCTS table is as seen in the illustration at the end of Exercise 8-1. If not, adjust the values as necessary.

1. Connect to the WEBSTORE schema using SQL Developer or SQL*Plus.

2. Update a single row, identified by primary key:

```
update products set product_description='DBA1 Exam Guide'
where product_id=102;
```

This statement should return the message "1 row updated."

3. Update a set of rows, using a subquery to select the rows and to provide values:

```
update products
set product_id=(1+(select max(product_id) from products where product_id <> 102))
where product_id=102;
```

This statement should return the message "1 row updated."

4. Confirm the state of the rows:

```
select * from products;
```

5. Commit the changes made:

```
commit;
```

DELETE

Previously inserted rows can be removed from a table with the DELETE command. The command will remove one row or a set of rows from the table, depending on a WHERE clause. If there is no WHERE clause, every row in the table will be removed (which can be a little disconcerting if you left out the WHERE clause by mistake).

 TIP There are no "warning" prompts for any SQL commands. If you instruct the database to delete a million rows, it will do so. Immediately. There is none of that "Are you sure?" business that some environments offer.

A deletion is all or nothing. It is not possible to nominate columns. When rows are inserted, you can choose which columns to populate. When rows are updated, you can choose which columns to update. But a deletion applies to the whole row—the only choice is which rows in which table. This makes the DELETE command syntactically simpler than the other DML commands. The syntax is as follows:

```
DELETE FROM table [WHERE condition];
```

This is the simplest of the DML commands, particularly if the condition is omitted. In that case, every row in the table will be removed with no prompt. The only complication is in the condition. This can be a simple match of a column to a literal:

```
delete from employees where employee_id=206;
delete from employees where last_name like 'S%';
delete from employees where department_id=&Which_department;
delete from employees where department_id is null;
```

The first statement identifies a row by primary key. One row only will be removed—or no row at all, if the value given does not find a match. The second statement uses a nonequality predicate that could result in the deletion of many rows: every employee whose surname begins with an uppercase "S." The third statement uses an equality predicate but not on the primary key. It prompts for a department number with a substitution variable, and all employees in that department will go. The final statement removes all employees who are not currently assigned to a department.

The condition can also be a subquery:

```
delete from employees where department_id in
(select department_id from departments where location_id in
  (select location_id from locations where country_id in
    (select country_id from countries where region_id in
      (select region_id from regions where region_name='Europe')
    )
  )
)
```

This example uses a subquery for row selection that navigates the HR geographical tree (with more subqueries) to delete every employee who works for any department that is based in Europe. The same rule for the number of values returned by the subquery applies as for an UPDATE command: if the row selection is based on an equality predicate (as in the preceding example) the subquery must be scalar, but if it uses IN the subquery can return several rows.

If the DELETE command finds no rows to delete, this is not an error. The command will return the message "0 rows deleted" rather than an error message because the statement did complete successfully—it just didn't find anything to do.

Exercise 8-3: Use the DELETE Command   In this exercise, use various techniques to delete rows in a table. It is assumed that the WEBSTORE.PRODUCTS table has been modified during the previous two exercises. If not, adjust the values as necessary.

1. Connect to the WEBSTORE schema using SQL Developer or SQL*Plus.

2. Remove one row, using the equality predicate on the primary key:

   ```
   delete from products where product_id=3;
   ```

   This should return the message "1 row deleted."

3. Attempt to remove every row in the table by omitting a WHERE clause:

   ```
   delete from products;
   ```

   This will fail, due to a constraint violation because there are child records in the ORDER_ITEMS table that reference PRODUCT_ID values in the PRODUCTS table via the foreign key constraint FK_PRODUCT_ID.

4. Commit the deletion:

   ```
   commit;
   ```

To remove rows from a table, there are two options: the DELETE command and the TRUNCATE command. DELETE is less drastic, in that a deletion can be rolled back whereas a truncation cannot be. DELETE is also more controllable, in that it is possible to choose which rows to delete, whereas a truncation always affects the whole table. DELETE is, however, a lot slower and can place a lot of strain on the database. TRUNCATE is virtually instantaneous and effortless.

TRUNCATE

The TRUNCATE command is not a DML command; it is a DDL command. The difference is enormous. When DML commands affect data, they insert, update, and delete rows as part of transactions. Transactions are defined later in this chapter, in the section "Control Transactions." For now, let it be said that a transaction can be controlled, in the sense that the user has the choice of whether to make the work done in a transaction permanent, or whether to reverse it. This is very useful but forces the database to do additional work behind the scenes that the user is not aware of. DDL commands are not user transactions (though within the database, they are in fact implemented as transactions—but developers cannot control them), and there is no choice about whether to make them permanent or to reverse them. Once executed, they are done. However, in comparison to DML, they are very fast.

 EXAM TIP Transactions, consisting of INSERT, UPDATE, and DELETE (or even MERGE) commands, can be made permanent (with a COMMIT) or reversed (with a ROLLBACK). A TRUNCATE command, like any other DDL command, is immediately permanent: it can never be reversed.

From the user's point of view, a truncation of a table is equivalent to executing a DELETE of every row: a DELETE command without a WHERE clause. But whereas a deletion may take some time (possibly hours, if there are many rows in the table), a truncation will go through instantly. It makes no difference whether the table contains one row or billions; a TRUNCATE will be virtually instantaneous. The table will still exist, but it will be empty.

PART II

TIP DDL commands, such as TRUNCATE, will fail if there is any DML command active on the table. A transaction will block the DDL command until the DML command is terminated with a COMMIT or a ROLLBACK.

 EXAM TIP TRUNCATE completely empties the table. There is no concept of row selection, as there is with a DELETE.

One part of the definition of a table as stored in the data dictionary is the table's physical location. When first created, a table is allocated a single area of space, of fixed size, in the database's datafiles. This is known as an *extent* and will be empty. Then, as rows are inserted, the extent fills up. Once it is full, more extents will be allocated to the table automatically. A table therefore consists of one or more extents, which hold the rows. As well as tracking the extent allocation, the data dictionary also tracks how much of the space allocated to the table has been used. This is done with the *high water mark*. The high water mark is the last position in the last extent that has been used; all space below the high water mark has been used for rows at one time or another, and none of the space above the high water mark has been used yet.

Note that it is possible for there to be plenty of space below the high water mark that is not being used at the moment; this is because of rows having been removed with a DELETE command. Inserting rows into a table pushes the high water mark up. Deleting them leaves the high water mark where it is; the space they occupied remains assigned to the table but is freed up for inserting more rows.

Truncating a table resets the high water mark. Within the data dictionary, the recorded position of the high water mark is moved to the beginning of the table's first extent. As Oracle assumes that there can be no rows above the high water mark, this has the effect of removing every row from the table. The table is emptied and remains empty until subsequent insertions begin to push the high water mark back up again. In this manner, one DDL command, which does little more than make an update in the data dictionary, can annihilate billions of rows in a table.

The syntax to truncate a table couldn't be simpler:

```
TRUNCATE TABLE table;
```

Figure 8-2 shows access to the TRUNCATE command through the SQL Developer navigation tree, but of course it can also be executed from SQL*Plus.

MERGE

There are many occasions where you want to take a set of data (the source) and integrate it into an existing table (the target). If a row in the source data already exists in the target table, you may want to update the target row, or you may want to replace it completely, or you may want to leave the target row unchanged. If a row in the source does not exist in the target, you will want to insert it. The MERGE command lets you do this. A MERGE passes through the source data, for each row attempting to locate a matching row in the target. If no match is found, a row can be inserted; if a match is

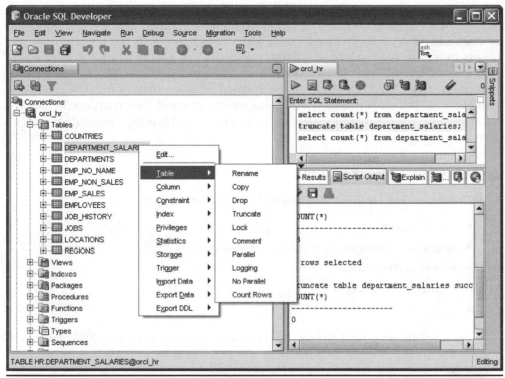

Figure 8-2 The TRUNCATE command in SQL Developer, from the command line and from the menus

found, the matching row can be updated. The release 10g enhancement means that the target row can even be deleted, after being matched and updated. The end result is a target table into which the data in the source has been merged.

A MERGE operation does nothing that could not be done with INSERT, UPDATE, and DELETE statements—but with one pass through the source data, it can do all three. Alternative code without a MERGE would require three passes through the data, one for each command.

The source data for a MERGE statement can be a table or any subquery. The condition used for finding matching rows in the target is similar to a WHERE clause. The clauses that update or insert rows are as complex as an UPDATE or an INSERT command. It follows that MERGE is the most complicated of the DML commands, which is not unreasonable, as it is (arguably) the most powerful. Use of MERGE is not on the OCP syllabus, but for completeness here is a simple example:

```
merge into employees e using new_employees n
  on (e.employee_id = n.employee_id)
when matched then
  update set e.salary=n.salary
when not matched then
  insert (employee_id,last_name,salary)
  values (n.employee_id,n.last_name,n.salary);
```

The preceding statement uses the contents of a table NEW_EMPLOYEES to update or insert rows in EMPLOYEES. The situation could be that EMPLOYEES is a table of all staff, and NEW_EMPLOYEES is a table with rows for new staff and for salary changes for existing staff. The command will pass through NEW_EMPLOYEES and, for each row, attempt to find a row in EMPLOYEES with the same EMPLOYEE_ID. If there is a row found, its SALARY column will be updated with the value of the row in NEW_EMPLOYEES. If there is not such a row, one will be inserted. Variations on the syntax allow the use of a subquery to select the source rows, and it is even possible to delete matching rows.

DML Statement Failures

Commands can fail for many reasons, including the following:

- Syntax errors
- References to nonexistent objects or columns
- Access permissions
- Constraint violations
- Space issues

Figure 8-3 shows several attempted executions of a statement with SQL*Plus.

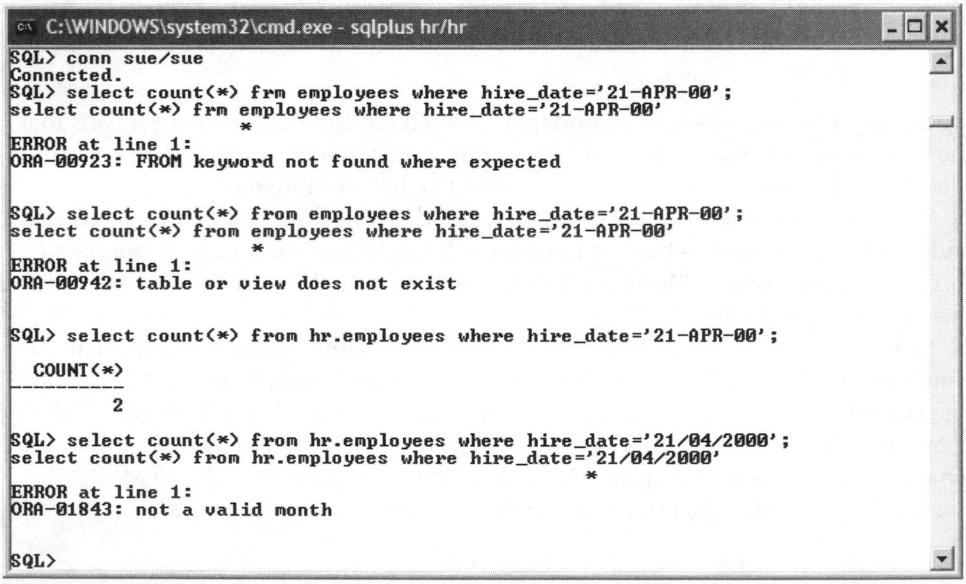

```
C:\WINDOWS\system32\cmd.exe - sqlplus hr/hr                              _ □ ×

SQL> conn sue/sue
Connected.
SQL> select count(*) frm employees where hire_date='21-APR-00';
select count(*) frm employees where hire_date='21-APR-00'
                    *
ERROR at line 1:
ORA-00923: FROM keyword not found where expected


SQL> select count(*) from employees where hire_date='21-APR-00';
select count(*) from employees where hire_date='21-APR-00'
                    *
ERROR at line 1:
ORA-00942: table or view does not exist


SQL> select count(*) from hr.employees where hire_date='21-APR-00';

  COUNT(*)
----------
         2

SQL> select count(*) from hr.employees where hire_date='21/04/2000';
select count(*) from hr.employees where hire_date='21/04/2000'
                                                   *
ERROR at line 1:
ORA-01843: not a valid month

SQL>
```

Figure 8-3   Some examples of statement failure

In Figure 8-3, a user connects as SUE (password, SUE—not an example of good security) and queries the EMPLOYEES table. The statement fails because of a simple syntax error, correctly identified by SQL*Plus. Note that SQL*Plus never attempts to correct such mistakes, even when it knows exactly what you meant to type. Some third-party tools may be more helpful, offering automatic error correction.

The second attempt to run the statement fails with an error stating that the object does not exist. This is because it does not exist in the current user's schema; it exists in the HR schema. Having corrected that, the third run of the statement succeeds—but only just. The value passed in the WHERE clause is a string, '21-APR-2000', but the column HIRE_DATE is not defined in the table as a string, it is defined as a date. To execute the statement, the database had to work out what the user really meant and cast the string as a date. In the last example, the typecasting fails. This is because the string passed is formatted as a European-style date, but the database has been set up as American: the attempt to match "21" to a month fails. The statement would have succeeded if the string had been '04/21/2007'.

If a statement is syntactically correct and has no errors with the objects to which it refers, it can still fail because of access permissions. If the user attempting to execute the statement does not have the relevant permissions on the tables to which it refers, the database will return an error identical to that which would be returned if the object did not exist. As far as the user is concerned, it does not exist.

Errors caused by access permissions are a case where SELECT and DML statements may return different results: it is possible for a user to have permission to see the rows in a table, but not to insert, update, or delete them. Such an arrangement is not uncommon; it often makes business sense. Perhaps more confusingly, permissions can be set up in such a manner that it is possible to insert rows that you are not allowed to see. And, perhaps worst of all, it is possible to delete rows that you can neither see nor update. However, such arrangements are not common.

A constraint violation can cause a DML statement to fail. For example, an INSERT command can insert several rows into a table, and for every row the database will check whether a row already exists with the same primary key. This occurs as each row is inserted. It could be that the first few rows (or the first few million rows) go in without a problem, and then the statement hits a row with a duplicate value. At this point it will return an error, and the statement will fail. This failure will trigger a reversal of all the insertions that had already succeeded. This is part of the SQL standard: a statement must succeed in total, or not at all. The reversal of the work is a *rollback*. The mechanisms of a rollback are described in the next section of this chapter, titled "Control Transactions."

If a statement fails because of space problems, the effect is similar. A part of the statement may have succeeded before the database ran out of space. The part that did succeed will be automatically rolled back. Rollback of a statement is a serious matter. It forces the database to do a lot of extra work and will usually take at least as long as the statement has taken already (sometimes much longer).

Control Transactions

The concepts behind a *transaction* are a part of the relational database paradigm. A transaction consists of one or more DML statements, followed by either a ROLLBACK or a COMMIT command. It is possible to use the SAVEPOINT command to give a degree of control within the transaction. Before going into the syntax, it is necessary to review the concept of a transaction. A related topic is read consistency; this is automatically implemented by the Oracle server, but to a certain extent programmers can manage it by the way they use the SELECT statement.

Database Transactions

Oracle's mechanism for assuring transactional integrity is the combination of undo segments and redo log files: this mechanism is undoubtedly the best of any database yet developed and conforms perfectly with the international standards for data processing. Other database vendors comply with the same standards with their own mechanisms, but with varying levels of effectiveness. In brief, any relational database must be able to pass the ACID test: it must guarantee atomicity, consistency, isolation, and durability.

A is for Atomicity

The principle of *atomicity* states that either all parts of a transaction must successfully complete or none of them. (The reasoning behind the term is that an atom cannot be split—now well known to be a false assumption.) For example, if your business analysts have said that every time you change an employee's salary you must also change the employee's grade, then the atomic transaction will consist of two updates. The database must guarantee that both go through or neither. If only one of the updates were to succeed, you would have an employee on a salary that was incompatible with his grade: a data corruption, in business terms. If anything (anything at all!) goes wrong before the transaction is complete, the database itself must guarantee that any parts that did go through are reversed; this must happen automatically. But although an atomic transaction sounds small (like an atom), it can be enormous. To take another example, it is logically impossible for an accounting suite nominal ledger to be half in August and half in September: the end-of-month rollover is therefore (in business terms) one atomic transaction, which may affect millions of rows in thousands of tables and take hours to complete (or to roll back, if anything goes wrong). The rollback of an incomplete transaction may be manual (as when you issue the ROLLBACK command), but it must be automatic and unstoppable in the case of an error.

C is for Consistency

The principle of *consistency* states that the results of a query must be consistent with the state of the database at the time the query started. Imagine a simple query that averages the value of a column of a table. If the table is large, it will take many minutes to pass through the table. If other users are updating the column while the query is in progress, should the query include the new or the old values? Should it include rows that were inserted or deleted after the query started? The principle of consistency requires that the database ensure that changed values are not seen by the query; it will give you an average of the column as it was when the query started, no matter how long the query takes or what other activity is occurring on the tables concerned. Oracle guarantees that if a query succeeds, the result will be consistent. However, if the database administrator has not configured the database appropriately, the query may not succeed: there is a famous Oracle error, "ORA-1555 snapshot too old," that is raised. This used to be an extremely difficult problem to fix with earlier releases of the database, but with recent versions the database administrator should always be able to prevent this.

I is for Isolation

The principle of *isolation* states that an incomplete (that is, uncommitted) transaction must be invisible to the rest of the world. While the transaction is in progress, only the one session that is executing the transaction is allowed to see the changes; all other sessions must see the unchanged data, not the new values. The logic behind this is, first, that the full transaction might not go through (remember the principle of atomicity and automatic or manual rollback?) and that therefore no other users should be allowed to see changes that might be reversed. And second, during the progress of a transaction the data is (in business terms) incoherent: there is a short time when the employee has had their salary changed but not their grade. Transaction isolation requires that the database must conceal transactions in progress from other users: they will see the preupdate version of the data until the transaction completes, when they will see all the changes as a consistent set. Oracle guarantees transaction isolation: there is no way any session (other than that making the changes) can see uncommitted data. A read of uncommitted data is known as a *dirty read*, which Oracle does not permit (though some other databases do).

D is for Durability

The principle of *durability* states that once a transaction completes, it must be impossible for the database to lose it. During the time that the transaction is in progress, the principle of isolation requires that no one (other than the session concerned) can see the changes it has made so far. But the instant the transaction completes, it must be broadcast to the world, and the database must guarantee that the change is never lost; a relational database is not allowed to lose data. Oracle fulfills this requirement by writing out all change vectors that are applied to data to log files as the changes are done. By applying this log of changes to backups taken earlier, it is possible to repeat any work done in the event of the database being damaged. Of course, data can be lost through user error such as inappropriate DML, or dropping or truncating tables. But as far as Oracle and the DBA are concerned, such events are transactions like any other: according to the principle of durability, they are absolutely nonreversible.

Executing SQL Statements

The entire SQL language consists of only a dozen or so commands. The ones we are concerned with here are: SELECT, INSERT, UPDATE, and DELETE.

Executing a SELECT Statement

The SELECT command retrieves data. The execution of a SELECT statement is a staged process: the server process executing the statement will first check whether the blocks containing the data required are already in memory, in the database buffer cache. If they are, then execution can proceed immediately. If they are not, the server process must locate them on disk and copy them into the database buffer cache.

 EXAM TIP Always remember that server processes read blocks from datafiles into the database buffer cache, DBWn writes blocks from the database buffer cache to the datafiles.

Once the data blocks required for the query are in the database buffer cache, any further processing (such as sorting or aggregation) is carried out in the PGA of the session. When the execution is complete, the result set is returned to the user process.

How does this relate to the ACID test just described? For consistency, if the query encounters a block that has been changed since the time the query started, the server process will go to the undo segment that protected the change, locate the old version of the data, and (for the purposes of the current query only) roll back the change. Thus any changes initiated after the query commenced will not be seen. A similar mechanism guarantees transaction isolation, though this is based on whether the change has been committed, not only on whether the data has been changed. Clearly, if the data needed to do this rollback is no longer in the undo segments, this mechanism will not work. That is when you get the "snapshot too old" error.

Figure 8-4 shows a representation of the way a SELECT statement is processed.

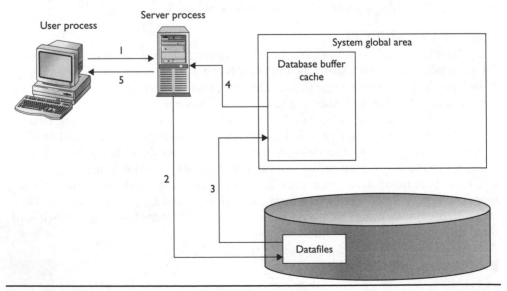

Figure 8-4 The stages of execution of a SELECT

In the figure, Step 1 is the transmission of the SELECT statement from the user process to the server process. The server will search the database buffer cache to determine if the necessary blocks are already in memory, and if they are, proceed to Step 4. If they are not, Step 2 is to locate the blocks in the datafiles, and Step 3 is to copy them into the database buffer cache. Step 4 transfers the data to the server process, where there may be some further processing before Step 5 returns the result of the query to the user process.

Executing an UPDATE Statement

For any DML operation, it is necessary to work on both data blocks and undo blocks, and also to generate redo: the A, C, and I of the ACID test require generation of undo; the D requires generation of redo.

 EXAM TIP Undo is not the opposite of redo! Redo protects *all* block changes, no matter whether it is a change to a block of a table segment, an index segment, or an undo segment. As far as redo is concerned, an undo segment is just another segment, and any changes to it must be made durable.

The first step in executing DML is the same as executing SELECT: the required blocks must be found in the database buffer cache, or copied into the database buffer cache from the datafiles. The only change is that an empty (or *expired*) block of an undo segment is needed too. From then on, things are a bit more complicated.

First, locks must be placed on any rows and associated index keys that are going to be affected by the operation. This is covered later in this chapter.

Then the redo is generated: the server process writes to the log buffer the change vectors that are going to be applied to the data blocks. This generation of redo is applied both to table block changes and to undo block changes: if a column of a row is to be updated, then the rowid and the new value of the column are written to the log buffer (which is the change that will be applied to the table block), and also the old value (which is the change that will be applied to the undo block). If the column is part of an index key, then the changes to be applied to the index are also written to the log buffer, together with a change to be applied to an undo block to protect the index change.

Having generated the redo, the update is carried out in the database buffer cache: the block of table data is updated with the new version of the changed column, and the old version of the changed column is written to the block of undo segment. From this point until the update is committed, all queries from other sessions addressing the changed row will be redirected to the undo data. Only the session that is doing the update will see the actual current version of the row in the table block. The same principle applies to any associated index changes.

Executing INSERT and DELETE Statements

Conceptually, INSERT and DELETE are managed in the same fashion as an UPDATE. The first step is to locate the relevant blocks in the database buffer cache, or to copy them into it if they are not there.

Redo generation is exactly the same: all change vectors to be applied to data and undo blocks are first written out to the log buffer. For an INSERT, the change vector to be applied to the table block (and possibly index blocks) is the bytes that make up the new row (and possibly the new index keys). The vector to be applied to the undo block is the rowid of the new row. For a DELETE, the change vector to be written to the undo block is the entire row.

A crucial difference between INSERT and DELETE is in the amount of undo generated. When a row is inserted, the only undo generated is writing out the new rowid to the undo block. This is because to roll back an INSERT, the only information Oracle requires is the rowid, so that this statement can be constructed:

```
delete from table_name where rowid=rowid_of_the_new_row ;
```

Executing this statement will reverse the original change.

For a DELETE, the whole row (which might be several kilobytes) must be written to the undo block, so that the deletion can be rolled back if need be by constructing a statement that will insert the complete row back into the table.

The Start and End of a Transaction

A session begins a transaction the moment it issues any DML. The transaction continues through any number of further DML commands until the session issues either a COMMIT or a ROLLBACK statement. Only committed changes will be made permanent and become visible to other sessions. It is impossible to nest transactions. The SQL standard does not allow a user to start one transaction and then start another before terminating the first. This can be done with PL/SQL (Oracle's proprietary third-generation language), but not with industry-standard SQL.

The explicit transaction control statements are COMMIT, ROLLBACK, and SAVEPOINT. There are also circumstances other than a user-issued COMMIT or ROLLBACK that will implicitly terminate a transaction:

- Issuing a DDL or DCL statement
- Exiting from the user tool (SQL*Plus or SQL Developer or anything else)
- If the client session dies
- If the system crashes

If a user issues a DDL (CREATE, ALTER, or DROP) or DCL (GRANT or REVOKE) command, the transaction in progress (if any) will be committed: it will be made permanent and become visible to all other users. This is because the DDL and DCL commands are themselves transactions. As it is not possible to nest transactions in SQL, if the user already has a transaction running, the statements the user has run will be committed along with the statements that make up the DDL or DCL command.

If you start a transaction by issuing a DML command and then exit from the tool you are using without explicitly issuing either a COMMIT or a ROLLBACK, the transaction will terminate—but whether it terminates with a COMMIT or a ROLLBACK is entirely dependent on how the tool is written. Many tools will have different behavior, depending on how the tool is exited. (For instance, in the Microsoft Windows environment, it is common to be able to terminate a program either by selecting the File | Exit options from a menu on the top left of the window, or by clicking an "X" in the top-right corner. The programmers who wrote the tool may well have coded different logic into these functions.) In either case, it will be a controlled exit, so the programmers should issue either a COMMIT or a ROLLBACK, but the choice is up to them.

If a client's session fails for some reason, the database will always roll back the transaction. Such failure could be for a number of reasons: the user process can die or be killed at the operating system level, the network connection to the database server may go down, or the machine where the client tool is running can crash. In any of these cases, there is no orderly issue of a COMMIT or ROLLBACK statement, and it is up to the database to detect what has happened. The behavior is that the session is killed, and an active transaction is rolled back. The behavior is the same if the failure is on the server side. If the database server crashes for any reason, when it next starts up all transactions from any sessions that were in progress will be rolled back.

Transaction Control: COMMIT, ROLLBACK, SAVEPOINT, SELECT FOR UPDATE

Oracle's implementation of the relational database paradigm begins a transaction implicitly with the first DML statement. The transaction continues until a COMMIT or ROLLBACK statement. The SAVEPOINT command is not part of the SQL standard and is really just an easy way for programmers to back out some statements, in reverse order. It need not be considered separately, as it does not terminate a transaction.

COMMIT

Commit processing is where many people (and even some experienced DBAs) show an incomplete, or indeed completely inaccurate, understanding of the Oracle architecture. When you say COMMIT, all that happens physically is that LGWR flushes the log buffer to disk. DBWn does absolutely nothing. This is one of the most important performance features of the Oracle database.

 EXAM TIP What does DBWn do when you issue a COMMIT command? Answer: absolutely nothing.

To make a transaction durable, all that is necessary is that the changes that make up the transaction are on disk: there is no need whatsoever for the actual table data to be on disk, in the datafiles. If the changes are on disk, in the form of multiplexed redo log files, then in the event of damage to the database the transaction can be reinstantiated by restoring the datafiles from a backup taken before the damage occurred and applying the changes from the logs. This process is covered in detail in later chapters—for now, just hang on to the fact that a COMMIT involves nothing more than flushing the log buffer to disk, and flagging the transaction as complete. This is why a transaction involving millions of updates in thousands of files over many minutes or hours can be committed in a fraction of a second. Because LGWR writes in very nearly real time, virtually all the transaction's changes are on disk already. When you say COMMIT, LGWR actually does write in real time: your session will hang until the write is complete. This delay will be the length of time it takes to flush the last bit of redo from the log buffer to disk, which will take milliseconds. Your session is then free to continue, and from then on all other sessions will no longer be redirected to the undo blocks when they address the changed table, unless the principle of consistency requires it.

The change vectors written to the redo log are all the change vectors: those applied to data blocks (tables and indexes) and those applied to undo segments.

 EXAM TIP The redo log stream includes all changes: those applied to data segments and to undo segments, for both committed and uncommitted transactions.

Where there is often confusion is that the stream of redo written out to the log files by LGWR will contain changes for both committed and uncommitted transactions. Furthermore, at any given moment DBWn may or may not have written out changed blocks of data segments or undo segments to the datafiles for both committed and uncommitted transactions. So in principle, your database on disk is corrupted: the datafiles may well be storing uncommitted work, and be missing committed changes. But in the event of a crash, the stream of redo on disk always has enough information to reinstantiate any committed transactions that are not in the datafiles (by use of the changes applied to data blocks), and to reinstantiate the undo segments (by use of the changes applied to undo blocks) needed to roll back any uncommitted transactions that are in the datafiles.

 EXAM TIP Any DDL command, or a GRANT or REVOKE, will commit the current transaction.

ROLLBACK

While a transaction is in progress, Oracle keeps an image of the data as it was before the transaction. This image is presented to other sessions that query the data while the transaction is in progress. It is also used to roll back the transaction automatically if anything goes wrong, or deliberately if the session requests it. The syntax to request a rollback is as follows:

```
ROLLBACK [TO SAVEPOINT savepoint] ;
```

The optional use of savepoints is detailed in the section following.

The state of the data before the rollback is that the data has been changed, but the information needed to reverse the changes is available. This information is presented to all other sessions, in order to implement the principle of isolation. The rollback will discard all the changes by restoring the prechange image of the data; any rows the transaction inserted will be deleted, any rows the transaction deleted will be inserted back into the table, and any rows that were updated will be returned to their original state. Other sessions will not be aware that anything has happened at all; they never saw the changes. The session that did the transaction will now see the data as it was before the transaction started.

SAVEPOINT

Savepoints allow a programmer to set a marker in a transaction that can be used to control the effect of the ROLLBACK command. Rather than rolling back the whole transaction and terminating it, it becomes possible to reverse all changes made after a particular point but leave changes made before that point intact. The transaction itself remains in progress: still uncommitted, still able to be rolled back, and still invisible to other sessions.

The syntax is as follows:

```
SAVEPOINT savepoint;
```

This creates a named point in the transaction that can be used in a subsequent ROLLBACK command. The following table illustrates the number of rows in a table at various stages in a transaction. The table is a very simple table called TAB, with one column.

Command	Rows Visible to the User	Rows Visible to Others
truncate table tab;	0	0
insert into tab values ('one');	1	0
savepoint first;	1	0
insert into tab values ('two');	2	0
savepoint second;	2	0
insert into tab values ('three');	3	0
rollback to savepoint second;	2	0
rollback to savepoint first;	1	0
commit;	1	1
delete from tab;	0	1
rollback;	1	1

The example in the table shows two transactions: the first terminated with a COMMIT, the second with a ROLLBACK. It can be seen that the use of savepoints is visible only within the transaction: other sessions see nothing that is not committed.

SELECT FOR UPDATE

One last transaction control statement is SELECT FOR UPDATE. Oracle, by default, provides the highest possible level of concurrency: readers do not block writers, and writers do not block readers. Or in plain language, there is no problem with one session querying data that another session is updating, or one session updating data that another session is querying. However, there are times when you may wish to change this behavior and prevent changes to data that is being queried.

It is not unusual for an application to retrieve a set of rows with a SELECT command, present them to a user for perusal, and prompt them for any changes. Because Oracle is a multiuser database, it is not impossible that another session has also retrieved the same rows. If both sessions attempt to make changes, there can be some rather odd effects. The following table depicts such a situation.

First User	Second User
select * from regions;	select * from regions;
	delete from regions where region_id=5;
	commit;
update regions set region_name='GB'where region_id=5;	

This is what the first user will see, from a SQL*Plus prompt:

```
SQL> select * from regions;
 REGION_ID REGION_NAME
---------- ------------------------
         5 UK
         1 Europe
         2 Americas
         3 Asia
         4 Middle East and Africa
SQL> update regions set region_name='GB' where region_id=5;
0 rows updated.
```

This is a bit disconcerting. One way around this problem is to lock the rows in which one is interested:

```
select * from regions for update;
```

The FOR UPDATE clause will place a lock on all the rows retrieved. No changes can be made to them by any session other than that which issued the command, and therefore the subsequent updates will succeed: it is not possible for the rows to have been changed. This means that one session will have a consistent view of the data (it won't change), but the price to be paid is that other sessions will hang if they try to update any of the locked rows (they can, of course, query them).

The locks placed by a FOR UPDATE clause will be held until the session issuing the command issues a COMMIT or ROLLBACK. This must be done to release the locks, even if no DML commands have been executed.

The So-Called "Autocommit"

To conclude this discussion of commit processing, it is necessary to remove any confusion about what is often called *autocommit*, or sometimes *implicit commit*. You will often hear it said that in some situations Oracle will autocommit. One of these situations is when doing DDL, which is described in the preceding section; another is when you exit from a user process such as SQL*Plus.

Quite simply, there is no such thing as an automatic commit. When you execute a DDL statement, there is a perfectly normal COMMIT included in the source code that implements the DDL command. But what about when you exit from your user process? If you are using SQL*Plus on a Windows terminal and you issue a DML statement followed by an EXIT, your transaction will be committed. This is because built into the SQL*Plus EXIT command there is a COMMIT statement. But what if you click in the top-right corner of the SQL*Plus window? The window will close, and if you log in again, you will see that the transaction has been rolled back. This is because the programmers who wrote SQL*Plus for Microsoft Windows included a ROLLBACK statement in the code that is executed when you close the window. The behavior of SQL*Plus on other platforms may well be different; the only way to be sure is to test it. So whether you get an "autocommit" when you exit from a program in various ways is entirely dependent on how your programmers wrote your user process. The Oracle server will simply do what it is told to do.

There is a SQL*Plus command SET AUTOCOMMIT ON. This will cause SQL*Plus to modify its behavior: it will append a COMMIT to every DML statement issued. So all statements are committed immediately as soon as they are executed and cannot be rolled back. But this is happening purely on the user process side; there is still no autocommit in the database, and the changes made by a long-running statement will be isolated from other sessions until the statement completes. Of course, a disorderly exit from SQL*Plus in these circumstances, such as killing it with an operating system utility while the statement is running, will be detected by PMON and the active transaction will always be rolled back.

Exercise 8-4: Manage Data Using DML In this exercise, you will demonstrate transaction isolation and control. Use two SQL*Plus sessions (or SQL Developer if you prefer), each connected as user SYSTEM. Run the commands in the steps that follow in the two sessions in the correct order.

Step	In Your First Session	In Your Second Session
1	create table t1 as select * from all_users;	
2	select count(*) from t1;	select count(*) from t1;

Results are the same in both sessions.

3	delete from t1;	
4	select count(*) from t1;	select count(*) from t1;

Results differ because transaction isolation conceals the changes.

5	rollback;	
6	select count(*) from t1;	select count(*) from t1;

Results are the same in both sessions.

7	delete from t1;	
8	select count(*) from t1;	select count(*) from t1;
9	create view v1 as select * from t1;	
10	select count(*) from t1;	select count(*) from t1;
11	rollback;	
12	select count(*) from t1;	select count(*) from t1;

Oh dear! The DDL statement committed the DELETE, so it can't be rolled back.

13	drop view v1;
14	drop table t1;

Identify and Administer PL/SQL Objects

PL/SQL is Oracle's proprietary third-generation language that runs within the database. You can use it to retrieve and manipulate data with SQL, while using procedural constructs such as IF . . . THEN . . . ELSE or FOR or WHILE. The PL/SQL code can be stored on a client machine and sent to the server for execution, or it can be stored within the database as a named block of code.

 EXAM TIP PL/SQL always executes within the database, no matter where it is stored. Java can run either within the database or on the user machine.

Stored and Anonymous PL/SQL

PL/SQL runs within the database, but it can be stored on either the client or the server. PL/SQL code can also be entered interactively from a SQL*Plus prompt. *Stored* PL/SQL is loaded into the database and stored within the data dictionary as a named PL/SQL object. When it is saved to the database, it is compiled: the compilation process checks for syntactical errors and also picks up errors relating to the data objects the code addresses. This saves time when the code is actually run, and means that programmers should pick up errors at compilation time, before users encounter them. Code stored remotely, or ad hoc code issued at the SQL*Plus prompt, is called *anonymous* PL/SQL. It is compiled dynamically; which impacts on performance, and it also raises the possibility that unexpected errors might occur.

Figure 8-5 shows an example of running an anonymous PL/SQL block and of creating and running a stored procedure.

The anonymous block in Figure 8-5 creates a variable called INCREASE with the DECLARE statement and sets it to 10. Then the procedural code (within the BEGIN . . .

Figure 8-5

Anonymous and stored PL/SQL

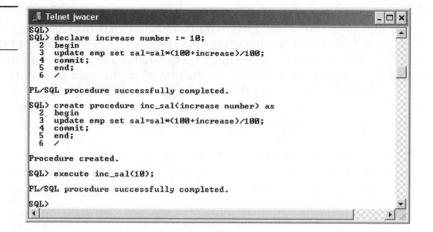

```
Telnet jwacer                                        _□×
SQL>
SQL> declare increase number := 10;
  2   begin
  3   update emp set sal=sal*(100+increase)/100;
  4   commit;
  5   end;
  6   /

PL/SQL procedure successfully completed.

SQL> create procedure inc_sal(increase number) as
  2   begin
  3   update emp set sal=sal*(100+increase)/100;
  4   commit;
  5   end;
  6   /

Procedure created.

SQL> execute inc_sal(10);

PL/SQL procedure successfully completed.

SQL>
```

END statements) uses the variable within a SQL statement that updates a column of a table.

The second example in the figure creates a procedure called INC_SAL, stored within the data dictionary. It takes a numeric argument called INCREASE and uses this in a SQL UPDATE statement. Then the procedure is invoked with the EXECUTE command, passing in a value for the argument.

These examples are very simple, but they should illustrate how anonymous PL/SQL runs just once and therefore must be compiled at execution time, whereas stored PL/SQL can be compiled in advance and then executed many times.

PL/SQL Objects

There are six commonly used types of PL/SQL objects: Procedure, Function, Package, Package body, Trigger, and Type body.

All are schema objects stored within the data dictionary. Procedures and functions are subprograms usually intended for performing repetitive instructions. Packages are collections of procedures and functions, grouped together for manageability. Triggers cannot be packaged: they are associated with tables and run whenever an appropriate DML statement is executed against the tables. Object types are beyond the scope of the OCP examinations.

TIP SQL*Plus and Database Control are only suitable for small-scale PL/SQL development. For real work, your programmers will need a proper IDE (integrated development environment) tool that will assist with syntax checking, debugging, and source code management.

Procedures and Functions

A *procedure* is a block of code that carries out some action. It can, optionally, be defined with a number of arguments. These arguments are replaced with the actual parameters given when the procedure is invoked. The arguments can be IN arguments, meaning that they are used to pass data into the procedure, or OUT arguments, meaning that they are modified by the procedure and after execution the new values are passed out of the procedure. Arguments can also be IN-OUT, where the one variable serves both purposes. Within a procedure, you can define any number of variables that, unlike the arguments, are private to the procedure. To run a procedure, either call it from within a PL/SQL block or use the interactive EXECUTE command.

A function is similar in concept to a procedure, but it does not have OUT arguments and cannot be invoked with EXECUTE. It returns a single value, with the RETURN statement.

Anything that a function can do, a procedure could do also. Functions are generally used for relatively simple operations: small code blocks that will be used many times. Procedures are more commonly used to divide code into modules, and may contain long and complex processes.

Packages

To group related procedures and functions together, your programmers create packages. A package consists of two objects: a specification and a body. A package specification lists the functions and procedures in the package, with their call specifications: the arguments and their data types. It can also define variables and constants accessible to all the procedures and functions in the package. The package body contains the PL/SQL code that implements the package: the code that creates the procedures and functions.

To create a package specification, use the CREATE PACKAGE command. For example,

```
SQL> create or replace package numbers
  2  as
  3  function odd_even(v1 number) return varchar2;
  4  procedure ins_ints(v1 in number);
  5  end numbers;
  6  /
Package created.
```

Then to create the package body, use the CREATE OR REPLACE PACKAGE BODY statement to create the individual functions and procedures.

There are several hundred PL/SQL packages provided as standard with the Oracle database. These supplied packages are, for the most part, created when you create a database. To invoke a packaged procedure, you must prefix the procedure name with the package name. For example,

```
SQL> exec numbers.odd_even(5);
```

This will run the ODD_EVEN procedure in the NUMBERS package. The package must exist in the schema to which the user is connected, or it would be necessary to prefix the package name with the schema name. The user would also need to have the EXECUTE privilege on the package.

Database Triggers

Database *triggers* are a special category of PL/SQL object, in that they cannot be invoked manually. A trigger runs (or "fires") automatically, when a particular action is carried out, or when a certain situation arises; this is the triggering event. There are a number of possible triggering events. For many of them the trigger can be configured to fire either before or after the event. It is also possible to have both before and after triggers defined for the same event. The DML triggers, that fire when rows are inserted, updated, or deleted, can be configured to fire once for each affected row, or once per statement execution.

All triggers have one factor in common: their execution is completely beyond the control of the user who caused the triggering event. The user may not even know that the trigger fired. This makes triggers admirably suited to auditing user actions and implementing security.

The following table describes the commonly used triggering events.

Event	Before or After?

DML triggers:
   INSERT
   UPDATE
   DELETE
	Before and/or after
	
	 Can fire once per statement, or once per row. A MERGE command will fire whatever triggers are appropriate to the action carried out.

DDL triggers:
   CREATE
   ALTER
   DROP
   TRUNCATE
	Before and/or after

Database operations:
   SERVERERROR
   LOGON
   LOGOFF
   STARTUP
   SHUTDOWN
	
	 After
	 After
	 Before
	 After
	 Before

SUSPEND	After Fires after a resumable operation is suspended because of a space error.

Note that there is no such thing as a trigger on SELECT, though Chapter 6 showed how fine-grained auditing can be used to produce a similar effect.

There are numerous uses for triggers. These might include:

- **Auditing users' actions**   A trigger can capture full details of what was done and who did it, and write them out to an audit table.

- **Executing complex edits**   An action on one row may, in business terms, require a number of associated actions on other tables. The trigger can perform these automatically.

- **Security**   A trigger can check the time, the user's IP address, the program they are running, and any other factors that should limit what the session can do.

- **Enforcing complex constraints**   An action may be fine in terms of the constraints on one table but may need to be validated against the contents of several other tables.

EXAM TIP It is impossible to run a trigger by any means other than its triggering event.

Exercise 8-5: Create PL/SQL Objects   In this exercise, you will use Database Control to create PL/SQL objects, and execute them with SQL*Plus.

1. Connect to your database as user SYSTEM with SQL*Plus.

2. Create a table to be used for this exercise:

```
create table integers(c1 number, c2 varchar2(5));
```

3. Connect to your database as user SYSTEM with Database Control.

4. From the database home page, take the Schema tab and then the Packages link in the Programs section. Click CREATE.

5. In the Create Package window, enter **NUMBERS** as the package name, and the source code for the package as shown in the next illustration. Click OK to create the package.

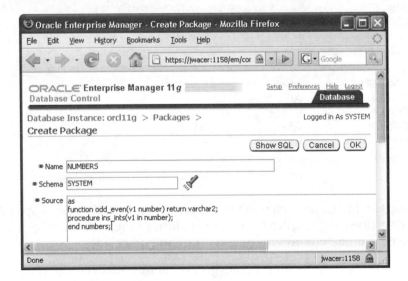

6. From the database home page, take the Schema tab and then the Packages Bodies link in the Programs section. Click CREATE.

7. In the Create Package Body window, enter **NUMBERS** as the package name, and the source code for the package body as in the next illustration. Click OK to create the package body.

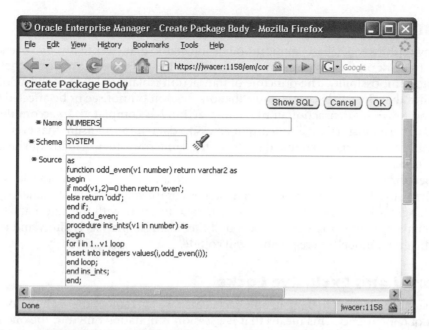

8. In your SQL*Plus session, describe the package, execute the procedure, and check the results, as in this illustration:

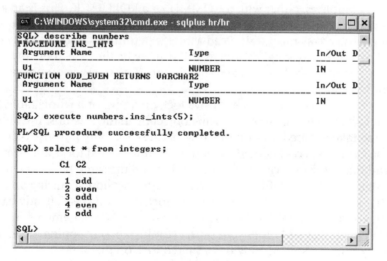

9. Tidy up by dropping the package and table:

```
drop package numbers;
drop table integers;
```

Note that this first DROP will COMMIT the insert of the rows.

Monitor and Resolve Locking Conflicts

In any multiuser database application it is inevitable that, eventually, two users will wish to work on the same row at the same time. The database must ensure that it is a physical impossibility. The principle of transaction isolation—the I of the ACID test—requires that the database guarantee that one session cannot see or be affected by another session's transaction until the transaction has completed. To accomplish this, the database must serialize concurrent access to data; it must ensure that even though multiple sessions have requested access to the same rows, they actually queue up, and take turns.

Serialization of concurrent access is accomplished by record and table locking mechanisms. Locking in an Oracle database is completely automatic. Generally speaking, problems only arise if software tries to interfere with the automatic locking mechanism with poorly written code, or if the business analysis is faulty and results in a business model where sessions will collide.

Shared and Exclusive Locks

The standard level of locking in an Oracle database guarantees the highest possible level of concurrency. This means that if a session is updating one row, the one row is locked; nothing else. Furthermore, the row is only locked to prevent other sessions from updating it—other sessions can read it at any time. The lock is held until the transaction completes, either with a COMMIT or a ROLLBACK. This is an *exclusive* lock: the first session to request the lock on the row gets it, and any other sessions requesting write access must wait. Read access is permitted—though if the row has been updated by the locking session, as will usually be the case, then any reads will involve the use of undo data to make sure that reading sessions do not see any uncommitted changes.

Only one session can take an exclusive lock on a row, or a whole table, at a time—but *shared* locks can be taken on the same object by many sessions. It would not make any sense to take a shared lock on one row, because the only purpose of a row lock is to gain the exclusive access needed to modify the row. Shared locks are taken on whole tables, and many sessions can have a shared lock on the same table. The purpose of taking a shared lock on a table is to prevent another session acquiring an exclusive lock on the table: you cannot get an exclusive lock if anyone else already has a shared lock. Exclusive locks on tables are required to execute DDL statements. You cannot issue a statement that will modify an object (for instance, dropping a column of a table) if any other session already has a shared lock on the table.

To execute DML on rows, a session must acquire exclusive locks on the rows to be changed, and shared locks on the tables containing the rows. If another session already has exclusive locks on the rows, the session will hang until the locks are released by a COMMIT or a ROLLBACK. If another session already has a shared lock on the table and exclusive locks on other rows, that is not a problem. An exclusive lock on the table would be, but the default locking mechanism does not lock whole tables unless this is necessary for DDL statements.

All DML statements require at least two locks: an exclusive lock on each row affected, and a shared lock on the table containing the row. The exclusive lock prevents another session from interfering with the row, and the shared lock prevents another session from changing the table definition with a DDL statement. These locks are requested automatically. If a DML statement cannot acquire the exclusive row locks it needs, then it will hang until it gets them.

To execute DDL commands requires an exclusive lock on the object concerned. This cannot be obtained until all DML transactions against the table have finished, thereby releasing both their exclusive row locks and their shared table locks. The exclusive lock required by any DDL statement is requested automatically, but if it cannot be obtained—typically, because another session already has the shared lock granted for DML—then the statement will terminate with an error immediately.

The Enqueue Mechanism

Requests for locks are queued. If a session requests a lock and cannot get it because another session already has the row or object locked, the session will wait. It may be that several sessions are waiting for access to the same row or object—in that case, Oracle will keep track of the order in which the sessions requested the lock. When the session with the lock releases it, the next session will be granted it, and so on. This is known as the *enqueue* mechanism.

If you do not want a session to queue up if it cannot get a lock, the only way to avoid this is to use the WAIT or NOWAIT clauses of the SELECT . . . FOR UPDATE command. A normal SELECT will always succeed, because SELECT does not require any locks—but a DML statement will hang. The SELECT . . . FOR UPDATE command will select rows and lock them in exclusive mode. If any of the rows are locked already, the SELECT . . . FOR UPDATE statement will be queued and the session will hang until the locks are released, just as a DML statement would. To avoid sessions hanging, use either SELECT . . . FOR UPDATE NOWAIT or SELECT . . . FOR UPDATE WAIT <n>, where <n> is a number of seconds. Having obtained the locks with either of the SELECT . . . FOR UPDATE options, you can then issue the DML commands with no possibility of the session hanging.

 TIP It is possible to append the keywords SKIP LOCKED to a SELECT FOR UPDATE statement, which will return and lock only rows that are not already locked by another session. This command existed with earlier releases but is only supported from release 11g.

Lock Contention

When a session requests a lock on a row or object and cannot get it because another session has an exclusive lock on the row or object, it will hang. This is lock contention, and it can cause the database performance to deteriorate appallingly as all the sessions queue up waiting for locks. Some lock contention may be inevitable, as a result of normal activity: the nature of the application may be such that different users will require access to the same data. But in many cases, lock contention is caused by program and system design.

The Oracle database provides utilities for detecting lock contention, and it is also possible to solve the problem in an emergency. A special case of lock contention is the *deadlock*, which is always resolved automatically by the database itself.

The Causes of Lock Contention

It may be that the nature of the business is such that users do require write access to the same rows at the same time. If this is a limiting factor in the performance of the system, the only solution is business process reengineering, to develop a more efficient business model. But although some locking is a necessary part of business data processing, there are some faults in application design that can exacerbate the problem.

Long-running transactions will cause problems. An obvious case is where a user updates a row and then does not commit the change. Perhaps the user even goes off to lunch, leaving the transaction unfinished. You cannot stop this happening if users have access to the database with tools such as SQL*Plus, but it should never occur with well-written software. The application should take care that a lock is only imposed just before an update occurs, and released (with a COMMIT or ROLLBACK) immediately afterward.

Third-party user process products may impose excessively high locking levels. For example, there are some application development tools that always do a SELECT . . . FOR UPDATE to avoid the necessity of requerying the data and checking for changes. Some other products cannot do row-level locking: if a user wants to update one row, the tool locks a group of rows—perhaps dozens or even hundreds. If your application software is written with tools such as these, the Oracle database will simply do what it is told to do: it will impose numerous locks that are unnecessary in business terms. If you suspect that the software is applying more locks than necessary, investigate whether it has configuration options to change this behavior.

Detecting and Resolving Lock Contention

There are views that will tell you what is going on with locking in the database, but this is one case where even very experienced DBAs will often prefer to use the graphical tools. To reach the Database Control lock manager, take the Performance tab from the database home page, then the Instance Locks link in the Additional Monitoring Links section. Figure 8-6 shows the Instance Locks window, with Blocking Locks selected. There may be any number of locks within the database, but it is usually only the locks that are causing sessions to hang that are of interest. These are known as *blocking* locks.

In Figure 8-6, there are two problems. Session number 116, logged on as user SCOTT, is holding an exclusive lock on one or more rows of the table HR.EMPLOYEES. This session is not hanging—it is operating normally. But session number 129, logged on as user MPHO, is blocked—it is waiting for an exclusive lock on one or more of the rows locked by session 116. Session 129 is hanging at this moment and will continue to hang until session 116 releases its lock(s) by terminating its transaction, with a COMMIT or a ROLLBACK. The second problem is worse: JON is blocking two sessions, those of ISAAC and ROOP.

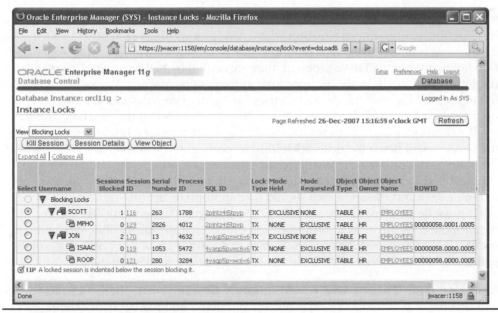

Figure 8-6   Showing locks with Database Control

Lock contention is a natural consequence of many users accessing the same data concurrently. The problem can be exacerbated by badly designed software, but in principle lock contention is part of normal database activity. It is therefore not possible for the DBA to resolve it completely—he can only identify that it is a problem, and suggest to system and application designers that they bear in mind the impact of lock contention when designing data structures and programs.

If locks are becoming an issue, as in Figure 8-6, they must be investigated. Database Control can provide the necessary information. Clicking the values in the "SQL ID" column will let you see what statements being executed caused the lock contention. In the figure, SCOTT and MPHO have both executed one statement. JON, ISAAC, and ROOP have executed another. The "ROWID" column can be used to find the exact row for which the sessions are contending. You cannot drill down to the row from this window, but the rowid can be used in a SELECT statement to retrieve the row in another (unblocked) session. When the code and the rows that cause the contention are known, a solution can be discussed with the system designers and developers.

In an emergency, however, it is possible for the DBA to solve the problem—by terminating the session, or sessions, that are holding too many locks for too long. When a session is terminated forcibly, any locks it holds will be released as its active transaction is rolled back. The blocked sessions will then become free and can continue.

To terminate a session, either use Database Control, or the ALTER SYSTEM KILL SESSION command. In the preceding example, if you decided that the SCOTT session is holding its lock for an absurd period of time, you would select the radio button for the session and click the KILL SESSION button. SCOTT's transaction will be rolled back, and MPHO's session will then be able to take the lock(s) it requires and continue working. In the case of the second problem in the figure, killing JON's session would free up ISAAC, who would then be blocking ROOP.

Deadlocks

It is possible to encounter a situation where two sessions block each other in such a fashion that both will hang, each waiting for the other to release its lock. This is a *deadlock*. Deadlocks are not the DBA's problem; they are caused by bad program design and resolved automatically by the database itself. Information regarding deadlocks is written out to the alert log, with full details in a trace file—part of your daily monitoring will pick up the occurrence of deadlocks and inform your developers that they are happening.

If a deadlock occurs, both sessions will hang—but only for a brief moment. One of the sessions will detect the deadlock within seconds, and it will roll back the statement that caused the problem. This will free up the other session, returning the message "ORA-00060 Deadlock detected." This message must be trapped by your programmers in their exceptions clauses, which should take appropriate action.

It must be emphasized that deadlocks are a program design fault. They occur because the code attempts to do something that is logically impossible. Well-written code will always request locks in a sequence that cannot cause deadlocks to occur, or will test whether incompatible locks already exist before requesting them.

Exercise 8-6: Detect and Resolve Lock Contention   In this exercise, you will first use SQL*Plus to cause a problem, and detect and solve it with Database Control.

1. Using SQL*Plus, connect to your database in two sessions as user WEBSTORE.

2. In your first session, lock all the rows in the PRODUCTS table:

   ```
   select * from products for update;
   ```

3. In your second session, attempt to update a row. The session will hang:

   ```
   update products set stock_count=stock_count-1;
   ```

4. Connect to your database as user SYSTEM with Database Control.

5. Navigate to the Instance Locks window, by taking the Performance tab from the database home page, and then the Database Locks link in the Additional Monitoring Links section.

6. Observe that the second SYSTEM session is shown as waiting for an EXCLUSIVE lock. Select the radio button for the first, blocking, session and click KILL SESSION.

7. In the confirmation window, click SHOW SQL. This will show a command something like

   ```
   ALTER SYSTEM KILL SESSION '120,1318' IMMEDIATE
   ```

8. Click RETURN and YES to execute the KILL SESSION command.

9. Returning to your SQL*Plus sessions, you will find that the second session is now working, but that the first session can no longer run any commands.

Overview of Undo

Undo data is the information needed to reverse the effects of DML statements. It is often referred to as *rollback data*, but try to avoid that term. In earlier releases of Oracle, the terms rollback data and undo data were used interchangeably, but from 9*i* onward they are different: their function is the same, but their management is not. Whenever a transaction changes data, the preupdate version of the data is written out to a rollback segment or to an undo segment. The difference is crucial. Rollback segments can still exist in an 11*g* database, but with release 9*i* of the database Oracle introduced the undo segment as an alternative. Oracle strongly advises that all databases should use undo segments—rollback segments are retained for backward compatibility, but they are not referenced in the OCP exam and are therefore not covered in this book.

To roll back a transaction means to use data from the undo segments to construct an image of the data as it was before the transaction occurred. This is usually done automatically to satisfy the requirements of the ACID test, but the flashback query capability (detailed in Chapter 19) leverages the power of the undo mechanism by giving you the option of querying the database as it was at some time in the past. And of course, any user can use the ROLLBACK command interactively to back out any DML statements that were issued and not committed.

The ACID test requires, first, that the database should keep preupdate versions of data in order that incomplete transactions can be reversed—either automatically in the case of an error or on demand through the use of the ROLLBACK command. This type of rollback is permanent and published to all users. Second, for consistency, the database must be able to present a query with a version of the database as it was at the time the query started. The server process running the query will go to the undo segments and construct what is called a *read-consistent* image of the blocks being queried, if they were changed after the query started. This type of rollback is temporary and only visible to the session running the query. Third, undo segments are also used for transaction isolation. This is perhaps the most complex use of undo data. The principle of isolation requires that no transaction can be in any way dependent upon another, incomplete transaction. In effect, even though a multiuser database will have many transactions in progress at once, the end result must be as though the transactions were executing one after another. The use of undo data combined with row and table locks guarantees transaction isolation: the impossibility of incompatible transactions. Even though several transactions may be running concurrently, isolation requires that the end result must be as if the transactions were serialized.

 EXAM TIP Use of undo segments is incompatible with use of rollback segments: it is one or the other, depending on the setting of the UNDO_ MANAGEMENT parameter.

Exercise 8-7: Use Undo Data   In this exercise, you will investigate the undo configuration and usage in your database. Use either SQL*Plus or SQL Developer.

1. Connect to the database as user SYSTEM.

2. Determine whether the database is using undo segments or rollback segments with this query:

```
select value from v$parameter where name='undo_management';
```

This should return the value AUTO. If it does not, issue this command, and then restart the instance:

```
alter system set undo_management=auto scope =spfile;
```

3. Determine what undo tablespaces have been created, and which one is being used with these two queries:

```
select tablespace_name from dba_tablespaces where contents='UNDO';
select value from v$parameter where name='undo_tablespace';
```

4. Determine what undo segments are in use in the database, and how big they are:

```
select tablespace_name,segment_name,segment_id,status from dba_rollback_segs;
select usn,rssize from v$rollstat;
```

Note that the identifying number for a segment has a different column name in the two views.

5. Find out how much undo data was being generated in your database in the recent past:

```
alter session set nls_date_format='dd-mm-yy hh24:mi:ss';
select begin_time, end_time,
(undoblks * (select value from v$parameter where  name='db_block_size'))
undo_bytes from  v$undostat;
```

Transactions and Undo Data

When a transaction starts, Oracle will assign it to one (and only one) undo segment. Any one transaction can only be protected by one undo segment—it is not possible for the undo data generated by one transaction to cut across multiple undo segments. This is not a problem, because undo segments are not of a fixed size. So if a transaction does manage to fill its undo segment, Oracle will automatically add another extent to the segment, so that the transaction can continue. It is possible for multiple transactions to share one undo segment, but in normal running this should not occur. A tuning problem common with rollback segments was estimating how many rollback segments would be needed to avoid excessive interleaving of transactions within rollback segments without creating so many as to waste space. One feature of undo management is that Oracle will automatically spawn new undo segments on demand, in an attempt to ensure that it is never necessary for transactions to share undo segments. If Oracle has found it necessary to extend its undo segments or to generate additional segments, when the workload drops Oracle will shrink and drop the segments, again automatically.

PART II

EXAM TIP No transaction can ever span multiple undo segments, but one undo segment can support multiple transactions.

As a transaction updates table or index data blocks, the information needed to roll back the changes is written out to blocks of the assigned undo segment. All this happens in the database buffer cache. Oracle guarantees absolutely the A, for atomicity, of the ACID test, meaning that all the undo data must be retained until a transaction commits. If necessary, the DBWn will write the changed blocks of undo data to the undo segment in the datafiles. By default, Oracle does not, however, guarantee the C, for consistency, of the ACID test. Oracle guarantees consistency to the extent that if a query succeeds, the results will be consistent with the state of the database at the time the query started—but it does not guarantee that the query will actually succeed. This means that undo data can be categorized as having different levels of necessity. *Active* undo is undo data that might be needed to roll back transactions in progress. This data can never be overwritten, until the transaction completes. At the other extreme, *expired* undo is undo data from committed transactions, which Oracle is no longer obliged to store. This data can be overwritten if Oracle needs the space for another active transaction. *Unexpired* undo is an intermediate category; it is neither active nor expired: the transaction has committed, but the undo data might be needed for consistent reads, if there are any long-running queries in progress. Oracle will attempt not to overwrite unexpired undo.

EXAM TIP Active undo can never be overwritten; expired undo can be overwritten. Unexpired undo can be overwritten, but only if there is a shortage of undo space.

The fact that undo information becomes inactive on commit means that the extents of undo segments can be used in a circular fashion. Eventually, the whole of the undo tablespace will be filled with undo data, so when a new transaction starts, or a running transaction generates some more undo, the undo segment will "wrap" around, and the oldest undo data within it will be overwritten—always assuming that this oldest data is not part of a long-running uncommitted transaction, in which case it would be necessary to extend the undo segment instead.

With the old manually managed rollback segments, a critical part of tuning was to control which transactions were protected by which rollback segments. A rollback segment might even be created and brought online specifically for one large transaction. Automatically managed undo segments make all of that unnecessary, because you as DBA have no control over which undo segment will protect any one transaction. Don't worry about this—Oracle does a better job that you ever could. But if you wish you can still find out which segment has been assigned to each transaction by querying the view V$TRANSACTION, which has join columns to V$SESSION and DBA_ROLLBACK_SEGS, thus letting you build up a complete picture of transaction activity in your database: how many transactions there are currently running, who is running them, which undo segments are protecting those transactions, when the transactions started, and how many blocks of undo each transaction has generated. A related dynamic performance view is V$ROLLSTAT, which gives information on the size of the segments.

Figure 8-7 shows queries to investigate transactions in progress. The first query shows that there are currently two transactions. JON's transaction has been assigned to the segment with SEGMENT_ID number 7 and is currently using 277 blocks of undo space. SCOTT's much smaller transaction is protected by segment 2. The second query shows the segment information. The size of each segment will depend on the size of the transactions that happen to have been assigned to them previously. Note that the join column to DBA_ROLLBACK_SEGS is called USN.

Managing Undo

A major feature of undo segments is that they are managed automatically, but you must set the limits within which Oracle will do its management. After considering the nature and volume of activity in your database, you set certain instance parameters and adjust the size of your undo tablespace in order to achieve your objectives.

Error Conditions Related to Undo

The principles are simple: first, there should always be sufficient undo space available to allow all transactions to continue, and second, there should always be sufficient undo data available for all queries to succeed. The first principle requires that your undo

```
Telnet jwacer                                                        _ □ ×
SQL> select t.start_time,t.used_ublk,s.username,r.segment_id,r.segment_name
  2  from v$transaction t, v$session s, dba_rollback_segs r
  3  where t.ses_addr=s.saddr and t.xidusn=r.segment_id;

START_TIME           USED_UBLK USERNAME SEGMENT_ID SEGMENT_NAME
-------------------- --------- -------- ---------- -------------------
01/01/08 12:18:32          277 JON               7 _SYSSMU7_1192467665$
01/01/08 12:15:47            1 SCOTT             2 _SYSSMU2_1192467665$

SQL>
SQL> select usn,rssize,extents,xacts from v$rollstat;

       USN    RSSIZE    EXTENTS      XACTS
---------- --------- ---------- ----------
         0    385024          6          0
         1   1171456          3          0
         2   3268608          5          1
         3   2220032          4          0
         4   2220032          4          0
         5   1171456          3          0
         6   2220032          4          0
         7   3268608          5          1
         8   2220032          4          0
         9   4317184          6          0
        10   3268608          5          0

11 rows selected.
```

Figure 8-7   Query showing details of transactions in progress

tablespace must be large enough to accommodate the worst case for undo demand. It should have enough space allocated for the peak usage of active undo data generated by your transaction workload. Note that this might not be during the highest number of concurrent transactions; it could be that during normal running you have many small transactions, but the total undo they generate might be less than that generated by a single end-of-month batch job. The second principle requires that there be additional space in the undo tablespace to store unexpired undo data that might be needed for read consistency.

If a transaction runs out of undo space, it will fail with the error ORA-30036, "unable to extend segment in undo tablespace." The statement that hit the problem is rolled back, but the rest of the transaction remains intact and uncommitted. The algorithm that assigns space within the undo tablespace to undo segments means that this error condition will only arise if the undo tablespace is absolutely full of active undo data.

EXAM TIP If a DML statement runs out of undo space, it will be rolled back. The rest of the transaction that had already succeeded remains intact and uncommitted.

If a query encounters a block that has been changed since the query started, it will go to the undo segment to find the preupdate version of the data. If, when it goes to the undo segment, that bit of undo data has been overwritten, the query fails on consistent read with a famous Oracle error ORA-1555, "snapshot too old."

If the undo tablespace is undersized for the transaction volume and the length of queries, Oracle has a choice: either let transactions succeed and risk queries failing with ORA-1555, or let queries succeed and risk transactions failing with ORA-30036. The default behavior is to let the transactions succeed: to allow them to overwrite unexpired undo.

Parameters for Undo Management, and Retention Guarantee

There are three parameters controlling undo: UNDO_MANAGEMENT, UNDO_TABLESPACE, and UNDO_RETENTION.

UNDO_MANAGEMENT defaults to AUTO with release 11g. It is possible to set this to MANUAL, meaning that Oracle will not use undo segments at all. This is for backward compatibility, and if you use this, you will have to do a vast amount of work creating and tuning rollback segments. Don't do it. Oracle Corporation strongly advises setting this parameter to AUTO, to enable use of undo segments. This parameter is static, meaning that if it is changed the change will not come into effect until the instance is restarted. The other parameters are dynamic—they can be changed while the running instance is executing.

If you are using UNDO_MANAGEMENT=AUTO, you must also specify UNDO_TABLESPACE. This parameter nominates a tablespace, which must have been created as an undo tablespace, as the active undo tablespace. All the undo segments within it will be brought online (that is, made available for use) automatically.

Lastly, UNDO_RETENTION, set in seconds, is usually optional. It specifies a target for keeping inactive undo data and determines when it becomes classified as expired rather than unexpired. If, for example, your longest running query is thirty minutes, you would set this parameter to 1800. Oracle will then attempt to keep all undo data for at least 1800 seconds, and your query should therefore never fail with ORA-1555. If, however, you do not set this parameter, or set it to zero, Oracle will still keep data for as long as it can anyway. The algorithm controlling which expired undo data is overwritten first will always choose to overwrite the oldest bit of data; therefore, UNDO_RETENTION is always at the maximum allowed by the size of the tablespace.

Where the UNDO_RETENTION parameter is not optional is if you have configured guaranteed undo retention. The default mode of operation for undo is that Oracle will favor transactions over queries. If the sizing of the undo tablespace is such that a choice has to be made between the possibility of a query failing with ORA-1555 and the certainty of a transaction failing with ORA-30036, Oracle will choose to let the transaction continue by overwriting undo data that a query might need. In other words, the undo retention is only a target that Oracle will try to achieve. But there may be circumstances when successful queries are considered more important than successful transactions. An example might be the end-of-month billing run for a utilities company, when it might be acceptable to risk transactions being blocked for a few hours while the reports are generating. Another case is if you are making use of flashback queries, which rely on undo data.

Guaranteed undo retention, meaning that undo data will never be overwritten until the time specified by the undo retention has passed, is enabled at the tablespace level. This attribute can be specified at tablespace creation time, or an undo tablespace can be altered later to enable it. Once you activate an undo tablespace for which retention guarantee has been specified, all queries will complete successfully, provided they finish within the undo retention time; you will never have "snapshot too old" errors again. The downside is that transactions may fail for lack of undo space.

If the UNDO_RETENTION parameter has been set, and the datafile(s) making up the undo tablespace is set to autoextend, then Oracle will increase the size of the datafile automatically if necessary to keep to the undo retention target. This combination of guaranteed undo retention and autoextending datafiles means that both queries and transactions will always succeed—assuming you have enough disk space. If you don't, the automatic extension will fail.

A database might have one tablespace used in normal operations where undo retention is not guaranteed, and another to be used during month-end reporting where retention is guaranteed.

Sizing and Monitoring the Undo Tablespace

The undo tablespace should be large enough to store the worst case of all the undo generated by concurrent transactions, which will be active undo, plus enough unexpired undo to satisfy the longest running query. In an advanced environment, you may also have to add space to allow for flashback queries as well. The algorithm is simple: calculate the rate at which undo is being generated at your peak workload, and multiply by the length of your longest query.

The V$UNDOSTAT view will tell you all you need to know. There is also an advisor within Database Control that will present the information in an immediately comprehensible way.

Figure 8-8 shows the undo management screen of Database Control. To reach this, take the Server tab from the database home page, then the Automatic Undo Management link in the Database Configuration section.

The configuration section of the screen shows that the undo tablespace currently in use is called UNDO1, and it is 100MB in size. Undo guarantee has not been set, but the datafile(s) for the tablespace is auto-extensible. Making your undo datafiles auto-extensible will ensure that transactions will never run out of space, but Oracle will not extend them merely to meet the UNDO_RETENTION target; it is therefore still possible for a query to fail with "snapshot too old." However, you should not rely on the auto-extend capability; your tablespace should be the correct size to begin with. The Change Tablespace button will issue an ALTER SYSTEM command to activate an alternative undo tablespace.

Further information given on the System Activity tab, shown in Figure 8-9, tells you that the peak rate for undo generation was only 1664KB per minute, and the

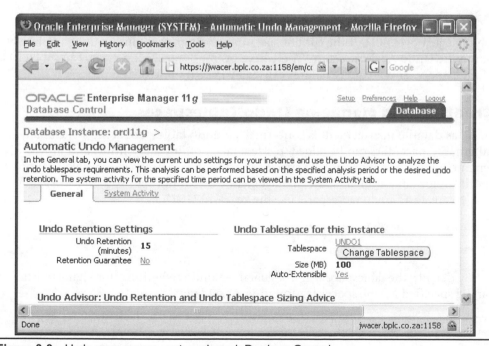

Figure 8-8   Undo management settings, through Database Control

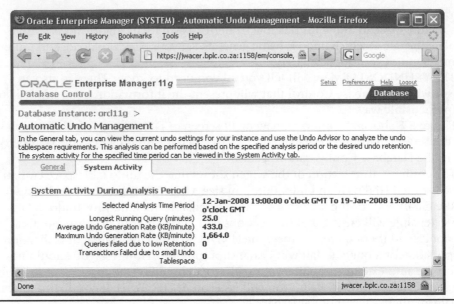

Figure 8-9 Undo activity, summarized by Database Control

longest running query was 25 minutes. It follows that the minimum size of the undo tablespace to be absolutely sure of preventing errors would be, in kilobytes,

```
1664 * 25 = 40265
```

which is just over 40M. If the current size were less than that, this would be pointed out in the Undo Advisor section. There have been no transaction errors caused by lack of undospace, and no query failures caused by lack of undo data.

Creating and Managing Undo Tablespaces

So far as datafile management is concerned, an undo tablespace is the same as any other tablespace: files can be added, resized, taken online and offline, and moved or renamed. But it is not possible to specify any options regarding storage: you cannot specify automatic segment space management, you cannot specify a uniform extent size. To create an undo tablespace, use the keyword UNDO:

```
CREATE UNDO TABLESPACE tablespace_name
DATAFILE datafile_name SIZE size
 [ RETENTION NOGUARANTEE | GUARANTEE ] ;
```

By default, the tablespace will not guarantee undo retention. This characteristic can be specified at tablespace creation time, or set later:

```
ALTER TABLESPACE tablespace_name
retention [ GUARANTEE | NOGUARANTEE ] ;
```

EXAM TIP Unless specified at creation time in the datafile clause, the datafile(s) of an undo tablespace will not be set to autoextend. But if your database is created with DBCA, it will enable automatic extension for the undo tablespace's datafile with maximum size unlimited. Automatic extension can be enabled or disabled at any time, as it can be for any datafile.

It is not possible to create segments in an undo tablespace, other than the undo segments that will be created automatically. Initially, there will be a pool of ten undo segments created in an undo tablespace. More will be created if there are more than ten concurrent transactions. Oracle will monitor the concurrent transaction rate and adjust the number of segments as necessary.

No matter how many undo tablespaces there may be in a database, generally speaking only one will be in use at a time. The undo segments in this tablespace will have a status of *online* (meaning that they are available for use); the segments in any other undo tablespaces will have status *offline*, meaning that they will not be used. If the undo tablespace is changed, all the undo segments in the old undo tablespace will be taken offline, and those in the new undo tablespace will be brought online. There are two exceptions to this:

- In a RAC database, every instance opening the database must have its own undo tablespace. This can be controlled by setting the UNDO_TABLESPACE parameter to a different value for each instance. Each instance will bring its own undo segments online.

- If the undo tablespace is changed by changing the UNDO_TABLESPACE parameter, any segments in the previously nominated tablespace that were supporting a transaction at the time of the change will remain online until the transaction finishes.

Two-Minute Drill

Describe Each Data Manipulation Language (DML) Statement

- INSERT enters rows into a table.
- UPDATE adjusts the values in existing rows.
- DELETE removes rows.
- MERGE can combine the functions of INSERT, UPDATE, and DELETE.
- Even though TRUNCATE is not DML, it does remove all rows in a table.
- It is possible for an INSERT to enter rows into multiple tables.
- Subqueries can be used to generate the rows to be inserted, updated, or deleted.
- An INSERT, UPDATE, or DELETE is not permanent until it is committed.

- TRUNCATE removes every row from a table.
- A TRUNCATE is immediately permanent: it cannot be rolled back.

Control Transactions

- A transaction is a logical unit of work, possibly comprising several DML statements.
- Transactions are invisible to other sessions until committed.
- Until committed, transactions can be rolled back.
- A SAVEPOINT lets a session roll back part of a transaction.

Manage Data Using DML

- All DML commands generate undo and redo.
- Redo protects all changes to segments—undo segments, as well as data segments.
- Server processes read from datafiles; DBWn writes to datafiles.

Identify and Administer PL/SQL Objects

- Anonymous PL/SQL is stored on the client; stored PL/SQL in the data dictionary.
- Procedures and functions can be packaged; triggers cannot be packaged.
- PL/SQL code can call SQL code.

Monitor and Resolve Locking Conflicts

- The default level of locking is row level.
- Locks are required for all DML commands and are optional for SELECT.
- A DML statement requires shared locks on the objects involved and exclusive locks on the rows involved.
- A DDL lock requires an exclusive lock on the object it affects.
- Deadlocks are resolved automatically.

Overview of Undo

- All DML statements generate undo data.
- Undo data is used for transaction rollback and isolation and to provide read consistency, and also for flashback queries.
- Automatic undo management using undo segments is the default with release 11*g*.

Transactions and Undo Data

- Undo data will always be kept until the transaction that generated it completes with a COMMIT or a ROLLBACK. This is *active* undo.

- Undo data will be retained for a period after it becomes inactive to satisfy any read consistency requirements of long running queries; this is *unexpired* undo.

- *Expired* undo is data no longer needed for read consistency and may be overwritten at any time as space in undo segments is reused.

Managing Undo

- An instance will use undo segments in one, nominated, undo tablespace.

- More undo tablespaces may exist, but only one will be used at a time.

- The undo tablespace should be large enough to take into account the maximum rate of undo generation and the longest running query.

- Undo tablespace datafiles are datafiles like any others.

Self Test

1. Which of the following commands can be rolled back? (Choose all correct answers.)

   A. COMMIT

   B. DELETE

   C. INSERT

   D. MERGE

   E. TRUNCATE

   F. UPDATE

2. If an UPDATE or DELETE command has a WHERE clause that gives it a scope of several rows, what will happen if there is an error partway through execution? The command is one of several in a multistatement transaction. (Choose the best answer.)

   A. The command will skip the row that caused the error and continue.

   B. The command will stop at the error, and the rows that have been updated or deleted will remain updated or deleted.

   C. Whatever work the command had done before hitting the error will be rolled back, but work done already by the transaction will remain.

   D. The whole transaction will be rolled back.

3. Study the result of this SELECT statement:

```
SQL> select * from t1;
         C1         C2         C3         C4
---------- ---------- ---------- ----------
          1          2          3          4
          5          6          7          8
```

If you issue this statement:

```
insert into t1 (c1,c2) values(select c1,c2 from t1);
```

why will it fail? (Choose the best answer.)

A. Because values are not provided for all the table's columns: there should be NULLs for C3 and C4.

B. Because the subquery returns multiple rows: it requires a WHERE clause to restrict the number of rows returned to one.

C. Because the subquery is not scalar: it should use MAX or MIN to generate scalar values.

D. Because the VALUES keyword is not used with a subquery.

E. It will succeed, inserting two rows with NULLs for C3 and C4.

4. You want to insert a row and then update it. What sequence of steps should you follow? (Choose the best answer.)

A. INSERT, UPDATE, COMMIT

B. INSERT, COMMIT, UPDATE, COMMIT

C. INSERT, SELECT FOR UPDATE, UPDATE, COMMIT

D. INSERT, COMMIT, SELECT FOR UPDATE, UPDATE, COMMIT

5. Which of these commands will remove every row in a table? (Choose one or more correct answers.)

A. A DELETE command with no WHERE clause

B. A DROP TABLE command

C. A TRUNCATE command

D. An UPDATE command, setting every column to NULL and with no WHERE clause

6. User JOHN updates some rows and asks user ROOPESH to log in and check the changes before he commits them. Which of the following statements is true? (Choose the best answer.)

A. ROOPESH can see the changes but cannot alter them because JOHN will have locked the rows.

B. ROOPESH will not be able to see the changes.

C. JOHN must commit the changes so that ROOPESH can see them and, if necessary, roll them back.

D. JOHN must commit the changes so that ROOPESH can see them, but only JOHN can roll them back.

7. There are several steps involved in executing a DML statement. Place these in the correct order:

   A. Apply the change vectors to the database buffer cache.

   B. Copy blocks from datafiles into buffers.

   C. Search for the relevant blocks in the database buffer cache.

   D. Write the change vectors to the log buffer.

8. When a COMMIT is issued, what will happen? (Choose the best answer.)

   A. All the change vectors that make up the transaction are written to disk.

   B. DBWn writes the change blocks to disk.

   C. LGWR writes the log buffer to disk.

   D. The undo data is deleted, so that the changes can no longer be rolled back.

9. What types of segment are protected by redo? (Choose all correct answers.)

   A. Index segments

   B. Table segments

   C. Temporary segments

   D. Undo segments

10. Which of these commands will terminate a transaction? (Choose all correct answers.)

    A. CREATE

    B. GRANT

    C. SAVEPOINT

    D. SET AUTOCOMMIT ON

11. What type of PL/SQL objects cannot be packaged? (Choose the best answer.)

    A. Functions

    B. Procedures

    C. Triggers

    D. All PL/SQL objects can be packaged, except anonymous blocks

12. If several sessions request an exclusive lock on the same row, what will happen? (Choose the best answer.)

    A. The first session will get the lock; after it releases the lock there is a random selection of the next session to get the lock.

    B. The first session will get an exclusive lock, and the other sessions will get shared locks.

    C. The sessions will be given an exclusive lock in the sequence in which they requested it.

    D. Oracle will detect the conflict and roll back the statements that would otherwise hang.

13. When a DML statement executes, what happens? (Choose the best answer.)

    A. Both the data and the undo blocks on disk are updated, and the changes are written out to the redo stream.

    B. The old version of the data is written to an undo segment, and the new version is written to the data segments and the redo log buffer.

    C. Both data and undo blocks are updated in the database buffer cache, and the updates also go to the log buffer.

    D. The redo log buffer is updated with information needed to redo the transaction, and the undo blocks are updated with information needed to reverse the transaction.

14. Your undo tablespace consists of one datafile on one disk, and transactions are failing for lack of undo space. The disk is full. You have enabled retention guarantee. Any of the following options could solve the problem, but which would cause downtime for your users? (Choose the best answer.)

    A. Create another, larger, undo tablespace and use `alter system set undo_tablespace= . . .` to switch to it.

    B. Move the datafile to a disk with more space, and use `alter database resize datafile . . .` to make it bigger.

    C. Reduce the undo_retention setting with `alter system set undo_retention= . . . .`

    D. Disable retention guarantee with `alter tablespace . . . retention guarantee.`

15. Examine this query and result set:

```
SQL> select BEGIN_TIME,END_TIME,UNDOBLKS,MAXQUERYLEN from V$UNDOSTAT;
BEGIN_TIME        END_TIME            UNDOBLKS MAXQUERYLEN
---------------   -----------------   -------- -----------
02-01-08:11:35:55 02-01-08:11:41:33     14435          29
02-01-08:11:25:55 02-01-08:11:35:55    120248         296
02-01-08:11:15:55 02-01-08:11:25:55    137497          37
02-01-08:11:05:55 02-01-08:11:15:55    102760        1534
02-01-08:10:55:55 02-01-08:11:05:55    237014         540
02-01-08:10:45:55 02-01-08:10:55:55    156223        1740
02-01-08:10:35:55 02-01-08:10:45:55    145275         420
02-01-08:10:25:55 02-01-08:10:35:55     99074         120
```

The blocksize of the undo tablespace is 4KB. Which of the following would be the optimal size for the undo tablespace? (Choose the best answer.)

    A. 1GB

    B. 2GB

    C. 3GB

    D. 4GB

Chapter 8: DML and Concurrency

365

PART II

Self Test Answers

1. ☑ **B, C, D**, and **F**. These are the DML commands: they can all be rolled back.

   ☒ **A** and **E**. COMMIT terminates a transaction, which can then never be rolled back. TRUNCATE is a DDL command and includes a built-in COMMIT.

2. ☑ **C**. This is the expected behavior: the statement is rolled back, and the rest of the transaction remains uncommitted.

   ☒ **A, B**, and **D**. A is wrong because, while this behavior is in fact configurable, it is not enabled by default. B is wrong because, while this is in fact possible in the event of space errors, it is not enabled by default. D is wrong because only the one statement will be rolled back, not the whole transaction.

3. ☑ **D**. The syntax is wrong: use either the VALUES keyword or a subquery, but not both. Remove the VALUES keyword, and it will run. C3 and C4 would be populated with NULLs.

   ☒ **A, B, C**, and **E**. A is wrong because there is no need to provide values for columns not listed. B and C are wrong because an INSERT can insert a set of rows, so there is no need to restrict the number with a WHERE clause or by using MAX or MIN to return only one row. E is wrong because the statement is not syntactically correct.

4. ☑ **A**. This is the simplest (and therefore the best) way.

   ☒ **B, C**, and **D**. All these will work, but they are all needlessly complicated: no programmer should use unnecessary statements.

5. ☑ **A** and **C**. The TRUNCATE will be faster, but the DELETE will get there too.

   ☒ **B** and **D**. B is wrong because this will remove the table as well as the rows within it. D is wrong because the rows will still be there—even though they are populated with NULLs.

6. ☑ **B**. The principle of isolation means that only JOHN can see his uncommitted transaction.

   ☒ **A, C**, and **D**. A is wrong because transaction isolation means that no other session will be able to see the changes. C and D are wrong because a committed transaction can never be rolled back.

7. ☑ **C, B, D**, and **A**. This is the sequence. All others are wrong.

8. ☑ **C**. A COMMIT is implemented by placing a COMMIT record in the log buffer, and LGWR flushing the log buffer to disk.

   ☒ **A, B**, and **D**. A is wrong because many of the change vectors (perhaps all of them) will be on disk already. B is wrong because DBWn does not participate in commit processing. D is wrong because the undo data may well persist for some time; a COMMIT is not relevant to this.

9. ☑ **A**, **B**, and **D**. Changes to any of these will generate redo.

☒ **C**. Changes to temporary segments do not generate redo.

10. ☑ **A** and **B**. Both DDL and access control commands include a COMMIT.

☒ **C** and **D**. **C** is wrong because a savepoint is only a marker within a transaction. **D** is wrong because this is a SQL*Plus command that acts locally on the user process; it has no effect on an active transaction.

11. ☑ **C**. Triggers cannot be packaged.

☒ **A**, **B**, and **D**. **A** and **B** are wrong because functions and procedures can be packaged. **D** is wrong because neither anonymous blocks nor triggers can be packaged.

12. ☑ **C**. This correctly describes the operation of the enqueue mechanism.

☒ **A**, **B**, and **D**. **A** is wrong because locks are granted sequentially, not randomly. **B** is wrong because the shared locks apply to the object; row locks must be exclusive. **D** is wrong because this is more like a description of how deadlocks are managed.

13. ☑ **C**. All DML occurs in the database buffer cache, and changes to both data block and undo blocks are protected by redo.

☒ **A**, **B**, and **D**. **A** is wrong because writing to disk is independent of executing the statement. **B** and **D** are incomplete: redo protects changes to both data blocks and undo blocks.

14. ☑ **B**. This is the option that would require downtime, because the datafile would have to taken offline during the move and you cannot take it offline while the database is open.

☒ **A**, **C**, and **D**. These are wrong because they are all operations that can be carried out during normal running without end users being aware.

15. ☑ **C**. To calculate, take the largest figure for UNDBLKS, which is for a ten-minute period. Divide by 600 to get the rate of undo generation in blocks per second, and multiply by the block size to get the figure in bytes. Multiply by the largest figure for MAXQUERYLEN, to find the space needed if the highest rate of undo generation coincided with the longest query, and divide by a billion to get the answer in gigabytes:
237014 / 600 * 4192 * 1740 = 2.9 (approximately)

☒ **A**, **B**, and **D**. The following algorithm should be followed when sizing an undo tablespace: Calculate the rate at which undo is being generated at your peak workload, and multiply by the length of your longest query.

CHAPTER 9

Retrieving, Restricting, and Sorting Data Using SQL

Exam Objectives

In this chapter you will learn to

This chapter contains several sections that are not directly tested by the exam but are considered prerequisite knowledge for every student. Two tools used extensively for exercises are SQL*Plus and SQL Developer, which are covered in Chapter 2. Oracle specialists use these every day in their work. The exercises and many of the examples are based on two demonstration sets of data. The first, known as the HR schema, is supplied by Oracle, while the second, the WEBSTORE schema, is designed, created, and populated later in this chapter. There are instructions on how to launch the tools and create the demonstration schemas.

The exam-testable sections include the concepts behind the relational paradigm and normalizing of data into relational structures and of retrieving data stored in relational tables using the SELECT statement. The statement is introduced in its basic form and is progressively built on to extend its core functionality. This chapter also discusses the *WHERE* clause, which specifies one or more conditions that the Oracle server evaluates to restrict the rows returned by the statement. A further language enhancement is introduced by the ORDER BY clause, which provides data sorting capabilities. The chapter closes by discussing ampersand substitution: a mechanism that provides a way to reuse the same statement to execute different queries by substituting query elements at runtime.

List the Capabilities of SQL SELECT Statements

Knowing how to retrieve data in a set format using a query language is the first step toward understanding the capabilities of SELECT statements. Describing the relations involved provides a tangible link between the theory of how data is stored in tables and the practical visualization of the structure of these tables. These topics form an important precursor to the discussion of the capabilities of the SELECT statement. The three primary areas explored are as follows:

- Introducing the SQL SELECT statement
- The DESCRIBE table command
- Capabilities of the SELECT statement

Introducing the SQL SELECT Statement

The SELECT statement from Structured Query Language (SQL) has to be the single most powerful nonspoken language construct. It is an elegant, flexible, and highly extensible mechanism created to retrieve information from a database table. A database would serve little purpose if it could not be queried to answer all sorts of interesting questions. For example, you may have a database that contains personal financial records like your bank statements, your utility bills, and your salary statements. You could easily ask the database for a date-ordered list of your electrical utility bills for the last six months or query your bank statement for a list of payments made to a certain account over the same period. The beauty of the SELECT statement is encapsulated in its simple, English-like format that allows questions to be asked of the database in a natural manner.

The DESCRIBE Table Command

To get the answers one seeks, one must ask the correct questions. An understanding of the terms of reference, which in this case are relational tables, is essential for the formulation of the correct questions. A structural description of a table is useful to establish what questions can be asked of it. The Oracle server stores information about all tables in a special set of relational tables called the *data dictionary*, in order to manage them. The data dictionary is quite similar to a regular language dictionary. It stores definitions of database objects in a centralized, ordered, and structured format. The data dictionary is discussed in detail in Chapter 1.

A clear distinction must be drawn between storing the definition and the contents of a table. The definition of a table includes information like table name, table owner, details about the columns that compose the table, and its physical storage size on disk. This information is also referred to as *metadata*. The contents of a table are stored in rows and are referred to as *data*.

The structural metadata of a table may be obtained by querying the database for the list of columns that compose it using the *DESCRIBE* command. The general form of the syntax for this command is intuitively

```
DESC[RIBE] <SCHEMA>.tablename
```

This command shall be systematically unpacked. The DESCRIBE keyword can be shortened to DESC. All tables belong to a schema or owner. If you are describing a table that belongs to the schema to which you have connected, the <SCHEMA> portion of the command may be omitted. Figure 9-1 shows how the EMPLOYEES table is described from SQL*Plus after connecting to the database as the HR user with the DESCRIBE EMPLOYEES command and how the DEPARTMENTS table is described using the shorthand notation: DESC HR.DEPARTMENTS. The HR. notational prefix could be omitted, since the DEPARTMENTS table belongs to the HR schema. The HR schema (and every other schema) has access to a special table called *DUAL*, which belongs to the SYS schema. This table can be structurally described with the command DESCRIBE SYS.DUAL.

Describing tables yields interesting and useful results. You know which columns of a table can be selected, since their names are exposed. You also know the nature of the data contained in these columns, since the column data type is exposed. Chapter 7 details column types.

Mandatory columns, which are forced to store data for each row, are exposed by the *"Null?"* column output produced by the DESCRIBE command having the value *NOT NULL*. You are guaranteed that any column restricted by the NOT NULL constraint contains some data. It is important to note that NULL has special meaning for the Oracle server. NULL refers to an absence of data. Blank spaces do not count as NULL, since they are present in the row and have some length even though they are not visible.

```
Command Prompt - SQLPLUS HR

SQL> DESCRIBE EMPLOYEES;
 Name                                      Null?    Type
 ----------------------------------------- -------- ----------------------------

 EMPLOYEE_ID                               NOT NULL NUMBER(6)
 FIRST_NAME                                         VARCHAR2(20)
 LAST_NAME                                 NOT NULL VARCHAR2(25)
 EMAIL                                     NOT NULL VARCHAR2(25)
 PHONE_NUMBER                                       VARCHAR2(20)
 HIRE_DATE                                 NOT NULL DATE
 JOB_ID                                    NOT NULL VARCHAR2(10)
 SALARY                                             NUMBER(8,2)
 COMMISSION_PCT                                     NUMBER(2,2)
 MANAGER_ID                                         NUMBER(6)
 DEPARTMENT_ID                                      NUMBER(4)

SQL> DESC HR.DEPARTMENTS
 Name                                      Null?    Type
 ----------------------------------------- -------- ----------------------------

 DEPARTMENT_ID                             NOT NULL NUMBER(4)
 DEPARTMENT_NAME                           NOT NULL VARCHAR2(30)
 MANAGER_ID                                         NUMBER(6)
 LOCATION_ID                                        NUMBER(4)

SQL> DESC SYS.DUAL
 Name                                      Null?    Type
 ----------------------------------------- -------- ----------------------------

 DUMMY                                              VARCHAR2(1)
```

Figure 9-1 Describing EMPLOYEES, DEPARTMENTS, and DUAL tables

Capabilities of the SELECT Statement

Relational database tables are built on a mathematical foundation called *relational theory*. In this theory, relations or tables are operated on by a formal language called *relational algebra*. Relational algebra uses some specialized terms: relations store tuples, which have attributes. Or in Oracle-speak, tables store rows, which have columns. SQL is a commercial interpretation of the relational algebra constructs. Three concepts from relational theory encompass the capability of the SELECT statement: projection, selection, and joining.

Projection refers to the restriction of columns selected from a table. When requesting information from a table, you can ask to view all the columns. You can retrieve all data from the HR.DEPARTMENTS table with a simple SELECT statement. This query will return DEPARTMENT_ID, DEPARTMENT_NAME, MANAGER_ID, and LOCATION_ID information for every department record stored in the table. What if you wanted a list containing only the DEPARTMENT_NAME and MANAGER_ID columns? Well, you would request just those two columns from the table. This restriction of columns is called *projection*.

Selection refers to the restriction of the rows selected from a table. It is often not desirable to retrieve every row from a table. Tables may contain many rows, and instead of requesting all of them, selection provides a means to restrict the rows returned. Perhaps you have been asked to identify only the employees who belong to department 30. With *selection* it is possible to limit the results set to those rows of data with a DEPARTMENT_ID value of 30.

Joining, as a relational concept, refers to the interaction of tables with each other in a query. *Third normal form* presents the notion of separating different types of data into autonomous tables to avoid duplication and maintenance anomalies and to associate related data using primary and foreign key relationships. These relationships provide the mechanism to join tables with each other (discussed in Chapter 12).

Assume there is a need to retrieve the e-mail addresses for employees who work in the Sales department. The EMAIL column belongs to the EMPLOYEES table, while the DEPARTMENT_NAME column belongs to the DEPARTMENTS table. *Projection* and *selection* from the DEPARTMENTS table may be used to obtain the DEPARTMENT_ID value that corresponds to the Sales department. The matching rows in the EMPLOYEES table may be *joined* to the DEPARTMENTS table based on this common DEPARTMENT_ID value. The EMAIL column may then be *projected* from this set of results.

The SQL SELECT statement is mathematically governed by these three tenets. An unlimited combination of projections, selections, and joins provides the language to extract the relational data required.

EXAM TIP The three concepts of projection, selection, and joining, which form the underlying basis for the capabilities of the SELECT statement, are usually measured in the exam. You may be asked to choose the correct three fundamental concepts or to choose a statement that demonstrates one or more of these concepts.

Data Normalization

The process of modeling data into relational tables is known as *normalization*. There are commonly said to be three levels of normalization: the first, second, and third normal forms. There are higher levels of normalization: fourth and fifth normal forms are well defined, but not commonly used. It is possible for SQL to address un-normalized data, but this will usually be inefficient, as that is not what the language is designed to do. In most cases, data stored in a relational database and accessed with SQL should be normalized to the third normal form.

TIP There are often several possible normalized models for an application. It is important to use the most appropriate—if the systems analyst gets this wrong, the implications can be serious for performance, storage needs, and development effort.

As an example of normalization, consider an un-normalized table called BOOKS that stores details of books, authors, and publishers, using the ISBN number as the primary key. A *primary key* is the one attribute (or attributes) that can uniquely identify a record. These are two entries:

ISBN	Title	Authors	Publisher
12345	Oracle 11g OCP SQL Fundamentals 1 Exam Guide	John Watson, Roopesh Ramklass	McGraw-Hill, Spear Street, San Francisco, CA 94105
67890	Oracle 11g New Features Exam Guide	Sam Alapati	McGraw-Hill, Spear Street, San Francisco, CA 94105

Storing the data in this table gives rise to several anomalies. First, here is the insertion anomaly: it is impossible to enter details of authors who are not yet published, because there will be no ISBN number under which to store them. Second, a book cannot be deleted without losing the details of the publisher: a deletion anomaly. Third, if a publisher's address changes, it will be necessary to update the rows for every book it has published: an update anomaly. Furthermore, it will be very difficult to identify every book written by one author. The fact that a book may have several authors means that the "author" field must be multivalued, and a search will have to search all the values. Related to this is the problem of having to restructure the table if a book comes along with more authors than the original design can handle. Also, the storage is very inefficient due to replication of address details across rows, and the possibility of error as this data is repeatedly entered is high. Normalization should solve all these issues.

The first normal form is to remove the repeating groups, in this case, the multiple authors: pull them out into a separate table called AUTHORS. The data structures will now look like the following.

Two rows in the BOOKS table:

ISBN	TITLE	PUBLISHER
12345	Oracle 11g OCP SQL Fundamentals 1 Exam Guide	McGraw-Hill, Spear Street, San Francisco, California
67890	Oracle 11g New Features Exam Guide	McGraw-Hill, Spear Street, San Francisco, California

And three rows in the AUTHORS table:

NAME	ISBN
John Watson	12345
Roopesh Ramklass	12345
Sam Alapati	67890

The one row in the BOOKS table is now linked to two rows in the AUTHORS table. This solves the insertion anomaly (there is no reason not to insert as many unpublished authors as necessary), the retrieval problem of identifying all the books by one author (one can search the AUTHORS table on just one name) and the problem of a fixed maximum number of authors for any one book (simply insert as many AUTHORS as are needed).

This is the first normal form: no repeating groups.

The second normal form removes columns from the table that are not dependent on the primary key. In this example, that is the publisher's address details: these are dependent on the publisher, not the ISBN. The BOOKS table and a new PUBLISHERS table will then look like this:

BOOKS		
ISBN	TITLE	PUBLISHER
12345	Oracle 11g OCP SQL Fundamentals 1 Exam Guide	McGraw-Hill
67890	Oracle 11g New Features Exam Guide	McGraw-Hill

PUBLISHERS			
PUBLISHER	**STREET**	**CITY**	**STATE**
McGraw-Hill	Spear Street	San Francisco	California

All the books published by one publisher will now point to a single record in PUBLISHERS. This solves the problem of storing the address many times, and it also solves the consequent update anomalies and the data consistency errors caused by inaccurate multiple entries.

Third normal form removes all columns that are interdependent. In the PUBLISHERS table, this means the address columns: the street exists in only one city, and the city can be in only one state; one column should do, not three. This could be achieved by adding an address code, pointing to a separate address table:

PUBLISHERS			
PUBLISHER	**ADDRESS CODE**		
McGraw-Hill	123		
ADDRESSES			
ADDRESS CODE	**STREET**	**CITY**	**STATE**
123	Spear Street	San Francisco	California

One characteristic of normalized data that should be emphasized now is the use of primary keys and foreign keys. A *primary key* is the unique identifier of a row in a table, either one column or a concatenation of several columns (known as a *composite* key). Every table should have a primary key defined. This is a requirement of the relational paradigm. Note that the Oracle database deviates from this standard: it is possible to define tables without a primary key—though it is usually not a good idea, and some other RDBMSs do not permit this.

A *foreign key* is a column (or a concatenation of several columns) that can be used to identify a related row in another table. A foreign key in one table will match a primary key in another table. This is the basis of the *many-to-one relationship*. A many-to-one relationship is a connection between two tables, where many rows in one table refer to a single row in another table. This is sometimes called a parent-child relationship: one parent can have many children. In the BOOKS example so far, the keys are as follows:

TABLE	KEYS
BOOKS	Primary key: ISBN Foreign key: Publisher
AUTHORS	Primary key: Name + ISBN Foreign key: ISBN
PUBLISHERS	Primary key: Publisher Foreign key: Address code
ADDRESSES	Primary key: Address code

These keys define relationships such as that one book can have several authors.

There are various standards for documenting normalized data structures, developed by different organizations as structured formal methods. Generally speaking, it really doesn't matter which method one uses as long as everyone reading the documents understands it. Part of the documentation will always include a listing of the attributes that make up each entity (also known as the columns that make up each table) and an entity-relationship diagram representing graphically the foreign to primary key connections. A widely used standard is as follows:

- Primary key columns identified with a hash (#)
- Foreign key columns identified with a backslash (\)
- Mandatory columns (those that cannot be left empty) with an asterisk (*)
- Optional columns with a lowercase "o"

The second necessary part of documenting the normalized data model is the *entity-relationship diagram*. This represents the connections between the tables graphically. There are different standards for these; Figure 9-2 shows the entity-relationship diagram for the BOOKS example using a very simple notation limited to showing the direction of the one-to-many relationships, using what are often called *crow's feet* to indicate which sides of the relationship are the many and the one. It can be seen that one BOOK can have multiple AUTHORS, one PUBLISHER can publish many books. Note that the diagram also states that both AUTHORS and PUBLISHERS have exactly one ADDRESS. More complex notations can be used to show whether the link is required or optional, information that will match that given in the table columns listed previously.

This is a very simple example of normalization, and it is not in fact complete. If one author were to write several books, this would require multiple values in the ISBN column of the AUTHORS table. That would be a repeating group, which would have to be removed because repeating groups break the rule for first normal form. A challenging exercise with data normalization is ensuring that the structures can handle all possibilities.

A table in a real-world application may have hundreds of columns and dozens of foreign keys. Entity-relationship diagrams for applications with hundreds or thousands of entities can be challenging to interpret.

Figure 9-2
An entity-relationship diagram relating AUTHORS, BOOKS, PUBLISHERS, and ADDRESSES

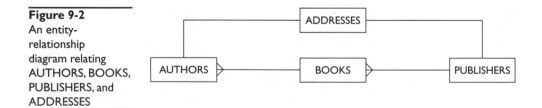

Create the Demonstration Schemas

Throughout this book, there are many examples of SQL code that run against tables. The examples use tables in the HR schema, which is sample data that simulates a simple human resources application, and the WEBSTORE schema, which simulates an order entry application.

The HR schema can be created when the database is created; it is an option presented by the Database Configuration Assistant. If they do not exist, they can be created later by running some scripts that will exist in the database Oracle Home.

The HR and WEBSTORE Schemas

The HR demonstration schema consists of seven tables, linked by primary key to foreign key relationships. Figure 9-3 illustrates the relationships between the tables, as an entity-relationship diagram.

Two of the relationships shown in Figure 9-3 may not be immediately comprehensible. First, there is a many-to-one relationship from EMPLOYEES to EMPLOYEES. This is what is known as a *self-referencing foreign key*. This means that many employees can be connected to one employee, and it's based on the fact that

Figure 9-3
The HR entity-relationship diagram

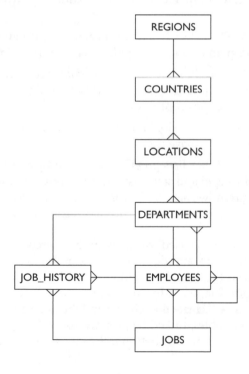

many employees may have one manager, but the manager is also an employee. The relationship is implemented by the column manager_id being a foreign key to employee_id, which is the table's primary key.

The second relationship that may require explanation is between DEPARTMENTS and EMPLOYEES, which is bidirectional. The one department–to–many employees relationship simply states that there may be many staff members in each department, based on the EMPLOYEES department_id column being a foreign key to the DEPARTMENTS primary key department_id column. The one employee–to–many departments relationship shows that one employee could be the manager of several departments and is implemented by the manager_id column in DEPARTMENTS being a foreign key to the primary key employee_id column in EMPLOYEES.

Table 9-1 shows the columns of each table in the HR schema, using the notation described in the earlier section "Data Normalization" to indicate primary keys (#), foreign keys (\), and whether columns are optional (o) or mandatory (*).

The tables are as follows:

- REGIONS has rows for major geographical areas.

- COUNTRIES has rows for each country, which are optionally assigned to a region.

- LOCATIONS includes individual addresses, which are optionally assigned to a country.

- DEPARTMENTS has a row for each department, optionally assigned to a location and optionally with a manager (who must exist as an employee).

- EMPLOYEES has a row for every employee, each of whom must be assigned to a job and optionally to a department and to a manager. The managers must themselves be employees.

- JOBS lists all possible jobs in the organization. It is possible for many employees to have the same job.

- JOB_HISTORY lists previous jobs held by employees, uniquely identified by employee_id and start_date; it is not possible for an employee to hold two jobs concurrently. Each job history record will refer to one employee, who will have had one job at that time and may have been a member of one department.

This HR schema is used for many of the exercises and examples embedded in the chapters of this book and does need to be available.

The WEBSTORE schema might already have been created if you worked through this book from Chapter 1. In this chapter, the entities and their relationships will be defined and we will create the schema and the necessary objects. The WEBSTORE schema consists of four tables, linked by primary key to foreign key relationships. Figure 9-4 illustrates the relationships between the tables, as an entity-relationship diagram.

Table 9-1	Table	Columns	
The Tables and Columns on the HR Schema	REGIONS	#*	region_id
		o	region_name
	COUNTRIES	#*	country_id
		o	country_name
		\o	region_id
	LOCATIONS	#*	location_id
		o	street_address
		o	postal_code
		*	city
		o	state_province
		\o	country_id
	DEPARTMENTS	#*	department_id
		*	department_name
		\o	manager_Id
		\o	location_id
	EMPLOYEES	#*	employee_id
		o	first_name
		*	last_name
		*	e-mail
		o	phone_number
		*	hire_date
		*	job_id
		o	salary
		o	commission_pct
		\o	manager_id
		\o	department_id
	JOBS	#*	job_id
		*	job_title
		o	min_salary
		o	max_salary
	JOB_HISTORY	#*	employee_id
		#*	start_date
		*	end_date
		*	job_id
		\o	department_id

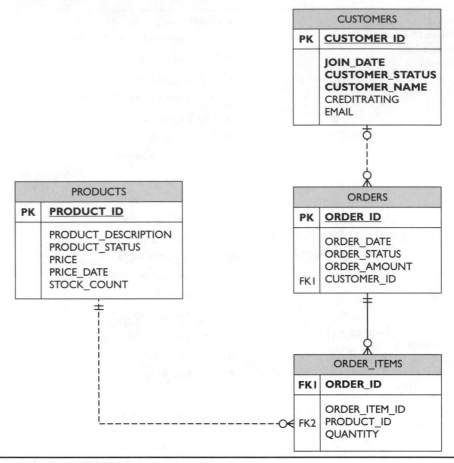

Figure 9-4 The WEBSTORE entity-relationship diagram

The store maintains product, customer, and order details in the appropriately named tables. Each order may consist of multiple products with various quantities, and these records are stored in the ORDER_ITEMS table. Each table has a primary key except for the ORDER_ITEMS table. The order_item_id column stores line item numbers for each distinct product that is part of the order, but each order is associated with one or more records from the ORDER_ITEMS table.

The tables are as follows:

- PRODUCTS has rows for each item, including description, status, price, and stock information. ORDER_ITEMS may be associated with only one product. A foreign key relationship exists between these tables, ensuring that only valid products can appear in records in the ORDER_ITEMS table.

- CUSTOMERS stores information for each customer.

- ORDERS stores customer order information. One customer may be associated with many orders. A foreign key constraint governs this relationship, ensuring that orders cannot be placed by nonexistent customers.
- ORDER_ITEMS stores the detail line items associated with each order.

Demonstration Schema Creation

If the database you are using was created specifically for studying for the OCP SQL examination, the demonstration schemas should have been created already. They are an option presented by the Database Configuration Assistant when it creates a database.

If the schemas were not created at database creation time, they can be created by running scripts installed into the Oracle Home of the database. These scripts will need to be run from SQL*Plus or SQL Developer as a user with SYSDBA privileges. The script will prompt for certain values as it runs. For example, on Linux, first launch SQL*Plus from an operating system prompt:

```
sqlplus / as sysdba
```

There are various options for this connection, but the preceding syntax will usually work if the database is running on the same machine where you are running SQL*Plus. Then invoke the script from the SQL> prompt:

```
SQL> @?/demo/schema/human_resources/hr_main.sql
```

The "?" character is a variable that SQL*Plus will expand into the path to the Oracle Home directory. The script will prompt for HR's password, default tablespace, and temporary tablespace; the SYS password; and a destination for the logfile of the script's running. Typical values for the default tablespace and temporary tablespace are USERS and TEMP, but these will have to have been created already. After completion, you will be connected to the database as the new HR user. To verify this, run this statement:

```
SQL> show user;
```

You will see that you are currently connected as HR; then run

```
SQL> select table_name from user_tables;
```

You will see a list of the seven tables in the HR schema.

To create the WEBSTORE schema (if it does not already exist), run the following statements to create the necessary objects and insert a dataset that will be used in later exercises and examples:

```
sqlplus / as sysdba
create user webstore identified by admin123
default tablespace users temporary tablespace temp quota unlimited on users;
grant create session, create table, create sequence to webstore;
connect webstore/admin123
```

```
create table customers(
customer_id  number(8) not null constraint pk_customer_id primary key,
join_date date default sysdate not null,
customer_status  varchar2(8) not null, customer_name    varchar2(20) not null,
creditrating     varchar2(10) not null, email varchar2(50) not null);

create table products(
product_id number(8) not null constraint pk_product_id primary key,
product_description  varchar2(20) not null,
product_status varchar2(8) not null, price number(10,2) not null,
price_date date not null, stock_count number(8) not null);

create table orders(
order_id      number(8) not null constraint pk_order_id primary key,
order_date    date not null, order_status  varchar2(8) not null,
order_amount  number(10,2) not null,
customer_id   number(8) constraint fk_customer_id references customers (customer_id));

create table order_items(
order_item_id  number(8) not null,
order_id       number(8) constraint fk_order_id references orders(order_id),
product_id     number(8) constraint fk_prod_id references products(product_id),
quantity       number);

create sequence cust_seq;

create sequence order_seq;

create sequence prod_seq;
```

Once these schema objects are created, use the following INSERT statements that make use of substitution variables to populate (or seed) the tables with several rows of data based on the sample data in Table 9-2.

```
insert into customers
(customer_id, customer_status, customer_name, creditrating, email) values
(cust_seq.nextval, '&cust_status', '&cust_name', '&creditrating', '&email');

insert into products(product_id, product_description,
product_status, price, price_date, stock_count)
values (prod_seq.nextval, '&product_description',
'&product_status', &price, sysdate, &stock_count);

insert into orders(order_id, order_date, order_status,
order_amount, customer_id)
values (order_seq.nextval, sysdate, '&order_status',
&order_amount, &customer_id);

insert into order_items values (&item_id, &order_id, &product_id, &quantity);
```

Table:	Customers		
Customer Status	*Customer Name*	*Credit Rating*	*Email*
NEW	Ameetha	Platinum	ameetha@largecorp.com
OLD	Sid	Gold	sid@mediumcorp.com
OLD	Coda	Bronze	coda@largecorp.com
Table:	Products		
Product Description	*Product Status*	*Price*	*Stock Count*
11G SQL Exam Guide	ACTIVE	60	20
11G All-in-One Guide	ACTIVE	100	40
Table:	Orders		
Order Status	*Order Amount*	*Customer Id*	
COMPLETE	680	2	
PENDING	400	3	
Table:	Order Items		
Order Item Id	*Order Id*	*Product Id*	*Quantity*
1	1	2	5
2	1	1	3
1	2	2	4

Table 9-2   Sample Data for the WEBSTORE Schema

Execute a Basic SELECT Statement

The practical capabilities of the SELECT statement are realized in its execution. The key to executing any query language statement is a thorough understanding of its syntax and the rules governing its usage. You will learn more about this topic first, then about the execution of a basic query, and finally about expressions and operators, which exponentially increase the utility of data stored in relational tables. Next, the concept of a null value is demystified, as its pitfalls are exposed. These topics are covered in the following four sections:

- Syntax of the primitive SELECT statement
- Rules are meant to be followed
- SQL expressions and operators
- NULL is nothing

Syntax of the Primitive SELECT Statement

In its most primitive form, the SELECT statement supports the projection of columns and the creation of arithmetic, character, and date expressions. It also facilitates the elimination of duplicate values from the results set. The basic SELECT statement syntax is as follows:

```
SELECT *|{[DISTINCT] column|expression [alias],...}
FROM table;
```

The special keywords or reserved words of the SELECT statement syntax appear in uppercase. When using the commands, however, the case of the reserved words in your query statement does not matter. Reserved words cannot be used as column names or other database object names. SELECT, DISTINCT, and FROM are three keywords. A SELECT statement always contains two or more clauses. The two mandatory clauses are the SELECT clause and the FROM clause. The pipe symbol (|) is used to denote OR. So you can read the first form of the preceding SELECT statement as

```
SELECT *
FROM table;
```

In this format, the asterisk symbol (*) is used to denote all columns. SELECT * is a succinct way of asking Oracle to return all possible columns. It is used as a shorthand, time-saving symbol instead of typing in SELECT *column1*, *column2*, *column3*, *column4*,...,*columnX*, to select all the columns. The FROM clause specifies which table to query to fetch the columns requested in the SELECT clause.

You can issue the following SQL command to retrieve all the columns and all the rows from the REGIONS table in the HR schema:

```
select * from regions;
```

When this command is executed, it returns all the rows of data and all the columns belonging to this table. Use of the asterisk in a SELECT statement is sometimes referred to as a "blind" query because the exact columns to be fetched are not specified.

The second form of the basic SELECT statement has the same FROM clause as the first form, but the SELECT clause is different:

```
SELECT {[DISTINCT] column|expression [alias],…}FROM table;
```

This SELECT clause can be simplified into two formats:

```
SELECT column1 (possibly other columns or expressions) [alias optional]
OR
SELECT DISTINCT column1 (possibly other columns or expressions) [alias op-
tional]
```

An *alias* is an alternative name for referencing a column or expression. Aliases are typically used for displaying output in a user-friendly manner. They also serve as shorthand when referring to columns or expressions to reduce typing. Aliases will be discussed in detail later in this chapter. By explicitly listing only the relevant columns in the SELECT clause you, in effect, *project* the exact subset of the results you wish to retrieve. The following statement will return just the REGION_NAME column of the REGIONS table:

```
select region_name from regions;
```

You may be asked to obtain all the job roles in the organization that employees have historically fulfilled. For this you can issue the command: SELECT * FROM JOB_ HISTORY. However, in addition, the SELECT * construct returns the EMPLOYEE_ID, START_DATE, and END_DATE columns. The uncluttered results set containing only the JOB_ID and DEPARTMENT_ID columns can be obtained with the following statement:

```
select job_id,department_id from job_history;
```

Using the DISTINCT keyword allows duplicate rows to be eliminated from the results set. In numerous situations a unique set of rows is required. It is important to note that the criterion employed by the Oracle server in determining whether a row is unique or distinct depends entirely on what is specified after the DISTINCT keyword in the SELECT clause. Selecting distinct JOB_ID values from the JOB_HISTORY table with the following query will return the eight distinct job types.

```
select distinct job_id from job_history;
```

An important feature of the DISTINCT keyword is the elimination of duplicate values from *combinations* of columns.

Rules Are Meant to Be Followed

SQL is a fairly strict language in terms of syntax rules, but it remains simple and flexible enough to support a variety of programming styles. This section discusses some of the basic rules governing SQL statements.

Uppercase or Lowercase

It is a matter of personal taste about the case in which SQL statements are submitted to the database. Many developers, including the authors of this book, prefer to write their SQL statements in lowercase. There is also a common misconception that SQL reserved words need to be specified in uppercase. Again, this is up to you. Adhering to a consistent and standardized format is advised.

There is one caveat regarding case sensitivity. When interacting with literal values, case does matter. Consider the JOB_ID column from the JOB_HISTORY table. This column contains rows of data that happen to be stored in the database in uppercase; for example, SA_REP and ST_CLERK. When requesting that the results set be restricted by a literal column, the case is critical. The Oracle server treats the request for the rows in the JOB_HISTORY table that contain a value of St_Clerk in the JOB_ID column differently from the request for rows that have a value of ST_CLERK in JOB_ID column.

Metadata about different database objects is stored by default in uppercase in the data dictionary. If you query a database dictionary table to return a list of tables owned by the HR schema, it is likely that the table names returned will be stored in uppercase. This does not mean that a table cannot be created with a lowercase name; it can be. It is just more common and the default behavior of the Oracle server to create and store tables, columns, and other database object metadata in uppercase in the database dictionary.

EXAM TIP SQL statements may be submitted to the database in any case. You must pay careful attention to case when interacting with character literal data and aliases. Requesting a column called JOB_ID or job_id returns the same column, but asking for rows where the JOB_ID value is PRESIDENT is different from asking for rows where the value is President.

Statement Terminators

Semicolons are generally used as SQL statement terminators. SQL*Plus always requires a statement terminator, and usually a semicolon is used. A single SQL statement or even groups of associated statements are often saved as script files for future use. Individual statements in SQL scripts are commonly terminated by a line break (or carriage return) and a forward slash on the next line, instead of a semicolon. You can create a SELECT statement, terminate it with a line break, include a forward slash to execute the statement, and save it in a script file. The script file can then be called from within SQL*Plus. Note that SQL Developer does not require a statement terminator if only a single statement is present, but it will not object if one is used. It is good practice to always terminate your SQL statements with a semicolon. Several examples of SQL*Plus statements follow:

```
select country_name, country_id, location_id from countries;

select city, location_id,
       state_province, country_id
from locations
/
```

The first example demonstrates two important rules. First, the statement is terminated by a semicolon. Second, the entire statement is written on one line. It is entirely acceptable for a SQL statement either to be written on one line or to span multiple lines as long as no words in the statement span multiple lines. The second sample of code demonstrates a statement that spans three lines that is terminated by a new line and executed with a forward slash.

Indentation, Readability, and Good Practice

Consider the following query:

```
select city, location_id,
       state_province, country_id
from locations
/
```

This example highlights the benefits of indenting your SQL statement to enhance the readability of your code. The Oracle server does not object if the entire statement is written on one line without indentation. It is good practice to separate different clauses of the SELECT statement onto different lines. When an expression in a clause is particularly complex, it often enhances readability to separate that term of the statement onto a new line. When developing SQL to meet your reporting needs, the process is often iterative. The SQL interpreter is far more useful during development if complex expressions are isolated on separate lines, since errors are usually thrown in the format of: "ERROR at line X:" This makes the debugging process much simpler.

Exercise 9-1: Answer Your First Questions with SQL   In this step-by-step exercise, you make a connection using SQL*Plus as the HR user to answer two questions using the SELECT statement.

Question 1: How many unique departments have employees currently working in them?

1. Start SQL*Plus and connect to the HR schema.

2. You may initially be tempted to find the answer in the DEPARTMENTS table. A careful examination reveals that the question asks for information about employees. This information is contained in the EMPLOYEES table.

3. The word "unique" should guide you to use the DISTINCT keyword.

4. Combining Steps 2 and 3, you can construct the following SQL statement:

```
select distinct department_id
from employees;
```

5. As shown in the following illustration, this query returns 12 rows. Notice that the third row is empty. This is a null value in the DEPARTMENT_ID column.

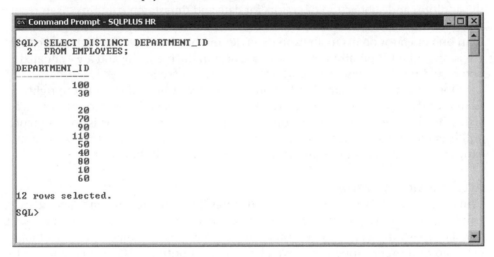

6. The answer to the first question is therefore: Eleven unique departments have employees working in them, but at least one employee has not been assigned to a department.

Question 2: How many countries are there in the Europe region?

1. This question comprises two parts. Consider the REGIONS table, which contains four regions each uniquely identified by a REGION_ID value, and the COUNTRIES table, which has a REGION_ID column indicating which region a country belongs to.

2. The first query needs to identify the REGION_ID of the Europe region. This is accomplished by the SQL statement, which shows that the Europe region has a REGION_ID value of 1.

```
select * from regions;
```

3. To identify which countries have 1 as their REGION_ID, you can execute the SQL query

```
select region_id, country_name from countries;
```

4. Manually counting the country rows with a REGION_ID of 1 returned shows that there are eight countries in the Europe region as far as the HR data model is concerned.

SQL Expressions and Operators

The general form of the SELECT statement introduced the notion that columns and expressions are selectable. An expression usually consists of an operation being performed on one or more column values or expressions. The operators that can act upon values to form an expression depend on the underlying data type. They are the four cardinal arithmetic operators (addition, subtraction, multiplication, and division) for numeric columns; the concatenation operator for character or string columns; and the addition and subtraction operators for date and timestamp columns. As in regular arithmetic, there is a predefined order of evaluation (operator precedence) when more than one operator occurs in an expression. Round brackets have the highest precedence. Division and multiplication operations are next in the hierarchy and are evaluated before addition and subtraction, which have lowest precedence.

Operators with the same level of precedence are evaluated from left to right. Round brackets may therefore be used to enforce nondefault operator precedence. Using brackets generously when constructing complex expressions is good practice and is encouraged. It leads to readable code that is less prone to error. Expressions expose a large number of useful data manipulation possibilities.

Arithmetic Operators

Consider the JOB_HISTORY table, which stores the start date and end date of an employee's term in a previous job role. It may be useful for tax or pension purposes to calculate how long an employee worked in that role. This information can be obtained using an arithmetic expression. Several elements of both the SQL statement and the results returned from Figure 9-5 warrant further discussion.

The SELECT clause specifies five elements. The first four are regular columns of the JOB_HISTORY table, while the latter provides the source information required to calculate the number of days that an employee filled a particular position. Consider employee number 176 on the ninth row of output. This employee started as a Sales Manager on January 1, 1999, and ended employment on December 31, 1999. Therefore, this employee worked for exactly one year, which, in 1999, consisted of 365 days.

PART II

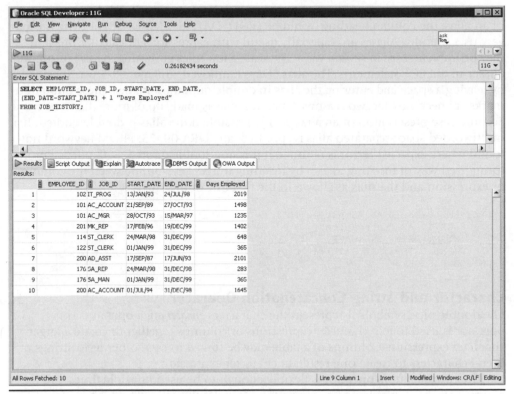

Figure 9-5 Arithmetic expression to calculate number of days worked

The number of days for which an employee was employed can be calculated by using the fifth element in the SELECT clause, which is an expression. This expression demonstrates that arithmetic performed on columns containing date information returns numeric values that represent a certain number of days.

To enforce operator precedence of the subtraction operation, the subexpression *end_date-start_date* is enclosed in round brackets. Adding 1 makes the result inclusive of the final day.

 TIP As you practice SQL on your test database environment, you may encounter two infamous Oracle errors: "ORA-00923: FROM keyword not found where expected" and "ORA-00942: table or view does not exist." These usually indicate spelling or punctuation errors, such as missing enclosing quotes around character literals.

Expression and Column Aliasing

Figure 9-5 introduced a new concept called column aliasing. Notice that the expression has a meaningful heading named Days Employed. This heading is an alias. An *alias* is an alternate name for a column or an expression. If this expression did not make use of an alias, the column heading would be (END_DATE-START_DATE)+1, which is not very user friendly. Aliases are especially useful with expressions or calculations and may be implemented in several ways. There are a few rules governing the use of column aliases in SELECT statements. The alias "Days Employed" in Figure 9-5 was specified by leaving a space and entering the alias in double quotation marks. These quotation marks are necessary for two reasons. First, this alias is made up of more than one word. Second, case preservation of an alias is only possible if the alias is double quoted. If a multiworded space-separated alias is specified, an "ORA-00923: FROM keyword not found where expected" error is returned if it is not double quoted. SQL offers a more formalized way of inserting aliases by inserting the *AS* keyword between the column or expression and the alias as shown in the first line of this query:

```
SELECT EMPLOYEE_ID AS "Employee ID",
       JOB_ID AS "Occupation",
       START_DATE, END_DATE,
       (END_DATE-START_DATE)+1 "Days Employed"
FROM JOB_HISTORY;
```

Character and String Concatenation Operator

The double pipe symbols || represent the character *concatenation* operator. This operator is used to join character expressions or columns together to create a larger character expression. Columns of a table may be linked to each other or to strings of literal characters to create one resultant character expression.

The concatenation operator is flexible enough to be used multiple times and almost anywhere in a character expression. Consider the following query:

```
SELECT 'THE '||REGION_NAME||' region is on Planet Earth' "Planetary Location",
FROM REGIONS;
```

Here, the character literal "The" is concatenated to the contents of the REGION_NAME column. This new string of characters is further concatenated to the character literal "region is on Planet Earth", and the entire expression is aliased with the friendly heading "Planetary Location".

Literals and the DUAL Table

Literals are commonly used in expressions and refer to numeric, character, or date and time values found in SELECT clauses that do not originate from any database object. Concatenating character literals to existing column data can be useful, but what about processing literals that have nothing to do with existing column data? To ensure relational consistency, Oracle offers a clever solution to the problem of using the database to evaluate expressions that have nothing to do with any tables or columns. To get the database to evaluate an expression, a syntactically legal SELECT statement must be submitted. What if you wanted to know the sum of two numeric literals? Oracle solves the problem of relational interaction with the database operating on literal expressions by providing a special single-rowed, single-columned table called DUAL.

Recall the DUAL table described in Figure 9-1. It contains one column called DUMMY of the character data type. You can execute the query SELECT * FROM DUAL, and the data value "X" is returned as the contents of the DUMMY column. Testing complex expressions during development, by querying the dual table, is an effective method to evaluate whether these expressions are correct. Literal expressions can be queried from any table, but remember that the expression will be processed for every row in the table, while querying the DUAL table returns only one row.

```
select 'literal '||'processing using the REGIONS table'
from regions;

select 'literal '||'processing using the DUAL table'
from dual;
```

The first statement will return four lines in the results set, since there are four rows of data in the REGIONS table, while the second returns only one row.

Two Single Quotes or the Alternative Quote Operator

The literal character strings concatenated so far have been singular words prepended and appended to column expressions. These character literals are specified using single quotation marks. For example:

```
select 'I am a character literal string' from dual;
```

What about character literals that contain single quotation marks? Plurals pose a particular problem for character literal processing. Consider the following statement:

```
select 'Plural's have one quote too many' from dual;
```

Executing this statement causes an ORA-00923 Oracle error to be generated. So, how are words that contain single quotation marks dealt with? There are essentially two mechanisms available. The most popular of these is to add an additional single quotation mark next to each naturally occurring single quotation mark in the character string. The following statement demonstrates how the previous error is avoided by replacing the character literal 'Plural's with the literal 'Plural''s.

```
select 'Plural''s have one quote too many' from dual;
```

Using two single quotes to handle each naturally occurring single quote in a character literal can become messy and error prone as the number of affected literals increases. Oracle offers a neat way to deal with this type of character literal in the form of the alternative quote (q) operator. The problem is that Oracle chose the single quote character as the special symbol with which to enclose or wrap other character literals. These character-enclosing symbols could have been anything other than single quotation marks.

Bearing this in mind, consider the alternative quote (q) operator. The q operator enables you to choose from a set of possible pairs of wrapping symbols for character literals as alternatives to the single quote symbols. The options are any single-byte or multibyte character or the four brackets: (round brackets), {curly braces}, [square brackets], or <angle brackets>. Using the q operator, the character delimiter can effectively be changed from a single quotation mark to any other character, as shown here:

```
SELECT q'<Plural's can also be specified with alternate quote operators>' "q<>"
FROM DUAL;

SELECT  q'[Even square brackets' [] can be used for Plural's]' "q[]"
FROM DUAL;

SELECT  q'XWhat about UPPER CASE X for Plural'sX' "qX"
FROM DUAL;
```

The syntax of the alternative quote operator is as follows:

```
q'delimiter character literal which may include single quotes delimiter'
```

where *delimiter* can be any character or bracket. The first and second examples show the use of angle and square brackets as character delimiters, while the third example demonstrates how an uppercase "X" has been used as the special character delimiter symbol through the alternative quote operator. Note that the "X" character can itself be included in the string—so long as it is not followed by a quotation mark.

NULL Is Nothing

Null refers to an absence of data. A row that contains a null value lacks data for that column. Null is formally defined as a value that is unavailable, unassigned, unknown, or inapplicable. Failure to heed the special treatment that null values require will almost certainly lead to an error, or worse, an inaccurate answer. This section focuses on interacting with null column data with the SELECT statement and its impact on expressions.

Not Null and Nullable Columns

Tables store rows of data that are divided into one or more columns. These columns have names and data types associated with them. Some of them are constrained by database rules to be mandatory columns. It is compulsory for some data to be stored in the NOT NULL columns in each row. When columns of a table, however, are not compelled by the database constraints to hold data for a row, these columns run the risk of being empty.

 TIP Any arithmetic calculation with a NULL value always returns NULL.

Oracle offers a mechanism for interacting arithmetically with NULL values using the general functions discussed in Chapter 10. Division by a null value results in null, unlike division by zero, which results in an error. When a null is encountered by the character concatenation operator, however, it is simply ignored. The character concatenation operators ignore null, while the arithmetic operations involving null values always result in null.

Foreign Keys and Nullable Columns

Data model design sometimes leads to problematic situations when tables are related to each other via a primary and foreign key relationship, but the column that the foreign key is based on is nullable.

The DEPARTMENTS table has, as its primary key, the DEPARTMENT_ID column. The EMPLOYEES table has a DEPARTMENT_ID column that is constrained by its foreign key relationship to the DEPARTMENT_ID column in the DEPARTMENTS table. This means that no record in the EMPLOYEES table is allowed to have in its DEPARTMENT_ID column a value that is not in the DEPARTMENTS table. This referential integrity forms the basis for third normal form and is critical to overall database integrity.

But what about NULL values? Can the DEPARTMENT_ID column in the DEPARTMENTS table contain nulls? The answer is *no*. Oracle insists that any column that is a primary key is implicitly constrained to be mandatory. But what about implicit constraints on foreign key columns? This is a quandary for Oracle, since in order to remain flexible and cater to the widest audience, it cannot insist that columns related through referential integrity constraints must be mandatory. Further, not all situations demand this functionality.

The DEPARTMENT_ID column in the EMPLOYEES table is actually nullable. Therefore, the risk exists that there are records with null DEPARTMENT_ID values present in this table. In fact, there are such records in the EMPLOYEES table. The HR data model allows employees, correctly or not, to belong to no department. When performing relational joins between tables, it is entirely possible to miss or exclude certain records that contain nulls in the join column. Chapter 12 discusses ways to deal with this challenge.

Exercise 9-2: Construct Expressions   In this exercise you will construct two queries to display results with an appropriate layout, one from the WEBSTORE schema and the other from the HR schema.

1. Query the WEBSTORE.CUSTOMERS table to retrieve a list of the format: X has been a member for Y days, where X is the CUSTOMER_NAME and Y is the number of days between today and the day the customer joined. Alias the expression: Customer Loyalty.

2. Add a character string expression that concatenates string literals around the CUSTOMER_NAME value and the date expression. A possible solution is

   ```
   select customer_name||' has been a member for: '||(sysdate-join_date)||'
   days.' "Customer Loyalty" from customers;
   ```

3. Query the HR.JOBS table and return a single expression of the form The Job Id for the <job_title's> job is: <job_id>. Take note that the job_title should have an apostrophe and an "s" appended to it to read more naturally. A sample of this output for the organization president is: "The Job Id for the

President's job is: AD_PRES". Alias this column expression: Job Description using the AS keyword. There are multiple solutions to this problem. The approach chosen here is to handle the naturally occurring single quotation mark with an additional single quote. You could make use of the alternate quote operator to delimit the naturally occurring quote with another character.

4. A single expression aliased as Job Description is required; you may construct it by concatenating the literal "The Job Id for the" to the JOB_TITLE column. This string is then concatenated to the literal "'s job is: ", which is further concatenated to the JOB_ID column. An additional single quotation mark is added to yield the SELECT statement that follows:

```
select 'The Job Id for the '||job_title||'''s job is: '||job_id
AS "Job Description" from jobs;
```

Limit the Rows Retrieved by a Query

One of the cornerstone principles in relational theory is selection. Selection is actualized using the WHERE clause of the SELECT statement, sometimes referred to as the *predicate*. Conditions that restrict the dataset returned take many forms and operate on columns as well as expressions. Only rows that conform to these conditions are returned. Conditions restrict rows using comparison operators in conjunction with columns and literal values. Boolean operators provide a mechanism to specify multiple conditions to restrict the rows returned. Boolean, conditional, concatenation, and arithmetic operators are discussed to establish their order of precedence when they are encountered in a SELECT statement.

The WHERE Clause

The WHERE clause extends the SELECT statement by providing the ability to restrict rows returned based on one or more conditions. Querying a table with just the SELECT and FROM clauses results in every row of data stored in the table being returned. Using the DISTINCT keyword, duplicate values are excluded, and the resultant rows are restricted to some degree. What if very specific information is required from a table, for example, only the data where a column contains a specific value? How would you retrieve the countries that belong to the Europe region from the COUNTRIES table? What about retrieving just those employees who work as sales representatives? These questions are answered using the WHERE clause to specify exactly which rows must be returned. The format of the SQL SELECT statement that includes the WHERE clause is

```
SELECT *|{[DISTINCT] column|expression [alias],...}
FROM table
[WHERE condition(s)];
```

The WHERE clause always follows the FROM clause. The square brackets indicate that the WHERE clause is optional. One or more conditions may be simultaneously applied to restrict the result set. A condition is specified by comparing two terms using a conditional operator. These terms may be column values, literals, or expressions. The *equality* operator is most commonly used to restrict result sets. An example of using a WHERE clause is shown next:

```
select country_name
from countries
where region_id=3;
```

This example projects the COUNTRY_NAME column from the COUNTRIES table. Instead of selecting every row, the WHERE clause restricts the rows returned to only those containing a 3 in the REGION_ID column.

Numeric-Based Conditions

Conditions must be formulated appropriately for different column data types. The conditions restricting rows based on numeric columns can be specified in several different ways. Consider the SALARY column in the EMPLOYEES table. This column has a data type of NUMBER(8,2). The SALARY column can be restricted as follows:

```
select last_name, salary from employees where salary = 10000;
```

The LAST_NAME and SALARY values of the employees who earn $10,000 are retrieved, since the data types on either side of the operator match and are compatible.

A numeric column can be compared to another numeric column in the same row to construct a WHERE clause condition, as the following query demonstrates:

```
select last_name, salary from employees
where salary = department_id;
```

This WHERE clause is too restrictive and results in no rows being selected because the range of SALARY values is 2100 to 999999.99, and the range of DEPARTMENT_ID values is 10 to 110. Since there is no overlap in the range of DEPARTMENT_ID and SALARY values, there are no rows that satisfy this condition and therefore nothing is returned.

WHERE clause conditions may also be used to compare numeric columns and expressions or to compare expressions to other expressions:

```
select last_name, salary from employees
where salary = department_id*100;

select last_name, salary from employees
where salary/10 = department_id*10;
```

The first example compares the SALARY column with DEPARTMENT_ID*100 for each row. The second example compares two expressions. Notice that the conditions in both examples are algebraically identical, and the same dataset is retrieved when both are executed.

Character-Based Conditions

Conditions determining which rows are selected based on character data are specified by enclosing character literals in the conditional clause, within single quotes. The JOB_ID column in the EMPLOYEES table has a data type of VARCHAR2(10). Suppose you wanted a list of the LAST_NAME values of those employees currently employed as sales representatives. The JOB_ID value for a sales representative is SA_REP. The following statement produces such a list:

```
select last_name from employees where job_id='SA_REP';
```

If you tried specifying the character literal without the quotes, an Oracle error would be raised. Remember that character literal data is case sensitive, so the following WHERE clauses are not equivalent.

> *Clause 1:* where job_id=SA_REP
> *Clause 2:* where job_id='Sa_Rep'
> *Clause 3:* where job_id='sa_rep'

Clause 1 generates an "ORA-00904: 'SA_REP': invalid identifier" error, since the literal SA_REP is not wrapped in single quotes. Clause 2 and Clause 3 are syntactically correct but not equivalent. Further, neither of these clauses yields any data, since there are no rows in the EMPLOYEES table having JOB_ID column values that are either Sa_Rep or sa_rep.

Character-based conditions are not limited to comparing column values with literals. They may also be specified using other character columns and expressions. Character-based expressions may form either one or both parts of a condition separated by a conditional operator. These expressions can be formed by concatenating literal values with one or more character columns. The following four clauses demonstrate some of the options for character-based conditions:

> *Clause 1:* where 'A '||last_name||first_name = 'A King'
> *Clause 2:* where first_name||' '||last_name = last_name||' '||first_name
> *Clause 3:* where 'SA_REP'||'King' = job_id||last_name
> *Clause 4:* where job_id||last_name ='SA_REP'||'King'

Clause 1 concatenates the string literal "A" to the LAST_NAME and FIRST_NAME columns. This expression is compared to the literal "A King". Clause 2 demonstrates that character expressions may be placed on both sides of the conditional operator. Clause 3 illustrates that literal expressions may also be placed on the left of the conditional operator. It is logically equivalent to clause 4, which has swapped the operands in clause 3 around. Both clauses 3 and 4 identically restrict the results.

Date-Based Conditions

DATE columns are useful for storing date and time information. Date literals must be enclosed in single quotation marks just like character data. When used in conditional WHERE clauses, date columns may be compared to other date columns, literals, or expressions. The literals are automatically converted into DATE values based on the default date format, which is DD-MON-RR. If a literal occurs in an expression involving a DATE column, it is automatically converted into a date value using the default format mask. DD represents days, MON represents the first three letters of a month, and RR represents a Year 2000–compliant year (that is, if RR is between 50 and 99, then the Oracle server returns the previous century, or else it returns the current century). The full four-digit year, YYYY, can also be specified. Consider the following four WHERE clauses:

Clause 1: `where start_date = end_date;`
Clause 2: `where start_date = '01-JAN-2001';`
Clause 3: `where start_date = '01-JAN-01';`
Clause 4: `where start_date = '01-JAN-99';`

The first clause tests equality between two DATE columns. Rows that contain the same values in their START_DATE and END_DATE columns will be returned. Note, however, that DATE values are only equal to each other if there is an exact match between all their components, including day, month, year, hours, minutes, and seconds. Chapter 10 discusses the details of storing DATE values. Until then, don't worry about the hours, minutes, and seconds components. In the second WHERE clause, the START_DATE column is compared to the character literal: '01-JAN-2001'. The entire four-digit year component (YYYY) has been specified. This is acceptable to the Oracle server. The third condition is equivalent to the second, since the literal '01-JAN-01' is converted to the date value 01-JAN-2001. This is due to the RR component being less than 50, so the current (twenty-first) century, 20, is prefixed to the year RR component to provide a century value. The century component for the literal '01-JAN-99' becomes the previous century (19) and is converted to a date value of 01-JAN-1999 for the fourth condition, since the RR component, 99, is greater than 50.

Date arithmetic using the addition and subtraction operators is supported. An expression like END_DATE – START_DATE returns the number of days between START_DATE and END_DATE. START_DATE + 30 returns a date 30 days later than START_DATE.

 EXAM TIP Conditional clauses compare two terms using comparison operators. Knowing the data types of the terms is important so that they can be enclosed in single quotes, if necessary.

Comparison Operators

The *equality* operator is generally used to illustrate the concept of restricting rows using a WHERE clause. There are several alternative operators that may also be used. The *inequality* operators like "less than" or "greater than or equal to" may be used to return rows conforming to inequality conditions. The *BETWEEN* operator facilitates range-based comparison to test whether a column value lies between two values. The *IN* operator tests set membership, so a row is returned if the column value tested in the condition is a member of a set of literals. The pattern matching comparison operator *LIKE* is extremely powerful, allowing components of character column data to be matched to literals conforming to a specific pattern. The last comparison operator discussed in this section is the *IS NULL* operator, which returns rows where the column value contains a null value. These operators may be used in any combination in the WHERE clause.

Equality and Inequality

Limiting the rows returned by a query involves specifying a suitable WHERE clause. If the clause is too restrictive, then few or no rows are returned. If the conditional clause is too broadly specified, then more rows than are required are returned. Exploring the different available operators should equip you with the language to request exactly those rows you are interested in. Testing for *equality* in a condition is both natural and intuitive. Such a condition is formed using the "is equal to" (=) operator. A row is returned if the equality condition is true for that row. Consider the following query:

```
select last_name, salary from employees where job_id='SA_REP';
```

The JOB_ID column of every row in the EMPLOYEES table is tested for equality with the character literal SA_REP. For character information to be equal, there must be an exact case-sensitive match. When such a match is encountered, the values for the projected columns, LAST_NAME and SALARY, are returned for that row. Note that although the conditional clause is based on the JOB_ID column, it is not necessary for this column to be projected by the query.

Inequality-based conditions enhance the WHERE clause specification. Range and pattern matching comparisons are possible using inequality and equality operators, but it is often preferable to use the BETWEEN and LIKE operators for these comparisons. The inequality operators are described in Table 9-3.

Inequality operators allow range-based queries to be fulfilled. You may be required to provide a set of results where a column value is *greater than* another value. The following query may be issued to obtain a list of LAST_NAME and SALARY values for employees who earn more that $5000:

```
select last_name, salary from employees where salary > 5000;
```

The *composite inequality operators* (made up of more than one symbol) are utilized in the following clauses:

Clause 1: `where salary <= 3000;`
Clause 2: `where salary <> department_id;`

Clause 1 returns those rows that contain a SALARY value that is less than or equal to 3000. Clause 2 demonstrates one of the two forms of the "not equal to" operators. Clause 2 returns the rows that have SALARY column values that are not equal to the DEPARTMENT_ID values.

Table 9-3 Inequality Operators	Operator	Description
	<	Less than
	>	Greater than
	<=	Less than or equal to
	>=	Greater than or equal to
	<>	Not equal to
	!=	Not equal to

Numeric inequality is naturally intuitive. The comparison of character and date terms, however, is more complex. Testing character inequality is interesting because the strings being compared on either side of the inequality operator are converted to a numeric representation of its characters. Based on the database character set and NLS (National Language Support) settings, each character string is assigned a numeric value. These numeric values form the basis for the evaluation of the inequality comparison. Consider the following statement:

```
select last_name from employees where last_name < 'King';
```

The character literal 'King' is converted to a numeric representation. Assuming a US7ASCII database character set with AMERICAN NLS settings, the literal 'King' is converted into a sum of its ordinal character values: K + i + n + g = (75+105+110+103=393). For each row in the EMPLOYEES table, the LAST_NAME column data is similarly converted to a numeric value. If this value is less than 393, then the row is selected. The same process for comparing numeric data using the inequality operators applies to character data.

Inequality comparisons operating on date values follow a similar process to character data. The Oracle server stores dates in an internal numeric format, and these values are compared within the conditions. Consider the following query:

```
select last_name from employees where hire_date < '01-JAN-2000';
```

This query retrieves each employee record containing a HIRE_DATE value that is earlier than '01-JAN-2000'.

Range Comparison with the BETWEEN Operator

The BETWEEN operator tests whether a column or expression value falls within a range of two boundary values. The item must be at least the same as the lower boundary value or at most the same as the higher boundary value or fall within the range, for the condition to be true.

Suppose you want the last names of employees who earn a salary in the range of $3400 and $4000. A possible solution using the BETWEEN operator is as follows:

```
select last_name from employees where salary between 3400 and 4000;
```

Conditions specified with the BETWEEN operator can be equivalently denoted using two inequality-based conditions:

```
select last_name from employees where salary >=3400 and salary <=4000;
```

It is shorter and simpler to specify the range condition using the BETWEEN operator.

Set Comparison with the IN Operator

The IN operator tests whether an item is a member of a set of literal values. The set is specified by comma-separating the literals and enclosing them in round brackets. If the literals are character or date values, then these must be delimited using single quotes. You may include as many literals in the set as you wish. Consider the following example:

```
select last_name from employees where salary in (1000,4000,6000);
```

PART II

The SALARY value in each row is compared for equality to the literals specified in the set. If the SALARY value equals 1000, 4000, or 6000, the LAST_NAME value for that row is returned. The following two statements demonstrate use of the IN operator with DATE and CHARACTER data.

```
select last_name from employees
where last_name in ('Watson','Garbharran','Ramklass');

select last_name from employees
where hire_date in ('01-JAN-1998','01-DEC-1999');
```

Pattern Comparison with the LIKE Operator

The LIKE operator is designed exclusively for character data and provides a powerful mechanism for searching for letters or words. LIKE is accompanied by two wildcard characters: the percentage symbol (%) and the underscore character (_). The percentage symbol is used to specify zero or more wildcard characters, while the underscore character specifies one wildcard character. A wildcard may represent any character.

You can use the following query to provide a list of employees whose first names begin with the letter "A":

```
select first_name from employees where first_name like 'A%';
```

The character literal that the FIRST_NAME column is compared to is enclosed in single quotes like a regular character literal. In addition, it has a percentage symbol, which has a special meaning in the context of the LIKE operator. The percentage symbol substitutes zero or more characters appended to the letter "A". The wildcard characters can appear at the beginning, the middle, or the end of the character literal. They can even appear alone, as in

```
where first_name like '%';
```

In this case, every row containing a FIRST_NAME value that is not null will be returned. Wildcard symbols are not mandatory when using the LIKE operator. In such cases, LIKE behaves as an equality operator testing for exact character matches; so the following two WHERE clauses are equivalent:

```
where last_name like 'King';
where last_name = 'King';
```

The underscore wildcard symbol substitutes exactly one other character in a literal. Consider searching for employees whose last names are four letters long, begin with a "K," have an unknown second letter, and end with an "ng." You may issue the following statement:

```
where last_name like 'K_ng';
```

As Figure 9-6 shows, the two wildcard symbols can be used independently, together, or even multiple times in a single WHERE condition. The first query retrieves those records where COUNTRY_NAME begins with the letter "I" followed by one or more characters, one of which must be a lowercase "a."

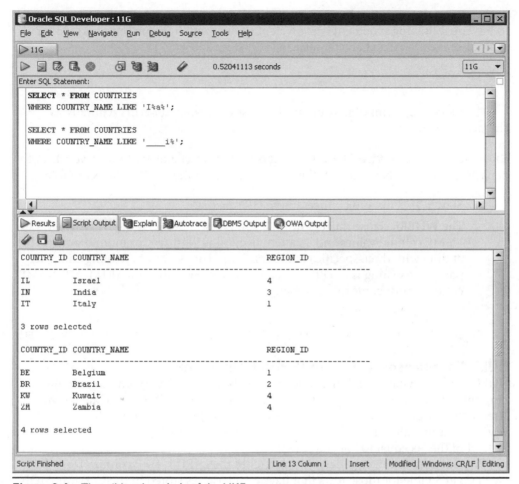

Figure 9-6 The wildcard symbols of the LIKE operator

The second query retrieves those countries whose names contain the letter "i" as its fifth character. The length of the COUNTRY_NAME values and the letter they begin with are unimportant. The four underscore wildcard symbols preceding the lowercase "i" in the WHERE clause represent exactly four characters (which could be any characters). The fifth letter must be an "i," and the percentage symbol specifies that the COUNTRY_NAME can have zero or more characters from the sixth character onward.

What about when you are searching for a literal that contains a percentage or underscore character? A naturally occurring underscore character may be escaped (or treated as a regular nonspecial symbol) using the ESCAPE identifier in conjunction with an ESCAPE character. In the following example, any JOB_ID values that begin with the three characters "SA_" will be returned:

```
select job_id from jobs
where job_id like 'SA\_%' escape '\';
```

Traditionally, the ESCAPE character is the backslash symbol, but it does not have to be. The following statement is equivalent to the preceding one but uses a dollar symbol as the ESCAPE character instead.

```
select job_id from jobs
where job_id like 'SA$_%' escape '$';
```

The percentage symbol may be similarly escaped when it occurs naturally as character data.

Exercise 9-3: Use the LIKE Operator   Construct a query to retrieve a list of department names that end with the letters "ing" from the DEPARTMENTS table.

1. Start SQL*Plus and connect to the HR schema.

2. The WHERE clause must perform a comparison between the DEPARTMENT_ NAME column values and a pattern beginning with zero or more characters but ending with three specific characters, "ing". The operator enabling character pattern matching is the LIKE operator. The pattern the DEPARTMENT_NAME column must conform to is '%ing'.

3. Thus, the correct query is

```
select department_name from departments where department_name like '%ing';
```

NULL Comparison with the IS NULL Operator

NULL values inevitably find their way into database tables. It is sometimes required that only those records that contain a NULL value in a specific column are sought. The *IS NULL* operator selects only the rows where a specific column value is NULL. Testing column values for equality to NULL is performed using the IS NULL operator instead of the "is equal to" operator (=).

Consider the following query, which fetches the LAST_NAME column from the EMPLOYEES table for those rows that have NULL values stored in the COMMISSION_ PCT column:

```
select last_name from employees
where commission_pct is null;
```

This WHERE clause reads naturally and retrieves only the records that contain NULL COMMISSION_PCT values.

Boolean Operators

Boolean or *logical* operators enable multiple conditions to be specified in the WHERE clause of the SELECT statement. This facilitates a more refined data extraction capability. Consider isolating those employee records with FIRST_NAME values that begin with the letter "J" and that earn a COMMISSION_PCT greater than 10 percent. First, the data in the EMPLOYEES table must be restricted to FIRST_NAME values like "J%", and second, the COMMISSION_PCT values for the records must be tested to ascertain if they are larger than 10 percent. These two separate conditions may be associated using the Boolean AND operator and are applied consecutively in a WHERE clause. A result set conforming to any or all conditions or to the negation of one or more conditions may be specified using the OR, AND, and NOT Boolean operators respectively.

The AND Operator

The *AND* operator merges conditions into one large condition to which a row must conform to be included in the results set. If two conditions specified in a WHERE clause are joined with an AND operator, then a row is tested consecutively for conformance to both conditions before being retrieved. If it conforms to neither or only one of the conditions, the row is excluded. Employee records with FIRST_NAME values beginning with the letter "J" and COMMISSION_PCT greater than 10 percent can be retrieved using the following query:

```
select first_name, last_name, commission_pct, hire_date from employees
where first_name like 'J%' and commission_pct > 0.1;
```

Notice that the WHERE clause now has two conditions, but only one WHERE keyword. The AND operator separates the two conditions. To specify further mandatory conditions, simply add them and ensure that they are separated by additional AND operators. You can specify as many conditions as you wish. Remember, though, the more AND conditions specified, the more restrictive the query becomes.

The OR Operator

The *OR* operator separates multiple conditions, at least one of which must be satisfied by the row selected to warrant inclusion in the results set. If two conditions specified in a WHERE clause are joined with an OR operator, then a row is tested consecutively for conformance to either or both conditions before being retrieved. Conforming to just one of the OR conditions is sufficient for the record to be returned. If it conforms to none of the conditions, the row is excluded. Retrieving employee records having FIRST_NAME values beginning with the letter "B" or those with a COMMISSION_PCT greater than 35 percent can be written as:

```
select first_name, last_name, commission_pct, hire_date from employees
where first_name like 'B%' or commission_pct > 0.35;
```

Notice that the two conditions are separated by the OR keyword. All employee records with FIRST_NAME values beginning with an uppercase "B" will be returned regardless of their COMMISSION_PCT values, even if they are NULL. Records with COMMISSION_PCT values greater that 35 percent (regardless of what letter their FIRST_NAME begins with) are also returned.

Further OR conditions may be specified by separating them with an OR operator. The more OR conditions you specify, the less restrictive your query becomes.

The NOT Operator

The *NOT* operator negates conditional operators. A selected row must conform to the logical opposite of the condition in order to be included in the results set. Conditional operators may be negated by the NOT operator as shown by the WHERE clauses listed in Table 9-4.

Positive	Negative
where last_name='King'	where NOT (last_name='King')
where first_name LIKE 'R%'	where first_name NOT LIKE 'R%'
where department_id IN (10,20,30)	where department_id NOT IN (10,20,30)
where salary BETWEEN 1 and 3000	where salary NOT BETWEEN 1 and 3000
where commission_pct IS NULL	where commission_pct IS NOT NULL

Table 9-4 Conditions Negated by the NOT Operator

The NOT operator negates the comparison operator in a condition, whether it's an equality, inequality, range-based, pattern matching, set membership, or null testing operator.

Precedence Rules

Arithmetic, character, comparison, and Boolean expressions were examined in the context of the WHERE clause. But how do these operators interact with each other? The precedence hierarchy for the previously mentioned operators is shown in Table 9-5.

Operators at the same level of precedence are evaluated from left to right if they are encountered together in an expression. When the NOT operator modifies the LIKE, IS NULL, and IN comparison operators, their precedence level remains the same as the positive form of these operators.

Consider the following SELECT statement that demonstrates the interaction of various different operators:

```
select last_name,salary,department_id,job_id,commission_pct
from employees
where last_name like '%a%' and salary > department_id * 200
or
job_id in ('MK_REP','MK_MAN') and commission_pct is not null
```

Precedence Level	Operator Symbol	Operation
1	()	Parentheses or brackets
2	/,*	Division and multiplication
3	+,-	Addition and subtraction
4	||	Concatenation
5	=,<,>,<=,>=	Equality and inequality comparison
6	[NOT] LIKE, IS [NOT] NULL, [NOT] IN	Pattern, null, and set comparison
7	[NOT] BETWEEN	Range comparison
8	!=,<>	Not equal to
9	NOT	NOT logical condition
10	AND	AND logical condition
11	OR	OR logical condition

Table 9-5 Operator Precedence Hierarchy

The LAST_NAME, SALARY, DEPARTMENT_ID, JOB_ID, and COMMISSION_PCT columns are projected from the EMPLOYEES table based on two discrete conditions. The first condition retrieves the records containing the character "a" in the LAST_NAME field AND with a SALARY value greater than 200 times the DEPARTMENT_ID value. The product of DEPARTMENT_ID and 200 is processed before the inequality operator, since the precedence of multiplication is higher than the inequality comparison.

The second condition fetches those rows with JOB_ID values of either MK_MAN or MK_REP in which COMMISSION_PCT values are not null. For a row to be returned by this query, either the first OR second conditions need to be fulfilled. Changing the order of the conditions in the WHERE clause changes its meaning due to the different precedence of the operators. Consider the following query:

```
select last_name,salary,department_id,job_id,commission_pct
from employees
where last_name like '%a%' and salary > department_id * 100 and commission_pct is not
null
or
job_id = 'MK_MAN'
```

There are two composite conditions in this query. The first condition retrieves the records with the character "a" in the LAST_NAME field AND a SALARY value greater than 100 times the DEPARTMENT_ID value AND where the COMMISSION_PCT value is not null. The second condition fetches those rows with JOB_ID values of MK_MAN. A row is returned by this query, if it conforms to either condition one OR condition two, but not necessarily to both.

 EXAM TIP Boolean operators OR and AND allow multiple WHERE clause conditions to be specified while the NOT operator negates a conditional operator and may be used several times within the same condition. The equality, inequality, BETWEEN, IN, and LIKE comparison operators test two terms within a single condition. Only one comparison operator is used per conditional clause.

Sort the Rows Retrieved by a Query

The usability of the retrieved datasets may be significantly enhanced with a mechanism to order or sort the information. Information may be sorted alphabetically, numerically, and chronologically in ascending or descending order. Further, the data may be sorted by one or more columns, including columns that are not listed in the SELECT clause. Sorting is usually performed once the results of a SELECT statement have been fetched. The sorting parameters do not influence the records returned by a query, just the presentation of the results. Exactly the same rows are returned by a statement including a sort clause as are returned by a statement excluding a sort clause. Only the ordering of the output may differ. Sorting the results of a query is accomplished using the ORDER BY clause.

The ORDER BY Clause

The ORDER BY clause is always the last clause in a SELECT statement. As the full syntax of the SELECT statement is progressively exposed, you will observe new clauses added, but none of them will be positioned after the ORDER BY clause. The format of the ORDER BY clause in the context of the SQL SELECT statement is as follows:

```
SELECT *|{[DISTINCT] column|expression [alias],...}
FROM table
[WHERE condition(s)]
[ORDER BY {col(s)|expr|numeric_pos} [ASC|DESC] [NULLS FIRST|LAST]];
```

Ascending and Descending Sorting

Ascending sort order is natural for most types of data and is therefore the default sort order used whenever the ORDER BY clause is specified. An ascending sort order for numbers is lowest to highest, while it is earliest to latest for dates and alphabetically for characters. The first form of the ORDER BY clause shows that results of a query may be sorted by one or more columns or expressions:

```
ORDER BY col(s)|expr;
```

Suppose that a report is requested that must contain an employee's LAST_NAME, HIRE_DATE, and SALARY information, sorted alphabetically by the LAST_NAME column for all sales representatives and marketing managers. This report could be extracted with

```
select last_name, hire_date, salary from employees
where job_id in ('SA_REP','MK_MAN')
order by last_name;
```

The data selected may be ordered by any of the columns from the tables in the FROM clause, including those that do not appear in the SELECT list. By appending the keyword DESC to the ORDER BY clause, rows are returned sorted in descending order. The optional NULLS LAST keywords specify that if the sort column contains null values, then these rows are to be listed last after sorting the remaining NOT NULL values. To specify that rows with null values in the sort column should be displayed first, append the NULLS FIRST keywords to the ORDER BY clause. A dataset may be sorted based on an expression as follows:

```
select last_name, salary, hire_date, sysdate-hire_date tenure
from employees order by tenure;
```

The smallest TENURE value appears first in the output, since the ORDER BY clause specifies that the results will be sorted by the expression alias. Note that the results could be sorted by the explicit expression and the alias could be omitted, but using aliases renders the query easier to read.

Several implicit default options are selected when you use the ORDER BY clause. The most important of these is that unless DESC is specified, the sort order is assumed to be ascending. If null values occur in the sort column, the default sort order is assumed to be NULLS LAST for ascending sorts and NULLS FIRST for descending sorts. If no ORDER BY clause is specified, the same query executed at different times may return the same set of results in different row order, so no assumptions should be made regarding the default row order.

Positional Sorting

Oracle offers an alternate shorter way to specify the sort column or expression. Instead of specifying the column name, the position of the column as it occurs in the SELECT list is appended to the ORDER BY clause. Consider the following example:

```
select last_name, hire_date, salary from employees order by 2;
```

The ORDER BY clause specifies the numeric literal 2. This is equivalent to specifying ORDER BY HIRE_DATE, since that is the second column in the SELECT clause. *Positional sorting* applies only to columns in the SELECT list.

Composite Sorting

Results may be sorted by more than one column using *composite sorting*. Multiple columns may be specified (either literally or positionally) as the composite sort key by comma-separating them in the ORDER BY clause. To fetch the JOB_ID, LAST_NAME, SALARY, and HIRE_DATE values from the EMPLOYEES table such that the results must be sorted in reverse alphabetical order by JOB_ID first, then in ascending alphabetical order by LAST_NAME, and finally in numerically descending order based on the SALARY column, you can run the following query:

```
select job_id, last_name, salary, hire_date from employees
where job_id in ('SA_REP','MK_MAN') order by job_id desc, last_name, 3 desc;
```

Exercise 9-4: Use the ORDER BY Clause   The JOBS table contains descriptions of different types of jobs an employee in the organization may occupy. It contains the JOB_ID, JOB_TITLE, MIN_SALARY, and MAX_SALARY columns. You are required to write a query that extracts the JOB_TITLE, MIN_SALARY, and MAX_SALARY columns, as well as an expression called VARIANCE, which is the difference between the MAX_SALARY and MIN_SALARY values, for each row. The results must include only JOB_TITLE values that contain either the word "President" or "Manager." Sort the list in descending order based on the VARIANCE expression. If more than one row has the same VARIANCE value, then, in addition, sort these rows by JOB_TITLE in reverse alphabetic order.

1. Start SQL Developer and connect to the HR schema.

2. Sorting is accomplished with the ORDER BY clause. Composite sorting is required using both the VARIANCE expression and the JOB_TITLE column in descending order.

3. Executing this statement returns a set of results matching the request:

```
SELECT JOB_TITLE, MIN_SALARY, MAX_SALARY, (MAX_SALARY - MIN_SALARY) VARIANCE
FROM JOBS WHERE JOB_TITLE LIKE '%President%' OR JOB_TITLE LIKE '%Manager%'
ORDER BY VARIANCE DESC, JOB_TITLE DESC;
```

Ampersand Substitution

As you develop and perfect SQL statements, they may be saved for future use. It is sometimes desirable to have a generic form of a statement that has a variable or placeholder defined that can be substituted at runtime. Oracle offers this functionality in the form of *ampersand substitution*. Every element of the SELECT statement may be substituted, and the reduction of queries to their core elements to facilitate reuse can save you hours of tedious and repetitive work. This section examines substitution variables and the DEFINE and VERIFY commands.

Substitution Variables

Substitution variables may be regarded as placeholders. A SQL query is composed of two or more clauses. Each clause can be divided into subclauses, which are in turn made up of character text. Any text, subclause, or clause element is a candidate for substitution.

Single Ampersand Substitution

The most basic and popular form of SQL element is *single ampersand substitution*. The ampersand character (&) is the symbol chosen to designate a substitution variable in a statement and precedes the variable name with no spaces between them. When the statement is executed, the Oracle server processes the statement, notices a substitution variable, and attempts to resolve this variable's value in one of two ways. First, it checks whether the variable is *defined* in the user session. (The DEFINE command is discussed later in this chapter.) If the variable is not defined, the user process prompts for a value that will be substituted in place of the variable. Once a value is submitted, the statement is complete and is executed by the Oracle server. The *ampersand substitution* variable is resolved at execution time and is sometimes known as *runtime binding* or *runtime substitution*.

You may be required to look up contact information like PHONE_NUMBER data given either LAST_NAME or EMPLOYEE_ID values. This generic query may be written as

```
select employee_id, last_name, phone_number from employees
where last_name = &LASTNAME or employee_id = &EMPNO;
```

When running this query, Oracle prompts you to input a value for the variable called LASTNAME. You enter an employee's last name, if you know it, for example, 'King'. If you don't know the last name but know the employee ID number, you can type in any value and press the ENTER key to submit the value. Oracle then prompts you to enter a value for the EMPNO variable. After typing in a value, for example, 0, and hitting ENTER, there are no remaining substitution variables for Oracle to resolve and the following statement is executed:

```
select employee_id, last_name, phone_number from employees
where last_name = 'King' or employee_id = 0;
```

Variables can be assigned any alphanumeric name that is a valid identifier name. The literal you substitute when prompted for a variable must be an appropriate data type for that context; otherwise, an "ORA-00904: invalid identifier" error is returned. If the variable is meant to substitute a character or date value, the literal needs to be enclosed in single quotes. A useful technique is to enclose the *ampersand substitution* variable in single quotes when dealing with character and date values. In this way, the user is required to submit a literal value without worrying about enclosing it in quotes.

Double Ampersand Substitution

When a substitution variable is referenced multiple times in the same query, Oracle will prompt you to enter a value for every occurrence of the single ampersand substitution variable. For complex scripts, this can be very inefficient and tedious. The following statement retrieves the FIRST_NAME and LAST_NAME data from the EMPLOYEES table for those rows that contain the same set of characters in both these fields:

```
select first_name, last_name from employees
where last_name like '%&SEARCH%' and first_name like '%&SEARCH%';
```

The two conditions are identical but apply to different columns. When this statement is executed, you are first prompted to enter a substitution value for the SEARCH variable used in the comparison with the LAST_NAME column. Thereafter, you are prompted to enter a substitution value for the SEARCH variable used in the comparison with the FIRST_NAME column. This poses two problems. First, it is inefficient to enter the same value twice, but second and more important, typographical errors may confound the query, since Oracle does not verify that the same literal value is entered each time substitution variables with the same name are used. In this example, the logical assumption is that the contents of the variables substituted should be the same, but the fact that the variables have the same name has no meaning to the Oracle server, and it makes no such assumption. The first example in Figure 9-7 shows the results of running the preceding query and submitting two distinct values for the SEARCH substitution variable. In this particular example, the results are incorrect since the requirement was to retrieve FIRST_NAME and LAST_NAME pairs that contained the identical string of characters.

When a substitution variable is referenced multiple times in the same query and your intention is that the variable must have the same value at each occurrence in the statement, it is preferable to make use of *double ampersand substitution*. This involves prefixing the first occurrence of the substitution variable that occurs multiple times in a query, with two ampersand symbols instead of one. When Oracle encounters a double ampersand substitution variable, a session value is defined for that variable and you are not prompted to enter a value to be substituted for this variable in subsequent references.

The second example in Figure 9-7 demonstrates how the SEARCH variable is preceded by two ampersands in the condition with the FIRST_NAME column and thereafter is prefixed by one ampersand in the condition with the LAST_NAME column. When the statement is executed, you are prompted to enter a value to be substituted for the SEARCH variable only once for the condition with the FIRST_NAME column. This value is then automatically resolved from the session value of the variable in subsequent references to it, as in the condition with the LAST_NAME column. To undefine the SEARCH variable, you need to use the UNDEFINE command described later in this chapter.

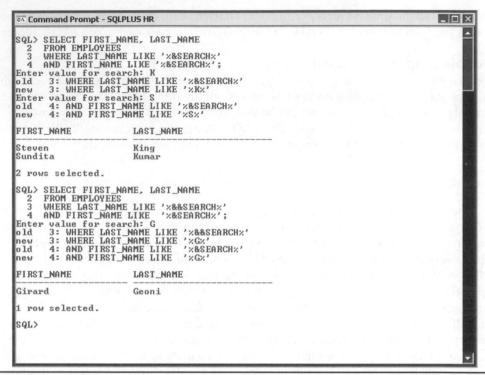

Figure 9-7　Double ampersand substitution

TIP　Whether you work as a developer, database administrator, or business end user, all SQL queries you encounter may be broadly classified as either ad hoc or repeated queries. Ad hoc queries are usually one-off statements written during some data investigation exercise that are unlikely to be reused. The repeated queries are those that are run frequently or periodically, which are usually saved as script files and run with little to no modification whenever required. Reuse prevents costly redevelopment time and allows these consistent queries to potentially benefit from Oracle's native automatic tuning features geared toward improving query performance.

Substituting Column Names

Literal elements of the WHERE clause have been the focus of the discussion on substitution thus far, but virtually any element of a SQL statement is a candidate for substitution. In the following statement, the FIRST_NAME and JOB_ID columns are static and will always be retrieved, but the third column selected is variable and specified as a substitution variable named COL. The result set is further sorted by this variable column in the ORDER BY clause:

```
select first_name, job_id, &&col
from employees
where job_id in ('MK_MAN','SA_MAN')
order by &col;
```

Unlike character and date literals, column name references do not require single quotes either when explicitly specified or when substituted via ampersand substitution.

Substituting Expressions and Text

Almost any element of a SQL statement may be substituted at runtime. The constraint is that Oracle requires at least the first word to be static. In the case of the SELECT statement, at the very minimum, the SELECT keyword is required and the remainder of the statement may be substituted as follows:

```
select &rest_of_statement;
```

When the statement is executed, you are prompted to submit a value for the variable called REST_OF_STATEMENT, which when appended to the SELECT keyword, is any legitimate query. Useful candidates for ampersand substitution are statements that are run multiple times and differ slightly from each other.

Define and Verify

Double ampersand substitution is used to avoid repetitive input when the same variable occurs multiple times in a statement. When a double ampersand substitution occurs, the variable is stored as a session variable. As the statement executes, all further occurrences of the variable are automatically resolved using the stored session variable. Any subsequent executions of the statement within the same session automatically resolve the substitution variables from stored session values. This is not always desirable and indeed limits the usefulness of substitution variables. Oracle does, however, provide a mechanism to *UNDEFINE* these session variables. The *VERIFY* command is specific to SQL*Plus and controls whether or not substituted elements are echoed on the user's screen prior to executing a SQL statement that uses substitution variables.

The DEFINE and UNDEFINE Commands

Session-level variables are implicitly created when they are initially referenced in SQL statements using double ampersand substitution. They persist or remain available for the duration of the session or until they are explicitly undefined. A session ends when the user exits their client tool like SQL*Plus or when the user process is terminated.

The problem with persistent session variables is they tend to detract from the generic nature of statements that use ampersand substitution variables. Fortunately, these session variables can be removed with the UNDEFINE command. Within a script or at the command line of SQL*Plus or SQL Developer, the syntax to undefine session variables is

```
UNDEFINE variable;
```

Consider a simple generic example that selects a static and variable column from the EMPLOYEES table and sorts the output based on the variable column:

```
select last_name, &&COLNAME
from employees where department_id=30 order by &COLNAME;
```

The first time this statement executes, you are prompted to supply a value for the COLNAME variable. Assume you enter SALARY. This value is substituted and the statement executes. A subsequent execution of this statement within the same session does not prompt for any COLNAME values, since it is already defined as SALARY in the context of this session and can only be undefined with the UNDEFINE COLNAME command. Once the variable has been undefined, the next execution of the statement prompts the user for a value for the COLNAME variable.

The DEFINE command serves two purposes. It can be used to retrieve a list of all the variables currently defined in your SQL session; it can also be used to explicitly define a value for a variable referenced as a substitution variable by one or more statements during the lifetime of that session. The syntax for the two variants of the DEFINE command are as follows:

```
DEFINE;
DEFINE variable=value;
```

As Figure 9-8 demonstrates, a variable called EMPNAME is defined explicitly to have the value 'King'. The stand-alone DEFINE command in SQL*Plus then returns a number of session variables prefixed with an underscore character as well as other

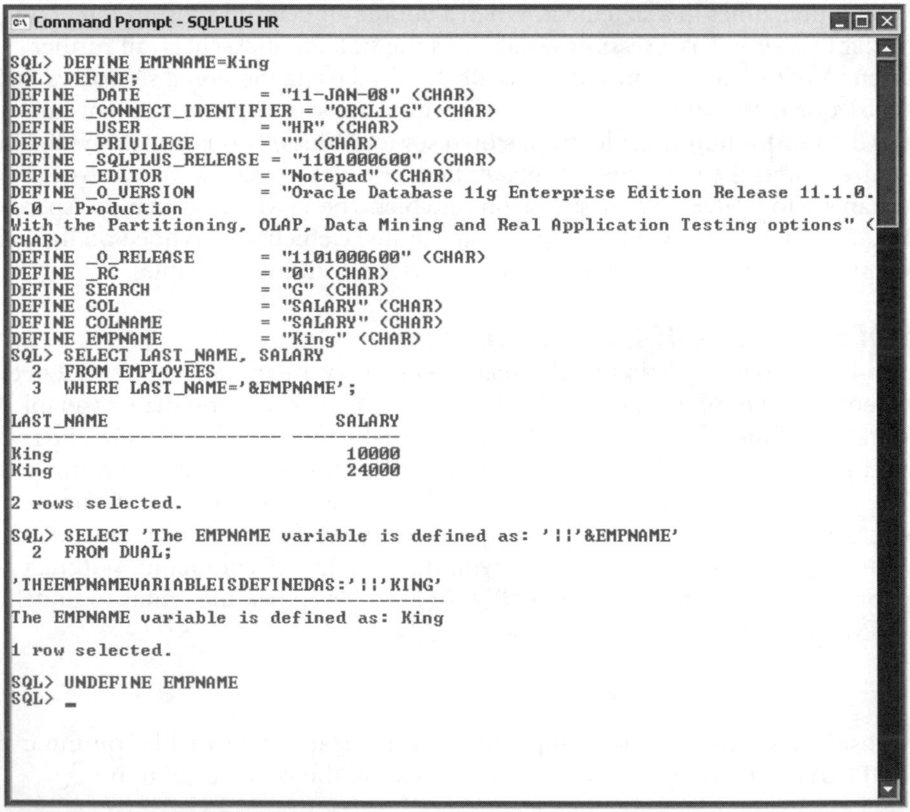

```
Command Prompt - SQLPLUS HR

SQL> DEFINE EMPNAME=King
SQL> DEFINE;
DEFINE _DATE            = "11-JAN-08" (CHAR)
DEFINE _CONNECT_IDENTIFIER = "ORCL11G" (CHAR)
DEFINE _USER            = "HR" (CHAR)
DEFINE _PRIVILEGE       = "" (CHAR)
DEFINE _SQLPLUS_RELEASE = "1101000600" (CHAR)
DEFINE _EDITOR          = "Notepad" (CHAR)
DEFINE _O_VERSION       = "Oracle Database 11g Enterprise Edition Release 11.1.0.
6.0 - Production
With the Partitioning, OLAP, Data Mining and Real Application Testing options" (
CHAR)
DEFINE _O_RELEASE       = "1101000600" (CHAR)
DEFINE _RC              = "0" (CHAR)
DEFINE SEARCH           = "G" (CHAR)
DEFINE COL              = "SALARY" (CHAR)
DEFINE COLNAME          = "SALARY" (CHAR)
DEFINE EMPNAME          = "King" (CHAR)
SQL> SELECT LAST_NAME, SALARY
  2    FROM EMPLOYEES
  3   WHERE LAST_NAME='&EMPNAME';

LAST_NAME                     SALARY
-----------------------    ----------
King                           10000
King                           24000

2 rows selected.

SQL> SELECT 'The EMPNAME variable is defined as: '||'&EMPNAME'
  2    FROM DUAL;

'THEEMPNAMEVARIABLEISDEFINEDAS:'||'KING'
--------------------------------------------------
The EMPNAME variable is defined as: King

1 row selected.

SQL> UNDEFINE EMPNAME
SQL> _
```

Figure 9-8   The DEFINE command

substitution variables defined earlier. Two different but simple queries are executed, and the explicitly defined substitution variable EMPNAME is referenced by both queries. Finally, the variable is UNDEFINED.

Support of session-persistent variables may be switched off and on as required using the *SET DEFINE OFF* command. The SET command is not a SQL language command, but rather a SQL environment control command. When you specify SET DEFINE OFF, the client tool (for example, SQL*Plus) does not save session variables or attach special meaning to the ampersand symbol. This allows the ampersand symbol to be used as an ordinary literal character if necessary. The SET DEFINE ON|OFF command therefore determines whether or not ampersand substitution is available in your session. The following query uses the ampersand symbol as a literal value. When it is executed, you are prompted to submit a value for bind variable SID.

```
select 'Coda & Sid' from dual;
```

By turning off the ampersand substitution functionality, this query may be executed without prompts:

```
SET DEFINE OFF
select 'Coda & Sid' from dual;
SET DEFINE ON
```

Once the statement executes, the SET DEFINE ON command may be used to switch the substitution functionality back on. If DEFINE is OFF and the context that an ampersand is used in a statement cannot be resolved literally, Oracle returns an error.

The VERIFY Command

Two categories of commands are available when dealing with the Oracle server: SQL language commands and the SQL client control commands. The SELECT statement is a language command, while the SET command controls the SQL client environment. There are many different language and control commands available, but the control commands relevant to substitution are DEFINE and VERIFY.

The *VERIFY* command controls whether the substitution variable submitted is displayed onscreen so that you can *verify* that the correct substitution has occurred. A message is displayed showing the *old* clause followed by the *new* clause containing the substituted value. The VERIFY command is switched ON and OFF with the command SET VERIFY ON|OFF. If VERIFY is first switched OFF and a query that uses ampersand substitution is executed, you are prompted to input a value. The value is then substituted, the statement runs, and its results are displayed. If VERIFY is then switched ON and the same query is executed, once you input a value but before the statement commences execution, Oracle displays the clause containing the reference to the substitution variable as the *old* clause with its line number and, immediately below this, the *new* clause displays the statement containing the substituted value.

Exercise 9-5: Using Ampersand Substitution   You are required to write a reusable query using the current tax rate and the EMPLOYEE_ID number as inputs and return the EMPLOYEE_ID, FIRST_NAME, SALARY, ANNUAL SALARY (SALARY * 12),

TAX_RATE, and TAX (TAX_RATE * ANNUAL SALARY) information for use by the HR department clerks.

1. Start SQL*Plus and connect to the HR schema.

2. The select list must include the four specified columns as well as two expressions. The first expression, aliased as ANNUAL SALARY, is a simple calculation, while the second expression, aliased as TAX, depends on the TAX_RATE. Since the TAX RATE may vary, this value must be substituted at runtime.

3. A possible solution is

```
SELECT &&EMPLOYEE_ID, FIRST_NAME, SALARY, SALARY * 12 AS "ANNUAL SALARY",
&&TAX_RATE, (&TAX_RATE * (SALARY * 12)) AS "TAX"
FROM EMPLOYEES WHERE EMPLOYEE_ID = &EMPLOYEE_ID;
```

4. The double ampersand preceding EMPLOYEE_ID and TAX_RATE in the SELECT clause stipulates to Oracle that when the statement is executed, the user must be prompted to submit a value for each substitution variable that will be used wherever they are subsequently referenced as &EMPLOYEE_ID and &TAX_RATE, respectively.

Two-Minute Drill

List the Capabilities of SQL SELECT Statements

- The three fundamental operations that SELECT statements are capable of are projection, selection, and joining.

- Projection refers to the restriction of columns selected from a table. Using projection, you retrieve only the columns of interest and not every possible column.

- Selection refers to the extraction of rows from a table. Selection includes the further restriction of the extracted rows based on various criteria or conditions. This allows you to retrieve only the rows that are of interest and not every row in the table.

- Joining involves linking two or more tables based on common attributes. Joining allows data to be stored in third normal form in discrete tables, instead of in one large table.

- The DESCRIBE command lists the names, data types, and nullable status of all columns in a table.

Execute a Basic SELECT Statement

- The SELECT clause determines the *projection* of columns. In other words, the SELECT clause specifies which columns are included in the results returned.

- The DISTINCT keyword preceding items in the SELECT clause causes duplicate combinations of these items to be excluded from the returned results set.

- Expressions and regular columns may be aliased using the AS keyword or by leaving a space between the column or expression and the alias.

- Naturally occurring single quotes in a character literal can be selected by making use of either an additional single quote per naturally occurring quote or the alternative quote operator.

Limit the Rows Retrieved by a Query

- One or more conditions constitute a WHERE clause. These conditions specify rules to which the data in a row must conform to be eligible for selection.

- For each row tested in a condition, there are terms on the left and right of a comparison operator. Terms in a condition can be column values, literals, or expressions.

- Comparison operators may test two terms in many ways. Equality or inequality tests are very common, but range, set, and pattern comparisons are also available.

- Boolean operators include the AND, OR, and NOT operators. The AND and OR operators enable multiple conditional clauses to be specified. These are sometimes referred to as multiple WHERE clauses.

- The NOT operator negates the comparison operator involved in a condition.

Sort the Rows Retrieved by a Query

- Results are sorted using the ORDER BY clause. Rows retrieved may be ordered according to one or more columns by specifying either the column names or their numeric position in the SELECT clause.

- The sorted output may be arranged in descending or ascending order using the DESC or ASC modifiers after the sort terms in the ORDER BY clause.

Ampersand Substitution

- Ampersand substitution facilitates SQL statement reuse by providing a means to substitute elements of a statement at runtime. The same SQL statement may therefore be run multiple times with different input parameters.

- Session-persistent variables may be set explicitly using the DEFINE command. The UNDEFINE command may be used to unset both implicitly (double ampersand substitution) and explicitly defined session variables.

- The VERIFY environmental setting controls whether SQL*Plus displays the old and new versions of statement lines that contain substitution variables.

Self Test

1. Which query will create a projection of the DEPARTMENT_NAME and LOCATION_ID columns from the DEPARTMENTS table? (Choose the best answer.)

    A. SELECT DISTINCT DEPARTMENT_NAME, LOCATION_ID
       FROM DEPARTMENTS;

    B. SELECT DEPARTMENT_NAME, LOCATION_ID
       FROM DEPARTMENTS;

    C. SELECT DEPT_NAME, LOC_ID
       FROM DEPT;

    D. SELECT DEPARTMENT_NAME AS "LOCATION_ID"
       FROM DEPARTMENTS;

2. After describing the EMPLOYEES table, you discover that the SALARY column has a data type of NUMBER(8,2). Which SALARY value(s) will not be permitted in this column? (Choose the best answers.)

    A. SALARY=12345678

    B. SALARY=123456.78

    C. SALARY=1234567.8

    D. SALARY=123456

    E. SALARY=12.34

3. After describing the JOB_HISTORY table, you discover that the START_DATE and END_DATE columns have a data type of DATE. Consider the expression "END_DATE – START_DATE". Choose two correct statements regarding this expression.

    A. A value of DATE data type is returned.

    B. A value of type NUMBER is returned.

    C. A value of type VARCHAR2 is returned.

    D. The expression is invalid, since arithmetic cannot be performed on columns with DATE data types.

    E. The expression is valid, since arithmetic can be performed on columns with DATE data types.

4. Which statement reports on unique JOB_ID values from the EMPLOYEES table? (Choose the best answer.)

    A. SELECT JOB_ID FROM EMPLOYEES;

    B. SELECT UNIQUE JOB_ID FROM EMPLOYEES;

    C. SELECT DISTINCT JOB_ID, EMPLOYEE_ID FROM EMPLOYEES;

    D. SELECT DISTINCT JOB_ID FROM EMPLOYEES;

5. Choose the two illegal statements. The two correct statements produce identical results. The two illegal statements will cause an error to be raised:

   A. SELECT DEPARTMENT_ID|| ' represents the '|| DEPARTMENT_NAME||'
      Department' as "Department Info"
      FROM DEPARTMENTS;

   B. SELECT DEPARTMENT_ID|| ' represents the || DEPARTMENT_NAME||'
      Department' as "Department Info"
      FROM DEPARTMENTS;

   C. select department_id|| ' represents the '||department_name||
      ' Department' "Department Info"
      from departments;

   D. SELECT DEPARTMENT_ID represents the DEPARTMENT_NAME
      Department as "Department Info"
      FROM DEPARTMENTS;

6. Which two clauses of the SELECT statement facilitate selection and projection? (Choose the best answer.)

   A. SELECT, FROM

   B. ORDER BY, WHERE

   C. SELECT, WHERE

   D. SELECT, ORDER BY

7. Choose the WHERE clause that extracts the DEPARTMENT_NAME values containing the character literal "er" from the DEPARTMENTS table. The SELECT and FROM clauses are SELECT DEPARTMENT_NAME FROM DEPARTMENTS. (Choose the best answer.)

   A. WHERE DEPARTMENT_NAME IN ('%e%r');

   B. WHERE DEPARTMENT_NAME LIKE '%er%';

   C. WHERE DEPARTMENT_NAME BETWEEN 'e' AND 'r';

   D. WHERE DEPARTMENT_NAME CONTAINS 'e%r'

8. Which of the following conditions are equivalent to each other? (Choose all correct answers.)

   A. WHERE SALARY <=5000 AND SALARY >=2000

   B. WHERE SALARY IN (2000,3000,4000,5000)

   C. WHERE SALARY BETWEEN 2000 AND 5000

   D. WHERE SALARY > 2000 AND SALARY < 5000

   E. WHERE SALARY >=2000 AND <=5000

9. Choose one false statement about the ORDER BY clause. (Choose the best answer.)

   A. When using the ORDER BY clause, it always appears as the last clause in a SELECT statement.

   B. The ORDER BY clause may appear in a SELECT statement that does not contain a WHERE clause.

   C. The ORDER BY clause specifies one or more terms by which the retrieved rows are sorted. These terms can only be column names.

   D. Positional sorting is accomplished by specifying the numeric position of a column as it appears in the SELECT list, in the ORDER BY clause.

10. When using ampersand substitution variables in the following query, how many times will you be prompted to input a value for the variable called JOB the first time this query is executed?
    SELECT FIRST_NAME, '&JOB'
    FROM EMPLOYEES
    WHERE JOB_ID LIKE '%'||&JOB||'%'
    AND '&&JOB' BETWEEN 'A' AND 'Z';

    (Choose the best answer.)

    A. 0

    B. 1

    C. 2

    D. 3

Self Test Answers

1. ☑ **B.** A projection is an intentional restriction of the columns returned from a table.

   ☒ **A, C,** and **D. A** is eliminated since the question has nothing to do with duplicates, distinctiveness, or uniqueness of data. **C** incorrectly selects nonexistent columns called DEPT_NAME and LOC_ID from a nonexistent table called DEPT. **D** returns just one of the requested columns: DEPARTMENT_NAME. Instead of additionally projecting the LOCATION_ID column from the DEPARTMENTS table, it attempts to alias the DEPARTMENT_NAME column as LOCATION_ID.

2. ☑ **A and C.** Columns with the NUMBER(8,2) data type can store at most eight digits, of which at most two of those digits are to the right of the decimal point. Although **A** and **C** are the correct answers, note that since the question is phrased in the negative, these values are *not* allowed to be stored in such a column. **A** and **C** are not allowed because they contain eight and seven whole number digits respectively, but the data type is constrained to store six whole number digits and two fractional digits.

☒ **B, D,** and **E. B, D,** and **E** can legitimately be stored in this data type and, therefore, are the incorrect answers to this question. **D** shows that numbers with no fractional part are legitimate values for this column, as long as the number of digits in the whole number portion does not exceed six digits.

3. ☑ **B** and **E.** The result of arithmetic between two date values represents a certain number of days.

☒ **A, C,** and **D.** It is a common mistake to expect the result of arithmetic between two date values to be a date as well, so **A** may seem plausible, but it is false.

4. ☑ **D.** Unique JOB_ID values are projected from the EMPLOYEES table by applying the DISTINCT keyword to just the JOB_ID column.

☒ **A, B,** and **C. A** returns an unrestricted list of JOB_ID values including duplicates; **B** makes use of the UNIQUE keyword in the incorrect context; and **C** selects the distinct combination of JOB_ID and EMPLOYEE_ID values. This has the effect of returning all the rows from the EMPLOYEES table, since the EMPLOYEE_ID column contains unique values for each employee record. Additionally, **C** returns two columns, which is not what was originally requested.

5. ☑ **B** and **D. B** and **D** represent the two illegal statements that will return syntax errors if they are executed. This is a tricky question because it asks for the illegal statements and not the legal statements. **B** is illegal because it is missing a single quote enclosing the character literal "represents the". **D** is illegal because it does not make use of single quotes to enclose its character literals.

☒ **A** and **C. A** and **C** are the legal statements and, therefore, in the context of the question, are the incorrect answers. **A** and **C** appear to be different, since the SQL statements differ in case and **A** uses the alias keyword AS, whereas **C** just leaves a space between the expression and the alias. Yet both **A** and **C** produce identical results.

6. ☑ **C.** The SELECT clause facilitates projection by specifying the list of columns to be projected from a table, while the WHERE clause facilitates selection by limiting the rows retrieved based on its conditions.

☒ **A, B,** and **D. A, B,** and **D** are incorrect because the FROM clause specifies the source of the rows being projected and the ORDER BY clause is used for sorting the selected rows.

7. ☑ **B.** The LIKE operator tests the DEPARTMENT_NAME column of each row for values that contain the characters "er". The percentage symbols before and after the character literal indicate that any characters enclosing the "er" literal are permissible.

☒ **A, C,** and **D. A** and **C** are syntactically correct. **A** uses the IN operator, which is used to test set membership. **C** tests whether the alphabetic value of the DEPARTMENT_NAME column is between the letter "e" and the letter "r." Finally, **D** uses the word "contains," which cannot be used in this context.

8. ☑ A and C. Each of these conditions tests for SALARY values in the range of $2000 to $5000.

☒ B, D, and E. B excludes values like $2500 from its set. D excludes the boundary values of $2000 and $5000, and E is illegal since it is missing the SALARY column name reference after the AND operator.

9. ☑ C. The terms specified in an ORDER BY clause can include column names, positional sorting, numeric values, and expressions.

☒ A, B, and D are true.

10. ☑ D. The first time this statement is executed, two single ampersand substitution variables are encountered before the third double ampersand substitution variable. If the first reference on line one of the query contained a double ampersand substitution, you would only be prompted to input a value once.

☒ A, B, and C. These are incorrect since you are prompted three times to input a value for the JOB substitution variable. In subsequent executions of this statement in the same session, you will not be prompted to input a value for this variable.

CHAPTER 10

Single-Row and Conversion Functions

Exam Objectives

In this chapter you will learn to

- 051.3.1   Describe Various Types of Functions Available in SQL
- 051.3.2   Use Character, Number, and Date Functions in SELECT Statements
- 051.4.1   Describe Various Types of Conversion Functions That Are Available in SQL
- 051.4.2   Use the TO_CHAR, TO_NUMBER, and TO_DATE Conversion Functions
- 051.4.3   Apply Conditional Expressions in a SELECT Statement

The functions discussed in this chapter are commonly used built-in PL/SQL programs, packaged and supplied by Oracle. Some operate on numeric, date, and character data, while others convert data between the different scalar data types. Functions can be nested, and some functions are aimed at simplifying interactions with NULL. The conditional functions CASE and DECODE have the ability to display different results depending on data values, which provide *if-then-else* logic in the context of a SQL query.

Describe and Use Character, Number, and Date Functions in SQL

SQL functions are broadly divided into those that calculate and return a value for every row in a data set and those that return a single aggregated value for all rows. The character case conversion functions will be examined, followed by the character manipulation, numeric, and date functions.

Defining a Function

A *function* is a program written to optionally accept input parameters, perform an operation, and return a single value. A function returns only one value per execution.

Three important components form the basis of defining a function. The first is the input parameter list. It specifies zero or more arguments that may be passed to a function as input for processing. These arguments or parameters may be optional and of differing data types. The second component is the data type of its resultant value. Upon execution, only one value of a predetermined data type is returned by the function. The third encapsulates the details of the processing performed by the function and contains the program code that optionally manipulates the input parameters, performs calculations and operations, and generates a return value.

A function is often described as a *black box* that takes an input, performs a calculation, and returns a value. Instead of focusing on their implementation details, it is more useful to concentrate on the features that built-in functions provide.

Functions may be *nested* within other functions, such as F1(x, y, F2(a, b), z), where F2 takes two input parameters, a and b, and forms the third of four parameters submitted to F1. Functions can operate on any data type; the most common are character, date, and numeric data. These operands may be columns or expressions.

As an example, consider a function that calculates a person's age. The AGE function takes one date input parameter, which is their birthday. The result returned by the AGE function is a number representing a person's age. The *black box* calculation involves obtaining the difference in years between the current date and the birthday input parameter.

Types of Functions

Functions can be broadly divided into two categories: those that operate on a single row at a time and those that process multiple rows. This distinction is vital to understanding the larger context in which functions are used.

Single-Row Functions

There are several categories of *single-row* functions, including character, numeric, date, conversion, and general. These are functions that operate on one row of a dataset at a time. If a query selects ten rows, the function is executed ten times, once per row with the values from that row as input to the function.

This query selects two columns of the REGIONS table along with an expression using the LENGTH function with the REGION_NAME column:

```
select region_id, region_name, length(region_name) from regions;
```

The length of the REGION_NAME column is calculated for each of the four rows in the REGIONS table; the function executes four separate times, returning one result per row.

Single-row functions manipulate the data items in a row to extract and format them for display purposes. The input values to a single-row function can be user-specified constants or literals, column data, variables, or expressions optionally supplied by other nested single-row functions. The nesting of single-row functions is a commonly used technique. Functions can return a value with a different data type from its input parameters. The preceding query shows how the LENGTH function accepts one character input parameter and returns a numeric output.

Apart from their inclusion in the SELECT list of a SQL query, single-row functions may be used in the WHERE and ORDER BY clauses.

Multiple-Row Functions

As the name suggests, this category of functions operates on more than one row at a time. Typical uses of *multiple-row* functions include calculating the sum or average of the numeric column values or counting the total number of records in sets. These are sometimes known as *aggregation* or *group* functions and are explored in Chapter 11.

Using Case Conversion Functions

Numerous sources, including application interfaces and batch programs, may save character data in tables. It is not safe to assume that character data has been entered in a case-consistent manner. The character *case conversion* functions serve two important purposes. They may be used, first, to modify the appearance of a character data item for display purposes and, second, to render them consistent for comparison operations. It is simpler to search for a string using a consistent case format instead of testing every permutation of uppercase and lowercase characters that could match the string. Remember that these functions do not alter the data stored in tables. They still form part of the read-only SQL query.

These functions expect string parameters that may consist of string literals, character column values, character expressions, or numeric and date values (which are implicitly converted into strings).

The LOWER Function

The LOWER function replaces the uppercase characters in a string with their lowercase equivalents. Its syntax is LOWER(*s*). The following query illustrates the usage of this function:

```
select lower(100+100), lower('SQL'), lower(sysdate) from dual
```

Assume that the current system date is 17-DEC-2007. The strings "200", "sql", and "17-dec-2007" are returned. The numeric and date expressions are evaluated and implicitly converted into character data before the LOWER function is executed.

The LOWER function is used in the following condition to locate the records with the letters "U" and "R", in any case, adjacent to each other in the LAST_NAME field:

```
select first_name, last_name, lower(last_name) from employees
where lower(last_name) like '%ur%';
```

Consider writing an alternative query to return the same results without using a case conversion function. It could be done as follows:

```
select first_name, last_name from employees
where last_name like '%ur%' or last_name like '%UR%'
or last_name like '%uR%' or last_name like '%Ur%'
```

This query works but is cumbersome, and the number of OR clauses required increases exponentially as the length of the search string increases.

The UPPER Function

The UPPER function is the logical opposite of the LOWER function and replaces the lowercase characters in a given string with their uppercase equivalents. Its syntax is UPPER(*s*). The following query illustrates the usage of this function:

```
select * from countries where upper(country_name) like '%U%S%A%';
```

This query extracts the rows from the COUNTRIES table where the COUNTRY_NAME values contain the letters "U," "S," and "A" (in any case) in that order.

The INITCAP Function

The INITCAP function converts a string of characters into capitalized case. It is often used for data presentation purposes. The first letters of each word in the string are converted to their uppercase equivalents, while the remaining letters of each word are converted to their lowercase equivalents. A word is usually a string of adjacent characters separated by a space or underscore, but other characters such as the percentage symbol, exclamation mark, or dollar sign are valid word separators. Punctuation or special characters are regarded as valid word separators.

The INITCAP function can take only one parameter. Its syntax is INITCAP(*s*). The following query illustrates the usage of this function:

```
select initcap('init cap or init_cap or init%cap') from dual
```

The query returns Init Cap Or Init_Cap Or Init%Cap.

Exercise 10-1: Use the Case Conversion Functions   Construct a query to retrieve a list of all FIRST_NAME and LAST_NAME values from the EMPLOYEES table where FIRST_NAME contains the character string "li".

1. Start SQL Developer or SQL*Plus and connect to the HR schema.

2. The WHERE clause must compare the FIRST_NAME column values with a pattern of characters containing all possible case combinations of the string "li". Therefore, if the FIRST_NAME contains the character strings "LI", "Li", "lI", or "li", that row must be retrieved.

3. The LIKE operator is used for character matching, and four combinations can be extracted with four WHERE clauses separated by the OR keyword. However, the case conversion functions can simplify the condition. If the LOWER function is used on the FIRST_NAME column, the comparison can be done with one WHERE clause condition. The UPPER or INITCAP functions could also be used.

4. Executing this statement returns employees' names containing the characters "li":

```
select first_name, last_name from employees where lower(first_name) like '%li%'
```

Using Character Manipulations Functions

The *character manipulation* functions are possibly some of the most powerful features to emerge from Oracle. Their usefulness in data manipulation is almost without peer, and many seasoned technical professionals whip together a quick script to massage data items using these functions. Nesting these functions is common. The concatenation operator (||) is generally used instead of the CONCAT function. The LENGTH, INSTR, SUBSTR, and REPLACE functions are often used together, as are RPAD, LPAD, and TRIM.

The CONCAT Function

The CONCAT function joins two character literals, columns, or expressions to yield one larger character expression. The CONCAT function takes two parameters. Its syntax is CONCAT(*s1*, *s2*), where *s1* and *s2* represent string literals, character column values, or expressions resulting in character values. The following query illustrates the usage of this function:

```
select concat('Today is:',SYSDATE) from dual
```

The second parameter to the CONCAT function is SYSDATE, which returns the current system date. This value is implicitly converted to a string to which the literal in the first parameter is concatenated. If the system date is 17-DEC-2007, the query returns the string "Today is:17-DEC-2007".

Consider using the CONCAT function to join three terms to return one character string. Since CONCAT takes only two parameters, it is only possible to join two terms with one instance of this function. The solution is to nest the CONCAT function within another CONCAT function, as shown here:

```
select concat('Outer1 ', concat('Inner1',' Inner2')) from dual;
```

The first CONCAT function has two parameters: the first is the literal "Outer1", while the second is a nested CONCAT function. The second CONCAT function takes two parameters: the first is the literal "Inner1", while the second is the literal "Inner2". This query results in the following string: Outer1 Inner1 Inner2. Nested functions are described in a later section.

The LENGTH Function

The LENGTH function returns the number of characters that constitute a character string. Blank spaces, tabs, and special characters are all counted by the LENGTH function. The LENGTH function takes only one string parameter. Its syntax is LENGTH(*s*). Consider the query:

```
select * from countries where length(country_name) > 10;
```

The LENGTH function is used to extract the COUNTRY_NAME values with lengths greater than ten characters from the COUNTRIES table.

The LPAD and RPAD Functions

The LPAD and RPAD functions, also known as left pad and right pad functions, return a string padded with a specified number of characters to the left or right of a given string respectively. The character strings used for padding include character literals, column values, expressions, blank spaces (the default), tabs, and special characters.

The LPAD and RPAD functions take three parameters. Their syntaxes are LPAD(*s, n, p*) and RPAD(*s, n, p*), where *s* represents the source string, *n* represents the final length of the string returned, and *p* specifies the character string to be used as padding. If LPAD is used, the padding characters *p* are added to the left of the source string *s* until it reaches length *n*. If RPAD is used, the padding characters *p* are added to the right of the source string *s* until it reaches length *n*. Note that if the parameter *n* is smaller than or equal to the length of the source string *s*, then no padding occurs and only the first *n* characters of *s* are returned. Consider the queries shown in Figure 10-1.

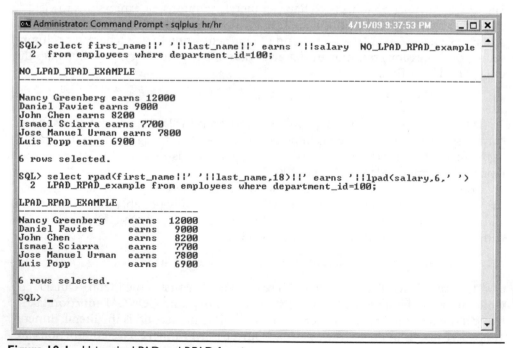

Figure 10-1 Using the LPAD and RPAD functions

The first query does not pad the data, and the results are not as readable as the output from the second query. RPAD is used to add spaces where necessary to the concatenation of first_name and last_name until each name is 18 characters long, while LPAD adds spaces to the beginning of the salary value until each salary is 6 characters long.

The TRIM Function

The TRIM function removes characters from the beginning or end of character values to yield a potentially shorter item. The TRIM function takes a parameter made up of a mandatory component and an optional one. Its syntax is TRIM([*trailing*|*leading*|*both*] *trimstring* from *s*). The string to be trimmed (*s*) is mandatory. The following points list the rules governing the use of this function:

- TRIM(*s*) removes spaces from both sides of the input string.

- TRIM(*trailing trimstring* from *s*) removes all occurrences of *trimstring* from the end of string *s* if it is present.

- TRIM(*leading trimstring* from *s*) removes all occurrences of *trimstring* from the beginning of string *s* if it is present.

- TRIM(*both trimstring* from *s*) and TRIM(*trimstring* from *s*) remove all occurrences of *trimstring* from the beginning and end of string *s* if it is present.

```
select trim(both '*' from '****Hidden****'),
trim(leading '*' from '****Hidden****'),
trim(trailing '*' from '****Hidden****') from dual;
```

The preceding query returns the strings "Hidden", "Hidden****", and "****Hidden". Note that although one trim character is specified, multiple occurrences will be trimmed if they are consecutively present.

The INSTR Function (In-string)

The INSTR function locates the position of a search string within a given string. It returns the numeric position at which the *n*th occurrence of the search string begins, relative to a specified start position. If the search string is not present, the INSTR function returns zero.

The INSTR function takes two optional and two mandatory parameters. The syntax is INSTR(*source string*, *search string*, [*search start position*], [*nth occurrence*]). The default value for the *search start position* is 1 or the beginning of the *source string*. The default value for the *nth* occurrence is 1 or the first occurrence. Consider the following queries:

Query 1: `select instr('1#3#5#7#9#', '#') from dual;`
Query 2: `select instr('1#3#5#7#9#', '#' ,5) from dual;`
Query 3: `select instr('1#3#5#7#9#', '#', 3, 4) from dual;`

Query 1 searches from the start of the source string for the first occurrence of the hash and returns position 2. Query 2 searches for the hash from position 5 and finds the next occurrence at position 6. Query 3 searches for the hash from position 3 and finds the fourth occurrence at position 10.

TIP The INSTR function is often used in combination with the SUBSTR function in utility programs designed to extract encoded data from electronic data streams.

The SUBSTR Function (Substring)

The SUBSTR function extracts a substring of a specified length from the source string beginning at a given position. If the start position is larger than the length of the source string, null is returned. If the number of characters to extract from a given start position is greater than the length of the source string, the segment returned is the substring from the start position to the end of the string.

The SUBSTR function takes three parameters, with the first two being mandatory. Its syntax is SUBSTR(*source string, start position,* [*number of characters to extract*]). The default number of characters to extract is equal to the number of characters from the *start position* to the end of the *source string.* Consider the following queries:

```
Query 1: select substr('1#3#5#7#9#', 5) from dual;
Query 2: select substr('1#3#5#7#9#', 5, 3) from dual;
Query 3: select substr('1#3#5#7#9#', -3, 2) from dual;
```

Query 1 extracts the substring beginning at position 5. Since the third parameter is not specified, the default extraction length is equal to the number of characters from the start position to the end of the source string, which is 6. Accordingly for query 1 the substring returned is "5#7#9#". Query 2 returns the three characters occupying positions 5–7, which form the substring "5#7". Query 3 starts at position –3. The negative start position parameter instructs Oracle to commence searching three characters from the end of the string. Therefore the start position is three characters from the end of the string, which is position 8. The third parameter is 2, which results in the substring "#9" being returned.

The REPLACE Function

The REPLACE function replaces all occurrences of a search item in a source string with a replacement term. If the length of the replacement term is different from that of the search item, then the lengths of the returned and source strings will be different. If the search string is not found, the source string is returned unchanged. The REPLACE function takes three parameters, with the first two being mandatory. Its syntax is REPLACE(*source string, search item,* [*replacement term*]). If the *replacement term* parameter is omitted, each occurrence of the *search item* is removed from the *source string.* In other words, the *search item* is replaced by an empty string. Consider the following queries:

```
Query 1: select replace('1#3#5#7#9#','#','->') from dual
Query 2: select replace('1#3#5#7#9#','#') from dual
```

The hash in query 1 is specified as the search character, and the replacement string is specified as "->". The hash symbol occurs five times in the source, and the resultant string is "1->3->5->7->9->". Query 2 does not specify a replacement string. The default behavior is therefore to replace the search string with an empty string; this, in effect, removes the search character completely from the source, resulting in the string "13579" being returned.

Using Numeric Functions

There is a range of built-in *numeric functions* provided by Oracle that rivals the mathematical toolboxes of popular spreadsheet packages. A significant differentiator between numeric and other functions is that they accept and return only numeric data. Oracle provides numeric functions for solving trigonometric, exponentiation, and logarithmic problems, among others. This guide focuses on three *numeric single-row functions*: ROUND, TRUNC, and MOD.

The Numeric ROUND Function

The ROUND function performs a rounding operation on a numeric value based on the decimal precision specified. The value returned is rounded either up or down, depending on the numeric value of the significant digit at the specified decimal precision position. If the specified decimal precision is *n*, the digit significant to the rounding is found (*n* + 1) places to the RIGHT of the decimal point. If it is negative, the digit significant to the rounding is found *n* places to the LEFT of the decimal point. If the numeric value of the significant digit is greater than or equal to 5, a "round up" occurs; otherwise, a "round down" occurs.

The ROUND function takes two parameters. Its syntax is ROUND(*source number, decimal precision*). The source number parameter represents any numeric value. The decimal precision parameter specifies the degree of rounding and is optional. If the decimal precision parameter is absent, the default degree of rounding is zero, which means the source is rounded to the nearest whole number.

Consider the decimal degrees listed in Table 10-1 for the number 1601.916. The negative decimal precision values are located to the left of the decimal point, while the positive values are found to the right.

If the decimal precision parameter is one, then the source number is rounded to the nearest tenth. If it is two, then the source is rounded to the nearest hundredth, and so on. The following queries illustrate the usage of this function:

Query 1: select round(1601.916, 1) from dual;
Query 2: select round(1601.916, 2) from dual;
Query 3: select round(1601.916, -3) from dual;
Query 4: select round(1601.916) from dual;

Decimal Precision	Significant Rounding Digit for Number: 1601.916	Decimal Position
−4	1	Thousands ($n \times 1000$)
−3	6	Hundreds ($n \times 100$)
−2	0	Tens ($n \times 10$)
−1	1	Units ($n \times 1$)
1	9	Tenths ($n \div 10$)
2	1	Hundredths ($n \div 100$)
3	6	Thousandths ($n \div 1000$)

Table 10-1 Decimal Precision Descriptions

Query 1 has a decimal precision parameter (*n*) of 1, which implies that the source number is rounded to the nearest tenth. Since the hundredths (*n* + 1) digit is 1 (less than 5), rounding down occurs and the number returned is 1601.9. The decimal precision parameter in query 2 is 2, so the source number is rounded to the nearest hundredth. Since the thousandths unit is 6 (greater than 5), rounding up occurs and the number returned is 1601.92. The decimal precision parameter of the query 3 is –3. Since it is negative, the digit significant for rounding is found 3 places to the left of the decimal point, at the hundreds digit, which is 6. Since the hundreds unit is 6, rounding up occurs and the number returned is 2000. Query 4 has dispensed with the decimal precision parameter. This implies that rounding is done to the nearest whole number. Since the tenth unit is 9, the number is rounded up and 1602 is returned.

The Numeric TRUNC Function (Truncate)

The TRUNC function performs a truncation operation on a numeric value based on the decimal precision specified. A numeric truncation is different from rounding in that it drops the numbers beyond the decimal precision specified and does not attempt to round up or down if the decimal precision is positive. However, if the decimal precision (*n*) is negative, the input value is zeroed down from the *n*th decimal position.

The TRUNC function takes two parameters. Its syntax is TRUNC(*source number, decimal precision*). Source number represents any numeric value. Decimal precision specifies the degree of truncation and is optional. If the decimal precision parameter is absent, the default decimal precision is zero, which means the source number is truncated to an integer value.

If the decimal precision parameter is 1, then the source number is truncated at its tenths unit. If it is 2, it is truncated at its hundredths unit, and so on. The following queries illustrate the usage of this function:

```
Query 1: select trunc(1601.916, 1) from dual;
Query 2: select trunc(1601.916, 2) from dual;
Query 3: select trunc(1601.916, -3) from dual;
Query 4: select trunc(1601.916) from dual;
```

Query 1 has a decimal precision parameter of 1, which implies that the source number is truncated at its tenths unit and the number returned is 1601.9. The decimal precision parameter (*n*) in query 2 is 2, so the source number is truncated at its hundredths unit and the number returned is 1601.91. Note that this result would be different if a rounding operation were performed, since the digit in position (*n* + 1) is 6 (greater than 5). Query 3 specifies a negative number (–3) as its decimal precision. Three places to the left of the decimal point implies that the truncation happens at the hundreds digit as shown earlier in Table 10-1. Therefore, the source number is zeroed down from its hundreds digit (6) and the number returned is 1000. Finally, query 4 does not have a decimal precision parameter, implying that truncation is done at the whole number degree of precision. The number returned is 1601.

The MOD Function (Modulus)

The MOD function returns the numeric remainder of a division operation. Two numbers, the dividend (number being divided) and the divisor (number to divide by), are provided, and a division operation is performed. If the divisor is a factor of the dividend, MOD returns zero, since there is no remainder. If the divisor is zero, no division by zero error is returned and the MOD function returns the dividend instead. If the divisor is larger than the dividend, then the MOD function returns the dividend as its result. This is because it divides zero times into the divisor, leaving the remainder equal to the dividend.

The MOD function takes two parameters. Its syntax is MOD(*dividend, divisor*). The *dividend* and *divisor* parameters represent a numeric literal, column, or expression, which may be negative or positive. The following queries illustrate the usage of this function:

```
Query 1: select mod(6, 2) from dual
Query 2: select mod(5, 3) from dual
Query 3: select mod(7, 35) from dual
Query 4: select mod(5.2, 3) from dual
```

Query 1 divides 6 by 2 perfectly, yielding 0 as the remainder. Query 2 divides 5 by 3, yielding 1 with remainder 2. Query 3 attempts to divide 7 by 35. Since the *divisor* is larger than the *dividend*, the number 7 is returned as the modulus value. Query 4 has a decimal fraction as the *dividend*. Dividing 5.2 by 3 yields 1 with remainder 2.2.

TIP Any even number divided by 2 naturally has no remainder, but odd numbers divided by 2 always have a remainder of 1. Therefore, the MOD function is often used to distinguish between even and odd numbers.

Working with Dates

The *date* functions provide a convenient way to solve date-related problems without needing to keep track of leap years or the number of days in particular months. We first describe storage of dates and the default date format masks before examining the SYSDATE function. We then discuss date arithmetic and the *date manipulation functions*: ADD_MONTHS, MONTHS_BETWEEN, LAST_DAY, NEXT_DAY, ROUND, and TRUNC.

Date Storage in the Database

The database stores dates internally in a numeric format that supports the storage of century, year, month, and day details, as well as time information such as hours, minutes, and seconds. When accessing date information from a table, the default format of the results comprises two digits that represent the day, a three-letter abbreviation of the month, and two digits representing the year component.

The SYSDATE Function

The SYSDATE function takes no parameters and returns the current system date and time according to the database server. By default the SYSDATE function returns the DD-MON-RR components of the current server system date. If the database server is located in a different time zone from a client querying the database, the date and time returned by SYSDATE will differ from the local time on the client machine. Here is a query to retrieve the database server date:

```
select sysdate from dual
```

Date Arithmetic

The following equation illustrates an important principle regarding *date arithmetic*: *Date1 – Date2 = Num1*.

A date can be subtracted from another date. The difference between two date items represents the number of days between them. Any number, including fractions, may be added to or subtracted from a date item. In this context the number represents a number of days. The sum or difference between a number and a date item always returns a date item. This principle implies that adding, multiplying, or dividing two date items is not permitted.

The MONTHS_BETWEEN Function

The MONTHS_BETWEEN function returns the number of months between two mandatory date parameters. Its syntax is MONTHS_BETWEEN(*date1*, *date2*). The function computes the difference in 31-day months between *date1* and *date2*. If *date1* occurs before *date2*, a negative number is returned. The difference between the two date parameters may consist of a whole number that represents the number of months between the two dates and a fractional component that represents the days and time remaining (based on a 31-day month) after the integer difference between years and months is calculated. A whole number with no fractional part is returned if the day components of the dates being compared are either the same or the last day of their respective months.

The following queries illustrate the MONTHS_BETWEEN function:

```
Query 1: select months_between(sysdate, sysdate-31) from dual;
Query 2: select months_between('29-mar-2008', '28-feb-2008')
from dual;
Query 3: select months_between('29-mar-2008', '28-feb-2008')
* 31 from dual;
```

Assume that the current date is 16-APR-2009. Query 1 returns 1 as the number of months between 16-APR-2009 and 16-MAR-2009. Query 2 implicitly converts the date literals into date items of the format DD-MON-YYYY. Since no time information is provided, Oracle assumes the time to be midnight on both days. The MONTHS_BETWEEN function returns approximately 1.03225806. The whole number component indicates that there is one month between these two dates. Closer examination of the fractional component interestingly reveals that there is exactly one month between 28-MAR-2008 and 28-FEB-2008. The fractional component must therefore represent the one-day difference. It would include differences in hours, minutes, and seconds as well, but for this example, the time components are identical. Multiplying 0.03225806 by 31 returns 1, since the fractional component returned by MONTHS_BETWEEN is based on a 31-day month. Similarly, query 3 returns the whole number 32.

EXAM TIP A common mistake is to assume that the return data type of single-row functions is the same as the category the function belongs to. This is only true of the numeric functions. Character and date functions can return values of any data type. For example the INSTR character function and the MONTHS_BETWEEN date function both return a number. It is also common to erroneously assume that the difference between two dates is a date, when in fact it is a number.

The ADD_MONTHS Function

The ADD_MONTHS function returns a date item calculated by adding a specified number of months to a given date value. The ADD_MONTHS function takes two mandatory parameters. Its syntax is ADD_MONTHS(*start date, number of months*). The function computes the target date after adding the specified number of months to the *start date*. The number of months may be negative, resulting in a target date earlier than the start date being returned. The number of months may be fractional, but the fractional component is ignored and the integer component is used. These three queries illustrate the ADD_MONTHS function:

```
Query 1: select add_months('07-APR-2009', 1) from dual;
Query 2: select add_months('31-DEC-2008', 2.5) from dual;
Query 3: select add_months('07-APR-2009', -12) from dual;
```

Query 1 returns 07-MAY-2009, since the day component remains the same if possible and the month is incremented by one. The second query has two interesting dimensions. The parameter specifying the number of months to add contains a fractional component, which is ignored. Therefore, it is equivalent to ADD_MONTHS ('31-DEC-2008', 2). Adding two months to the date 31-DEC-2008 should return the date 31-FEB-2009, but there is no such date, so the last day of the month, 28-FEB-2009, is returned. Since the number of months added in the third query is –12, the date 07-APR-2008 is returned, which is 12 months prior to the start date.

The NEXT_DAY Function

The NEXT_DAY function returns the date when the next occurrence of a specified day of the week occurs. It takes two mandatory parameters and has the syntax NEXT_DAY(*start date, day of the week*). The function computes the date on which the *day of the week* parameter next occurs after the *start date*. The *day of the week* parameter may be either a character value or an integer value. The acceptable values are determined by the NLS_DATE_LANGUAGE database parameter, but the default values are at least the first three characters of the day name or integer values, where 1 represents Sunday, 2 represents Monday, and so on. The character values representing the days of the week may be specified in any case. The short name may be longer than three characters;

for example, Sunday may be referenced as sun, sund, sunda, or Sunday. Consider the following queries:

Query 1: `select next_day('01-JAN-2009', 'tue') from dual;`
Query 2: `select next_day('01-JAN-2009', 'WEDNE') from dual;`
Query 3: `select next_day('01-JAN-2009', 5) from dual;`

Here, 01-JAN-2009 is a Thursday. Therefore, the next time a Tuesday occurs will be five days later, on 06-JAN-2009. The second query specifies the character literal WEDNE, which is interpreted as Wednesday. The next Wednesday after 01-JAN-2009 is 07-JAN-2009. The third query uses the integer form to specify the fifth day of the week. Assuming your session is set to American defaults, where Sunday is represented by the number 1, the fifth day is Thursday. The next time another Thursday occurs after 01-JAN-2009 is 08-JAN-2009.

The LAST_DAY Function

The LAST_DAY function returns the date of the last day in the month to which the given day belongs. It takes a single mandatory parameter and has the syntax LAST_DAY(*start date*). The function extracts the month that the *start date* parameter belongs to and calculates the date of the last day of that month. The following query returns the date 31-JAN-2009:

```
select last_day('01-JAN-2009') from dual;
```

The Date ROUND Function

The date ROUND function performs a rounding operation on a value based on a specified date precision format. The value returned is rounded either up or down to the nearest date precision format. This function takes one mandatory parameter and one optional parameter and has the syntax ROUND(*source date*, [*date precision format*]). The *source date* parameter represents any date item. The *date precision format* parameter specifies the degree of rounding and is optional. If it is absent, the default degree of rounding is *day*. The *date precision formats* include *century* (CC), *year* (YYYY), *quarter* (Q), *month* (MM), *week* (W), *day* (DD), *hour* (HH), and *minute* (MI).

Rounding up to *century* is equivalent to adding one to the current century. Rounding up to the next month occurs if the *day* component is greater than 16, or else rounding down to the beginning of the current month occurs. If the month falls between one and six, then rounding to *year* returns the date at the beginning of the current year; if not, it returns the date at the beginning of the following year. Consider the following query and its results:

```
SQL> select round(sysdate) day, round(sysdate,'w') week,
  2         round(sysdate,'month') month, round(sysdate,'year') year
  3  from dual;

DAY       WEEK      MONTH     YEAR
--------- --------- --------- ---------
17-APR-09 15-APR-09 01-MAY-09 01-JAN-09
```

Assume this query was run on 17-APR-2009 at 00:05. The first item rounds the date to the nearest day. Since the time is 00:05, which is after midnight, the date is not rounded up. The second item rounds the date to the same day of the week as the first day of the month. Since 01-APR-2009 is a Wednesday, the date returned is the Wednesday of the week in which this date occurs. Remember that, by default, the first day of the week is a Sunday. Therefore, the first Wednesday in the week beginning 12-APR-2009 is 15-APR-2009. The third item rounds the date to the beginning of the following month, since the day component is 17 and returns 01-MAY-2009. The fourth item is rounded up to the date at the beginning of the current year, since the month component is 4, and 01-JAN-2009 is returned.

The Date TRUNC Function

The date TRUNC function performs a truncation operation on a date value based on a specified date precision format.

The date TRUNC function takes one mandatory parameter and one optional parameter. Its syntax is TRUNC(*source date*, [*date precision format*]). The *source date* parameter represents any date item. The *date precision format* parameter specifies the degree of truncation and is optional. If it is absent, the default degree of truncation is *day*. This means that any time component of the *source date* is set to midnight or 00:00:00 (00 hours, 00 minutes, and 00 seconds). Truncating at the month level sets the date of the *source date* to the first day of the month. Truncating at the year level returns the date at the beginning of the current year. The following query and results show four items in the SELECT list, each truncating a date literal to a different degree of precision:

```
SQL> select trunc(sysdate) day, trunc(sysdate,'w') week,
  2         trunc(sysdate,'month') month, trunc(sysdate,'year') year
  3  from dual;

DAY       WEEK      MONTH     YEAR
--------- --------- --------- ---------
17-APR-09 15-APR-09 01-APR-09 01-JAN-09
```

Assume this query was run on 17-APR-2009 at 12:05am. The first item sets the time component of 00:05 to 00:00 and returns the current day. The second item truncates the date to the same day of the week as the first day of the month (Wednesday) and returns the Wednesday in its week: 15-APR-2009. The third item truncates the date to the beginning of the current month and returns 01-APR-2009. The fourth item truncates the date to the beginning of the current year and returns 01-JAN-2009.

Exercise 10-2: Use the Character Manipulation Functions   Connect to the WEBSTORE schema and construct a query that extracts the unique e-mail hostname from the CUSTOMERS.EMAIL column.

1. Start SQL Developer and connect to the WEBSTORE schema.

2. A typical CUSTOMERS.EMAIL entry looks as follows: sid@mediumcorp.com. The hostname begins immediately after the @ symbol and ends before the

dot com. The SUBSTR function may be used to extract this value. However, the start position and the length are still unknown. The INSTR function may be used to locate the position of the first occurrence of the @ symbol and the characters ".com".

3. A possible solution is

```
select distinct substr(email, instr(email,'@')+1, instr(email, '.com')) hostname
from customers;
```

Describe Various Types of Conversion Functions Available in SQL

SQL conversion *functions* are single-row functions designed to alter the nature of the data type of a column value, expression, or literal. *TO_CHAR, TO_NUMBER,* and *TO_DATE* are the three most widely used conversion functions. TO_CHAR converts numeric and date information into characters, while TO_NUMBER and TO_DATE convert character data into numbers and dates, respectively.

Conversion Functions

Oracle allows columns to be defined with ANSI, DB2, and SQL/DS data types. These are converted internally to Oracle data types. Each column has an associated data type that constrains the nature of the data it can store. A NUMBER column cannot store character information. A DATE column cannot store random characters or numbers. However, the character equivalents of both number and date information can be stored in a VARCHAR2 field.

If a function that accepts a character input parameter finds a number instead, Oracle automatically converts it into its character equivalent. If a function that accepts a number or a date parameter encounters a character value, there are specific conditions under which automatic data type conversion occurs. Although implicit data type conversions are available, it is generally more reliable to explicitly convert values from one data type to another using single-row conversion functions.

Implicit Data Type Conversion

Values that do not share identical data types with function parameters are *implicitly converted* to the required format if possible. VARCHAR2 and CHAR data types are collectively referred to as character types. Character fields are flexible and allow the storage of almost any type of information. Therefore, DATE and NUMBER values can easily be converted to their character equivalents. These conversions are known as *number to character* and *date to character* conversions. Consider the following queries:

Query 1: `select length(1234567890) from dual`
Query 2: `select length(SYSDATE) from dual`

Both queries use the LENGTH function, which takes a character string parameter. The number 1234567890 in query 1 is implicitly converted into a character string,

'1234567890', before being evaluated by the LENGTH function, which returns 10. Query 2 first evaluates the SYSDATE function, which is assumed to be 07-APR-38. This date is implicitly converted into the character string '07-APR-38', and the LENGTH function returns the number 9.

It is uncommon for character data to be implicitly converted into numeric data types, since the only condition under which this can occur is if the character data represents a valid number. The character string '11' will be implicitly converted to a number, but '11.123.456' will not be, as the following queries demonstrate:

Query 3: `select mod('11', 2) from dual`
Query 4: `select mod('11.123', 2) from dual`
Query 5: `select mod('11.123.456', 2) from dual`
Query 6: `select mod('$11', 2) from dual`

Queries 3 and 4 implicitly convert the character strings '11' and '11.123' into the numbers 11 and 11.123, respectively, before the MOD function evaluates them and returns the results 1 and 1.123. Query 5 returns the error "ORA-1722: invalid number," when Oracle tries to perform an implicit *character to number* conversion because the string '11.123.456' is not a valid number. Query 6 also fails with the invalid number error, since the dollar symbol cannot be implicitly converted into a number.

Implicit *character to date* conversion is possible when the character string conforms to the following date patterns: [D|DD] *separator1* [MON|MONTH] *separator2* [R|RR|YY|YYYY]. D and DD represent single-digit and two-digit days of the month. MON is a three-character abbreviation, while MONTH is the full name for a month. R and RR represent single- and two-digit years. YY and YYYY represent two- and four-digit years, respectively. The *separator1* and *separator2* elements may be most punctuation marks, spaces, and tabs. Table 10-2 demonstrates implicit character to date conversion, listing several function calls and the results SQL Developer returns. These results assume that your system makes use of the American session defaults.

Function Call	Format	Results
`add_months('24-JAN-09', 1)`	DD-MON-RR	24/FEB/09
`add_months('1\january/8'', 1)`	D\MONTH/R	01/FEB/08
`months_between('13*jan*8', '13/feb/2008')`	DD*MON*R, DD/MON/ YYYY	−1
`add_months('01$jan/08', 1)`	DD$MON/RR	01/FEB/08
`add_months('13!jana08', 1)`	JANA is an invalid month	ORA-1841: (full) year must be between −4713 and +9999 and not be 0
`add_months('24-JAN-09 18:45', 1)`	DD-MON-RR HH24:MI	ORA-1830: date format picture ends before converting entire input string

Table 10-2 Examples of Implicit Character to Date Conversion

TIP Although implicit data type conversions are available, it is more reliable to convert values explicitly from one data type to another using single-row conversion functions. Converting character information to NUMBER and DATE relies on format masks.

Explicit Data Type Conversion

Functions that convert items from one data type to another are known as *explicit* data type conversion functions. These return a value guaranteed to be the type required and offer a safe and reliable method of converting data items.

NUMBER and DATE items can be converted explicitly into character items using the TO_CHAR function. A character string can be explicitly changed into a NUMBER using the TO_NUMBER function. The TO_DATE function is used to convert character strings into DATE items. Oracle's format masks enable a wide range of control over character to number and character to date conversions.

EXAM TIP Your understanding of commonly used format models or masks will be practically tested with questions like: Predict the result of a function call such as TO_CHAR(TO_DATE('01-JAN-00','DD-MON-RR'),'Day').

Use the TO_CHAR, TO_NUMBER, and TO_DATE Conversion Functions

This certification objective contains a systematic description of the TO_NUMBER, TO_DATE, and TO_CHAR functions, with examples. The discussion of TO_CHAR is divided into the conversion of date items to characters and numbers to characters. This separation is warranted by the availability of different format masks for controlling conversion to character values. These conversion functions exist alongside many others but are the most widely used.

Using the Conversion Functions

Many situations demand the use of conversion functions. They may range from formatting DATE fields in a report to ensuring that numeric digits extracted from character fields are correctly converted into numbers before applying them in an arithmetic expression.

Table 10-3 illustrates the syntax of the single-row explicit data type conversion functions.

`TO_NUMBER(char1, [format mask], [nls_parameters]) = num1`	`TO_CHAR(num1, [format mask], [nls_parameters]) = char1`
`TO_DATE(char1, [format mask], [nls_parameters]) = date1`	`TO_CHAR(date1, [format mask], [nls_parameters]) = char1`

Table 10-3 Syntax of Explicit Data Type Conversion Functions

Optional national language support parameters (nls_parameters) are useful for specifying the language and format in which the names of date and numeric elements are returned. These parameters are usually absent, and the default values for elements such as day or month names and abbreviations are used. As Figure 10-2 shows, there is a publicly available view called NLS_SESSION_PARAMETERS that contains the NLS parameters for your current session. The default NLS_CURRENCY value is the dollar symbol, but this can be changed at the user session level. For example, to change the currency to the three-character-long string GBP, the following command may be issued:

```
ALTER SESSION set NLS_CURRENCY='GBP';
```

Converting Numbers to Characters Using the TO_CHAR Function

The TO_CHAR function returns an item of data type VARCHAR2. When applied to items of type NUMBER, several formatting options are available. Its syntax is

```
TO_CHAR(num, [format], [nls_parameter]),
```

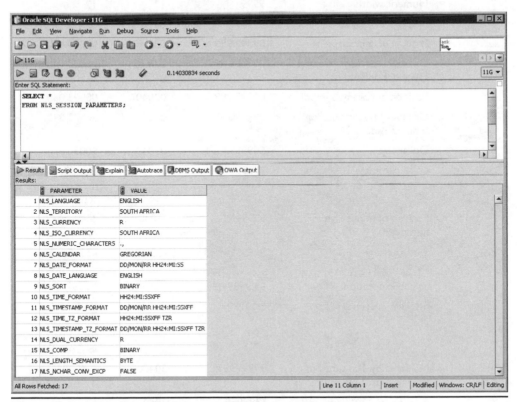

Figure 10-2 National Language Support (NLS) session parameters

The *num* parameter is mandatory and must be a numeric value. The optional *format* parameter may be used to specify numeric formatting information like width, currency symbol, the position of a decimal point, and group (or thousands) separators and must be enclosed in single quotation marks. There are other formatting options for numbers being converted into characters, some of which are listed in Table 10-4. Consider the following two queries:

Query 1: `select to_char(00001)||' is a special number' from dual;`

Query 2: `select to_char(00001, '0999999')||' is a special number' from dual;`

Query 1 evaluates the number 00001, removes the leading zeros, converts the number 1 into the character '1', and returns the character string '1 is a special number'. Query 2 applies the numeric format mask '0999999' to the number 00001, converting

Format Element	Description of Element	Format	Number	Character Result
9	Numeric width	9999	12	12
0	Displays leading zeros	09999	0012	00012
.	Position of decimal point	09999.999	030.40	00030.400
D	Decimal separator position (period is default)	09999D999	030.40	00030.400
,	Position of comma symbol	09999,999	03040	00003,040
G	Group separator position (comma is default)	09999G999	03040	00003,040
$	Dollar sign	$099999	03040	$003040
L	Local currency	L099999	03040	GBP003040 if nls_currency is set to GBP
MI	Position of minus sign for negatives	99999MI	-3040	3040-
PR	Wrap negatives in parentheses	99999PR	-3040	<3040>
EEEE	Scientific notation	99.99999EEEE	121.976	1.21976E+02
U	nls_dual_currency	U099999	03040	CAD003040 if nls_dual_currency is set to CAD
V	Multiplies by 10n times (n is the number of nines after V)	9999V99	3040	304000
S	+ or − sign is prefixed	S999999	3040	+3040

Table 10-4 Numeric Format Masks

it into the character string '0000001'. After concatenation to the character literals, the string returned is '0000001 is a special number'. The zero and the six nines in the format mask indicate to the TO_CHAR function that leading zeros must be displayed and that the display width must be set to seven characters. Therefore, the string returned by the TO_CHAR function contains seven characters.

 TIP Converting numbers into characters is a reliable way to ensure that functions and general SQL syntax, which expects character input, do not return errors when numbers are encountered. Converting numbers into character strings is common when numeric data must be formatted for reporting purposes. The format masks that support currency, thousands separators, and decimal point separators are frequently used when presenting financial data.

Converting Dates to Characters Using the TO_CHAR Function

You can take advantage of a variety of format models to convert DATE items into almost any character representation of a date using TO_CHAR. Its syntax is

```
TO_CHAR(date1, [format], [nls_parameter]),
```

Only the *date1* parameter is mandatory; it must take the form of a value that can be implicitly converted to a date. The optional *format* parameter is case sensitive and must be enclosed in single quotes. The format mask specifies which date elements are extracted and whether the element should be described by a long or an abbreviated name. The names of days and months are automatically padded with spaces. These may be removed using a modifier to the format mask called the fill mode (*fm*) operator. By prefixing the format model with the letters *fm*, you instruct Oracle to trim all spaces from the names of days and months. There are many formatting options for dates being converted into characters, some of which are listed in Table 10-5. Consider the following three queries:

> *Query 1:* select to_char(sysdate)||' is today''s date' from dual;
> *Query 2:* select to_char(sysdate,'Month')||'is a special time' from dual;
> *Query 3:* select to_char(sysdate,'fmMonth')||'is a special time' from dual;

If the current system date is 03/JAN/09 and the default display format is DD/MON/RR, then query 1 returns the character string '03/JAN/09 is today's date'. There are two notable components in query 2. First, only the month component of the current system date is extracted for conversion to a character type. Second, since the format mask is case sensitive and 'Month' appears in title case, the string returned is 'January is a special time'. There is no need to add a space in front of the literal 'is a special time', since the TO_CHAR function automatically pads the name of the month with a space. If the format mask in query 2 was 'MONTH', the string returned would be 'JANUARY is a special time'. The *fm* modifier is applied to query 3, and the resultant string is 'Januaryis a special time'. Note there is no space between January and the literal 'is a special time'. In Table 10-5, assume the elements are operating on the date 02-JUN-1975 and the current year is 2009.

The date format elements pertaining to weeks, quarters, centuries, and other less commonly used format masks are listed in Table 10-6. The result column is obtained by evaluating the TO_CHAR function using the date 24-SEP-1000 BC, with the format mask from the format element column in the table.

The time component of a date time data type is extracted using the format models in Table 10-7. The result is obtained by evaluating the TO_CHAR function using the date including its time component 27-JUN-2010 21:35:13, with the format mask in the format element column in Table 10-7.

Several miscellaneous elements that may be used in date time format models are listed in Table 10-8. Punctuation marks are used to separate format elements. Three types of suffixes exist to format components of date time elements. Furthermore, character literals may be included in a date format model if they are enclosed in double quotation marks. The results in Table 10-8 are obtained by applying the TO_CHAR function using the date 12/SEP/08 14:31 with the format masks listed in the description and format mask column.

Format Element	Description	Result
Y	Last digit of year	5
YY	Last two digits of year	75
YYY	Last three digits of year	975
YYYY	Four-digit year	1975
RR	Two-digit century-aware year	75
YEAR, year, Year	Case-sensitive English spelling of year	NINETEEN SEVENTY FIVE, nineteen seventy five, Nineteen Seventy Five
MM	Two-digit month	06
MON, mon, Mon	Three-letter abbreviation of month	JUN, jun, Jun
MONTH, month, Month	Case-sensitive English spelling of month	JUNE, june, June
D	Day of the week	2
DD	Two-digit day of month	02
DDD	Day of the year	153
DY, dy, Dy	Three-letter abbreviation of day	MON, mon, Mon
DAY, day, Day	Case-sensitive English spelling of day	MONDAY, monday, Monday

Table 10-5 Date Format Masks for Days, Months, and Years

Format Element	Description	Result
W	Week of month	4
WW	Week of year	39
Q	Quarter of year	3
CC	Century	10
S preceding CC, YYYY, or YEAR	If date is BC, a minus is prefixed to result	–10, –1000, or –ONE THOUSAND
IYYY, IYY, IY, I	ISO dates of four, three, two, and one digit, respectively	1000, 000, 00, 0
BC, AD, B.C. and A.D.	BC or AD and period-spaced B.C. or A.D.	BC
J	Julian day—days since 31 December 4713 BC	1356075
IW	ISO standard week (1 to 53)	39
RM	Roman numeral month	IX

Table 10-6   Less Commonly Used Date Format Masks

Format Element	Description	Result
AM, PM, A.M., and P.M.	Meridian indicators	PM
HH, HH12, and HH24	Hour of day, 1–12 hours, and 0–23 hours	09, 09, 21
MI	Minute (0–59)	35
SS	Second (0–59)	13
SSSSS	Seconds past midnight (0–86399)	77713

Table 10-7   Date Format Mask for Time Components

Format Element	Description and Format Mask	Result
– / . , ? # !	Punctuation marks: 'MM.YY'	09.08
"any character literal"	Character literals: '"Week" W "of" Month'	Week 2 of September
TH	Positional or ordinal text: 'DDth "of" Month'	12TH of September
SP	Spelled out number: 'MmSP Month Yyyysp'	Nine September Two Thousand Eight
THSP or SPTH	Spelled-out positional or ordinal number: 'hh24SpTh'	Fourteenth

Table 10-8   Miscellaneous Date Format Masks

The JOB_HISTORY table keeps track of jobs occupied by employees in the company. The query in Figure 10-3 retrieves a descriptive sentence about the quitting date for each employee based on their END_DATE, EMPLOYEE_ID, and JOB_ID fields. A character expression is concatenated to a TO_CHAR function call with a format model of "fmDay "the "ddth "of" Month YYYY'. The *fm* modifier is used to trim blank spaces that trail the names of the shorter days and shorter months. The two character literals enclosed in double quotation marks are the words "the" and "of". The 'th' format model is applied to the 'dd' date element to create an ordinal day such as the 17th or 31st. The 'Month' format model displays the full name of the month element of the END_DATE column in title case. Finally, the YYYY format mask retrieves the four-digit year component.

Although the century component of a date is not displayed by default, it is stored in the database when the date value is inserted or updated and is available for retrieval. The DD-MON-RR format mask is the default for display and input. When inserting or updating date values, the century component is obtained from the SYSDATE function if it is not supplied. The RR date format mask differs from the YY format mask in that it may be used to specify different centuries based on the current and specified years. The century component assigned to a date with its year specified with the RR date format may be better understood by considering the following principles:

- If the two digits of the current year and the specified year lie between 0 and 49, the current century is returned. Suppose the present date is 02-JUN-2007. The century returned for the date 24-JUL-04 in DD-MON-RR format is 20.

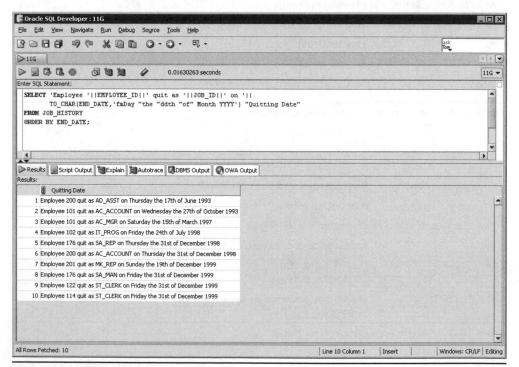

Figure 10-3 TO_CHAR function with dates

- If the two digits of the current year lie between 0 and 49 and the specified year falls between 50 and 99, the previous century is returned. Suppose the current date is 02-JUN-2007. The century returned for 24-JUL-94 is 19.

- If the two digits of the current and specified years lie between 50 and 99, the current century is returned by default. Suppose the current date is 02-JUN-1975; the century returned for 24-JUL-94 is 19.

- If the two digits of the current year lie between 50 and 99 and the specified year falls between 0 and 49, the next century is returned. Suppose the current date is 02-JUN-1975; the century returned for 24-JUL-07 is 20.

Converting Characters to Dates Using the TO_DATE Function

The TO_DATE function returns an item of type DATE. Character strings converted to dates may contain all or just a subset of the date time elements composing a DATE. When strings with only a subset of the date time elements are converted, Oracle provides default values to construct a complete date. Components of character strings are associated with different date time elements using a format model or mask. Its syntax is

```
TO_DATE(string1, [format], [nls_parameter]),
```

Only *string1* is mandatory, and if no format mask is supplied, *string1* must be implicitly convertible into a date. The optional *format* parameter is almost always used and is specified in single quotation marks. The format masks are identical to those listed in Tables 10-5, 10-6, and 10-7. The TO_DATE function has an *fx* modifier, which is similar to *fm* used with the TO_CHAR function. The *fx* modifier specifies an exact match for *string1* and the format mask. When the *fx* modifier is specified, character items that do not exactly match the format mask yield an error. Consider the following five queries:

```
Query 1: select to_date('25-DEC-2010') from dual;
Query 2: select to_date('25-DEC') from dual;
Query 3: select to_date('25-DEC', 'DD-MON') from dual;
Query 4: select to_date('25-DEC-2010 18:03:45', 'DD-MON-YYYY
HH24:MI:SS') from dual;
Query 5: select to_date('25-DEC-10', 'fxDD-MON-YYYY') from dual;
```

Query 1 evaluates the string 25-DEC-2010 and has sufficient information to convert it implicitly into a DATE item with a default mask of DD-MON-YYYY. The hyphen separator could be substituted with another punctuation character. Since no time components are provided, the time for this converted date is set to midnight, or 00:00:00. Query 2 cannot implicitly convert the string into a date because there is insufficient information and an ORA-01840: input value is not long enough for date format; an error is returned. By supplying a format mask DD-MON to the string 25-DEC in query 3, Oracle can match the number 25 to DD and the abbreviated month name DEC to the MON component. Year and time components are absent, so the current year returned by the SYSDATE function is used and the time is set to midnight. If the current year is 2009, query 3 returns the date 25/DEC/09 00:00:00. Query 4 performs a complete conversion of a string with all the date time elements present, and no default values are supplied by Oracle. Query 5 uses the *fx* modifier in its format mask. Since the year component of the string is 10 and the corresponding format mask is YYYY, the *fx* modifier results in an ORA-01862 error being returned: "the numeric value does not match the length of the format item."

Converting Characters to Numbers Using the TO_NUMBER Function

The TO_NUMBER function returns an item of type NUMBER. Character strings converted into numbers must be suitably formatted so that any nonnumeric components are translated or stripped away with an appropriate format mask. The syntax is

```
TO_NUMBER(string1, [format], [nls_parameter]),
```

Only the *string1* parameter is mandatory, and if no *format* mask is supplied, it must be a value that can be implicitly converted into a number. The optional *format* parameter is specified in single quotation marks. The format masks are identical to those listed in Table 10-4. Consider the following two queries:

Query 1: `select to_number('$1,000.55') from dual;`
Query 2: `select to_number('$1,000.55','$999,999.99') from dual;`

Query 1 cannot perform an implicit conversion to a number because of the dollar sign, comma, and period; it returns the error ORA-1722: invalid number. Query 2 matches the dollar symbol, comma, and period from the string to the format mask, and although the numeric width is larger than the string width, the number 1000.55 is returned.

 EXAM TIP The TO_NUMBER function converts character items into numbers. If you convert a number using a shorter format mask, an error is returned. If you convert a number using a longer format mask, the original number is returned. Be careful not to confuse TO_NUMBER conversions with TO_CHAR. For example, TO_NUMBER(123.56,'999.9') returns an error, while TO_CHAR(123.56,'999.9') returns 123.6.

Apply Conditional Expressions in a SELECT Statement

Nested functions were introduced earlier, but we offer you a formal discussion of this concept in this section. We also describe conditional functions that work with NULL values and support conditional logic in expressions.

Nested Functions

Nested functions use the output from one function as the input to another. Functions always return exactly one result. Therefore, you can reliably consider a function call in the same way as you would a literal value, when providing input parameters to a function. Single-row functions can be nested to any level of depth. The general form of a function is

```
Function1(parameter1, parameter2,...) = result1
```

Substituting function calls as parameters to other functions may lead to an expression such as

```
F1( param1.1, F2( param2.1, param2.2, F3( param3.1)), param1.3)
```

Nested functions are first evaluated before their return values are used as parametric input to other functions. They are evaluated from the innermost to outermost levels. The preceding expression is evaluated as follows:

1. F3(*param3.1*) is evaluated, and its return value provides the third parameter to function F2 and may be called *param2.3*.

2. F2(*param2.1, param2.2, param2..3*) is evaluated, and its return value provides the second parameter to function F1 and is *param1.2*.

3. F1(*param1.1, param1.2, param1.3*) is evaluated, and the result is returned to the calling program.

Function F3 is nested three levels deep in this example.
Consider the following query:

```
select next_day(last_day(sysdate)-7, 'tue') from dual;
```

There are three functions in the SELECT list, which, from inner to outer levels, are SYSDATE, LAST_DAY, and NEXT_DAY. The query is evaluated as follows:

1. The innermost function is evaluated first. SYSDATE returns the current date. Assume that today's date is 28-OCT-2009.

2. The second innermost function is evaluated next. LAST_DAY('28-OCT-2009') returns the date of the last day in October, which is 31-OCT-2009.

Finally, the NEXT_DAY('24-OCT-2009', 'tue') function is evaluated, and the query returns the number of the last Tuesday of the month, which in this example is 27-OCT-2009.

TIP It is tempting to dive in and construct a complex expression comprising many nested function calls, but this approach evolves with practice and experience. Conceptualize a solution to a query and break it down into the component function calls. The DUAL table is useful for ad hoc testing and debugging of separate function calls. Test and debug smaller components and iteratively assemble these until the final expression is formed.

Conditional Functions

Conditional logic, also known as *if-then-else* logic, refers to choosing a path of execution based on data values meeting certain conditions. *Conditional functions* return different values based on evaluating comparison conditions. Functions within this category simplify working with null values and include the *NVL, NVL2, NULLIF,* and *COALESCE* functions. Generic conditional logic is implemented by the DECODE function and the CASE expression. The DECODE function is specific to Oracle, while the CASE expression is ANSI SQL compliant.

The NVL Function

The NVL function evaluates whether a column or expression of any data type is null. If the term is null, it returns an alternative not-null value; otherwise, the original term is returned.

The NVL function takes two mandatory parameters; its syntax is *NVL(original, ifnull)*, where *original* represents the term being tested and *ifnull* is the result returned if the *original* term evaluates to null. The data types of the *original* and *ifnull* parameters must always be compatible. Either they must be of the same type, or it must be possible to implicitly convert *ifnull* to the type of the *original* parameter. The NVL function returns a value with the same data type as the *original* parameter. Consider the following three queries:

Query 1: `select nvl(1234) from dual;`
Query 2: `select nvl(null, 1234) from dual;`
Query 3: `select nvl(substr('abc', 4), 'No substring exists')`
`from dual;`

Since the NVL function takes two mandatory parameters, query 1 returns the error ORA-00909: invalid number of arguments. Query 2 returns 1234 after the null keyword is tested and found to be null. Query 3 involves a nested SUBSTR function that attempts to extract the fourth character from a three-character string that returns null, leaving the outer function NVL(null,'No substring exists') to execute, which then returns the string 'No substring exists'.

 TIP The NVL function is invaluable for converting null numeric values to zero, so that arithmetic on them doesn't return null.

The NVL2 Function

The NVL2 function provides an enhancement to NVL but serves a very similar purpose. It evaluates whether a column or expression of any data type is null or not. If the first term is not null, the second parameter is returned, or else the third parameter is returned. Recall that the NVL function is different, since it returns the original term if it is not null.

The NVL2 function takes three mandatory parameters with the syntax NVL2(*original, ifnotnull, ifnull*), where *original* represents the term being tested. *ifnotnull* is returned if *original* is not null, and *ifnull* is returned if *original* is null. The data types of the *ifnotnull* and *ifnull* parameters must be compatible, and they cannot be of type LONG. Either they must be of the same type, or it must be possible to convert *ifnull* to the type of the *ifnotnull* parameter. The data type returned by the NVL2 function is the same as that of the *ifnotnull* parameter. Consider the following queries:

```
Query 1: select nvl2(1234, 1, 'a string') from dual;
Query 2: select nvl2(null, 1234, 5678) from dual;
Query 3: select nvl2(substr('abc', 2), 'Not bc', 'No
substring') from dual;
```

The *ifnotnull* term in query 1 is a number, and the *ifnull* parameter is a string. Since there is a data type incompatibility between them, an "ORA-01722: invalid number" error is returned. Query 2 returns the *ifnull* parameter, which is 5678. Query 3 extracts the characters "bc" using the SUBSTR function and the NVL2('bc','Not bc','No Substring') function is evaluated and the *ifnotnull* parameter, 'Not bc', is returned.

The NULLIF Function

The NULLIF function tests two terms for equality. If they are equal, the function returns a null, or else it returns the first of the two terms tested.

The NULLIF function takes two mandatory parameters of any data type. Its syntax is NULLIF(*ifunequal, comparison_term*), where the parameters *ifunequal* and *comparison_term* are compared. If they are identical, then NULL is returned. If they differ, the *ifunequal* parameter is returned. Consider the following queries:

```
Query 1: select nullif(1234, 1234) from dual;
Query 2: select nullif('24-JUL-2009', '24-JUL-09') from dual;
```

Query 1 returns a null, since the parameters are identical. The character literals in query 2 are not implicitly converted to DATE items and are compared as two character strings by the NULLIF function. Since the strings are of different lengths, the *ifunequal* parameter 24-JUL-2009 is returned.

Figure 10-4 shows how NULLIF is nested as a parameter to the NVL2 function. The NULLIF function itself has the SUBSTR and UPPER character functions embedded in the expression used as its *ifunequal* parameter. The EMAIL column is compared with an expression, formed by concatenating the first character of the FIRST_NAME to the uppercase equivalent of the LAST_NAME column, for employees with four-character-long first names. When these terms are equal, NULLIF returns a null, or else it returns the evaluated *ifunequal* parameter. This is used as a parameter to NVL2. The NVL2 function provides descriptive text classifying rows as matching the pattern or not.

The COALESCE Function

The COALESCE function returns the first not-null value from its parameter list. If all its parameters are null, then null is returned.

The COALESCE function takes two mandatory parameters and any number of optional parameters. The syntax is COALESCE(*expr1, expr2, . . . , exprn*), where *expr1* is returned if it is not null, else *expr2* if it is not null, and so on. COALESCE is a general form of the NVL function, as the following two equations illustrate:

```
COALESCE(expr1, expr2) = NVL(expr1, expr2)
COALESCE(expr1,expr2,expr3) = NVL(expr1,NVL(expr2,expr3))
```

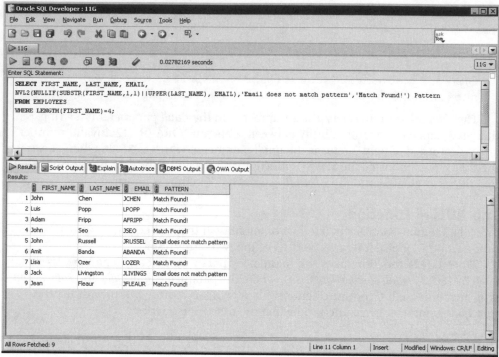

Figure 10-4   The NVL2 and NULLIF functions

The data type returned by COALESCE, if a not-null value is found, is the same as that of the first not-null parameter. To avoid an "ORA-00932: inconsistent data types" error, all not-null parameters must have data types compatible with the first not-null parameter. Consider the following three queries:

Query 1: `select coalesce(null, null, null, 'a string') from dual;`
Query 2: `select coalesce(null, null, null) from dual;`
Query 3: `select coalesce(substr('abc', 4), 'Not bc', 'No substring') from dual;`

Query 1 returns the fourth parameter: a string, since this is the first not-null parameter encountered. Query 2 returns null because all its parameters are null. Query 3 evaluates its first parameter, which is a nested SUBSTR function, and finds it to be null. The second parameter is not null, so the string 'Not bc' is returned.

EXAM TIP The parameters of the general function NVL2 can be confusing if you are already familiar with NVL. NVL(*original, ifnull*) returns *original* if it is not null, or else *ifnull* is returned. The NVL2(*original, ifnotnull, ifnull*) function returns *ifnotnull* if *original* is not null, or else *ifnull* is returned. The confusion may arise because the second parameter in the NVL function is *ifnull,* while the second parameter in the NVL2 function is *ifnotnull.* Be mindful of the meaning of the parameter positions in functions.

The DECODE Function

The DECODE function implements *if-then-else* conditional logic by testing its first two terms for equality and returns the third if they are equal and optionally returns another term if they are not.

The DECODE function takes at least three mandatory parameters, but it can take many more. The syntax of the function is DECODE(*expr1, comp1, iftrue1, [comp2, iftrue2 . . . [compN, iftrueN]], [iffalse]*). These parameters are evaluated as shown in the following pseudocode example:

```
If expr1 = comp1 then return iftrue1
    else if expr1 = comp2 then return iftrue2
         . . .
         . . .
            else if expr1 = compN then return iftrueN
    else return null | iffalse;
```

Here, *expr1* is compared with *comp1*. If they are equal, then *iftrue1* is returned. If *expr1* is not equal to *comp1*, then what happens next depends on whether the optional parameters *comp2* and *iftrue2* are present. If they are, then *expr1* is compared to *comp2*. If they are equal, then *iftrue2* is returned. If not, what happens next depends on whether further *compn, iftrueN* pairs exist, and the cycle continues until no comparison terms remain. If no matches have been found and if the *iffalse* parameter is defined, then *iffalse* is returned. If the *iffalse* parameter does not exist and no matches are found, a null is returned.

All parameters to the DECODE function may be expressions. The return data type is the same as that of the first matching comparison item. The expression *expr1* is implicitly converted to the data type of the first comparison parameter *comp1*. As the other comparison parameters *comp2 . . . compn* are evaluated, they too are implicitly converted to the same data type as *comp1*. DECODE considers two nulls to be equivalent, so if *expr1* is null and *comp3* is the first null comparison parameter encountered, then the corresponding result parameter *iftrue3* is returned. Consider the following queries:

Query 1: select decode(1234, 123, '123 is a match') from dual;
Query 2: select decode(1234, 123, '123 is a match', 'No match') from dual;
Query 3: select decode('search', 'comp1', 'true1', 'comp2', 'true2', 'search', 'true3', substr('2search', 2, 6), 'true4', 'false') from dual;

Query 1 compares the number 1234 with the first comparison term 123. Since they are not equal, the first result term cannot be returned. Further, as there is no default *iffalse* parameter defined, a null is returned. Query 2 is identical to the first except that an *iffalse* parameter is defined. Therefore, since 1234 is not equal to 123, the string 'No match' is returned. Query 3 searches through the comparison parameters for a match. The strings comp1 and comp2 are not equal to search, so the results true1 and true2 are not returned. A match is found in the third comparison term *comp3* (parameter 6), which contains the string search. Therefore, the third result term *iftrue3* (parameter 7) containing the string 'true3' is returned. Note that since a match has been found, no further searching takes place. So, although the fourth comparison term (parameter 8) is also a match to *expr1*, this expression is never evaluated, because a match was found in an earlier comparison term.

The CASE Expression

Virtually all third- and fourth-generation programming languages implement a *case* construct. Like the DECODE function, the CASE expression facilitates *if-then-else* conditional logic. There are two variants of the CASE expression. The *simple* CASE expression lists the conditional search item once, and equality to the search item is tested by each comparison expression. The *searched* CASE expression lists a separate condition for each comparison expression.

The CASE expression takes at least three mandatory parameters but can take many more. Its syntax depends on whether a simple or a searched CASE expression is used. The syntax for the simple CASE expression is as follows:

```
CASE search_expr
 WHEN comparison_expr1 THEN iftrue1
 [WHEN comparison_expr2 THEN iftrue2
 ...
 WHEN comparison_exprN THEN iftrueN
 ELSE iffalse]
END
```

The simple CASE expression is enclosed within a CASE . . . END block and consists of at least one WHEN . . . THEN statement. In its simplest form, with one WHEN . . . THEN statement, the *search_expr* is compared with the *comparison_expr1*. If they are equal, then the result *iftrue1* is returned. If not, a null value is returned unless an ELSE component is defined, in which case, the default *iffalse* value is returned. When more than one WHEN . . . THEN statement exists in the CASE expression, searching for a matching comparison expression continues until a match is found.

The search, comparison, and result parameters can be column values, expressions, or literals but must all be of the same data type. Consider the following query:

```
select
 case substr(1234, 1, 3)
  when '134' then '1234 is a match'
  when '1235' then '1235 is a match'
  when concat('1', '23') then concat('1', '23')||' is a match'
  else 'no match'
 end
from dual;
```

The search expression derived from the SUBSTR(1234, 1, 3) is the character string 123. The first WHEN . . . THEN statement compares the string 134 with 123. Since they are not equal, the result expression is not evaluated. The second WHEN . . . THEN statement compares the string 1235 with 123 and, again, they are not equal. The third WHEN . . . THEN statement compares the results derived from the CONCAT('1','23') expression, which is 123, to the search expression. Since they are identical, the third results expression, '123 is a match', is returned.

The LAST_NAME and HIRE_DATE columns for employees with DEPARTMENT_ID values of 10 or 60 are retrieved along with two numeric expressions and one CASE expression, as shown in Figure 10-5.

Assume that SYSDATE is 01-JAN-2008. The numeric expression aliased as YEARS returns a truncated value obtained by dividing the months of service by 12. Five categories of loyalty classification based on years of service are defined by truncating the quotient obtained by dividing the months of service by 60. This forms the search expression in the CASE statement. None of the rows in the dataset matches the comparison expression in the first WHEN . . . THEN statement, but as Figure 10-5 shows, five rows met the remaining WHEN . . . THEN statements and one row is caught by the ELSE statement.

The syntax for the searched CASE expression is as follows:

```
CASE
 WHEN condition1 THEN iftrue1
 [WHEN condition2 THEN iftrue2
 ...
 WHEN conditionN THEN iftrueN
 ELSE iffalse]
END
```

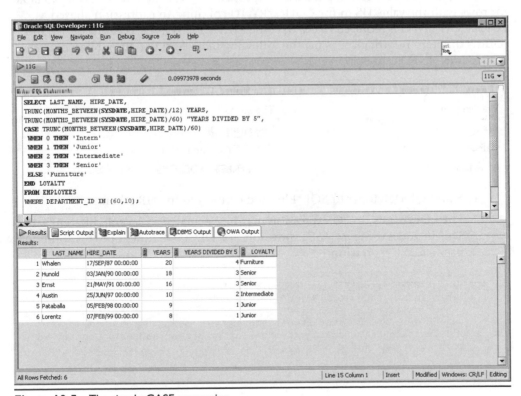

Figure 10-5 The simple CASE expression

The searched CASE expression is enclosed within a CASE . . . END block and consists of at least one WHEN . . . THEN statement. In its simplest form with one WHEN . . . THEN statement, *condition1* is evaluated; if it is true, then the result *iftrue1* is returned. If not, a null value is returned unless an ELSE component is defined, in which case the default *iffalse* value is returned. When more than one WHEN . . . THEN statement exists in the CASE expression, searching for a matching comparison expression continues until one is found. The query to retrieve the identical set of results to those obtained in Figure 10-5, using a searched CASE expression, is

```
select last_name, hire_date,
trunc(months_between(sysdate, hire_date)/12) years,
trunc(months_between(sysdate, hire_date)/60) "Years divided by 5",
case
 when trunc(months_between(sysdate, hire_date)/60) < 1 then 'Intern'
 when trunc(months_between(sysdate, hire_date)/60) < 2 then 'Junior'
 when trunc(months_between(sysdate, hire_date)/60) < 3 then 'Intermediate'
 when trunc(months_between(sysdate, hire_date)/60) < 4 then 'Senior'
 else 'Furniture'
end Loyalty
from employees
where department_id in (60,10);
```

Exercise 10-3: Use the DECODE Function   Query the HR.LOCATIONS table for rows with the value US in the COUNTRY_ID column. An expression aliased as LOCATION_INFO is required to evaluate the STATE_PROVINCE column values and returns different information as per the following table. Sort the output based on the LOCATION_INFO expression.

If STATE_PROVINCE Is	The Value Returned Is
Washington	The string 'Headquarters'
Texas	The string 'Oil Wells'
California	The CITY column value
New Jersey	The STREET_ADDRESS column value

1. Start SQL Developer or SQL*Plus and connect to the HR schema.

2. The LOCATION_INFO expression may be calculated in several different ways. This includes using a CASE expression or a DECODE function. This solution uses a CASE expression:

```
select case state_province
 when 'Washington' then 'Headquarters'
 when'Texas' then 'Oil Wells'
 when 'California' then city
 when 'New Jersey' then street_address
end location_info, state_province, city, street_address, country_id
from locations where country_id='US' order by location_info;
```

Two-Minute Drill

Describe Various Types of Functions Available in SQL

- Functions accept zero or more input parameters but always return one result of a predetermined data type.
- Single-row functions execute once for each row selected, while multiple-row functions execute once for the entire set of rows queried.
- Character functions are either case-conversion or character-manipulation functions.

Use Character, Number, and Date Functions in SELECT Statements

- The INITCAP function accepts a string of characters and returns each word in title case.
- The function that computes the number of characters in a string, including spaces and special characters, is the LENGTH function.
- The INSTR function returns the positional location of the nth occurrence of a specified string of characters in a source string.
- The SUBSTR function extracts and returns a segment from a given source string.
- The REPLACE function substitutes each occurrence of a search item in the source string with a replacement term and returns the modified source string.
- A modulus operation returns the remainder of a division operation and is available via the MOD function.
- The numeric ROUND function rounds numbers either up or down to the specified degree of precision.
- The SYSDATE function is commonly executed against the DUAL table and returns the current date and time of the database server.
- The difference between two date items is always a number that represents the number of days between these two items.
- The MONTHS_BETWEEN function computes the number of months between two given date parameters and is based on a 31-day month.
- The LAST_DAY function is used to obtain the last day in a month given any valid date item.

Describe Various Types of Conversion Functions Available in SQL

- Explicit conversion occurs when a function like TO_CHAR is invoked to change the data type of a value. The TO_CHAR function performs date to character and number to character data type conversions.

- Character items are explicitly transformed into date values using the TO_DATE conversion function.

- Character items are changed into number values using the TO_NUMBER conversion function.

Use the TO_CHAR, TO_NUMBER, and TO_DATE Conversion Functions

- The TO_CHAR function returns an item of type VARCHAR2.

- Format models or masks prescribe patterns that character strings must match to facilitate accurate and consistent conversion into number or date items.

- Character terms, like month and day names, extracted from dates with the TO_CHAR function are automatically padded with spaces that may be trimmed by prefixing the format mask with the *fm* modifier.

- The TO_DATE function has an *fx* modifier that specifies an exact match for the character string to be converted and the date format mask.

Apply Conditional Expressions in a SELECT Statement

- Nested functions use the output from one function as the input to another.

- The NVL function returns either the original item unchanged or an alternative item if the initial term is null.

- The NVL2 function returns a new *if-null* item if the original item is null or an alternative *if-not-null* item if the original term is not null.

- The NULLIF function tests two terms for equality. If they are equal, the function returns null, or else it returns the first of the two terms tested.

- The COALESCE function returns the first not-null value from its parameter list. If all its parameters are null, then a null is returned.

- The DECODE function and the simple CASE and searched CASE expressions are used to facilitate *if-then-else* conditional logic.

Self Test

1. Which statements regarding single-row functions are true? (Choose all that apply.)

   A. They may return more than one value.

B. They execute once for each row processed.

C. They may have zero or more input parameters.

D. They must have at least one mandatory parameter.

2. What value is returned after executing the following statement:
```
SELECT SUBSTR('How_long_is_a_piece_of_string?', 5, 4)
FROM DUAL;
```
(Choose the best answer.)

A. long

B. _long

C. ring?

D. None of the above

3. What value is returned after executing the following statement:
```
SELECT INSTR('How_long_is_a_piece_of_string?','_', 5, 3)
FROM DUAL;
```
(Choose the best answer.)

A. 4

B. 14

C. 12

D. None of the above

4. What value is returned after executing the following statement:
```
SELECT MOD(14, 3) FROM DUAL;
```
(Choose the best answer.)

A. 3

B. 42

C. 2

D. None of the above

5. What value is returned after executing the following statement? Take note that 01-JAN-2009 occurred on a Thursday.
```
SELECT NEXT_DAY('01-JAN-2009', 'wed') FROM DUAL;
```
(Choose the best answer.)

A. 07-JAN-2009

B. 31-JAN-2009

C. Wednesday

D. None of the above

6. Assuming SYSDATE=30-DEC-2007, what value is returned after executing the following statement:
   ```
   SELECT TRUNC(SYSDATE, 'YEAR') FROM DUAL;
   ```
   (Choose the best answer.)

   A. 31-DEC-2007

   B. 01-JAN-2008

   C. 01-JAN-2007

   D. None of the above

7. Choose any incorrect statements regarding conversion functions. (Choose all that apply.)

   A. TO_CHAR may convert date items to character items.

   B. TO_DATE may convert character items to date items.

   C. TO_CHAR may convert numbers to character items.

   D. TO_DATE may convert date items to character items.

8. If SYSDATE returns 12-JUL-2009, what is returned by the following statement?
   ```
   SELECT TO_CHAR(SYSDATE, 'fmDDth MONTH') FROM DUAL;
   ```
   (Choose the best answer.)

   A. 12TH JULY

   B. 12th July

   C. TWELFTH JULY

   D. None of the above

9. What value is returned after executing the following statement?
   ```
   SELECT NVL2(NULLIF('CODA', 'SID'), 'SPANIEL', 'TERRIER')
   FROM DUAL;
   ```
   (Choose the best answer.)

   A. SPANIEL

   B. TERRIER

   C. NULL

   D. None of the above

10. If SYSDATE returns 12-JUL-2009, what is returned by the following statement?
    ```
    SELECT DECODE(TO_CHAR(SYSDATE, 'MM'), '02', 'TAX DUE',
    'PARTY') FROM DUAL;
    ```
    (Choose the best answer.)

    A. TAX DUE

    B. PARTY

    C. 02

    D. None of the above

Self Test Answers

1. ☑ **B and C.** Single-row functions execute once for every record selected in a dataset and may take either no input parameters, like SYSDATE, or many input parameters.

   ☒ **A and D.** A function by definition returns only one result and there are many functions with no parameters.

2. ☑ **A.** The SUBSTR function extracts a four-character substring from the given input string starting with and including the fifth character. The characters at positions 1 to 4 are "How_". Starting with the character at position 5, the next four characters form the word "long".

   ☒ **B, C, and D.** B is a five-character substring beginning at position 4, while "ring?", which is also five characters long, starts five characters from the end of the given string.

3. ☑ **B.** The INSTR function returns the position that the *n*th occurrence of the search string may be found after starting the search from a given start position. The search string is the underscore character, and the third occurrence of this character starting from position 5 in the source string occurs at position 14.

   ☒ **A, C, and D.** Since position 4 is the first occurrence of the search string and position 12 is the third occurrence if the search began at position 1.

4. ☑ **C.** When 14 is divided by 3, the answer is 4 with remainder 2.

   ☒ **A, B, and D.**

5. ☑ **A.** Since the first of January 2009 falls on a Thursday, the date of the following Wednesday is six days later.

   ☒ **B, C, and D.** B returns the last day of the month in which the given date falls, and C returns a character string instead of a date.

6. ☑ **C.** The date TRUNC function does not perform rounding, and since the degree of truncation is YEAR, the day and month components of the given date are ignored and the first day of the year it belongs to is returned.

   ☒ **A, B, and D.** A returns the last day in the month in which the given date occurs, and B returns a result achieved by rounding instead of truncation.

7. ☑ **D.** Dates are only converted into character strings using TO_CHAR, not the TO_DATE function.

   ☒ **A, B, and C.** A, B, and C are correct statements.

8. ☑ **A.** The DD component returns the day of the month in uppercase. Since it is a number, it does not matter, unless the 'th' mask is applied, in which case that component is specified in uppercase. MONTH returns the month spelled out in uppercase.

☒ **B, C,** and **D.** B would be returned if the format mask was 'fmddth Month', and C would be returned if the format mask was 'fmDDspth MONTH'.

9. ☑ **A.** The NULLIF function compares its two parameters, and since they are different, the first parameter is returned. The NVL2('CODA', 'SPANIEL','TERRIER') function call returns SPANIEL, since its first parameter is not null.

☒ **B, C,** and **D.**

10. ☑ **B.** The innermost function TO_CHAR(SYSDATE, 'MM') results in the character string '07' being returned. The outer function is DECODE('07','02','TAX DUE','PARTY'). Since '07' is not equal to '02', the else component 'PARTY' is returned.

☒ **A, C,** and **D.** A would only be returned if the month component extracted from SYSDATE was '02'.

CHAPTER 11

Group Functions

Exam Objectives

In this chapter you will learn to

- 051.5.1 Identify the Available Group Functions
- 051.5.2 Describe the Use of Group Functions
- 051.5.3 Group Data by Using the GROUP BY Clause
- 051.5.4 Include or Exclude Grouped Rows by Using the HAVING Clause

Single-row functions, explored in Chapter 10, return a single value for each row in a set of results. *Group* or *aggregate* functions operate on multiple rows. They are used to count the number of rows or to find the average of specific column values in a dataset. Many statistical operations, such as calculating standard deviation, medians, and averages, depend on executing functions against grouped data and not just single rows.

You will examine group functions in two stages. A discussion of their purpose and syntax precedes a detailed analysis of the AVG, SUM, MIN, MAX, and COUNT functions. Grouping or segregating data based on one or more column values is examined before the *GROUP BY* clause is introduced. The WHERE clause restricts rows in a dataset before grouping, while the *HAVING* clause restricts them after grouping. This chapter concludes with a discussion of the HAVING clause.

The Group Functions

This section defines SQL *group functions* and discusses the different variants. The syntax and examples demonstrating the selected group functions are provided along with a discussion of their data types and the effect of the DISTINCT keyword and null values.

Definition of Group Functions

Group functions operate on aggregated data and return a single result per group. These groups usually consist of zero or more rows of data. Single-row functions are defined with the formula: $F(x, y, z, \ldots) = result$, where $x, y, z \ldots$ are input parameters. The function F executes on one row of the dataset at a time and returns a result for each row. Group functions may be defined using the following formula:

$$F(g1, g2, g3, \ldots, gn) = result1, result2, result2, \ldots, resultn;$$

The group function executes once for each cluster of rows and returns a single result per group. These rows within these groups are associated using a common value or attribute. If a table is presented as one group to the *group function* in its entirety, then one result is returned. One or more group functions may appear in the SELECT list as follows:

```
SELECT group_function(column or expression),...
FROM table [WHERE ...] [ORDER BY...]
```

Consider the EMPLOYEES table. There are 107 rows in this table. Groups may be created based on the common values that rows share. For example, the rows that share the same DEPARTMENT_ID value may be clustered together. Thereafter, *group functions* are executed separately against each unique group.

Figure 11-1 shows 12 distinct DEPARTMENT_ID values in the EMPLOYEES table, including a null value. The rows are distributed into 12 groups based on common DEPARTMENT_ID values. The *COUNT* function executes 12 times, once for each group. Notice that the distinct groups do not contain the same number of rows.

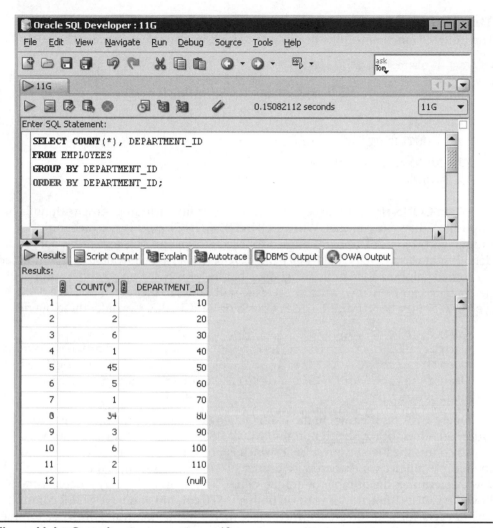

Figure II-I   Group functions operating on 12 groups

 TIP *Group functions* aggregate a number of values from multiple rows into a single result. They are widely used for reporting purposes, providing sum totals, averages, and counts. They are also known as summary or aggregate functions.

Using Group Functions

AVG, SUM, MIN, MAX, and COUNT demonstrate the practical application of *group functions*. These group functions all return numeric results. Additionally, the MIN and MAX functions may return character and date results. These functions operate on non-null values, but unlike the others, the COUNT function call also counts rows with null values under certain conditions.

The COUNT Function

The *COUNT* function counts the number of rows in a group. Its syntax is

```
COUNT({*|[DISTINCT|ALL] expr}) ;
```

This syntax may be deconstructed into the following forms:

1. COUNT(*)
2. COUNT(DISTINCT expr)
3. COUNT(ALL expr)
4. COUNT(expr)

When COUNT(*) is invoked, all rows in the group, including those with nulls or duplicate values, are counted. When COUNT(DISTINCT *expr*) is executed, only unique occurrences of *expr* are counted for each group. The ALL keyword is part of the default syntax, so COUNT(ALL *expr*) and COUNT(*expr*) are equivalent. If *expr* is based on named columns, then nulls are ignored, but if *expr* is based on anything else, it will be evaluated for every row, whether there are null values in the row or not. The data type of *expr* may be NUMBER, DATE, CHAR, or VARCHAR2. Consider these queries:

Query 1: `select count(*) from employees;`
Query 2: `select count(commission_pct), count(1) from employees;`
Query 3: `select count(distinct commission_pct) from employees;`
Query 4: `select count(hire_date), count(manager_id) from employees;`

Query 1 counts the rows in the EMPLOYEES table and returns the integer 107. Query 2 counts the rows with non-null COMMISSION_PCT values and returns 35. It also counts the literal expression 1, which is not based on a named column and is therefore evaluated for every row, returning 107. Query 3 considers the 35 non-null rows, determines the number of unique values, and returns 7. Query 4 demonstrates how the COUNT function is used on both a DATE column and a NUMBER column. The integers 107 and 106 are returned, since there are 107 non-null HIRE_DATE values and 106 non-null MANAGER_ID values in the group.

The SUM Function

The *SUM* function returns the aggregated total of the non-null numeric values in a group. It has this syntax:

```
SUM([DISTINCT|ALL] expr) ;
```

This syntax may be deconstructed into the following forms:

1. SUM(DISTINCT expr)
2. SUM(ALL expr)
3. SUM(expr)

SUM(DISTINCT *expr*) provides a total by adding all the unique values returned after *expr* is evaluated for each row in the group. SUM(*expr*) and SUM(ALL *expr*) provide a total by adding *expr* for each row in the group. Null values are ignored. The *expr* parameter must be a numeric value. Consider the following queries:

Query 1: `select sum(2) from employees;`
Query 2: `select sum(salary) from employees;`
Query 3: `select sum(distinct salary) from employees;`
Query 4: `select sum(commission_pct) from employees;`

There are 107 rows in the EMPLOYEES table. Query 1 adds the number 2 across 107 rows and returns 214. Query 2 takes the SALARY column value for every row in the group, which in this case is the entire table, and returns the total salary amount of 691400. Query 3 returns a total of 397900, since many employees get paid the same salary and the DISTINCT keyword only adds unique values in the column to the total. Query 4 returns 7.8 after adding the non-null COMMISSION_PCT values.

The AVG Function

The *average* value of a column or expression is obtained by dividing the sum by the number of non-null rows in the group. The *AVG* function has this syntax:

```
AVG([DISTINCT|ALL] expr) ;
```

This syntax may be deconstructed into the following forms:

1. `AVG(DISTINCT expr)`
2. `AVG(ALL expr)`
3. `AVG(expr)`

When AVG(DISTINCT *expr*) is invoked, the distinct values of *expr* are summed and divided by the number of unique occurrences of *expr*. AVG(ALL *expr*) and AVG(*expr*) add the non-null values of *expr* for each row and divide the sum by the number of non-null rows in the group. The *expr* parameter must be a numeric value. Consider the queries:

Query 1: `select avg(2) from employees;`
Query 2: `select avg(salary) from employees;`
Query 3: `select avg(distinct salary) from employees;`
Query 4: `select avg(commission_pct) from employees;`

There are 107 rows in the EMPLOYEES table. Query 1 adds the number 2 across 107 rows and divides the total by the number of rows to return the number 2. Numeric literals submitted to the AVG function are returned unchanged. Query 2 adds the SALARY value for each row to obtain the total salary amount of 691400, which is divided by the rows with non-null SALARY values (107) to return the average 6461.68224. There are 57 unique salary values, which when added, yield a total of 397900. Dividing 397900 by 57 returns 6980.70175 as the average of the distinct salary values, which is returned by the third query. Adding the non-null COMMISSION_PCT values produces a total of 7.8. Dividing this by the employee records with non-null COMMISSION_PCT values (35) yields 0.222857143, which is returned by query 4.

The MAX and MIN Functions

The *MAX* and *MIN* functions return the maximum (largest) and minimum (smallest) *expr* value in a group. The MAX and MIN functions operate on NUMBER, DATE, CHAR, and VARCHAR2 data types. They return a value of the same data type as their input arguments, which are either the largest or smallest items in the group. When applied to DATE items, MAX returns the latest date and MIN returns the earliest one. Character strings are converted to numeric representations of their constituent characters based on the NLS settings in the database. When the MIN function is applied to a group of character strings, the word that appears first alphabetically is returned, while MAX returns the word that would appear last. The MAX and MIN functions have this syntax:

```
MAX([DISTINCT|ALL] expr); MIN([DISTINCT|ALL] expr)
```

This syntax may be deconstructed into the following forms:

1. MAX(DISTINCT expr); MIN(DISTINCT expr)
2. MAX(ALL expr); MIN(ALL expr)
3. MAX(expr); MIN(expr);

MAX(*expr*), MAX(ALL *expr*), and MAX(DISTINCT *expr*) examine the values for *expr* in a group of rows and return the largest value. Null values are ignored. MIN(*expr*), MIN(ALL *expr*), and MIN(DISTINCT *expr*) examine the values for *expr* in a group of rows and return the smallest value. Consider these queries:

Query 1: select min(commission_pct), max(commission_pct) from employees
Query 2: select min(start_date),max(end_date) from job_history
Query 3: select min(job_id),max(job_id) from employees

Query 1 returns 0.1 and 0.4 for the minimum and maximum COMMISSION_PCT values in the EMPLOYEES table. Notice that null values for COMMISSION_PCT are ignored. Query 2 evaluates a DATE column and indicates that the earliest START_DATE in the JOB_HISTORY table is 17-SEP-1987 and the latest END_DATE is 31-DEC-1999. Query 3 returns AC_ACCOUNT and ST_MAN as the JOB_ID values appearing first and last alphabetically in the EMPLOYEES table.

 EXAM TIP There are two fundamental rules to remember when studying group functions. First, they always operate on a single group of rows at a time. The group may be one of many groups a dataset has been segmented into, or it may be an entire table. The group function executes once per group. Second, rows with nulls occurring in group columns or expressions are ignored by all group functions, except the COUNT(*) form of the COUNT function.

Exercise 11-1: Use the Group Functions   The COUNTRIES table stores a list of COUNTRY_NAME values. You are required to calculate the average length of all the country names. Any fractional components must be rounded to the nearest whole number.

1. Start SQL*Plus or SQL Developer and connect to the HR schema.

2. The length of the country name value for each row is to be calculated using the LENGTH function. The average length may be determined using the AVG function. It may be rounded to the nearest whole number using the ROUND function. A possible solution is

```
select round(avg(length(country_name))) average_country_name_length
from countries;
```

3. Executing this statement shows that the average length of all the country names in the COUNTRIES table is eight characters.

Group Data Using the GROUP BY Clause

The *group functions* discussed earlier use groups of rows making up the entire table. This section explores partitioning a set of data into groups using the *GROUP BY* clause. Group functions may be applied to these subsets or clusters of rows.

Creating Groups of Data

A table has at least one column and zero or more rows of data. In many tables data requires analysis to transform it into useful information. It is a common reporting requirement to calculate statistics from a set of data divided into groups using different attributes. Previous examples using group functions operated against all the rows in a table. The entire table was treated as one large group. Groups of data within a set are created by associating rows with common attributes with each other. Thereafter, group functions can execute against each of these groups. Groups of data include entire rows and not specific columns.

Consider the EMPLOYEES table. It comprises 11 columns and 107 rows. You could create groups of rows that share a common DEPARTMENT_ID value. The SUM function may then be used to create salary totals per department. Another possible set of groups may share common JOB_ID column values. The AVG group function may then be used to identify the average salary paid to employees in different jobs.

A group is defined as a subset of the entire dataset sharing one or more common attributes. These attributes are typically column values but may also be expressions. The number of groups created depends on the distinct values present in the common attribute.

As Figure 11-2 shows, there are 12 unique DEPARTMENT_ID values in the EMPLOYEES table. If rows are grouped using common DEPARTMENT_ID values, there will be 12 groups. If a group function is executed against these groups, there will be 12 values returned, as it will execute once for each group.

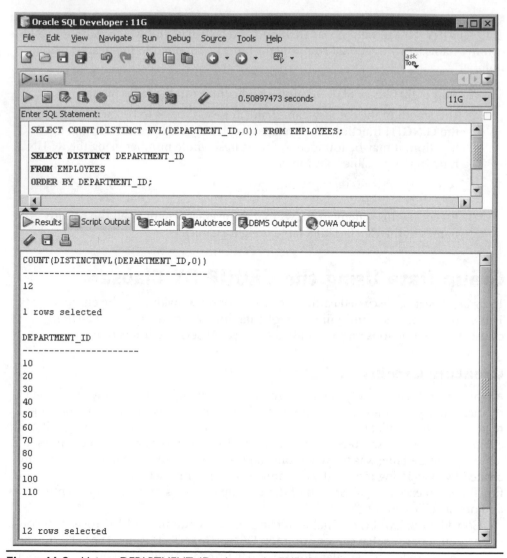

Figure 11-2   Unique DEPARTMENT_ID values in the EMPLOYEES table

TIP   Grouping data and using summary functions are widely utilized for reporting purposes. It is valuable to practice the segmentation of a set of data into different groups. Oracle provides the analytical language to deconstruct datasets into groups, divide these into further subgroups, and so on. Aggregate grouping functions can then be executed against these groups and subgroups.

The GROUP BY Clause

The SELECT statement is enhanced by the addition of the GROUP BY clause. This clause facilitates the creation of groups. It appears after the WHERE clause but before the ORDER BY clause, as follows:

```
SELECT column|expression|group_function(column|expression [alias]),...}
FROM table
[WHERE condition(s)]
[GROUP BY {col(s)|expr}]
[ORDER BY {col(s)|expr|numeric_pos} [ASC|DESC] [NULLS FIRST|LAST]];
```

The column or expression specified in the GROUP BY clause is also known as the *grouping attribute* and is the component that rows are grouped by. The dataset is segmented according to the grouping attribute. Consider the following query:

```
select max(salary), count(*)
from employees
group by department_id
order by department_id;
```

The grouping attribute in this example is the DEPARTMENT_ID column. The dataset, on which the group functions in the SELECT list must operate, is divided into 12 groups, one for each department. For each group (department), the maximum salary value and the number of rows are returned. Since the results are sorted by DEPARTMENT_ID, the third row in the set of results contains the values 11000 and 6. This indicates that 6 employees have a DEPARTMENT_ID value of 30. Of these 6, the highest earner has a SALARY value of 11000. This query demonstrates that the grouping attribute does not have to be included in the SELECT list.

It is common to see the grouping attribute in the SELECT list alongside grouping functions. If an item that is not a group function appears in the SELECT list and there is no GROUP BY clause, an "ORA-00937: not a single-group group function" error is raised. If a GROUP BY clause is present but that item is not a grouping attribute, then an "ORA-00979: not a GROUP BY expression" error is returned.

 EXAM TIP Any item in the SELECT list that is not a group function must be a grouping attribute of the GROUP BY clause.

If a group function is placed in a WHERE clause, an "ORA-00934: group function is not allowed here" error is returned. Imposing group-level conditions is achieved using the HAVING clause discussed later in this chapter. Group functions may, however, be used as part of the ORDER BY clause.

The first query in Figure 11-3 raises an error because the END_DATE column is in the SELECT list with a group function and there is no GROUP BY clause. An ORA-00979 error is returned from the second query, since the START_DATE item is listed in the SELECT clause, but it is not a grouping attribute.

The third query divides the JOB_HISTORY rows into groups based on the four-digit year component from the END_DATE column. Four groups are created using this grouping attribute. These represent different years when employees ended their jobs. The COUNT shows the number of employees who quit their jobs during each of these years. The results are listed in descending order based on the "Number of Employees" expression. Note that the COUNT group function is present in the ORDER BY clause.

```
Command Prompt - SQLPLUS HR/HR                            _ □ ✕
SQL> SELECT   END_DATE ,COUNT(*)
  2  FROM JOB_HISTORY;
SELECT   END_DATE ,COUNT(*)
         *
ERROR at line 1:
ORA-00937: not a single-group group function


SQL> SELECT   END_DATE, START_DATE, COUNT(*)
  2  FROM JOB_HISTORY
  3  GROUP BY END_DATE;
SELECT   END_DATE, START_DATE, COUNT(*)
                   *
ERROR at line 1:
ORA-00979: not a GROUP BY expression


SQL> SELECT   TO_CHAR(END_DATE,'YYYY') "Year" ,
  2           COUNT(*) "Number of Employees"
  3  FROM JOB_HISTORY
  4  GROUP BY TO_CHAR(END_DATE,'YYYY')
  5  ORDER BY COUNT(*) DESC;

Year Number of Employees
---- -------------------
1999                   4
1998                   3
1993                   2
1997                   1
```

Figure 11-3 The GROUP BY clause

EXAM TIP A dataset is divided into groups using the GROUP BY clause. The grouping attribute is the common key shared by members of each group. The grouping attribute is usually a single column but may be multiple columns or an expression that cannot be based on group functions. Note that only grouping attributes and group functions are permitted in the SELECT clause when using GROUP BY.

Grouping by Multiple Columns

A powerful extension to the GROUP BY clause uses multiple grouping attributes. Oracle permits datasets to be partitioned into groups and allows these groups to be further divided into subgroups using a different grouping attribute. Consider the following two queries:

> *Query 1:* `select department_id, sum(commission_pct)`
> `from employees where commission_pct is not null`
> `group by department_id;`
> *Query 2:* `select department_id, job_id, sum(commission_pct)`
> `from employees where commission_pct is not null`
> `group by department_id, job_id;`

Query 1 restricts the rows returned from the EMPLOYEES table to the 35 rows with non-null COMMISSION_PCT values. These rows are then divided into two groups: 80 and NULL based on the DEPARTMENT_ID grouping attribute. The result set contains two rows, which return the sum of the COMMISSION_PCT values for each group.

Query 2 is similar to the first one except it has an additional item: JOB_ID in both the SELECT and GROUP BY clauses. This second grouping attribute decomposes the two groups by DEPARTMENT_ID into the constituent JOB_ID components belonging to the rows in each group. The distinct JOB_ID values for rows with DEPARTMENT_ID=80 are SA_REP and SA_MAN. The distinct JOB_ID value for rows with null DEPARTMENT_ID is SA_REP. Therefore, query 2 returns two groupings, one that consists of two subgroups, and the other with only one, as shown in Figure 11-4.

Exercise 11-2: Group Data Based on Multiple Columns   Analysis of staff turnover is a common reporting requirement. You are required to create a report that contains the number of employees who left their jobs, grouped by the year in which they left. The jobs they performed is also required. The results must be sorted in descending order based on the number of employees in each group. The report must list the year, the JOB_ID, and the number of employees who left a particular job in that year.

1. Start SQL Developer and connect to the HR schema.

2. The JOB_HISTORY table contains the END_DATE and JOB_ID columns, which constitute the source data for this report.

3. The year component may be extracted using the TO_CHAR function. The number of employees who quit a particular job in each year may be obtained using the COUNT(*) function.

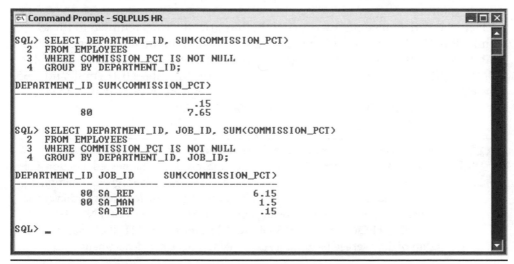

Figure 11-4   The GROUP BY clause with multiple columns

4. Executing the following statement returns the staff turnover report as requested:

```
select  to_char(end_date,'yyyy') "Quitting Year" ,job_id,
count(*) "Number of Employees"
from job_history
group by to_char(end_date,'yyyy'), job_id
order by count(*) desc;
```

Nested Group Functions

Recall that single-row functions may be nested or embedded to any level of depth. *Group functions may only be nested two levels deep.* Three formats using group functions are shown here:

G1(*group_item*) = result
G1(G2(*group_item*) = result
G1(G2(G3(*group_item*))) is NOT allowed.

Group functions are represented by the letter G followed by a number. The first simple form contains no nested functions. Examples include the SUM(*group_item*) or AVG(*group_item*) functions that return a single result per group. The second form supports two nested group functions, like SUM(AVG(*group_item*)). In this case, a GROUP BY clause is necessary because the average value of the *group_item* per group is calculated before being aggregated by the SUM function.

The third form is disallowed by Oracle. Consider an expression that nests three group functions. If the MAX function is applied to the previous example, the expression MAX(SUM(AVG(*group_item*))) is formed. The two inner group functions return a *single value* representing the sum of a set of average values. This expression becomes MAX(*single value*), which is not sensible, since a group function cannot be applied to a single value.

Figure 11-5 demonstrates two queries. Both restrict the rows returned to those with DEPARTMENT_ID values of null, 40, and 80. These are then partitioned by their DEPARTMENT_ID values into three groups. The first query calculates the sum of the COMMISSION_PCT values for each group and returns the values 0.15, null, and 7.65. Query 2 contains the nested group functions, which may be evaluated as follows: AVG(SUM(COMMISSION_PCT)) = (0.15 + 7.65) /2 = 3.9.

EXAM TIP Single-row functions may be nested to any level, but group functions may be nested to at most two levels deep. The nested function call COUNT(SUM(AVG(X))) returns the error "ORA-00935: group function is nested too deeply." It is acceptable to nest single-row functions within group functions. Consider the following query: SELECT SUM(AVG(LENGTH(LAST_NAME))) FROM EMPLOYEES GROUP BY DEPARTMENT_ID. It calculates the sum of the average length of LAST_NAME values per department.

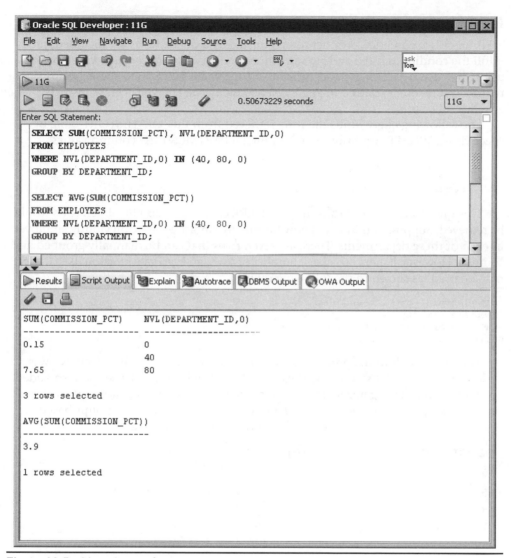

Figure 11-5 Nested group functions

Include or Exclude Grouped Rows Using the HAVING Clause

Creating groups of data and applying aggregate functions is very useful. A refinement to these features is the ability to include or exclude results based on group-level conditions. This section introduces the *HAVING* clause. A clear distinction is made between the WHERE clause and the HAVING clause.

Restricting Group Results

WHERE clause conditions restrict rows returned by a query. Rows are included if they fulfill the conditions listed and are sometimes known as *row-level results*. Clustering rows using the GROUP BY clause and applying an aggregate function to these groups returns results often referred to as *group-level results*. The HAVING clause restricts group-level results.

The following query limits the rows retrieved from the JOB_HISTORY table by specifying a WHERE condition based on the DEPARTMENT_ID column values.

```
select department_id
from job_history
where department_id in (50,60,80,110);
```

This query returns seven rows. If the WHERE clause were absent, all ten rows would be retrieved. Suppose you want to know how many employees were previously employed in each of these departments. There are seven rows that can be manually grouped and counted. However, if there are a large number of rows, an aggregate function like COUNT may be used, as shown in the following query:

```
select department_id, count(*)
from job_history
where department_id in (50,60,80,110)
group by department_id;
```

This query adds to the previous statement. The aggregate function COUNT was added to the SELECT list, and a GROUP BY DEPARTMENT_ID clause was also added. Four rows with their aggregate row count are returned, and it is clear that the original seven rows restricted by the WHERE clause were clustered into four groups based on common DEPARTMENT_ID values, as shown in the following table:

DEPARTMENT_ID	COUNT(*)
50	2
60	1
80	2
110	2

Suppose you wanted to restrict this list to only those departments with more than one employee. The HAVING clause limits or restricts the group-level rows as required. This query must perform the following steps:

1. Consider the entire row-level dataset.
2. Limit the dataset by any WHERE clause conditions.
3. Segment the data into one or more groups using the grouping attributes specified in the GROUP BY clause.
4. Apply any aggregate functions to create a new group-level dataset. Each row may be regarded as an aggregation of its source row-level data based on the groups created.

5. Limit or restrict the group-level data with a HAVING clause condition. Only group-level results matching these conditions are returned.

 TIP Choosing the appropriate context to use a WHERE or a HAVING clause depends on whether actual rows or group-level rows are to be restricted. When actual (physical) rows are restricted, one or more conditions are imposed using a WHERE clause. When these rows are grouped together, one or more aggregate functions may be applied, yielding one or more group-level rows that may be restricted using a HAVING clause.

The HAVING Clause

The general form of the SELECT statement is further enhanced by the addition of the HAVING clause and becomes

```
SELECT column|expression|group_function(column|expression [alias]),...}
FROM table
[WHERE condition(s)]
[GROUP BY {col(s)|expr}]
[HAVING group_condition(s)]
[ORDER BY {col(s)|expr|numeric_pos} [ASC|DESC] [NULLS FIRST|LAST]];
```

An important difference between the HAVING clause and the other SELECT statement clauses is that it may only be specified if a GROUP BY clause is present. This dependency is sensible, since group-level rows must exist before they can be restricted. The HAVING clause can occur before the GROUP BY clause in the SELECT statement. However, it is more common to place the HAVING clause after the GROUP BY clause. All grouping is performed and group functions are executed prior to evaluating the HAVING clause.

The following query shows how the HAVING clause is used to restrict an aggregated dataset. Records from the JOB_HISTORY table are divided into four groups. The rows that meet the HAVING clause condition (contributing more than one row to the group row count) are returned:

```
select department_id, count(*)
from job_history
where department_id in (50,60,80,110)
group by department_id
having count(*)>1
```

Three rows with DEPARTMENT_ID values of 50, 80, and 110, each with a COUNT(*) value of 2, are returned.

Figure 11-6 shows three queries. Query 1 divides the 107 records from the EMPLOYEES table into 19 groups based on common JOB_ID values. The average salary for each JOB_ID group and the aggregate row count are computed. Query 2 refines the results by conditionally excluding those aggregated rows where the average salary is less than or equal to 10000, using a HAVING clause. Query 3 demonstrates that the Boolean operators may be used to specify multiple HAVING clause conditions.

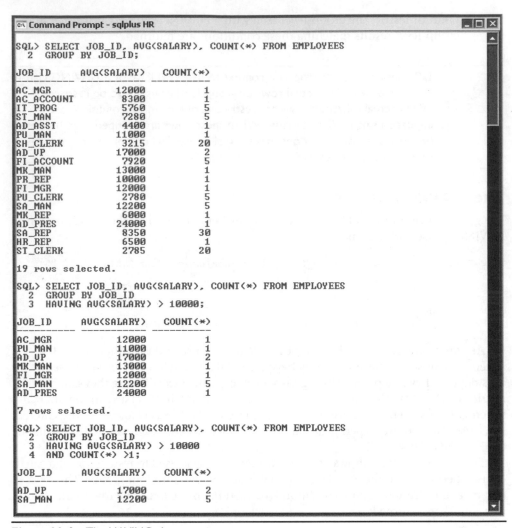

```
Command Prompt - sqlplus HR                                      _ □ ✕

SQL> SELECT JOB_ID, AVG(SALARY), COUNT(*) FROM EMPLOYEES
  2   GROUP BY JOB_ID;

JOB_ID      AVG(SALARY)    COUNT(*)
----------  -----------    --------
AC_MGR            12000           1
AC_ACCOUNT         8300           1
IT_PROG            5760           5
ST_MAN             7280           5
AD_ASST            4400           1
PU_MAN            11000           1
SH_CLERK           3215          20
AD_VP             17000           2
FI_ACCOUNT         7920           5
MK_MAN            13000           1
PR_REP            10000           1
FI_MGR            12000           1
PU_CLERK           2780           5
SA_MAN            12200           5
MK_REP             6000           1
AD_PRES           24000           1
SA_REP             8350          30
HR_REP             6500           1
ST_CLERK           2785          20

19 rows selected.

SQL> SELECT JOB_ID, AVG(SALARY), COUNT(*) FROM EMPLOYEES
  2   GROUP BY JOB_ID
  3   HAVING AVG(SALARY) > 10000;

JOB_ID      AVG(SALARY)    COUNT(*)
----------  -----------    --------
AC_MGR            12000           1
PU_MAN            11000           1
AD_VP             17000           2
MK_MAN            13000           1
FI_MGR            12000           1
SA_MAN            12200           5
AD_PRES           24000           1

7 rows selected.

SQL> SELECT JOB_ID, AVG(SALARY), COUNT(*) FROM EMPLOYEES
  2   GROUP BY JOB_ID
  3   HAVING AVG(SALARY) > 10000
  4   AND COUNT(*) >1;

JOB_ID      AVG(SALARY)    COUNT(*)
----------  -----------    --------
AD_VP             17000           2
SA_MAN            12200           5
```

Figure 11-6 The HAVING clause

EXAM TIP The HAVING clause may only be specified when a GROUP BY clause is present. A GROUP BY clause can be specified without a HAVING clause.

Exercise 11-3: Use the HAVING Clause The company is planning a recruitment drive and wants to identify which days of the week 20 or more staff members were hired. Your report must list the days and the number of employees hired on each of them.

1. Start SQL*Plus or SQL Developer and connect to the HR schema.

2. Divide EMPLOYEES records into groups based on the day component of the HIRE_DATE column. You can obtain the number of employees per group

using the COUNT function. Use the HAVING clause to restrict these rows to only those where the count is greater than or equal to 20.

3. A possible solution is the following statement, which returns the days of the week on which 20 or more employees were hired:

```
select to_char(hire_date,'Day') hire_day, count(*)
from employees
group by to_char(hire_date,'Day')
having count(*)>=20;
```

Two-Minute Drill

Describe the Group Functions

- Group functions are also known as multiple-row, aggregate, or summary functions. They execute once for each group of data and aggregate the data from multiple rows into a single result for each group.

- Groups may be entire tables or portions of a table grouped together by a common grouping attribute.

Identify the Available Group Functions

- The COUNT of a column or an expression returns an integer value representing the number of rows in a group, where the specified column or expression is not null.

- The SUM function returns an aggregated total of all the non-null numeric values in a group.

- The AVG function divides the sum of a column or expression by the number of non-null rows in a group.

- The MAX and MIN functions operate on NUMBER, DATE, CHAR, and VARCHAR2 data types. They return a value that is either the largest or smallest item in the group.

- Group functions may be nested at most two levels deep.

Group Data Using the GROUP BY Clause

- The GROUP BY clause specifies the grouping attribute rows must have in common for them to be clustered together.

- The GROUP BY clause facilitates the creation of groups within a selected set of data and appears after the WHERE clause but before the ORDER BY clause.

- Any item on the SELECT list that is not a group function must be a grouping attribute.

- Group functions may not be placed in a WHERE clause.

- Datasets may be partitioned into groups and further divided into subgroups based on multiple grouping attributes.

Include or Exclude Grouped Rows Using the HAVING Clause

- Clustering rows using a common grouping attribute with the GROUP BY clause and applying an aggregate function to each of these groups returns *group-level results.*

- The HAVING clause provides the language to limit the group-level results returned.

- The HAVING clause may only be specified if there is a GROUP BY clause present.

- All grouping is performed and group functions are executed prior to evaluating the HAVING clause.

Self Test

1. What result is returned by the following statement?
   ```
   SELECT COUNT(*) FROM DUAL;
   ```
   (Choose the best answer.)

   A. NULL

   B. 0

   C. 1

   D. None of the above

2. Choose one correct statement regarding group functions.

   A. Group functions may only be used when a GROUP BY clause is present.

   B. Group functions can operate on multiple rows at a time.

   C. Group functions only operate on a single row at a time.

   D. Group functions can execute multiple times within a single group.

3. What value is returned after executing the following statement?
   ```
   SELECT SUM(SALARY) FROM EMPLOYEES;
   ```
   Assume there are ten employee records and each contains a SALARY value of 100, except for one, which has a null value in the SALARY field. (Choose the best answer.)

   A. 900

   B. 1000

   C. NULL

   D. None of the above

4. Which values are returned after executing the following statement?
   ```
   SELECT COUNT(*), COUNT(SALARY) FROM EMPLOYEES;
   ```

Assume there are ten employee records and each contains a SALARY value of 100, except for one, which has a null value in their SALARY field. (Choose all that apply.)

A. 10 and 10

B. 10 and NULL

C. 10 and 9

D. None of the above

5. What value is returned after executing the following statement?
```
SELECT AVG(NVL(SALARY,100)) FROM EMPLOYEES;
```
Assume there are ten employee records and each contains a SALARY value of 100, except for one employee, who has a null value in the SALARY field. (Choose the best answer.)

A. NULL

B. 90

C. 100

D. None of the above

6. What value is returned after executing the following statement?
```
SELECT SUM((AVG(LENGTH(NVL(SALARY,0)))))
FROM EMPLOYEES
GROUP BY SALARY;
```
Assume there are ten employee records and each contains a SALARY value of 100, except for one, which has a null value in the SALARY field. (Choose the best answer.)

A. An error is returned

B. 3

C. 4

D. None of the above

7. How many rows are returned by the following query?
```
SELECT SUM(SALARY), DEPARTMENT_ID FROM EMPLOYEES
GROUP BY DEPARTMENT_ID;
```
Assume there are 11 non-null and 1 null unique DEPARTMENT_ID values. All records have a non-null SALARY value. (Choose the best answer.)

A. 12

B. 11

C. NULL

D. None of the above

8. What values are returned after executing the following statement?
   `SELECT JOB_ID, MAX_SALARY FROM JOBS GROUP BY MAX_SALARY;`
   Assume that the JOBS table has ten records with the same JOB_ID value of DBA and the same MAX_SALARY value of 100. (Choose the best answer.)

   A. One row of output with the values DBA, 100

   B. Ten rows of output with the values DBA, 100

   C. An error is returned

   D. None of the above

9. How many rows of data are returned after executing the following statement?
   `SELECT DEPT_ID, SUM(NVL(SALARY,100)) FROM EMP`
   `GROUP BY DEPT_ID HAVING SUM(SALARY) > 400;`
   Assume the EMP table has ten rows and each contains a SALARY value of 100, except for one, which has a null value in the SALARY field. The first five rows have a DEPT_ID value of 10 while the second group of five rows, which includes the row with a null SALARY value, has a DEPT_ID value of 20. (Choose the best answer.)

   A. Two rows

   B. One row

   C. Zero rows

   D. None of the above

10. How many rows of data are returned after executing the following statement?
    `SELECT DEPT_ID, SUM(SALARY) FROM EMP GROUP BY DEPT_ID`
    `HAVING SUM(NVL(SALARY,100)) > 400;`
    Assume the EMP table has ten rows and each contains a SALARY value of 100, except for one, which has a null value in the SALARY field. The first five rows have a DEPT_ID value of 10, while the second five rows, which include the row with a null SALARY value, have a DEPT_ID value of 20. (Choose the best answer.)

    A. Two rows

    B. One row

    C. Zero rows

    D. None of the above

Self Test Answers

1. ☑ C. The DUAL table has one row and one column. The COUNT(*) function returns the number of rows in a table or group.

   ☒ A, B, and D.

2. ☑ B. By definition, group functions can operate on multiple rows at a time, unlike single-row functions.

☒ **A, C,** and **D.** A group function may be used without a GROUP BY clause. In this case, the entire dataset is operated on as a group. The COUNT function is often executed against an entire table, which behaves as one group. **D** is incorrect. Once a dataset has been partitioned into different groups, any group functions execute once per group.

3. ☑ **A.** The SUM aggregate function ignores null values and adds non-null values. Since nine rows contain the SALARY value 100, 900 is returned.

☒ **B, C,** and **D. B** would be returned if SUM(NVL(SALARY,100)) were executed. **C** is a tempting choice, since regular arithmetic with NULL values returns a NULL result. However, the aggregate functions, except for COUNT(*), ignore NULL values.

4. ☑ **C.** COUNT(*) considers all rows, including those with NULL values, while COUNT(SALARY) only considers the non-null rows.

☒ **A, B,** and **D.**

5. ☑ **C.** The NVL function converts the one NULL value into 100. Thereafter, the average function adds the SALARY values and obtains 1000. Dividing this by the number of records returns 100.

☒ **A, B,** and **D. B** would be returned if AVG(NVL(SALARY,0)) were selected. It is interesting to note that if AVG(SALARY) were selected, 100 would have also been returned, since the AVG function would sum the non-null values and divide the total by the number of rows with non-null SALARY values. So AVG(SALARY) would be calculated as: 900/9=100.

6. ☑ **C.** The dataset is segmented by the SALARY column. This creates two groups: one with SALARY values of 100 and the other with a null SALARY value. The average length of SALARY value 100 is 3 for the rows in the first group. The NULL salary value is first converted into the number 0 by the NVL function, and the average length of SALARY is 1. The SUM function operates across the two groups adding the values 3 and 1, returning 4.

☒ **A, B,** and **D. A** seems plausible, since group functions may not be nested more than two levels deep. Although there are four functions, only two are group functions, while the others are single-row functions evaluated before the group functions. **B** would be returned if the expression SUM(AVG(LENGTH(SALARY))) were selected.

7. ☑ **A.** There are 12 distinct DEPARTMENT_ID values. Since this is the grouping attribute, 12 groups are created, including 1 with a null DEPARTMENT_ID value. Therefore 12 rows are returned.

☒ **B, C,** and **D.**

8. ☑ **C.** For a GROUP BY clause to be used, a group function must appear in the SELECT list.

☒ **A, B,** and **D.** These are incorrect, since the statement is syntactically inaccurate and is disallowed by Oracle. Do not mistake the column named MAX_SALARY for the MAX(SALARY) function.

9. ☑ **B.** Two groups are created based on their common DEPT_ID values. The group with DEPT_ID values of 10 consists of five rows with SALARY values of 100 in each of them. Therefore, the SUM(SALARY) function returns 500 for this group, and it satisfies the HAVING SUM(SALARY) > 400 clause. The group with DEPT_ID values of 20 has four rows with SALARY values of 100 and one row with a NULL SALARY. SUM(SALARY) only returns 400 and this group does not satisfy the HAVING clause.

☒ **A, C,** and **D.** Beware of the SUM(NVL(SALARY,100)) expression in the SELECT clause. This expression selects the format of the output. It does not restrict or limit the dataset in any way.

10. ☑ **A.** Two groups are created based on their common DEPT_ID values. The group with DEPT_ID values of 10 consists of five rows with SALARY values of 100 in each of them. Therefore the SUM(NVL(SALARY,100)) function returns 500 for this group and satisfies the HAVING SUM(NVL(SALARY,100))>400 clause. The group with DEPT_ID values of 20 has four rows with SALARY values of 100 and one row with a null SALARY. SUM(NVL(SALARY,100)) returns 500, and this group satisfies the HAVING clause. Therefore, two rows are returned.

☒ **B, C,** and **D.** Although the SELECT clause contains SUM(SALARY), which returns 500 and 400 for the two groups, the HAVING clause contains the SUM(NVL(SALARY,100)) expression, which specifies the inclusion or exclusion criteria for a group-level row.

CHAPTER 12

SQL Joins

Exam Objectives

In this chapter you will learn to

- 051.6.1 Write SELECT Statements to Access Data from More Than One Table Using Equijoins and Nonequijoins
- 051.6.2 Join a Table to Itself Using a Self-Join
- 051.6.3 View Data That Does Not Meet a Join Condition Using Outer Joins
- 051.6.4 Generate a Cartesian Product of All Rows from Two or More Tables

The three pillars of relational theory are selection, projection, and joining. This chapter focuses on the practical implementation of *joining*. Rows from different tables or views are associated with each other using *joins*. Support for joining has implications for the way data is stored, and many data models such as third normal form or star schemas have emerged to exploit this feature.

Tables may be joined in several ways. The most common technique is called an *equijoin*, where a row is associated with one or more rows in another table based on the *equality* of column values or expressions. Tables may also be joined using a *nonequijoin*, where a row is associated with one or more rows in another table if its column values fall into a range determined by inequality operators.

A less common technique is to associate rows with other rows in the same table. This association is based on columns with logical and usually hierarchical relationships with each other and is called a *self-join*. Rows with null or differing entries in common *join columns* are excluded when equijoins and nonequijoins are performed. An *outer join* is available to fetch these *one-legged* or *orphaned* rows, if necessary.

A cross join or *Cartesian* product is formed when every row from one table is joined to all rows in another. This join is often the result of missing or inadequate join conditions but is occasionally intentional.

Write SELECT Statements to Access Data from More Than One Table Using Equijoins and Nonequijoins

This section introduces the different types of *joins* in their primitive forms, outlining the broad categories that are available before delving into an in-depth discussion of the various *join* clauses. The modern ANSI-compliant and traditional Oracle syntaxes are discussed, but emphasis is placed on the modern syntax. This section concludes with a discussion of nonequijoins and additional join conditions. Joining is described by focusing on the following eight areas:

- Types of joins
- Joining tables using SQL:1999 syntax
- Qualifying ambiguous column names
- The NATURAL JOIN clause
- The natural JOIN USING clause
- The natural JOIN ON clause
- N-way joins and additional join conditions
- Nonequijoins

Types of Joins

Two basic joins are the *equijoin* and the *nonequijoin*. Joins may be performed between multiple tables, but much of the following discussion will use two hypothetical tables to illustrate the concepts and language of joins. The first table is called the *source*, and the second is called the *target*. Rows in the source and target tables comprise one or more columns. As an example, assume that the *source* and *target* are the COUNTRIES and REGIONS tables from the HR schema, respectively.

The COUNTRIES table comprises three columns named COUNTRY_ID, COUNTRY_NAME, and REGION_ID, while the REGIONS table comprises two columns named REGION_ID and REGION_NAME. The data in these two tables is related via the common REGION_ID column. Consider the following queries:

Query 1: `select * from countries where country_id='CA';`
Query 2: `select region_name from regions where region_id='2';`

Query 1 retrieves the column values associated with the row from the COUNTRIES table with COUNTRY_ID='CA'. The REGION_ID value of this row is 2. Query 2 fetches Americas as the region name from the REGIONS table for the row with REGION_ID=2, thus identifying the one region in which Canada lies. Joining facilitates the retrieval of column values from multiple tables using a single query.

The source and target tables can be swapped, so the REGIONS table could be the source and the COUNTRIES table could be the target. Consider the following two queries:

Query 1: `select * from regions where region_name='Americas';`
Query 2: `select country_name from countries where region_id='2';`

Query 1 fetches one row with a REGION_ID value of 2. Joining in this reversed manner allows the following question to be asked: What countries belong to the Americas region? The answers from the second query are five countries named: Argentina, Brazil, Canada, Mexico, and the United States of America. These results may be obtained from a single query that joins the tables together.

Natural Joins

The natural join is implemented using three possible *join clauses* that use the following keywords in different combinations: *NATURAL JOIN, USING,* and *ON.*

When the source and target tables share identically named columns, it is possible to perform a natural join between them without specifying a join column. This is sometimes referred to as a *pure natural join.* In this scenario, columns with the same names in the source and target tables are automatically associated with each other. Rows with matching column values in both tables are retrieved. The REGIONS and COUNTRIES table both share a commonly named column: REGION_ID. They may be naturally joined without specifying join columns, as shown in the first two queries in Figure 12-1.

The NATURAL JOIN keywords instruct Oracle to identify columns with identical names between the source and target tables. Thereafter, a join is implicitly performed between them. In the first query, the REGION_ID column is identified as the only commonly named column in both tables. REGIONS is the source table and appears after the FROM clause. The target table is therefore COUNTRIES. For each row in the REGIONS table, a match for the REGION_ID value is sought from all the rows in the COUNTRIES table. An interim result set is constructed containing rows matching the join condition. This set is then restricted by the WHERE clause. In this case, because the COUNTRY_NAME must be Canada, the REGION_NAME Americas is returned.

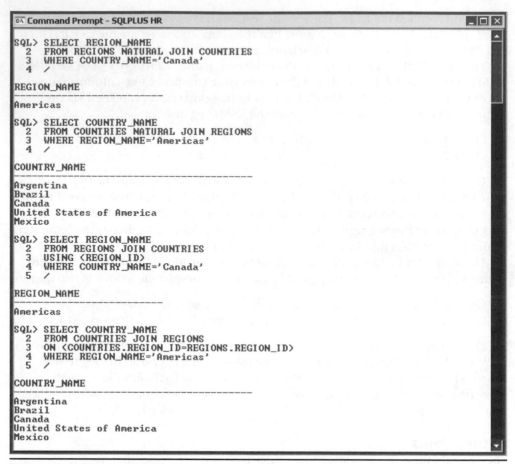

```
Command Prompt - SQLPLUS HR                                    _ □ ×
SQL> SELECT REGION_NAME
  2  FROM REGIONS NATURAL JOIN COUNTRIES
  3  WHERE COUNTRY_NAME='Canada'
  4  /

REGION_NAME
--------------------------------
Americas

SQL> SELECT COUNTRY_NAME
  2  FROM COUNTRIES NATURAL JOIN REGIONS
  3  WHERE REGION_NAME='Americas'
  4  /

COUNTRY_NAME
------------------------------------------------
Argentina
Brazil
Canada
United States of America
Mexico

SQL> SELECT REGION_NAME
  2  FROM REGIONS JOIN COUNTRIES
  3  USING (REGION_ID)
  4  WHERE COUNTRY_NAME='Canada'
  5  /

REGION_NAME
--------------------------------
Americas

SQL> SELECT COUNTRY_NAME
  2  FROM COUNTRIES JOIN REGIONS
  3  ON (COUNTRIES.REGION_ID=REGIONS.REGION_ID)
  4  WHERE REGION_NAME='Americas'
  5  /

COUNTRY_NAME
------------------------------------------
Argentina
Brazil
Canada
United States of America
Mexico
```

Figure 12-1   Natural joins

The second query shows a natural join where COUNTRIES is the source table. The REGION_ID value for each row in the COUNTRIES table is identified and a search for a matching row in the REGIONS table is initiated. If matches are found, the interim results are limited by any WHERE conditions. The COUNTRY_NAME from rows with Americas as their REGION_NAME is returned.

Sometimes more control must be exercised regarding which columns to use for joins. When there are identical column names in the source and target tables you want to exclude as join columns, the *JOIN . . . USING* format may be used. Remember that Oracle does not impose any rules stating that columns with the same name in two discrete tables must have a relationship with each other. The third query explicitly specifies that the REGIONS table be joined to the COUNTRIES table based on common values in their REGION_ID columns. This syntax allows natural joins to be formed on specific columns instead of on all commonly named columns.

The fourth query demonstrates the *JOIN . . . ON* format of the natural join, which allows join columns to be explicitly stated. This format does not depend on the columns in the source and target tables having identical names. This form is more general and is the most widely used natural join format.

TIP Be wary when using pure natural joins, since database designers may assign the same name to key or unique columns. These columns may have names like ID or SEQ_NO. If a pure natural join is attempted between such tables, ambiguous and unexpected results may be returned.

Outer Joins

Not all tables share a perfect relationship, where every record in the source table can be matched to at least one row in the target table. It is occasionally required that rows with nonmatching join column values also be retrieved by a query. Suppose the EMPLOYEES and DEPARTMENTS tables are joined with common DEPARTMENT_ID values. EMPLOYEES records with null DEPARTMENT_ID values are excluded along with values absent from the DEPARTMENTS table. An *outer join* fetches these rows.

Cross Joins

A *cross join* or *Cartesian product* derives its names from mathematics, where it is also referred to as a cross product between two sets or matrices. This join creates one row of output for every combination of source and target table rows.

If the source and target tables have three and four rows, respectively, a cross join between them results in ($3 \times 4 = 12$) rows being returned. Consider the row counts retrieved from the queries in Figure 12-2.

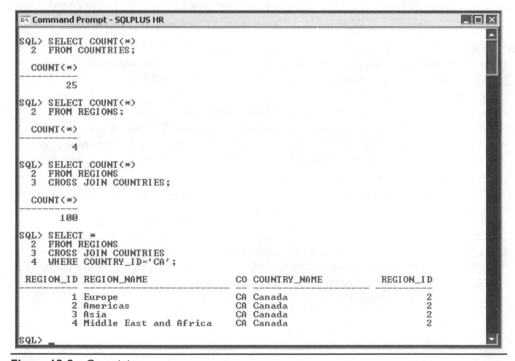

Figure 12-2 Cross join

The first two row counts are performed on the COUNTRIES and REGIONS tables, yielding 25 and 4 rows respectively. The third query counts the number of rows returned from a cross join of these tables and yields 100. Query 4 would return 100 records if the WHERE clause were absent. Each of the four rows in the REGIONS table is joined to the one row from the COUNTRIES table. Each row returned contains every column from both tables.

Oracle Join Syntax

A proprietary Oracle join syntax has evolved that is stable and understood by millions of users. This traditional syntax is supported by Oracle and is present in software systems across the world. This syntax performs a Cartesian product, and then filters the result with a WHERE clause while the ANSI syntax joins the tables first, and then any separate WHERE clause conditions are applied to the joined results set. You will no doubt encounter the traditional Oracle join syntax that is now making way for the standardized ANSI-compliant syntax discussed in this chapter.

The traditional Oracle join syntax supports natural joining, outer joins, and Cartesian joins, as shown in the following queries:

```
Query 1: select regions.region_name, countries.country_name
from regions, countries
where regions.region_id=countries.region_id;
Query 2: select last_name, department_name
from employees, departments
where employees.department_id (+) = departments.department_id;
Query 3: select * from regions,countries;
```

Query 1 performs a natural join by specifying the join as a condition in the WHERE clause. This is the most significant difference between the traditional and ANSI SQL join syntaxes. Take note of the column aliasing using the TABLE.COLUMN_NAME notation to disambiguate the identical column names. This notation is discussed later in this chapter. Query 2 specifies the join between the source and target tables as a WHERE condition with a plus symbol enclosed in brackets (+) to the *left* of the equal sign that indicates to Oracle that a *right outer join* must be performed. This query returns employees' LAST_NAME and their matching DEPARTMENT_NAME values. In addition, the outer join retrieves DEPARTMENT_NAME from the rows with DEPARTMENT_ID values not currently assigned to any employee records. Query 3 performs a Cartesian or cross join by excluding the join condition.

 EXAM TIP The traditional Oracle join syntax is widely used. However, the exam assesses your understanding of joins and the ANSI SQL forms of its syntax. Be prepared, though: some questions may tap your knowledge of the traditional syntax.

Joining Tables Using SQL:1999 Syntax

Prior to Oracle 9*i*, the traditional join syntax was the only language available to join tables. Since then, Oracle has introduced a new language that is compliant to the ANSI SQL:1999 standards. It offers no performance benefits over the traditional syntax. Natural, outer, and cross joins may be written using both SQL:1999 and traditional Oracle SQL.

The general form of the SELECT statement using ANSI SQL:1999 syntax is as follows:

```
SELECT table1.column, table2.column
    FROM table1
    [NATURAL JOIN table2] |
    [JOIN table2 USING (column_name)] |
    [JOIN table2 ON (table1.column_name = table2.column_name)] |
    [LEFT | RIGHT | FULL OUTER JOIN table2
    ON (table1.column_name = table2.column_name)] |
    [CROSS JOIN table2];
```

This is dissected and examples are explained in the following sections. The general form of the traditional Oracle-proprietary syntax relevant to joins is as follows:

```
SELECT table1.column, table2.column
    FROM table1, table2
    [WHERE (table1.column_name = table2.column_name)] |
    [WHERE (table1.column_name(+)= table2.column_name)] |
    [WHERE (table1.column_name)= table2.column_name) (+)] ;
```

If no joins or fewer than *N* – 1 joins are specified in the WHERE clause conditions, where N refers to the number of tables in the query, then a Cartesian or cross join is performed. If an adequate number of join conditions is specified, then the first optional conditional clause specifies an equijoin, while the second two optional clauses specify the syntax for right and left outer joins.

Qualifying Ambiguous Column Names

Columns with the same names may occur in tables involved in a join. The columns named DEPARTMENT_ID and MANAGER_ID are found in both the EMPLOYEES and DEPARTMENTS tables. The REGION_ID column is present in both the REGIONS and COUNTRIES tables. Listing such columns in a query becomes problematic when Oracle cannot resolve their origin. Columns with unique names across the tables involved in a join cause no ambiguity, and Oracle can easily resolve their source table.

The problem of ambiguous column names is addressed with dot notation. A column may be prefixed by its table name and a dot or period symbol to designate its origin. This differentiates it from a column with the same name in another table. Dot notation may be used in queries involving any number of tables. Referencing some columns using dot notation does not imply that all columns must be referenced in this way.

Dot notation is enhanced with table aliases. A *table alias* provides an alternate, usually shorter name for a table. A column may be referenced as *TABLE_NAME* .*COLUMN_NAME* or *TABLE_ALIAS.COLUMN_NAME*. Consider the query shown in Figure 12-3.

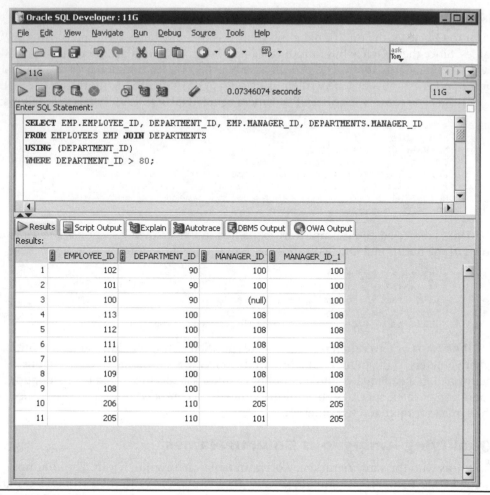

Figure 12-3   Dot notation

The EMPLOYEES table is aliased with the short name EMP, while the DEPARTMENTS table is not. The SELECT clause references the EMPLOYEE_ID and MANAGER_ID columns as EMP.EMPLOYEE_ID and EMP.MANAGER_ID. The MANAGER_ID column from the DEPARTMENTS table is referred to as DEPARTMENTS.MANAGER_ID. Qualifying the EMPLOYEE_ID column using dot notation is unnecessary because there is only one column with this name between the two tables. Therefore, there is no ambiguity.

The MANAGER_ID column must be qualified to avoid ambiguity because it occurs in both tables. Since the JOIN . . . USING format is applied, only DEPARTMENT_ID is used as the join column. If a NATURAL JOIN was employed, both the DEPARTMENT_ID and MANAGER_ID columns would be used. If the MANAGER_ID column was not qualified, an "ORA-00918: column ambiguously defined" error would be returned. If DEPARTMENT_ID was aliased, an "ORA-25154: column part of USING clause cannot have qualifier" error would be raised.

SQL Developer provides the heading MANAGER_ID to the first reference made in the SELECT clause. The string "_1" is automatically appended to the second reference, creating the heading MANAGER_ID_1.

TIP Qualifying column references with dot notation to indicate a column's table of origin has a performance benefit. Time is saved because Oracle is directed instantaneously to the appropriate table and does not have to resolve the table name.

The NATURAL JOIN Clause

The general syntax for the NATURAL JOIN clause is as follows:

```
SELECT table1.column, table2.column
    FROM table1
    NATURAL JOIN table2;
```

The pure natural join identifies the columns with common names in *table1* and *table2* and implicitly joins the tables using all these columns. The columns in the SELECT clause may be qualified using dot notation unless they are one of the join columns. Consider the following queries:

Query 1: select * from locations natural join countries;
Query 2: select * from locations, countries
where locations.country_id = countries.country_id;
Query 3: select * from jobs natural join countries;
Query 4: select * from jobs, countries;

In query 1, COUNTRY_ID occurs in both tables and becomes the join column. Query 2 is written using traditional Oracle syntax and retrieves the same rows as query 1. Unless you are familiar with the columns in the source and target tables, natural joins must be used with caution, as join conditions are automatically formed between all columns with shared names.

Query 3 performs a natural join between the JOBS and COUNTRIES tables. There are no columns with identical names and this results in a Cartesian product. Query 4 is equivalent to query 3, and a Cartesian join is performed using traditional Oracle syntax.

The natural join is simple but prone to a fundamental weakness. It suffers the risk that two columns with the same name might have no relationship and may not even have compatible data types. Figure 12-4 describes the COUNTRIES, REGIONS, and SALE_REGIONS tables. The SALES_REGIONS table was constructed to illustrate the following important point: Although it has REGION_ID in common with the COUNTRIES table, it cannot be naturally joined to it because their data types are

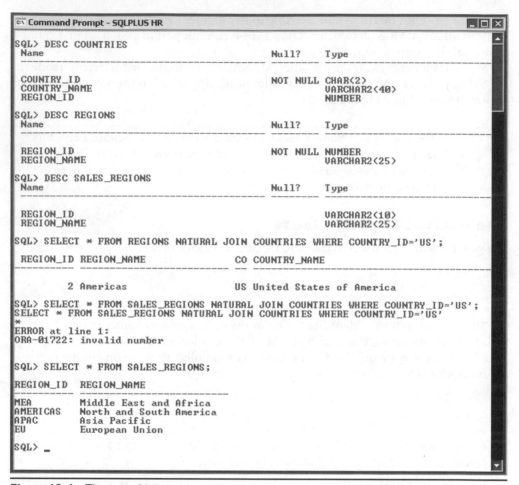

```
Command Prompt - SQLPLUS HR                                            _ □ ×

SQL> DESC COUNTRIES
Name                                        Null?    Type
--------------------------------------      -------  -------------------

COUNTRY_ID                                  NOT NULL CHAR(2)
COUNTRY_NAME                                         VARCHAR2(40)
REGION_ID                                            NUMBER

SQL> DESC REGIONS
Name                                        Null?    Type
--------------------------------------      -------  -------------------

REGION_ID                                   NOT NULL NUMBER
REGION_NAME                                          VARCHAR2(25)

SQL> DESC SALES_REGIONS
Name                                        Null?    Type
--------------------------------------      -------  -------------------

REGION_ID                                            VARCHAR2(10)
REGION_NAME                                          VARCHAR2(25)

SQL> SELECT * FROM REGIONS NATURAL JOIN COUNTRIES WHERE COUNTRY_ID='US';

 REGION_ID REGION_NAME                  CO COUNTRY_NAME
---------- --------------------------   -- ------------------------------

         2 Americas                     US United States of America

SQL> SELECT * FROM SALES_REGIONS NATURAL JOIN COUNTRIES WHERE COUNTRY_ID='US';
SELECT * FROM SALES_REGIONS NATURAL JOIN COUNTRIES WHERE COUNTRY_ID='US'
*
ERROR at line 1:
ORA-01722: invalid number


SQL> SELECT * FROM SALES_REGIONS;

REGION_ID  REGION_NAME
---------  ---------------------------
MEA        Middle East and Africa
AMERICAS   North and South America
APAC       Asia Pacific
EU         European Union

SQL> _
```

Figure 12-4 The natural join

incompatible. The data types of the COUNTRIES.REGION_ID and SALES_REGIONS.
REGION_ID columns are NUMBER and VARCHAR2, respectively. The character data
cannot be implicitly converted into numeric data and an "ORA-01722: invalid number"
error is raised. The REGIONS.REGION_ID column is of type NUMBER, and its data is
related to the data in the COUNTRIES table. Therefore, the natural join between the
REGIONS and COUNTRIES table works perfectly.

Exercise 12-1: Use the NATURAL JOIN The JOB_HISTORY table shares
three identically named columns with the EMPLOYEES table: EMPLOYEE_ID, JOB_
ID, and DEPARTMENT_ID. Describe the tables and fetch the EMPLOYEE_ID, JOB_ID,
DEPARTMENT_ID, LAST_NAME, HIRE_DATE, and END_DATE values for all rows

retrieved using a pure natural join. Alias the EMPLOYEES table as EMP and the JOB_HISTORY table as JH and use dot notation where necessary.

1. Start SQL*Plus and connect to the HR schema.

2. The tables are described and the columns with identical names and their data types may be examined using

```
desc employees;
desc job_history;
```

3. The FROM clause is
   FROM JOB_HISTORY JH

4. The JOIN clause is
   NATURAL JOIN EMPLOYEES EMP

5. The SELECT clause is
   SELECT EMP.LAST_NAME, EMP.HIRE_DATE, JH.END_DATE

6. Executing the following statement returns a single row with the same EMPLOYEE_ID, JOB_ID, and DEPARTMENT_ID values in both tables and is shown in the following illustration:

```
select employee_id, job_id, department_id,
emp.last_name, emp.hire_date, jh.end_date
from job_history jh natural join employees emp;
```

```
Command Prompt - SQLPLUS HR                                    _ □ ×

SQL> DESC EMPLOYEES
 Name                                       Null?    Type
 ------------------------------------       -------- --------------

 EMPLOYEE_ID                                NOT NULL NUMBER(6)
 FIRST_NAME                                          VARCHAR2(20)
 LAST_NAME                                  NOT NULL VARCHAR2(25)
 EMAIL                                      NOT NULL VARCHAR2(25)
 PHONE_NUMBER                                        VARCHAR2(20)
 HIRE_DATE                                  NOT NULL DATE
 JOB_ID                                     NOT NULL VARCHAR2(10)
 SALARY                                              NUMBER(8,2)
 COMMISSION_PCT                                      NUMBER(2,2)
 MANAGER_ID                                          NUMBER(6)
 DEPARTMENT_ID                                       NUMBER(4)

SQL> DESC JOB_HISTORY
 Name                                       Null?    Type
 ------------------------------------       -------- --------------

 EMPLOYEE_ID                                NOT NULL NUMBER(6)
 START_DATE                                 NOT NULL DATE
 END_DATE                                   NOT NULL DATE
 JOB_ID                                     NOT NULL VARCHAR2(10)
 DEPARTMENT_ID                                       NUMBER(4)

SQL> SELECT EMPLOYEE_ID, JOB_ID, DEPARTMENT_ID,
  2         EMP.LAST_NAME, EMP.HIRE_DATE, JH.END_DATE
  3  FROM JOB_HISTORY JH
  4  NATURAL JOIN EMPLOYEES EMP;

EMPLOYEE_ID JOB_ID      DEPARTMENT_ID LAST_NAME              HIRE_DATE END_DATE
----------- ----------- ------------- ---------------------- --------- ---------
        176 SA_REP                 80 Taylor                 24-MAR-98 31-DEC-98

SQL> _
```

The Natural JOIN USING Clause

The format of the syntax for the natural JOIN USING clause is as follows:

```
SELECT table1.column, table2.column
FROM table1
JOIN table2 USING (join_column1, join_column2...);
```

While the pure natural join contains the NATURAL keyword in its syntax, the JOIN . . . USING syntax does not. An error is raised if the keywords NATURAL and USING occur in the same join clause. The JOIN . . . USING clause allows one or more equijoin columns to be explicitly specified in brackets after the USING keyword. This avoids the shortcomings associated with the pure natural join. Many situations demand that tables be joined only on certain columns, and this format caters to this requirement. Consider the following queries:

Query 1: `select * from locations join countries using (country_id);`
Query 2: `select * from locations, countries where locations.country_id = countries.country_id;`
Query 3: `select * from jobs join countries using ;`

Query 1 specifies that the LOCATIONS and COUNTRIES tables must be joined on common COUNTRY_ID column values. All columns from these tables are retrieved for the rows with matching join column values. Query 2 shows a traditionally specified query that retrieves the same rows as query 1. Query 3 illustrates that a Cartesian join cannot be accidentally specified with the JOIN . . . USING syntax since only columns with shared names are permitted after the USING keyword. The join columns cannot be qualified using table names or aliases when they are referenced. Since this join syntax potentially excludes some columns with identical names from the join clause, these must be qualified if they are referenced to avoid ambiguity.

As Figure 12-5 shows, the JOB_HISTORY and EMPLOYEES tables were joined based on the presence of equal values in their JOB_ID and EMPLOYEE_ID columns. Rows conforming to this join condition are retrieved. These tables share three identically named columns. The JOIN . . . USING syntax allows the specification of only two of these as join columns. Notice that although the third identically named column is DEPARTMENT_ID, it is qualified with a table alias to avoid ambiguity. However, the join columns in the USING clause cannot be qualified with table aliases.

The Natural JOIN ON Clause

The format of the syntax for the natural JOIN ON clause is as follows:

```
SELECT table1.column, table2.column
FROM table1
JOIN table2 ON (table1.column_name = table2.column_name);
```

The pure natural join and the JOIN . . . USING clauses depend on join columns with identical column names. The JOIN . . . ON clause allows the explicit specification

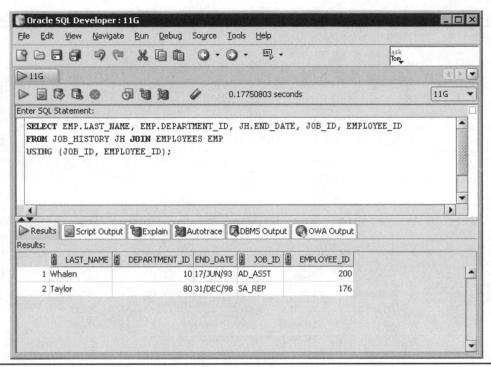

Figure 12-5   Natural join using the JOIN ... USING clause

of join columns, regardless of their column names. This is the most flexible and widely used form of the join clauses. The equijoin columns are fully qualified as *table1.column1 = table2.column2* and are optionally specified in brackets after the ON keyword. The following queries illustrate the JOIN . . . ON clause:

```
Query 1: select * from departments d
join employees e on (e.employee_id=d.department_id);
Query 2: select * from employees e, departments d
where e.employee_id=d.department_id;
```

Query 1 retrieves all column values from both the DEPARTMENTS and EMPLOYEES tables for the rows that meet the equijoin condition that is fulfilled by EMPLOYEE_ID values matching DEPARTMENT_ID values from the DEPARTMENTS table. The traditional Oracle syntax in query 2 returns the same results as query 1. Notice the similarities between the traditional join condition specified in the WHERE clause and the join condition specified after the ON keyword.

The START_DATE column in the JOB_HISTORY table is joined to the HIRE_DATE column in the EMPLOYEES table in Figure 12-6. This equijoin retrieves the details of employees who worked for the organization and changed jobs.

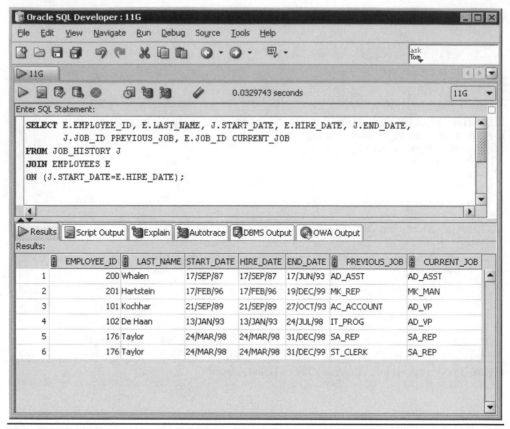

Figure 12-6 Natural join using the JOIN ... ON clause

Exercise 12-2: Use the NATURAL JOIN ... ON Clause Each record in the DEPARTMENTS table has a MANAGER_ID column matching an EMPLOYEE_ID value in the EMPLOYEES table. You are required to produce a report with one column aliased as Managers. Each row must contain a sentence of the format FIRST_NAME LAST_NAME is manager of the DEPARTMENT_NAME department. Alias the EMPLOYEES table as E and the DEPARTMENTS table as D and use dot notation where possible.

1. Start SQL Developer and connect to the HR schema.

2. The expression aliased as Managers may be constructed by concatenating the required items and separating them with spaces.

3. Executing the following statement returns 11 rows describing the managers of each department:

```
select e.first_name||' '||e.last_name||' is manager of the
'||d.department_name||'department.' "Managers" from employees e
join departments d on (e.employee_id=d.manager_id);
```

N-Way Joins and Additional Join Conditions

The joins just discussed were demonstrated using two tables. There is no restriction on the number of tables that may be related using joins. Third normal form consists of a set of tables connected through a series of primary and foreign key relationships. Traversing these relationships using joins enables consistent and reliable retrieval of data. When multiple joins exist in a statement, they are evaluated from left to right. Consider the following query using pure natural joins:

```
select r.region_name, c.country_name, l.city, d.department_name
from departments d natural join locations l
natural join countries c natural join regions r;
```

The join between DEPARTMENTS and LOCATIONS creates an interim result set consisting of 27 rows. These tables provide the DEPARTMENT_NAME and CITY columns. This set is naturally joined to the COUNTRIES table. Since the interim set does not contain the COUNTRY_ID column, a Cartesian join is performed. The 27 interim rows are joined to the 25 rows in the COUNTRIES table, yielding a new interim results set with 675 (27 × 25) rows and three columns: DEPARTMENT_ NAME, CITY, and COUNTRY_NAME. This set is naturally joined to the REGIONS table. Once again, a Cartesian join occurs because the REGION_ID column is absent from the interim set. The final result set contains 2700 (675 × 4) rows and four columns. Using pure natural joins with multiple tables is error prone and not recommended.

The JOIN . . . USING and JOIN . . . ON syntaxes are better suited for joining multiple tables. The following query joins correctly these four tables using the pure natural join syntax, by including the required join columns in the SELECT clause.

```
select region_id, country_id, c.country_name, l.city, d.department_name
from departments d natural join locations l
natural join countries c natural join regions r;
```

This query correctly yields 27 rows in the final results set. The following query demonstrates how the JOIN . . . ON clause is used to fetch the same 27 rows. A join condition can reference only columns in its scope. In the following example, the join from DEPARTMENTS to LOCATIONS may not reference columns in the COUNTRIES or REGIONS tables, but the join between COUNTRIES and REGIONS may reference any column from the four tables involved in the query.

```
select r.region_name, c.country_name, l.city, d.department_name
from departments d
join locations l on (l.location_id=d.location_id)
join countries c on (c.country_id=l.country_id)
join regions r on (r.region_id=c.region_id);
```

The JOIN . . . USING clause can also be used to join these four tables as follows:

```
select r.region_name, c.country_name, l.city, d.department_name
from departments d
join locations l using (location_id)
join countries c using (country_id)
join regions r using (region_id);
```

The WHERE clause is used to specify conditions that restrict the results set of a query whether it contains joins or not. The JOIN . . . ON clause is also used to specify conditions that limit the results set created by the join. Consider the following two queries:

Query 1: `select d.department_name from departments d`
`join locations l on (l.LOCATION_ID=d.LOCATION_ID)`
`where d.department_name like 'P%';`
Query 2: `select d.department_name from departments d`
`join locations l on`
`(l.LOCATION_ID=d.LOCATION_ID and d.department_name like`
`'P%');`

Query 1 uses a WHERE clause to restrict the 27 rows created by equijoining the DEPARTMENTS and LOCATIONS tables based on their LOCATION_ID values to the three that contain DEPARTMENT_ID values beginning with the letter "P." Query 2 implements the condition within the brackets of the ON subclause and returns the same three rows.

Five tables are joined in Figure 12-7, resulting in a list describing the top earning employees and geographical information about their departments.

 EXAM TIP There are three natural join formats. The pure natural join uses the NATURAL JOIN clause and joins two tables based on all columns with shared names. The other two formats use the JOIN . . . USING and JOIN . . . ON clauses and are also referred to as natural joins. They do not use the NATURAL keyword.

Nonequijoins

Nonequijoins match column values from different tables based on an inequality expression. The value of the join column in each row in the source table is compared to the corresponding values in the target table. A match is found if the expression used in the join, based on an inequality operator, evaluates to true. When such a join is constructed, a nonequijoin is performed.

A nonequijoin is specified using the JOIN . . . ON syntax, but the join condition contains an inequality operator instead of an equal sign.

The format of the syntax for a nonequijoin clause is as follows:

```
SELECT table1.column, table2.column
    FROM table1
    [JOIN table2 ON (table1.expr1< table2.expr2)]|
    [JOIN table2 ON (table1.expr1 > table2.expr2)]|
    [JOIN table2 ON (table1.expr1 <= table2.expr2)]|
    [JOIN table2 ON (table1.expr1 >= table2.expr2)]|
    [JOIN table2 ON (table1.expr1 BETWEEN table2.expr2 AND table2.expr3)]|
    [JOIN table2 ON (table1.expr1 LIKE table2. expr2)]
```

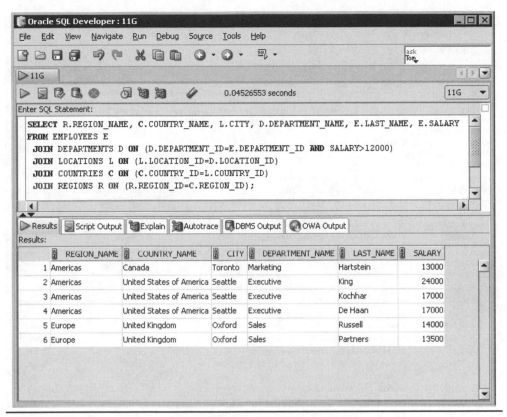

Figure 12-7 N-way joins and additional join conditions

Consider the first 15 rows returned by the query in Figure 12-8. The EMPLOYEES table is nonequijoined to the JOBS table based on the inequality join condition (2*E .SALARY < J.MAX_SALARY). The JOBS table stores the salary range for different jobs in the organization. The SALARY value for each employee record is doubled and compared with all MAX_SALARY values in the JOBS table. If the join condition evaluates to true, the row is returned.

The first two rows display the employee with a LAST_NAME of Abel who currently has a JOB_ID value of SA_REP and earns a SALARY of 11000. These are the only two rows in the JOBS table that satisfy the inequality join condition (2*E.SALARY < J.MAX_SALARY) for this employee record.

TIP Nonequijoins are not commonly used. The BETWEEN range operator often appears with nonequijoin conditions, since it is simpler to use one BETWEEN operator in a condition than two nonequijoin conditions based on (<=) and (>=) operators.

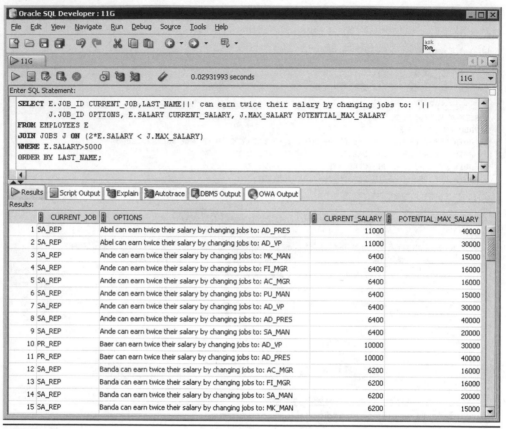

Figure 12-8 Nonequijoins

Join a Table to Itself Using a Self-Join

Storing hierarchical data in a single relational table is accomplished by allocating at least two columns per row. One column stores an identifier of the row's parent record and the second stores the row's identifier. Associating rows with each other based on a hierarchical relationship requires Oracle to *self-join* a table to itself.

Joining a Table to Itself Using the JOIN . . . ON Clause

Suppose there is a need to store a family tree in a relational table. There are several approaches one could take. One option is to use a table called FAMILY with columns named ID, NAME, MOTHER_ID, and FATHER_ID, where each row stores a person's name, unique ID number, and the ID values for their parents.

When two tables are joined, each row from the source table is subjected to the join condition with rows from the target table. If the condition evaluates to true, then the joined row, consisting of columns from both tables, is returned.

When the join columns originate from the same table, a self-join is required. Conceptually, the source table is duplicated to create the target table. The self-join works like a regular join between these tables. Note that, internally, Oracle does not duplicate the table and this description is merely provided to explain the concept of self-joining. Consider the following three queries:

Query 1: `select id, name, father_id from family;`
Query 2: `select name from family where id=&father_id;`
Query 3: `select f1.name Dad, f2.name Child`
`from family f1 join family f2 on (f1.id=f2.father_id)`

To identify someone's father in the FAMILY table, you could use query 1 to get their ID, NAME, and FATHER_ID. In query 2, the FATHER_ID value obtained from the first query can be substituted to obtain the father's NAME value. Notice that both queries 1 and 2 source information from the FAMILY table.

Query 3 performs a self-join with the JOIN . . . ON clause by aliasing the FAMILY table as f1 and f2. Oracle treats these as different tables even though they point to the same physical table. The first occurrence of the FAMILY table, aliased as f1, is designated as the source table, while the second, aliased as f2, is assigned as the target table. The join condition in the ON clause is of the format *source.child_id=target.parent_id*. Figure 12-9 shows a sample of FAMILY data and demonstrates a three-way self-join to the same table.

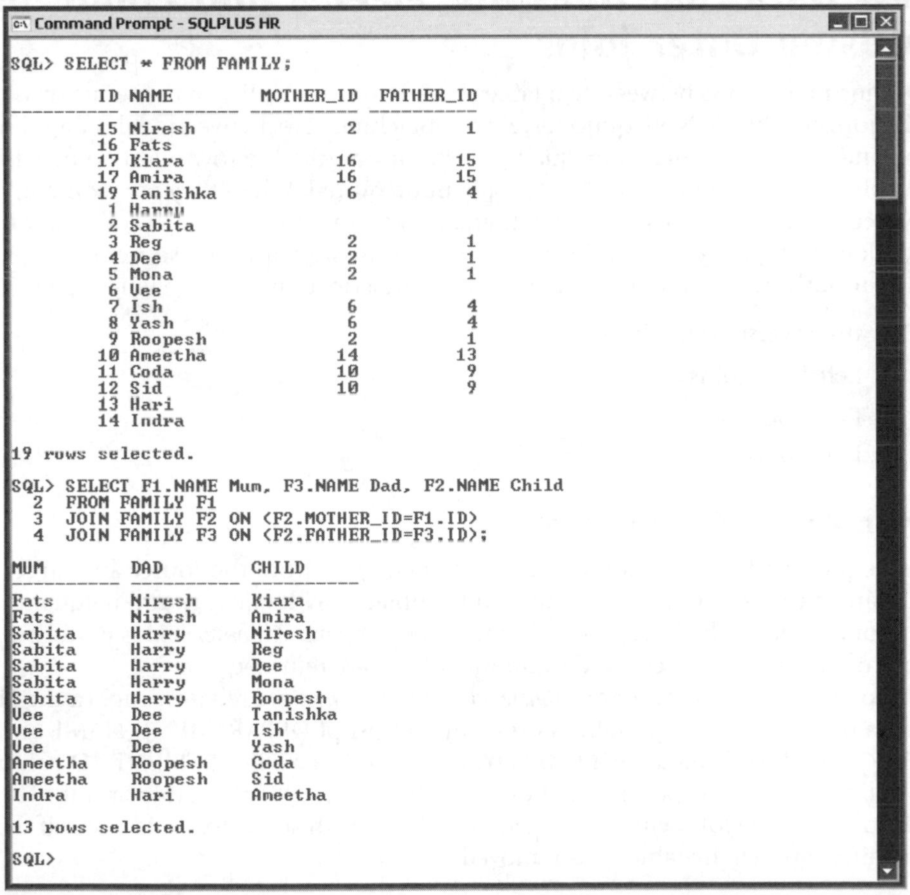

```
Command Prompt - SQLPLUS HR

SQL> SELECT * FROM FAMILY;

        ID NAME        MOTHER_ID  FATHER_ID
---------- ---------- ---------- ----------
        15 Niresh              2          1
        16 Fats
        17 Kiara              16         15
        17 Amira              16         15
        19 Tanishka            6          4
         1 Harry
         2 Sabita
         3 Reg                 2          1
         4 Dee                 2          1
         5 Mona                2          1
         6 Vee
         7 Ish                 6          4
         8 Yash                6          4
         9 Roopesh             2          1
        10 Ameetha            14         13
        11 Coda               10          9
        12 Sid                10          9
        13 Hari
        14 Indra

19 rows selected.

SQL> SELECT F1.NAME Mum, F3.NAME Dad, F2.NAME Child
  2  FROM FAMILY F1
  3  JOIN FAMILY F2 ON (F2.MOTHER_ID=F1.ID)
  4  JOIN FAMILY F3 ON (F2.FATHER_ID=F3.ID);

MUM        DAD         CHILD
---------- ----------- ----------
Fats       Niresh      Kiara
Fats       Niresh      Amira
Sabita     Harry       Niresh
Sabita     Harry       Reg
Sabita     Harry       Dee
Sabita     Harry       Mona
Sabita     Harry       Roopesh
Vee        Dee         Tanishka
Vee        Dee         Ish
Vee        Dee         Yash
Ameetha    Roopesh     Coda
Ameetha    Roopesh     Sid
Indra      Hari        Ameetha

13 rows selected.

SQL>
```

Figure 12-9   Self-join

Exercise 12-3: Perform a Self-Join   There is a hierarchical relationship between employees and their managers. For each row in the EMPLOYEES table, the MANAGER_ID column stores the EMPLOYEE_ID of every employee's manager. Using a self-join on the EMPLOYEES table, you are required to retrieve the employee's LAST_NAME, EMPLOYEE_ID, manager's LAST_NAME, and employee's DEPARTMENT_ID for the rows with DEPARMENT_ID values of 10, 20, or 30. Alias the EMPLOYEES table as E and the second instance of the EMPLOYEES table as M. Sort the results based on the DEPARTMENT_ID column.

1. Start SQL Developer or SQL*Plus and connect to the HR schema.

2. Execute the following statement to return nine rows describing the managers of each employee in these departments:

```
select e.last_name employee, e.employee_id, e.manager_id, m.last_name
manager, e.department_id
from employees e join employees m on (e.manager_id=m.employee_id)
where e.department_id in (10,20,30)
order by e.department_id;
```

View Data That Does Not Meet a Join Condition by Using Outer Joins

Equijoins match rows between two tables based on the equality of the terms involved in the join condition. Nonequijoins rely on matching rows between tables based on a join condition containing an inequality operator. Target table rows with no matching join column in the source table are usually not required. When they are required, however, an *outer join* is used to fetch them. Several variations of outer joins may be used, depending on whether join column data is missing from the source or target tables or both. These outer join techniques are described in the following topics:

- Inner versus outer joins
- Left outer joins
- Right outer joins
- Full outer joins

Inner Versus Outer Joins

When equijoins and nonequijoins are performed, rows from the source and target tables are matched using a join condition formulated with equality and inequality operators, respectively. These are referred to as *inner joins*. An *outer join* is performed when rows, that are not retrieved by an inner join, are returned.

Two tables sometimes share a *master-detail* or *parent-child* relationship. In the HR schema the DEPARTMENTS table stores a master list of DEPARTMENT_NAME and DEPARTMENT_ID values. Each EMPLOYEES record has a DEPARTMENT_ID column constrained to be either a value that exists in the DEPARTMENTS table or null. This leads to one of the following three scenarios. The fourth scenario could occur if the constraint between the tables was removed.

1. An employee row has a DEPARTMENT_ID value that matches a row in the DEPARTMENTS table.

2. An employee row has a null value in its DEPARTMENT_ID column.

3. There are rows in the DEPARTMENTS table with DEPARTMENT_ID values that are not stored in any employee records.

4. An employee row has a DEPARTMENT_ID value that is not featured in the DEPARTMENTS table.

Rows matching the first scenario are retrieved using a natural inner join between the two tables. The second and third scenarios cause many problems, as these rows are excluded by inner joins. An outer join can be used to include these orphaned rows in the results set. The fourth scenario should rarely occur in a well-designed database, because foreign key constraints would prevent the insertion of child records with no parent values. Since this row will be excluded by an inner join, it may be retrieved using an outer join.

A left outer join between the source and target tables returns the results of an inner join as well as rows from the source table excluded by that inner join. A right outer join between the source and target tables returns the results of an inner join as well as rows from the target table excluded by that inner join. If a join returns the results of an inner join as well as rows from both the source and target tables excluded by that inner join, then a full outer join has been performed.

Left Outer Joins

The format of the syntax for the LEFT OUTER JOIN clause is as follows:

```
SELECT table1.column, table2.column
FROM table1
LEFT OUTER JOIN table2
ON (table1.column = table2.column);
```

A left outer join performs an inner join of *table1* and *table2* based on the condition specified after the ON keyword. Any rows from the table on the *left* of the JOIN keyword excluded for not fulfilling the join condition are also returned. Consider the following two queries:

Query 1: select e.employee_id, e.department_id EMP_DEPT_ID,
d.department_id DEPT_DEPT_ID, d.department_name
from departments d left outer join employees e
on (d.DEPARTMENT_ID=e.DEPARTMENT_ID)
where d.department_name like 'P%';
Query 2: select e.employee_id, e.department_id EMP_DEPT_ID,
d.department_id DEPT_DEPT_ID, d.department_name
from departments d join employees e
on (d.DEPARTMENT_ID=e.DEPARTMENT_ID)
where d.department_name like 'P%';

Queries 1 and 2 are identical except for the join clauses, which have the keywords LEFT OUTER JOIN and JOIN, respectively. Query 2 performs an inner join and seven rows are returned. These rows share identical DEPARTMENT_ID values in both tables. Query 1 returns the same seven rows and one additional row. This extra row is obtained from the table to the left of the JOIN keyword, which is the DEPARTMENTS table. It is the row containing details of the Payroll department. The inner join does not include this row, since no employees are currently assigned to the department.

A left outer join is shown in Figure 12-10. The inner join produces 27 rows with matching LOCATION_ID values in both tables. There are 43 rows in total, which implies that 16 rows were retrieved from the LOCATIONS table, which is on the *left* of the JOIN keyword. None of the rows from the DEPARTMENTS table contain any of these 16 LOCATION_ID values.

```
Command Prompt - SQLPLUS HR                                              _ □ ✕

SQL> SELECT CITY, L.LOCATION_ID "L.LOCATION_ID", D.LOCATION_ID "D.LOCATION_ID"
  2    FROM LOCATIONS L LEFT OUTER JOIN DEPARTMENTS D
  3    ON (L.LOCATION_ID=D.LOCATION_ID);

CITY                            L.LOCATION_ID D.LOCATION_ID
------------------------------- ------------- -------------
Roma                                     1000
Venice                                   1100
Tokyo                                    1200
Hiroshima                                1300
Southlake                                1400          1400
South San Francisco                      1500          1500
South Brunswick                          1600
Seattle                                  1700          1700
Seattle                                  1700          1700
Seattle                                  1700          1700
Seattle                                  1700          1700
Seattle                                  1700          1700
Seattle                                  1700          1700
Seattle                                  1700          1700
Seattle                                  1700          1700
Seattle                                  1700          1700
Seattle                                  1700          1700
Seattle                                  1700          1700
Seattle                                  1700          1700
Seattle                                  1700          1700
Seattle                                  1700          1700
Seattle                                  1700          1700
Seattle                                  1700          1700
Seattle                                  1700          1700
Seattle                                  1700          1700
Seattle                                  1700          1700
Seattle                                  1700          1700
Toronto                                  1800          1800
Whitehorse                               1900
Beijing                                  2000
Bombay                                   2100
Sydney                                   2200
Singapore                                2300
London                                   2400          2400
Oxford                                   2500          2500
Stretford                                2600
Munich                                   2700          2700
Sao Paulo                                2800
Geneva                                   2900
Bern                                     3000
Utrecht                                  3100
Mexico City                              3200

43 rows selected.
```

Figure 12-10   Left outer join

PART II

Right Outer Joins

The format of the syntax for the RIGHT OUTER JOIN clause is as follows:

```
SELECT table1.column, table2.column
FROM table1
RIGHT OUTER JOIN table2
ON (table1.column = table2.column);
```

A right outer join performs an inner join of *table1* and *table2* based on the join condition specified after the ON keyword. Rows from the table to the *right* of the JOIN keyword, excluded by the join condition, are also returned. Consider the following query:

```
select e.last_name, d.department_name from departments d
right outer join employees e
on (e.department_id=d.department_id)
where e.last_name like 'G%';
```

The inner join produces seven rows containing details for the employees with LAST_NAME values that begin with "G." The EMPLOYEES table is to the *right* of the JOIN keyword. Any employee records that do not conform to the join condition are included, provided they conform to the WHERE clause condition. In addition, the right outer join fetches one EMPLOYEE record with a LAST_NAME of Grant. This record currently has a null DEPARTMENT_ID value. The inner join excludes the record, since no DEPARTMENT_ID is assigned to this employee.

A right outer join between the JOB_HISTORY and EMPLOYEES tables is shown in Figure 12-11. The EMPLOYEES table is on the right of the JOIN keyword. The DISTINCT keyword eliminates duplicate combinations of JOB_ID values from the tables. The results show the jobs that employees have historically left. The jobs that no employees have left are also returned.

 EXAM TIP There are three types of outer join formats. Each of them performs an inner join before including rows the join condition excluded. If a left outer join is performed, then rows excluded by the inner join, to the left of the JOIN keyword, are also returned. If a right outer join is performed, then rows excluded by the inner join, to the right of the JOIN keyword, are returned as well.

Full Outer Joins

The format of the syntax for the FULL OUTER JOIN clause is as follows:

```
SELECT table1.column, table2.column
FROM table1
FULL OUTER JOIN table2
ON (table1.column = table2.column);
```

A *full outer join* returns the combined results of a left and right outer join. An inner join of *table1* and *table2* is performed before rows excluded by the join condition from both tables are merged into the results set.

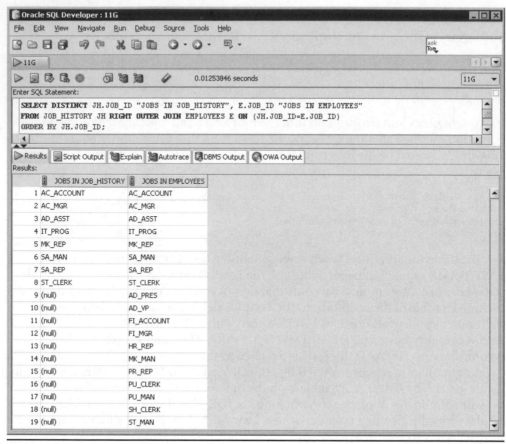

Figure 12-11   Right outer join

The traditional Oracle join syntax does not support a full outer join, which is typically performed by combining the results from left and right outer joins using the UNION set operator described in Chapter 13. Consider the full outer join shown in Figure 12-12. The WHERE clause restricting the results to rows with NULL DEPARTMENT_ ID values shows the orphan rows in both tables. There is one record in the EMPLOYEES table that has no DEPARTMENT_ID values, and there are 16 departments to which no employees belong.

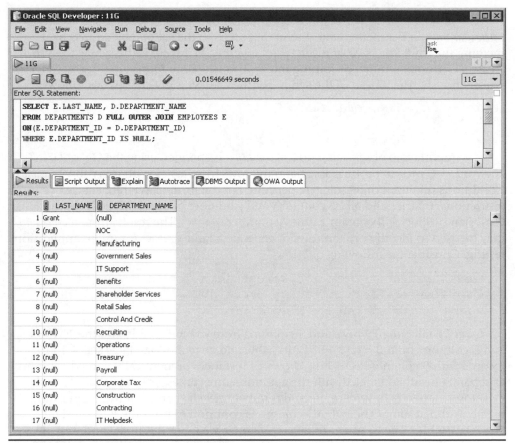

Figure 12-12 Full outer join

Generate a Cartesian Product of Two or More Tables

A *Cartesian product* of two tables is created by joining each row of the source table with every row in the target table. The number of rows in the result set created by a Cartesian product is equal to the number of rows in the source table multiplied by the number of rows in the target table. Cartesian products may be formed intentionally using the ANSI SQL:1999 *cross join* syntax. This technique is described in the next section.

Creating Cartesian Products Using Cross Joins

Cartesian product is a mathematical term that refers to the set of data created by merging the rows from two or more tables together. *Cross join* is the syntax used to create a Cartesian product by joining multiple tables. Both terms are often used synonymously. The format of the syntax for the CROSS JOIN clause is as follows:

```
SELECT table1.column, table2.column
FROM table1
CROSS JOIN table2;
```

It is important to observe that no *join condition* is specified using the ON or USING keyword. A Cartesian product associates the rows from *table1* with every row in *table2*. Conditions that limit the results are permitted in the form of WHERE clause restrictions. If *table1* and *table2* contain x and y number of rows, respectively, the Cartesian product will contain x times y number of rows. The results from a *cross join* may be used to identify orphan rows or generate a large dataset for use in application testing. Consider the following queries:

> *Query 1:* `select * from jobs cross join job_history;`
> *Query 2:* `select * from jobs j cross join job_history jh`
> `where j.job_id='AD_PRES';`

Query 1 takes the 19 rows and 4 columns from the JOBS table and the 10 rows and 5 columns from the JOB_HISTORY table and generates one large set of 190 records with 9 columns. SQL*Plus shows all instances of identically named columns as separate headings labeled with the column name (unless they are aliased). SQL Developer appends an underscore and number to each shared column name and uses it as the heading. The JOB_ID column is common to both the JOBS and JOB_HISTORY tables. The headings in SQL Developer are labeled JOB_ID and JOB_ID_1, respectively. Query 2 generates the same Cartesian product as the first, but the 190 rows are constrained by the WHERE clause condition and only 10 rows are returned.

Figure 12-13 shows a *cross join* between the REGIONS and COUNTRIES tables. There are 4 rows in REGIONS and 25 rows in COUNTRIES. Since the WHERE clause limits the REGIONS table to 2 of 4 rows, the Cartesian product produces 50 (25 × 2) records. The results are sorted alphabetically, first on the REGION_NAME and then on the COUNTRY_NAME. The first record has the pair of values, Asia and Argentina. When the REGION_NAME changes, the first record has the pair of values, Africa and Argentina. Notice that the COUNTRY_NAME values are repeated for every REGION_NAME.

 EXAM TIP When using the *cross join* syntax, a Cartesian product is intentionally generated. Inadvertent Cartesian products are created when there are insufficient join conditions in a statement. Joins that specify fewer than $N - 1$ *join conditions* when joining N tables or that specify invalid *join conditions* may inadvertently create Cartesian products. A *pure natural join* between two tables sharing no identically named columns results in a Cartesian join, since two tables are joined but less than one condition is available.

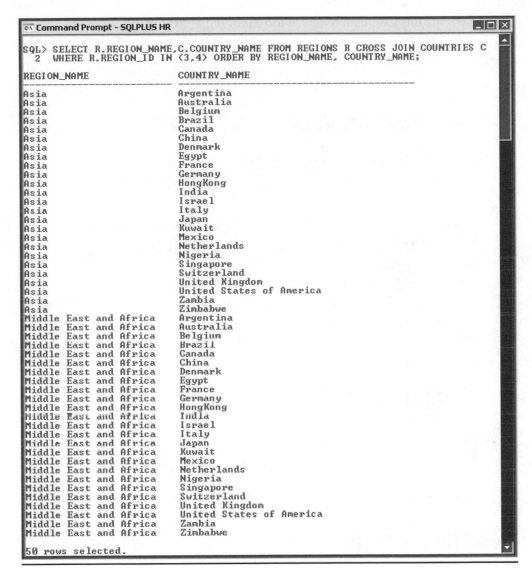

Figure 12-13   The cross join

Exercise 12-4: Work with Joins   Using SQL Developer or SQL*Plus, connect to the WEBSTORE schema and produce a report of customers who purchased the 11G All-in-One Guide (PRODUCT_ID=2). The report must contain the customer's name, the product description, and the quantity ordered. There are several approaches to solving this question. Your approach may differ from this solution.

1. Start SQL*Plus and connect to the WEBSTORE schema.

2. Execute this statement to return the report required as shown in the following illustration:

```
select customer_name, product_description, quantity
from customers join orders using (customer_id) join order_items using (oder_id)
join products using (product_id) where product_id=2;
```

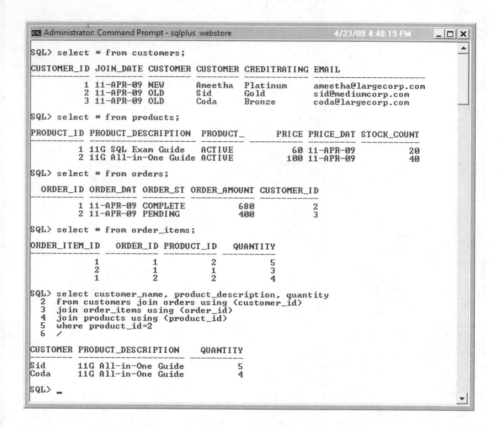

Two-Minute Drill

Write SELECT Statements to Access Data from More Than One Table Using Equijoins and Nonequijoins

- Equijoining occurs when one query fetches column values from multiple tables in which the rows fulfill an equality-based join condition.

- A pure natural join is performed using the NATURAL JOIN syntax when the source and target tables are implicitly equijoined using all identically named columns.

- The JOIN . . . USING syntax allows a natural join to be formed on specific columns with shared names.

- Dot notation refers to qualifying a column by prefixing it with its table name and a dot or period symbol. This designates the table a column originates from and differentiates it from identically named columns from other tables.

- The JOIN . . . ON clause allows the explicit specification of join columns regardless of their column names. This provides a flexible joining format.

- The ON, USING, and NATURAL keywords are mutually exclusive and therefore cannot appear together in a join clause.

- A nonequijoin is performed when the values in the join columns fulfill the join condition based on an inequality operator.

Join a Table to Itself Using a Self-Join

- A self-join is required when the join columns originate from the same table. Conceptually, the source table is duplicated and a target table is created. The self-join then works as a regular join between two discrete tables.

- Storing hierarchical data in a relational table requires a minimum of two columns per row. One column stores an identifier of the row's parent record, and the second stores the row's identifier.

View Data That Does Not Meet a Join Condition Using Outer Joins

- When equijoins and nonequijoins are performed, rows from the source and target tables are matched. These are referred to as inner joins.

- An outer join is performed when rows that are not retrieved by an inner join are included for retrieval.

- A left outer join between the source and target tables returns the results of an inner join and the missing rows it excluded from the source table.

- A right outer join between the source and target tables returns the results of an inner join and the missing rows it excluded from the target table.

- A full outer join returns the combined results of a left outer join and a right outer join.

Generate a Cartesian Product of Two or More Tables

- A Cartesian product is sometimes called a cross join and refers to the set of data created by merging the rows from two or more tables with each other.

- The count of the rows returned from a Cartesian product is equal to the number of rows in the source table multiplied by the number of rows in the target table.

- Joins that specify fewer than $N - 1$ join conditions when joining N tables, or that specify invalid join conditions, inadvertently create Cartesian products.

Self Test

1. The EMPLOYEES and DEPARTMENTS tables have two identically named columns: DEPARTMENT_ID and MANAGER_ID. Which of these statements joins these tables based only on common DEPARTMENT_ID values? (Choose all that apply.)

   A. SELECT * FROM EMPLOYEES NATURAL JOIN DEPARTMENTS;

   B. SELECT * FROM EMPLOYEES E NATURAL JOIN DEPARTMENTS D ON E.DEPARTMENT_ID=D.DEPARTMENT_ID;

   C. SELECT * FROM EMPLOYEES NATURAL JOIN DEPARTMENTS USING (DEPARTMENT_ID);

   D. None of the above

2. The EMPLOYEES and DEPARTMENTS tables have two identically named columns: DEPARTMENT_ID and MANAGER_ID. Which statements join these tables based on both column values? (Choose all that apply.)

   A. SELECT * FROM EMPLOYEES NATURAL JOIN DEPARTMENTS;

   B. SELECT * FROM EMPLOYEES JOIN DEPARTMENTS USING (DEPARTMENT_ID,MANAGER_ID);

   C. SELECT * FROM EMPLOYEES E JOIN DEPARTMENTS D ON E.DEPARTMENT_ID=D.DEPARTMENT_ID AND E.MANAGER_ID=D.MANAGER_ID;

   D. None of the above

3. Which join is performed by the following query?
   ```
   SELECT E.JOB_ID ,J.JOB_ID FROM EMPLOYEES E
   JOIN JOBS J ON (E.SALARY < J.MAX_SALARY);
   ```
   (Choose the best answer.)

   A. Equijoin

   B. Nonequijoin

   C. Cross join

   D. Outer join

4. Which of the following statements are syntactically correct? (Choose all that apply.)

   A. SELECT * FROM EMPLOYEES E JOIN DEPARTMENTS D USING (DEPARTMENT_ID);

   B. SELECT * FROM EMPLOYEES JOIN DEPARTMENTS D USING (D.DEPARTMENT_ID);

    C. SELECT D.DEPARTMENT_ID FROM EMPLOYEES JOIN DEPARTMENTS D
       USING (DEPARTMENT_ID);

    D. None of the above

5. Which of the following statements are syntactically correct? (Choose all that
   apply.)

    A. SELECT E.EMPLOYEE_ID, J.JOB_ID PREVIOUS_JOB, E.JOB_ID
       CURRENT_JOB FROM JOB_HISTORY J CROSS JOIN EMPLOYEES E ON
       (J.START_DATE=E.HIRE_DATE);

    B. SELECT E.EMPLOYEE_ID, J.JOB_ID PREVIOUS_JOB, E.JOB_ID
       CURRENT_JOB FROM JOB_HISTORY J JOIN EMPLOYEES E ON
       (J.START_DATE=E.HIRE_DATE);

    C. SELECT E.EMPLOYEE_ID, J.JOB_ID PREVIOUS_JOB, E.JOB_ID
       CURRENT_JOB FROM JOB_HISTORY J OUTER JOIN EMPLOYEES E ON
       (J.START_DATE=E.HIRE_DATE);

    D. None of the above

6. Choose one correct statement regarding the following query:

```
SELECT * FROM EMPLOYEES E
JOIN DEPARTMENTS D ON (D.DEPARTMENT_ID=E.DEPARTMENT_ID)
JOIN LOCATIONS L ON (L.LOCATION_ID =D.LOCATION_ID);
```

    A. Joining three tables is not permitted.

    B. A Cartesian product is generated.

    C. The JOIN   ON clause may be used for joins between multiple tables.

    D. None of the above.

7. How many rows are returned after executing the following statement?

```
SELECT * FROM REGIONS R1 JOIN REGIONS R2 ON (R1.REGION_
ID=LENGTH(R2.REGION_NAME)/2);
```

   The REGIONS table contains the following row data. (Choose the best answer.)

REGION_ID	REGION_NAME
1	Europe
2	Americas
3	Asia
4	Middle East and Africa

    A. 2

    B. 3

    C. 4

    D. None of the above

8. Choose one correct statement regarding the following query:
   ```
   SELECT C.COUNTRY_ID
   FROM LOCATIONS L RIGHT OUTER JOIN COUNTRIES C
   ON (L.COUNTRY_ID=C.COUNTRY_ID) WHERE L.COUNTRY_ID is NULL;
   ```
   A. The rows returned represent those countries for which there are no locations.

   B. The rows returned represent those locations that have no COUNTRY_ID.

   C. The rows returned represent the COUNTRY_ID values for all the rows in the LOCATIONS table.

   D. None of the above.

9. Which of the following statements are syntactically correct? (Choose all that apply.)
   A. SELECT JH.JOB_ID FROM JOB_HISTORY JH RIGHT OUTER JOIN JOBS J ON JH.JOB_ID=J.JOB_ID

   B. SELECT JOB_ID FROM JOB_HISTORY JH RIGHT OUTER JOIN JOBS J ON (JH.JOB_ID=J.JOB_ID)

   C. SELECT JOB_HISTORY.JOB_ID FROM JOB_HISTORY OUTER JOIN JOBS ON JOB_HISTORY.JOB_ID=JOBS.JOB_ID

   D. None of the above

10. If the REGIONS table, which contains 4 rows, is cross joined to the COUNTRIES table, which contains 25 rows, how many rows appear in the final results set? (Choose the best answer.)
    A. 100 rows

    B. 4 rows

    C. 25 rows

    D. None of the above

Self Test Answers

1. ☑ D. The queries in B and C incorrectly contain the NATURAL keyword. If this is removed, they will join the DEPARTMENTS and EMPLOYEES tables based on the DEPARTMENT_ID column.

   ☒ A, B, and C. A performs a pure natural join that implicitly joins the two tables on all columns with identical names, which, in this case, are DEPARTMENT_ID and MANAGER_ID.

2. ☑ A, B, and C. These clauses demonstrate different techniques to join the tables on both the DEPARTMENT_ID and MANAGER_ID columns.

   ☒ D.

3. ☑   **B.** The join condition is an expression based on the *less than* inequality operator. Therefore, this join is a nonequijoin.

   ☒   **A, C,** and **D. A** would be correct if the operator in the join condition expression was an equality operator. The CROSS JOIN keywords or the absence of a join condition would result in **C** being true. **D** would be true if one of the OUTER JOIN clauses was used instead of the JOIN . . . ON clause.

4. ☑   **A.** This statement demonstrates the correct usage of the JOIN . . . USING clause.

   ☒   **B, C,** and **D. B** is incorrect because only nonqualified column names are allowed in the brackets after the USING keyword. **C** is incorrect because the column in brackets after the USING keyword cannot be referenced with a qualifier in the SELECT clause.

5. ☑   **B** demonstrates the correct usage of the JOIN . . . ON clause.

   ☒   **A, C,** and **D. A** is incorrect since the CROSS JOIN clause cannot contain the ON keyword. **C** is incorrect since the OUTER JOIN keywords must be preceded by the LEFT, RIGHT, or FULL keyword.

6. ☑   **C.** The JOIN . . . ON clause and the other join clauses may all be used for joins between multiple tables. The JOIN . . . ON and JOIN . . . USING clauses are better suited for N-way table joins.

   ☒   **A, B,** and **D. A** is false, since you may join as many tables as you wish. A Cartesian product is not created, since there are two join conditions and three tables.

7. ☑   **B.** Three rows are returned. For the row with a REGION_ID value of 2, the REGION_NAME is Asia and half the length of the REGION_NAME is also 2. Therefore this row is returned. The same logic results in the rows with REGION_ID values of 3 and 4 and REGION_NAME values of Europe and Americas being returned.

   ☒   **A, C,** and **D.**

8. ☑   **A.** The right outer join fetches the COUNTRY.COUNTRY_ID values that do not exist in the LOCATIONS table in addition to performing an inner join between the tables. The WHERE clause then eliminates the inner join results. The rows remaining represent those countries for which there are no locations.

   ☒   **B, C,** and **D.**

9. ☑   **A.** This statement demonstrates the correct use of the RIGHT OUTER JOIN . . . ON clause.

☒   **B, C,** and **D.** The JOB_ID column in the SELECT clause in **B** is not qualified and is therefore ambiguous, since the table from which this column comes is not specified. **C** uses an OUTER JOIN without the keywords LEFT, RIGHT, or FULL.

10. ☑   **A.** The cross join associates every four rows from the REGIONS table 25 times with the rows from the COUNTRIES table, yielding a result set that contains 100 rows.

☒   **B, C,** and **D.**

CHAPTER 13

Subqueries and Set Operators

Exam Objectives

In this chapter you will learn to

- 051.7.1   Define Subqueries
- 051.7.2   Describe the Types of Problems That the Subqueries Can Solve
- 051.7.3   List the Types of Subqueries
- 051.7.4   Write Single-Row and Multiple-Row Subqueries
- 051.8.1   Describe Set Operators
- 051.8.2   Use a Set Operator to Combine Multiple Queries into a Single Query
- 051.8.3   Control the Order of Rows Returned

515

The previous chapters have dealt with the SELECT statement in considerable detail, but in every case the SELECT statement has been a single, self-contained command. This chapter shows how two or more SELECT commands can be combined into one statement. The first technique is the use of *subqueries*. A subquery is a SELECT statement whose output is used as input to another SELECT statement (or indeed to a DML statement, as done in Chapter 8). The second technique is the use of set operators, where the results of several SELECT commands are combined into a single result set.

Define Subqueries

A subquery is a query that is nested inside a SELECT, INSERT, UPDATE, or DELETE statement or inside another subquery. A subquery can return a set of rows or just one row to its parent query. A *scalar* subquery returns exactly one value: a single row, with a single column. Scalar subqueries can be used in most places in a SQL statement where you could use an expression or a literal value.

The places in a query where a subquery may be used are

- In the SELECT list used for column projection
- In the FROM clause
- In the WHERE clause
- In the HAVING clause

A subquery is often referred to as an *inner* query, and the statement within which it occurs is then called the *outer* query. There is nothing wrong with this terminology, except that it may imply that you can only have two levels, inner and outer. In fact, the Oracle implementation of subqueries does not impose any practical limits on the level of nesting: the depth of nesting permitted in the FROM clause of a statement is unlimited, and that in the WHERE clause is up to 255.

EXAM TIP Subqueries can be nested to an unlimited depth in a FROM clause but to "only" 255 levels in a WHERE clause. They can be used in the SELECT list and in the FROM, WHERE, and HAVING clauses of a query.

A subquery can have any of the usual clauses for selection and projection. The following are required clauses:

- A SELECT list
- A FROM clause

The following are optional clauses:

- WHERE
- GROUP BY
- HAVING

The subquery (or subqueries) within a statement must be executed before the parent query that calls it, in order that the results of the subquery can be passed to the parent.

Exercise 13-1: Try Out Types of Subquery   In this exercise, you will write code that demonstrates the places where subqueries can be used. Use either SQL*Plus or SQL Developer. All the queries should be run when connected to the HR schema.

1. Log on to your database as user HR.

2. Write a query that uses subqueries in the column projection list. The query will report on the current numbers of departments and staff:

```
select sysdate Today,
(select count(*) from departments) Dept_count,
(select count(*) from employees) Emp_count
from dual;
```

3. Write a query to identify all the employees who are managers. This will require using a subquery in the WHERE clause to select all the employees whose EMPLOYEE_ID appears as a MANAGER_ID:

```
select last_name from employees where
(employee_id in (select manager_id from employees));
```

4. Write a query to identify the highest salary paid in each country. This will require using a subquery in the FROM clause:

```
select max(salary),country_id from
 (select e.salary,department_id,location_id,l.country_id
  from employees e join departments d using (department_id)
                   join locations l using (location_id))
group by country_id;
```

Describe the Types of Problems That the Subqueries Can Solve

There are many situations where you will need the result of one query as the input for another.

Use of a Subquery Result Set for Comparison Purposes

Which employees have a salary that is less than the average salary? This could be answered by two statements, or by a single statement with a subquery. The following example uses two statements:

```
select avg(salary) from employees;
select last_name from employees where salary < result_of_previous_query ;
```

Alternatively, this example uses one statement with a subquery:

```
select last_name from employees
where salary < (select avg(salary) from employees);
```

In this example, the subquery is used to substitute a value into the WHERE clause of the parent query: it returns a single value, used for comparison with the rows retrieved by the parent query.

The subquery could return a set of rows. For example, you could use the following to find all departments that do actually have one or more employees assigned to them:

```
select department_name from departments where department_id in
(select distinct(department_id) from employees);
```

In the preceding example, the subquery is used as an alternative to an inner join. The same result could have been achieved with the following:

```
select department_name from departments join employees
on employees.department_id = departments.department_id
group by department_name;
```

If the subquery is going to return more than one row, then the comparison operator must be able to accept multiple values. These operators are IN, NOT IN, ANY, and ALL. If the comparison operator is any of the scalar equality or inequality operators (which each can only accept one value), the parent query will fail.

 TIP Using NOT IN is fraught with problems because of the way SQL handles NULLs. As a general rule, do not use NOT IN unless you are certain that the result set will not include a NULL.

Generate a Table from Which to SELECT

Subqueries can also be used in the FROM clause, where they are sometimes referred to as *inline views*. Consider another problem based on the HR schema: employees are assigned to a department, and departments have a location. Each location is in a country. How can you find the average salary of staff in a country, even though they work for different departments? Like this:

```
select avg(salary),country_id from
   (select salary,department_id,location_id,l.country_id
    from employees join departments d using (department_id)
    join locations l using (location_id))
group by country_id;
```

The subquery constructs a table with every employee's salary and the country in which their department is based. The parent query then addresses this table, averaging the SALARY and grouping by COUNTRY_ID.

Generate Values for Projection

The third place a subquery can go is in the SELECT list of a query. How can you identify the highest salary and the highest commission rate and thus what the maximum commission paid would be if the highest salaried employee also had the highest commission rate? Like this, with two subqueries:

```
select
(select max(salary) from employees) *
(select max(commission_pct) from employees)
from dual;
```

In this usage, the SELECT list used to project columns is being populated with the results of the subqueries. A subquery used in this manner must be scalar, or the parent query will fail with an error.

Generate Rows to Be Passed to a DML Statement

DML statements are covered in Chapter 8. Consider these examples:

```
insert into sales_hist select * from sales where date > sysdate-1;
update employees set salary = (select avg(salary) from employees);
delete from departments
where department_id not in (select department_id from employees);
```

The first example uses a subquery to identify a set of rows in one table that will be inserted into another. The second example uses a subquery to calculate the average salary of all employees and passes this value (a scalar quantity) to an UPDATE statement. The third example uses a subquery to retrieve all DEPARTMENT_IDs that are in use and passes the list to a DELETE command, which will remove all departments that are not in use.

Note that it is not legal to use a subquery in the VALUES clause of an INSERT statement; this is fine:

```
insert into dates select sysdate from dual;
```

But this is not:

```
insert into dates (date_col) values (select sysdate from dual);
```

 EXAM TIP A subquery can be used to select rows for insertion but not in a VALUES clause of an INSERT statement.

Exercise 13-2: Write More Complex Subqueries   In this exercise, you will write more complicated subqueries. Use either SQL*Plus or SQL Developer. All the queries should be run when connected to the HR schema.

1. Log on to your database as user HR.
2. Write a query that will identify all employees who work in departments located in the United Kingdom. This will require three levels of nested subqueries:

   ```
   select last_name from employees where department_id in

   (select department_id from departments
   where location_id in
   ```

```
(select location_id from locations
where country_id =

(select country_id from countries
where country_name='United Kingdom')
)
);
```

3. Check that the result from Step 2 is correct by running the subqueries independently. First, find the COUNTRY_ID for the United Kingdom:

```
select country_id from countries where country_name='United Kingdom';
```

The result will be UK. Then find the corresponding locations:

```
select location_id from locations where country_id = 'UK';
```

The LOCATION_IDs returned will be 2400, 2500, and 2600. Then find the DEPARTMENT_IDs of departments in these locations:

```
select department_id from departments where location_id in (2400,2500,2600);
```

The result will be two departments, 40 and 80. Finally, find the relevant employees:

```
select last_name from employees where department_id in (40,80);
```

4. Write a query to identify all the employees who earn more than the average and who work in any of the IT departments. This will require two subqueries that are not nested:

```
select last_name from employees
where department_id in
(select department_id from departments where department_name like 'IT%')
and salary > (select avg(salary) from employees);
```

List the Types of Subqueries

There are three broad divisions of subquery:

- Single-row subqueries
- Multiple-row subqueries
- Correlated subqueries

Single- and Multiple-Row Subqueries

The *single-row* subquery returns one row. A special case is the scalar subquery, which returns a single row with one column. Scalar subqueries are acceptable (and often very useful) in virtually any situation where you could use a literal value, a constant, or an expression. *Multiple-row* subqueries return sets of rows. These queries are commonly used to generate result sets that will be passed to a DML or SELECT statement for further processing. Both single-row and multiple-row subqueries will be evaluated once, before the parent query is run.

Single- and multiple-row subqueries can be used in the WHERE and HAVING clauses of the parent query, but there are restrictions on the legal comparison operators. If the comparison operator is any of the ones in the following table, the subquery must be a single-row subquery:

Symbol	Meaning
=	Equal
>	Greater than
>=	Greater than or equal
<	Less than
<=	Less than or equal
<>	Not equal
!=	Not equal

If any of the operators in the preceding table are used with a subquery that returns more than one row, the query will fail. The operators in the following table can use multiple-row subqueries:

Symbol	Meaning
IN	Equal to any member in a list
NOT IN	Not equal to any member in a list
ANY	Returns rows that match any value on a list
ALL	Returns rows that match all the values in a list

 EXAM TIP The comparison operators valid for single-row subqueries are =, >, >=, <, <=, <> and !=. The comparison operators valid for multiple-row subqueries are IN, NOT IN, ANY, and ALL.

Correlated Subqueries

A *correlated subquery* has a more complex method of execution than single- and multiple-row subqueries and is potentially much more powerful. If a subquery references columns in the parent query, then its result will be dependent on the parent query. This makes it impossible to evaluate the subquery before evaluating the parent query. Consider this statement, which lists all employees who earn less than the average salary:

```
select last_name from employees
where salary < (select avg(salary) from employees);
```

The single-row subquery need be executed only once, and its result substituted into the parent query. But now consider a query that will list all employees whose salary is less than the average salary of their department. In this case, the subquery must be run for each employee to determine the average salary for their department; it is necessary to pass the employee's department code to the subquery. This can be done as follows:

```
select p.last_name, p.department_id from employees p
where p.salary < (select avg(s.salary) from employees s
where s.department_id=p.department_id);
```

In this example, the subquery references a column, `p.department_id`, from the select list of the parent query. This is the signal that, rather than evaluating the subquery once, must be evaluated for every row in the parent query. To execute the query, Oracle will look at every row in EMPLOYEES and, as it does so, run the subquery using the DEPARTMENT_ID of the current employee row.

The flow of execution is as follows:

1. Start at the first row of the EMPLOYEES table.

2. Read the DEPARTMENT_ID and SALARY of the current row.

3. Run the subquery using the DEPARTMENT_ID from Step 2.

4. Compare the result of Step 3 with the SALARY from Step 2, and return the row if the SALARY is less than the result.

5. Advance to the next row in the EMPLOYEES table.

6. Repeat from Step 2.

A single-row or multiple-row subquery is evaluated once, before evaluating the outer query; a correlated subquery must be evaluated once for every row in the outer query. A correlated subquery can be single- or multiple-row, if the comparison operator is appropriate.

TIP Correlated subqueries can be a very inefficient construct, due to the need for repeated execution of the subquery. Always try to find an alternative approach.

Exercise 13-3: Investigate the Different Types of Subquery

In this exercise, you will demonstrate problems that can occur with different types of subqueries. Use either SQL*Plus or SQL Developer. All the queries should be run when connected to the HR schema: it is assumed that the EMPLOYEES table has the standard sets of rows.

1. Log on to your database as user HR.

2. Write a query to determine who earns more than Mr. Tobias:

```
select last_name from employees where
salary > (select salary from employees where last_name='Tobias')
order by last_name;
```

This will return 86 names, in alphabetical order.

3. Write a query to determine who earns more than Mr. Taylor:

```
select last_name from employees where
salary > (select salary from employees where last_name='Taylor')
order by last_name;
```

This will fail with the error: "ORA-01427: single-row subquery returns more than one row." Determine why the query in Step 2 succeeded but the one in Step 3 failed. The answer lies in the data:

```
select count(last_name) from employees where last_name='Tobias';
select count(last_name) from employees where last_name='Taylor';
```

The following illustration shows the error followed by the output of the queries from Step 3, executed with SQL*Plus. The use of the "greater than" operator in the queries for Steps 2 and 3 requires a single-row subquery, but the subquery used may return any number of rows, depending on the search predicate used.

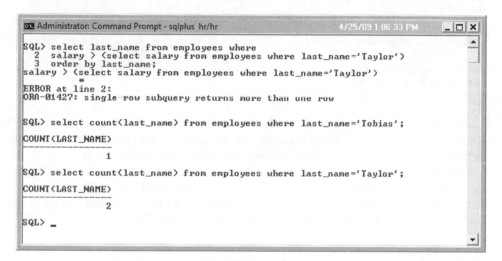

4. Fix the code in Steps 2 and 3 so that the statements will succeed no matter what LAST_NAME is used. There are two possible solutions: one uses a different comparison operator that can handle a multiple-row subquery; the other uses a subquery that will always be single-row.

The first solution:

```
select last_name from employees where
salary > all (select salary from employees where last_name='Taylor')
order by last_name;
```

The second solution:

```
select last_name from employees where
salary > (select max(salary) from employees where last_name='Taylor')
order by last_name;
```

Write Single-Row and Multiple-Row Subqueries

Following are examples of single- and multiple-row subqueries. They are based on the HR schema.

How would you figure out which employees have a manager who works for a department based in the United Kingdom? This is a possible solution, using multiple-row subqueries:

```
select last_name from employees
where manager_id in
(select employee_id from employees where department_id in
 (select department_id from departments where location_id in
  (select location_id from locations where country_id='UK')));
```

In the preceding example, subqueries are nested three levels deep. Note that the subqueries use the IN operator because it is possible that the queries could return several rows.

You have been asked to find the job with the highest average salary. This can be done with a single-row subquery:

```
select job_title from jobs natural join employees group by job_title
having avg(salary) =
(select max(avg(salary)) from employees group by job_id);
```

The subquery returns a single value: the maximum of all the average salary values that was determined per JOB_ID. It is safe to use the equality operator for this subquery because the MAX function guarantees that only one row will be returned.

The ANY and ALL operators are supported syntax, but their function can be duplicated with other more commonly used operators combined with aggregations. For example, these two statements, which retrieve all employees whose salary is above that of anyone in department 80, will return identical result sets:

```
select last_name from employees where salary > all
(select salary from employees where department_id=80);
select last_name from employees where salary >
(select max(salary) from employees where department_id=80);
```

The following table summarizes the equivalents for ANY and ALL:

Operator	Meaning
< ANY	Less than the highest
> ANY	More than the lowest
= ANY	Equivalent to IN
> ALL	More than the highest
< ALL	Less than the lowest

Describe the Set Operators

All SELECT statements return a set of rows. The set operators take as their input the results of two or more SELECT statements and from these generate a single result set. This is known as a *compound query*. Oracle provides three set operators: UNION, INTERSECT, and MINUS. UNION can be qualified with ALL. There is a significant deviation from the ISO standard for SQL here, in that ISO SQL uses EXCEPT where Oracle uses MINUS, but the functionality is identical. The Oracle set operators are

- **UNION**   Returns the combined rows from two queries, sorting them and removing duplicates.
- **UNION ALL**   Returns the combined rows from two queries without sorting or removing duplicates.
- **INTERSECT**   Returns only the rows that occur in both queries' result sets, sorting them and removing duplicates.
- **MINUS**   Returns only the rows in the first result set that do not appear in the second result set, sorting them and removing duplicates.

These commands are equivalent to the standard operators used in mathematics set theory, often depicted graphically as Venn diagrams.

Sets and Venn Diagrams

Consider groupings of living creatures, classified as follows:

- **Creatures with two legs**   Humans, parrots, bats
- **Creatures that can fly**   Parrots, bats, bees
- **Creatures with fur**   Bears, bats

Each classification is known as a *set*, and each member of the set is an *element*. The *union* of the three sets is humans, parrots, bats, bees, and bears. This is all the elements in all the sets, without the duplications. The *intersection* of the sets is all elements that are common to all three sets, again removing the duplicates. In this simple example, the intersection has just one element: bats. The intersection of the two-legged set and the flying set has two elements: parrots and bats. The *minus* of the sets is the elements of one set without the elements of another, so the two-legged creatures set minus the flying creatures set results in a single element: humans. These sets can be represented graphically as the Venn diagram shown in Figure 13-1.

The circle in the top left of the figure represents the set of two-legged creatures; the circle top right is creatures that can fly; the bottom circle is furry animals. The unions, intersections, and minuses of the sets are immediately apparent by observing the elements in the various parts of the circles that do or do not overlap. The diagram in the figure also includes the universal set, represented by the rectangle. The universal set is all elements that exist but are not members of the defined sets. In this case, the universal set would be defined as all living creatures that evolved without developing fur, two legs, or the ability to fly (such as fish).

Figure 13-1
A Venn diagram,
showing three sets
and the universal set

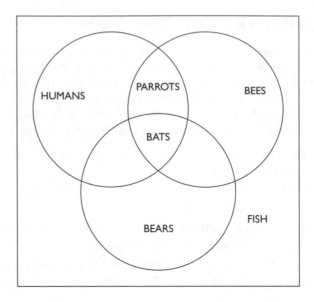

Set Operator General Principles

All set operators make compound queries by combining the result sets from two or more queries. If a SELECT statement includes more than one set operator (and therefore more than two queries), they will be applied in the order the programmer specifies: top to bottom and left to right. Although pending enhancements to ISO SQL will give INTERSECT a higher priority than the other set operators, there is currently no priority of one operator over another. To override this precedence based on the order in which the operators appear, you can use parentheses: operators within brackets will be evaluated before passing the results to operators outside the brackets.

 TIP Given the pending change in operator priority, it may be good practice always to use parentheses. This will ensure that the code's function won't change when run against a later version of the database.

Each query in a compound query will project its own list of selected columns. These lists must have the same number of elements, be nominated in the same sequence, and be of broadly similar data type. They do not have to have the same names (or column aliases), nor do they need to come from the same tables (or subqueries). If the column names (or aliases) are different, the result set of the compound query will have columns named as they were in the first query.

 EXAM TIP The columns in the queries that make up a compound query can have different names, but the output result set will use the names of the columns in the first query.

While the selected column lists do not have to be exactly the same data type, they must be from the same data type group. For example, the columns selected by one query could be of data types DATE and NUMBER, and those from the second query could be TIMESTAMP and INTEGER. The result set of the compound query will have columns with the higher level of precision: in this case, they would be TIMESTAMP and NUMBER. Other than accepting data types from the same group, the set operators will not do any implicit type casting. If the second query retrieved columns of type VARCHAR2, the compound query would throw an error even if the string variables could be resolved to legitimate date and numeric values.

EXAM TIP The corresponding columns in the queries that make up a compound query must be of the same data type group.

UNION, MINUS, and INTERSECT will always combine the result sets of the input queries, then sort the results to remove duplicate rows. The sorting is based on all the columns, from left to right. If all the columns in two rows have the same value, then only the first row is returned in the compound result set. A side effect of this is that the output of a compound query will be sorted. If the sort order (which is ascending, based on the order in which the columns happen to appear in the select lists) is not the order you want, it is possible to put a single ORDER BY clause at the end of the compound query. It is not possible to use ORDER BY in any of the queries that make up the whole compound query, as this would disrupt the sorting that is necessary to remove duplicates.

EXAM TIP A compound query will by default return rows sorted across all the columns, from left to right. The only exception is UNION ALL, where the rows will not be sorted. The only place where an ORDER BY clause is permitted is at the end of the compound query.

UNION ALL is the exception to the sorting-no-duplicates rule: the result sets of the input queries will be concatenated to form the result of the compound query. But you still can't use ORDER BY in the individual queries; it can only appear at the end of the compound query, where it will be applied to the complete result set.

Exercise 13-4: Describe the Set Operators In this exercise, you will see the effect of the set operators. Either SQL*Plus or SQL Developer can be used.

1. Connect to your database as user WEBSTORE.

2. Run these queries:

```
select * from customers;
select * from orders;
```

Note the result, in particular the order of the rows. If these tables are as created in Chapter 9, there will be three customers' details and two orders returned. The CUSTOMER_ID values are returned in the order: 1,2,3 and 2,3 respectively.

3. Perform a union between the set of customers.customer_id and orders .customer_id values:

```
select customer_id from customers union select customer_id from orders;
```

Only the distinct customer_id values are returned sorted as: 1,2,3.

4. This time, use UNION ALL:

```
select customer_id from customers union all select customer_id from orders;
```

There will be five rows, and they will not be sorted.

5. An intersection will retrieve rows common to two queries:

```
select customer_id from customers intersect select customer_id from orders;
```

Two rows are common, and the result is sorted.

6. A MINUS will remove common rows:

```
select customer_id from customers minus select customer_id from orders;
```

The first set (1,2,3) minus (2,3) yields a single row.

All queries in this exercise are shown in the following illustration.

Use a Set Operator to Combine Multiple Queries into a Single Query

Compound queries are two or more queries, linked with one or more set operators. The end result is a single result set.

The examples that follow are based on two tables, OLD_DEPT and NEW_DEPT. The table OLD_DEPT is intended to represent a table created with an earlier version of Oracle, when the only data type available for representing date and time data was DATE, the only option for numeric data was NUMBER, and character data was fixed-length CHAR. The table NEW_DEPT uses the more tightly defined INTEGER numeric data type (which Oracle implements as a NUMBER of up to 38 significant digits but no decimal places), the more space-efficient VARCHAR2 for character data, and the TIMESTAMP data type, which can by default store date and time values with six decimals of precision on the seconds. There are two rows in each table.

The UNION ALL Operator

A UNION ALL takes two result sets and concatenates them together into a single result set. The result sets come from two queries that must select the same number of columns, and the corresponding columns of the two queries (in the order in which they are specified) must be of the same data type group. The columns do not have to have the same names.

Figure 13-2 demonstrates a UNION ALL operation from two tables. The UNION ALL of the two tables converts all the values to the higher level of precision: the dates are returned as timestamps (the less precise DATEs padded with zeros), the character data is the more efficient VARCHAR2 with the length of the longer input column, and the numbers (though this is not obvious due to the nature of the data) will accept decimals. The order of the rows is the rows from the first table in whatever order they happen to be stored followed by the rows from the second table in whatever order they happen to be stored.

Figure 13-2
A UNION ALL with data type conversions

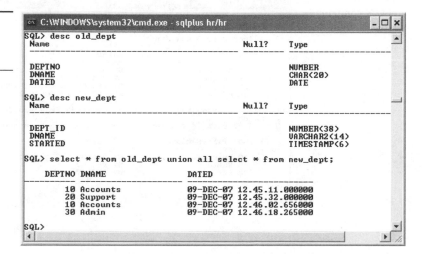

EXAM TIP A UNION ALL will return rows grouped from each query in their natural order. This behavior can be modified by placing a single ORDER BY clause at the end.

The UNION Operator

A UNION performs a UNION ALL and then sorts the result across all the columns and removes duplicates. The first query in Figure 13-3 returns all four rows because there are no duplicates. However, the rows are now in order. It may appear that the first two rows are not in order because of the values in DATED, but they are: the DNAME in the table OLD_DEPTS is 20 bytes long (padded with spaces), whereas the DNAME in NEW_DEPTS, where it is a VARCHAR2, is only as long as the name itself. The spaces give the row from OLD_DEPT a higher sort value, even though the date value is less.

The second query in Figure 13-3 removes any leading or trailing spaces from the DNAME columns and chops off the time elements from DATED and STARTED. Two of the rows thus become identical, and so only one appears in the output.

Because of the sort, the order of the queries in a UNION compound query makes no difference to the order of the rows returned.

 TIP If, as a developer, you know that there can be no duplicates between two tables, then always use UNION ALL. It saves the database from doing a lot of sorting. Your DBA will not be pleased with you if you use UNION unnecessarily.

The INTERSECT Operator

The intersection of two sets is the rows that are common to both sets, as shown in Figure 13-4.

Figure 13-3
UNION compound queries

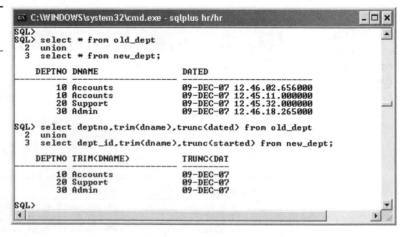

Figure 13-4
INTERSECT
and MINUS

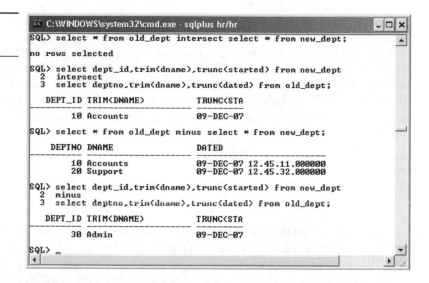

```
SQL> select * from old_dept intersect select * from new_dept;

no rows selected

SQL> select dept_id,trim(dname),trunc(started) from new_dept
  2  intersect
  3  select deptno,trim(dname),trunc(dated) from old_dept;

   DEPT_ID TRIM(DNAME)            TRUNC(STA
---------- ---------------------- ---------
        10 Accounts               09-DEC-07

SQL> select * from old_dept minus select * from new_dept;

    DEPTNO DNAME                  DATED
---------- ---------------------- -----------------------
        10 Accounts               09-DEC-07 12.45.11.000000
        20 Support                09-DEC-07 12.45.32.000000

SQL> select dept_id,trim(dname),trunc(started) from new_dept
  2  minus
  3  select deptno,trim(dname),trunc(dated) from old_dept;

   DEPT_ID TRIM(DNAME)            TRUNC(STA
---------- ---------------------- ---------
        30 Admin                  09-DEC-07

SQL> _
```

PART II

The first query shown in Figure 13-4 returns no rows, because every row in the two tables is different. Next, applying functions to eliminate some of the differences returns the one common row. In this case, only one row is returned; had there been several common rows, they would be in order. The order in which the queries appear in the compound query has no effect on this.

The MINUS Operator

A MINUS runs both queries, sorts the results, and returns only the rows from the first result set that do not appear in the second result set.

The third query in Figure 13-4 returns all the rows in OLD_DEPT because there are no matching rows in NEW_DEPT. The last query forces some commonality, causing one of the rows to be removed. Because of the sort, the rows will be in order irrespective of the order in which the queries appear in the compound query.

More Complex Examples

If two queries do not return the same number of columns, it may still be possible to run them in a compound query by generating additional columns with NULL values. For example, consider a classification system for animals: all animals have a name and a weight, but the birds have a wingspan whereas the cats have a tail length. A query to list all the birds and cats might be

```
select name,tail_length,to_char(null) from cats
union all
select name,to_char(null),wing_span from birds;
```

Note the use of TO_CHAR(NULL) to generate the missing values.

A compound query can consist of more than two queries, in which case operator precedence can be controlled with parentheses. Without parentheses, the set operators will be applied in the sequence in which they are specified. Consider the situation where there is a table PERMSTAFF with a listing of all permanent staff members and a table CONSULTANTS with a listing of consultant staff. There is also a table BLACKLIST of people blacklisted for one reason or another. The following query will list all the permanent and consulting staff in a certain geographical area, removing those on the blacklist:

```
select name from permstaff where location = 'Germany'
union all
select name from consultants where work_area = 'Western Europe'
minus
select name from blacklist;
```

Note the use of UNION ALL, because is assumed that no one will be in both the PERMSTAFF and the CONSULTANTS tables; a UNION would force an unnecessary sort. The order of precedence for set operators is the order specified by the programmer, so the MINUS operation will compare the names from the BLACKLIST set with the result of the UNION ALL. The result will be all staff (permanent and consulting) who do not appear on the blacklist. If the blacklisting could be applied only to consulting staff and not to permanent staff, there would be two possibilities. First, the queries could be listed in a different order:

```
select name from consultants where work_area = 'Western Europe'
minus
select name from blacklist
union all
select name from permstaff where location = 'Germany';
```

This would return consultants who are not blacklisted and then append all permanent staff. Alternatively, parentheses could control the precedence explicitly:

```
select name from permstaff where location = 'Germany'
union all
(select name from consultants where work_area = 'Western Europe'
minus
select name from blacklist);
```

This query will list all permanent staff and then append all consultant staff who are not blacklisted.

These two queries will return the same rows, but the order will be different because the UNION ALL operations list the PERMSTAFF and CONSULTANTS tables in a different sequence. To ensure that the queries return identical result sets, there would need to be an ORDER BY clause at the foot of the compound queries.

 TIP The two preceding queries will return the same rows, but the second version could be considered better code because the parentheses make it more self-documenting. Furthermore, relying on implicit precedence based on the order of the queries works at the moment, but future releases of SQL may include set operator precedence.

Control the Order of Rows Returned

By default, the output of a UNION ALL compound query is not sorted at all: the rows will be returned in groups in the order of which query was listed first and within the groups in the order that they happen to be stored. The output of any other set operator will be sorted in ascending order of all the columns, starting with the first column named.

It is not syntactically possible to use an ORDER BY clause in the individual queries that make up a compound query. This is because the execution of most compound queries has to sort the rows, which would conflict with the ORDER BY.

There is no problem with placing an ORDER BY clause at the end of the compound query, however. This will sort the entire output of the compound query. The default sorting of rows is based on all the columns in the sequence they appear. A specified ORDER BY clause has no restrictions: it can be based on any columns (and functions applied to columns) in any order. For example:

```
SQL> select deptno,trim(dname) name from old_dept
  2  union
  3  select dept_id,dname from new_dept
  4  order by name;
    DEPTNO NAME
---------- --------------------
        10 Accounts
        30 Admin
        20 Support
```

Note that the column names in the ORDER BY clause must be the name(s) (or, in this case, the alias) of the columns in the first query of the compound query.

Two-Minute Drill

Define Subqueries

- A subquery is a SELECT statement embedded within another SQL statement.
- Subqueries can be nested within each other.
- With the exception of the correlated subquery, subqueries are executed once, before the outer query within which they are embedded.

Describe the Types of Problems That the Subqueries Can Solve

- Selecting rows from a table with a condition that depends on the data from another query can be implemented with a subquery.
- Complex joins can sometimes be replaced with subqueries.
- Subqueries can add values to the outer query's output that are not available in the tables the outer query addresses.

List the Types of Subqueries

- Multiple-row subqueries can return several rows, possibly with several columns.
- Single-row subqueries return one row, possibly with several columns.
- A scalar subquery returns a single value; it is a single-row, single-column subquery.
- A correlated subquery is executed once for every row in the outer query.

Write Single-Row and Multiple-Row Subqueries

- Single-row subqueries should be used with single-row comparison operators.
- Multiple-row subqueries should be used with multiple-row comparison operators.
- The ALL and ANY operators can be alternatives to use of aggregations.

Describe the Set Operators

- UNION ALL concatenates the results of two queries.
- UNION sorts the results of two queries and removes duplicates.
- INTERSECT returns only the rows common to the result of two queries.
- MINUS returns the rows from the first query that do not exist in the second query.

Use a Set Operator to Combine Multiple Queries into a Single Query

- The queries in the compound query must return the same number of columns.
- The corresponding columns must be of compatible data types.
- The set operators have equal precedence and will be applied in the order they are specified.

Control the Order of Rows Returned

- It is not possible to use ORDER BY in the individual queries that make a compound query.
- An ORDER BY clause can be appended to the end of a compound query.
- The rows returned by a UNION ALL will be in the order they occur in the two source queries.
- The rows returned by a UNION will be sorted across all their columns, left to right.

Self Test

1. Consider this generic description of a SELECT statement:

```
SELECT select_list
FROM table
WHERE condition
GROUP BY expression_1
HAVING expression_2
ORDER BY expression_3 ;
```

Where could subqueries be used? (Choose all correct answers.)

A. *select_list*

B. *table*

C. *condition*

D. *expression_1*

E. *expression_2*

F. *expression_3*

2. A query can have a subquery embedded within it. Under what circumstances could there be more than one subquery? (Choose the best answer.)

A. The outer query can include an inner query. It is not possible to have another query within the inner query.

B. It is possible to embed a single-row subquery inside a multiple-row subquery, but not the other way round.

C. The outer query can have multiple inner queries, but they must not be embedded within each other.

D. Subqueries can be embedded within each other with no practical limitations on depth.

3. Consider this statement:

```
select employee_id, last_name from employees where
salary > (select avg(salary) from employees);
```

When will the subquery be executed? (Choose the best answer.)

A. It will be executed before the outer query.

B. It will be executed after the outer query.

C. It will be executed concurrently with the outer query.

D. It will be executed once for every row in the EMPLOYEES table.

4. Consider this statement:

```
select o.employee_id, o.last_name from employees o where
o.salary > (select avg(i.salary) from employees i
where i.department_id=o.department_id);
```

When will the subquery be executed? (Choose the best answer.)

A. It will be executed before the outer query.

B. It will be executed after the outer query.

C. It will be executed concurrently with the outer query.

D. It will be executed once for every row in the EMPLOYEES table.

5. Consider the following statement:

```
select last_name from employees join departments
on employees.department_id = departments.department_id
where department_name='Executive';
```

and this statement:

```
select last_name from employees where department_id in
(select department_id from departments where department_name='Executive');
```

What can be said about the two statements? (Choose two correct answers.)

A. The two statements should generate the same result.

B. The two statements could generate different results.

C. The first statement will always run successfully; the second statement will fail if there are two departments with DEPARTMENT_NAME 'Executive'.

D. Both statements will always run successfully, even if there are two departments with DEPARTMENT_NAME 'Executive'.

6. What are the distinguishing characteristics of a scalar subquery? (Choose two correct answers.)

A. A scalar subquery returns one row.

B. A scalar subquery returns one column.

C. A scalar subquery cannot be used in the SELECT list of the parent query.

D. A scalar subquery cannot be used as a correlated subquery.

7. Which comparison operator cannot be used with multiple-row subqueries? (Choose the best answer.)

A. ALL

B. ANY

C. IN

D. NOT IN

E. All of the above can be used

8. Consider this statement:

```
select last_name, (select count(*) from departments) from employees
where salary = (select salary from employees);
```

What is wrong with it? (Choose the best answer.)

A. Nothing is wrong—the statement should run without error.

B. The statement will fail because the subquery in the SELECT list references a table that is not listed in the FROM clause.

C. The statement will fail if the conditional subquery returns more than one row.

D. The statement will run but is extremely inefficient because of the need to run the second subquery once for every row in EMPLOYEES.

9. Which of the following statements are equivalent? (Choose two answers.)

A. `select employee_id from employees where salary < all (select salary from employees where department_id=10);`

B. `select employee_id from employees where salary < (select min(salary) from employees where department_id=10);`

C. `select employee_id from employees where salary not >= any (select salary from employees where department_id=10);`

D. `select employee_id from employees e join departments d on e.department_id=d.department_id where e.salary < (select min(salary) from employees) and d.department_id=10;`

10. Consider this statement, which is intended to prompt for an employee's name and then find all employees who have the same job as the first employee:

```
select last_name,employee_id from employees where job_id =
(select job_id from employees where last_name = '&Name');
```

What would happen if a value were given for &Name that did not match with any row in EMPLOYEES? (Choose the best answer.)

A. The statement would fail with an error.

B. The statement would return every row in the table.

C. The statement would return no rows.

D. The statement would return all rows where JOB_ID is NULL.

11. Which of these set operators will not sort the rows? (Choose the best answer.)

A. INTERSECT

B. MINUS

C. UNION

D. UNION ALL

12. Which of these operators will remove duplicate rows from the final result? (Choose all that apply.)

A. INTERSECT

B. MINUS

C. UNION

D. UNION ALL

13. If a compound query contains both a MINUS and an INTERSECT operator, which will be applied first? (Choose the best answer.)

    A. The INTERSECT, because INTERSECT has a higher precedence than MINUS.

    B. The MINUS, because MINUS has a higher precedence than INTERSECT.

    C. The precedence is determined by the order in which they are specified.

    D. It is not possible for a compound query to include both MINUS and INTERSECT.

14. There are four rows in the REGIONS table. Consider the following statements and choose how many rows will be returned for each: 0, 4, 8, or 16.

    A. `select * from regions union select * from regions`

    B. `select * from regions union all select * from regions`

    C. `select * from regions minus select * from regions`

    D. `select * from regions intersect select * from regions`

15. Consider this compound query:

```
select empno, hired from emp
union all
select emp_id,hired,fired from ex_emp;
```

The columns EMP.EMPNO and EX_EMP.EMP_ID are integer; the column EMP.HIRED is timestamp; the columns EX_EMP.HIRED and EX_EMP.FIRED are date. Why will the statement fail? (Choose the best answer.)

    A. Because the columns EMPNO and EMP_ID have different names

    B. Because the columns EMP.HIRED and EX_EMP.HIRED are different data types

    C. Because there are two columns in the first query and three columns in the second query

    D. For all of the reasons above

    E. The query will succeed

16. Which line of this statement will cause it to fail? (Choose the best answer.)

    A. `select ename, hired from current_staff`

    B. `order by ename`

    C. `minus`

    D. `select ename, hired from current staff`

    E. `where deptno=10`

    F. `order by ename;`

17. Study this statement:

```
select ename from emp union all select ename from ex_emp;
```

In what order will the rows be returned? (Choose the best answer.)

    A. The rows from each table will be grouped and within each group will be sorted on ENAME.

B. The rows from each table will be grouped but not sorted.

C. The rows will not be grouped, but will all be sorted on ENAME.

D. The rows will be neither grouped nor sorted.

Self Test Answers

1. ☑ A, B, C, and E. Subqueries can be used at all these points.
   ☒ D and F. A subquery cannot be used in the GROUP BY and ORDER BY clauses of a query.

2. ☑ D. Subquery nesting can be done to many levels.
   ☒ A, B, and C. A and C are incorrect because subqueries can be nested. B is incorrect because the number of rows returned is not relevant to nesting subqueries, only to the operators being used.

3. ☑ A. The result set of the inner query is needed before the outer query can run.
   ☒ B, C, and D. B and C are not possible because the result of the subquery is needed before the parent query can start. D is incorrect because the subquery is only run once.

4. ☑ D. This is a correlated subquery, which must be run for every row in the table.
   ☒ A, B, and C. The result of the inner query is dependent on a value from the outer query; it must therefore be run once for every row.

5. ☑ A and D. The two statements will deliver the same result, and neither will fail if the name is duplicated.
   ☒ B and C. B is incorrect because the statements are functionally identical, though syntactically different. C is incorrect because the comparison operator used, IN, can handle a multiple-row subquery.

6. ☑ A and B. A scalar subquery can be defined as a query that returns a single value.
   ☒ C and D. C is incorrect because a scalar subquery is the only subquery that can be used in the SELECT list. D is incorrect because scalar subqueries can be correlated.

7. ☑ E. ALL, ANY, IN, and NOT IN are the multiple-row comparison operators.
   ☒ A, B, C, and D. All of these can be used.

8. ☑ C. The equality operator requires a single-row subquery, and the conditional subquery could return several rows.
   ☒ A, B, and D. A is incorrect because the statement will fail in all circumstances except the unlikely case where there is zero or one employee. B is incorrect because this is not a problem; there need be no relationship between the source of data for the inner and outer queries. D is incorrect because the subquery will only run once; it is not a correlated subquery.

9. ☑   A and B are identical.

☒   C is logically the same as A and B but syntactically is not possible; it will give an error. D will always return no rows, because it asks for all employees who have a salary lower than all employees. This is not an error but can never return any rows. The filter on DEPARTMENTS is not relevant.

10. ☑   C. If a subquery returns NULL, then the comparison will also return NULL, meaning that no rows will be retrieved.

☒   A, B, and D. A is incorrect because this would not cause an error. B is incorrect because a comparison with NULL will return nothing, not everything. D is incorrect because a comparison with NULL can never return anything, not even other NULLs.

11. ☑   D. UNION ALL returns rows in the order that they are delivered by the queries that make up the compound query.

☒   A, B, and C. INTERSECT, MINUS, and UNION all use sorting as part of their execution.

12. ☑   A, B, and C. INTERSECT, MINUS, and UNION all remove duplicate rows.

☒   D. UNION ALL returns all rows, duplicates included.

13. ☑   C. All set operators have equal precedence, so the precedence is determined by the sequence in which they occur.

☒   A, B, and D. A and B are incorrect because set operators have equal precedence—though this may change in future releases. D is incorrect because many set operators can be used in one compound query.

14. ☑   A = 4; B = 8; C = 0; D = 4.

☒   Note that 16 is not used; that would be the result of a Cartesian product query.

15. ☑   C. Every query in a compound query must return the same number of columns.

☒   A, B, D, and E. A is incorrect because the columns can have different names. B is incorrect because the two columns are of the same data type group, which is all that is required. It therefore follows that D and E are also incorrect.

16. ☑   B. You cannot use ORDER BY for one query of a compound query; you may only place a single ORDER BY clause at the end.

☒   A, C, D, E, and F. All these lines are legal.

17. ☑   B. The rows from each query will be grouped together, but there will be no sorting.

☒   A, C, and D. A is not possible with any syntax. C is incorrect because that would be the result of a UNION, not a UNION ALL. D is incorrect because UNION ALL will return the rows from each query grouped together.

PART III

Advanced Database Administration

CHAPTER 14

Configuring the Database for Backup and Recovery

Exam Objectives

In this chapter you will learn to

Perhaps the most important aspect of a database administrator's job is to ensure that the database does not lose data. The mechanisms of redo and undo ensure that it is absolutely impossible to corrupt the database no matter what the DBA does or does not do. After working through the section of this chapter titled "Instance Recovery," you will be able to prove this. However, it is possible for an Oracle database to lose data because of physical damage if the DBA does not take appropriate precautions. From release 9i onward, an Oracle database can be configured so that no matter what happens the database will never lose a single row of committed data. It is also possible to configure an environment for 100 percent availability. This chapter will go through the concepts behind Oracle's backup and recovery mechanisms: the enabling structure within which you will configure whatever level of data security and availability is demanded by your organization.

Backup and Recovery Issues

This is an area where the DBA cannot work in isolation. The amount of downtime and data loss that an organization can stand is a matter for the business analysts, not the DBA. The business analysts in conjunction with the end users will determine the requirement, and the DBA will then configure the database appropriately. To do this, you will require the cooperation of the system administrators and other support staff. Sometimes there will be budget constraints to consider: a zero data loss and 100 percent uptime environment will be far more expensive to configure than an environment that does not have such guarantees. Performance may also tend to degrade as the uptime and data loss requirements become more demanding.

The end result of considering the business requirements, performance, and financial considerations is often a compromise. It is vitally important that this be documented, usually in the form of a service level agreement that details exactly what is being done, and what the effects will be of various types of failure. For you as the DBA, there is no such thing as "good" or "bad" database administration in this environment; there is only whether the procedures you are following confirm to the service level agreement, or not. This protects the DBA from criticism (you can't be fired for doing what it has been agreed that you will do) and guarantees the end users the level of service that they have agreed they require. The three areas of a service level agreement relevant to backup and recovery are the mean time between failures (the MTBF), the mean time to recover (the MTTR), and loss of data. Your objective as DBA is to increase the MTBF while reducing the MTTR and data loss.

MTBF refers to how frequently the database becomes unavailable. For some organizations, the database must be available all the time. Real-time systems, such as satellite flight control or process control in an oil refinery, must run all the time; even a few minutes' failure can be catastrophic. Oracle provides two advanced options that can contribute to 100 percent availability: RAC and Streams. A *RAC*, or clustered, database consists of one physical database opened by multiple instances on multiple computers. If any one computer or instance fails, the database remains open for use through a surviving instance. RAC protects against hardware, operating system, and software failure. The Streams environment consists of two or more databases on separate computers, which may be geographically widely separated. The Streams mechanism takes care of keeping the two databases synchronized, in real time if necessary. Users can connect to either, and changes made on each database are published to the other database. If one database becomes unavailable for any reason, work can continue on the other. Streams goes further than RAC for fault tolerance, because it protects against disk and network failure as well as hardware, operating system, and software failure.

MTTR refers to the length of downtime following a failure. For many organizations, this is actually more significant than losing data. For example, every minute that the billing system for a telco is unavailable could mean subscribers are getting free cell phone calls, and extended downtime could cost a lot more money than losing a few minutes of data. Clearly the ideal is to have the system available all the time, but when it does fail, it is your duty to bring it back up with minimal delay. A critical part of reducing MTTR is practice. When a database crashes, you will be under enormous pressure to open it as soon as possible. It is vital to be prepared. You do not want to be looking up things in manuals before taking appropriate action. Practice, practice, practice—if you can't test recovery on a live system, test on a backup system. Run simulations of all possible types of failure, and prepare for all eventualities.

The third objective is to minimize data loss. Some organizations cannot stand any data loss whatsoever. For example, a stock trading system must not lose a trade. It might be preferable to have no trades taking place—temporarily close the exchange—than to take the risk of losing a transaction. In other environments it may be acceptable to lose a few hours of data, but make sure that this is documented. From release 9i onward, an Oracle database can be configured for zero data loss, under any circumstances whatsoever. This is done through Data Guard. In a Data Guard system the live database, known as the primary, is protected by one or more standby databases. The standby is continually updated with all the changes applied to the primary. These changes can be propagated in real time if necessary.

These three advanced options—RAC, Streams, and Data Guard—all have performance implications (which may be for better or for worse, depending on how things are set up and what the objective is) and should not be embarked upon lightly. They are beyond the scope of the OCP examinations, but knowledge of them is required for Oracle University's more advanced qualifications.

Any fault-tolerant environment will rely heavily on hardware redundancy. This is where you cannot work independently of the system administrators. If a datafile becomes unavailable because of a disk failure, your database will also (at least partially) become unavailable. Your objective of increasing the MTBF must be aligned with your system administrators' targets for disk redundancy and replacement. Similarly, you are totally dependent on the network. If your users cannot connect, they will not care whether the reason is that a router has failed or the database has crashed. Your targets for the database must be set with the whole IT environment in mind, and the service level agreements must make this clear. Your role as DBA is to ensure that you can meet the agreed standards for uptime and data loss, no matter what the nature of the failure.

TIP You will find that the DBA is expected to know about everything. Not just the database, but also the hardware, the network, the operating system, the programming language, and the application. Sometimes only the DBA can see the totality of the environment, but no one can know it all; so work with the appropriate specialists, and build up a good relationship with them.

Categories of Failures

Failures can be divided into a few broad categories. For each type of failure, there will be an appropriate course of action to resolve it. Each type of failure may well be documented in a service level agreement; certainly the steps to be followed should be documented in a procedures manual.

Statement Failure

An individual SQL statement can fail for a number of reasons, not all of which are within the DBA's domain—but even so, he/she must be prepared to fix them. The first level of fixing will be automatic. Whenever a statement fails, the server process executing the statement will detect the problem and roll back the statement. Remember that a statement might attempt to update many rows, and fail partway through execution; all the rows that were updated before the failure will have their changes reversed through the use of undo. This will happen automatically. If the statement is part of a multistatement transaction, all the statements that have already succeeded will remain intact, but uncommitted. Ideally, the programmers will have included exceptions clauses in their code that will identify and manage any problems, but there will always be some errors that get through the error handling routines.

A common cause of statement failure is invalid data, usually a format or constraint violation. A well-written user program will avoid format problems, such as attempting to insert character data into a numeric field, but these can often occur when doing batch jobs with data coming from a third-party system. Oracle itself will try to solve formatting problems by doing automatic typecasting to convert data types on the fly, but this is not very efficient and shouldn't be relied upon. Constraint violations will be detected, but Oracle can do nothing to solve them. Clearly, problems caused by invalid data are not the DBA's fault, but you must be prepared to deal with them by working with the users to validate and correct the data, and with the programmers to try to automate these processes.

A second class of non-DBA-related statement failure is logic errors in the application. Programmers may well develop code that in some circumstances is impossible for the database to execute. A perfect example is the deadlock described in Chapter 8: the code will run perfectly, until through bad luck two sessions happen to try to do the same thing at the same time to the same rows. A deadlock is not a database error; it is an error caused by programmers writing code that permits an impossible situation to arise.

Space management problems are frequent, but they should never occur. A good DBA will monitor space usage proactively and take action before problems arise. Space-related causes of statement failure include inability to extend a segment because the tablespace is full; running out of undo space; insufficient temporary space when running queries that use disk sorts or working with temporary tables; a user hitting their quota limit; or an object hitting its maximum extents limit. Database Control gives access to the undo advisor, the segment advisor, the Automatic Database Diagnostic Monitor, and the alert mechanism, all described in chapters to come, which will help to pick up space-related problems before they happen. The effect of space problems that slip through can perhaps be alleviated by setting datafiles to autoextend, or by enabling resumable space allocation, but ideally space problems should never arise in the first place.

 TIP Issue the command `alter session enable resumable` and from then on the session will not show errors on space problems but instead hang until the problem is fixed. You can enable *resumable* for the whole instance with the RESUMABLE_TIMEOUT parameter.

Statements may fail because of insufficient privileges. Remember from Chapter 6 how privileges let a user do certain things, such as select from a table or execute a piece of code. When a statement is parsed, the server process checks whether the user executing the statement has the necessary permissions. This type of error indicates that the security structures in place are inappropriate, and the DBA (in conjunction with the organization's security manager) should grant appropriate system and object privileges.

 EXAM TIP If a statement fails, it will be rolled back. Any other DML statements will remain intact and uncommitted.

Figure 14-1 shows some examples of statement failure: a data error, a permissions error, a space error, and a logic error.

User Process Failure

A user process may fail for any number of reasons, including the user exiting abnormally instead of logging out; the terminal rebooting; or the program causing an address violation. Whatever the cause of the problem, the outcome is the same. The PMON background process periodically polls all the server processes, to ascertain the state of the session. If a server process reports that it has lost contact with its user process, PMON will tidy up. If the session were in the middle of a transaction, PMON will roll back the transaction and release any locks held by the session. Then it will terminate the server process and release the PGA back to the operating system.

This type of problem is beyond the DBA's control, but you should watch for any trends that might indicate a lack of user training, badly written software, or perhaps network or hardware problems.

 EXAM TIP If a session terminates abnormally, an active transaction will be rolled back automatically.

```
Telnet jwacer.bplc.co.za                                             _ □ ×

SQL> --invalid data: there is already a department 10
SQL> insert into dept values (10,'Sales','UK');
insert into dept values (10,'Sales','UK')
*
ERROR at line 1:
ORA-00001: unique constraint (SCOTT.PK_DEPT) violated


SQL> --insufficient privileges: no insert privilege on hr.regions
SQL> insert into hr.regions values (99,'British Isles');
insert into hr.regions values (99,'British Isles')
            *
ERROR at line 1:
ORA-00942: table or view does not exist


SQL> --space problem: insufficient quota
SQL> create table too_big (c1 varchar2(10)) storage (initial 1000m);
create table too_big (c1 varchar2(10)) storage (initial 1000m)
*
ERROR at line 1:
ORA-01536: space quota exceeded for tablespace 'USERS'


SQL> --logic problem: the code can't handle two Taylors:
SQL> declare v_sal number;
  2  begin
  3  select salary into v_sal from hr.employees where last_name='Taylor';
  4  end;
  5  /
declare v_sal number;
*
ERROR at line 1:
ORA-01422: exact fetch returns more than requested number of rows
ORA-06512: at line 3


SQL> _
```

Figure 14-1   Examples of statement failures

Network Failure

In conjunction with the network administrators, it should be possible to configure Oracle Net such that there is no single point of failure. The three points to consider are listeners, network interface cards, and routes.

A database listener is unlikely to crash, but there are limits to the amount of work that one listener can do. A listener can service only one connect request at a time, and it does take an appreciable amount of time to launch a server process and connect it to a user process. If your database experiences high volumes of concurrent connection requests, users may receive errors when they try to connect. You can avoid this by configuring multiple listeners, each on a different address/port combination.

At the operating system and hardware levels, network interfaces can fail. Ideally, your server machine will have at least two network interface cards, for redundancy as well as performance. Create at least one listener for each card.

Routing problems or localized network failures can mean that even though the database is running perfectly, no one can connect to it. If your server has two or more network interface cards, they should ideally be connected to physically separate subnets. Then on the client side configure connect time fault tolerance by listing multiple addresses in the ADDRESS_LIST section of the TNS_NAMES.ORA entry. This will permits the user processes to try a series of routes until they find one that is working.

TIP The network fault tolerance for a single-instance database is only at connect time; a failure later on will disrupt currently connected sessions, and they will have to reconnect. In a RAC environment, it is possible for a session to fail over to a different instance, and the user may not even notice.

User Errors

Historically, *user errors* were undoubtedly the worst errors to manage. Recent releases of the database improve the situation dramatically. The problem is that user errors are not errors as far as the database is concerned. Imagine a conversation along these lines:

> User: "I forgot to put a WHERE clause on my UPDATE statement, so I've just updated a million rows instead of one."
> DBA: "Did you say COMMIT?"
> User: "Of course."
> DBA: "Um . . ."

As far as Oracle is concerned, this is a transaction like any other. The *D* for "Durable" of the ACID test states that once a transaction is committed, it must be immediately broadcast to all other users, and be absolutely nonreversible. But at least with DML errors such as the one dramatized here, the user would have had the chance to roll back their statement if they realized that it was wrong before committing. But DDL statements don't give you that option. For example, if a programmer drops a table believing that it is in the test database, but the programmer is actually logged on to the production database, there is a COMMIT built into the DROP TABLE command. That table is gone—you can't roll back DDL.

TIP Never forget that there is a COMMIT built into DDL statements that will include any preceding DML statements.

The ideal solution to user errors is to prevent them from occurring in the first place. This is partly a matter of user training, but more importantly of software design: no user process should ever let a user issue an UPDATE statement without a WHERE clause, unless that is exactly what is required. But even the best-designed software cannot prevent users from issuing SQL that is inappropriate to the business. Everyone makes mistakes. Oracle provides a number of ways whereby you as DBA may be able to correct user errors, but this is often extremely difficult—particularly if the error isn't reported for some time. The possible techniques include flashback query, flashback drop, and flashback database (described in Chapter 19) and incomplete recovery (described in Chapters 16 and 18).

Flashback query involves running a query against a version of the database as at some time in the past. The read-consistent version of the database is constructed, for your session only, through the use of undo data.

Figure 14-2 shows one of many uses of flashback query. The user has "accidentally" deleted every row in the EMP table, and committed the delete. Then the rows are retrieved with a subquery against the table as it was five minutes previously.

```
Telnet jwacer.bplc.co.za                                    _ □ ✕
SQL> delete from emp;
14 rows deleted.
SQL> commit;
Commit complete.
SQL> select count(*) from emp;
  COUNT(*)
----------
         0
SQL> insert into emp (select * from emp as of timestamp(sysdate - 5/1440));
14 rows created.
SQL> commit;
Commit complete.
SQL> select count(*) from emp;
  COUNT(*)
----------
        14
```

Figure 14-2 Correcting user error with flashback query

Flashback drop reverses the effect of a DROP TABLE command. In previous releases of the database, a DROP command did what it says: it dropped all references to the table from the data dictionary. There was no way to reverse this. Even flashback query would fail, because the flashback query mechanism does need the data dictionary object definition. But from release 10g the implementation of the DROP command has changed: it no longer drops anything; it just renames the object so that you will never see it again, unless you specifically ask to. Figure 14-3 illustrates the use of flashback drop to recover a table.

Figure 14-3
Correcting user
error with flashback
drop

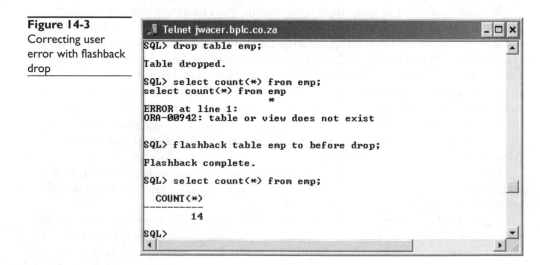

```
Telnet jwacer.bplc.co.za                                    _ □ ✕
SQL> drop table emp;
Table dropped.
SQL> select count(*) from emp;
select count(*) from emp
                     *
ERROR at line 1:
ORA-00942: table or view does not exist

SQL> flashback table emp to before drop;
Flashback complete.
SQL> select count(*) from emp;
  COUNT(*)
----------
        14
SQL>
```

Incomplete recovery and flashback database are much more drastic techniques for reversing user errors. With either tool, the whole database is taken back in time to before the error occurred. The other techniques that have been described let you reverse one bad transaction, while everything else remains intact. But if you ever do an incomplete recovery, or a flashback of the whole database, you will lose all the work previously done after the time to which the database was returned—not just the bad transaction.

Media Failure

Media failure means damage to disks, and therefore the files stored on them. This is not your problem (it is something for the system administrators to sort out), but you must be prepared to deal with it. The point to hang on to is that damage to any number of any files is no reason to lose data. With release 9*i* and later, you can survive the loss of any and all of the files that make up a database without losing any committed data—if you have configured the database appropriately. Prior to 9*i*, complete loss of the machine hosting the database could result in loss of data; the Data Guard facility, not covered in the OCP curriculum, can even protect against that.

Included in the category of "media failure" is a particular type of user error: system or database administrators accidentally deleting files. This is not as uncommon as one might think (or hope).

 TIP On Unix systems, the `rm` command has been responsible for any number of appalling mistakes. You might want to consider, for example, aliasing the `rm` command to `rm -i` to gain a little peace of mind.

When a disk is damaged, one or more of the files on it will be damaged, unless the disk subsystem itself has protection through RAID. Remember that a database consists of three file types: the control file, the online redo logs, and the datafiles. The control file and the online logs should always be protected through multiplexing. If you have multiple copies of the control file on different disks, then if any one of them is damaged, you will have a surviving copy. Similarly, having multiple copies of each online redo log means that you can survive the loss of any one. Datafiles can't be multiplexed (other than through RAID, at the hardware level); therefore, if one is lost the only option is to *restore* it from a backup. To restore a file is to extract it from wherever it was backed up, and put it back where it is meant to be. Then the file must be *recovered*. The restored backup will be out of date; recovery means applying changes extracted from the redo logs (both online and archived) to bring it forward to the state it was in at the time the damage occurred.

Recovery requires the use of archived redo logs. These are the copies of online redo logs, made after each log switch. After restoring a datafile from backup, the changes to be applied to it to bring it up to date are extracted, in chronological order, from the archive logs generated since the backup was taken. Clearly, you must look after your archive logs because if any are lost, the recovery process will fail. Archive logs are initially created on disk, and because of the risks of using disk storage they, just like the controlfile and the online log files, should be multiplexed: two or more copies on different devices.

So to protect against media failure, you must have multiplexed copies of the controlfile, the online redo log files, and the archive redo log files. You will also take backups of the controlfile, the data files, and the archive log files. You do not back up the redo logs—they are, in effect, backed up when they are copied to the archive logs. Datafiles cannot be protected by multiplexing; they need to be protected by hardware redundancy—either conventional RAID systems, or Oracle's own Automatic Storage Management (ASM).

Instance Failure

An *instance failure* is a disorderly shutdown of the instance, popularly referred to as a crash. This could be caused by a power cut, by switching off or rebooting the server machine, or by any number of critical hardware problems. In some circumstances one of the Oracle background processes may fail—this will also trigger an immediate instance failure. Functionally, the effect of an instance failure, for whatever reason, is the same as issuing the SHUTDOWN ABORT command. You may hear people talking about "crashing the database" when they mean issuing a SHUTDOWN ABORT command.

After an instance failure, the database may well be missing committed transactions and storing uncommitted transactions. This is a definition of a corrupted or inconsistent database. This situation arises because the server processes work in memory: they update blocks of data and undo segments in the database buffer cache, not on disk. DBWn then, eventually, writes the changed blocks down to the datafiles. The algorithm the DBWn uses to select which dirty buffers to write is oriented toward performance and results in the blocks that are least active getting written first—after all, there would be little point in writing a block that is being changed every second. But this means that at any given moment there may well be committed transactions that are not yet in the datafiles and uncommitted transactions that have been written: there is no correlation between a COMMIT and a write to the datafiles. But of course, all the changes that have been applied to both data and undo blocks are already in the redo logs.

Remember the description of commit processing detailed in Chapter 8: when you say COMMIT, all that happens is that LGWR flushes the log buffer to the current online redo log files. DBWn does absolutely nothing on COMMIT. For performance reasons, DBWn writes as little as possible as rarely as possible—this means that the database is always out of date. But LGWR writes with a very aggressive algorithm indeed. It writes as nearly as possible in real time, and when you (or anyone else) say COMMIT, it really does write in real time. This is the key to instance recovery. Oracle accepts the fact that the database will be corrupted after an instance failure, but there will always be enough information in the redo log stream on disk to correct the damage.

Instance Recovery

The rules to which a relational database must conform, as formalized in the ACID test, require that it may never lose a committed transaction and never show an uncommitted transaction. Oracle conforms to the rules perfectly. If the database is corrupted—meaning that it does contain uncommitted data or is missing committed data—Oracle will detect the inconsistency and perform instance recovery to remove the corruptions. It will reinstate any committed transactions that had not been saved to the datafiles at the time of the crash, and roll back any uncommitted transactions that had been written to the datafiles. This instance recovery is completely automatic—you can't stop it, even if you wanted to. If the instance recovery fails, which will only happen if there is media failure as well as instance failure, you cannot open the database until you have used media recovery techniques to restore and recover the damaged files. The final step of media recovery is automatic instance recovery.

The Mechanics of Instance Recovery

Because instance recovery is completely automatic, it can be dealt with fairly quickly, unlike media recovery, which will take a whole chapter. In principle, instance recovery is nothing more than using the contents of the online log files to rebuild the database buffer cache to the state it was in before the crash. This rebuilding process replays all changes extracted from the redo logs that refer to blocks that had not been written to disk at the time of the crash. Once this has been done, the database can be opened. At that point, the database is still corrupted—but there is no reason not to allow users to connect, because the instance (which is what users see) has been repaired. This phase of recovery, known as the roll forward, reinstates all changes—changes to data blocks and changes to undo blocks—for both committed and uncommitted transactions. Each redo record has the bare minimum of information needed to reconstruct a change: the block address and the new values. During roll forward, each redo record is read, the appropriate block is loaded from the datafiles into the database buffer cache, and the change is applied. Then the block is written back to disk.

Once the roll forward is complete, it is as though the crash had never occurred. But at that point, there will be uncommitted transactions in the database—these must be rolled back, and Oracle will do that automatically in the rollback phase of instance recovery. However, that happens after the database has been opened for use. If a user connects and hits some data that needs to be rolled back and hasn't yet been, this is not a problem—the roll forward phase will have populated the undo segment that was protecting the uncommitted transaction, so the server can roll back the change in the normal manner for read consistency.

Instance recovery is automatic and unavoidable—so how do you invoke it? By issuing a STARTUP command. Remember from Chapter 3, on starting an instance, the description of how SMON opens a database. First, it reads the controlfile when the database transitions to mount mode. Then in the transition to open mode, SMON checks the file headers of all the datafiles and online redo log files. At this point, if there had been an instance failure, it is apparent because the file headers are all out of sync. So SMON goes into the instance recovery routine, and the database is only actually opened after the roll forward phase has completed.

 TIP You never have anything to lose by issuing a STARTUP command. After any sort of crash, try a STARTUP and see how far it gets. It might get all the way.

554

The Impossibility of Database Corruption

It should now be apparent that there is always enough information in the redo log stream to reconstruct all work done up to the point at which the crash occurred, and furthermore that this includes reconstructing the undo information needed to roll back transactions that were in progress at the time of the crash. But for the final proof, consider this scenario.

User JOHN has started a transaction. He has updated one row of a table with some new values, and his server process has copied the old values to an undo segment. Before these updates were done in the database buffer cache, his server process wrote out the changes to the log buffer. User ROOPESH has also started a transaction. Neither has committed; nothing has been written to disk. If the instance crashed now, there would be no record whatsoever of either transaction, not even in the redo logs. So neither transaction would be recovered—but that is not a problem. Neither was committed, so they should not be recovered: uncommitted work must never be saved.

Then user JOHN commits his transaction. This triggers LGWR to flush the log buffer to the online redo log files, which means that the changes to both the table and the undo segments for both JOHN's transaction and ROOPESH's transaction are now in the redo log files, together with a commit record for JOHN's transaction. Only when the write has completed is the "commit complete" message returned to JOHN's user process. But there is still nothing in the datafiles. If the instance fails at this point, the roll forward phase will reconstruct both the transactions, but when all the redo has been processed, there will be no commit record for ROOPESH's update; that signals SMON to roll back ROOPESH's change but leave JOHN's in place.

But what if DBWn has written some blocks to disk before the crash? It might be that JOHN (or another user) was continually requerying his data, but that ROOPESH had made his uncommitted change and not looked at the data again. DBWn will therefore decide to write ROOPESH's changes to disk in preference to JOHN's; DBWn will always tend to write inactive blocks rather than active blocks. So now, the datafiles are storing ROOPESH's uncommitted transaction but missing JOHN's committed transaction. This is as bad a corruption as you can have. But think it through. If the instance crashes now—a power cut, perhaps, or a SHUTDOWN ABORT—the roll forward will still be able to sort out the mess. There will always be enough information in the redo stream to reconstruct committed changes; that is obvious, because a commit isn't completed until the write is done. But because LGWR flushes *all* changes to *all* blocks to the log files, there will also be enough information to reconstruct the undo segment needed to roll back ROOPESH's uncommitted transaction.

So to summarize, because LGWR always writes ahead of DBWn, and because it writes in real time on commit, there will always be enough information in the redo stream to reconstruct any committed changes that had not been written to the datafiles, and to roll back any uncommitted changes that had been written to the data files. This instance recovery mechanism of redo and rollback makes it absolutely impossible to corrupt an Oracle database—so long as there has been no physical damage.

EXAM TIP Can a SHUTDOWN ABORT corrupt the database? Absolutely not! It is impossible to corrupt the database.

Tuning Instance Recovery

A critical part of many service level agreements is the MTTR—the *mean time to recover* after various events. Instance recovery guarantees no corruption, but it may take a considerable time to do its roll forward before the database can be opened. This time is dependent on two factors: how much redo has to be read, and how many read/write operations will be needed on the datafiles as the redo is applied. Both these factors can be controlled by checkpoints.

A checkpoint guarantees that as of a particular time, all data changes made up to a particular SCN, or System Change Number, have been written to the datafiles by DBWn. In the event of an instance crash, it is only necessary for SMON to replay the redo generated from the last checkpoint position. All changes, committed or not, made before that position are already in the datafiles; so clearly, there is no need to use redo to reconstruct the transactions committed prior to that. Also, all changes made by uncommitted transactions prior to that point are also in the datafiles—so there is no need to reconstruct undo data prior to the checkpoint position either; it is already available in the undo segment on disk for the necessary rollback.

The more up to date the checkpoint position is, the faster the instance recovery. If the checkpoint position is right up to date, no roll forward will be needed at all—the instance can open immediately and go straight into the rollback phase. But there is a heavy price to pay for this. To advance the checkpoint position, DBWn must write changed blocks to disk. Excessive disk I/O will cripple performance. But on the other hand, if you let DBWn get too far behind, so that after a crash SMON has to process many gigabytes of redo and do billions of read/write operations on the datafiles, the MTTR following an instance failure can stretch into hours.

Tuning instance recovery time used to be largely a matter of experiment and guesswork. It has always been easy to tell how long the recovery actually took—just look at your alert log, and you will see the time when the STARTUP command was issued and the time that the startup completed, with information about how many blocks of redo were processed—but until release 9i of the database it was almost impossible to calculate accurately in advance. Release 9i introduced a new parameter, FAST_START_MTTR_TARGET, that makes controlling instance recovery time a trivial exercise. You specify it in seconds, and Oracle will then ensure that DBWn writes out blocks at a rate sufficiently fast that if the instance crashes, the recovery will take no longer than that number of seconds. So the smaller the setting, the harder DBWn will work in an attempt to minimize the gap between the checkpoint position and real time. But note that it is only a target—you can set it to an unrealistically low value, which is impossible to achieve no matter what DBWn does. Database Control also provides an MTTR advisor, which will give you an idea of how long recovery would take if the instance failed. This information can also be obtained from the view V$INSTANCE_RECOVERY.

The MTTR Advisor and Checkpoint Auto-Tuning

The parameter FAST_START_MTTR_TARGET defaults to zero. This has the effect of maximizing performance, with the possible cost of long instance recovery times after an instance failure. The DBWn process will write as little as it can get away with, meaning that the checkpoint position may be a long way out of date and that therefore a large amount of redo would have to be applied to the datafiles in the roll forward phase of instance recovery.

Setting FAST_START_MTTR_TARGET to a nonzero value has two effects. First, it sets a target for recovery, as described in the preceding section. But there is also a secondary effect: enabling *checkpoint auto-tuning*. The checkpoint auto-tuning mechanism inspects statistics on machine utilization, such as the rate of disk I/O and CPU usage, and if it appears that there is spare capacity, it will use this capacity to write out additional dirty buffers from the database buffer cache, thus pushing the checkpoint position forward. The result is that even if the FAST_START_MTTR_TARGET parameter is set to a high value (the highest possible is 3600 seconds—anything above that will be rounded down), actual recovery time may well be much less.

 TIP Enabling checkpoint auto-tuning with a high target should result in your instance always having the fastest possible recovery time that is consistent with maximum performance.

Database Control has an interface to the parameter. From the database home page, take the Advisor Central link, and then the MTTR advisor to get a window that displays the current estimated recovery time (this is the advisor) and gives the option of adjusting the parameter. More complete information can be gained from querying the V$INSTANCE_RECOVERY view, described here:

```
SQL> desc v$instance_recovery;
 Name                                     Null?    Type
 ---------------------------------------- -------- ------------
 RECOVERY_ESTIMATED_IOS                            NUMBER
 ACTUAL_REDO_BLKS                                  NUMBER
 TARGET_REDO_BLKS                                  NUMBER
 LOG_FILE_SIZE_REDO_BLKS                           NUMBER
 LOG_CHKPT_TIMEOUT_REDO_BLKS                       NUMBER
 LOG_CHKPT_INTERVAL_REDO_BLKS                      NUMBER
 FAST_START_IO_TARGET_REDO_BLKS                    NUMBER
 TARGET_MTTR                                       NUMBER
 ESTIMATED_MTTR                                    NUMBER
 CKPT_BLOCK_WRITES                                 NUMBER
 OPTIMAL_LOGFILE_SIZE                              NUMBER
 ESTD_CLUSTER_AVAILABLE_TIME                       NUMBER
 WRITES_MTTR                                       NUMBER
 WRITES_LOGFILE_SIZE                               NUMBER
 WRITES_LOG_CHECKPOINT_SETTINGS                    NUMBER
 WRITES_OTHER_SETTINGS                             NUMBER
 WRITES_AUTOTUNE                                   NUMBER
 WRITES_FULL_THREAD_CKPT                           NUMBER
```

The critical columns are described in Table 14-1.

 TIP Tracking the value of the ESTIMATED_MTTR will tell you if you are keeping to your service level agreement for crash recovery time; WRITES_ MTTR tells you the price you are paying for demanding a fast recovery time.

Column	Meaning
RECOVERY_ESTIMATED_IOS	The number of read/write operations that would be needed on datafiles for recovery if the instance crashed now
ACTUAL_REDO_BLOCKS	The number of OS blocks of redo that would need to be applied to datafiles for recovery if the instance crashed now
ESTIMATED_MTTR	The number of seconds it would take to open the database if it crashed now
TARGET_MTTR	The setting of FAST_START_MTTR_TARGET
WRITES_MTTR	The number of times DBWn had to write, in addition to the writes it would normally have done, to meet the TARGET_MTTR
WRITES_AUTOTUNE	The number of writes DBWn did that were initiated by the auto-tuning mechanism

Table 14-1   Some Columns of the V$INSTANCE_RECOVERY View

 EXAM TIP   Checkpoint auto-tuning is enabled if FAST_START_MTTR_TARGET is set to a nonzero value.

Checkpointing

As discussed in the preceding section, the checkpoint position (the point in the redo stream from which instance recovery must start following a crash) is advanced automatically by the DBWn. This process is known as *incremental* checkpointing. In addition, there may be *full checkpoints* and *partial checkpoints*.

A full checkpoint occurs when all dirty buffers are written to disk. In normal running, there might be several hundred thousand dirty buffers, but the DBWn would write just a few hundred of them for the incremental checkpoint. For a full checkpoint, it will write the lot. This will entail a great deal of work: very high CPU and disk usage while the checkpoint is in progress, and reduced performance for user sessions. Full checkpoints are bad for business. Because of this, there will never be a full checkpoint except in two circumstances: an orderly shutdown, or at the DBA's request.

When the database is shut down with the NORMAL, IMMEDIATE, or TRANSACTIONAL option, there is a checkpoint: all dirty buffers are flushed to disk by the DBWn before the database is closed and dismounted. This means that when the database is opened again, no recovery will be needed. A clean shutdown is always desirable and is necessary before some operations (such as enabling the archivelog mode or the flashback database capability). A full checkpoint can be signaled at any time with this command:

```
alter system checkpoint;
```

A partial checkpoint is necessary and occurs automatically as part of certain operations. Depending on the operation, the partial checkpoint will affect different buffers, as shown in Table 14-2.

Operation	What Buffers Will Be Flushed from the Cache
Taking a tablespace offline	All blocks that are part of the tablespace
Taking a datafile offline	All blocks that are part of the datafile
Dropping a segment	All blocks that are part of the segment
Truncating a table	All blocks that are part of the table
Putting a tablespace into backup mode	All blocks that are part of the tablespace

Table 14-2   Events That Will Trigger a Partial Checkpoint

 EXAM TIP Full checkpoints occur only with an orderly shutdown or by request. Partial checkpoints occur automatically as needed.

 TIP Manually initiated checkpoints should never be necessary during normal operation, though they can be useful when you want to test the effect of tuning. There is no checkpoint following a log switch. This has been the case since release 8i, though to this day many DBAs do not realize this.

Preparing the Database for Recoverability

To guarantee maximum recoverability for a database, the controlfiles must be multiplexed; the online redo logs must be multiplexed; the database must be running in archivelog mode, with the archive log files also multiplexed; and finally there must be regular backups, which are the subject of Chapters 15 and 18.

Protecting the Controlfile

The controlfile is small but vital. It is used to mount the database, and while the database is open, the controlfile is continually being read and written. If the controlfile is lost, it is possible to recover; but this is not always easy, and you should never be in that situation, because there should always be at least two copies of the controlfile, on different physical devices.

 EXAM TIP You can have up to eight multiplexed copies of the controlfile.

In an ideal world, not only will each copy of the controlfile be on a different disk, but each of the disks will be on a different channel and controller if your hardware permits this. However, even if your database is running on a computer with just one disk (on a small PC, for instance), you should still multiplex the controlfile to different directories. There is no general rule saying that two copies is too few, or eight copies is too many, but there will be rules set according to the business requirements for fault tolerance.

 TIP Your organization will have standards, such as "every production database will have three controlfiles on three different disks." If your organization does not have such standards, someone should agree to write them. Perhaps this person should be you.

Provided that the controlfile is multiplexed, recovering from media damage that results in the loss of a controlfile is a trivial matter. Oracle ensures that all copies of the controlfile are identical, so just copy a surviving controlfile over the damaged or missing one. But damage to a controlfile does result in downtime. The moment that Oracle detects that a controlfile is damaged or missing, the instance will terminate immediately with an instance failure.

If you create a database with the DBCA, by default you will have three controlfile copies, which is probably fine; but they will all be in the same directory, which is not so good. To move or add a controlfile copy, first shut down the database. No controlfile operations can be done while the database is open. Second, use an operating system command to move or copy the controlfile. Third, edit the CONTROL_FILES parameter to point to the new locations. If you are using a static initSID.ora parameter file, just edit it with any text editor. If you are using a dynamic spfileSID.ora parameter file, start up the database in NOMOUNT mode, and issue an `alter system` command with the scope set to spfile (necessary because this is a static parameter) to bring the new copy into use the next time the database is mounted. Fourth, shut down and open the database as normal. Figure 14-4 show the complete routine for adding a controlfile copy on a Windows system.

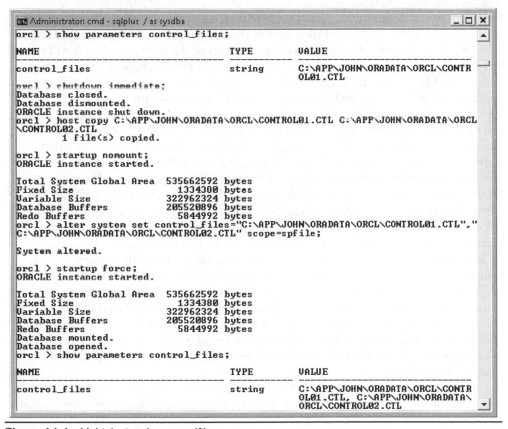

Figure 14-4   Multiplexing the controlfile

TIP There are no restrictions on naming for controlfile copies other than whatever is a legal name for your operating system, but you should adhere to some standard. Your organization may well have a standard for this already.

Protecting the Online Redo Log Files

Remember that an Oracle database requires at least two online log file groups to function, so that it can switch between them. You may need to add more groups for performance reasons, but two are required. Each group consists of one or more members, which are the physical files. Only one member per group is required for Oracle to function, but at least two members per group are required for safety.

TIP Always have at least two members in each log file group, for security. This is not just data security; it is job security, too.

The one thing that a DBA is not allowed to do is to lose all copies of the current online log file group. If that happens, you will lose data. The only way to protect against data loss when you lose all members of the current group is to configure a Data Guard environment for zero data loss, which is not a trivial exercise. Why is it so critical that you do not lose all members of the current group? Think about instance recovery. After a crash, SMON will use the contents of the current online log file group for roll forward recovery, to repair any corruptions in the database. If the current online log file group is not available, perhaps because it was not multiplexed and media damage has destroyed the one member, then SMON cannot do this. And if SMON cannot correct corruptions with roll forward, you cannot open the database.

Just as with multiplexed copies of the controlfile, the multiple members of a log file group should ideally be on separate disks, on separate controllers. But when considering disk strategy, think about performance as well as fault tolerance. In the discussion of commit processing in Chapter 8, it was made clear that when a COMMIT is issued, the session will hang until LGWR has flushed the log buffer to disk. Only then is "commit complete" returned to the user process, and the session allowed to continue. This means that writing to the online redo log files is one of the ultimate bottlenecks in the Oracle environment: you cannot do DML faster than LGWR can flush changes to disk. So on a high-throughput system, make sure that your redo log files are on your fastest disks served by your fastest controllers.

If a member of a redo log file group is damaged or missing, the database will remain open if there is a surviving member. This contrasts with the controlfile, where damage to any copy will crash the database immediately. Similarly, groups can be added or removed and members of groups can be added or moved while the database is open, as long as there are always at least two groups, and each group has at least one valid member.

If you create a database with DBCA, by default you will have three groups, but they will have only one member each. You can add more members (or indeed whole groups) either through Database Control or from the SQL*Plus command line. There are two views that will tell you the state of your redo logs. V$LOG will have one row per group, and V$LOGFILE will have one row per log file member. Figure 14-5 shows an example of online redo log configuration.

The first query shows that this database has three log file groups. The current group—the one LGWR is writing to at the moment—is group 2; the other groups are inactive, meaning first that the LGWR is not writing to them, and second that in the event of an instance failure, SMON would not require them for instance recovery. In other words, the checkpoint position has advanced into group 2. The SEQUENCE# column tells us that there have been 200 log switches since the database was created. This number is incremented with each log switch. The MEMBERS column shows that each group consists of only one member—seriously bad news, which should be corrected as soon as possible.

The second query shows the individual online redo log files. Each file is part of one group (identified by GROUP#, which is the join column back to V$LOG) and has a unique name. The STATUS column should always be null, as shown. If the member has not yet been used, typically because the database has only just been opened and no log switches have occurred, the status will be STALE; this will only be there until the first log switch. If the status is INVALID, you have a problem.

 TIP As with the controlfile, Oracle does not enforce any naming convention for log files, but most organizations will have standards for this.

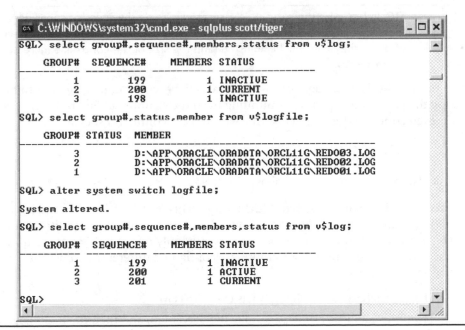

```
C:\WINDOWS\system32\cmd.exe - sqlplus scott/tiger

SQL> select group#,sequence#,members,status from v$log;

    GROUP#  SEQUENCE#    MEMBERS STATUS
---------- ---------- ---------- ----------------
         1        199          1 INACTIVE
         2        200          1 CURRENT
         3        198          1 INACTIVE

SQL> select group#,status,member from v$logfile;

    GROUP# STATUS  MEMBER
---------- ------- ------------------------------------------------
         3         D:\APP\ORACLE\ORADATA\ORCL11G\REDO03.LOG
         2         D:\APP\ORACLE\ORADATA\ORCL11G\REDO02.LOG
         1         D:\APP\ORACLE\ORADATA\ORCL11G\REDO01.LOG

SQL> alter system switch logfile;

System altered.

SQL> select group#,sequence#,members,status from v$log;

    GROUP#  SEQUENCE#    MEMBERS STATUS
---------- ---------- ---------- ----------------
         1        199          1 INACTIVE
         2        200          1 ACTIVE
         3        201          1 CURRENT

SQL>
```

Figure 14-5   Online redo log configuration

Then there is a command to force a log switch:

```
alter system switch logfile;
```

The log switch would happen automatically, eventually, if there were any DML in progress.

The last query shows that after the log switch, group 3 is now the current group that LGWR is writing to, at log switch sequence number 201. The previously current group, group 2, has status ACTIVE. This means that it would still be needed by SMON for instance recovery if the instance failed now. In a short time, as the checkpoint position advances, it will become INACTIVE. Issuing an

```
alter system checkpoint;
```

command would force the checkpoint position to come up to date, and group 2 would then become inactive immediately.

The number of members per group is restricted by settings in the controlfile, determined at database creation time. Turn back to Chapter 2, and the CREATE DATABASE command called by the `CreateDB.sql` script; the MAXLOGFILES directive limits the number of groups that this database can have, and the MAXLOGMEMBERS directive limits the maximum number of members of each group. The DBCA defaults for these (sixteen and three, respectively) may well be suitable for most databases, but if they prove to be inappropriate, it is possible to recreate the controlfile with different values. However, as with all controlfile operations, this will require downtime.

 TIP In fact, with the current release, the limits on the redo log specified in the controlfile are only soft limits: if you create groups and members in excess of these, the limits will be adjusted (and the size of the controlfile increased) automatically.

To protect the database against loss of data in the event of damage to an online redo log file group, multiplex it. Continuing from the example in Figure 14-5, to add multiplexed copies to the online log, one would use a command such as this:

```
alter database add logfile member
'D:\APP\ORACLE\ORADATA\ORCL11G\REDO01A.log' to group 1;
```

or it can also be done through Database Control.

Exercise 14-1: Multiplex the Redo Log This exercise will add a member to each redo log group through Database Control and then confirm the addition from SQL*Plus. The assumption is that there is currently only one member per group, and that you have three groups; if your groups are configured differently, adjust the instructions accordingly.

1. Using Database Control, log on as user SYSTEM.
2. From the database home page, take the Server tab, and then the Redo Log Groups link in the Storage section.
3. Select the first group, and click EDIT.

4. In the Redo Log Members section, click ADD. The Add Redo Log Member page appears.

5. Enter a filename **REDO01b.LOG** for the new member for group 1.

6. Click CONTINUE.

7. Click SHOW SQL and study the command that will be executed, and then click RETURN.

8. Click APPLY to execute the command—or REVERT if you would rather return to Step 4.

9. Take the Redo Log Groups link at the top of the screen to the Redo Log Groups window, and repeat Steps 3–8 for the other groups.

10. Using SQL*Plus, connect as user SYSTEM and issue these queries to confirm the creation of the new members:

```
SQL> select group#,sequence#,members,status from v$log;
SQL> select group#,status,member from v$logfile;
```

The result will show the new members with status INVALID. This is not a problem; it happens merely because they have never been used.

11. Issue the following command three times, to cycle through all your log file groups:

```
SQL> alter system switch logfile;
```

12. Reissue the second query in Step 10 to confirm that the status of all your log file group members is now null.

Archivelog Mode and the Archiver Process

Oracle guarantees that your database is never corrupted by any instance failure, through the use of the online redo log files to repair any inconsistencies caused by an instance failure. This is automatic, and unavoidable, no matter what caused the failure: perhaps a power cut, rebooting the server machine, or issuing a SHUTDOWN ABORT command. But to guarantee no loss of data following a media failure, it is necessary to have a record of all changes applied to the database since the last backup of the database; this is not enabled by default.

The online redo log files are overwritten as log switches occur; the transition to archivelog mode ensures that no online redo log file group is overwritten unless it has been copied as an archive log file first. Thus there will be a series of archive log files that represent a complete history of all changes ever applied to the database. If a datafile is damaged at any time, it will then be possible to restore a backup of the datafile and apply the changes from the archive log redo stream to bring it up-to-date.

By default, a database is created in noarchivelog mode; this means that online redo log files are overwritten by log switches with no copy being made first. It is still impossible to corrupt the database, but data could be lost if the datafiles are damaged by media failure. Once the database is transitioned to archivelog mode, it is impossible to lose data as well—provided that all the archive log files generated since the last backup are available.

Once a database is converted to archivelog mode, a new background process will start, automatically. This is the archiver process, ARCn. By default Oracle will start four of these processes (named ARC0, ARC1, ARC2, and ARC3), but you can have up to thirty. In earlier releases of the database it was necessary to start this process either with a SQL*Plus command or by setting the initialization parameter LOG_ARCHIVE_ START, but an 11g instance will automatically start the archiver if the database is in archivelog mode.

 TIP In archivelog mode, recovery is possible with no loss of data up to and including the last commit. Most production databases are run in archivelog mode.

The archiver will copy the online redo log files to an archive log file after each log switch, deriving a unique name each time, thus generating a continuous chain of log files that can be used for recovering a backup. The name and location of these archive log files is controlled by initialization parameters. For safety the archive log files can and should be multiplexed, just as the online log files can be multiplexed, but eventually they should migrated to offline storage, such as a tape library. The Oracle instance takes care of creating the archive logs with the ARCn process, but the migration to tape must be controlled by the DBA, either through operating system commands or by using the recovery manager utility RMAN (described in later chapters) or another third-party backup software package.

The transition to archivelog mode can be done only while the database is in MOUNT mode after a clean shutdown, and it must be done by a user with a SYSDBA connection. It is also necessary to set the initialization parameters that control the names and locations of the archive logs generated. Clearly, these names must be unique, or archive logs could be overwritten by other archive logs. To ensure unique filenames, it is possible to embed variables such as the log switch sequence number in the archive log filenames (see Table 14-3).

The minimum archiving necessary to ensure that recovery from a restored backup will be possible is to set one archive destination. But for safety, it will usually be a requirement to multiplex the archive log files by specifying two or more destinations, ideally on different disks served by different controllers.

Variable	Description
%d	A unique database identifier, necessary if multiple databases are being archived to the same directories.
%t	The thread number, visible as the THREAD# column in V$INSTANCE. This is not significant, except in a RAC database.
%r	The incarnation number. This is important if an incomplete recovery has been done, as described in Chapters 16 and 18.
%s	The log switch sequence number. This will guarantee that the archives from any one database do not overwrite each other.

Table 14-3 Variables That May Be Used to Embed Unique Values in Archive Log File Names

From 9*i* onward, it is possible to specify up to ten archive destinations, giving you ten copies of each filled online redo log file. This is perhaps excessive for safety. One archive destination? Good idea. Two destinations? Sure, why not. But *ten*? This is to do with Data Guard. For the purposes of this book and the OCP exam, an archive log destination will always be a directory on the machine hosting the database, and two destinations on local disks will usually be sufficient. But the destination can be an Oracle Net alias, specifying the address of a listener on a remote computer. This is the key to zero data loss: the redo stream can be shipped across the network to a remote database, where it can be applied to give a real-time backup. Furthermore, the remote database can (if desired) be configured and opened as a data warehouse, meaning that all the query processing can be offloaded from the primary database to a secondary database optimized for such work.

Exercise 14-2: Transition the Database to Archivelog Mode   Convert your database to archivelog mode, and set parameters to enable archiving to two destinations. The instructions for setting parameters in Step 3 assume that you are using a dynamic spfile; if your instance is using a static pfile, make the edits manually instead.

1. Create two directories with appropriate operating system commands. For example, on Windows,

   ```
   c:\> md c:\oracle\archive1
   c:\> md c:\oracle\archive2
   ```

   or on Unix,

   ```
   $ mkdir /oracle/archive1
   $ mkdir /oracle/archive2
   ```

2. Connect with SQL*Plus as user SYS with the SYSDBA privilege:

   ```
   SQL> connect / as sysdba
   ```

3. Set the parameters to nominate two destination directories created in Step 1 and to control the archive log file names. Note that it is necessary to include a trailing slash character on the directory names (a backslash on Windows).

   ```
   SQL> alter system set log_archive_dest_1='location=/oracle/archive1/' scope=spfile;
   SQL> alter system set log_archive_dest_2='location=/oracle/archive2/' scope=spfile;
   SQL> alter system set log_archive_format='arch_%d_%t_%r_%s.log' scope=spfile;
   ```

4. Shut down the database cleanly:

   ```
   SQL> shutdown immediate;
   ```

5. Start up in mount mode:

   ```
   SQL> startup mount;
   ```

6. Convert the database to archivelog mode:

   ```
   SQL> alter database archivelog;
   ```

7. Open the database:

   ```
   SQL> alter database open;
   ```

PART III

8. Confirm that the database is in archivelog mode and that the archiver is running with these two queries:

```
SQL> select log_mode from v$database;
SQL> select archiver from v$instance;
```

9. Force a log switch:

```
SQL> alter system switch logfile;
```

10. The log switch will have forced an archive to both the destinations. Confirm this from within the Oracle environment with this query:

```
SQL> select name from v$archived_log;
```

and then from an operating system prompt confirm that the files listed by this query were in fact created.

Protecting the Archive Redo Log Files

The LOG_ARCHIVE_DEST_n instance parameters can be used to specify up to ten locations in which copies of archive log files will be generated. At least one of these must be a local disk device (either a directory on a file system, or an ASM device); the other nine can be local disks or remote standby databases.

Each archive log destination can be specified as being *optional* (the default) or *mandatory.* This setting is related to another instance parameter: LOG_ARCHIVE_MIN_SUCCEED_DEST, which defaults to 1. Consider these settings:

```
log_archive_dest_1='location=/u02/orcl/arch1/ mandatory'
log_archive_dest_2='location=/u03/orcl/arch2/ optional'
log_archive_dest_3='location=/u03/orcl/arch3/ optional'
log_archive_min_succeed_dest=2
```

These parameter settings will make it impossible to overwrite an online redo log file group unless it has been successfully archived to the first destination, and to at least one of the second and third destinations. This guarantees two copies of every filled redo log, which is often said to be the minimum necessary for safety. Note that by default (as is the situation following Exercise 14-2) only one copy is required.

Archive log destinations can also be specified with two older parameters:

LOG_ARCHIVE_DEST

LOG_ARCHIVE_DUPLEX_DEST

These date back to earlier versions of the database and can specify just two destinations. However, if only the standard edition of the database has been licensed, then it is these that must be used: the LOG_ARCHIVE_DEST_n parameters, that allow up to ten destinations, are only legal in the Enterprise Edition.

If the ARCn process encounters a problem writing archive log files, eventually the database may hang. This will be dependent on the number of destinations, the number specified as the minimum that must succeed, and whether the destination with a problem is mandatory. A typical reason for archiving to fail is that the destination is full: it is necessary to monitor the progress of archiving, and to migrate archive log files from the disk destination to tape, thus freeing up space for more archives. In any case, all archive logs should be backed up to tape on a regular basis. This can be done manually, or with RMAN.

The Flash Recovery Area

The flash recovery area is a default location for all recovery-related files. The flash recovery area can be located in either a file system directory (Oracle will create its own subdirectories within this) or an ASM disk group. The flash recovery area can only be a disk destination. You must monitor its space usage, and back it up to tape.

Using a flash recovery area can simplify the management of files needed for restore and recovery by enabling a degree of automation in their generation and removal. The flash recovery area is not enabled by default, unless the database is created with the Database Configuration Assistant (DBCA).

Recovery Files

The files that can be stored in the flash recovery area are either permanent or transient. The permanent files are

- Controlfile multiplexed copies
- Online redo log file multiplexed copies

The use of the flash recovery area for the permanent occupants can be automatic. If it has been defined at database creation time, and neither the CONTROL_FILES parameter nor the DB_CREATE_FILE_DEST parameter was set, then a controlfile copy will be created automatically in the flash recovery area. Similarly, if the DB_CREATE_ONLINE_LOG_DEST_N parameter(s) were not set and the CREATE DATABASE command did not specify locations for the online redo log file group members, online redo log file members will be created in the flash recovery area.

The transient occupants of the flash recovery area are

- Archive redo log files
- RMAN backups
- RMAN copies
- Controlfile auto-backups
- Flashback log files

All these files can be redirected elsewhere if you wish, except for the flashback logs; the DBA has no control over these, and a flash recovery area must be defined if Flashback Database is enabled (as described in Chapter 19). The transient occupants can be deleted automatically by the RMAN Recovery Manager if the flash recovery area is full, if space is needed for more recent transient files, and if the policies in effect permit this.

PART III

If none of the LOG_ARCHIVE_DEST_n parameters have been set, then transitioning the database to archivelog mode will internally set LOG_ARCHIVE_DEST_10 to the flash recovery area, if it has been configured.

Configure the Flash Recovery Area

The flash recovery area is controlled by two instance parameters:

- DB_RECOVERY_FILE_DEST
- DB_RECOVERY_FILE_DEST_SIZE

The first of these parameters nominates the location. This can be a file system directory or an ASM disk group. It is possible for several databases to share a common destination; each database will have its own directory structure (created automatically) in the destination. The second parameter limits the maximum amount of space in the destination that the database will take up; it says nothing about how much space is actually available in the destination. It is not possible to set the location, if the size has not been set already.

EXAM TIP You must set DB_RECOVERY_FILE_DEST_SIZE before attempting to set DB_RECOVERY_FILE_DEST.

If a database is created with the DBCA defaults, the location will be set to a directory named flash_recovery_area in the directory specified by the ORACLE_BASE environment variable. The size will be set to 2GB. Both the parameters are dynamic, and the size parameter will almost certainly need to be changed to a much higher value.

TIP How large should the flash recovery area be? Oracle Corporation's advice is that the flash recovery area should be greater than the sum of the sizes of the database, all incremental backups since the last full backup, and all archive redo log files that have not been backed up to tape.

The DB_RECOVERY_FILE_DEST parameter is dynamic, but if it is changed, Oracle is still aware of the existence of files in the previously specified location. These views all include a column IS_RECOVERY_DEST_FILE, as well as a column for the name and directory of the file:

V$CONTROLFILE

V$LOGFILE

V$ARCHIVED_LOG

V$BACKUP_PIECE

The value of the DB_RECOVERY_FILE_DEST_SIZE will be applied to the current setting of DB_RECOVERY_FILE_DEST. If it is increased, more files can be written to the flash recovery area before automatic deletions occur; if it is reduced, then some files considered to be obsolete according to the defined retention policy may be deleted.

Flash Recovery Area Space Usage

RMAN, the Recovery Manager, can manage space within the flash recovery area: it can delete files that are no longer needed according to its configured policies for retaining copies and backups of files, if the flash recovery area space limit has been reached. In an ideal situation, the flash recovery area will be large enough to store a complete copy of the database, plus any archive logs and incremental backups that would be necessary to recover the copy if necessary.

The database backup routines should also include backing up the flash recovery area to tape, thus implementing a strategy of primary, secondary, and tertiary storage:

- Primary storage is the live database, on disk.

- Secondary storage is a copy of the database plus files needed for fast recovery.

- Tertiary storage is long-term backups in a tape library.

RMAN can manage the whole cycle: backup of the database from primary to secondary, and migration of backups from secondary to tertiary storage. Such a system can be implemented in a fashion that will allow near-instant recovery following a failure, combined with the ability to take the database back in time if this is ever necessary.

To monitor the space usage, query the dynamic performance view V$FLASH_RECOVERY_AREA_USAGE:

```
orcl > desc v$flash_recovery_area_usage
 Name                                    Null?    Type
 --------------------------------------- -------- -----------------
 FILE_TYPE                                        VARCHAR2(20)
 PERCENT_SPACE_USED                               NUMBER
 PERCENT_SPACE_RECLAIMABLE                        NUMBER
 NUMBER_OF_FILES                                  NUMBER
```

This view will show, for each type of file that can reside in the flash recovery area, how much space the files are occupying and how much could be reused, expressed as a percentage of the current setting of the DB_RECOVERY_FILE_DEST_SIZE parameter.

Exercise 14-3: Investigate the Flash Recovery Area Configuration In this exercise, you will investigate the configuration of the flash recovery area using Database Control.

1. From the database home page, take the Availability tab, then the Recovery Settings link in the Backup/Recovery section.

2. Navigate to the bottom part of the Recovery Settings window, which shows the flash recovery area configuration, as shown in this illustration:

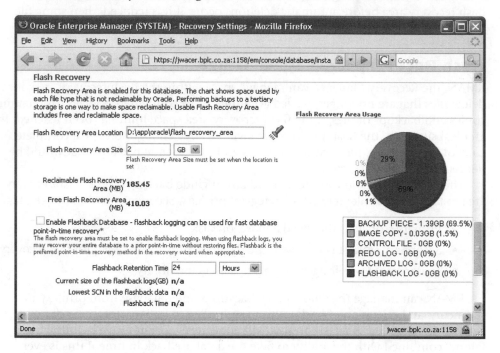

3. Interpret the display: note the settings for the instance parameters DB_RECOVERY_FILE_DEST and DB_RECOVERY_FILE_DEST_SIZE. These are `D:\app\oracle\flash_recovery_area` and 2GB in the illustration. Note the space free and the space reclaimable: 410MB and 185MB in the illustration. Note the allocation of space: in the illustration, 69 percent of the flash recovery area is taken up with backup pieces, 1.5 percent with image copies.

4. If the flash recovery area parameters are not set, set them now. The directory must be one on which the operating system account that owns the Oracle software has full permissions, and the size should be at least 2GB.

Two-Minute Drill

Identify the Types of Failure That Can Occur in an Oracle Database

- Instance failure results in automatic instance recovery on the next startup.
- Session failures are managed automatically by the PMON process.
- User errors can be reversed using a number of techniques.
- Recovering from media failures requires use of backups and archive logs.

Describe Ways to Tune Instance Recovery

- Instance recovery is automatic and unstoppable.
- Instance recovery applies change vectors from the online redo log files, since the last incremental checkpoint position.
- The time taken for instance recovery is dependent on the amount of redo to be applied, and the number of I/Os on datafiles needed to apply it.
- The FAST_START_MTTR_TARGET parameter sets a maximum time for recovery, using a self-tuning mechanism.
- If FAST_START_MTTR_TARGET is set, it will also enable the checkpoint auto-tuning process to reduce recovery time further.

Identify the Importance of Checkpoints, Redo Log Files, and Archived Log Files

- Full checkpoints occur only on orderly shutdown or on demand.
- Partial checkpoints occur automatically when necessary.
- Incremental checkpoints advance the point in the redo stream from which recovery must begin after an instance failure.
- The redo log consists of the disk structures for storing change vectors. The online log is essential for instance recovery.
- The archive log consists of copies of online log file members, created as they are filled. These are essential for datafile recovery after media failure.

Configure ARCHIVELOG Mode

- In ARCHIVELOG mode, an online log file member cannot be overwritten until it has been archived.
- Archive processes start automatically when ARCHIVELOG mode is enabled.
- The mode can only be changed when the database is mounted.

Configure Multiple Archive Log File Destinations to Increase Availability

- The instance parameter(s) LOG_ARCHIVE_DEST_n enable up to ten archive log destinations.
- If LOG_ARCHIVE_DEST_n is not specified, the tenth destination will default to the flash recovery area.
- If Enterprise Edition is not available, there can only be two destinations. These are specified with LOG_ARCHIVE_DEST and LOG_ARCHIVE_DUPLEX_DEST.
- Archive logs can go to a local disk directory, to an ASM device, or (through Oracle Net) to a remote standby database.

- If the number of successful archives does not reach the LOG_ARCHIVE_MIN_ SUCCEED_DEST setting, eventually the database will hang as it cannot overwrite filled online log files.

Overview of the Flash Recovery Area

- The flash recovery area is a default location for all recovery-related files.
- The flash recovery area can be on a local disk file system or an ASM device.
- Permanent occupants of the flash recovery area are controlfile copies and online redo log file members.
- Transient occupants of the flash recovery area are RMAN backups and copies, archive log files, controlfile autobackups, and flashback logs.

Configure the Flash Recovery Area

- The initialization parameter DB_RECOVERY_FILE_DEST specifies the location of the flash recovery area.
- The initialization parameter DB_RECOVERY_FILE_DEST_SIZE specifies the maximum size of the flash recovery area.
- When the flash recovery area is configured, the initialization parameter LOG_ ARCHIVE_DEST_10 is automatically set to the flash recovery area location.
- The recommended size of the flash recovery area is the sum of the database size, the size of incremental backups, and the size of all archived log files that have not been copied to tape or to another disk location.

Use the Flash Recovery Area

- The initialization parameters DB_RECOVERY_FILE_DEST_SIZE and DB_ RECOVERY_FILE_DEST are dynamic.
- The dynamic performance view V$RECOVERY_FILE_DEST shows the total used and reclaimable space on the destination file system or flash recovery area.
- Oracle performs some automatic management of the space in the flash recovery area and keeps track of which files are no longer needed for recovery or other flashback functions.

Self Test

1. Different errors require different actions for recovery. Match these types of failure (a) through (d) to the appropriate recovery process A through D:

    (a) Server machine reboots

    (b) Client machine reboots

(c) Statement causes a constraint violation

(d) Datafile damaged

A. PMON

B. RMAN

C. Session server process

D. SMON

2. What instance parameter must be set to enable the checkpoint auto-tuning capability? (Choose the best answer.)

    A. DBWR_IO_SLAVES

    B. FAST_START_MTTR_TARGET

    C. LOG_CHECKPOINT_INTERVAL

    D. STATISTICS_LEVEL

3. Which redo log files may be required for instance recovery? (Choose the best answer.)

    A. Only the current online redo log file

    B. Only the active online redo file(s)

    C. Both current and active online redo log file(s)

    D. Current and active online redo log files, and possibly archive redo log files

4. When will a full checkpoint occur? (Choose all correct answers.)

    A. As part of a NORMAL shutdown

    B. As part of an IMMEDIATE shutdown

    C. When a tablespace is taken offline

    D. When a log switch occurs

5. Which of these operations cannot be accomplished while the database is open? (Choose all correct answers.)

    A. Adding a controlfile copy

    B. Adding an online log file member

    C. Changing the location of the flash recovery area

    D. Changing the archivelog mode of the database

6. How can you use checkpointing to improve performance?

    A. Frequent checkpoints will reduce the workload on the DBWn.

    B. Enabling checkpoint auto-tuning will optimize disk I/O.

    C. Reducing the MTTR will reduce disk I/O.

    D. Increasing the MTTR will reduce disk I/O.

7. What file types will, by default, be stored in the flash recovery area if it has been defined? (Choose all correct answers.)

   A. Archive redo log files

   B. Background process trace files

   C. RMAN backup sets

   D. RMAN image copies

   E. Undo data

8. There are several steps involved in transitioning to archivelog mode. Put these in the correct order:

   1   alter database archivelog

   2   alter database open

   3   alter system archive log start

   4   full backup

   5   shutdown immediate

   6   startup mount

   A. 5, 6, 1, 2, 4; 3 not necessary

   B. 5, 4, 6, 1, 2, 3

   C. 6, 1, 3, 5, 4, 2

   D. 1, 5, 4, 6, 2; 3 not necessary

   E. 5, 6, 1, 2, 3; 4 not necessary

9. What conditions must hold before an online log file member can be reused if the database is operating in archivelog mode? (Choose all correct answers.)

   A. It must be inactive.

   B. It must be multiplexed.

   C. It must be archived.

   D. The archive must be multiplexed.

10. If the database is in archivelog mode, what will happen if the archiving fails for any reason? (Choose the best answer.)

   A. The instance will abort.

   B. All non-SYSDBA sessions will hang.

   C. DML operations will hang.

   D. The database will revert to noarchivelog mode.

Self Test Answers

1. ☑ **A, B, C,** and **D. A** – b: PMON releases resources of failed sessions. **B** – d: RMAN
   manages media recovery. **C** – c: the server process rolls back failed statements.
   D – a: SMON performs instance recovery.
   ☒ All other combinations.

2. ☑ **B.** If FAST_START_MTTR_TARGET is set to a nonzero value, then
   checkpoint auto-tuning will be in effect.
   ☒ **A, C,** and **D. A** is wrong because DBWR_IO_SLAVES is for simulating
   asynchronous disk I/O. **C** is wrong because LOG_CHECKPOINT_INTERVAL
   will disable the self-tuning mechanism. **D** is wrong because STATISTICS_
   LEVEL is not relevant to checkpoint auto-tuning.

3. ☑ **C.** Instance recovery will always require the current online redo log file,
   and if any others were active, it will need them as well.
   ☒ **A, B,** and **D. A** and **B** are wrong because they are not sufficient. **D** is wrong
   because instance recovery never needs an archive redo log file.

4. ☑ **A** and **B.** Any orderly shutdown will trigger a full checkpoint.
   ☒ **C,** and **D. C** is wrong because this would trigger only a partial checkpoint.
   D is wrong because log switches do not trigger checkpoints.

5. ☑ **A** and **D.** Anything to do with the controlfile can only be done in
   nomount or shutdown modes. Changing the archivelog mode can only
   be done in mount mode.
   ☒ **B** and **C. B** is wrong because the online redo log can be configured while
   the database is open. **C** is wrong because DB_RECOVERY_FILE_DEST is a
   dynamic parameter.

6. ☑ **D.** Setting a longer FAST_START_MTTR_TARGET, or not setting it at all,
   will reduce the need for DBWn to write dirty buffers to disk, which should
   improve performance.
   ☒ **A, B,** and **C. A** and **C** are both wrong because they describe the
   opposite effect. **B** is wrong because the auto-tuning capability does not affect
   performance, though it will reduce recovery time after instance failure.

7. ☑ **A, C,** and **D.** These will go to the flash recovery area, unless directed
   elsewhere.
   ☒ **B** and **E. B** is wrong because background trace files will go to a directory
   in the DIAGNOSTIC_DEST directory. **E** is wrong because undo data is stored
   in the undo tablespace.

8. ☑ **A.** This is the correct sequence.

☒ **B, C, D,** and **E. B, C,** and **D** are wrong because enabling archiving is not necessary (it will occur automatically). **E** is wrong because a backup is a necessary part of the procedure.

9. ☑ **A** and **C.** These are the two conditions.

☒ **B** and **D.** While these are certainly good practice, they are not requirements.

10. ☑ **C.** Once all the online log files need archiving, DML commands will be blocked.

☒ **A, B,** and **D. A** is wrong because the instance will remain open. **B** is wrong because only sessions that attempt DML will hang; those running queries can continue. **D** is wrong because this cannot happen automatically.

CHAPTER 15

Back Up with RMAN

Exam Objectives

In this chapter you will learn to

- 051.15.1   Create Consistent Database Backups
- 052.15.2   Back Up Your Database Without Shutting It Down
- 052.15.3   Create Incremental Backups
- 052.15.4   Automate Database Backups
- 052.15.5   Manage Backups, View Backup Reports, and Monitor the Flash Recovery Area
- 053.2.2   Define, Apply, and Use a Retention Policy
- 053.5.1   Create Image File Backups
- 053.5.2   Create a Whole Database Backup
- 053.5.3   Enable Fast Incremental Backup
- 053.5.4   Create Duplex Backups and Back Up Backup Sets
- 053.5.5   Create an Archival Backup for Long-Term Retention
- 053.5.6   Create a Multisection, Compressed, and Encrypted Backup
- 053.5.7   Report on and Maintain Backups
- 053.4.1   Configure Backup Settings
- 053.4.2   Allocate Channels to Use in Backing Up
- 053.4.3   Configure Backup Optimization

Oracle's recommended backup and recovery tool is RMAN, the Recovery Manager. Using RMAN is not compulsory: Oracle Corporation still supports backups created with operating system utilities (as described in Chapter 18), but RMAN has functionality that is simply not available with other products. It is possible to use RMAN out of the box, but most DBAs will need the more advanced facilities and will carry out a considerable amount of configuration to make these easier to use. There is an RMAN interface in Database Control that can be used to generate simple RMAN jobs and to schedule their execution, and there is also a command-line interface that gives access to all the facilities. However, the most common technique for running RMAN is undoubtedly through scripts. These and other advanced capabilities will be dealt with in Chapter 17.

Backup Concepts and Terminology

A backup carried out with operating system commands is known as a *user-managed backup*. A backup carried out by RMAN is known as a *server-managed backup*. There are three decisions to make before carrying out a server-managed backup. Should it be

- Closed or open?
- Whole or partial?
- Full or incremental?

A *closed* backup is carried out when the database is shut down; alternative terms for closed are cold, consistent, and offline. An *open* backup is carried out while the database is in use; alternative terms are hot, inconsistent, and online. An open backup can only be made if the database is in archivelog mode. A *whole* backup is a backup of all the datafiles and the control files. A *partial* backup is a backup of a subset of these. In most circumstances, partial backups can only be made if the database is in archivelog mode. A *full* backup includes all used blocks of the files backed up. An *incremental* backup includes only those blocks that have been changed since the last backup. An incremental backup can be cumulative (including all blocks changed since the last full backup) or differential (including all blocks changed since the last incremental backup).

 EXAM TIP An open backup can only be made if the database is in archivelog mode. If the database is in noarchivelog mode, only closed backups are possible and (if using RMAN) the database must be in mount mode, following a clean shutdown.

Any combination of these is possible. Many sites perform closed, whole, full backups during weekly or monthly maintenance slots, and open, whole, incremental backups daily. Partial backups are often carried out more frequently for particularly volatile files, or following direct load operations that do not generate redo.

The file types that can be backed up by RMAN are

- Datafiles
- Controlfile

- Archive redo log files
- SPFILE
- Backup set pieces

Files that cannot be backed up by RMAN include

- Tempfiles
- Online redo log files
- Password file
- Static PFILE
- Oracle Net configuration files

RMAN can generate three types of backup:

- A *backup set* is a proprietary format that can contain several files and will not include blocks of a datafile that are not currently part of a segment.
- A *compressed backup set* has the same content as a backup set, but RMAN will apply a compression algorithm as it writes out the backup set.
- An *image copy* is a backup file that is identical to the input file. An image copy is immediately interchangeable with its source, whereas to extract a file from a backup set requires an RMAN restore operation.

Backup sets (compressed or not) can be full or incremental; an image copy, by its very nature, can be only full. A backup set is a logical structure containing one or more input files; physically, it consists of one or more *pieces*, which are the output files of a backup operation.

RMAN backup and restore operations are carried out by server processes known as *channels*. A channel is either of type disk (meaning that it can read and write backups on disk) or of type SBT_TAPE (meaning that it is capable of reading and writing backups stored on a tape device).

The RMAN *repository* is metadata about backups: the names and locations of the pieces that make up the backup sets, and the files contained within them, and the names and locations of image copies. The repository is the key to automating restore and recovery operations: RMAN reads it to work out the most efficient way of restoring and recovering damaged datafiles. The repository is stored in the controlfile of the target database, and optionally in a set of tables created in a *catalog* database. Use of a catalog substantially enhances RMAN's capabilities.

RMAN operations are launched, monitored, and controlled with the RMAN executable. This is a user process that can establish sessions against several databases concurrently. First, the RMAN executable will always connect to the *target* database. The target is the database that is going to be backed up, or restored and recovered. Second, the RMAN executable can connect to a repository in a catalog database—if this has been configured. Third, RMAN can connect to an *auxiliary* database. An auxiliary database is a database that will be created from a backup of a target database.

PART III

Using the RMAN BACKUP Command to Create Backups

All the types of backup that RMAN can create are launched with the BACKUP command. Previous versions have a COPY command, used to create image copies, which is still supported for backward compatibility, but the functionality of this has now been subsumed into the BACKUP command. Backups can be made interactively with the RMAN executable or Database Control, but generally speaking they will be automated, by using an operating system scheduler to run jobs, or by using the Enterprise Manager job scheduling system, or by using the database job scheduler. This last technique is described in Chapter 22.

Server-Managed Consistent Backups

An *offline* backup is a backup taken while the database is closed. You may hear offline backups referred to as *closed, cold,* or *consistent* backups. The term "closed" is self-explanatory and "cold" is just slang, but "consistent" requires an understanding of the Oracle architecture. For a datafile to be consistent, every block in the datafile must have been checkpointed, and the file closed by the operating system. In normal running, the datafiles are inconsistent: there will be a number of blocks that have been copied into the database buffer cache, updated, and not yet written back to disk. The datafile itself, on disk, is therefore not consistent with the real-time state of the database; some parts of it will be out-of-date. To make a datafile consistent, all changed blocks must be flushed to disk, and the datafile closed. As a general rule, this only happens when the database is shut down cleanly—with the IMMEDIATE, TRANSACTIONAL, or NORMAL shutdown options.

An RMAN-consistent backup can be accomplished only when the database is in mount mode. This is because RMAN needs to read the controlfile in order to find the datafiles. If a user-managed operating system backup were attempted in mount mode, it would be invalid (though the DBA wouldn't realize this until attempting to restore) because even in mount mode the controlfile might be written to while being copied. The copy would then be inconsistent, and therefore useless. RMAN avoids the problem by taking a read-consistent snapshot of the controlfile and backing that up.

An RMAN backup is launched from the RMAN executable. The RMAN executable is a tool supplied by Oracle and installed into the Oracle Home. RMAN logs on to the database (like any other user process) and then launches additional server processes to copy files. In general, there are three techniques for using RMAN: an interactive interface, for performing ad hoc tasks; a script interface, for running jobs through the operating system's scheduler; and an Enterprise Manager interface, for generating scripts and defining jobs to be scheduled by Enterprise Manager.

This is an RMAN script for performing an offline whole full backup:

```
run {
shutdown immediate;
startup mount;
allocate channel d1 type disk;
```

```
backup as backupset database
format 'd:\backup\offline_full_whole.bus';
alter database open;
}
```

The first two commands within the `run{}` block perform a clean shutdown and then bring the database back up in mount mode. Then the script launches a server process, known as a *channel*, to perform the backup. In this case, the channel is a disk channel because the backup is being directed to disk; the alternative channel type is SBT_TAPE (or type SBT is also syntactically acceptable), which is used for backups directed to a tape device. The next command launches a backup operation. This will be of type BACKUPSET. Backup sets are an RMAN-proprietary structure that can combine many input files into one output file. Backup sets have other advantages, such as compression (not enabled in this example) and the ability to reduce the size of the backup by ignoring blocks in the input datafiles that have never been used, or are not in use at the moment. The keyword DATABASE instructs RMAN to back up the entire set of datafiles and the controlfile. RMAN will never back up online redo log file members or tempfiles. The FORMAT keyword names the file that will contain the backup set: the backup piece. Finally, the script opens the database.

 EXAM TIP RMAN will never back up the online redo log files, or the tempfiles. It will back up datafiles, archivelog files, the controlfile, and the spfile.

The script could be entered and executed interactively, from an RMAN prompt. Alternatively, if the script were written with an editor (such as vi on Unix or the Windows Notepad) and saved to a file `offline_full_whole.rman`, an operating system command that could be scheduled to run this script is

```
rman target sys/oracle@orcl11g @offline_full_whole.rman
```

This command launches the RMAN executable, with the SYS login (necessary because of the SHUTDOWN and STARTUP commands) to a target database identified by the Oracle Net alias orcl11g, and then specifies the name of the script, which must be preceded by an "@" symbol.

Exercise 15-1: Automate a Consistent Backup   In this exercise, use the Database Control job scheduling system to perform an automated offline backup.

1. Connect to the database with Database Control as user SYS.

2. On the Availability tab, take the Schedule Backup link in the Manage section.

3. In the Schedule Backup window, select the radio button for Whole Database and enter an operating username and password for host credentials, if these have not already been saved as Preferred Credentials. The username should have read and write permissions on the ORACLE_BASE directory structure. Click the SCHEDULE CUSTOMIZED BACKUP button.

4. In the Schedule Customized Backup: Options window, select the radio buttons and check boxes for Full Backup, "Use as the base of an incremental backup strategy," Offline Backup, and "Also backup all archived logs on disk." Click NEXT.

5. In the Schedule Customized Backup: Settings window, note that the default destination is to the flash recovery area. Click NEXT.

6. In the Schedule Customized Backup: Schedule window, accept the default schedule, which will run the backup immediately. Click NEXT.

7. In the Schedule Customized Backup: Review window, observe the RMAN commands that will be run, and click SUBMIT JOB.

8. The job will take a few minutes to run, during which the database will be shut down and restarted.

9. To confirm the success of the operation, reconnect to Database Control and from the database home page on the Availability tab, take the Backup Reports link in the Manage section.

10. In the View Backup Report window, click the links for the name of the job and the status to see the full details of the job.

Server-Managed Open Backups

An absolutely reliable open backup can be made using RMAN with a two-word command issued at the RMAN prompt: BACKUP DATABASE. This command relies on configured defaults for the destination of the backup (disk or tape library), the names of the backup files generated, the number of server channels to launch to carry out the backup, and the type of backup (image copies of the files, backup sets, or compressed backup sets).

This RMAN script performs a full whole online backup of the database and the archive log files:

```
run {
allocate channel t1 type sbt_tape;
allocate channel t2 type sbt_tape;
backup as compressed backupset filesperset 4 database;
backup as compressed backupset archivelog all delete all input;
}
```

The script launches two channels that will write to the tape library. The device driver for the tape library (supplied by the hardware vendor) must have been installed. The use of multiple channels (possibly related to the number of tape drives in the library) will parallelize the backup operation, which should make it run faster. The first backup command backs up the complete database (all the databases and the controlfile) but rather than putting every file into one huge (even though compressed) backup set, it instructs RMAN to divide the database into multiple backup sets, each containing no more than four files; this can make restore operations faster than if all the files are in one backup set. The second backup command will back up all the archive log files (by default, into one backup set) removing them from disk as it does so. The commands do not specify how many pieces each backup set should consist of: by default, only one.

TIP Some RMAN commands can be run independently from the RMAN prompt; others must be included within a `run {}` block of several commands.

When making an open backup, it is possible that RMAN could attempt to copy a block of a file at the same time as the DBWn is writing to the block: this results in what is called a *fractured* block. A fractured block would be useless in a backup, because copying it while it was being updated would make the copy internally inconsistent. RMAN detects fractured blocks if they occur, and will retry the block copy until it gets a consistent version. To obtain a read-consistent version of the controlfile, RMAN creates a read-consistent snapshot copy of the controlfile, and that is what is actually backed up.

EXAM TIP When creating backup sets, or compressed backup sets, RMAN will never back up blocks that have not been allocated to a segment. This results in considerable space savings.

An open or closed backup can be made of the entire database, one tablespace, or an individual file, as in these examples:

```
backup as backupset format '/backup/orcl/df_%d_%s_%p' tablespace gl_tabs;
backup as compressed backupset datafile 4;
backup as backupset archivelog like '/u01/archive1/arch_1%';
```

The first example here will back up all the datafiles making up the GL_TABS tablespace, and the backup set piece will be uniquely named using these format specifiers:

- `%d` is the database ID.
- `%s` is the backup set number, which increments with every set created.
- `%p` is the piece number, starting at 1 for each set.

The second example nominates one datafile, by number. Datafiles can be addressed by name or number.

The third example uses a wildcard (the percentage character) to identify all archivelogs in a certain directory whose names begin with a certain string.

Incremental Backups

Why should you consider incremental backups? There are three major reasons: time, space, and the impact on end users. The time for a backup to complete may not be important to the users, but it can be very important to the system administrators. Automated tape libraries are very expensive pieces of equipment and may well be used for backing up systems other than the Oracle databases. If the time required for an RMAN backup can be reduced, there will be savings in the tape library resources needed. Even though the default operation of RMAN is to scan the whole datafile when backing it up incrementally in order to identify which blocks have changed, there will still be time savings because in virtually all cases it is the writing to tape that is the bottleneck, not the reading of the files. By enabling block change tracking (detailed later in this section), which obviates the need to scan the whole file, the time for the backup can be reduced dramatically. The volume of an incremental backup will usually be substantially less than the volume of a full backup. As discussed previously, backup sets are always smaller than the source files, or image copies, because they never include empty blocks that have never been written to and can, optionally, be compressed. But incremental backups may well be just a small fraction of the size of a full backup set. This will reduce the impact on the tape library or the disk resources needed. The impact on users is largely dependent on the excessive disk I/O needed for a full backup. When block change tracking is enabled, an incremental backup can directly access changed blocks, which will reduce the strain on disk I/O resources substantially.

Incremental backups can be made with server-managed backups, but not with user-managed backups. As far as an operating system utility is concerned, the granularity of the backup is the datafile: an operating system utility cannot look inside the datafile to extract changed blocks incrementally. Incremental backups must always be as backup sets or compressed backup sets. It is logically impossible to make an image copy incremental backup, because an incremental backup can never be identical to the source file. If it were, it wouldn't be incremental.

An incremental backup relies on a starting point that contains all blocks: this is known as the *incremental level 0* backup. Then an *incremental level 1* backup will extract all blocks that have changed since the last level 1 backup, or the last level 0 backup if there have been no intervening level 1 backups. A *cumulative* backup will extract all blocks that have changed since the last level 0 backup, irrespective of whether there have been any level 1 backups in the meantime.

An RMAN command to make a level 0 backup is

```
backup as backupset incremental level 0 database;
```

This command relies on configured defaults for launching channels, for the number of files to place in each backup set, and to where the backup set will be written. The backup set will contain all blocks that have ever been used. Many sites will make an incremental level 0 backup every weekend. Then a level 1 backup can be made with this command:

```
backup as backupset incremental level 1 database;
```

This command could be run daily, to extract all blocks changed since the last level 1 (or, the first time it is run, the level 0) backup. A cumulative incremental backup might be run midweek:

```
backup as backupset incremental level 1 cumulative database;
```

This will extract all blocks changed since the level 0 backup.

EXAM TIP If there is no level 0 backup, then the first level 1 differential or cumulative backup will in fact perform a level 0 backup.

 TIP You can specify incremental levels higher than 1, but they don't have any effect and are permitted only for backward compatibility. Earlier releases of RMAN made use of them.

Incremental backups will always be smaller than full backups, but the time saving may not be as great as you might expect. This is because the default behavior of an incremental backup is to scan the entire datafile being backed up in order to determine which blocks need to be extracted. There is an advantage to this: it allows RMAN to check for block corruption. But there are many occasions when you would prefer that the incremental backup proceed much faster. This can be done by enabling block change tracking.

Block change tracking relies on starting an additional background process: the Change Tracking Writer, or CTWR. This process records the address of each block that has been changed in a file called the *change tracking file*. If block change tracking has been enabled, then RMAN will read the change tracking file when doing an incremental backup to determine which blocks need to be backed up. This is far faster than scanning the whole file.

The change tracking file will be created in a location specified by the DBA, or by default it will go to the DB_CREATE_FILE_DEST directory if this has been defined. It is initially sized at 10MB and will grow in 10MB increments, but unless the database is terabyte sized, 10MB will be adequate. The change tracking file is in the form of a bitmap, with each bit covering 32 blocks of the database. There may be a minimal performance overhead to enabling block change tracking, but experience shows that this is not significant. To enable block change tracking and nominate the name and location of the tracking file, use a command such as this:

```
alter database enable block change tracking using file
'/u01/app/oracle/oradaa/orcl/change_tracking.dbf';
```

To monitor the effectiveness of block change tracking, query the view V$BACKUP_DATAFILE. This view is populated every time a datafile is backed up into a backup set: the column DATAFILE_BLOCKS is the size of the datafile, and BLOCKS READ is the number of blocks read by the last backup. The ratio of these will show that block change tracking is reducing the number of blocks that must be read to carry out an incremental backup:

```
select file#, datafile_blocks, (blocks_read / datafile_blocks) * 100
as pct_read_for backup from v$backup_datafile
where used_change_tracking-'YES' and incremental_level > 0;
```

Monitoring the results of a query such as this following level 0 and level 1 cumulative and differential backups will give an indication of how effective an incremental strategy is: if the ratio increases, perhaps backups should be carried out more frequently.

Exercise 15-2: Open Incremental Backup with RMAN In this exercise you will perform an open incremental backup of the database, using the RMAN executable.

1. From an operating system prompt, launch the RMAN executable and connect to the target database, identified by the ORACLE_SID environment variable, using operating system authentication. The program is `$ORACLE_HOME/bin/rman` on Unix, `%ORACLE_HOME%\bin\rman.exe` on Windows:

   ```
   rman target /
   ```

2. Run the command to make a level 1 incremental backup:

   ```
   backup incremental level 1 database;
   ```

3. As the backup proceeds, observe the steps:

   A. A channel of type disk is launched.

   B. The datafiles are identified.

   C. The channel writes out a backup set of a single piece, containing the datafiles.

   D. The controlfile and spfile go into a second backup set, also of one piece.

   The illustration shows this operation, performed on Windows.

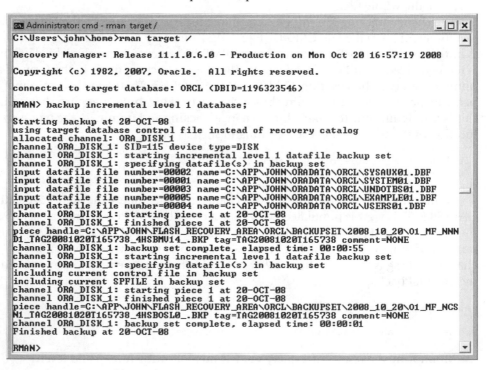

```
Administrator: cmd - rman target /                                        _ □ X
C:\Users\john\home>rman target /

Recovery Manager: Release 11.1.0.6.0 - Production on Mon Oct 20 16:57:19 2008

Copyright (c) 1982, 2007, Oracle.  All rights reserved.

connected to target database: ORCL (DBID=1196323546)

RMAN> backup incremental level 1 database;

Starting backup at 20-OCT-08
using target database control file instead of recovery catalog
allocated channel: ORA_DISK_1
channel ORA_DISK_1: SID=115 device type=DISK
channel ORA_DISK_1: starting incremental level 1 datafile backup set
channel ORA_DISK_1: specifying datafile(s) in backup set
input datafile file number=00002 name=C:\APP\JOHN\ORADATA\ORCL\SYSAUX01.DBF
input datafile file number=00001 name=C:\APP\JOHN\ORADATA\ORCL\SYSTEM01.DBF
input datafile file number=00003 name=C:\APP\JOHN\ORADATA\ORCL\UNDOTBS01.DBF
input datafile file number=00005 name=C:\APP\JOHN\ORADATA\ORCL\EXAMPLE01.DBF
input datafile file number=00004 name=C:\APP\JOHN\ORADATA\ORCL\USERS01.DBF
channel ORA_DISK_1: starting piece 1 at 20-OCT-08
channel ORA_DISK_1: finished piece 1 at 20-OCT-08
piece handle=C:\APP\JOHN\FLASH_RECOVERY_AREA\ORCL\BACKUPSET\2008_10_20\01_MF_NNN
D1_TAG20081020T165738_4HSBMU14_.BKP tag=TAG20081020T165738 comment=NONE
channel ORA_DISK_1: backup set complete, elapsed time: 00:00:55
channel ORA_DISK_1: starting incremental level 1 datafile backup set
channel ORA_DISK_1: specifying datafile(s) in backup set
including current control file in backup set
including current SPFILE in backup set
channel ORA_DISK_1: starting piece 1 at 20-OCT-08
channel ORA_DISK_1: finished piece 1 at 20-OCT-08
piece handle=C:\APP\JOHN\FLASH_RECOVERY_AREA\ORCL\BACKUPSET\2008_10_20\01_MF_NCS
N1_TAG20081020T165738_4HSBOSL0_.BKP tag=TAG20081020T165738 comment=NONE
channel ORA_DISK_1: backup set complete, elapsed time: 00:00:01
Finished backup at 20-OCT-08

RMAN>
```

4. Still within RMAN, run this command to list your backups:

   ```
   list backup of database;
   ```

You will see the first backup, made in Exercise 15-1, is incremental level 0 and will be over 1GB. The second backup is incremental level 1, and only a few megabytes. This is because very little data has been changed between the two backups. But note that the time taken did not drop proportionately.

5. Connect to the database as user SYS with SQL*Plus.

6. Enable block change tracking, nominating the tracking file to be created. For example:

```
alter database enable block change tracking using file
'/u01/app/oracle/product/11.1.0/oradata/orcl/change_tracking.dbf';
```

7. Confirm that the file has been created, and check the size:

```
select * from v$block_change_tracking;
```

8. Confirm that the change tracking writer process has started:

```
select program from v$process where program like '%CTWR%';
```

The next illustration demonstrates Steps 6, 7, and 8 on a Windows system.

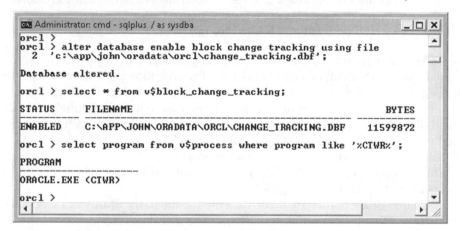

9. Confirm that the file has been created, and check the size:

```
select * from v$block_change_tracking;
```

10. Confirm that the change tracking writer process has started.

11. Connect to the database with the RMAN executable, and make new level 0 and level 1 incremental backups:

```
backup incremental level 0 database;
backup incremental level 1 database;
```

If either backup fails with errors relating to space in the flash recovery area, increase its size with a command such as this, issued from SQL*Plus:

```
alter system set db_recovery_file_dest_size=4G;
```

12. From your RMAN session, rerun the query from Step 4. Note that implementing block change tracking has reduced the time taken for the incremental level 1 backup substantially.

Image Copies

An image copy of a file is a byte-for-byte identical copy of an individual datafile, controlfile, or archive log file. The result is exactly as though the file had been copied with an operating system utility, though the mechanism is different: RMAN reads and writes in Oracle blocks, not operating system blocks. This means that many of the great features of backup sets (such as incremental backup, compression, writing directly to tape, or controlling the size of the output pieces) cannot be used. But it does mean that a restore can be very fast, because there is no need to extract the file from a backup set. The target database controlfile can be updated to address the image copy instead of the damaged file; in effect, no restore is actually needed if a recent image copy is available. Oracle Corporation's advice is to keep a whole image copy of the database, plus archive logs made since the backup was taken, available in the flash recovery area; this will mean that a full restore is virtually instantaneous, and recovery will be fast as well. However, the economics of disk storage may not make this possible.

 EXAM TIP An image copy can be used immediately, without a restore operation. Files backed up into backup sets must be restored from the backup set by RMAN before they can be used.

Tape channels cannot be used for image copies, but if multiple files are to be copied, then parallelism can be considered. However, thought needs to be put into the degree of parallelism to be used. If all the copies are going to a single nonstriped disk, then there is little point in launching more than one disk channel. Also, the speed of backup to disk can have a negative impact on your users. A full-speed image copy will take up a significant amount of CPU and I/O capacity; this can be avoided by deliberately slowing down the backup process.

Image copies can be made of datafiles, the controlfile, and archive logs. Image copies cannot be made of the spfile.

Although image copies are made on a file-for-file basis, RMAN does let you copy many files with one command. To back up the entire database,

```
RMAN> backup as copy database;
```

If the configured defaults are unchanged, this command will launch one disk channel and copy all the datafiles and the controlfile to the flash recovery area. The follow-up command would be

```
RMAN> backup as copy archivelog all delete all input;
```

which will move all the archive log files to the flash recovery area.

Protect Your Backups

RMAN can back up your live database and its archive log files, and it can also back up its own backups. These can in any case be protected with backup duplexing. Consider this command:

```
backup as backupset device type disk copies 2 database plus archivelog;
```

This will back up the entire database and any archivelogs to the default disk destination (the flash recovery area) using the default number of channels (one). However, there will be two backup sets generated, each consisting (by default) of one piece, and each containing the entire database and its archivelogs. Multiplexing the backups on disk in this manner gives a degree of protection, but it will be essential to transfer the backups to tape eventually. This could be accomplished as follows:

```
backup device type sbt_tape backupset all delete all input;
```

TIP The keyword SBT is interchangeable with SBT_TAPE. It stands for System Backup to Tape, and refers to a nondisk backup device.

This command will locate the pieces of all known backup sets on disk and copy them into another backup set in the tape library, removing them from disk as it does so. An alternative technique is to use one of these commands, which are only valid if a tape library is available:

```
backup recovery area;
backup recovery files;
```

The first command backs up the flash recovery area (both current and any previous locations) to tape, using defaults for the number of channels, sets, and pieces. The files included in the backup are full and incremental backup sets; controlfile autobackups; datafile and archive log image copies; and archive redo logs. The second command backs up all these recovery related files, even if they are not in the flash recovery area.

This structure lets you create a three-tiered backup strategy:

- Primary storage is the live database, on disk.
- Secondary storage is the flash recovery area, on disk.
- Tertiary storage is the tape library.

A simple script to implement a backup strategy using three tiers of storage would be

```
run {backup recovery files delete all input;
backup database plus archivelog all delete all input;}
```

The first command will move all existing backups to tape, and the second command will create a new backup of the database and any archive logs, while removing the logs from the LOG_ARCHIVE_DEST_n locations.

TIP The DELETE ALL INPUT clause will not be applied to the live database; it only applies to archive logs and backups.

The script relies on defaults for the number of channels and the size and naming of the backup sets and pieces.

Parallelizing Backup Operations

Every time RMAN is used, there will be at least two sessions launched against the target database: these are known as the *default session* and the *polling session*. The default session is the session that invokes the kernelized PL/SQL (kernelized PL/SQL is PL/SQL that is available to the instance before a database has been mounted or opened) that implements RMAN; the polling session monitors the progress of RMAN operations. Whenever RMAN reads or writes a disk or tape, it will need a third session: a channel.

A database of many gigabytes will take a long time to back up, even if the backup is a fast incremental. To reduce the time taken, parallelize the backup by launching multiple channels. The degree of parallelism achieved will be constrained by the lowest of these factors:

- The number of channels
- The number of backup sets
- The number of input files

Each channel reads one or more files and writes one or more backups; the number of channels is therefore a hard limit on parallelism. However, parallelism is applied within a backup command, not across several backup commands, so if the command itself limits the number of backup sets generated, this may limit the degree of parallelism. Finally, it is not possible for the degree of parallelism to exceed the number of input files—unless the multisection backup capability is enabled.

Consider this script:

```
run {allocate channel t1 type sbt;
allocate channel t2 type sbt;
allocate channel t3 type sbt;
allocate channel t4 type sbt;
backup database files per set 8;}
```

The first four lines launch four arbitrarily named channels. The backup command then forces RMAN to count the number of files in the database, and distribute them into backup sets containing no more than eight files each. If the database consists of 100 datafiles plus the controlfile, 13 backup sets will be generated: the first 12 will each contain 8 files, the thirteenth will have the remaining 5 files. The degree of parallelism will be 4: constrained by the number of channels. However, if the database had only 20 datafiles, there would be only 3 backup sets produced, and the degree of parallelism would be 3; one channel would be idle. If the database had only 4 datafiles, all would go into one backup set produced serially.

If a file is many gigabytes (or terabytes), then it will be desirable to parallelize the backup of this one file. Normally, only one channel can read a file, but by using the multisection keyword this behavior can be changed:

```
run {allocate channel t1 type sbt;
allocate channel t2 type sbt;
```

```
allocate channel t3 type sbt;
allocate channel t4 type sbt;
backup as compressed backupset datafile 16 section size 10g;}
```

This script will launch four channels, each of which will read a series of 10GB sections of datafile 16. Each channel will generate pieces (separate physical files) containing the backup of a section. If the file is 200GB, there will be 20 such pieces, generated four at a time. Without the SECTION SIZE keywords, the degree of parallelism would have been one (i.e., serial) and one channel would have carried out the entire operation.

Exercise 15-3: Back Up Using Multiple Channels In this exercise, you will use a command block to launch multiple channels and parallelize a backup operation.

1. Connect to the database with the RMAN executable, using operating system authentication:

   ```
   rman target /
   ```

2. In another window, connect to the database with SQL*Plus, using operating system authentication:

   ```
   sqlplus / as sysdba
   ```

3. With SQL*Plus, investigate the number of sessions against the instance:

   ```
   select username,program from v$session order by program;
   ```

   You will see that there are two sessions connected as user SYS using the RMAN executable as their user process: these are the default session and the polling session.

4. At the RMAN prompt, create a command block by entering RUN followed by a series of commands within braces:

   ```
   run {
   allocate channel d1 type disk;
   allocate channel d2 type disk;
   backup as compressed backupset database;
   }
   ```

5. While the backup is in progress, rerun the query from Step 3. You will see that there are now four RMAN sessions: the default session, the polling session, and two channel sessions.

6. In the RMAN window, observe the progress of the backup; note how the files are divided between the two channels, each of which generates its own backup set.

Encrypting Backups

In some environments there is a requirement for data to be encrypted. This can be particularly important for backups, because they may be stored on removable media over which the DBA has little or no control. RMAN can encrypt backups, but there are two provisos:

- To create encrypted backups on disk, the Advanced Security Option must be enabled. This is a separately licensed option that must be purchased on top of the Enterprise Edition database license.
- To write encrypted backups directly to tape, the tape library must be accessed through the Oracle Secure Backup SBT interface, which is a separate product that must be licensed and configured for the tape library.

Encryption can be transparent or password based. Transparent data encryption, which is the default, is based on the use of a wallet. This is a file containing the keys used to encrypt and decrypt data, and is itself protected with a password. However, the wallet can be configured to open automatically when needed. The wallet must be available to the RMAN channel processes when creating or restoring backups; it is therefore most useful when backups will always be created and restored on the database on the same machine. A password-encrypted backup can be restored anywhere, so long as the password is known. Each backup uses a different, randomly generated key. This key is itself encrypted with either the specified password, or the database master key stored in the wallet.

The available encryption algorithms are AES with keys of length 128 (the default), 192, or 256 bits. To create a backup with password encryption, first set the algorithm and the password and then make the backup. For example,

```
set encryption algorithm 'aes256' identified by pa55word;
backup as compressed backupset database format '/u01/mnt/backups/orcl_enc.bkp';
```

Before attempting to restore using the backup, set the password again:

```
set decryption identified by pa55word;
```

If the restore operation might require many backups encrypted using different passwords, run a series of set decryption commands to specify them all.

 EXAM TIP The default encryption requires a wallet and will be AES128. Alternatively, a password or longer keys can be specified.

Configuring RMAN Defaults

The Recovery Manager is meant to be easy to use out of the box, but the defaults may well not be appropriate for any one site. By configuring the defaults, RMAN's operations can be customized to your environment.

Figure 15-1 shows the use of the SHOW command, followed by three CONFIGURE commands.

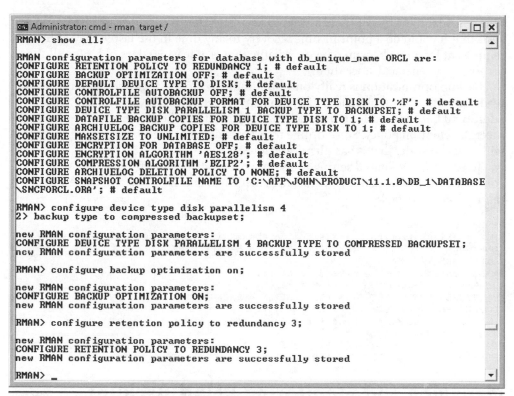

Figure 15-1 Use of SHOW and CONFIGURE to set defaults

The SHOW command displays RMAN's configured defaults. In the figure, they are all on their default values. These are hard-coded. To adjust these defaults, use the CONFIGURE command. The first CONFIGURE command instructs RMAN to always launch four channels when backing up to disk unless a different number of channels is specified, and to always write out compressed backup sets unless some other form of backup is specified. The second CONFIGURE command enables optimization. This allows RMAN not to back up certain files if it considers that it already has sufficient copies of the files. Optimization is related to the retention policy. The default retention policy is 1, meaning that RMAN will attempt to have at least one copy of everything. The third CONFIGURE command changes the retention policy to REDUNDANCY 3, meaning that RMAN will attempt to keep three copies of everything. The result of the configuration adjustments shown in Figure 15-1 could be seen by running SHOW ALL again.

There are two possible retention policies that can be configured. A redundancy level specifies a number of copies of files that should be kept. If set to 3, then when RMAN makes a fourth backup of a file, it will consider the first backup to be redundant, and a candidate for deletion. The alternative strategy is to set a recovery window:

```
RMAN> configure retention policy to recovery window of 90 days;
```

This command instructs RMAN always to keep backups of datafiles and archive logs such that it could do a point-in-time recovery to any time in the last 90 days. This requires at least one backup of every datafile that is at least 90 days old, plus all the archive logs generated since then.

Backup optimization is really only applicable to archive logs and the datafiles of read-only or offline tablespaces. If optimization is enabled, RMAN will not create additional backups of files if it already has sufficient identical copies of the files to meet its retention policy. Since online read-write datafiles are always changing, RMAN will never consider that it has identical copies.

To return a configured setting to its out-of-the-box default, use the CLEAR command, as in this example, which uses SHOW to check values, and CLEAR to return them to default:

```
RMAN> show device type;
RMAN configuration parameters for database with db_unique_name ORCL are:
CONFIGURE DEVICE TYPE DISK PARALLELISM 4 BACKUP TYPE TO
COMPRESSED BACKUPSET;
RMAN> configure device type disk clear;
old RMAN configuration parameters:
CONFIGURE DEVICE TYPE DISK PARALLELISM 4 BACKUP TYPE TO
COMPRESSED BACKUPSET;
RMAN configuration parameters are successfully reset to default value
RMAN> show device type;
RMAN configuration parameters for database with db_unique_name ORCL are:
CONFIGURE DEVICE TYPE DISK PARALLELISM 1 BACKUP TYPE TO BACKUPSET; # default
```

Managing and Monitoring RMAN Backups

The RMAN executable provides commands for reporting on what backups have been made and what backups are required. The same information can also be obtained through the Database Control interface, or it is possible to query the RMAN repository directly by querying various views that are populated from it. If you are using a Recovery Catalog, this is another source of information. RMAN can also physically remove backups from tape and disk.

The LIST, REPORT, and DELETE Commands

As a general rule, LIST tells you about backups that have been made, whereas REPORT tells you what needs to be backed up. The following table shows some examples of LIST:

Command	Function
RMAN> list backup;	List all your backup sets.
RMAN> list copy;	List all your image copies.
RMAN> list backup of database;	List all your whole database backup sets, whether full or incremental.
RMAN> list backup of datafile 1; RMAN> list backup of tablespace users;	List the backup sets that include datafile 1 and the backups that include the USERS tablespace.

Command	Function
RMAN> list backup of archivelog all;	List all archive log backup set backups. Use this command or the next to investigate backups of archive logs.
RMAN> list copy of archivelog from time='sysdate - 7';	List all image copies of archive logs generated in the last seven days.
RMAN> list backup of archivelog from sequence 1000 until sequence 1050;	List all backup sets containing archive logs of log switch sequence numbers 1000–1050.

To change the format of the dates and times in the output of LIST, set the environment variable NLS_DATE_FORMAT before launching the RMAN executable. For example, on Unix,

```
$ export NLS_DATE_FORMAT=dd-mm-yy hh24:mi:ss
```

or on Windows,

```
C:\> set NLS_DATE_FORMAT=dd-mm-yy hh24:mi:ss
```

will change the date/time display to the European standard.

The REPORT command interrogates the target database to determine what needs to be backed up. This requires contrasting the physical structure of the database and the archived logs that have been generated with the backup sets and copies as recorded in the repository, and applying a retention policy. The retention policy can be that configured as a default, or it can be specified as part of the REPORT command. This table shows some examples:

Command	Function
RMAN> report schema;	List the datafiles (but not the controlfile or archived logs) that make up the database.
RMAN> report need backup;	Apply the configured retention policy and list all the datafiles and archive log files that need at least one backup to conform to the policy.
RMAN> report need backup days 3;	List all objects that haven't been backed up for three days. Use this command or the next to ignore the configured retention policy.
RMAN> report need backup redundancy 3;	List all files of which there are not at least three backups.

RMAN has a retention policy. This is a database-wide setting, which controls how many backups of each file RMAN will attempt to keep.

The REPORT OBSOLETE command takes things a step further: it contrasts the RMAN backups that have been taken with the retention policy and lists all those that can be deleted because they are no longer required. This command works in conjunction with DELETE OBSOLETE, which will remove the records of any such backups from the repository and physically remove the backup files from disk or tape. For example,

```
RMAN> report obsolete;
```

will apply the configured retention policy and list all copies and backup sets that are no longer required. Then,

```
RMAN> delete obsolete;
```

will remove the backups deemed surplus to requirements.

```
RMAN> report obsolete redundancy 2;
```

lists all backups that take the number of backups of an object to three or more. Then to remove the superfluous backups,

```
RMAN> delete obsolete redundancy 2;
```

The DELETE command can also be used to remove individual backups, by number or by tag:

```
RMAN> delete backupset 4;
RMAN> delete copy of datafile 6 tag file6_extra;
```

Archival Backups

In Oracle terminology, an *archival backup* is a backup that you want to keep long term, possibly forever. It will not usually be necessary to recover from an archival backup: it should be possible to restore it in order to recreate the database as it was at the time the backup was made, but you won't want to apply archived logs to it to bring it further forward in time. Often, archival backups are made purely to satisfy legislation regarding retention of records; they have little or no technical significance. An archival backup does not count toward compliance with the configured retention policy, and neither will it be deleted automatically by a DELETE OBSOLETE command.

Even though it will not usually be necessary to keep the archive logs needed to recover an archival backup up to the present day, if the archival backup is an open backup then it will be necessary to keep all the archive logs generated while the backup was being taken. This is because they will be needed to make the open backup consistent, in the event of having to restore it.

The syntax to create an archival backup is

```
BACKUP ... KEEP { FOREVER | UNTIL TIME 'date_expr' }
[ RESTORE POINT rsname ] ;
```

The clause defining what to back up can be anything: a datafile, a tablespace, the whole database, incremental, compressed, encrypted, and so on. It can be directed to either tape or disk. However, usually, the only sensible backup target is a full backup of the whole database, and it will probably be directed through a tape channel to a tape library. The date expression can be an actual date or a calculation. An example is

```
backup database as compressed backup set keep until time 'sysdate + 90'
restore point quarterly_backup ;
```

This command will write out a compressed backup, which will be considered obsolete (and therefore deletable) after 90 days. If the database is open at the time, the relevant archivelogs will be included.

The Dynamic Performance Views

A number of views populated from the target database controlfile can be used to report on RMAN's backups. By querying these, you can develop your own reports, rather than relying on RMAN's LIST command.

View	Displays
v$backup_files	One row for each file that has been backed up, which may be a datafile, the spfile, the controlfile, or an archive log. Also, one row for each piece that RMAN has created. The column FILE_TYPE distinguishes which type of file the row refers to.
v$backup_set	One row per backup set
v$backup_piece	One row per backup piece
v$backup_redolog	One row for each archived log that has been backed up
v$backup_spfile	One row for each backup that has been made of the spfile
v$backup_datafile	One row for backup of a datafile
v$backup_device	Names of SBT devices that have been linked to RMAN
v$rman_configuration	One row for every configuration setting, excluding all those on default

Join columns in the various views will let you construct comprehensive reports on what has been backed up, where the backups are located, and the size and type of each backup.

Crosschecking Backups

The information used by the RMAN commands REPORT and LIST, and the information displayed in the dynamic performance views, is drawn from the RMAN repository: data stored in the controlfile of the target database. It says nothing about reality—whether the backup files actually still exist. To confirm that the backups do exist, use the CROSSCHECK command. For example:

```
RMAN> crosscheck backup of database;
using channel ORA_DISK_1
crosschecked backup piece: found to be 'AVAILABLE'
backup piece handle=/u01/app/oracle/flash_recovery_area/orcl/backupset/2008_10_20/
o1_mf_nnnd0_backup_orcl_000002_1_4hs9zcn8_.bkp RECID=5 STAMP=668623611
crosschecked backup piece: found to be 'AVAILABLE'
backup piece handle=/u01/app/oracle/flash_recovery_area/orcl/backupset/2008_10_21/
o1_MF_nnnd1_tag20081020t165738_4hsbmv14_.bkp RECID=8 STAMP=668624267
Crosschecked 2 objects
```

This command queries the repository to find details of what whole backups have been made of the database, and then goes to the storage device(s) to see if the pieces do in fact exist. For pieces on disk, the disk directory is read and the file header validated; for pieces on tape, only the tape directory is read. Any pieces that no longer exist are flagged in the repository as EXPIRED. An expired backup will not be considered by RMAN when it works out how to carry out a restore and recover operation. In some circumstances (such as if a file system or a tape drive is taken offline), a crosscheck may mark many backups as expired; rerunning the crosscheck when the device is brought back into use will reset their status to AVAILABLE.

A related command is

```
RMAN> delete expired;
```

This command will not delete any files from disk. It will, however, remove from the repository all references to backups previously marked EXPIRED by a crosscheck. At many installations, the tape library will automatically delete files according to their age: if this is happening, then a crosscheck followed by DELETE EXPIRED will update the RMAN repository to make it aware of what has happened.

 EXAM TIP A DELETE EXPIRED command does not delete any files, it only updates the RMAN repository. A DELETE OBSOLETE will delete files and update the repository accordingly.

Exercise 15-4: Manage Backups   After putting the RMAN configured settings back to defaults, use the BACKUP, LIST, REPORT, and DELETE commands to create and remove backups.

1. Connect to your database with SQL*Plus, and query the state of your flash recovery area:

```
select * from v$flash_recovery_area_usage;
```

2. Connect to your database with RMAN using operating system authentication:

```
rman target /
```

3. Ensure that your retention policy is set to the default, REDUNDANCY 1:

```
RMAN> configure retention policy clear;
```

4. Delete all your backup sets and image copies:

```
RMAN> delete backupset all;
RMAN> delete copy all;
```

If any backups are listed, enter YES to confirm deletion.

5. List the items that need backing up, according to the configured retention policy:

```
RMAN> report need backup;
```

This will list all your datafiles.

6. Choose a datafile, and back it up. In the example that follows, file 6 has been chosen:

```
RMAN> backup datafile 6;
```

Repeat the command to take a second backup of the same file.

7. Repeat the command from Step 4. The file that has been backed up will not be listed.

8. In your SQL*Plus session, rerun the query from Step 1 and note that there is some reclaimable space.

9. List your backups with

```
RMAN> list backup;
```

10. Report and delete the backup that is unnecessary according to the configured retention policy:

```
RMAN> report obsolete;
RMAN> delete obsolete;
```

This will remove the first backup made in Step 5, because it is redundant following the creation of the second backup.

11. In your SQL*Plus session, rerun the query from Step 1 and note the difference in usage.

Two-Minute Drill

Create Consistent Database Backups

- If the database is in noarchivelog mode, then whole consistent backups (full or incremental) are the only type of backup possible.

- An RMAN-consistent backup is taken with the database in mount mode, following a clean shutdown.

Back Up Your Database Without Shutting It Down

- An open backup of the database must also include a backup of the archivelog files, either included in the same backup set or in a separate backup set.

- Open backups, for which the database must be in archivelog mode, can be whole or partial, full or incremental.

Create Incremental Backups

- A level 1 incremental or cumulative backup cannot be based on a full backup, only a level 0 incremental backup.

- Unless block change tracking is enabled, an incremental backup must scan the entire database.

- An RMAN backup set, whether full or incremental, never includes unused blocks.

Automate Database Backups

- Oracle Enterprise Manager (Database Control or Grid Control) can schedule the running of backup jobs.

Manage Backups, View Backup Reports, and Monitor the Flash Recovery Area

- The LIST command shows what backups have been made, and the REPORT command shows what backups are needed or are redundant.
- The flash recovery area is the default destination for RMAN disk backups.
- RMAN can automatically delete files considered to be obsolete from the flash recovery area.

Define, Apply, and Use a Retention Policy

- The backup retention policy may be based on redundancy (keeping a certain number of copies) or recovery window (guaranteeing the possibility of point-in-time recovery).
- Backups considered obsolete according to the retention policy can be automatically deleted.

Create Image File Backups

- An image copy is identical to the source file.
- Image copies can be directed only to disk.
- Image copies can be made of datafiles, the controlfile, and archivelog files.

Create a Whole Database Backup

- A whole RMAN backup is the full set of datafiles, the spfile, and the controlfile.
- RMAN does not back up online logs, tempfiles, or the password file.

Enable Fast Incremental Backup

- Changed blocks are tracked by the change tracking writer process, the CTWR.
- The change tracking file is automatically managed; the DBA can choose only its name and location.

Create Duplex Backups and Back Up Backup Sets

- The COPIES keyword instructs RMAN to create multiple copies of backup sets or images.
- Backup sets can be backed up into more backup sets with BACKUP BACKUPSET.

- The BACKUP RECOVERY AREA and BACKUP RECOVERY FILES commands can only write to a tape destination.

Create an Archival Backup for Long-Term Retention

- The KEEP keyword creates a backup to which the retention policy will not be applied.
- If the archival backup is an open backup, all necessary archive logs will be automatically included.

Create a Multisection, Compressed, and Encrypted Backup

- The SECTION keyword lets multiple channels back up one file concurrently.
- Backup sets can be compressed (unlike image copies), by default with the BZIP2 algorithm.
- Encryption can be enabled using either a wallet or a password.

Report on and Maintain Backups

- RMAN will automatically delete backups from the flash recovery area considered to be obsolete, if the flash recovery area is full.
- The DELETE OBSOLETE command will delete all backups considered obsolete, whether in the flash recovery area or not.

Configure Backup Settings

- RMAN's default behavior is modified with the CONFIGURE command.
- Configured defaults are stored in the target database's controlfile, as part of the RMAN repository.

Allocate Channels to Use in Backing Up

- Channels are of type disk or SBT (or SBT_TAPE). SBT channels are only available if a suitable device driver has been installed.
- Parallelize backups by launching multiple channels, using ALLOCATE CHANNEL commands within a run block or by configuring a default.

Configure Backup Optimization

- Optimization only applies to identical files: archivelogs, or datafiles that are either offline or read-only.
- Optimization is not enabled by default, and if enabled is reliant upon the retention policy currently in effect.

PART III

Self Test

1. What file types can be backed up by RMAN? (Choose four answers.)

   A. Archive log files

   B. Controlfile

   C. Online log files

   D. Password file

   E. Permanent tablespace datafiles

   F. Server parameter file

   G. Static parameter file

   H. Temporary tablespace tempfiles

2. If your database is in noarchivelog mode, which of the following is possible? (Choose the best answer.)

   A. Online backups

   B. Partial backups

   C. Incremental backups

   D. All of the above, but only if you use RMAN

3. RMAN backup sets are smaller than RMAN image copies because . . . . (Choose the best answer.)

   A. They always use compression.

   B. They always skip unused blocks.

   C. They never include tempfiles.

   D. They can be written directly to tape.

4. Which of the following statements are correct about RMAN offline backup? (Choose all correct answers.)

   A. The database must be in NOMOUNT mode.

   B. The database must be in MOUNT mode.

   C. The backup will fail if the shutdown mode was SHUTDOWN IMMEDIATE.

   D. Noarchivelog databases can only be backed up offline.

   E. Archivelog databases cannot be backed up offline.

   F. Offline backups can be incremental.

5. You need to back up the control file while the database is open. What will work? (Choose the best answer.)

   A. The controlfile can be included in an RMAN backup set, but not backed up as an image copy.

B. The ALTER DATABASE BACKUP CONTROLFILE TO TRACE command will make an image copy of the controlfile.

C. You cannot back up the controlfile while it is in use—it is protected by multiplexing.

D. None of the above.

6. You perform a full backup on Sunday, an incremental level 0 backup on Monday, an incremental level 1 differential backup on Tuesday, an incremental level 1 cumulative backup on Wednesday, and an incremental level 1 cumulative backup on Thursday. Which blocks will be included in the Thursday backup? (Choose the best answer.)

A. All blocks changed since Sunday

B. All blocks changed since Monday

C. All blocks changed since Tuesday

D. All blocks changed since Wednesday

7. If you issue this RMAN command,

```
backup incremental level 1;
```

and there is no level 0 backup, what will happen? (Choose the best answer.)

A. The command will fail.

B. The incremental backup will be based on the most recent full backup.

C. RMAN will perform a level 0 backup.

D. RMAN will perform a level 1 cumulative backup of all blocks that have ever been changed.

8. What processes must be running if an RMAN backup scheduled within the Oracle environment is to run? (Choose two correct answers.)

A. The database instance processes must be running, in MOUNT or OPEN mode.

B. The database instance processes must be running, in at least NOMOUNT mode.

C. The Enterprise Manager processes (either Database Control or the Grid Control agent) must be running.

D. The operating system scheduler must be running.

9. What is true about the CROSSCHECK command? (Choose the best answer.)

A. CROSSCHECK will check the validity of the backup pieces.

B. CROSSCHECK will delete references to files that no longer exist.

C. CROSSCHECK will verify the existence of backup set pieces.

D. CROSSCHECK only works with backup sets, not image copies.

10. If the volume of data in the flash recovery area has reached the limit defined by DB_RECOVERY_FILE_DEST_SIZE, what will happen when RMAN attempts to write more data to it? (Choose the best answer.)

A. If AUTOEXTEND has been enabled and the MAXSIZE has not been reached, the flash recovery area will extend as necessary.

B. The operation will fail.

C. This will depend on whether warning and critical alerts have been enabled for the flash recovery area.

D. RMAN will automatically delete OBSOLETE backups.

E. RMAN will automatically delete EXPIRED backups.

Self Test Answers

1. ☑ A, B, E, and F. These are the database file types that the Recovery Manager can back up and restore.

☒ C, D, G, and H. RMAN will never back up online redo logs or tempfiles because it is not necessary to back them up, and it cannot back up a static parameter file or the external password file.

2. ☑ C. RMAN can make incremental backups no matter what mode the database is in.

☒ A, B, and D. Whatever method you use, backups of a noarchivelog mode database cannot be either partial or online.

3. ☑ B. A backup set will never include blocks that have never been used.

☒ A, C, and D. A is wrong because compression is an option, not enabled by default. C is wrong because it applies to image copies as well as backup sets. D is wrong because it is not relevant: an image copy can't go to tape, because if it did, it wouldn't be an image.

4. ☑ B, D, and F. Offline backups must be done in mount mode. This is the only backup type for a noarchivelog mode database, but it can be incremental.

☒ A, C, and E. A is wrong because the database must be mounted, or RMAN won't be able to connect to its repository or find the location of the datafiles. C is wrong because an IMMEDIATE shutdown is clean—it is only an ABORT that would cause problems. E is wrong because an archivelog mode database can certainly be backed up offline—it just isn't necessary.

5. ☑ D. A, B, and C are all incorrect.

   ☒ A, B, and C. A is wrong because a copy of the controlfile can be created while the database is open, via a read-consistent snapshot. B is wrong because this command will generate a CREATE CONTROLFILE script, not a file copy. C is wrong because the file multiplexing is an additional precaution, not the only one.

6. ☑ B. A cumulative backup will include all blocks changed since the last level 0 backup.

   ☒ A, C, and D. A is wrong because the full backup cannot be used as a base for an incremental backup. C and D are wrong because cumulative backups always go back to the most recent level 0 backup.

7. ☑ C. RMAN will revert to level 0 in this circumstance.

   ☒ A, B, and D. A is wrong because the backup will succeed—though perhaps not in the way you wanted. B is wrong because no incremental backup can be based on a full backup. D is wrong because although the effect described is correct, it will not be recorded as a cumulative backup but as a level 0 backup.

8. ☑ A and C. The Enterprise Manager processes will run the backup, and the database must be mounted or RMAN will not be able to connect to the repository.

   ☒ B, and D. B is wrong because NOMOUNT mode is not enough. D is wrong because Oracle-scheduled backups do not use the operating system scheduler.

9. ☑ C. The CROSSCHECK command verifies that the repository does accurately reflect reality.

   ☒ A, B, and D. A is wrong because CROSSCHECK does not validate whether the backups are good—only whether they exist. B is wrong because CROSSCHECK doesn't delete references to missing backups; it only flags them as expired. D is wrong because CROSSCHECK confirms the existence of both backup sets and image copies.

10. ☑ D. Backups that are OBSOLETE according to RMAN's retention policy will be removed.

    ☒ A, B, C, and E. A is wrong because this describes datafiles, not the flash recovery area. B is wrong because the operation will not necessarily fail—it may be possible to free up space automatically. C is wrong because the alert system will only report the problem; it won't fix it. E is wrong because EXPIRED refers to the status of the backup record in the repository, not the backup itself.

CHAPTER 16

Restore and Recover with RMAN

Exam Objectives

In this chapter you will learn to

In principle, restore and recovery (Oracle uses these terms very precisely) following a failure are simple. To *restore* a damaged file is to extract it from a previously made backup; to *recover* it is to apply change vectors extracted from the redo stream, thus bringing it up to date. Recovery can be complete (meaning no loss of data) or incomplete (meaning that you do, deliberately, lose data). However, there are many variations, depending on the nature of the damage and the downtime that can be tolerated. Using Recovery Manager automates the process, which can make restore and recovery operations much faster than using manual techniques and also eliminates the possibility of making mistakes. There is also a Data Recovery Advisor Wizard, which can diagnose problems and recommend the best action to take.

The Data Recovery Advisor

The Data Recovery Advisor (the DRA) is a facility for diagnosing and repairing problems with a database. There are two interfaces: the RMAN executable and Enterprise Manager. The DRA is capable of generating scripts to repair damage to datafiles and (in some circumstances) the controlfile: it does not advise on problems with the spfile or with the online redo log files. It is dependent on the Automatic Diagnostic Repository (the ADR) and the Health Monitor. The information the Health Monitor gathers and the advice the DRA gives follow the same diagnosis and repair methods that the DBA would follow without them—but they make the process quicker and less prone to error.

The Health Monitor and the ADR

The Health Monitor is a set of checks that run automatically when certain error conditions arise, or manually in response to the DBA's instructions. The results of the checks are not stored in the database, but in the file system. This is because the nature of some errors is such that the database is not available: it is therefore essential to have an external repository for the Health Monitor results. This repository is the Automatic Diagnostic Repository (the ADR), which is located in the directory specified by the DIAGNOSTIC_DEST instance parameter.

Different Health Monitor checks can run only at various stages:

- In nomount mode, only the "DB Structure Integrity" check can run, and it can only check the integrity of the controlfile.

- In mount mode, the "DB Structure Integrity" check will check the integrity of the controlfile, and of the online redo log files and the datafile headers. The "Redo Integrity Check" can also run, which will check the online and archive log files for accessibility and corruption.

- In open mode, it is possible to run checks that will scan every data block for corruption, and check the integrity of the data dictionary and the undo segments.

The interfaces that will allow manual running of Health Monitor checks are available only when the database is open. There are two interfaces: using SQL*Plus to invoke procedures in the DBMS_HM PL/SQL package, and Database Control. Figure 16-1 shows the Database Control interface. To reach this window, from the database home page take the Advisor Central link in the Related Links section, and then the Checkers tab.

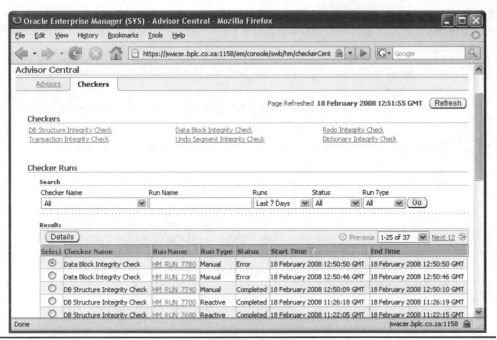

Figure 16-1 The Database Control interface to the Health Monitor

From the window shown in Figure 16-1, you can see the results of all Health Monitor runs (runs in reaction to errors and manual runs) and also run checks on demand.

The Capabilities and Limitations of the DRA

The DRA can do nothing unless the instance is in nomount mode, or higher. It follows that it cannot assist if there is a problem with the initialization file. In nomount mode, it can diagnose problems with the controlfile and generate scripts to restore it, either by using an existing valid copy or (if none is available) by extracting a copy from a backup set—provided it can find one. Once the database reaches mount mode, the DRA can diagnose problems with missing or damaged datafiles and missing online log file groups, and generate repair scripts.

The DRA (in the current release) only supports single-instance databases. If a fault brings down a RAC database, you can mount it in single-instance mode, use the DRA to repair the damage, and then shut it down and reopen it in RAC mode. This technique may not be able to repair damage that is local to one instance. The DRA cannot repair failures on a primary database by using blocks or files from a standby database, and neither can it repair failures on a standby database.

 EXAM TIP The DRA will function only for a single-instance database. It cannot work with a RAC clustered database, nor with a Data Guard standby database.

Exercise 16-1: Use the DRA to Diagnose and Advise Upon Problems   In this exercise, you will cause a problem with the database, and use the DRA to report on it.

1. From an operating system prompt, launch the RMAN executable:

   ```
   rman target /
   ```

2. Confirm that there is a whole full backup of the SYSAUX tablespace:

   ```
   list backup of tablespace sysaux;
   ```

   If this does not return at least one backup set of type FULL, create one:

   ```
   backup as backupset tablespace sysaux;
   ```

3. Shut down the instance and exit from RMAN:

   ```
   shutdown immediate;
   exit;
   ```

4. Using an operating system utility, delete the datafile(s) for the SYSAUX tablespace that were listed in Step 2. If using Windows, you may have to stop the Windows service under which the instance is running to release the Windows file lock before the deletion is possible.

5. Connect to the database with SQL*Plus, and attempt a startup:

   ```
   startup;
   ```

   This will stop in mount mode, with an error regarding the missing file. If using Windows, make sure the service has been started.

6. Launch the RMAN executable and connect, as in Step 1.

7. Diagnose the problem:

   ```
   list failure;
   ```

   This will return a message to the effect that one or more non-system datafiles are missing.

8. Generate advice on the failure:

   ```
   advise failure;
   ```

   This will suggest that you should restore and recover the datafile, and generate a repair script. Open the script with any operating system editor, and study its contents.

Using the Data Recovery Advisor

The Data Recovery Advisor makes use of information gathered by the Health Monitor to find problems, and then it constructs RMAN scripts to repair them. As with any RMAN-based utility, the instance must be started. To start an instance in nomount mode, all that is required is a parameter file. RMAN is in fact capable of starting an instance without a parameter file, using the ORACLE_SID environment variable as a default for the one parameter for which there is no default value: the DB_NAME parameter. This ability may mean that is possible to bootstrap a restore and recovery operation from nothing.

The flow for using the DRA is as follows:

- **Assess data failures** The Health Monitor, running reactively or on demand, will write error details to the ADR.

- **List failures** The DRA will list all failures, classified according to severity.

- **Advise on repair** The DRA will generate RMAN scripts to repair the damage.

- **Execute repair** Run the scripts.

The commands can be run from the RMAN executable, or through Database Control. The advice will only be generated for errors previously listed and still open. No advice will be generated for additional errors that have occurred since the listing, or for errors fixed since the listing.

 TIP If one or more failures exist, then you should typically use `LIST FAILURE` to show information about the failures and then use `ADVISE FAILURE` in the same RMAN session to obtain a report of your repair.

Figure 16-2 shows a DRA session, launched from the RMAN executable. The situation is that the instance started and mounted the database, but failed to open.

Figure 16-2   A DRA session, using the Recovery Manager

The first command in the figure launches the RMAN executable, from an operating system prompt. The connection succeeds, but RMAN reports that the database is not open.

The second command lists all current failures: there is one nonsystem datafile missing. If this step were omitted, the next step would not return anything.

The third command generates advice on fixing the failure. The first suggestion is that some error by the system administrators could be responsible for the problem and could be fixed manually. Then there is an automatic repair involving restore and recovery. This is in the form of an RMAN script. The contents of the script (not shown in the figure) were

```
# restore and recover datafile
restore datafile 4;
recover datafile 4;
```

To run the script, the command would be

```
repair failure;
```

Following this, the database can be opened.

 TIP The DRA works, but you can often do better. For example, it does not generate scripts that will minimize downtime by opening the database before doing the restore and recovery (which would be possible in the example).

On connecting with Database Control to a damaged database, there will always be a button named PERFORM RECOVERY. Figure 16-3 shows the window this will produce for the same situation shown in Figure 16-2.

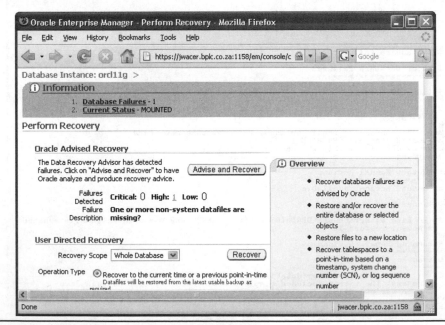

Figure 16-3   The Database Control interface to the DRA

The Information section seen in Figure 16-3 shows that there is one failure, and that the database is mounted. The ADVISE AND RECOVER button will launch a wizard that will list details of the failure, generate the repair script, and then submit it as a job to the Enterprise Manager job system, and finally prompt you to open the database.

 EXAM TIP The DRA will not generate any advice if you have not first asked it to list failures. Any failures occurring since the last listing, or fixed since the last listing, will not be advised upon.

The DRA can generate scripts to restore a missing or damaged controlfile copy and to rebuild a missing online log file group and to restore and recover missing or damaged datafiles. It will not take any action if a member of a multiplexed log file group is damaged.

Exercise 16-2: Repair a Fault with the DRA   In this exercise, you will diagnose and repair the problem caused in Exercise 16-1 using Database Control.

1. Using a browser, attempt to connect to Database Control. This will present a window stating that the database is mounted, with buttons for STARTUP and PERFORM RECOVERY.

2. Click STARTUP. Enter operating system and database credentials and follow the prompts to open the database. This will fail, so click PERFORM RECOVERY.

3. In the Perform Recovery window, click ADVISE AND REPAIR to enter the DRA Wizard.

4. In the View And Manage Failures window, click ADVISE.

5. In the Manual Actions window, click CONTINUE WITH ADVICE.

6. In the Recovery Advice window, observe the script and click CONTINUE.

7. In the Review window, click SUBMIT RECOVERY JOB.

8. When the job completes, use either Database Control or SQL*Plus to open the database. It is possible that Database Control will have gotten confused as a result of this exercise, and may have trouble determining what state the database is in. If this appears to be the case, close the browser and restart the Database Control processes from an operating system prompt with the commands:

```
emctl stop dbconsole;
emctl start dbconsole;
```

Reconnect with the browser, and confirm that the database is now open.

Database Restore and Recovery

Some files are *critical*. Damage to a critical file will mean that the database instance will terminate if it is open, and cannot be reopened until the damage is repaired. Other files are *noncritical*: if these are damaged, the database can remain open or be opened if it is closed. In either case, there is no reason to lose data: you should be able to perform a complete recovery from any form of damage, provided that you

have a backup and the necessary archivelog files. The one exception to this rule is if you lose all copies of the current online log files.

The critical files are

- Any copy of the controlfile
- A datafile that is part of the SYSTEM tablespace
- A datafile that is part of the current undo tablespace

Noncritical files are

- Multiplexed online log files
- Tempfiles
- Datafiles that are not part of the SYSTEM or current undo tablespaces

As a general rule, damage to any number of datafiles should be repaired with a *complete recovery*: no loss of data. Restore the damaged file(s), and apply redo to bring them right up to date. *Incomplete recovery* means to restore the database (the entire database) and apply redo only up to a certain point. All work done after that point will be lost. Why would one do this? Usually for one reason only: user error. If a mistake is serious enough, it will be necessary to take the whole database back in time to before the error was made so that the work can be redone, correctly. A second reason for incomplete recovery is because a complete recovery was attempted, but failed. This will happen if archive log files are missing, or if all copies of the current online log file group are lost.

There are four steps for complete recovery:

- Take the damaged data file(s) offline.
- Restore the damaged file(s).
- Recover the restored files(s).
- Bring the recovered file(s) online.

Complete Recovery from Data File Loss Using RMAN

Media failure resulting in damage to one or more datafiles requires use of restore and recover routines: a backup of the datafile must be restored, and then archive redo logs applied to it to synchronize it with the rest of the database. There are various options available, depending on whether the database is in archivelog mode or not, and whether the file damaged is one that is critical to Oracle's ongoing operation or if it is a noncritical file containing "only" user data.

Recovery of Datafiles in Noarchivelog Mode

There is no supported technique for recovery when in noarchivelog mode, because the archive log files needed for recovery do not exist. Therefore, only a restore can be done. But if a restored datafile is not synchronized with the rest of the database by application of archive redo log files, it cannot be opened. The only option when in noarchivelog mode is therefore to restore the whole database: all the datafiles and the controlfile. Provided that all these files are restored from a whole offline backup, after the restore you will have a database where all these files are synchronized, and thus a database that can be opened. But you will have lost all the work done since the backup was taken.

Once the full restore has been done, the database will still be missing its online redo log files, because they were never backed up. For this reason, the post-restore startup will fail, with the database being left in mount mode. While in mount mode, issue ALTER DATABASE CLEAR LOGFILE GROUP <group number> commands to recreate all the log file groups. Then open the database. If you do the restore through the Database Control interface to RMAN, this process will be fully automatic.

In noarchivelog mode, loss of any one of possibly hundreds of datafiles can be corrected only by a complete restore of the last backup. The whole database must be taken back in time, with the loss of users' work. Furthermore, that last backup must have been a whole, offline backup, which will have entailed downtime. It should by now be apparent that the decision to operate your database in noarchivelog mode should not be taken lightly.

TIP Virtually all databases (including test and development systems) should run in archivelog mode. Even if the service level agreement says that data can be lost, if any work is ever lost, your users will not be happy.

EXAM TIP If in noarchivelog mode, your only options following loss of any datafile are either a whole database restore, or to drop the relevant tablespace. There can be no recovery.

The RMAN commands to restore a database in noarchivelog mode are

```
shutdown abort;
startup mount;
restore database;
alter database open resetlogs;
```

The first command will terminate the instance. This will not be necessary if the damaged file is part of either the SYSTEM or currently active undo tablespaces, because in that case it would have aborted already. The second command brings the database up in mount mode; this can be done only if all copies of the controlfile are available—if they are not, the controlfile must first be restored (as described in Chapter 18). The third command will restore all datafiles from the most recent full, or incremental level 0, backup. The fourth command will recreate the online log file members, set the log sequence number to 1, and open the database.

If you are using incremental backups, there is a minor variation in restoring a database in noarchivelog mode: the RECOVER command is needed, to apply the incremental backups. After the restore and before opening the database, run this command:

```
recover database noredo;
```

This command will locate all cumulative and differential incremental level 1 backups and apply them. The NOREDO qualifier is needed to instruct RMAN not to attempt to apply any redo data—because, in noarchivelog mode, there is none to apply.

Recovery of a Noncritical File in Archivelog Mode

In an Oracle database, the datafiles that make up the SYSTEM tablespace and the currently active undo tablespace (as specified by the UNDO_TABLESPACE parameter) are considered to be "critical." Damage to any of these will result in the instance terminating immediately. Furthermore, the database cannot be opened again until the damage has been repaired by a restore and recover exercise. Damage to the other datafiles, which make up tablespaces for user data, will not as a rule result in the instance crashing. Oracle will take the damaged files offline, making their contents inaccessible, but the rest of the database should remain open. How your application software will react to this will depend on how it is structured and written.

TIP Is it safe to run your application with part of the database unavailable? This is a matter for discussion with your developers and business analysts, and an important point to consider when deciding on how to spread your segments across tablespaces.

If your backups were done with RMAN, the restore and recovery operation of a damaged datafile will be completely automatic. RMAN will carry out the restore in the most efficient manner possible, making intelligent use of full and incremental backups and then applying the necessary archive logs. If RMAN is linked to a tape library through SBT channels, it will load the tapes automatically to extract the files it needs.

The restore and complete recovery of a datafile can succeed only if all the archive log files generated since the last backup of the datafile are available. Either they must still be on disk in the archive log destination directories, or if they have been migrated to tape, they must be restored during the recovery operation. RMAN will do the extract from a backup set and restore to disk automatically. If for some reason an archive log file is missing or corrupted, the recovery will fail, but since archive log destinations and RMAN backup sets can and should be multiplexed, you should never find yourself in this situation. If you do, the only option is a complete restore, and an incomplete recovery up to the missing archive, which will mean loss of all work done subsequently.

Exercise 16-3: Recover from Loss of a Noncritical Datafile with Database Control First, create a tablespace and a segment within it, and back it up. Then simulate damage to the datafile. Diagnose the problem and resolve it. The database will stay open for use throughout the whole exercise. At various points you will be asked to supply host operating system credentials, if you have not saved them in previous exercises: give a suitable Windows or Unix login, such as the Oracle owner.

1. Connect to your database as user SYSTEM using SQL*Plus, and create a tablespace. For example, on Windows,

```
SQL> create tablespace noncrit
datafile 'C:\APP\ORACLE\ORADATA\ORCL\noncrit.dbf' size 2m;
```

or on Unix,

```
SQL> create tablespace noncrit
datafile '/app/oracle/oradata/orcl/noncrit.dbf' size 2m;
```

2. Create a table within the new tablespace and insert a row into it:

```
SQL> create table ex16 (c1 date) tablespace noncrit;
SQL> insert into ex16 values(sysdate);
SQL> commit;
```

3. Using Database Control, connect to your database as user SYSTEM.

4. From the database home page, take the Availability tab, then the Schedule Backup link in the Manage section.

5. In the Schedule Backup window, select the Tablespaces radio button in the Customized Backup section. Click SCHEDULE CUSTOMIZED BACKUP.

6. In the Schedule Backup: Tablespaces window, click ADD.

7. In the Tablespaces: Available Tablespaces window, select the radio button for your new NONCRIT tablespace, and click SELECT.

8. In the Schedule Customized Backup: Tablespaces window, click NEXT.

9. In the Schedule Customized Backup: Options window, leave everything on defaults and click NEXT.

10. In the Schedule Customized Backup: Settings window, leave everything on defaults and click NEXT.

11. In the Schedule Customized Backup: Schedule window, select One Time (Immediately) radio button and click NEXT.

12. In the Schedule Customized Backup: Review window, study the script and click SUBMIT JOB to run the backup.

13. Simulate a disk failure by corrupting the new datafile. On Windows, open the file with Windows Notepad, delete a few lines from the beginning of the file, and save it; it is important to use Notepad because it is one of the few Windows utilities that will ignore the file lock that Oracle places on datafiles. On Unix you can use any editor you please, such as vi. Make sure that the characters deleted are at the start of the file, to ensure that the file header is damaged.

14. Flush the buffer cache, so that the next read of ex16 will need to read from disk:

```
alter system flush buffer_cache;
```

15. Confirm that the file is damaged by attempting to query the table:

```
SQL> select * from ex16;
select * from ex16
              *
ERROR at line 1:
ORA-01578: ORACLE data block corrupted (file # 7, block # 9)
ORA-01110: data file 7: 'C:\APP\ORACLE\ORADATA\ORCL\NONCRIT.DBF'
```

16. In your Database Control session, take the Availability tab from the database home page, and then the Perform Recovery link in the Manage section.

17. In the Perform Recovery: Type window, take the link for Datafiles With Error.

18. In the Perform Object Level Recovery: Datafiles window, the new datafile will be listed. Select it, and click NEXT.

19. In the Perform Object Level Recovery: Rename window, click NEXT.

20. In the Perform Object Level Recovery: Review window, click SUBMIT.

21. In the Perform Recovery: Result window, study the output of the operation, as shown in the illustration.

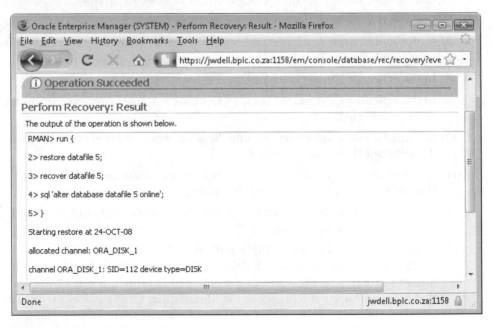

22. Confirm that the tablespace and the tables within it are now usable, with no loss of data.

```
SQL> select * from ex16;
C1
---------
21-OCT-08
```

Of the four steps for complete recovery, the first step (taking the damaged file offline) will be automatic if the file is noncritical. The following two steps (restore and recovery) are accomplished with RMAN commands, and the final step (bringing the datafile online) can be done with either SQL*Plus or RMAN. The scripts generated by Database Control automate the entire procedure.

If an incremental backup strategy has been used, a restore and recover operation will make use of a level 0 incremental backup, then apply any incremental level 1 backups that may be available, and then apply redo data to complete the recovery. The logic behind this method (which keeps use of redo to a minimum) is that it is always faster to apply an incremental backup than to apply redo, because an incremental backup can be applied in a single sequential pass through the datafile, whereas applying redo (which consists of change vectors in chronological order) will involve random access to the datafile. The presence or absence of incremental backups does not lead to any syntactical difference in the use of the RECOVER command; RMAN, by interrogating its repository, will work out the best way to perform the operation.

EXAM TIP RMAN will always apply incremental backups in preference to applying redo data, if they are available.

Recovering from Loss of a Critical Datafile

The datafiles that make up the SYSTEM and currently active undo tablespace are considered critical by Oracle, meaning that it is not possible to keep the database open if they are damaged. If any portion of the SYSTEM tablespace were not available, parts of the data dictionary would be missing. Oracle cannot function without a complete data dictionary. If parts of the undo tablespace were not available, it would be possible that undo data required for maintaining transactional integrity and isolation would not be available, and Oracle can't take that chance either. Therefore, damage to these datafiles will cause the instance to terminate immediately.

TIP The critical datafiles should be on disk systems with hardware redundancy, such as RAID level 1 disk mirroring, so that in the case of media failure the files will survive and the database will remain open.

If the database does crash because of damage to critical datafiles, as ever, the first action is to attempt a startup. This will stop in mount mode, with error messages written to the alert log showing the extent of the damage. To recover, follow the same routine as that for a noncritical file, and then open the database. The restore and recover process is identical to that for a noncritical file, but it must be carried out in mount mode. Of the four steps for complete recovery, if the damaged file is a critical file only the second and third steps are necessary: as the database cannot be opened, there is no need to take the damaged file offline and bring it back online afterward.

EXAM TIP Loss of a critical data file will not mean loss of data, but it will mean loss of time.

Incomplete Recovery

An incomplete recovery means losing data. The whole database is taken back in time by a restore of all the datafiles, and then it is not completely recovered. Rather than applying all the redo generated since the backup was taken, you deliberately stop the application of redo at some point, to produce a version of the database that is not up-to-date. All work done from that point is lost. There are only two reasons for performing an incomplete recovery: either complete recovery is impossible or you deliberately decide to lose data.

Complete recovery will not be possible unless all archive logs generated from the time of the backup are available, as well as the online redo logs. If an archive log is missing or corrupted, then recovery will stop at that point. Complete recovery should never fail because of missing archive or online log files, as both file types can and should be multiplexed to different devices, making their total loss impossible, but it can happen. If so, incomplete recovery up to the point at which the missing or damaged redo data occurs is your only option.

EXAM TIP Incomplete recovery is necessary if there is a missing archive log, or if all copies of the current online redo log file group are missing.

To decide to lose data deliberately is a course of action taken after user error. It may be that a user has committed a transaction that is inappropriate to the business requirements. Such errors could include perfectly normal mistakes—we all make mistakes—while using package software, but more commonly they are errors made using tools such as SQL*Plus. Omitting a WHERE clause when issuing an UPDATE or DELETE statement will result in the whole table being affected, not just one row; if this change is committed, perhaps by exiting from the tool, then the changes are irreversible. As far as Oracle is concerned, it is a committed transaction and can never be rolled back. Worse still is issuing DDL commands. These include an implicit COMMIT statement. It is frighteningly easy, for example, to drop a table or even a schema when you think you are connected to the development database when in fact you are connected to production.

Following a user error, you can restore the whole database and recover it up to the point just before the error, thus producing a version of the database without the mistake, but also, without all the correct work done since.

TIP There are several "flashback" technologies that may make it possible to recover from user errors without resorting to an incomplete recovery.

EXAM TIP It is not possible to skip the recovery of a bad transaction and recover all other work.

A special case of incomplete recovery is recovery of the controlfile. Ideally, all recovery operations will be conducted using the current controlfile, but there are circumstances when this isn't possible and a backup of the controlfile must be restored. There are two possible reasons for this: either all copies of the current controlfile have been lost and it is not possible to run a CREATE CONTROLFILE command to recreate it, or the current controlfile does not accurately describe the version of the database you want to restore, typically, because changes such as dropping tablespaces have occurred since taking the backup.

There are four steps for incomplete recovery:

- Mount the database.
- Restore all the datafiles.
- Recover the database until a certain point.
- Open the database with reset logs.

The first contrast with complete recovery is that complete recovery can be done with the database open, unless the damaged files are critical. Incomplete recovery can be done only in mount mode.

Second, for a complete recovery, you restore only the damaged datafiles; incomplete recovery operations begin with a restore of all datafiles. The datafiles do not have to be restored from the same backup, but they must all be older than the point to which you wish to recover. The controlfile will have to be restored as well as the datafiles if the physical structure of the current database is different from the structure of the version being restored. For example, if a tablespace has been accidentally dropped, the current controlfile will know nothing about it. Restoring the datafiles that make up the tablespace won't help: the current controlfile will ignore them, and not include them in the recovery. Do not restore the controlfile unless you have to; it may complicate matters if you do.

The third step is to apply redo from archive and (if necessary) online logs to the desired point. This contrasts with complete recovery, where you apply all the redo to bring the database right up-to-date; for incomplete recovery, you stop the recovery at whatever point you want prior to the latest time. There are several options for specifying the point to which you want to recover.

Finally, open the database with RESETLOGS. This will reinitialize the online redo log files, creating a new incarnation of the database. An incarnation of a database is a version of the database with a new thread of redo, beginning at log sequence number 1. This is the final contrast with complete recovery. After a complete recovery, the database is exactly as it was before the problem occurred, but after an incomplete recovery it is a different incarnation. Backups and archive logs are specific to an incarnation and those generated by one incarnation must be kept separate from those generated by a previous incarnation.

 EXAM TIP You must be connected AS SYSDBA to do an incomplete recovery. No normal user, and not even a SYSOPER user, can do this.

Having mounted the database and restored all the datafiles and (if necessary) the controlfile, you have three options for incomplete recovery:

- Until time
- Until system change number (SCN)
- Until log sequence number

The UNTIL TIME option will apply redo to roll the datafiles forward until a particular time. The precision is to the second. This option would usually be used to correct user error. If a user made an irreversible mistake and the time the mistake was made is known, then a time-based recovery to just before the mistake may be the best option.

The UNTIL SCN option can be used if the exact system change number when the error was made is known. By using advanced tools such as the Log Miner utility or by using the Flashback capability to be detailed in Chapter 19, it may be possible to identify exactly the SCN at which a transaction was committed. The recovery can be stopped precisely before the problem, thus losing the minimum possible amount of data.

The UNTIL SEQUENCE option is used if an archive log file or an online log file group is missing; it will recover all work up to the log switch into the missing file or group.

 EXAM TIP The syntax for incomplete recovery differs between SQL*Plus and RMAN. SQL*Plus uses UNTIL CANCEL and UNTIL CHANGE, where RMAN would use UNTIL SEQUENCE and UNTIL SCN. They both use UNTIL TIME.

By default, RMAN will restore the most recent backup, and apply all available redo. Incomplete recovery must modify this behavior: the restore must be from backups that are older than the point in time to which the recovery is to be made, and the recovery must be stopped at that time. To ensure that the restore and recover both use the same UNTIL TIME, it is considered best practice to execute both commands within a single run block. For example,

```
1  run {startup mount;
2  set until time = "to_date('27-10-08 10:00:00','dd-mm-yy hh24:mi:ss')";
3  restore database;
4  recover database;
5  alter database open resetlogs;}
```

This example, with line numbers added for clarity, shows the four steps for incomplete recovery:

- **Line 1**   The database must be started in mount mode. It is of no significance whether the preceding shutdown were orderly or an abort.
- **Line 2**   The SET UNTIL command specifies a time that will be applied to all subsequent commands. The example includes a format string that will eliminate any ambiguity in interpreting the date and time. An alternative is

to rely on matching the NLS_DATE_FORMAT environment variable. Note the use of double quotes around the entire string, and single quotes within it.

- **Line 3**   The RESTORE command will extract datafiles from backups that are at least as old as the time specified in the SET UNTIL command.

- **Line 4**   The RECOVER command will apply redo from archive log files and (if necessary) online log files, stopping at the specified time.

- **Line 5**   The RESETLOGS clause instructs Oracle to initialize the online redo log files and reset the log switch sequence number.

An alternative syntax is to specify the UNTIL value with each command. For example,

```
restore database until time 'sysdate - 7';
recover database until time '27-OCT-08';
```

The first of these commands instructs RMAN to restore the database from backups that are at least seven days old. The second command will perform an incomplete recovery up to the beginning of October 27, 2008, assuming that the NLS_DATE_FORMAT environment variable is set to dd-MON-rr.

Autobackup and Restore of the Controlfile

For a complete recovery, it should always be possible to use the current controlfile. The only case where this will not be possible is if all copies have been lost—typically, because it was not multiplexed and the one copy was damaged. The database is critically dependent on the controlfile: it will crash if the controlfile is damaged. RMAN makes the situation even worse: the RMAN repository, which stores details of all backups, is stored in the controlfile. So if the controlfile is damaged, the database will crash—but RMAN will not be able to restore it, because the information it needs will not be available. There are two ways around this recursive problem: either use an RMAN catalog database (as described in Chapter 17) or enable the AUTOBACKUP facility.

Because the controlfile is vital not only to the running database but also to RMAN, an automatic backup can be enabled. From the RMAN prompt,

```
configure controlfile autobackup on;
```

Having executed this command, every RMAN operation will conclude with an automatic backup of the controlfile and the spfile into a backup set stored in a well-known location. Then if necessary, with the database in nomount mode, you can use this:

```
restore controlfile from autobackup;
```

This command instructs RMAN to go to the well-known filename in a well-known location and extract the controlfile from the most recent autobackup. The restore will be to the locations given in the spfile. Then mount the database using the restored controlfile, and RMAN will be able to locate the backups needed to restore the rest of the database. The well-known location will be in the flash recovery area if this has been enabled. The well-known filename is based on the DBID; the DBID (a ten-digit number) should be part of your most basic documentation, and will have been displayed whenever you connect to the database with RMAN. It is also visible as the column DBID in the V$DATABASE view.

If the spfile has also been lost, start the instance with a dummy initialization file: a pfile with just one parameter, DB_NAME. Then connect with RMAN, and issue these commands, substituting your DBID number for that given:

```
set dbid 1234567890;
restore spfile from autobackup;
```

The restore of an spfile will be to the default location, in $ORACLE_HOME/dbs for Unix or %ORACLE_HOME%\database for Windows. Then restart the instance in nomount mode, which will use the restored spfile, and restore the controlfile. Mount the controlfile, and RMAN will then have access to its repository and can locate and restore the datafile backups.

EXAM TIP The commands restore controlfile from autobackup and restore spfile from autobackup can be executed in nomount mode. All other RMAN commands can be executed only in mount or open mode.

Exercise 16-4: Enable Controlfile Autobackup   In this exercise, enable the controlfile autobackup facility and observe it in operation.

1. Connect to the database with RMAN:

   ```
   rman target /
   ```

2. Confirm that autobackup is not enabled:

   ```
   show controlfile autobackup;
   ```

   This will show that autobackup is not enabled.

3. Enable autobackup, and confirm:

   ```
   configure autobackup on;
   show all;
   ```

   Note that the default format for autobackups is '%F'.

4. Carry out a backup operation:

   ```
   backup datafile 1;
   ```

   Observe that following the requested backup, there is a second backup set created for the controlfile and the spfile.

5. Determine the location of autobackup of the controlfile and the spfile:

   ```
   list backup of controlfile;
   list backup of spfile;
   ```

In both cases, the most recent backup set listed will be to a file in the flash recovery area. This can be overridden by configuring a format other than the '%F' shown in Step 3, but if this is done, the automatic location of the autobackups will no longer function.

This script accomplishes the complete restore and recovery of a database, assuming that everything was lost:

```
1   run{startup nomount pfile=dummy.pfile;
2   set dbid=1196323546;
3   restore spfile from autobackup;
4   shutdown abort;
5   startup nomount;
6   restore controlfile from autobackup;
7   alter database mount;
8   restore database;
9   recover database;
10  alter database open resetlogs;}
```

Taking this script line by line,

1	Start the instance, using a dummy parameter file with just one parameter: DB_NAME.
2	Tell RMAN the DBID of the database on which you are working.
3	Extract the spfile from the most recent autobackup, relying on defaults for its name and location.
4	Abort the instance, because (having been started with a dummy pfile) it is not of any further use.
5	Start the instance, using the restored spfiles.
6	Extract the controlfile from the most recent autobackup.
7	Mount the controlfile.
8	Restore all the datafiles.
9	Carry out a complete recovery by applying any incremental backups, followed by archive log files and online log files.
10	Open the database, and reinitialize the online redo log files. A RESETLOGS is always required after restoring the controlfile.

Exercise 16-5: Perform Incomplete Recovery with RMAN, Using a Backup Controlfile In this exercise, which continues from Exercise 16-3, you will drop a tablespace and then perform an incomplete recovery to a time just before it was dropped. This is possibly the most complex operation that may ever be necessary. It must be performed in several stages: first a version of the controlfile that dates from the time the tablespace existed must be restored, and the database must be mounted with this controlfile. Only then can the rest of the database be restored and recovered.

Before launching RMAN or SQL*Plus, ensure that your operating system date format is set to a known value. For example, on Windows:

```
set NLS_DATE_FORMAT=dd-mm-yy hh24:mi:ss
```

PART III

or on Unix or Linux:

```
export NLS_DATE_FORMAT=dd-mm-yy hh24:mi:ss
```

1. Connect to the database with RMAN, and perform a full whole backup:

```
rman target /
RMAN> backup as compressed backupset database;
```

2. Connect to the database with SQL*Plus as user SYSTEM, and force a few log switches and archives by executing this command a few times:

```
alter system switch logfile;
```

3. Connect to the database with RMAN, and back up the archive logs while removing them from the archivelog destinations:

```
backup archivelog all delete all input;
```

4. Repeat Step 2.

5. Note the current time:

```
select sysdate from dual;
```

6. Wait a few seconds, and insert a second row into the ex16 table:

```
insert into ex16 values(sysdate);
commit;
```

7. Drop the tablespace, and attempt to query the ex16 table:

```
drop tablespace noncrit including contents and datafiles;
select * from ex16;
```

8. In your RMAN session, execute this run block to restore the controlfile, substituting the time you noted in Step 5 for that shown, and using a suitable name for the restored controlfile:

```
run {shutdown abort;
startup mount;
set until time = '26-10-08 15:35:33';
restore controlfile to '/u01/app/oracle/oradata/orcl/control04.ctl';}
```

It is not possible to restore the controlfile over the current controlfile copies, because they are already in use to mount the database.

9. In your SQL*Plus session, adjust the CONTROL_FILES parameter so that the restored controlfile will be used for the next mount:

```
SQL> alter system set
control_files='/u01/app/oracle/oradata/orcl/control04.ctl'
scope=spfile;
SQL> shutdown abort;
SQL> startup mount;
```

10. In your RMAN session,

```
run {allocate channel d1 type disk;
allocate channel d2 type disk;
set until time = '26-10-08 15:35:33';
restore database;
```

```
recover database;
alter database open resetlogs};
```

11. Study the output of running the block in Step 8. In particular, note these points:

    - Two channels were used, to parallelize the operation.

    - The date given must conform to that specified by the NLS_DATE_FORMAT environment variable.

    - The restore will have been from the most recent backup earlier than the UNTIL time.

    - The recovery uses a combination of archive logs on disk, and archive logs extracted from a backup set.

12. Connect to the database with SQL*Plus as user SYSTEM, and confirm that while the restore and recovery has succeeded, the row inserted after the UNTIL time is gone:

    ```
    select * from ex16;
    ```

13. Confirm that the log sequence number has been reset to 1:

    ```
    select * from v$log;
    ```

Using Image Copies for Recovery

If your backup strategy includes creating image copies as well as (or instead of) backup sets, then you have another option available for restore operations: do not restore at all. As an image copy is byte-for-byte the same as the source datafile, it can be used immediately if it is still available on disk. All that is necessary is to tell the database the location of the image copy, and then recover the copy. This can result in massive time savings when compared with the delays involved in extracting a datafile from a backup set.

To facilitate the use of image copies, use the following RMAN command:

```
RMAN> backup as copy database;
```

This command will copy every datafile to the flash recovery area, as image copies.

To use an image copy, first take the original datafile offline (which will have happened automatically in many cases) and then update the controlfile to point to the copy, and recover it. For example, if a copy has been made as follows:

```
RMAN> backup as copy datafile 4 format '/u02/df_copies/users.dbf';
```

Then it can be brought into use like this:

```
RMAN> run {sql 'alter database datafile 4 offline';
set newname for datafile 4 to '/u02/df_copies/users.dbf';
switch datafile 4;
recover datafile 4;
sql 'alter database datafile 4 online';}
```

This accomplishes a complete recovery, without actually needing to restore. The SWITCH command is equivalent to the ALTER DATABASE RENAME FILE command that can be executed in SQL*Plus. If the whole database has been copied to the flash recovery area then the whole database can be "restored" with one command:

```
RMAN> switch database to copy;
```

EXAM TIP Any SET commands, such as SET UNTIL, SET NEWNAME, and SET DBID, can be executed only within a run block, never as stand-alone commands at the RMAN prompt.

TIP Maintaining a reasonably up-to-date image copy of the database will mean that the downtime involved in any restore and recover operation is substantially reduced. If you have the disk space available, you should consider doing this.

Another use of image copies is to update them by applying incremental backups. This technique of updating copies with incremental backups takes a full copy as its starting point, and then rolls the copy forward by applying the incrementals. This requires as a starting point a complete copy of the database (which can be made while the database is open), followed by creating incremental backups with the syntax that will permit them to be applied to the copy. This simple script, just two commands, can accomplish the entire process:

```
run {
backup incremental level 1 for recover of copy with tag 'inc_copy' database;
recover copy of database with tag 'inc_copy' ;
}
```

The first time the script is run, the BACKUP command will attempt a level 1 backup, but as there is no level 0 backup on which to base the level 1, it will perform a level 0 backup instead. The syntax will cause RMAN to make this as a copy, rather than as a backup set. The RECOVER command will fail, because there will be neither a copy of the database nor an incremental backup to apply. The second time the script is run, the first command will perform a level 1 backup, extracting all changed blocks since the first run. The second command will apply this incremental backup to the copy. This behavior will continue for all subsequent runs.

A strategy based on incrementally updated backups can result in very fast recovery times, with minimal backup workload on the live database: there is only ever one full backup, and (if the script is run daily) the worst case is that the copy would be one day behind. It will be necessary to back up the copy (with, for example, BACKUP RECOVERY AREA if the copy has been directed to the flash recovery area) and the archive log files, because without this a point-in-time recovery to any time earlier than the most recent run of the script will be impossible.

Block Recovery

In all the restore and recover operations described so far in the chapter, the granularity of the restore has been the file: every example has restored a complete file, and recovered it. While this is necessary if a file has been completely destroyed (by accidental deletion, perhaps), in many cases damage is limited to just a small range of blocks: the file remains usable, but certain blocks will have been corrupted. In this case, the file will remain online, and the end users may not be aware that there is a problem. They will only find out when they attempt to read the damaged blocks: if a session hits a corrupted block, it will return an error to the user process, and a message will be written to the alert log. RMAN can also detect corrupted blocks, and furthermore it can repair them.

Detection of Corrupt Blocks

RMAN will detect corrupt blocks as it performs backup operations. Unless instructed otherwise, it will terminate the backup as soon as it hits a corrupt block. If you wish, you can run RMAN backups that specify a tolerance for corrupted blocks. If this is done, then rather than throwing an error and terminating the backup immediately when a corruption is detected, RMAN will continue to back up the datafile but will record the addresses of any corruptions it encounters in its repository. This example instructs RMAN to continue a backup as long as no more than 100 corrupt blocks are encountered:

```
RMAN> run {
set maxcorrupt for datafile 7 to 100;
backup datafile 7;}
```

The details of corrupt blocks are visible in two places. The view V$DATABASE_BLOCK_CORRUPTION shows the address of the cause of the problem: the datafile file number and block number. The address of the block in the backup is also visible in V$BACKUP_CORRUPTION for corruptions encountered by backup set backups, or in V$COPY_CORRUPTION if the backup were to an image copy. In normal running, you would not use the SET MAXCORRUPT keywords. Without them, the backup will fail and you will thus be made aware of the problem immediately. Then rerun the backup with SET MAXCORRUPT and after completion query the views to determine the extent of the damage.

By default, RMAN will always check for physical corruption, known as "media corruption" in the non-RMAN world. An example of this would be a block that Oracle cannot process at all: an invalid checksum, or a block full of zeros. RMAN can also be instructed to check for logical corruption, also known as "software corruption," as well. These checks will occur whenever a file is backed up, whether as an image copy or into a backup set. To override the defaults,

```
RMAN> backup nochecksum datafile 7;
```

will not check for physical corruption, but

```
RMAN> backup check logical datafile 6;
```

will check for logical as well as physical corruption.

Block Media Recovery

If RMAN has detected a block corruption, it can do Block Media Recovery, or BMR. BMR changes the granularity of a restore and recover operation from the datafile to just the damaged blocks. This has two huge advantages over file restore and recover: first, the file does not have to be taken offline; normal DML can continue. Second, the mean time to recover is much reduced, since only the damaged blocks are involved in the operation, not the whole file. The only downtime that will occur is if a session happens to hit a block that is actually damaged and has not yet been recovered.

The BMR mechanism provides RMAN with a list of one of more blocks that need recovery. RMAN will extract backups of these blocks from a backup set or an image copy and write them to the datafile. Then RMAN will pass through the archive logs generated since the backup and extract redo records relevant to the restored blocks and apply them. The recovery will always be complete—it would be logically impossible to do an incomplete recovery; incomplete recovery of just one block would leave the database in an inconsistent state. If a session hits a corrupted block before the BMR process has completed, then it will still receive an ORA-01578 error, but it is quite possible that the BMR operation will be complete before any users are aware of the problem.

The BLOCK RECOVER Command

The BLOCK RECOVER command always specifies a list of one or more blocks to be restored and recovered, and it optionally specifies the backup from which the restore should be made. For example, this command,

```
RMAN> block recover datafile 7 block 5;
```

instructs RMAN to restore and recover the one specified block from the most recent backup set or image copy of the file. The syntax would also accept a list of blocks in several files:

```
RMAN> block recover datafile 7 block 5,6,7 datafile 9 block 21,25;
```

There may be doubt regarding the integrity of the backups. In that case, you can instruct RMAN to restore the block(s) from a backup that is known to be good:

```
RMAN> block recover datafile 7 block 5 from backupset 1093;
```

will restore from the nominated backup set, which could also be specified by a tag:

```
RMAN> block recover datafile 7 block 5 from tag monthly_whole;
```

If the damage is more extensive, then two other options for BMR will simplify the process. First, provided that RMAN has populated the view V$DATABASE_BLOCK_CORRUPTION by running a backup with MAXCORRUPT set to greater than zero, then the CORRUPTION LIST option will instruct RMAN to restore and recover every block listed in the view. Second, to ensure that the backup(s) used for the restore are from a time before the corruption occurred, there is the UNTIL option. For example,

```
RMAN> block recover corruption list until time sysdate - 7;
```

instructs RMAN to restore and recover every block that has been discovered to be damaged by a previous backup operation, using only backups made at least one week ago.

 TIP In the BMR context, the keyword UNTIL does not denote an incomplete recovery! It means that the restore must be from a backup made before a particular date (or sequence number or SCN).

Two-Minute Drill

Describe the Data Recovery Advisor

- The Automatic Diagnostic Repository (ADR) is a set of files in the DIAGNOSTIC_DEST directory.
- The DRA can repair damage to datafiles and controlfile, and replace missing log file groups.
- Restore and recovery of the controlfile or a critical datafile can be done only in mount mode.
- Restore and recovery of a noncritical datafile can be done while the database is open.

Use the Data Recovery Advisor to Perform Recovery (Control File, Redo Log File, and Datafile)

- Failures must be listed before they can be advised upon.
- The DRA can be accessed through the RMAN executable or with Enterprise Manager.
- The DRA is available in all modes: in nomount mode it can repair the controlfile; in mount or open mode it can repair datafiles.

Perform Complete Recovery from a Critical or Noncritical Data File Loss Using RMAN

- Only the datafiles that make up the SYSTEM and the current undo tablespaces are critical. Damage to other datafiles will not cause the database to crash.

- Restore and complete recovery of noncritical datafiles can be carried out with the database open; critical datafiles must be restored and recovered in mount mode.
- RMAN will recover by applying incremental backups if possible, and archive log files when necessary.

Perform Incomplete Recovery Using RMAN

- Incomplete recovery can be accomplished only in mount mode.
- If all copies of the current online log file group are lost, an incomplete recovery will be required.
- The complete set of datafiles must be restored.
- Recovery will be stopped by use of the UNTIL clause, up to (but not including) a nominated time, archive log sequence number, or system change number.
- Following incomplete recovery, the database must be opened with RESETLOGS to reinitialize the online log files.

Recover Using Incrementally Updated Backups

- An image copy of a datafile (or the whole database) can be updated by applying incremental backups.
- The incremental backup must be made with the syntax: BACKUP INCREMENTAL LEVEL 1 FOR RECOVER OF COPY
- The incremental backup can be applied with the syntax: RECOVER COPY OF

Switch to Image Copies for Fast Recovery

- Image copies are immediately usable; there is no need to restore them.
- The SET NEWNAME command informs RMAN that the copy is to be used; the SWITCH command updates the target database controlfile accordingly.

Recover Using a Backup Control File

- A backup controlfile must be used if an incomplete recovery is to a time when the physical structure was different from that at present.
- If all copies of the controlfile are lost, the controlfile can be restored, in nomount mode, from an autobackup.
- If no datafiles or online log files are damaged, complete recovery using a backup controlfile is possible—but an OPEN RESETLOGS will be necessary.

Perform Block Media Recovery

- A backup operation will fail if it encounters a corrupt block, unless SET MAXCORRUPT has been specified.

- BMR can be accomplished with the database open and the datafile online.

- Corrupted blocks detected by RMAN will be visible in the V$DATABASE_BLOCK_CORRUPTION view.

- The BLOCK RECOVER command can recover a nominated list of blocks, or all blocks listed the V$DATABASE_BLOCK_CORRUPTION view.

Self Test

1. Loss of which of these files will cause an open database to crash? (Choose all correct answers.)

   A. A multiplexed controlfile

   B. A multiplexed online log file

   C. A multiplexed archive log file

   D. An active undo tablespace datafile

   E. An active temporary tablespace tempfile

   F. A datafile from the SYSAUX tablespace

   G. A datafile from the SYSTEM tablespace

   H. A datafile containing critical user data

2. You issue the command ALTER DATABASE CLEAR LOGFILE GROUP 2, and it fails with the message "ORA-01624: log 2 needed for crash recovery of instance orcl11g (thread 1)." What could be an explanation for this? (Choose the best answer.)

   A. Log file group 2 is active.

   B. Log file group 2 is being used for recovery.

   C. The database has not been checkpointed.

   D. The group is not multiplexed.

3. Your database is in noarchivelog mode, and you lose a noncritical datafile. What can you do to minimize loss of data? (Choose the best answer.)

   A. Restore the one damaged file, and leave the rest of the database up-to-date.

   B. Restore all the datafiles, but leave the controlfile up-to-date.

   C. Restore the whole database, and clear the online redo logs.

   D. Restore the one damaged file, and apply the online redo logs.

4. What sequence will allow you to add a multiplexed controlfile copy? (Choose the best answer.)

   1. Adjust the CONTROL_FILES parameter.

   2. Copy the controlfile.

   3. Mount the database.

   4. Open the database.

   5. Recover the controlfile.

   6. Recover the database.

   7. Shut down the database.

   A. 7, 2, 1, 3, 4 (5 and 6 not necessary)

   B. 7, 1, 3, 2, 6, 4 (5 not necessary)

   C. 2, 1, 5 (3, 4, 6 and 7 not necessary)

   D. 7, 1, 6, 3, 4 (2 and 5 not necessary)

5. These are three DRA commands:

   ADVISE FAILURE;

   LIST FAILURE;

   REPAIR FAILURE;

   In what order must they be run to fix a problem? (Choose the best answer.)

   A. ADVISE, LIST, REPAIR

   B. LIST, ADVISE, REPAIR

   C. LIST, REPAIR (ADVISE is not necessary)

   D. ADVISE, REPAIR (LIST is not necessary)

6. On what type or state of database can the DRA not be used? (Choose all correct answers.)

   A. A single-instance database that is shut down

   B. A single-instance database in nomount mode

   C. A single-instance database in mount mode

   D. An open RAC database

   E. A mounted standby database

7. Where is the Automatic Diagnostic Repository stored? (Choose the best answer.)

   A. In the Automatic Workload Repository

   B. In the SYSAUX tablespace

   C. In the data dictionary

   D. In operating system files

   E. In the Enterprise Manager repository

8. If you issue the LIST FAILURE command with the DRA and then another failure occurs, when you run ADVISE FAILURE for what will you receive advice? (Choose the best answer.)

    A. For the original failures only

    B. For the new failure only

    C. For all the failures

    D. For none of the failures until you run a new LIST FAILURES

9. Which file types can be repaired while the database is open? (Choose the best answer.)

    A. A damaged multiplexed controlfile copy

    B. A current multiplexed online log file

    C. A damaged noncritical datafile, if the database is in archivelog mode

    D. All of the above, if the DRA is used and server-managed backups are available

10. It is now 15:00, on Tuesday. A bad transaction was committed in your database at about 14:30. Investigation shows that the tables and indexes affected were in just two tablespaces: the rest of the database is fine. The two tablespaces and several others were backed up last night, but some tablespaces are backed up only on the weekend. Your database is in archivelog mode, with log switches about every 10 minutes. Which of the following statements is correct? (Choose the best answer.)

    A. You can do an incomplete restore and recovery to 14:29, of just the two tablespaces. The loss of data will be about 30 minutes of work in those tablespaces.

    B. You must restore the whole database from the weekend backup and recover to 14:29. You will lose about 30 minutes of work.

    C. You must restore the whole database and do an incomplete recovery canceling the application of the archive log that was active at 14:30. You will lose about 10 minutes of work.

    D. You can restore some tablespaces from last night, the others from the weekend, and recover to 14:29. You will lose about 30 minutes of work.

11. Under which of the following circumstances is an incomplete recovery necessary? (Choose two answers.)

    A. You lose all copies of your current online log file group.

    B. You lose a critical tablespace: SYSTEM, and/or the currently active UNDO tablespace.

    C. A user makes a bad transaction, and the instance crashes before he can issue the ROLLBACK statement.

    D. A datafile is created, used, and destroyed before it gets backed up.

    E. You back up a tablespace, drop it, and then want to get to the objects that were in it.

PART III

12. To do an incomplete recovery, what mode must the database be in? (Choose the best answer.)

   A. Incomplete recovery can be done only with the database SHUTDOWN.

   B. Incomplete recovery can be done only in NOMOUNT mode.

   C. Incomplete recovery can be done only in MOUNT mode.

   D. Incomplete recovery can be in OPEN mode, if the database is in archivelog mode.

   E. SQL*Plus can do incomplete recovery only in CLOSED mode; RMAN can do it in any mode.

13. When using RMAN to restore a controlfile autobackup, what piece of information might you need to supply? (Choose the best answer.)

   A. The database name

   B. The approximate time of the latest backup

   C. The database ID

   D. The instance name

   E. The instance number

14. You are using RMAN to perform incomplete recovery. Which of the following is the best sequence to follow? (Choose the best answer.)

   A. shutdown abort / startup mount / restore / recover / open resetlogs

   B. shutdown immediate / startup mount / restore / open resetlogs / recover

   C. shutdown immediate / restore / recover / open resetlogs

   D. shutdown immediate / startup nomount / restore / recover / open resetlogs

15. After a RESETLOGS, what will have changed? (Choose all that apply.)

   A. There will be a new database incarnation number.

   B. The system change number will be reset.

   C. The log switch sequence number will be reset.

   D. The database ID will be changed.

   E. The instance number will be changed.

   F. All previous backups and archivelogs will be invalid.

16. Which of the following statements are correct about block media recovery (BMR)? (Choose two answers.)

   A. BMR can be performed only with RMAN.

   B. BMR can be performed only with SQL*Plus.

   C. Both RMAN and SQL*Plus can be used for BMR.

   D. BMR is always a complete recovery.

   E. BMR is always an incomplete recovery.

   F. BMR can be either complete or incomplete; the DBA decides.

17. If, during an RMAN backup, a corrupt block is encountered, what will happen? (Choose the best answer.)

   A. The backup will fail.

   B. The backup will succeed.

   C. It depends on the MAXCORRUPT setting.

   D. If the corruption is in the SYSTEM tablespace, the backup will fail; otherwise, it will continue, but the address of the corrupt block will be written to the RMAN repository.

18. To what file types is BMR applicable? (Choose the best answer.)

   A. Archive log files

   B. Controlfiles

   C. Datafiles

   D. Online log files

   E. Tempfiles

   F. All of the above

19. What will be the effect of issuing this command:

```
blockrecover corruption list until time sysdate - 7;
```

   (Choose the best answer.)

   A. The recovery will be up to but not including the system change number of the time specified.

   B. The recovery will be up to and including the system change number of the time specified.

   C. The recovery will be complete, but the restore will be from before the time specified.

   D. The recovery will be of all blocks entered onto the corruption list before the time specified.

   E. The recovery will be of all blocks entered onto the corruption list after the time specified.

Self Test Answers

1. ☑ **A, D, and G.** Damage to any controlfile copy will terminate the instance, as will damage to the critical tablespaces: SYSTEM and the current undo tablespace.

   ☒ **B, C, E, F, and H.** All these are noncritical files, damage to which will not cause the instance to terminate.

2. ☑ **A.** An active log file group contains change vectors referring to blocks that have not yet been written to the datafiles by the DBWn, and cannot be cleared.

☒ **B, C,** and **D.** B is wrong because you cannot issue a CLEAR command while a recovery is progress, and D because multiplexing is not relevant to this. C is relevant because following a checkpoint the group would no longer be active, but this is not the best answer.

3. ☑ **C.** This is the only option in noarchivelog mode.

☒ **A, B,** and **D.** These are all attempts at a partial restore, which is not possible in noarchivelog mode.

4. ☑ **A.** This is a sequence that will work.

☒ **B, C,** and **D.** None of these sequences is feasible.

5. ☑ **B.** This is a sequence that will work.

☒ **A, C,** and **D.** Advice will be generated only for problems discovered by a previous List command, and repair scripts will be generated by the Advise stage.

6. ☑ **A, D,** and **E.** The DRA cannot run against a database that is shut down, nor against any RAC or Data Guard standby database.

☒ **B** and **C.** The DRA can run against a single instance database that is in nomount, mount, or open mode.

7. ☑ **D.** The repository exists as operating system files in the location specified by the DIAGNOSTIC_DEST instance parameter.

☒ **A, B, C,** and **E.** The repository is not stored in any database tables, nor by Enterprise Manager.

8. ☑ **A.** The ADVISE FAILURE will refer only to failures previously listed.

☒ **B, C,** and **D.** ADVISE FAILURE can run only following LIST FAILURE in the same session, and will refer to the information gathered at that time.

9. ☑ **C.** Noncritical datafiles can be restored and recovered while the database is open, if it is running in archivelog mode.

☒ **A, B,** and **D.** Damage to any controlfile copy will cause the instance to terminate, and it cannot be mounted or opened until the damage is repaired. A current multiplexed online log file cannot be repaired, though it can be cleared when no longer current or active. The DRA cannot repair anything—it can only advise.

10. ☑ D. An incomplete recovery is required, and the restore can be from the most recent backup of each datafile.

   ☒ A, B, and C. A is wrong because an incomplete recovery can follow only a restore of the complete set of datafiles (though in this case, a TSPITR might also have been an option). B is wrong because while it will work, it is less efficient than A: the recovery would take longer because more redo would have to be applied. C is wrong because there is no way to cancel the application of one archive log file, and then continue.

11. ☑ A and E. Loss of all copies of the current log file group necessitates an incomplete recovery, as does the reversion of the database to a time when a dropped tablespace still existed.

   ☒ B, C, and D. The SYSTEM and UNDO tablespaces can be completely recovered, even though they are critical to the running of the database. An uncommitted transaction can never be recovered—it will always be rolled back.

12. ☑ C. Incomplete recovery can be accomplished only in MOUNT mode.

   ☒ A, B, D, and E. MOUNT is necessary, whether you are using RMAN or SQL*Plus.

13. ☑ C. The DBID will be needed to allow RMAN to identify an autobackup of that particular database.

   ☒ A, B, D, and E. The database name will be read from the controlfile, as will details of the last backup. The instance name and number are not relevant.

14. ☑ A. This is the correct sequence. An IMMEDIATE shutdown would be acceptable but would take longer.

   ☒ B, C, and D. These sequences are not possible.

15. ☑ A and C. A RESETLOGS generates a new database incarnation number and returns the log sequence number to zero.

   ☒ B, D, E, and F. The SCN continues to increment following a RESET LOGS, and the DBID remains the same. The instance number is not relevant. Previous backups and archive logs will still be usable (though this was not the case with releases prior to 10g).

16. ☑ A and D. The BMR capability is a strong reason for using RMAN, but it must be complete.

   ☒ B, C, E, and F. SQL*Plus cannot do BMR, and an incomplete BMR is not possible.

17. ☑ **C.** The MAXCORRUPT setting can be used to allow a backup to skip over one or more corrupted blocks.

☒ **A, B,** and **D.** By default, a corrupt block will cause a backup to fail, but this behavior can be changed. It makes no difference in which tablespace the corrupt block is found.

18. ☑ **C.** Only datafile blocks can be recovered with BMR.

☒ **A, B, D, E,** and **F.** Neither log files (of any kind) nor tempfiles can be recovered. BMR cannot be applied to the controlfile: it must be restored and recovered as a whole.

19. ☑ **C.** The UNTIL clause in this context determines the latest backup that may be restored.

☒ **A, B, D,** and **E. A** and **B** are wrong because BMR can be only complete. **D** and **E** are wrong because the entire corruption list is always restored and recovered by this command.

CHAPTER 17

Advanced RMAN Facilities

Exam Objectives

In this chapter you will learn to

- 053.3.1   Identify Situations That Require an RMAN Recovery Catalog
- 053.3.2   Create and Configure a Recovery Catalog
- 053.3.3   Synchronize the Recovery Catalog
- 053.3.4   Create and Use RMAN Stored Scripts
- 053.3.5   Back Up the Recovery Catalog
- 053.3.6   Create and Use a Virtual Private Catalog
- 053.8.1   Create a Duplicate Database
- 053.8.2   Use a Duplicate Database
- 053.7.5   Restore a Database onto a New Host
- 053.7.7   Perform Disaster Recovery
- 053.9.1   Identify the Situations That Require TSPITR
- 053.9.2   Perform Automated TSPITR
- 053.10.1   Monitor RMAN Sessions and Jobs
- 053.10.2   Tune RMAN
- 053.10.3   Configure RMAN for Asynchronous I/O

Using RMAN for basic backup, restore, and recovery operations has been covered in Chapters 15 and 16. This chapter deals with some more advanced capabilities. First is the recovery catalog: a storage structure for the RMAN repository that, while not essential, will make many operations much simpler. Second, there are facilities for creating databases. Third is tablespace point-in-time recovery: a technique for performing an incomplete recovery on just a part of the database. Finally, we'll cover some considerations regarding performance and monitoring.

The Recovery Catalog

RMAN requires a *repository* in which to store details of all the backups it has made. The repository is a store of metadata about the target database and its backups. It contains details of the physical structure of the database: the locations of the datafiles; details of all the backups that have been made; and RMAN's persistent configuration settings. The repository is always stored in the controlfile of the target database, and optionally in a recovery catalog as well.

 EXAM TIP The RMAN repository always exists in the target database controlfile, but it only has data going back as far as the CONTROLFILE_ RECORD_KEEP_TIME parameter. The recovery catalog is an additional store that can retain data indefinitely.

If the repository is lost, then RMAN is crippled. Your backups will be fine, but RMAN won't know where they are. However, it should still be possible to rebuild the repository and continue to work, provided appropriate precautions have been taken.

 TIP To avoid dependency on the target database controlfile, use a recovery catalog, or if this is not possible, you must enable the controlfile autobackup facility.

The Need for a Recovery Catalog

RMAN's repository is always written to the target database's controlfile, but it can also be written out to a schema in a separate Oracle database. This database is known as the recovery catalog. Using RMAN with a recovery catalog enhances its capabilities substantially.

First, and perhaps most important, with a recovery catalog you are no longer dependent upon the target database controlfile. What if all copies of the controlfile are destroyed? Your backups are perfect, but without a repository, RMAN will never be able to find them. In fact, it may be possible to survive this situation: you can instruct RMAN to scan your backup devices and locate and identify any backups, but a far preferable situation is to have the repository always available in a recovery catalog database, on a separate machine from the target.

Second, the recovery catalog can store RMAN scripts. Without a recovery catalog, you can still use scripts but they have to be stored as operating system files on the machine where you are running the RMAN executable.

Third, if you are supporting many databases, one recovery catalog can be used to store metadata about all of them. It becomes a centralized repository of all your backup and restore information. Note that one catalog can be used with databases on any platform. You could, for example, run the RMAN executable on a Windows PC and connect to a recovery catalog in a database on a Unix host, and then connect to a series of target databases on Windows, Unix, Open VMS, and any other platform.

Fourthly, some operations are greatly simplified with a recovery catalog. For example, the target database need not be in MOUNT mode, as is required for all RMAN operations otherwise (with the one exception of RESTORE . . . FROM AUTOBACKUP). While connected to a recovery catalog, RMAN can locate backups of the spfile and controlfile and restore them, greatly simplifying the bootstrapping process of recovering a severely damaged database. Related to this is the ability to create a new database from a backup of the original.

And last, there is no limit to the length of time for which a recovery catalog can retain this metadata. The controlfile-based repository will retain data for only the time specified by the instance parameter CONTROL_FILE_RECORD_KEEP_TIME. This defaults to just seven days. You can certainly increase the value of this parameter, but to increase it to, for example, several months would be to use the controlfile for a purpose for which it was never intended: it is meant to be a store of currently relevant information, not a long-term storage place.

The recovery catalog database will usually not be a particularly large or busy database, and it will not have very demanding resource requirements, but it will improve RMAN functionality significantly.

Creating and Connecting to the Catalog

The RMAN executable can connect, concurrently, to up to three database instances:

- A target database, to which a backup or restore and recover operation will be applied
- A recovery catalog database, where metadata describing the target and all available backups is stored
- An auxiliary database, which is a database to be created using backups of the target

The catalog must be created. This entails identifying (or creating) a database to use and then creating a tablespace where the catalog objects will be stored and a user to whose schema they will belong. The user should be granted the RECOVERY_CATALOG_ OWNER role, which includes the necessary object privileges. For example, run these commands in the database to be used for the catalog:

```
create tablespace rmancat datafile 'rmancat01.dbf' size 200m;
create user rman identified by rman default tablespace rmancat
quota unlimited on rmancat;
grant recovery_catalog_owner to rman;
```

TIP There is nothing special about the RECOVERY_CATALOG_OWNER role: it is just a few system privileges. Run this query to see what it can do:
```
select privilege from dba_sys_privs where
GRANTEE='RECOVERY_CATALOG_OWNER';
```

Then to create the catalog, connect with the RMAN executable and run the CREATE CATALOG command, as in Figure 17-1.

The first command in Figure 17-1 runs the RMAN executable from an operating system prompt, specifying that the connection should be to a database containing an RMAN catalog. The connection will be made as the user RMAN identified by the password rman, through a TNS connect string catdb. The first command executed at the RMAN prompt is CREATE CATALOG. This will generate the catalog objects. If there were already a catalog in that schema, the command would return an error. The second command at the RMAN prompt connects to a target database as user SYS, using the TNS connect string ORCL. The third RMAN command registers the target in the catalog: the registration process copies all relevant information from the target database's controlfile into the catalog; if the target database were already registered, this would return an error. From this point it is possible to connect to both catalog and target with one command from an operating system prompt:

```
rman target / catalog rman/rman@catdb
```

 EXAM TIP RMAN connections to a target will usually be as SYS because of the common need to issue startup and shutdown commands. There is no need to specify AS SYSDBA—this is assumed by the tool.

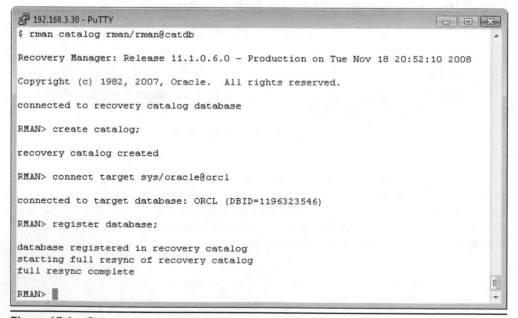

Figure 17-1 Creating a catalog and registering a database

The syntax in the preceding example is the most commonly used. It uses operating system authentication to connect as user SYS to a local database, and then connects to a remote catalog database as user RMAN using Oracle Net. The RMAN executable must be the same release as the target database, which will always be the case if it is run locally from the target, using the same Oracle Home. The RMAN executable need not be the same version as the RMAN catalog, so there will not be a problem with connecting to it across a network. Alternative syntax would be

```
rman target sys/oracle@orcl catalog rman/rman
```

This syntax connects to the target as SYS using password file authentication and Oracle Net, and to the catalog in a local database as user RMAN. This will often work but is not always advisable because of the possibility of version incompatibilities between the executable and target.

The catalog must be created with a version of RMAN that is equal to or higher than the version of any database that will be registered in it. It is therefore possible to create a single catalog of version 11.1.0.6 (11*g* release 1 patch set 6, the first production release of 11*g*) and use this to register 11*g*, 10*g*, and 9*i* databases. For each target, use the version of the RMAN executable installed in the target's Oracle Home.

 EXAM TIP The RMAN executable must be the same version as the target database, and less than or equal to the version of RMAN used to create the catalog.

The Virtual Private Catalog

One catalog can register details of all databases in an organization, but in some circumstances it will be desirable to create one or more *virtual private catalogs*. Security rules may require a separation of duties: some DBAs will be responsible for some databases; other DBAs will be responsible for other databases. To assist in this, RMAN has the capacity to create virtual private catalogs: as a DBA, you can register your own databases in what appears to be your own, private, catalog, and you will not be able to see any databases registered in any other private catalogs. This feature allows the consolidation of several catalogs into one, without compromising security.

The steps to create and use virtual private catalogs are

1. Create the catalog as normal.
2. Create an additional schema, and grant it the RECOVERY_CATALOG_OWNER role and the CREATE_SESSION system privilege.
3. Connect to the catalog as the catalog owner with RMAN, and issue this command:

   ```
   grant register database to vpcowner;
   ```

   where *vpcowner* is the name of the user created in Step 2. This will allow *vpcowner* to register his own databases.

4. If you wish the new user to have privileges on databases already registered, issue this command:

```
grant catalog for database dbname to vpcowner;
```

where *dbname* is the name of an already registered database that you wish vpcowner to manage.

5. As vpcowner, connect to the catalog with RMAN, and issue the command

```
create virtual catalog;
```

6. Using RMAN, connect to the catalog as *vpcowner* and to the target as SYS, register the target (if was not previously registered), and then carry out backup and restore operations as normal.

The owner of a virtual private catalog will have no access to backups relating to databases not registered in their domain, and need have no object or tablespace privileges in the catalog database, nor any system privileges beyond those granted in Step 2.

 TIP A GRANT REGISTER DATABASE will insert a row in VPC_USERS, a table in the catalog owner's schema. A GRANT CATALOG FOR DATABASE will insert a row in the VPC_DATABASES table. The virtual catalog owner has synonyms that allow these tables, which are used to filter access to be seen.

Protecting and Rebuilding the Catalog

If the recovery catalog is not available, RMAN can still function—but it will be crippled. Because the RMAN repository is always stored in the target databases' controlfiles, loss (temporary or permanent) of the catalog is not disastrous. But the controlfile-based repository will only hold a relatively small amount of information—all data older than the CONTROLFILE_RECORD_KEEP_TIME parameter will be overwritten. So while backups can still be performed, any restore and recover operations will be much harder. Backup sets and image copies going back weeks may be available, but RMAN will not be able to find them. Furthermore, any stored scripts will also be unavailable. It is therefore necessary to protect the catalog database. And worst of all, if all copies of the controlfile itself are lost, then RMAN will be useless—unless the controlfile autobackup facility has been enabled (which it should always be).

There is a recursive problem with backing up the catalog database. If you back it up with RMAN, then if it needs to be restored, RMAN will not be able to do the job. So, unless you have a second catalog database and use this to register the first, you will have to use a user-managed backup technique. These are fully described in Chapter 18.

The catalog schema is not very big, nor very busy. Even if the catalog is supporting hundreds of databases, it will usually be only a few gigabytes. It may therefore be feasible to make full whole offline backups regularly: simply shut it down, and copy it. This, together with the archive logs (as with any production database, the catalog database should be run in ARCHIVELOG mode), will be an adequate backup—if you can stand the downtime. Alternatively, it may be possible to make a logical backup, using the export/import utilities or the newer Data Pump facility (described in Chapter 23).

If backups are made without connecting to the catalog for any reason (such as the catalog being unavailable—perhaps because it was down for a cold backup), then the catalog repository must be resynchronized with the controlfile repository. This will happen automatically the next time RMAN connects to both the target and the catalog. The resync operation transfers all information from the controlfile repository into the catalog, thus bringing it up to date. Data about backups will therefore only be lost if the period without a resync exceeds the CONTROLFILE_RECORD_KEEP_TIME.

 TIP All backup events that occur while not connected to the catalog, as well as information regarding archive log generation and physical changes such as datafile creation, are transferred into the catalog by an automatic resync at the next connection. You can also force a resync from the RMAN prompt with the RESYNC CATALOG command.

But what if the controlfile and perhaps other parts of the target database are lost, and the catalog is lost too? The backups (backup sets and image copies) may be perfect, but RMAN will not be able to find them. Of course, it should be possible to restore the catalog—but assume that it is not. The first step is to connect to the target with the RMAN executable, and start it in NOMOUNT mode. Even if there is no parameter file, this will succeed because RMAN will start the instance with a dummy parameter file; Figure 17-2 shows this procedure. Of course, the startup will stop in NOMOUNT mode: there will be no controlfile to mount.

Once the instance is started, if you know where the backups of the controlfile and spfile are located, instruct RMAN to restore them from this location; or if autobackup had been enabled, use the technique described in Chapter 16. Then restart the instance with the restored spfile, and mount the database with the restored controlfile. Then, if

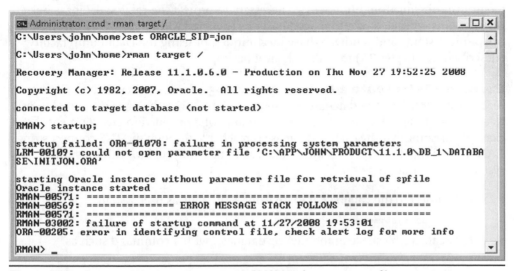

Figure 17-2 Starting a Windows instance, with RMAN and no parameter file

you know where the other backup sets are stored, register them in the controlfile-based repository with the CATALOG command. For example,

```
catalog datafilecopy '/u02/dfcopies/example01/dbf';
catalog backuppiece '/u02/backupsets/TAG20081028T174426_4JGMW1R9_.BKP';
catalog start with '/u01/app/oracle/flash_recovery_area';
```

The first of these commands registers an image copy of a datafile, which could have been made either by RMAN or by a user-managed backup. Similar syntax can register copies of the controlfile and of archive log files. The second command registers a backup set piece. Note that in neither case is it necessary to tell RMAN what the copy or backup set contains: RMAN can work this out by inspecting the file contents. The third command is the most powerful: it instructs RMAN to go to a directory (in the example, the root of the flash recovery area) and navigate down all subdirectories cataloging every copy and backup set piece that it finds. By giving a tape device as the path, RMAN can rebuild an entire repository. Follow up the catalog commands by connecting to each target database. The automatic RESYNC operation will populate the catalog with any information from the repositories in each controlfile that has not already been inserted.

While it is possible to create a new, empty, RMAN catalog and then populate it (always assuming that you know where the backups are) with the CATALOG and RESYNC CATALOG commands, it is far more preferable to back up your catalog so that if it is damaged, you can restore it.

By all means back up your catalog database with RMAN. Connect to it as a target, and back it up as you would any other target. Be sure to enable the autobackup facility. But do not back up your recovery catalog database only with RMAN! If it is damaged, there could be a recursive problem with any attempt to restore: if either the controlfile or the tablespace containing the catalog were damaged, any attempt to open the database and then connect to it as a catalog must fail. The autobackup will help you to survive this situation, but it will be necessary to protect the catalog database by other means—perhaps user-managed backups (detailed in Chapter 18), or using operating system– and hardware-based techniques, or using the Data Pump facility (described in Chapter 23) to make a logical backup.

Exercise 17-1: Create a Recovery Catalog   In this exercise, you will create a recovery catalog. Use any database you have available, even the one you intend to use as a target—though this would not be acceptable for a production environment. The examples assume that the catalog database is reachable through the TNS connect string CATDB, and that the target is a local database to be connected to with operating system authentication.

1. Connect to the catalog database using SQL*Plus as user system:

   ```
   sqlplus system/oracle@rman
   ```

2. Create a tablespace in the catalog database, with a command such as

   ```
   create tablespace rman datafile '/u01/oradata/orcl/rman01.dbf' size 50m;
   ```

3. Create a schema to hold the catalog, using the new tablespace as the default tablespace:

```
create user rman identified by rman default tablespace rman;
```

4. Grant privileges to the new schema:

```
grant recovery_catalog_owner to rman;
alter user rman quota unlimited on rman;
```

5. From an operating system prompt, launch the RMAN executable and connect to the catalog database as the new user:

```
rman catalog rman/rman@catdb
```

6. Create the catalog:

```
create catalog;
```

7. Exit from RMAN, and from an operating system prompt connect concurrently to both the catalog and the target:

```
rman catalog rman/rman@catdb target /
```

8. Register the target and see if any RMAN backups have been made:

```
register database;
list backup of database;
```

If no backups are listed, perform a full backup (as detailed in Chapter 15).

9. Exit from RMAN, and use SQL*Plus to query some views that will confirm that the target has been registered and that backups have been made:

```
sqlplus rman/rman@catdb
SQL> select dbid,name from rc_database;
SQL> select db_id,bs_key,backup_type from rc_backup_set;
```

Stored Scripts

RMAN scripts can be stored as operating system files, and invoked from the command line. For example, if these two commands are saved into a file named rman_script.rmn,

```
run {backup database plus archivelog delete all input;
delete obsolete;}
```

then the script can be invoked from an operating system prompt as follows:

```
rman target / catalog rman/rman@catdb @rman_script.rmn
```

However, if you have a catalog, you can use it to store scripts. There are six script-related commands:

```
create [ global ] script
replace [ global ] script
print [ global ] script
list [ global ] script names
execute [ global ] script
delete [ global ] script
```

TIP There is no command to edit a script. However, you can query the views RC_STORED_SCRIPT and RC_STORED_SCRIPT_LINE to view scripts, and edit them by using DML against these views. Of course, you bypass all the syntax checking if you do this. The views will not show global scripts.

The commands are all self-explanatory. By default, scripts are database-specific. If you want to run the same script against many targets, you must connect to each target and create it many times. But if the GLOBAL keyword is used, then the script will be visible to all targets. While global scripts are very useful, care must be taken to ensure that they will run against any target you wish. For example, if a script includes a FORMAT clause to name the backup pieces, the path element of the piece name would have to be different for Unix targets and Windows targets because of the different form of the directory delimiter on these operating systems. Extensive use of the CONFIGURE command will allow more use of global scripts, because the scripts behavior will then be modified transparently by each target.

 TIP You can convert RMAN scripts stored as operating system files to scripts stored within the catalog with this command:
```
create script script_name from file 'file_name';
```

Figure 17-3 demonstrates the creation and running of a stored script. Note the automatic resync of the recovery catalog: this will update the catalog with any changes

```
oracle@vblin1:~
RMAN> create script inc_backup_plus_logs
2> {backup incremental level 1 database;
3> backup archivelog all delete all input;}

created script inc_backup_plus_logs

RMAN> run {execute script inc_backup_plus_logs;}

executing script: inc_backup_plus_logs

Starting backup at 18-DEC-08
starting full resync of recovery catalog
full resync complete
using channel ORA_DISK_1
channel ORA_DISK_1: starting incremental level 1 datafile backup set
channel ORA_DISK_1: specifying datafile(s) in backup set
input datafile file number=00001 name=/u01/app/oracle/oradata/orcl/system01.dbf
input datafile file number=00002 name=/u01/app/oracle/oradata/orcl/sysaux01.dbf
input datafile file number=00003 name=/u01/app/oracle/oradata/orcl/undotbs01.dbf
input datafile file number=00005 name=/u01/app/oracle/oradata/orcl/example01.dbf
input datafile file number=00006 name=/u01/app/oracle/oradata/orcl/rman01.dbf
input datafile file number=00004 name=/u01/app/oracle/oradata/orcl/users01.dbf
channel ORA_DISK_1: starting piece 1 at 18-DEC-08
```

Figure 17-3 Creating and executing an RMAN stored script

that have occurred since the last resync, such as datafile adjustments and archivelog generation, so that the catalog will be aware of the current state of the database.

Using RMAN to Create Databases

To clarify some naming conventions, the *target database* is the existing database you want to copy. The *auxiliary database* is the new database created from the target. The target and the auxiliary may be on the same server or on different machines. The examples that follow assume that you are duplicating a database and instance named orcl to a database and instance named newdb.

Here are the general steps to follow to create a duplicate database:

1. Install the Oracle Home on the node that will host the auxiliary database.
2. Create a password file for the auxiliary instance.
3. Ensure network connectivity to the auxiliary instance.
4. Create an initialization parameter file for the auxiliary instance.
5. Start the auxiliary instance as NOMOUNT.
6. Start the target database in MOUNT or OPEN mode.
7. Create backups or copy existing backups and archived redo log files to a location accessible to the auxiliary instance, unless you are using active database duplication.
8. Allocate auxiliary channels if necessary.
9. Run the RMAN DUPLICATE command.
10. Open the auxiliary instance.

You must create a password file in the Oracle home for the auxiliary database. For example,

```
orapwd file=$ORACLE_HOME/dbs/oranewdb password=oracle1 entries=3
```

Note that the location for all database password files is $ORACLE_HOME/dbs on Unix, or %ORACLE_HOME%\database on Windows. The file itself must be named ora<SID> on Unix, and PWD<SID>.ora on Windows, where <SID> is the new instance name.

You must ensure network connectivity to the auxiliary. This will entail launching a listener process if the auxiliary is on a different server, and in any case configuring a tnsnames.ora file entry that will connect to the new instance.

The next step is to create an initialization parameter file for the auxiliary instance, in the same location as the password file. Only DB_NAME must be specified; all other parameters are optional, depending on whether you use Oracle Managed Files or you want to specify an alternative location for one or more file destinations. Table 17-1 lists the parameters you can specify in the auxiliary initialization file along with their descriptions and under what circumstances they are required.

Initialization Parameter	Value(s)	Required?
DB_NAME	The name you specify in the DUPLICATE command, which must be unique among databases in the destination ORACLE_HOME.	Yes
CONTROL_FILES	All controlfile locations.	Yes, unless you use Oracle-Managed Files (OMF)
DB_BLOCK_SIZE	The block size for the duplicate database. This size must match the source database.	Yes, if not using the default (which is 2KB)
DB_FILE_NAME_CONVERT	Pairs of strings for converting datafile and tempfile names.	No
LOG_FILE_NAME_CONVERT	Pairs of strings to rename online redo log files.	No
DB_CREATE_FILE_DEST	Location for OMF datafiles.	No, unless using OMF
DB_CREATE_ONLINE_LOG_DEST_n	Location for OMF online redo log files.	No, unless using OMF
DB_RECOVERY_FILE_DEST	Location of the flash recovery area.	No

Table 17-1 Auxiliary Instance Initialization Parameters

Note that the DB_FILE_NAME_CONVERT parameter can be specified when you run the DUPLICATE command. Here is an initialization parameter file for an auxiliary instance, using the CONVERT parameters to map the names of the target files to those to be used in the auxiliary:

```
DB_NAME=NEWDB
DB_BLOCK_SIZE=8192
CONTROL_FILES=('/u01/app/oracle/oradata/newdb/control01.ctl',
               '/u01/app/oracle/oradata/newdb/control02.ctl',
               '/u01/app/oracle/oradata/newdb/control03.ctl')
DB_FILE_NAME_CONVERT=('/u01/app/oracle/oradata/orcl/',
                      '/u01/app/oracle/oradata/newdb/')
LOG_FILE_NAME_CONVERT=('/u01/app/oracle/oradata/orcl/',
                       '/u01/app/oracle/oradata/newdb/',
                       '/u06/app/oracle/oradata/orcl/',
                       '/u06/app/oracle/oradata/newdb/')
```

Using the initialization parameter file you just created, start the instance in NOMOUNT mode. Set your ORACLE_SID environment variable to the name of the new instance, and start it in NOMOUNT mode using the new parameter file. On Unix:

```
export ORACLE_SID=newdb
```

Or on Windows,

```
set ORACLE_SID=newdb
```

and then treat the Windows service:

```
oradim -new -sid newdb
```

and then,

```
sqlplus / as sysdba
startup nomount
```

If the target database is not already open, start it in MOUNT or OPEN mode.

All datafile backups of the target, including incremental backups and archived redo log files, must be available on a file system accessible by the auxiliary instance. Alternatively, you can perform an active database duplication, in which case you do not have to create or copy backups for the operation in advance. Either way, the directories in which the auxiliary database files will be created must exist.

Now use RMAN to connect concurrently to both the target database and to the newly started auxiliary instance. Allocate channels (possibly several, which may reduce the time needed) against both, and execute the DUPLICATE command. This must be done within a run block:

```
rman target sys/oracle@orcl auxiliary sys/oracle@newdb

run { allocate auxiliary channel a1 device type disk;
     allocate auxiliary channel a2 device type disk;
     allocate channel t1 type disk;

     allocate channel t2 type disk;
     duplicate target database to newdb;}
```

This example will create the new database from existing backups. Alternative syntax to use the live database as the source rather than a backup is

```
duplicate target database to newdb from active database;
```

In summary, here is what the DUPLICATE command does:

- Creates a controlfile for the duplicate database.
- Restores the target datafiles to the duplicate database or copies directly from the running database.
- Performs incomplete recovery up to the last archived redo log file.
- Shuts down and restarts the auxiliary instance.
- Opens the auxiliary database with the RESETLOGS option to create the online redo log files.
- Generates a new DBID for the auxiliary database.

PART III

The generation of a new DBID is critical: RMAN distinguishes databases by their DBID, not by their DB_NAME, and if a new DBID were not generated, RMAN would not be able to tell the two databases apart.

A duplicate database can be used for many things, including the following:

- Test backup and recovery procedures without disrupting the production database.
- Create development and UAT systems.
- Generate reports that would otherwise have a detrimental effect on the response time for an online transaction processing (OLTP) production system.
- Export a table from the duplicate database that was inadvertently dropped from the production database, and then import it back into the production database.

Tablespace Point-in-Time Recovery (TSPITR)

Tablespace point-in-time recovery, or TSPITR, is a technique for performing incomplete recovery on just a part of the database. Incomplete recovery must, as a general rule, be applied to the whole database: as described in Chapter 16, all the datafiles must be restored, and rolled forward together. The TSPITR technique creates an auxiliary database from a subset of the tablespaces of the target database, performs an incomplete recovery on just this subset, and then replaces the tablespaces in the target database with those from the auxiliary. The end result appears as though just the subset has been restored and recovered, leaving the remainder of the target database up-to-date. Doing this manually would be a nontrivial task.

The TSPITR Methodology

RMAN facilitates automatic TSPITR, making it easy to restore the contents of one or more tablespaces to a previous point in time without affecting other tablespaces or other objects in the database. TSPITR is a useful recovery tool for these scenarios:

- Corruption or deletion of rows in key tables that occur in a logically isolated tablespace; in other words, no indexes or parent/child relationships from objects in other tablespaces
- Incorrect Data Definition Language (DDL) changes the structure of one or more tables in a tablespace, such that Flashback Table is not available to recover these tables
- A table dropped with the PURGE option

TSPITR is not a cure-all for all tablespace disasters. For example, you cannot use it to recover a dropped tablespace. You also cannot recover a renamed tablespace to a point in time before it was renamed.

First, some terminology:

- **Target time**   The point in time or SCN to which the tablespace(s) will be recovered
- **Recovery set**   The group of datafiles containing the tablespace(s) to be recovered
- **Auxiliary set**   Other datafiles required to recover the tablespace(s), such as the datafiles for the SYSTEM, UNDO, and TEMP tablespaces
- **Auxiliary destination**   A temporary location to store the auxiliary set of files, including online and archived redo log files, and a copy of the controlfile created during the recovery process

The key to TSPITR is an auxiliary instance to facilitate the recovery process, as covered earlier in this chapter. The auxiliary instance does the work of restoring a backup controlfile from before the desired point in time, restores the recovery set and the auxiliary set from the target database, and finally recovers the database for the auxiliary instance to the desired point in time. Here is a complete list of steps that RMAN performs during TSPITR:

1. Starts an auxiliary instance with a randomly generated name.
2. Restores a controlfile to the auxiliary instance, and mounts the auxiliary database.
3. Restores the datafiles for the recovery set to the auxiliary database.
4. Restores the datafiles for the auxiliary set to the auxiliary database.
5. Recovers the auxiliary database to the desired point in time.
6. Exports the dictionary metadata for the recovered tablespace from the auxiliary database.
7. Imports the dictionary metadata for the recovered tablespace into the target database.
8. Deletes all auxiliary files.

Steps 6 and 7 are critical. The export process writes out the definitions of all objects in the auxiliary tablespace set as they are at the point in time to which the recovery was made; the import process then reads this information into the target database, replacing all current definitions. This completes the process of taking the affected tablespace(s) back to a previous point in time, while leaving the remainder of the target database current. There is one final step that must be performed manually: bringing the recovered tablespace online.

Perform Automated TSPITR

Performing a TSPITR with RMAN is simple—but there are a few steps to be done before and after to ensure a successful operation.

Verifying Tablespace Dependencies

Other tablespaces may have objects with dependencies on objects in the tablespace to be recovered. The rules for TSPITR state that the tablespace(s) to be recovered must be self-contained, with no dependencies on objects in other tablespaces that are not to be recovered. For example, if a table has indexes they too must be recovered. Use the data dictionary view TS_PITR_CHECK to identify any dependencies, as in this example, which checks whether objects in the tablespace named INTERFACE have any dependent objects in other tablespaces, and whether objects in other tablespaces have dependent objects in the INTERFACE tablespace:

```
SQL> select obj1_owner, obj1_name, ts1_name,
  2         obj2_owner, obj2_name, ts2_name
  3  from ts_pitr_check
  4  where
  5  ts1_name = 'INTERFACE' and ts2_name != 'INTERFACE')
  6    or (ts1_name != 'INTERFACE' and ts2_name = 'INTERFACE')
  7  ;

no rows selected

SQL>
```

The view is populated with rows defining one-to-one relationships, where an object in the tablespace TS1_NAME has a dependent object in the tablespace TS2_NAME. The view also lists objects that cannot be included in a point-in-time recovery, such as advanced queue tables. This are indicated by the value '-1' in the TS2_NAME column.

To resolve any issues found, you can either temporarily remove the dependencies or add the tablespace containing objects with dependencies to the recovery set. You are better off with the latter, however, to ensure that your tables remain logically consistent with one another.

Identifying Objects Lost after TSPITR

In addition to resolving any dependencies with the tablespace to be recovered, you also need to identify any objects created after the target time that will be lost if you recover the tablespace. You can use the data dictionary view TS_PITR_OBJECTS_TO_BE_DROPPED to determine which objects you will lose after your target recovery time, as in this example:

```
SQL> select owner, name,

  2      to_char(creation_time, 'yyyy-mm-dd:hh24:mi:ss') create_time
  3  from ts_pitr_objects_to_be_dropped
  4  where tablespace_name = 'INTERFACE'
  5    and creation_time >
  6          to_date('2008-07-19:21:55:00','yyyy-mm-dd:hh24:mi:ss')
  7  ;

OWNER         NAME                      CREATE_TIME
-----------   ------------------------  -------------------
RJB           SALES_RESULTS_2007_TEMP   2008-07-19:22:00:56

SQL>
```

To resolve these issues, you can export individual objects before the recovery operation and then import them after recovery is complete.

Performing Automated TSPITR with RMAN

The most straightforward method for running TSPITR is through RMAN, though it is also possible to carry out the eight steps listed previously manually. Connect to the target database (and to a catalog, if you have one) and run a command such as

```
recover tablespace interface until time '18-12-08 09:01:00'
auxiliary destination '/u01/app/oracle/oradata/auxdata' ;
```

This will perform an incomplete recovery on the tablespace INTERFACE to the nominated time using the nominated auxiliary destination for the storage. The tablespace will be left offline, so to complete the procedure, bring the tablespace online. With SQL*Plus:

```
alter tablespace interface online;
```

Or with RMAN:

```
sql 'alter tablespace interface online';
```

Exercise 17-2: Perform a Tablespace Point-in-Time Recovery   In this exercise, you will set up a situation that requires a tablespace point-in-time recovery and perform this with RMAN.

1. Create a tablespace with a command such as

   ```
   create tablespace pitr datafile
   '/u01/app/oracle/oradata/orcl/pitr01.dbf' size 20m;
   ```

2. Create a table in the tablespace, and insert a row:

   ```
   create table t1 (c1 date) tablespace pitr;
   insert into t1 values (sysdate);
   commit;
   ```

3. From an operating system prompt, set the environment variable that will control the date format. Use this operating system session from now on, to ensure that dates are interpreted correctly.

   On Windows:

   ```
   C:\> set nls_date_format=dd-mm-yy hh24:mi:ss
   ```

   On Unix:

   ```
   $ export nls_date_format=dd-mm-yy hh24:mi:ss
   ```

4. Launch RMAN, and from the RMAN prompt back up the new tablespace:

   ```
   RMAN> backup tablespace pitr;
   ```

5. Using SQL*Plus, check the time and then drop the table:

   ```
   SQL> select sysdate from dual;
   SQL> drop table t1;
   ```

6. From the RMAN prompt, perform TSPITR:

```
RMAN> recover tablespace pitr until time '18-12-08 09:01:00'
auxiliary destination '/u01/app/oracle/oradata/auxdata' ;
```

Use the time retrieved in Step 5 as the UNTIL TIME. You can nominate any convenient directory as the auxiliary destination, but it must exist and the Oracle user must have read/write permissions on it.

7. Study the output of Step 6, relating this to the eight steps enumerated previously.

8. Using SQL*Plus, bring the tablespace online and then confirm that the table is now available again.

RMAN Performance and Monitoring

RMAN is implemented in PL/SQL. As a rule, PL/SQL is stored in the data dictionary and is therefore not available unless the database is open. If this were the case with the RMAN PL/SQL, it would be useless if the database were sufficiently damaged that it could not be opened; for that reason, the RMAN PL/SQL is kernelized, meaning that it is compiled and linked into the Oracle executable code, and so available even in NOMOUNT mode. All RMAN work is carried out by database sessions. Every RMAN operation will require at least two: the default session, which invokes the kernelized PL/SQL, and a polling session that reports back to the RMAN user process. The channels are further sessions that actually do the work. So tuning and monitoring RMAN becomes an exercise in tuning and monitoring the work being done by these various sessions.

Monitoring RMAN Sessions and Jobs

At any given point in time, you may have multiple backup jobs running, each with one or more channels. Each channel utilizes one operating system process. If you want to identify which channel is using the most CPU or I/O resources at the operating system level, you can join the dynamic performance views V$SESSION and V$PROCESS to identify the operating system processes associated with each RMAN channel.

In addition to identifying the processes associated with each RMAN job, you can also determine the progress of a backup or restore operation. You can use the dynamic performance view V$SESSION_LONGOPS to identify how much work an RMAN session has completed and the estimated total amount of work.

Finally, RMAN provides troubleshooting information in a number of ways, above and beyond the command output at the RMAN> prompt, when something goes wrong. You can also enable enhanced debugging to help you and Oracle Support identify the cause of a serious RMAN problem.

In the following sections, you'll be introduced to the dynamic performance views V$SESSION, V$PROCESS, and V$SESSION_LONGOPS that can help you identify and monitor RMAN backup and restore jobs. Also, you'll learn where to look when a backup or restore job fails.

Using V$SESSION and V$PROCESS

The dynamic performance view V$PROCESS contains a row for each operating system process connected to the database instance. V$SESSION contains additional information about each session connected to the database, such as the current SQL command and the Oracle username executing the command. These sessions include RMAN sessions. As a result, you can monitor RMAN sessions using these views as well.

RMAN populates the column V$SESSION.CLIENT_INFO with the string rman and the name of the channel. Remember that each RMAN channel corresponds to a server process, and therefore V$SESSION will have one row for each channel.

To retrieve information from V$SESSION and V$PROCESS about current RMAN sessions, join the views V$SESSION and V$PROCESS on the PADDR and ADDR columns, as you will see in the exercise.

Exercise 17-3: Monitor RMAN Channels   In this exercise, you will start an RMAN job that uses two or more channels and retrieve the channel names from V$SESSION and V$PROCESS.

1. Create an RMAN job that backs up the USERS tablespace using two disk channels:

```
RMAN> run {
2>         allocate channel ch1 type disk;
3>         allocate channel ch2 type disk;
4>         backup as compressed backupset tablespace users;
5>         }

starting full resync of recovery catalog
full resync complete
released channel: ORA_DISK_1
allocated channel: ch1
channel ch1: SID=130 device type=DISK
starting full resync of recovery catalog
full resync complete

allocated channel: ch2
channel ch2: SID=126 device type=DISK
. . .
Finished Control File and SPFILE Autobackup at 27-JUL-08
released channel: ch1
released channel: ch2

RMAN>
```

2. While the RMAN job is running, join the views V$PROCESS and V$SESSION to retrieve the CLIENT_INFO column contents:

```
SQL> select sid, spid, client_info
  2  from v$process p join v$session s on (p.addr = s.paddr)
  3  where client_info like '%rman%'
  4  ;

     SID SPID                     CLIENT_INFO
---------- ------------------------ ------------------------
     126 25070                    rman channel=ch2
     130 7732                     rman channel=ch1

SQL>
```

Note that RMAN's user processes will still exist in V$SESSION until you exit RMAN or start another backup operation.

If you have multiple RMAN jobs running, some with two or more channels allocated, it might be difficult to identify which process corresponds to which RMAN backup or recovery operation. To facilitate the desired differentiation, you can use the SET COMMAND ID command within an RMAN RUN block, as in this example:

```
run {
        set command id to 'bkup users';
        backup tablespace users;
    }
```

When this RMAN job runs, the CLIENT_INFO column in V$SESSION contains the string id=bkup users to help you identify the session for each RMAN job.

Exercise 17-4: Monitor Multiple RMAN Jobs   In this exercise, you'll start two RMAN jobs and identify each job in V$SESSION and V$PROCESS using the SET COMMAND option in RMAN.

1. Create two RMAN jobs (in two different RMAN sessions) that back up the USERS and CHGTRK tablespaces and use the SET COMMAND option:

```
/* session 1 */
RMAN> run {
2>          set command id to 'bkup users';
4>          backup as compressed backupset tablespace users;
5>      }
. . .
/* session 2 */
RMAN> run {
2>          set command id to 'bkup chgtrk';
4>          backup as compressed backupset tablespace users;
5>      }
```

2. While the RMAN job is running, join the views V$PROCESS and V$SESSION to retrieve the CLIENT_INFO column contents:

```
SQL> select sid, spid, client_info
  2  from v$process p join v$session s on (p.addr = s.paddr)
  3  where client_info like '%id=%';

       SID SPID                        CLIENT_INFO
---------- ------------------------    ------------------------
       141 19708                       id=bkup users
        94 19714                       id=bkup chgtrk

SQL>
```

Using V$SESSION_LONGOPS

The dynamic performance view V$SESSION_LONGOPS isn't specific to RMAN either. Oracle records any operations that run for more than six seconds (in absolute time), including RMAN backup and recovery operations, statistics gathering, and long queries in V$SESSION_LONGOPS.

RMAN populates two different types of rows in V$SESSION_LONGOPS: detail rows and aggregate rows. Detail rows contain information about a single RMAN job step, such as creating a single backup set. Aggregate rows apply to all files referenced in a single RMAN command, such as BACKUP DATABASE. As you might expect, aggregate rows are updated less frequently than detail rows.

 EXAM TIP The initialization parameter STATISTICS_LEVEL must be set to TYPICAL or ALL before the view V$SESSION_LONGOPS will contain information about long-running RMAN jobs. The default value for STATISTICS_LEVEL is TYPICAL.

This example initiates a full database backup, and while the backup is running, both detail and aggregate rows for active RMAN jobs are shown:

```
SQL> select sid, serial#, opname, sofar, totalwork
  2  from v$session_longops
  3  where opname like 'RMAN%'
  4    and sofar <> totalwork
  5  ;


    SID    SERIAL# OPNAME                              SOFAR  TOTALWORK
------- ---------- ------------------------- ---------- ----------
    130      39804 RMAN: aggregate output         97557          0
     94      47546 RMAN: aggregate input         191692     331808
    155       1196 RMAN: full datafile backup    219980     331808
    155       1196 RMAN: full datafile backup    121172          0

SQL>
```

The SID and SERIAL# are the same columns you see in V$SESSION. The OPNAME column is a text description of the operation monitored in the row, and for RMAN, it contains the prefix RMAN:.

The column SOFAR is, as you might expect, a measure of the progress of a step. Its value differs depending on the type of operation:

- For image copies, it is the number of blocks read.
- For backup input rows, it is the number of blocks read from the files being backed up.
- For backup output rows (backup set or image copy), it is the number of blocks written so far to the backup piece.
- For restore operations, it is the number of blocks processed so far to the destination files.
- For proxy copies (copy operations from a media manager to or from disk), it is the number of files that have been copied so far.

The column TOTALWORK has a similar definition, except that it estimates the total amount of work required during the step:

- For image copies, it is the total number of blocks in the file.
- For backup input rows, it is the total number of blocks to be read from all files in the step.

- For backup output rows, it is always zero because RMAN does not know how many blocks will be written into a backup piece until it is done.

- For restore operations, it is the total number of blocks in all files restored in a single job step or aggregate.

- For proxy copies, it is the total number of files to be copied in the job step.

To calculate the progress of an RMAN step as a percentage, you can divide SOFAR by TOTALWORK as follows and add this expression to the SELECT statement:

```
round(sofar/totalwork*100,1)
```

Tuning RMAN

You can tune RMAN operations in many ways. You can tune the overall throughput of a backup by using multiple RMAN channels and assigning datafiles to different channels. Each channel is assigned to a single process, so parallel processing can speed the backup process. Conversely, you can multiplex several backup files to the same backup piece. For a particular channel, you can use the MAXPIECESIZE and MAXOPENFILES parameters to maximize throughput to a specific output device. The BACKUP command uses these parameters in addition to FILESPERSET and BACKUP DURATION to optimize your backup operation. You can also use BACKUP DURATION to minimize the effect of the backup on response time if your database must be continuously available and you have to contend with stringent SLAs. Finally, you can also use database initialization parameters to optimize backup and recovery performance, especially for synchronous I/O operations.

If you understand how each tuning method works, you can keep the user response time fast, optimize your hardware and software environment, and potentially delay upgrades when budgets are tight (which is almost always). A throughput *bottleneck* will almost always exist somewhere in your environment. A bottleneck is the slowest step or task during an RMAN backup.

The next section reviews the basic steps that a channel performs during a backup operation. The techniques presented in the following sections will help you identify where the bottleneck is within the channel's tasks and how to minimize its impact on backup and recovery operations.

Identifying Backup and Restore Steps

RMAN backup performs its tasks within a channel in one of three main phases:

1. *Read phase:* The channel reads data blocks into the input buffers.

2. *Copy phase:* The channel copies blocks from the input buffers to the output buffers and performs additional processing, if necessary:

   - **Validation**   Check blocks for corruption, which is not CPU-intensive.

   - **Compression**   Use BZIP2 or ZLIB to compress the block, which is CPU-intensive.

- **Encryption** Use an encryption algorithm (transparent, password-protected, or both) to secure the data, which is CPU-intensive.

3. *Write phase:* The channel writes the blocks from the output buffers to the output device (disk or tape).

Using dynamic performance views, you can identify which phase of which channel operation is the bottleneck and address it accordingly.

In some scenarios, you may want to increase the backup time to ensure that the recovery time will be short. Creating image copies and recovering the image copies on a daily or hourly basis will add to the backup time but will dramatically reduce recovery time.

Parallelizing Backup Sets

One of the simplest ways to improve RMAN performance is to allocate multiple channels (either disk or tape). The number of channels you allocate should be no larger than the number of physical devices; allocating two or more channels (and therefore processes) for a single physical device will not improve performance and may even decrease performance. If you're writing to a single Automatic Storage Management (ASM) disk group or a file system striped by the operating system, you can allocate more channels and improve throughput, since the logical ASM disk group or striped file system maps to two or more physical disks. You can allocate up to 255 channels, and each channel can read up to 64 datafiles in parallel. Each channel writes to a separate backup copy or image copy.

If the number of datafiles in your database is relatively constant, you can allocate a fixed number of channels and assign each datafile to a specific channel. Here is an example:

```
run {
    allocate channel dc1 device type disk;
    allocate channel dc2 device type disk;
    allocate channel dc3 device type disk;
    backup as compressed backupset incremental level 0
      (datafile 1,2,9    channel dc1)
      (datafile 3,5,8    channel dc2)
      (datafile 4,6,7    channel dc3)
      ;
}
```

Note also that you can specify the path name for a datafile instead of the datafile number, as in this example:

```
(datafile '/u01/oradata/users02.dbf' channel dc2)
```

To automate this process further, you can use the CONFIGURE command to increase the parallelism for each device type. Here is the default RMAN configuration for disk device channels:

```
CONFIGURE DEVICE TYPE DISK PARALLELISM 1 BACKUP TYPE TO BACKUPSET; # default
```

TIP It is generally said that the number of channels should not exceed the number of devices. However, experience on some hardware shows that allocating several channels per device may speed up RMAN operations. Experiment, and find out what works best for your environment.

Understanding RMAN Multiplexing

You can improve RMAN performance and throughput by *multiplexing* backup and recovery operations. Multiplexing enables RMAN to read from multiple files simultaneously and write the data blocks to the same backup piece.

Using multiplexing as an RMAN tuning method is one way to reduce bottlenecks in backup and recovery operations. The level of multiplexing is primarily controlled by two parameters: FILESPERSET and MAXOPENFILES.

The FILESPERSET parameter of the RMAN BACKUP command determines the number of datafiles to put in each backup set. If a single channel backs up 10 datafiles and the value of FILESPERSET is 4, RMAN will back up only 4 files per backup set. The parameter FILESPERSET defaults to 64.

The level of multiplexing (the number of input files that are read and written to the same backup piece) is the minimum of MAXOPENFILES and the number of files in each backup set. The default value for MAXOPENFILES is 8. Here is an equation that may make the calculation easier to understand:

```
multiplexing_level =
        min(MAXOPENFILES, min(FILESPERSET, files_per_channel))
```

This example backs up 10 datafiles in one channel, the value for MAXOPENFILES is 12, and the value for FILESPERSET is at the default value of 64. Therefore, the multiplexing level is calculated as follows:

```
multiplexing_level = min(12, min(64, 10)) = 10
```

RMAN allocates a different number and size of disk I/O buffers depending on the level of multiplexing in your RMAN job. Once the level of multiplexing is derived by RMAN using the FILESPERSET and MAXOPENFILES parameters using the aforementioned equation, you can use the information in Table 17-2 to find out how many and what size buffers RMAN needs to perform the backup.

Oracle recommends that the value FILESPERSET should be 8 or less to optimize recovery performance. In other words, putting too many input files into a single backup

Level of Multiplexing	Size of Input Disk Buffer
<= 4	16 buffers of 1MB each divided among all input files
5–8	A variable number of 512MB buffers to keep total buffer size under 16MB
> 8	Total of 4 buffers of 128KB for each (512KB) for each input file

Table 17-2 RMAN Datafile Buffer Sizing

set will slow down a recovery operation because the RESTORE or RECOVER command will still have to read a large number of unneeded blocks in the backup set when all you may need is to recover a single datafile.

Tuning the BACKUP Command

Just like the CONFIGURE CHANNEL command, the BACKUP command has parameters that can help you improve performance or limit the computing resources that a channel uses for an RMAN backup. Here are the key tuning parameters for the BACKUP command:

- MAXPIECESIZE: The maximum size of a backup piece per channel
- FILESPERSET: The maximum number of files per backup set
- MAXOPENFILES: The maximum number of input files that a channel can have open at a given time
- BACKUP DURATION: Decrease or increase the time to complete the backup

You've seen the parameters MAXPIECESIZE, FILESPERSET, and MAXOPENFILES before. Note that MAXPIECESIZE and MAXOPENFILES have the same purpose as in the CHANNEL commands, except that they apply to all channels in the backup.

BACKUP DURATION specifies an amount of time to complete the backup. You can qualify this option with MINIMIZE TIME to run the backup as fast as possible or MINIMIZE LOAD to use the entire timeframe specified in the BACKUP DURATION window. In addition, you can use the PARTIAL option, as you might expect, to save a partial backup that was terminated due to time constraints. For example, to limit a full database backup to two hours, run it as fast as possible, and save a partial backup, you may use this command:

```
RMAN> backup duration 2:00 partial database;
```

If the backup does not complete in the specified time frame, the partial backup is still usable in a recovery scenario after a successive BACKUP command finishes the backup and you use the PARTIAL option. Without the PARTIAL option, the backup would terminate with an error.

Configure RMAN for Asynchronous I/O

Whether you use synchronous or asynchronous I/O in your RMAN environment depends on several factors. These factors include the type of device you use for backup sets (disk or tape) and whether the output device or host operating system supports synchronous or asynchronous I/O. Even if the host operating system or device does not support native asynchronous I/O, you can configure RMAN to simulate asynchronous I/O using initialization parameters such as DBWR_IO_SLAVES.

After you review the key differences between asynchronous and synchronous I/O, you will learn how to monitor the performance of each type of I/O using dynamic performance views, identify where the throughput bottleneck is, and adjust RMAN parameters accordingly.

PART III

Understanding Asynchronous and Synchronous I/O

When RMAN reads or writes data, the I/O operations are either *synchronous* or *asynchronous*. A synchronous I/O operation limits a server process from performing more than one operation at a time. It must wait for one operation to finish before another can start. As you might expect, an asynchronous operation can initiate an I/O operation and immediately perform other operations, including initiating another I/O operation.

You can use initialization parameters to control the type of I/O operations. For tape backups, you can set BACKUP_TAPE_IO_SLAVES to TRUE to configure backups for asynchronous operations. Otherwise, set it to FALSE for synchronous operations. The default is FALSE.

For disk backups, most modern operating systems support native asynchronous I/O. However, if your operating system does not support it, you can still set BACKUP_TAPE_IO_SLAVES to TRUE and direct Oracle to simulate asynchronous I/O by setting DBWR_IO_SLAVES to a nonzero value. This allocates four backup disk I/O slaves to simulate RMAN asynchronous I/O operations.

Monitoring Asynchronous I/O

To monitor asynchronous I/O operations, you use the dynamic performance view V$BACKUP_ASYNC_IO. The key columns to watch are the following:

- IO_COUNT   Number of I/Os performed on the file
- LONG_WAITS   Number of times the backup or restore process had to tell the OS to wait for the I/O to complete
- SHORT_WAIT_TIME_TOTAL   Total time, in hundredths of a second, taken for nonblocking polling for I/O completion
- LONG_WAIT_TIME_TOTAL   Total time, in hundredths of a second, taken while blocking waits for I/O completion

The largest ratio of LONG_WAITS to IO_COUNT is a likely bottleneck in the backup process. SHORT_WAIT_TIME_TOTAL and LONG_WAIT_TIME_TOTAL are also indicators of a bottleneck if they are nonzero.

This example identifies two input files with nonzero ratios:

```
SQL> select long_waits / io_count waitcountratio, filename
  2  from v$backup_async_io
  3  where long_waits / io_count > 0
  4  order by long_waits / io_count desc
  5  ;

WAITCOUNTRATIO FILENAME
-------------- ----------------------------------------
    .248201439 /u01/oradata/bkup/6bjmt1e3_1_1
            .2 /u01/app/oracle/flash_recovery_area/HR/a
               utobackup/2008_07_31/o1_mf_s_661554862_%
               u_.bkp
SQL>
```

For these two files, you may consider increasing the multiplexing to decrease or eliminate the wait times when backing them up.

Monitoring Synchronous I/O

The dynamic performance view V$BACKUP_SYNC_IO will help you identify bottlenecks in synchronous I/O operations, as well as the progress of backup jobs. You use the column DISCRETE_BYTES_PER_SECOND to view the I/O rate of the operation. You then compare that rate to the maximum rate of the output device, such as a tape drive. If the rate is significantly lower, you can tune the process to improve the throughput of the backup operation by parallelization or increasing the level of multiplexing for the channel.

 EXAM TIP If you are using synchronous I/O but you have set BACKUP_ DISK_IO_SLAVES to TRUE, then the I/O performance is monitored in V$BACKUP_ASYNC_IO.

Two-Minute Drill

Identify Situations That Require an RMAN Recovery Catalog

- If you have several databases to back up, and you want to use stored scripts, then a recovery catalog is highly recommended based on Oracle best practices.

- Having a centralized metadata repository permits easy backup reporting because you can use one set of RC_ views in one database to query backup information.

- There is no limit to the time for which a catalog will store metadata regarding backups: this makes it possible to automate restore operations involving backups taken at any time in the past.

Create and Configure a Recovery Catalog

- The three basic steps for creating a recovery catalog are 1) choose a new or existing database, 2) create the recovery catalog owner, and 3) create the catalog itself.

- The predefined role RECOVERY_CATALOG_OWNER includes all privileges necessary to manage a recovery catalog, such as ALTER SESSION, CREATE SESSION, and CREATE TABLE.

- You use the CREATE CATALOG command to create the recovery catalog.

Synchronize the Recovery Catalog

- The initial synchronization of the recovery catalog uses the target database controlfile.

- Each database to be backed up needs to be registered with the recovery catalog using the REGISTER DATABASE command.

- The catalog will resync with the controlfile-based repository automatically as necessary.

Create and Use RMAN Stored Scripts

- You create stored scripts with either the CREATE SCRIPT or CREATE GLOBAL SCRIPT command.
- Local scripts are available only for the target database.
- Global scripts are available for any target database or even when you are not connected to any target database.
- You execute a global or local script within a RUN block.
- You execute scripts with the EXECUTE [GLOBAL] SCRIPT command.

Back Up the Recovery Catalog

- The recovery catalog database is backed up like any other database in your environment.

Create and Use a Virtual Private Catalog

- A virtual private catalog facilitates the separation of duties among several DBAs.
- One or more virtual private catalogs share the same base recovery catalog.
- You grant the RECOVERY_CATALOG_OWNER role to each Oracle user account that will own a virtual private catalog.
- The base recovery catalog owner can grant permissions on existing registered databases to virtual private catalog owners using the GRANT CATALOG command.
- Once you grant a user the RECOVERY_CATALOG_OWNER role, the user creates the virtual catalog with the CREATE VIRTUAL CATALOG command.
- The virtual private catalog owner uses REGISTER DATABASE to register a new database, just as a base recovery catalog user would.
- You can query the DBINC data dictionary view to determine the databases accessible to the virtual private catalog owner.

Create a Duplicate Database

- The database connected to as the target will be duplicated to the database connected to as the auxiliary.
- Preparing to create a duplicate database includes creating a password file, ensuring network connectivity, and creating an initialization parameter file for the auxiliary instance.

- The initialization parameter DB_FILE_NAME_CONVERT specifies the file system mapping for datafile and tempfile names; the initialization parameter LOG_FILE_NAME_CONVERT specifies the file system mapping for online redo log files.

- The RMAN command for performing database duplication is DUPLICATE TARGET DATABASE. You can specify FROM ACTIVE DATABASE in the DUPLICATE command to create the copy from an online database instead of from a database backup.

- The duplicate database has a new DBID, even if it has the same database name as the source database.

Use a Duplicate Database

- A duplicate database can be used to test backup and recovery procedures without affecting the availability of the source database.

- You can use a duplicate database to test a database upgrade or test performance of application upgrades.

- You can export one or more tables from a duplicate database and import it back into the production database as a secondary recovery method.

Restore a Database onto a New Host

- The instance must be started in NOMOUNT mode, possible with a dummy parameter file.

- The backups and archivelogs must be available on the new host.

Perform Disaster Recovery

- The Oracle home must be installed at the DR site.

- If the current online redo log files cannot be transferred to the DR site, an incomplete recovery must be performed.

Identify the Situations That Require TSPITR

- TSPITR is useful when one or more corrupt or missing tables are isolated to a single tablespace and have minimal or no dependencies with objects in other tablespaces.

- You cannot use TSPITR to recover a dropped tablespace or to recover a renamed tablespace to a point in time before it was renamed.

Perform Automated TSPITR

- The recovery set is the group of datafiles containing the tablespaces to be recovered; the auxiliary set is a set of other datafiles required to recover the datafiles in the recovery set, such as the SYSTEM tablespace.

- The auxiliary destination is a temporary work area used by RMAN to store auxiliary set files, log files, and a copy of the controlfile.

- RMAN drops the auxiliary instance and deletes all auxiliary files at the completion of TSPITR.

- You use the data dictionary view TS_PITR_CHECK to discover dependencies between the objects in the tablespace to be recovered and objects in other tablespaces, and the data dictionary view TS_PITR_OBJECTS_TO_BE_DROPPED to determine objects you will lose after TSPITR completes.

- You perform TSPITR in RMAN using the RECOVER TABLESPACE command with the UNTIL TIME and AUXILIARY DESTINATION clauses.

- After TSPITR is complete, you need to bring the tablespace back online.

Monitor RMAN Sessions and Jobs

- You can join V$SESSION with V$PROCESS to identify the operating system processes associated with each RMAN channel.

- The RMAN command SET COMMAND ID helps you to distinguish processes for different backup jobs in V$SESSION.

- Use V$SESSION_LONGOPS to monitor the status of RMAN jobs that run for more than six seconds; the view contains both detail rows and aggregate rows for each RMAN job.

- You must set the initialization parameter STATISTICS_LEVEL to TYPICAL or ALL before RMAN will record job status information in V$SESSION_LONGOPS.

Tune RMAN

- You can allocate up to 255 channels per RMAN session, and each channel can read up to 64 datafiles in parallel.

- You can calculate the level of multiplexing by using this formula: min(MAXOPENFILES, min(FILESPERSET, files_per_channel))

- You tune the BACKUP command by using the MAXPIECESIZE, FILESPERSET, MAXOPENFILES, and BACKUP DURATION parameters.

- The BACKUP parameter BACKUP DURATION can be set to MINIMIZE TIME to perform the backup as quickly as possible or MINIMIZE LOAD to reduce the I/O demands on the database.

Configure RMAN for Asynchronous I/O

- You set the initialization parameter BACKUP_TAPE_IO_SLAVES to TRUE to configure tape backups for asynchronous operations.

- Setting the initialization parameter DBWR_IO_SLAVES allocates four backup disk I/O slave process to simulate RMAN asynchronous I/O operations.

- Use the dynamic performance view V$BACKUP_ASYNC_IO to monitor asynchronous RMAN operations.

Self Test

1. Which of the following are good reasons to use a recovery catalog instead of the target database controlfile? (Choose three.)

   A. You can keep stored scripts in the recovery catalog.

   B. You save space in the controlfile of the target database used for RMAN backup information.

   C. A recovery catalog is easier to maintain than a controlfile in each target database.

   D. The recovery catalog can report on the tablespaces and datafiles in the target database at any point in time since the recovery catalog was created.

   E. A recovery catalog can be used to manage RMAN information for more than one database.

2. If you do not use a recovery catalog, what data dictionary or dynamic performance views must you query to retrieve RMAN backup information? (Choose the best answer.)

   A. The V$ views on each target such as V$BACKUP_SET and V$DATAFILE_COPY

   B. The RC_ views on each target

   C. The DBA_ views on each target

   D. V$CONTROLFILE

3. Which statement is true about RMAN local and global scripts? (Choose the best answer.)

   A. A local script is available only for a single target database.

   B. A global script references a list of commands in an external file.

   C. A local script references a list of commands in an external file.

   D. A global script can execute commands against many target databases simultaneously.

   E. A local script is available only to the user that created it. A global script is available to all users.

4. You create and execute a stored local script using the following commands:

```
create script full_backup
{
    backup as compressed backupset database;
    delete noprompt obsolete;
}
execute script full_backup;
```

What happens when you run these commands? (Choose the best answer.)

A. The script does not run because it must be executed within a RUN block.

B. A full backup occurs and all previous backups and archived redo logs outside of the retention period or retention policy are deleted.

C. The script creation step fails because you must explicitly allocate one or more channels with a stored script.

D. The script does not run because you must specify a target database when you use a local script.

5. The virtual catalog database owner VPC1 has the RECOVERY_CATALOG_OWNER privilege on the database CATDB2 in addition to the RMAN REGISTER DATABASE privilege. Which of the following sets of commands will allow an 11g RMAN client to create a virtual catalog, register a new database DW, and create a full database backup?

A. RMAN> connect catalog vpc1/vpc1pwd@dw
   RMAN> create virtual catalog;
   RMAN> connect target system/syspwd@catdb2;
   RMAN> register database;
   RMAN> backup database;

B. RMAN> connect catalog vpc1/vpc1pwd@catdb2
   RMAN> exec
    catowner.dbms_rcvcat.create_virtual_catalog;
   RMAN> connect target system/syspwd@dw;
   RMAN> register database;
   RMAN> backup database;

C. RMAN> connect catalog vpc1/vpc1pwd@catdb2
   RMAN> create virtual catalog;
   RMAN> connect target system/syspwd@dw;
   RMAN> grant catalog for database DW to vpc1;
   RMAN> backup database;

D. RMAN> connect catalog vpc1/vpc1pwd@catdb2
   RMAN> create virtual catalog;
   RMAN> connect target system/syspwd@dw;
   RMAN> register database;
   RMAN> backup database;

6. To create a duplicate database, put the following steps in the correct order:

    1. Start the auxiliary instance as NOMOUNT.
    2. Allocate auxiliary channels if necessary.
    3. Run the RMAN DUPLICATE command.
    4. Create a password file for the auxiliary instance.
    5. Ensure network connectivity to the auxiliary instance.
    6. Open the auxiliary instance.
    7. Start the source database in MOUNT or OPEN mode.
    8. Create an initialization parameter file for the auxiliary instance.
    9. Create backups or copy existing backups and archived log files to a common location accessible by the auxiliary instance.

    A. 5, 4, 8, 1, 7, 9, 3, 2, 6

    B. 4, 5, 8, 1, 7, 9, 2, 3, 6

    C. 4, 5, 8, 1, 7, 9, 3, 2, 6

    D. 5, 4, 1, 8, 7, 9, 2, 3, 6

7. You can use TSPITR for which of the following scenarios? (Choose two answers.)

    A. You accidentally drop the USERS tablespace.

    B. You dropped two columns in a table.

    C. You renamed a tablespace and want to recover the tablespace with the old name.

    D. A user deleted most of the rows in a table that does not have any dependencies on objects in other tablespaces.

8. Identify the step you must perform manually after using automated TSPITR in RMAN. (Choose the best answer.)

    A. Bring the recovered tablespace(s) online.

    B. Resync the recovery catalog.

    C. Delete the temporary files created in the auxiliary location.

    D. Create a text-based initialization parameter file for the auxiliary instance.

9. Which of the following two dynamic performance views can you use to identify the relationship between Oracle server sessions and RMAN channels? (Choose two answers.)

    A. V$PROCESS and V$SESSION

    B. V$PROCESS and V$BACKUP_SESSION

    C. V$PROCESS and V$BACKUP_ASYNC_IO

    D. V$BACKUP_ASYNC_IO and V$SESSION

    E. V$BACKUP_SYNC_IO and V$BACKUP_ASYNC_IO

10. The initialization parameters in your database are set as follows:

```
BACKUP_TAPE_IO_SLAVES = TRUE
LARGE_POOL_SIZE = 50M
JAVA_POOL_SIZE = 75M
PGA_AGGREGATE_TARGET = 20M
```

Identify the correct statement regarding where RMAN allocates the memory buffers for tape backup. (Choose the best answer.)

A. RMAN uses the Java pool in the SGA.

B. RMAN uses the shared pool in the SGA.

C. RMAN allocates memory from the large pool in the PGA.

D. RMAN allocates memory from the large pool in the SGA.

Self Test Answers

1. ☑ **A, D,** and **E.** Using a recovery catalog allows you to create and maintain stored scripts. In addition, it keeps a running history of all changes to the database tablespaces and datafiles because the recovery catalog was created. Finally, you can store recovery information for more than one database in a recovery catalog.

   ☒ **B** and **C.** **B** is not a good reason to use a recovery catalog because the RMAN repository information is always stored in the controlfile even if you use a recovery catalog. **C** is also not a good reason, because a recovery catalog requires more setup and maintenance in addition to a backup of another database. Also, the controlfile is simpler to manage, and its size can be controlled with the parameter `CONTROL_FILE_RECORD_KEEP_TIME`. It is much simpler to export a copy of the controlfile whenever the database structure changes using `ALTER DATABASE BACKUP CONTROLFILE TO TRACE`.

2. ☑ **A.** When you do not use a recovery catalog, information about RMAN backups is available on each individual target in dynamic performance views such as `V$BACKUP_SET` and `V$DATAFILE_COPY`. These views are sourced from the target database controlfile.

   ☒ **B, C,** and **D.** **B** is wrong because the `RC_` views exist only in the database containing the recovery catalog. **C** is wrong because the `DBA_` views do not maintain RMAN information. **D** is wrong because `V$CONTROLFILE` contains only the locations of each copy of the target database's controlfile.

3. ☑ **A.** A local script is available only to the connected target database at the time the script was created.

   ☒ **B, C, D,** and **E. B** and **C** are wrong because both global and local scripts are stored in the recovery catalog. **D** is wrong because any script operates on one database at a time. **E** is wrong because both local and global scripts are available to any user that authenticates with the recovery catalog.

4. ☑ **A.** Stored scripts, whether they are local or global, must be run within a RUN block as follows:

```
run {execute script full_backup;}
```

☒ **B, C,** and **D. B** is wrong because a script must be enclosed in a RUN block. **C** is wrong because you can include a channel allocation or use the default channel in the RUN command containing the EXECUTE SCRIPT command. **D** is wrong because both local and global scripts apply only to the currently connected target database.

5. ☑ **D.** To create the virtual catalog, you connect to the base catalog, create the virtual catalog, connect to the target database, register the database, and finally back it up. You need to create the virtual catalog only once, and each target database needs to be registered only once. Subsequent backup operations can occur after connecting to the base catalog and the target database.

☒ **A, B,** and **C. A** is wrong because the base catalog and virtual catalog are on the instance with the service name CATDB2, not the target database DW. **B** is wrong because EXEC CATOWNER.DBMS_RCVCAT.CREATE_VIRTUAL_ CATALOG is only for pre-11*g* clients and must be run by the virtual catalog owner at a SQL> prompt. **C** is wrong because GRANT CATALOG FOR DATABASE DW TO VPC1 must be run by the base catalog owner and only if the database is already registered in the base catalog.

6. ☑ **B.** These steps are in the correct order.

☒ **A, C,** and **D** are in the wrong order.

7. ☑ **B** and **D.** You can use TSPITR to recover from DDL changes to a table; in addition, you can recover a table that has corrupted or erroneously altered rows. TSPITR is also useful if the table is dropped with the PURGE option and therefore not reclaimable from the recycle bin.

☑ **A** and **C. A** is wrong because you cannot use TSPITR for dropped tablespaces. **C** is wrong because you cannot use TSPITR to recover the tablespace with a previous name; in other words, the tablespace was renamed at some point in the past.

8. ☒ **A.** This step must be performed manually after RMAN completes the automated portion of TSPITR.

☑ **B, C,** and **D. B** is wrong because the resync will occur automatically when necessary. **C** is wrong because RMAN automatically shuts down the auxiliary instance and removes all temporary files used for the recovery operation. **D** is wrong because you need to manually create a text-based initialization parameter file for duplicating a database, but not for TSPITR.

9. ☑ **A.** You join the views `V$PROCESS` and `V$SESSION` on the `ADDR` and `PADDR` columns and select rows where the beginning of the column `CLIENT_INFO` contains the string `RMAN`.

☒ **B, C, D,** and **E. B** is wrong because there is no such view as `V$BACKUP_SESSION`. **C, D,** and **E** are wrong because you use `V$BACKUP_ASYNC_IO` and `V$BACKUP_SYNC_IO` to monitor performance of RMAN jobs for asynchronous and synchronous I/O, respectively.

10. ☑ **D.** If you set `BACKUP_TAPE_IO_SLAVES` to `TRUE`, then RMAN allocates tape buffers from the shared pool unless the initialization parameter `LARGE_POOL_SIZE` is set, in which case RMAN allocates tape buffers from the large pool.

☒ **A, B,** and **C.** The parameters `JAVA_POOL_SIZE` and `PGA_AGGREGATE_TARGET` have no effect on the location of the RMAN buffers.

CHAPTER 18

User-Managed Backup, Restore, and Recovery

Exam Objectives

In this chapter you will learn to

The backup tool recommended by Oracle Corporation is RMAN, the Recovery Manager. However, there may be circumstances where it is not the best solution. In some cases (such as damage to a controlfile copy or an online log file) it may be quicker to repair damage using manual techniques, and in some environments there may be hardware- and operating system–based backup facilities available that cannot easily be brought into the RMAN server-managed backup system.

That having been said, always consider using RMAN and always question recommendations not to use it. There is often a political problem with backups: historically, backup and restore often fell within the system administration domain, not the database administration domain; using RMAN can involve a transfer of responsibilities that may not be welcome. This can mean that the decision is not informed solely by technical considerations and may not be made in the best interests of the database users.

User-managed (as opposed to *server-managed*, meaning RMAN) backup, restore, and recovery techniques are fully supported by Oracle, and all database administrators must practice them diligently. They are tested in the OCP examinations.

Backup and Recovery in One Page

Figure 18-1 summarizes user-managed backup and recovery.

Backup can be offline (meaning that the database is shut down) or online (meaning that it is available for use). Restore and recovery can be complete (meaning no loss of data) or incomplete (meaning that you do lose data). Most of this chapter is variations on the steps shown in Figure 18-1.

User-Managed Database Backup

User-managed backup is accomplished with whatever operating system facilities happen to be available and SQL*Plus commands. These may be as simple as the `copy` command on Windows, or `cp` on Unix. The significance of archivelog mode for the backup techniques available is the same for user-managed backup as for server-managed backup: in noarchivelog mode, backup must be closed and whole; in archivelog mode, it can be open and partial. In neither case is an incremental backup possible: operating system facilities are not Oracle aware and will not be capable of identifying blocks that have changed since the last backup, in the way that RMAN can. The granularity of any user-managed backup or restore operation is the datafile, not the individual blocks.

Backup in Noarchivelog Mode

Strictly speaking, there are two file types to consider: the datafiles and the controlfile. There is no necessity to back up tempfiles, because in the event of damage they can always be recreated with no loss of data, and there is no necessity to back up the online redo log files, because (provided the database is shut down cleanly before

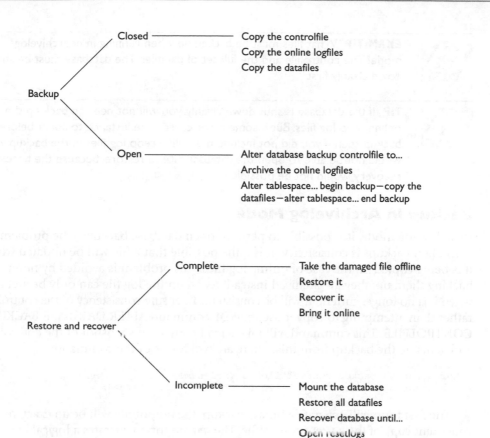

Figure 18-1 The one-page guide to backup and recovery

a backup) they too can be re-created if necessary. However, most DBAs will include tempfiles and online log files in a backup, as this can make restore simpler. The technique is simply to shut down the database cleanly and copy it.

These are examples of SQL commands that will generate a set of Unix commands to be executed from an operating system prompt to perform a whole backup:

```
select 'cp ' || name || ' /u01/backups' from v$controlfile;
select 'cp ' || name || ' /u01/backups' from v$datafile;
select 'cp ' || name || ' /u01/backups' from v$tempfile;
select 'cp ' || member || ' /u01/backups' from v$logfile;
```

TIP It is important to use scripts to generate backup commands. If you rely on naming conventions and standard file locations (such as an assumption that all datafiles are suffixed lowercase ".dbf" and reside in a subdirectory of the ORACLE_BASE), then you will miss any files that happened to be created without following those rules.

EXAM TIP What files must be backed up when running in noarchivelog mode? The controlfile and the full set of datafiles. The database must be shut down cleanly first.

TIP If the database is shut down cleanly, you will not need to back up the online redo log files. But if some error caused the instance to abort before the backup, then if you did not include the online redo log files in the backup you would not be able to open the database after a restore, because the necessary recovery would not be possible.

Backup in Archivelog Mode

In archivelog mode, it is possible to perform open database backups. The problem with open backups is consistency: it is quite possible that a file will be updated while it is being copied. In the case of online log files, this problem is avoided by never backing them up: they are archived instead. As on online log file can only be archived when it is no longer current, it will be consistent. To ensure consistency of the controlfile, rather than attempting to copy it use the SQL command ALTER DATABASE BACKUP CONTROLFILE. This command will take a read-consistent snapshot of the controlfile and generate the backup from this. There are two forms of the command:

```
alter database backup controlfile to <filename> ;
alter database backup controlfile to trace as <filename> ;
```

The first form will generate a binary backup: the output file will be an exact, read-consistent copy of the current controlfile. The second form generates a logical backup: in the nominated file there will be a set of SQL commands that can be used to create a new controlfile that contains the same information on the physical structures of the database as the current controlfile. The CREATE CONTROLFILE command, which must be executed in nomount mode, will generate a new controlfile in the locations specified by the CONTROL_FILES parameter; to run this successfully, you must know the names of all the datafiles and the online redo log files.

EXAM TIP Following a CREATE CONTROLFILE OPERATION, the new controlfile will contain only data regarding physical structures; data regarding, for example, RMAN backups will be lost.

It is not possible to ensure consistency of the datafiles. The problem is the granularity of the operating system's copying. Whatever copy utility is used, it will copy files one operating system block at a time. But when the DBWn process writes to a datafile, it will write an Oracle block. Typically, the operating system block will be different from the Oracle block, in size or in boundaries or both. Consider the case where the operating system block size is 1KB (the Linux default) and the Oracle block is 8KB (the DBCA default): when you launch an operating system copy command, the operating system will bring the command onto CPU, and it will start work. Perhaps it has time to copy four operating system blocks (half an Oracle block) before the operating system's preemptive multitasking algorithm takes the command off CPU. Then the operating system might give some CPU time to the DBWn process, which could overwrite the Oracle block with a new version from the database buffer cache. Then the operating system puts the copy command back onto CPU, and it continues to copy the remainder of the Oracle block—which will be from the new version. In the copied file, this block will be *fractured*—internally inconsistent, because it was updated while being copied. Fractured blocks are useless. Of course, you might be lucky: the copy could go through without encountering this problem. But you cannot rely on this. Note that RMAN, being aware of the Oracle block formatting, can detect if a block was changed while being copied, and will retry until it gets a consistent version.

When making an open backup of a datafile, the tablespace must be put into *backup mode*. In backup mode, the datafile header is frozen, the datafiles are checkpointed, and the redo generation algorithm is adjusted. In normal running, redo is limited to the minimal change vector applied to a block; in backup mode, no matter how small the change vector is, the entire block is written out to the redo stream. This version of the block in the redo stream will be read consistent. This means that if the datafile copy has fractured blocks, they can be replaced with the read-consistent versions of the blocks in the redo stream, which will be available in the archived log files. So when making an open backup, you accept that the datafile copies may be damaged, but this doesn't matter because the information necessary to repair them is available elsewhere.

While a tablespace is in backup mode, the rate of redo generation for all DML against objects in the tablespace will increase substantially. A change that might normally generate only a hundred bytes of redo will generate a full block (perhaps 8KB) instead; you will find that the database is log-switching much more frequently— perhaps every couple of minutes instead of every half hour. For this reason it is good practice to place tablespaces in backup mode one at a time, for the shortest possible period.

The commands to enable and disable backup mode for a tablespace are

```
alter tablespace <tablespace_name> begin backup ;
alter tablespace <tablespace_name> end backup ;
```

A tablespace's datafiles can be copied safely between the two commands. Or to enable backup mode for all tablespaces at once,

```
alter database begin backup ;
alter database end backup;
```

Changes made to blocks of temporary tablespaces are not protected by redo, and it is therefore not possible to back them up safely while the database is open.

EXAM TIP There is no difference between backing up tablespaces of user data, and backing up the SYSTEM, SYSAUX, or UNDO tablespaces: just copy the datafiles while the tablespace is in backup mode. But you cannot backup temporary tablespaces: you can't even put them into backup mode.

Exercise 18-1: Carry Out a User-Managed Backup In this exercise, you will first create a tablespace and a table within it, and then make a backup of the tablespace and of the controlfile.

1. Create a tablespace, with a command such as this for Unix:

```
create tablespace ex181 datafile '/u01/app/oracle/oradata/orcl/ex181.dbf'
size 10m extent management local segment space management auto;
```

or this for Windows:

```
create tablespace ex181 datafile 'c:\app\oracle\oradata\orcl\ex181.dbf'
size 10m extent management local segment space management auto;
```

2. Create a table in the new tablespace:

```
create table t1 (c11 date) tablespace ex181;
```

3. Put the tablespace into backup mode:

```
alter tablespace ex181 begin backup;
```

4. Back up the datafile, using a command such as this for Unix:

```
cp /u01/app/oracle/oradata/orcl/ex181.dbf /tmp/ex181.dbf.bak
```

or this for Windows:

```
ocopy c:\app\oracle\oradata\orcl\ex181.dbf c:\temp\ex181.dbf.bak
```

Note the use of the ocopy.exe utility here: this is a program provided by Oracle (you will find it in %ORACLE_HOME%\bin) that can copy open files, unlike some of the standard Windows utilities.

5. Take the tablespace out of backup mode:

```
alter tablespace ex181 end backup;
```

6. Make a binary backup of the controlfile, nominating any suitable destination, for example:

```
alter database backup controlfile to '/tmp/cf.bin';
```

7. Make a logical backup of the controlfile, nominating any suitable destination, for example:

```
alter database backup controlfile to trace as 'c:\temp\cf.log';
```

8. Inspect the file generated in Step 7. Study all the commands and read all the comments. Many of the commands will be investigated shortly.

Backup of the Password and Parameter Files

It is possible (though, it must be said, unlikely) that consistency issues could affect backup of the password file and of the dynamic parameter file; they could be updated by the instance while being copied. So to be certain, they too should be backed up in a way that will ensure that they can be restored with no problems: a simple copy of the files may not be adequate.

To back up the password file, keep a copy of the command used to create it. For example, on Unix,

```
orapwd file=$ORACLE_HOME/dba/orapwd<SID> password=oracle users=5
```

or on Windows,

```
orapwd file=%ORACLE_HOME%\database\PWD<SID>.ora password=oracle users=5
```

where <SID> is the instance name. If the password file should ever be damaged, simply run the script to recreate it.

To back up the spfile, from a SQL*Plus prompt generate a text file. For example,

```
create pfile='init<SID>.ora' from spfile;
```

If the dynamic parameter file should ever be damaged, recreate it with this command, which can be executed even while the instance is shut down, before nomount mode:

```
create spfile from pfile='init<SID>.ora' ;
```

A static parameter file can be safely backed up with a simple operating system copy command, because by its nature it will be consistent; the instance cannot write to it.

Media Failure That Does Not Affect Datafiles

The technique to restore and recover following media failure resulting in damage to one or more files is dependent on the type of file or files damaged. In some cases, there will be no downtime—the end users may not even be aware that a problem ever occurred—and in most cases, provided the database is operating in archivelog mode, there will be no loss of data.

Recovery from Loss of a Multiplexed Controlfile

As long as a surviving multiplexed copy of the controlfile exists, recovery from loss of a controlfile is simple. Just replace it with a surviving copy of the controlfile. To restore the damaged or missing controlfile copy from a backup would be useless in these circumstances, because all copies of the controlfile must be identical; clearly, a restored copy would not be synchronized with the surviving copies, nor with the rest of the database.

Virtually the moment the damage occurs, the instance will terminate. As ever, the DBA's first reaction to a crashed instance should be to attempt a startup. This will fail, in NOMOUNT mode, with an appropriate error message. The alert log will state which controlfile copy is missing, and also—in the section listing the nondefault initialization parameters—how many controlfile copies there actually are, and where they are. At this point, you have three options. First, you could edit the parameter file to remove the reference to the missing or damaged controlfile copy, as shown in Figure 18-2.

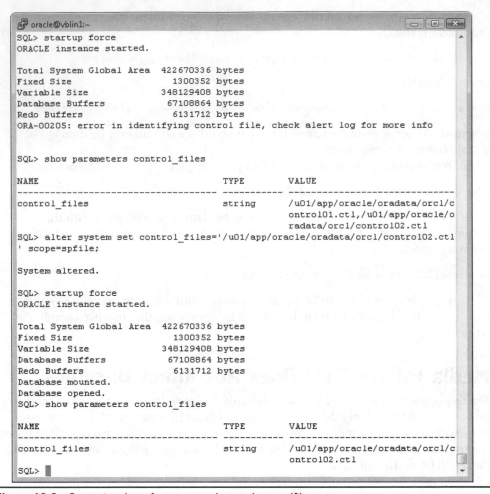

Figure 18-2 Removing the reference to a damaged controlfile

This is fine, but your database will now be running on one less multiplexed copy, which will presumably be in breach of your security guidelines. A better option is therefore to replace the damaged file with a copy made from a surviving copy or indeed to change the CONTROL_FILES initialization parameter to replace the reference to the damaged file with a reference to a brand new file, which is a copy of one of the surviving controlfiles made when the instance is completely shut down.

 EXAM TIP Recovering from loss of a controlfile will entail downtime. It cannot be done online.

Exercise 18-2: Recover from Loss of a Controlfile   In this exercise, you will simulate the loss of a multiplexed controlfile and replace it with a copy.

1. Connect to your database with SQL*Plus, and ensure that your controlfile is multiplexed with this query:

   ```
   SQL> select * from v$controlfile;
   ```

   This query must return at least two rows. If it does not, multiplex your controlfile by following the instructions given in Chapter 14, illustrated in Figure 14-4.

2. Simulate damage to a controlfile by crashing the database (shutdown abort) and renaming one of your controlfiles. Note that on Windows you may have to stop the Windows service before Windows will let you rename the file, and start it again afterward.

3. Issue a startup command. The startup will stop in nomount mode, with an "ORA-00205: error in identifying controlfile, check alert log for more info" error message.

4. Copy your surviving controlfile to the name and location of the file you renamed.

5. Issue another startup command, which will be successful.

TIP Many DBAs do not like to copy a surviving controlfile over a damaged one, because it is all too easy to copy accidentally the damaged controlfile over the surviving one. Do not laugh at this. It is safer to copy the surviving controlfile to a new file, and edit the CONTROL_FILES parameter to change the reference to the damaged file to the new file.

Recovery from Loss of a Multiplexed Online Redo Log File

Provided that the online redo log files are multiplexed, loss of one member will not cause any downtime, but there will be messages in the alert log telling you that there is a problem. If you can tolerate the downtime, you can shut down the database and copy a surviving member of the group over the damaged or missing member, but clearly this is not an option if the database must remain open.

For open recovery, use the ALTER DATABASE CLEAR LOGFILE command to delete the existing files (or at least, those that still exist) and create new ones. This can be done only if the log file is inactive. If you attempt to clear the current log file group, or the previous one that is still active, you will receive an error (as shown in Figure 18-3). Furthermore, if the database is in archivelog mode, the log file group must have been archived.

TIP Recovery from loss of a multiplexed online redo log file can be done while the database is open, and therefore does not entail any downtime.

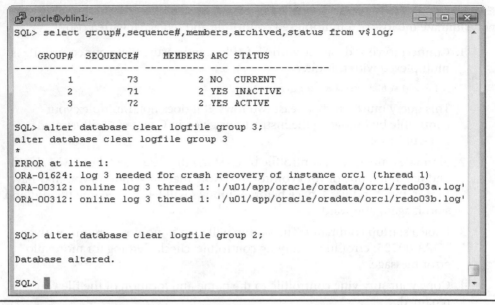

```
oracle@vblin1:~
SQL> select group#,sequence#,members,archived,status from v$log;

    GROUP#   SEQUENCE#    MEMBERS ARC STATUS
---------- ---------- ---------- --- ----------------
         1         73          2 NO  CURRENT
         2         71          2 YES INACTIVE
         3         72          2 YES ACTIVE

SQL> alter database clear logfile group 3;
alter database clear logfile group 3
*
ERROR at line 1:
ORA-01624: log 3 needed for crash recovery of instance orcl (thread 1)
ORA-00312: online log 3 thread 1: '/u01/app/oracle/oradata/orcl/redo03a.log'
ORA-00312: online log 3 thread 1: '/u01/app/oracle/oradata/orcl/redo03b.log'


SQL> alter database clear logfile group 2;

Database altered.

SQL>
```

Figure 18-3   Clearing a log file group with SQL*Plus

Exercise 18-3: Recover a Lost Multiplexed Online Log File   This exercise will simulate loss of a log file member and then, while the database is open, diagnose the problem and clear it.

1. Using SQL*Plus, connect to your database as user SYS with SYSDBA privilege:

   ```
   SQL> connect / as sysdba;
   ```

2. Observe the state of your online logs with the following query:

   ```
   SQL> select group#,status,member from v$logfile order by 1,3;
        GROUP# STATUS   MEMBER
   ---------- ------- ----------------------------------------
            1          /u01/app/oracle/oradata/orcl/redo01a.log
            1          /u01/app/oracle/oradata/orcl/redo01b.log
            2          /u01/app/oracle/oradata/orcl/redo02a.log
            2          /u01/app/oracle/oradata/orcl/redo02b.log
            3          /u01/app/oracle/oradata/orcl/redo03a.log
            3          /u01/app/oracle/oradata/orcl/redo03b.log
   6 rows selected.
   ```

   Confirm that you do have at least two members of each group and that all the members have the STATUS column on NULL, as in the example here. If any groups do not have two members, multiplex them immediately by following the steps provided in Chapter 14, Exercise 14-1. If any members do not have a STATUS of NULL, execute the command

   ```
   SQL> alter system switch logfile;
   ```

   a few times to cycle through the groups, and then rerun the query.

3. Shut down the database:

   ```
   SQL> shutdown immediate;
   ```

4. Using an operating system command, simulate media failure by deleting one of the members. For example, on Windows,

```
SQL> host del C:\ORACLE\PRODUCT\11.1.0\ORADATA\ORCL\REDO01A.LOG
```

or on Unix,

```
SQL> host rm /u01/app/oracle/oradata/orcl/redo01a.log
```

5. Start up the database and simulate user activity by performing a few log switches:

```
SQL> startup;
SQL> alter system switch logfile;
SQL> alter system switch logfile;
SQL> alter system switch logfile;
```

6. Check the state of your log file members:

```
SQL> select group#,status,member from v$logfile order by 1,3;
     GROUP# STATUS  MEMBER
---------- ------- ------------------------------------------
         1 INVALID /u01/app/oracle/oradata/orcl/redo01a.log
         1         /u01/app/oracle/oradata/orcl/redo01b.log
         2         /u01/app/oracle/oradata/orcl/redo02a.log
         2         /u01/app/oracle/oradata/orcl/redo02b.log
         3         /u01/app/oracle/oradata/orcl/redo03a.log
         3         /u01/app/oracle/oradata/orcl/redo03b.log
```

Note that the missing file is now marked as being INVALID, but that the database opened without (apparently) any problem.

7. Connect to your database as user SYSTEM, using Database Control.

8. From the database home page, take the Server tab, and then the Redo Log Groups link in the Storage section to bring up the window shown in the illustration.

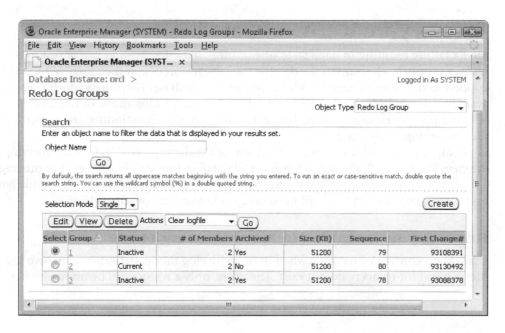

9. If the group with the problem (group number 1 in the example shown) is not INACTIVE, use the Switch Logfile choice in the Actions drop-down list and click Go to force log switches until it is inactive.

10. Clear the log file group by selecting its radio button using the Clear Logfile choice in the Actions drop-down list, and clicking Go.

11. In your SQL*Plus session, confirm that the problem has been fixed by running the query from Step 6.

 EXAM TIP Damage to a multiplexed online log file results in neither downtime nor data loss; damage to a nonmultiplexed log file group (or every member of a multiplexed group) may result in both.

Recovery from Loss of a Tempfile

If a tempfile is damaged, the database will remain open. It can also be opened, if the damage occurred while the database was closed. Users will only become aware of the problem when they attempt to use the tempfile: when their server process finds it necessary to write some temporary data, because of insufficient space in the session's PGA. As a DBA, you should, however, be aware of any such damage: it will be reported in the alert log. To fix a problem with a tempfile, add another tempfile to the temporary tablespace and drop the original:

```
alter tablespace temp add tempfile
'/u01/app/oracle/oradata/orcl/temp02.dbf' size 50m;
alter tablespace temp drop tempfile
'/u01/app/oracle/oradata/orcl/temp01.dbf';
```

Recovery from Loss of Datafiles

Media failure resulting in damage to one or more datafiles requires use of restore and recover routines: a backup of the datafile must be restored, and then archive redo logs applied to it to synchronize it with the rest of the database. There are various options available, depending on whether the database is in archivelog mode or not, and whether the file damaged is one that is critical to Oracle's functioning or a noncritical file containing "only" user data.

In all cases you must determine the extent of the damage. This is done by querying the view V$RECOVER_FILE, which will list all datafiles found to be damaged or missing. This view is available when the database is in mount mode (necessary if a critical file has been damaged) or open mode (if the damage is limited to noncritical files).

Recovery of Datafiles in Noarchivelog Mode

There is no concept of recovery when in noarchivelog mode, because the archive log files needed for recovery do not exist. Therefore, only a restore can be done. But if a restored datafile is not synchronized with the rest of the database by application of archive redo log files, it cannot be opened. The only option when in noarchivelog mode is therefore to restore the whole database: all the datafiles, and the controlfile. Provided that all these files are restored from a whole offline backup, after the restore you will have a database where all these files are synchronized, and thus a database that can be opened. But you will have lost all the work done since the backup was taken.

Once the full restore has been done, the database will still be missing its online redo log files, unless they were backed up and restored as well. For this reason, the post-restore startup will fail, with the database being left in mount mode. While in mount mode, issue ALTER DATABASE CLEAR LOGFILE GROUP <group number> commands to recreate all the log file groups. Then open the database.

In noarchivelog mode, loss of any one of possibly hundreds of datafiles can be corrected only by a complete restore of the last backup. The whole database must be taken back in time, with the loss of users' work. Furthermore, that last backup must have been a whole, offline backup, which will have entailed downtime. It should by now be apparent that the decision to operate your database in noarchivelog mode should not be taken lightly.

EXAM TIP If in noarchivelog mode, your only option following loss of a datafile is a whole database restore. There can be no recovery.

Recovery of a Noncritical Datafile in Archivelog Mode

In an Oracle database, the datafiles that make up the SYSTEM tablespace and the currently active undo tablespace (as specified by the UNDO_TABLESPACE parameter) are considered to be "critical." Damage to any of these will result in the instance terminating immediately. Furthermore, the database cannot be opened again until the damage has been repaired by a restore and recover exercise. Damage to the other datafiles, which make up tablespaces for user data, will not as a rule result in the instance crashing. Oracle will take the damaged files offline, making their contents inaccessible, but the rest of the database should remain open. How your application software will react to this will depend on how it is structured and written.

TIP Is it safe to run your application with part of the database unavailable? This is a matter for discussion with your developers and business analysts, and an important point to consider when deciding on how to spread your segments across tablespaces.

The restore and complete recovery of a datafile can succeed only if all the archive log files generated since the last backup of the datafile are available. If for some reason an archive log file is missing or corrupted, the recovery will fail and the only option is a complete restore, and an incomplete recovery up to the missing archive, which will mean loss of all work done subsequently.

There are four steps for open recovery of a noncritical datafile:

1. Take the damaged file offline.
2. Restore the file.
3. Recover the file.
4. Bring the file online.

Exercise 18-4: Recover from Loss of a Noncritical Datafile In this exercise you will restore and recover the datafile created in Exercise 18-1.

1. Simulate a disk failure by corrupting the new datafile. On Windows, open the file with Windows Notepad, delete a few lines from the beginning of the file, and save it; it is important to use Notepad because it is one of the few Windows utilities that will ignore the file lock that Oracle places on datafiles. On Unix you can use any editor you please, such as vi. Make sure that the characters deleted are at the start of the file, to ensure that the file header is damaged.

2. Confirm that the file is damaged by attempting to query the table created in the tablespace:

```
SQL> select * from t1;
select * from
             *
ERROR at line 1:
ORA-01578: ORACLE data block corrupted (file # 7, block # 9)
ORA-01110: data file 7: '/u01/app/oracle/oradata/orcl/ex181.dbf'
```

3. From a SQL*Plus prompt, take the file offline:

```
alter database datafile '/u01/app/oracle/oradata/orcl/ex181.dbf' offline;
```

4. From an operating system prompt, restore the backup made in Exercise 18-1. For example, on Unix,

```
cp /tmp/ex181.dbf.bak /u01/app/oracle/oradata/orcl/ex181.dbf
```

5. Issue the `recover` command:

```
recover datafile '/u01/app/oracle/oradata/orcl/ex181.dbf';
```

When prompted, hit the ENTER key to apply the archived redo logs from their default locations. The number to apply will depend on how you completed the previous exercises, but eventually you will see the message "Media recovery complete."

6. Bring the file online:

```
alter database datafile '/u01/app/oracle/oradata/orcl/ex181.dbf' online;
```

7. Confirm that the table is now accessible by running the query from Step 2.

Recovering a Critical Datafile in Archivelog Mode

The datafiles that make up the SYSTEM and the currently active undo tablespace are considered critical by Oracle, meaning that it is not possible to keep the database open if they are damaged. The recovery technique is the same as that for a noncritical datafile, with the exception that the recovery must be done in mount mode because the database will have crashed and it will not be possible to open it. It is not necessary to offline the damaged file. The steps are therefore:

1. Mount the database.
2. Restore the file.
3. Recover the file.
4. Open the database.

Another scenario where complete recovery can be done only in mount mode is if the entire database needs to be recovered. This would be the case if the damage were so extensive that a large proportion of the datafiles had to be restored. The syntax for this, in mount mode, is

```
recover database;
```

This command will roll all the restored datafiles forward in parallel, prompting for archive log files as necessary.

User-Managed Incomplete Recovery

There are four steps to incomplete recovery:

1. Mount the database.
2. Restore all the datafiles (and the controlfile if necessary).
3. Recover the database until a certain point.
4. Open the database with resetlogs.

At Step 2, only restore the controlfile if the current physical structure of the database does not correspond to the physical structure at the time from which the restore is made. If the physical structure is still the same (that is, no tablespaces have created or dropped), then do not restore the controlfile; using the current controlfile, which is aware of all recent log switches and archives, will make recovery simpler. Do not under any circumstances restore the online redo log files: data from the current online log files will be needed if the recovery is to be up to a very recent time.

At Step 3, you have three options: stop the recovery at a certain time, at a certain SCN (system change number), or at a certain log switch sequence number. The time option is most commonly used. The SCN option would usually only be used for instantiating a copy of a database to an exact point for some reason, such as establishing a streamed (replicated) database. The last option would usually be used only if an archive log file is missing or damaged, making it impossible to recover further. Examples of the commands are

```
recover database until time '2008-12-21:13:50:00' ;
recover database until change 93228650 ;
recover database until cancel;
```

PART III

Points to note are, first, that there is no permitted variation in the date format. It must be yyyy-mm-dd:hh24:mi:ss no matter what your SQL*Plus session has its NLS_DATE_FORMAT set to. Second, the syntax for recovery up to a certain archive log file does not allow you to specify which log file: you must stop the recovery interactively, when prompted for the log file that you do not wish to (or cannot) apply. Third, in all cases the recovery will be to the change vector immediately before that requested stopping point: the nominated SCN will not be applied. Finally, if the recovery includes applying changes for transactions that had not been committed at the point at which recovery ceases, these changes will be rolled back.

 EXAM TIP A RECOVER DATABASE UNTIL . . . will stop immediately before applying the change vector of the nominated time or SCN, not immediately after.

If RMAN has been configured, then a user-managed incomplete recovery must be terminated with a fifth step: updating the RMAN repository with details of the RESETLOGS operation. The problem is that without this, RMAN will observe that the log switch sequence number recorded in the controlfile has dropped to 1, and will not know if this is because you deliberately reset it (in which case RMAN should do nothing) or because you have restored an old controlfile (in which case RMAN should recover it). From an RMAN prompt, the command to do this is RESET DATABASE.

Exercise 18-5: Perform an Incomplete Recovery In this exercise, back up your database; drop the tablespace created in Exercise 18-1; and perform an incomplete recovery to a point just before this—thus restoring the tablespace. Then the final step: inform RMAN of what you have done.

1. Connect to your database with SQL*Plus, and put the whole database into backup mode:

   ```
   SQL> alter database begin backup;
   ```

2. Identify all the datafiles:

   ```
   select name from v$datafile;
   ```

3. Copy the datafiles to some safe destination, using whatever operating system utility you wish.

4. Take the database out of backup mode:

   ```
   alter database end backup;
   ```

5. Simulate some user activity by executing this command a few times to force some log switches and archives:

   ```
   alter system switch logfile;
   ```

6. Determine the exact time:

   ```
   select to_char(sysdate,'yyyy-mm-dd:hh24:mi:ss') from dual;
   ```

7. Drop the tablespace:

   ```
   drop tablespace ex181 including contents and datafiles;
   ```

Confirm that the tablespace is gone by attempting to query the table t1.

8. Terminate the instance:

```
shutdown abort
```

9. Using an operating system utility, restore all the datafiles from the backup made in Step 3. Note that under Windows, you may need to stop and start the Windows service in order to release file locks.

10. Start up the database in mount mode:

```
startup mount
```

11. Recover the database until the time identified in Step 6. Remember that there are no options regarding the format. For example,

```
recover database until time '2008-12-21:18:20:45';
```

You will receive several prompts for archive log files (the number will depend on Step 5). You can press ENTER each time, or enter AUTO to allow Oracle to attempt to locate the archive logs automatically. This will succeed, unless you have deliberately moved them.

12. Open the database, with the RESETLOGS option:

```
alter database open resetlogs;
```

13. Confirm that the tablespace has been restored, by querying the table t1.

14. Launch RMAN, and connect to both the target and the catalog. From an operating system prompt:

```
rman target / catalog rman/rman@catdb
```

15. Update the repository:

```
RMAN> reset database;
```

Two-Minute Drill

Recover from a Lost TEMP File

- A temporary tablespace cannot be placed in backup mode.
- Tempfiles would not usually be restored—it is quicker to drop and recreate them.

Recover from a Lost Redo Log Group

- Damaged log file members, or entire groups, can be dropped and recreated, or cleared (which comes down to the same thing).
- Online redo log files must not be backed up for an open backup, and they need not be backed up for a closed backup—if the database is shut down cleanly.

Recover from the Loss of a Password File

- As a rule, the password file need not be backed up. Keep a copy of the command used to create it, and recreate if necessary.

Perform User-Managed Complete Database Recovery

- The SQL*Plus command is RECOVER DATAFILE (in open mode, unless the datafile is critical) or RECOVER DATABASE (in mount mode only).
- The steps for complete recovery of a noncritical datafile are
  Take the file offline.
  Restore the file.
  Recover the file.
  Bring the file online.
- The steps for complete recovery of a critical datafile are
  Mount the database.
  Restore the file.
  Recover the file.
  Open the database.

Perform User-Managed Incomplete Database Recovery

- The options are
  Until a specified time
  Until an SCN
  Until the cancel command is submitted at the recovery prompt
- The steps are
  Mount the database.
  Restore all datafiles (and the controlfile if necessary).
  Recover the database UNTIL . . . .
  Open the database with RESETLOGS.
- If using RMAN, the repository must be updated with RESET DATABASE.

Perform User-Managed Backups

- In noarchivelog mode, a complete backup while the database is shut down is the only option.
- In archive log mode, there are three steps to an open backup:
  ALTER DATABASE BACKUP CONTROLFILE.
  Archive the online redo logs.
  Copy the datafiles, while their tablespace is in backup mode.

Identify the Need for Backup Mode

- In backup mode, datafiles can be safely copied.
- When backup mode is enabled:
  The datafile header is frozen.
  The tablespace is checkpointed.
  The redo generation algorithm switches from change vectors to complete blocks.
- An open backup may contain fractured blocks, but these can be replaced with read-consistent blocks from the redo stream.

Back Up and Recover a Controlfile

- Unless the database is closed, the controlfile can only be backed up with the ALTER DATABASE BACKUP CONTROLFILE command.
- The easiest way to recover from the loss of a controlfile copy is to use another copy.
- A binary backup of the controlfile can be restored.
- A controlfile can be recreated with the CREATE CONTROLFILE command, if all the relevant information regarding datafiles and online redo log files is available.

Self Test

1. How could you diagnose problems with a multiplexed online log file group member? (Choose the best answer.)

   A. Query the V$LOG view.

   B. Query the V$LOGFILE view.

   C. Query the V$LOGFILE_MEMBER view.

   D. You do not need to diagnose it; the instance will crash when the problem occurs.

2. You issue the command ALTER DATABASE CLEAR LOGFILE GROUP 2 and it fails with the message "ORA-01624: log 2 needed for crash recovery of instance ocp11g (thread 1)." What could be an explanation for this? (Choose the best answer.)

   A. Log file group 2 has not been archived.

   B. Log file group 2 is being used for recovery.

   C. Log file group 2 is active.

   D. The group is not multiplexed.

3. During a recovery, it becomes apparent that an archive log is missing. What will be the result?

 A. The recovery will succeed, but some data will be missing.

 B. The recovery will fail.

 C. The recovery will continue, if the damaged file was not from the SYSTEM tablespace or the active undo tablespace.

 D. You must issue an ALTER DATABASE CLEAR ARCHIVE LOG FILE command to regenerate the missing archive.

4. If you lose all of the tempfiles from your temporary tablespace, what is the most likely result noticed by your users?

 A. The database becomes unavailable and users cannot connect.

 B. The users can't perform SELECT statements.

 C. The users cannot add or delete rows in any table.

 D. The users can't use ORDER BY or GROUP BY in their queries.

5. Which is the best method for recovering a tempfile? (Choose the best answer.)

 A. Drop the TEMP tablespace and re-create it with a datafile in a new location.

 B. Add another tempfile to the TEMP tablespace and drop the corrupted or missing tempfile while the database is running.

 C. Shut down the database, restore the tempfile from a backup, and recover it using archived and online redo log files.

 D. Add another tempfile to the TEMP tablespace and drop the corrupted or missing tempfile after the database has been shut down and restarted in MOUNT mode.

6. To restore and recover a datafile that is part of the active undo tablespace, arrange these steps in the correct order:

 1   Bring the file online.

 2   Open the database.

 3   Recover the damaged file.

 4   Restore the damaged file.

 5   Start the database in mount mode.

 6   Start the database in nomount mode.

 7   Take the damaged file offline.

 A. 6,7,4,5,3,1,7

 B. 5,7,2,4,3,1 (6 not needed)

 C. 5,7,4,3,1,2 (6 not needed)

 D. 5,4,3,2 (1,6,7 not needed)

Self Test Answers

1. ☑ **B.** The V$LOGFILE view shows information about each log file group member.

   ☒ **A, C,** and **D.** V$LOG show information for groups, not group members. There is no V$LOGFILE_MEMBER view, and damage to a multiplexed log file member will not cause the instance to crash.

2. ☑ **C.** This is the error generated if you attempt to clear a log file group before it has become inactive.

   ☒ **A, B,** and **D.** A would give a different error, stating that you cannot clear an unarchived log. **B** is not possible because it is archive logs that are used for recovery, and **D** is not relevant to clearing.

3. ☑ **B.** This should never happen, though, if you have multiplexed archive log destinations, as you should.

   ☒ **A, C,** and **D.** A and **C** are wrong because it is not possible to skip over a missing archive log file during a recovery. **D** is wrong because CLEAR applies only to online log files, not archive log files.

4. ☑ **D.** Temporary tablespaces provide sort space for queries that use ORDER BY and GROUP BY when the sort operation will not fit in memory.

   ☒ **A, B,** and **C.** A is wrong because the database remains available for some queries and most DML activity even if the TEMP tablespace is unavailable. **B** is wrong because users can still perform SELECT statements that don't need sorting or the sort operation will fit into memory. **C** is a wrong answer because most DML activity does not require the TEMP tablespace.

5. ☑ **B.** Once the missing tempfile is dropped and a new one added, the TEMP tablespace is automatically available to users.

   ☒ **A, C,** and **D.** A is wrong because dropping the tablespace is not necessary, and you cannot drop the default temporary tablespace. **C** is wrong because you cannot recover a temporary tablespace; there are no permanent objects in a temporary tablespace. **D** is wrong because the database does not need to be shut down to recover a temporary tablespace.

6. ☑ **D.** This is the best (that is to say, the fastest) sequence for recovering a critical datafile.

   ☒ **A, B, C.** A is wrong because no datafile operations can be accomplished in nomount mode. **B** is the sequence for open recovery of a noncritical datafile. **C** would work but includes unnecessary steps.

PART III

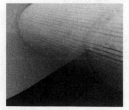

CHAPTER 19

Flashback

Exam Objectives

In this chapter you will learn to

- 053.11.1 Restore Dropped Tables from the Recycle Bin
- 053.11.2 Perform Flashback Query
- 053.11.3 Use Flashback Transaction
- 053.12.1 Perform Flashback Table Operations
- 053.12.2 Configure and Monitor Flashback Database and Perform Flashback Database Operations
- 053.12.3 Set Up and Use a Flashback Data Archive

A long time ago (in a galaxy far away . . . also known as Oracle 5) every version of every data block could be logged to a Before Image file. This provided the rollback function, which was handled at the block level rather than the transaction level. It did provide the capability to "roll back" the entire database but the performance overhead was generally unacceptable, so Oracle 6 introduced row level before image logging in rollback (nowadays, "undo") segments. The option of block-level logging was reintroduced in release 10g as Flashback Database, but in a fashion that has minimal performance overhead. The Flashback Database capability lets you "rewind" the database to some point in the past, by backing out (in reverse chronological order) all the changes made to the datafiles.

This chapter also covers the other flashback technologies available in an Oracle 11g database. These are not as extreme as Flashback Database in that they do not entail either downtime or loss of data. They are still, however, very powerful techniques for recovering from errors by backing out changes that you would prefer not to have been committed. These technologies are Flashback Drop, various forms of Flashback Query, and (an 11g new feature) the Flashback Data Archive.

The Different Flashback Technologies

There are four distinct flashback technologies available, each implemented with a different underlying architecture. Each technology has different capabilities and limitations, but there is overlapping functionality between them. The typical reason for using any type of flashback technology is to correct mistakes—it is vital to understand what type of flashback technology is appropriate for correcting different types of errors.

Flashback Database

Flashback Database is, by analogy, like pressing a rewind button on the database. The current database is taken as the starting point, and it is taken back in time, change by change, reversing all work done sequentially. The end result is as if you had done an incomplete recovery: all work subsequent to the flashback point is lost, and indeed the database must be opened with RESETLOGS. Clearly, this is a very drastic thing to do. It allows you to back out changes that resulted in logical corruptions (in a business sense): inappropriate transactions, such as running your year-end archive-and-purge routines before running your end-of-year reports.

If you have experienced physical corruption within the database or loss of media, Flashback Database will not help—for that, you must use traditional, complete, recovery methods. Flashback Database is an alternative to incomplete recovery following user error—perhaps a more flexible and much faster alternative.

 EXAM TIP Flashback Database will not back out physical corruption, only logical corruption caused by user error.

Flashback Query, Transaction, and Table

Three flashback techniques are based on the use of undo segments. The first flashback capability was initially introduced with release 9i of the database and has been substantially enhanced subsequently.

Flashback Query (the release 9i feature) lets you query the database as it was at some time in the past, either for one select statement or by taking your session temporarily back in time so that all its queries will be against a previous version of the database. This can be used to see the state of the data before a set of transactions was committed. What did the tables look like half an hour ago? This can be invaluable in tracking down the cause of business data corruptions, and can also be used to correct some mistakes: by comparing the current and previous versions of a table, you can identify what was done that was wrong. It is even possible to select all versions of a row over a period of time, to show a history of what has happened to the row, when it happened, who did it, and the identifiers of the transactions that made each change.

Flashback Transaction automates the repair process. Once you have used Flashback Query to identify which transaction it was that caused the problem, Oracle can construct SQL statements that will reverse the changes. This is not the same as rolling back a committed transaction! It is impossible to roll back a committed change, because the rules of a relational database do not permit this. But it is possible to construct another transaction that will reverse the effect of the first, erroneous transaction. Unlike Flashback Database, Flashback Transaction does not imply data loss: all other work done remains in effect, and the database stays current.

The third flashback technique based on undo data is Flashback Table. Having determined that inappropriate work has been committed against one table, you can instruct Oracle to reverse all changes made to that table since a particular point in time, while leaving all other tables current.

Throughout any Flashback Query, Transaction, or Table operation, the database remains open and all objects (including those involved in the flashback) are available for use. Transactional integrity and constraints are always enforced, which means that the flashback operation might fail. For example, if a flashback of a transaction requires an insert into a primary key column, that value must not be in use. Flashing back one table may not be possible if it has foreign key constraints—you will have to flash back all the related tables in one operation.

 EXAM TIP Flashback query, in its three variations, relies on the use of UNDO segments.

Flashback Drop

It is now possible to "un-drop" a table. This is implemented by mapping the DROP command onto a RENAME command. Rather than dropping the table, it is renamed to a system-generated name, and only actually dropped later, when its storage space is needed for a live object. If necessary, and if its storage space has not been reused, the object can be renamed back to its original name and thus restored. Without this capability, the only way to get a table back after a drop would be to do an incomplete recovery to the point in time just before the table was dropped. This was usually time-consuming, and it meant the loss of all work done subsequently. The new Flashback Database capability achieves the same result as incomplete recovery and should be much faster, but work done on other tables following the drop is lost and the database will be unavailable until the operation is completed.

Flashback Drop lets you reinstate the table as it was at the time that it was dropped, with no loss of data whatsoever; the database remains current. This does not require any use of backups, and neither is there any downtime for users. Note that Flashback Drop is specifically for the DROP command; you cannot flash back a TRUNCATE command. Along with the table itself, any associated indexes and permissions will also be restored.

 EXAM TIP You cannot flash back a table truncation, only a table drop.

Flashback Data Archive

Release 11g of the Oracle Database includes a feature sometimes referred to as Total Recall, which is implemented with a Flashback Data Archive. This is the ability to view tables as they were at any time in the past. The forms of flashback described so far all have time limits: Flashback Database is restricted by the size of the flashback logs, flashback query by the undo retention, and flashback drop by the available space in tablespaces. A Flashback Data Archive can be configured to store before-images of rows indefinitely.

Enabling a table for Flashback Data Archive creates another table (and a few other objects) that will store all previous versions of rows: storing them forever if desired. When DML is committed against the table, a background process called the Flashback Data Archive process (the FBDA) will capture the necessary data and save it to the archive. From there, it can be queried with the same syntax used for a regular flashback query—but the flashback can go back years.

When a Flashback Data Archive is created, you specify a time limit (which may be years) and the FBDA will make sure that all data is saved until that time has passed, and will then remove it. The FBDA is responsible for creating the objects in the archive, populating them with rows as necessary, and purging data that has passed the expiry date.

When to Use Flashback Technology

Human error has always been the most difficult type of error from which to recover. This is because as far as the database is concerned, human error is not an error at all. The "error" is just another committed transaction, and the rules of a relational database (the "D" for "Durable" of the ACID test) do not allow Oracle to back out committed transactions. Depending on the nature of the error, the different Flashback technologies may help you to recover, while minimizing downtime and loss of data.

The most drastic flashback technique is Flashback Database. Consider using this only when you would also consider using incomplete recovery—the effect is the same, though the downtime will typically be much less. Examples would include dropping a user or a tablespace on the production system when you thought you were connected to the test system. A critical table truncation (though not a table drop) would also be a time to use Flashback Database.

Flashback Drop will restore a table (together with its indexes and grants) to the state it was in at the time of the drop. Note that this will not restore a truncated table—only one that has been completely dropped. There is no downtime involved, other than the obvious fact that until the table is undropped, no one can get to it, and no work will be lost. Unlike Flashback Database, Flashback Drop does not require any configuration—it is always available, unless you specifically disable it.

For finer granularity of recovery, consider Flashback Table and Flashback Transaction. These should not affect the users at all, other than that the work reversed is gone—which is presumably the desired outcome. Like Flashback Drop, the Flashback Query, Transaction, and Table facilities are always available without any configuration other than granting appropriate privileges. They may, however, require some tuning of undo management.

The Flashback Data Archive is for long-term storage. Typically, this will be for legal reasons: in many jurisdictions there are requirements for keeping data for years, and then for destroying it (sometimes known as "digital shredding"). A Flashback Data Archive can enable this transparently. The DBA can thus guarantee legal compliance without the need for any programming effort.

In some cases, you will have a choice of Flashback technologies. Consider an example where a batch job is run twice. Perhaps you import a few hundred thousand invoices into your accounting system from your billing system every day, and through some mistake and lack of validation the same billing run is imported twice. If the import is done as one huge transaction, then Flashback Transaction will reverse it. But if it is done as many small transactions, rather than reversing them all it may be easier to do a table-level flashback of all the tables affected. It may be that some of the billing system interface tables are dropped after the run—Flashback Drop will recover them. But if the run involves a truncation, the only option is Flashback Database. Also, it may be that the error was not discovered for some time and a significant amount of work has been done based on the erroneously imported data; then Flashback Database may be the only way to ensure that you end up with a database that is consistent in business terms.

When choosing a Flashback technique, always remember that Oracle will guarantee transactional integrity, but that the results in business terms may not be what you want. Flashback Database, or indeed incomplete recovery, is the only way to guarantee absolutely the integrity of the database and conformity with your business rules—but the price in lost time and data may be very high.

 EXAM TIP In the case of media damage, such as losing a datafile, no Flashback technology can help. That is what the standard backup, restore, and recovery procedures are for.

Flashback Database

To flash back an entire database is functionally equivalent to an incomplete recovery, but the method and the enabling technology are completely different.

Flashback Database Architecture

Once Flashback Database is enabled, images of altered blocks are copied from time to time from the database buffer cache to a new memory area within the SGA, the flashback buffer. This flashback buffer is flushed to disk, to the flashback logs, by a new background process: the Recovery Writer, or RVWR. There is no change to the usual routine of writing changes to the log buffer, which the LGWR then flushes to disk; flashback logging is additional to this. Unlike the redo log, flashback logging is not a log of changes—it is a log of complete block images.

 EXAM TIP Unlike redo logs, the flashback logs cannot be multiplexed and are not archived. They are created and managed automatically.

Critical to performance is that not every change is copied to the flashback buffer—only a subset of changes. If all changes to all blocks were copied to the buffer, then the overhead in terms of memory usage and the amount of extra disk I/O required to flush the buffer to disk would be crippling for performance. Internal algorithms limit which versions of which blocks are placed in the flashback buffer, in order to restrict its size and the frequency with which it will fill and be written to disk. These algorithms are intended to ensure that there will be no negative performance hit when enabling Flashback Database: they guarantee that even very busy blocks are logged only infrequently.

When conducting a database flashback, Oracle will read the flashback logs to extract the versions of each changed database block, and copy these versions back into the datafiles. As these changes are applied to the current database in reverse chronological order, this has the effect of taking the database back in time, by reversing the writes that the DBWn process has done.

Since not every version of every changed block is copied into the flashback buffer and hence to the flashback logs, it is not possible to flash back to an exact point in time. It may be that a block was changed many times, but that the flashback log has only a subset of these changes. Consider the case where block A was changed at 10:00 and again at 10:05, but that only the 10:00 version is in the flashback log. Block B was changed at 10:05 and at 10:20, and both versions are in the flashback log. All the changes have been committed. It is now 11:00, and you want to flash back to 10:15. The flashback operation will restore the 10:00 version of block A and the 10:05 version of block B: it will take each changed block back as close as it can to, but no later than, the desired time. Thus Flashback Database constructs a version of the datafiles that is just before the time you want. This version of the datafiles may well be totally inconsistent: as in this example, different blocks will be at different system change numbers, depending on what happened to be available in the flashback log.

To complete the flashback process, Oracle then uses the redo log. It will recover all the blocks to the exact time requested (in the example, only block A needs recovery), thus synchronizing all the datafiles to the same SCN. The final stage is to roll back any transactions that were uncommitted at the point, exactly as occurs at the last stage of an incomplete recovery.

So Flashback Database is in fact a combination of several processes and data structures. First, you must allocate some memory in the SGA (which will be automatic— you cannot control how large the buffer is) and some space on disk to store the flashback data, and start the RVWR process to enable flashback logging. When doing a flashback, Oracle will use the flashback logs to take the database back in time to before the time you want, and then apply redo logs (using whatever archive redo log files and online redo log files are necessary) in the usual fashion for incomplete recovery to bring the datafiles forward to the exact time you want. Then the database can be opened with a new incarnation, in the same manner as following a normal incomplete recovery.

 EXAM TIP Flashback Database requires archivelog mode and the use of ALTER DATABASE OPEN RESETLOGS to create a new incarnation of the database.

Flashback Database requires archivelog mode, because without the availability of the archive log stream it would not be possible to convert the inconsistent version of the database produced by the application of flashback logs to a consistent version that can be opened. So what is the benefit of Flashback Database over incomplete recovery, which also requires archive log mode? It is in the speed and convenience with which you can take the database back in time.

An incomplete recovery is always time-consuming, because part of the process is a full restore. The time for an incomplete recovery is to a large extent proportional to the size of the database. By contrast, the time needed for a database flashback is largely proportional to the number of changes that need to be backed out. In any normal environment, the volume of changed data will be tiny when compared to the total volume of data, so a flashback should be many times faster. Furthermore, Flashback Database is very easy to use. Once configured, flashback logging will proceed completely unattended and a database can be flashed back very easily with one command. There are none of the possibilities for error inherent in a traditional restore and recover operation.

Configuring Flashback Database

Configuring a database to enable Flashback Database does require downtime: there is a command that can only be issued while the database is in mount mode. To configure Flashback Database, follow these steps:

1. Ensure that the database is in archivelog mode.

   Archive log mode is a prerequisite for enabling Flashback Database. Confirm this by querying the V$DATABASE view:

   ```
   SQL> select log_mode from v$database;
   ```

2. Set up a flash recovery area.

The flash recovery area is the location for the flashback logs. You have no control over them other than setting the flash recovery area directory and limiting its size. It is controlled with two instance parameters: DB_RECOVERY_FILE_DEST specifies the destination directory and DB_RECOVERY_FILE_DEST_SIZE restricts the maximum amount of space in bytes that it can take up. Remember that the flash recovery area is used for purposes other than flashback logs, and it will need to be sized appropriately. For example,

```
SQL> alter system set db_recovery_file_dest='/flash_recovery_area';
SQL> alter system set db_recovery_file_dest_size=8G;
```

3. Set the flashback retention target.

This is controlled by the DB_FLASHBACK_RETENTION_TARGET instance parameter, which is in minutes, and the default is one day. The flashback log space is reused in a circular fashion, older data being overwritten by newer data. This parameter instructs Oracle to keep flashback data for a certain number of minutes before overwriting it:

```
SQL> alter system set db_flashback_retention_target=240;
```

It is only a target (four hours in the preceding example) and if the flash recovery area is undersized, Oracle may not be able to keep to it. But in principle, you should be able to flash back to any time within this target.

4. Cleanly shut down and mount the database.

```
SQL> shutdown immediate;
SQL> startup mount;
```

5. Enable flashback logging.

While in mount mode,

```
SQL> alter database flashback on;
```

will start the RVWR process and allocate a flashback buffer in the SGA. The process startup will be automatic from now on.

6. Open the database.

```
SQL> alter database open;
```

Logging of data block images from the database buffer cache to the flashback buffer will be enabled from now on.

These steps configure Flashback Database using SQL*Plus. It can also be done through Database Control.

Exercise 19-1: Configure Flashback Database with Database Control   Use Database Control to enable Flashback Database.

1. Connect to your database with Database Control as user SYS.

2. From the database home page, take the Maintenance tab, then the Configure Recovery Settings link in the Backup/Recovery section.

3. In the Flash Recovery Area section, nominate a directory for the flash recovery area and a maximum size. Check the Enable Flashback Database logging check box, and specify a flashback retention time, as in this illustration:

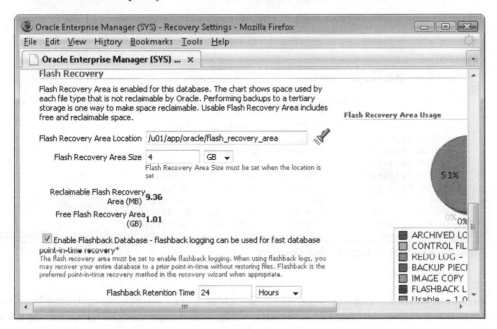

4. Click APPLY. This will lead to a prompt to restart the database, which you must accept to complete the configuration.

Monitoring Flashback Database

The flashback retention target is only a target—there is no guarantee that you could actually flash back to a time within it. Conversely, you might be able to flash back to beyond the target. The possible flashback period is a function of how much flashback logging information is being generated per second, and how much space is available to store this information before overwriting it with more recent data.

The most basic level of flashback monitoring is to confirm that it is actually enabled:

```
SQL> select flashback_on from v$database;
```

On Unix you can see the RVWR process as an operating system process; on Windows it will be another thread within ORACLE.EXE.

To monitor the current flashback capability and estimate the space needed for flashback logs to meet your target, query the V$FLASHBACK_DATABASE_LOG view. V$FLASHBACK_DATABASE_STAT gives a historical view of the rate of disk I/O for the datafiles, the online redo log files, and the flashback log files.

In Figure 19-1, the first query shows the setting for the retention target in minutes, as specified by the DB_FLASHBACK_RETENTION_TARGET instance parameter; this is

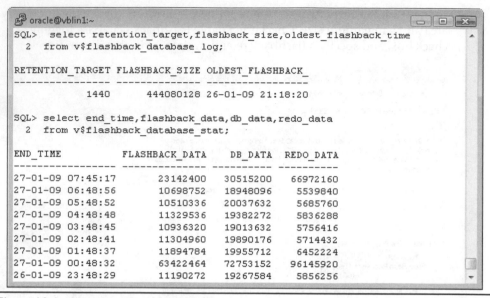

```
oracle@vblin1:~
SQL>  select retention_target,flashback_size,oldest_flashback_time
  2   from v$flashback_database_log;

RETENTION_TARGET FLASHBACK_SIZE OLDEST_FLASHBACK_
---------------- -------------- -----------------
            1440      444080128 26-01-09 21:18:20

SQL>  select end_time,flashback_data,db_data,redo_data
  2   from v$flashback_database_stat;

END_TIME          FLASHBACK_DATA    DB_DATA  REDO_DATA
----------------- -------------- ---------- ----------
27-01-09 07:45:17       23142400   30515200   66972160
27-01-09 06:48:56       10698752   18948096    5539840
27-01-09 05:48:52       10510336   20037632    5685760
27-01-09 04:48:48       11329536   19382272    5836288
27-01-09 03:48:45       10936320   19013632    5756416
27-01-09 02:48:41       11304960   19890176    5714432
27-01-09 01:48:37       11894784   19955712    6452224
27-01-09 00:48:32       63422464   72753152   96145920
26-01-09 23:48:29       11190272   19267584    5856256
```

Figure 19-1   Monitoring Flashback Database

on the default of one day. Then there is the actual space being taken up by the flashback log files, and the exact time to which the flashback logs could take the database back. If the flash recovery area is sized appropriately and the retention target is realistic, then there will be a sensible relationship between the time shown in this query and the current time less the retention target.

The second query shows the price you are paying for enabling Flashback Database, in terms of the bytes of I/O that it necessitates per hour. The top row will always be an incomplete hour, up to the current time. In the example, the database was generating about 10MB of flashback data per hour through the night, with higher rates in the late evening and morning. The impact of this on performance will need to be discussed with your system administrators, bearing in mind whether the system is I/O bound or not. For comparison, the view also shows the I/O related to normal database activity. The view will have one row per hour.

The size of the flashback buffer is outside the DBA's control, but to see the current size, you can query the V$SGASTAT view:

```
SQL> select * from v$sgastat where name = 'flashback generation buff';
POOL          NAME                           BYTES
------------- ------------------------------ ----------
shared pool   flashback generation buff       3981204
```

Flashback Database can also be monitored through Database Control. Navigate to the Configure Recovery Settings window as in Exercise 19-1, and you will see the equivalent information, with the exception of the flashback buffer size.

Using Flashback Database

There are three interfaces to Flashback Database: SQL*Plus, RMAN, and Database Control. Whichever tool you choose to use, the method is the same:

- Shut down the database.
- Mount the database.
- Flash back to a time, an SCN, or a log switch sequence number.
- Open the database with RESETLOGS.

Provided that all archive logs required are available, a flashback operation will proceed completely automatically.

Flashback with SQL*Plus

The SQL*Plus flashback syntax will accept either a timestamp or a system change number argument—unlike RMAN, it will not accept a date nor a log switch sequence number.

If you are not sure exactly what time you need to go back to (you will be very fortunate if you know the exact timestamp or SCN), you can have several attempts, by combining flashback with recovery. Consider this scenario:

It is 20 December 2008. At about 10:00 a junior DBA dropped an important schema on the production database. This is terrifyingly easy to do: perhaps during an upgrade of software on a development system—when connected to the production database by mistake. The error is noticed within ten minutes, but it is a big busy database in a call center, used for taking orders, and every second of processing counts. The first step is to shut down the database:

```
SQL> shutdown abort;
```

There is no point in using any other type of shutdown—all work in progress is going to be lost anyway, and you need to minimize the downtime. Then take the database back to 10:00 as follows:

```
SQL> startup mount;
SQL> flashback database to timestamp
to_timestamp('20-12-08 10:00:00','dd-mm-yy hh24:mi:ss');
SQL> alter database open read only;
```

Note that unlike RECOVER DATABASE UNTIL TIME, this command is sensitive to NLS settings for the timestamp format. While in READ ONLY mode, you can run a query against the dropped schema. If you discover that the schema is still there, perhaps you can recover a bit more user data:

```
SQL> shutdown abort;
SQL> startup mount;
SQL> recover database until time '2008-12-20:10:02:00';
SQL> alter database open read only;
```

You run your test query again, and you discover that after recovering two more minutes of data the schema is gone: it must have been dropped between 10:00 and 10:02. So you split the difference:

```
SQL> shutdown abort;
SQL> startup mount;
SQL> flashback database to timestamp
to_timestamp('20-12-08 10:01:00','dd-mm-yy hh24:mi:ss');
SQL> alter database open read only;
```

If the schema is not there now, flash back a few seconds earlier. If it is there, do a few seconds of recovery. You can repeatedly issue flashback and recover commands until you find the time that you want, testing by running queries while in read-only mode. When you get to a point you are satisfied with, do one final shutdown and open with RESETLOGS to create a new incarnation of the database that can be opened for normal use:

```
SQL> shutdown abort;
SQL> startup mount;
SQL> alter database open resetlogs;
```

This method will minimize the loss of data, and it may take only a few minutes. An incomplete recovery might take hours, particularly if you need to have several tries before you get to the right time.

 TIP Many sites name machines following conventions such as sun1p1 for the production server; sun1d1 for the development server; sun1t1 for the test server; and so on. The various databases and instances may have exactly the same names. Get one key wrong, and you are connected to the wrong database. Always check where you are before doing anything.

Flashback with RMAN

Within the Recovery Manager environment you have three options: you can flash back to a time, to an SCN, or to a log switch sequence number, as in these examples:

```
RMAN> flashback database to time =
to_date('20-12-08 10:00:00','yy-mm-dd hh24:mi:ss');
RMAN> flashback database to scn=2728665;
RMAN> flashback database to sequence=2123 thread=1;
```

Apart from the minor changes in syntax, RMAN flashback is the same as SQL*Plus flashback. In particular, you can use the same technique of repeatedly applying flashback and recovery until you find the optimal point to open the database.

Flashback with Database Control

If Flashback Database has been enabled, then Database Control will be aware of this. If you request a point-in-time recovery, Database Control will suggest flashback by default if there is sufficient information in the flashback logs, but you can elect to do an incomplete recovery instead if you wish. The assumption is that flashback is generally much faster than incomplete recovery.

The options for database flashback are to a time, an SCN, or a log switch sequence number. The only limitation to be aware of is that the granularity of the time-based flashback with Database Control is only to the minute, whereas RMAN can flash back to a second and SQL*Plus can flash back to a timestamp—which can be to a millionth of a second.

Exercise 19-2: Use Flashback Database with Database Control

Simulate a bad transaction against a table, and flash back the database to before the transaction. This exercise assumes that Exercise 19-1 has been completed, so that flashback logging is running.

1. Connect to your database with SQL*Plus as user SYSTEM.

2. Create a table, and count the rows within it:

```
SQL> create table test as select * from all_users;
SQL> select count(*) from test;
```

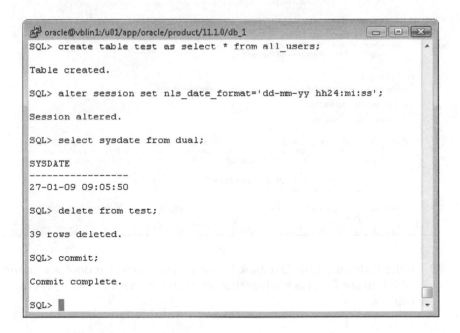

3. Note the current system time, and delete all rows from the table, as shown in the illustration.

4. Connect to your database with Database Control as user SYS.

5. From the database home page take the Availability tab, and click the Perform Recovery link in the Manage section.

6. In the Perform Recovery window, select Whole Database in the Recovery Scope drop-down box, and the "Recover to the current time or a previous point-in-time" radio button. Click RECOVER to continue.

7. Accept the request to restart the database, and repeat Step 6. As your database is now in mount mode, you will be able to click PERFORM RECOVERY to continue.

8. In the Perform Whole Database Recovery: Point-In-Time window, review the details regarding flashback. Select the "Recover to a prior point-in-time" radio button, and enter the time noted in Step 3, as in the illustration. Click NEXT to continue.

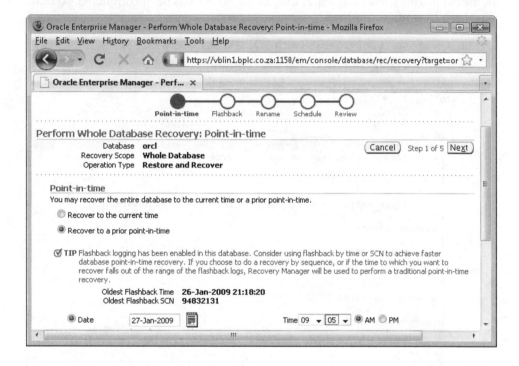

9. In the Perform Whole Database Recovery: Flashback: window, accept the default to use flashback rather than incomplete recovery. Click NEXT to continue.

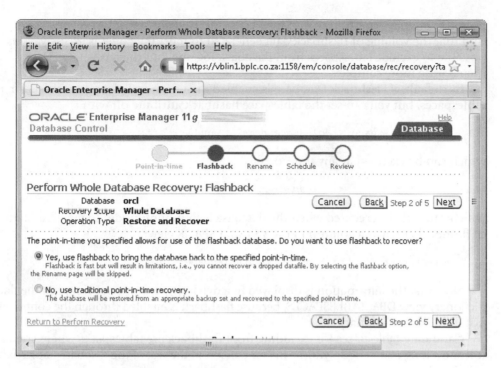

10. In the Perform Recovery: Review window, study the RMAN script that will be executed. This will be very simple. For example:

```
run { flashback database
to time "to_date('2009-01-27 09:05:58', 'YYYY-MM-DD HH24:MI:SS')";}
```

and click SUBMIT.

11. When the flashback is finished, click OPEN DATABASE to complete the operation with RESETLOGS.

12. Return to your SQL*Plus session and rerun the query in Step 2 to confirm that the table is as it was before the bad transaction.

Limiting the Amount of Flashback Data Generated

Enabling Flashback Database may have an effect on online performance. The algorithm Oracle uses to restrict the amount of data written out to the flashback logs is designed to minimize the impact on performance, but (particularly on a system that is I/O bound) you may want to restrict it further. In some circumstances, you could also find that the volume of flashback data generated to meet the target is excessive. It is possible to exclude tablespaces from flashback logging, but the recovery process is then a little more complex.

By default, if Flashback Database is enabled then flashback data is recorded for all tablespaces, but you can set the tablespace flashback attribute off with

```
SQL> alter tablespace <tablespace_name> flashback off;
```

which can be executed at any time, or

```
SQL> alter tablespace <tablespace_name> flashback on;
```

which can only be executed when the database is in mount mode. To view the status of flashback, there is a column in the V$TABLESPACE view:

```
SQL> select name,flashback_on from v$tablespace;
```

Note that the information is displayed in a dynamic performance view, not the data dictionary view DBA_TABLESPACES, because flashback is enabled through the controlfile, not in the data dictionary.

Candidate tablespaces for excluding from flashback are tablespaces where you can tolerate a long period of downtime in comparison to the rest of the database; tablespaces you can drop whenever you please; or tablespaces that can be restored and recovered very quickly.

If one or more tablespaces are not generating flashback data, then before carrying out a flashback operation the files making up the tablespaces must be taken offline. Then the flashback, including the implicit recovery, can proceed as normal. Remember that offline datafiles are ignored by RECOVER—it is the same with FLASHBACK.

You will not be able to open the database (with or without RESETLOGS) until you have either dropped the datafiles making up the off-lined tablespaces, or restored and recovered them to the same point as the flashback. To drop them is a drastic action, but if it is a tablespace that you can just drop and recreate, and reinstantiate the objects within it, then this will minimize the downtime. Otherwise, after the flashback bring the datafiles making up the tablespace online. Then restore them, and do an incomplete recovery up to the time to which you flashed back. This will synchronize all the datafiles, and you can then open them with RESETLOGS.

 TIP Excluding some tablespaces from flashback logging will help with online performance, but the price you pay is that you will have to do a partial restore as part of the recovery process. This will generally still be quicker than the full restore needed for an incomplete recovery.

Flashback Drop

Accidentally dropping a table is very easy to do. It is not just that you can drop the wrong table because of a typing error—it could be the right table, but you are connected to the wrong schema, or logged on to the wrong instance. You can reduce the likelihood of this by setting your SQL*Plus prompt, for example,

```
SQL> set sqlprompt "_user'@'_connect_identifier>"
SYSTEM@orcl11g>
```

TIP To set your sqlprompt automatically for all SQL*Plus sessions, put the preceding command into the glogin.sql file, in the ORACLE_HOME/sqlplus/admin directory.

Flashback Drop lets you reinstate a previously dropped table (but not a truncated table!) exactly as it was before the drop. All the indexes will also be recovered, and also any triggers and grants. Unique, primary key, and not-null constraints will also be recovered—but not foreign key constraints.

EXAM TIP The Flashback Drop command applies only to tables, but all associated objects will also be recovered—except for foreign key constraints.

The Implementation of Flashback Drop

Up to and including release 9i of the Oracle Database, when a table was dropped all references to it were removed from the data dictionary. If it were possible to see the source code for the old DROP TABLE command, you would see that it was actually a series of DELETE commands against the various tables in the SYS schema that define a table and its space usage, followed by a COMMIT. There was no actual clearing of data from disk, but the space used by a dropped table was flagged as being unused, and thus available for reuse. Even though the blocks of the table were still there, there was no possible way of getting to them, because the data dictionary would have no record of which blocks were part of the dropped table. The only way to recover a dropped table was to do a point-in-time recovery, restoring a version of the database from before the drop when the data dictionary still knew about the table.

From release 10g onward of the Oracle Database, the implementation of the DROP TABLE command has been completely changed. Tables are no longer dropped at all; they are renamed.

In Figure 19-2, you can see that a table, OLD_NAME, occupies one extent of 64KB, which starts 38281 blocks into file four. After the rename to NEW_NAME, the storage is exactly the same—therefore the table is the same. Querying the view DBA_OBJECTS .OBJECT_ID would show that the table's object number had not changed either.

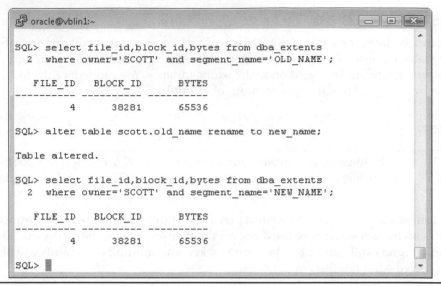

```
oracle@vblin1:~

SQL> select file_id,block_id,bytes from dba_extents
  2  where owner='SCOTT' and segment_name='OLD_NAME';

   FILE_ID    BLOCK_ID        BYTES
---------- ----------- ------------
        4       38281        65536

SQL> alter table scott.old_name rename to new_name;

Table altered.

SQL> select file_id,block_id,bytes from dba_extents
  2  where owner='SCOTT' and segment_name='NEW_NAME';

   FILE_ID    BLOCK_ID        BYTES
---------- ----------- ------------
        4       38281        65536

SQL>
```

Figure 19-2   Renaming tables with SQL*Plus

The DROP TABLE command has been mapped internally onto a RENAME command, which affects the table and all its associated indexes, triggers, and constraints, with the exception of foreign key constraints, which are dropped. Foreign key constraints have to be physically dropped. If they were maintained, even with a different name, then DML on the nondropped parent table would be constrained by the contents of a dropped table, which would be absurd.

Grants on tables do not have names, so they can't be renamed. When you grant an object privilege, you specify the object by name and the underlying storage of the grant references the object by its object number. As the object numbers don't get changed by a RENAME operation, the grants remain valid.

As far as normal SELECT and DML statements are concerned, a dropped table is definitely dropped. There is no change to any other commands, and all your software will assume that a dropped table really is gone. But now that DROP is in fact RENAME, it becomes possible to undrop—by renaming the table back to its original name. However, this is not guaranteed to succeed. It may be that the space occupied by the dropped table has been reused. There are also complications if in the interim period another table has been created, reusing the same name as the dropped table.

The dropped objects can be queried, by looking at the "recycle bin" to obtain their new names. This is a listing of all objects that have been dropped, mapping the original table and index names onto the system-generated names of the dropped objects. There is a recycle bin for each user, visible in the USER_RECYCLEBIN data dictionary view, or for a global picture you can query DBA_RECYCLEBIN. The space occupied by the recycle bin objects will be reused automatically when a tablespace comes under space pressure (after which time the objects cannot be recovered), or you can manually force Oracle to really drop the objects with the PURGE command.

TIP There are no guarantees of success with Flashback Drop, but it may well work. The sooner you execute it, the greater the likelihood of success.

Using Flashback Drop

Consider the example in Figure 19-3. This is the most basic use of Flashback Drop. The DROP command renames the table to a system-generated name, and Flashback Drop brings it back. Variations in syntax are

```
SQL> drop table <table_name> purge;
SQL> flashback table <table_name> to before drop rename to <new_name> ;
```

The first command really will drop the table. The PURGE keyword instructs Oracle to revert to the original meaning of DROP: all references to the table are deleted, and it can never be brought back. The second command will flash back the table but give it a new name. This would be essential if, between the drop and the flashback, another table had been created with the same name as the dropped table. Note that although

Figure 19-3
Using Flashback
Drop

```
oracle@vblin1:~

SQL> create table drop_tab (c1 date);

Table created.

SQL> insert into drop_tab values(sysdate);

1 row created.

SQL> commit;

Commit complete.

SQL> drop table drop_tab;

Table dropped.

SQL> select * from drop_tab;
select * from drop_tab
              *
ERROR at line 1:
ORA-00942: table or view does not exist


SQL> flashback table drop_tab to before drop;

Flashback complete.

SQL> select * from drop_tab;

C1
---------
27-JAN-09

SQL>
```

a table can be renamed during a flashback, it cannot change schemas: all flashback operations occur within the schema to which the object belongs. The indexes, triggers, and constraints that are flashed back along with the table keep their recycle bin names. If you want to return them to their original names, you must rename them manually after the flashback.

There are two points to emphasize here. First, Flashback Drop can only recover from a DROP. It cannot recover from a TRUNCATE. Second, if you drop a user with, for example,

```
SQL> drop user scott cascade;
```

you will not be able to recover any of SCOTT's tables with flashback. The drop of the schema means that Oracle cannot maintain the objects at all, even in the recycle bin, because there is no user to whom to connect them.

Database Control also has an interface to Flashback Drop. From the database home page, take the Availability tab and then Perform Recovery in the Manage section. In the drop-down box for Recovery Scope, select TABLES, and then the radio button for Flashback Dropped Tables. This will take you to the Perform Object Level Recovery: Dropped Objects Selection window (shown in Figure 19-4), where you can

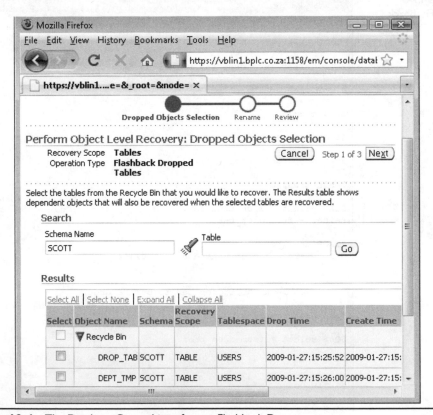

Figure 19-4 The Database Control interface to Flashback Drop

view all the dropped tables in your database. From here you can select from the dropped tables, or go on to recover (and, optionally, rename) them.

The SQL*Plus command SHOW RECYCLEBIN will display the dropped objects, with their original names and their recycle bin names. The view DBA_RECYCLEBIN provides the same information, and more.

If a table is dropped, and then another table is created with the same name and then also dropped, there will be two tables in the recycle bin. They will have different recycle bin names, but the same original name. By default, a Flashback Drop command will always recover the most recent version of the table, but if this is not the version you want, you can specify the recycle bin name of the version you want recovered, rather than the original name. For example,

```
SQL> flashback table "BIN$sn0WEwXuTum7c1Vx4d0caA==$0" to before drop;
```

Exercise 19-3: Use Flashback Drop with SQL*Plus   Create a new schema, and a table within it. Drop the table, and then recover it with Flashback Drop.

1. Connect to your database as user SYSTEM with SQL*Plus.

2. Create a user for this exercise:

```
SQL> create user dropper identified by dropper;
SQL> grant create session, resource to dropper;
SQL> connect dropper/dropper;
```

3. Create a table, with an index and a constraint, and insert a row:

```
SQL> create table names (name varchar2(10));
SQL> create index name_idx on names(name);
SQL> alter table names add (constraint name_u unique(name));
SQL> insert into names values ('John');
SQL> commit;
```

4. Confirm the contents of your schema:

```
SQL> select object_name,object_type from user_objects;
SQL> select constraint_name,constraint_type,table_name from
user_constraints;
```

5. Drop the table:

```
SQL> drop table names;
```

6. Rerun the queries from Step 4. Note that the objects have been removed from USER_OBJECTS, but the constraint does still exist with a system-generated name.

7. Query your recycle bin to see the mapping of the original name to the recycle bin names:

```
SQL> select object_name,original_name,type from user_recyclebin;
```

Note that this view does not show the constraint.

8. Demonstrate that it is possible to query the recycle bin but that you cannot do DML against it, as the next illustration shows. Note that the table name must

be enclosed in double quotes to allow SQL*Plus to parse the nonstandard characters correctly.

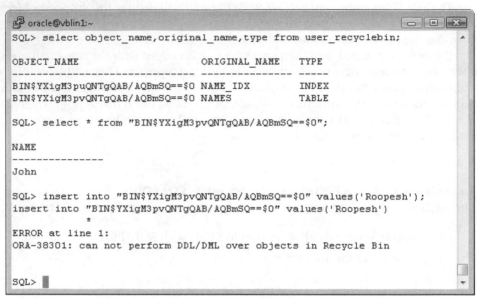

```
oracle@vblin1:~
SQL> select object_name,original_name,type from user_recyclebin;

OBJECT_NAME                              ORIGINAL_NAME    TYPE
---------------------------------------- ---------------- -----
BIN$YXigM3puQNTgQAB/AQBmSQ==$0 NAME_IDX                   INDEX
BIN$YXigM3pvQNTgQAB/AQBmSQ==$0 NAMES                      TABLE

SQL> select * from "BIN$YXigM3pvQNTgQAB/AQBmSQ==$0";

NAME
---------------
John

SQL> insert into "BIN$YXigM3pvQNTgQAB/AQBmSQ==$0" values('Roopesh');
insert into "BIN$YXigM3pvQNTgQAB/AQBmSQ==$0" values('Roopesh')
                *
ERROR at line 1:
ORA-38301: can not perform DDL/DML over objects in Recycle Bin

SQL>
```

9. Recover the table with Flashback Drop:

   ```
   SQL> flashback table names to before drop;
   ```

10. Rerun the queries from Steps 4 and 7. Note that the index and the constraint have retained their recycle bin names.

11. Rename the index and constraint to the original names. In the examples that follow, substitute your own recycle bin names:

    ```
    SQL> alter index "BIN$YXigM3puQNTgQAB/AQBmSQ==$0" rename to name_idx;
    SQL> alter table names rename constraint
    "BIN$YXigM3ptQNTgQAB/AQBmSQ==$0" to name_u;
    ```

12. Confirm the success of the operation by rerunning the queries from Step 10.

13. Connect as user SYSTEM, and drop the DROPPER schema:

    ```
    SQL> connect system/oracle;
    SQL> drop user dropper cascade;
    ```

14. Query the DBA_RECYCLEBIN view to demonstrate that all the objects owned by user DROPPER really are gone:

    ```
    SQL> select count(*) from dba_recyclebin where owner='DROPPER';
    ```

Managing the Recycle Bin

The recycle bin is a term given to the storage space used by dropped objects. You can ignore the recycle bin completely—its management is automatic, both in terms of transferring objects into it when they are dropped, and removing them permanently when the space is needed in the tablespace for live objects. But there may be circumstances when you will need to be aware of the contents of the recycle bin and how much space they are taking up.

The recycle bin can be disabled with the instance parameter RECYCLEBIN. This defaults to ON, meaning that all schemas will have a recycle bin. The parameter is dynamic, and can be set to OFF for a session or for the entire system.

Querying the Recycle Bin

Each user has their own recycle bin, and can always view dropped tables in their own schema. The simplest way is the SHOW RECYCLEBIN command:

```
SQL> show recyclebin;
ORIGINAL NAME RECYCLEBIN NAME                    OBJECT TYPE  DROP TIME
------------- ------------------------------     ------------ ----------
DROP_TAB      BIN$vWMhmt3sTcqJ9WhSREM29g==$0 TABLE        2008-12-27:09:18:42
TEMP_DEPT     BIN$OLp3r9zPRRe6KSjs7Ee3gQ==$0 TABLE        2008-12-27:11:15:50
TEMP_EMPS     BIN$DKaQ10DDSty8hXQH2Xniwg==$0 TABLE        2008-12-27:11:15:36
```

This shows that the current user has three dropped tables: their original names, their recycle bin names, and the time they were dropped. For more detailed information, query the data dictionary view USER_RECYCLEBIN, or DBA_RECYCLEBIN for a global view:

```
SQL> select owner,original_name,type,droptime,can_undrop, space from  dba_recyclebin;
OWNER       ORIGINAL_NAME    TYPE    DROPTIME             CAN  SPACE
----------- ---------------- ------- -------------------- ---  -------
SYS         T1               TABLE   2008-12-04:12:44:05  YES     8
DROPPED     T1               TABLE   2008-12-27:11:23:21  YES     8
HR          DROP_TAB         TABLE   2008-12-27:09:18:42  YES     8
HR          TEMP_EMPS        TABLE   2008-12-27:11:15:36  YES     8
HR          TEMP_DEPT        TABLE   2008-12-27:11:15:50  YES     8
```

The critical column is CAN_UNDROP. Oracle is under no obligation to keep dropped tables or indexes: the Flashback Drop facility is purely a convenience that Oracle provides; it is not part of the relational database standard. If Oracle needs the space being occupied by a dropped object to allocate more space to a live object, it will take it—from that point, the dropped object can no longer be recovered with Flashback Drop and it will be removed from the view. The SPACE column (in units of datafile blocks) shows how much space is taken up by the dropped object.

Having identified the dropped table's name in the recycle bin, it can be queried like any other table, though you will have to enclose its name in double quotes because of the nonstandard characters used in recycle bin names. But always remember that you have a limited (and unpredictable) time during which you can do this. If you think it is likely that a dropped table will be needed, you should undrop it immediately.

EXAM TIP Flashback Drop is not enabled for tables stored in the SYSTEM tablespace: such tables will not be reported by the queries described here, because they are dropped and purged immediately.

Reclaiming Space from the Recycle Bin

Space taken up by dropped objects is in an ambiguous state: it is assigned to the object, but Oracle can overwrite it at will. The normal diagnostics regarding space usage will ignore space occupied by the recycle bin. This means that your "tablespace percent full" alerts will not fire until the warning and critical space usage levels are reached by live objects. Furthermore, if your datafiles have the AUTOEXTEND attribute enabled, Oracle will not in fact autoextend the datafiles until all space occupied by dropped objects has been reassigned: it will overwrite the recycle bin in preference to increasing the datafile size.

Consider this example: a 1MB tablespace, called SMALL, has been completely filled by one table—called LARGE. The space usage alerts will have fired, and querying DBA_FREE_SPACE reports no space available. Then the table is dropped. The alert will clear itself and DBA_FREE_SPACE will report that the whole tablespace is empty, but querying the recycle bin, or indeed DBA_SEGMENTS, reveals the truth—as in Figure 19-5.

This apparently contradictory state is resolved by Oracle reusing space as it needs it. If space is required in the tablespace for a new segment, then it will be taken—and it will no longer be possible to retain the dropped table. If there are many deleted objects in the recycle bin, Oracle will overwrite the object that had been in there for

```
oracle@vblin1:~                                                          □  ▣  ✕

SQL> select sum(bytes) from dba_free_space where tablespace_name='SMALL';

SUM(BYTES)
----------


SQL> select segment_name,bytes from dba_segments
  2  where tablespace_name='SMALL';

SEGMENT_NAME                           BYTES
------------------------------- ----------
LARGE                                 983040

SQL> drop table large;

Table dropped.

SQL> select sum(bytes) from dba_free_space where tablespace_name='SMALL';

SUM(BYTES)
----------
    983040

SQL> select segment_name,bytes from dba_segments
  2  where tablespace_name='SMALL';

SEGMENT_NAME                           BYTES
------------------------------- ----------
BIN$YXoZt4LEtjjgQAB/AQBszA==$0        983040

SQL>
```

Figure 19-5   Recycle bin space usage

the longest time. This FIFO, or First In First Out, algorithm assumes that objects dropped recently are the most likely candidates for a flashback.

It is also possible to remove deleted objects permanently using the PURGE command in its various forms:

```
drop table <table_name> purge ;
```

drop the table and do not move it to the recycle bin.

```
purge table <table_name> ;
```

remove the table from the recycle bin. If there are several objects with the same original name, the oldest is removed. Avoid this confusion by specifying the recycle bin name instead.

```
purge index <index_name> ;
```

remove an index from the recycle bin—again, you can specify either the original name or the recycle bin name.

```
purge tablespace <tablespace_name> ;
```

remove all dropped objects from the tablespace.

```
purge tablespace <tablespace_name> user <user_name> ;
```

remove all dropped objects belonging to one user from the tablespace.

```
purge user_recyclebin ;
```

remove all your dropped objects.

```
purge dba_recyclebin ;
```

remove all dropped objects. You will need DBA privileges to execute this.

Flashback Query

The basic form of Flashback Query has been available since release 9i of the Oracle Database: you can query the database as it was at some time in the past. The principle is that your query specifies a time, which is mapped onto a system change number and an SCN, and whenever the query hits a block that has been changed since that SCN, it will go to the undo segments to extract the undo data needed to roll back the change. This rollback is strictly temporary, and only visible to the session running the flashback query. Clearly, for a Flashback Query to succeed, the undo data must be available.

In subsequent releases of the database, Flashback Query has been enhanced substantially, and it can now be used to retrieve all versions of a row, to reverse individual transactions, or to reverse all the changes made to a table since a certain time. It is also possible to guarantee that a flashback will succeed—but there is a price to be paid for enabling this: it may cause transactions to fail.

EXAM TIP All forms of Flashback Query rely on undo data to reconstruct data as it was at an earlier point in time.

Basic Flashback Query

Any select statement can be directed against a previous version of a table. Consider this example:

```
ocp10g> select sysdate from dual;
SYSDATE
-----------------
27-12-08 16:54:06
SQL> delete from regions where region_name like 'A%';
2 rows deleted.
SQL> commit;
Commit complete.
SQL> select * from regions;
REGION_ID REGION_NAME
--------- ------------------------
        1 Europe
        4 Middle East and Africa
SQL> select * from regions as of timestamp to_timestamp('27-12-08
16:54:06','dd-mm-yy hh24:mi:ss');
REGION_ID REGION_NAME
--------- ------------------------
        1 Europe
        2 Americas
        3 Asia
        4 Middle East and Africa
SQL> select * from regions as of timestamp to_timestamp('27-12-08
16:54:06','dd-mm-yy hh24:mi:ss') minus select * from regions;
REGION_ID REGION_NAME
--------- ------------------------
        2 Americas
        3 Asia
```

First, note the time. Then delete some rows from a table, and commit the change. A query confirms that there are only two rows in the table, and no rows where the REGION_NAME begins with "A." The next query is directed against the table as it was at the earlier time: back then there were four rows, including those for "Asia" and "Americas." Make no mistake about this—the two rows beginning with "A" are gone; they were deleted, and the delete was committed. It cannot be rolled back. The deleted rows you are seeing have been constructed from undo data. The final query combines real-time data with historical data, to see what rows have been removed. The output of this query could be used for repair purposes, to insert the rows back into the table.

While being able to direct one query against data as of an earlier point in time may be useful, there will be times when you want to make a series of selects. It is possible to take your whole session back in time by using the DBMS_FLASHBACK package:

```
SQL> execute dbms_flashback.enable_at_time(-
> to_timestamp('27-12-08 16:54:06','dd-mm-yy hh24:mi:ss'));
PL/SQL procedure successfully completed.
SQL>
```

From this point on, all queries will see the database as it was at the time specified. All other sessions will see real-time data—but this one session will see a frozen version of the database, until the flashback is canceled:

```
SQL> execute dbms_flashback.disable;
PL/SQL procedure successfully completed.
SQL>
```

While in flashback mode, it is impossible to execute DML commands. They will throw an error. Only SELECT statements are possible.

How far back you can take a flashback query (either one query, or by using DBMS_FLASHBACK) is dependent on the contents of the undo segments. If the undo data needed to construct the out-of-date result set is not available, then the query will fail with an ORA-08180, "No snapshot found based on specified time," error.

The syntax for enabling flashback query will accept either a timestamp or an SCN. If you use an SCN, then the point to which the flashback goes is precise. If you specify a time, it will be mapped onto an SCN with a precision of three seconds.

 EXAM TIP You can query the database as of an earlier point in time, but you can never execute DML against the older versions of the data.

Flashback Table Query

Conceptually, a table flashback is simple. Oracle will query the undo segments to extract details of all rows that have been changed, and then construct and execute statements that will reverse the changes. The flashback operation is a separate transaction, which will counteract the effect of all the previous transactions—if possible. The database remains online and normal work is not affected, unless row locking is an issue. This is not a rollback of committed work, it is a new transaction designed to reverse the effects of committed work. All indexes are maintained, and constraints enforced: a table flashback is just another transaction, and the usual rules apply. The only exception to normal processing is that by default triggers on the table are disabled for the flashback operation.

A table flashback will often involve a table that is in a foreign key relationship. In that case, it is almost inevitable that the flashback operation will fail with a constraint violation. To avoid this problem, the syntax permits flashback of multiple tables with one command, which will be executed as a single transaction with the constraint checked at the end.

The first step to enabling table flashback is to enable row movement on the tables. This is a flag set in the data dictionary that informs Oracle that row IDs may change. A row ID can never actually change—but a flashback operation may make it appear as though it has. For instance, in the case of a row that is deleted, the flashback operation will insert it back into the table: it will have the same primary key value, but a different row ID.

In the example that follows, there are two tables: EMP and DEPT. There is a foreign key relationship between them, stating that every employee in EMP must be a member of a department in DEPT.

First, insert a new department and an employee in that department, and note the time:

```
SQL> insert into dept values(50,'SUPPORT','LONDON');
1 row created.
SQL> insert into emp values(8000,'WATSON','ANALYST',7566,'27-DEC-
08',3000,null,50);
1 row created.
SQL> commit;
Commit complete.
SQL> select sysdate from dual;
SYSDATE
------------------
27-12-08 18:30:11
```

Next delete the department and the employee, taking care to delete the employee first to avoid a constraint violation:

```
SQL> delete from emp where empno=8000;
1 row deleted.
SQL> delete from dept where deptno=50;
1 row deleted.
SQL> commit;
Commit complete.
```

Now attempt to flash back the tables to the time when the department and employee existed:

```
SQL> flashback table emp to timestamp to_timestamp('27-12-08 18:30:11',
'dd-mm-yy hh24:mi:ss');
flashback table emp to timestamp to_timestamp('27-12-08 18:30:11','dd-mm-yy
hh24:mi:ss')
                    *
ERROR at line 1:
ORA-08189: cannot flashback the table because row movement is not enabled
```

This fails because by default row movement, which is a prerequisite for table flashback, is not enabled for any table—so enable it, for both tables:

```
SQL> alter table dept enable row movement;
Table altered.
SQL> alter table emp enable row movement;
Table altered.
```

and now try the flashback again:

```
SQL> flashback table emp to timestamp to_timestamp('27-12-08 18:30:11',
'dd-mm-yy hh24:mi:ss');
flashback table emp to timestamp to_timestamp('27-12-08 18:30:11',
'dd-mm-yy hh24:mi:ss')
*
```

```
ERROR at line 1:
ORA-02091: transaction rolled back
ORA-02291: integrity constraint (SCOTT.FK_DEPTNO) violated -
parent key not found
```

This time the flashback fails for a more subtle reason. The flashback is attempting to reverse the deletion of employee 8000 by inserting him—but employee 8000 was in department 50, which has been deleted and so does not exist. Hence the foreign key violation. You could avoid this problem by flashing back the DEPT table first, which would insert department 50. But if your flashback involves many tables and many DML statements, it may be logically difficult to find a sequence that will work. The answer is to flash back both tables together:

```
SQL> flashback table emp,dept to timestamp to_timestamp('27-12-00
18:30:11','dd-mm-yy hh24:mi:ss');
Flashback complete.
```

This succeeds because both the tables are flashed back in one transaction, and the constraints are only checked at the end of that transaction—by which time, the data is logically consistent.

The flashback could still fail for other reasons:

- Primary key violations will occur if a key value has been reused between a delete and the flashback.

- An ORA-08180, "No snapshot found based on specified time," will be raised if there is not enough undo information to go back to the time requested.

- If any rows affected by the flashback are locked by other users, the flashback will fail with ORA-00054: "Resource busy and acquire with NOWAIT specified."

- The table definitions must not change during the period concerned—flashback cannot go across DDLs. Attempting to do this will generate ORA-01466: "Unable to read data—table definition has changed."

- Flashback does not work for tables in the SYS schema. Try to imagine the effect of flashing back part of the data dictionary . . . .

If a table flashback fails for any reason, the flashback operation will be canceled: any parts of it that did succeed will be rolled back, and the tables will be as they were before the flashback command was issued.

Variations in the syntax allow flashback to a system change number, and firing of DML triggers during the operation:

```
SQL> flashback table emp,dept to scn 6539425 enable triggers;
```

Table flashback can also be initiated by Database Control. From the database home page, take the Availability tab and then the Perform Recovery link in the Manage section. Select Tables in the Recovery Scope drop-down box, and then the Flashback Existing Tables radio button to invoke the Flashback Table Wizard.

Flashback Versions Query

A row may have changed several times during its life. Flashback Versions Query lets you see all the committed versions of a row (but not any uncommitted versions), including the timestamps for when each version was created and when it ended. You can also see the transaction identifier of the transaction that created any given version of a row, which can then be used with Flashback Transaction Query. This information is exposed by a number of pseudocolumns that are available with every table. Pseudocolumns are columns appended to the row by Oracle internally: they are not part of the ISO standards for a relational database, but they can be very useful. One pseudocolumn is the row ID: the unique identifier for every row in the database, that is used in indexes as the pointer back to the table. The pseudocolumns relevant to flashback are

- **VERSIONS_STARTSCN** The SCN at which this version of the row was created, either by INSERT or by UPDATE
- **VERSIONS_STARTTIME** The timestamp at which this version of the row was created
- **VERSIONS_ENDSCN** The SCN at which this version of the row expired, because of either DELETE or UPDATE
- **VERSIONS_ENDTIME** The timestamp at which this version of the row expired
- **VERSIONS_XID** The unique identifier for the transaction that created this version of the row
- **VERSIONS_OPERATIONS** The operation done by the transaction to create this version of the row, either INSERT or UPDATE or DELETE

To see these pseudocolumns, you must include the VERSIONS BETWEEN keywords in your query. For example, Figure 19-6 shows all versions of the row for employee 8000.

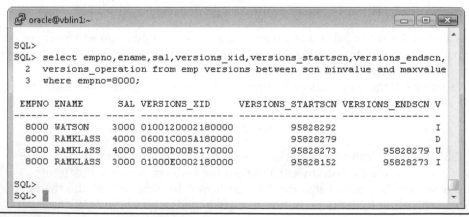

Figure 19-6 Flashback Versions Query

The versions are sorted in descending order of existence: they must be read from the bottom up. The bottom row shows that employee 8000 was inserted (the "I" in the last column) at SCN 95828152 by transaction number 01000E0002180000. The employee was given the ENAME of RAMKLASS and the SAL of 3000. This version of the row existed until SCN 95828273, which takes us to the third row. At this SCN, the row was updated (the "U" in the last column) with a new salary. This version of the row persisted until SCN 95828279, when it was deleted, as shown in the second row. The VERSIONS_ENDSCN column is always null for a deletion. The top row of the result set shows a new insertion, which reuses the employee number. For this row, the VERSIONS_ENDSCN is also null, because the row still exists, in that version, as at the end of the time range specified in the query.

In the example in Figure 19-6, the VERSIONS BETWEEN clause uses two constants for the SCN. MINVALUE instructs Oracle to retrieve the earliest information in the undo segments; MAXVALUE will be the current SCN. In other words, the query as written will show all versions that can possibly be retrieved, given the information available. The syntax will also accept a range specified with two timestamps:

```
SQL> select empno,ename,sal,versions_xid,versions_starttime,
versions_endtime,versions_operation from emp versions between
timestamp (systimestamp - 1/24) and systimestamp
where empno=8000;
```

The preceding example will select all versions of employee number 8000 that existed during the last hour.

 EXAM TIP Flashback Version Query cannot work against external tables, temporary tables, or V$ views. Why not? Because none of these objects generates undo.

Flashback Transaction Query

Flashback Table Query and Flashback Versions Query use undo data for an object. Flashback Transaction Query analyzes the undo by a different dimension: it will retrieve all the undo data for a transaction, no matter how many objects it affects. The critical view is FLASHBACK_TRANSACTION_QUERY, described here:

```
ocp11g> describe flashback_transaction_query
 Name                               Null?    Type
 ---------------------------------- -------- --------------------
 XID                                         RAW(8)
 START_SCN                                   NUMBER
 START_TIMESTAMP                             DATE
 COMMIT_SCN                                  NUMBER
 COMMIT_TIMESTAMP                            DATE
 LOGON_USER                                  VARCHAR2(30)
 UNDO_CHANGE#                                NUMBER
 OPERATION                                   VARCHAR2(32)
 TABLE_NAME                                  VARCHAR2(256)
 TABLE_OWNER                                 VARCHAR2(32)
 ROW_ID                                      VARCHAR2(19)
 UNDO_SQL                                    VARCHAR2(4000)
```

Because the data in this view may be sensitive, it is protected by a privilege: you must be granted SELECT ANY TRANSACTION before you can query it. By default, this privilege is granted to SYS and to the DBA role. There will be one or more rows in this view for every transaction whose undo data still exists in the undo segments, and every row will refer to one row affected by the transaction. The table that follows describes the columns.

XID	The transaction identifier. This is the join column to the pseudocolumn VERSIONS_XID displayed in a Flashback Versions Query
START_SCN	The system change number at the time the transaction started
START_TIMESTAMP	The timestamp at the time the transaction started
COMMIT_SCN	The system change number at the time the transaction was committed
COMMIT_TIMESTAMP	The timestamp at the time the transaction was committed
LOGON_USER	The Oracle username of the session that performed the transaction
UNDO_CHANGE#	The undo system change number. This is not likely to be relevant to most work
OPERATION	The DML operation applied to the row: INSERT, UPDATE, or DELETE
TABLE_NAME	The table to which the row belongs
TABLE_OWNER	The schema to which the table belongs
ROW_ID	The unique identifier of the row affected
UNDO_SQL	A constructed statement that will reverse the operation. For example, if the OPERATION were a DELETE, then this will be an INSERT

A one-line SQL statement might generate many rows in FLASHBACK_TRANSACTION_QUERY. This is because SQL is a set-oriented language: one statement can affect many rows. But each row affected will have its own row in the view. The view will show committed transactions and also transactions in progress. For an active transaction, the COMMIT_SCN and COMMIT_TIMESTAMP columns are NULL. Rolled-back transactions are not displayed.

Take an example where a salary was multiplied by eleven, rather than being incremented by ten percent:

```
SQL> update emp set sal = sal*11 where empno=7902;
1 row updated.
SQL> commit;
Commit complete.
```

Later, it is suspected that a mistake was made. So query the versions of the row:

```
SQL> select ename,sal,versions_xid from emp versions between scn
  2  minvalue and maxvalue where empno=7902;
ENAME           SAL VERSIONS_XID
---------- ---------- ----------------
FORD         33000 06002600B0010000
FORD          3000
```

This does indicate what happened, and gives enough information to reverse the change. But what if the transaction affected other rows in other tables? To be certain, query FLASHBACK_TRANSACTION_QUERY, which will have one row for every row affected by the transaction. A minor complication is that the XID column is type RAW, whereas the VERSIONS_XID pseudocolumn is hexadecimal, so you must use a type casting function to make the join:

```
SQL> select operation,undo_sql from flashback_transaction_query
where xid=hextoraw('06002600B0010000');
OPERATION   UNDO_SQL
----------  --------------------------------------------------------
UPDATE      update "SCOTT"."EMP" set "SAL" = '3000' where ROWID =
            'AAAM+yAAEAAAAAeAAM';
```

This query returns only one row, which confirms that there was indeed only one row affected by the transaction and provides a statement that will reverse the impact of the change. Note the use of a ROWID in the UNDO_SQL statement. Provided that there has been no reorganization of the table, this will guarantee that the correct row is changed.

The view FLASHBACK_TRANSACTION_QUERY will construct undo statements to reverse a transaction, but executing them individually would be an awful task for a large transaction. This is where the DBMS_FLASHBACK package is again useful: it includes procedures to back out transactions. In order to execute the transaction backout procedures, you must have been granted the FLASHBACK ANY TABLE privilege.

Consider this example:

```
ocp11g> execute dbms_flashback.transaction_backout(-
numtxns=>2,-
xids=>sys.xid_array('0900010059100000','02000700920F0000'),
 options=>dbms_flashback.cascade);
```

This procedure call will reverse all the work done by the two nominated transactions. Taking the arguments in order:

- NUMTXNS is the number of transactions that should be reversed, in this example, two.

- XIDS is a list of transaction identifiers, passed as an XID_ARRAY variable. This list would have been identified with a flashback query.

- OPTIONS can take various values, in the form of package constants. The CASCADE option will attempt to order the changes to avoid conflicts.

It is impossible to roll back a committed transaction. The rules of a relational database forbid this. So when the backout procedure reverses one or more transactions, it must construct and attempt to execute more DML, in another transaction, which will reverse the effect of the original transaction(s). This process is fraught with difficulty, because of the possibility of dependencies between the transactions and conflicts with work done subsequently. This will typically show up as constraint violations. The

OPTIONS argument controls what to do if there is a problem. These are the possible values:

- NOCASCADE (the default) will apply undo changes with no attempt to identify dependencies. This may well fail if, for instance, the transactions listed affect tables in foreign key relationships.

- CASCADE attempts to undo the transactions logically such that constraint violations will not occur.

- NONCONFLICT_ONLY backs out only changes to rows that do not cause problems. The database will remain consistent, but some transactions may be incomplete.

- NOCASCADE_FORCE will undo SQL statements in reverse order of commit times.

Whatever changes the DBMS_FLASHBACK.BACKOUT_TRANSACTION manages to accomplish are left uncommitted. This gives you an opportunity to investigate what it managed to achieve before committing (or rolling back).

Figure 19-7 shows an example of combining flashback query with flashback transaction. The first query shows a row, which is then updated and committed. A flashback versions query retrieves the identifier of the transaction that made the change, and passing this to DBMS_FLASHBACK.BACKOUT_TRANSACTION reverses the change. Finally, the reversal must be committed.

```
Administrator: cmd - sqlplus jon/jon                              _ □ ×
orcl > select * from regions where region_id=1;

 REGION_ID REGION_NAME
---------- -------------------------
         1 Europe

orcl > update regions set region_name='United Kingdom' where region_id=1;

1 row updated.

orcl > commit;

Commit complete.

orcl > select region_name,versions_xid from regions
  2  versions between scn minvalue and maxvalue where region_id=1;

REGION_NAME                 VERSIONS_XID
--------------------------- ----------------
United Kingdom              070002000C0C0000
Europe                     0A000C00650C0000

orcl > execute dbms_flashback.transaction_backout(-
> numtxns=>1,xids=>sys.xid_array('070002000C0C0000'));

PL/SQL procedure successfully completed.

orcl > select * from regions where region_id=1;

 REGION_ID REGION_NAME
---------- -------------------------
         1 Europe

orcl > commit;

Commit complete.
```

Figure 19-7   Using the flashback transaction facility

Exercise 19-4: Use Flashback Query with Database Control   Create a table, execute some DML, and then investigate and reverse the changes.

1. Connect to your database as user SYSTEM using SQL*Plus.

2. Create a table and enable row movement for it:

```
SQL> create table countries (name varchar2(10));
SQL> alter table countries enable row movement;
```

3. Insert some rows as follows:

```
SQL> insert into countries values('Zambia');
SQL> insert into countries values('Zimbabwe');
SQL> insert into countries values ('Zamibia');
SQL> commit;
```

Correct the spelling mistake, but omit the WHERE clause:

```
SQL> update countries set name= 'Namibia';
SQL> commit;
```

4. Connect to your database as user SYSTEM with Database Control.

5. From the database home page, take the Availability tab and then the Perform Recovery link in the Manage section to reach the Perform Recovery window.

6. In the Recovery Scope drop-down box, choose Tables, and select the Flashback Existing Tables radio button. Click RECOVER to reach the Perform Object Level Recovery: Point-In-Time window.

7. Select the "Evaluate row changes and transactions to decide on a point in time" radio button, and enter **SYSTEM.COUNTRIES** as the table, as in the next illustration, and click NEXT to reach the Perform Recovery: Flashback Versions Query Filter window.

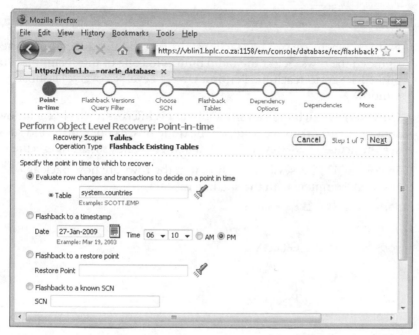

8. In the Step 1 section, highlight the column NAME and click the Move link to select it for the query. In the Step 2 section, enter

```
WHERE NAME LIKE '%'
```

in order to see all rows. In the Step 3 section, select the Show All Row History radio button.

9. Click NEXT to reach the Perform Object Level Recovery: Choose SCN window.

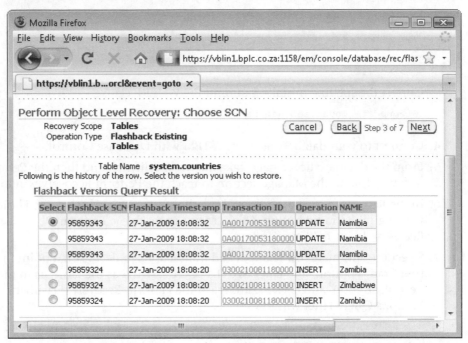

10. Note that there are two transactions: the first did the three inserts; the second updated the rows. Select the radio button for one of the "Namibia" rows, and click NEXT to reach the Perform Object Level Recovery: Flashback Tables window.

11. Click NEXT to reach the Perform Object Level Recovery: Review window. Click SHOW ROW CHANGES to see what will be done by this operation, and SHOW SQL to see the actual FLASHBACK TABLE statement. Click SUBMIT to execute it.

12. In your SQL*Plus session, confirm that the rows are now back as when first inserted, complete with the spelling mistake:

```
SQL> select * from countries;
```

13. Tidy up:

```
SQL> drop table countries;
```

Flashback and Undo Data

Flashback query in its various forms relies entirely on undo data. You are asking Oracle to present you a version of the data as it was some time ago: if the data has been changed since that time, Oracle must roll back the changes. To do this, Oracle needs the undo data that protected the change. Whether the query will succeed will depend on whether that undo data is still available. Consider Figure 19-8.

The first query asks for a view of the table as it was 40 minutes ago, and it succeeds. This is because there is at least 40 minutes of undo data available in the undo segments. The second query attempts to go back 40 days, and it fails. In virtually all databases, it would be completely unrealistic to expect flashback query to work over such a long period. You would probably need an undo tablespace the size of Jupiter to store that much undo data.

Undo data is generated as necessary according to the transaction workload: at busy times of day you may be generating many megabytes of undo per second, at other times you may be generating virtually no undo at all. As undo data can be overwritten once the transaction is completed, the age of the oldest undo data available in the undo tablespace will vary depending on workload. A comprehensive discussion of this was included in Chapter 12 with reference to the ORA-1555 "snapshot too old" error, and this is equally relevant to flashback query.

To guarantee that a flashback query will always succeed for a given period, set the RETENTION GUARANTEE attribute for the undo tablespace, in conjunction with the UNDO_RETENTION instance parameter. This will ensure that you can always flash back the number of seconds specified—but the price you will pay is that if your undo tablespace is not sized adequately for the transaction workload, then the database may hang while performing DML. As discussed in Chapter 12, you must monitor the V$UNDOSTAT view to calculate the necessary size.

```
Administrator: cmd - sqlplus / as sysdba                          _ □ X
orcl >
orcl >
orcl > select count(*) from regions as of timestamp(systimestamp - 40/1440);

  COUNT(*)
----------
        4

orcl > select count(*) from regions as of timestamp(systimestamp - 40);
select count(*) from regions as of timestamp(systimestamp - 40)
                                                 *
ERROR at line 1:
ORA-08180: no snapshot found based on specified time


orcl >
```

Figure 19-8 Flashback query and undo data

The Flashback Data Archive

The three flashback technologies discussed so far (Flashback Database, Flashback Drop, and the various forms of Flashback Query) can be useful, but they all have limited flashback capability. A Flashback Data Archive can be configured to guarantee the ability to flash back a table to any time—perhaps to a time years ago. It can also guarantee that data is removed when it has expired.

Architecturally, Flashback Data Archive requires one or more tablespaces, various segments for each protected table, and a new background process: the FBDA process. The DBA must create the tablespace(s) and the archive(s) within them, specifying a retention period for each archive, and then nominate tables to be protected by an archive. The necessary segments will be created automatically, and the FBDA will start when required. Users and application software will not be aware of any change so far as DML is concerned. Some DDL commands (such as DROP and TRUNCATE) will not be usable against protected tables, as they would remove information from the data dictionary needed to interpret information in the archive. Flashback query commands (such as a SELECT with the AS OF clause) will execute successfully against versions of the table within the time frame specified for the archive protecting the table.

To use the Total Recall facility, implemented by Flashback Data Archives, first create a tablespace. It is technically possible to create the archive(s) in a preexisting tablespace, but it makes sense to separate them from regular data. Then create the archive, specifying a tablespace, a retention time, and (optionally) a quota. For example,

```
create flashback archive default hrarch tablespace fbda1
quota 10g retention 5 year;
```

This command includes the DEFAULT keyword, which means that it will be used as the archive for all tables unless specified otherwise. The default archive can also be set later:

```
alter flashback archive hrarch set default;
```

The QUOTA clause limits the space the archive can occupy in the tablespace. If an archive fills, more space can be added either in the original tablespace or in another tablespace. For example, this command will extend the archive into another tablespace:

```
alter flashback archive hrarch add tablespace fbda2 quota 10g;
```

It is also possible to adjust the retention:

```
alter flashback archive hrarch modify retention 7 year;
```

Data is removed from an archive automatically by the FBDA background process once it is older than the nominated retention period, but it can be removed manually before the period has expired. For example,

```
alter flashback archive hrarch
purge before timestamp to_timestamp('01-01-2009','dd-mm-yyyy');
```

As there will often be legal implications to the ability to manage an archive, it is protected by privileges. The FLASHBACK ARCHIVE ADMINISTER system privilege grants the ability to create, alter, or drop an archive, and control the retention and purging. You must grant FLASHBACK ARCHIVE on the archive to a user who will nominate tables to be archived:

```
grant flashback archive administer to fbdaadmin;
grant flashback archive on hrarch to hr;
```

Finally, to enable archive protection for a table, use this command:

```
alter table hr.employees flashback archive hrarch;
```

There are three data dictionary views that document the Flashback Data Archive configuration:

- **DBA_FLASHBACK_ARCHIVE**   Describes the configured archives.
- **DBA_FLASHBACK_ARCHIVE_TS**   Shows the quotas assigned per archive per tablespace.
- **DBA_FLASHBACK_ARCHIVE_TABLES**   Lists the tables for which archiving is enabled.

Exercise 19-5: Create a Flashback Data Archive   In this exercise you will investigate the structures of a Flashback Data Archive.

1. Create a tablespace to be used for the Flashback Data Archive:

   ```
   create tablespace fda datafile 'fda1.dbf' size 10m;
   ```

2. Create a Flashback Data Archive in the tablespace, with a retention of seven years:

   ```
   create flashback archive fla1 tablespace fda retention 7 year;
   ```

3. Create a schema to use for this exercise, and grant it the DBA role:

   ```
   grant dba to fbdauser identified by fbdauser;
   ```

4. Grant the user the necessary privilege on the archive:

   ```
   grant flashback archive on fla1 to fbdauser;
   ```

5. Connect as the FBDAUSER. Create a table, and enable the Flashback Data Archive for this table:

   ```
   connect fbdauser/fbdauser
   create table t1 as select * from all_users;
   alter table t1 flashback archive fla1;
   ```

6. Run these queries to determine the objects created by the archive. You may have to wait several minutes, because the objects are not created immediately.

The illustration shows an example of the result, but the names will be unique to your environment.

```
select object_name,object_type from user_objects;
select segment_name,segment_type from dba_segments
where tablespace_name='FDA';
```

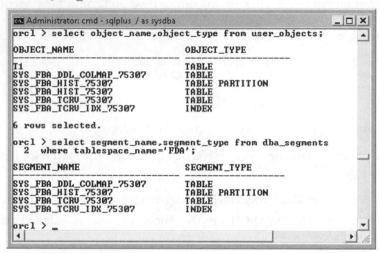

7. Perform some DML against the protected table:

```
delete from t1;
commit;
```

8. Perform a flashback query against the protected table using standard flashback query syntax, and then query the history table in the archive. The history table's name will have been displayed in Step 6. This illustration shows this step:

9. Attempt some DDL commands against the protected table:

```
alter table t1 drop column created;
truncate table t1;
drop table t1;
```

Connect AS SYSDBA, and attempt these:

```
drop user fbdauser cascade;
drop tablespace fda including contents and datafiles;
```

Note that these commands all generate errors related to the existence of the archive and the protected table.

10. Remove the archive protection from the table:

```
alter table fbdauser.t1 no flashback archive;
```

11. Drop the Flashback Data Archive:

```
drop flashback archive fla1;
```

12. Rerun all the commands from Step 9.

Two-Minute Drill

Restore Dropped Tables from the Recycle Bin

- Dropped tables can be restored with FLASHBACK TABLE <table_name> TO BEFORE DROP, if the space they occupy has not been reused.

- Flashback drop cannot function if the owning schema or the tablespace has been dropped.

- Dependent indexes, triggers, and grants will also be restored, as will all constraints except foreign key constraints.

- Dropped tables can be viewed, but you cannot perform DML or DDL against them.

- Space occupied by dropped objects does not impact on quotas or trigger space shortage alerts.

Perform Flashback Query

- Flashback Query relies on data in the undo segments.

- The AS OF clause must be used to give access to the pseudocolumns that identify different versions of a row.

- The point to which the flashback should go can be specified as a timestamp or an SCN.

Use Flashback Transaction

- The SELECT ANY TRANSACTION and FLASHBACK ANY TABLE privileges must be granted to users who will use the flashback transaction facility.

- Transactions can be viewed in the FLASHBACK_TRANSACTION_QUERY view, the UNDO_SQL column being a construction of a statement to reverse the change.

PART III

- A transaction flashback may not succeed, because of conflicts caused (typically) by constraint violations.

Perform Flashback Table Operations

- A table flashback attempts to reverse all changes applied to one or more tables.
- The necessary changes, no matter over what time or how many tables, are applied as one transaction.
- Row movement must be enabled on tables before attempting a table flashback.

Configure and Monitor Flashback Database and Perform Flashback Database Operations

- A database flashback is functionally equivalent to an incomplete recovery.
- Flashback logs exist in the flash recovery area, and the flashback buffer exists in the shared pool; both are automatically managed.
- A database flashback operation is accomplished in mount mode and terminated with a RESETLOGS.
- Both flashback log files and redo log files are needed during a flashback. The database must be running in archivelog mode.

Set Up and Use a Flashback Data Archive

- An archive exists in one or more tablespaces.
- Once a table is nominated for archiving, some DDL commands will no longer be possible.
- The FBDA background process captures before-images of rows and saves them to the archive, and purges the archive of data that has passed its retention period.

Self Test

1. Under which of these circumstances might Flashback Database be of use? (Choose the best answer.)

   A. To recover a dropped table

   B. To recover a dropped schema

   C. To recover a damaged datafile

   D. To reverse a bad transaction

   E. All of the above

2. Which of the following is correct about Flashback Database? (Choose two correct answers.)

   A. You should set the FLASHBACK_BUFFER_SIZE parameter.

   B. You must create the flashback log files.

   C. You must set the DB_RECOVERY_FILE_DEST parameter.

   D. You must issue ALTER SYSTEM FLASHBACK ON.

   E. You must issue ALTER DATABASE FLASHBACK ON.

3. Why is archivelog mode required to enable Flashback Database? (Choose the best answer.)

   A. Because the redo log data is needed to reverse changes

   B. To recover to an exact time after flashback

   C. Because ARCn processes are needed to write flashback data

   D. Because archivelog mode is optional, not required

4. What state must the database be in to turn on the Flashback Database feature? (Choose the best answer.)

   A. Shutdown

   B. Nomount

   C. Mount

   D. Open

5. Which of the following commands is not necessary for a Flashback Database operation? (Choose all that apply.)

   A. Alter database open readonly

   B. Alter database open resetlogs

   C. Flashback database to . . .

   D. Recover database until . . .

   E. Shutdown

   F. Startup mount

6. What tool(s) can be used to perform a database flashback? (Choose the best answer.)

   A. Database Control and RMAN

   B. Database Control and SQL*Plus

   C. RMAN and SQL*Plus

   D. Database Control, RMAN, and SQL*Plus

7. You have set the DB_FLASHBACK_RETENTION_TARGET to one day, but the flash recovery area does not have room for this much flashback data. What will happen? (Choose the best answer.)

   A. The database will hang until space is freed up.

   B. It will depend on whether AUTOEXTEND has been enabled for the flash recovery area.

   C. The database will continue to function, but flashback operations may fail.

   D. If there are any backups in the flash recovery area not needed according the retention policy, they will be automatically removed.

8. A user error has occurred, but the effects are limited to one tablespace. You want to flash back this one tablespace, but not the others. What must you do? (Choose the best answer.)

   A. Execute ALTER TABLESPACE . . . FLASHBACK OFF for all the other tablespaces, then flash back the database.

   B. Take the other datafiles offline, flash back the database, and bring the other datafiles online.

   C. Flash back the whole database, then do complete recovery of the other tablespaces.

   D. It is not possible to flash back one tablespace and leave the rest of the database current.

9. You have enabled Flashback Database, but you suspect that flashback logging is impacting adversely on performance. What could you do? (Choose the best answer.)

   A. Reduce the DB_FLASHBACK_RETENTION_TARGET parameter.

   B. Tune the frequency of RVWR writes.

   C. Stop flashback logging for some tablespaces.

   D. Investigate the flashback log multiplexing and archiving strategy.

   E. Tune the flashback buffer.

10. When you drop a table, what objects will go into the recycle bin? (Choose two answers.)

    A. The table

    B. Grants on the table

    C. Indexes on the table

    D. All constraints on the table

    E. All constraints on the table except foreign key constraints

11. After dropping a table, how can you access the rows within it? (Choose the best answer.)

    A. Query the table using the AS OF syntax.

B. Query the table using the BEFORE DROP syntax.

C. Query the table using its recycle bin name.

D. You can't query it until it has been recovered.

12. If a table has been dropped and then another table created with the same name, which of the following statements are correct? (Choose two answers.)

A. You can rename the new table, before you flash back the dropped one.

B. You can flash back the dropped table, if you specify a new name for it.

C. You can flash back the dropped table into a different schema.

D. You must drop the new table before flashing back the old one.

13. Under which of the following circumstances will Flashback Drop work? (Choose the best answer.)

A. When a table has been truncated

B. When a table has been purged

C. When a user has been dropped

D. When an index has been dropped

E. None of the above

14. There are two tables in the recycle bin with the same original name. What will happen if you issue a FLASHBACK TABLE *<original_name>* TO BEFORE DROP command? (Choose the best answer.)

A. The command will return an error.

B. The oldest recycle bin table will be recovered.

C. The newest recycle bin table will be recovered.

D. You can't have two tables in the recycle bin with the same original name.

15. If a Flashback Table operation violates a constraint, what will happen? (Choose the best answer.)

A. The row concerned will not be flashed back, but the rest of the operation will succeed.

B. The flashback operation will hang until the problem is fixed.

C. The flashback operation will be rolled back.

D. You must disable constraints before a table flashback.

16. What is the best technique to flash back two tables in a foreign key relationship? (Choose the best answer.)

A. Flash back the child table, then the parent table.

B. Flash back the parent table, then the child table.

C. Flash back both tables in one operation.

D. This is not an issue—foreign key constraints are not protected by flashback.

PART III

17. Why and when must you enable row movement on a table before a flashback operation? (Choose the best answer.)

    A. Flashback Drop requires row movement, because all the rows in the table will have different object numbers.

    B. Flashback Query requires row movement, because the rows will have new ROWIDs picked up from the undo segment.

    C. Flashback Transaction requires row movement, because any affected rows may be moved as the transaction is reversed.

    D. Flashback Table requires row movement, because any affected rows may be moved as the changes are reversed.

18. Which process is responsible for writing before-images of rows to a Flashback Data Archive? (Choose the best answer.)

    A. FBDA, Flashback Data Archiver Process

    B. RVWR, Recovery Writer

    C. CTWR, Change Tracking Writer

    D. ARCn, Archiver process

19. Which of these operations cannot be executed against a table for which archiving has been enabled? (Choose all correct answers.)

    A. DROP

    B. TRUNCATE

    C. Add a column

    D. Drop a column

    E. None of the above

Self Test Answers

1. ☑ B. The only way to recover a dropped schema (other than incomplete recovery) is Flashback Database.

    ☒ A, C, D, and E. No flashback technology will help with physical corruption, so C and E are wrong. A would be better fixed with Flashback Table, and D with Flashback Transaction.

2. ☑ C and E. The flash recovery area must be configured, and flashback enabled within the database.

    ☒ A, B, and D. There is no such parameter as FLASHBACK_BUFFER_SIZE, and the flashback logs are created automatically, so A and B are wrong. Remember that flashback is an attribute of the database, not the instance, so D is also wrong.

3. ☑ **B.** Flashback is only approximate; redo is needed to reach the precise point required—so **B** is correct.

☒ **A, C,** and **D. A** is wrong because redo can never be used to reverse changes, only to redo them. **C** is wrong because the flashback data is written by the RVWR process, not by the archiver processes. **D** is wrong because archivelog mode is necessary.

4. ☑ **C.** Mount mode is necessary.

☒ **A, B,** and **D.** As with the transition to archivelog mode, the database must be mounted.

5. ☑ **A** and **D.** These steps are optional (but possibly useful).

☒ **B, C, E,** and **F.** These steps are all required.

6. ☑ **D.** All three tools are usable.

☒ **A, B,** and **C.** A database flashback can be initiated with SQL*Plus, or RMAN, or Database Control.

7. ☑ **C.** The retention target is only a target, and Oracle will continue to function even if it cannot be met—but your flashbacks may fail.

☒ **A, B,** and **D. A** is what happens if it is not possible to archive logs. **B** is an attribute that can be applied to datafiles, not the flash recovery area. **D** will only happen if you instruct RMAN to do it.

8. ☑ **D.** One tablespace cannot be flashed back (though a TSPITR operation would give that result).

☒ **A, B,** and **C. A** restricts tablespaces from generating flashback data. **B** and **C** can't work because the other datafiles would not be synchronized.

9. ☑ **C.** This might reduce the workload involved in flashback logging.

☒ **A, B, D,** and **E. A** will not have an effect on performance, only on how far you can flash back. **B** and **E** are impossible—Oracle controls these. **D** is wrong because flashback logs cannot be multiplexed or archived.

10. ☑ **A** and **C.** The only items that go into the recycle bin are the table and its indexes.

☒ **B, D,** and **E.** Grants are preserved, but they remain in the data dictionary. The same is true of constraints, except for foreign key constraints, which are dropped.

11. ☑ **C.** You can query the table using its system-generated name.

☒ **A, B,** and **D.** AS OF is the syntax for flashback query, and BEFORE DROP is the syntax to flash back the drop.

12. ☑ A and B. Both these approaches are reasonable.

☒ C and D. C is impossible. D would work, but at the price of losing your current table.

13. ☑ E. Flashback drop is not applicable to any of these scenarios.

☒ A, B, C, and D. A will not put anything in the recycle bin, B will remove the table from the recycle bin. C bypasses the recycle bin. D is wrong because even though indexes do go into the recycle bin when you drop their table, they do not go in there if they are dropped individually.

14. ☑ C. Flashback drop will recover the most recent table.

☒ A, B and D. If tables have the same original name, they are recovered on a last-in-first-out basis.

15. ☑ C. Table flashbacks are implemented as one transaction, which (like any other transaction) will be rolled back if it hits a problem.

☒ A, B, and D. A and B are wrong because a table flashback must succeed in total, or not at all. D would be a way around the difficulty, but it is certainly not a requirement for flashback, and probably not a good idea.

16. ☑ C. This is the only way to guarantee success.

☒ A, B, and D. A and B could both fail, depending on the nature of the changes. D confuses Flashback Table, when foreign key constraints are maintained, with Flashback Drop, where they are dropped.

17. ☑ D. It is only Flashback Table that requires row movement.

☒ A, B, and C. A is wrong because the object number is preserved through the DROP and FLASHBACK . . . TO BEFORE DROP operations. B is wrong because ROWIDs always refer to the table the row is a part of. C is wrong because flashback of one transaction can proceed without row movement being required.

18. ☑ A. The FBDA manages the contents of Flashback Data Archives.

☒ B, C, and D. RVWR writes to the flashback logs; CTWR records changed blocks addresses for RMAN fast incremental backups; the ARCn process(es) write archive log files.

19. ☑ A, B and D. A and B would remove necessary information from the data dictionary, and D would not generate the undo needed for archiving.

☒ C and E. Columns can be added to archive-enabled tables.

CHAPTER 20

Automatic Storage Management

Exam Objectives

In this chapter you will learn how to

- 053.1.1 Describe Automatic Storage Management (ASM)
- 053.1.2 Set Up Initialization Parameter Files for ASM and Database Instances
- 053.1.3 Start Up and Shut Down ASM Instances
- 053.1.4 Administer ASM Disk Groups

Automatic Storage Management, or ASM, is a facility provided with the Oracle database for managing your disks. It is an Oracle-aware logical volume manager, or LVM, that can stripe and mirror database files and recovery files across a number of physical devices. This is an area where the database administration domain overlaps with the system administration domain.

Many databases will not use ASM: they will store their files on the volumes provided by the operating system, which may well be managed by an LVM. But if you do not have a proper LVM, as will probably be the case with low-end systems running on, for example, Linux or Windows, then ASM provides an excellent (and bundled) alternative to purchasing and installing one. On high-end systems, ASM can work with whatever LVM is provided by the operating system, or can obviate the requirement for one. In all cases, ASM has been proven to deliver spectacular performance and should always be considered as a viable option for database storage.

Before going into the details of ASM architecture and configuration, the following is a brief discussion of logical and physical volume management. This is not intended to be any sort of comprehensive treatment (which is not necessary for the OCP exam) but rather the minimum information needed to appreciate the purpose of ASM.

The Purpose of a Logical Volume Manager

Your database server machine will have one or more disks, either internal to the computer or in external disk arrays. These disks are the physical volumes. In virtually all modern computer installations, there is a layer of abstraction between these physical volumes and the logical volumes. Logical volumes are virtual disks, or file systems, that are visible to application software, such as the Oracle database. Physical volumes are presented to the software as logical volumes by the operating system's LVM.

Even the simplest computer nowadays will probably be using some sort of LVM, though it may be extremely limited in its capabilities. In the case of a Windows PC, you may well have only one disk, partitioned into two logical drives: perhaps a C: drive formatted with the FAT32 file system, and a D: drive formatted with the NTFS file system. Thus one physical volume is presented to you by Windows as two logical volumes. Larger installations may have dozens or hundreds of disks. By using an LVM to put these physical volumes into arrays that can be treated as one huge disk area and then partitioned into as many (or as few) logical volumes as you want, your system administrators can provide logical volumes of whatever size, performance, and fault tolerance is appropriate.

RAID Levels

If the physical volumes are mapped one-to-one onto logical volumes, the performance and fault tolerance of the logical volumes is exactly that of the physical volumes. RAID (or *redundant array of inexpensive discs*—not a term that has any meaning nowadays) in its various levels is intended to enhance performance and fault tolerance by exploiting the presence of multiple physical volumes. There are four levels to consider in most environments.

RAID level 0 is optimal for performance but suboptimal for fault tolerance. A RAID 0 array consists of one or more logical volumes cut (or striped) across two or more physical volumes. Theoretically, this will improve logical disk I/O rates and decrease fault tolerance by a proportion equal to the number of physical volumes. For example, if the array consists of four disks, then it will be possible to read from and write to all of them concurrently; a given amount of data can be transferred to the logical volume in a quarter of the time it would take if the logical volume were on only one disk. But if any of the four disks is damaged, the logical volume will be affected, so it is four times more likely to fail than if it were on only one disk.

RAID level 1 is optimal for fault tolerance. There may be performance gains, but that is not why you use it. Where RAID 1 is definitely suboptimal is cost. A RAID 1 array consists of one or more logical volumes mirrored across two or more disks: whenever data is written to the logical volume, copies of it will be written concurrently to two or more physical volumes. If any one physical volume is lost, the logical volume will survive because all data on the lost physical volume is available on another physical volume. There may be a performance improvement for read operations if it is possible to read different data from the mirrors concurrently; this will depend on the capabilities of the LVM. The cost problem is simply that you will require double the disk capacity—more than double, if you want a higher degree of mirroring. In the four-disk example, the logical volume will be equivalent in size to only two of the physical disks, but you can lose any one disk, and possibly two disks, before the logical volume is damaged.

RAID level 5 is a compromise between the performance of RAID 0 and the fault tolerance of RAID 1. The logical volume is cut across multiple physical volumes (so concurrent read and writes are possible), and a checksumming algorithm writes out enough information to allow reconstruction of the data on any one physical volume, if it gets damaged. Thus you do not get all the performance gain of RAID 0, because of the checksumming overhead; in particular, write operations can be slow because each write operation needs to calculate the checksum before the write can take place. You do not get all the fault tolerance of RAID 1, because you can survive the loss of only one disk. In the four-disk example, the logical volume will be equivalent in size to three physical volumes, and if any one of the four is lost, the logical volume will survive.

RAID 0+1 is optimal for both fault tolerance and performance: you mirror your striped disks. In the four-disk example, your system administrators would create one logical volume striped across two of the physical disks and mirror this to the other two disks. This should result in double the performance and double the safety (and double the price) of mapping one logical volume directly onto one physical volume.

Volume Sizes

Physical volumes have size restrictions. A disk is a certain size, and this cannot be changed. Logical volumes may have no size restrictions at all. If your LVM allows you to put a hundred disks of 100GB each into a RAID 0 array, then your logical volume will be 10TB big. (It will also perform superbly, but it will not be very tolerant against disk failure.) Furthermore, logical volumes can usually be resized at will, while the system is running.

Choice of RAID Level

Many system administrators will put all their physical volumes into RAID 5 arrays. This is simple to do and provides a certain amount of fault tolerance and perhaps a small performance improvement, but this may not be the best practice for an Oracle database. As the DBA, you should take control of the RAID strategy and apply different levels to different file types.

Some files are critical to the database remaining open: the files that make up the SYSTEM tablespace, the active UNDO tablespace, and the controlfile copies. Damage to any of these will cause the database to crash. Some files are critical for performance: the online redo log files and the controlfiles. I/O on these can be a serious bottleneck. By considering the characteristics of each file, a RAID strategy should become apparent. For example, the SYSTEM and UNDO tablespaces should be on RAID 1 volumes, so that they will always be available. The online redo logs are protected by multiplexing, so you don't have to worry about hardware fault tolerance, but performance is vital, so put them on RAID 0 volumes. The controlfile copies are critical for performance, but if any copy is damaged, the database will crash; thus, RAID 0+1 could be appropriate. Your other datafiles could perhaps go on RAID 5 volumes, unless they are particularly important or volatile.

ASM Compared with Third-Party LVMs

ASM has a huge advantage over other logical volume managers: it is aware of the nature of Oracle database files, and it performs striping and mirroring at the file level, not the volume level. This means it can make more intelligent decisions about how to manage the files than a third-party product.

First, when a logical volume is cut across several physical volumes in what are called "stripes," a decision must be made on the size of the stripe. Different file types will perform better with different stripe sizes: ASM is aware of this and will stripe them appropriately.

Second, ASM can handle files individually, whereas all other LVMs work at the volume level: they are not aware of the files within the volume. So with a third-party LVM, you have to specify RAID attributes per volume. ASM can specify the attributes per file, so you can, for instance, have three-way mirroring for your SYSTEM tablespace datafiles but no mirroring at all for your temporary tablespaces' tempfiles, all within the same logical volume.

Third, ASM is in principle the same on all platforms, and it is bundled with the database. You do not have to learn (and perhaps purchase) different volume managers for different platforms. Any configuration you do is portable, within the limits of device naming conventions.

Fourth, there is the question of availability. Some operating systems come with an LVM as standard. With AIX on IBM hardware, for example, use of the LVM is not an option—it is compulsory. With other vendors' operating systems, the LVM may be a separately licensed option, or there may not be one at all—you will have to buy a third-party product. ASM is always available and should bring significant performance and manageability benefits to systems that do not have an LVM; on those that do, it will add an extra, Oracle-aware, layer to space management that will further enhance performance while reducing the management workload.

The ASM Architecture

Implementing ASM requires a change in the instance architecture. It even requires another instance. There is an instance parameter: INSTANCE_TYPE, which defaults to RDBMS. An RDBMS instance is a normal instance, used for opening a database and accepting user sessions. Setting this parameter to ASM will start an Automatic Storage Management instance, which is very different. An ASM instance is not used by end users; it controls access to ASM files stored on ASM disk groups, on behalf of the RDBMS instances. These files are functionally the same as non-ASM database files: they are datafiles, controlfiles, log files, and recovery files, but they are stored in the ASM logical volume manager environment, not in the file systems provided by your operating system.

The Oracle cluster services are needed on the host in order to set up communication between the RDBMS instances and the ASM instance. The cluster services are the same services used to enable a RAC (or Real Application Clusters) environment, where several instances on several hosts open a shared database.

The Cluster Synchronization Service

Oracle Corporation provides a suite of clusterware. This is intended for setting up a RAC: a group of instances on several machines opening a database on shared disks. Oracle clusterware can be used as a replacement for clusterware that you would otherwise buy from your hardware and operating system vendor. However, the cluster services are also used in a single-instance environment to set up the communications between ASM and RDBMS instances.

 EXAM TIP ASM is not required for RAC (because you can use a third-party clustered volume manager for the shared database files), nor is it only for RAC (because it works very well for single-instance, nonclustered databases too).

In a RAC environment, the cluster services require a separate installation and will run off their own Oracle home. In a single-instance environment, the small part of the cluster services that is needed to enable ASM is installed into and runs from the database Oracle home; this is the CSSD, or Cluster Services Synchronization Daemon. Under Windows, the CSSD runs as a service; on Unix, it is a daemon launched by an entry in the /etc/inittab file.

The ASM Disks and Disk Groups

An ASM *disk group* is a pool of ASM disks managed as one logical unit. As with any other LVM, ASM takes a number of physical volumes and presents them to Oracle as one or more logical volumes. The physical volumes can be actual disks or partitions of disks, or they can be volumes managed by a volume manager that is part of your operating system. Either way, they will not be formatted with any file system; they must be raw devices. ASM will take the raw devices and put them into a number of ASM disk groups. A disk group is the logical volume.

EXAM TIP ASM disks must be raw devices, without a file system, but they do not need to be actual disks. They can be disks, partitions of a disk, or logical volumes managed by an LVM.

TIP It is possible to set up ASM using files instead of raw disks, but this is totally unsupported and suitable only for training or demonstration systems.

For example, on a Linux system you might have six SCSI disks of 72GB each. You could decide to use one of them, /dev/sda, for the root file system and utilities. Then use /dev/sdb for the $ORACLE_HOME directories, and then /dev/sdc, /dev/sdd, /dev/sde, and /dev/sdf for the database files. You would create a file system on each disk and format it—probably as ext3—and then mount the file systems onto directory mount points in the root file system. This is all very well, but you are wasting the performance potential of the machine. It will be extremely difficult to balance the I/O evenly across the four disks used for the database, and you will have to monitor which files have the most activity and try to keep them separate. Also, one disk may fill up while the others have plenty of space.

The equivalent Windows example would be drive C: for Windows itself, and drive D: for the ORACLE_HOME. Then drives E:, F:, G:, and H: would be dedicated to database files. Probably all the disks would be formatted as NTFS.

If you were to put the four disks dedicated to the database into one RAID 0 logical volume, you would get better performance, and a system that requires much less monitoring and management. But it may be that you do not have a logical volume manager. Enter ASM . . . .

To use ASM, you would not format the four disks to be used for database files. The root file system and the ORACLE_HOME file system must be managed as normal; you cannot use ASM volumes for anything other than database and recovery files. Then you would launch an ASM instance and set instance parameters such that it will find the four raw volumes and place them into one ASM disk group. This group will contain the database, with whatever RAID characteristics you want.

EXAM TIP You can use ASM only for database and recovery files, not for your Oracle Home or for anything else. The definition of "database file" is quite broad, but does not include trace files, the alert log, the password file, or a static parameter file.

The size of the ASM disk group is the sum of the size of the ASM disks less a small amount, but depending on what degree of fault tolerance is specified, the size available for use will be less. The default fault tolerance is single mirror, meaning that, to continue our example, the end result will be close to 144GB of space available for the database, with single mirrors for fault tolerance and four times the native disk performance. This degree of mirroring can be changed for the whole group, or for individual files within it; the striping is automatic and cannot be disabled.

EXAM TIP ASM mirroring defaults to single mirror, but can set to none or double; striping cannot be disabled.

Disks can be added and removed from a disk group dynamically, within certain limits. In general, if the operating system and hardware can handle adding or removing disks while the computer is running, then ASM can handle this as well.

Figure 20-1 illustrates the ASM storage structure, represented as an entity-relationship diagram. One ASM instance can support multiple RDBMS instances, and it is possible (though in practice never done) to run more than one ASM instance to which the RDBMS instance could connect: this potential many-to-many relationship between the instance types is resolved by the Cluster Services. Another many-to-many relationship is between files and disks: one disk may store parts of many files, and one file can be distributed across many disks; this is resolved by the allocation units.

The ASM Instance

When using non-ASM files, an RDBMS instance will locate and open its files itself. In the ASM environment, these tasks are carried out by an ASM instance on behalf of the RDBMS instance. But even in an ASM environment, the RDBMS instance will always do its own I/O; its server processes will read the datafiles, its DBWn process will write to the datafiles, and the LGWR will write to the online redo log files.

EXAM TIP Normal disk activity does not go through the ASM instance. ASM is a management and control facility that makes the files available; it does not do the actual I/O work.

Figure 20-1
The components
of ASM

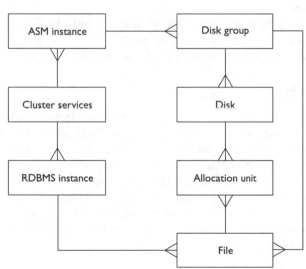

In some respects, an ASM instance is an instance like any other. It has an SGA and some of the usual background processes. But it cannot mount or open a database; all it can do is locate and manage ASM disks. Many instance parameters are not legal for an ASM instance. Usually, the parameter file (which may be a dynamic spfile or a static pfile) will have only half a dozen parameters. Because it cannot mount or open a database, it will never be able to read a data dictionary; for this reason, you can only connect to it with password file or operating system authentication, as SYSOPER or as SYSDBA, or as SYSASM. SYSASM is a role introduced with release 11g, to permit a separation of duties between the database administrator and the ASM administrator.

It is possible to have more than one ASM instance running on one computer, but there is no value in doing this. You should create one ASM instance per computer and use it to manage all the ASM disks available to that computer on behalf of all the RDBMS instances running on the computer.

An ASM instance will have two background processes in addition to the usual processes. These are the RBAL and the ARBn processes, used to handle rebalancing activity—the movement of data between ASM disks in an ASM disk group, in response to adding or removing a disk to or from the group. If a new device is added to a group, ASM will detect this and initiate an operation to bring the disk into use. This will mean moving data onto the disk, to take account of the increased possibilities for striping and to include the new disk in spreading the I/O workload evenly. The RBAL process coordinates this rebalancing, and the ARBn processes (several of these may be launched automatically) do the work. Also, if a disk leaves an ASM disk group, either by design or because of a hardware failure, a rebalancing operation is necessary to reestablish mirrors. In either case, the redistribution of data will occur without users being aware of the problem or the activity.

 EXAM TIP A rebalancing operation will start automatically in response to disk group reconfiguration.

To create and configure disk groups, you must first connect to the ASM instance and start it. Once you have created and mounted the groups, the ASM instance will then wait for requests from RDBMS instances for access to files.

The RDBMS Instance

An RDBMS instance that is using ASM files functions as normal, except that it will have two additional background processes: RBAL and ASMB. The RBAL process opens the ASM disks, which it will locate through the ASM instance. The ASMB process connects to the ASM instance by creating a session against it, via a server process. This session is responsible for the continuing communication between the RDBMS instance and the ASM instance; in effect, the RDBMS instance becomes a client to the ASM server. The information passed over this session will be requests for physical changes, such as file creation, deletion, or resizing, and also various statistics and status messages.

It is not necessary to inform the RDBMS instance of the name of the ASM instance. When an ASM instance starts, it registers its name and the names of the ASM disk groups it is managing with the Cluster Synchronization Service. This is why the Oracle cluster services must be running, even if the node and instance are not clustered. The RDBMS instance does know the names of the disk groups that it is using; these names are embedded in the ASM filenames stored (like any other filenames) in the RDBMS instance's controlfile, and this lets the ASMB process instance locate the ASM instance managing those groups by interrogating the Cluster Synchronization Service. It can then make an IPC connection to the ASM instance.

Commonly, an RDBMS instance will require access to only two disk groups: one for its live database files, the other for its flash recovery area.

The ASM Files

Files in ASM disk groups are managed by the ASM instance on behalf of the RDBMS instances. They are created, read, and written by the RDBMS instances. The files types that will commonly be stored as ASM files include any or all of these:

- Controlfile
- Dynamic initialization parameter file, the spfile
- Online redo log files
- Archive redo log files
- Datafiles
- Tempfiles
- RMAN backup sets
- RMAN image copies
- Flashback logs
- Controlfile autobackups
- Data Pump dump files

As this list shows, the whole database can be stored on ASM disks, as can all recovery-related files. You can direct the flash recovery area to an ASM disk group.

 EXAM TIP ASM does not manage the Oracle binaries, nor the alert log, trace files, and password file.

All ASM files are striped across all the ASM disks in the group. The allocation of space is by *allocation unit*, or *AU*. The standard AU size is 1MB, and for files where data access tends to take the form of reasonably large disk I/O operations, such as datafiles or archive log files, the striping is also in 1MB units. This is known as "coarse" striping. For files where read and write requests are generally for smaller units of I/O, such as online logs and the controlfile, the AUs themselves are striped across the disks in

128KB stripes, in what is known as "fine" striping. Thus there will be lower latency in satisfying the (typically, small) requests for reads and writes of these file types, because the one small request can be split up into several even smaller requests directed to each disk in the group in parallel.

The syntax for creating and managing ASM files is exactly the same as for file system–based files. All ASM files are created and managed by the RDBMS instance, using the usual commands. The only difference is in the filename: when creating a database file, you specify only the name of the disk group to which the file should be directed, and ASM will generate the actual filename and manage the physical locations.

There is a one-to-one relationship between a database file and an ASM file. If your database has 200 datafiles using conventional file system storage, it will still have 200 datafiles when you convert to ASM. But they will no longer exist as individual files that you can see with operating system utilities. In fact, normal operating system commands will not be able to see anything at all within the ASM disks, because they are not formatted with a file system. This means that the only way to get at ASM files is through Oracle utilities. This is not a problem at all, but it does mean that you must use RMAN to back up your ASM datafiles, archive logs, and controlfiles.

ASM files can coexist with files stored within file systems. There is no reason why a tablespace should not consist of one ASM file and one conventional file, but there would be no purpose in such an arrangement. However, this does mean that it is possible to migrate a database to ASM over time, by moving the various files whenever convenient. Because you cannot write to an ASM disk group with any operating system tools, for datafiles this move must be accomplished with RMAN through a backup and restore operation. To move online logs, create new members in an ASM disk group and drop the old members.

Creating Raw Devices

Your system administrators will be responsible for creating the raw devices to be given to ASM. These may be whole disks, partitions of a disk, or RAID devices provided by a logical volume manager. Whatever they are, there will be some operating system syntax that lets Oracle address them: a Unix raw device will be addressed through a block device driver in the /dev directory; Windows will address it through a \\.\ path name. On a Windows PC, you could use the Microsoft Management Console Disk Management snap-in to create the devices. On a Linux PC, you could use the fdisk utility. Larger systems will have an LVM, either part of the operating system or a third-party product such as Veritas.

Exercise 20-1: Create Raw Devices   If you can create raw devices on your system, or have a system administrator who can provide them, you will need to do so now for the purposes of the exercises that follow. They do not need to be particularly large—a few hundred megabytes will do. If you cannot create raw devices, it is possible to simulate raw devices by using files. Creating simulated raw devices is the purpose of this exercise. There are two sets of instructions: first for Linux, then for Windows.

1. Linux:

   Use the dd command to create empty two empty files, of 1GB each, in a directory of your choice. For example,

   ```
   dd if=/dev/zero of=/u01/app/oracle/raw1.disk bs=1024 count=1000000
   dd if=/dev/zero of=/u01/app/oracle/raw2.disk bs=1024 count=1000000
   ```

   The files raw1.disk and raw2.disk will consist of one million blocks, each containing 1KB of nothing.

2. Windows:

   Locate any large file, which is a multiple of 1024 bytes, and copy it twice to a directory of your choice. In this example, the file happens to be an ISO image of a compact disc:

   ```
   copy \tmp\oel5\d1.iso \app\oracle\raw1.disk
   copy \tmp\oel5\d1.iso \app\oracle\raw2.disk
   ```

   The files created will be formatted by ASM when they are assigned to a disk group. ASM will make some checks (it will not, for example, accept a copy of an Oracle datafile) but pretty much any file should do as the source. If you have a problem, try again with a different file.

Creating, Starting, and Stopping an ASM Instance

An ASM instance is controlled by an instance parameter file, as is an RDBMS instance, but there are strict limits on the parameters that can be included. Many will cause an ASM instance to have errors on startup, so keep the parameter file as small as possible. The parameters most likely to be needed (and often all that are required) are listed in Table 20-1.

Parameter	Required?	Description
instance_type	Yes	Must be ASM for an ASM instance. Default is RDBMS.
instance_name	No	Must be prefixed with "+". Defaults to the ORACLE_SID environment variable.
asm_power_limit	No	Controls the number of ASMB processes to be used for rebalancing operations. Default is 1, the lowest.
asm_diskstring	Yes	List of paths identifying the disks to be given to ASM.
asm_diskgroups	No	Disk groups to be mounted on startup. Default is NULL.

Table 20-1 Common ASM Initialization Parameters

PART III

An ASM parameter file for Windows might take this form:

```
instance_name='+asm'
instance_type='asm'
asm_diskstring='\\.\*:'
asm_diskgroups=dgroupA,dgroupB
```

The instance name must be prefixed with a "+" symbol, on all platforms. On Windows, this must also be specified when creating the Windows service for the instance. The syntax for the ASM_DISKSTRING will be platform specific. In the example, Oracle will find every device, as indicated by the "\\.\" characters, that includes the ":" character in its name. All Windows disk devices that have been assigned a drive letter will have a ":" in their name, so this string will find all devices that have been assigned a drive letter. The two nominated disk groups, dgroupA and dgroupB, must exist; if this is the first startup of the ASM instance, omit this parameter and set it only after the groups have been created. Many databases will require only two disk groups: one for the live database files, the other for the flash recovery area. Wildcard characters (such as the asterisk in the preceding example) can be used to let ASM find a number of devices without having to name them all individually.

A Linux parameter file might look like this:

```
instance_name='+asm'
instance_type='asm'
asm_diskstring='/dev/md2','/dev/md3','/dev/md4','/dev/md5'
asm_diskgroups=dgroupA,dgroupB
remote_login_passwordfile=exclusive
```

This time the disk string has four distinct values, rather than using wildcards, which will let it find four named RAID devices. The two nominated disk groups must exist and be composed of the RAID volumes named in diskstring. In this example, there are no wildcards, but they could be used if desired. For example, if using Solaris this would let ASM find all disks on the second and third controllers:

```
asm_disk_string='/dev/rdsk/c2*','/dev/rdsk/c3*'
```

To start the instance, you must connect to it as SYSASM and issue a STARTUP command. The connection can be made by setting the ORACLE_SID environment variable to the instance name (not forgetting that it must be prefixed with a "+" symbol), or if a password file has been created and enabled as in the preceding example, you can connect with password file authentication. The startup will first go through NOMOUNT, where the instance is built in memory and the disks identified by the ASM_DISKSTRING parameter are discovered. Then the instance will mount the disk groups specified by ASM_DISKGROUPS. There is no MOUNT or OPEN mode for an ASM instance; disk groups can be mounted or unmounted.

 TIP The size of an ASM instance can, as in the preceding examples, be left completely on default. This will result in an instance of about 160MB. In most circumstances this is both sufficient and necessary.

RDBMS instances use files in disk groups managed by the ASM instance. If the ASM instance has not started and mounted the disk groups, then the RDBMS instances cannot open. It is therefore necessary to ensure, through your operating system utilities, that the ASM instance starts before the RDBMS instances that are dependent upon it. If the ASM instance terminates, then the dependent RDBMS instances will terminate also. If, when a SHUTDOWN command is issued to an ASM instance, one or more RDBMS instances have opened files in one of its disk groups, then you will receive this message:

```
ORA-15097: cannot SHUTDOWN ASM instance with connected RDBMS instance
```

The exception is a SHUTDOWN ABORT, which will terminate the ASM instance and thus cause the termination of the RDBMS instance(s).

TIP If an RDBMS instance fails, the ASM instance will not be affected. If an ASM instance fails, the dependent RDBMS instances will abort.

Exercise 20-2: Create an ASM Instance   Create a parameter file and use it to start an ASM instance. All steps in this exercise should be done from an operating system prompt. The examples assume that you are using simulated raw disks, as created in Exercise 20-1. If you have real raw devices, substitute their names accordingly, and omit the hidden parameter. Note that Step 2 is applicable only to Windows

1. Configure the Cluster Synchronization Services Daemon. This requires running the `localconfig` utility, in the `ORACLE_HOME`/bin directory. On Unix, this must be run as the root user:

   ```
   localconfig add
   ```

   On Windows, you will see that a service has been created and put on automatic start called OracleCSService; on Unix, you will see an entry in the `/etc/inittab` file that will respawn the `init.cssd` process at run levels 3 and 5.

2. From an operating system prompt, run the ORADIM utility to create a Windows service for the ASM instance.

   ```
   C:\> oradim -new -asmsid +ASM -startmode manual
   ```

   This will create and start the ASM service. Subsequently, it must be started either from the Control Panel Services, or with this command from the operating system prompt:

   ```
   C:\> net start oracleasmservice+ASM
   ```

3. If using Windows, use the Notepad to create a file named INIT+ASM.ORA in the ORACLE_HOME\database directory, with just these four lines:

   ```
   instance_name='+asm'
   instance_type='asm'
   asm_diskstring='c:\app\oracle\raw*.disk'
   _asm_allow_only_raw_disks=false
   ```

If using Linux, use an editor such as vi to create a file named init+asm.ora in the ORACLE_HOME/dbs directory with these five lines:

```
instance_name='+asm'
instance_type='asm'
asm_diskstring='/u01/app/oracle/raw*.disk'

_asm_allow_only_raw_disks=false
memory_target=0
```

Note the use of the parameter _ASM_ALLOW_ONLY_RAW_DISKS. This is a "hidden" parameter (use of which is not supported) that will allow ASM to use files rather than raw devices for the purposes of this exercise. The last parameter disables automatic memory management, which is necessary on some Linux systems depending on how shared memory has been configured.

4. Set your ORACLE_SID environment variable to the ASM instance name.

5. Connect to the ASM instance with SQL*Plus as SYSASM, and start the instance.

6. Confirm that ASM has found the disks with this SQL statement:

```
select path,os_mb from v$asm_disk;
```

The illustration shows Steps 3, 4, and 5 executed on a Windows system.

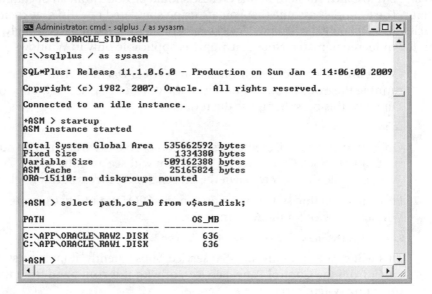

Creating ASM Disk Groups

Disk groups are created by an ASM instance and then used by an RDBMS instance. To create a disk group, as a minimum, give the group a name and a list of disks that have been discovered by the ASM disk string and are therefore visible in the V$ASM_DISK view:

```
SQL> create diskgroup dg1 disk '/dev/sdc', '/dev/sdd', '/dev/sde', '/dev/sdf';
```

If you nominate a disk that is already part of a disk group, the command will fail. The default level of redundancy provided by ASM is "normal" redundancy, meaning that each AU is mirrored once. All files will be striped across all the disks for maximum performance. For normal redundancy, the group must have at least two disks, and the effective size of the group will be half the total space allocated.

In the preceding example, which continues the Linux four-SCSI-disk example discussed earlier, the result will be a disk group with an effective size of 144GB (less a small amount). Every file created in the group will (unless specified otherwise) be striped and mirrored with RAID 0+1. The stripe size will be selected by ASM according to the type of file: online redo log files and controlfile copies will be fine striped; datafiles and archive logs will be coarse striped.

To override the default NORMAL redundancy, meaning single mirror, add the keywords HIGH REDUNDANCY or EXTERNAL REDUNDANCY to the CREATE DISKGROUP command. HIGH REDUNDANCY will create three copies of every allocation unit (and therefore requires a minimum of three disks), and EXTERNAL REDUNDANCY will not mirror at all: the assumption is that there is an underlying LVM that is doing whatever level of RAID is deemed appropriate.

Redundancy can be taken a step further by putting ASM disks within a disk group into failure groups. When ASM mirrors extents, it will never mirror an extent to another disk in the same failure group. This means that you are better protected against the failure of multiple disks. By default, each disk is considered to be its own failure group; this gives ASM complete freedom to mirror that disk's data onto any other disk in the group. However, if some disks are connected at the hardware level, typically by being attached to the same controller, you would not want ASM to mirror between them. Using failure groups forces ASM to create mirrors on a different subset of the disks within the group. An example of this is

```
SQL> create diskgroup dgroupa normal redundancy
failgroup controller2 disk '/dev/rdsk/c2*'
failgroup controller3 disk '/dev/rdsk/c3*';
```

This command creates a disk group consisting of all the disk devices matched by the wildcards given, which is all the disks hanging off the second and third controllers. But the use of failure groups (their names are not significant) instructs ASM never to mirror data between two disks that are on the same controller.

Exercise 20-3: Create a Disk Group Use the ASM instance created in Exercise 20-2 to create a disk group with the two raw volumes created in Exercise 20-1.

1. From an operating system prompt, set your ORACLE_SID environment variable to the ASM instance.

2. Connect to your ASM instance with SQL*Plus with the SYSASM privilege using operating system authentication, and start the instance.

3. Create a disk group, nominating the two raw volumes listed in Step 5 of Exercise 20-2.

```
create diskgroup dg1
disk 'C:\APP\ORACLE\RAW1.DISK', 'C:\APP\ORACLE\RAW2.DISK';
```

4. Confirm the creation of the group by querying the relevant views.

```
select name,group_number,type,state,total_mb from v$asm_diskgroup;
```

Note that the group has NORMAL redundancy, so the total space available will be effectively halved. The group is MOUNTED, meaning that it is available for use.

The illustration shows Steps 1 through 4 on a Linux system.

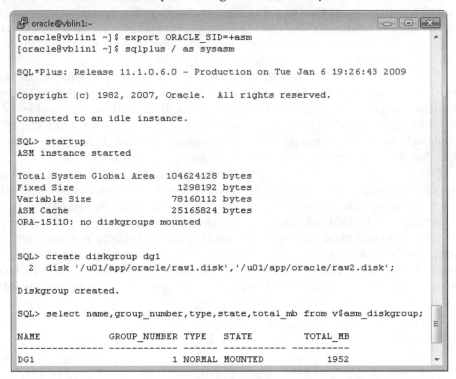

```
oracle@vblin1:~
[oracle@vblin1 ~]$ export ORACLE_SID=+asm
[oracle@vblin1 ~]$ sqlplus / as sysasm

SQL*Plus: Release 11.1.0.6.0 - Production on Tue Jan 6 19:26:43 2009

Copyright (c) 1982, 2007, Oracle.  All rights reserved.

Connected to an idle instance.

SQL> startup
ASM instance started

Total System Global Area  104624128 bytes
Fixed Size                  1298192 bytes
Variable Size              78160112 bytes
ASM Cache                  25165824 bytes
ORA-15110: no diskgroups mounted

SQL> create diskgroup dg1
  2  disk '/u01/app/oracle/raw1.disk','/u01/app/oracle/raw2.disk';

Diskgroup created.

SQL> select name,group_number,type,state,total_mb from v$asm_diskgroup;

NAME            GROUP_NUMBER TYPE   STATE       TOTAL_MB
--------------- ------------ ------ ----------- ----------
DG1                        1 NORMAL MOUNTED          1952
```

5. To ensure that the disk group is mounted automatically when the ASM instance starts, add this line to the ASM instance parameter file created in Exercise 20-2, Step 3:

```
asm_diskgroups=dg1
```

If this is not done, you will have to mount the disk group manually every time you start the ASM instance:

```
alter diskgroup dg1 mount;
```

Creating and Using ASM Files

The ASM disk groups are created in the ASM instance; the ASM files are created in the RDBMS instance. The normal commands for creating datafiles, tempfiles, and log files can all take a disk group name in place of a filename. For example,

```
SQL> create tablespace new_tbs datafile '+dg1' size 100m;
SQL> alter tablespace system add datafile '+system_dg' size 1000m;
SQL> alter database add logfile group 4 '+dg_log1','+dg_log2' size 100m;
```

The first of these commands creates a new tablespace with one datafile in the disk group DG1. The second command adds a datafile to the SYSTEM tablespace, in a disk group created specially for the SYSTEM datafiles; this will probably be a disk group created with HIGH redundancy. The third command creates a new online log file group, with two members in different disk groups; these will likely be groups with EXTERNAL redundancy, because you can rely on the multiplexing to provide fault tolerance.

To direct archive logs to ASM, set the LOG_ARCHIVE_DEST parameters to point to disk groups:

```
SQL> alter system set log_archive_dest_1='location=+dg_arc1';
SQL> alter system set log_archive_dest_2='location=+dg_arc2';
```

It is also possible to direct the flash recovery area to an ASM disk group:

```
SQL> alter system set db_recovery_file_dest='+dg_flash';
```

In all these examples, you do not specify a filename, only a disk group. ASM will generate the actual filenames according to its own conventions. If you wish, you can see the names by querying views such as V$DATAFILE, V$LOGFILE, or V$ARCHIVED_LOG, but there is little value in this. A feature of ASM is that it gives you complete independence from the physical storage: there is no reason for you to want to know the actual filenames. It is possible to interpret the system-generated names, but they are not any sort of physical path.

Exercise 20-4: Use ASM for Datafiles   Create a tablespace in the disk group created in Exercise 20-3.

1. Connect to your RDBMS instance with SQL*Plus as user SYSTEM. Ensure that your ORACLE_SID environment variable is set to the name of your RDBMS instance first.

2. Create a tablespace with a datafile in your ASM disk group.

   ```
   SQL> create tablespace new_tbs datafile '+dg1' size 100m;
   ```

3. Find the filename of the new datafile.

   ```
   SQL> select file_name from dba_data_files where tablespace_name='NEW_TBS';
   FILE_NAME
   ---------------------------------------
   +DG1/orcl/datafile/new_tbs.256.675459139
   ```

ASM and RMAN

Since ASM files are created on raw devices managed by Oracle, there is no way that you can back up ASM files with operating system utilities: no regular operating system command or utility can see the contents of an ASM disk, because it has no file system installed upon it. You must use RMAN. The RMAN backup and restore and recover commands do not change at all when using ASM; wherever you would use a filename, enter the ASM filename. If your backup scripts specify tablespace names, or the whole database, then they will run unchanged.

Apart from being required for regular backup and recovery procedures, RMAN is also the only tool available for migrating a database from conventional file system storage to ASM storage. The examples that follow assume that you have three disk groups: group dg1 is for your datafiles; groups dg2 and dg3 are for controlfiles and online redo log files.

To migrate the controlfile, change the CONTROLFILES instance parameter to point toward your disk groups and then shut down the database and start it in NOMOUNT mode:

```
SQL> alter system set controlfiles='+dg2','+dg3' scope=spfile;
SQL> shutdown immediate;
SQL> startup nomount;
```

Then launch RMAN, and restore the controlfile from its original location:

```
RMAN> restore controlfile from
'/u01/app/oracle/oradata/orcl/control01.ctl';
```

You can now mount and open the database, using the controlfile on the ASM device.

From an RMAN prompt, this script will migrate all your datafiles to an ASM disk group:

```
shutdown immediate;
startup mount;
backup as copy database format '+dg1';
switch database to copy;
alter database open;
```

To migrate the redo logs, create new members in your disk groups and drop the old members:

```
SQL> alter database add logfile member '+dg2','+dg3' to group 1;
SQL> alter database drop logfile member '/u01/app/oracle/oradata/orcl/redo01a.log',
'/u01/app/oracle/oradata/orcl/redo01b.log ';
```

Finally, you must move your temporary tablespace tempfiles. Since these cannot be backed up, the technique is to drop them and create new files on a disk group. It may be simpler just to create a new temporary tablespace, and drop the original temporary tablespace:

```
create temporary tablespace tempasm tempfile '+dg1' size 1g;
alter database default temporary tablespace tempasm;
drop tablespace temp including contents and datafiles;
```

 EXAM TIP RMAN is the only tool you can use to back up ASM files. User-managed backups are not possible, because operating system utilities cannot see ASM files.

The ASMCMD Utility

In order to make administration of ASM files simpler, Oracle provides a command-line utility that gives a Unix-like interface to ASM. This is the ASMCMD utility, named `%ORACLE_HOME%\bin\asmcmd.bat` on Windows and `$ORACLE_HOME/bin/asmcmd` on Unix. To run the tool, you must first set your ORACLE_SID environment variable to the name of the ASM instance, and then a set of commands are available with functionality and syntax similar to that of a Unix file system. The commands are summarized in Table 20-2.

Most of the ASMCMD commands are self-explanatory and follow standard (although much simplified) Unix in their syntax. Two do require special attention: the `md_backup` and `md_restore` commands. These let you recreate a disk group. They do not back up or restore any files in the disk group (the files must be protected by other means, usually RMAN), but they do make it possible to extract the metadata describing the disk groups and the disks of which they are composed. This would be necessary in the event of a disaster recovery operation. If the machine hosting the ASM instance and its attached disks were lost and had to be replaced, then after creating an ASM instance on a replacement machine (which should ideally have the same disk configuration), restoring the metadata would recreate the disk groups. Then using RMAN, the files themselves could be restored.

Command	Description
help	View available commands and usage
cd	Navigate around the ASM directory structure
cp	Copy a file
du	Return the space used in a directory
find	Find a file
ls	List contents of a directory
lsct	List connected RDBMS instances
lsdg	List the disk groups
mkalias	Create an alias name for a file
mkdir	Create a directory
pwd	Display the current ASM directory
rm	Delete a file
rmalias	Delete a file alias
md_backup	Back up the metadata describing a disk group
md_restore	Restore the metadata describing a disk group
lsdsk	List the discovered disks
remap	Attempt to repair damaged disk blocks

Table 20-2 ASMCMD Commands

The syntax of the `md_backup` command is

```
md_backup [-b location_of_backup] [-g dgname]
```

The location of the output file will default to a file named AMBR_BACKUP_ INTERMEDIATE_FILE in the directory from which ASMCMD was launched, and if no disk groups are specified, all mounted disk groups will be included.

Exercise 20-5: Use the ASMCMD Utility   In this exercise you will use the ASMCMD utility to investigate the files in the ASM disk group created in Exercise 20-4.

1. At an operating system prompt, set your ORACLE_SID environment variable to the name of the ASM instance, and launch the ASMCMD utility. On Windows:

```
set ORACLE_SID=+asm
asmcmd.bat
```

Or on Unix:

```
export ORACLE_SID=+asm
asmcmd
```

2. Display details of your disk group.

```
lsdg
```

Note the difference between the values for Usable_file_MB space and Free_MB: this is because the Type of the disk group is "NORMAL", which is mirrored.

3. Use the `cd` and `ls` commands to navigate to the directory and display the datafile shown in Step 3 of Exercise 20-4.

```
cd +DG1/orcl/datafile
ls -l
```

4. Create a backup of the ASM metadata, relying on the defaults, which will back up all mounted disk groups to a file in your current operating system directory.

```
md_backup
```

5. Exit from the ASMCMD utility, and inspect the generated file AMBR_BACKUP_ INTERMEDIATE_FILE with any editor. It will be readable but should not be edited. Observe the details of your disk group and disks.

6. Launch SQL*Plus. Connect to the ASM instance as SYSASM, and query views that describe your ASM files and disk groups.

```
select * from v$asm_file;
select * from v$asm_diskgroup;
```

Note the correspondence with the results of Steps 2 and 3.

Two-Minute Drill

Describe Automatic Storage Management (ASM)

- ASM is a logical volume manager, providing striping and (optionally) mirroring of Oracle database files.

- The files that can be stored on ASM devices include datafiles; tempfiles; the controlfile; online and archive redo log files; the spfile; RMAN backup sets; and image copies.

- You cannot use ASM devices for the Oracle binaries or diagnostic and trace files.

- ASM will always stripe files across all disks in a disk group, but mirroring is optional.

- The default mirroring is NORMAL REDUNDANCY (meaning two copies of each allocation unit), but this can be adjusted to EXTERNAL REDUNDANCY (one copy only), or to HIGH REDUNDANCY (three copies) if the group has at least three disks.

- The cluster services are required (even in a non-RAC environment) to set up the connections between RDBMS instances and an ASM instance.

- No data ever passes through an ASM instance. ASM is responsible only for managing the storage structures; the RDBMS instance(s) perform the I/O operations.

Set Up Initialization Parameter Files for ASM and Database Instances

- The parameter INSTANCE_TYPE must be set to either RDBMS (the default) or ASM to control whether the instance is a database instance or an ASM instance.

- An ASM instance should have the ASM_DISKSTRING and ASM_DISKGROUP parameters set to identify the disks that the ASM instance may use and the disk groups it should mount. These parameters are illegal in an RDBMS instance.

- Very few parameters are legal in an ASM instance. Usually INSTANCE_TYPE, INSTANCE_NAME, and the ASM prefixed parameters are all that are needed.

Start Up and Shut Down ASM Instances

- You can connect to an ASM instance only with operating system or password file authentication, as SYSDBA or SYSASM (though SYSDBA is only supported for backward compatibility).

- An ASM instance can be started only in NOMOUNT mode. It will never mount a controlfile nor open any datafiles—though it will mount disk groups to make them available to RDBMS instances.

- An ASM instance cannot be shut down (other than with an ABORT) if an RDBMS instance has opened files in disk groups it is managing.

Administer ASM Disk Groups

- Disk groups are made up of one or more discovered disks.

- Files created in ASM disk groups consist of 1MB allocation units, distributed across all the disks in the group.

- ASM files can be backed up only with RMAN; operating system utilities cannot see the files in a disk group.
- Disks can be added to and removed from a disk group dynamically. The allocation units of the files will be restriped by an automatic rebalancing operation to take advantage of any new disks, or to reestablished mirrors if a disk is removed.
- Disk groups can be mounted manually with the ALTER DISKGROUP MOUNT command, or automatically by nominating them in the ASM_DISKGROUPS parameter.

Self Test

1. What file types and directories can be stored with ASM? (Choose all that apply.)
   A. Alert log
   B. Controlfiles
   C. Datafiles
   D. Online redo log files
   E. Oracle Home directory
   F. Tempfiles

2. Which of the following recovery files can be stored with ASM? (Choose all that apply.)
   A. Archive redo log files
   B. RMAN backup sets
   C. RMAN image copies
   D. User-managed backups
   E. The flash recovery area

3. Which of the following parameters is required for an ASM instance? (Choose the best answer.)
   A. ASM_DISKGROUPS
   B. ASM_POWER_LIMIT
   C. INSTANCE_NAME
   D. INSTANCE_TYPE

4. How should you migrate your online redo log files to ASM storage? (Choose the best answer.)
   A. Copy the files to an ASM disk group, and use RENAME to update the controlfile.
   B. Use RMAN to transfer them to an ASM disk group, and SWITCH to update the controlfile.

C. Create new members in an ASM disk group, and drop the old members.

D. Online logs cannot use ASM storage.

5. If you abort an ASM instance, what will be the effect on RDBMS instances that make use of disk groups managed by the aborted instance? (Choose the best answer.)

A. ASM is a single point of failure, and therefore the RDBMS instances will also abort.

B. The RDBMS instances will remain open, but any ASM datafiles will be inaccessible.

C. RDBMS instances that have already opened ASM files will not be affected, but no new RDBMS instances will be able to open.

D. The RDBMS instances will hang until the ASM instance is restarted.

E. You will receive a message stating that you cannot abort the instance because it is in use.

6. What are the default characteristics of ASM files? (Choose the best answer.)

A. The files will be striped for performance but not mirrored for safety.

B. The files will be mirrored for safety but not striped for performance.

C. The files will be both striped and mirrored.

D. The files will be neither striped nor mirrored.

7. What happens when you open an ASM instance? (Choose the best answer.)

A. The ASM disk groups are made available to RDBMS instances.

B. The ASM disks are opened.

C. The ASM files are opened.

D. You cannot open an ASM instance.

8. What statement is correct about ASM and logical volume managers (LVMs)? (Choose the best answer.)

A. ASM is itself an LVM and cannot work with a third-party LVM.

B. ASM can use LVM volumes, if they are formatted with a file system.

C. You can use ASM for striping, and the LVM for mirroring.

D. You can use ASM for mirroring, and the LVM for striping.

9. What does the RBAL process do? (Choose the best answer.)

A. It rebalances data across the disks in an ASM disk group when a disk is added or removed.

B. It coordinates rebalancing activity.

C. It opens and closes ASM disks.

D. It depends on whether it is the RBAL process of an ASM instance or of an RDBMS instance.

10. Which of the following techniques is valid for backing up files on ASM disks? (Choose all that apply.)

    A. If the files are mirrored, split the mirror, back up the split copy, and reinstantiate the mirror.

    B. Put the tablespaces into hot backup mode, and copy the ASM datafiles.

    C. Connect to the ASM instance with RMAN, and back up as normal.

    D. Connect to the RDBMS instance with RMAN, and back up as normal.

11. How can you connect to an ASM instance? (Choose the best answer.)

    A. By using operating system authentication only

    B. By using password file authentication only

    C. By using data dictionary authentication only

    D. None of the above are correct

12. What does ASM stripe? (Choose the best answer.)

    A. Files across all disk groups

    B. Disks across all disk groups

    C. Disk groups across all disks

    D. Files across all disks in a group

13. Some operations can only be carried out when connected to an ASM instance, while others can only be carried out when connected to an RDBMS instance. Mark each of these operations as being "ASM" or "RDBMS."

    A. Creating ASM datafiles

    B. Creating ASM disk groups

    C. Backing up ASM datafiles

    D. Backing up volume group metadata

14. If an RDBMS instance that is using ASM files crashes, what will the ASM instance do? (Choose the best answer.)

    A. The ASM instance will abort.

    B. The ASM instance will recover the files that the RDBMS instance had open, and remain available for other RDBMS instances.

    C. The ASM instance will recover the files that the RDBMS instance had open, and shut down cleanly.

    D. Nothing.

Self Test Answers

1. ☑ **B, C, D**, and **F**. You can use ASM for database files, such as the controlfile, the datafiles, the tempfiles, and the online log files.

   ☒ **A** and **E**. Your Oracle Home and the alert and trace files must be on conventional storage.

2. ☑ **A, B, C**, and **E**. Archive logs, RMAN backups, and indeed the whole flash recovery area can be on ASM.

   ☒ **D**. You cannot direct user-managed backups to ASM, because operating system utilities cannot write to ASM devices.

3. ☑ **D**. The only essential parameter is INSTANCE_TYPE.

   ☒ **A, B**, and **C**. These are not mandatory. It would, however, be good practice to set these parameters too.

4. ☑ **C**. The only method is to create new files.

   ☒ **A, B**, and **D**. ASM can certainly be used for online log file, but you can't copy to an ASM disk group, and RMAN cannot back up online log files.

5. ☑ **A**. The ABORT command will terminate the instance, and all dependent RDBMS instance will then terminate also.

   ☒ **B, C, D**, and **E**. All RDBMS instances that are using files in disk groups managed by the ASM instance will abort immediately. An ABORT is the only shutdown method that will succeed—all others will generate an error message if the ASM instance is in use.

6. ☑ **C**. By default, files are both striped and mirrored.

   ☒ **A, B**, and **D**. You can disable the mirroring by using the EXTERNAL REDUNDANCY option when you create the disk group, or by specifying this for any particular file. You cannot disable the striping (and you would not want to).

7. ☑ **D**. You cannot open an ASM instance.

   ☒ **A, B**, and **C**. ASM will open the disks when it starts, and the disk groups will be available to RDBMS instances when they are mounted. ASM files are opened by RDBMS instances, not the ASM instance.

8. ☑ **C**. This is probably the best way to use ASM: to rely on an LVM to provide fault tolerance, and ASM to provide Oracle-aware striping.

   ☒ **A, B**, and **D**. ASM can use any devices presented by the operating system, even LVM devices, but they should not be formatted by a file system. You can use an LVM to mirror volumes, and then ASM will stripe files on top of this.

9. ☑ **D.** There is an RBAL process in both an ASM instance and the RDBMS instances that are using it, but they perform different functions.

☒ **A, B,** and **C. A** describes the ARBn process, **B** is RBAL in an ASM instance, and **C** is RBAL in an RDBMS instance.

10. ☑ **D.** Absolutely normal RMAN backups, when you are connected to the RDBMS instance as the target, are the only way to back up ASM files.

☒ **A, B,** and **C. A** and **B** are variations on user-managed backups, which are not possible. **C** makes the mistake of thinking that the backup would be done through the ASM instance, not the RDBMS instance.

11. ☑ **D.** Both password file and operating system authentication will work.

☒ **A, B,** and **C.** ASM instances do not open a database, so you cannot use data dictionary authentication, but both other methods are available.

12. ☑ **D.** ASM stripes files across all disks in the group.

☒ **A, B,** and **C.** ASM striping is managed per file, not per disk or disk group.

13. ☑ **A** and **C,** RDBMS; **B** and **D,** ASM. Files are created and backed up with normal commands issued from SQL*Plus or RMAN from the RDBMS instance. Operations related to the disk groups can be accomplished only from the ASM instance.

14. ☑ **D.** An ASM need do nothing when a dependent RDBMS instance fails.

☒ **A, B,** and **C.** An ASM instance operates independently of the RDBMS instances that are using it. If any file recovery is needed, it is done through the RDBMS instance.

CHAPTER 21

The Resource Manager

Exam Objectives

In this chapter you will learn to
- 053.17.1   Understand the Database Resource Manager
- 053.17.2   Create and Use Database Resource Manager Components

Many computer systems will have several groups of users, each with different standards for the level of service they require. If the system as a whole is highly stressed, it may be impossible to deliver the desired level of service to all groups. But if a priority structure can be negotiated, then it should be possible to guarantee a certain level of service to certain groups—perhaps at the expense of other groups.

In a mainframe environment, the operating system itself handles allocating resources to tasks. A *transaction processing (TP)* monitor will ensure that high-priority jobs get the processing power they need. But simpler operating systems such as Unix or Windows may not have proper resource scheduling capabilities. Oracle's Resource Manager brings mainframe-style resource management capabilities to all supported Oracle platforms, meaning that you as DBA can guarantee that certain groups of database users will always receive a certain level of service, no matter what the overall workload on the database may be.

The Need for Resource Management

Operating systems like Unix or Windows use a very simple algorithm to assign resources to different processes: round-robin time slicing. To the operating system, there is really no difference between any of the background processes that make up the Oracle instance and any of the many server processes that support user sessions: as far as the operating system is concerned, a process is a process; it will be brought onto CPU, given a few cycles of CPU time, and then switched off CPU so that the next process can be brought on. The operating system has no way of knowing that one server process is supporting a session doing completely trivial work, while another server process is supporting a session doing work critical to the survival of the organization. A more immediate problem that all DBAs come across is that one bad SQL statement can kill the database. The Resource Manager provides a mechanism whereby the operating system's time-slicing algorithm can be adjusted, to ensure that some users receive more processing capacity than others—and to ensure that any single query does not destroy performance for everyone else. The underlying mechanism is to place a cooperative multitasking layer controlled by Oracle on top of the operating system's preemptive multitasking system.

Throughout this chapter, the environment is assumed to be that of a telesales organization. There are several groups of users: of particular interest are the data entry clerks and the management accountants.

There may be 200 data entry clerks in the call center, taking orders over the telephone. If their database sessions are running slowly, this is disastrous for the company. Customers will dial in only to be told "you are number 964 in the queue, your call is important to us, please do not hang up . . . ." This is happening because the data entry clerks cannot process calls fast enough: they take an order, they click the Submit button, and then they wait . . . and wait . . . and wait . . . for the system to respond. This is costing money.

On the other hand, the management accountants' work is not so urgent. Perhaps an advertisement has been run on one local radio station, and the response in terms of sales inquiries needs to be evaluated before running the advertisement nationwide.

This is important work, but it doesn't have to be real time. If the reports take ten minutes to run instead of five, does it really matter?

 TIP Do not adjust the priorities of Oracle processes by using the Unix `renice` command, or the Windows equivalent. Oracle assumes that the operating system is treating all processes equally, and if you interfere with this there may be unexpected (and disastrous) side effects.

What is needed is a technique for ensuring that if the database sessions supporting the data entry clerks need computing resources, they get them—no matter what. This could mean that at certain times of day when the call center is really busy, the clerks need 100 percent of computing resources. The Resource Manager can handle this, and during that time of peak usage the sessions supporting the management accountants may hang completely. But during other times of day, when the call center is not busy, there will be plenty of resources available to be directed to the management accountants' work.

At month end, another task will become top priority: the end-of-month billing runs, and the rollover of the ledgers into the next accounting period. The Resource Manager needs to be versatile enough to manage this, too.

Clearly, the Resource Manager is only necessary in highly stressed systems, but when you need it, there is no alternative. In fact, you are using the Resource Manager whether you know it or not; it is configured by default in all databases from release 8i onward, but the default configuration has no effect on normal work.

The Resource Manager Architecture

Users are placed in Resource Manager consumer groups, and Resource Manager plans, consisting of a set of directives, control the allocation of resources across the groups. Each session is assigned to a group, depending upon attributes defined when the session was established and possibly modified subsequently. The underlying architecture places a cooperative multitasking layer on top of the preemptive multitasking provided by the operating system. The server process of a session in a low-priority group will, when brought onto CPU by a context switch, voluntarily relinquish the CPU earlier than it would have done if relying purely on the operating system's preemptive multitasking algorithm.

Consumer Groups

A Resource Manager consumer group is a set of users with similar resource requirements. One group may contain many users, and one user may be a member of many groups, but at any given moment, each session will have one group as its effective group. When a user first creates a session, his default consumer group membership will be active, but if he is a member of multiple groups, he can switch to another group, activating his membership of that group. The switch can be manual or automatic, depending on a number of factors.

In the telesales example, the two hundred data entry clerks could be in a group called OLTP, and the half-dozen management accountants could be in a group called DSS. Some users could be in both groups; depending on what work they are doing, they will activate the appropriate group membership. Other groups might be BATCH, to be given top priority for month-end processing, and LOW for people who happen to have accounts on the system but are of no great significance.

There are fourteen groups created by default when a database is created:

- **SYS_GROUP** This is a group intended for the database administrators. By default, only the SYS and SYSTEM users are in this group.

- **DEFAULT_CONSUMER_GROUP** This is a group for all users that have not been specifically assigned to any other group. By default, all sessions other than SYS and SYSTEM are in this group, and this membership is active when they first create a session.

- **OTHER_GROUPS** This is a group that all users are members of, used as a catch-all for any sessions that are in groups not listed in the active Resource Manager plan.

- **LOW_GROUP** This group is intended for low-priority sessions.

- **BATCH_GROUP, INTERACTIVE_GROUP** These are preconfigured groups intended for sessions doing certain types of work.

- **The AUTOTASK groups** There are seven groups associated with the automatic tasks, such as gathering statistics and running advisors. These are intended to prevent the auto-tasks from impacting adversely on end-user sessions.

- **ORA$DIAGNOSTICS** A group for running diagnostic tasks.

To view the groups in your database, query the views DBA_RSRC_CONSUMER_ GROUPS and DBA_USERS. The latter shows the initial consumer group set for each session at connect time (see Figure 21-1).

Resource Manager Plans

A Resource Manager plan is of a certain type. The most basic (and most common) type of plan is one that allocates CPU resources, but there are other resource allocation methods. Many plans can exist within the database, but only one plan is active at any one time. This plan applies to the whole instance: all sessions are controlled by it.

The resources that can be controlled by a plan are

- Total CPU usage for all sessions in a group

- Degree of parallelism available to each session in a group

- Number of active sessions permitted per group

- Volume of undo space permitted per group

- Time before terminating idle sessions

- Maximum length of execution time for a call in a session, which can also trigger the switch of a session into another group

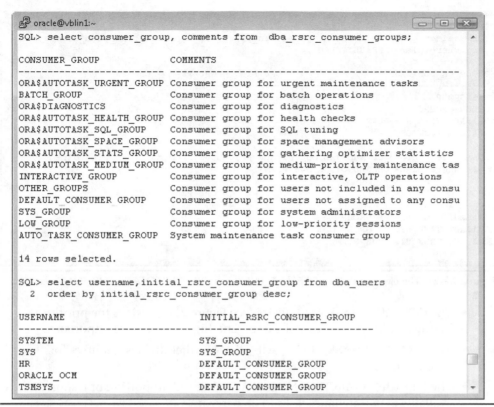

```
oracle@vblin1:~
SQL> select consumer_group, comments from  dba_rsrc_consumer_groups;

CONSUMER_GROUP           COMMENTS
------------------------ --------------------------------------------------
ORA$AUTOTASK_URGENT_GROUP Consumer group for urgent maintenance tasks
BATCH_GROUP              Consumer group for batch operations
ORA$DIAGNOSTICS         Consumer group for diagnostics
ORA$AUTOTASK_HEALTH_GROUP Consumer group for health checks
ORA$AUTOTASK_SQL_GROUP  Consumer group for SQL tuning
ORA$AUTOTASK_SPACE_GROUP  Consumer group for space management advisors
ORA$AUTOTASK_STATS_GROUP  Consumer group for gathering optimizer statistics
ORA$AUTOTASK_MEDIUM_GROUP Consumer group for medium-priority maintenance tas
INTERACTIVE_GROUP       Consumer group for interactive, OLTP operations
OTHER_GROUPS            Consumer group for users not included in any consu
DEFAULT_CONSUMER_GROUP  Consumer group for users not assigned to any consu
SYS_GROUP               Consumer group for system administrators
LOW_GROUP               Consumer group for low-priority sessions
AUTO_TASK_CONSUMER_GROUP System maintenance task consumer group

14 rows selected.

SQL> select username,initial_rsrc_consumer_group from dba_users
  2  order by initial_rsrc_consumer_group desc;

USERNAME                     INITIAL_RSRC_CONSUMER_GROUP
---------------------------- ----------------------------
SYSTEM                       SYS_GROUP
SYS                          SYS_GROUP
HR                           DEFAULT_CONSUMER_GROUP
ORACLE_OCM                   DEFAULT_CONSUMER_GROUP
TSMSYS                       DEFAULT_CONSUMER_GROUP
```

Figure 21-1   Resource Manager consumer groups

In the telesales example, there could be three plans based on CPU usage. A daytime plan would give top priority to the OLTP group. At times of peak activity, with the system working to full capacity, it is possible that the sessions of users in other groups would hang. At night, a different plan would be activated that would guarantee that the DSS jobs would run, though perhaps still not with the priority of the OLTP group. A month-end plan would give 100 percent of resources to the BATCH group.

A plan consists of a number of directives. Each directive assigns resources to a particular group at a particular priority level. Seven plans are configured at database creation time:

- The INTERNAL_PLAN is not for normal use—it disables the Resource Manager.
- The DEFAULT_PLAN has four directives (see Figure 21-2). The first states that at priority level 1, the highest priority, the session connected to the SYS_GROUP consumer group can take 100 percent of CPU resources. At level 2, OTHER_ GROUPS can have 90 percent, the ORA$DIAGNOSTICS can have 5 percent, and a subplan can have the remaining 5 percent. This plan ensures that if SYS or SYSTEM needs to do something, it will get whatever resources it needs to do it. Any resources it does not need will "trickle down" to the groups at level 2.

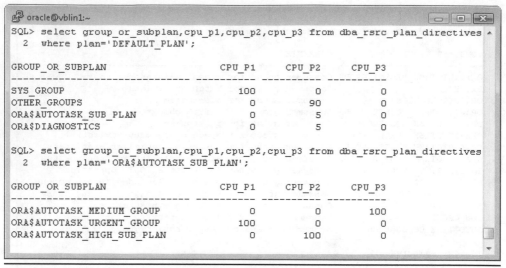

```
oracle@vblin1:~                                                    ___ ___ ___

SQL> select group_or_subplan,cpu_p1,cpu_p2,cpu_p3 from dba_rsrc_plan_directives
  2  where plan='DEFAULT_PLAN';

GROUP_OR_SUBPLAN                      CPU_P1      CPU_P2      CPU_P3
-----------------------------     ----------  ----------  ----------
SYS_GROUP                               100           0           0
OTHER_GROUPS                              0          90           0
ORA$AUTOTASK_SUB_PLAN                     0           5           0
ORA$DIAGNOSTICS                           0           5           0

SQL> select group_or_subplan,cpu_p1,cpu_p2,cpu_p3 from dba_rsrc_plan_directives
  2  where plan='ORA$AUTOTASK_SUB_PLAN';

GROUP_OR_SUBPLAN                      CPU_P1      CPU_P2      CPU_P3
-----------------------------     ----------  ----------  ----------
ORA$AUTOTASK_MEDIUM_GROUP                 0           0         100
ORA$AUTOTASK_URGENT_GROUP               100           0           0
ORA$AUTOTASK_HIGH_SUB_PLAN                0         100           0
```

Figure 21-2 The directives of the DEFAULT_PLAN and ORA$AUTOTASK_SUB_PLAN plans

- The ORA$AUTOTASK_SUB_PLAN (see Figure 21-2) assigns the priorities between tasks considered to be of urgent, high, or medium importance.

- The ORA$AUTOTASK_HIGH_SUB_PLAN further divides resources for automatic jobs.

- The DEFAULT_MAINTENANCE_PLAN raises the proportion of resources available to maintenance tasks to 25 percent.

- The INTERNAL_QUIESCE plan has a particular purpose covered at the end of the chapter: it will freeze all sessions except those of the SYS_GROUP members.

- The MIXED_WORKLOAD_PLAN (shown in Figure 21-3) gives top priority to the SYS_GROUP, then the INTERACTIVE_GROUP, and then the BATCH_GROUP.

To enable a plan, set the RESOURCE_MANAGER_PLAN instance parameter. This can be set automatically by the Scheduler (described in Chapter 22), manually with an ALTER SYSTEM command, or programmatically with the DBMS_RESOURCE_MANAGER.SWITCH_PLAN procedure. Following creation of a database with DBCA, the Scheduler will be configured to activate the DEFAULT_PLAN during normal working hours, and the DEFAULT_MAINTENANCE_PLAN at night and weekends. It is assumed that these plans will be appropriate for most sites: they give the DBA staff top priority, followed by users, and restrict the resources that can be taken by maintenance jobs.

 EXAM TIP The instance parameter RESOURCE_LIMITS has nothing to do with the Resource Manager. It pertains to the older method of controlling resources, through database profiles.

Resource Manager Configuration Tools

There is a PL/SQL API that can be used to administer the Resource Manager; as well as a Database Control interface. The API consists of two packages: DBMS_RESOURCE_

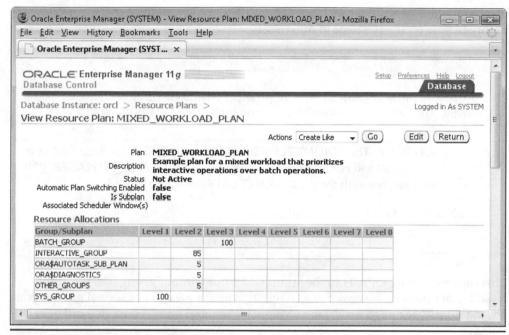

Figure 21-3   The MIXED_WORKLOAD_PLAN, shown in Database Control

MANAGER_PRIVS and DBMS_RESOURCE_MANAGER. DBMS_RESOURCE_MANAGER_
PRIVS is used to put users into consumer groups and also to grant the system privilege
necessary to administer the Resource Manager (see Figure 21-4).

```
oracle@vblin1:~
SQL> desc dbms_resource_manager_privs;
PROCEDURE GRANT_SWITCH_CONSUMER_GROUP
 Argument Name                     Type                    In/Out Default?
 --------------------------------- ----------------------- ------ --------
 GRANTEE_NAME                      VARCHAR2                IN
 CONSUMER_GROUP                    VARCHAR2                IN
 GRANT_OPTION                      BOOLEAN                 IN
PROCEDURE GRANT_SYSTEM_PRIVILEGE
 Argument Name                     Type                    In/Out Default?
 --------------------------------- ----------------------- ------ --------
 GRANTEE_NAME                      VARCHAR2                IN
 PRIVILEGE_NAME                    VARCHAR2                IN     DEFAULT
 ADMIN_OPTION                      BOOLEAN                 IN
PROCEDURE REVOKE_SWITCH_CONSUMER_GROUP
 Argument Name                     Type                    In/Out Default?
 --------------------------------- ----------------------- ------ --------
 REVOKEE_NAME                      VARCHAR2                IN
 CONSUMER_GROUP                    VARCHAR2                IN
PROCEDURE REVOKE_SYSTEM_PRIVILEGE
 Argument Name                     Type                    In/Out Default?
 --------------------------------- ----------------------- ------ --------
 REVOKEE_NAME                      VARCHAR2                IN
 PRIVILEGE_NAME                    VARCHAR2                IN     DEFAULT
```

Figure 21-4   The DBMS_RESOURCE_MANAGER_PRIVS package

To give user JOHN the capability of administering the Resource Manager, with the ability to pass on the privilege to other users:

```
SQL> execute dbms_resource_manager_privs.grant_system_privilege(-
grantee_name=>'JOHN',admin_option=>true);
```

This procedure call will grant the system privilege ADMINISTER RESOURCE MANAGER. You can see this grant by querying the DBA_SYS_PRIVS view.

EXAM TIP The ADMINISTER RESOURCE MANAGER system privilege can be granted and revoked only with the DBMS_RESOURCE_MANAGER_PRIVS package, not with the usual GRANT and REVOKE commands.

To add a user to a group, use a call such as this:

```
SQL> exec dbms_resource_manager_privs.grant_switch_consumer_group(-
grantee_name=>'ROOPESH',consumer_group=>'OLTP',grant_option=>false);
```

This call will add ROOPESH to the group OLTP, but without giving him the ability to add other users to the group. If ROOPESH is now a member of several groups, you should nominate one as his default group. This requires a procedure in a different package:

```
exec dbms_resource_manager.set_initial_consumer_group(-
user=>'ROOPESH',consumer_group=>'OLTP');
```

DBMS_RESOURCE_MANAGER is used to create consumer groups, plans, and directives. It is also used to create the "pending area." Before any work can be done with Resource Manager objects, you must create a pending area. This is an area of memory in the SGA, used for storing the objects while they are being configured. A plan may consist of many directives, and each directive is created independently; it would therefore be possible to create a totally impossible plan: one that might, for example, allocate 500 percent of CPU. The pending area is provided to prevent this possibility: the plan is created in the pending area, and then when complete it is validated to check that it does make sense. Only then does the plan get saved to the data dictionary.

To reach the Database Control interface to the Resource Manager, from the database home page take the Server tab, and then follow the links in the Resource Manager section. To configure the Resource Manager with the APIs is an extremely laborious process, and in virtually all circumstances Database Control will be a far superior method. At all stages in the Database Control windows there will be a SHOW SQL button: this will show all the API calls, including those that create and validate the pending area.

TIP When using Database Control, keep copies of the API calls revealed by the SHOW SQL button. These will let you recreate (and possibly debug) the Resource Manager environment as necessary.

Managing Users and Consumer Groups

A pending area is needed to create consumer groups, but not to put users into groups. If you use Database Control, the pending area will be managed for you; if you use the API directly, you must explicitly create it. Database Control does itself use the API, but the GUI front end makes it much simpler to use and has validations that should make it impossible to create a logically inconsistent Resource Manager environment.

At connect time, a session will pick up the initial consumer group assigned to that user. If the user is a member of multiple consumer groups, the session can be switched to a different consumer group later on. This can be done either manually or by using more advanced techniques automatically according to the work that the session is doing.

Any user can switch their active consumer group to any of the groups of which they are a member by using the SWITCH_CURRENT_CONSUMER_GROUP procedure in the DBMS_SESSION package. Alternatively, a user with the privilege to administer the Resource Manager can switch another session over, by using one of two procedures in the DBMS_RESOURCE_MANAGER package. The SWITCH_CONSUMER_GROUP_FOR_USER procedure will switch all sessions logged on with a particular user name, or SWITCH_CONSUMER_GROUP_FOR_SESS will switch one particular session, identified by SID and SERIAL#:

```
SQL> exec dbms_resource_manager.switch_consumer_group_for_sess(-
session_id=>209,session_serial=>10223,consumer_group=>'OLTP');
```

 EXAM TIP The DBMS_RESOURCE_MANAGER_PRIVS package includes the procedure to put someone in a group, but it is procedures in DBMS_SESSION and DBMS_RESOURCE_MANAGER that can change a user's active consumer group.

Resource Manager Plans

A plan consists of a set of directives that divide resources among consumer groups. There are several principles that can be used to control this:

- CPU method
- Number of active sessions
- Degree of parallelism
- Operation execution time
- Idle time
- Volume of undo data

It is also possible to enable automatic consumer group switching by combining operation execution time with CPU usage: a session that initiates a long-running job that will impact adversely on other users can be downgraded to a lower priority. The CPU method is known as an "emphasis" method, because the effect will vary depending on system activity. The other methods are "absolute" methods, meaning that you define a hard limit, which is always enforced exactly as written.

CPU Method

Continuing the telesales example, the daytime plan would give maximum resources to the OLTP group. All other sessions will hang, if the OLTP users really do need the whole machine. The only exception is the SYS_GROUP. You should always give the SYS_GROUP priority over anything else: if you, the DBA, need to do something on the production system (such as rebuilding a broken index, or doing a restore and recover), then you should be able to do it as fast as possible. The plan could look like this:

Priority Level	Group	CPU %
1	SYS_GROUP	100
2	OLTP	100
3	DSS	50
	BATCH	50
4	OTHER_GROUPS	100

There are eight possible priority levels; this plan uses four of them. All CPU resources not used at one level trickle down to the next level. When this plan is active, the SYS_GROUP at level 1 can, if necessary, take over the whole machine; all other sessions will hang. But this shouldn't happen; in normal running, no CPU cycles will be taken by the SYS_GROUP, so the whole machine will be available at level 2, where the OLTP users can use it all. Any CPU resources they do not need drop down to level 3, where they are divided 50/50 between the DSS and the BATCH sessions. If, after they have taken what they need, there is still some capacity left, it will be available to members of other groups. It is possible, at times when the OLTP users are working nonstop and CPU usage has hit 100 percent, that the DSS and BATCH sessions will hang.

 EXAM TIP The total CPU allocated at each level cannot exceed 100 percent. If it does, the pending area will fail to validate and the plan will not be saved to the data dictionary. It is possible to have a plan that allocates less than 100 percent at a level, but there is little purpose in doing this.

The nighttime plan will have different settings:

Priority Level	Group	CPU %
1	SYS_GROUP	100
2	OLTP	50
	DSS	25
	BATCH	25
3	OTHER_GROUPS	100

As with the daytime plan, if the SYS_GROUP needs to do something, it will get top priority. But at level 2, the DSS and BATCH users are guaranteed processing time. They still do not have as high a priority as the OLTP group, but their sessions will not hang. The month-end plan might change this further:

Priority Level	Group	CPU %
1	SYS_GROUP	100
2	BATCH	100
3	DSS	50
	OLTP	50
4	OTHER_GROUPS	100

When this plan is active, the BATCH jobs will take priority over everyone else, taking the whole machine if necessary. This would be advisable if the month-end processing actually means that the system is not usable, so it is vital to get it done as fast as possible.

TIP If the CPU is not running at 100 percent usage, then these plans will have no effect. They have an impact only if the CPU capacity cannot satisfy the demands upon it.

A variation on the CPU method is that the "group" can itself be a plan. It is possible by this method to set up a hierarchy, where a top-level plan allocates resources between two or more subplans. These subplans can then allocate resources among consumer groups. A case where this might be applicable would be an application service provider. Perhaps you have installed an application such as an accounting suite, and you lease time on it to several customers. Each customer will have its own groups of users. Your top-level plan will divide resources between subplans for each customer, perhaps according to the amount it is paying for access to the service. Then within that division, the customers can each allocate resources among their consumer groups. The DEFAULT_PLAN uses this method to assign resources to the various automatic tasks.

EXAM TIP Every plan must include a directive for the group OTHER_ GROUPS; otherwise, the validation will fail and you cannot save the plan from the pending area to the data dictionary.

To create a plan such as the daytime plan just described requires a series of procedure calls through the API. The first step is to create the pending area:

```
SQL> exec dbms_resource_manager.create_pending_area;
```

You then create the plan:

```
SQL> exec dbms_resource_manager.create_plan(-
plan=>'DAYTIME',comment=>'plan for normal working hours');
```

and the directives within it:

```
SQL> exec dbms_resource_manager.create_plan_directive(-
plan=>'DAYTIME',group_or_subplan=>'SYS_GROUP',cpu_p1=>100,-
comment=>'give sys_group users top priority');
SQL> exec dbms_resource_manager.create_plan_directive(-
plan=>'DAYTIME',group_or_subplan=>'OLTP',cpu_p2=>100,-
```

```
comment=>'give oltp users next priority');
SQL> exec dbms_resource_manager.create_plan_directive(-
plan=>'DAYTIME',group_or_subplan=>'DSS',cpu_p3=>50,-
comment=>'dss users have half at level 3');
SQL> exec dbms_resource_manager.create_plan_directive(-
plan=>'DAYTIME',group_or_subplan=>'BATCH',cpu_p3=>50,-
comment=>'batch users have half at level 3');
SQL> exec dbms_resource_manager.create_plan_directive(-
plan=>'DAYTIME',group_or_subplan=>'OTHER_GROUPS',cpu_p4=>100,-
comment=>'if there is anything left, the others can have it');
```

Finally, validate the pending area and (if the validation returns successfully) save the plan to the data dictionary:

```
SQL> exec dbms_resource_manager.validate_pending_area;
SQL> exec dbms_resource_manager.submit_pending_area;
```

To activate the plan,

```
SQL> alter system set resource_manager_plan=daytime;
```

This plan will be displayed in Database Control as in Figure 21-5.

TIP The DBMS_RESOURCE_MANAGER.CREATE_PLAN_DIRECTIVE procedure has the arguments CPU_Pn, where n ranges from 1 to 8. These are in fact deprecated: you should use the alternative MGMT_Pn arguments instead. But Database Control still generates code that refers to the old CPU_Pn arguments.

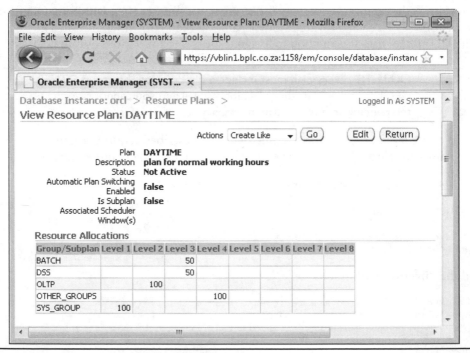

Figure 21-5 The daytime plan, using the CPU method

Exercise 21-1: Manage Users and Plans Create some users and consumer groups, view the configuration, and test the consumer group switching for a user who is a member of multiple groups.

1. Connect to your database as user SYSTEM using SQL*Plus.

2. Create some users and grant them the CONNECT role:

```
SQL> grant connect to clerk identified by clerk;
SQL> grant connect to acct identified by acct;
SQL> grant connect to batch identified by batch;
SQL> grant connect to mgr identified by mgr;
```

3. Connect to your database as user SYSTEM using Database Control.

4. From the database home page, take the Server tab, and then the Consumer Groups link in the Resource Manager section, to see the default groups.

5. Click CREATE to reach the Create Resource Consumer Group window.

6. Enter **OLTP** for the consumer group name, and **group for telesales clerks** as the description. Click ADD to display a listing of all users in the database.

7. Check the selection boxes for users CLERK and MGR, and click SELECT to return to the Create Resource Consumer Group window.

8. Click SHOW SQL, and study the output. Note the use of the pending area. Click ENTER to return to the Create Resource Consumer Group window.

9. Click OK to create the group, and assign the users to it.

10. Create two more groups, with users as follows:

    Group DSS, members ACCT and MGR

    Group BATCH, members BATCH and MGR

    From your SQL*Plus session check the groups and the memberships, with a query such as that shown in the illustration.

```
 oracle@vblin1:~                                          ▢ ▣ ▣
SQL> select consumer_group,comments,grantee from
  2  dba_rsrc_consumer_groups join dba_rsrc_consumer_group_privs
  3  on consumer_group=granted_group order by consumer_group;

CONSUMER_GROUP                  COMMENTS              GRANTEE
------------------------        ---------------       ---------------
BATCH                           group for batch jobs  BATCH
BATCH                           group for batch jobs  MGR
DEFAULT_CONSUMER_GROUP          Consumer group for u  PUBLIC
DSS                             group for management  ACCT
DSS                             group for management  MGR
LOW_GROUP                       Consumer group for l  PUBLIC
OLTP                            group for telesales   CLERK
OLTP                            group for telesales   MGR
SYS_GROUP                       Consumer group for s  SYSTEM

9 rows selected.

SQL>
```

11. Set the initial consumer groups:

```
SQL> exec dbms_resource_manager.set_initial_consumer_group-
> ('CLERK','OLTP');
SQL> exec dbms_resource_manager.set_initial_consumer_group-
> ('ACCT','DSS');
SQL> exec dbms_resource_manager.set_initial_consumer_group-
> ('BATCH','BATCH');
SQL> exec dbms_resource_manager.set_initial_consumer_group-
> ('MGR','OLTP');
```

12. From the database home page, select the Server tab, and then the Plans link in the Resource Manager section, to see the default plans.

13. Click CREATE a new plan. Name it DAYTIME, and click the Activate This Plan check box.

14. Click MODIFY to reach the Select Groups/Subplans window.

15. Select the BATCH, DSS, OLTP, and SYS_GROUP groups and click MOVE, and then OK.

16. Select the Advanced radio button, and set the percentages for each level as in Figure 21-5.

17. Click the SHOW SQL button and study the procedure calls. Note in particular the final call to DBMS_RESOURCE_MANAGER.SWITCH_PLAN, which will activate the new plan. Click ENTER.

18. Click OK to complete the operation.

19. In a second SQL*Plus session, connect as user CLERK.

20. In the first session, confirm that CLERK's effective consumer group is OLTP:

```
SQL> select username,resource_consumer_group from v$session;
```

21. In the second session, connect as user MGR and run this code block to activate your membership of the DSS group:

```
SQL> declare old_grp varchar2(30);
  2  begin
  3  dbms_session.switch_current_consumer_group('DSS',old_grp,TRUE);
  4  end;
  5  /
```

22. In the first session, repeat the query of Step 20 to confirm that MGR is in the DSS group.

23. In the first session, switch the MGR user over to the OLTP group.

```
SQL> execute
dbms_resource_manager.switch_consumer_group_for_user('MGR','BATCH');
```

24. In the first session, repeat the query of Step 20 to confirm that MGR has been switched over to the BATCH group.

Use of the Ratio CPU Method

There is an alternative technique for allocating CPU resources. Rather than coding CPU usage as a percentage, you can specify ratios—and let Oracle work out the percentages.

In the telesales example in the preceding section, the CPU resources at level 2 for the nighttime plan were

OLTP 50%
DSS 25%
BATCH 25%

If you decide to add a fourth group (call it WEB) and want to make it equal in priority to OLTP, and to double DSS and BATCH, you will have to change all the directives to achieve this:

OLTP 33%
WEB 33%
DSS 17%
BATCH 17%

The ratio method lets you specify proportions. The absolute values have no significance. For example, the original ratios could have been

OLTP 20
DSS 10
BATCH 10

and now, to add the WEB group with a priority equal to OLTP, you only have to add one new directive,

WEB 20

and leave the others unchanged.

The Active Session Pool Method

It may be that investigation has shown that a certain number of jobs can be run concurrently by one group of users with no problems, but that if this number is exceeded, then other groups will have difficulties. For example, it might be that the telesales company has six management accountants, logging on with Oracle usernames in the DSS group. If one, two, or even three of them generate reports at the same time, everything is fine, but if four or more attempt to run reports concurrently, then the OLTP users begin to suffer.

The active session pool method of the Resource Manager lets the DBA limit the number of statements that will run concurrently for one group, without restricting the actual number of logins. To continue the example, all six accountants can be connected, and if three of them submit reports, they will all run, but if a fourth submits a job, it will be queued until one of the other three finishes. The nighttime plan would remove all restrictions of this nature.

An *active session* is defined as a session that is running a query, or a session that is in an uncommitted transaction. If parallel processing has been enabled, the individual parallel processors do not count against the session pool; rather, the entire parallel operation counts as one active session. By default, a session will be queued indefinitely, but if you wish, you can set a time limit. If a session from the pool does not become available within this limit, the statement is aborted and an error returned to the session that issued it.

EXAM TIP A session that is not actually doing anything will still count against the active session pool for the group if it has made a change and not committed it.

To enable the active session pool, either use the API directly or go through Database Control, as in Figure 21-6. In this example, when the daytime plan is active, BATCH users are limited to only one active session. If a second BATCH user issues any kind of SQL statement before the first has completed, it will be queued until the first statement has finished. DSS users are limited to three active sessions, but they are queued for only five minutes. If a session waits longer than that, an error will be returned.

To monitor the effect of the active session pool, a column CURRENT_QUEUE_DURATION in V$SESSION will show for every queued session the number of seconds it has been waiting. The view V$RSRC_CONSUMER_GROUP gives a global picture, showing how many sessions for each group are queued at any given moment.

What if the active session pool were set to zero for all groups? The result would be that all sessions would hang. This is in fact a very useful capability, and it is used by the command ALTER SYSTEM QUIESCE RESTRICTED.

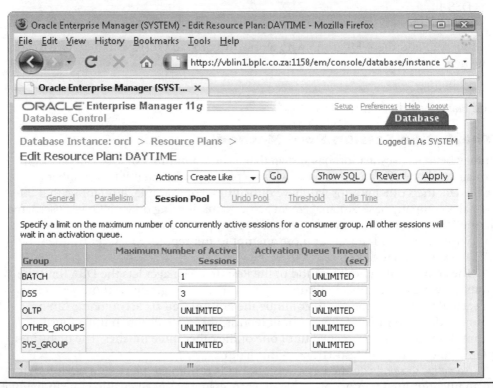

Figure 21-6 Enabling active session pools

This command activates the Resource Manager plan INTERNAL_QUIESCE, which sets the active session pool for all groups other than the SYS_GROUP to zero. The effect is that statements in progress will continue until they finish, but that no one (other than members of the SYS_GROUP) can issue any more statements. If they do, the session will hang. In effect, the database is frozen for all but the administrators. This can be invaluable to get a stable system for a moment of maintenance work.

To cancel the quiesce, issue ALTER SYSTEM UNQUIESCE.

 TIP Quiesce is invaluable for DDL operations that require a very short exclusive object lock, such as an online index rebuild: quiesce the database, launch the operation, and then unquiesce. The rebuild operation will continue, and users may not have noticed that they were ever blocked.

Limiting the Degree of Parallelism

Parallel processing, both for SELECT statements and for DML, can greatly enhance the performance of individual statements, but the price you pay may be an impact on other users. To enable parallel processing, you must, as a minimum,

- Create a pool of parallel execution servers, with the PARALLEL_MAX_SERVERS instance parameter.
- Enable parallelism for each table, with the ALTER TABLE <*table name*> PARALLEL command.
- Enable parallel DML for your session with ALTER SESSION ENABLE PARALLEL DML (parallel query will be enabled automatically for the session, if parallelism is set for the table).

The problem is that once you enable parallel processing, you cannot stop anyone from using it. It may be that your management accountants have discovered that if they run a query with the degree of parallelism set to 50 (and you cannot control this—it is done by hints in the code they write), then the report generates faster. But do you really want one session to take 50 parallel execution servers from the pool? That may not leave enough for other work. Furthermore, the query may now run faster but cripple the performance of the rest of the database. The Resource Manager can control this, by setting a hard limit on the number of parallel processors that each session of any one group is allowed to use. In the daytime plan, for instance, you might limit the DSS and BATCH groups to no more than four per session, even if they ask for 50, and not permit OTHER_GROUPS sessions to use parallel processing at all. The nighttime plan could remove these restrictions.

As with all Resource Manager limits, this can be set through the API or through Database Control, as Figure 21-7 illustrates.

PART III

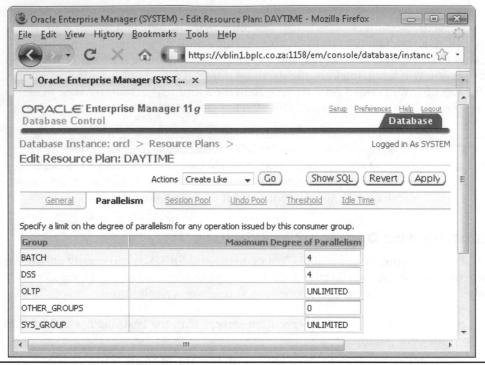

Figure 21-7 Restricting parallelism

Controlling Jobs by Execution Time

The problem of one large job killing performance for everyone else is well known in the database world. The Resource Manager solves this by providing a mechanism whereby large jobs can be completely eliminated from the system at certain times.

In Figure 21-8, for the daytime plan, severe limits have been placed on the maximum execution time of statements submitted by all users except the SYS_GROUP. Any jobs submitted by the DSS or BATCH users will be canceled if they would not complete in one minute. An even more severe restriction is applied to the OLTP group. Because OLTP has been given a much higher priority at the CPU level, a large job submitted by an OLTP user would be much more serious than one submitted by other users (the OLTP sessions are meant to be used for running small, fast queries and transactions), so this setting will eliminate any job that would take more than ten seconds to complete. The tightest restriction is on OTHER_GROUPS sessions: if they submit a request that takes more than ten seconds, the session will be terminated.

The nighttime plan would remove these restrictions, so that the long-running queries and batch jobs could go through when online performance is less important.

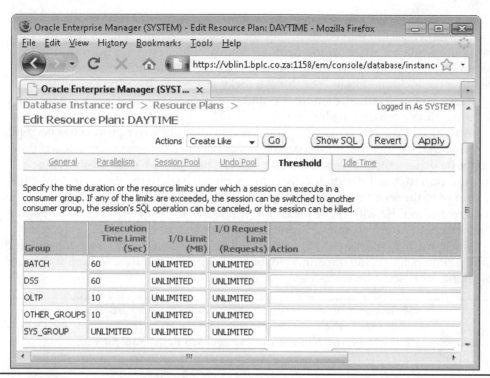

Figure 21-8   Controlling execution times

Terminating Sessions by Idle Time

Sessions that are not doing anything waste machine resources. Every session consists, on the server side, of a server process and a PGA. Even if the session is not executing a statement, the operating system must still bring it onto the CPU according to its round-robin time-slicing algorithm. This is known as a *context switch*. Every context switch forces the computer to do a lot of work as registers are loaded from main memory, the state of the session checked, and then the registers cleared again. If the PGA has been paged to disk, that too must be reloaded into main memory. The shared server mechanism, detailed in Chapter 4, will help to reduce idle processes, but it can't do anything about the number of sessions. The UGAs (in the SGA, remember) will still be taking up memory, and Oracle still has to check the state of the session on a regular basis.

The Resource Manager can disconnect sessions that are not working, according to two criteria. The first is simply based on idle time: how long is it since the session executed a statement? The second is more sophisticated: it not only checks how long since a session executed a statement, but also whether the session is holding any record or table locks that are blocking other sessions, which is a much more serious problem.

Remember from Chapter 8 that a record lock enqueue held by one session will cause another session that needs to lock the same row to hang indefinitely; this can cause the whole database to stop working if the problem escalates from session to session. It is possible for the DBA to detect this problem, identify the session that is holding the lock, and kill it—but this is a tricky procedure. By using the Resource Manager, you can configure automatic killing of any sessions that block other sessions for more than a certain length of time.

An important point is that "idle time" is time that the server process has been idle, not time that the user process has been idle. For example, your management accountant might be using a spreadsheet as his user process: he will have downloaded some information to it, to work on locally before saving it back to the database. While this is going on, the server process is indeed idle, but the user could be working flat-out in the spreadsheet. He will not be pleased if, when tries to pass the information back, he finds that you have disconnected him and perhaps lost all his work in progress.

In Figure 21-9, all groups except SYS_GROUPS have been given reasonable amounts of idle time before being disconnected, but much more aggressive settings if they are blocking other sessions.

 TIP It is also possible to disconnect sessions by using profiles assigned to named users, which you must enable with the instance parameter RESOURCE_ LIMITS. However, the Resource Manager is a better tool for this.

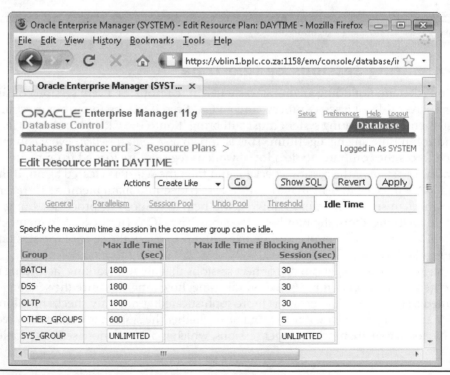

Figure 21-9 Configuring idle time disconnection with Database Control

Restricting Generation of Undo Data

Management of undo data was covered in Chapter 8. All DML statements must generate undo data, and this data must be stored until the transaction has been committed or rolled back. Oracle has no choice about this; it is according to the rules of a relational database. If you have configured the UNDO_RETENTION instance parameter and set the RETENTION GUARANTEE attribute for your undo tablespace, then the undo data may well be kept for some considerable time after the transaction has committed.

All your undo data will be written to a single undo tablespace, unless (against Oracle Corporation's advice) you are using the outdated rollback segment method of undo management. This means that transactions from all users are sharing a common storage area. A potential problem is that one badly designed transaction could fill this storage area, the undo tablespace.

Programmers should not design large, long-running transactions. In business terms, though, huge transactions may be necessary to preserve the integrity of the system. For example, an accounting suite's nominal ledger cannot be partly in one accounting period, and partly in the next: this is an impossibility in accountancy. So the rollover from one period to the next could mean updating millions of rows in thousands of tables over many hours, and then committing. This will require a huge undo tablespace and will also cause record-locking problems as the big transaction blocks other work. The answer is to break up the one business transaction into many small database transactions programmatically. If this is a problem, go back to the developers; there is nothing you as DBA can do to fix it.

As DBA, however, you can prevent large transactions by one group of users from filling up the undo tablespace. If your batch routines do not commit regularly, they will write a lot of undo data that cannot be overwritten. If too many of these batch jobs are run concurrently, the undo tablespace can fill up with active undo. This will cause all transactions to cease, and no more transactions can start, until one of them commits. The Resource Manager provides a mechanism whereby the undo tablespace can in effect be partitioned into areas reserved for different consumer groups.

Your calculations on undo generated per second and your desired undo retention (as derived from the V$UNDOSTAT view, and your requirements for long running queries and the flashback query capability) might show that the undo tablespace should be, for example, 8GB. To be safe, you size it at 12GB. But to ensure that the small OLTP transactions will always have room for their undo data, you can limit the space used by the BATCH group to, say, 6GB during normal working hours by assigning an undo pool in a Resource Manager plan. To calculate the undo space necessary for individual transactions, you can query the view V$TRANSACTION while the transaction is in progress. The column USED_UBLK shows how much undo is being used by each active transaction.

EXAM TIP The undo pool per group has nothing to do with tablespace quotas, which are assigned per user. You cannot even grant quotas on undo tablespaces.

When the amount of active undo data generated by all sessions of a certain consumer group hits its pool limit (which you can set through Database Control, as shown in Figure 21-10), it will no longer be possible for members of that group to add more undo to current transactions or to start new transactions: they will hang until one transaction commits, thus freeing up space within the pool. Meanwhile, other groups can continue working in the remainder of the undo tablespace. This restricts the effect of generating too much undo to one group, rather than having it impact on all users.

Automatic Consumer Group Switching

In the discussion of consumer groups, you saw that one user can be a member of multiple groups, and that either the user or the system administrator can switch a user's session from one consumer group to another.

Why would one wish to do this? From the user's point of view, they will presumably want to activate their membership in the group that has the highest priority at any given time. So if the daytime plan gives priority to OLTP and the nighttime plan gives priority to DSS, then if you are a member of both groups, you will switch between them as the different plans are activated. So whichever plan is enabled, you will always have the highest priority available to you.

The DBA may wish to switch users' sessions for a very different reason: to reduce the impact one session is having on others. This will mean identifying sessions that are causing problems and downgrading them, rather than upgrading them, which is what the typical user would like. It may well be that a job that kills the database if run

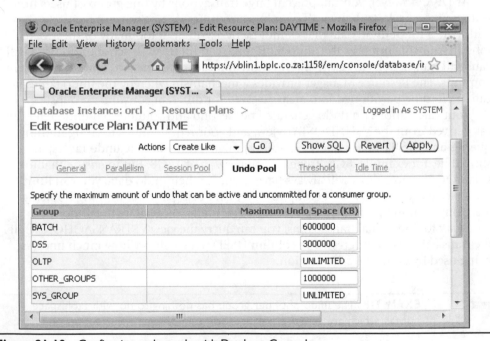

Figure 21-10 Configuring undo pools with Database Control

at normal priority can run without impacting other sessions if its priority is reduced. Of course, it will take longer to complete, but that may not be a problem (at least, not to everyone else). To do this manually would be extremely difficult, requiring continuous monitoring of sessions and workload. This is exactly what the Resource Manager can do.

Automatic consumer group switching can switch a session permanently, or just for one call. The former technique might be acceptable in a client-server environment where each end user has a dedicated session, but the latter technique will be preferable in cases where a large number of users are connected to an application server that is funneling their application server sessions through a small number of shared database sessions. In this environment, each user will issue a series of commands through the application server, which may be picked up by any of the database sessions; there is not a persistent link between any one application server session and any one database session, so it becomes preferable to manage group switches at the call level.

Automatic consumer group switching can be based on the amount of CPU time or the amount of I/O (measured in megabytes or I/O requests). If the threshold is time based, it is possible to switch the session before the call starts if the optimizer estimates that the call might exceed the threshold.

 TIP Enabling the switch-on-estimate capability places great faith in the accuracy of the optimizer's estimate. This accuracy (or lack thereof) will be dependent on many factors, the accuracy of the object statistics in particular.

Adaptive Consumer Group Mapping

The default method for assigning sessions to consumer groups is through the Oracle username, as specified by the INITIAL_RSRC_CONSUMER_GROUP displayed in DBA_USERS. The initial group can be changed at any time, either manually or by the automatic consumer group switching capability based on the workload of the statements being executed. While this is useful if users have their own schema login, in many environments this is not good enough for one simple reason: in large systems, it is common for all users to connect to the same schema. Partly this is an administrative convenience (in an environment with hundreds or thousands of users, to manage security through the schema mechanism would be an impossible workload for the DBA) and for web applications it is an architectural limitation. In an application server environment, a large number of users will connect to the application server using the stateless HTTP web protocol; the application server will connect to the database with a relatively small number of persistent database sessions. The application server distributes the workload of requests from the users across the pool of database sessions, which are all connected as the same database user.

In an environment where many users share one schema, the schema identity is not sufficient to distinguish between them and allocate them to appropriate resource manager consumer groups. For this reason, there are a number of other attributes of a session that can be used to map it (either permanently or temporarily) to a consumer group.

Table 21-1 lists all the attributes, in their default order of priority: the first to match is applied. Thus, an explicit setting will always take precedence, but if that has not been done (either manually or automatically), then the Resource Manager will try them in order until it finds one that has been configured.

To use either MODULE or ACTION as the mapping attribute, your programmers must embed calls in their code to the DBMS_APPLICATION_INFO package to name the modules and the actions within them; typically, a PL/SQL package would be assigned a module name, and the procedures and functions within it could be named as actions. Thus, a session can be given a certain priority when it runs certain blocks of code.

To use the SERVICE as the mapping attribute, you must ensure that some users connect through one database service, and some through another. This will require setting up multiple service names in the SERVICE_NAMES instance parameter (or programmatically, by using the DBMS_SERVICE package to create and start the services) and configuring the client side of Oracle Net such that different users will request a different service. Then users who connect through one service (such as DSS) could be assigned to a lower priority group than users connecting through another service (such as OLTP).

The three CLIENT_* attributes are visible as the columns PROGRAM, OSUSER, and MACHINE in the V$SESSION dynamic performance view. These will assign a consumer group according to the user process being used (perhaps so that a data mining tool could have low priority), or the operating system ID on the client

1	EXPLICIT	Switch to a group either by using the API or by using automatic consumer group switching.
2	SERVICE_MODULE_ACTION	Switch to a group according to the action name being executed, the program module, and the service used to connect.
3	SERVICE_MODULE	Switch to a group according to the service name used to connect and the program module.
4	MODULE_NAME_ACTION	Switch to a group according to the program module and the action within it being executed.
5	MODULE_NAME	Switch to a group according to the program module.
6	SERVICE_NAME	Activate a group at login according to the service name used to connect.
7	ORACLE_USER	Activate a group at login according to Oracle user ID used to connect.
8	CLIENT_PROGRAM	Activate a group at login according to the user process being used to connect.
9	CLIENT_OS_USER	Activate a group at login according to the operating system ID on the client machine.
10	CLIENT_MACHINE	Activate a group at login according to the name of the client machine.

Table 21-1 Session Attributes

machine, or the machine itself (perhaps so that sessions from different application servers could be assigned to different groups).

The order of the attributes in the preceding table is critical, and it can be changed. Consider a user connected to Oracle from a PC in the management accountants' office (with the machine name DSS_PC1) as Oracle user CLERK. You can use the Resource Manager API to map both the Oracle username and the machine name to a consumer group:

```
SQL> exec dbms_resource_manager.set_consumer_group_mapping(-
dbms_resource_manager.oracle_user,'CLERK','OLTP');
SQL> exec dbms_resource_manager.set_consumer_group_mapping(-
dbms_resource_manager.client_machine,'DSS_PC1','DSS');
```

By default, according to the preceding table, the user will be assigned to the OLTP group, because his Oracle username takes precedence over the location he has connected from. This could be changed by swapping the order around:

```
SQL> exec dbms_resource_manager.set_consumer_group_mapping_pri(-
EXPLICIT => 1, -
SERVICE_MODULE_ACTION => 2, -
SERVICE_MODULE => 3, -
MODULE_NAME_ACTION => 4, -
MODULE_NAME => 5, -
SERVICE_NAME => 6, -
ORACLE_USER => 10, -
CLIENT_PROGRAM => 8, -
CLIENT_OS_USER => 9, -
CLIENT_MACHINE => 7,);
```

From now on, the machine that the user is working from will determine his active Resource Manager group, no matter what Oracle username he logs in as. The current order of precedence is displayed in the view DBA_RSRC_MAPPING_PRIORITY. The session could then be switched dynamically after the session has been established according to which block of code he happens to be running.

To manage mapping through Database Control, take the Resource Consumer Group Mappings link in the Resource Manager section under the Administration tab.

TIP The Resource Manager is a very powerful facility, but it is a mission to set up. Make use of the graphical tools (because the APIs are not a lot of fun) and always copy the output of Show SQL, so that you can recreate the environment if necessary.

Exercise 21-2: Configure and Test Automatic Consumer Group Switching
Set up a mechanism that will automatically downgrade all large jobs to a low priority. Do this with Database Control, but whenever possible click the SHOW SQL button and study the API calls being generated.

1. Connect to your database as user SYSTEM with Database Control.

2. Choose the Server tab on the database home page, and then the Consumer Groups link in the Resource Manager section.

3. Click CREATE to reach the Create Resource Consumer Group window.

4. Enter **HIGH** as the name of the group, and click ADD to display a list of all users.

5. Select the check boxes for the four users you created earlier: ACCT, BATCH, CLERK, and MGR. Click SELECT.

6. Click OK to create the group and return to the Consumer Groups window.

7. Select the new group, and click CREATE LIKE to create another group. Name it **MEDIUM**, and allocate your four users as members of the group. Create a third group called **LOW**, and again allocate your four users as members of this group.

8. From the database home page, choose the Server tab; then click the Users link in the Security section.

9. Select each of the four users ACCT, BATCH, CLERK, and MGR in turn, and click EDIT. On the Consumer Group Privileges tab, set the Default Consumer Group for each user to HIGH.

10. Navigate to the Resource Plans window, and click CREATE to reach the Create Resource Plan window. Enter **AUTO_SWITCH** as the name of the plan, select the Activate This Plan check box, and click MODIFY to reach the Select Groups/ Subplans window.

11. Select your HIGH, MEDIUM, and LOW groups and move them to the Resource Allocations section. Click OK to return to the Create Resource Plan window.

12. Enter priorities for the consumer groups at level 1, as shown in the illustration.

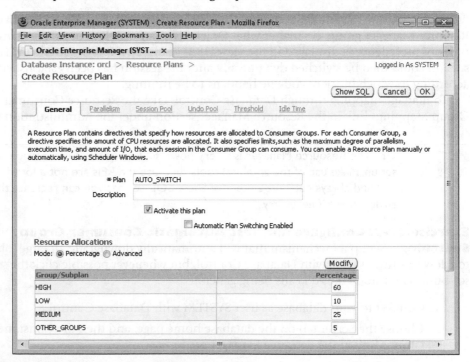

13. Choose the Threshold tab, and configure switching as in the illustration. This will switch users from their initial group of HIGH down to MEDIUM if a job takes more than five seconds, and then down to LOW priority if it takes more than ten seconds at MEDIUM.

14. Click OK to execute the configuration, and return to the Resource Plans window.
15. In a SQL*Plus session, connect as user CLERK.
16. In a second SQL*Plus session, connect as user SYSTEM and confirm that CLERK's active group is HIGH:

```
SQL> select resource_consumer_group from v$session where username='CLERK';
```

17. In the CLERK session, simulate launching a large job by running a query that does a Cartesian join based on a view with many rows, for example:

```
SQL> select count(*) from all_objects,all_objects;
```

18. While the query is running, in your second session reissue the query in Step 16 a few times, and you will see the CLERK session being downgraded from HIGH to MEDIUM after five seconds, and then to LOW after a further ten seconds.
19. Tidy up by using Database Control to activate the Default Plan.

Two-Minute Drill

Understand the Database Resource Manager

- The Resource Manager enables you to prioritize sessions.
- Users are assigned to consumer groups, and plans allocate resources to these groups.

- Resources can be controlled by emphasis (CPU usage) and absolute methods (such as parallelism or execution time).
- Sessions can be switched between groups manually, or automatically according to execution time or various session attributes.

Create and Use Database Resource Manager Components

- A pending area must be created in memory before working with the Resource Manager.
- Users must be granted membership of consumer groups.
- A plan can be activated by setting the RESOURCE_MANAGER_PLAN parameter manually, or with the DBMS_RESOURCE_MANAGER.SWITCH_PLAN procedure call, or automatically by the Scheduler.
- All sessions must have an active consumer group, which defaults to DEFAULT_CONSUMER_GROUP.
- Every plan must have a directive for the consumer group OTHER_GROUPS.

Self Test

1. There are several steps involved in setting up the Resource Manager:
   a. Assign users to consumer groups.
   b. Create consumer groups
   c. Create directives
   d. Create the pending area
   e. Create the plan
   f. Submit the pending area
   g. Validate the pending area

   What is the correct order for accomplishing these steps? (Choose the best answer.)
   A. d-e-g-f-c-b-a
   B. d-b-a-e-c-g-f
   C. d-b-a-c-e-g-f
   D. d-b-a-v-e-f-g
   E. b-a-d-e-c-f-g

2. Which of the following statements, if any, are correct about users and consumer groups? (Choose all correct answers.)

A. One user can only be a member of one consumer group.

B. One user can be a member of many consumer groups.

C. The SYS_GROUP is reserved for the user SYS.

D. By default, the initial group for all users is DEFAULT_CONSUMER_GROUP.

3. Some actions in the Resource Manager API are done with procedures in the package DBMS_RESOURCE_MANAGER_PRIVS, and others with procedures in the package DBMS_RESOURCE_MANAGER. Mark the following actions accordingly:

A. Granting the privilege to administer the Resource Manager

B. Placing users in groups

C. Removing users from groups

D. Switching a session's effective group

E. Creating consumer groups

F. Configuring how to map sessions to groups

4. Resource Manager plans can use a number of methods to control resources. Which of the following are possible? (Choose three correct answers.)

A. CPU usage

B. Tablespace quota usage

C. Number of active sessions

D. Number of idle sessions

E. Volume of redo data generated

F. Volume of undo data generated

5. A CPU method plan allocates resources at two levels as follows:

1.   Level 1: SYS_GROUP, 50% OLTP, 50%

2.   Level 2: DSS,50% BATCH, 50%

If the only users logged on are from the BATCH group, what percentage of CPU can they use? (Choose the best answer.)

A. 12.5%

B. 25%

C. 50%

D. 100%

E. The plan will not validate because it attempts to allocate 200% of CPU resources.

6. You create a Resource Manager plan limiting the active session pool for the group DSS to 3. What will happen if three members of the group are logged on, and a fourth member attempts to connect? (Choose the best answer.)

   A. The new session will not be able to connect until an existing session disconnects.

   B. The new session will be able to connect but will hang immediately.

   C. The new session will be able to connect but will only be able to run queries, not DML statements.

   D. Any statements the new session issues may hang, depending on other activity.

7. If the active Resource Manager plan specifies that sessions belonging to a particular group may only have four parallel execution servers, what will happen if a session in that group issues a statement that requests six parallel execution servers? (Choose the best answer.)

   A. The statement will not run.

   B. The statement will run with four parallel servers.

   C. It will depend on the setting of the PARALLEL_MIN_PERCENT instance parameter.

   D. It will depend on the setting of the PARALLEL_AUTOMATIC_TUNING instance parameter.

8. When you use the Resource Manager to define an undo pool, what happens? (Choose the best answer.)

   A. If a user exceeds their quota on the undo tablespace, their session will hang.

   B. If a user exceeds their quota on the undo tablespace, the statement running will be rolled back but the rest of the statement will remain intact.

   C. If a group fills its undo pool, all the group's transactions will hang until one session commits, rolls back, or is terminated.

   D. The effect depends on whether RETENTION GUARANTEE is enabled for the undo tablespace.

9. Which of the following statements are correct regarding adaptive consumer group switching? (Choose two answers.)

   A. If a group exceeds its permitted CPU usage, one or more of its sessions will be downgraded.

   B. Switching can be triggered by transient session attributes.

   C. Switching can be triggered by SQL statement execution time or volume of I/O.

   D. You can configure whether the switch is permanent, or for one statement.

10. The pending area is an area of memory used to configure the Resource Manager before saving the configuration to the data dictionary. For which

of these operations must you create, validate, and submit a pending area? (Choose the best answer.)

A. Adding users to consumer groups

B. Creating consumer groups

C. Using the CREATE_SIMPLE_PLAN procedure

D. None of the above

11. There are a number of session attributes that can be used to map a session to a particular consumer group, other than the Oracle username. Which of the following is not a valid attribute for this purpose? (Choose the best answer.)

A. The operating system ID on the client machine

B. The name of the program module being executed

C. The time of the session logon

D. The user process

Self Test Answers

1. ☑ C. This is the correct sequence, though d-b-e-c-g-f-a will also work.
   ☒ A, B, D, and E. None of these sequences will work, because the pending area must be active when working with groups and plans, and cannot be validated after it has been submitted.

2. ☑ B. One user can be a member of many groups, though only one membership is active at any time.
   ☒ A, C, and D. A is wrong because there can be a many-to-many relationship between users and groups. C is wrong because it is possible to put other users in the SYS group. D is wrong because SYS and SYSTEM are, by default, in the SYS_GROUP group.

3. ☑ DBMS_RESOURCE_MANAGER_PRIVS: A, B, C
   DBMS_RESOURCE_MANAGER: D, E, F
   The DBMS_RESOURCE_MANAGER_PRIVS package handles security, while the DBMS_RESOURCE_MANAGER package manages everything else.
   ☒ All other possibilities.

4. ☑ A, C, and F. The emphasis method controls CPU usage. Active sessions and volume of undo data are two of the absolute methods.
   ☒ B, D, and E. Tablespace usage can be limited by quotas, not by the Resource Manager. Idle sessions can be timed out, but not limited in number. Redo volume is not a possible limit.

5. ☑ D. If no other sessions are connected, then all CPU resources will be available to the connected sessions.

☒ A, B, C, and E. A, B, and C misinterpret the "trickle down" nature of resource allocation. E fails to appreciate that CPU is allocated at each priority level, not across priority levels.

6. ☑ D. The session pool does not limit the number of sessions, only the number of active sessions.

☒ A, B, and C. A is wrong because it describes the effect of session limits in profiles, not the Resource Manager. B is wrong because this result would only occur if the active session pool were full. C is wrong because the Resource Manager makes no distinction between the types of SQL statements.

7. ☑ B. The limit will override the request.

☒ A, C, and D. A is wrong because the intent of the Resource Manager is not to block statements, but to control them. C and D refer to the instance parameters that drive the optimizer, not the Resource Manager.

8. ☑ C. Undo pools refer to whole groups, not to individual users or sessions. If a group fills its pool, all sessions that are part of the group will hang until one issues a COMMIT or a ROLLBACK.

☒ A, B, and D. Tablespace quotas are relevant to neither undo in general, nor the Resource Manager. Retention Guarantee does not apply either.

9. ☑ B and C. A session's group membership is reevaluated whenever certain attributes change, and can be triggered by execution time or I/O.

☒ A and D. A is wrong because CPU usage is used for the emphasis method, not for the absolute methods that can trigger a group change. D is wrong because the whole point of adaptive switching is that it should be temporary.

10. ☑ B. Any creation or modification of Resource Manager objects requires a pending area.

☒ A, C, and D. A is wrong because placing users in groups is a modification to the user, not the Resource Manager. C is wrong because the CREATE_SIMPLE_PLAN procedure automates the whole process, and so it does not require explicitly creating a pending area. D is wrong because group creation is impossible without a pending area.

11. ☑ C. The time can control the plan, not users' effective groups.

☒ A, B, and D. All of these are valid attributes for initial consumer group mapping.

CHAPTER 22

The Scheduler

Exam Objectives

In this chapter you will learn to

- 053.18.1   Create a Job, Program, and Schedule
- 053.18.1   Use a Time-Based or Event-Based Schedule for Executing Scheduler Jobs
- 053.18.1   Create Lightweight Jobs
- 053.18.1   Use Job Chains to Perform a Series of Related Tasks
- 053.19.1   Create Windows and Job Classes
- 053.19.2   Use Advanced Scheduler Concepts to Prioritize Jobs

There will be many occasions when you as DBA, or your users, need to automate the scheduling and running of jobs. These jobs could be of many kinds—for example, maintenance work, such as database backups; data loading and validation routines; report generation; collecting optimizer statistics; or executing business processes. The Scheduler is a facility that can be used to specify tasks to be run at some point (or points) in the future. The jobs can run within the database, on the machine hosting the database instance, or even on a remote machine.

The Scheduler can be coupled to the Resource Manager. It can activate Resource Manager plans and run jobs with the priorities assigned to various Resource Manager consumer groups.

The Scheduler was introduced in release 10*g* of the Oracle database and is substantially enhanced in release 11*g*. In earlier releases of the database, job scheduling capabilities were provided through the DBMS_JOB facility. This is still supported for backward compatibility, but it is not as versatile as the Scheduler.

The Scheduler Architecture

The data dictionary includes a table that is the storage point for all Scheduler jobs. You can query this table through the DBA_SCHEDULER_JOBS view. The job queue coordinator background process, the CJQ0 process, monitors this table and when necessary launches job queue processes, the J*nnn* processes, to run the jobs. The CJQ0 process is launched automatically if there are any defined and active Scheduler jobs. The J*nnn* processes are launched on demand, though the maximum number is limited by the JOB_QUEUE_PROCESSES instance parameter, which can have any value from zero to a thousand (the default). If set to zero, the Scheduler will not function.

The job queue coordinator picks up jobs from the job queue table and passes them to job queue processes for execution. It also launches and terminates the job queue processes on demand. To see the processes currently running, query the V$PROCESS view:

```
SQL> select program from v$process where program like '%J%';
PROGRAM
------------------------------------------------
oracle@vblin1.bplc.co.za (CJQ0)
oracle@vblin1.bplc.co.za (J000)
oracle@vblin1.bplc.co.za (J001)
```

This query shows that the job queue coordinator and two job queue processes are running. In a Unix instance, the processes will be separate operating system processes (as in this query); in a Windows instance they execute as threads within the ORACLE.EXE process.

 EXAM TIP The JOB_QUEUE_PROCESSES instance parameter must be greater than zero or the Scheduler cannot run. It is 1000 by default. The job queue coordinator will always be running if there any defined and active jobs.

Jobs defined as procedures run within the database. Jobs can also be defined as operating system commands or shell scripts: these will run as external operating system tasks. The triggering factor for a job can be a time or an event. Time-based jobs may run once, or repeatedly according to a schedule. Event-based jobs run when certain conditions arise. There are some preconfigured events, or you can use user-defined events. Jobs can be connected into a chain, using simple rules for branching depending on a job's success or failure.

An advanced feature of the Scheduler is to associate it with the Resource Manager. It may be that certain jobs should be run with certain priorities, and this can be achieved by linking a job to a Resource Manager consumer group. It is also possible to use the Scheduler to activate a Resource Manager plan, rather than having to activate a plan manually by changing the RESOURCE_MANAGER_PLAN instance parameter or using the DBMS_RESOURCE_MANAGER.SWITCH_PLAN procedure call.

The Scheduler can be configured with an API—the DBMS_SCHEDULER package—and monitored through a set of data dictionary views, or it can be managed with Database Control.

Scheduler Objects

The most basic object in the Scheduler environment is a *job*. A job can be completely self-contained: it can define the action to be taken, and when to take it. In a more advanced configuration, the job is only a part of the structure consisting of a number of Scheduler objects of various types.

Jobs

A job specifies what to do, and when to do it.

The "what" can be an anonymous PL/SQL block (which could consist of just a single SQL statement), a PL/SQL stored procedure (which could invoke a Java stored procedure or an external procedure), or any executable file stored in the server's file system: either a binary executable or a shell script. A particularly powerful capability (beyond the scope of the OCP curriculum) is the remote external job, which runs on a separate machine.

The "when" specifies either the timestamp at which to launch the job and a repeat interval for future runs, or the triggering event.

There are several options when creating a job, as can be seen from looking at the DBMS_SCHEDULER.CREATE_JOB procedure. This procedure is overloaded; it has no less than six forms. Figure 22-1 shows part of the output from a DESCRIBE of the DBMS_SCHEDULER package, showing the first three forms of CREATE_JOB.

All forms of the CREATE_JOB procedure must specify a JOB_NAME. This must be unique within the schema in which the job is created. Note that jobs are schema objects.

Then, taking the first form of the procedure, the JOB_TYPE must be one of PLSQL_BLOCK, STORED_PROCEDURE, EXECUTABLE, or CHAIN. If JOB_TYPE is PLSQL_BLOCK, then JOB_ACTION can be either a single SQL statement or a PL/SQL block. If the JOB_TYPE is STORED_PROCEDURE, then JOB_ACTION must

```
oracle@vblin1:~                                                  ☐ ▫ ✕

PROCEDURE CREATE_JOB
  Argument Name                  Type                     In/Out Default?
  ------------------------       ----------------------   ------ --------
  JOB_NAME                       VARCHAR2                 IN
  JOB_TYPE                       VARCHAR2                 IN
  JOB_ACTION                     VARCHAR2                 IN
  NUMBER_OF_ARGUMENTS            BINARY_INTEGER           IN      DEFAULT
  START_DATE                     TIMESTAMP WITH TIME ZONE IN      DEFAULT
  REPEAT_INTERVAL                VARCHAR2                 IN      DEFAULT
  END_DATE                       TIMESTAMP WITH TIME ZONE IN      DEFAULT
  JOB_CLASS                      VARCHAR2                 IN      DEFAULT
  ENABLED                        BOOLEAN                  IN      DEFAULT
  AUTO_DROP                      BOOLEAN                  IN      DEFAULT
  COMMENTS                       VARCHAR2                 IN      DEFAULT
PROCEDURE CREATE_JOB
  Argument Name                  Type                     In/Out Default?
  ------------------------       ----------------------   ------ --------
  JOB_NAME                       VARCHAR2                 IN
  JOB_TYPE                       VARCHAR2                 IN
  JOB_ACTION                     VARCHAR2                 IN
  NUMBER_OF_ARGUMENTS            BINARY_INTEGER           IN      DEFAULT
  START_DATE                     TIMESTAMP WITH TIME ZONE IN      DEFAULT
  EVENT_CONDITION                VARCHAR2                 IN
  QUEUE_SPEC                     VARCHAR2                 IN
  END_DATE                       TIMESTAMP WITH TIME ZONE IN      DEFAULT
  JOB_CLASS                      VARCHAR2                 IN      DEFAULT
  ENABLED                        BOOLEAN                  IN      DEFAULT
  AUTO_DROP                      BOOLEAN                  IN      DEFAULT
  COMMENTS                       VARCHAR2                 IN      DEFAULT
PROCEDURE CREATE_JOB
  Argument Name                  Type                     In/Out Default?
  ------------------------       ----------------------   ------ --------
  JOB_NAME                       VARCHAR2                 IN
  PROGRAM_NAME                   VARCHAR2                 IN
  SCHEDULE_NAME                  VARCHAR2                 IN
  JOB_CLASS                      VARCHAR2                 IN      DEFAULT
  ENABLED                        BOOLEAN                  IN      DEFAULT
  AUTO_DROP                      BOOLEAN                  IN      DEFAULT
  COMMENTS                       VARCHAR2                 IN      DEFAULT
  JOB_STYLE                      VARCHAR2                 IN      DEFAULT
```

Figure 22-1   The specification of the CREATE_JOB procedure

name a stored procedure, which can be anything that conforms to the PL/SQL call specification: a PL/SQL stored procedure, a Java stored procedure, or an external procedure written in C. If the JOB_TYPE is EXECUTABLE, then the JOB_ACTION can be anything that could be run from an operating system command-line prompt: an individual command, an executable binary file, or a shell script or batch file. If the JOB_TYPE is CHAIN, then the steps of the chain will be defined separately. The NUMBER_OF_ARGUMENTS parameter states how many arguments the JOB_ACTION should take.

The first form of the procedure, shown in Figure 22-1, continues with details of when and how frequently to run the job. The first execution will be on the START_DATE; the REPEAT_INTERVAL defines a repeat frequency, such as daily, until END_DATE. JOB_CLASS has to do with priorities and integration of the Scheduler with the

Resource Manager. The ENABLED argument determines whether the job can actually be run. Perhaps surprisingly, this defaults to FALSE. If a job is not created with this argument on TRUE, it cannot be run (either manually, or through a schedule) without enabling it first. Finally, AUTO_DROP controls whether to drop the job definition after the END_TIME. This defaults to TRUE. If a job is created with no scheduling information, it will be run as soon as it is enabled, and then dropped immediately if AUTO_DROP is on TRUE, which is the default.

The second form of CREATE_JOB shown in Figure 22-1 creates an event-based job. The EVENT_CONDITION is an expression based on the definition of the messages enqueued to the queue table nominated by the QUEUE_SPEC argument. Between the start and end dates, Oracle will monitor the queue and launch the job whenever a message arrives that conforms to the condition.

The third form of the CREATE_JOB procedure has the job details replaced with a PROGRAM_NAME that points to a program, which will provide these details, and the scheduling details replaced with a SCHEDULE_NAME that points to a schedule, which will manage the timing of the runs.

Programs

Programs provide a layer of abstraction between the job and the action it will perform. They are created with the DBMS_SCHEDULER.CREATE_PROGRAM procedure:

```
PROCEDURE CREATE_PROGRAM
Argument Name            Type                  In/Out Default?
----------------------   --------------------  ------ --------
PROGRAM_NAME             VARCHAR2              IN
PROGRAM_TYPE             VARCHAR2              IN
PROGRAM_ACTION           VARCHAR2              IN
NUMBER_OF_ARGUMENTS      BINARY_INTEGER       IN     DEFAULT
ENABLED                  BOOLEAN              IN     DEFAULT
COMMENTS                 VARCHAR2             IN     DEFAULT
```

By pulling the "what" of a job out of the job definition itself and defining it in a program, it becomes possible to reference the same program in different jobs, and thus to associate it with different schedules and job classes, without having to define it many times. Note that (as for a job) a program must be ENABLED before it can be used; the default for this is FALSE.

Schedules

A *schedule* is a specification for when and how frequently a job should run. The basic principle of a schedule is to pull out the "when" portion of a job out of a job, thus associating it with different jobs. It is created with the DBMS_SCHEDULER.CREATE_ SCHEDULE procedure:

```
PROCEDURE CREATE_SCHEDULE
Argument Name       Type                           In/Out Default?
----------------    -------------------------      ------ --------
SCHEDULE_NAME       VARCHAR2                       IN
START_DATE          TIMESTAMP WITH TIME ZONE       IN     DEFAULT
REPEAT_INTERVAL     VARCHAR2                       IN
END_DATE            TIMESTAMP WITH TIME ZONE       IN     DEFAULT
COMMENTS            VARCHAR2                       IN     DEFAULT
```

PART III

The START_DATE defaults to the current date and time. This is the time that any jobs associated with this schedule will run. The REPEAT_INTERVAL specifies how frequently the job should run, until the END_DATE. Schedules without a specified END_DATE will run forever.

The REPEAT_INTERVAL argument can take a wide variety of calendaring expressions. These consist of up to three elements: a frequency, an interval (defaulting to 1), and possibly several specifiers. The frequency may be one of these values:

YEARLY
MONTHLY
WEEKLY
DAILY
HOURLY
MINUTELY
SECONDLY

The specifiers can be one of these:

BYMONTH
BYWEEKNO
BYYEARDAY
BYMONTHDAY
BYHOUR
BYMINUTE
BYSECOND

Using these elements of a REPEAT_INTERVAL makes it possible to set up schedules that should satisfy any requirement. For example,

```
repeat_interval=>'freq=hourly; interval=12'
```

will run the job every 12 hours, starting at the START_DATE. The next example,

```
repeat_interval=>'freq=yearly; bymonth=jan,apr,jul,oct; bymonthday=2'
```

will run the job on the second day of each of the named four months, starting as early in the day as resources permit. A final example,

```
repeat_interval=>'freq=weekly; interval=2; byday=mon; byhour=6; byminute=10'
```

will run the job at ten past six on alternate Mondays.

Using programs and schedules normalizes the job structure, allowing reuse of predefined programs and schedules for many jobs, as shown in Figure 22-2.

Job Classes

A job class is used to associate one or more jobs with a Resource Manager consumer group, and also to control logging levels. Create a class with the DBMS_SCHEDULER .CREATE_JOB_CLASS procedure:

```
PROCEDURE CREATE_JOB_CLASS
Argument Name                  Type                In/Out Default?
------------------------       ------------------  ------ --------
JOB_CLASS_NAME                 VARCHAR2            IN
RESOURCE_CONSUMER_GROUP        VARCHAR2            IN     DEFAULT
SERVICE                        VARCHAR2            IN     DEFAULT
LOGGING_LEVEL                  BINARY_INTEGER      IN     DEFAULT
LOG_HISTORY                    BINARY_INTEGER      IN     DEFAULT
COMMENTS                       VARCHAR2            IN     DEFAULT
```

The JOB_CLASS_NAME is the name to be referenced by the JOB_CLASS argument of the CREATE_JOB procedure. The RESOURCE_CONSUMER_GROUP nominates the group whose resource allocations should be applied to the running job, as determined by the Resource Manager plan in effect whenever the job happens to run. The SERVICE has significance only in a RAC database: you can restrict the job to run only on an instance offering a particular service name. The details of logging can also be specified per class.

Windows

A *schedule* specifies exactly when a job should be launched. *Windows* extend the concept of schedules, by giving Oracle more freedom to decide when to run the job. A window opens at a certain time and closes after a certain duration: jobs specified to run in a window may be launched, at Oracle's discretion, at any time during the window. The window itself can open repeatedly according to a schedule. Use of windows is of particular value when combined with classes and the Resource Manager: Oracle can schedule jobs to run within a window according to their relative priorities. Windows also activate Resource Manager plans.

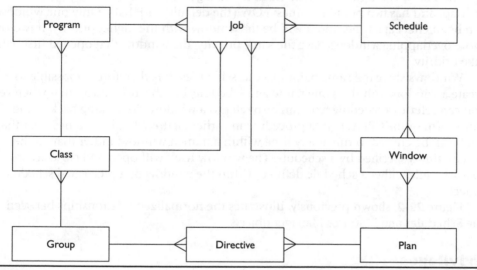

Figure 22-2   The relationships between Scheduler and Resource Manager objects

Create windows with the DBMS_SCHEDULER.CREATE_WINDOW procedure:

```
PROCEDURE CREATE_WINDOW
Argument Name          Type                          In/Out Default?
-------------------    ------------------------      ------ --------
WINDOW_NAME            VARCHAR2                       IN
RESOURCE_PLAN          VARCHAR2                       IN
START_DATE             TIMESTAMP WITH TIME ZONE IN          DEFAULT
REPEAT_INTERVAL        VARCHAR2                       IN
END_DATE               TIMESTAMP WITH TIME ZONE IN          DEFAULT
DURATION               INTERVAL DAY TO SECOND         IN
WINDOW_PRIORITY        VARCHAR2                       IN    DEFAULT
COMMENTS               VARCHAR2                       IN    DEFAULT
```

The RESOURCE_PLAN nominates the Resource Manager plan that will be activated when the window opens. The window will open on the START_DATE and reopen according to the REPEAT_INTERVAL until the END_DATE. The procedure is overloaded; there is a second form that lets you nominate a precreated schedule rather than specifying the schedule here with these three arguments.

The DURATION is an INTERVAL DAY TO SECOND datatype. This will allow a time span to be specified in days, hours, minutes, and seconds. The basic syntax for an INTERVAL DAY TO SECOND column is

```
'<days> <hours>:<minutes>:<seconds>'
```

Note that there is a space between the days and the hours, and colons between the hours, minutes, and seconds. So this,

```
'1 2:3:4'
```

specifies a time gap of one day, two hours, three minutes, and four seconds.

The PRIORITY argument is intended to manage circumstances where windows overlap, and has two possible values: LOW (the default) or HIGH. Only one window can be in effect at a time, and it will be the window with the higher priority. If two or more overlapping windows have the same priority, the window that opened first will take priority.

Windows share the same namespace as schedules. It is therefore impossible to create a window with the same name as a schedule, but this does mean that wherever you can refer to a schedule, you can also refer to a window. So looking back to the third form of the CREATE_JOB procedure in earlier Figure 22-1, it becomes clear that a job can be created to run at any time within a named window, rather than at the precise times specified by a schedule. The window itself will open and close according to a schedule, either a schedule defined within the window or a precreated schedule object.

Figure 22-2, shown previously, illustrates the normalized relationships between the Scheduler and Resource Manager objects.

Privileges

All Scheduler privileges are granted and revoked with the usual GRANT and REVOKE syntax. There are a number of Scheduler-related privileges:

- CREATE JOB
- CREATE ANY JOB
- CREATE EXTERNAL JOB
- EXECUTE ANY PROGRAM
- EXECUTE ANY CLASS
- MANAGE SCHEDULER
- EXECUTE ON <job, program, or class>
- ALTER ON <job, program, or schedule>
- ALL ON <job, program, schedule, or class>

Before a user can create any jobs, schedules, or programs, they must be granted the CREATE JOB privilege; this includes the ability to create and use their own programs and schedules. To create jobs in other schemas, the user will need CREATE ANY JOB. External jobs require a separate privilege. To use Scheduler objects in other schemas, you need the EXECUTE privilege on them. The MANAGE SCHEDULER privilege is needed to create job classes and windows, and to force windows to open or close irrespective of their schedules.

The ready-made role SCHEDULER_ADMIN includes the first six privileges just listed. It is granted to SYSTEM with ADMIN by default.

Creating and Scheduling Jobs

Time-driven jobs can be independent, or tied to a program and a schedule. Event driven jobs are launched by some triggering event. Jobs can be linked together, with dependencies, into a chain. An advanced concept is that of the *lightweight job*: a technique for creating many jobs very fast, without the overhead of standard jobs.

A Self-Contained Job

To create and schedule a job with one procedure call, use the CREATE_JOB procedure. For example,

```
begin
dbms_scheduler.create_job(
job_name=>'hr.refresh_sums',
job_type=>'stored_procedure',
job_action=>'hr.refresh_summaries',
start_date=>trunc(sysdate)+23/24,
repeat_interval=>'freq=weekly;byday=mon,tue,wed,thu,fri;byhour=23',
enabled=>true,
auto_drop=>false,
comments=>'update summary tables');
end;
```

This will create an enabled job that will call the procedure HR.REFRESH_SUMMARIES at eleven o'clock every weekday evening, starting today. The job is created in the HR schema.

Exercise 22-1: Create a Job with the Scheduler API   Use the DBMS_
SCHEDULER package to create a job, and confirm that it is working.

1. Connect to your database as user SYSTEM using SQL*Plus.

2. Create a table to store times, and set your date format to show the date and time.

```
SQL> create table times (c1 date);
SQL> alter session set nls_date_format='dd-mm-yy hh24:mi:ss';
```

3. Create a job to insert the current time into the table every minute.

```
SQL> begin
  2   dbms_scheduler.create_job(
  3    job_name=>'savedate',
  4    job_type=>'plsql_block',
  5    job_action=>'insert into times values(sysdate);',
  6    start_date=>sysdate,
  7    repeat_interval=>'freq=minutely;interval=1',
  8    enabled=>true,
  9    auto_drop=>false);
 10   end;
 11  /
PL/SQL procedure successfully completed.
```

4. Query the job and times tables a few times to see that the job is scheduled
and running:

```
SQL> select job_name,enabled,
to_char(next_run_date,'dd-mm-yy hh24:mi:ss'),run_count from
user_scheduler_jobs;
SQL> select * from times;
```

5. Disable the job.

```
SQL> exec dbms_scheduler.disable('savedate');
```

6. Rerun the queries from Step 4 to confirm that the job is disabled, and that no
more inserts are occurring.

7. Drop the job:

```
SQL> exec dbms_scheduler.drop_job('savedate');
```

Using Programs and Schedules

Programs and schedules enable you to reuse Scheduler components for similar tasks.
Rather than defining each job as a self-contained entity, you create programs and
schedules, each of which can be used by many jobs.

The job created in Exercise 22-1 could be split up into a job, a program, and a
schedule. To do this through Database Control, from the database home page select
the Server tab. Then in the Oracle Scheduler section select the Programs link, click
CREATE, and enter the code you want executed as in Figure 22-3. This can be as long
and complicated as you want, within the 32K limit of the PL/SQL VARCHAR2 datatype.

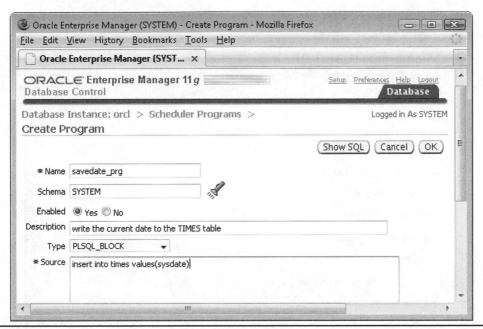

Figure 22-3 Creating a program with Database Control

TIP Keep your JOB_ACTIONs and PROGRAM_ACTIONs as short as possible, preferably just one statement. Do all the work in a procedure invoked by that statement. This will be far easier to maintain than having a large amount of SQL or PL/SQL in your job and program definitions.

If you create a program with the CREATE_PROGRAM procedure, then (just as with jobs) the program will be disabled by default. Change this default either by specifying the ENABLED argument as TRUE when you create the program or by using the ENABLE procedure subsequently:

```
SQL> exec dbms_scheduler.enable('myprogram');
```

To create a schedule, choose the Schedules link from the Oracle Scheduler section, and click CREATE to view the page shown in Figure 22-4. The GUI interface does not give access to some of the more complicated interval possibilities, such as every third Tuesday, which would be

```
'freq=weekly;interval=3;byday=tue'
```

but it gives access to all that will usually be required.

Figure 22-4   Creating a schedule with Database Control

To create a job, select the Jobs link. The initial window (shown in Figure 22-5) assumes that the job is a PL/SQL block. Select the CHANGE COMMAND TYPE button to nominate your program. The Schedule link lets you tie the job to a precreated schedule, rather than defining the schedule within the job. Note that Database Control by default reverses the values for ENABLED and AUTO DROP from the actual defaults.

 TIP Programs share the same namespace as jobs: you cannot have a program with the same name as a job. The same is true for schedules and windows.

It is also possible to run a job independently of a schedule, by using the RUN_JOB procedure:

```
SQL> exec dbms_scheduler.run_job('savedate');
```

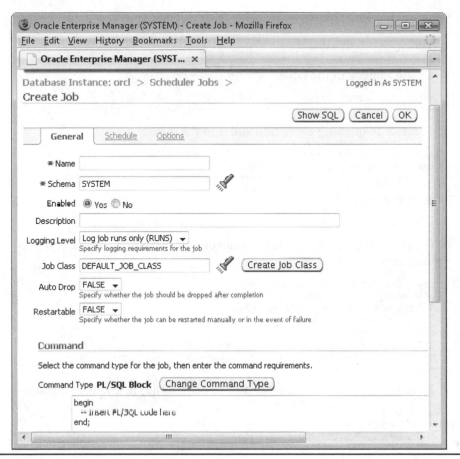

Figure 22-5 Creating a job with Database Control

Event-Driven Jobs

The event that launches an event-driven job takes the form of a message delivered to a queue. The Oracle Database's Advanced Queuing facility is a means for managing the asynchronous delivery of messages. The queue exists within a table, one column of which is a user-defined object that carries the payload of the message; the other columns are used by the Advanced Queuing control structures. The flow is that a process (or possibly several processes) should place messages on the queue. The Scheduler will monitor the queue and, depending on the content of messages, launch particular jobs.

A full treatment of this is beyond the scope of the OCP examinations, but an appreciation of how an event can launch a job is required. This is a summary of the steps with examples of the necessary code to implement a job that will run when a file has been delivered:

1. Create an abstract data type to define the events:

```
create type incoming_t as object(event_type number);
```

2. Create a queue table to store queues that use this object type:

```
exec dbms_aqadm.create_queue_table(queue_table=>'incoming_qt',-
queue_payload_type=>'incoming_t',multiple_consumers=>true);
```

3. Create a queue in the table:

```
exec dbms_aqadm.create_queue(-
queue_name=>'incoming_q',queue_table=>'incoming_qt');
```

4. Create a de-queuing agent, and add it to the queue:

```
exec dbms_aqadm.create_aq_agent('inc_agent');
exec dbms_aqadm.add_subscriber(-
'incoming_q',sys.aq$_agent('inc_agent',null,null));
```

5. Start the queue:

```
exec dbms_aqadm.start_queue(queue_name=>'incoming_q');
```

6. Create a job that will monitor the queue and run when a certain event is enqueued:

```
exec dbms_scheduler.create_job(-
job_name => 'load_data',-
job_type => 'stored_procedure',-
job_action => 'read_file',-
start_date => systimestamp,-
queue_spec => 'incoming_q,inc_agent',-
event_condition => 'tab.user_data.event_type=1',-
enabled => true);
```

7. Include code in the event generating application(s) to enqueue messages:

```
declare
enqueue_options dbms_aq.enqueue_options_t;
message_properties dbms_aq.message_properties_t;
msgid raw(16);
payload incoming_t;
begin
payload := incoming_t(1);
dbms_aq.enqueue(queue_name => 'incoming_q',
enqueue_options => enqueue_options,
message_properties => message_properties,
payload => payload,
msgid => msgid);
commit;
end;
```

8. Confirm that the job was launched:

```
select actual_start_date,status from dba_scheduler_job_run_details
where job_name='LOAD_DATA';
```

This very simple example is intended to illustrate a mechanism whereby the arrival of a file could trigger the running of a job. The code in Step 7 would be executed by the process that generates, or detects, the file: it enqueues a message with the value of the payload's single attribute set to 1. This value will be checked by the Scheduler, which will then run the LOAD_DATA job.

Job Chains

A chain represents a set of linked programs with execution dependencies. The steps to follow to use job chains are

1. Create a chain object.
2. Define the steps (the individual programs) of the chain.
3. Define the rules connecting the steps.
4. Enable the chain.
5. Create a job to launch the chain.

This code fragment demonstrates the first four steps:

```
exec dbms_scheduler.create_chain(chain_name=>'mychain');
exec dbms_scheduler.define_chain_step(chain_name => 'mychain',-
step_name => 'step1',program_name => 'prg1');
exec dbms_scheduler.define_chain_step(chain_name => 'mychain',-
step_name => 'step2',program_name => 'prg2');
exec dbms_scheduler.define_chain_step(chain_name => 'mychain',-
step_name => 'step3',program_name => 'prg3');
exec dbms_scheduler.define_chain_rule(chain_name => 'mychain',-
rule_name => 'rule1',condition => 'step1 succeeded',-
action => 'start step2');
exec dbms_scheduler.define_chain_rule(chain_name => 'mychain',-
rule_name => 'rule2',condition => 'step1 failed',-
action => 'start step3');
exec dbms_scheduler.enable('mychain');
```

These commands create and enable a very simple chain of three steps. The execution of either the second or third step is dependent on the outcome of the first step. The syntax for creating rules permits the use of keywords such as SUCCEEDED and FAILED, which will test the outcome of another step. Figure 22-6 shows the result of running the preceding code, as seen through Database Control.

To launch the chain, you must create a job. This could be based on a schedule, or an event. This job will run the chain on the last Tuesday of alternate months:

```
exec dbms_scheduler.create_job(job_name=>'run_mychain',-
job_type=>'chain',job_action=>'mychain',-
start_date=>next_day(last_day(sysdate)-7,'tuesday'),-
repeat_interval=>'freq=monthly;interval=2',-
enabled=>true);
```

Lightweight Jobs

Creating and launching a job involves a certain amount of activity within the data dictionary. This may make it impossible to create a large number (perhaps hundreds) of jobs in a short time (perhaps a few seconds). To get around this problem, it is possible to create *lightweight jobs*. A lightweight job is a simpler construct than a regular job. It must be based on a program, and can have only a limited range of attributes: for example, AUTO_DROP is always TRUE. A lightweight job can be created individually, but there is little value in this. The real value comes with the ability to create an array of job definitions (perhaps hundreds) and submit them all simultaneously.

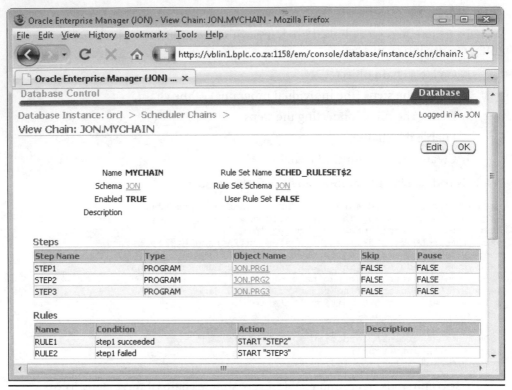

Figure 22-6 A job chain, created in the schema JON

TIP It is not possible to create lightweight jobs with Database Control; the option is not visible in any of the windows. You must therefore use the DBMS_ SCHEDULER API.

To create a single lightweight job, use a version of the CREATE_JOB procedure call that specifies a program and set the JOB_STYLE argument to LIGHTWEIGHT. For example:

```
SQL>  exec dbms_scheduler.create_job(-
> job_name=>'lw21',program_name=>'prg1',-
> enabled=>true,job_style=>'lightweight',-
> end_date=>to_timestamp(sysdate+1),repeat_interval=>'freq=hourly');
```

This will create a lightweight job that will run the program PRG1 every hour for the next 24 hours.

Study the code in Figure 22-7, which creates and executes an array of 100 lightweight jobs.

```
oracle@vblin1:~
SQL> declare
  2  lw_job sys.job;
  3  lw_job_array sys.job_array;
  4  begin
  5  lw_job_array := sys.job_array();
  6  lw_job_array.extend(100);
  7  for i in 1..100 loop
  8  lw_job := sys.job(job_name=>'lw_job'||to_char(i),job_style=>'lightweight',
  9  job_template=>'prg1',enabled=>true);
 10  lw_job_array(i) := lw_job;
 11  end loop;
 12  dbms_scheduler.create_jobs(lw_job_array,'transactional');
 13  end;
 14  /

PL/SQL procedure successfully completed.

SQL> select job_name from user_scheduler_jobs;

no rows selected

SQL> select job_name,status from user_scheduler_job_log
  2  where job_name like 'LW_JOB%';

JOB_NAME        STATUS
------------    ---------------------------
LW_JOB1         SUCCEEDED
LW_JOB10        SUCCEEDED
LW_JOB100       SUCCEEDED
LW_JOB11        SUCCEEDED
LW_JOB15        SUCCEEDED
```

Figure 22-7   Creating lightweight jobs with the PL/SQL API

The following table describes each line in the anonymous PL/SQL block in Figure 22-7.

Line 2	Define a variable named LW_JOB of type SYS.JOB.
Line 3	Define an array of LW_JOBs.
Line 4	Begin the executable code.
Line 5	Initialize the array using the SYS.JOB_ARRAY function.
Line 6	Extend the array to 100 elements.
Line 7	Open a loop, to be iterated 100 times.
Lines 8 & 9	Populate the LW_JOB variable with values that will create an enabled lightweight job named by the loop counter and using the program PRG1.
Line 10	Insert the new job into the array.
Line 11	Close the loop.
Line 12	Create all the jobs defined in the array, in a single transaction.
Line 13	End the executable code.
Line 14	Run anonymous block.

The first query in the figure shows that there are no jobs. This is because AUTO_DROP is always TRUE for lightweight jobs, and END_DATE will have defaulted to the current timestamp. So once the jobs have run, they will be dropped. Since the jobs were created with ENABLED set to TRUE, they will have been run immediately as they were created. The second query (output truncated) proves that the jobs were created and did indeed run, successfully.

In this example, the only difference between the jobs is their names, which include a suffix generated by the loop counter. The array could, however, consist of jobs that run different programs, and if they were set up to take arguments, these could be different as well.

 TIP When would you use lightweight jobs? Perhaps to parallelize a business operation consisting of many distinct tasks. After changing your web sales price list, for example, you may need to refresh a vast number of web pages cached on your application server. As each would be identified with a different URL, you would have to send many distinct messages. You would want to send them in as short a time as possible.

Using Classes, Windows, and the Resource Manager

The more advanced capabilities of the Scheduler enable you to integrate it with the Resource Manager, to control and prioritize jobs. These are the relevant components:

- **Job classes** Jobs can be assigned a class, and a class can be linked to a Resource Manager consumer group. Classes also control the logging level for their jobs.

- **Consumer groups** Resource Manager consumer groups are restricted in the resources they can use, being limited in, for instance, CPU usage or the number of active sessions.

- **Resource plans** A Resource Manager plan defines how to apportion resources to groups. Only one plan is active in the instance at any one time.

- **Windows** A window is a defined (probably recurring) period of time, during which certain jobs will run and a certain plan will be active.

- **Window groups** It is possible to combine windows into window groups, for ease of administration.

Prioritizing jobs within a window is done at two levels. Within a class, jobs can be given different priorities by the Scheduler, but because all jobs in a class are in the same consumer group, the Resource Manager will not distinguish between them. But if jobs in different classes are scheduled within the same window, the Resource Manager will assign resources to each class according to the consumer groups for that class.

Using Job Classes

Create a class with Database Control, or through the API. For example,

```
SQL> exec dbms_scheduler.create_job_class(-
job_class_name=>'daily_reports',-
resource_consumer_group=>'dss',-
logging_level=>dbms_scheduler.logging_full);
```

Then assign the jobs to the class, either at job creation time by specifying the JOB_CLASS attribute, or by modifying the job later. To assign a job to a class with the API, you must use the SET_ATTRIBUTE procedure. To put the job REPORTS_JOB into the class just created,

```
SQL> exec dbms_scheduler.set_attribute(-
name=>'reports_job',-
attribute=>'job_class',-
value=>'daily_reports');
```

If there are several jobs in the one class, prioritize them with further SET_ATTRIBUTE calls:

```
SQL> exec dbms_scheduler.set_attribute(-
name=>'reports_job',-
attribute->'job_priority',-
value=>2);
```

If several jobs in the same class are scheduled to be executed at the same time, the job priority determines the order in which jobs from that class are picked up for execution by the job coordinator process. It can be a value from 1 through 5, with 1 being the first to be picked up for job execution. The default for all jobs is 3. This could be critical if, for example, the class's consumer group has an active session pool that is smaller than the number of jobs: those jobs with the highest priority will run first, while the others are queued.

TIP To set priorities with Database Control, on the Options tab of the Create Job window set the priority to one of "Very high," "High," "Medium," "Low," and "Very low," These are mapped onto the numeric values 1 to 5.

EXAM TIP It is not possible to assign priorities when creating jobs with the CREATE_JOB procedures—you must use the SET_ATTRIBUTE procedure of the API subsequently.

Logging levels are also controlled by the job's class. There are three options:

- **DBMS_SCHEDULER.LOGGING_OFF** No logging is done for any jobs in this class.

- **DBMS_SCHEDULER.LOGGING_RUNS**   Information is written to the job log regarding each run of each job in the class, including when the run was started and whether the job ran successfully.
- **DBMS_SCHEDULER.LOGGING_FULL**   In addition to logging information about the job runs, the log will also record management operations on the class, such as creating new jobs.

To view logging information, query the DBA_SCHEDULER_JOB_LOG view:

```
SQL> select job_name,log_date,status from dba_scheduler_job_log;
JOB_NAME      LOG_DATE                        STATUS
------------  ------------------------------  ------------
PURGE_LOG     16-JAN-05 13-00-03              SUCCEEDED
TEST_JOB      16-JAN-05 11-00-00              FAILED
NIGHT_INCR    16-JAN-05 01-00-13              SUCCEEDED
NIGHT_ARCH    16-JAN-05 01-00-00              SUCCEEDED
```

More detailed information is written to the DBA_SCHEDULER_JOB_RUN_DETAILS view, including the job's run duration and any error code it returned.

Logging information is cleared by the automatically created PURGE_LOG job. By default, this runs daily according to the preconfigured schedule DAILY_PURGE_SCHEDULE and will remove all logging information more than 30 days old.

Using Windows

Create windows either through Database Control or with the CREATE_WINDOW procedure. For example,

```
SQL> exec dbms_scheduler.create_window(-
window_name=>'daily_reporting_window',-
resource_plan=>'night_plan',-
schedule_name=>'weekday_nights',-
duration=>'0 08:00:00',-
window_priority=>'low',-
comments=>'for running regular reports');
```

This window activates a Resource Manager plan called NIGHT_PLAN. This might be a plan that gives priority to the DSS consumer groups over the OLTP group. It opens according to the schedule WEEKDAY_NIGHTS, which might be Monday through Friday at 20:00. The window will remain open for eight hours; the DURATION argument accepts an INTERVAL DAY TO SECOND value, as does the REPEAT_INTERVAL for a schedule. Setting the priority to LOW means that if this window overlaps with another window, then the other window will be allowed to impose its Resource Manager plan. This would be the case if you created a different window for your end-of-month processing, and the end-of-month happened to be on a weekday. You could give the end-of-month window HIGH priority, to ensure that the end-of-month Resource Manager plan, which could give top priority to the BATCH group, does come into effect.

 EXAM TIP Even if a job has priority 1 within its class, it might still only run after a job with priority 5 in another class—if the second job's class is in a consumer group with a higher Resource Manager priority.

If two windows with equal priority overlap, the window with longest to run will open (or remain open). If both windows have the same time to run, the window currently open will remain open.

 TIP Oracle Corporation advises that you should avoid using overlapping windows.

Exercise 22-2: Use Scheduler Windows to Control the Resource Manager
In this exercise, you will use the Scheduler to automate the activation of the Resource Manager plan DAYTIME created in Exercise 21-1.

1. Connect to your database as user SYSTEM with SQL*Plus.

2. Run this query to determine which window is currently open:

   ```
   select WINDOW_NAME,ACTIVE from dba_scheduler_windows;
   ```

3. Run this query to determine which Resource Manager plan is currently active:

   ```
   select * from v$rsrc_plan;
   ```

   You will see that one of the preconfigured plans (DEFAULT or DEFAULT_ MAINTENANCE) and its subplans are active.

4. Temporarily clear whatever Resource Manager plan may be currently active:

   ```
   alter system set resource_manager_plan='' scope=memory;
   ```

5. Confirm that there is no Resource Manager plan active:

   ```
   select * from v$rsrc_plan;
   ```

   This will return no rows.

6. Execute this procedure call to create a window named DAYTIME that will activate the DAYTIME plan:

   ```
   exec dbms_scheduler.create_window(-
   window_name=>'daytime',resource_plan=>'daytime',-
   start_date=>trunc(systimestamp) + 6/24,repeat_interval=>'freq=daily',-
   duration=>'0 12:00:00',comments=>'daily at 6AM');
   ```

   This will open the window from now onward every morning at 6 o'clock, for 12 hours.

7. Force the database to open the new window immediately:

   ```
   exec dbms_scheduler.open_window(-
   window_name=>'daytime',duration=>'0 00:05:00',force=>true);
   ```

   This procedure call will open the window immediately and activate its plan, but only for five minutes.

8. Rerun the query from Step 3 or 5 to confirm that the DAYTIME window is open and the DAYTIME plan is active.

9. After five minutes, repeat Step 8. You will see that the window has closed and that no plan is active. This situation will persist until the next scheduled opening of a window.

10. Tidy up with Database Control: connect as SYSTEM.

11. From the database home page take the Server tab, then the Windows link in the Oracle Scheduler section. Select the DAYTIME window, and click DELETE.

Two-Minute Drill

Create a Job, Program, and Schedule

- A job can specify what to do and when to do it, or it can point to a program and/or a schedule.
- A job (or its program) can be an anonymous PL/SQL block, a stored procedure, or an external operating system command or script.
- Either Database Control or the DBMS_SCHEDULER API can be used to manage the Scheduler environment.

Use a Time-Based or Event-Based Schedule for Executing Scheduler Jobs

- A time-based schedule has start and end dates, and a repeat interval.
- The repeat interval can be a date expression, or a calendaring expression consisting of a frequency, an interval, and possibly several specifiers.
- An event-based schedule uses an agent to query an Advanced Queue, and launches jobs depending on the content of the queued messages.

Create Lightweight Jobs

- A lightweight job has less overhead in the data dictionary than a regular job, and therefore large numbers of them can be created much faster than an equivalent number of regular jobs.
- Lightweight jobs do not have the full range of attributes that regular jobs have.

Use Job Chains to Perform a Series of Related Tasks

- A chain object consists of a number of steps.
- Each step can launch a program.
- Simple logic (such as the success or failure of a previous step) can control the flow of execution through a job chain with branching steps.

Create Windows and Job Classes

- A window is a defined period during which certain jobs may run, that will itself open according to an embedded schedule or a preexisting schedule object.

- A window can activate a Resource Manager plan.

- Only one window can be open at once.

- If windows overlap, the open window will be determined by which has HIGH or LOW priority.

- A job class associates the jobs in the class with a Resource Manager consumer group.

Use Advanced Scheduler Concepts to Prioritize Jobs

- Jobs can be prioritized at two levels: the Resource Manager will allocate resources via consumer groups to all the jobs in a class, and the class will prioritize the jobs within it according to the job priority set by the Scheduler.

- Scheduler priority varies between levels 1 to 5 (highest to lowest).

Self Test

1. When a job is due to run, what process will run it? (Choose the best answer.)

    A. A CJQ*n* process

    B. A J*nnn* process

    C. A server process

    D. A background process

2. Which of the following is a requirement if the Scheduler is to work? (Choose the best answer.)

    A. The instance parameter JOB_QUEUE_PROCESSES must be set.

    B. A Resource Manager plan must be enabled.

    C. A schedule must have been created.

    D. All of the above.

    E. None of the above.

3. A Scheduler job can be of several types. Choose all that apply:

    A. An anonymous PL/SQL block

    B. An executable operating system file

    C. A PL/SQL stored procedure

    D. A Java stored procedure

    E. An operating system command

    F. An operating system shell script (Unix) or batch file (Windows)

4. You create a job with this syntax:

```
exec dbms_scheduler.create_job(-
job_name=>'j1',-
program_name=>'p1',-
schedule_name=>'s1',-
job_class=>'c1');
```

and find that it is not running when expected. What might be a reason for this? (Choose the best answer.)

A. The schedule is associated with a window, which has not opened.

B. The job has not been enabled.

C. The class is part of a Resource Manager consumer group with low priority.

D. The permissions on the job are not correct.

5. What are the possible priority levels of a job within a class? (Choose the best answer.)

A. 1 to 5

B. 1 to 999

C. HIGH or LOW

D. It depends on the Resource Manager plan in effect

6. You want job to run every 30 minutes. Which of the following possibilities for the REPEAT_INTERVAL argument are correct syntactically and will achieve this result? (Choose two answers.)

A. `'freq=minutely;interval=30'`

B. `'freq=hourly;interval=1/2'`

C. `'0 00:30:00'`

D. `'freq=minutely;byminute=30'`

E. `'freq=byminute;interval=30'`

7. You create a job class, and you set the LOGGING_LEVEL argument to LOGGING_RUNS. What will be the result? (Choose the best answer.)

A. There will be a log entry for each run of each job in the class, but no information on whether the job was successful.

B. There will be a log entry for each run of each job in the class, and information on whether the job was successful.

C. There will be a single log entry for the class whenever it is run.

D. You cannot set logging per class, only per job.

8. Which of the following statements (if any) are correct regarding how Scheduler components can be used together? (Choose all that apply.)

A. A schedule can be used by many jobs.

B. A job can use many programs.

PART III

C. A class can have many programs.

D. Job priorities can be set within a class.

E. Consumer groups control priorities within a class.

F. A Resource Manager plan can be activated by a schedule.

9. Which view will tell you about jobs configured with the Scheduler? (Choose the best answer.)

A. DBA_JOBS

B. DBA_SCHEDULER

C. DBA_SCHEDULED_JOBS

D. DBA_SCHEDULER_JOBS

10. If two windows are overlapping and have equal priority, which window(s) will be open? (Choose the best answer.)

A. Both windows will be open.

B. Windows cannot overlap.

C. Whichever window opened first will remain open; the other will remain closed.

D. Whichever window opened first will be closed, and the other will open.

E. It will depend on which window has the longest to run.

Self Test Answers

1. ☑ B. Jobs are run by job queue processes.

   ☒ A, C, and D. The job queue coordinator does not run jobs; it assigns them to job queue processes. These are not classed as background processes, and they are not server processes.

2. ☑ E. The Scheduler is available, by default, with no preconfiguration steps needed.

   ☒ A, B, C, and D. A is wrong because (in release 11g) the JOB_QUEUE_PROCESSES instance parameter defaults to 1000; therefore, it does not need to be set. B and C are wrong because the Resource Manager is not required, and neither is a schedule.

3. ☑ A, B, C, D, E, and F. The JOB_TYPE can be PLSQL_BLOCK, or STORED_PROCEDURE (which can be PL/SQL or Java), or EXECUTABLE (which includes executable files, OS commands, or shell scripts).

   ☒ All the answers are correct.

4. ☑ B. The job will, by default, not be enabled and therefore cannot run.

☒ A, C, and D. A is wrong because the job is not controlled by a window, but by a schedule. C is wrong because while the Resource Manager can control job priority, it would not in most circumstances block a job completely. D is wrong because while permissions might cause a job to fail, they would not stop it from running.

5. ☑ A. Job priorities are 1 to 5 (highest to lowest).

☒ B, C, and D. B is wrong because it is the incorrect range. C is the choice for window priority, not job priority. D is wrong because the Resource Manager controls priorities between classes, not within them.

6. ☑ A and B. Both will provide a half-hour repeat interval.

☒ C, D, and E. C is the syntax for a window's duration, not a repeat interval. D and E are syntactically wrong: there is no such specifier as BYMINUTE (though such a specifier might be useful).

7. ☑ B. With logging set to LOGGING_RUNS, you will get records of each run of each job, including the success or failure.

☒ A, C, and D. A is wrong because LOGGING_RUNS will include the success or failure. C and D are wrong because even though logging is set at the class level, it is applied at the job level. Note that logging can also be set at the job level.

8. ☑ A and D. Many jobs can be controlled by one schedule, and Scheduler priorities are applied to jobs within classes.

☒ B, C, E, and F. B and C both misunderstand the many-to-one relationships of Scheduler objects. E is wrong because consumer groups control priorities between classes, not within them. F is wrong because plans are activated by windows, not schedules.

9. ☑ D. The DBA_SCHEDULER_JOBS view externalizes the data dictionary jobs table, with one row per scheduled job.

☒ A, B, and C. A is wrong because DBA_JOBS describes the jobs scheduled through the old DBMS_JOB system. B and C refer to views that do not exist.

10. ☑ E. Other things being equal, the window with the longest to run will open (or remain open).

☒ A, B, C, and D. Only one window can be open at once, and windows can overlap. The algorithms that manage overlapping windows are not well documented, but neither C nor D is definitively correct.

CHAPTER 23

Moving and Reorganizing Data

Exam Objectives

In this chapter you will learn to

- 052.17.1 Describe and Use Methods to Move Data
  (Directory Objects, SQL*Loader, External Tables)
- 052.17.2 Explain the General Architecture of Oracle Data Pump
- 052.17.3 Use Data Pump Export and Import to Move Data Between
  Oracle Databases
- 053.16.2 Describe the Concepts of Transportable Tablespaces and Databases
- 053.16.1 Manage Resumable Space Allocation
- 053.16.3 Reclaim Wasted Space from Tables and Indexes by Using the Segment
  Shrink Functionality

831

There are many situations where bulk transfers of data into a database or between databases are necessary. Common cases include populating a data warehouse with data extracted from transaction processing systems, or copying data from live systems to test or development environments. As entering data with standard INSERT statements is not always the best way to do large-scale operations, the Oracle database comes with facilities designed for bulk operations. These are SQL*Loader and Data Pump. There is also the option of reading data without ever actually inserting it into the database; this is accomplished through the use of external tables.

Data loading operations, as well as DML, may fail because of space problems. This can be an appalling waste of time. The resumable space allocation mechanism can provide a way to ameliorate the effect of space problems. There are also techniques to reclaim space that is inappropriately assigned to objects and make it available for reuse.

SQL*Loader

In many cases you will be faced with a need to do a bulk upload of datasets generated from some third-party system. This is the purpose of SQL*Loader. The input files may be generated by anything, but as long as the layout conforms to something that SQL*Loader can understand, it will upload the data successfully. Your task as DBA is to configure a SQL*Loader controlfile that can interpret the contents of the input datafiles; SQL*Loader will then insert the data.

Architecturally, SQL*Loader is a user process like any other: it connects to the database via a server process. To insert rows, it can use two techniques: *conventional* or *direct path*. A conventional insert uses absolutely ordinary INSERT statements. The SQL*Loader user process constructs an INSERT statement with bind variables in the VALUES clause and then reads the source datafile to execute the INSERT once for each row to be inserted. This method uses the database buffer cache and generates undo and redo data: these are INSERT statements like any others, and normal commit processing makes them permanent.

The direct path load bypasses the database buffer cache. SQL*Loader reads the source datafile and sends its contents to the server process. The server process then assembles blocks of table data in its PGA and writes them directly to the datafiles. The write is above the *high water mark* of the table and is known as a *data save*. The high water mark is a marker in the table segment above which no data has ever been written: the space above the high water mark is space allocated to the table that has not yet been used. Once the load is complete, SQL*Loader shifts the high water mark up to include the newly written blocks, and the rows within them are then immediately visible to other users. This is the equivalent of a COMMIT. No undo is generated, and if you wish, you can switch off the generation of redo as well. For these reasons, direct path loading is extremely fast, and furthermore it should not impact on your end users, because interaction with the SGA is kept to a minimum.

Direct path loads are very fast, but they do have drawbacks:

- Referential integrity constraints must be dropped or disabled for the duration of the operation.
- INSERT triggers do not fire.

- The table will be locked against DML from other sessions.

- It is not possible to use direct path for clustered tables.

These limitations are a result of the lack of interaction with the SGA while the load is in progress.

 EXAM TIP Only UNIQUE, PRIMARY KEY, and NOT NULL constraints are enforced during a direct path load; INSERT triggers do not fire; the table is locked for DML.

SQL*Loader uses a number of files. The *input datafiles* are the source data that it will upload into the database. The *controlfile* is a text file with directives telling SQL*Loader how to interpret the contents of the input files, and what to do with the rows it extracts from them. *Log files* summarize the success (or otherwise) of the job, with detail of any errors. Rows extracted from the input files may be rejected by SQL*Loader (perhaps because they do not conform to the format expected by the controlfile) or by the database (for instance, insertion might violate an integrity constraint); in either case they are written out to a *bad file*. If rows are successfully extracted from the input but rejected because they did not match some record selection criterion, they are written out to a *reject file*.

The controlfile is a text file instructing SQL*Loader on how to process the input datafiles. It is possible to include the actual data to be loaded on the controlfile, but you would not normally do this; usually, you will create one controlfile and reuse it, on a regular basis, with different input datafiles. The variety of input formats that SQL*Loader can understand is limited only by your ingenuity in constructing a controlfile.

Consider this table:

```
SQL> desc dept;
 Name                                    Null?    Type
 ----------------------------------      -------- ---------------
 DEPTNO                                  NOT NULL NUMBER(2)
 DNAME                                            VARCHAR2(14)
 LOC                                              VARCHAR2(13)
```

And this source datafile, named DEPTS.TXT:

```
60,CONSULTING,TORONTO
70,HR,OXFORD
80,EDUCATION,
```

A SQL*Loader controlfile to load this data is DEPTS.CTL:

```
1       load data
2       infile 'depts.txt'
3       badfile 'depts.bad'
4       discardfile 'depts.dsc'
5       append
6       into table dept
7       fields terminated by ','
8       trailing nullcols
9       (deptno integer external(2),
10       dname,
11       loc)
```

To perform the load, from an operating system prompt run this command:

```
sqlldr userid=scott/tiger control=depts.ctl direct=true
```

This command launches the SQL*Loader user process, connects to the local database as user SCOTT password TIGER, and then performs the actions specified in the controlfile DEPTS.CTL. The DIRECT=TRUE argument instructs SQL*Loader to use the direct path rather than conventional insert (which is the default). Taking the controlfile line by line:

Line	Purpose
1	Start a new load operation.
2	Nominate the source of the data.
3	Nominate the file to write out any badly formatted records.
4	Nominate the file to write out any unselected records.
5	Add rows to the table (rather than, for example, truncating it first).
6	Nominate the table for insertion.
7	Specify the field delimiter in the source file.
8	If there are missing fields, insert NULL values.
9, 10, 11	The columns into which to insert the data.

This is a very simple example. The syntax of the controlfile can handle a wide range of formats with intelligent parsing to fix any deviations in format such as length or data types. In general you can assume that it is possible to construct a controlfile that will understand just about any input datafile. However, do not think that it is always easy.

TIP It may be very difficult to get a controlfile right, but once you have it, you can use it repeatedly, with different input datafiles for each run. It is then the responsibility of the feeder system to produce input datafiles that match your controlfile, rather than the other way around.

External Tables

An external table is visible to SELECT statements as any other table, but you cannot perform DML against it. This is because it does not exist as a segment in the database: it exists only as a data dictionary construct, pointing toward one or more operating system files. Using external files is an alternative to using SQL*Loader, and is often much more convenient.

The operating system files of external tables are located through Oracle directory objects. Directories are also a requirement for Data Pump, discussed later in this chapter.

Directories

Oracle directories provide a layer of abstraction between the user and the operating system: you as DBA create a directory object within the database, which points to a physical path on the file system. Permissions on these Oracle directories can then be granted to individual database users. At the operating system level, the Oracle user will need permissions against the operating system directories to which the Oracle directories refer.

Directories can be created either from a SQL*Plus prompt or from within Database Control. To see information about directories, query the view DBA_DIRECTORIES. Each directory has a name, an owner, and the physical path to which it refers. Note that Oracle does not verify whether the path exists when you create the directory—if it does not, or if the operating system user who owns the Oracle software does not have permission to read and write to it, you will only get an error when you actually use the directory. Having created a directory, you must give the Oracle database user(s) who will be making use of the directory permission to read from and write to it, just as your system administrators must give the operating system user permission to read from and write to the physical path.

 EXAM TIP Directories are always owned by user SYS, but any user to whom you have granted the CREATE ANY DIRECTORY privilege can create them.

Figure 23-1 demonstrates how to create directories, using SQL*Plus. In the figure, user SCOTT attempts to create a directory pointing to his operating system home directory on the database server machine. This fails because, by default, users do not have permission to do this. After being granted permission, he tries again. As the directory creator, he will have full privileges on the directory. He then grants read permission on the directory (and therefore any files within it) to all users, and read and write permission to one user. The query against ALL_DIRECTORIES shows that the directory (like all directories) is owned by SYS: directories are not schema objects. This is why SCOTT cannot drop the directory, even though he created it.

Using External Tables

A common use of external tables is to avoid the necessity to use SQL*Loader to read data into the database. This can give huge savings in the ETL (extract-transform-load) cycle typically used to update a DSS system with data from a feeder system. Consider the case where a feeder system regularly generates a dataset as a flat ASCII file, which should be merged into existing database tables. One approach would be to use SQL*Loader to load the data into a staging table, and then a separate routine to merge the rows from the staging table into the DSS tables. This second routine cannot start until the load is finished. Using external tables, the merge routine can read the source data from the operating system file(s) without having to wait for it to be loaded.

PART III

Figure 23-1

Managing directories with SQL*Plus

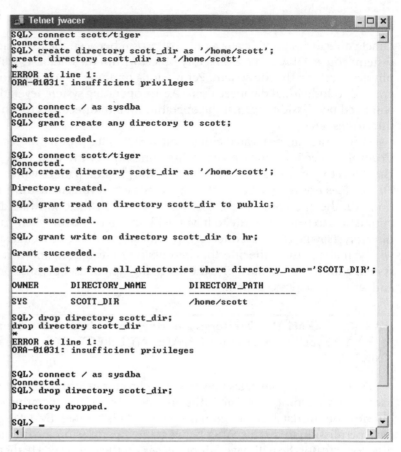

```
Telnet jwacer                                                    _ □ ×
SQL> connect scott/tiger
Connected.
SQL> create directory scott_dir as '/home/scott';
create directory scott_dir as '/home/scott'
*
ERROR at line 1:
ORA-01031: insufficient privileges


SQL> connect / as sysdba
Connected.
SQL> grant create any directory to scott;

Grant succeeded.

SQL> connect scott/tiger
Connected.
SQL> create directory scott_dir as '/home/scott';

Directory created.

SQL> grant read on directory scott_dir to public;

Grant succeeded.

SQL> grant write on directory scott_dir to hr;

Grant succeeded.

SQL> select * from all_directories where directory_name='SCOTT_DIR';

OWNER        DIRECTORY_NAME        DIRECTORY_PATH
----------   -----------------     --------------------
SYS          SCOTT_DIR             /home/scott

SQL> drop directory scott_dir;
drop directory scott_dir
*
ERROR at line 1:
ORA-01031: insufficient privileges


SQL> connect / as sysdba
Connected.
SQL> drop directory scott_dir;

Directory dropped.

SQL> _
```

To create an external table, use the CREATE TABLE command with the keywords ORGANIZATION EXTERNAL. These tell Oracle that the table does not exist as a segment. Then specify the layout and location of the operating system file. For example,

```
create table new_dept
  (deptno number(2),
  dname varchar2(14),
  loc varchar2(13))
organization external (
  type oracle_loader
  default directory jon_dir
  access parameters
    (records delimited by newline
    badfile 'depts.bad'
    discardfile 'depts.dsc'
    log file 'depts.log'
    fields terminated by ','
    missing field values are null)
  location ('depts.txt'));
```

This command will create an external table that will be populated by the DEPTS. TXT file shown in the section "SQL*Loader" earlier in this chapter. The syntax for the

ACCESS PARAMETERS is virtually identical to the SQL*Loader controlfile syntax and is used because the TYPE has been set to ORACLE_LOADER. The specification for the DEFAULT DIRECTORY gives the Oracle directory where Oracle will look for the source datafile, and where it will write the log and other files.

External tables can be queried in exactly the same way as internal tables. Any SQL involving a SELECT will function against an external table: they can be used in joins, views, and subqueries. They cannot have indexes, constraints, or triggers.

Exercise 23-1: Use SQL*Loader and External Tables   In this exercise, you will install and use SQL*Loader to insert data into a table, and also to generate the CREATE TABLE script for an external table.

1. Connect to your database as user SYSTEM (in the examples, the SYSTEM password is ORACLE) with SQL*Plus.

2. Create a table to use for the exercise:

   ```
   create table names(first varchar2(10),last varchar2(10));
   ```

3. Using any editor that will create plain text files, create a file names.txt with these values (or similar):

   ```
   John,Watson
   Roopesh,Ramklass
   Sam,Alapati
   ```

4. Using the editor, create a controlfile names.ctl with these settings:

   ```
   load data
   infile 'names.txt'
   badfile 'names.bad'
   truncate
   into table names
   fields terminated by ','
   trailing nullcols
   (first,last)
   ```

   This controlfile will truncate the target file before carrying out the insert.

5. From an operating system prompt, run SQL*Loader as follows:

   ```
   sqlldr system/oracle control=names.ctl
   ```

6. Study the log file names.log that will have been generated.

7. With SQL*Plus, confirm that the rows have been inserted:

   ```
   select * from names;
   ```

8. To generate a statement that will create an external table, you can use SQL*Loader and an existing controlfile:

   ```
   sqlldr userid=system/oracle control=names.ctl external_table=generate_only
   ```

9. This will have generated a CREATE TABLE statement in the log file names.log, which will look something like this:

   ```
   CREATE TABLE "SYS_SQLLDR_X_EXT_NAMES"
   (
     "FIRST" VARCHAR2(10),
   ```

PART III

```
        "LAST" VARCHAR2(10)
)
ORGANIZATION external
(
  TYPE oracle_loader
  DEFAULT DIRECTORY SYS_SQLLDR_XT_TMPDIR_00000
  ACCESS PARAMETERS
  (
    RECORDS DELIMITED BY NEWLINE CHARACTERSET WE8MSWIN1252
    BADFILE 'SYS_SQLLDR_XT_TMPDIR_00000':'names.bad'
    Log file 'names.log_xt'
    READSIZE 1048576
    FIELDS TERMINATED BY "," LDRTRIM
    MISSING FIELD VALUES ARE NULL
    REJECT ROWS WITH ALL NULL FIELDS
    (
      "FIRST" CHAR(255)
        TERMINATED BY ",",
      "LAST" CHAR(255)
        TERMINATED BY ","
    )
  )
  location
  (
    'names.txt'
  )
)REJECT LIMIT UNLIMITED
```

10. From your SQL*Plus session, create an Oracle directory pointing to the operating system directory where your `names.txt` file is. For example,

    ```
    create directory system_dmp as '/home/oracle';
    ```

11. Make any edits you wish to the command shown in Step 9. For example, you might want to change the name of the table being created ("SYS_SQLLDR_X_EXT_NAMES" isn't very useful) to something more meaningful. You will need to change both the DEFAULT DIRECTORY and BADFILE settings to point to the directory created in Step 10.

12. Run the statement created in Step 11 from your SQL*Plus session.

13. Query the table with a few SELECT and DML statements. You will find that a log file is generated for every SELECT, and that DML is not permitted.

14. Tidy up: delete the `names.txt` and `names.ctl` files; drop the tables; as SYS, drop the directory.

Data Pump

In the normal course of events, SELECT and DML commands are used to extract data from the database and to insert data into it, but there are occasions when you will need a much faster method for bulk operations. For many reasons it may be desirable to extract a large amount of data and the associated object definitions from a database in a form that will allow it to be easily loaded into another. One obvious purpose for extracting large amounts of data is for backups, but there are others, such as archiving of historical data before deleting it from the live system, or to transfer data between production and test environments, or between an online system and a data warehouse. Data Pump (introduced with release 10g and enhanced with 11g) is a tool for large-scale, high-speed data transfer between Oracle databases.

Data Pump Architecture

Data Pump is a server-side utility. You initiate Data Pump jobs from a user process, either SQL*Plus or through Enterprise Manager, but all the work is done by server processes. This improves performance dramatically over the old Export/Import utilities, because the Data Pump processes running on the server have direct access to the datafiles and the SGA; they do not have to go via a session. Also, it is possible to launch a Data Pump job and then detach from it, leaving it running in the background. You can reconnect to the job to monitor its progress at any time.

There are a number of processes involved in a Data Pump job, two queues, a number of files, and one table. First, the processes:

The user processes are `expdp` and `impdp` (for Unix) or `expdp.exe` and `impdp.exe` (Windows). These are used to launch, control, and monitor Data Pump jobs. Alternatively, there is an Enterprise Manager interface. The `expdp` or `impdp` user process establishes a session against the database through a normal server process. This session then issues commands to control and monitor Data Pump jobs. When a Data Pump job is launched, at least two processes are started: a Data Pump Master process (the DMnn) and one or more worker processes (named DWnn). If multiple Data Pump jobs are running concurrently, each will have its own DMnn process, and its own set of DWnn processes. As the name implies, the master process controls the workers. If you have enabled parallelism, then each DWnn may make use of two or more parallel execution servers (named Pnnn).

Two queues are created for each Data Pump job: a control queue and a status queue. The DMnn divides up the work to be done and places individual tasks that make up the job on the control queue. The worker processes pick up these tasks and execute them—perhaps making use of parallel execution servers. This queue operates on a deliver-exactly-once model: messages are enqueued by the DMnn and dequeued by the worker that picks them up. The status queue is for monitoring purposes: the DMnn places messages on it describing the state of the job. This queue operates on a publish-and-subscribe model: any session (with appropriate privileges) can query the queue to monitor the job's progress.

The files generated by Data Pump come in three forms: SQL files, dump files, and log files. SQL files are DDL statements describing the objects included in the job. You can choose to generate them (without any data) as an easy way of getting this information out of the database, perhaps for documentation purposes or as a set of scripts to recreate the database. Dump files contain the exported data. This is formatted with XML tags. The use of XML means that there is a considerable overhead in dump files for describing the data. A small table like the REGIONS table in the HR sample schema will generate a 94KB dump file, but while this overhead may seem disproportionately large for a tiny table like that, it becomes trivial for larger tables. The log files describe the history of the job run.

EXAM TIP Remember the three Data Pump file types: SQL files, log files, and dump files.

Finally, there is the control table. This is created for you by the DMnn when you launch a job, and is used both to record the job's progress and to describe it. It is included in the dump file as the final item of the job.

Directories and File Locations

Data Pump always uses Oracle directories. These are needed to locate the files that it will read or write, and its log files. One directory is all that is needed, but often a job will use several. If the amount of data is many gigabytes to be written out in parallel to many files, you may want to spread the disk activity across directories in different file systems.

If a directory is not specified in the Data Pump command, there are defaults. Every 11g database will have an Oracle directory that can be used. This is named DATA_PUMP_ DIR. If the environment variable ORACLE_BASE has been set at database creation time, the operating system location will be the ORACLE_BASE/admin/*database_name*/ dpdump directory. If ORACLE_BASE is not set, the directory will be ORACLE_HOME/ admin/*database_name*/dpdump (where *database_name* is the name of the database). To identify the location in your database, query the view DBA_DIRECTORIES. However, the fact that this Oracle directory exists does not mean it can be used; any user wishing to use Data Pump will have to be granted read and/or write permissions on it first.

Specifying the directory (or directories) to use for a Data Pump job can be done at four levels. In decreasing order of precedence, these are

- A per-file setting within the Data Pump job
- A parameter applied to the whole Data Pump job
- The DATA_PUMP_DIR environment variable
- The DATA_PUMP_DIR directory object

So it is possible to control the location of every file explicitly, or a single Oracle directory can be nominated for the job, or an environment variable can be used, or failing all of these, Data Pump will use the default directory. The environment variable should be set on the client side but will be used on the server side. An example of setting it on Unix is

```
DATA_PUMP_DIR=SCOTT_DIR; export DATA_PUMP_DIR
```

or on Windows:

```
set DATA_PUMP_DIR=SCOTT_DIR
```

Direct Path or External Table Path?

Data Pump has two methods for loading and unloading data: the direct path and the external table path. The direct path bypasses the database buffer cache. For a direct path export, Data Pump reads the datafile blocks directly from disk, extracts and formats the content, and writes it out as a dump file. For a direct path import, Data Pump reads the dump file, uses its content to assemble blocks of table data, and writes them directly to the datafiles. The write is above the "high water mark" of the table, with the same benefits as those described earlier for a SQL*Loader direct load.

The external table path uses the database buffer cache. Even though Data Pump is manipulating files that are external to the database, it uses the database buffer cache as though it were reading and writing an internal table. For an export, Data Pump reads blocks from the datafiles into the cache through a normal SELECT process. From there, it formats the data for output to a dump file. During an import, Data Pump constructs standard INSERT statements from the content of the dump file and executes them by reading blocks from the datafiles into the cache, where the INSERT is carried out in the normal fashion. As far as the database is concerned, external table Data Pump jobs look like absolutely ordinary (though perhaps rather large) SELECT or INSERT operations. Both undo and redo are generated, as they would be for any normal DML statement. Your end users may well complain while these jobs are in progress. Commit processing is absolutely normal.

So what determines whether Data Pump uses the direct path or the external table path? You as DBA have no control; Data Pump itself makes the decision based on the complexity of the objects. Only simple structures, such as heap tables without active triggers, can be processed through the direct path; more complex objects such as clustered tables force Data Pump to use the external table path because it requires interaction with the SGA in order to resolve the complexities. In either case, the dump file generated is identical.

 EXAM TIP The external table path insert uses a regular commit, like any other DML statement. A direct path insert does not use a commit; it simply shifts the high water mark of the table to include the newly written blocks. Data Pump files generated by either path are identical.

Using Data Pump Export and Import

Data Pump is commonly used for extracting large amounts of data from one database and inserting it into another, but it can also be used to extract other information such as PL/SQL code or various object definitions. There are several interfaces: command-line utilities, Enterprise Manager, and a PL/SQL API. Whatever purpose and technique are used, the files are always in the Data Pump proprietary format. It is not possible to read a Data Pump file with any tool other than Data Pump.

Capabilities

Fine-grained object and data selection facilities mean that Data Pump can export either the complete database or any part of it. It is possible to export table definitions with or without their rows; PL/SQL objects; views; sequences; or any other object type. If exporting a table, it is possible to apply a WHERE clause to restrict the rows exported (though this may make direct path impossible) or to instruct Data Pump to export a random sample of the table expressed as a percentage.

Parallel processing can speed up Data Pump operations. Parallelism can come at two levels: the number of Data Pump worker processes, and the number of parallel execution servers each worker process uses.

An estimate facility can calculate the space needed for a Data Pump export, without actually running the job.

The Network Mode allows transfer of a Data Pump data set from one database to another without ever staging it on disk. This is implemented by a Data Pump export job on the source database writing oe data over a database link to the target database, where a Data Pump import job reads the data from the database link and inserts it.

Remapping facilities mean that objects can be renamed or transferred from one schema to another and (in the case of data objects) moved from one tablespace to another as they are imported.

When exporting data, the output files can be compressed and encrypted.

Using Data Pump with the Command-Line Utilities

The executables `expdb` and `impdp` are installed into the `ORACLE_HOME/bin` directory. Following are several examples of using them. Note that in all cases the command must be a single one-line command; the line breaks are purely for readability.

To export the entire database,

```
expdp system/manager@orcl11g full=y
parallel =4
dumpfile=datadir1:full1_%U.dmp,
        datadir2:full2_%U.dmp,
        datadir3:full3_%U.dmp,
        datadir4:full4_%U.dmp,
filesize=2G
compression=all
```

This command will connect to the database as user SYSTEM and launch a full Data Pump export, using four worker processes working in parallel. Each worker will generate its own set of dump files, uniquely named according to the %U template, which generates strings of eight unique characters. Each worker will break up its output into files of 2GB (perhaps because of underlying file system restrictions) of compressed data.

A corresponding import job (which assumes that the files generated by the export have all been placed in one directory) would be

```
impdb system/manager@dev11g full=y
directory=data_dir
parallel=4
dumpfile=full1_%U.dmp,full2_%U.dmp,full3_%U.dmp,full4_%U.dmp
```

This command makes a selective export of the PL/SQL objects belonging to two schemas:

```
expdp system/manager schemas=hr,oe
directory=code_archive
dumpfile=hr_oe_code.dmp
include=function,include=package,include=procedure,include=type
```

This command will extract everything from a Data Pump export that was in the HR schema, and import it into the DEV schema:

```
impdp system/manager
directory=usr_data
dumpfile=usr_dat.dmp
schema=hr
remap_schema=hr:dev
```

Using Data Pump with Database Control

The Database Control interface to Data Pump generates the API calls that are invoked by the `expdp` and `impdp` utilities, but unlike the utilities it makes it possible to see the scripts and if desired copy, save, and edit them. To reach the Data Pump facilities, from the database home page select the Data Movement tab. In the Move Row Data section, there are four links that will launch wizards:

- **Export to Export Files**   Define Data Pump export jobs.
- **Import from Export Files**   Define Data Pump import jobs.
- **Import from Database**   Define a Data Pump network mode import.
- **Monitor Export and Import Jobs**   Attach to running jobs to observe their progress, to pause or restart them, or to modify their operation.

The final stage of each wizard gives the option to see the PL/SQL code that is being generated. The job is run by the Enterprise Manager job system, either immediately or according to a schedule. Figure 23-2 shows this final step of scheduling a simple export job of the HR.REGIONS table.

Figure 23-2
The final step of the Database Control Data Pump Export Wizard

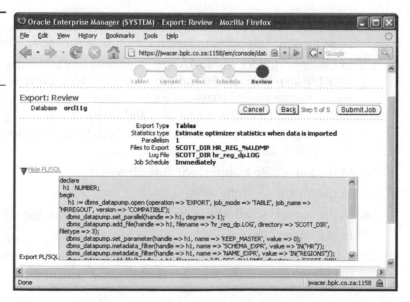

Exercise 23-2: Perform a Data Pump Export and Import In this exercise, you will carry out a Data Pump export and import using Database Control.

1. Connect to your database as user SYSTEM with SQL*Plus, and create a table to use for the exercise:

```
create table ex232 as select * from all_users;
```

2. Connect to your database as user SYSTEM with Database Control. Navigate to the Export Wizard: select the Data Movement tab from the database home page, then the Export To Export Files link in the Move Row Data section.

3. Select the radio button for Tables. Enter your operating system username and password for host credentials (if these have not already been saved as preferred credentials) and click CONTINUE.

4. In the Export: Tables window, click ADD and find the table SYSTEM.EX232. Click NEXT.

5. In the Export: Export Options window, select the directory SYSTEM_DMP (created in Exercise 23-1) as the Directory Object for Optional Files. Click NEXT.

6. In the Export: Files window, choose the directory SYSTEM_DMP and click NEXT.

7. In the Export: Schedule window, give the job a name and click NEXT to run the job immediately.

8. In the Review window, click SUBMIT JOB.

9. When the job has completed, study the log file that will have been created in the operating directory mapped onto the Oracle directory SYSTEM_DMP. Note the name of the Data Pump file EXPDAT01.DMP produced in the directory.

10. Connect to the database with SQL*Plus, and drop the table:

```
drop table system.ex232;
```

11. In Database Control, select the Data Movement tab from the database home page, then the Import from Export Files link in the Move Row Data section.

12. In the Import: Files window, select your directory and enter the filename noted in Step 9. Select the radio button for Tables. Enter your operating system username and password for host credentials (if these have not already been saved as preferred credentials) and click CONTINUE.

13. In the Import: Tables window, click ADD. Search for and select the SYSTEM.EX232 table. Click SELECT and NEXT.

14. In the Import: Re-Mapping window, click NEXT.

15. In the Import: Options window, click NEXT.

16. In the Import: Schedule window, give the job a name and click NEXT.

17. In the Import: Review window, click SUBMIT JOB.

18. When the job has completed, confirm that the table has been imported by querying it from your SQL*Plus session.

Tablespace Export and Import

A variation on Data Pump export/import is the *tablespace transport* capability. This is a facility whereby entire tablespaces and their contents can be copied from one database to another. This is the routine:

1. Make the source tablespace(s) read only.
2. Use Data Pump to export the metadata describing the tablespace(s) and the contents.
3. Copy the datafile(s) and Data Pump export file to the destination system.
4. Use Data Pump to import the metadata.
5. Make the tablespace(s) read-write on both source and destination.

An additional step that may be required when transporting tablespaces from one platform to another is to convert the *endian* format of the data. A big-endian platform (such as Solaris on SPARC chips) stores a multibyte value such as a 16-bit integer with the most significant byte first. A little-endian platform (such as Windows on Intel chips) stores the least significant byte first. To transport tablespaces across platforms with a different endian format requires converting the datafiles: you do this with the RMAN command CONVERT.

To determine the platform on which a database is running, query the column PLATFORM_NAME in V$DATABASE. Then to see the list of currently supported platforms and their endian-ness, query the view V$TRANSPORTABLE_PLATFORM:

```
orcl > select * from v$transportable_platform order by platform_name;
PLATFORM_ID PLATFORM_NAME                     ENDIAN_FORMAT
----------- ------------------------------- --------------
          6 AIX-Based Systems (64-bit)      Big
         16 Apple Mac OS                    Big
         19 HP IA Open VMS                  Little
         15 HP Open VMS                     Little
          5 HP Tru64 UNIX                   Little
          3 HP-UX (64-bit)                  Big
          4 HP-UX IA (64-bit)               Big
         18 IBM Power Based Linux           Big
          9 IBM zSeries Based Linux         Big
         13 Linux 64-bit for AMD            Little
         10 Linux IA (32-bit)               Little
         11 Linux IA (64-bit)               Little
         12 Microsoft Windows 64-bit for AMD Little
          7 Microsoft Windows IA (32-bit)   Little
          8 Microsoft Windows IA (64-bit)   Little
         20 Solaris Operating System (AMD64) Little
         17 Solaris Operating System (x86)  Little
          1 Solaris[tm] OE (32-bit)         Big
          2 Solaris[tm] OE (64-bit)         Big
19 rows selected.
```

Database Control has a wizard that takes you through the entire process of transporting a tablespace (or several). From the database home page, select the Data Movement tab and then the Transport Tablespaces link in the Move Database Files section. From the Transport Tablespaces window you can launch either a wizard to generate a set of files (the Data Pump dump file and copies of the datafiles) that can be moved to another database, or a wizard to integrate a previously created set of files into the database. Tablespaces can also be transported using RMAN (RMAN can extract the necessary datafiles from a backup if necessary) or by using the `impdp` and `expdp` utilities.

When transporting tablespaces, there are certain restrictions:

- The tablespace(s) should be *self-contained*. This means that the objects within the tablespace(s) must be complete: not dependent on any other objects. For instance, if tables are in one tablespace and indexes on the tables in another, both tablespaces must be included in the set to be transported.

- The destination database must use the same (or a compatible) character set as the source database.

- The schemas that own the objects in the tablespace(s) must exist in the destination database, or the operation will fail.

- Any objects in the destination database with the same owner and object name as objects in the transportable tablespace set will not be lost: they will be ignored during the import.

- A tablespace of the same name must not already exist. Remember that is possible to rename tablespaces.

Figure 23-3 shows the steps to generate a transport set.

In Figure 23-3, the first command is the PL/SQL procedure call to confirm that a set of tablespaces (in the example, just one tablepsace: TS1) is self-contained. Then the tablespace is made read only. The Data Pump job, launched with the `expdp`

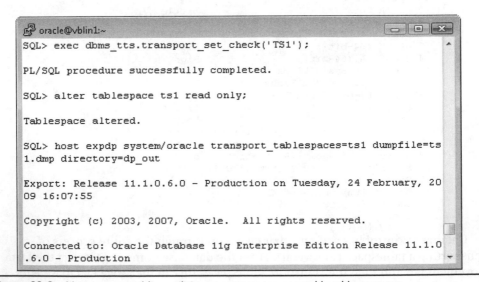

```
oracle@vblin1:~
SQL> exec dbms_tts.transport_set_check('TS1');

PL/SQL procedure successfully completed.

SQL> alter tablespace ts1 read only;

Tablespace altered.

SQL> host expdp system/oracle transport_tablespaces=ts1 dumpfile=ts
1.dmp directory=dp_out

Export: Release 11.1.0.6.0 - Production on Tuesday, 24 February, 20
09 16:07:55

Copyright (c) 2003, 2007, Oracle.  All rights reserved.

Connected to: Oracle Database 11g Enterprise Edition Release 11.1.0
.6.0 - Production
```

Figure 23-3 Using command-line utilities to create a transportable tablespace set

command-line utility, connects as user SYSTEM and then specifies the tablespace to be transported. This will generate a dump file with metadata describing the contents of the TS1 tablespace in the Oracle directory DP_OUT. Then, while the tablespace is still read only, copy its datafiles and the Data Pump dump file to a suitable location on the destination database server.

If the destination database is on a platform with a different endian-ness from the source, connect to the destination database with RMAN and run a command such as this:

```
RMAN> convert datafile '/u02/ttsfiles/ts1.dbf'
from platform='Linux IA (32-bit)' format '/u02/ttsfiles/ts1conv.dbf';
```

This command will read the nominated datafile, and convert it from the named platform format to a new file in the format that is required for the destination database.

To import the tablespace(s) on the destination system, use a command such as that shown in Figure 23-4.

The `impdp` command in Figure 23-4 reads a dump file to determine the name and contents of the tablespace consisting of the nominated datafile (previously converted, if necessary).

TIP Do not forget the final step: make the tablespace read/write, in both the source and the destination databases.

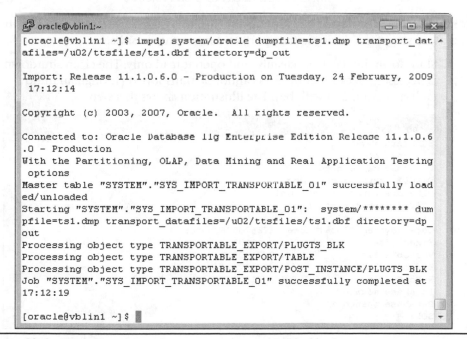

Figure 23-4 Using the `impdp` utility to import a transported tablespace

A generalization of the transportable tablespace feature makes it possible to transport an entire database from one machine to another. As discussed in Chapter 17, RMAN can create a database. This is a useful capability, but the new database can be only on the same platform as the source database; the technique leverages RMAN backup and restore, which cannot work across platforms. The transportable database feature leverages the transportable tablespace capability, which can go across platforms. The technique is to copy all the datafiles to the new machine with appropriate conversion, start an instance with a new parameter file, and create a new controlfile and online log files.

Transporting a database from one machine (and possibly one platform) to another does not involve any technology not already discussed in this chapter and previous chapters on backup and recovery, but it does involve many steps. To ease the process, there is an RMAN command that will automate (almost) the whole process: it will convert the datafiles, generate a parameter file, and generate a script to be run on the destination machine that will create the controlfile and open the database with a RESETLOGS (necessary to create the online redo log files). The script will not, however, transfer any files that are external to the database (such as BFILEs or external table files), and it will not create a password file.

TIP After a database transport there will usually be some objects that must be adjusted manually, such as directories. Also, the transported database will have the same DBID as the source: you can change this with the DBNEWID utility, implemented as the executable `$ORACLE_HOME/bin/nid` on Unix or `%ORACLE_HOME%\bin\nid.exe` on Windows.

Exercise 23-3: Transport a Database   In this exercise you will carry out the preparatory steps for a database transport, and inspect the results.

1. Shut down the database cleanly, and open it read only. The clean shutdown is necessary, because undo data cannot be transported (though an undo tablespace can, and will, be). The illustration shows this step.

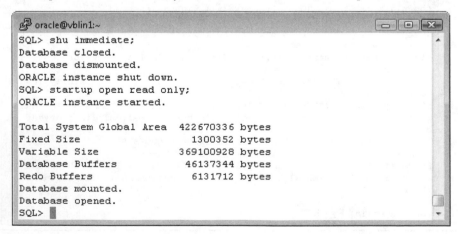

2. Connect to the database with the RMAN executable. If working on Windows, run a command to prepare for transport to a Linux system, nominating a suitable name for the SQL script and a suitable destination for the script, the converted datafiles, and the generated parameter file:

```
convert database transport script 'tran2linux.sql'
to platform 'Linux IA (32-bit)' format 'c:\tran2linux\%U';
```

The illustration shows this step on a Linux system, preparing for a transport to Windows.

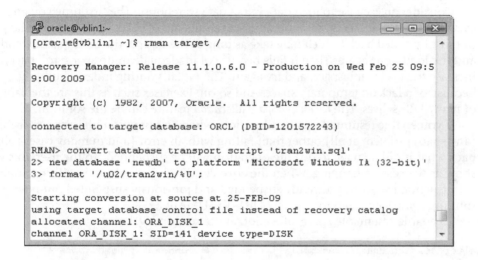

```
oracle@vblin1:~
[oracle@vblin1 ~]$ rman target /

Recovery Manager: Release 11.1.0.6.0 - Production on Wed Feb 25 09:5
9:00 2009

Copyright (c) 1982, 2007, Oracle.  All rights reserved.

connected to target database: ORCL (DBID=1201572243)

RMAN> convert database transport script 'tran2win.sql'
2> new database 'newdb' to platform 'Microsoft Windows IA (32-bit)'
3> format '/u02/tran2win/%U';

Starting conversion at source at 25-FEB-09
using target database control file instead of recovery catalog
allocated channel: ORA_DISK_1
channel ORA_DISK_1: SID=141 device type=DISK
```

3. Use an operating system utility to inspect the files generated in the nominated destination. These will be copies of the database's datafiles, a parameter file, and a SQL script.

4. Note the contents of the parameter file. It will include the phrase "Please change the values of the following parameters:" followed by a list of parameters that will usually need adjustment before transferring the files to the destination system.

5. Note the contents of the SQL script. This includes a number of commands that refer to operating system directories; these will usually require editing before running the script on the destination system.

6. Note that the generated files do not include a password file. If the database uses a password file (that is to say, if the instance parameter REMOTE_LOGIN_PASSWORDFILE has been set), this must be created on the destination system.

7. Shut down the source database, and open it normally.

Resumable Space Allocation

Many operations can fail for reasons of inadequate space. This typically shows up as an inability to add another extent to a segment, which itself can have several causes: a datafile could be full; an auto-extensible datafile or tempfile could be on a disk that is full; an undo segment could be in an undo tablespace that is full; an operation requiring temporary space could be using a temporary tablespace that is full; or a user could have reached their quota limit on a tablespace. Whatever the reason, space-related errors tend to be dreadfully time consuming.

Consider an exercise to load data into a data warehouse. The first time you attempt this, it fails because the destination tablespace runs out of space. The data that did go in must be rolled back (which may take as long as the insert), the tablespace extended, and the load done again. Then it fails because of inadequate undo space; roll back, increase the undo tablespace, and try again. Then it fails during index rebuilding, because of a lack on temporary space. And so on. Exercises such as this are the bane of many DBAs' lives. The *resumable space allocation* feature can be the solution.

If you enable resumable space allocation, when an operation hits a space problem (any space problem at all) rather than failing with an error (and in many cases rolling back what it did manage to do) the operation will be suspended. To the user, this will show as the session hanging. When the error condition is resolved, it will continue. All suspended sessions (currently suspended and previously suspended but now running again) are listed in the view DBA_RESUMABLE.

To enable resumable space allocation at the session level, the command is

```
alter session enable resumable [ timeout <seconds> ] [ name <opname> ] ;
```

The TIMEOUT option lets you specify for how long the statement should hang. If this time is reached without the problem being resolved, the error is returned and the statement fails. If there is no specified TIMEOUT, the session will hang indefinitely. The NAME option lets you specify a name that will be displayed in the DBA_RESUMABLE view, which can help you determine at which point in a multistatement process the space problem occurred.

TIP It is possible for a process to be suspended and resumed many times. The DBA_RESUMABLE view will show you details of the current or the last suspension.

It is also possible to enable resumable space for all sessions, by setting an instance parameter. This is a dynamic parameter. For example, to set a timeout of one minute:

```
alter system set resumable_timeout=60;
```

This will cause all sessions that hit a space problem to be suspended for up to one minute.

TIP The `expdb` and `impdp` Data Pump utilities have a command-line switch RESUMABLE=Y (the default is N) that will allow Data Pump jobs to suspend if they hit space problems.

EXAM TIP While a session is suspended, it will retain control of all the resources it is using, including: undo space, temporary space, PGA memory, and record locks.

There is little point in enabling resumable space allocation for a session or the instance if you don't do anything about the problem that caused a session to be suspended. Suspended sessions will, by default, be reported through the server alert system (fully described in Chapter 24), be displayed by Database Control, and be listed in the DBA_RESUMABLE data dictionary view. Having spotted a problem, you can fix it interactively from another session. Or you can create a trigger: an AFTER SUSPEND ON DATABASE trigger that will run whenever a session is suspended. This trigger could report the problem (perhaps by generating an e-mail), or it could include code to investigate the problem, and fix it automatically. For example, to send an e-mail:

```
create trigger detect_suspend
after suspend on database
begin
utl_mail.send(sender=>'dba@mycompany.com',
recipients=>'dba@mycompany.com',
subject=>'DB session suspended',
message=>'resumable space allocation event occurred');
end;
```

TIP If you create an AFTER SUSPEND ON DATABASE trigger that attempts to fix problems, remember that it might hit the same problem.

Exercise 23-4: Use Resumable Space Allocation   In this exercise you will set up a space allocation problem, and enable resumable space allocation to gain the opportunity to fix it without an error.

1. Connect to your database as user SYSTEM and create a tablespace to use for this exercise. With SQL*Plus:

   ```
   create tablespace small datafile 'small1.dbf' size 2m;
   ```

2. Create a table in the tablespace, with fixed-length rows. It will be impossible to insert 2000 rows without filling the tablespace:

   ```
   create table toobig(c1 char(1000)) tablespace small;
   ```

3. Run this anonymous PL/SQL block to force an error:

   ```
   begin
   for i in 1..2000 loop
   insert into toobig values ('a row');
   end loop;
   end;
   /
   ```

The illustration shows Steps 1, 2, and 3.

```
oracle@vblin1:/u02/tran2win                                        ⊡ ◻ ✕

SQL> create tablespace small datafile 'small1.dbf' size 2m;

Tablespace created.

SQL> create table toobig(c1 char(1000)) tablespace small;

Table created.

SQL> begin
  2   for i in 1..2000 loop
  3   insert into toobig values ('a row');
  4   end loop;
  5   end;
  6  /
begin
*
ERROR at line 1:
ORA-01653: unable to extend table SYSTEM.TOOBIG by 128 in tables
ace SMALL
ORA-06512: at line 3
```

4. Note the error: an ORA-01653.

5. Alter the session to enable resumable space allocation:

   ```
   alter session enable resumable name 'exercise 23-4';
   ```

6. Rerun the code from Step 3. The session will hang.

7. Start another SQL*Plus session, connected as SYSTEM, and run this query:

   ```
   select session_id,suspend_time,name ,sql_text,error_number
   from dba_resumable;
   ```

   Note that the ERROR_NUMBER column is reporting the error that would
   have been returned to the session, had it not been suspended.

8. Connect to the database with Database Control; you will see the problem
   reported on the database home page, in the Alerts section.

9. From your second SQL*Plus session, fix the problem:

   ```
   alter tablespace small add datafile 'small2.dbf' size 4m;
   ```

10. Observe that the procedure call of Step 6 will now complete successfully, with
    no intervention required.

11. Tidy up by dropping the tablespace:

    ```
    drop tablespace small including contents and datafiles;
    ```

Segment Reorganization

During typical database operation, rows will be inserted, updated, and deleted. This
will affect the table segments that store the rows themselves, and the index segments
associated with the tables. Chapter 5 included a discussion of extent management (how

space is allocated to segments within a tablespace) and segment space management (how rows are allocated to blocks within a segment). You are strongly advised to use locally managed tablespaces with automatic segment space management: these options are enabled by default in the current release of the database and rely on bitmaps to track extent allocation and block usage.

The bitmapped managed techniques are very efficient for allocating space as rows are inserted and segments grow, but UPDATE and DELETE statements can still result in problems that may make it necessary to reorganize the segments. Updates can cause row migration, and deletions can result in wasted space.

Row Chaining and Migration

A chained row is a row that is stored in more than one block. This will occur when the row is bigger than the block. If the block size is 4KB and the row is 5KB, there is no choice; the row will be stored in two blocks. At system design time, this should have been considered: the rows are too large for the blocks. This is sometimes a systems analysis problem, caused by incorrect normalization resulting in an unnecessary number of columns in the table, but it is often a design time problem. Perhaps the table uses columns of type CHAR or LONG rather than VARCHAR2 or BLOB, or perhaps the table could have been sliced vertically, into two or more tables. Whatever the cause, row chaining is not the DBA's problem. Row migration is a different matter.

Most of the Oracle primitive data types have variable length, and therefore most tables have rows of variable length. As rows are updated, their length may change. This means that the rows will get bigger.

The default settings for a table segment reserve 10 percent of each block as space for rows to expand. If rows are only ever inserted or deleted, then this 10 percent is in fact wasted space. But if rows are subjected to updates that make them bigger, then it may not be sufficient. If the 10 percent free space has already been used by previous updates and an update is made that will increase the size of another row, the entire row must be relocated to another block, where there is room for the new version of the row. This is a row migration. Clearly, this will impact on the performance of the UPDATE statement: it becomes in effect a DELETE and an INSERT. A worse problem arises with subsequent access to the row, because the index entries are not adjusted when a row is migrated: the index keys always point to the row's original location. When a row is migrated, a stub (think of it as a forwarding address) is left behind, which directs the session to the current location of the row. The result is that it takes two table block reads to get the row, not one. Worse still, if a row has been migrated once and is updated again, it may be migrated again. And again.

 EXAM TIP Row migration is caused by UPDATE statements. INSERT and DELETE can never cause row migration.

Row migration should be detected and fixed by the DBA. The ideal situation is to prevent it in the first place, by adjusting the table settings to reserve an appropriate amount of space for rows to expand. For example, if you know that on average the rows of a certain table will double in size during its lifetime, the percentage of space reserved should not be 10 percent but 50 percent. This can be set at table creation time, or later:

```
alter table <table_name> pctfree 50;
```

Many times the information needed to set the PCTFREE correctly is not available, so all you can do is correct the problem later. The simplest method is to move the table:

```
alter table <table_name> move [ <tablespace_name> ] ;
```

The underlying implementation of the MOVE command is a CREATE TABLE . . . AS SELECT * FROM . . . command followed by some data dictionary magic to rename the newly created table to the name of the original table, while maintaining the connections to dependent objects. The row migration problem is fixed, because the moved table will have all the rows freshly inserted. An INSERT can never cause row migration. The problem is that all dependent indexes will be broken, because the rows are in a new table, with new rowids; the indexes will have rowids that are now invalid. The indexes will have to be reorganized next.

 EXAM TIP Reorganizing a table with a MOVE will render all associated indexes unusable.

 TIP While a table move is in progress, the table can be queried but will be locked against DML. You cannot move a table if there is an uncommitted transaction against it.

A row migration problem can be detected with the ANALYZE command. This will pass through the table counting the rows that are chained or migrated. To see the result, query the CHAIN_CNT column in DBA_TABLES. To determine whether the rows are chained or migrated, look at the AVG_ROW_LEN column: if this is less than the block size, then the rows will be migrated rows; if it is greater, they will be chained rows.

 EXAM TIP For most purposes, tables should be analyzed with procedures in the DBMS_STATS package. An exception is counting chained and migrated rows: these are detected only with the ANALYZE command.

Exercise 23-5: Manage Row Migration In this exercise you will create, investigate, and fix a row migration problem.

1. Connect to your database as user SYSTEM with SQL*Plus.

2. Create a table with variable-length rows:

```
create table ex235 (c1 varchar2(20));
```

3. Run this PL/SQL code block to insert some rows:

```
begin
for i in 1..1000 loop
```

```
insert into ex235 values (null);
end loop;
end;
/
```

4. Analyze the table, and determine that no rows are migrated:

```
analyze table ex235 compute statistics;
select avg_row_len, chain_cnt from user_tables where table_name='EX235';
```

Steps 2, 3, and 4 are shown in the illustration.

```
Administrator: cmd - sqlplus system/oracle                              _ □ X
orcl > create table ex235 (c1 varchar2(20));

Table created.

orcl > begin
  2   for i in 1..1000 loop
  3     insert into ex235 values (null);
  4   end loop;
  5   end;
  6   /
PL/SQL procedure successfully completed.

orcl > analyze table ex235 compute statistics;

Table analyzed.

orcl > select avg_row_len,chain_cnt from user_tables where table_name='EX235';

AVG_ROW_LEN   CHAIN_CNT
-----------   ---------
          3           0

orcl > _
```

5. Update the rows by populating the (previously null) column:

```
update ex235 set c1='1234567890qwertyuiop';
```

6. Repeat Step 4. Note that the rows are longer, and that the majority of them are now migrated.

7. Fix the problem by moving the table:

```
alter table ex235 move;
```

8. Repeat Step 4. Note that the row migration problem has been solved.

9. Tidy up:

```
drop table ex235;
```

Segment Shrink

When a row is deleted, the space it was occupying in its block becomes available for reuse when another row is inserted. However, the nature of the activity against a table can result in a significant amount of wasted space within a table. This could be reclaimed with a MOVE operation: following a MOVE, all the blocks will be consecutively full of freshly reinserted rows. But during the MOVE, the table is locked and following it all the indexes must be rebuilt. For many environments, this makes use of MOVE to reorganize tables impossible. The SHRINK command, while not as effective as a MOVE, avoids these problems. It can be run without any impact on end users. A limitation is that the table's tablespace must have been created to use automatic segment space management. Tables in tablespaces that use the older freelist technique for managing segment space usage cannot be shrunk, because (unlike the new bitmap method) the freelist does not include sufficient information for Oracle to work out how full each block actually is.

The syntax of SHRINK is

```
alter <table_name> shrink space [ cascade ] [ compact ] ;
```

The underlying implementation of a table shrink is to relocate rows from the end of the table into blocks toward the beginning of the table, by means of matched INSERT and DELETE operations. Then when all possible moves have been done, to bring the high water mark of the table down to the last currently used block, release all the space above this point. There are two distinct phases: the *compact* phase moves the rows in a series of small transactions, through normal DML that generates both undo and redo and uses row locks. The second phase is a DDL command. As with any DDL command, this is a transaction against the data dictionary: it will execute almost instantaneously, but will require a very short table lock.

 EXAM TIP A table shrink operation generates undo and redo. Indexes are maintained, because the shrink is implemented as a set of DML transactions. There is no table lock during the compaction, but individual rows will be locked while they are being moved.

Using the keyword COMPACT carries out the first phase, but not the second: the rows are relocated, but the space is not actually released from the segment. The reason for using this is that while the compaction can occur during normal running hours (though it may take many hours to complete on a large table), it is possible that the DDL at the end will hang due to concurrency with other transactions. So it may be necessary to shrink the table with the COMPACT keyword first, and then again without COMPACT during a maintenance period: it will be fast, because the compaction will have already been done.

 EXAM TIP The SHRINK SPACE COMPACT command reorganizes the contents of the segment, but does not return space to the tablespace.

The CASCADE keyword instructs Oracle also to shrink dependent objects, such as indexes. Indexes do deteriorate as DML is executed: if a row is deleted, this will result in wasted space in the index. Oracle's index maintenance algorithm does not permit reuse of this space. It is logically impossible to reclaim this space by relocating other index keys because the index keys must always be stored in order. The best that can be done is to merge adjacent, partially used, leaf blocks of the index. If such a merge results in one completely empty block, then this block can be reused within the index. You can also shrink an index directly:

```
alter index <index_name> shrink space [ cascade ] [ compact ] ;
```

However, while this works syntactically, shrinking an index will not actually reduce its size. It may, however, stop it from getting bigger.

TIP Older DBAs will recognize that ALTER INDEX SHRINK SPACE is functionally equivalent to the ALTER INDEX COALESCE command. The latter command is still available, but may be deprecated in later releases.

Before a table can be shrunk, you must enable row movement for the table:

```
alter table <table_name> enable row movement;
```

Enabling row movement is necessary because the nature of the operation means that rowids will be changing. The same row (no change to primary key) will be in a different physical location, and therefore have a different rowid. This is something that Oracle will not permit unless row movement has been enabled.

EXAM TIP A table must be in a tablespace with automatic segment space management and row movement must have been enabled, or it cannot be shrunk. If these conditions have not been met, a MOVE may be the only way to reorganize the table.

To identify whether a table would benefit from a shrink space operation, you can analyze the table and then query the DBA_TABLES view to retrieve the amount of free space, on average, in each block. This query computes the ratio of free space as a proportion of the block size.

```
select
avg_space/(select value from v$parameter where name='db_block_size')
from user_tables where table_name = '<table_name>';
```

However, as there may be thousands of tables in the database and some may undergo very different patterns of activity, this information may not be sufficient to work out whether a shrink is necessary. For this reason, there is a supplied advisor: the Segment Advisor. The Segment Advisor inspects tables to detect "wasted" space but then makes use of information in the Automatic Workload Repository to make a decision on whether the space should be released by a reorganization, or if the historical pattern of activity against the table suggests that the space may be required again and should not therefore be released. The Segment Advisor runs, be default, every night. Figure 23-5 shows the results of an automatic run of the Segment Advisor, viewed in Database Control.

In Figure 23-5, the Segment Advisor has detected a table (which happens to be in the SYSMAN schema) that would benefit from a reorganization. This advice will be based on the current state of the table (it is six times as large as it needs to be) with previous activity taken into account. Clicking the SHRINK button will take you to the

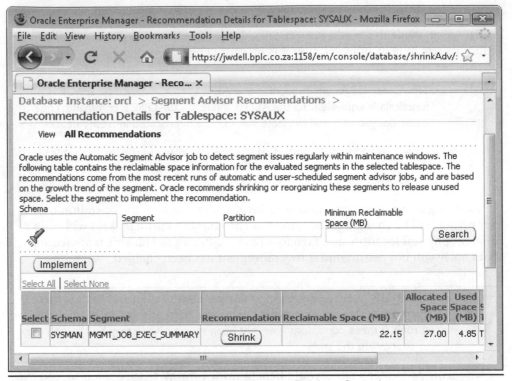

Figure 23-5   The Segment Advisor's recommendation in Database Control

window shown in Figure 23-6, where the wizard gives you the options of performing a complete shrink operation (the Compact Segments and Release Space radio button) or stopping after the compaction phase (the Compact Segments radio button). The wizard also generates statements to enable row movement on the table(s).

Note that it is not possible to shrink a table that has a column of type LONG. It is possible to shrink a table on which materialized views have been created (and if CASCADE is specified, the materialized views will be shrunk too) unless the materialized view is a *refresh on commit* materialized view. This restriction is because even though table shrink is implemented internally as a set of INSERT and DELETE commands, any DML triggers will be automatically disabled for the shrink operation. On-commit materialized views are in fact maintained by triggers and so would be broken by a shrink operation.

EXAM TIP You cannot shrink a table that is in a freelist-managed tablespace, that has a LONG column, or has a refresh-on-commit materialized view.

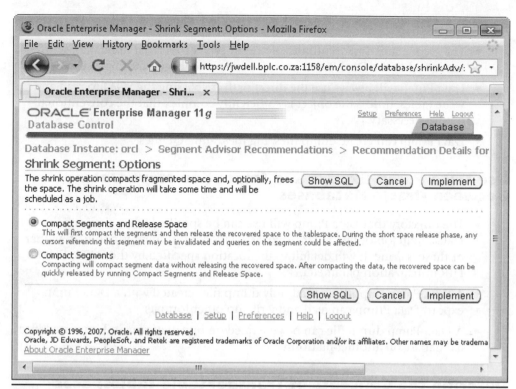

Figure 23-6 The Database Control interface to the shrink facility

Two-Minute Drill

Describe and Use Methods to Move Data (Directory Objects, SQL*Loader, External Tables)

- An Oracle directory is a database object that points to a physical path.

- Directories are not schema objects: no matter who creates them, they are owned by SYS.

- SQL*Loader is a client-server tool that connects over a normal session, and reads a text file to construct rows for insertion into tables.

- SQL*Loader can insert rows using normal INSERT statements, or can write blocks directly to datafiles. During a direct load, the table will be locked for DML.

- An external table exists as a data dictionary construct that points to an operating system file, in a directory.

- External tables can be read with SELECT but cannot be written to with DML commands.

Explain the General Architecture of Oracle Data Pump

- The `expdp` and `impdp` utilities are client-server tools that use database sessions, but the Data Pump processes are server background processes.
- Data Pump will always use the direct path (bypassing the SGA) to read and write tables, unless the object is sufficiently complex that the conventional path is necessary.
- Data Pump can create dump files, log files, and SQL files.

Use Data Pump Export and Import to Move Data Between Oracle Databases

- The directory that Data Pump will use can be specified when defining the Data Pump job or by the DATA_PUMP_DIR environment variable. If neither of these is done, it will default to the location specified by the DATA_PUMP_DIR initialization parameter.
- A Data Pump import can read only dump files created with a Data Pump export; Data Pump can read and write no other formats.
- A Data Pump dump file can be generated on one platform and imported into a database on another platform.

Describe the Concepts of Transportable Tablespaces and Databases

- Tablespace datafiles can be transported across platforms, but the databases must use the same character set. If the platforms are different endian, the datafiles must be converted with RMAN.
- A tablespace must be made read only before transport.
- Data Pump is used to export and import the metadata describing the contents of a tablespace transport set.
- A tablespace transport set must be self-contained: it cannot contain objects with dependencies on objects that are not in the set.
- Transporting an entire database involves creating a new controlfile with CREATE CONTROLFILE, new online redo log files with RESETLOGS, and transporting in the entire set of tablespaces.

Manage Resumable Space Allocation

- Resumable space allocation can be enabled for a session with ALTER SESSION ENABLE RESUMABLE or for all sessions with the RESUMABLE_TIMEOUT instance parameter.

- While a session is suspended, it will retain all resources taken, including row locks, undo space, temporary space, and PGA memory.

- Suspended sessions are visible in DBA_RESUMABLE and reported by Database Control.

- When a space error condition is cleared, the suspended session will resume work with no need for manual intervention.

Reclaim Wasted Space from Tables and Indexes by Using the Segment Shrink Functionality

- A table shrink is implemented as matched deletions and insertions, to move rows from the end of the table segment toward the beginning.

- DML locks are needed during a shrink, but a DDL lock is only needed for the final, very fast, step of moving the high water mark to release the freed space.

- The COMPACT keyword will move the rows, but not complete the operation by returning space to the tablespace.

- Only heap tables can be shrunk. This includes regular tables, and other objects that use heap tables for storage such as materialized views, materialized view logs, and partitions of heap tables.

- It is possible syntactically to shrink an index, but the implementation is a coalesce of free space that may be reused by the index. No space will be returned to the tablespace.

Self Test

1. You are using Data Pump to upload rows into a table, and you wish to use the direct path. Which of the following statements are correct? (Choose two answers.)

   A. You must include the "DIRECT" keyword in the Data Pump controlfile.

   B. This is not possible if the table is in a cluster.

   C. You have no control over this; Data Pump will use the direct path automatically if it can.

   D. Direct path is slower than the external table path because it doesn't cache data in memory.

2. Which of the following is not a Data Pump file type? (Choose the best answer.)

   A. Dump file

   B. Log file

   C. Controlfile

   D. SQL file

3. Which of the following is not a SQL*Loader file? (Choose the best answer.)

   A. Bad file

   B. Controlfile

   C. Discard file

   D. Good file

   E. Log file

4. You create a directory with the statement

   ```
   create directory dp_dir as 'c:\tmp';
   ```

   but when you try to use it with Data Pump, there is an error. Which of the following could be true? (Choose three answers.)

   A. The Oracle software owner has no permissions on c:\tmp.

   B. The Oracle database user has no permissions on dp_dir.

   C. The path c:\tmp does not exist.

   D. The path c:\tmp must exist, or the "create directory" statement would have failed.

   E. If you use Data Pump in network mode, then there will be no need for a directory.

   F. Issuing the command grant all on 'c:\tmp' to public; may solve some permission problems.

5. You run SQL*Loader on your PC, to insert data into a remote database. Which of the following is true? (Choose the correct answer.)

   A. The input datafiles must be on your PC.

   B. The input datafiles must be on the server.

   C. Direct load is possible only if the input datafiles are on the server.

   D. Direct load is only possible if you run SQL*Loader on the server, not on the PC.

6. How can you enable the suspension and resumption of statements that hit space errors? (Choose all the correct answers.)

   A. Issue an ALTER SESSION ENABLE RESUMABLE command.

   B. Issue an ALTER SYSTEM ENABLE RESUMABLE command.

   C. Set the instance parameter RESUMABLE_STATEMENTS.

   D. Set the instance parameter RESUMABLE_TIMEOUT.

   E. Use the DBMS_RESUMABLE.ENABLE procedure.

7. If a statement is suspended because of a space error, what will happen when the problem is fixed? (Choose the best answer.)

   A. After the resumable timeout has expired, the statement will continue executing from the point it had reached.

   B. After the resumable timeout has expired, the statement will start executing from the beginning again.

   C. The statement will start executing from the beginning immediately after the problem is fixed.

   D. The statement will continue executing from the point it had reached immediately after the problem is fixed.

8. You receive an alert warning you that a tablespace is nearly full. What actions could you take to prevent this becoming a problem, without any impact for your users? (Choose two correct answers.)

   A. Purge all recycle bin objects in the tablespace.

   B. Shrink the tables in the tablespace.

   C. Shrink the indexes in the tablespace.

   D. Move one or more tables to a different tablespace.

   E. Move one or more indexes to a different tablespace.

9. Which process is responsible for sending the alert when a tablespace usage critical threshold is reached? (Choose the best answer.)

   A. Database Control

   B. The DBMS_SERVER_ALERT package

   C. MMON, the manageability monitor process

   D. The server process of the session that detected the problem

   E. DBWn, the Database Writer, when it detects the problem

10. What must you do before executing a table shrink operation? (Choose the best answer.)

   A. Compact the table.

   B. Disable triggers on the table.

   C. Disable row movement for the table.

   D. Enable row movement for the table.

Self Test Answers

1. ☑ **B and C.** Clusters are complex structures that cannot be directly loaded. Data Pump determines whether a direct load is possible automatically.

   ☒ **A and D.** There is no DIRECT keyword because the choice is automatic. Direct is faster because it bypasses the SGA.

2. ☑ **C.** SQL*Loader can use a controlfile, Data Pump does not.

   ☒ **A, B, and D.** These are the file types that Data Pump can generate.

3. ☑ **D.** There is no "good" file—the acceptable rows are inserted.

   ☒ **A, B, C, and E.** These are the file types that SQL*Loader can generate.

4. ☑ **A, B,** and **C.** These conditions could all cause problems when using the directory, but not when creating it.

☒ **D, E,** and **F. D** is wrong because the existence of the directory is not checked at creation time. **E** is wrong because while network mode does not need a directory for the dump file(s) it will need a directory for the log file(s). **F** is wrong because it confuses the issue of Oracle permissions on directories with operating system permissions on physical paths.

5. ☑ **A.** SQL*Loader is a client-server process: the input files must be local to the user process.

☒ **B, C,** and **D. B** is wrong because the input files must be on the PC, accessible to the client-side process. **C** and **D** are wrong because direct load is not relevant to the location of the files.

6. ☑ **A** and **D.** These are the only two methods to enable resumable space allocation.

☒ **B, C,** and **E. B** and **C** are wrong because resumable space allocation is enabled at the system level with the instance parameter RESUMABLE_TIMEOUT. **E** is wrong because while there is a package DBMS_RESUMABLE, it does not (rather annoyingly) include a procedure to enable resumable space allocation.

7. ☑ **D.** As "suspended" implies, the statement will continue from the point at which it stopped.

☒ **A, B,** and **C.** The timeout controls how long the suspension can last before returning an error: it is the period during which the problem can be fixed.

8. ☑ **A** and **B.** Both purging dropped objects and shrinking tables will release space immediately, with no downtime.

☒ **C, D,** and **E.** An index can be shrunk, but this will release space within the index, not return it to the tablespace. Relocating either indexes or tables has implications for availability of the data.

9. ☑ **C.** The MMON background process raises alerts.

☒ **A, B, D,** and **E. A** is wrong because while Database Control reports alerts, it does not raise them. **B** is wrong because the DBMS_SERVER_ALERT API is used to configure the alert system; it does not implement it. **D** and **E** are wrong because foreground and background processes will encounter problems, not warn of their imminence.

10. ☑ **D.** Row movement is a prerequisite for a table shrink operation.

☒ **A, B,** and **C. A** is wrong because compaction is part of the shrink, not a prerequisite. **B** is wrong because there is no need to disable triggers—they will be disabled automatically. **C** is wrong because row movement must be enabled, not disabled.

CHAPTER 24

The AWR and the Alert System

Exam Objectives

In this chapter you will learn to

- 052.12.2 Use and Manage Automatic Workload Repository (AWR)
- 052.12.3 Use Advisory Framework
- 052.12.4 Manage Alerts and Thresholds

The manageability infrastructure provided with Oracle Database 11g can be used to automate a significant amount of the database administrator's day-to-day work. With earlier releases, monitoring the database in order to pick up developing problems before they became critical took too much time. Identifying and diagnosing performance issues was not only time-consuming but also required much skill. Use of the Alert system and the diagnostic advisors, installed as standard in every 11g database, frees the DBA from the necessity of devoting a large amount of effort to this work.

The Automatic Workload Repository

Oracle collects a vast amount of statistical information regarding performance and activity. This information is accumulated in memory and periodically written to the database: to the tables that make up the Automatic Workload Repository, the AWR. The AWR exists as a set of tables and other objects in the SYSAUX tablespace. The AWR is related to the data dictionary, but unlike the data dictionary, the AWR is not essential for the database to function (though it may be necessary for it to function well). Data is written to the AWR, stored for a while, and eventually overwritten with more recent information.

Gathering AWR Statistics

The level of statistics gathered is controlled by the instance parameter STATISTICS_LEVEL. This can be set to BASIC, or to TYPICAL (which is the default), or to ALL. The TYPICAL level will force the collection of all the statistics that are needed for normal tuning, without collecting any whose collection would impact adversely on performance. The BASIC level will disable virtually all statistics, with no appreciable performance benefit. The ALL level will collect extremely detailed statistics on SQL statement execution; these may occasionally be necessary if you are doing advanced SQL statement tuning, but they may cause a slight performance drop while being collected.

Statistics are accumulated in memory, in data structures within the SGA. This causes no performance impact, because the statistics merely reflect what the instance is doing anyway. Periodically (by default, once an hour) they are flushed to disk, to the AWR. This is known as an AWR *snapshot*. The flushing to disk is done by a background process: the Manageability Monitor, or MMON. This use of a background process is the key to the efficiency of the statistics collection process. In earlier releases of the database, accessing performance tuning statistics was only possible by running queries against various views—the dynamic performance V$ views. Populating these views was an expensive process. The DBA had to launch a session against the database and then issue a query. The query forced Oracle to extract data from the SGA and present it to the session in a view. This approach is still possible—all the old views, and many more, are still available—but the AWR approach is far more efficient.

 TIP No third-party tool can ever have the direct memory access to the instance that MMON has. If your instance is highly stressed, you should think carefully before using any tuning products other than those provided by Oracle.

The MMON has direct access to the memory structures that make up the SGA, and therefore the statistics within them. It can extract data from the SGA without the need to go via a session. The only overhead is the actual writing of the snapshot of the data to the AWR. By default this occurs only once an hour and should not therefore have a noticeable effect on runtime performance.

 EXAM TIP AWR statistics are saved as a snapshot to the AWR by the MMON process, by default every 60 minutes. By default, the snapshots are stored for eight days before being overwritten.

The AWR is a set of tables located in the SYSAUX tablespace—these tables cannot be relocated. They exist in the SYSMAN schema. You can log on to the database with tools such as SQL*Plus as user SYSMAN, but this should never be necessary, and indeed Oracle Corporation does not support access to the AWR tables with SQL*Plus, or with any tools other than the various APIs provided in the form of DBMS packages or through various views. The most straightforward way to access AWR information is through Enterprise Manager; both Enterprise Manager Database Control and Enterprise Manager Grid Control log on to the database as SYSMAN, using a password that is encrypted in their configuration files. This is why changing the SYSMAN password requires more than executing an ALTER USER SYSMAN IDENTIFIED BY . . . command; in addition to this, you must also use the EMCTL utility:

```
emctl setpasswd dbconsole
```

which will update the encrypted password in the appropriate file.

An AWR snapshot can be thought of as a copy of the contents of many V$ views at the time the snapshot was taken, but never forget that the mechanism for copying the information is not to query the V$ views: the information is extracted directly from the data structures that make up the instance. The process that makes the copy is MMON. In addition to information from the dynamic performance views, the AWR stores information otherwise visible in the DBA views, populated from the data dictionary. This category of information includes a history of object statistics. Without the AWR, the database would have no long-term record of how objects were changing. The statistics gathered with DBMS_STATS provide current information, but it may also be necessary to have a historical picture of the state of the database objects. The AWR can provide this.

Managing the AWR

Snapshots of statistics data are kept in the AWR, by default, for eight days. This period is configurable. As a rough guide for sizing, if the snapshot collection is left on every hour and the retention time is left on eight days, then the AWR may well require between 200MB and 300MB of space in the SYSAUX tablespace. But this figure is highly variable and will to a large extent depend on the number of sessions.

To administer the AWR with Database Control, from the database home page select the Server tab, then the Automatic Workload Repository link in the Statistics Management section. The Automatic Workload Repository window, as in Figure 24-1, shows the

PART III

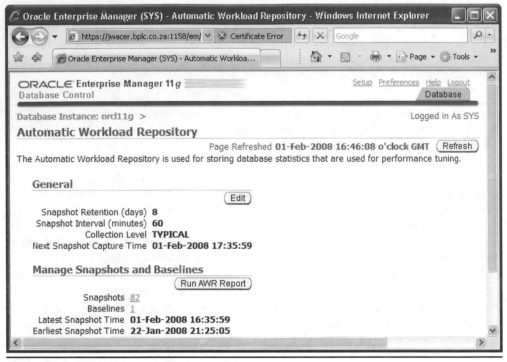

Figure 24-1 The AWR administration window

current settings for snapshot collection and retention and for the STATISTICS_LEVEL and lets you adjust them.

Adjusting the AWR settings to save snapshots more frequently will make problem diagnosis more precise. If the snapshots are several hours apart, you may miss peaks of activity (and consequent dips in performance). But gathering snapshots too frequently will increase the size of the AWR and could possibly impact performance due to the increased workload of collecting and saving the information.

 TIP It is important to monitor the size and growth of the SYSAUX tablespace and the AWR within it. The Alert system will assist with the first task, and the view V$SYSAUX_OCCUPANTS should be used for the second.

 EXAM TIP By default, AWR snapshots are taken every hour and saved for eight days. The AWR is located in the SYSAUX tablespace and cannot be relocated to anywhere else.

Statistics, Metrics, and Baselines

AWR snapshots contain statistics. What Oracle calls a *statistic* is a raw figure, which is meaningless by itself. To be useful, statistics must be converted into *metrics*. A metric is two or more statistics correlated together. For example, the number of disk reads is a statistic; perhaps the number is two billion. By itself, this is useless information. What the DBA needs to know are metrics such as disk reads per second, disk reads per transaction, disk reads per SQL statement, and disk reads per session. The DBA will also need to do further correlations. For example, disk reads per transaction is very useful; it will identify the transactions that are stressing the I/O system and perhaps should be tuned. But the DBA will need to observe this metric over time and see how it changes—perhaps as the SQL is rewritten or indexing structures are changed, the I/O workload will reduce. This introduces the *baseline*. A baseline is a stored set of statistics (and metrics) that can be used for comparisons across time.

As the MMON process saves an AWR snapshot, it automatically generates a large number of metrics from the statistics. Creating baselines must be done by the DBA. Snapshots are purged after a certain period—by default, after eight days. A baseline is a pair (possibly several pairs) of snapshots that will be kept indefinitely: until the baseline is deliberately dropped. The metrics derived from the baseline can then be compared with the metrics derived from current activity levels, assisting you with identifying changes in activity and behavior.

Baselines need to be created for specific events and for normal running. For example, if the database has regular end-of-month processing, it would make sense to store the AWR snapshots gathered during each month end as baselines so that throughout the year you can observe how the month-end processing activity is changing and determine whether any problems are apparent. It also makes sense to store baselines for periods of normal, satisfactory running so that if performance degrades at a later time, information will be available that will help identify what might have changed.

To create a baseline with Database Control, select the link next to "Baselines" shown in Figure 24-1. In the figure, this link is "1," indicating that at the moment there is only one baseline. This link will take you to the AWR Baselines window. From there, you can define periods to store as baselines.

The DBMS_WORKLOAD_REPOSITORY Package

Database Control has interfaces for managing the AWR, but it does so by invoking procedures in a PL/SQL package: DBMS_WORKLOAD_REPOSITORY. The procedures can adjust the frequency and persistence of snapshots, generate an ad hoc snapshot (additional to those generated by MMON), create and manipulate baselines, and generate reports on activity between any two snapshots. Figure 24-2 shows the use of some of the procedures in the package.

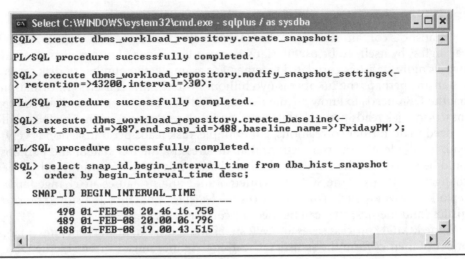

Figure 24-2 Use of the DBMS_WORKLOAD_REPOSITORY package

The first procedure call forces the MMON process to gather a snapshot immediately, in addition to its normal scheduled snapshots. This would typically be used just before and after launching a job of some kind, so that reports can be generated focusing on a particular time frame. The second procedure call adjusts the snapshot management, such that snapshots will be retained for 30 days and gathered by MMON every half hour (the units are minutes). The third procedure call nominates two snapshots to be stored indefinitely as a named baseline. Finally, the query lists all snapshots in the repository; note that in addition to the snapshots gathered automatically on the hour, there is also the ad hoc snapshot gathered by the first procedure call.

Exercise 24-1: Monitor the Automatic Workload Repository   In this exercise, you will determine the size of the AWR and monitor its growth as it stores more snapshots.

1. Connect to your database with SQL*Plus as user SYSTEM.

2. The view V$SYSAUX_OCCUPANTS shows all the components installed into the SYSAUX tablespace. Find out how much space the AWR is taking up:

   ```
   select occupant_desc,space_usage_kbytes from v$sysaux_occupants
   where occupant_name='SM/AWR';
   ```

   Note the size returned.

3. Gather an AWR snapshot:

   ```
   execute dbms_workload_repository.create_snapshot;
   ```

4. Rerun the query from Step 2, and calculate the increase in size caused by taking the manual snapshot.

5. Find out how many snapshots there are, and what date range they cover:

```
select min(begin_interval_time), max(begin_interval_time),
count(snap_id) from dba_hist_snapshot;
```

6. Connect to your database as user SYSTEM with Database Control.

7. Navigate to the Automatic Workload Repository window, shown in Figure 24-1: from the database home page select the Server tab, and then the Automatic Workload Repository link in the Statistics Management section. You will see figures corresponding to the results of the query in Step 5.

The Database Advisory Framework

The database comes preconfigured with a set of advisors. First among these is the Automatic Database Diagnostic Monitor, or ADDM. Studying ADDM reports, which are generated automatically whenever an AWR snapshot is taken, will usually be a regular part of the DBA's routine. The ADDM reports themselves are of great value and will highlight problems within the database and suggest solutions, but in many cases, its recommendations will include suggesting that you run one or more other advisors. These advisors can give much more precise diagnostic information and advice than the ADDM.

To use the advisors, in Database Control click the Advisor Central link in the Related Links section. The Advisor Central window gives you the options of viewing the results of previous advisor tasks, or of using any of the other advisors:

- The Automatic Database Diagnostic Monitor (the ADDM)
- The Memory Advisors
- The SQL Access, Tuning, and Repair Advisors
- The Automatic Undo Advisor
- The Mean Time to Recover (MTTR) Advisor
- The Data Recovery Advisor
- The Segment Advisor

The Automatic Database Diagnostic Monitor

The ADDM is run automatically by the MMON whenever a snapshot is taken. As with all the advisors, it takes statistics and other information from the AWR. The automatically generated ADDM reports always cover the period between the current snapshot and the previous one—so by default, you will have access to reports covering every hour. You can invoke the ADDM manually to generate a report covering the period between any two snapshots, if you want to span a greater period. The ADDM is triggered both by automatic snapshots and also if you gather a snapshot manually. The reports are purged by default after 30 days.

PART III

EXAM TIP ADDM reports are generated on demand, and whenever a snapshot is gathered. By default, they are stored for 30 days.

To view the ADDM reports with Database Control, click the Advisor Central link in the Related Links section of the database home page. The Advisor Central window will show you the most recent runs of each advisor, as in Figure 24-3.

Select the report's radio button and click View Result to see the summary of recent activity, as in Figure 24-4. In the figure, this shows that overall the database has seen very little activity since the previous evening, but that there were distinct spikes at about 23:00 and 07:00, as well as in the last hour since 14:00, which will be the period covered by this report.

The lower part of the ADDM window shows the results of the analysis. In the figure, ADDM has detected issues with virtual memory, with the SQL being executed, and with disk I/O. Clicking the links would show detail of the finding.

The ADDM will often recommend running another advisor. In the example shown in Figure 24-4, selecting the Top SQL By DB Time link shows the result in Figure 24-5, which identifies the SQL statements that were stressing the system and recommends running the SQL Tuning Advisor against them.

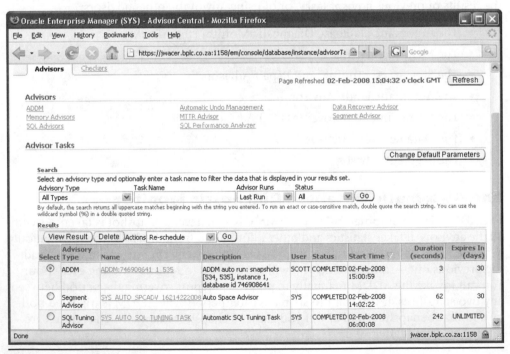

Figure 24-3 Advisor Central

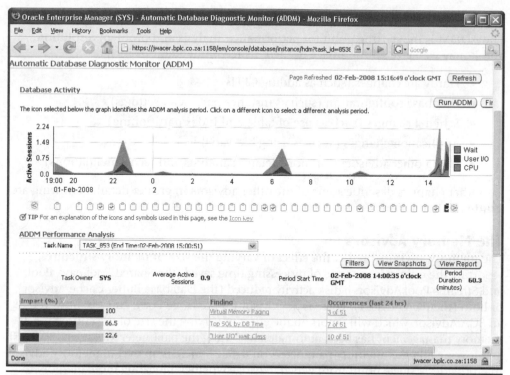

Figure 24-4 The ADDM report summary

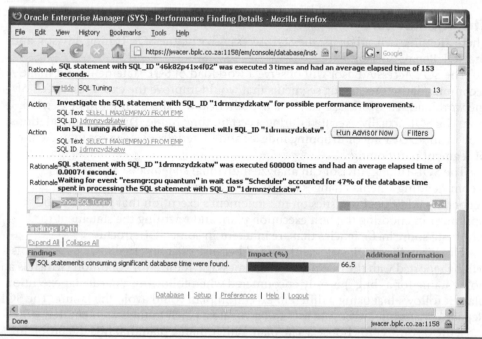

Figure 24-5 An ADDM recommendation to apply another advisor

The Advisors

The ADDM is the starting point for performance analysis and problem resolution, and it may well give all the advice needed. Its recommendations include

- Hardware changes (such as adding CPUs)
- Database configuration (such as instance parameter settings)
- Schema changes (such as use of table and index partitioning)
- Application changes (such as using bid variables)
- Using other advisors (for more detailed analysis and recommendations)

Other chapters describe some of the other advisors in greater detail. Following are summary descriptions.

The Memory Advisors

The memory advisors predict the effect of varying the size of memory structures, reporting the estimates in terms of processing time saved (the Shared Pool, Java Pool, and Streams Pool Advisors), disk activity reduced (the Database Buffer Cache Advisor), or both (the PGA Advisor). There is no advisor for the Large Pool. There is, however, an SGA Advisor, which will report on the effect of varying the size of the entire SGA. If memory management has been automated by setting the parameter MEMORY_TARGET and leaving all other memory parameters on default, there is an overall memory advisor that provides a single point from which to gauge whether allocating more memory to the instance would improve performance.

The SQL Advisors

There are three SQL advisors: the SQL Access Advisor, the SQL Tuning Advisor, and the SQL Repair Advisor.

The SQL Access Advisor will observe a workload of SQL statements and make recommendations regarding segments that would improve the execution speed of the workload. The workload can be a hypothetical workload, or it can be derived from the SQL actually executed during a certain time frame. The recommendations may include: creating or dropping indexes and materialized views, or to make use of segment partitioning.

The SQL Tuning Advisor can analyze individual statements; and as well as recommending schema changes (as the Access Advisor does), it can recommend generating additional statistics on the statement's execution that will assist the optimizer in choosing the best execution plan, and rewriting the statement to eliminate some inefficiencies that are inherent in some SQL structures.

Occasionally, a SQL statement can fail because of an internal Oracle error. This will be reported with the "ORA-600" error message. If the error condition (which is a polite name for a "bug") is only encountered when following a particular execution plan, it follows that using a different execution plan could avoid the failure. The SQL Repair Advisor can investigate this and generate a patch to the statement that will force the optimizer to choose a safe plan, rather than a plan that hits the problem.

The Automatic Undo Advisor

The Undo Advisor will observe the rate of undo data generation and the length of queries being run, and it will recommend a minimum size for the undo tablespace, which will ensure that queries do not fail with a "snapshot too old" error.

The Mean Time to Recover (MTTR) Advisor

The mechanism for instance recovery after a failure is detailed in Chapter 14. In summary, if the instance terminates in a disorderly fashion (such as a power cut or server reboot while the database was open, or just a SHUTDOWN ABORT), then on the next startup it is necessary to reinstate all work in progress that had not been written to the datafiles at the time of the crash. This will happen automatically, but until it is done, users cannot log on. The MTTR Advisor estimates how long this period of downtime for crash recovery will be, given the current workload.

The Data Recovery Advisor

If the database has been damaged in some way (such as files deleted or data blocks corrupted), it may take some time to identify the problem. There will often be several ways of recovering from the situation. For example, if a number of datafiles have been damaged by corruptions appearing on a disk, it will be necessary to find out which files and which blocks. A decision must then be made as to whether to restore entire files or only the damaged blocks. If the database is protected by a physical standby, switching over to that would also be a possibility.

Following a failure, any DBA (no matter how experienced) will need time to determine the nature and extent of the problem, and then more time to decide upon the course of action that will repair the damage with the minimum disruption to work. The Data Recovery Advisor follows an expert system to advise the DBA on this. The expert system is essentially what the DBA would follow anyway, but the advisor can do it much faster.

The Segment Advisor

Segments grow automatically. As rows are inserted into table segments and index keys are inserted into index segments, the segments fill—and then Oracle will allocate more extents as necessary. But segments do not shrink automatically as data is removed or modified with DELETE and UPDATE commands; this only happens when the segment is deliberately reorganized. The Segment Advisor observes tables and indexes, both their current state and their historical patterns of use, and recommends appropriate reorganization when necessary.

Automatic Maintenance Jobs

If the database is to run well, it is vital that the optimizer has access to accurate object statistics; that the tables and indexes are operating efficiently, without a large amount of wasted space and fragmentation; and that the high-load SQL statements have been tuned. The gathering of statistics and the running of the Segment Advisor and the SQL Tuning Advisor are, by default, automatic in an 11g database.

The Scheduler (described in Chapter 22) runs jobs automatically, at certain times and repeatedly at certain intervals. The jobs will usually be defined by the DBA, but following creation of a database with the DBCA, there will be three tasks configured within what is called the AutoTask system. These AutoTasks are

- Gathering optimizer statistics
- Running the Segment Advisor
- Running the SQL Advisor

The AutoTasks run within the Scheduler's *maintenance windows*. The maintenance windows are defined to open at 22:00 every weeknight and to close four hours later, at 02:00, and on Saturday and Sunday to open at 06:00, closing 20 hours later, at 02:00. The Scheduler is linked to another database facility: the Resource Manager, described in Chapter 21. The Resource Manager plan that is activated during the maintenance window is one that ensures that no more than 25 percent of machine resources are dedicated to the AutoTask jobs, meaning that running these tasks should not impact adversely on other work. If the maintenance window time frames are not suitable for your database workload, they are adjustable; if the maximum of 25 percent resource usage is too high and causes performance for other work to degrade, this too can be changed. The underlying assumption is that the AutoTasks will run at a time and with a priority that is unlikely to cause problems for regular work for end users.

 EXAM TIP There are three automated maintenance tasks: gathering optimizer statistics; the Segment Advisor; the SQL Tuning Advisor. The advisors run automatically, but the recommendations must be accepted (or ignored) manually. The tasks run in the maintenance windows, which by default open for 4 hours every weeknight at 22:00 and for 20 hours on Saturday and Sunday, opening at 06:00.

For any of the AutoTasks to run, the STATISTICS_LEVEL parameter must be set to TYPICAL (the default) or ALL. The simplest way to manage the scheduling of the AutoTask jobs is through Database Control. Select the Server tab from the database home page, then the Automated Maintenance Tasks link on the Scheduler section. The Automated Maintenance Tasks window, shown in Figure 24-6, displays the window for the next run (which opens at 06:00, because the figure was taken on a Saturday evening) with links for the results of the last two advisor runs. Clicking these links will show the recommendations (if any) with an option to implement them (implementing the recommendations is not automatic).

The Segment Advisor task relies on the history of object statistics built up by the daily running of the gather Optimizer Statistics Gathering. By observing these, the Segment Advisor can see not only how much unused space there is in the tables and indexes, but also whether this space is likely to be needed again, and if not advise that

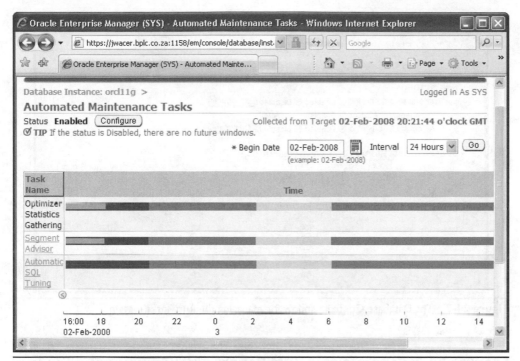

Figure 24-6 The Automated Maintenance Tasks window

the segments should be reorganized. The SQL Tuning Advisor task relies on the AWR statistics gathered by the MMON process. These statistics include figures on which SQL statements are being executed many times, perhaps millions of times an hour; which statements are responsible for a large amount of disk and memory I/O; and which statements are taking a long time to run. These are the high-load statements that will be subjected to tuning analysis.

To view and adjust the window schedule, click Configure. This will take you to the window shown in Figure 24-7, where there are radio buttons for enabling or disabling the jobs; buttons for configuring Optimizer Statistics Gathering and Automatic SQL Tuning jobs; links for editing the opening and closing times of the daily windows; and check boxes for selecting in which windows the various jobs will run.

TIP The default settings for the maintenance windows may well not be appropriate for you. In many Middle Eastern countries, for example, Saturday and Sunday are working days. Also, many databases support global organizations: just because it is the middle of the night for you, that doesn't mean it is for many of your end users.

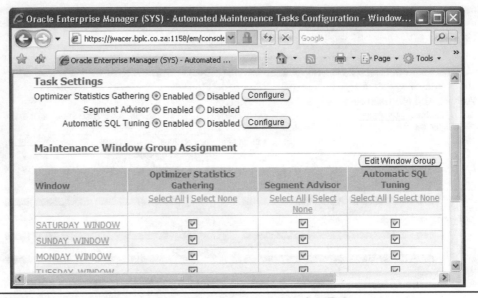

Figure 24-7 The Database Control window for managing the AutoTasks system

Exercise 24-2: Generate an ADDM Report In this exercise, you will generate an Automatic Database Diagnostic Monitor report on activity between two snapshots.

1. Connect to your database as user SYSTEM with SQL*Plus.

2. Force the creation of an AWR snapshot:

```
execute dbms_workload_repository.create_snapshot;
```

3. Simulate a workload by creating a table and running an anonymous PL/SQL block to generate some activity:

```
create table tmptab as select * from all_objects;
begin
for i in 1..10 loop
insert into tmptab select * from all_objects;
delete from tmptab;
end loop;
commit;
end;
/
```

4. Force the creation of an AWR snapshot, using the command in Step 2. This illustration shows Steps 2–4:

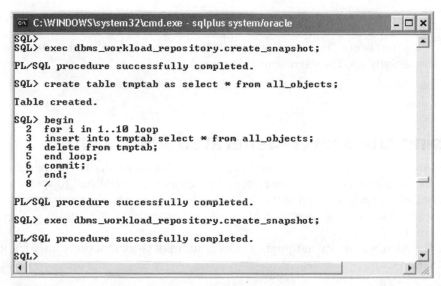

```
C:\WINDOWS\system32\cmd.exe - sqlplus system/oracle

SQL>
SQL> exec dbms_workload_repository.create_snapshot;

PL/SQL procedure successfully completed.

SQL> create table tmptab as select * from all_objects;

Table created.

SQL> begin
  2   for i in 1..10 loop
  3   insert into tmptab select * from all_objects;
  4   delete from tmptab;
  5   end loop;
  6   commit;
  7   end;
  8   /

PL/SQL procedure successfully completed.

SQL> exec dbms_workload_repository.create_snapshot;

PL/SQL procedure successfully completed.

SQL>
```

5. Connect to your database as user SYSTEM using Database Control.

6. Click the Advisor Central link in the Related Links section on the database home page. The first report listed will be the ADDM report generated as a result of the snapshot, as shown here:

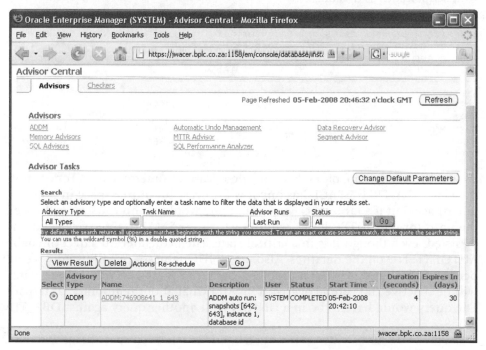

7. Select the radio button for the latest ADDM report, and click View Result. Study the report: it will show a spike of activity in the last few minutes, with a number of "Findings" beneath. Click the findings to see the nature of the activity and the statements that caused it.

8. To tidy up, drop the table from your SQL*Plus session:

```
drop table tmptab;
```

Using the Server-Generated Alert System

The Alert system is the reason why, from release 10g onward, the Oracle database can be described as *self-managing*. In earlier releases, the DBA had to spend a great deal of effort on humdrum work that was essential but not always that interesting. They also had to devise methods of picking up exceptional conditions as they occurred.

The Alert system can automate a large amount of work that previously fell into the DBA domain.

Alert Condition Monitoring and Notifications

A typical example of the humdrum work is space management: at its most basic, monitoring tablespaces to see when they are about to fill up. This could be done with scripts, such as this one:

```
SQL> select d.tablespace_name,sum(d.bytes) total,sum(f.bytes) free
  2  from dba_data_files d left outer join dba_free_space f
  3  on d.tablespace_name=f.tablespace_name
  4  group by d.tablespace_name;
TABLESPACE_NAME                      TOTAL       FREE
------------------------------  ----------  ----------
SYSAUX                           807337984    38928384
USERS                             24641536     1507328
SMALL                               401408
SYSTEM                          1509949440     4390912
EXAMPLE                          314572800    23396352
UNDO1                            209715200   208338944
```

But these scripts are prone to error—or at least, misinterpretation. For example, the view DBA_FREE_SPACE has one row for every bit of free space in every tablespace. But if a tablespace were full, there would be no rows at all; hence the need for the OUTER JOIN, without which the SMALL tablespace would not be listed, even though it is in a critical state. Then consider the effect of enabling AUTOEXTEND on the datafiles. Also, an UNDO tablespace will usually be 100 percent full—but this is not a problem, because a large part of the undo data will be inactive and can be overwritten. And what about temporary tablespaces? The query would have to be in a UNION with another query against DBA_TEMP_FILES.

Many DBAs have written suites of SQL code to report on space usage and raise warnings before error conditions occurred. Fine—but the scripts had to be written, they had to be run regularly, and they had to be updated to take account of changes in technology. Many companies have written and marketed tools to do the same thing.

The Alert system replaces a vast amount of this humdrum work. It will monitor many conditions that can cause problems, and will send notifications by a variety of methods. With regard to space management, it is by default configured to raise a warning alert when a tablespace reaches 85 percent full and a critical alert when a tablespace is 97 percent full, with account being taken of auto-extension and the nature of the contents.

Alerts comes in two forms. *Stateful* alerts are based on conditions that persist and can be fixed. Tablespace space usage is an example, or the number of sessions hanging, or the average time it is taking to complete a SQL statement execution. *Stateless* alerts are based on events; they happen and are gone. A query failing with "snapshot too old" or two transactions deadlocking are examples.

To configure the Alert system, you set thresholds. The thresholds are stored in the AWR. Then the MMON background process will monitor the database and the instance, in real time, and compare the current state with the thresholds. If a threshold is crossed, it will raise the alert. The mechanism by which an alert is raised is simply to put an entry on the alert queue. A queue is a table of messages that other processes can read. What happens to the alert message next is a matter for further configuration. The default behavior is that Enterprise Manager (either Database Control or Grid Control) will dequeue the message and display it on the database home page, but Enterprise Manager can be configured to send e-mails or SMS messages when it finds that an alert has been raised. You can also view the alerts by querying the view DBA_OUTSTANDING_ALERTS, and it is possible to write an alert handler that will dequeue the messages and take any action desired.

 EXAM TIP Alerts are raised by the MMON process, not by Enterprise Manager. Enterprise Manager reads alerts, as can other event handlers written by you or by third parties.

Setting Thresholds

There are over 200 metrics for which you can set thresholds. They are documented in the view V$METRICNAME, which gives the name of the metric and the units in which it is measured, and the ID number by which it is identified.

There is an API (the DBMS_SERVER_ALERT package) for setting thresholds. For example:

```
1     execute dbms_server_alert.set_threshold(-
2     metrics_id=>dbms_server_alert.redo_generated_sec,-
3     warning_operator=>dbms_server_alert.operator_ge,-
4     warning_value=>'1000000',-
5     critical_operator=>dbms_server_alert.operator_ge,-
6     critical_value=>'2000000',-
7     observation_period=>1,-
8     consecutive_occurrences=>5,-
9     instance_name=>'ORCL11G',-
10     object_type=>dbms_server_alert.object_type_system,-
11     object_name=>null);
```

Taking this PL/SQL execution call line by line:

1. The procedure SET_THRESHOLD will create or update an alert threshold.

2. The metric being set is the rate of redo generation, measured in bytes per second.

3. The comparison operator for the warning level, which is "greater than or equal to."

4. The value for a warning alert, which is 1MB a second.

5. The comparison operator for the critical level, which is "greater than or equal to."

6. The value for a critical alert, which is 2MB a second.

7. The observation period, in minutes.

8. The number of consecutive occurrences before the alert is raised.

9. The instance for which the alert is being configured.

10. The type of object to which the alert refers.

11. The name of the object to which the alert refers.

Note that not all the arguments are relevant for all alerts.

The preceding example configures an alert for the rate of redo generation; a warning will be raised if this exceeds 1MB a second, and a critical warning if it goes over 2MB a second. The observation period is set to a minute and consecutive occurrences to five; this means that if the redo generation happens to hit a high level just a couple of times, it will not be reported—but if it stays at a high level consistently (for five consecutive minutes), then it will be reported. As this metric is one that could vary between instances in a RAC environment, the instance name must be specified, but the object name is not relevant. If the alert were for tablespace usage, then the instance name would not be specified, the object type would be tablespace, and the object name would be set to the name of the tablespace.

To reach the graphical interface for setting thresholds, select the Metric And Policy Settings link in the Related Links section on the database home page. This will show all the metrics with their settings. Clicking the Edit symbol for a metric will take you to the window where the thresholds can be set. Figure 24-8 shows this for the "Redo Generated (per second)" metric, after executing the procedure call just described. The graphical interface does not give access to all the settings for all the metrics; in this case, you cannot specify an observation period (it is always set to one minute) and have no choice of comparison operators.

The Notification System

The default notification mechanism for stateful alerts is nothing more than displaying them in Enterprise Manager on the database home page, and writing them to the DBA_OUTSTANDING_ALERTS view. They will remain visible until they are cleared. They may be cleared because the DBA has fixed the problem, or in some cases the

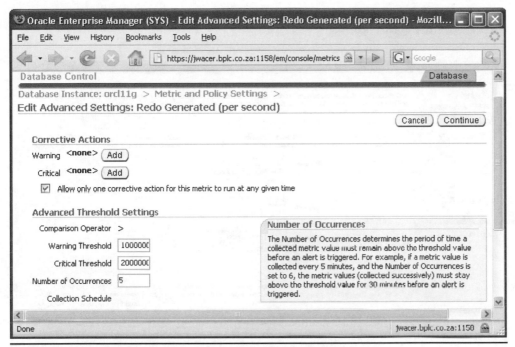

Figure 24-8 Setting thresholds with Database Control

problem will go away in the natural course of events. For instance, a tablespace-usage alert would usually require DBA action (such as adding another datafile), whereas an activity-related alert such the rate of redo generation might clear automatically when the activity reduces.

When an alert is cleared, within the database it is removed from the DBA_ OUTSTANDING_ALERTS view and written to the DBA_ALERT_HISTORY view. Stateless alerts go straight to the history view.

If any notification beyond the default is needed, this must be configured within Enterprise Manager. The Enterprise Manager notification system requires configuration at three levels:

- A notification method must be configured.
- A rule must be created to catch the event.
- An administrator must subscribe to the rule.

To set up notification methods in Database Control, click the Setup link visible in most Database Control windows at the top right and bottom center, and then the Notification Methods link in the left-hand side menu bar. From here, you specify the address of the SMTP server to which Database Control should send e-mail notifications, with authentication details and a reply address. From this window, shown in Figure 24-9, you can also define additional notification methods.

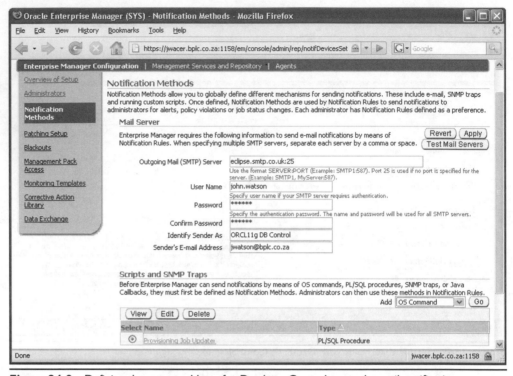

Figure 24-9 Defining the server address for Database Control to send e-mail notifications

The alternative notification methods can be seen at the bottom of Figure 24-9: operating system commands or scripts, PL/SQL procedures, or an SNMP trap (which lets Database Control integrate with any SNMP management system that may be available).

Having defined the notification method, create a rule. Select the Preferences link visible in most Database Control windows at the top right and bottom center, then the Rules link in the left-hand side menu bar. There are several preconfigured rules. To create a new one, click Create and give the rule a name; select the Public check box to make it available to other uses. Then click Metrics, if the rule is for a metric, and select which metrics the rule should monitor. Figure 24-10 shows adding the "Redo Generated (per second)" metric to a rule.

The final step is for a user to subscribe to the notifications. From the Setup link again, choose Administrators on the left-hand side menu bar. There will by default be three administrators: SYS, SYSMAN, and SYSTEM. A site making use of Enterprise Manager would usually have created additional users. Select the radio button for the user who is to subscribe to one or more rules, click Edit to make sure the user's e-mail address is set up, and then click Subscribe To Rules to reach a list of all the public rules, where the ones for which the user is to receive notifications by e-mail can be selected. Notifications sent with any of the other methods (PL/SQL, OS command, or SNMP) do not need this step; the code written to implement the PL/SQL

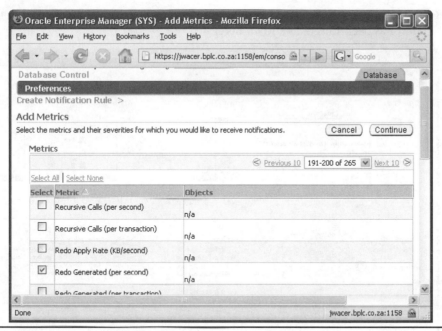

Figure 24-10   Adding a metric to a Database Control notification rule

procedure, the operating system script, or the SNMP trap should handle the
propagation of the notification.

Exercise 24-3: Configure Alerts   In this exercise, you will enable an alert for
the commit rate and demonstrate its use.

1. Connect to your database with Database Control as user SYSTEM.

2. From the database home page, click the Metric And Policy Settings link in the
   Related Links section.

3. Make sure that the View box is set to All Metrics, and scroll down to the User
   Commit (per second) metric.

4. Set the "Warning" and "Critical" thresholds to 1 and 4, respectively. These are
   artificially low thresholds that it will be simple to cross. Click OK to save this
   change.

5. Connect to your database as user SYSTEM with SQL*Plus, and issue the
   COMMIT command a few times quickly:

```
SQL> commit;
Commit complete.
SQL> /
Commit complete.
SQL> /
Commit complete.
SQL> /
Commit complete.
SQL> /
Commit complete.
```

6. In your Database Control session, within a few seconds you will see that the alert has been raised, as shown here:

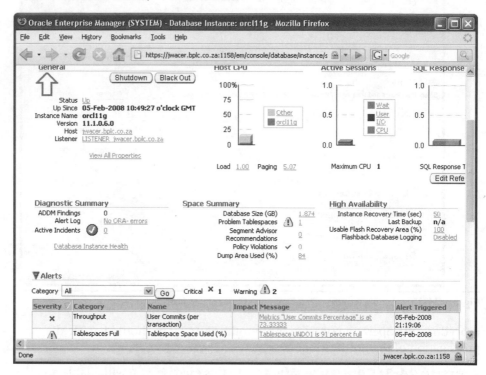

7. Tidy up, by returning to the Edit Thresholds window and clearing the threshold values.

Two-Minute Drill

Use and Manage the Automatic Workload Repository

- By default, snapshots are taken every hour and stored for eight days.
- Additional snapshots can be taken on demand.
- Snapshots can be preserved indefinitely if nominated for a baseline.
- MMON is responsible for creating snapshots and launching the ADDM.
- The AWR consists of tables (and related objects) in the SYSMAN schema, in the SYSAUX tablespace.

Use the Advisory Framework

- The ADDM runs automatically whenever a snapshot is taken, and manually on demand.

- ADDM reports will give advice directly and may recommend running other advisors.

- By default, the SQL Tuning Advisor and the Segment Advisor will run automatically in the maintenance windows.

- Setting STATISTICS_LEVEL to BASIC will disable gathering snapshots and running the advisors.

Manage Alerts and Thresholds

- Stateful alerts must be configured with thresholds.

- If a stateful alert is raised, it will remain until the situation is cleared; stateless alerts are reported and do not need to be cleared.

- Thresholds are stored in the AWR.

- It is the MMON background process that raises an alert, and (usually) Enterprise Manager that reports it.

Self Test

1. The AWR is located in the SYSAUX tablespace. If you suspect that it is growing to such a size that it will fill the SYSAUX tablespace, what actions could you take to reduce the likelihood of this happening? (Choose all correct answers.)

   A. Relocate the AWR to a tablespace created specifically for storing it.

   B. Reduce the time between snapshots, so that less data will be generated by each one.

   C. Increase the time between snapshots, so that fewer snapshots will be generated.

   D. Adjust the scheduling of the automatic maintenance tasks, so that they will run less frequently.

2. By default, snapshots are removed from the AWR on a regular basis, making comparisons of activity over a long period of time (such as contrasting this year's year-end processing with last year's) impossible. What should you do to make this possible? (Choose the best answer.)

   A. Save the year-end snapshots as a baseline.

   B. Adjust the snapshot retention period to the whole period: a little over a year.

   C. Set the datafile(s) that make up the SYSAUX tablespace to AUTOEXTEND, so that snapshots will not be purged.

   D. Disable purging of snapshots by setting STATISTICS_LEVEL to ALL.

3. When does the Automatic Database Diagnostic Monitor run? (Choose all correct answers.)

   A. Whenever a snapshot is taken by MMON

   B. Whenever a snapshot is taken by the DBA

   C. On demand

   D. When the automatic tasks run in the maintenance windows

   E. When triggered by the Alert system

4. Which advisors are run by the AutoTasks system in the maintenance windows? (Choose all correct answers.)

   A. The Automatic Database Diagnostic Monitor

   B. The memory advisors

   C. The Segment Advisor

   D. The SQL Access Advisor

   E. The SQL Tuning Advisor

   F. The Undo Advisor

5. With regard to the collection of monitoring information, put these steps in the correct order:

   A. Data accumulates in the SGA.

   B. MMON generates an ADDM report.

   C. MMON writes data to the AWR.

   D. Reports are purged.

   E. Snapshots are purged.

6. Which process raises alerts? (Choose the best answer.)

   A. MMON, the Manageability Monitor

   B. Enterprise Manager (Database Control or Grid Control)

   C. The server process that detects the problem

   D. SMON, the System Monitor

7. End users are complaining that they receive "snapshot too old" error messages when running long queries. You look at the DBA_OUTSTANDING_ALERTS view, and don't see any. Why might this be? (Choose the best answer.)

   A. The STATISTICS_LEVEL parameter is set to BASIC.

   B. The snapshots for the periods when the errors occurred have been purged.

   C. No alert has been configured for "snapshot too old."

   D. "Snapshot too old" is reported in DBA_ALERT_HISTORY.

Self Test Answers

1. ☑ C. Increasing the time between snapshots will reduce the number stored, and therefore the space needed.

   ☒ A, B, and D. A is wrong because it is not possible to relocate the AWR. B is wrong because the space needed to store a snapshot is not related to the snapshot frequency; this would actually have the opposite effect to that desired. D is wrong because the automatic maintenance tasks do not control snapshots, and it is snapshots that take up the bulk of the space in the AWR.

2. ☑ A. This is exactly the type of situation for which baselines are intended.

   ☒ B, C, and D. B would work, but you would need a SYSAUX tablespace the size of Jupiter; it is not a good solution. C is wrong because the available space has no effect on the retention time. D is wrong because STATISTICS_LEVEL controls how much information is gathered, not for how long it is kept.

3. ☑ A, B, and C. MMON will always generate an ADDM report when a snapshot is taken (whether automatically or manually), and the DBA can request a report at any time.

   ☒ D and E. D is wrong because the AutoTasks do not include running the ADDM. E is wrong because the Alert system signals real-time problems: it is not used to launch ADDM, which reports on activity after the events have occurred.

4. ☑ C and E. These run in every maintenance window, but implementing the recommendations is up to the DBA.

   ☒ A, B, D, and F. A is wrong because MMON invokes the ADDM. B, D, and F are wrong because they are advisors that must be invoked manually.

5. ☑ A, C, B, E, and D. This is the correct sequence.

   ☒ All other sequences are wrong.

6. ☑ A. MMON raises alerts.

   ☒ B, C, and D. B is wrong because Enterprise Manager does not raise alerts; it reports them. C and D are wrong because neither server sessions nor the SMON are part of the Alert system.

7. ☑ D. "Snapshot too old" is a stateless alert and so goes directly to the alert history.

   ☒ A, B, and C. A is wrong because the STATISTICS_LEVEL refers to statistics, not alerts. B is wrong because outstanding alerts do not get purged on any schedule, only by being resolved. C is wrong because "snapshot too old" is a stateless alert, and thresholds can only apply to stateful alerts.

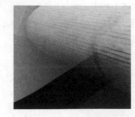

CHAPTER 25

Performance Tuning

Exam Objectives

In this chapter you will learn to

- 052.13.1   Use Automatic Memory Management
- 052.13.2   Use Memory Advisors
- 052.13.3   Troubleshoot Invalid and Unusable Objects
- 053.14.1   Implement Automatic Memory Management
- 053.14.2   Manually Configure SGA Parameters
- 053.14.3   Configure Automatic PGA Memory Management
- 053.15.1   Use the SQL Tuning Advisor
- 053.15.2   Use the SQL Access Advisor to Tune a Workload
- 053.15.3   Understand Database Replay

Performance management is a huge subject. The treatment given in the core OCP syllabus is little more than an introduction. There is an additional qualification (the "Oracle Database 11g Performance Tuning Certified Expert") that requires passing another exam that takes performance management further. But even after studying for and passing that, you aren't finished. As an Oracle DBA, you will study performance monitoring and enhancement techniques throughout your whole career. Indeed, you may want "Don't worry—I'll find the problem soon" inscribed on your tombstone.

The topics discussed here are tuning memory; tuning SQL; tuning segment access; identifying objects that are invalid or unusable; and using the Database Replay facility to generate workloads for testing.

Managing Memory

Memory usage in the Oracle instance falls into two categories: program global areas (the PGAs) that are private to each session, and the system global area (the SGA) that is shared by all the Oracle processes. From release 9i it has been possible to automate the management of the PGA. From release 10g it has been possible to automate the management of the SGA. Release 11g can manage both PGA and SGA together.

 TIP All Oracle memory usage is virtual memory. The Oracle processes have no way of knowing if the memory to which they are connecting is in RAM or has been swapped (or paged) to disk. However, swapping will cripple performance and should be avoided.

PGA Memory Management

A user session against an Oracle instance consists of a user process connected to a server process. The user process generates SQL statements and sends them to the server process for execution: this is the client-server split. Associated with the server process is a block of nonsharable memory: the PGA. When executing SQL, the server process makes use of the PGA to store session-specific data, including

- Temporary tables
- Sorting rows
- Merging bitmaps
- Variables
- The call stack

For some data in the PGA, use of memory is nonnegotiable. For example, if the session needs memory for its call stack, that memory must be made available. For other structures (such as temporary table storage) use of PGA is nice but not essential, because if necessary the data can be written out to a disk-based storage structure—though this will impact adversely on performance.

Every SQL statement uses memory in the SGA (specifically, the shared SQL area, in the shared pool) and also will require a minimum amount of PGA memory (sometimes referred to as the private SQL area), without which it cannot execute. Making more PGA memory available will often reduce execution time, but the reduction is not linear. Typically, there will be three stages of memory allocation: these are known as *optimal, one-pass,* and *multipass.* The optimal memory allocation will allow the statement to execute purely in memory, with no requirement to make use of temporary storage on disk. The optimal memory allocation is sufficient to accommodate all the input data and any auxiliary data structures that the statement must create. The one-pass memory allocation is insufficient for optimal execution and therefore forces an extra pass over the data. The multipass memory allocation is even smaller and means that several passes over the data will be needed.

As an example, consider a sort operation. The ideal situation is that all the rows to be sorted can be read into the PGA and sorted there. The memory required for this is the optimal memory allocation. If the optimal memory allocation is not available, then the rows must be separated into batches. Each batch will be read into memory, sorted, and written out to disk. This results in a set of sorted batches on disk, which must then be read back into memory and merged into a final sorted list of all the rows. The PGA memory needed for this is the one-pass allocation: the sort operation has had to become multiple sorts followed by a merge. If the one-pass memory allocation is not available, then the merge phase as well as the sort phase will require use of temporary disk storage. This is a multipass execution.

 EXAM TIP A statement's shared SQL area is in the shared pool of the SGA; its private SQL area is in the session's PGA.

The ideal situation is that all SQL statements should execute optimally, but this goal may be impossible to reach. In data warehouse operations, the optimal memory allocation can be many gigabytes if the queries are addressing vast tables. In such environments, one-pass executions may be the best that can be achieved. Multipass executions should be avoided if at all possible. For example, to sort 10GB of data may require something over 10GB of memory to run optimally, but only 40MB to run with one pass. Only if less than 40MB is available will the sort become multipass, and execution times will then increase substantially.

Managing PGA memory can be automatic, and Oracle Corporation strongly recommends that it should be. The older manual management techniques are supported only for backward compatibility and will not be discussed here. To implement automatic PGA memory management, you set a target for the total PGA memory allocation, summed up for all sessions. The Oracle instance will then pass out memory from this total to sessions on demand. When a session has finished executing its statement, the PGA it was using can be allocated to another session. This system relies on the fact that at any one moment only some of the connected sessions will need any negotiable PGA memory. They will all need a certain amount of PGA memory to retain the state of the session even when the session is idle, but this will leave enough from the total so that those sessions actually running statements can have what they need. At least, that is what one hopes.

 TIP It is sometimes impossible to achieve optimal memory allocations, because the memory requirements can be huge. One-pass executions are bad but may be unavoidable. Multipass executions are disastrous, and if these are occurring, you should talk to the system administrators about available hardware and to the programmers about tuning their SQL.

Automatic PGA memory management is enabled with two instance parameters:

- WORKAREA_SIZE_POLICY
- PGA_AGGREGATE_TARGET

The WORKAREA_SIZE_POLICY will default to AUTO, meaning that Oracle can assign PGA to sessions on demand, while attempting to keep the total allocated PGA within the PGA_AGGREGATE_TARGET. This parameter defaults to the greater of 10MB or 20 percent of the size of the SGA and should be adjusted upward until a satisfactory proportion of statements are executing optimally, but not set so high that memory is over-allocated and the operating system has to page virtual memory to disk.

 TIP For many systems, the default for PGA_AGGREGATE_TARGET will be far too low for optimal performance.

SGA Memory Management

The SGA contains several memory structures, which can be sized independently. These are

- The shared pool
- The database buffer cache
- The large pool
- The Streams pool
- The Java pool
- The log buffer

As a general rule, the memory allocation to the large pool, the Java pool, and the Streams pool is not a matter for negotiation—either the memory is needed or it isn't. If these structures are undersized, there will be errors; if they are oversized, there will be no performance improvement. The memory allocation to the shared pool, the database buffer cache, and the log buffer is negotiable: if less than optimal, there will not be errors but performance will degrade. The exception is the shared pool: if this is chronically undersized, there will be errors.

TIP Do not throw memory at Oracle unnecessarily. An oversized shared pool or log buffer is seriously bad for performance. An oversized buffer cache is less likely to be a problem, unless it is so oversized that the system is having to swap.

SGA memory management can be automatic (and Oracle Corporation advises that it should be) with the exception of the log buffer. The DBA sets a total size for the SGA, and the instance will apportion this total to the various structures, ensuring that there are no errors from undersizing of SGA components and that memory above this minimum is allocated where it will do the most good. The components will be resized on demand, so that if a component needs more memory, it will be taken from a component that can spare it. The log buffer is the one SGA component whose size is fixed at instance startup and that cannot be automatically managed.

The parameters for manual management of the SGA are

- SHARED_POOL_SIZE
- DB_CACHE_SIZE
- LARGE_POOL_SIZE
- STREAMS_POOL_SIZE
- JAVA_POOL_SIZE

To enable automatic SGA management, leave all of these on default (or set to zero) and set one parameter to enable automatic shared memory management (ASMM):

- SGA_TARGET

When using ASMM, the instance will monitor demand for memory in the various SGA components and pass out memory to the components as required, downsizing components if this is necessary to keep the total allocated memory within the target. Also included within the target is the log buffer. This is sized with the LOG_BUFFER parameter, which is static: the log buffer is created at instance startup and cannot be resized subsequently.

TIP The default for LOG_BUFFER is probably correct. You can set the parameter to higher than default, but this will often cause a degradation in performance. If you set it to less than the default, your setting will often be ignored.

EXAM TIP The log buffer is the only SGA structure that cannot be adjusted dynamically. It cannot therefore be automatically managed.

If you set any of the parameters that control the automatically managed SGA components, the value given will act as a minimum size below which ASMM will never reduce that component.

Automatic Memory Management

The Automatic Memory Management mechanism lets the Oracle instance manage server memory usage as a whole, by setting one parameter: MEMORY_TARGET. This takes the automatic PGA management (enabled with PGA_AGGREGATE_TARGET) and the automatic shared memory management (enabled with SGA_TARGET) a step further, by letting Oracle transfer memory between PGAs and SGA on demand.

TIP To enable automatic memory management, set the one parameter MEMORY_TARGET, and do not set any of the other parameters listed previously, with the exception of LOG_BUFFER—though this too can often be left on default.

Automatic memory management is not just a tool to make database administration easy. It will often give big performance benefits as well. Many databases will experience different patterns of activity at different times, which could benefit from different memory configurations. For example, it is not uncommon for a database used for order processing to experience a very light transaction processing workload during most of the month, and then a heavy query processing workload during month-end reporting runs. Transaction processing will typically not be demanding on PGA memory but will require a large database buffer cache. Query processing will often require large PGA allocations, but not much buffer cache.

EXAM TIP The MEMORY_TARGET parameter is dynamic—it can be adjusted without shutting down the instance—but only within a limit set by another parameter: MEMORY_MAX_TARGET. This is static, so it can only be raised by adjusting with the SCOPE=SPFILE clause and restarting the instance.

Manually transferring memory between SGA and PGA in response to changing patterns of activity is not a practical option, and many systems will not be able to allocate enough memory to both concurrently to satisfy their peak demands. Automatic memory management is able to transfer memory between SGA and PGA as necessary to optimize performance within an overall memory constraint. This overall constraint must be determined by the DBA and the system administrator together. There is little point in the DBA setting an upper limit that is so large that the operating system has to page SGA and PGA to a swap device; the system administrator will be able to advise on a suitable maximum value.

EXAM TIP If you set the parameter PGA_AGGREGATE_TARGET or SGA_TARGET when AMM is enabled, the values you specify will be a minimum size beneath which AMM will never reduce the PGA or SGA.

Exercise 25-1: Set the Memory Management Parameters In this exercise, you will disable Automatic Memory Management (if it is enabled) and set the SGA and PGA targets independently. Make all the changes using syntax that will only affect the running instance: do not propagate the changes to the spfile, unless you are prepared to reverse them later.

1. Connect to your database with SQL*Plus as user SYSTEM.

2. Ensure that none of the parameters for managing the dynamic SGA memory structures manually are set:

```
alter system set db_cache_size=0 scope=memory;
alter system set shared_pool_size=0 scope=memory;
alter system set large_pool_size=0 scope=memory;
alter system set java_pool_size=0 scope=memory;
```

3. Disable Automatic Memory Management:

```
alter system set memory_target=0 scope=memory;
```

4. Set the parameters to size PGA and SGA independently, using the lowest permitted values:

```
alter system set pga_aggregate_target=10m scope=memory;
alter system set sga_target=64m scope=memory;
```

The second command may take a few minutes to complete, and it may fail if Oracle cannot reduce the SGA to the requested value.

5. Determine the actual size of the currently allocated PGAs, by summing up the value for the statistic session pga memory across all sessions:

```
select sum(value) from v$sesstat natural join v$statname
where name='session pga memory';
```

The figure will be significantly in excess of the 10MB requested in Step 4. This is because 10MB is a value that is so low that Oracle cannot keep to it. The PGA target is only a target, not a hard limit.

6. Determine the actual size of the SGA:

```
select sum(bytes) from v$sgastat;
```

This figure too may be greater than that requested in Step 4.

The Memory Advisors

The Oracle instance collects a vast amount of information regarding activity and performance. These statistics enable the memory advisors. These are tools that will calculate the effect of varying the sizes of the SGA and PGA memory structures. The Automatic Memory Management facility uses the advisors to make decisions about memory allocation, and they are also visible to the DBA through various views and through Enterprise Manager. Figure 25-1 shows three queries that display memory advisor information.

The first query in Figure 25-1 shows the PGA advisor. The third selected column shows an estimate for the amount of disk I/O that would be needed if the PGA target were set to the figure shown in the first column. The second column expresses this figure as a proportion of the actual setting. The fifth row of the output is the current setting: a PGA_TARGET_FACTOR of 1. It can be seen that if another 30MB of memory

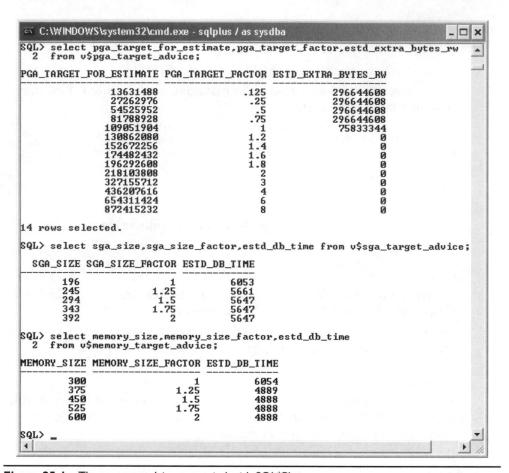

```
C:\WINDOWS\system32\cmd.exe - sqlplus / as sysdba                    _ □ ×
SQL> select pga_target_for_estimate,pga_target_factor,estd_extra_bytes_rw
  2  from v$pga_target_advice;

PGA_TARGET_FOR_ESTIMATE PGA_TARGET_FACTOR ESTD_EXTRA_BYTES_RW
----------------------- ----------------- -------------------
               13631488              .125           296644608
               27262976               .25           296644608
               54525952                .5           296644608
               81788928               .75           296644608
              109051904                 1            75833344
              130862080               1.2                   0
              152672256               1.4                   0
              174482432               1.6                   0
              196292608               1.8                   0
              218103808                 2                   0
              327155712                 3                   0
              436207616                 4                   0
              654311424                 6                   0
              872415232                 8                   0

14 rows selected.

SQL> select sga_size,sga_size_factor,estd_db_time from v$sga_target_advice;

  SGA_SIZE SGA_SIZE_FACTOR ESTD_DB_TIME
---------- --------------- ------------
       196               1         6053
       245            1.25         5661
       294             1.5         5647
       343            1.75         5647
       392               2         5647

SQL> select memory_size,memory_size_factor,estd_db_time
  2  from v$memory_target_advice;

MEMORY_SIZE MEMORY_SIZE_FACTOR ESTD_DB_TIME
----------- ------------------ ------------
        300                  1         6054
        375               1.25         4889
        450                1.5         4888
        525               1.75         4888
        600                  2         4888

SQL> _
```

Figure 25-1   The memory advisors, queried with SQL*Plus

were added to the target, less I/O would be needed, but that adding more than this would give no further benefit.

The second query in Figure 25-1 shows the SGA advisor. This relates the size of the SGA to a projected value for DB_TIME. DB_TIME is an overall figure for the amount of time taken by the database to execute SQL; minimizing DB_TIME is the overall objective of all tuning. It can be seen that if the SGA were raised from its current value of 196MB to 294MB, DB_TIME would reduce but there would be no point in going further.

The third query is against the memory target advisor, which gives advice on the total (SGA plus PGA) memory allocation. This shows that the optimal value is 450MB, as opposed to the current value of 300MB. If using Automatic Memory Management (enabled with the MEMORY_TARGET parameter), then this last query is all that need be used. It can be seen that virtually all of the DB_TIME saving could be achieved by raising the target to 375MB, and if the system administrators say sufficient memory is not available to allocate the optimal amount, then this is what the DBA should ask for.

EXAM TIP The advisors will not be enabled unless the STATISTICS_LEVEL parameter is set to TYPICAL or ALL.

Exercise 25-2: Use the Memory Advisors   In this exercise, you will gather advice about memory allocation using the advisors through Database Control.

1. Connect to your database as user SYS with Database Control.

2. From the database home page, click the Advisor Central link in the Related Links section. Then on the Advisors tab, click the Memory Advisors link in the Advisors section.

3. On the SGA tab, in the Current Allocation section you will see the current SGA memory usage, which will be the same total as that returned for the query in Exercise 25-1, Step 4, and the breakdown into the individual components.

4. Click ADVICE to see a graphical representation of a query against the V$SHARED_POOL_ADVICE view. The following illustration is an example, which shows that the optimal SGA would be nearly 200MB.

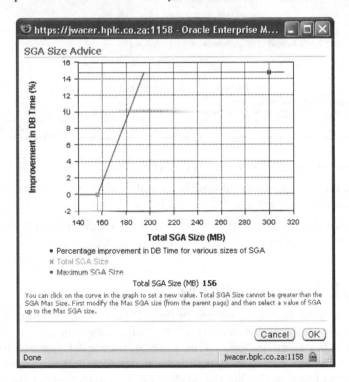

5. On the PGA tab, you will see the target (set to 10MB) and the actual allocated PGA, which will be higher. The ADVICE button will show a graphical representation of a query against V$PGA_TARGET_ADVICE.

6. Enable Automatic Memory Management by clicking the ENABLE button at the top of the Memory Advisors window. This will display the value of MEMORY_ MAX_TARGET, along with a possible memory size, and suggest a value for MEMORY_TARGET. In the following illustration, these values are 300MB and 166MB.

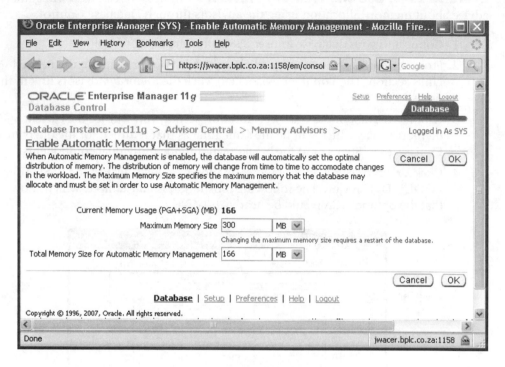

7. Leave the memory parameters on default, and click OK.

8. The memory advisor will now be available: click ADVICE to see the suggested value for the target.

9. Return the instance to the original memory configuration (as it was before Exercise 25-1) by shutting it down and restarting.

The SQL Tuning Advisor

The SQL Tuning Advisor analyzes one or more SQL statements, examining statistics, and potentially recommends creating a SQL Profile, new indexes, materialized views, or a revised SQL statement. You can run the SQL Tuning Advisor manually; however, it is run automatically during every maintenance window on the most resource-intensive SQL statements identified within the production workload. Optionally, you can specify that the analysis performed during the maintenance window automatically implements recommended SQL Profiles.

The Capabilities of the SQL Tuning Advisor

Whether the SQL Tuning Advisor runs automatically or you run it on one or more SQL statements, it performs the same types of analyses:

- **Statistics Analysis**   Check for stale or missing statistics, and recommend refreshing or creating them.
- **SQL Profiling**   Collect auxiliary statistics on a SQL statement along with partial execution statistics and store them in a SQL Profile.
- **Access Paths**   Analyze the impact of creating new indexes, creating materialized views, and partitioning.
- **Structure Analysis**   Restructure the SQL statements to see if better execution plans are generated.

From the preceding list, you can configure the Automatic SQL Tuning task to implement automatically SQL Profiles if the performance improvement improves by a factor of three. All other recommendations, and SQL Profile recommendations for minimal performance improvements, must be implemented manually after reviewing the Automatic SQL Tuning Report. When profiling a SQL statement, the optimizer partially runs the statement, experimenting with various execution plans. The execution statistics generated during this process update the profile. Information on how the statement actually ran can be used by the optimizer subsequently when the statement is encountered during normal database operation. Note that the SQL Tuning Advisor considers each SQL statement individually. If it recommends an index for a SELECT statement, it may help the performance of the query but may dramatically reduce the performance of DML activity against the table in a heavily OLTP environment. Thus, the SQL Access Advisor, discussed later in this chapter, may be a better analysis tool to analyze all operations against one or more tables in a workload.

The SQL Tuning Advisor can use a number of sources for its analysis:

- The SQL statements currently cached in the library cache of the shared pool
- A precreated set of statements
- Statements retrieved from the AWR
- An individual ad hoc statement

There is a graphical interface to the SQL Tuning Advisor, and also a set of PL/SQL APIs.

Using the SQL Tuning Advisor with Enterprise Manager

You can set the SQL Tuning Advisor options in Enterprise Manager. From the database home page, click the Advisor Central link in the Related Links section. Under the Advisors heading, click the SQL Advisors link. The SQL Advisors window shown in

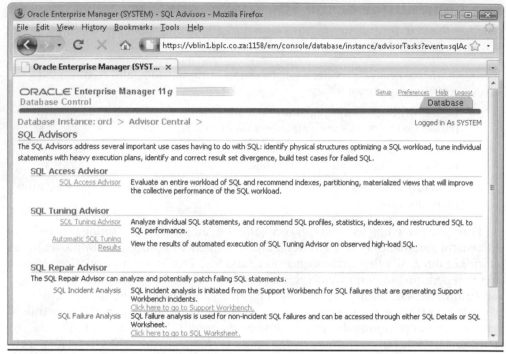

Figure 25-2   The SQL Advisors window

Figure 25-2 gives a choice between the SQL Access Advisor (described later in this chapter, the SQL Repair Advisor, and the SQL Tuning Advisor (described here), with a description of their capabilities.

Next, click the SQL Tuning Advisor link. On the page in Figure 25-3, you can specify the options for a manual invocation of the SQL Tuning Advisor. In this example, you specify a 30-minute time limit for the job, to be run immediately, with only limited analysis of each SQL statement. Using the limited analysis option does not generate any SQL profile recommendations. In this case, unless you have any existing SQL Tuning Sets, you cannot submit this job yet.

Therefore, you can navigate to one of the pages using the links in the Overview section of the page in Figure 25-3: Top Activity (statements from the library cache), Historical SQL (statements from an AWR snapshot), or SQL Tuning Sets (created previously). They can provide data sources that can be used to create a SQL Tuning

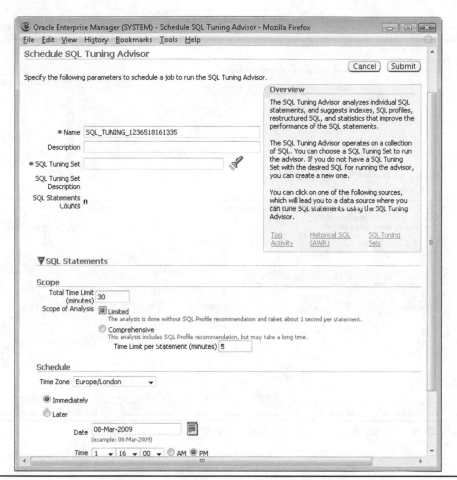

Figure 25-3 Schedule SQL tuning task in Database Control

Set as input to the SQL Tuning Advisor. When you click the Top Activity link in Figure 25-3, you see the Top Activity page in Figure 25-4.

At the bottom of the page, you see the Top SQL activity for the selected time period, which in this example is from about 1:14 P.M. to 1:19 P.M. The top SQL includes the execution of a PL/SQL package, an UPDATE statement, and an INSERT statement. Clicking the Select All link adds all three of these statements to a SQL

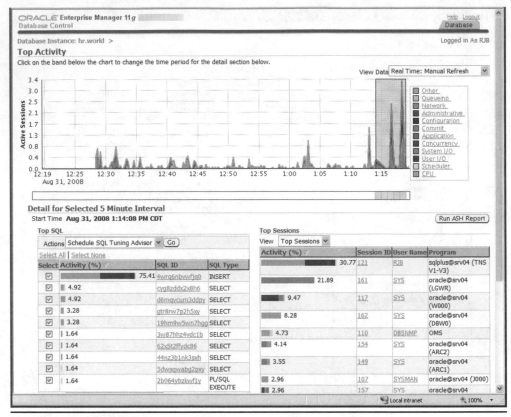

Figure 25-4 The Database Control Top Activity window

Tuning Set that you can use on the SQL Tuning Advisor page in Figure 25-3. After clicking the Select All link, click the GO button next to the Schedule SQL Tuning Advisor action in the drop-down menu. You will see the page in Figure 25-5 with a SQL Tuning Set created from the SQL statements you selected on the previous page.

In Figure 25-5, you schedule a comprehensive analysis of the selected SQL statements. You also want to run the job immediately. Clicking SUBMIT submits the job for processing. Figure 25-6 shows the job in progress.

After the job submitted in Figure 25-5 completes, you see the results of the analysis. You can also access the results from the Advisor Central page, as you can see in Figure 25-7.

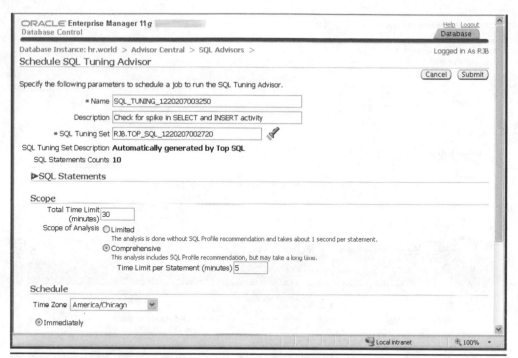

Figure 25-5   Schedule SQL Tuning Advisor with SQL Tuning Set

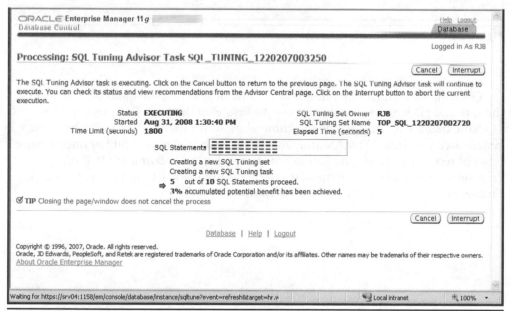

Figure 25-6   SQL Tuning Advisor job progress

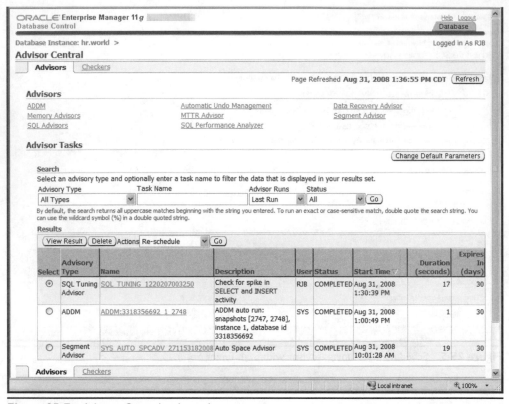

Figure 25-7   Advisor Central task results

Clicking the SQL Tuning Advisor task name or selecting the radio button next to the task and clicking VIEW RESULT, you see the results of the analysis in Figure 25-8.

Note that the results include recommendations for user SQL (e.g., RJB) and for system accounts (e.g., SYSMAN and DBSNMP). Each SQL statement has one or more types of recommendation, including statistics gathering, creating a SQL Profile, creating an index, or revising the SQL statement itself. You can implement the SQL Profile recommendation by clicking IMPLEMENT ALL PROFILES.

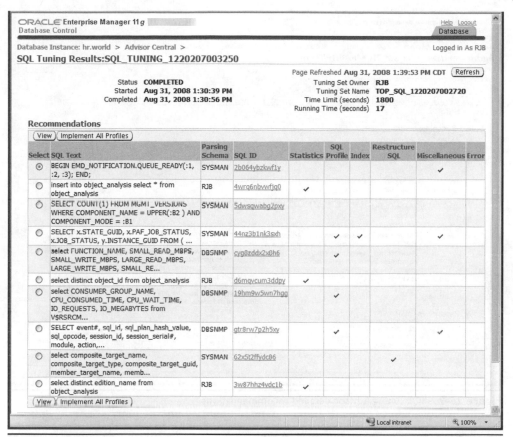

Figure 25-8 SQL Tuning Advisor recommendations summary

Selecting the radio button for the fourth SQL statement in Figure 25-8, you can see a detailed explanation of all recommendations for this SQL statement in Figure 25-9.

In Figure 25-9, you are advised to implement one of the recommendations, such as saving a SQL Profile for future executions or creating an index on one of the tables in the SQL query.

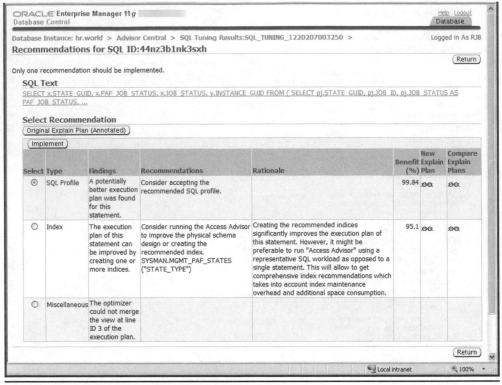

Figure 25-9   SQL Tuning Advisor detailed recommendations

The SQL Tuning Advisor API: the DBMS_SQLTUNE Package

If you need to have more control over your tuning tasks or want to run a specific set of tuning tasks repeatedly, you can use the DBMS_SQLTUNE PL/SQL package to create, run, and monitor a SQL Tuning Advisor job.

For a basic analysis of a SQL statement, you will use the following procedures within DBMS_SQLTUNE:

- **CREATE_TUNING_TASK**   Create a tuning task for a SQL statement or a SQL Tuning Set.
- **EXECUTE_TUNING_TASK**   Execute a tuning task created with **CREATE_TUNING_TASK**.
- **REPORT_TUNING_TASK**   Show the results and recommendations from the SQL Tuning Advisor.

In addition, you can use the following data dictionary views to query the name and status of tuning jobs:

- **DBA_ADVISOR_LOG**   Task names, status, and execution statistics for all tasks

- **DBA_/USER_ADVISOR_TASKS**   More detailed information about advisor tasks, such as advisor name, user-specified description, and execution type for the current user

- **V$ADVISOR_PROGRESS**   More detailed information about the completion status and time remaining for an advisor task

Exercise 25-3: Run the SQL Tuning Advisor for a SQL Statement   In this exercise, you will use DBMS_SQLTUNE to generate recommendations for one of the SQL statements in Figure 25-8.

1. Connect to the database with SQL*Plus as user SYSTEM, and create the table to be used in this exercise:

```
create table object_analysis as select * from all_objects;
```

2. These commands, executed at the SQL prompt, will create a variable to store the name of the task, create a task to tune one statement, and then run the task:

```
variable vtask varchar2(100);
execute :vtask := dbms_sqltune.create_tuning_task(-
sql_text=>'select distinct object_id from object_analysis');
execute dbms_sqltune.execute_tuning_task(:vtask);
```

3. Retrieve the recommendations from the tuning task, first setting up SQL*Plus to display them:

```
set long 10000
set longchunksize 10000
select dbms_sqltune.report_tuning_task(:vtask) from dual;
```

The illustration shows Steps 2 and 3.

```
oracle@vblin1:~
SQL> variable vtask varchar2(100);
SQL> execute :vtask := dbms_sqltune.create_tuning_task(-
> sql_text=>'select distinct object_id from object_analysis');

PL/SQL procedure successfully completed.

SQL> execute dbms_sqltune.execute_tuning_task(:vtask);

PL/SQL procedure successfully completed.

SQL> set long 10000
SQL> set longchunksize 10000
SQL> select dbms_sqltune.report_tuning_task(:vtask) from dual;
```

4. Study the output of the tuning task, as retrieved in Step 3. Following the detail of the task, there will be a recommendation to gather statistics on the table, and an example of a procedure call to do this.

5. Tidy up:

```
drop table object_analysis;
```

The SQL Access Advisor

The SQL Access Advisor performs an analysis of overall SQL performance using a workload specification, concentrating on the segment structures. The workload specification can be one of the following:

- A single SQL statement
- A SQL statement tuning set
- Current SQL cache contents
- A hypothetical workload imputed from the DDL of a set of objects

Recommendations from the SQL Access Advisor include new indexes, materialized views, and partitioning. There is a graphical interface through Enterprise Manager, and a PL/SQL API.

Using the SQL Access Advisor with Database Control

The four steps to create a set of recommendations are as follows:

1. Create a task.
2. Define the workload.
3. Generate the recommendations.
4. Review and implement the recommendations.

From the SQL Advisors window in Figure 25-2, click the SQL Access Advisor link. You will see the page shown in Figure 25-10, where you can perform one of two tasks: verify that existing structures such as indexes and materialized views are being used, or recommend new structures.

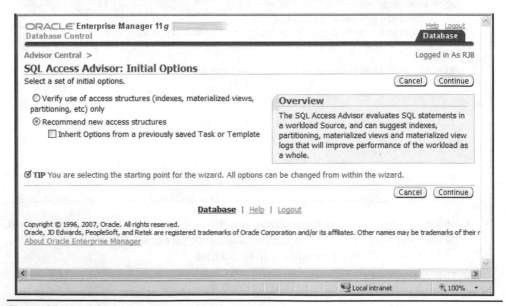

Figure 25-10 SQL Access Advisor options

For this example, you want to find new access structures, so you select the second radio button. If you select the Inherit Options check box, you can choose a template that may fit your environment, such as OLTP or data warehousing. When you click CONTINUE, you will see the first step of the wizard as in Figure 25-11.

For the source of the tuning activity, you can select one of three sources: recent SQL from the cache, an existing SQL Tuning Set (such as the SQL Tuning Set created in the SQL Tuning Advisor example earlier in this chapter), or a generated workload based on the type of queries that appear likely given the structure of the objects in one or more schemas. In this example, we want to analyze all current and recent SQL activity. Therefore click the corresponding radio button and then click NEXT.

The next page, in Figure 25-12, lets you select which types of access structures that the SQL Access Advisor should recommend: indexes, materialized views, and partitioning. In addition, you can direct the SQL Access Advisor to perform a limited analysis on just the high-cost statements—or perform a relatively time-consuming analysis on all relationships between the tables in the specified workload. The Advanced Options section lets you further refine the analysis based on disk space limitations as well as specify alternate locations for recommended indexes and materialized views. Select the Indexes and Materialized Views check boxes and select the Comprehensive radio button. Finally, click NEXT.

The next page, in Figure 25-13, specifies the scheduling options for the tuning task. As you can see, Enterprise Manager (EM) will automatically create the task for you.

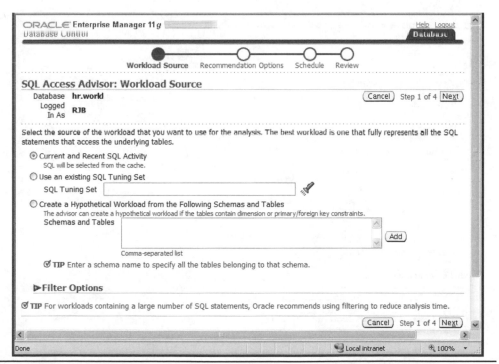

Figure 25-11   Specify SQL Access Advisor workload source

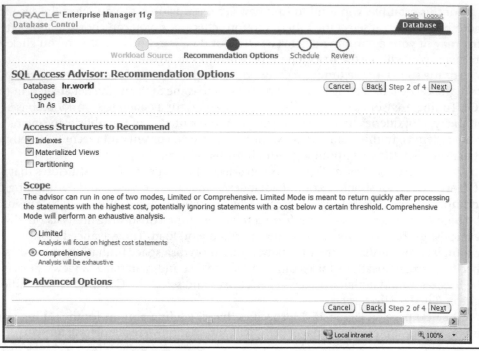

Figure 25-12 Specifying SQL Access Advisor recommendation options

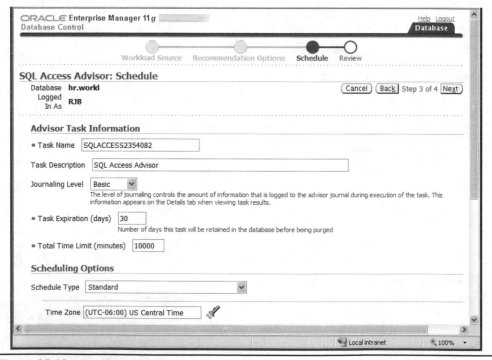

Figure 25-13 Specifying SQL Access Advisor scheduling options

Other options on this page include how much logging the SQL Access Advisor generates, how long the task will remain in the database, the total time allotted to this task, and when to start the task.

In Figure 25-13, accept the default options and click NEXT to proceed to Step 4 of the wizard, as you can see in Figure 25-14. Step 4 summarizes the options you have chosen and gives you a chance to revise the options before submitting the job.

Note the SHOW SQL button in Figure 25-14. This will show the API calls being generated by the wizard. This is a useful source of code for scripted tuning jobs that can be incorporated into a batch job, which includes other SQL commands or processes that you cannot easily perform repeatedly within EM.

Click the SUBMIT button shown in Figure 25-14 to start the analysis. From the Advisor Central page, you can monitor the progress of the job. When the job completes, select the job and click VIEW RESULT. The page in Figure 25-15 shows a summary of the improvements you can make if you implement the recommendations in the second tab. The SQL Statements tab shows you the statements analyzed and gives you the option to implement the recommendations. The Details tab recaps the options you chose to run this analysis. In this particular analysis, almost half of the recent SQL statements may benefit dramatically if the recommendations are implemented.

Using the SQL Access Advisor with DBMS_ADVISOR

Using the SQL Access Advisor via the DBMS_ADVISOR package can get quite complex. Using Enterprise Manager is an easier way to run most day-to-day analyses. There is, however, one procedure designed to make the job easy. DBMS_ADVISOR.

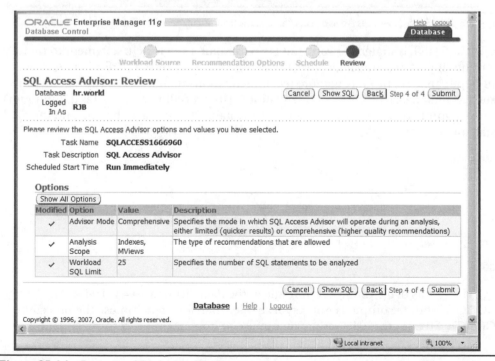

Figure 25-14   Reviewing SQL Access Advisor options

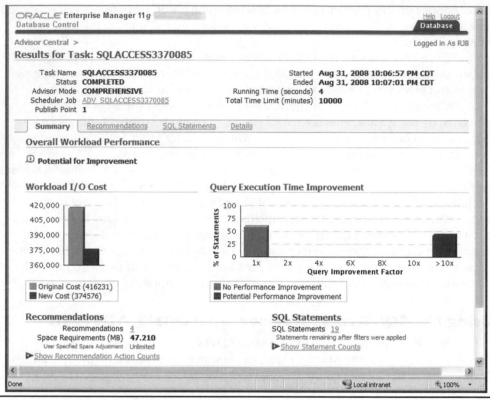

Figure 25-15   SQL Access Advisor recommendation summary

QUICK_TUNE is straightforward and takes as input a single SQL statement to tune. As a result, it performs much like the SQL Tuning Advisor but can perform a much more in-depth analysis, producing more recommendations than the SQL Tuning Advisor, such as materialized view recommendations. The procedure requires (as a minimum) three arguments: the name of the advisor, the name of the task to be run, and the statement. For example:

```
SQL> execute dbms_advisor.quick_tune(-
  3     dbms_advisor.sqlaccess_advisor,-
  4     'task1',-
  5     'select distinct object_id from object_analysis'-
  6     );-
  7  /

PL/SQL procedure successfully completed.

SQL>
```

The results of the tuning effort reside in the data dictionary view USER_ADVISOR_ ACTIONS, but the output is not very readable. Therefore, you can use the procedure CREATE_FILE to create the script you can use to implement the recommendations generated by the QUICK_TUNE procedure. First, create a directory object to point to a file system directory to hold the script:

```
SQL> create directory tune_scripts as '/u06/tune_scripts';

Directory created.

SQL>
```

Next, use CREATE_FILE to create the script containing the implementation recommendations:

```
SQL> begin
  2      dbms_advisor.create_file
  3          (dbms_advisor.get_task_script('task1'),
  4           'TUNE_SCRIPTS',
  5           'tune_fts.sql'
  6          );
  7  end;
  8  /

PL/SQL procedure successfully completed.

SQL>
```

In this example, the file `tune_fts.sql` looks like this:

```
Rem   SQL Access Advisor: Version 11.1.0.6.0 - Production
Rem
Rem   Username:         JON
Rem   Task:             task1
Rem   Execution date:
Rem

CREATE MATERIALIZED VIEW LOG ON
    "JON"."OBJECT_ANALYSIS"
    WITH ROWID, SEQUENCE("OBJECT_ID")
    INCLUDING NEW VALUES;

CREATE MATERIALIZED VIEW "JON"."MV$$_0BDC0000"
    REFRESH FAST WITH ROWID
    ENABLE QUERY REWRITE
    AS SELECT JON.OBJECT_ANALYSIS.OBJECT_ID C1, COUNT(*) M1
    FROM JON.OBJECT_ANALYSIS
    GROUP BY JON.OBJECT_ANALYSIS.OBJECT_ID;

begin
   dbms_stats.gather_table_stats
       ('"JON"','"MV$$_0BDC0000"',NULL,dbms_stats.auto_sample_size);
end;
/
```

The recommendations include creating a materialized view log, creating a materialized view that can be used for query rewrite, and collecting statistics on the materialized view.

Identifying and Fixing Invalid and Unusable Objects

First, the terminology. Ideally, all objects have a status of *valid*. PL/SQL objects and views can become *invalid*; indexes can become *unusable*. Depending on the reason for an object becoming invalid, it may become valid automatically when next accessed. Unusable indexes must be made valid by rebuilding, which does not occur automatically.

Invalid Objects

The code of named PL/SQL objects is stored within the data dictionary. These can be

- Procedures
- Functions
- Triggers
- Packages
- Object types

Most, if not all, of these procedural objects will refer to data objects, such as tables. When a procedural object is compiled, the compiler checks the data objects to which it refers in order to confirm that the definition is correct for the code. For example, if the code refers to a column, the column must exist or the code will not compile. If any of the data objects to which a procedural object refers changes after the procedural object has been compiled, then the procedure will be marked INVALID. Procedural objects may also be invalid for more mundane reasons: perhaps the programmer made a simple syntactical mistake. In that case, the object will be created INVALID and will be useless.

The same situation can occur with views. When created, they may be fine, but they may be invalidated if the detail tables on which they are based have their definitions changed.

 EXAM TIP Oracle will always attempt to recompile invalid PL/SQL objects and views automatically, but this may not succeed. You do not have to do it manually—though it may be advisable to do so.

Objects can be created invalid because of programmer error, or they can become invalid some time after creation. The view DBA_OBJECTS (and the derived views ALL_OBJECTS and USER_OBJECTS) has a column, STATUS, which should ideally always be VALID. To identify all invalid objects in the database, as user SYSTEM run the query

```
select owner,object_name,object_type from dba_objects
where status='INVALID';
```

If any objects are listed by this query, the first question to ask is whether the object was ever valid. It may never have worked and not be needed, in which case the best thing to do may be to drop it. But if, as is likely, you do not know if the object was ever valid, then a sensible first step is to attempt to compile it. The first time an invalid object is accessed, Oracle will attempt to compile it automatically—but if the compilation fails, the user will receive an error. Clearly, it is better for the DBA to compile it first; then, if there is an error, they can try to fix it before a user notices. Even if the object does compile when it is accessed, there may be a delay while the compilation takes place; it is better for perceived performance if this delay is avoided by proactive DBA work.

To repair invalid objects, first attempt to compile them. The syntax is

```
ALTER object_type object_name COMPILE ;
```

For example, the statement

```
SQL> alter procedure hr.add_reg compile;
```

will attempt to compile the procedure ADD_REG in the HR schema, and the statement

```
SQL> alter view rname compile;
```

will compile the view RNAME in your current schema. If the compilation succeeds, you have no further problems. If it fails, then you need to work out why. If a procedure does not compile, use the SQL*Plus command SHOW ERRORS to see why not (unfortunately, SHOW ERRORS is not supported for views).

Often a useful starting point in identifying the cause of compilation errors is to use the DBA_DEPENDENCIES view, described here:

```
SQL> desc dba_dependencies;
 Name                                   Null?    Type
 -------------------------------------- -------- -------------
 OWNER                                  NOT NULL VARCHAR2(30)
 NAME                                   NOT NULL VARCHAR2(30)
 TYPE                                            VARCHAR2(17)
 REFERENCED_OWNER                                VARCHAR2(30)
 REFERENCED_NAME                                 VARCHAR2(64)
 REFERENCED_TYPE                                 VARCHAR2(17)
 REFERENCED_LINK_NAME                            VARCHAR2(128)
 DEPENDENCY_TYPE                                 VARCHAR2(4)
```

For every object, identified by OWNER and NAME, there will be rows for each object on which it depends. For example, if a view retrieves columns from a dozen tables, they will each be listed as a REFERENCED_NAME. If a view does not compile, then investigating these tables would be sensible.

There will be occasions when you are faced with the need to recompile hundreds or thousands of invalid objects. Typically, this occurs after an upgrade to an application, or perhaps after applying patches. Rather than recompiling them individually, use the supplied utility script. On Unix,

```
SQL> @?/rdbms/admin/utlrp
```

or on Windows,

```
SQL> @?\rdbms\admin\utlrp
```

This script, which should be run when connected AS SYSDBA, will attempt to compile all invalid objects. If after running it there are still some invalid objects, you can assume that they have problems that should be addressed individually.

Unusable Indexes

If a procedural object, such as a stored PL/SQL function or a view, becomes invalid, the DBA does not necessarily have to do anything: the first time it is accessed, Oracle will attempt to recompile it—and this may well succeed. But if an index becomes unusable for any reason, it must always be repaired explicitly before it can be used.

An index consists of the index key values, sorted into order, each with the relevant rowid. The rowid is the physical pointer to the location of the row to which the index key refers. If the rowids of the table are changed, then the index will be marked as unusable. This could occur for a number of reasons. Perhaps the most common is that the table has been moved, with the ALTER TABLE . . . MOVE command. This will change the physical placement of all the rows, and therefore the index entries will be pointing to the wrong place. Oracle will be aware of this and will therefore not permit use of the index.

In earlier releases of the Oracle database, it was more than likely that users would detect unusable indexes because their sessions would return errors. When executing SQL statements, if the session attempted to use an unusable index, it would immediately return an error, and the statement would fail. From release 10g and higher the database changes this behavior. If a statement attempts to use an unusable index, the statement will revert to an execution plan that does not require the index. Thus, statements will always succeed—but perhaps at greatly reduced performance. This behavior is controlled by the instance parameter SKIP_UNUSABLE_INDEXES, which defaults to TRUE. The exception to this is if the index is necessary to enforce a constraint: if the index on a primary key column becomes unusable, the table will be locked for DML.

 TIP If you wish your database to react as earlier releases, where unusable indexes would cause errors, issue the command ALTER SYSTEM SET SKIP_UNUSABLE_INDEXES=FALSE;.

To detect indexes that have become unusable, query the DBA_INDEXES view:

```
SQL> select owner, index_name from dba_indexes where status='UNUSABLE';
```

Indexes are marked unusable if the rowid pointers are no longer correct. To repair the index, it must be recreated with the ALTER INDEX . . . REBUILD command. This will make a pass through the table, generating a new index with correct rowid pointers for each index key. When the new index is completed, the original, unusable index is dropped.

TIP While an index rebuild is in progress, additional storage space is required; plan ahead to make sure it is available.

The syntax of the REBUILD command has several options. The more important ones are TABLESPACE, ONLINE, and NOLOGGING. By default, the index will be rebuilt within its current tablespace, but by specifying a tablespace with the TABLESPACE keyword, it can be moved to a different one. Also by default, during the course of the rebuild the table will be locked for DML. This can be avoided by using the ONLINE keyword. The NOLOGGING keyword instructs Oracle not to generate redo for the index rebuild operation. This will make the rebuild proceed much faster, but it does mean that the tablespace containing the index should be backed up immediately. Until the tablespace is backed up, the index will not survive media damage requiring use of restore and recovery.

EXAM TIP NOLOGGING disables redo generation only for the index rebuild; all subsequent DML against the index will generate redo as normal. Unless ONLINE is specified, the table will be locked for DML while the rebuild is going on.

TIP Rebuilding indexes may also be necessary as part of normal database administration. Indexes become inefficient with time—particularly if there are many deletions, or updates that affect the key values of rows.

Exercise 25-4: Repair Invalid Objects and Unusable Indexes In this exercise, you will create some objects, break them, and repair them.

1. Using SQL*Plus, connect to your database as user SYSTEM.

2. Create a table to be used for the exercise:

   ```
   create table valid_t as select * from all_users;
   ```

3. Create some objects dependent on this table:

   ```
   create index valid_i on valid_t (username);
   create view valid_v as select * from valid_t;
   create procedure valid_p as begin
   insert into valid_t values ('name',99,sysdate);
   end;
   /
   ```

4. Confirm the status of the objects:

   ```
   select object_name,object_type,status from user_objects
   where object_name like 'VALID%';
   select status from user_indexes where index_name ='VALID_I';
   ```

They will all have the STATUS of VALID.

Steps 2, 3, and 4 are shown here:

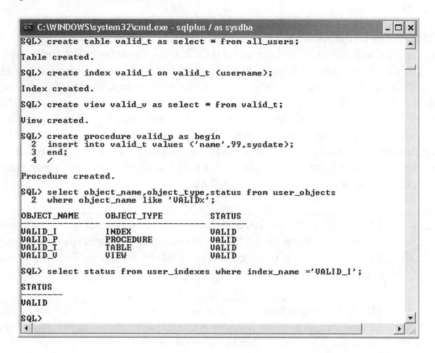

5. Perform the DDL command on the table that will break the objects:

```
alter table valid_t drop column created;
alter table valid_t move;
```

6. Rerun the queries from Step 4. Note that the procedure and the view are now INVALID, and the index is UNUSABLE.

7. Attempt to use the invalid objects:

```
execute valid_p;
select * from valid_v;
```

8. Attempt to correct the errors:

```
alter view valid_v compile;
alter procedure valid_p compile;
alter index valid_i rebuild online nologging;
```

The compilations will fail, because the table has been changed, but the index will rebuild: it was never INVALID, merely UNUSABLE because the table move had changed all the rowids.

9. Correct the errors by adding the column back to the table:

```
alter table valid_t add (created date);
```

10. Repeat Step 7. The statements will succeed.

11. Rerun the queries in Step 4. All the objects are fine now, because the attempts to use them forced an automatic recompilation.

12. Tidy up by dropping the objects:

```
drop table valid_t;
drop procedure valid_p;
drop view valid_v;
```

Database Replay

Changes occur in your software and hardware environment, whether it be upgrades to operating system, database, or application software—or increasing the number of CPUs. Less desirable changes may also occur: due to budgetary constraints, the server hosting your database may soon be part of a consolidation effort and new applications will be added to the server. In any case, you need to measure the impact of these changes. Database Replay will help to assess the change in performance on a test system by capturing the workload on the production server, and then replaying the workload on the test system. This way you can resolve performance problems and ensure that the new production environment will still run your database applications with the same results as the old production system, before the change is implemented.

Using Database Replay consists of four main steps:

1. Workload capture

2. Workload preprocessing

3. Workload replay

4. Analysis and reporting

Database Replay Workload Capture

The first step of the Database Replay process is to capture the workload. Depending on your environment, you may only need to capture a couple of hours or even a day or two. This depends on the mix of applications in your environment and what time during the day they run.

Included in the capture process are all external database calls from clients; database background activities and internal scheduler jobs are not captured. The client requests are recorded in platform-independent binary files that can be replayed on a database that is installed on a completely different hardware or software platform. As of Oracle Database 11g Release 2, you can even capture client requests on an Oracle Database 10g database and replay them on an Oracle Database 11g Release 2 platform to test a database software upgrade. Each recorded client request contains the following information:

- SQL text
- Bind values
- Transaction information

The transaction information includes timestamps as well. This gives you the option to replay the workload faster, slower, or at the same rate as the original workload. In any case, the timestamps ensure that a client request is replayed in the same relative chronological order to all other recorded requests.

Certain client requests are not captured in a workload. These requests include the following:

- Direct path load operations using SQL*Loader
- Oracle Streams operations
- Advanced Replication events
- Non-PL/SQL-based Advanced Queuing operations
- Flashback queries
- Oracle Call Interface object navigations
- Non-SQL-based object access
- Distributed transactions
- Remote DESCRIBE and COMMIT commands

Any distributed transactions will still be captured but will be replayed as if they were originally run as local transactions.

The recording process itself incurs minimal overhead on the production system. However, depending on how long you are capturing, you need to ensure that there is enough disk space to hold the captured workload. If you run out of disk space during a capture session, the capture stops.

If possible, start the workload capture when there are no active sessions. Any ongoing transactions will be captured but may not play back correctly because only part of each ongoing transaction will be played back in the target system. You can begin the capture process using the START_CAPTURE procedure in the PL/SQL package DBMS_WORKLOAD_CAPTURE. This requires a minimum of two arguments: a name for the capture, and an Oracle directory to which to save the capture. For example,

```
SQL> execute dbms_workload_capture.start_capture(-
'Data Warehouse Migration','REP_CAP_DIR');
```

Then run the application as normal. All the workload will be captured, until you terminate the capture:

```
SQL> execute dbms_workload_capture.finish_capture;
```

Database Replay Workload Preprocessing

After the capture operation is complete, the captured information must be preprocessed by transforming the captured data into replay files that can be easily replayed on any target system. The preprocessing step only needs to happen once for each capture operation. Once preprocessed, it can be replayed over and over on one or more target systems.

After moving the capture files to a location accessible to the replay system (which could be the original database), use the DBMS_WORKLOAD_REPLAY.PROCESS_CAPTURE procedure, which requires a single argument: the Oracle directory where the capture files exist. For example,

```
SQL> execute dbms_workload_replay.process_capture('REP_CAP_DIR');
```

Launch the Replay

During the replay phase, the preprocessed workload executes on the target system using the same timing, concurrency, and transaction dependencies as on the source system. You can, however, "speed up" or "slow down" one or more client requests, depending on the requirements of the new environment.

Database Replay uses one or more replay clients to recreate all client requests. You may only need one replay client, or you may need more replay clients than the original number of clients on the source database. Oracle provides a calibration tool that you run against a captured workload to calculate the number of replay clients you will need to ensure that the workload is played back at the desired rate.

EXAM TIP One replay client can replay the statements from many sessions.

Before running the first replay, you must perform some prerequisite checks:

- Ensure that the target system has access to the replay directory.
- Remap references to other production systems via database links, external tables, directory objects, URLs, and e-mail notifications.
- Remap connection strings to the replay system from the production system.

TIP Failing to remap all references to the production system could be disastrous, as your replay exercise might then update the production database.

By default, the order of all COMMIT statements is preserved, which is usually the best option to prevent data divergence. However, if most or all of the transactions are independent, you can turn off preservation of the COMMIT order to run the replay faster.

To launch a replay, in the target database run two procedures to prepare the database:

```
execute dbms_workload_replay.initialize_replay('replay 1','REP_CAP_DIR');
execute dbms_workload_replay.prepare_replay;
```

The INITIALIZE_REPLAY procedure requires two arguments (the name of the operation, and the directory containing the data) and puts the database into a state where a replay can be launched. The PREPARE_REPLAY procedure has optional arguments that will control how quickly the replay will run.

Having completed the preparatory work, the replay clients must now be started. These are independent operating system processes, launched by running an executable file in the $ORACLE_HOME/bin directory. This will launch a replay client. The basic syntax is

```
wrc <username> / <password>
```

Finally, the replay can be started:

```
SQL> execute dbms_workload_replay.start_replay;
```

This last procedure call will allow the connected clients to start running the statements in the captured workload.

Database Replay Analysis and Reporting

Database Replay generates a report detailing actual results of the replay, including all exception conditions such as data divergence due to incorrect or out-of-sync DML statements or SQL queries. Also included in the report are detailed time-based statistics such as total DB time and average session time. You can also use AWR reports to perform a detailed comparison between the captured workload and the replayed workload.

You can use the PL/SQL package DBMS_WORKLOAD_REPLAY to retrieve and generate a report, as in this example:

```
declare
    capture_dir_id      number;
    curr_replay_id      number;
    replay_report       clob;
begin
    /* retrieve pointer to all captured sessions  */
    /* in the replay directory                    */
    capture_dir_id :=
        dbms_workload_replay.get_replay_info(dir => 'REP_CAP_DIR');
    /* get latest replay session id */
    select max(id) into curr_replay_id
    from dba_workload_replays
    where capture_id = capture_dir_id;
    /* generate the report */
    replay_report :=
        dbms_workload_replay.report
            (replay_id => curr_replay_id,
             format => dbms_workload_replay.type_text);
end;
```

Note that you may have more than one report in the replay directory if you have performed the replay more than once. The SELECT statement in the PL/SQL block ensures that you retrieve the latest report. You can use DELETE_REPLAY_INFO to delete a report in the replay directory.

Exercise 25-5: Use Database Replay   In this exercise, you will generate and capture a workload, and replay it after adding an index. The report will show improved performance.

1. Using SQL*Plus, connect to your database as user SYSTEM. Create a user, a table, and a directory (substitute a path suitable for your environment) to be used for this exercise:

```
grant dba to player identified by player;
create table player.t1 as select * from all_objects;
create directory play_d as '/home/oracle/play_d';
grant all on directory play_d to public;
```

2. Start the capture:

```
exec dbms_workload_capture.start_capture('play capture','PLAY_D');
```

The illustration shows Steps 1 and 2.

```
oracle@vblin1:~
SQL> grant dba to player identified by player;

Grant succeeded.

SQL> create table player.t1 as select * from all_objects;

Table created.

SQL> create directory play_d as '/home/oracle/play_d';

Directory created.

SQL>  exec dbms_workload_capture.start_capture('play capture','PLAY_D');

PL/SQL procedure successfully completed.

SQL>
```

3. Connect as the new user, and run a PL/SQL block that will generate a workload on the database:

```
connect player / player
declare m number;
begin
for i in 1..1000 loop
select count(1) into m from t1 where object_id=1;
end loop;
end;
```

This illustration shows Step 3.

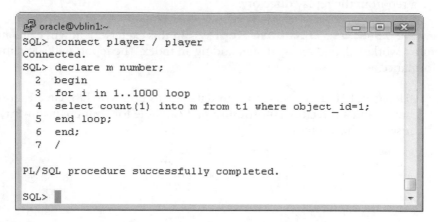

```
oracle@vblin1:~
SQL> connect player / player
Connected.
SQL> declare m number;
  2  begin
  3  for i in 1..1000 loop
  4  select count(1) into m from t1 where object_id=1;
  5  end loop;
  6  end;
  7  /

PL/SQL procedure successfully completed.

SQL>
```

4. Connect as SYSTEM. Terminate the capture, and process it:

```
execute dbms_workload_capture.finish_capture;
execute dbms_workload_replay.process_capture('PLAY_D');
```

5. Replay the workload. Note that when launching the replay client, you must specify the physical path, not the Oracle directory:

```
exec dbms_workload_replay.initialize_replay('play capture','PLAY_D');
exec dbms_workload_replay.prepare_replay;
```

In a separate window, launch the client from an operating system prompt:

```
wrc player/player replaydir=/home/oracle/play_d
```

In the SQL*Plus session, start the replay:

```
exec dbms_workload_replay.start_replay;
```

The illustrations show this step.

```
oracle@vblin1:~
SQL> exec dbms_workload_replay.initialize_replay('play capture','PLAY_D');

PL/SQL procedure successfully completed.

SQL> exec dbms_workload_replay.prepare_replay;

PL/SQL procedure successfully completed.

SQL> exec dbms_workload_replay.start_replay;

PL/SQL procedure successfully completed.

SQL>
```

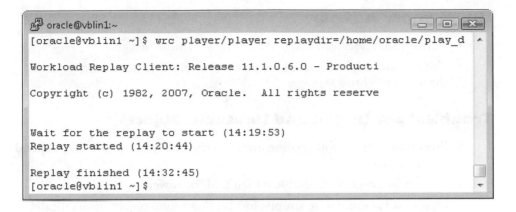

6. To retrieve the replay report, you must first obtain its ID number:
   ```
   select id,capture_id,directory,start_time,end_time
   from dba_workload_replays;
   ```
   Set the SQL*Plus buffer size, and retrieve the report:
   ```
   set long 100000
   select dbms_workload_replay.report(<id>,'TEXT') from dual;
   ```
   Study the report, and note the values of the DB Time for the Replay and the Capture: they will be similar.

7. Connected as PLAYER, add a primary key constraint to the table:
   ```
   alter table t1 add constraint t1_pk primary key (object_id);
   ```

8. Repeat Steps 5 and 6. You will observe a significant drop in the DB Time value, demonstrating the improvement in performance that follows from defining the constraint.

9. Tidy up:
   ```
   drop user player cascade;
   ```

Two-Minute Drill

Use Automatic Memory Management

- Automatic Shared Memory Management can be enabled with the parameter SGA_TARGET.

- Automatic PGA Management can be enabled with the parameter PGA_AGGREGATE_TARGET.

- Automatic Memory Management can be enabled with the parameter MEMORY_TARGET.

Use Memory Advisors

- There are advisors for PGA, SGA, and total memory usage.
- The advisors can be accessed by querying dynamic performance views, or through Enterprise Manager.

Troubleshoot Invalid and Unusable Objects

- Procedural objects will become invalid if the objects on which they depend are changed.
- Indexes will become unusable if their table is moved.
- Oracle will attempt to recompile invalid procedural object automatically.
- Unusable indexes must be rebuilt manually.
- Oracle will not attempt to use an unusable index, by default, so there will be no errors.

Implement Automatic Memory Management

- You configure AMM by setting the parameter MEMORY_TARGET.
- MEMORY_MAX_TARGET is an upper bound for MEMORY_TARGET. The former is not a dynamic parameter.
- When MEMORY_TARGET is set and both SGA_TARGET and PGA_AGGREGATE_TARGET are set, then SGA_TARGET and PGA_AGGREGATE_TARGET are used as minimum values.

Manually Configure SGA Parameters

- You can set MEMORY_TARGET to zero and SGA_TARGET to a nonzero value to exercise more control over SGA memory.
- Adjustments to automatically tuned SGA parameters are saved across instance restarts.
- ASMM uses the MMAN background process to coordinate changes in memory size.
- The five auto-tuned ASMM initialization parameters are SHARED_POOL_SIZE, LARGE_POOL_SIZE, JAVA_POOL_SIZE, DB_CACHE_SIZE, and STREAMS_POOL_SIZE.
- The manually tuned ASMM initialization parameters are DB_KEEP_CACHE_SIZE, DB_RECYCLE_CACHE_SIZE, DB_nK_CACHE_SIZE, and LOG_BUFFER.
- You can easily disable ASMM by setting SGA_TARGET to zero, but then the current auto-tuned ASMM initialization parameters are set to their current values.
- The static parameter SGA_MAX_SIZE is the upper limit for the value of SGA_TARGET.

Configure Automatic PGA Memory Management

- The parameter PGA_AGGREGATE_TARGET sets an upper limit for memory used by all server and background processes and enables auto-tuning of PGA memory.
- PGA memory areas include private SQL areas, named cursors, work areas for sorting operations, and session-specific memory variables.

Use the SQL Tuning Advisor

- The SQL Tuning Advisor performs statistics analysis, SQL Profile analysis, access path analysis, and structure analysis.
- The SQL Tuning Advisor can automatically implement SQL Profiles.
- The SQL Tuning Advisor tunes each SQL statement individually.
- You can specify a SQL Tuning Set, a workload, recent SQL activity, or a single SQL statement as input to the SQL Tuning Advisor.

Use the SQL Access Advisor to Tune a Workload

- A SQL Access Advisor workload can consist of a single SQL statement, a SQL Tuning Set, the current SQL cache contents, existing statistics, or a schema name.
- Recommendations from the SQL Access Advisor include new indexes, materialized views, and partitioning.
- The four steps composing a SQL Access Advisor session are: (1) creating the task, (2) defining the workload, (3) generating the recommendations, and (4) reviewing and implementing the recommendations.
- You can either review usage of existing structures or recommend new structures in a SQL Access Advisor session.

Understand Database Replay

- Database Replay consists of four steps: (1) workload capture, (2) workload preprocessing, (3) workload replay, and (4) analysis and reporting.
- Each recorded client request contains the SQL text, bind values, and transaction information—including a timestamp.
- Client requests such as SQL*Loader operations, Oracle Streams, flashback queries, distributed transactions, and remote DESCRIBE or COMMIT commands are not included in the capture operation.
- Captured replay information needs to be processed only once for any number of target environments, and for any number of replays on the target system.

PART III

Self Test

1. Where are private SQL areas stored? (Choose the best answer.)

    A. In each session's PGA, always

    B. In each session's PGA, unless a PGA Aggregate Target has been set

    C. In the PGA, unless Automatic Memory Management has been enabled

    D. In the shared pool of the SGA, always

2. Which memory structure is fixed in size at instance startup? (Choose the best answer.)

    A. The shared pool

    B. The large pool

    C. The Java pool

    D. The log buffer

    E. None are fixed, if Automatic Memory Management has been enabled

3. When Automatic Memory Management is enabled, what is not possible? (Choose the best answer.)

    A. Transfer of memory between sessions' PGAs

    B. Transfer of memory between structures within the SGA

    C. Transfer of memory from SGA to PGA, and vice versa

    D. Increasing the total memory usage after instance startup

    E. All of the above are possible

4. Storage of what structures can exist in the PGA? (Choose all correct answers.)

    A. Shared SQL areas

    B. Private SQL areas

    C. Global temporary tables

    D. Sort areas

    E. Bitmap merge areas

    F. Cached object definitions

5. Which instance parameter can disable the memory advisors? (Choose the best answer.)

    A. DB_CACHE_ADVICE

    B. MEMORY_TARGET

    C. STATISTICS_LEVEL

    D. TIMED_STATISTICS

6. Which of these parameters cannot be changed without an instance restart? (Choose all correct answers.)

   A. MEMORY_MAX_TARGET

   B. MEMORY_TARGET

   C. PGA_AGGREGATE_TARGET

   D. SGA_TARGET

7. If you create a table and a procedure that refers to it, and then change the definition of the table, what will happen when you try to run the procedure? (Choose the best answer.)

   A. The procedure will recompile automatically and run successfully.

   B. The procedure will fail until you recompile it.

   C. The procedure will run with reduced performance until you analyze the table.

   D. The procedure may or may not compile, depending on the nature of the change.

8. If a SELECT statement attempts to use an UNUSABLE index, what will happen? (Choose the best answer.)

   A. The statement will fail.

   B. The statement will succeed, but at reduced performance.

   C. The index will be rebuilt automatically if possible.

   D. It depends on the SKIP_UNUSABLE_INDEXES parameter.

9. You determine that an index is unusable, and decide to rebuild it. Which of the following statements, if any, are correct? (Choose all correct answers.)

   A. The NOLOGGING and ONLINE keywords cannot be used together when rebuilding the index.

   B. A rebuild may require double the disk space while it is in progress.

   C. If you do not use the ONLINE keyword during a rebuild, the table will be unavailable for SELECT and DML statements.

   D. The NOLOGGING keyword applied to a rebuild means that DML against the index will not generate redo.

10. If a primary key index becomes unusable, what will be the effect upon an application that uses it? (Choose the best answer.)

   A. SELECT will succeed, but perhaps at reduced performance.

   B. DML commands will succeed, but perhaps at reduced performance.

   C. The primary key constraint can no longer be enforced.

   D. The table may be locked for DML.

PART III

11. Identify the true statement about Automatic Memory Management (AMM). (Choose the best answer.)

    A. MEMORY_TARGET and MEMORY_MAX_TARGET must both be set to enable AMM.

    B. MEMORY_TARGET enables AMM, and it is a static parameter.

    C. MEMORY_MAX_TARGET enables AMM, and it is a static parameter.

    D. MEMORY_TARGET enables AMM, and it is a dynamic parameter.

12. The SQL Tuning Advisor performs all but which of the following analyses? (Choose the best answer.)

    A. Structure analysis

    B. SQL Profile analysis

    C. Access paths

    D. Changes to materialized views

    E. Statistics analysis

13. Which of the following can you use as input for the SQL Tuning Advisor? (Choose all that apply.)

    A. A single SQL statement provided by a user

    B. An existing SQL Tuning Set (STS)

    C. A preprocessed Database Replay workload

    D. A schema name

    E. A SQL statement identified in EM as using excessive resources

14. Which of the following procedures will run a SQL Tuning Advisor job against a SQL Tuning Set? (Choose the best answer.)

    A. DBMS_QUICKTUNE.EXECUTE_TUNING_TASK

    B. DBMS_SQLTUNE.EXECUTE_TUNING_TASK

    C. DBMS_SQLTUNE.RUN_TUNING_TASK

    D. DBMS_ADVISOR.EXECUTE_TUNING_TASK

15. Which of the following can you use as input for the SQL Access Advisor? (Choose all that apply.)

    A. A single SQL statement provided by a user

    B. An existing SQL Tuning Set (STS)

    C. A preprocessed Database Replay workload

    D. A schema name

    E. Current SQL cache contents

16. Which of the following changes can the SQL Access Advisor recommend? (Choose two answers.)

    A. Restructuring one or more SQL statements

    B. Gathering statistics for selected SQL statements

    C. Adding a materialized view log

    D. Enabling query rewrite

17. Which of the following procedures will run a SQL Access Advisor job against a single SQL statement? (Choose the best answer.)

    A. DBMS_QUICKTUNE.EXECUTE_TUNING_TASK

    B. DBMS_ADVISOR.EXECUTE_TUNING_TASK

    C. DBMS_SQLTUNE.RUN_TUNING_TASK

    D. DBMS_ADVISOR.QUICK_TUNE

    E. The SQL Access Advisor requires a workload, AWR snapshot, or STS and cannot analyze a single SQL statement

18. You want to remap your database links so that they do not reference production database objects. Within which Database Replay step do you perform the remapping? (Choose the best answer.)

    A. During the workload replay step

    B. During the workload preprocessing step

    C. During the workload capture step

    D. Before the workload capture starts

    E. You do not need to remap, since it happens automatically

19. Which of the following database client operations are captured during Database Replay? (Choose all that apply.)

    A. A flashback query

    B. Distributed transactions

    C. Oracle Streams operations

    D. A CREATE TABLE statement

    E. A transaction started before capturing begins

Self Test Answers

1. ☑ **A.** Private SQL areas are private to each session, in the session's PGA.
    ☒ **B, C,** and **D. B** is wrong because automatic PGA management is not relevant to where the private SQL area is stored, only to how it is managed. **C** and **D** are wrong because private SQL areas are always in the PGA.

2. ☑ **D.** The log buffer cannot be changed after startup.
    ☒ **A, B, C,** and **E. A, B,** and **C** are wrong because all these structures can be resized. **E** is wrong because not even Automatic Memory Management makes the log buffer resizable.

3. ☑ E. Memory can be transferred between all structures (except the log buffer), and the total can be increased.

☒ A, B, C, and D. These are wrong because all are possible—though D, the increase of total memory usage, is only possible up to the value specified by the MEMORY_MAX_TARGET parameter.

4. ☑ B, C, D, and E. These are all PGA memory structures, though they may spill to a temporary segment in the users' temporary tablespace.

☒ A and F. These are wrong because these structures both exist in the shared pool of the SGA.

5. ☑ C. STATISTICS_LEVEL must be on TYPICAL or FULL, or the advisors will not run.

☒ A, D, and B. A and D are wrong, because these parameters (which still exist only for backward compatibility) are controlled by STATISTICS_LEVEL. B is wrong because MEMORY_TARGET determines whether implementing the advice is automatic or manual.

6. ☑ A. MEMORY_MAX_TARGET is a static parameter: it cannot be changed without restarting the instance.

☒ B, C, and D. All these parameters are dynamic, meaning that they can be changed without restarting the instance.

7. ☑ D. Oracle will attempt recompilation, but this may not succeed.

☒ A, B, and C. A is wrong because this will not necessarily succeed if the nature of the change is such that the procedure needs to be rewritten. B is wrong because manual recompilation is not necessary (though it may be a good idea). C is wrong because it refers to object statistics, which are not relevant to a problem of this kind.

8. ☑ D. The SKIP_UNUSABLE_INDEXES parameter will control whether the statement produces an error or reverts to an alternative plan.

☒ A, B, and C. A and B are both wrong because they make an assumption about the SKIP_UNUSABLE_INDEXES parameter: A assumes it is false; B assumes it is true. C is wrong because indexes are never rebuilt automatically.

9. ☑ B. A rebuild requires additional space, as the new index is built before the original index is dropped.

☒ A, C, and D. A is wrong because NOLOGGING and ONLINE can be used together. C is wrong because without ONLINE the index is locked for DML, but not for SELECT. D is wrong because DML always generates redo—it is only the DDL that will not generate redo.

10. ☑ D. Loss of a primary key index means that DML against the constrained column(s) will be impossible.

☒ **A, B, and C. A** is wrong because this is not certain—it is dependent on the SKIP_UNUSABLE_INDEXES setting. **B** is wrong because DML commands will fail if they affect the constrained column(s). **C** is wrong because the constraint will be enforced—by locking the table.

11. ☑ **D.** MEMORY_TARGET enables AMM; it is a dynamic parameter and cannot be more than MEMORY_MAX_TARGET.

☒ **A, B, and C. A** is wrong because the MEMORY_MAX_TARGET can be left on default. **B** is wrong because MEMORY_TARGET is dynamic. **C** is wrong because while MEMORY_MAX_TARGET provides a limit for AMM, it does not enable it.

12. ☑ **D.** Only the SQL Access Advisor recommends changes to materialized views, including creating materialized view logs.

☒ **A, B, C, and E.** The SQL Tuning Advisor performs statistics analysis, SQL Profiling, access paths, and structure analysis.

13. ☑ **A, B, and E.** The SQL Tuning Advisor can use currently running SQL statements, a single statement provided by any user, an existing SQL Tuning Set, or historical SQL statements from AWR snapshots.

☒ **C and D. C** is wrong because you cannot use Database Replay workloads to specify SQL for the SQL Tuning Advisor. **D** is wrong because you cannot specify a schema or table names; you can only specify SQL statements.

14. ☑ **B.** DBMS_SQLTUNE.EXECUTE_TUNING_TASK runs a SQL Tuning Advisor task created with DBMS_SQLTUNE.CREATE_TUNING_TASK.

☒ **A, C, and D.** These are not valid packages or procedures.

15. ☑ **A, B, D, and E.** In addition to a single SQL statement (using QUICK_TUNE), an existing STS, a schema name, and current SQL cache contents, the SQL Access Advisor also uses statistics to analyze overall SQL performance.

☒ **C. C** is wrong because you cannot use the captured Database Replay information as a source for the SQL Access Advisor.

16. ☑ **C and D.** The SQL Access Advisor recommends materialized views, materialized view logs, and enabling query rewrite. In addition, the SQL Access Advisor will also recommend new indexes or partitions.

☒ **A and B.** The SQL Tuning Advisor recommends SQL statement restructuring and statistics gathering, not the SQL Access Advisor.

17. ☑ **D.** DBMS_ADVISOR.QUICK_TUNE runs an analysis on a single SQL statement. You provide the name of the tuning task, which the procedure automatically creates, along with the SQL to be tuned.

☒ **A, B, C, and E. A, B,** and **C** are wrong because these procedures do not exist. **E** is wrong because the SQL Access Advisor can run an analysis on a single SQL statement, just as the SQL Tuning Advisor can.

18. ☑   A. The database links, external tables, directory objects, and connection string remappings need to occur during the workload replay step immediately before replay is initiated.

☒   B, C, D, and E. B, C, and D are wrong because you do not perform the remapping during these steps. E is wrong because you need to perform the remapping manually.

19. ☑   B, D, and E. Most SQL statements are captured, including the SQL statement's text, bind values, and transaction information. Distributed transactions are captured but replayed as local transactions. Even transactions started before capturing begins are captured, but they may cause data divergence during replay. Thus, Oracle recommends restarting the instance before initiating capture.

☒   A and C. In addition to flashback queries and Oracle Streams operations, OCI object navigations, non-SQL-based object access, SQL*Loader operations, and remote COMMIT and DESCRIBE commands are not captured.

CHAPTER 26

Globalization

Exam Objectives

In this chapter you will learn to

- 053.20.1   Customize Language-Dependent Behavior for the Database
  and Individual Sessions
- 053.20.2   Work with Database and NLS Character Sets

The Oracle database has many capabilities grouped under the term *globalization* that will assist a DBA who must consider users of different nationalities. Globalization was known as National Language Support, or NLS, in earlier releases (you will still see the NLS acronym in several views and parameters), but globalization is more than linguistics: it is a comprehensive set of facilities for managing databases that must cover a range of languages, time zones, and cultural variations.

Globalization Requirements and Capabilities

Large database systems, and many small ones too, will usually have a user community that is distributed geographically, temporally, and linguistically. Consider a database hosted in Johannesburg, South Africa, with end users scattered throughout sub-Saharan Africa. Different users will be expecting data to be presented to them in Portuguese, French, and English, at least. They may be in three different time zones with different standards for the formats of dates and numbers. The situation becomes even more complex when the application is running in a three-tier environment: you may have a database in one location, several geographically distributed application servers, and users further distributed from the application servers.

It is possible for a lazy DBA to ignore globalization completely. Typically, such a DBA will take United States defaults for everything—and then let the programmers sort it out. But this is putting an enormous amount of work onto the programmers, and they may not wish to do it either. The result is an application that works but is detested by a portion of its users. But there is more to this than keeping people happy: there may well be financial implications too. Consider two competing e-commerce sites, both trying to sell goods all over the world. One has taken the trouble to translate everything into languages applicable to each customer; the other insists that all customers use American English. Which one is going to receive the most orders? Furthermore, dates and monetary formats can cause dreadful confusion when different countries have different standards. Such problems can be ignored or resolved programmatically, but a good DBA will attempt to resolve them through the facilities provided as standard within the database.

Character Sets

The data stored in a database must be coded into a character set. A *character set* is a defined encoding scheme for representing characters as a sequence of bits. Some products use the character sets provided by the host operating system. For example, Microsoft Word does not have its own character sets; it uses those provided by the Windows operating system. Other products provide their own character sets and are thus independent of whatever is provided by the host operating system. Oracle products fall into the latter group: they ship with their own character sets, which is one reason why Oracle applications are the same on all platforms, and why clients and servers can be on different platforms.

A character set consists of a defined number of distinct characters. The number of characters that a character set can represent is limited by the number of bits the character set uses for each character. A single-byte character set will use only one byte per character: eight bits, though some single-byte character sets restrict this even further by using only seven of the eight bits. A multibyte character set uses one, two, or even three bytes for each character. The variations here are whether the character set is fixed-width (for example, always using two bytes per character) or variable-width (where some characters will be represented in one byte, other characters in two or more).

How many characters are actually needed? Well, as a bare minimum, you need upper- and lowercase letters, the digits 0 through 9, a few punctuation marks, and some special characters to mark the end of a line, or a page break, for instance. A seven-bit character set can represent a total of 128 (2^7) characters. It is simply not possible to get more than that number of different bit patterns if you have only seven bits to play with. Seven-bit character sets are just barely functional for modern computer systems, but they are usually inadequate. They provide the characters just named, but very little else. If you need to do simple things like using box drawing characters, or printing a name that includes a letter with an accent, you may find that you can't do it with a seven-bit character set. Anything more advanced, such as storing and displaying data in Arabic or Chinese script, will be totally out of the question. Unfortunately, Oracle's default character sets are seven-bit ASCII or seven-bit EBCDIC, depending on the platform: even such widely used languages as French and Spanish cannot be written correctly in these character sets. This is a historical anomaly, dating back to the days when these character sets were pretty much the only ones in use. Eight-bit character sets can represent 256 (2^8) different characters. These will typically be adequate for any Western European language–based system, though perhaps not for some Eastern European languages, and definitely not for many Asian languages. For these more complex linguistic environments, it is necessary to use a multibyte character set.

EXAM TIP The default character set is seven bit, either ASCII or EBCDIC. If you use DBCA to create a database, it will pick up a default from the operating system. This will often be better, but may not be perfect.

Unicode character sets deserve a special mention. Unicode is an international standard for character encoding, which is intended to include every character that will ever be required by any computer system. Currently, Unicode has defined more than 32,000 characters.

TIP Oracle Corporation recommends AL32UTF8, a varying-width Unicode character set, for all new deployments.

Encoding Scheme	Example Character Sets
Single-byte seven-bit	US7ASCII. This is the default for Oracle on non-IBM systems.
	YUG7ASCII. Seven-bit Yugoslavian, a character set suitable for the languages used in much of the Balkans.
Single-byte eight-bit	WE8ISO8859P15. A Western European eight-bit ISO standard character set, which includes the Euro symbol (unlike WE8ISO8859P1).
	WE8DEC. Developed by Digital Equipment Corporation, widely used in the DEC (or Compaq) environment in Europe.
	I8EBCDIC1144. An EBCDIC character set specifically developed for Italian. EBCDIC is used on IBM platforms.
Fixed-width multibyte	AL16UTF16. This is a Unicode two-byte character set, and the only fixed-width Unicode character set supported by 11g.
Varying-width	JA16SJIS. Shift-JIS, a Japanese character set, where a shift-out control code is used to indicate that the following bytes are double-byte characters. A shift-in code switches back to single-byte characters.
	ZHT16CCDC. A traditional Chinese character set, where the most significant bit of the byte is used to indicate whether the byte is a single character or part of a multibyte character.
	AL32UTF8. A Unicode varying-width character set.

Table 26-1   Sample Oracle Database 11g Character Sets

Oracle Database 11*g* ships with more than 200 character sets. Table 26-1 includes just a few examples.

Language Support

The number of languages supported by Oracle depends on the platform, release, and patch level of the product. To determine the range available on any one installation, query the view V$NLS_VALID_VALUES, as follows:

```
SQL> select * from v$nls_valid_values where parameter='LANGUAGE';

PARAMETER              VALUE                 ISDEP
--------------------   --------------------  -----
LANGUAGE               AMERICAN              FALSE
LANGUAGE               GERMAN                FALSE
LANGUAGE               FRENCH                FALSE
LANGUAGE               CANADIAN FRENCH       FALSE
LANGUAGE               SPANISH               FALSE
. . .
```

```
LANGUAGE              ALBANIAN              FALSE
LANGUAGE              BELARUSIAN            FALSE
LANGUAGE              IRISH                 FALSE
67 rows selected.
SQL>
```

The language used will determine the language for error messages and also set defaults for date language and sort orders. The defaults are shown here:

Initialization Parameter	Default	Purpose
NLS_LANGUAGE	AMERICAN	Language for messages
NLS_DATE_LANGUAGE	AMERICAN	Used for day and month names
NLS_SORT	BINARY	Linguistic sort sequence

The default sort order—binary—is poor. Binary sorting may be acceptable for a seven-bit character set, but for character sets of eight bits or more the results are often inappropriate. For example, the ASCII value of a lowercase letter *a* is 97, and a lowercase letter *z* is 122. So a binary sort will place *a* before *z*, which is fine. But consider diacritic variations: a lowercase letter *a* with an umlaut, *ä*, is 132, which is way beyond *z*; so the binary sort order will produce "a,z,ä"—which is wrong in any language. The German sort order would give "a,ä,z"—which is correct. Figure 26-1 illustrates how a sort order is affected by the language setting, using German names.

Oracle provides many possible sort orders; there should always be one that will fit your requirements. Again, query V$NLS_VALID_VALUES to see what is available:

```
SQL> select * from v$nls_valid_values where parameter='SORT';
PARAMETER             VALUE                 ISDEP
--------------------  --------------------  -----
SORT                  BINARY                FALSE
SORT                  WEST_EUROPEAN         FALSE
SORT                  XWEST_EUROPEAN        FALSE
SORT                  GERMAN                FALSE
SORT                  XGERMAN               FALSE
SORT                  DANISH                FALSE
SORT                  XDANISH               FALSE
SORT                  SPANISH               FALSE
SORT                  XSPANISH              FALSE
SORT                  GERMAN_DIN            FALSE
. . .
SORT                  SCHINESE_STROKE_M     FALSE
SORT                  GBK                   FALSE
SORT                  SCHINESE_RADICAL_M    FALSE
SORT                  JAPANESE_M            FALSE
SORT                  KOREAN_M              FALSE

87 rows selected.
```

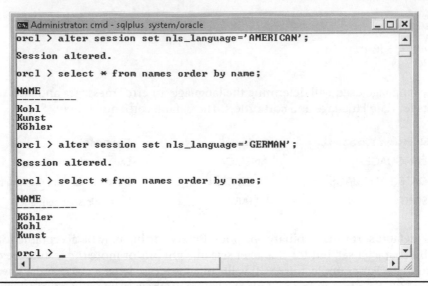

Figure 26-1 Linguistic sorting

Territory Support

The territory selected sets a number of globalization defaults. To determine the territories your database supports, again query V$NLS_VALID_VALUES:

```
SQL> select * from v$nls_valid_values where parameter='TERRITORY';

PARAMETER            VALUE                ISDEP
-------------------- -------------------- -----
TERRITORY            AMERICA              FALSE
TERRITORY            UNITED KINGDOM       FALSE
TERRITORY            GERMANY              FALSE
TERRITORY            FRANCE               FALSE
TERRITORY            CANADA               FALSE
TERRITORY            SPAIN                FALSE
TERRITORY            ITALY                FALSE
TERRITORY            THE NETHERLANDS      FALSE
TERRITORY            SWEDEN               FALSE
TERRITORY            NORWAY               FALSE
. . .
TERRITORY            BELARUS              FALSE

98 rows selected.
```

The territory selection sets defaults for day and week numbering, credit and debit symbols, date formats, decimal and group numeric separators, and currency symbols. Some of these can have profound effects on the way your application software will behave.

For example, in the U.S. the decimal separator is a point (.), but in Germany and many other countries it is a comma (,). Consider a number such as "10,001". Is this ten thousand and one, or ten and one thousandth? You certainly need to know. Of equal importance is day of the week numbering. In the U.S., Sunday is day 1 and Saturday is day 7, but in Germany (and indeed in most of Europe) Monday (or Montag, to take the example further) is day 1 and Sunday (Sonntag) is day 7. If your software includes procedures that will run according to the day number, the results may be disastrous if you do not consider this. Figure 26-2 illustrates some other territory-related differences in time settings.

These are the defaults for territory-related settings:

Variable	Default / Purpose
NLS_TERRITORY	AMERICA / Geographical location
NLS_CURRENCY	$ / Local currency symbol
NLS_DUAL_CURRENCY	$ / A secondary currency symbol for the territory
NLS_ISO_CURRENCY	AMERICA / Indicates the ISO territory currency symbol
NLS_DATE_FORMAT	DD-MM-RR / Format used for columns of data type DATE
NLS_NUMERIC_CHARACTERS	., / Decimal and group delimiters
NLS_TIMESTAMP_FORMAT	DD-MM-RRHH.MI.SSXFF AM / Format used for columns of data type TIMESTAMP
NLS_TIMESTAMP_TZ_FORMAT	DD-MM-RRHH.MI.SSXFF AM TZR / Format used for columns of data type TIMESTAMP WITH LOCAL TIMEZONE

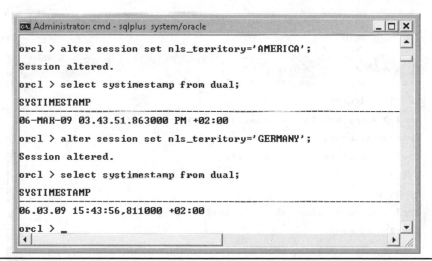

Figure 26-2   Date and time formats, on the sixth of March in the afternoon, in a time zone two hours ahead of Greenwich Mean Time (GMT)

Other NLS Settings

Apart from the language- and territory-related settings just described, there are a few more advanced settings that are less likely to cause problems:

Variable	Default / Purpose
NLS_CALENDAR	Gregorian / Allows use of alternative calendar systems
NLS_COMP	BINARY / The alternative of ANSI compares letters using their NLS value, not the numeric equivalent
NLS_LENGTH_SEMANTICS	BYTE / Allows one to manipulate multibyte characters as complete characters rather than bytes
NLS_NCHAR_CONV_EXCP	FALSE / Limits error messages generated when converting between VARCHAR2 and NVARCHAR

Figure 26-3 illustrates switching to the Japanese Imperial calendar (which counts the years from the ascension of Emperor Akihito to the throne), with an associated effect on the date display.

Using Globalization Support Features

Globalization can be specified at any and all of five levels:

- The database
- The instance
- The client environment
- The session
- The statement

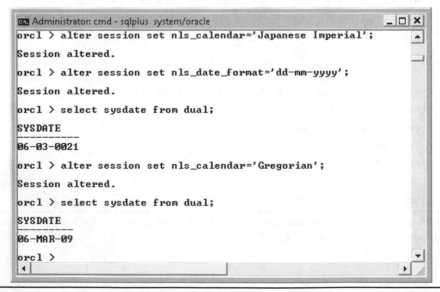

Figure 26-3   Use of the Japanese Imperial calendar

The levels are listed in ascending order of priority. Thus, instance settings take precedence over database settings, and so on. An individual statement can control its own globalization characteristics, thus overriding everything else.

EXAM TIP Remember the precedence of the various points where globalization settings can be specified. On the server side, instance settings take precedence over database settings, but all the server settings can be overridden on the client side: first by the environment, then at the session and statement levels.

Choosing a Character Set

At database creation time, choice of character set is one of the two most important decisions you make. When you create a database, two settings are vital to get right at creation time; everything else can be changed later. These two are the DB_BLOCK_SIZE parameter, which can never be changed, and the database character set, which it may be possible but not necessarily practicable to change. The difficulty with the DB_BLOCK_SIZE is that this parameter is used as the block size for the SYSTEM tablespace. You can't change that without re-creating the data dictionary: in other words, creating a new database. The database character set is used to store all the data in columns of type VARCHAR2, CLOB, CHAR, and LONG (although still supported, you should not be using LONG datatypes unless you need them for backward compatibility). If you change it, you may well destroy all the data in your existing columns of these types.

It is therefore vital to select, at creation time, a character set that will fulfill all your needs, present and future. For example, if you are going to have data in French or Spanish, a Western European character set is needed. If you are going have data in Russian or Czech, you should choose an Eastern European character set. But what if you may have both Eastern and Western European languages? Furthermore, what if you anticipate a need for Korean or Thai as well? Oracle provides two solutions to the problem: the National Character Set and the use of Unicode.

The National Character Set was introduced with release 8.0 of the database. This is a second character set, specified at database creation time, which is used for columns of data types NVARCHAR2, NCLOB, and NCHAR. So if the DBA anticipated that most of the information would be in English but that some would be Japanese, they could select a Western European character set for the database character set, and a Kanji character set as the National Character Set. With release 9i, the rules changed: from then on, the National Character Set can only be Unicode. This should not lead to any drop in functionality, because the promise of Unicode is that it can encode any character. Two types of Unicode are supported as the National Character Set: AL16UTF16 and UTF8. AL16UTF16 is a fixed-width, two-byte character set, and UTF8 is a variable-width character set. The choice between the two is a matter of space efficiency and performance, related to the type of data you anticipate storing in the NVARCHAR2 and NCLOB columns.

It may very well be that the majority of the data could in fact be represented in one byte, and only a few characters would need multiple bytes. In that case, AL16UTF16 will nearly double the storage requirements—quite unnecessarily, because one of the two bytes per character will be packed with zeros. This not only wastes space but also impacts on disk I/O. UTF8 will save a lot of space. But if the majority of the data cannot be coded in one byte, then UTF8 becomes much less efficient because the multibyte characters must be assembled, at runtime, from a number of single bytes, with a consequent performance hit. Also, UTF8 will often need three or even four bytes to store a character that AL16UTF16 can encode in two.

The second possibility for a fully multilingual database is to use Unicode as the actual database character set. The supported options are UTF8 and AL32UTF8, which are both variable-width multibyte character sets.

The only limitation on the database character set is that it must have either US7ASCII or EBCDIC as a subset. This is because the database character set is used to store SQL and PL/SQL source code, which is written in these characters.

Both the database character set and the National Character Set are specified in the CREATE DATABASE command. The defaults are US7ASCII and AL16UTF16. If you create a database using the Database Creation Assistant (DBCA), DBCA will provide a default for the database character set, which it will pick up from the character set of the host operating system where you are running DBCA. This may be more appropriate than the seven-bit Oracle default, but remember that your clients may be using terminals with a different operating system from the database server.

Changing Character Sets

There are many occasions when DBAs have wished that they could change the database character set. Typically, this is because the database was created using the default of US7ASCII, and later on a need arises for storing information using characters not included in that character set, such as a French name. Prior to release 9i there was no supported technique for changing the character set. From 9i onward, there is a supported technique, but there is no guarantee that it will work. It is your responsibility as DBA to carry out thorough checks that the change will not damage the data. The problem is simply that a change of character set does not reformat the data currently in the datafiles, but it will change the way the data is presented. For example, if you were to convert from a Western European character set to an Eastern European character set, many of the letters with the accents common in Western languages would then be interpreted as Cyrillic characters, with disastrous results.

There are two tools provided to assist with deciding on character set change: the Database Character Set Scanner and the Language and Character Set File Scanner. These are independently executable utilities, `csscan` and `lcsscan` on Unix, `csscan.exe` and `lcsscan.exe` on Windows.

The Database Character Set Scanner will log on to the database and make a pass through the datafiles, generating a report of possible problems. For example,

```
csscan system/systempassword full=y tochar=utf8
```

This command will connect to the database as user SYSTEM and scan through all the datafiles to check if conversion to UTF8 would cause any problems. A typical problem when going to UTF8 is that a character that was encoded in one byte in the original character set might require two bytes in UTF8, so the data might not fit in the column after the change. The scanner will produce a comprehensive report listing every row that will have problems with the new character set. You must then take appropriate action to fix the problems before the conversion, if possible.

TIP You must run the `csminst.sql` script to prepare the database for running the character set scanner.

The Language and Character Set File Scanner is a utility that will attempt to identify the language and character set used for a text file. It will function on plain text only; if you want to use it on, for example, a word processing document, you will have to remove all the control codes first. This scanner may be useful if you have to upload data into your database and do not know what the data is. The tool scans the file and applies a set of heuristics to make an intelligent guess about the language and character set of the data.

Having determined whether it is possible to change the character set without damage, execute the command ALTER DATABASE CHARACTER SET to make the change. The equivalent command to change the National Character Set is ALTER DATABASE NATIONAL CHARACTER SET. The only limitation with this command is that the target character set must be a superset of the original character set, but that does not guarantee that there will be no corruptions. That is the DBA's responsibility.

Globalization Within the Database

The database's globalization settings are fixed at creation time, according to the instance parameter settings in effect when the CREATE DATABASE command was issued and the character set was specified. They are visible in the view NLS_DATABASE_PARAMETERS as follows:

```
SQL> select * from nls_database_parameters;

PARAMETER                      VALUE
------------------------------ ----------------------------------------
NLS_LANGUAGE                   AMERICAN
NLS_TERRITORY                  AMERICA
NLS_CURRENCY                   $
NLS_ISO_CURRENCY               AMERICA
NLS_NUMERIC_CHARACTERS         .,
NLS_CHARACTERSET               WE8MSWIN1252
NLS_CALENDAR                   GREGORIAN
NLS_DATE_FORMAT                DD-MON-RR
NLS_DATE_LANGUAGE              AMERICAN
NLS_SORT                       BINARY
NLS_TIME_FORMAT                HH.MI.SSXFF AM
NLS_TIMESTAMP_FORMAT           DD-MON-RR HH.MI.SSXFF AM
NLS_TIME_TZ_FORMAT             HH.MI.SSXFF AM TZR
NLS_TIMESTAMP_TZ_FORMAT        DD-MON-RR HH.MI.SSXFF AM TZR
NLS_DUAL_CURRENCY              $
NLS_COMP                       BINARY
NLS_LENGTH_SEMANTICS           BYTE
NLS_NCHAR_CONV_EXCP            FALSE
NLS_NCHAR_CHARACTERSET         AL16UTF16
NLS_RDBMS_VERSION              11.1.0.6.0

20 rows selected.
```

PART III

Globalization at the Instance Level

Instance parameter settings will override the database settings. In a RAC environment, it is possible for different instances to have different settings, so that, for example, European and U.S. users could each log on to the database through an instance configured appropriately to their different needs. The settings currently in effect are exposed in the view NLS_INSTANCE_PARAMETERS, which has the same rows as NLS_DATABASE_PARAMETERS except for three rows to do with character sets and RDBMS version that do not apply to an instance.

The globalization instance parameters can be changed like any others, but as they are all static, it is necessary to restart the instance before any changes come into effect.

Client-Side Environment Settings

When an Oracle user process starts, it inspects the environment within which it is running to pick up globalization defaults. This mechanism means that it is possible for users who desire different globalization settings to configure their terminals appropriately to their needs, and then Oracle will pick up and apply the settings automatically, without the programmers or the DBA having to take any action. This feature should be used with care, as it can cause confusion because it means that the application software may be running in an environment that the programmers had not anticipated. The internal implementation of this is that the user process reads the environment variables and then generates a series of ALTER SESSION commands to implement them.

The key environment variable is NLS_LANG. The full specification for this is a language, a territory, and a character set. To use French as spoken in Canada with a Western European character set, an end user could set it to

```
NLS_LANG=FRENCH_CANADA.WEISO8859P1
```

and then, no matter what the database and instance globalization is set to, his user process will then display messages and format data according to Canadian French standards. When the user sends data to the server, he will enter it using Canadian French conventions, but the server will then store it according to the database globalization settings. The three elements (language, territory, and character set) of NLS_LANG are all optional.

 TIP The DBA has absolutely no control over what end users do with the NLS_LANG environment variable. If the application is globalization sensitive, the developers should take this into account and control globalization within the session instead.

The conversion between server-side and client-side globalization settings is done by Oracle Net. In terms of the OSI seven-layer model, any required conversion is a layer 6 (presentation layer) function that is accomplished by Oracle Net's Two-Task Common layer. Some conversion is perfectly straightforward and should always succeed. This is the case with formatting numbers, for instance. Other conversions are problematic. If the client and the server are using different character sets, it may not be possible for data to be converted. An extreme case would be a client process using a multibyte character set intended for an Oriental language, and a database created with US7ASCII. There is no way that the data entered on the client can be stored correctly in the much more limited character set available within the database, and data loss and corruption are inevitable.

Exercise 26-1: Make Globalization and Client Environment Settings
This exercise will demonstrate how you, acting as an end user, can customize your environment, in order to affect your Oracle sessions.

1. From an operating system prompt, set the NLS_LANG variable to (for example) Hungarian, and also adjust the date display from the default. Using Windows,

   ```
   C:\>set NLS_LANG=Hungarian
   C:\>set NLS_DATE_FORMAT=Day dd Month yyyy
   ```

   or on Unix,

   ```
   $ export NLS_LANG=Hungarian
   $ export NLS_DATE_FORMAT='Day dd Month yyyy'
   ```

2. From the same operating system session, launch SQL*Plus and connect as user SYSTEM.

3. Display the current date with

   ```
   select sysdate from dual;
   ```

The illustration shows the complete sequence of steps. Note that in the illustration the display is in fact incorrect: in Hungarian, "Friday" is "Pentek" and "March" is "Március". These errors are because the client-side settings cannot display the database character set correctly. Your date elements may differ from the illustration, depending on your server-side character set.

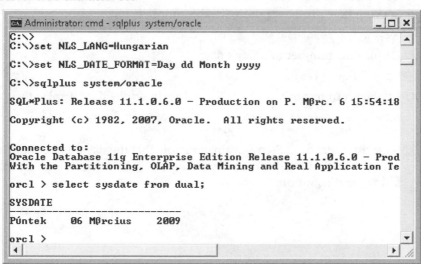

Session-Level Globalization Settings

Once connected, users can issue ALTER SESSION commands to set up their globalization preferences. Normally this would be done programmatically, perhaps by means of a logon trigger. The application will determine who the user is and configure the environment accordingly. An alternative to ALTER SESSION is the supplied package DBMS_SESSION. The following examples will each have the same effect:

```
SQL> alter session set nls_date_format='dd.mm.yyyy';
Session altered.
SQL> execute dbms_session.set_nls('nls_date_format','''dd.mm.yyyy''');
PL/SQL procedure successfully completed.
```

Specifications at the session level take precedence over the server-side database and instance settings and will also override any attempt made by the user to configure their session with operating system environment variables. The globalization settings currently in effect for your session are shown in the V$NLS_PARAMETERS view. The same information, with the exception of the character sets, is shown in the NLS_SESSION_PARAMETERS view.

Exercise 26-2: Control Globalization Within the Session   For this exercise, it is assumed that you have completed Exercise 26-1 and that you are working in the same SQL*Plus session. You will demonstrate how European and U.S. standards can cause confusion.

1. Confirm that your NLS_LANG environment variable is set to a European language. On Windows,

   ```
   SQL> host echo %NLS_LANG%
   ```

   or on Unix,

   ```
   SQL> host echo $NLS_LANG
   ```

2. Set your date display to show the day number:

   ```
   SQL> alter session set nls_date_format='D';
   ```

3. Display the number of today's day:

   ```
   SQL> select sysdate from dual;
   ```

4. Change your territory to the U.S., and again set the date display format:

   ```
   SQL> alter session set nls_territory=AMERICA;
   SQL> alter session set nls_date_format='D';
   ```

5. Issue the query from Step 3 again, and note that the day number has changed with the shift of environment from Europe to America as shown in the following illustration:

```
Administrator: cmd - sqlplus  system/oracle                    _ □ ×

orcl > host echo %NLS_LANG%
Hungarian

orcl > alter session set nls_date_format='D';

Session altered.

orcl > select sysdate  from dual;

S
-
5

orcl > alter session set nls_territory=AMERICA;

Session altered.

orcl > alter session set nls_date_format='D';

Session altered.

orcl > select sysdate  from dual;

S
-
6
```

Statement Globalization Settings

The tightest level of control over globalization is to manage it programmatically,
within each SQL statement. This entails using NLS parameters in SQL functions.
Figure 26-4 shows an example that presents the same data in two date languages.

```
Administrator: cmd - sqlplus  system/oracle                    _ □ ×

orcl >
orcl > select
  2    to_char(hiredate,'Day dd, Month YYYY','NLS_DATE_LANGUAGE=DUTCH'),
  3    to_char(hiredate,'Day dd, Month YYYY','NLS_DATE_LANGUAGE=GERMAN')
  4    from scott.emp;

TO_CHAR(HIREDATE,'DAYDD,MONT  TO_CHAR(HIREDATE,'DAYDD,MONTH

Woensdag   17, December  1900 Mittwoch    17, Dezember  1980
Vrijdag    20, Februari  1981 Freitag     20, Februar   1981
Zondag     22, Februari  1981 Sonntag     22, Februar   1981
Donderdag  02, April     1981 Donnerstag  02, April     1981
Maandag    28, September 1981 Montag      28, September 1981
Vrijdag    01, Mei       1981 Freitag     01, Mai       1981
Dinsdag    09, Juni      1981 Dienstag    09, Juni      1981
Zondag     19, April     1987 Sonntag     19, April     1987
Dinsdag    17, November  1981 Dienstag    17, November  1981
Dinsdag    08, September 1981 Dienstag    08, September 1981
Zaterdag   23, Mei       1987 Samstag     23, Mai       1987
```

Figure 26-4   Controlling date language within a SQL statement

The SQL functions to consider are the typecasting functions that convert between data types. Depending on the function, various parameters may be used.

Function	Globalization Parameters
TO_DATE	NLS_DATE_LANGUAGE
	NLS_CALENDAR
TO_NUMBER	NLS_NUMERIC_CHARACTERS
	NLS_CURRENCY
	NLS_DUAL_CURRENCY
	NLS_ISO_CURRENCY
	NLS_CALENDAR
TO_CHAR, TO_NCHAR	NLS_DATE_LANGUAGE
	NLS_NUMERIC_CHARACTERS
	NLS_CURRENCY
	NLS_DUAL_CURRENCY
	NLS_ISO_CURRENCY
	NLS_CALENDAR

Numbers, dates, and times can have a wide range of format masks applied for display. Within numbers, these masks allow embedding group and decimal separators, and the various currency symbols; dates can be formatted as virtually any combination of text and numbers; times can be shown with or without time zone indicators and as AM/PM or 24 hours. Refer to Chapter 10 for a discussion of conversion functions and format masks.

Languages and Time Zones

Once you have your NLS settings in place, you need to understand how they are used when sorting or searching. Depending on the language, the results of a sort on a name or address in the database will return the results in a different order.

Even with Oracle's robust support for character sets, there are occasions when you might want to create a customized globalization environment for a database, or tweak an existing locale. In a later section, a brief introduction to the Oracle Locale Builder is provided.

The chapter concludes with a discussion of time zones, and how Oracle supports them using initialization parameters at both the session and database levels, much like NLS parameters.

Linguistic Sorting and Selection

Oracle's default sort order is binary. The strings to be sorted are read from left to right, and each character is reduced to its numeric ASCII (or EBCDIC) value. The sort is done in one pass. This may be suitable for American English, but it may give incorrect results for other languages. Obvious problems are diacritics such as *ä* or *à* and diphthongs like *æ*, but there are also more subtle matters. For example, in traditional Spanish, *ch* is a character in its own right that comes after *c*; thus the correct order is "Cerveze, Cordoba, Chavez." To sort this correctly, the database must inspect the subsequent character as well as the current character, if it is a *c*.

TIP As a general rule, it is safe to assume that Oracle can handle just about any linguistic problem, but that you as DBA may not be competent to understand it. You will need an expert in whatever languages you are working in to advise.

Linguistic sorting means that rather than replacing each character with its numeric equivalent, Oracle will replace each character with a numeric value that reflects its correct position in the sequence appropriate to the language in use. There are some variations here, depending on the complexity of the environment.

A monolingual sort makes two passes through the strings being compared. The first pass is based on the *major* value of each character. The major value is derived by removing diacritic and case differences. In effect, each letter is considered as uppercase with no accents. Then a second comparison is made, using the *minor* values, which are case and diacritic sensitive. Monolingual sorts are much better than binary but are still not always adequate. For French, for example, Oracle provides the monolingual FRENCH sort order, and the multilingual FRENCH_M, which may be better if the data is not exclusively French.

A technique that may remove confusion is to use Oracle's case- and diacritic-insensitive sort options. For example, you may wish to consider these variations on a Scottish name as equivalent:

MacKay
Mackay
MACKAY

To retrieve all three with one query, first set the NLS_SORT parameter to GENERIC_BASELETTER as shown in Figure 26-5. This will ignore case and diacritic variations. Then set the NLS_COMP parameter away from the default of BINARY to ANSI. This instructs Oracle to compare values using the NLS_SORT rules, not the numeric value of the character. The GENERIC_BASELETTER sort order will also "correct" what may appear to some as incorrect ordering. A more complex example would require equating "McKay" with "MacKay"; that would require the Locale Builder.

Similarly, all the sort orders can be suffixed with _AI or _CI for accent-insensitive and case-insensitive sorting. For example,

```
SQL> alter session set nls_sort=FRENCH_CI;
```

will ignore upper- and lowercase variations but will still handle accented characters according to French standards.

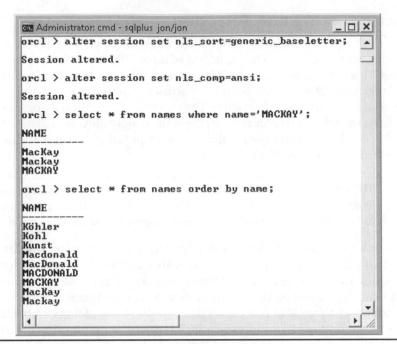

Figure 26-5 Case and accent insensitivity for SELECT and sorting

The Locale Builder

The globalization support provided as standard by Oracle Database 11g is phenomenal, but there may be circumstances that it cannot handle. The Locale Builder is a graphical tool that can create a customized globalization environment, by generating definitions for languages, territories, character sets, and linguistic sorting.

As an example, Oracle does not provide out-of-the-box support for Afrikaans; you could create a customized globalization to fill this gap, which might combine elements of Dutch and English standards with customizations common in Southern Africa such as ignoring the punctuation marks or spaces in names like O'Hara or Du Toit. To launch the Locale Builder, run

```
$ORACLE_HOME/nls/lbuilder/lbuilder
```

on Unix, or

```
%ORACLE_HOME%\nls\lbuilder\lbuilder.bat
```

on Windows to view the dialog box shown in Figure 26-6.

Using Time Zones

Businesses, and therefore databases, must work across time zones. From release 9*i* onward, the Oracle environment can be made time-zone aware. This is done by specifying a time zone in which the database operates, and then using the TIMESTAMP

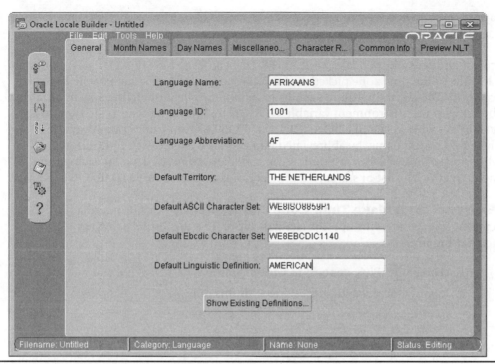

Figure 26-6   Creating a locale with the Locale Builder

WITH TIME ZONE and TIMESTAMP WITH LOCAL TIME ZONE data types. The former will be not be normalized to the database time zone when it is stored, but it will have a time zone indicator to show the zone to which it refers. The latter is normalized to the database time zone on storage but is subsequently converted to the client time zone on retrieval. The usual DATE and TIMESTAMP data types are always normalized to the database time zone on storage and displayed unchanged when selected.

As an example of when time zone processing is important, consider an e-mail database hosted in London, set to Greenwich Mean Time, GMT. A user in Harare (which is two hours ahead of GMT) sends an e-mail at his local time of 15:00; the mail is addressed to two recipients, one in Paris (Central European Time, CET: one hour ahead of GMT with daylight saving time in effect in the Northern Hemisphere summer) and the other in Bogotá (which is five hours behind GMT). How do you ensure that the recipients and the sender will all see the mail as having been sent correctly according their local time zone? If the column denoting when the mail was sent is of data type TIMESTAMP WITH LOCAL TIME ZONE, then when the mail is received by the database, the time will be normalized to GMT: it will be saved as 13:00. Then when the Bogotá user retrieves it, the time will be adjusted to 08:00 by his user process. When the Paris user retrieves the mail, they will see it as having been sent at either 14:00 or 15:00, depending on whether the date it was sent was in the period between March and October when daylight saving time is in effect. It is possible to do this type of work programmatically, but it requires a great deal of work as well as knowledge of all time zones and any local quirks for daylight saving. The database can do it all for you.

The database time zone can be set at creation time in the CREATE DATABASE command and adjusted later with ALTER DATABASE SET TIME_ZONE=. If not set, it defaults to the time zone picked up from the host operating system at the time of creation. The client time zone defaults to that of the client operating system, or it can be set with the environment variable ORA_STDZ. Within a session, the time zone can be set with ALTER SESSION SET TIME_ZONE=. Time zones can always be specified by full name, by abbreviated name, or as a fixed offset, in hours and minutes, from GMT. The last option cannot take account of daylight saving time adjustments. The list of supported time zones is displayed in V$TIMEZONE_NAMES.

Exercise 26-3: Make Time Zone Adjustments Confirm and adjust your current time zone, using appropriate data types. Test the results using appropriate formatting masks.

1. Using SQL*Plus, connect to your instance as user SYSTEM.

2. Identify the database time zone with this query:

```
select property_value from database_properties
where property_name = 'DBTIMEZONE';
```

   and note the result.

3. Create a table as follows:

```
create table times
    (date_std date,
     date_tz timestamp with time zone,
     date_ltz timestamp with local time zone);
```

4. View the list of supported time zones with this query:

```
select * from v$timezone_names;
```

5. Adjust your session time zone to something other than the database time zone, for example,

```
alter session set time_zone='Pacific/Tahiti';
```

6. Set your timestamp with time zone format to 24 hour clock, with abbreviated time zone names with daylight saving variations.

```
alter session set nls_timestamp_tz_format='YYYY-MM-DD HH24:MI:SS TZD';
```

7. Set your timestamp format to 24 hour clock.

```
alter session set nls_timestamp_format='YYYY-MM-DD HH24:MI:SS';
```

8. Set your date format to 24 hour clock.

```
alter session set nls_date_format='YYYY-MM-DD HH24:MI:SS';
```

9. Insert a row into the table created in Step 3.

```
insert into times values('2008-10-26 15:00:00',
'2008-10-26 15:00:00','2008-10-26 15:00:00');
```

10. Display the times.

```
select * from times;
```

Note that all times read 15:00.

11. Switch your session to the database time zone.

```
alter session set time_zone=DBTIMEZONE;
```

12. Repeat the query from Step 10, and note that the TIMESTAMP WITH LOCAL TIMEZONE has been adjusted to reflect that your session is now in a different zone.

13. Tidy up:

```
drop table times;
```

Two-Minute Drill

Customize Language-Dependent Behavior for the Database and Individual Sessions

- Globalization covers aspects of data presentation, calendars, and dates, including dates, numbers, and linguistic localizations.
- A *character set* is a defined encoding scheme for representing characters as a sequence of bits.
- The number of characters that a character set can represent is limited by the number of bits the character set uses for each character.
- The Unicode standards are an international standard for character encoding, which is intended to include every character that will ever be required by any computer system.
- The number of languages supported by Oracle depends on the platform, release, and patch level of the product.
- The language used will determine the language for error messages and also set defaults for date language and sort orders.
- Binary sorting may be acceptable for a seven-bit character set, but for character sets of eight bits or more the results are often inappropriate.
- Query V$NLS_VALID_VALUES to see the available character sets, sort orders, territories, and languages.
- Globalization can be specified at any and all of these five levels, in increasing order of priority: database, instance, client environment, session, and statement.
- The database character set is used to store all the data in columns of type VARCHAR2, CLOB, CHAR, and LONG.
- Two types of Unicode are supported as the National Character Set: AL16UTF16 and UTF8.

PART III

- There are two tools provided to assist with deciding on character set change: the Database Character Set Scanner and the Language and Character Set File Scanner.
- The key client-side environment variable is NLS_LANG. The full specification for this is a language, a territory, and a character set.

Work with Database and NLS Character Sets

- Oracle's default sort order is binary.
- Linguistic sorting means that rather than replacing each character with its numeric equivalent, Oracle will replace each character with a numeric value that reflects its correct position in the sequence appropriate to the language in use.
- The Locale Builder is a graphical tool that can create a customized globalization environment, by generating definitions for languages, territories, character sets, and linguistic sorting.
- Applications are made time-zone aware by specifying a time zone in which the database operates, and then using the TIMESTAMP WITH TIME ZONE and TIMESTAMP WITH LOCAL TIME ZONE data types.
- The usual DATE and TIMESTAMP data types are always normalized to the database time zone on storage and displayed unchanged when selected.
- The database time zone can be set at creation time in the CREATE DATABASE command and adjusted later with ALTER DATABASE SET TIME_ZONE.

Self Test

1. Your database was created with US7ASCII as the database character set, and you later find that this is inadequate. What can you do? (Choose the best answer.)

   A. Recreate the database.

   B. Issue an `alter database character set...` command.

   C. Issue an `alter system character set...` command.

   D. Generate a `create controlfile...` command, edit it to specify a different character set, and recreate the controlfile.

2. What are the options for the National Character Set? (Choose the best answer.)

   A. None. It must be AL16UTF16.

   B. It can be any Unicode character set.

   C. It can be either AL16UTF16 or UTF8.

   D. It can be any character set you require.

3. Match each character set with a type:

Character Set	Type
1. AL16UTF16	a. Seven-bit single-byte
2. US7ASCII	b. Eight-bit single-byte
3. UTF8	c. Fixed-width multibyte
4. WE8ISO8859P15	d. Variable-width

   A. 1-c; 2-b; 3-d; 4-a

   B. 1-d; 2-a; 3-c; 4-b

   C. 1-c; 2-d; 3-b; 4-a

   D. 1-c; 2-a; 3-d; 4-b

4. Which statements are correct about the TIMESTAMP WITH LOCAL TIME ZONE data type? (Choose two answers.)

   A. Data is saved with a local time zone indicator.

   B. Data is normalized to the database time zone when it is saved.

   C. On retrieval, data is normalized to the retrieving client's time zone.

   D. On retrieval, data is normalized to the time zone of the client that entered it.

5. Globalization can be set at various levels. Put these in order of precedence, lowest first:

   A. Client environment

   B. Database settings

   C. Instance parameters

   D. Session parameters

   E. Statements

6. The NLS_LANGUAGE and NLS_TERRITORY parameters set defaults for a number of other globalization parameters. Which of the following are controlled by NLS_LANGUAGE? (Choose two answers.)

   A. NLS_DATE_LANGUAGE

   B. NLS_DATE_FORMAT

   C. NLS_NUMERIC_CHARACTERS

   D. NLS_SORT

7. Choose the best description of the Character Set Scanner tool:

   A. It scans character sets to assess their suitability for a particular language.

   B. It scans files to determine the language and character set of the data in them.

   C. It scans datafiles to determine whether the character set can be changed.

   D. It reports on problems a character set change would cause.

8. If the database and the user process are using different character sets, how does data get converted? (Choose the best answer.)

 A. Data is not converted, which is why there may be corruptions if the character sets are incompatible.

 B. On data entry, the instance converts data to the database character set. On retrieval, the user process converts to the client character set.

 C. Oracle Net will convert, in both directions.

 D. It depends on various NLS parameters.

9. The database is set to GMT. A client in Buenos Aires (three hours behind GMT) executes these statements at 10:00:00 local time:

```
create table times(c1 timestamp,
c2 timestamp with local time zone);
insert into times values(to_timestamp('10:00:00'),
  to_timestamp('10:00:00'));
commit;
```

 A client in Nairobi (three hours ahead of GMT) executes these statements at 18:00:00 local time:

```
alter session set nls_timestamp_format='hh24:mi:ss';
select * from times;
```

 What will the Nairobi user see for the columns c1 and c2? (Choose the best answer.)

 A. 10:00:00 and 16:00:00

 B. 13:00:00 and 16:00:00

 C. 13:00:00 and 10:00:00

 D. 10:00:00 and 13:00:00

10. Study the result of this query:

```
SQL> select * from dates;
C1
--------
06-04-08
```

 C1 is a date-type column. How could you determine what the date returned actually means? (Choose three answers.)

 A. Query NLS_DATABASE_PARAMETERS.

 B. Query NLS_INSTANCE_PARAMETERS.

 C. Query NLS_SESSION_PARAMETERS.

 D. Set your NLS_DATE_FORMAT to a known value, and rerun the query.

 E. Change the query to use TO_CHAR with an NLS parameter.

11. How can you prevent users from causing confusion with, for instance, date and time formats by setting local globalization environment variables? (Choose the best answer.)

A. You can't; the users have control over this.

B. Write logon triggers to set the session environment.

C. Set instance globalization parameters to override client-side settings.

D. Configure Oracle Net to convert all data sent to and from the database appropriately.

12. Which view will tell you what languages can be supported by your installation? (Choose the best answer.)

A. NLS_DATABASE_PARAMETERS

B. NLS_INSTANCE_PARAMETERS

C. V$NLS_VALID_VALUES

D. V$NLS_LANGUAGES

13. You want to make the order in which sorted names are returned independent of whether the names include accented characters, upper- and lowercase characters, punctuation marks, or spaces. How can you do this? (Choose the best answer.)

A. Set the sort order to GENERIC_BASELETTER, which will ignore such variations.

B. Use the _AI and _CI versions of any of the supported sort orders.

C. Use the Locale Builder to design a custom sort order.

D. This cannot be done.

Self Test Answers

1. ☑ B. Use this command, but test with the character set scanner first.

☒ A, C, and D. A is wrong because you do not need to recreate the database to change the database character set. C is wrong because ALTER SYSTEM cannot be used to change the character set. D is wrong because changing the character set in the controlfile will not convert the database character set.

2. ☑ C. Either of these Unicode sets is currently allowed.

☒ All other answers are wrong because the only two options are AL16UTF16 or UTF8.

3. ☑ D. 1-c; 2-a; 3-d; 4-b

☒ A, B, and C. All other combinations are incorrect.

4. ☑ B and C. This is the data type that fully normalizes times to and from the database.

☒ A and D. Timestamp values are not saved with the time zone indicator, nor are they normalized when retrieved.

5. ☑ **B, C, A, D, and E.** The correct order is **B, C, A, D, E.** Instance parameters override the database parameters, and then on the client side environment variables can be overridden by ALTER SESSION commands, and then by individual statements.

☒ All other orders are incorrect.

6. ☑ **A and D.** NLS_DATE_LANGUAGE and NLS_SORT are the two parameters controlled by NLS_LANGUAGE.

☒ **B and C.** NLS_DATE_FORMAT and NLS_NUMERIC_CHARACTERS are controlled by NLS_TERRITORY.

7. ☑ **D.** It will, for instance, report if a changed encoding would prevent data from fitting into an existing column.

☒ **A, B, and C.** All other options are incorrect descriptions.

8. ☑ **C.** Oracle Net will do the best conversion possible.

☒ **A, B, and D.** All other conversion scenarios are incorrect.

9. ☑ **B.** The database will normalize the time 10:00:00 from the local time zone at the point of entry, GMT+3, to the database time zone, GMT. Thus both times are saved as 13:00:00 GMT. For retrieval, the timestamp column will be displayed as saved, 13:00:00, but the timestamp with local time zone column will adjust the time to that of the time zone of the client retrieving the data, which is GMT+3.

☒ **A, C, and D.** All other options are incorrect.

10. ☑ **C, D and E.** NLS_SESSION_PARAMETERS will show the format used so that you can interpret the output of the query correctly, or you could set the format to a sensible value, or control the format in the query.

☒ **A, and D.** You must query the session-specific version of the view to be sure of interpreting the output correctly.

11. ☑ **B.** The best option is to write logon triggers, which will prevent any possible confusion caused by the client configuration.

☒ **A, C, and D. A** is wrong because you can override the local settings with a logon trigger. **C** is wrong because client-side settings can override instance settings. **D** is wrong because you cannot configure Oracle Net to perform a specific conversion.

12. ☑ **C.** The view V$NLS_VALID_VALUES will show you the full range of supported languages, as well as all other globalization options.

☒ **A, B, and D. A** is wrong because NLS_DATABASE_PARAMETERS shows the permanent values for each database NLS-related initialization parameter. **B** is wrong because NLS_INSTANCE_PARAMETERS shows the changed NLS values since instance startup. **D** is wrong because there is no such view as V$NLS_LANGUAGES.

13. ☑   **C.** To remove punctuation marks and spaces as well, you will need to create your own variation with the Locale Builder.

☒   **A, B,** and **D.** Setting the sort order to GENERIC_BASELETTER or using the _AI or _CI versions of the sort orders does not remove punctuation marks and spaces.

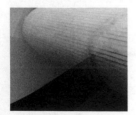

CHAPTER 27

The Intelligent Infrastructure

Exam Objectives

In this chapter you will learn to

- 052.18.1   Use the Enterprise Manager Support Workbench
- 052.18.2   Manage Patches
- 053.13.1   Set Up the Automatic Diagnostic Repository
- 053.13.2   Use Support Workbench

The Support Workbench and the Automatic Diagnostic Repository offer wizards for diagnosing and repairing problems, and for working with Oracle Support Services. This material is not extensively examined, but it is possible that general knowledge of procedures could be tested. If you do not have a MetaLink account, you cannot complete the exercises for this chapter—for this reason, it includes screen shots to illustrate every step in using Database Control to set up a job to download and apply a patch.

 TIP MetaLink has recently been rebadged as My Oracle Support, with an alternative user interface that requires the Adobe Flash player. Some Oracle professionals prefer the Flash interface, but others prefer the "classic" interface; try them both, and make up your own mind.

MetaLink is the external interface of Oracle Support Services: a searchable database containing millions of articles on technical issues, and facilities for locating and downloading patches and for raising SRs (Service Requests). An SR is a request for an Oracle Support Services analyst to assist with a problem. To raise an SR, you must have a MetaLink account associated with a valid CSI (Customer Support Identifier) number issued by Oracle Corporation.

The Enterprise Manager Support Workbench

The Enterprise Manager Support Workbench is a graphical tool giving access to the Automatic Diagnostic Repository (the ADR) with facilities for gathering information, packaging it, and sending it to Oracle Support Services.

The Automatic Diagnostic Repository (ADR)

The ADR is a central storage point for all diagnostic information. This includes various dumps and trace files, the alert log, and health monitor reports. It is a file-based repository. All instances (RDBMS instances and also ASM instances) create their own directory structure within the ADR.

The location of the ADR is determined by the instance parameter DIAGNOSTIC_ DEST. This will default to the ORACLE_BASE environment variable (which is a registry variable on Windows systems) or, if this has not been set, to the ORACLE_HOME/log directory. Within DIAGNOSTIC_DEST, there will be a directory for ADR_BASE: this is DIAGNOSTIC_DEST/diag. In ADR_BASE there are directories for each Oracle product, such as the RDBMS, or database listeners. Within each product directory, there will be directories for each instance of the product: this is ADR_HOME for the instance. For a database instance, ADR_HOME is

```
ORACLE_BASE/diag/rdbms/database_name/instance_name
```

where *database_name* is the name of the database and *instance_name* is the name of the instance. For example:

```
/u01/app/oracle/diag/rdbms/orcl11g/orcl11g
```

Within ADR_HOME there will be a directory structure for the various files that make up the ADR for the instance. Some of the files are formatted with XML tags and are not intended to be viewed directly with editors; some are binary data; others are plain text. The directory `ADR_HOME/trace` is used as the default value for the instance parameters USER_DUMP_DEST (trace files generated by user sessions) and BACKGROUND_DUMP_DEST (the alert log and trace files generated by background processes). There is another copy of the alert log, formatted with XML tags, in `ADR_HOME/alert`.

Problems and Incidents

A *problem* is a critical error in the database or the instance. Examples include internal Oracle errors (errors reported with the error code ORA-600) and operating system errors. Each problem has a problem key, which is a text string including the error code and any parameters.

An *incident* is an occurrence of a problem. Incidents are considered to have the same root cause if their problem keys match. When an incident occurs, it is reported in the alert log and Enterprise Manager gathers diagnostic data about the incident in the form of dump files (incident dumps) and stores these in an ADR subdirectory created for that incident.

An *incident package* is a collection of data regarding one or more incidents and problems, formatted for upload to Oracle Support Services as part of an SR.

The ADR Command-Line Interface (ADRCI)

There is a command-line tool for managing the ADR: the ADRCI. This tool can display details of all problems and incidents, and generate reports and incident packages. Figure 27-1 shows the launching of the ADRCI on Windows, and then running the HELP command.

In Figure 27-1, note that ADRCI has detected ADR_BASE. A simple ADRCI session might use these commands:

```
set home diag/rdbms/orcl11g/orcl11g
show problem
ips create package problem 8
```

The SET HOME command points the ADRCI toward one ADR_HOME, the path being relative to ADR_BASE. The SHOW PROBLEM command will list all known problems for that ADR_HOME, identified by PROBLEM_ID number. The IPS CREATE PACKAGE command will generate an incident package for the nominated problem in the directory `ADR_HOME/incpkg`.

In most cases, the ADRCI will not be needed: Database Control has an interface to the ADR that is usually easier to use.

```
C:\WINDOWS\system32\cmd.exe - adrci                        - □ ×

D:\>adrci

ADRCI: Release 11.1.0.6.0 - Beta on Tue Mar 11 12:39:49 2008

Copyright (c) 1982, 2007, Oracle.  All rights reserved.

ADR base = "d:\app\oracle"
adrci> help

 HELP [topic]
    Available Topics:
            CREATE REPORT
            ECHO
            EXIT
            HELP
            HOST
            IPS
            PURGE
            RUN
            SET BASE
            SET BROWSER
            SET CONTROL
            SET ECHO
            SET EDITOR
            SET HOMES | HOME | HOMEPATH
            SET TERMOUT
            SHOW ALERT
            SHOW BASE
            SHOW CONTROL
            SHOW HM_RUN
            SHOW HOMES | HOME | HOMEPATH
            SHOW INCDIR
            SHOW INCIDENT
            SHOW PROBLEM
            SHOW REPORT
            SHOW TRACEFILE
            SPOOL

 There are other commands intended to be used directly by Oracle, type
 "HELP EXTENDED" to see the list

adrci> _
```

Figure 27-1   The ADRCI utility

The Support Workbench

Enterprise Manager Database Control database home page displays all critical alerts. Clicking any of them will take you to the Support Workbench, shown in Figure 27-2.

Figure 27-2 shows that there have been eight problems with a total of 127 incidents, but only one problem is still active. This is the problem number 5, which generated an ORA-600 error. From the Support Workbench, you can select a problem, view the details, and create an incident package by clicking the appropriate buttons.

 TIP SRs used to be called TARs (Technical Assistant Requests), and you will still hear many DBAs using phrases such as "raising a tar."

To create an SR regarding a problem, select the problem's check box and click View to reach the Problem Details window, shown in Figure 27-3.

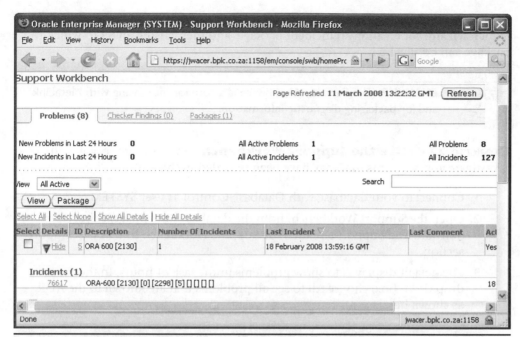

Figure 27-2 The Support Workbench

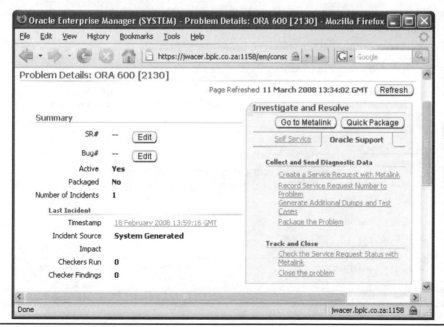

Figure 27-3 Problem Details, with links for using MetaLink

The links shown in the Oracle Support tab of the Problem Details window will launch wizards for creating an incident package, and then raising an SR to which the package can be attached.

EXAM TIP The Support Workbench is a tool for interfacing with MetaLink and for packaging diagnostic information.

Exercise 27-1: Use the Support Workbench   In this exercise, you will investigate any problems that may have been recorded in the ADR.

1. Connect to your database with Database Control as user SYSTEM.

2. Open the Support Workbench: from the database home page, choose the Software And Support tab, then the Support Workbench link in the Support section.

3. The default display is to show problems in the last 24 hours. In the View drop-down box, choose All to see all problems that are known to the ADR, as shown here:

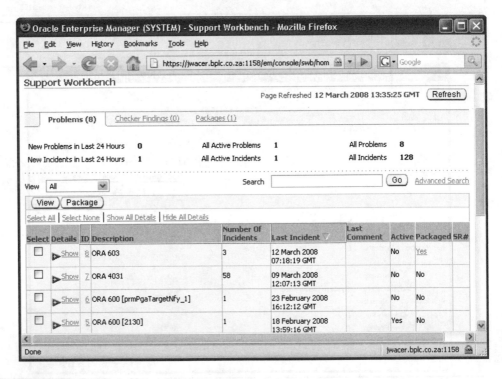

4. Investigate any problems shown by clicking the links to show the details of the problem.

Patches

In some environments, patching can take up a considerable amount of time. It is, however, a vital task. Some patches will be to fix problems in the Oracle code that cause some features not to work as documented: applying these is optional, only necessary if your installation happens to have hit the problem. Others are to fix security issues and are not optional at all. Patches can be applied using a command-line utility, or with Enterprise Manager.

Types of Patch

Patches are shipped in three forms:

- **Interim patches** These are written to fix one specific problem, for an exact release level of the database. They are not necessarily fully integration or regression tested.

- **CPU (Critical Patch Update) patches** These are cumulative patches for a specific release level and include all dependent patches. CPUs are fully integration and regression tested.

- **Patch sets** A patch set is a cumulative set of product fixes that will increment the release level of the product (as reported by a query against V$VERSION), for instance, from 11.1.0.6 to 11.1.0.7.

If you have hit a problem, and research with MetaLink and with other resources identifies the problem as a known bug with a patch to fix it, this patch can be installed as an interim patch. Otherwise, do not install interim patches. CPUs are usually issued every three months and will often include patches for security problems. These should be installed, particularly if your systems have to comply with security standards enforced by local jurisdictions. Applying a patch set is a much bigger operation that may change the behavior of the product, rather than merely fixing problems. Applying patch sets should not be embarked upon without full testing.

To apply patches, use the Opatch utility. This can be invoked from the command line, or through Database Control.

 TIP Many DBAs try to avoid installing interim patches. They will fix a problem, but applying several may be problematic because of the lack of integration testing. CPUs and patch sets are much safer.

Integration with MetaLink and the Patch Advisor

Database Control includes a Patch Advisor that will identify what CPUs and what Oracle-recommended patches should be applied to the database. This requires configuring a connection to MetaLink and scheduling a job to make the check. An account with MetaLink and an Internet connection from the server machine are prerequisites for doing this.

To configure MetaLink integration, click the Setup link at the top right of the Database Control database home page and then the Patching Setup link in the Overview Of Setup section. In the Patching Setup window, enter your MetaLink username and password. These will be associated with the username you used when connecting to Database Control. If there is a proxy server between the database server and the Internet, the Proxy And Connection Settings tab will let you configure this.

To schedule a job for checking what patches are needed, from the database home page click the Jobs link in the Related Links section. In the Create Job drop-down box choose Refresh From MetaLink and click GO. Give the job a name, schedule it to run with whatever frequency you think appropriate, and submit the job. Once the job has run, the Patch Advisor should be available.

To reach the Patch Advisor, from the database home page select the Software And Support tab, then the Patch Advisor link in the Database Software Patching section. This will show all the recommended patches for the database, as of the last time the job was run.

Applying Patches

Patches can be applied with the Opatch utility, or with Database Control; the Database Control method in fact uses Opatch behind the scenes. The Opatch utility is installed into the directory ORACLE_HOME/Opatch and launched by running the executable file opatch (or opatch.bat on Windows). The prerequisites are that the ORACLE_ HOME environment variable must be set (note that on Windows it is not sufficient to have this as a registry variable; it must be set within the operating system session); the Java Runtime Environment 1.4 or later must be available; a few standard operating system utilities must be available. To test the prerequisites, use the LSINVENTORY command as in Figure 27-4.

In Figure 27-4, Opatch is being run on a Windows system. The utility was invoked by specifying the full path, using the ORACLE_HOME environment variable, and the LSINVENTORY command. This shows summary information regarding what has been installed, including any interim patches (none, in the example). To obtain much more detailed information, use the -detail switch:

```
%ORACLE_HOME%\Opatch\opatch lsinventory -detail
```

All patches will come with a README.TXT file of instructions detailing how to install the patch. These instructions will include detail on whether the database should be open or shut down while the patch is applied. To apply a patch once it is downloaded from MetaLink and expanded (it will have come as a ZIP file), run Opatch as follows:

```
opatch apply path_to_patch
```

where *path_to_patch* is the directory where the patch was expanded.

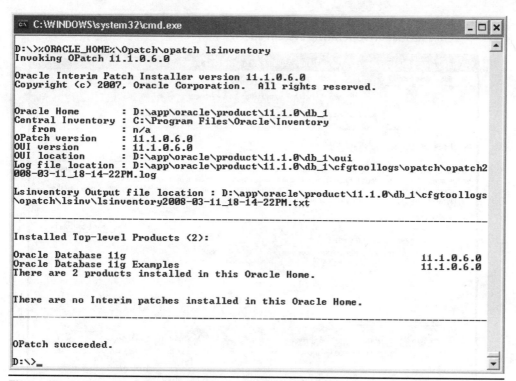

```
C:\WINDOWS\system32\cmd.exe                                            _ □ ×

D:\>%ORACLE_HOME%\Opatch\opatch lsinventory
Invoking OPatch 11.1.0.6.0

Oracle Interim Patch Installer version 11.1.0.6.0
Copyright (c) 2007, Oracle Corporation.  All rights reserved.


Oracle Home       : D:\app\oracle\product\11.1.0\db_1
Central Inventory : C:\Program Files\Oracle\Inventory
   from           : n/a
OPatch version    : 11.1.0.6.0
OUI version       : 11.1.0.6.0
OUI location      : D:\app\oracle\product\11.1.0\db_1\oui
Log file location : D:\app\oracle\product\11.1.0\db_1\cfgtoollogs\opatch\opatch2
008-03-11_18-14-22PM.log

Lsinventory Output file location : D:\app\oracle\product\11.1.0\db_1\cfgtoollogs
\opatch\lsinv\lsinventory2008-03-11_18-14-22PM.txt
------------------------------------------------------------------------------

Installed Top-level Products (2):

Oracle Database 11g                                          11.1.0.6.0
Oracle Database 11g Examples                                 11.1.0.6.0
There are 2 products installed in this Oracle Home.

There are no Interim patches installed in this Oracle Home.
------------------------------------------------------------------------------


OPatch succeeded.

D:\>_
```

Figure 27-4 Using Opatch to inspect the inventoried software

To apply a patch with Database Control, the patch must first be downloaded to a *staging area*. The staging area is a location where the patch is *staged*—stored locally, prior to application. To reach the wizard that will stage and apply the patch, from the database home page select the Software And Support tab, and then the Stage Patch link in the Database Software Patching section. This will launch a six-step wizard:

- Select patch
- Select destination
- Set credentials
- Stage or apply
- Schedule
- Summary

The wizard will connect to MetaLink using stored credentials, download the patch, and create a job to apply the patch. The illustrations that follow show examples of using the wizard to apply a patch.

1. First, enter the patch number and operating system (some patches come in versions that are operating system specific).

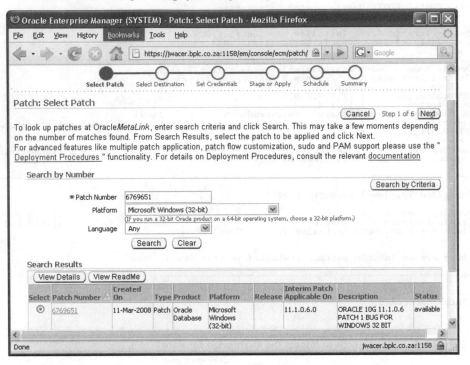

2. Choose the targets to which the patch should be applied. The choice will be limited to targets appropriate for the patch (in the example, database instances).

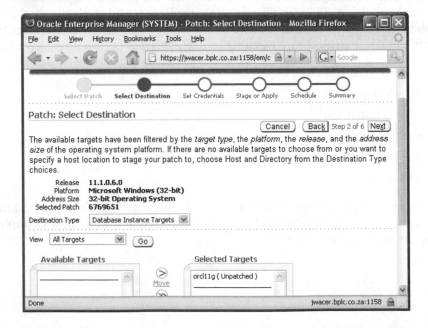

3. Provide credentials. These will be either operating system credentials, database credentials, or both depending on the patch.

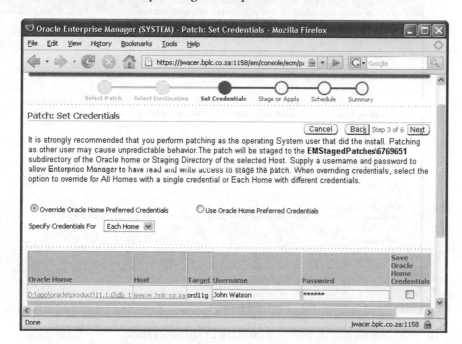

4. Decide whether to apply the patch or only stage it for future use.

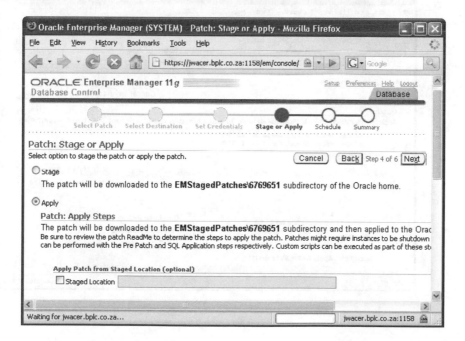

5. Schedule the job that will download and apply the patch.

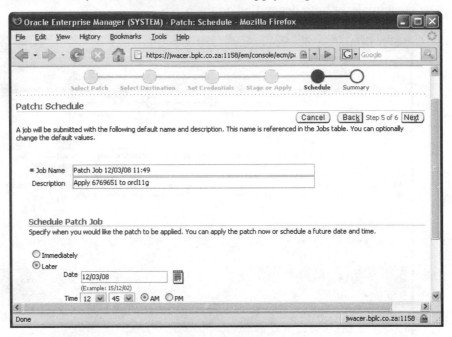

6. The final step is to view a summary of the operation.

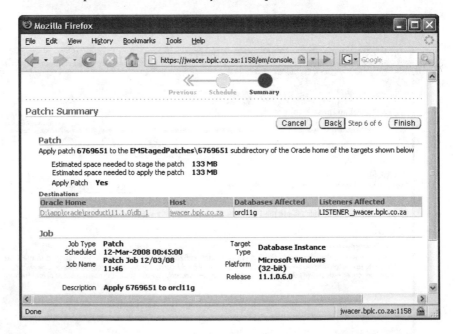

EXAM TIP Patches are applied with the Opatch utility—even when working with Database Control, you are still using Opatch.

Exercise 27-2: Download and Apply a Patch   In this exercise, you will download a patch and apply it. Oracle Corporation provides a dummy patch for this purpose. At the time of writing, this is only available for 32-bit Linux. If you are working on another operating system, don't worry—you will get practice in patching soon enough when you start working on a live database.

1. Log in to MetaLink.

2. Select the Patches & Updates tab, and then the Simple Search link.

3. When prompted for a Patch Number/Name, enter **6198642**. When prompted for a Platform Or Language, select Linux x86 from the drop-down box. Click GO.

4. Click the DOWNLOAD button, shown in the next illustration, to download the patch from MetaLink to an appropriate directory.

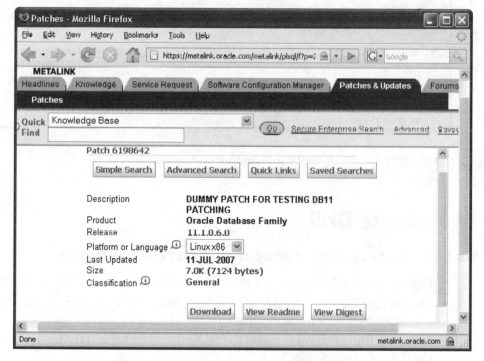

5. From an operating system prompt, unzip the patch. It will unzip into a directory named 6198642.

6. Shut down the database and the listener: Opatch will not proceed if these are running.

7. Apply the patch:

```
$ORACLE_HOME/OPatch/opatch apply patch_directory
```

where *patch_directory* is the directory into which the patch was unzipped. The next illustration shows this step, and the start of the output.

```
db11g@jwlnx1:~
[db11g@jwlnx1 ~]$
[db11g@jwlnx1 ~]$ $ORACLE_HOME/OPatch/opatch apply /home/db11g/patches/6198642
Invoking OPatch 11.1.0.6.0

Oracle Interim Patch Installer version 11.1.0.6.0
Copyright (c) 2007, Oracle Corporation.  All rights reserved.


Oracle Home       : /u02/app/db11g/product/11.1.0/db_1
Central Inventory : /u02/app/oraInventory
   from           : /etc/oraInst.loc
OPatch version    : 11.1.0.6.0
OUI version       : 11.1.0.6.0
OUI location      : /u02/app/db11g/product/11.1.0/db_1/oui
Log file location : /u02/app/db11g/product/11.1.0/db_1/cfgtoollogs/opatch/opatc
h2008-03-12_14-34-16PM.log

ApplySession applying interim patch '6198642' to OH '/u02/app/db11g/product/11.
1.0/db_1'

Running prerequisite checks...

OPatch detected non-cluster Oracle Home from the inventory and will patch the l
ocal system only.
```

8. Confirm the patch application with this command:

```
$ORACLE_HOME/OPatch/opatch lsinventory
```

Two-Minute Drill

Use the Enterprise Manager Support Workbench

- Database Control can connect to MetaLink and identify lists of advised patches.
- The Support Workbench can classify errors into named problems, each consisting of one or more incidents.
- Diagnostic information is stored in files in the ADR, located by default in the ORACLE_BASE directory.
- All diagnostic information in the ADR relevant to a problem can be packaged for transmission to Oracle Support Services.

Manage Patches

- Interim patches fix one problem.
- CPUs are bundled patches, often including security fixes.

- Patch sets raise the release level of the product.
- The Opatch utility installs patches and updates the inventory.

Set Up the Automatic Diagnostic Repository

- The ADR is a file-based repository, accessible no matter what the state of the instance and the database.
- The ADR location is determined by the DIAGNOSTIC_DEST instance parameter, which will default to the ORACLE_BASE environment variable.
- Maintenance of the ADR is automatic: the instance (and other processes, such as database listeners) will create their own directories and files in the ADR.

Self Test

1. If the system is behind a firewall proxy server, where must the proxy server be defined before the REFRESHFROMMETALINK job can run? (Choose the best answer.)

   A. In the browser

   B. In Database Control

   C. In both the browser and Database Control

   D. It is necessary to configure the firewall to allow a direct connection from the database server to the Internet

2. Where is the Automatic Diagnostic Repository? (Choose the best answer.)

   A. In the location specified by the ADR_BASE environment variable.

   B. In the flash recovery area.

   C. In the location specified by the DIAGNOSTIC_DEST instance parameter.

   D. In the location specified by the oraInst.loc file on Unix systems, or the INST_LOC registry variable on Windows systems.

3. If your database release level is at 11.1.0.6, application of what type of patch will raise this level? (Choose the best answer.)

   A. An interim patch

   B. A critical patch update

   C. A patch set

   D. Any patch installation will raise the reported level

4. What tool(s) can you use to install patches? (Choose all correct answers.)

   A. Database Control

   B. The Opatch utility

   C. The Oracle Universal Installer

   D. The Automatic Diagnostic Repository Command-Line Interface tool (the ADRCI)

5. What are the prerequisites for running the Opatch utility? (Choose all correct answers.)

    A. ORACLE_HOME must be set as an environment variable.

    B. MetaLink credentials must be either stored or entered at runtime.

    C. A Java Runtime Environment must be available.

    D. The database must be in NOMOUNT mode.

6. The value of the initialization parameter DIAGNOSTIC_DEST is NULL, the environment variable ORACLE_HOME is set to /u01/app/oracle/product/11.1.0/db_1, and the value of the environment variable ORACLE_BASE is set to /u01/app/oracle. At startup, what value is assigned by Oracle to DIAGNOSTIC_DEST? (Choose the best answer.)

    A. /u01/app/oracle/diag

    B. /u01/app/oracle/log

    C. /u01/app/oracle/product/11.1.0/db_1/log

    D. /u01/app/oracle

7. Which of the following tasks can you accomplish using the adrci command-line tool? (Choose the best answers.)

    A. Package incident information into a ZIP file to send to Oracle support.

    B. View diagnostic data within ADR.

    C. Perform a health check on the database while it is running.

    D. Run recommended fixes from the most recent health check on the database.

8. You can use the EM Support Workbench for which of the following tasks? (Choose all correct answers.)

    A. Run recommended repairs.

    B. Manually run a health check.

    C. Close problems and incidents.

    D. Generate additional SQL test cases to help Oracle support solve the problem.

    E. View problems and incidents.

Self Test Answers

1. ☑ **B.** Database Control must be able to make an outbound HTTP connection to MetaLink.

    ☒ **A, C,** and **D.** A and C are wrong because the browser does not make the connection to MetaLink—it makes a connection to Database Control. D is wrong because while this would work, it is not necessary.

2. ☑ C. The DIAGNOSTIC_DEST parameter specifies the directory used as the root of the ADR.

☒ A, B, and D. A is wrong because ADR_BASE is not an environment variable. B is wrong because the flash recovery area stores backup and recovery data, not problem diagnosis data. D is wrong because it confuses the ADR with the OUI Inventory.

3. ☑ C. Patch sets raise the fourth digit of the release level.

☒ A, B, and D. Interim patches and critical patch updates apply within a release level and cannot raise it.

4. ☑ A and B. Opatch (either invoked from the command line or through Database Control) is the tool to install patches.

☒ C and D. C is wrong because the OUI doesn't install patches—it installs or upgrades an Oracle Home, which is a much larger operation. D is wrong because the ADRCI uses the ADR to investigate problems; it doesn't install patches to fix them.

5. ☑ A and C. Opatch needs the ORACLE_HOME environment variable (the Windows registry variable is not enough) and a JRE.

☒ B and D. B is wrong because MetaLink is not needed to apply a patch, only to download it. D is wrong because (in most cases) the database should be shut down before applying patches.

6. ☑ D. The ADR root directory (also known as the ADR base) is set by the parameter DIAGNOSTIC_DEST. If it is not set, Oracle sets DIAGNOSTIC_DEST to the environment variable ORACLE_BASE. If ORACLE_BASE is not set, then the ADR root directory is set to $ORACLE_HOME/log.

☒ A, B, and C. All three locations are not assigned, given the values of DIAGNOSTIC_DEST, ORACLE_BASE, and ORACLE_HOME.

7. ☑ A and B. The `adrci` command-line tool allows you to view diagnostic information in the ADR root directory in addition to packaging both problem and incident information for Oracle support.

☒ C and D. The `adrci` command-line tool cannot initiate health checks nor run fixes recommended by other Oracle diagnostic tools.

8. ☑ B, C, D, and E. You can use the Support Workbench for viewing problems and incidents, manually running health checks, generating additional dumps and test cases for Oracle support, creating and tracking a service request to Oracle support, collecting all data related to a problem and packaging it, and closing the problem when it has been resolved.

☒ A. The EM support workbench cannot run recommended repairs. However, you can initiate advisors that recommend repairs.

PART III

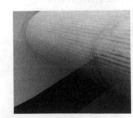

APPENDIX

About the CD

The CD-ROM included with this book comes complete with MasterExam and the electronic version of the book. The software is easy to install on any Windows 2000/XP/Vista computer and must be installed to access the MasterExam feature. You may, however, browse the electronic book directly from the CD without installation. To register for the bonus MasterExam, simply click the Bonus MasterExam link on the main launch page and follow the directions to the free online registration.

System Requirements

Software requires Windows 2000 or higher and Internet Explorer 6.0 or above and 20MB of hard disk space for full installation. The electronic book requires Adobe Acrobat Reader.

Installing and Running MasterExam

If your computer CD-ROM drive is configured to autorun, the CD-ROM will automatically start up upon inserting the disk. From the opening screen you may install MasterExam by clicking the MasterExam link. This will begin the installation process and create a program group named LearnKey. To run MasterExam, use Start | All Programs | LearnKey | MasterExam. If the autorun feature did not launch your CD, browse to the CD and click the LaunchTraining.exe icon.

MasterExam

MasterExam provides you with a simulation of the actual exams. The number of questions, the type of questions, and the time allowed are intended to be an accurate representation of the exam environment. You have the option to take an open-book exam, including hints, references, and answers, a closed-book exam, or the timed MasterExam simulation.

When you launch MasterExam, a digital clock display will appear in the bottom right-hand corner of your screen. The clock will continue to count down to zero unless you choose to end the exam before the time expires.

Electronic Book

The entire contents of the All-in-One Exam Guide are provided in PDF. Adobe's Acrobat Reader has been included on the CD.

Help

A help file is provided through the help button on the main page in the lower left-hand corner. An individual help feature is also available through MasterExam.

Removing Installation(s)

MasterExam is installed to your hard drive. For best results removing programs, use the Start | All Programs | LearnKey| Uninstall option to remove MasterExam.

Technical Support

For questions regarding the content of the electronic book or MasterExam, please visit www.mhprofessional.com or e-mail customer.service@mcgraw-hill.com. For customers outside the 50 United States, e-mail international_cs@mcgraw-hill.com.

LearnKey Technical Support

For technical problems with the software (installation, operation, removing installations), please visit www.learnkey.com, e-mail techsupport@learnkey.com, or call toll free at 1-800-482-8244.

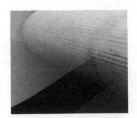

Glossary

A

ACID   Atomicity, Consistency, Isolation, and Durability. Four characteristics that a relational database must be able to maintain for transactions.

ADDM   Automatic Database Diagnostic Monitor. A tool that generates performance tuning reports based on snapshots in the AWR.

ADR   Automatic Diagnostic Repository. The default location for the alert log, trace files, and other information useful for fault finding.

ADRCI   The ADR command-line interface.

AES   Advanced Encryption Standard. A widely used data encryption method.

AL16UTF16   A Unicode fixed-width two-byte character set, commonly specified for the NLS character set used for NVARCHAR2, NCHAR, and NCLOB data types.

alias   In Oracle Net, a pointer to a connect string. An alias must be resolved into the address of a listener and the name of a service or instance.

ANSI   American National Standards Institute. A U.S. body that defines a number of standards relevant to computing.

API Application programming interface. A defined method for manipulating data, typically implemented as a set of PL/SQL procedures in a package.

ARBn Background processes that perform extent movement between disks in an Automatic Storage Management (ASM) disk group during the rebalancing process triggered by adding a disk to or removing a disk from the group.

ASA Automatic Segment Advisor. An Oracle advisory tool that can recommend segments (tables or indexes) that are candidates for segment shrink.

ASCII American Standard Code for Information Interchange. A standard (with many variations) for coding letters and other characters as bytes.

ASH Active session history. A category of information in the AWR that records details of session activity.

ASM Automatic Storage Management. A logical volume manager (LVM) provided with the Oracle database.

ASMM Automatic Shared Memory Management. A technique for automating the allocation of memory to both the SGA and PGA structures.

ASSM Automatic segment space management. The method of managing space within segments by use of bitmaps.

attribute One element of a tuple (aka a column).

AVG A function that divides the sum of a column or expression by the number of nonnull rows in a group.

AWR Automatic Workload Repository. A set of tables in the SYSAUX tablespace, populated with tuning data gathered by the MMON process.

B

background process A process that is part of the instance: launched at startup.

BFILE A large object data type that is stored as an operating system file. The value in the table column is a pointer to the file.

bind variable A value passed from a user process to a SQL statement at statement execution time.

BLOB Binary large object. A LOB data type for binary data, such as photographs and video clips. BLOBs do not undergo character set conversion when passed between a session's user process and server process.

block The units of storage into which datafiles are formatted. The size can be 2KB, 4KB, 8KB, 16KB, 32KB, or 64KB. Some platforms will not permit all these sizes.

BMR   Block media recovery. An RMAN technique for restoration and recovery of individual data blocks, rather than complete datafiles.

C

Cartesian product   Sometimes called a cross join. A mathematical term that refers to the set of data created by multiplying the rows from two or more tables together: every row is joined to every other row.

CET   Central European Time. A time zone used in much of Europe (though not Great Britain) that is one hour ahead of UTC, with daylight saving time in effect during the summer months.

character set   The encoding system for representing data within bytes. Different character sets can store different characters and may not be suitable for all languages. Unicode character sets can store any character.

check constraint   A simple rule enforced by the database that restricts the values that can be entered into a column.

checkpoint   An event that forces the DBWn to write all dirty buffers from the database buffer cache to the datafiles.

CKPT   The checkpoint process. The background process responsible for recording the current redo byte address—the point in time up to which the DBWn has written changed data blocks to disk—and for signaling checkpoints, which force DBWn to write all changed blocks to disk immediately.

client-server architecture   A processing paradigm where the application is divided into client software that interacts with the user and server software that interacts with the data.

CLOB   Character large object. A LOB data type for character data, such as text documents, stored in the database character set.

cluster   A hardware environment where more than one computer shares access to storage. A RAC database consists of several instances on several computers opening one database on the shared storage.

cluster segment   A segment that can contain one or more tables, denormalized into a single structure.

COALESCE   A function that returns the first nonnull value from its parameter list. If all its parameters are null, then a null value is returned.

column   An element of a row: tables are two-dimensional structures, divided horizontally into rows and vertically into columns.

commit   To make a change to data permanent.

complete recovery   Following a restore of damaged database files, a complete recovery applies all redo to bring the database up to date with no loss of data.

connect identifier   An Oracle Net alias.

connect role   A preseeded role retained only for backward compatibility.

connect string   The database connection details needed to establish a session: the address of the listener and the service or instance name.

consistent backup   A backup made while the database is closed.

constraint   A mechanism for enforcing rules on data: that a column value must be unique, or may only contain certain values. A primary key constraint specifies that the column must be both unique and not null.

control file   The file containing pointers to the rest of the database, critical sequence information, and the RMAN repository.

CPU   Central processing unit. The chip that provides the processing capability of a computer, such as an Intel Pentium or a Sun SPARC.

CTWR   Change Tracking Writer. The optional background process that records the addresses of changed blocks, to enable fast incremental backups.

D

data blocks   The units into which datafiles are formatted, made up of one or more operating system blocks.

data dictionary   The tables and views owned by SYS in the SYSTEM tablespace that define the database and the objects within it.

data dictionary views   Views on the data dictionary tables that let the DBA investigate the state of the database.

Data Guard   A facility whereby a copy of the production database is created and updated (possibly in real time) with all changes applied to the production database.

Data Pump   A facility for transferring large amounts of data at high speed into, out of, or between databases.

database buffer cache   An area of memory in the SGA used for working on blocks copied from datafiles.

database link   A connection from one database to another, based on a username and password and a connect string.

Database Replay   An Oracle feature that can help assess the performance impact of a workload captured from one system and replayed on another.

datafile   The disk-based structure for storing data.

DBA   Database administrator. The person responsible for creating and managing Oracle databases—this could be you.

DBA role   A preseeded role in the database provided for backward compatibility that includes all the privileges needed to manage a database, except that needed to start up or shut down.

DBCA   The Database Configuration Assistant. A GUI tool for creating, modifying, and dropping instances and databases.

DBID   Database identifier. A unique number for every database, visible in the DBID column of the V$DATABASE dynamic performance view.

DBMS   Database management system, often used interchangeably with RDBMS.

DBWn or DBWR   The Database Writer. The background process responsible for writing changed blocks from the database buffer cache to the datafiles. An instance may have up to 20 database writer processes, DBW0 through DBWj.

DDL   Data Definition Language. The subset of SQL commands that change object definitions within the data dictionary: CREATE, ALTER, DROP, and TRUNCATE.

deadlock   A situation where two sessions block each other, such that neither can do anything. Deadlocks are detected and resolved automatically by the DIA0 background process.

DECODE   A function that implements if-then-else conditional logic by testing two terms for equality and returning the third term if they are equal or, optionally, returning some other term if they are not.

DHCP   Dynamic Host Configuration Protocol. The standard for configuring the network characteristics of a computer, such as its IP address, in a changing environment where computers may be moved from one location to another.

DIA0   The diagnosability process that detects hang and deadlock situations.

DIAG   The diagnosability process that generates diagnostic dumps.

direct path   A method of I/O on datafiles that bypasses the database buffer cache.

directory object   An Oracle directory: a object within the database that points to an operating system directory.

dirty buffer   A buffer in the database buffer cache that contains a copy of a data block that has been updated in memory and not yet written back to the datafile.

DMnn   Data Pump Master process. The process that controls a Data Pump job—one will be launched for each job that is running.

DML   Data Manipulation Language. The subset of SQL commands that change data within the database: INSERT, UPDATE, DELETE, and MERGE.

DNS   Domain Name Service. The TCP mechanism for resolving network names into IP addresses.

domain   The set of values an attribute is allowed to take. Terminology: tables have rows; rows have columns with values. Or: relations have tuples; tuples have attributes with values taken from their domain.

DSS   Decision Support System. A database, such as a data warehouse, optimized for running queries as opposed to OLTP work.

DWnn   Data Pump Worker process. There will be one or more of these launched for each Data Pump job that is running.

E

easy connect   A method of establishing a session against a database by specifying the address on the listener and the service name, without using an Oracle Net alias.

EBCDIC   Extended Binary Coded Decimal Interchange Code. A standard developed by IBM for coding letters and other characters in bytes.

environment variable   A variable set in the operating system shell that can be used by application software and by shell scripts.

equijoin   A join condition using an equality operator.

F

fact table   The central table in a star schema, with columns for values relevant to the row and columns used as foreign keys to the dimension tables.

FGA   Fine-grained auditing. A facility for tracking user access to data, based on the rows that are seen or manipulated.

flash recovery area   A default location for all recovery-related files.

Flashback Data Archive   A database container object that retains historical data for one or more database objects for a specified retention period.

Flashback Database   A flashback feature that recovers the entire database to a prior point in time using Flashback Database logs.

Flashback Database logs   Changed database blocks that are stored in the flash recovery area and used for Flashback Database.

Flashback Drop   A flashback feature that makes it easy to recover dropped tables if they are still in the recycle bin.

Flashback Query   A flashback feature that enables you to view table rows at a prior point in time.

Flashback Table   A Flashback Query that recovers a single table and its associated objects to a prior point in time.

full backup   A backup containing all blocks of the files backed up, not only those blocks changed since the last backup.

G

GMT   Greenwich Mean Time. Now referred to as UTC, this is the time zone of the meridian through Greenwich Observatory in London.

grid computing   An architecture where the delivery of a service to end users is not tied to certain server resources but can be provided from anywhere in a pool of resources.

GROUP BY   A clause that specifies the grouping attribute rows must have in common for them to be clustered together.

GUI   Graphical user interface. A layer of an application that lets users work with the application through a graphical terminal, such as a PC with a mouse.

H

HTTP   Hypertext Transfer Protocol. The protocol that enables the World Wide Web (both invented at the European Organization for Nuclear Research in 1989)—this is a layered protocol that runs over TCP/IP.

HWM   High water mark. This is the last block of a segment that has ever been used—blocks above this are part of the segment but are not yet formatted for use.

I

I/O   Input/output. The activity of reading from or writing to disks—often the slowest point of a data processing operation.

image copy   An RMAN copy of a file.

inconsistent backup   A backup made while the database was open.

incremental backup   A backup containing only blocks that have been changed since the last backup was made.

INITCAP   A function that accepts a string of characters and returns each word in title case.

inner join   When equijoins and nonequijoins are performed, rows from the source and target tables are matched. These are referred to as inner joins.

instance recovery   The automatic repair of damage caused by a disorderly shutdown of the database.

INSTR   A function that returns the positional location of the *n*th occurrence of a specified string of characters in a source string.

IOT   Index-organized table. A table type where the rows are stored in the leaf blocks of an index segment.

IP   Internet Protocol. Together with the Transmission Control Protocol, TCP/IP: the de facto standard communication protocol used for client/server communication over a network.

IPC   Inter-Process Communications protocol. The platform-specific protocol, provided by your OS vendor, used by processes running on the same machine to communicate with each other.

ISO   International Organization for Standardization. A group that defines many standards, including SQL.

J

J2EE   Java 2 Enterprise Edition. The standard for developing Java applications.

JOIN . . . ON   A clause that allows the explicit specification of join columns regardless of their column names. This provides a flexible joining format.

JOIN . . . USING   A syntax that allows a natural join to be formed on specific columns with shared names.

joining   Involves linking two or more tables based on common attributes. Joining allows data to be stored in third normal form in discrete tables, instead of in one large table.

JVM   Java Virtual Machine. The runtime environment needed for running code written in Java. Oracle provides a JVM within the database, and there will be one provided by your operating system.

L

large pool   A memory structure within the SGA used by certain processes: principally shared server processes and parallel execution servers.

LAST_DAY   A function used to obtain the last day in a month given any valid date item.

LDAP   Lightweight Directory Access Protocol. The TCP implementation of the X25 directory standard, used by the Oracle Internet Directory for name resolution, security, and authentication. LDAP is also used by other software vendors, including Microsoft and IBM.

LENGTH   A function that computes the number of characters in a string, including spaces and special characters.

LGWR   The Log Writer. The background process responsible for flushing change vectors from the log buffer in memory to the online redo log files on disk.

library cache   A memory structure within the shared pool, used for caching SQL statements parsed into their executable form.

listener   The server-side process that listens for database connection requests from user processes and launches server processes to establish sessions.

LOB   Large object. A data structure that is too large to store within a table. LOBs (Oracle supports several types) are defined as columns of a table but physically are stored in a separate segment.

log switch   The action of closing one online logfile group and opening another: triggered by the LGWR process filling the first group.

LRU   Least recently used. LRU lists are used to manage access to data structures, using algorithms that ensure that the data that has not been accessed for the longest time is the data that will be overwritten.

LVM   Logical Volume Manager. A layer of software that abstracts the physical storage within your computer from the logical storage visible to an application.

M

MMAN   The Memory Manager background process, which monitors and reassigns memory allocations in the SGA for automatically tunable SGA components.

MML   Media Management Layer. Software that lets RMAN make use of automated tape libraries and other SBT devices.

MMNL   Manageability Monitor Light. The background process responsible for flushing ASH data to the AWR, if MMON is not doing this with the necessary frequency.

MMON   The Manageability Monitor is a background process that is responsible for gathering performance monitoring information and raising alerts.

MOD   The modulus operation, a function that returns the remainder of a division operation.

MONTHS_BETWEEN   A function that computes the number of months between two given date parameters and is based on a 31-day month.

mounted database   A situation where the instance has opened the database controlfile, but not the online redo log files or the datafiles.

MTBF   Mean time between failures. A measure of the average length of running time for a database between unplanned shutdowns.

MTS   Multi-Threaded Server. Since release 9*i*, renamed to Shared Server. This is the technique whereby a large number of sessions can share a small pool of server processes, rather than requiring one server each.

MTTR   Mean time to recover. The average time it takes to make the database available for normal use after a failure.

multiplexing   To maintain multiple copies of files (particularly controlfiles and redo log files).

N

namespace   A logical grouping of objects within which no two objects may have the same name.

natural join   A join performed using the NATURAL JOIN syntax when the source and target tables are implicitly equijoined using identically named columns.

NCLOB   National character large object. A LOB data type for character data, such as text documents, stored in the alternative national database character set.

NetBEUI   NetBIOS Extended User Interface. An enhanced version of NETBIOS.

NetBIOS   Network Basic Input Output System. The network communications protocol that was burnt onto the first network card that IBM ever produced.

NLS   National Language Support. The capability of the Oracle database to support many linguistic, geographical, and cultural environments—now usually referred to as Globalization.

node   A computer attached to a network.

nonequijoin   Performed when the values in the join columns fulfill the join condition based on an inequality expression.

null   The absence of a value, indicating that the value is not known, missing, or inapplicable.

NULLIF   A function that tests two terms for equality. If they are equal, the function returns null; else it returns the first of the two terms tested.

NVL   A function that returns either the original item unchanged or an alternative item if the initial term is null.

NVL2   A function that returns a new if-null item if the original item is null or an alternative if-not-null item if the original term is not null.

O

OC4J   Oracle Containers for J2EE. The control structure provided by the Oracle Internet Application Server for running Java programs.

OCA   Oracle Certified Associate.

OCI   Oracle Call Interface. An API, published as a set of C libraries, that programmers can use to write user processes that will use an Oracle database.

OCP   Oracle Certified Professional. The qualification you are working toward at the moment.

ODBC   Open Database Connectivity. A standard developed by Microsoft for communicating with relational databases. Oracle provides an ODBC driver that will allow clients running Microsoft products to connect to an Oracle database.

offline backup   A backup made while the database is closed.

OLAP   Online analytical processing. Selection-intensive work involving running queries against a (usually) large database. Oracle provides OLAP capabilities as an option, in addition to the standard query facilities.

OLTP   Online transaction processing. A pattern of activity within a database typified by a large number of small, short transactions.

online backup   A backup made while the database is open.

online redo log   The files to which change vectors are streamed by the LGWR.

Oracle Net   Oracle's proprietary communications protocol, layered on top of an industry-standard protocol.

ORACLE_BASE   The root directory into which Oracle products are installed.

ORACLE_HOME   The root directory of any one Oracle product.

OS   Operating system. Typically, in the Oracle environment, this will be a version of Unix (perhaps Linux) or Microsoft Windows.

outer join   A join performed when rows, which are not retrieved by an inner join, are included for retrieval.

P

parse   To convert SQL statements into a form suitable for execution.

PGA   Program global area. The variable-sized block of memory used to maintain the state of a database session. PGAs are private to the session and controlled by the session's server process.

PL/SQL   Procedural Language / Structured Query Language. Oracle's proprietary programming language, which combines procedural constructs, such as flow control, and user interface capabilities with SQL.

PMON   The Process Monitor. The background process responsible for monitoring the state of user's sessions against an instance.

primary key   The column (or combination of columns) whose value(s) can be used to identify each row in a table.

projection   The restriction of columns selected from a table. Using projection, you retrieve only specific columns.

R

RAC   Real Application Clusters. Oracle's clustering technology, which allows several instances in different machines to open the same database for scalability, performance, and fault tolerance.

RAID   Redundant Array of Inexpensive Disks. Techniques for enhancing performance and/or fault tolerance by using a volume manager to present a number of physical disks to the operating system as a single logical disk.

RAM   Random access memory. The chips that make up the real memory in your computer hardware, as against the virtual memory presented to software by the operating system.

raw device   An unformatted disk or disk partition.

RDBMS   Relational database management system, often used interchangeably with DBMS.

referential integrity   A rule defined on a table specifying that the values in a column (or columns) must map onto those of a row in another table.

relation   A two-dimensional structure consisting of tuples with attributes (aka a table).

REPLACE   A function that substitutes each occurrence of a search item in the source string with a replacement term and returns the modified source string.

RMAN   Recovery Manager. Oracle's backup and recovery tool.

rowid   The unique identifier of every row in the database, used as a pointer to the physical location of the row. The rowid datatype is proprietary to Oracle Corporation, not part of the SQL standard.

RVWR   The Recovery Writer background process, an optional process responsible for flushing the flashback buffer to the flashback logs.

S

SBT   System backup to tape. An RMAN term for a tape device, interchangeable with SBT_TAPE.

schema   The objects owned by a database user.

SCN   System change number. The continually incrementing number used to track the sequence and exact time of all events within a database.

segment   A database object, within a schema, that stores data.

selection   The extraction of rows from a table. Selection includes the further restriction of the extracted rows based on various criteria or conditions. This allows you to retrieve only specific rows.

self-join   A join required when the join columns originate from the same table. Conceptually, the self-join works as a regular join between the source table and itself.

sequence   A database object, within a schema, that can generate consecutive numbers.

service name   A logical name registered by an instance with a listener, which can be specified by a user process when it issues a connect request. A service name will be mapped onto a SID by the listener when it establishes a session.

session   A user process and a server process, connected to the instance.

SGA   System global area. The block of shared memory that contains the memory structures that make up an Oracle instance.

SID   Either: System Identifier. The name of an instance, which must be unique on the computer the instance is running on. Users can request a connection to a named SID, or to a logical service and let the listener choose an appropriate SID.
   Or: Session Identifier. The number used to identify uniquely a session logged on to an Oracle instance.

SMON   The System Monitor. The background process responsible for opening a database and monitoring the instance.

spfile   The server parameter file: the file containing the parameters used to build an instance in memory.

SQL   Structured Query Language. An international standard language for extracting data from and manipulating data in relational databases.

SSL   Secure Sockets Layer. A standard for securing data transmission, using encryption, checksumming, and digital certificates.

SUBSTR   A function that extracts and returns a segment from a given source string.

SUM   A function that returns an aggregated total of all the nonnull numeric expression values in a group.

synonym   An alternative name for a database object.

Sysasm   The privilege that lets a user connect to an ASM instance with operating system or password file authentication, and start up and shut down the instance.

Sysdba   The privilege that lets a user connect with operating system or password file authentication, and create or start up and shut down a database.

Sysoper   The privilege that lets a user connect with operating system or password file authentication, and start up and shut down (but not create) a database.

System   A preseeded schema used for database administration purposes.

T

table   A logical two-dimensional data storage structure, consisting of rows and columns.

tablespace   The logical structure that abstracts logical data storage in tables from physical data storage in datafiles.

TCP   Transmission Control Protocol. Together with the Internet Protocol, TCP/IP: the de facto standard communication protocol used for client/server communication over a network.

TCPS   TCP with SSL. The secure sockets version of TCP.

tempfile   The physical storage that makes up a temporary tablespace, used for storing temporary segments.

TNS   Transparent Network Substrate. The heart of Oracle Net, a proprietary layered protocol running on top of whatever underlying network transport protocol you choose to use—probably TCP/IP.

TO_CHAR   A function that performs date to character and number to character data type conversions.

TO_DATE   A function that explicitly transforms character items into date values.

TO_NUMBER   A function that changes character items into number values.

transaction   A logical unit of work, which will complete in total or not at all.

TSPITR   Tablespace Point in Time Recovery. A recovery method that is ideal for recovering a set of objects isolated to a single tablespace.

tuple   A one-dimensional structure consisting of attributes (aka a row).

U

UGA   User global area. The part of the PGA that is stored in the SGA for sessions running through shared servers.

UI   User interface. The layer of an application that communicates with end users—nowadays, frequently graphical; a GUI.

URL   Uniform Resource Locator. A standard for specifying the location of an object on the Internet, consisting of a protocol; a host name and domain; an IP port number; a path and filename; and a series of parameters.

UTC   Coordinated Universal Time, previously known as Greenwich Mean Time (GMT). UTC is the global standard time zone; all others relate to it as offsets, ahead or behind.

X

X Window System   The standard GUI environment used on most computers, except those made by Apple and those that run Microsoft Windows.

XML   Extensible Markup Language. A standard for data interchange using documents, where the format of the data is defined by tags within the document.

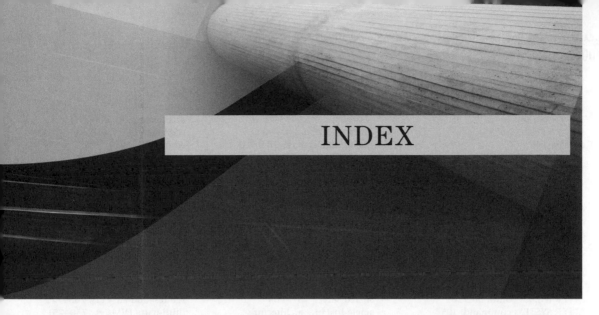

INDEX

GET YOUR FREE SUBSCRIPTION
TO *ORACLE MAGAZINE*

Oracle Magazine is essential gear for today's information technology professionals. Stay informed and increase your productivity with every issue of *Oracle Magazine*. Inside each free bimonthly issue you'll get:

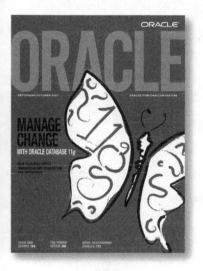

- Up-to-date information on Oracle Database, Oracle Application Server, Web development, enterprise grid computing, database technology, and business trends
- Third-party news and announcements
- Technical articles on Oracle and partner products, technologies, and operating environments
- Development and administration tips
- Real-world customer stories

If there are other Oracle users at your location who would like to receive their own subscription to *Oracle Magazine*, please photocopy this form and pass it along.

Three easy ways to subscribe:

① **Web**
Visit our Web site at **oracle.com/oraclemagazine**
You'll find a subscription form there, plus much more

② **Fax**
Complete the questionnaire on the back of this card and fax the questionnaire side only to **+1.847.763.9638**

③ **Mail**
Complete the questionnaire on the back of this card and mail it to **P.O. Box 1263, Skokie, IL 60076-8263**

ORACLE®

Want your own FREE subscription?

To receive a free subscription to *Oracle Magazine*, you must fill out the entire card, sign it, and date it (incomplete cards cannot be processed or acknowledged). You can also fax your application to +1.847.763.9638. **Or subscribe at our Web site at oracle.com/oraclemagazine**

○ **Yes, please send me a FREE subscription** *Oracle Magazine*.   ○ No.

○ From time to time, Oracle Publishing allows our partners exclusive access to our e-mail addresses for special promotions and announcements. To be included in this program, please check this circle. If you do not wish to be included, you will only receive notices about your subscription via e-mail.

○ Oracle Publishing allows sharing of our postal mailing list with selected third parties. If you prefer your mailing address not to be included in this program, please check this circle.

If at any time you would like to be removed from either mailing list, please contact Customer Service at +1.847.763.9635 or send an e-mail to oracle@halldata.com. If you opt in to the sharing of information, Oracle may also provide you with e-mail related to Oracle products, services, and events. If you want to completely unsubscribe from any e-mail communication from Oracle, please send an e-mail to: unsubscribe@oracle-mail.com with the following in the subject line: REMOVE [your e-mail address]. For complete information on Oracle Publishing's privacy practices, please visit oracle.com/html/privacy/html

X	
signature (required)	date

name _____   title _____

company _____   e-mail address _____

street/p.o. box _____

city/state/zip or postal code _____   telephone _____

country _____   fax _____

Would you like to receive your free subscription in digital format instead of print if it becomes available? ○ Yes ○ No

---

YOU MUST ANSWER ALL 10 QUESTIONS BELOW.

① WHAT IS THE PRIMARY BUSINESS ACTIVITY OF YOUR FIRM AT THIS LOCATION? (check one only)

- ☐ 01 Aerospace and Defense Manufacturing
- ☐ 02 Application Service Provider
- ☐ 03 Automotive Manufacturing
- ☐ 04 Chemicals
- ☐ 05 Media and Entertainment
- ☐ 06 Construction/Engineering
- ☐ 07 Consumer Sector/Consumer Packaged Goods
- ☐ 08 Education
- ☐ 09 Financial Services/Insurance
- ☐ 10 Health Care
- ☐ 11 High Technology Manufacturing, OEM
- ☐ 12 Industrial Manufacturing
- ☐ 13 Independent Software Vendor
- ☐ 14 Life Sciences (biotech, pharmaceuticals)
- ☐ 15 Natural Resources
- ☐ 16 Oil and Gas
- ☐ 17 Professional Services
- ☐ 18 Public Sector (government)
- ☐ 19 Research
- ☐ 20 Retail/Wholesale/Distribution
- ☐ 21 Systems Integrator, VAR/VAD
- ☐ 22 Telecommunications
- ☐ 23 Travel and Transportation
- ☐ 24 Utilities (electric, gas, sanitation, water)
- ☐ 98 Other Business and Services _____

② WHICH OF THE FOLLOWING BEST DESCRIBES YOUR PRIMARY JOB FUNCTION? (check one only)

CORPORATE MANAGEMENT/STAFF
- ☐ 01 Executive Management (President, Chair, CEO, CFO, Owner, Partner, Principal)
- ☐ 02 Finance/Administrative Management (VP/Director/ Manager/Controller, Purchasing, Administration)
- ☐ 03 Sales/Marketing Management (VP/Director/Manager)
- ☐ 04 Computer Systems/Operations Management (CIO/VP/Director/Manager MIS/IS/IT, Ops)

IS/IT STAFF
- ☐ 05 Application Development/Programming Management
- ☐ 06 Application Development/Programming Staff
- ☐ 07 Consulting
- ☐ 08 DBA/Systems Administrator
- ☐ 09 Education/Training
- ☐ 10 Technical Support Director/Manager
- ☐ 11 Other Technical Management/Staff
- ☐ 98 Other

③ WHAT IS YOUR CURRENT PRIMARY OPERATING PLATFORM (check all that apply)

- ☐ 01 Digital Equipment Corp UNIX/VAX/VMS
- ☐ 02 HP UNIX
- ☐ 03 IBM AIX
- ☐ 04 IBM UNIX
- ☐ 05 Linux (Red Hat)
- ☐ 06 Linux (SUSE)
- ☐ 07 Linux (Oracle Enterprise)
- ☐ 08 Linux (other)
- ☐ 09 Macintosh
- ☐ 10 MVS
- ☐ 11 Netware
- ☐ 12 Network Computing
- ☐ 13 SCO UNIX
- ☐ 14 Sun Solaris/SunOS
- ☐ 15 Windows
- ☐ 16 Other UNIX
- ☐ 98 Other
- 99 ☐ None of the Above

④ DO YOU EVALUATE, SPECIFY, RECOMMEND, OR AUTHORIZE THE PURCHASE OF ANY OF THE FOLLOWING? (check all that apply)

- ☐ 01 Hardware
- ☐ 02 Business Applications (ERP, CRM, etc.)
- ☐ 03 Application Development Tools
- ☐ 04 Database Products
- ☐ 05 Internet or Intranet Products
- ☐ 06 Other Software
- ☐ 07 Middleware Products
- 99 ☐ None of the Above

⑤ IN YOUR JOB, DO YOU USE OR PLAN TO PURCHASE ANY OF THE FOLLOWING PRODUCTS? (check all that apply)

SOFTWARE
- ☐ 01 CAD/CAE/CAM
- ☐ 02 Collaboration Software
- ☐ 03 Communications
- ☐ 04 Database Management
- ☐ 05 File Management
- ☐ 06 Finance
- ☐ 07 Java
- ☐ 08 Multimedia Authoring
- ☐ 09 Networking
- ☐ 10 Programming
- ☐ 11 Project Management
- ☐ 12 Scientific and Engineering
- ☐ 13 Systems Management
- ☐ 14 Workflow

HARDWARE
- ☐ 15 Macintosh
- ☐ 16 Mainframe
- ☐ 17 Massively Parallel Processing

- ☐ 18 Minicomputer
- ☐ 19 Intel x86(32)
- ☐ 20 Intel x86(64)
- ☐ 21 Network Computer
- ☐ 22 Symmetric Multiprocessing
- ☐ 23 Workstation Services

SERVICES
- ☐ 24 Consulting
- ☐ 25 Education/Training
- ☐ 26 Maintenance
- ☐ 27 Online Database
- ☐ 28 Support
- ☐ 29 Technology-Based Training
- ☐ 30 Other
- 99 ☐ None of the Above

⑥ WHAT IS YOUR COMPANY'S SIZE? (check one only)

- ☐ 01 More than 25,000 Employees
- ☐ 02 10,001 to 25,000 Employees
- ☐ 03 5,001 to 10,000 Employees
- ☐ 04 1,001 to 5,000 Employees
- ☐ 05 101 to 1,000 Employees
- ☐ 06 Fewer than 100 Employees

⑦ DURING THE NEXT 12 MONTHS, HOW MUCH DO YOU ANTICIPATE YOUR ORGANIZATION WILL SPEND ON COMPUTER HARDWARE, SOFTWARE, PERIPHERALS, AND SERVICES FOR YOUR LOCATION? (check one only)

- ☐ 01 Less than $10,000
- ☐ 02 $10,000 to $49,999
- ☐ 03 $50,000 to $99,999
- ☐ 04 $100,000 to $499,999
- ☐ 05 $500,000 to $999,999
- ☐ 06 $1,000,000 and Over

⑧ WHAT IS YOUR COMPANY'S YEARLY SALES REVENUE? (check one only)

- ☐ 01 $500, 000, 000 and above
- ☐ 02 $100, 000, 000 to $500, 000, 000
- ☐ 03 $50, 000, 000 to $100, 000, 000
- ☐ 04 $5, 000, 000 to $50, 000, 000
- ☐ 05 $1, 000, 000 to $5, 000, 000

⑨ WHAT LANGUAGES AND FRAMEWORKS DO YOU USE? (check all that apply)

- ☐ 01 Ajax
- ☐ 02 C
- ☐ 03 C++
- ☐ 04 C#
- ☐ 13 Python
- ☐ 14 Ruby/Rails
- ☐ 15 Spring
- ☐ 16 Struts
- ☐ 05 Hibernate
- ☐ 06 J++/J#
- ☐ 07 Java
- ☐ 08 JSP
- ☐ 09 .NET
- ☐ 10 Perl
- ☐ 11 PHP
- ☐ 12 PL/SQL
- ☐ 17 SQL
- ☐ 18 Visual Basic
- ☐ 98 Other

⑩ WHAT ORACLE PRODUCTS ARE IN USE AT SITE? (check all that apply)

ORACLE DATABASE
- ☐ 01 Oracle Database 11*g*
- ☐ 02 Oracle Database 10*g*
- ☐ 03 Oracle9*i* Database
- ☐ 04 Oracle Embedded Database (Oracle Lite, Times Ten, Berkeley)
- ☐ 05 Other Oracle Database Release

ORACLE FUSION MIDDLEWARE
- ☐ 06 Oracle Application Server
- ☐ 07 Oracle Portal
- ☐ 08 Oracle Enterprise Manager
- ☐ 09 Oracle BPEL Process Manager
- ☐ 10 Oracle Identity Management
- ☐ 11 Oracle SOA Suite
- ☐ 12 Oracle Data Hubs

ORACLE DEVELOPMENT TOOLS
- ☐ 13 Oracle JDeveloper
- ☐ 14 Oracle Forms
- ☐ 15 Oracle Reports
- ☐ 16 Oracle Designer
- ☐ 17 Oracle Discoverer
- ☐ 18 Oracle BI Beans
- ☐ 19 Oracle Warehouse Builder
- ☐ 20 Oracle WebCenter
- ☐ 21 Oracle Application Express

ORACLE APPLICATIONS
- ☐ 22 Oracle E-Business Suite
- ☐ 23 PeopleSoft Enterprise
- ☐ 24 JD Edwards EnterpriseOne
- ☐ 25 JD Edwards World
- ☐ 26 Oracle Fusion
- ☐ 27 Hyperion
- ☐ 28 Siebel CRM

ORACLE SERVICES
- ☐ 28 Oracle E-Business Suite On Demand
- ☐ 29 Oracle Technology On Demand
- ☐ 30 Siebel CRM On Demand
- ☐ 31 Oracle Consulting
- ☐ 32 Oracle Education
- ☐ 33 Oracle Support
- ☐ 98 Other
- 99 ☐ None of the Above

08014004